INTRODUCTION TO
MANAGEMENT SCIENCE

INTRODUCTION TO

MANAGEMENT SCIENCE

Second Edition

William J. Stevenson
College of Business
Rochester Institute of Technology

IRWIN

Homewood, IL 60430
Boston, MA 02116

This book is dedicated to you.

Senior sponsoring editor: Richard T. Hercher, Jr.
Developmental editor: Joanne Dorff
Project editor: Susan Trentacosti
Production manager: Carma W. Fazio
Interior designer: Maureen McCutcheon
Cover designer: Larry J. Cope
Cover illustrator: Alice B. Thiede
Compositor: Better Graphics, Inc.
Typeface: 10/12 Times Roman
Printer: R. R. Donnelley & Sons Company

Library of Congress Cataloging-in Publication Data

Stevenson, William J.
Introduction to management science/William J. Stevenson.—2nd ed.
p. cm.
Includes bibliographical references and index.
ISBN 0-256-08809-8
1. Management science. I. Title
T56.S82 1992
658'.001'51—dc20 91-28759

Printed in the United States of America
1 2 3 4 5 6 7 8 9 0 DOC 7 6 5 4 3 2 1

Preface

OVERVIEW

This book is about the use of quantitative models in decision making. Most chapters describe the purpose of a particular model, how to formulate the model, procedures for solving the model, and how managers can interpret and use the solutions to improve their decision making.

Throughout my career in college teaching, I have observed that many students do not like quantitative courses because they find the material to be difficult, frustrating, and boring. I have also observed that students rely heavily on the instructor and their textbook for guidance and assistance. In writing this book, I have tried to address these observations in a meaningful way. The feedback I received from users of the first edition, and my own classroom experience, suggest that the book is achieving its objectives.

Every effort has been made to develop a textbook that is readable and interesting. The writing style is light and informal. Material is presented assuming that readers have no prior knowledge of the subject matter. The subject matter is developed in a logical format, usually beginning with an overview so that readers can immediately see where the discussion will lead. Explanations are clear and simple, and often intuitive, and examples are sprinkled liberally throughout the text. Solved problems are provided at the end of all chapters. Students use them as guides for solving the end-of-chapter problems. Answers for many of the problems are provided in the Appendix.

The prerequisites for being able to understand the material in this book are basic algebra and introductory statistics.

Extensive checking for errors in examples and answers has been done, as there is nothing more frustrating to students than encountering errors.

PEDAGOGICAL FEATURES

Much attention has been devoted to pedagogy. This book has a number of features designed to enhance learning. The features include the following:

- ☐ Every chapter begins with a chapter outline and a list of behavioral objectives. These provide the reader with a topical overview of the chapter and a guide as to what the reader should expect to learn from the chapter. Every chapter includes a summary, and some chapters also have interim summaries.
- ☐ There are numerous examples throughout the chapters and a set of solved problems at the end of each chapter that serve as a resource guide for solving problems.
- ☐ The end-of-chapter problems are plentiful and they are progressively graduated in difficulty. The problem types parallel the sequence of topics within the chapter. Answers to many problems are provided in the Appendix. Students find these extremely valuable in confirming their solutions, or indicating when more effort is needed.
- ☐ The writing style is a key feature of this book. It is light and informal, and concentrates primarily on key concepts and ideas; it does not spend a lot of time with fine points and minor details. Explanations are clear and logical. Every effort has been made to present an interesting, readable book.
- ☐ Key terms are highlighted in **boldface type** the first time they appear, and a glossary of these key terms is provided at the end of every chapter.
- ☐ Many chapters have "theme" problems that are used to illustrate procedures used to solve problems and interpret the results. These add interest to the material as well as continuity. The same theme problem is used in Chapters 2, 3, 4, and 6.
- ☐ Many chapters include a management dialogue that provides a forum for answering typical questions managers often raise about a particular subject.

INSTRUCTIONAL SUPPORT

This book has a number of instructional aids:

Instructor's Manual The manual provides complete solutions for all end-of-chapter problems as well as any discussion questions and case problems. It also has suggestions for alternate course outlines.

Software Decision Support System for Management Science/Operations Research (DSS) by Vahid Lotfi and Carl Pegels provides PC users with computational support for most of the models in this textbook.

Test Bank A test bank written by David Anyiwo is available. It provides true-false and multiple-choice questions that are graded according to difficulty. Tests based on the test bank are available from Irwin using the teletest service that will generate a master test from test items you choose. For details, call 1-800-331-5094, ext. 2742.

Acetates This series of approximately 80 transparencies covers the key topics throughout the text. Many transparencies are taken directly from the text in order to provide a direct link with the material presented in the book.

Study Guide A study guide (Stevenson and Van Ness) is available that contains a number of useful features. Among them are a list of key concepts for each chapter, study tips, and problems with complete solutions.

ACKNOWLEDGMENTS

This book has benefited greatly from the suggestions of reviewers and from student comments during class testing. I want to thank all of those individuals who shared their ideas with me. Among the reviewers of the first edition were:

Salvatore Belardo, State University of New York at Albany; C. Randall Byars, University of Idaho; James J. Cochran, Wright State University; Robert B. Fetter, Yale University; Thomas Foote, (formerly) San Diego State University; Donald W. Kroeber, Radford University; David M. Lyth, Western Michigan University; Jeffrey L. Ringuest, Boston College; Carol Lee Stamm, Western Michigan University; Wilban Terpening, Gonzaga University; Richard A. Toelle, University of Idaho; Paul D. Van Ness, Rochester Institute of Technology; and Ted Weston, Colorado State University.

Reviewers of the second edition were:

David Anyiwo, Hampton University; Gordon Buhrer, Old Dominion University; Jonathan Furdek, Purdue University, Calumet; Charles Gallagher, Barry University; Ed Gillenwater, University of Mississippi; Eugene Kartchner, Utah State University; Joseph Kearny, Davenport College; James Leonard, Elmhurst College; Charles Lienert, Metropolitan State University; Ming-te Lu, St. Cloud State University; Theresa McGlone, Eastern Kentucky University; George Mitchell, Southwest State University; Richard Newman, Indiana University Northwest; Robert Robinson, Southwest Missouri State; Robert Rubin, St. Leo College; and Larry Sunn, University of Redlands.

A special thank you to Yar M. Ebadi at Kansas State University and Nicholas G. Hall at Ohio State University for their extremely thorough problem checking. They spent many hours solving every problem in the text in order to ensure the text's accuracy.

William J. Stevenson

Note to Students

Many students approach quantitative courses with a certain amount of apprehension. Sometimes, knowing what lies ahead can reduce some of this. You should know that this book is student-oriented. Much thought and careful planning went into it, with you in mind, and many of the following features were designed to help you learn.

Every chapter begins with an outline that provides you with an overview of the organization of information that is to be presented in the chapter. There is also a set of objectives at the beginning of each chapter. These tell you what you can expect to accomplish after you have read the chapter and have worked some end-of-chapter problems. There are numerous examples throughout most chapters that help to reinforce important concepts and illustrate the use of formulas and solution techniques. Then, at the end of most chapters, there is a set of solved problems that further illustrate problem solving. Each chapter also includes a glossary of key terms. The end-of-chapter problems are organized to parallel presentation of related material in the chapter. And the answers to many of the end-of-chapter problems are printed at the end of the book.

Problem solving is emphasized throughout the book. Problem-solving skills that you learn and/or sharpen here will serve you in other courses, in your career, and in your personal life. The ability to organize facts and combine them with basic tools of analysis to solve problems can be a tremendous asset.

A study guide is also available. It contains study tips, a summary of important concepts, and problems with complete solutions.

I hope that you will find this book satisfactory. If you have any comments or suggestions, drop me a line. You can write to me either at the Rochester Institute of Technology, College of Business, Rochester, NY 14623–0887, or in care of Richard D. Irwin, Inc., 1818 Ridge Road, Homewood, IL 60430.

W. J. S.

Contents in Brief

Contents

Chapter 1
Introduction

Chapter Outline

Learning Objectives

After completing this chapter, you should be able to answer these and similar questions:

1. What is management science?
2. What advantages does a quantitative approach to problem solving offer?
3. Why is it important to be knowledgeable about management science?
4. What is a model, and how are models used in management science?
5. What benefits and risks should a manager be aware of when using models?
6. What types of models are most useful in management science?
7. What is the management science approach to problem solving?
8. Why are computers important in management science?

Bob Doyle is the owner of a very successful baking company. The company supplies near-finished baked goods to supermarkets which then complete the baking in order to offer fresh baked goods to their customers. The company supplies frozen rolls, pies, cinnamon buns, and similar items, which are delivered weekly.

The company is a family-run operation, having been started by Bob's father during the mid-60s. Bob took over when his father retired in 1989, and with the help of a cousin, (Big) John Talley, he has managed to achieve a dramatic increase in business. Plans have been made to expand operations to a number of other cities and to substantially increase the size of the work force.

Although Bob attended college and received a degree in business administration, neither he nor Big John, who went to work right out of high school, have had much experience with formal methods of management, especially as they pertain to the use of computers and quantitative techniques for decision making. However, just recently, Bob was invited to attend a seminar on the use of management science techniques to improve decision making. Bob is excited because he has noticed that as the business has grown, his intuitive style of management has caused him to second-guess a number of decisions that have been made, and he is hoping that the seminar will help him to make better decisions.

(Later in the chapter, you'll be able to read about a conversation that took place between Bob Doyle and the leader of the seminar about the potential benefits of Bob's firm using some management science techniques.)

Management science is a discipline devoted to solving certain managerial-type problems using quantitative models. This quantitative approach is widely employed in business. Areas of application include forecasting, capital budgeting, capacity planning, scheduling, inventory management, project management, and production planning.

In this first chapter, some of the basics of management science are covered, including the answers to such questions as: What is management science? Who uses it? Why use a quantitative approach? What are models, and why are they used? What are the different types of models? How are models used? Why are computers important in management science?

INTRODUCTION

Management science uses a logical approach to problem solving. The problem is viewed as the focal point of analysis, and quantitative models are the vehicles by which solutions are obtained.

A Problem Focus

By adopting a problem focus, a decision maker has the advantage of directing attention to the essence of an analysis: to solve a specific problem. The problem in question may pertain to a current condition or it may relate more to the future. An example of a current condition would be customers complaining to the manager of a bank about the amount of time they have to wait in line for a teller. It is hoped that these kinds of problems can be kept to a minimum; a manager cannot be productive if he or she spends very much time putting out fires.

Often, problems result from inadequate planning. Hence, an ideal use of a manager's time, and of management science models, is to plan for the future. An example of that kind of problem would be deciding where to locate a warehouse to minimize future shipping costs. Another example would be choosing a plan for assigning jobs to machines that will minimize the total time needed to complete the jobs. Still other examples include predicting future demand so that intelligent decisions can be made about production levels, work force levels, capacity, and inventory; selecting the combination of product output quantities that will maximize profits; and identifying appropriate levels of inventory.

Use of a Quantitative Approach

Problem solving can be either qualitative or quantitative. In qualitative problem solving, intuition and subjective judgment are used. Past experience with similar problems is often an important factor in choosing a qualitative approach, as is the complexity and importance of a problem. Managers tend to use a qualitative approach to problem solving when:

1. The problem is fairly simple.
2. The problem is familiar.
3. The costs involved are not great.
4. Immediate decisions are needed.

Conversely, managers tend to use a quantitative approach when one or more of the following conditions exist:

1. The problem is complex.
2. The problem is not familiar.
3. The costs involved are substantial.
4. Enough time is available to analyze the problem.

Generally speaking, decisions based on quantitative analysis tend to be more objective than those based on a purely qualitative analysis. On the other hand, a purely quantitative analysis will include only information that can be quantified. Therefore, the results of models should be followed routinely only for the simplest and best understood cases; otherwise, the results should be questioned and analyzed. As a general rule, the results of a mathematical analysis should be reviewed by management for reasonableness and feasibility.

The use of quantitative analysis is not new. Quantitative methods of problem solving can be traced back to ancient times. Who would doubt that the great pyramids of Egypt were designed and built using quantitative methods? In similar fashion, the movements and supply requirements of Roman armies, the construction of ancient canals and waterways, and the ancient shipbuilding processes undoubtedly benefited from the use of quantitative methods.

Many of the early uses involved engineering applications. However, there were very few *managerial* applications of mathematical analysis before the Industrial Revolution, particularly with respect to problem solving. Even then, management science as we now know it did not exist.

A key period in the development of the use of the quantitative approach to problem solving came during World War II when teams of scientists were brought together to help solve complex military problems on deploying troops, searching the seas, supplying troops, and so on. A typical team would consist of a mathematician, a physicist, an engineer, and a psychologist. These interdisciplinary teams were the beginnings of the *operations research* field, which is closely related to management science. After the war, many of the techniques used by the operations research teams were adapted to business applications, and management science began to emerge as a discipline. Previously developed quantitative techniques were added along with newly developed techniques to form an expanding body of knowledge that had important business applications.

One difficulty that early practitioners faced was the burdensome computational requirements that often were required to solve even fairly simple problems. It is not surprising, then, that increasing use of management science has accompanied advances in computer technology, both in hardware and software. Today, access to computers, both mainframe and personal, puts the power of management science within the reach of virtually all managers.

The combination of access to computers and computer codes for solving management problems, continuing developments in management science models, and successful applications have contributed to the respectability of management science as a discipline. Successful applications of management science and new developments in this field are reported regularly in such journals as *Management Science, Decision Sciences, Interfaces,* and *Operations Research.*

Finally, it should be noted that although the field of management science is not entirely quantitative, the preponderance of management science applications falls under the heading of quantitative analysis. For that reason, this book emphasizes applications involving quantitative models.

MODELS

A **model** is an abstraction of reality. It is a simplified, and often idealized, representation of reality. An equation, an outline, a diagram, and a map are each an example of a model. By its very nature a model is incomplete: A good model will capture the important details of reality without including innumerable minor details that would obscure rather than illuminate. You could think of a model as a selective abstraction because only those details that are considered to be important for the problem at hand are included in the model. For example, suppose the problem involved aerodynamic properties of a new automotive design. Important details that come to mind are weight, shape, size, and height. Unimportant details include color, interior design, type of radio, and so on. Thus, it is important to carefully decide which aspects of reality to include in a model.

Models provide a manager or analyst with an alternative to working directly with reality. This allows the person using the model greater freedom in terms of experimenting with different ideas, controlling certain aspects of the situation, and investigating alternative solutions. It also reduces the cost of mistakes if mistakes can be corrected within the realm of the model.

In practice, models are employed in a variety of ways. In order to gain a better perspective about models and the ways they are used, let's consider some of the different kinds of models and the reasons for their use.

Model Types

Models can be classified in a number of ways. One way uses these categories:

1. Iconic.
2. Analog.
3. Symbolic.

The three model types differ with respect to level of abstraction, form, and the way they are used.

Iconic models are the least abstract models; they are physical models that look like reality. Thus, a scale model of a car, ship, or airplane would be an iconic model. A primary reason for using iconic models is that they convey important physical characteristics to such audiences as potential investors or buyers, senior managers (for approval), designers, and employees who, ultimately, will be responsible for producing or building the actual object or item.

Analog models are also physical models, but they are more abstract than iconic models: Instead of replicating physical appearance as iconic models do, these models substitute some physical analogy for important aspects of reality. For example, a graph is an analog model. A graph of demand uses a line to represent the amount of demand in various time periods. The height of the line represents demand at a point in time, and up and down movements in the line represent changes in demand over time. Other examples of analog models include an ordinary clock with a minute and an hour hand, a thermometer, a barometer, a blueprint, a chart, and a sketch. Analog models often have visual features that make them intuitively appealing and easy to understand, which explains why they are widely used for instructional purposes. Moreover, they can be modified more easily than iconic models, making it easier to explore "What if . . . ?" kinds of questions. Very often, these models tend to be less costly to construct and change than iconic models. Even so, some analog models are fairly complex, and it may require a certain level of expertise to use and interpret them. This would be the case, for example, in reading blueprints and translating them into instructions for machine operations.

Symbolic models are the most abstract: they incorporate numbers and algebraic symbols to represent important aspects of a problem, often in equation form. These numbers and symbols are then manipulated to solve for unknown values of key variables.

From a visual standpoint, these symbolic, or **mathematical, models** are the least appealing; they do not look like a physical entity. However, in certain respects, mathematical models are far superior to their physical cousins, the iconic and analog models. Altering a symbolic model can be as simple as changing a "5" to a "6." Moreover, mathematical models lend themselves to the computational power inherent in calculators and computers.

Consider this simple mathematical model:

$$\text{Profit} = 5x$$

where

$$x = \text{pounds of material sold}$$

The number 5 represents the profit per unit of material, and the symbol x represents the quantity of a certain material; profit is the product of the profit per unit and the number of units sold. Thus, if 15 units are sold, the profit is $5(15) = \$75$.

A slightly more complex version of this model is the following:

$$\text{Profit} = 5x_1 + 8x_2 + 4x_3$$

where

$$x_1 = \text{pounds of material 1 sold}$$
$$x_2 = \text{pounds of material 2 sold}$$
$$x_3 = \text{pounds of material 3 sold}$$

Thus, if $x_1 = 10$, $x_2 = 20$, and $x_3 = 30$, the total profit would be:

$$5(10) + 8(20) + 4(30) = \$330$$

Mathematical models are made up of constants and variables; constants are fixed or known quantities not subject to variation, whereas **variables** can take on different values. Constants generally are represented by numbers and the variables by letters.

Thus, in the model Profit $= 5x_1 + 8x_2 + 4x_3$, the unit profits (5, 8, and 4) are the constants, and the quantities of materials 1, 2, and 3 (i.e., x_1, x_2, and x_3) are the variables. In this example, the variables are **decision variables.** The manager or analyst would want to know what values to set these at (i.e., how much of each to produce) in order to obtain the highest profit. Decision variables, therefore, are under the control of a decision maker and can be set at a desired level. Another kind of variable that is often encountered is an **uncontrollable variable.** An example would be the weather: Although it is beyond the control of a manager, weather sometimes is a factor that can have some bearing on profits. For instance, a mild, rainy winter can substantially reduce profits at ski resorts. Similarly, rainy weather and flooding can slow down a construction project. Other examples of uncontrollable variables include government decisions (for example, revision of the tax code, pollution regulations), competitors' decisions (e.g., product design, advertising, pricing), and consumer decisions.

Thus, models that are used for problem solving include constants, decision variables, and uncontrollable variables. The challenge for the manager or analyst who is developing a model is to determine the levels of the decision variables that will best serve the goals of the manager, given the constants and uncontrollable variables.

You may have realized by now that mathematical models are the ones most often used in management science. Iconic models are rarely used because they are not well suited to management science problems. Analog models, particularly graphs, are used sometimes, although much of that use pertains to instructional purposes rather than applications in practice. Graphs are especially useful for helping to convey various important concepts, although as problem-solving tools, they lack the generality needed to solve most large-scale problems. Even so, an analyst may use a graph to clarify a point relating to a model and then shift to a symbolic model to complete the analysis. Hence, the models used in this book will be a blend of mathematical and graphical models: The graphical models will help to illustrate important concepts and help you to develop an intuitive understanding of various models, whereas the mathematical models will enable you to determine solutions for a wide range of problems.

Benefits and Risks of Using Models

Models have numerous benefits for problem solvers, but there also are certain risks for the users. Obviously, the benefits generally must tend to outweigh the risks, or models would not be used.

An important benefit of using a model is that it allows an analyst to strip away many unimportant details of reality and thereby focus attention on a small number of important aspects of a problem. The risk in doing this is that one or more of the important aspects of a problem may be inadvertently left out. If this happens, it is highly unlikely that the analyst will be able to successfully solve the real-world problem using the model.

Another benefit of using quantitative models is that they force the analyst to quantify information. The risk is that nonquantitative information may be downplayed or ignored because it is difficult or impossible to include that type of information in a quantitative model.

A third benefit of models is the structure they provide for analyzing a problem in terms of what information is needed and how to organize information. One risk is that an inexperienced analyst may attempt to force a problem to fit the model. In effect, chances of obtaining a good solution would be diminished.

The process of developing a model can generate tremendous insight about reality. Care must be taken, however, so that modeling does not become an end in itself. In fact, it is easy to get carried away with modeling and to end up with a model that is more complex and powerful than what is needed to solve the problem.

Another benefit of models is that they compress time. They usually are also less costly than a real-life situation would be, and they permit users the luxury of experimentation without dangers that would be inherent in a real-life setting. However, due to their abstract nature, models sometimes do not adequately portray relationships that exist in reality. A consequence of this kind of error is that solutions obtained from the model fail under the harsh light of reality. One way to reduce this risk is to give careful consideration to the assumptions on which the model is based.

Assumptions of Models

All models are based on assumptions (that is, conditions that are assumed to exist). Some of these will be technical, such as "the relationship is linear;" others will be operational, such as "the budget is $25,000;" and still others may be political, such as "Marketing will support the proposal."

It is usually wise to write out the assumptions that can be identified before developing the model. This will increase the chances of developing a workable and acceptable model. Moreover, those who are in a position to approve or reject a solution (e.g., manager, customer, potential investor) may want to know what assumptions were made, why they were made, how realistic they are, and so on.

In terms of studying management science, assumptions in the technical category will be most relevant. As each new model is introduced, make note of the assumptions and what impact they have on the model. Recognize that many assumptions simplify; they reduce the complexity that would be inherent in reality. Using simplifying assumptions in practice always involves evaluating the trade-offs: The simpler the model, the easier it will be to understand and use it in order to obtain solutions, but the greater the risk will be that the solutions based on the model will not apply to reality.

Optimizing versus Predictive Models

Some models can be used to determine an optimal, or best, solution to a problem, whereas other models are used to predict approximate, or average, future outcomes. The choice between these two kinds of models depends primarily on the *degree of certainty* that can be assigned to the information available to the analyst.

Optimizing models are used for problems in which information is known with a high degree of certainty. For instance, in a problem involving production times, if the production times are known and are constant (that is, the same time is required for every repetition of the process), an optimizing model could be used to determine an optimal solution to the problem. Conversely, when it cannot be determined precisely what value will occur (usually in the future), a **predictive model** that incorporates *probabilities* is appropriate. For example, choosing the size of a warehouse to build depends on how large future demand will be. If, because of contractual commitments from a buyer, a manager knows what demand to plan for, an optimal size warehouse could be determined. However, such cases are quite rare. Instead, managers usually are faced with situations in which future demand is subject to variability (i.e., it cannot be predicted exactly, but only approximately). Then the goal is to minimize the error in predictions; without complete knowledge, it is virtually impossible to specify an optimal solution.

It should be noted that an optimal solution is generally optimal only in the context of a model and not necessarily in the larger context of reality. This is because all models are simplified versions of reality; that is, they do not and cannot incorporate all of the details and factors that comprise reality. Consequently, it is debatable whether any solution is truly optimal in the purest sense of the word. Therefore, when the term *optimal* is employed in this text, and in management science in general, it refers to the conditions contained in a mathematical model. This is not to say that optimal solutions are unacceptable in reality or that they are not good solutions. On the contrary, such solutions may not only be very good, they also may be much better than solutions generated in less scientific ways. Nonetheless, it would be incorrect to believe that optimal solutions obtained from models will be truly optimal when applied to reality. Because of this, a manager should review all but the most routine solutions before implementing them, and should decide whether to implement the solution as it stands or to first modify it because of some other subjective considerations.

THE MANAGEMENT SCIENCE APPROACH

Although management science incorporates quantitative analysis in its approach to problem solving, it would be a mistake to regard management science as merely a collection of techniques. It is as much a *philosophy* of problem solving as it is the use of quantitative methods.

The management science approach is quite similar to the **scientific approach** commonly used in the physical sciences. Both involve a logical sequence that includes careful definition of the problem, use of models, and analysis leading to solution of the problem. The management science approach is outlined in Figure 1–1.

Problem Definition

The first step in problem solving is *careful* problem definition. It is important to resist the temptation to rush through this stage in order to begin working on the

FIGURE 1-1 The Management Science Approach

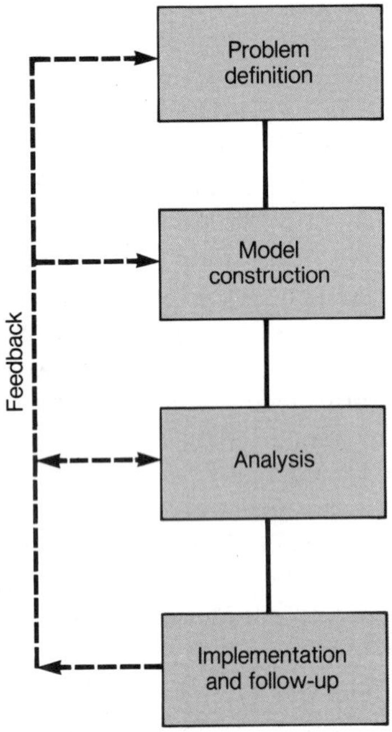

model and the solution. Unfortunately, exactly the opposite occurs in many cases. When that happens, the solution is less likely to solve the problem, and it may create additional problems. Furthermore, senior managers may become disillusioned in the process, and they may turn to other, less objective, methods for handling problems.

Good problem definition may involve observing a currrent situation or process in order to better understand it. Almost always, it is highly desirable to talk with the people who are closely involved (e.g., workers, supervisors, salespeople, staff). Not only do such people usually possess considerable knowledge and insight that enable them to suggest potential solutions, they also are the ones who must live with the solution. By including them in the process, they are less likely to resist the solution because they will feel that they contributed to it.

Once the problem has been reasonably defined, it is time to construct a model. However, it is wise to leave room for possible future redefinition of the problem. It is quite common to gain new insights and raise additional questions as modeling progresses. These often lead to refining, or even modifying, the initial problem definition.

Model Construction

The goal of modeling should be to achieve an accurate, yet relatively simple, representation of reality. Hence, the model should reflect the major aspects of the problem as simply as possible. Often, this requires trade-offs because simplicity and accuracy rarely go hand in hand. Therefore, the model builder must decide on an appropriate balance between a model that is highly accurate in its portrayal of reality (and consequently, complex) and one that is relatively simple. Usually, the more complex the model, the more costly and time-consuming it is to build and the more difficult it is to understand. Conversely, a model that is too simple may not provide an adequate portrayal of reality, thereby decreasing the chances of finding a reasonable solution to the problem. Ideally, a model will enable the analyst or manager to study a problem in a quasi-laboratory environment that will lead to a clearer understanding of the problem and a solution.

Although model building requires abstraction of reality, it is important to obtain accurate information about the problem. This may relate to production times, machine times, or other technical aspects of the problem. In many instances, this information will come from three main sources: the accounting department, those directly involved (for example, managers, other employees), and direct observation. After the model has been constructed, it is generally prudent to confirm the results with people who are more closely involved and to use common sense in evaluating the results before proceeding very far into the analysis stage. This will help to identify any inadequacies in the model.

One mistake that inexperienced model builders often make is failing to take a broad perspective of the problem. That is, they do not take into account other dimensions of reality that a solution may have an impact on. For instance, in dealing with the optimal capacity of a department, the model builder should include the ability to assess the impact that the capacity will have on *other* departments within the organization as well as on external factors (e.g., will the suppliers be able to meet the resulting demands on them?). To accomplish this broad perspective, a model builder should adopt a *systems approach* to model building and should focus not only on the immediate problem but also on the interrelationships that exist within and outside the organization and how these relationships will be affected.

An important aspect of model building is collecting and preparing data. Because information obtained from the data is the foundation for the model, errors or missed information can have a negative impact on the validity of model results.

Model Analysis

The nature of the analysis will depend on the type of model that is used. For instance, models that portray a situation that has a high degree of certainty lend themselves to *algorithms* (solution techniques) that generally help to identify optimal solutions. However, in some instances, no algorithms exist for identifying optimal solutions. Instead, *search techniques* may be used to identify acceptable solutions. In less certain situations, models may be used to identify approximate solutions.

In order to identify optimal or acceptable solutions, the analyst uses a **measure of effectiveness** such as profit, revenue, time, or cost to evaluate alternative solutions. Thus, if profit is the measure of effectiveness, the solution chosen will be the one that is projected to yield the highest profit. The measure of effectiveness that is used usually will come from the objective of the manager who is responsible for solving the problem. If the objective is not obvious or known, it will be necessary to solicit it from the manager or other appropriate person.

Very often, the size of a problem and its computational requirements necessitate using a computer. Consequently, the user of a management science model usually will become involved with examining and interpreting computer output. Therefore, in order to be successful, the manager or other analyst must understand the basics of such techniques as well as how to interpret computer output.

An important part of model analysis, whether done manually or by using a computer, is determining how sensitive a particular solution is to changes in one or more of the constants in the model. This is referred to as **sensitivity analysis.** A manager can use sensitivity analysis to learn if changes in the values of certain constants used in the model will have any effect on the solution, and if so, what that effect would be. One reason for examining possible changes is that the manager has acquired new information indicating that the value of a constant may be different than that used in the model, and the manager wants to know if that will change the results. Another reason for using sensitivity analysis is to answer "What if . . . ?" type questions. For example, a manager may be able to purchase an additional amount of some raw material used in a production process. The question is, would it be profitable to obtain additional amounts of the raw material, and if so, how much?

Implementation and Follow-Up

Once an appropriate solution has been identified, it must be implemented. This may involve reporting the recommended solution to the appropriate manager (e.g., the manager who requested the analysis) or it may mean making a presentation to senior managers (i.e., selling it to them). Presentations of results based on quantitative models to senior managers can seem more difficult than the analysis itself. One reason is that these people often ask probing questions. Another is that they have the power to approve or reject the solution. One obstacle that can be encountered is that senior managers may lack quantitative skills. This means that the presenter must explain the model and the results in layman's terms, a feat some find difficult. For these reasons, it is wise to carefully prepare the presentation lest all the work that preceded it be in vain.

Not all solutions will be implemented. Some, of course, will be judged as not solving the problem. Others may be judged as too costly or they may be unacceptable for other reasons. One other reason might be that the goals of management have changed during the problem-solving interval. For instance, a new manager who has different experiences, priorities, and perspectives may have replaced the previous manager. Then too, certain aspects of the problem may have changed (for example, there may be new or different constraints, different legal requirements, new technology, and so on). In some cases, the problem may have corrected itself, or the organization may have decided to abandon that phase of the operation.

If a solution is implemented, it is important to carefully monitor that implementation. One reason for this is to make sure that the recommended solution is applied correctly. Consider the advice of a physician: "Take two every four hours." Unfortunately, the patient takes *four* every *two* hours and ends up in the emergency room. Also, the solution could be implemented correctly but the desired results may not be realized. This usually will require that the user investigate the cause or causes. A reasonable checklist would include questions such as: Were there mistakes in the implementation? Did the analysis support the solution? Was the analysis correct? Were there errors in the model? Was the problem correctly and completely defined?

In some cases, only minor corrections will be needed to achieve the desired results, whereas in other cases, major reworking will be called for. The chances of needing major reworking will be less if each step of the management science process is given careful attention. Continuing feedback at every phase of the process can help uncover inadequacies that can then be corrected, thereby avoiding such pitfalls as working on the wrong problem, working with an incorrect model, using misleading data, and so on. Feedback allows for continual evaluation and corrective action throughout the process.

COMPUTERS IN MANAGEMENT SCIENCE

Computers are an important tool in management science. The use of quantitative models lends itself to computerized solutions. Moreover, the nature of many management science models is such that substantial calculations are required to solve everyday problems. Consequently, illustration and discussion of computer output will be covered throughout the book where appropriate.

It is important to recognize that for instructional purposes, manual solutions are demonstrated in each chapter. These will provide you with a basic understanding of the important concepts related to the various models that are discussed and insights on how the models can be used to generate solutions. Both are important parts to the learning process. Hence, it is important to devote a reasonable amount of time and energy to manual solutions. Once you have mastered the important concepts of a model, you will be in a better position to use and *understand* computer output.

TABLE 1–1 Overview of the Book

Chapter	Title	Brief Description
Part I	**Linear Programming**	
2	Introduction to Linear Programming	Covers basics of linear programming: What it is. How to recognize problems and formulate models.
3	Linear Programming: Graphical Solutions	How to solve simple linear programming problems graphically.
4	Linear Programming: The Simplex Method	How to set up and solve linear programming problems using the general-purpose simplex algorithm, and how to interpret computer output.
5	Simplex: Maximization with Mixed Constraints and Minimization	How to set up and solve maximization problems that have mixed constraints and minimization problems.
6	Postoptimality Analysis	Sensitivity analysis of linear programming models. Shows how to determine the impact of potential changes to a linear programming model on the optimal solution.
7	Transportation and Assignment Problems	Two special-purpose linear programming models.
8	Integer Programming	How to obtain optimal solutions when decision variables are restricted to integer values.
9	Goal Programming	How to handle problems with multiple objectives (goal programming).
Part II	**Decision Theory**	
10	Decision Theory	A general approach for handling problems that have multiple alternatives and a discrete set of possible outcomes.
Part III	**Forecasting and Inventory Models**	
11	Forecasting	Describes basic forecasting techniques.
12	Inventory Models I	Introduces basic concepts of inventory management, shows how to determine optimum order sizes and when to reorder inventory.
13	Inventory Models II	Covers special inventory models and describes methods used by Japanese manufacturers.
Part IV	**Network Models**	
14	Networks	Models used to find shortest routes to multiple locations or the maximum possible flow through a system.
15	PERT/CPM	Describes methods used to plan projects.
Part V	**Stochastic Models**	
16	Queuing Models	Analysis of waiting lines.
17	Simulation	Describes an important class of models that can be used to help managers answer "What if . . . ?" questions.
18	Markov Analysis	Covers special purpose analysis of systems intended to reveal both short-term and long-term behavior.
Part VI	**Calculus Methods**	
19	Calculus-Based Optimization	Optimization of nonlinear models.
Part VII	**Decision Making and Information Systems**	
20	Decision Making and Information Systems	Describes computerized information systems that combine a database and model and have the capability for generating management reports.

PLAN OF THE BOOK

The book is organized into seven parts.

Table 1–1 provides a brief overview of the parts and chapters.

MANAGEMENT SCIENCE IN PRACTICE

Management science techniques are widely used in today's businesses. A number of surveys have revealed the extent of usage and the importance assigned to the usefulness of management science tools by managers.

One such survey was conducted by Shannon, Long, and Buckles. They surveyed individuals in universities, government, and industry on the extent of usage, and the importance for decision making, of various management science techniques. Table 1–2 summarizes a portion of their results. Not all of the techniques they surveyed in their study correspond to the techniques described in this book. Those that did not apply were not listed in the first column of the table. Consequently, the utility ranks for the unlisted techniques are not represented.

The results show that techniques such as linear programming and simulation are used very often, and that these two techniques are ranked the highest in terms of their usefulness. Moreover, most of the techniques are widely used.

Other surveys have found similar results. Moreover, experience suggests that these techniques are being increasingly integrated into the managerial decision process. And increasingly, computers and statistical analysis are being used at all levels of organizations.

The implication of these results is that quantitative tools and computers are becoming increasingly important factors in decision making, so that it behooves decision makers to be well grounded in understanding and using them.

TABLE 1–2 Survey Results on the Usage and Importance of Management Science Techniques

Technique	Usage (percent)	Utility (rank)
Linear programming	84%	2
Simulation	80	1
Network analysis	58	4
Queuing theory	55	7
Decision trees	55	3
Integer programming	39	6
Dynamic programming	32	11
Markov analysis	32	10
Goal programming	20	8

Source: Adapted from *AIIE Transactions,* December 1980. Copyright Institute of Industrial Engineers, 25 Technology Park/Atlanta, Norcross, GA 30092. Printed by permission.

MANAGER DIALOGUE

At the beginning of this chapter, a baking company that supplied near-finished baked goods to supermarkets was described. The owner, Bob Doyle, wondered if the use of management science techniques would be desirable given the rate at which the company was growing. What follows is part of a conversation Bob had with the leader of a seminar he attended, Ann Marie.

Bob: I really enjoyed the seminar, and I was amazed at the wide variety of applications of management science techniques. It seems as if my firm could really benefit from using them, but I wonder if I am being overly optimistic about what these techniques can accomplish.

Ann: I'm not sure exactly what you are saying. Could you elaborate a bit?

Bob: Well, for one thing, I've been managing so far without any knowledge of these techniques, and the business has been fairly successful. My dad used to say, "If it ain't broken, don't fix it." So maybe by trying to use these techniques, I'll end up actually making things worse instead of better.

Ann: It's been my experience that small firms tend to be able to operate successfully if their owners or managers are good, intuitive, decision makers. I think it is because the business is small enough that they can manage the entire operation by themselves. However, in larger companies, or when small firms expand, the operation is too large to be managed by one person. The complexities of operations of larger firms tend to diminish the value of purely intuitive decision making, and that is where management science tools can really help managers to make good decisions.

Bob: And my firm may be at that point now. But I wonder, is it really necessary to use computers, or can these techniques be performed manually?

Ann: Let me answer you in this way. It is certainly possible to do most of the computations manually. In fact, for my consulting firm, all of my people go through a training program that requires them to perform computations manually to insure that they fully understand how the techniques generate solutions to problems. However, most problems they become involved with are fairly large, meaning that manual computations would not be feasible. Moreover, we have computer

SUMMARY

Management science is the discipline devoted to the solution of management problems using a scientific approach. The focus is on problem solving using quantitative models. The approach is to define the problem, construct a model that reflects the important aspects of the problem, analyze the model to identify an

(concluded)

packages that can handle computations for all of the management science techniques I mentioned in my seminar. And they are so quick and easy to use that there is no need to do any manual computations. Having said that, it seems to me that in your case, you might want to explore using some of these techiques in your company using manual methods just to get an idea of how they work, and to integrate them into your decision making. Then, if you do decide to go that route on a larger scale, you can obtain software for your personal computer that will enable you to use the techniques that are best suited for your problems.

Bob: That sounds great, but I also wonder about surrendering decision making to a computer. I worry about losing control.

Ann: Well, that is a mistake that occurs all too often; people think that a computer can, and even should, in some cases, make decisions. But that is not how computers, or even management science techniques, should be used. Instead, these are tools to *help* make better decisions, not to actually *make* the decisions. That remains the responsibility of the manager. Computers help by removing the burden of calculations; they are quick and efficient, and don't make errors in computations. Management science techniques provide structure that can help managers to better understand complex problems and guide their problem solving. But it is not always possible or practical to include all the information that is available to a manager in a model. Consequently, when a manager obtains a solution using a management science technique, with or without the use of a computer, the manager must decide whether to implement that exact solution, or modify it slightly to allow for other factors, or even to reject the solution and return to the drawing board, so to speak. So, you can see, the manager remains very much the main player in decision making.

Other than that, I have one additional suggestion, which is for you to think carefully about where in your decision-making process you really feel the need for help, and to then explore the use of management science models in those areas. In other words, try to use the tools where they will truly help decision making, and not just for the sake of using them.

appropriate solution to the problem, implement the solution, and check to see that the problem has been solved.

The core of management science is the scientific approach to problem solving. An important part of this is the use of quantitative models. Models are abstractions of reality: Ideally, a model will capture the important aspects of a situation without including all of the minor details that would increase complexity and, thereby, reduce the chances of finding a solution to the problem.

There are a variety of model types that are employed in decision-making environments; management science models fall under the heading of symbolic models (that is, numbers and symbols are used to form mathematical models). Using these models tends to be a more objective approach than using qualitative models, although in symbolic models the more important qualitative aspects of a problem may be ignored. Furthermore, quantitative models enable users to take advantage of the tremendous computational abilities of computers and calculators.

GLOSSARY

Analog Model A model that substitutes certain physical properties for actual properties, such as using distance to represent time.

Decision Variable A variable whose value can be set by a decision maker; the purpose of modeling is to determine appropriate values for decision variables.

Deterministic Model A model in which all numerical values are known with certainty.

Iconic Model A physical model that looks like the entity it represents (e.g., a miniature boat).

Management Science A discipline devoted to the use of quantitative models for solving managerial-type problems.

Measure of Effectiveness A basis for evaluating the desirability of a particular solution. Common measures include profits, costs, and revenues.

Mathematical Model A symbolic model; uses numbers and symbols.

Model A selective abstraction of reality.

Optimizing Model A model that is intended to find the best solution to a problem.

Predictive Model A model used to predict future outcomes, often in terms of an expected outcome plus a range of probable variation for that outcome.

Probabilistic Model A model that incorporates probability to reflect inherent randomness in certain variables.

Scientific Approach A logical approach to problem solving that includes defining the problem, constructing a model, analyzing the model, and solving and implementing the solution.

Sensitivity Analysis Determining the degree to which possible changes in various model dimensions will affect the result of model analysis.

Symbolic Model A model that uses numbers and algebraic symbols to represent selected aspects of reality.

Uncontrollable Variable A variable that influences the results of a model, but one that cannot be controlled by the analyst.

Variable A portion of a model that can take on different values (e.g., the speed of a vehicle, the number of newspapers sold per day).

DISCUSSION AND REVIEW QUESTIONS

1. Explain what is meant by the term *management science.*
2. Suppose you have just been hired by a small firm. Ater being on the job for a few weeks, you realize that most problem solving is done on an informal basis—quantitative models are not being used. You share your reservations about this with your manager, and after a certain amount of discussion, your manager asks you to outline your reasoning on why the firm should adopt a more quantitative approach to problem solving. What would the main points of your response be?
3. Suppose that senior management has asked you to give a presentation that will enlighten them on the use of models for problem solving. Specifically, they want to know what a model is, what types of models there are, how models can lead to good solutions, and any potential pitfalls to be aware of. Outline your presentation.
4. You are faced with making a choice between two models. One is a fairly simple model that will provide an approximate answer to the problem; the other is a much more complex model that can be expected to provide a much more precise answer to the problem.
   a. Under what circumstances would you choose the simple model?
   b. Under what circumstances would the more sophisticated model be your choice?
5. Briefly describe the management science approach to problem solving.
6. Briefly describe the following model types and give an example of each: iconic, analog, and symbolic.
7. Contrast *optimizing* and *predictive* models, and indicate the conditions under which each type would be appropriate.
8. How would you respond to a student who says, ''Why should I have to study management science, my major is marketing?''
9. Suppose that after a considerable amount of time and effort, the solution obtained from a model is not implemented.
   a. List some possible reasons for this.
   b. Would you say that the time and effort was, therefore, probably wasted? Explain your answer.
10. What does the phrase ''modeling can become an end in itself'' mean? Is this necessarily bad?
11. Why might a solution that is optimal in a model not be optimal in reality? How might the gap be closed? What risks might there be in attempting to close the gap?
12. How and why are computers an integral part of management science?

Chapter 1 Supplement
Break-Even Analysis

Supplement Outline

Learning Objectives

After completing this supplement, you should be able to:

1. Describe the basic nature of break-even analysis.
2. List, and briefly explain, each of the components of break-even analysis.
3. Explain how break-even analysis can be useful to management.
4. List the assumptions of the break-even model.
5. Solve typical problems.

INTRODUCTION

One of the simplest quantitative models used by managers is the break-even model. Break-even analysis, which is sometimes referred to as cost-volume analysis, is concerned with the interrelationship of costs, volume (quantity of output or sales), and profit. Break-even analysis provides managers with answers to questions such as:

1. What profit can be expected if sales are 6,000 units this month?
2. Would it be profitable to produce this product if annual demand is 50,000 units?
3. How many units must be sold in order to cover costs?
4. What costs will result if 3,000 units are made?

The basic relationship that underlies break-even analysis is summarized by the following formula:

$$\text{Profit} = \text{Total revenue} - \text{Total cost} \qquad (1S\text{–}1)$$

We can see from this equation that profit will be positive if total revenue exceeds total cost, and negative (a loss) if total cost exceeds total revenue. If total revenue and total cost are equal, profit will be zero; the organization will just "break even."

COMPONENTS OF BREAK-EVEN ANALYSIS

In order to understand break-even analysis, it is necessary to understand the components of the analysis: volume, revenue, and cost.

Volume

Volume is the level of output of a machine, department, or organization, or the quantity of sales. Generally, it is expressed as the *number of units* that are produced or sold, although occasionally, it is expressed in terms of dollar volume (e.g., sales of $32,000).

Revenue

Revenue is the income generated by the sale of a product. **Total revenue** is equal to the revenue per unit (selling price per unit) multiplied by the number of units (volume) sold. Thus, if revenue per unit is $10 and the volume sold is 2,000 units, the total revenue is $10(2,000) = $20,000.

If the selling price per unit remains the same regardless of the number sold (i.e., there are no quantity discounts), then total revenue will increase linearly as volume increases. A graph of total revenue is illustrated in Figure 1S–1.

FIGURE 1S–1 Total Revenue Increases Linearly as Volume Increases

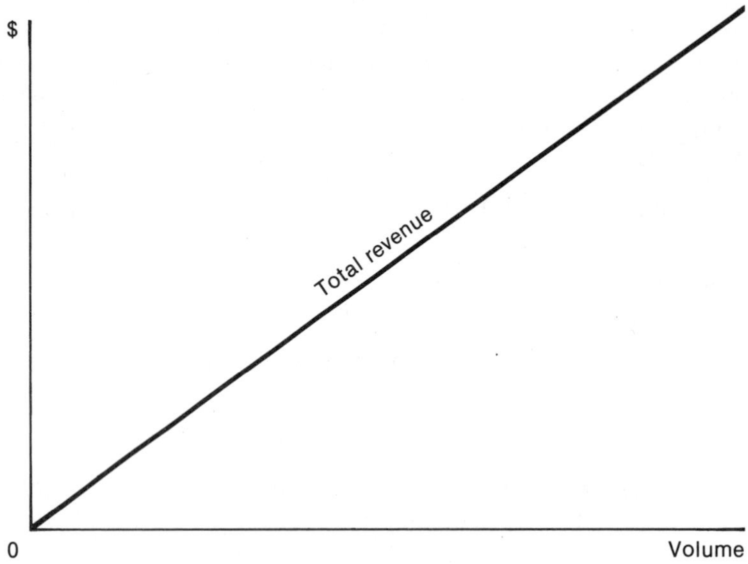

Costs

There are usually a number of different costs that must be taken into account in order to determine profit. A useful way of thinking about them is by classifying them either as *fixed* or *variable*. **Fixed costs** are costs that are not related (at least within reasonable limits) to the volume of output. Consequently, fixed costs remain the same regardless of volume. Examples of fixed costs include such expenses as:

- Rent/leasing costs for plant and equipment.
- Administrative costs.
- Heat, light, and air conditioning.
- Maintenance.
- Janitorial services.
- Insurance.
- Depreciation on plant and equipment.

Fixed costs are the sum of these and other costs that do not vary with level of output. Figure 1S–2 illustrates fixed costs.

FIGURE 1S-2 Fixed Costs

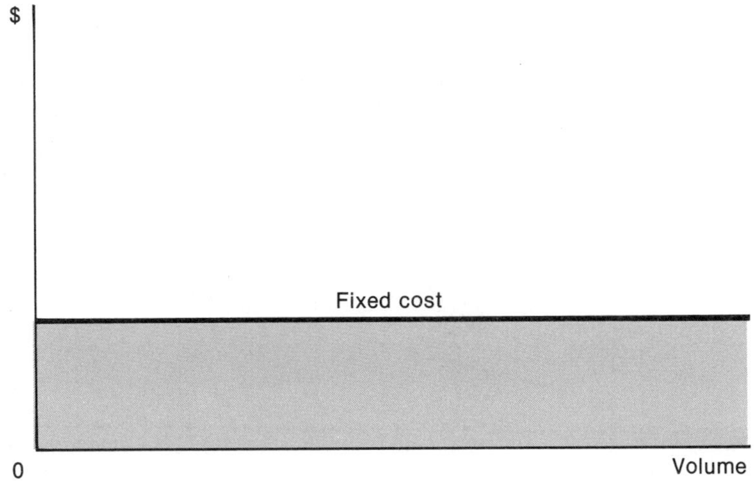

Variable costs are expenses that vary with volume; each unit produced requires certain inputs (e.g., material) that add to the cost. Typical examples of variable costs include such expenses as:

- Raw materials and purchased parts.
- Direct labor.
- Packaging and shipping costs.

Total variable cost is equal to the product of variable cost per unit and the volume that is produced. Thus, if the variable cost per unit is \$5 and the volume is 2,000 units, the total variable cost is \$5(2,000) = \$10,000. Total variable cost is illustrated in Figure 1S-3.

Total cost is the sum of fixed cost and total variable cost. Thus, if fixed cost *for the period during which the 2,000 units were produced* was \$7,000, then total cost (*TC*) would be:

$$TC = \$7,000 + \$5(2,000) = \$17,000$$

The computation of total cost is summarized by the following formula:

$$TC = F + VQ \quad \text{(1S-2)}$$

FIGURE 1S–3 Total Variable Cost

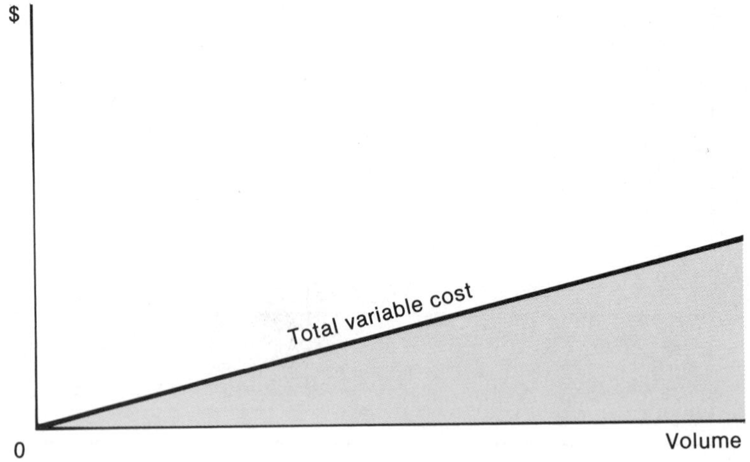

where

F = fixed cost assigned
V = variable cost per unit
Q = volume or quantity

Total cost is illustrated in Figure 1S–4.

Profit

Recall that profit is the difference between total revenue and total cost. Using the preceding illustrations where

Fixed cost	=	\$7,000
Total variable cost	=	\$10,000
Total revenue	=	\$20,000

we can determine that profit is \$3,000:

$$\begin{aligned} \text{Profit} &= \text{Total revenue} - (\text{Fixed cost} + \text{Total variable cost}) \\ &= \$20{,}000 - (\$7{,}000 + \$10{,}000) \\ &= \$3{,}000 \end{aligned} \qquad (1S\text{–}3)$$

We can write Equation 1S–3 in a slightly different form in order to clearly indicate how each of the components is included in the computation of profit:

FIGURE 1S–4

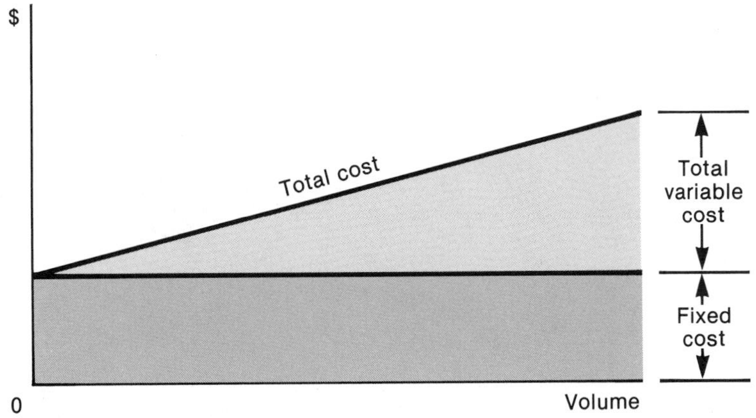

$$\text{Profit} = RQ - (F + VQ) \tag{1S–4}$$

where

R = revenue per unit
Q = quantity or volume
V = variable cost per unit
F = fixed cost assigned

Figure 1S–5 incorporates total revenue and total cost on the same graph. Note that profit is the vertical difference between the total revenue line and the total cost line for any given volume. Moreover, notice that if total cost exceeds total revenue, there is a loss (negative profit). If total cost and total revenue are equal, profit is zero. The volume or quantity at which that occurs is called the break-even point (BEP).

THE BREAK-EVEN POINT

The **break-even point (BEP)** is the volume for which total revenue and total cost are equal. Knowledge of that volume is useful because it reveals to management where the dividing line is between profit and loss; a volume of sales that is higher than the break-even point will result in a profit, while a volume of sales that is lower than the break-even point will result in a loss.

FIGURE 1S–5 Profit and the Break-Even Point

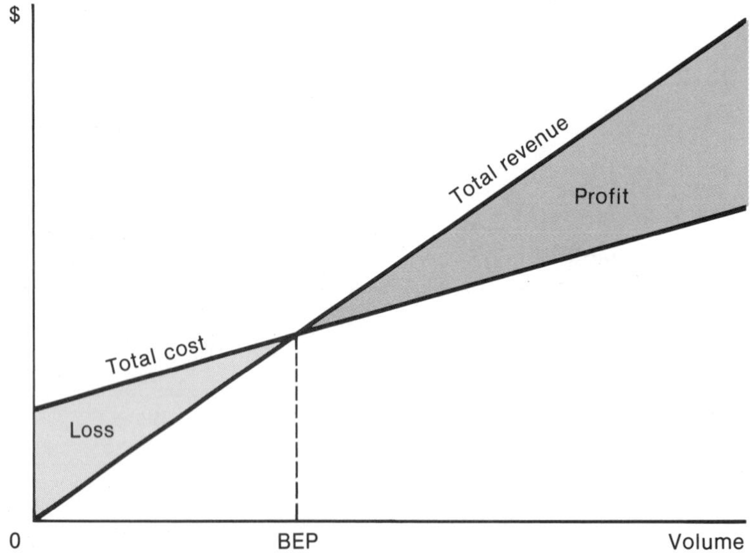

We can obtain an expression that will enable us to calculate the break-even quantity by turning to Formula 1S–4. If we set profit equal to zero and then solve for Q, we have an expression for the break-even point:

$$Q_{\text{BEP}} = \frac{F}{R - V} \tag{1S–5}$$

■

EXAMPLE Given this information on costs and revenue:

F = \$60,000
V = \$20 per unit
R = \$30 per unit

determine each of the following:

a. Profit (loss) at a volume of 5,000 units
b. Profit (loss) at a volume of 10,000 units.
c. The break-even point.

Solution

Profit = $RQ - (F + VQ)$

a. Q = 5,000 units.

Profit = \$30(5,000) − [\$60,000 + \$20(5,000)] = −\$10,000

Hence, there is a loss of \$10,000; total cost exceeds total revenue by that amount.

b. Q = 10,000 units.

Profit = \$30(10,000) − [\$60,000 + \$20(10,000)] = \$40,000

c. $$Q_{BEP} = \frac{F}{R - V} = \frac{\$60{,}000}{\$30 \text{ per unit} - \$20 \text{ per unit}} = 6{,}000 \text{ units}$$

Hence, if 6,000 units are sold, revenues will just cover costs; if a smaller quantity is sold, there will be a loss, but if a larger quantity is sold, there will be a profit.

ASSUMPTIONS OF BREAK-EVEN ANALYSIS

The appropriateness of any model in a given situation depends on how well the assumptions of the model are satisfied by the situation. In the case of the break-even model, the key assumptions are:

1. The revenue per unit is the same for all volumes. This would not be the case if quantity discounts caused revenue per unit to decrease as the quantity sold increased.
2. The variable cost per unit is the same for all volumes. This would not be the case if learning was a factor, so that the labor cost per unit decreased as the level of production increased.
3. Fixed cost is the same for all levels of volume. This would not be the case if a volume was called for that exceeded current capacity, so that additional capacity at a different fixed cost had to be added.
4. Only one product is involved. This is a simplifying assumption that avoids having to combine revenues and costs for multiple items.
5. All output is sold. This means that the volume used to compute total revenue is the same as the volume used to compute total variable cost. If this assumption is not met, we must be careful to use each volume as appropriate in computing profit.
6. All relevant costs have been accounted for, and have been correctly assigned to either the fixed cost category or the variable cost category.

SUMMARY

Break-even analysis focuses on the interrelationship among cost, revenue, volume of sales, and profit. It is useful to managers in a number of ways, but particularly in helping to identify the level of sales for which total revenue will cover total cost. More generally, break-even formulas can be used to answer "What if . . . ?" questions related to selection of a level of volume of output and/or sales.

GLOSSARY

Break-Even Point The volume of sales for which total revenue equals total cost; profit is zero at the break-even point.

Fixed Costs Costs that do not vary with the level of output or sales. An example would be monthly rent on a facility.

Revenue Income received from sale of a product or service.

Total Revenue Revenue per unit multiplied by number of units sold.

Total Variable Cost Variable cost per unit multiplied by the number of units produced.

Variable Costs Costs associated with producing units of a product (e.g., typewriters) that are related to the number of units produced. Typical examples are labor and materials costs.

Volume The quantity of units produced and/or sold.

PROBLEMS

1. The Exxoff Corporation produces an automotive lubricant that is sold to wholesale distributors for $25 a case. Fixed costs are $80,000 and variable costs are $15 per case.
   a. What profit or loss would result if 4,000 cases are sold?
   b. What profit or loss would result if 10,000 cases are sold?
   c. What is the break-even volume in cases?
2. The Greene Daisy Company offers a spring tune-up service for power lawn mowers at a price of $24.95. Labor and supplies cost an average of $10 per tune-up, and overhead charged to the operation is $5,000 a month. Determine:
   a. The monthly volume needed to break even.
   b. The profit that would result if 375 tune-ups are performed per month.

3. A company that produces cleaning products is considering a proposal to begin production of a new detergent that would cost $1 a bottle to make and distribute, and retail for $2.19 a bottle. Fixed cost for the operation would be $3,000 a week. Assume that all output can be sold.
   a. What would the total cost, total revenue, and profit (or loss) be for a weekly volume of 10,000 bottles?
   b. What is the break-even volume?

4. Fast-Lube operates a chain of shops that offer a 20-minute oil change and lubrication service for passenger cars and light trucks. The shops have an overhead of $1,000 per day. Labor and materials cost $5 per job, and customers are charged $19.95 for the service. Determine:
   a. The number of jobs per day that a shop needs in order to cover all of its costs.
   b. The profit or loss that would result if 35 cars were serviced in a day.
   c. Suppose two workers work together in a shop and each receives $20 a day in pay and benefits plus $1 per job, and material costs $3 per job, what is the break-even volume for the shop? (Hint: $20 is a fixed cost.)

5. Schmaltz, Ltd., produces a variety of specialty beverages. One of its products is made in a separate facility for which monthly rent, administrative costs, and equipment leasing is $80,000. The facility has a monthly capacity of 50,000 cases of the specialty beverage. Eight workers handle production and shipping. Each receives salary and fringe benefits of $2,500 per month. Packaging and distribution costs are $.30 per case, and ingredients cost $1.10 per case. The product is sold for $5.89 a case. Determine the following:
   a. The profit or loss on sales of 40,000 cases.
   b. The break-even volume. Hint: note carefully which costs are truly variable.
   c. The profit or loss that would result from sales of 60,000 cases.

6. Lamb, Stew is a fledgling catering firm that serves the meat-and-potato segment of the market. The co-owners want to expand their successful operations to include a neighboring town. After investigating their options, they have narrowed their choices to two. One option is to have a capacity of 10 events per month. This would result in a cost of $1,600 a month plus a cost of $250 per event. The other option would have a capacity of 20 events per month, a cost of $3,200 a month, and a cost of $200 per event. The firm would charge $450 for each event.
   a. Determine the break-even volume for each option.
   b. What profit (or loss) would each option produce if monthly demand is 10 events?
   c. If monthly demand is 14 events, which option would yield the greater profit?

7. The construction firm of Smagglewhetsy & Kid must decide whether to continue to perform payroll functions in-house or to subcontract those services. In-house costs are $2,000 a month plus $30 per employee. The same services can be performed by a contractor for $50 per employee plus a monthly service fee of $1,200.

   a. If the construction firm has 30 employees, which option would provide the lowest cost?

   b. Suppose the firm is undergoing an expansion, adding two new employees to its payroll each month. At this rate, in how many months should the firm consider doing its own payroll?

8. The law firm of Smith, Jones, Greene, Smith-Jones, Browne, White, Peabody, Jones-White, & Greene-Peabody provides accounting services for some of its clients. The person who handles this service and her secretary cost the firm an average of $80,000 a year in salary and benefits. Clients are charged a fixed rate of $300 a year for these services, and the firm is billed $50 per client for computer time, postage, and supplies. Now, a local acounting firm has offered to provide comparable service for a fee of $600 per client.

   a. What profit or loss would the firm realize if 300 clients use its accounting service each year?

   b. Assuming 300 clients a year, would the law firm be better off using its own staff, or using the outside accounting firm?

   c. At what level of client usage would the two alternatives produce the same profit?

Part I
Linear Programming

The chapters in Part I cover one of the most widely used, and most powerful, tools of management science: *linear programming*. Linear programming models are used to find optimal solutions to a special class of management science problems known as *constrained optimization:* finding the best solution to a problem given certain constraints in the problem that must be satisfied by the solution.

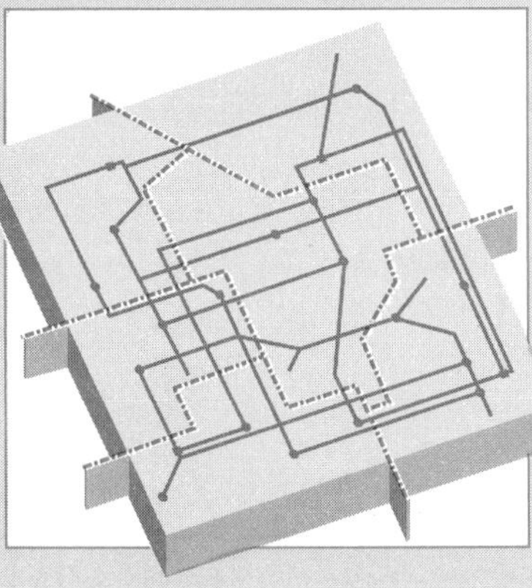

The part begins with a general introduction to the topic of linear programming, including terminology, the use of linear programming models, and the formulation of models. Graphical solutions to simple linear programming problems, with a supplement on graphical sensitivity analysis, follows. The simplex method, a general-purpose, algebraic technique for solving linear programming problems, is discussed. Other linear programming aspects covered are computer solutions; dual and sensitivity analysis of solutions; the special-purpose transportation and assignment models; integer programming techniques, used when optimal integer solutions to problems are needed; and goal programming.

Part Outline

Chapter 2
Introduction to Linear Programming

Chapter Outline

Learning Objectives

After completing this chapter, you should be able to:

1. Explain what is meant by the term *constrained optimization.*
2. Explain what *linear programming* is.
3. List and briefly explain the components and the assumptions of linear programming models.
4. Recognize problems that can be solved using linear programming models.
5. Formulate linear programming models.
6. Describe several problem types that lend themselves to solutions using linear programming models.

The manager of a company that assembles computer equipment and computers is about to begin production of two new microcomputers. Each type of microcomputer will require assembly time, inspection time, and storage space. The amounts of these resources that can be allocated daily to microcomputers is limited. The manager would like to be able to determine how many of each type of microcomputer to produce each day in order to maximize the profits obtained from the sale of these computers. The manager wonders if linear programming can be used to solve this problem.

INTRODUCTION

This chapter begins our coverage of linear programming, which is one of the most popular tools of management science. Linear programming (LP) models enable users to find optimal solutions to certain problems in which the solution must satisfy a given set of requirements, or constraints.

The purpose of this chapter is to provide you with an introduction to linear programming models. Emphasis is placed on familiarization with terminology, problem recognition, model formulation, and examples of applications of linear programming. The chapter is designed to help you to develop two very important skills:

1. The ability to *recognize* problems that can be solved using LP models.
2. The ability to set up, or *formulate,* an LP model in mathematical terms.

Constrained Optimization

A commonly encountered form of decision making involves situations in which the set of acceptable solutions is somehow restricted. The restrictions may be imposed internally or externally. For example, an internal restriction might be the amount of raw material that a department has available to produce its products. This would impose a limit on the amount of product that could be produced. Other internal restrictions can include availability of labor time, machine time, technical requirements (for example, drying times, curing times), and budgets. An external restriction might be labor regulations (e.g., safety equipment, training requirements, overtime) that limit the options open to decision makers.

The restrictions are referred to as *constraints* for purposes of linear programming. The goal in linear programming is to find the best solution given the constraints imposed by the problem; hence, the term **constrained optimization.**

Linear Programming

In 1947, George Dantzig developed the use of linear algebra for determining solutions to problems that involved the optimal allocation of scarce resources. In spite of numerous potential applications in business, response to this new technique was low, primarily because of the substantial computational burden it required. Subsequent advances that were made during the last three decades in computer technology and related computer software have removed the computational burden. This has led to widespread use of linear programming in business.

Although computers often are used to solve linear programming problems, computer programming is not required to obtain computer solutions: Preprogrammed packages are used that require the user to input the problem. The *programming* aspect of linear programming refers to the use of *algorithms*. An **algorithm** is a well-defined sequence of steps that will lead to a solution. The term *linear* refers to straight-line relationships. LP models are based on linear relationships. Taken as a whole, the term **linear programming** refers to a family of mathematical techniques that can be used to find solutions to constrained optimization problems.

LINEAR PROGRAMMING MODELS

Linear programming models are mathematical representations of LP problems. Some models have a specialized format, whereas others have a more generalized format. In this chapter, the generalized format is discussed. Later chapters will cover specialized formats.

Linear programming models have certain characteristics in common. Knowledge of these characteristics enables us to recognize problems that are amenable to a solution using LP models. Moreover, that same knowledge is necessary for us to be able to correctly formulate an LP model. Thus, it is essential to understand the characteristics of LP models. The characteristics can be grouped into two categories: components and assumptions. The components relate to the structure of a model, whereas the assumptions reveal the conditions under which the model is valid. The characteristics are listed in Table 2–1. A discussion of the charac-

TABLE 2–1 Characteristics of LP Models

Components	
1. Objective 2. Decision variables 3. Constraints 4. Parameters	Model structure
Assumptions	
1. Proportionality 2. Additivity 3. Divisibility 4. Certainty 5. Non-negativity	Model validity

teristics will provide insight into the nature of linear programming problems and models.

Components of LP Models

The *objective* in problem solving is the criterion by which all decisions are evaluated. As such, it provides the focus for problem solving.

In linear programming models, a single, *quantifiable* objective must be specified by the decision maker. For example, the objective might relate to profits, *or* costs, *or* market share, but to only *one* of these. Moreover, because we are dealing with optimization, the objective will be either maximization or minimization. Hence, every LP problem will be either a maximization (max) problem or a minimization (min) problem. Maximization problems often involve profit, revenue, market share, or return on investment, whereas minimization problems often involve cost, time, or distance. Once the objective is specified, it becomes the measure of effectiveness against which alternate solutions are judged. For example, the optimal solution will be the one that yields the highest profit or the one that provides the lowest cost.

The decision maker can control the value of the objective, which is achieved through choices in the levels of **decision variables.** Decision variables represent choices available to a decision maker, usually with respect to the amount or *quantity* of either an input to a process or an output from a process. For instance, a problem may involve maximizing the profit obtained from the sale of three products, each with its own unit profit (i.e., profit per unit). If we assume that all the output can be sold, the problem facing the decision maker is to determine how much of each product to produce in order to obtain the greatest profit. In terms of the LP model, the decision variables represent those unknown quantities.

The ability of a decision maker to select values of the decision variables in an LP program is subject to certain restrictions or limits. These can come from a variety of sources. The restrictions may reflect availabilities of resources (e.g., raw materials, labor time, machine time, work space, or storage space), legal or contractual requirements (e.g., product or work standards), technological requirements (e.g., necessary compressive strength or tensile strength), or they may reflect other limits based on forecasts, customer orders, company policies, and so on. In an LP model, the restrictions are referred to as **constraints.** Only solutions that satisfy all constraints in a model are acceptable. These are referred to as **feasible solutions.** The **optimal solution** is the feasible solution that yields the best value in terms of the objective.

An LP model consists of a mathematical statement of the objective, called the **objective function,** and a set of mathematical statements of the restrictions (the constraints). The objective function and the constraints consist of symbols that represent the decision variables (for example, x_1, x_2, x_3) and numerical values called **parameters.** The parameters are fixed values that specify the impact that one unit of each decision variable will have on the objective and on any constraint it pertains to as well as to the numerical value of each constraint. For example, if the profit per unit on Product 1 is $4, the 4 is a parameter. Similarly, if each unit of Product 1 requires 1.5 hours of labor, the 1.5 is a parameter. And, if there are 200 hours of labor available, the 200 is also a parameter.

The components are the building blocks of an LP model. We can better understand their meaning by examining a simple LP model. Example 1 illustrates such a model.

■

EXAMPLE 1 This simple example illustrates the components of LP models.

Decision variables:
x_1 = quantity of Product 1
x_2 = quantity of Product 2
x_3 = quantity of Product 3

maximize $4x_1 + 7x_2 + 5x_3$ (profit) ← Objective function

subject to

1	$2x_1 + 3x_2 + 6x_3 \leq 300$ labor hours	System constraints
2	$5x_1 + 4x_3 \leq 200$ lb. raw material A	System constraints
3	$3x_1 + 5x_2 + 2x_3 \leq 360$ lb. raw material B	System constraints
4	$x_1 = 30$ units	Individual constraints
5	$x_2 \geq 40$ units	Individual constraints

x_1, x_2, and $x_3 \geq 0$ ← Non-negativity constraints

First, the decision variables are listed and defined. In this case, each of the three decision variables represents the quantity of a different product that can be produced.

Next we see a statement of the objective: to maximize the total profit obtained from the sale (after production) of the three products. The objective function indicates that each unit of the product represented by the symbol x_1 will contribute $4 to profit, each unit of the product represented by x_2 will contribute $7 to profit, and each unit of the product represented by x_3 will contribute $5 to profit. Any solution to the problem will specify a quantity for each decision variable. Given those quantities, the value of the objective function can be determined. For example, if $x_1 = 30$, $x_2 = 50$, and $x_3 = 0$, the value of the objective function would be:

$$4(30) + 7(50) + 5(0) = \$470$$

The remainder of the model lists the constraints that must be satisfied by the solution. For discussion purposes, they have been arranged into three groups: system constraints, individual constraints, and non-negativity constraints. **System**

constraints involve more than one decision variable, whereas **individual constraints** involve only one decision variable. Thus, the first three are system constraints. In contrast, the fourth and fifth constraints pertain to a single decision variable; therefore, each is an individual constraint. The last set of constraints, arranged on a single line, are the **non-negativity constraints.** They specify that no variable will be allowed to take on a negative value. The non-negativity constraints typically apply in an LP model, whether they are explicitly stated or not.

Generally speaking, a constraint has four elements:

1. A right-hand side (RHS) quantity that specifies the limit for that constraint. It must be a constant, not a variable.
2. An algebraic sign that indicates whether the limit is an upper bound (≤), a lower bound (≥), or an equality (=) that must be met exactly.
3. The decision variables to which the constraint applies.
4. The impact that one unit of each decision variable will have on the right-hand side quantity of the constraint.

The constraints in this LP model illustrate three inequality/equality relationships: greater than or equal to (≥), less than or equal to (≤), and equal to (=). The ≥ type of constraint imposes a minimum limit that is acceptable. Examples include "employees must work a minimum of six hours per shift," and "the cottage cheese must contain at least 4 percent butterfat." The ≤ type of constraint sets an upper limit that is not to be exceeded. Often such limits pertain to the amount of some resource that will be available. Other examples include an upper limit on demand, technological limits, and managerial preferences. The = type of constraint is the most specific of the three types. Whereas the other two types can be satisfied by a *range* of values (for example, ≤ 30 can be satisfied by any value from 0 to 30), an equality constraint must be met *exactly*. Therefore, the constraint $x_1 = 30$ means that the only acceptable value of x_1 is 30.

Strictly speaking, two other relationships are possible: constraints with less than (<) signs or greater than (>) signs. They permit values that approach, but do not exactly equal, the right-hand side amount. For variables that are continuous, the distinction may be unimportant. Moreover, there are other ways of dealing with discrete data (e.g., integer programming). Consequently, these less than and greater than constraints will not be employed in this text.

Consider the first constraint in the example. The right-hand side quantity is 300 hours, and the ≤ sign tells us that this is an upper limit on the availability of labor time. The left side of the inequality reveals that each of the three products requires some labor time: Product 1 requires 2 hours per unit, Product 2 requires 3 hours per unit, and Product 3 requires 6 hours per unit.

The second constraint pertains to the availability of raw material A: 200 pounds is available. Hence, this constraint is also an upper bound. Note that x_2 does not appear in this constraint; evidently Product 2 does not require any of raw material

A. The third constraint pertains to the availability of raw material B. It is an upper limit, and all three products require it. The fourth constraint indicates that the only acceptable value of x_1 is 30 units, whereas the fifth constraint indicates that x_2 must be at least 40 units.

Assumptions of LP Models

Table 2–1 lists five basic assumptions of LP models:

1. Proportionality.
2. Additivity.
3. Divisibility.
4. Certainty.
5. Non-negativity.

The **proportionality** requirement is that each decision variable have a *linear* impact in the objective function and in each constraint in which it appears. This means, for example, that if the profit of x_1 is \$4 per unit, that same figure must hold regardless of the quantity of x_1: It must be true over the entire range of possible values of x_1. This also applies to each of the constraints: It is required that the same coefficient (for example, 2 lb. per unit) apply over the entire range of possible values of the decision variable.

In terms of a mathematical model, a function or equation is linear when the variables included are all to the power 1 (that is, not squared, cubed, square root, etc.) and no products (e.g., x_1x_2) appear. Thus, this constraint is linear:

$$2x_1 + x_2 = 40$$

These constraints are not linear:

$$2x_1^2 + x_2 \leq 40 \qquad (x_1 \text{ is squared})$$
$$2x_1 + x_1x_2 \leq 40 \qquad (\text{the second term is a product of variables})$$

The **additivity** assumption requires that terms of the objective function be additive (e.g., the total profit must equal the sum of the profits from each decision variable) and the terms of each constraint be additive (e.g., the total amount of resource used must equal the sum of the resources used by each of the decision variables).

The **divisibility** requirement pertains to potential values of decision variables. It is assumed that noninteger values are acceptable. For instance, $x_1 = 3.5$ is presumed to be an acceptable value. If a problem concerns the quantity of sugar to mix in a recipe, 3.5 pounds would be acceptable. However, if the problem concerns the optimal number of houses to construct, 3.5 does not appear to be acceptable. Instead, that type of problem would seem to require strictly integer solutions. In such cases, *integer programming* methods should be used. These are discussed in a later chapter. It should be noted, however, that some obvious integer-type situations can be handled under the assumption of divisibility. For instance, suppose 3.5 is determined to be the optimal number of television sets to produce per hour. This would result in 7 sets every two hours, which would be acceptable. Another possibility exists when the items are relatively inexpensive (e.g., nuts, bolts, nails, or small pieces of plastic). For example, a model might yield an optimal solution of 210.3 units to be produced. That quantity could easily be rounded to 210 units, and it would still result in a solution that probably is within a few pennies of equaling the (unattainable) optimal value of the objective function.

Thus, the divisibility assumption is that noninteger values will be acceptable. We have seen that in the strictest sense this holds only if the variables are measured on a continuous scale (such as time, distance, weight, volume, etc.), but that in certain cases, little harm is done if the items are measured on a discrete basis (i.e., by counting, such as number of cars, number of television sets, and number of tables).

The **certainty** requirement involves two aspects of LP models. One aspect relates to the model parameters (i.e., the numerical values). It is assumed that these values are known and constant. For instance, if $2x_1$ appears in a labor constraint with hours as the unit of measure, it is assumed that each unit of x_1 will require exactly 2 hours of labor. If the right-hand side of the constraint is 300 labor hours, it is assumed that this quantity will remain at 300. In practice, production times and other parameters may not be truly constant. Therefore, the model builder must make an assessment as to the degree to which the certainty requirement is met. Small departures may not have a significant effect on the model; large departures almost surely will.

Certainty has another aspect in LP models. It is the assumption that all relevant constraints have been identified and represented in the model. For example, if there is a limit on the demand for some item, that limit should be recorded as a constraint (e.g., $x_1 \leq 100$).

The **non-negativity** requirement is that negative values of variables are unrealistic and, therefore, will not be considered in any potential solutions; only positive values and zero will be allowed. For instance, in a problem involving the number of houses to construct, an answer of -2 would imply that two houses that have already been constructed should be torn down! Consider another negative solution that requires preparing -3 apple pies. Neither of these makes sense. For that reason, the non-negativity assumption is inherent in LP models.[1]

---

[1] In the strictest sense, non-negativity is not a theoretical requirement, although certain LP algorithms do require it. However, such unrestricted variables ordinarily would not be found in business applications. For that reason, the discussion here treats non-negativity as an assumption of LP models.

FORMULATING LP MODELS

Once a problem has been defined, the attention of the analyst shifts to formulating a model. Just as it is important to carefully define a problem, it is important to carefully formulate the model that will be used to solve the problem. Linear programming algorithms (solution techniques) are widely used and understood, and computer packages are readily available for solving LP problems. Consequently, *obtaining* solutions is not the real issue. In fact, the ease with which solutions can be obtained may tempt an analyst or decision maker to rush through the formulation phase in order to get a quick idea of what the solution will look like. Too often, though, the analyst fails to check that all constraints have been accounted for and have been correctly formulated. This is unfortunate because if a model is ill-structured, it can easily lead to poor decisions.

Formulating linear programming models involves the following steps:

1. Define the decision variables.
2. Determine the objective function.
3. Identify the constraints.
4. Determine appropriate values for parameters and determine whether an upper limit, lower limit, or equality is called for.
5. Use this information to build a model.
6. Validate the model.

In practice, the first step is usually straightforward. In many cases, the decision variables are obvious; in others, a brief discussion with the appropriate manager is necessary. However, identifying the constraints and then determining appropriate values for the parameters can require considerable time and effort on the part of the analyst. Potential sources of information include historical records, interviews with managers and staff, and data collection. Obtaining parameters for the objective function is usually not difficult; accounting records or personnel can generally provide that information. Once the information about constraints and parameters has been obtained, constructing an appropriate model becomes the focus. This can be both demanding and time-consuming, especially for large problems. Validating the model will involve a critical review of the output, perhaps under a variety of inputs, in order to decide if the results are reasonable. This typically involves checking with people who are familiar with the situation (managers and staff) about the reasonableness of the results.

Decision Variables

Decision variables are quantities whose values are to be determined by solving a linear programming model. Typical decision variables relate to products, stocks or bonds, raw materials, shipping routes, locations, and so on. In general, the decision variable will be defined in terms of a *quantity* or amount, such as: "x_1 = the quantity of Product 1 to produce," or "x_1 = the quantity of red dye to include in the mixture." If a problem involves shipping routes, the decision variables would represent the quantity to be shipped over a particular route.

In LP models, decision variables have unit profits, revenues, costs, or a similar measure associated with them.

Objective Function

Once the variables have been identified, the objective function usually can be specified. It is necessary to decide if the problem is a maximization or a minimization problem and the coefficients of each decision variable. Obviously, we want to *maximize* profits, revenue, and so on, and we want to *minimize* costs, time, and so on.

If a problem concerns maximizing profits, the profit per unit for each variable either may be given or it may have to be derived by finding the difference between revenue per unit and cost per unit for each decision variable. For instance, if the revenue is $50 per unit for a product and the cost is $30 per unit, the profit per unit is $50 − $30 = $20.

Note that the units of all the coefficients in the objective function must be the same (e.g., all in dollars, all in hours). In addition, all terms in the objective function must include a variable. And some computer software packages require that all decision variables be represented in the objective function.

Constraints

Constraints describe the restrictions of an LP problem. Constraints on individual variables are usually not difficult to recognize, if there are any. They are also usually simple to formulate (for example, "at least 10 units of Product 1 must be made" leads to $x_1 \geq 10$). If multiple restrictions are placed on a variable, such as "at least 10 units of Product 1 must be made, but no more than 20 can be sold," a separate expression will be needed for each restriction. Thus, both $x_1 \geq 10$ and $x_1 \leq 20$ will be needed to describe the case just mentioned.

Formulating system constraints can require more effort than that required for individual constraints. This is due primarily to the need to deal with interrelationships among decision variables. For instance, one type of relationship pertains to one variable relative to the others (e.g., the mixture must have at least 10 percent of Ingredient A). Another type specifies a ratio between two of the variables (e.g., the ratio of Ingredient A to Ingredient B must be 3:1).

It is usually helpful when dealing with system constraints to begin by naming and listing the constraints (e.g., labor, machine time, raw material, material A, x_1 proportion, ratio x_1/x_2, and so on). This not only serves as a reference, it also focuses attention on the specific system constraints.

Finally, it is common practice to write constraints in such a way that the variables are on the left side of the expression while a constant alone is placed on the right side of the expression. For example, the expression $x_1 \geq x_2$ would be written as $x_1 - x_2 \geq 0$. (Note that subtracting an equal amount, such as x_2, from both sides of an equality does not change the direction of the inequality.)

The non-negativity constraints can be listed on a single line (for example, $x_1, x_2, x_3, x_4 \geq 0$). It is a good practice to show these.

The Microcomputer Problem

At the beginning of this chapter, a problem involving production of microcomputers was briefly described. The issue was whether the decision of how much of each type of computer to make could be made using linear programming. The problem is shown with added detail in Example 2.

In determining whether the problem can be solved using linear programming, we can first note that there are *restrictions* on assembly time, inspection time, and storage space. We also can note that the manager has an *objective,* which is to maximize profit. Thus, it would appear that this is a *constrained optimization* problem.

EXAMPLE 2 **The Microcomputer Problem**

General description A firm that assembles computers and computer equipment is about to start production of two new microcomputers. Each type of microcomputer will require assembly time, inspection time, and storage space. The amounts of each of these resources that can be devoted to the production of the microcomputers is limited. The manager of the firm would like to determine the quantity of each microcomputer to produce in order to maximize the profit generated by sales of these microcomputers.

Additional information In order to develop a suitable model of the problem, the manager has met with design and manufacturing personnel. As a result of those meetings, the manager has obtained the following information:

	Type 1	Type 2
Profit per unit	\$60	\$50
Assembly time per unit	4 hours	10 hours
Inspection time per unit	2 hours	1 hour
Storage space per unit	3 cubic feet	3 cubic feet

The manager also has acquired information on the availability of company resources. These (daily) amounts are:

Resource	Amount Available
Assembly time	100 hours
Inspection time	22 hours
Storage space	39 cubic feet

The manager also met with the firm's marketing manager and learned that demand for the microcomputers was such that whatever combination of these two types of microcomputers is produced, all of the output can be sold.

In terms of meeting the assumptions, it would appear that the relationships are *linear:* The contribution to profit per unit of each type of computer and the time and storage space per unit of each type of computer is the same regardless of the quantity produced. Therefore, the total impact of each type of computer on the profit and each constraint is a linear function of the quantity of that variable. There may be a question of *diversibility* because, presumably, only whole units of computers will be sold. However, because this is a recurring process (i.e., the computers will be produced daily, a noninteger solution such as 3.5 computers per day will result in 7 computers every other day), this does not seem to pose a problem. The question of *certainty* cannot be explored here; in practice, the manager could be questioned to determine if there are any other possible constraints and whether the values shown for assembly times, and so forth are known with certainty. For the purposes of discussion, we will assume certainty. Lastly, the assumption of *non-negativity* seems justified; negative values for production quantities would not make sense.

Because we have concluded that linear programming is appropriate, let us now turn our attention to constructing a model of the microcomputer problem. First, we must define the decision variables. Based on the statement, "The manager . . . would like to determine the quantity of each microcomputer to produce," the decision variables are the quantities of each type of computer. Thus:

x_1 = quantity of Type 1 to produce
x_2 = quantity of Type 2 to produce

Next, we can formulate the objective function. The profit per unit of Type 1 is listed as \$60, and the profit per unit of Type 2 is listed as \$50, so the appropriate objective function is:

maximize $\quad Z = 60x_1 + 50x_2$

where Z is the value of the objective function, given values of x_1 and x_2. Theoretically, a mathematical function requires such a variable for completeness. However, in practice, the objective function often is written without the Z, as sort of a shorthand version. That approach is underscored by the fact that computer input does not call for Z: It is understood. The output of a computerized model does include a Z, though. The approach taken in this text is generally to omit the Z from problems and models as an input, except for a handful of instances when illustration can benefit from its inclusion.

Now for the constraints. There are three resources with limited availability: assembly time, inspection time, and storage space. The fact that availability is limited means that these constraints will all be $\leq$ constraints. Suppose we begin with the assembly constraint. The Type 1 microcomputer requires 4 hours of assembly time per unit, whereas the Type 2 microcomputer requires 10 hours of assembly time per unit. Therefore, with a limit of 100 hours available, the assembly constraint is:

$$4x_1 + 10x_2 \leq 100 \text{ hours}$$

Similarly, each unit of Type 1 requires 2 hours of inspection time, and each unit of Type 2 requires 1 hour of inspection time. With 22 hours available, the inspection constraint is:

$$2x_1 + 1x_2 \leq 22$$

(Note, the coefficient of 1 for x_2 need not be shown. Thus, an alternative form for this constraint is: $2x_1 + x_2 \leq 22$.) The storage constraint is determined in a similar manner. It is:

$$3x_1 + 3x_2 \leq 39$$

There are no other system or individual constraints. The non-negativity constraints are:

$$x_1, x_2 \geq 0$$

In summary, the mathematical model of the microcomputer problem is:

x_1 = quantity of Type 1 to produce
x_2 = quantity of Type 2 to produce

maximize $\quad 60x_1 + 50x_2$

subject to

Assembly	$4x_1 + 10x_2 \leq 100$ hours
Inspection	$2x_1 + 1x_2 \leq 22$ hours
Storage	$3x_1 + 3x_2 \leq 39$ cubic feet
	$x_1, x_2 \geq 0$

Now that we have seen an example of how LP models are formulated, let's turn our attention to some applications of LP models.

LINEAR PROGRAMMING APPLICATIONS

There are a wide range of problems that lend themselves to solution by linear programming techniques. This section briefly describes some of those problem types. The discussion is not meant to be all-inclusive. Rather, its purpose is to give you a sense of the importance of LP techniques for managerial decision making and the apparent diversity of situations to which linear programming can be applied.

Product Mix

Organizations often produce similar products or offer similar services that use the same resources (for example, labor, equipment, time, materials). Because of limits in the amounts of these resources that are available during any time period, a decision must be made concerning how much of each product to produce, or service to make available, during the time period that will be consistent with the goals of the organization. The basic question that can be answered using linear programming is: What mix of output (or service) will maximize profit (revenue, etc.) given the availability of scarce resources? The microcomputer problem described in this chapter is an example of a product mix problem.

Diet Problems

Diet problems usually involve the mixing of raw materials or other ingredients to obtain an end product that has certain characteristics. For instance, food processors and dieticians generally are concerned with meeting dietary needs in food products. There may be specific requirements pertaining to nutrients, calories, sodium content, and so on. The general question to be answered by linear programming is: What mix of inputs (e.g., different food types) will achieve the desired results for the least cost? The following example illustrates this type of problem.

■

EXAMPLE 3 A cereal manufacturer is investigating the possibility of introducing a new cereal. It would be composed of wheat, rice, and corn flakes. The cost per ounce and dietary requirements are shown in the following table:

	Wheat	Rice	Corn	Requirements per 12-Ounce Box
Protein (grams per ounce)	4	2	2	At least 27 grams
Carbohydrates (grams per ounce)	20	25	21	At least 240 grams
Calories per ounce	90	110	100	No more than 1,260 calories
Cost per ounce	$.03	.05	.02	

Formulate an LP model for this problem that will determine the optimal quantities of wheat, rice, and corn per box that will achieve the requirements at minimum cost.

Solution

x_1 = ounces of wheat per box
x_2 = ounces of rice per box
x_3 = ounces of corn per box

minimize $.03x_1 + .05x_2 + .02x_3$

subject to

Protein	$4x_1 + 2x_2 + 2x_3 \geq 27$ grams
Carbohydrates	$20x_1 + 25x_2 + 21x_3 \geq 240$ grams
Calories	$90x_1 + 110x_2 + 100x_3 \leq 1{,}260$ calories
Box size	$x_1 + x_2 + x_3 = 12$ ounces
	$x_1, x_2, \text{ and } x_3 \geq 0$

Note the box size constraint, which is needed to assure that the quantities of inputs per box equal the box size.

Other kinds of applications that fall into this category include mixing feed for livestock, mixing pet foods, mixing building materials (concrete, mortar, paint), and so on.

Blending Problems

Blending problems are very similar to diet problems. In fact, diet and blending problems could be lumped into the same category. Strictly speaking, though, blending problems have an additional requirement: to achieve a mix that has a specific consistency, as illustrated in the next example.

EXAMPLE 4 Formulate the appropriate model for this blending problem: The sugar content of three juices, orange, banana, and pineapple, is 10, 15, and 20 percent, respectively. How many quarts of each must be mixed together to achieve one gallon (four quarts) that has a sugar content of at least 17 percent of minimum cost? The cost per quart is 20 cents for orange juice, 30 cents for banana juice, and 40 cents for pineapple juice.

Solution

O = quantity of orange juice
B = quantity of banana juice
P = quantity of pineapple juice

minimize $.20O + .30B + .40P$

subject to

Sugar content $.10O + .15B + .20P \geq .17(O + B + P)$
Total amount $O + B + P = 4$ quarts

The sugar constraint must be rewritten so that the decision variables are on the left side and the constant is on the right side. Thus, expanding the right side results in:

$$.10O + .15B + .20P = .17O + .17B + .17P$$

Then, subtracting the left side amounts from both sides gives us

$$-.07O - .02B + .03P = 0$$

Portfolio Selection

Portfolio selection problems generally involve allocating a fixed dollar amount (e.g., $100,000) among a variety of investments such as bonds, stocks, real estate, and so on. Usually the goal is to maximize income or total return. The problems take on an added dimension when certain other requirements are specified (for instance, no more than 40 percent of the portfolio can be invested in bonds). The next example illustrates this kind of problem.

EXAMPLE 5 A conservative investor has $100,000 to invest. The investor has decided to use three vehicles for generating income: municipal bonds, a certificate of deposit (CD), and a money market account. After reading a financial newsletter, the investor has also identified several additional restrictions on the investments:

1. No more than 40 percent of the investment should be in bonds.
2. The proportion allocated to the money market account should be at least double the amount in the CD.

The annual return will be 8 percent for bonds, 9 percent for the CD, and 7 percent for the money market account. Assume the entire amount will be invested.

Formulate the LP model for this problem, ignoring any transaction costs and the potential for different investment lives. Assume that the investor wants to maximize the total annual return.

Solution

x_1 = amount invested in bonds
x_2 = amount invested in the CD
x_3 = amount invested in the money market account

The annual return from each investment is the product of the rate of return and the amount invested. Thus, the objective function is:

$$\text{maximize} \quad .08x_1 + .09x_2 + .07x_3$$

The requirement that no more than 40 percent be in bonds produces this constraint:

$x_1 \leq .40(\$100{,}000)$, which becomes $x_1 \leq \$40{,}000$

The requirement that the proportion invested in the money market account be at least double the amount in the CD leads to: $x_3 \geq 2x_2$. Then, subtracting $2x_2$ from both sides gives us: $x_3 - 2x_2 \geq 0$, which can be rearranged so that x_2 comes before x_3: $-2x_2 + x_3 \geq 0$. Finally, the investor must recognize that the amounts invested in bonds, the CD, and the money market account must equal \$100,000. This gives us:

$$x_1 + x_2 + x_3 = \$100{,}000$$

In sum, the model is:

$$\text{maximize} \quad .08x_1 + .09x_2 + .07x_3$$

subject to

Amount in bonds	$x_1 \leq \$\ 40{,}000$
Money/CD	$-2x_2 + x_3 \geq 0$
Investment	$x_1 + x_2 + x_3 = \$100{,}000$
	$x_1, x_2, \text{ and } x_3 \geq 0$

Note: If the problem had stated that the investor did not necessarily want to invest the entire \$100,000, the investment constraint would have been a less-than-or-equal-to constraint:

$$x_1 + x_2 + x_3 \leq \$100{,}000$$

MANAGER DIALOGUE

Kim Hansen has just completed her junior year in the School of Management at a large eastern university. She is currently working as an intern in a consulting firm as a summer job. Her main activities involve developing quantitative models based on a consultant's written description of a problem and gathering data that are used in the models. Because she is new at it, she is still encountering difficulties in formulating the models. The following is a condensation of a recent discussion Kim had with her mentor, Mark Tompkins.

Kim: I still seem to be having trouble with my modeling. It is not always clear to me what the decision variables are and what the constraints are. And even when I do identify the constraints, the units are not always right. Can you give me some suggestions?

Mark: Let me assure you, you are not alone. Many people have the same difficulties getting started in formulating models. Mostly, it's just a matter of experience, but I do have a few suggestions that may help you.

Kim: I'm all ears.

Mark: First, when you read the problem description, try to get a sense of purpose of the model. For example, you might find that the manager wants to maximize profits, or minimize costs. Then, look for the variables that have profits or costs associated with them. These will be the decision variables. Thus, if profit maximization is the purpose, and *A*, *B*, and *C* have profits of \$2 per unit, \$3 per unit, and \$5 per unit, *A*, *B*, and *C* are the decision variables.

Kim: That seems easy enough. Then why am I having trouble with it?

Mark: One possibility is that you are letting yourself become overwhelmed by the amount of information contained in a problem description. I always try to break up a problem into small pieces. I do this by using as a framework the structure of a model. That is, I know the elements of a model, and I try to relate the information in the description to those elements: objective, decision variables, constraints, and parameters.

In addition, the bond constraint would be affected because the amount in bonds is related to the amount invested. The bond constraint would have been:

$$x_1 \le .40(x_1 + x_2 + x_3)$$

which would be rearranged to:

$$.60x_1 - .40x_2 - .40x_3 \le 0$$

(concluded)

Kim: So what I'm hearing is that you look the problem over in order to learn its purpose, and then you identify the variables that relate to that purpose. What then?

Mark: I define the decision variables (e.g., A = the quantity of Product A, B = the quantity of Product B, etc.). And, if it isn't obvious, I include in the definition the *units* of the decision variables, such as pounds, dollars, boxes, or whatever. Then, I formulate the objective function.

Kim: What about the constraints? Do you have any suggestions on how to identify them, and how to formulate them?

Mark: One thing I always look for is a statement or a listing that indicates something has limited availability, such as "there are 40 pounds of material available," or "the machine department has two hours of processing time available." This tells me that material and machine time are less-than-or-equal-to constraints. These are typical of maximization problems. Minimization problems may also have this type of constraint, but they must also have either equal-to or greater-than-or-equal-to constraints that specify minimum levels that must be achieved, such as in a diet problem where the amount of some nutrient in a diet must be achieved (e.g., at least 20 grams of protein per serving).

Once I've identified a constraint, I assign a name to it, such as labor, material, protein. This helps me to relate to the problem.

Aside from that, you need to remember that the units must be the same on both sides of a constraint (e.g., if the units on the right side are *hours*, then the units of the parameters on the left side must be *hours* per unit; it would be wrong to have minutes on the left side and hours on the right side. However, the units on different constraints do not have to be the same: One constraint might be in pounds, another in hours, and another in minutes. The only requirement is that *within* a constraint, all units must be the same.

Kim: These suggestions are really helpful. I can't wait to try them on the new problems I've just been given. Thanks, Mark.

Other Applications

The preceding examples illustrate some of the frequently encountered applications of LP models to real-world problems. There are, however, many other applications of linear programming models, including the following:

- *Transportation problems.* A typical problem might involve a set of factories that produce the same product and a set of warehouses to which the product is to be shipped. The objective is to determine a distribution plan that will minimize total distribution cost given the capacities of the various factories and the needs of the warehouses.

- □ *Assignment problems.* A typical problem might include a set of jobs to be performed, a set of machines that can perform the jobs, and a cost per job for each job/machine combination. The objective is to assign the jobs to machines in such a way that the total cost of performing the jobs is minimized. Variations of this problem include minimizing total time for a set of assignments and maximizing profits from a set of assignments.
- □ *Project management problems.* A typical problem might involve finding the minimum time for project completion given times for the tasks required and specified precedence relationships among tasks. A variation may involve shortening project duration given costs to shorten various project tasks. The objective would be to minimize total cost: project costs and shortening costs.
- □ *Marketing research problems.* A typical problem might be to determine the number of households of each of several income categories to survey in order to obtain desired information at minimum cost.

SUMMARY

Linear programming models are used to find optimal solutions to constrained optimization problems. In order for linear programming models to be used, the problems must involve a single objective, a linear objective function and linear constraints, and have known and constant numerical values.

Linear programming models are composed of decision variables and numerical values that are arranged into an objective function and a set of constraints. The constraints are restrictions that can pertain to any decision variable or to a combination of decision variables. In general, variables are not allowed to have negative values. These restrictions are referred to as non-negativity constraints.

Linear programming models are widely used. Among the applications of these models are problems that involve product mix, blending, portfolio selection, distribution, assignments, and marketing research.

This chapter illustrates model formulation. The following chapters illustrate procedures for finding optimal solutions to LP models.

GLOSSARY

Additivity A requirement of LP models that both the terms of the objective function and the terms of the constraints be additive.

Algorithm A solution technique; a sequence of steps that will lead to a solution.

Constrained Optimization Finding the optimal solution to a problem given that certain constraints must be satisfied by the solution.

Constraint A restriction that must be satisfied by a solution.

Decision Variable A variable that is under the control of the decision maker.

Divisibility The assumption in LP models that noninteger values are acceptable solutions for decision variables.

Feasible Solution Any solution that satisfies all of a problem's constraints.

Individual Constraint A restriction on a decision variable.

Linear Programming A family of mathematical techniques that can be used for constrained optimization problems with linear relationships.

Non-Negativity Constraints Variables are not allowed to have negative values.

Objective Function A mathematical expression that incorporates the contribution per unit of each variable.

Optimal Solution The best solution to a problem; no other solution will yield a better value for the objective function and still satisfy the given set of constraints of the problem.

Parameters Numerical values that appear in the objective function and constraints; assumed known and constant in LP models.

Proportionality A requirement of LP models that the impact or contribution of every decision variable in the objective function, and each constraint in which it appears, be linear.

System Constraint A constraint that pertains to more than one decision variable.

SOLVED PROBLEMS

Problem 1. A toy manufacturer makes three versions of a toy robot. The first version requires 10 minutes each for fabrication and packaging and 2 pounds of plastic, the second version requires 12 minutes for fabrication and packaging and 3 pounds of plastic, and the third version requires 15 minutes for fabrication and packaging and 4 pounds of plastic. There are 8 hours of fabrication and packaging time available and 200 pounds of plastic available for the next production cycle. The unit profits are \$1 for each Version 1, \$5 for each Version 2, and \$6 for each Version 3. A minimum of 10 units of each must be made to fill previous orders.

Formulate an LP model that will determine the optimal production quantities for profit maximization.

Solution

a. Identify the decision variables:

x_1 = number of Version 1 robots
x_2 = number of Version 2 robots
x_3 = number of Version 3 robots

b. Identify the constraints by name:

Fabrication and packaging time
Quantity of plastic
Quantity of Version 1 robots (minimum of 10)
Quantity of Version 2 robots (minimum of 10)
Quantity of Version 3 robots (minimum of 10)

c. Write the objective function:

maximize $1x_1 + 5x_2 + 6x_3$

d. Write the constraints:

Note that fabrication and packaging times are given in minutes per unit, but that available time is given in hours. It is necessary that both sides of a constraint have the same units. This can be accomplished by converting 8 hours to 480 minutes.

The constraints are:

Fabrication and packaging	$10x_1 + 12x_2 + 15x_3 \leq$	480 minutes
Plastic	$2x_1 + 3x_2 + 4x_3 \leq$	200 pounds
Version 1	$x_1 \geq$	10 robots
Version 2	$x_2 \geq$	10 robots
Version 3	$x_3 \geq$	10 robots

$$x_1,\ x_2,\ \text{and}\ x_3 \geq 0$$

Problem 2. A soup company wants to determine the optimal ingredients for its vegetable soup. The main ingredients are:

Vegetables:
- Potatoes
- Carrots
- Onions

Meat
Water
Flavorings

The soup must meet these specifications:

a. No more than half of the soup can be vegetables.

b. The ratio of water to meat should be 8:1.

c. The amount of meat should be between 5 and 6 percent of the soup.

d. The flavorings should weigh no more than ½ ounce.

The cost per ounce of the ingredients is \$.02 for the vegetables, \$.05 for the meat, \$.001 for the water, and \$.05 for the flavorings.

Formulate an LP model that will determine the optimal amounts of the various ingredients to achieve 15-ounce cans of soup at minimum cost.

Solution

Identify the decision variables:

x_1 = quantity of potatoes
x_2 = quantity of carrots
x_3 = quantity of onions
x_4 = quantity of meat
x_5 = quantity of water
x_6 = quantity of flavorings

Write the objective function:

$$\text{minimize} \quad .02x_1 + .02x_2 + .02x_3 + .05x_4 + .001x_5 + .05x_6$$

Write constraints for each specification:

a. $x_1 + x_2 + x_3 \leq .50(15 \text{ oz.})$. Thus:

$$x_1 + x_2 + x_3 \leq 7.5 \text{ ounces}$$

b. $\frac{x_5}{x_4} = \frac{8}{1}$. Cross-multiplying yields $x_5 = 8x_4$. Then, subtracting $8x_4$ from both sides in order to have all variables on the left side yields:

$$-8x_4 + x_5 = 0$$

c. This requires *two* constraints:

$$x_4 \geq .05(15), \text{ which is } x_4 \geq .75 \text{ ounce}$$
$$x_4 \leq .06(15), \text{ which is } x_4 \leq .90 \text{ ounce}$$

d. $x_6 \leq .5$ ounce.

There is one additional constraint: The ingredients must add up to 15 ounces, the weight of a can of soup. Thus:

$$x_1 + x_2 + x_3 + x_4 + x_5 + x_6 = 15 \text{ ounces}$$

Finally, there are the non-negativity constraints:

All variables ≥ 0

PROBLEMS

1. A furniture company produces a variety of products. One department specializes in wood tables, chairs, and bookcases. These are made using three resources: labor, wood, and machine time. The department has 60 hours of labor available each day, 16 hours of machine time, and 400 board feet of wood. A consultant has developed a linear programming model for the department:

x_1 = quantity of tables
x_2 = quantity of chairs
x_3 = quantity of bookcases

maximize $40x_1 + 30x_2 + 45x_3$ (profit)

subject to

Labor	$2x_1 + 1x_2 + 2.5x_3 \leq$	60 hours
Machine	$.8x_1 + .6x_2 + 1.0x_3 \leq$	16 hours
Wood	$30x_1 + 20x_2 + 30x_3 \leq$	400 board-feet
Tables	$x_1 \geq$	10 board-feet

$$x_1, x_2, x_3 \geq 0$$

Answer these questions posed by department manager Barbara Brady:

a. What is the main purpose of the model?
b. What are the decision variables?
c. What are the system constraints (name them)?
d. What is the meaning of the number 2.5 in the labor constraint?
e. Explain what is meant by $x_1 \geq 10$.
f. What does the term $40x_1$ in the objective function represent?

2. The Stone Company produces three sizes of window fans: small, medium, and large. The manager has formulated an LP model for fan production:

maximize $6x_1 + 8x_2 + 5x_3$ (profit)

subject to

Labor	$3x_1 + 4x_2 + 5x_3 \leq 160$ hours
Metal	$1x_1 + 2x_2 + 3x_3 \leq 100$ pounds
Plastic	$2x_1 + 2x_2 + 2x_3 \leq 110$ pounds
Large fan	$x_3 \geq 18$
	$x_1, x_2, x_3 \geq 0$

Briefly explain or define each of these parts of the model:

a. x_1, x_2, and x_3.

b. The 6 in the objective function.

c. The product of the 8 and x_2 in the objective function.

d. The terms *labor, metal*, and *plastic*.

e. The 5 in the labor constraint.

f. The 160 hours.

g. $x_3 \geq 18$.

h. The product of 5 and x_3 in the labor constraint.

i. $x_1, x_2, x_3 \geq 0$.

j. What two key questions can be answered using this model?

3. A confectionary company produces two sizes of its popular dark chocolate bars: a 3.5-ounce size and a 6-ounce size. The 3.5-ounce bar costs $.22 to make and sells for $.35, whereas the 6-ounce bar costs $.40 to make and sells for $.55. The company has 15,000 ounces of chocolate in stock, and the manager wants to use it all on the next production run. In addition, the manager has specified that a minimum of 1,000 of the 3.5-ounce bars and 1,200 of the 6-ounce bars should be made.

   a. What are the decision variables in this problem?

   b. What are the constraints?

   c. Formulate a linear programming model that will enable the manager to determine how many of each size bar to produce in order to satisfy the conditions specified with maximum profit.

4. The Mantell Company makes softballs and baseballs. In order to make each type of ball, leather, nylon, wood chips, and machine time and labor are needed. The requirements for each item and the resources available are shown in the following table:

Item	Softball	Baseball	Available
Leather	6	4	6,000 ounces
Nylon	8	3	5,000 yards
Wood chips	10	2	5,000 ounces
Labor	3	2	3,600 minutes
Machine	1	1	2,000 minutes

Softballs sell for $17 each, and baseballs sell for $15 each. Formulate a linear programming model that can be used to determine the number of each type of ball to produce in order to maximize revenue.

5. Sharon Smith is the marketing manager of a large savings and loan association that has branches throughout the state. She would like to mail a promotional piece to prospective borrowers. Sharon has selected three regions in which to do a mailing. A marketing agency can supply lists of prospective borrowers in each region, as shown in the following table:

Region	List Size	Cost per Name
I	10,000	$.11
II	20,000	.12
III	30,000	.13

Sharon would like to have a pool of 15,000 names and would like the mail to contain at least 10 percent of the people on each list. Formulate an LP model that will accomplish these requirements for the least cost. Assume that there is no overlap among lists, and that any quantity can be ordered from each list.

6. Aviation Electronics produces three types of switching devices. Each type involves a two-step assembly operation. The assembly times are shown in the following table:

	Assembly Time per Unit (minutes)	
	Station 1	Station 2
Model A	2.5	3.0
Model B	1.8	1.6
Model C	2.0	2.2

Each workstation has a daily working time of 7.5 hours. Manager Bob Parkes wants to obtain the greatest possible profit during the next five working days. Model A yields a profit of $8.25 per unit, Model B a profit of $7.50 per unit, and Model C a profit of $7.80 per unit. Assume that the firm can sell all it produces during this time, but it must fill outstanding orders for 20 units of each model type.

Formulate the linear programming model of this problem.

7. A manager of an automobile dealership must decide how many cars to order for the end of the model year. Midsize cars yield an average profit of $500 each, and compact cars yield an average profit of $400 each. Either type of

car will cost the dealership \$8,000 each, and no more than \$720,000 can be invested. The manager wants at least 10 of each type, but no more than 50 of the midsize cars and no more than 60 of the compact cars. Formulate the linear programming model of this problem.

8. Petfoods makes dog food using a blend of three ingredients: K9, K8, and K1. The company has a regular blend, an extra blend, and puppy delite. The regular blend consists of one third of each ingredient, the extra blend is 50 percent K9, and 25 percent each of K8 and K1. The puppy delite is 10 percent K8 and the rest K1. The dog food is produced in one-pound cans. There are 1,500 pounds of K9, and 1,000 pounds of each of the other ingredients available. The regular blend yields a profit of \$.20 per can, the extra blend yields \$.18 per can, and the puppy delite a profit of \$.25 per can. Formulate an LP model that can be used to determine the maximum profit combination of the different types of dog food.

9. A manufacturer of lawn and garden equipment makes two basic types of lawn mowers: a push-type and a self-propelled model. The push-type requires 9 minutes to assemble and 2 minutes to package; the self-propelled mower requires 12 minutes to assemble and 6 minutes to package. Each type has an engine. The company has 12 hours of assembly time available, 75 engines, and 5 hours of packing time. Profits are \$70 for the self-propelled model, and \$45 for the push-type mower, per unit. Formulate a linear programming model that will enable the manager to determine how many mowers of each type to make in order to maximize total profit.

10. A farm consists of 600 acres of land, of which 500 acres will be planted with corn, soybeans, and wheat, according to these conditions:

    1. At least half of the planted acreage should be in corn.
    2. No more than 200 acres should be soybeans.
    3. The ratio of corn to wheat planted should be 2:1.

    It costs \$20 an acre to plant corn, \$15 an acre to plant soybeans, and \$12 an acre to plant wheat.

    a. Formulate this problem as an LP model that will minimize planting cost while achieving the specified conditions.

    b. How would the model change if the acreage to be planted was *at least* 500?

11. A client has approached a stockbroker with the following request: Invest \$100,000 for maximum annual income under these conditions:

    1. Spread the investment over no more than three different stocks.
    2. Put no more than 40 percent of the money into any one stock.
    3. Put a minimum of \$10,000 into oil stock.

    The broker has identified three stocks for investing the funds. Their estimated annual returns and price per share are shown in the following table:

Stock	Price per Share	Estimated Annual Return per Share
Oil	$120	$11
Auto	52	4
Health	18	2

Formulate an LP model of the problem.

12. A high school dietician is planning menus for the upcoming month. A new item will be spaghetti with sauce. The dietician wants each serving to contain at least 10 grams of protein and at least 40 grams of carbohydrates. Spaghetti contains 5 grams of protein and 32 grams of carbohydrates per cup, and the sauce contains 4 grams of protein and 5 grams of carbohydrates per cup. For aesthetic reasons, the dietician wants the ratio of spaghetti to sauce to be 4:1.

    Spaghetti costs $.30 per cup to buy and prepare, and sauce costs $.40 per cup to buy and prepare. The dietician wants to minimize the cost per serving and keep the calories per serving to 330 or less. The sauce contains 100 calories per cup, and the spaghetti contains 160 calories per cup.

    Formulate a linear programming model for this problem.

13. A fuel oil company intends to distribute a new gasoline that has an octane rating of 94. The company has three fuels that can be blended to achieve a range of octanes. The cost per gallon and the octane ratings of these fuels are shown in the following table.

Fuel	Cost per Gallon	Octane
A10	$.45	87
B11	.55	90
C12	.60	98

Due to technical reasons, the ratio of C12 to A10 cannot be more than 3:1.

Prepare an LP model that will achieve the desired octane rating at minimum cost. Assume the octanes mix linearly. Hint: See Example 4.

14. The trust department of a commercial bank must make frequent decisions on customer portfolios. A typical case might involve a portfolio of $120,000. The bank's policy is to use conservative investments such as treasury notes, municipal bonds, and blue-chip stocks. Treasury notes have an annual return of 9 percent, municipal bonds a return of 8 percent, and blue-chip stocks a return of 10 percent. The bank also has a policy of not placing more of a portfolio into stocks than into treasury notes and bonds combined.

Formulate an LP model that will yield the largest annual return for the $120,000 portfolio, given the bank's policies. Ignore transaction costs, fees, tax consequences, and so on.

15. A meat packing company makes pork sausage in 2,000 pound batches. The sausage is made from pork, beef, and filler. The cost of pork is $2.50 per pound, the cost of beef is $1.80 per pound, and the cost of filler is $1.00 per pound. Each batch must contain the following:

    1. At least 800 pounds of pork.
    2. No more than 30 percent filler.
    3. At least 300 pounds of beef.

    The manager wants to know the mix of ingredients that will minimize cost. Formulate an LP model for this problem.

16. A pharmaceutical company is investigating the possibility of marketing a new dietary supplement that would contain iron, calcium, and phosphorous. The supplement would be made by mixing together three inputs, which the company refers to as T5, N1, and T4. The amounts of the three minerals (mg. per ounce) contained in each input, the minimum and maximum levels of each mineral per 12-ounce bottle, and the cost per ounce of the inputs are shown in the table below.

Cost per Ounce:	**$.75**	**$.60**	**$.55**	**Minimum**	**Maximum**
Input:	**T5**	**N1**	**T4**	**per Bottle**	**per Bottle**
Mineral					
Iron	10	16	12	100 mg.	150 mg.
Calcium	400	600	800	6,000 mg.	8,000 mg.
Phosphorous	800	550	500	6,000 mg.	8,000 mg.

The manager would like to know what the lowest cost combination of inputs is that would achieve the desired dietary ranges for the three minerals on a per bottle basis. Formulate this problem as an LP model.

17. A small specialty shop, Nuts-to-You, sells a variety of candy and nuts. The owner is concerned with the problem of how to package nuts. The shop carries four types of nuts, which are sold in one-pound bags. It also sells one-pound bags of its own special mix, which consists of 40 percent peanuts and equal parts of the other three types of nuts. The shop has a limited supply of nuts on hand, and the owner believes that before the next shipment of nuts arrives, the current supply can be sold. However, the owner recognizes that different combinations of nuts (individual bags versus bags of the special mix) will yield different profits. The owner would like to know how much of the current supply to allocate to the mix and how much to each individual type in order to maximize profits.

    The current supply and cost per pound of each nut type are:

Nut	Cost per Pound	Pounds Available
Peanuts	$1.00	600
Cashews	3.00	360
Walnuts	2.50	500
Pecans	3.50	400

The selling price of the packaged nuts are:

Package	Price
Mix	$4.00
Peanuts	1.50
Cashews	4.80
Walnuts	4.60
Pecans	5.00

Assume that mixing costs are negligible.

Formulate this linear programming problem.

18. The AGC Company supplies fruit juice and juice blends to wholesale grocers in the northeast. A list of the firm's products and revenue per ounce is shown in the following table:

Product	Revenue per Ounce
Apple juice	$.03
Grape juice	.06
Cranberry juice	.05
Apple-grape juice	.07
Apple-cranberry juice	.08
All-in-one juice	.10

The apple-grape juice is 70 percent apple juice and 30 percent grape juice. The apple-cranberry juice is 60 percent apple juice and 40 percent cranberry juice, and the all-in-one is 50 percent apple juice, 20 percent grape juice, and the rest cranberry juice.

The company has 200 gallons of apple juice, 100 gallons of grape juice, and 150 gallons of cranberry juice on hand, and the owner wants to know how many containers of each product to prepare in order to maximize profit. Cost per ounce for apple juice is $.02, for grape juice, $.04, and for cranberry juice, $.03.

All products are sold in 64-ounce (two-quart) containers. The apple-cranberry juice is also sold in a one-quart size. *Hint:* Use quarts rather than ounces.

The company has an order for 10 containers of apple juice and 12 containers of the apple-cranberry one-quart size that must be filled from current supplies.

Formulate the linear programming model of this problem.

19. A small shop located on the edge of a large city sells a variety of dried fruits and nuts. The shop caters to travelers of all types; it sells one-pound boxes of individual items, such as dried bananas, as well as one-pound boxes of mixed fruits and nuts, although its popular trail mix is sold only in the two-pound size.

Because of complaints from customers about long lines at the counters, the manager has decided to prepare boxes ahead of time and place them on shelves for self-service. The manager has specified that 50 percent of current supplies should be prepackaged, and the rest should be unpackaged. The amounts of current supplies are listed in the following table:

Item	Supply (pounds)
Dried bananas	800
Dried apricots	600
Coconut pieces	500
Raisins	700
Walnuts	900

The selling prices of the various types of boxes offered are shown in the next table:

Type	Price per Box
Trail mix	$7.00
Subway mix	3.00
Dried bananas	2.80
Dried apricots	3.25
Coconut pieces	3.60
Raisins	3.50
Walnuts	5.50

The manager would like to obtain as much revenue as possible from prepackaged sales. The manager has stipulated that no more than 30 percent of the prepackaged stock should be allocated to the mixes. The trail mix consists of equal parts of all individual items, whereas the subway mix consists of two parts walnuts and one part each of dried bananas, raisins, and coconut pieces.

Formulate the linear programming model for this problem.

20. A financial adviser recently received a call from a client who wanted to invest a portion of a $150,000 inheritance. The client wanted to realize an annual income, but also wanted to spend some of the money. After discussing the matter, the client and the adviser agreed that a mutual fund, corporate bonds, and a money market account would make suitable investments. The client was willing to leave allocation of the funds among these investment vehicles to the financial adviser, but with these provisions:

 1. At least 20 percent of the amount invested should be in the money market account.
 2. The investment must produce at least $12,000 annually.
 3. The uninvested portion should be as large as possible.

 The annual returns would be 11 percent for the mutual fund, 8 percent for the bonds, and 7 percent for the money market. Formulate an LP model that will achieve the client's requests. Ignore transaction costs, the adviser's fee, and so on. (Hint: All terms in the objective function must include a variable.)

21. Wineco produces wine coolers and sells them to retail distributors. One popular blend consists of wine, apple juice, and grape juice. Operators must adhere to certain guidelines when preparing the wine cooler:

 1. At least 10 percent of the mix must be grape juice.
 2. The ratio of apple juice to grape juice must be 2½:1.
 3. The mix must contain between 20 percent and 25 percent wine.

 The company pays $1.20 per gallon for wine, $1.40 per gallon for grape juice, and $.60 per gallon for apple juice.

 Formulate an LP model that will help the owner to determine how much wine cooler to mix each day if the capacity of the mixing equipment is 200 gallons per day and the wine cooler is sold for $4 a gallon. The owner wants to maximize profits. Ignore mixing and bottling costs.

22. The planning committee of a bank makes monthly decisions on the amount of funds to allocate to loans and to government securities. Some of the loans are secured (backed by collateral such as a home or an automobile), and some are unsecured. A list of the various types of loans and their annual rates of return are shown in the following table:

Type of Loan	Annual Rate of Return
Secured	
Residential mortgage	11
Commercial mortgage	12
Automobile	15
Home improvement	13
Unsecured	
Vacation	17
Student	10

The current rate on government securities is 9 percent.

In making its decision, the planning committee must satisfy certain legal requirements and bank policies. These can be summarized by the following set of conditions:

1. The amount allocated to secured loans must be at least four times the amount allocated to unsecured loans.
2. Auto and home loans should be no more than 20 percent of all secured loans.
3. Student loans should be no more than 30 percent of unsecured loans.
4. The amount allocated to government securities should be at least 10 percent, but no more than 20 percent, of available funds.
5. The amount allocated to vacation loans must not exceed 10 percent of all loans.

The bank has $5 million dollars available for loans and investments in the next month. Formulate a linear programming model that will enable the planning committee to determine the optimal allocation of funds if the objective is to maximize the annual return, given the preceding list of conditions.

23. A classic linear programming problem involves minimizing trim loss. Here is one version of the problem:

A mill cuts 20-foot pieces of wood into several different lengths: 8-foot, 10-foot, and 12-foot. The mill has a certain amount of 20-foot stock on hand and orders for the various sizes. The objective is to fill the orders with as little waste as possible. For example, if two 8-foot lengths are cut from a 20-foot piece, there will be a loss of 4 feet, the leftover amount.

Currently, the mill has 350 20-foot pieces of wood on hand and the following orders, which must be filled from stock on hand:

Size in feet	Number Ordered
8	275
10	100
12	250

a. Formulate an LP model that will enable the mill operator to satisfy the orders with minimum trim loss. (Hint: list the different ways the 20-foot pieces could be cut into the desired sizes.)

b. Using your notation from ***a***, write an equation for:

(1) The amount of waste that would result given a solution.

(2) The number of pieces of each size (8-foot, 10-foot, and 12-foot).

Chapter 2 Case

Direct Marketing

A direct marketing agency has been asked by a client to do a lead-generation mailing. The purpose of the mailing will be to offer prospective investors long-term notes at preferred rates. Names and addresses for the mailing will be obtained from three lists: CPAs, real estate developers, and personal investors. The cost and response rates for these are shown in the following table:

List	Cost per 1,000	Expected Response Rate
CPAs	$ 85	2%
Real estate developers	110	3
Personal investors	95	6

The conversion of leads into sales is expected to be 1 in 20. Moreover, the client has stipulated several additional conditions:

1. Between 10 and 20 percent of the mailing should be to CPAs.
2. No fewer than 10,000 pieces should go to real estate developers.

For purposes of analysis, assume that the lists are large enough to support the mailing sizes that will be called for and assume that the amount of duplication in the lists is negligible. However, assume that 5 percent of the names on a list will be unusable because of deaths, changes in address, and so on. Lists can be ordered in any amount.

The account executive in charge of the mailing wants to answer these questions before deciding whether to approve the mailing:

1. What size mailing will be needed?
2. How many names from each list will be needed?
3. What will be the list cost?
4. What will be the expected response rate?
5. What will be the cost per lead?

Required:

Prepare a report that addresses the following points:

1. Formulate this as an LP model that will minimize cost assuming the client wants to achieve at least 250 responses.
2. Formulate this as an LP model that will maximize expected responses given a budget of $20,000.
3. For each of the questions posed in the problem, write an equation that can be used to answer the question.

Chapter 3 Linear Programming

Graphical Solutions

Chapter Outline

Learning Objectives

After completing this chapter, you should be able to:

1. Identify LP problems that are amenable to graphical solution.
2. Define or explain terms such as *optimal solution, feasible solution space, corner point, redundant constraint, slack,* and *surplus*.
3. Solve two-variable LP problems graphically and interpret your answers.
4. Recognize problems that have multiple solutions, problems that have no feasible solutions, and unbounded problems.

INTRODUCTION

Graphical linear programming is a relatively straightforward method for determining the optimal solution to certain linear programming problems. In practical terms, this method can be used only to solve problems that involve two decision variables. However, most linear programming applications involve situations that have more than two decision variables, so graphical linear programming methods cannot be used to solve them. Even so, much can be gained from studying the graphical approach, particularly in terms of the insight it generates about important concepts of models and solutions. Graphical methods provide a visual portrayal of many important concepts. Moreover, they provide a framework for intuitive explanations of other LP techniques that are covered in later chapters. Viewed from this perspective, graphical LP is a valuable learning tool.

In order to demonstrate the graphical method, the microcomputer problem that was formulated in the preceding chapter will be solved. The model is:

x_1 = quantity of Type 1 computers to produce per day
x_2 = quantity of Type 2 computers to produce per day

maximize $60x_1 + 50x_2$

subject to

Assembly	$4x_1 + 10x_2 \leq$	100 hours
Inspection	$2x_1 + 1x_2 \leq$	22 hours
Storage	$3x_1 + 3x_2 \leq$	39 cubic feet
	$x_1, x_2 \geq 0$	

GRAPHING THE MODEL

The first step in the graphical method is to graph the model. Graphing consists of several distinct steps:

1. Plot each of the constraints.
2. Determine the region or area that contains all of the points that satisfy the entire *set* of constraints.
3. Determine the optimal solution.

Let's examine each of these steps as we solve the microcomputer problem.

Plotting the Constraints

We begin by plotting the non-negativity constraints, as shown in Figure 3–1. For purposes of illustration, the area of feasibility for these two constraints (i.e., the area that satisfies both constraints) has been shaded in. However, as a general rule, the shading would be done after all constraints have been plotted.

FIGURE 3-1 A Graph Showing the Non-Negativity Constraints

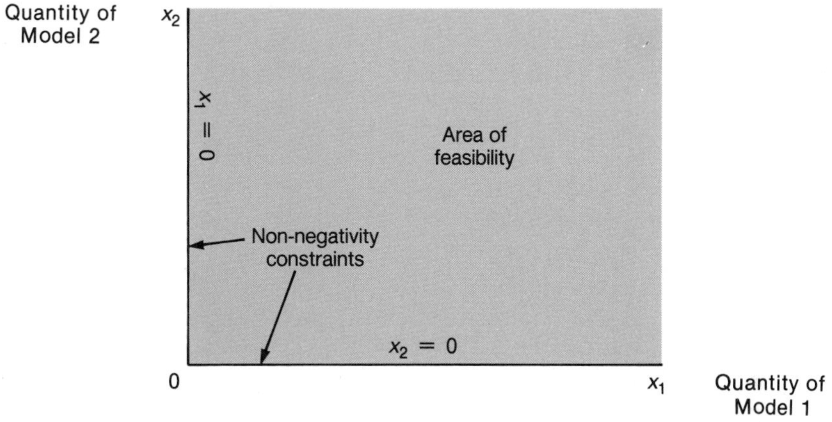

The procedure for graphing each of the remaining constraints relies on the fact that a straight line can be plotted if any two points on that line can be identified. Of course, the constraints in this problem are all inequalities rather than lines. As such, they describe a region or area that will satisfy them. However, the boundary of that area of feasibility is represented by the "equal" portion of the "less than or equal to" constraint. Recognizing this, we can deal with the task of graphing a constraint in two parts. First, treat the constraint as an equality and plot the straight line that is the boundary of the feasible region; then, shade in the feasible region.

Consider the assembly time constraint:

$$4x_1 + 10x_2 \leq 100$$

Removing the inequality portion of the constraint produces this straight line:

$$4x_1 + 10x_2 = 100$$

There are a number of different ways to determine the coordinates of two points on the line. Perhaps the easiest two points to identify and work with are the points where the line intersects each axis (i.e., where $x_1 = 0$ and where $x_2 = 0$). We can solve for those points, first by setting $x_2 = 0$ and solving for x_1, and then setting $x_1 = 0$ and solving for x_2. Thus with $x_2 = 0$, we find:

$$4x_1 + 10(0) = 100$$

Solving, we find that $4x_1 = 100$, so $x_1 = 25$ when $x_2 = 0$. Similarly, we can solve the equation for x_2 when $x_1 = 0$:

$$4(0) + 10x_2 = 100$$

Solving for x_2, we find $x_2 = 10$ when $x_1 = 0$.

FIGURE 3–2 A Plot of the First Constraint (assembly time)

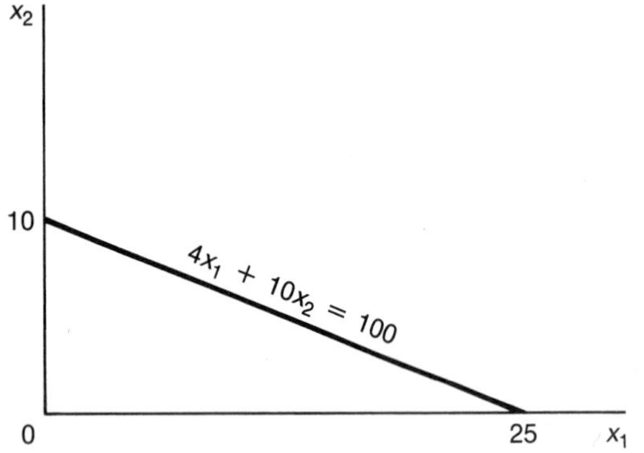

FIGURE 3–3 The Feasible Region, Given the First Constraint and the Non-Negativity Constraints

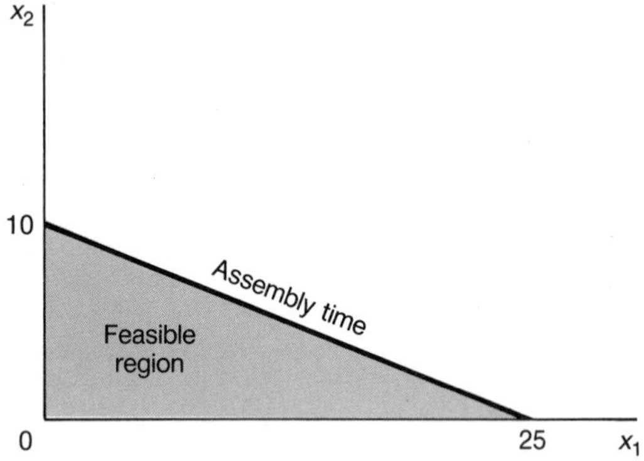

Thus, we have two points: $x_1 = 0, x_2 = 10$, and $x_1 = 25, x_2 = 0$. We can now add this line to our graph of the non-negativity constraints by connecting these two points (see Figure 3–2).

Next we must determine which side of the line represents points that are less than 100. To do this, we can select a test point that is not on the line, and we can substitute the x_1 and x_2 values of that point into the left side of the equation of the line. If the result is less than 100, this tells us that all points on that side of the line are less than the value of the line (e.g., 100). Conversely, if the result is greater than 100, this indicates that the other side of the line represents the set of points that will yield values that are less than 100. A relatively simple test point to use is the origin (i.e., $x_1 = 0$, $x_2 = 0$). Substituting these values into the equation yields:

$$4(0) + 10(0) = 0$$

Obviously this is less than 100. Hence, the side of the line closest to the origin represents the "less than" area.

The feasible region for this constraint and the non-negativity constraints then becomes the shaded portion shown in Figure 3–3.

For the sake of illustration, suppose we try one other point, say $x_1 = 10$, $x_2 = 10$. Substituting these values into the assembly constraint yields:

$$4(10) + 10(10) = 140$$

Clearly this is greater than 100. Therefore, all points on this side of the line are greater than 100 (see Figure 3–4).

FIGURE 3–4 The Point 10, 10 is above the Constraint Line

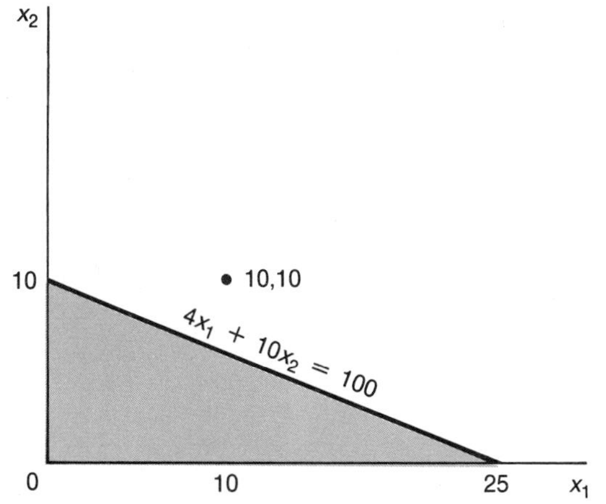

FIGURE 3–5 A Partially Completed Graph of the Microcomputer Problem Showing the Assembly, Inspection, and Non-Negativity Constraints

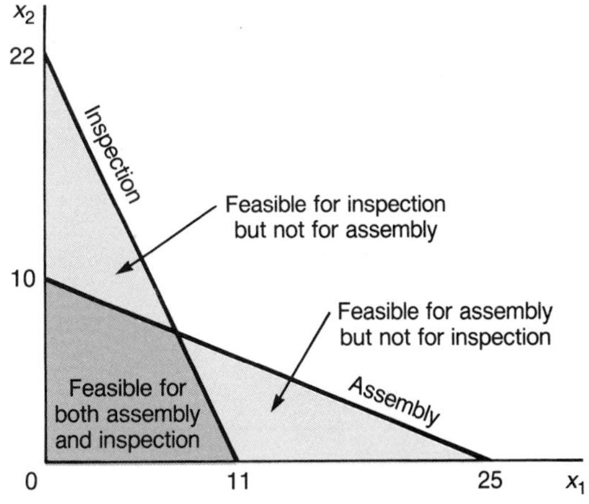

Continuing with the problem, we can add the two remaining constraints to the graph. For the inspection constraint:

1. Convert the constraint into the equation of a straight line by replacing the inequality sign with an equality sign:

   $$2x_1 + 1x_2 \leq 22 \quad \text{becomes} \quad 2x_1 + 1x_2 = 22$$

2. Set x_1 equal to zero and solve for x_2:

   $$2(0) + 1x_2 = 22$$

   Solving, we find $x_2 = 22$. Thus, the line will intersect the x_2 axis at 22.
3. Next, set x_2 equal to zero and solve for x_1:

   $$2x_1 + 1(0) = 22$$

   Solving, we find $x_1 = 11$. Thus, the other end of the line will intersect the x_1 axis at 11.
4. Add the line to the graph (see Figure 3–5).
5. Note that the area of feasibility for this constraint is below the line. Again the area of feasibility at this point is shaded in for illustration, although when graphing problems, it is more practical to refrain from shading in the **feasible solution space** until all constraint lines have been drawn. However, because constraints are plotted one at a time, using a small arrow for each to indicate the direction of feasibility can be helpful.

FIGURE 3–6 Completed Graph of the Microcomputer Problem Showing All of the Constraints and the Feasible Solution Space

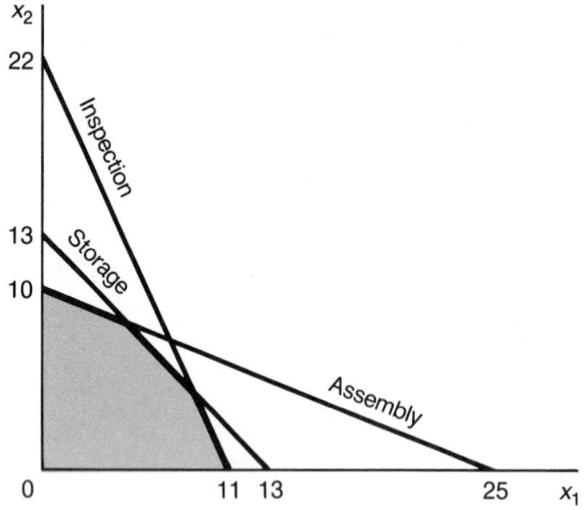

The storage constraint is handled in the same manner:

1. Convert it into an equality:

$$3x_1 + 3x_2 = 39$$

2. Set x_1 equal to zero and solve for x_2:

$$3(0) + 3x_2 = 39$$

Solving, $x_2 = 13$. Thus, $x_2 = 13$ when $x_1 = 0$.

3. Set x_2 equal to zero and solve for x_1:

$$3x_1 + 3(0) = 39$$

Solving, $x_1 = 13$. Thus, $x_1 = 13$ when $x_2 = 0$.

4. Add the line to the graph (see Figure 3–6).
5. Determine the feasible solution space—the area that satisfies all of the constraints—and shade it in (see Figure 3–6).

FINDING THE OPTIMAL SOLUTION

Once the constraints have been graphed and the area of feasibility has been identified, it is possible to obtain the optimal solution to the problem. Two different approaches to obtaining the solution will be demonstrated. One involves examining points at the edge of the feasible solution space where constraints meet, and the other involves graphing the objective function. The extreme point approach will be demonstrated first.

The Extreme Point Approach

The **extreme point** approach involves finding the coordinates of each corner point that borders the feasible solution space, and then determining which corner point provides the best value of the objective function (i.e., the highest value for a maximization problem or the lowest value for a minimization problem). An important mathematical theorem provides the rationale for this approach: The **extreme point theorem** states that if a problem has an **optimal solution,** at least one optional solution will occur at a corner point of the feasible solution space. Note that not every problem has an optimal solution; for example, some do not have a feasible solution space. Also note that the extreme point theorem does not exclude the occurrence of an optimal solution somewhere else on the border of the feasible solution space (solutions will *only* occur on the border, never at an internal point of the feasible solution space). In fact, problems that have *multiple* optimal solutions will have solutions that occur at points along a border of the feasible solution space *as well as* at a corner point. In other words, an optimal solution to *every* LP problem that has an optimal solution will occur at a corner point. Therefore, an approach that examines every corner point of the feasible solution space will be able to identify the optimal solution. Note, too, that corner points represent *intersections* of constraints; so finding the corner points involves finding the coordinates of intersections of constraints. Let us now see how this approach works.

The necessary steps are:

1. Graph the problem.
2. Determine the values of the decision variables at each corner point. Sometimes, this can be done by inspection; usually, it is done using simultaneous equations.
3. Substitute the values of the decision variables at each corner point into the objective function to obtain its value at each corner point.
4. After all corner points have been so evaluated, select the one with the highest value of the objective function (for a maximization problem) or lowest value (for a minimization problem) as the optimal solution.

We can use the extreme point approach to verify the optimal solution for the microcomputer problem that will be obtained in the next section using the objective function approach.

The extreme point solution can be obtained by following the steps outlined above. Figure 3–7 repeats the graph of the problem that was constructed previously in Figure 3–6, with each of the extreme points now labeled for discussion purposes. Note that 0,0 is included as an extreme point, even though it will not yield any profit because both decision variables are equal to zero.

Table 3–1 summarizes the approach used to obtain each point and its profit.

FIGURE 3–7 Graph of Microcomputer Problem with Extreme Points of the Feasible Solution Space Indicated

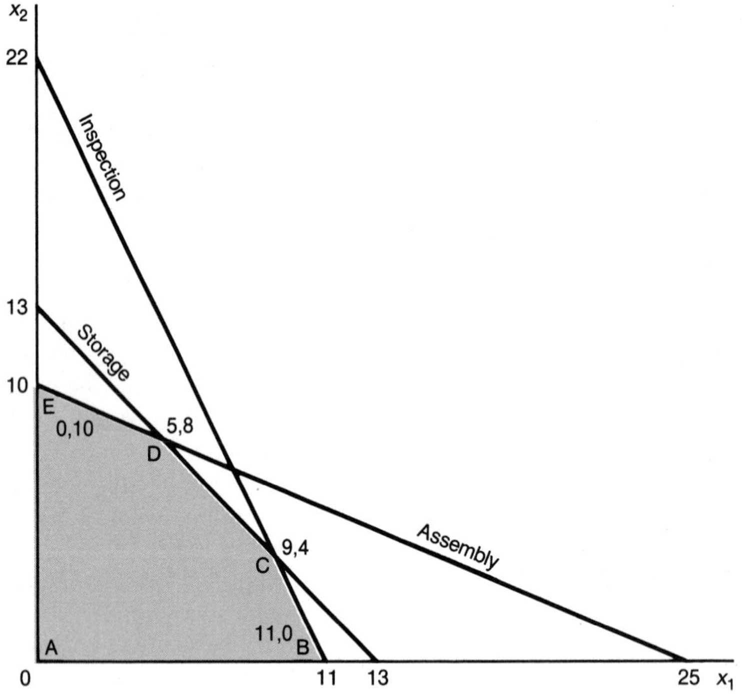

TABLE 3–1 Extreme Point Solutions for the Microcomputer Problem

Point	Coordinates x_1	x_2	How Determined	Value of the Objective Function
A	0	0	Inspection	\$60(0) + \$50(0) = \$0
B	11	0	Inspection	\$60(11) + \$50(0) = \$660
C	9	4	Simultaneous equations	\$60(9) + \$50(4) = \$740 (largest)
D	5	8	Simultaneous equations	\$60(5) + \$50(8) = \$700
E	0	10	Inspection	\$60(0) + \$50(10) = \$500

Note that the coordinates of points A, B, and E were determined by inspection. The coordinates of the origin are obvious. In addition, the x_1 intercept of the inspection constraint and the x_2 intercept of the assembly constraint were known by having determined them in the course of plotting the constraints. The coordinates of point C and point D can be determined by the solution of simultaneous equations. Using point D to illustrate, we can solve simultaneously for the intersection of the assembly and storage lines (see Figure 3–7):

$$\begin{array}{lrcl} \text{Assembly} & 4x_1 + 10x_2 & = & 100 \\ \text{Storage} & 3x_1 + 3x_2 & = & 39 \end{array}$$

As usual, there are a number of ways for obtaining a common solution to this set of equations. One way would be to multiply each coefficient of the assembly constraint by $\frac{3}{4}$, thereby resulting in a new x_1 coefficient of 3, which would lead to the elimination of x_1. Thus:

$$\frac{3}{4}(4x_1 + 10x_2 = 100) = 3x_1 + 7.5x_2 = 75$$

Subtracting the storage line from this new line results in one equation with x_2 the only variable:

$$\begin{array}{lrcl} \text{New} & 3x_1 + 7.5x_2 & = & 75 \\ \text{Storage} & -(3x_1 + 3x_2 & = & 39) \\ \hline & 4.5x_2 & = & 36 \quad \text{Solving, } x_2 = 8 \end{array}$$

By substituting $x_2 = 8$ into either of the original lines, or the new line, the value of x_1 at intersection D can be determined. If the original assembly equation is used, we find:

$$4x_1 + 10(8) = 100$$

Solving, $x_1 = 5$. Hence, the coordinates of point D are $x_1 = 5$ and $x_2 = 8$.

The profit at each corner point can be computed by substituting the coordinates of the point into the objective function. Point C ($x_1 = 9$, $x_2 = 4$) represents the optimal solution because it yields the largest profit for the extreme points (see Table 3–1).

The Objective Function Approach

The objective function approach avoids the need to determine the coordinates of all of the corner points of the feasible solution space. Instead, this approach directly identifies the optimal corner point, so only the coordinates of the optimal point need to be determined. It accomplishes this by adding the objective function to the graph and then using it to determine which point is optimal. Let's see how the objective function approach works.

FIGURE 3–8 Microcomputer Problem with $300 Profit Line Added

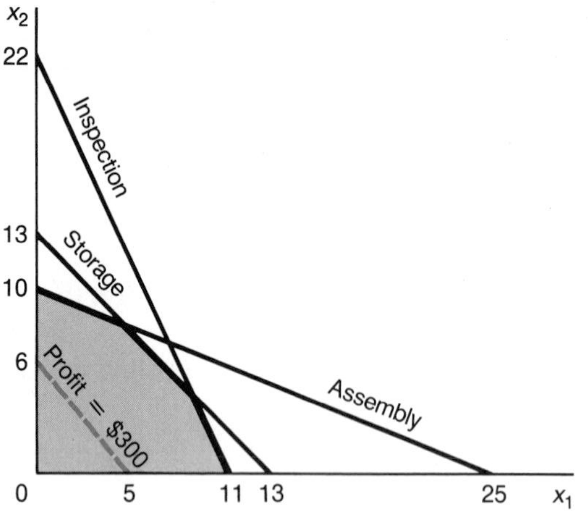

FIGURE 3–9 The Microcomputer Problem with Profit Lines of $300 and $600

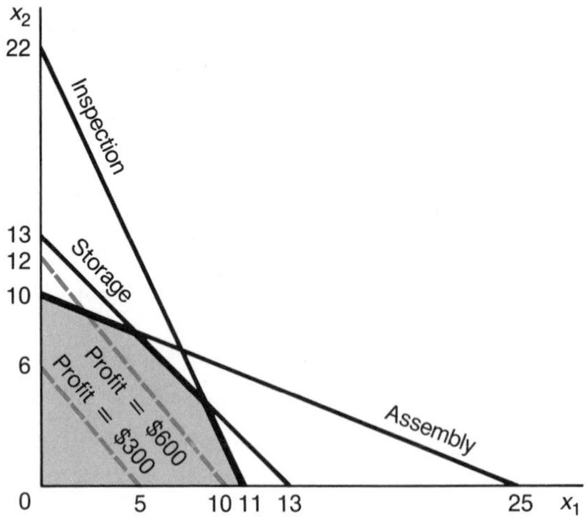

The first step is to plot the objective function. Plotting an objective function line involves the same logic as plotting a constraint line: Determine where the line intersects each axis. Recall that the objective function for the microcomputer problem is:

$$60x_1 + 50x_2$$

Now, this is not an equation because it does not include an equal sign. We can get around this by simply setting it equal to some quantity. Any quantity will do, although one that is evenly divisible by both coefficients is desirable.

Suppose we decide to set the objective function equal to 300. That is:

$$60x_1 + 50x_2 = 300$$

We can now plot the line of our graph. As before, we can determine the x_1 and x_2 intercepts of the line by setting one of the two variables equal to zero, solving for the other, and then reversing the process. Thus, with $x_1 = 0$, we have:

$$60(0) + 50x_2 = 300$$

Solving, we find $x_2 = 6$. Similarly, with $x_2 = 0$, we have:

$$60x_1 + 50(0) = 300$$

Solving, we find $x_1 = 5$.

This line is plotted in Figure 3–8.

The profit line can be interpreted in the following way. Every point on the line (i.e., every combination of x_1 and x_2 that lies on the line) will provide a profit of $300. We can see from the graph many combinations that are both on the $300

FIGURE 3–10 The Microcomputer Problem with Profit Lines of \$300, \$600, and \$900

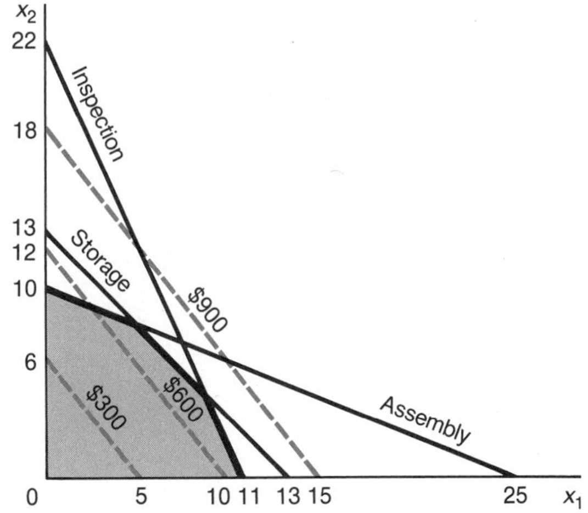

profit line and within the feasible solution space. In fact, considering noninteger as well as integer solutions, the possibilities are infinite.

Suppose we now consider another line, say the \$600 line. To do this, we set the objective function equal to this amount. Thus:

$$60x_1 + 50x_2 = 600$$

Solving for the x_1 and x_2 intercepts yields these two points:

x_1 intercept	x_2 intercept
$x_1 = 10$	$x_1 = 0$
$x_2 = 0$	$x_2 = 12$

This line is plotted in Figure 3–9, along with the previous \$300 line for purposes of comparison.

Two things are evident in Figure 3–9 regarding the profit lines. One is that the \$600 line is *farther* from the origin than the \$300 line; the other is that the two lines are *parallel*. The lines are parallel because they both have the same slope. The slope is not affected by the right side of the equation. Rather, it is determined solely by the coefficients 60 and 50. It would be correct to conclude that regardless of the quantity we select for the value of the objective function, the resulting line will be parallel to these two lines. Moreover, if the amount is greater than 600, the line will be even farther away from the origin than the \$600 line. If the value is less than 300, the line will be closer to the origin than the \$300 line. And if the value is between 300 and 600, the line will fall between the \$300 and \$600 lines.

Now consider a third line, one with the profit equal to \$900. That line is shown in Figure 3–10 along with the previous two profit lines. As expected, it is parallel

FIGURE 3–11 Finding the Optimal Solution to the Microcomputer Problem

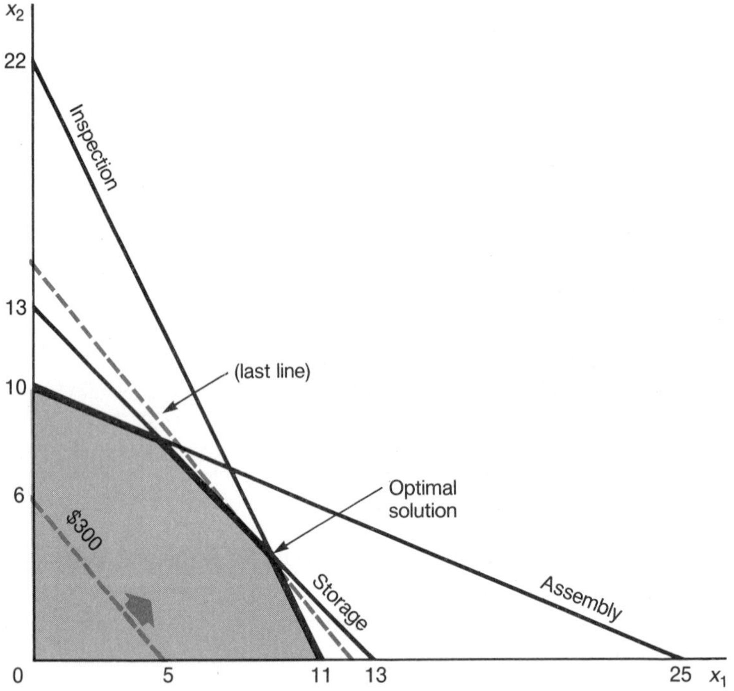

to the other two, and even farther away from the origin. However, the line does not touch the feasible solution space at all. Consequently, there is no feasible combination of x_1 and x_2 that will yield that amount of profit. Evidently, the maximum possible profit is an amount between $600 and $900, which we can see by referring to Figure 3–10. We could continue to select profit lines in this manner, and eventually, we could determine an amount that would yield the greatest profit. However, there is a much simpler alternative. We can plot just one line, say the $300 line. We know that all other lines will be parallel to it. Consequently, by moving this one line parallel to itself we can represent other profit lines. We also know that as we move away from the origin, the profits get larger. What we want to know is how far the line can be moved out from the origin and still be touching the feasible solution space, and the values of the decision variables at that point of greatest profit (i.e., the optimal solution). We can locate this point on the graph by placing a straight edge along the $300 line (or any other convenient line) and sliding it away from the origin, being careful to keep it parallel to the $300 line. This approach is illustrated in Figure 3–11.

Once we have determined where the optimal solution is in the feasible solution space, we must determine what the values of the decision variables are at that point. Then, we can use that information to compute the profit for that combination.

Note that the optimal solution is at the intersection of the inspection boundary and the storage boundary (see Figure 3–10). In other words, the optimal combination of x_1 and x_2 must satisfy both boundary (equality) conditions. We can determine those values by solving the two equations *simultaneously*. The equations are:

Inspection	$2x_1 + 1x_2 = 22$
Storage	$3x_1 + 3x_2 = 39$

The idea behind solving two **simultaneous equations** is to algebraically eliminate one of the unknown variables (i.e., to obtain an equation with a single unknown). This can be accomplished by multiplying the constants of one of the equations by a fixed amount and then adding (or subtracting) the modified equation from the other. (Occasionally, it is easier to multiply each equation by a fixed quantity.) For example, we can eliminate x_2 by multiplying the inspection equation by 3 and then subtracting the storage equation from the modified inspection equation. Thus:

$$3(2x_1 + 1x_2 = 22) \quad \text{becomes} \quad 6x_1 + 3x_2 = 66$$

Subtracting the storage equation from this produces:

$$\begin{array}{r} 6x_1 + 3x_2 = 66 \\ -(3x_1 + 3x_2 = 39) \\ \hline 3x_1 + 0x_2 = 27 \end{array}$$

Solving the resulting equation yields $x_1 = 9$. The value of x_2 can be found by substituting $x_1 = 9$ into either of the original equations or the modified inspection equation. Suppose we use the original inspection equation. We have:

$$2(9) + 1x_2 = 22$$

Solving, we find $x_2 = 4$.

Hence, the optimal solution to the microcomputer problem is to produce nine Type 1 computers and four Type 2 computers per day. We can substitute these values into the objective function to find the optimal profit. Thus:

$$\$60(9) + \$50(4) = \$740$$

Hence, the last line—the one that would last touch the feasible solution space as we moved away from the origin parallel to the $300 profit line—would be the line where profit equaled $740.

In this problem, the optimal values for both decision variables are integers. Now this will not always be the case—one or both of the decision variables may turn out to be non-integer. In some situations non-integer values would be of little consequence. This would be the case if the decision variables were measured on a continuous scale, such as the amount of water, sand, sugar, fuel oil, time, or distance needed for optimality, or if the contribution per unit (profit, cost, etc.) were small, as would be the case with the number of nails or ball bearings to make. In some cases, the answer would simply be rounded down (maximization problems) or up (minimization problems) with very little impact on the objective function. In this chapter and the following two chapters, it will be assumed that non-integer answers are acceptable as such. Chapter 8 on integer programming will discuss how to obtain optimal integer solutions.

Note that the solution to this problem occurred where two constraint lines intersected. These intersections are called **corner points,** or *extreme points,* of the feasible solution space. The optimal solution to an LP problem will always occur at a corner point because as the objective function line is moved in the direction that will improve its value (e.g., away from the origin in a maximization problem), it will last touch one of these intersections of constraints. (In fact, this is the basis for the extreme point approach to finding the optimal solution that was demonstrated in the previous section.)

Let's review the procedure for finding the optimal solution using the objective function approach:

1. Graph the constraints.
2. Identify the feasible solution space.
3. Set the objective function equal to some amount that is divisible by each of the objective function coefficients. This will yield integer values for the x_1 and x_2 intercepts and, thereby, simplify plotting the line. Often, the product of the two objective function coefficients will provide a satisfactory line. Ideally, the line selected will cross the feasible solution space close to the optimal point, in which case it would not be necessary to slide a straight edge: The optimal solution can be readily identified visually.
4. After identifying the optimal point, determine which two constraints intersect there. Solve their equations simultaneously to obtain the values of x_1 and x_2 at the optimum.
5. Substitute the values obtained in the previous step into the objective function to determine the value of the objective function at the optimum.

SLACK

Slack is the amount of scarce resource that is *unused* by a given solution. This amount can range from zero, for a case in which all of a particular resource is used, to the original amount of the resource that was available (i.e., none of it is used).

Let's see what slack remains for the optimal solution to the microcomputer problem. The amount of unused resource can be computed by substituting the

TABLE 3–2 Computing the Amount of Slack for the Optimal Solution to the Microcomputer Problem

Constraint	Amount Used with $x_1 = 9$ and $x_2 = 4$	Originally Available	Amount of Slack (Available − Used)
Assembly	4(9) + 10(4) = 76	100	100 − 76 = 24 hours
Inspection	2(9) + 1(4) = 22	22	22 − 22 = 0 hours
Storage	3(9) + 3(4) = 39	39	39 − 39 = 0 cubic feet

values of the decision variables into each constraint and subtracting the result from the original right-hand side amount. Thus, the original constraints were:

Assembly time $4x_1 + 10x_2 \leq 100$ hours
Inspection time $2x_1 + 1x_2 \leq 22$ hours
Storage space $3x_1 + 3x_2 \leq 39$ cubic feet

The optimal values of the decision variables were:

$x_1 = 9, x_2 = 4$

Substituting these values into the constraints yields the results shown in Table 3–2.

We can see that 24 hours of assembly time will be unused given the optimal solution, but that all of the inspection time and storage space will be used. Recall our graphical solution to the problem (see Figure 3–10). The optimal solution was at the corner point where the inspection and storage constraint line intersected (i.e., at those boundaries), which implied that all of those resources would be used. Constraints that have no slack are sometimes referred to as **binding constraints** since they limit, or bind, the solution. Because the assembly boundary was not involved, we would expect that some assembly time would remain, although we cannot easily tell from the graph how much assembly time would be unused. If the optimal solution had been at the point where the assembly and storage constraints met, assembly and storage slacks would have been zero, although some unused inspection time would have remained.

Knowledge of unused capacity can be useful for planning. A manager may be able to use the remaining assembly time for other products, or, perhaps, to schedule equipment maintenance, safety seminars, training sessions, or other activities. In still another vein, it may be profitable to consider the acquisition of additional amounts of the two other resources to allow for greater use of the assembly resource and, thereby, to increase profits by increasing the size of the feasible solution space. This topic is discussed in the chapter supplement and in Chapter 6.

Slack can potentially exist in a $\leq$ constraint. Moreover, it can be useful to represent slack in a constraint. This is accomplished using a *slack variable, s,* which carries a subscript that denotes which constraint it applies to. For instance, s_1 refers to the amount of slack in the first constraint, s_2 to the amount of slack in the second constraint, and so on. When slack variables are added to the constraints, they are no longer inequalities because the slack variable accounts for any difference between the left- and right-hand sides of the expression. Hence, once slack variables are added to the constraints, they become *equalities.* Furthermore, every variable in a model must be represented in the objective function. However, since slack does not provide any real contribution to the objective, each slack variable is assigned a coefficient of zero in the objective function. With slack variables included, the microcomputer problem would appear as follows:

maximize

$$60x_1 + 50x_2 + 0s_1 + 0s_2 + 0s_3$$

subject to

Assembly	$4x_1 + 10x_2 + s_1$	$= 100$
Inspection	$2x_1 + 1x_2 \quad s_2$	$= 22$
Storage	$3x_1 + 3x_2 + s_3$	$= 39$

All variables ≥ 0

Note that all variables, including slack variables, must be non-negative.

When all of the constraints are written as equalities, the linear program is said to be in **standard form.**

A MINIMIZATION EXAMPLE

Graphical solutions to minimization problems are very similar to solutions to maximization problems. There are a few differences that will be highlighted in this section. The main differences are that the constraints, in general, are the greater than or equal to variety, which causes the feasible solution space to be restricted to an area away from the origin, instead of close to the origin, as in a maximization problem, and the optimum is the point with the smallest possible value of the objective function, instead of the largest. These contrasts are illustrated in Figure 3–12.

■

EXAMPLE 1 Determine the values of decision variables x_1 and x_2 that will yield the minimum cost in the following problem. Solve using the objective function approach.

FIGURE 3–12 A Comparison of Maximization and Minimization Problems

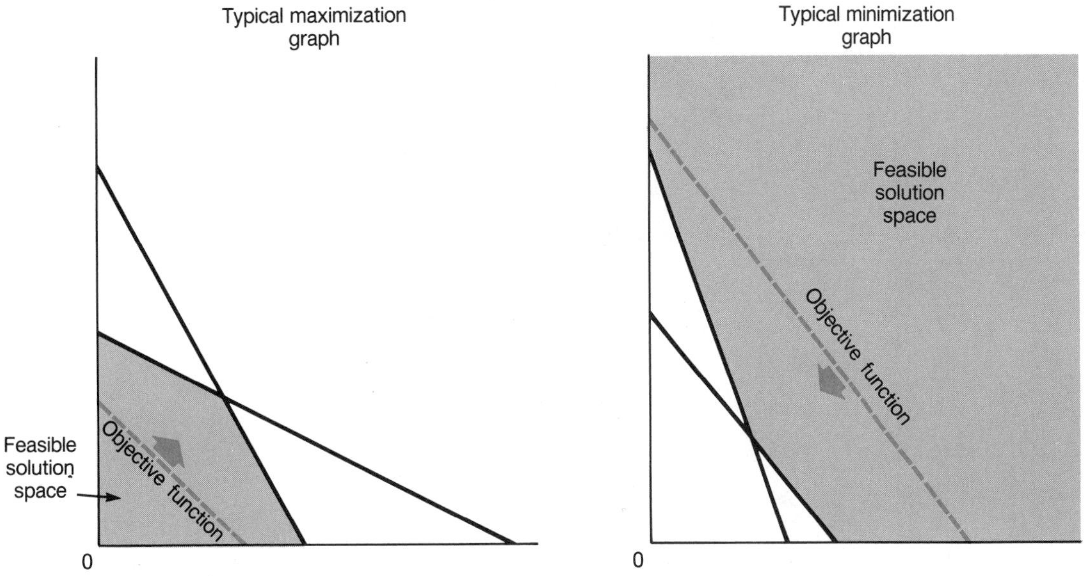

$$
\begin{array}{lrl}
\text{minimize} & .10x_1 + .07x_2 & \\
\text{subject to} & & \\
\quad \text{Constraint 1} & 6x_1 + \;\; 2x_2 \geq & 18 \\
\quad \text{Constraint 2} & 8x_1 + 10x_2 \geq & 40 \\
\quad \text{Constraint 3} & x_2 \geq & 1 \\
 & x_1 \text{ and } x_2 \geq 0 &
\end{array}
$$

Solution

Graph the constraints using this procedure:

1. Treat each constraint as an equality.
2. For the first two constraints, find the x_1 intercept by setting x_2 equal to 0 and solving for x_1, and then find the x_2 intercept by setting x_1 equal to 0 and solving for x_2. For the third constraint, x_2 is simply equal to 1.
3. Plot these constraints.

Shade in the feasible solution space. (See Figure 3–13.)

Using the objective function approach, we would next plot the objective function on the graph. To do so, we must select an amount to set the objective function equal to. The product of the two cost coefficients is .10(.07) = .007, which would have an x_1 intercept of .07 and an x_2 intercept of .10. Unfortunately, these intercepts are so close

FIGURE 3–13 A Graph of the Constraints and the Feasible Solution Space for Example 1

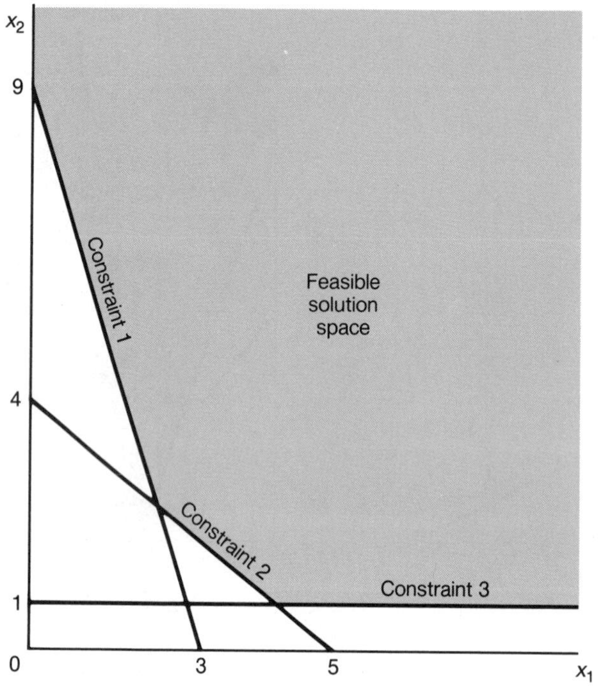

to the origin that they will not provide a good indication of the objective function. Suppose we increase our cost function by a factor of 100, to .70. This results in an objective function of:

$$.10x_1 + .07x_2 = .70$$

The x_1 intercept would now be 7 and the x_2 intercept would be 10. This line is much more acceptable because it crosses the feasible solution space in the region close to what we now perceive as the optimal solution. (See Figure 3–14.)

Because the solution is at the intersection of constraints 1 and 2, we can solve their equations simultaneously to determine the optimal values of x_1 and x_2. As before, the approach is to multiply the constants in one equation by some amount that will cause one of the two variables to drop out when the modified equation is added to, or subtracted from, the other. In this case, the coefficient of x_2 in the second constraint is 5 times the value of the x_2 coefficient in the first constraint, so multiplying the first equation by 5 and then subtracting the second from the first equation will eliminate x_2. Thus:

$$5(6x_1 + 2x_2 = 18) \quad \text{becomes} \quad 30x_1 + 10x_2 = 90$$

FIGURE 3-14 Using the Objective Function to Find the Optimum for Example 1

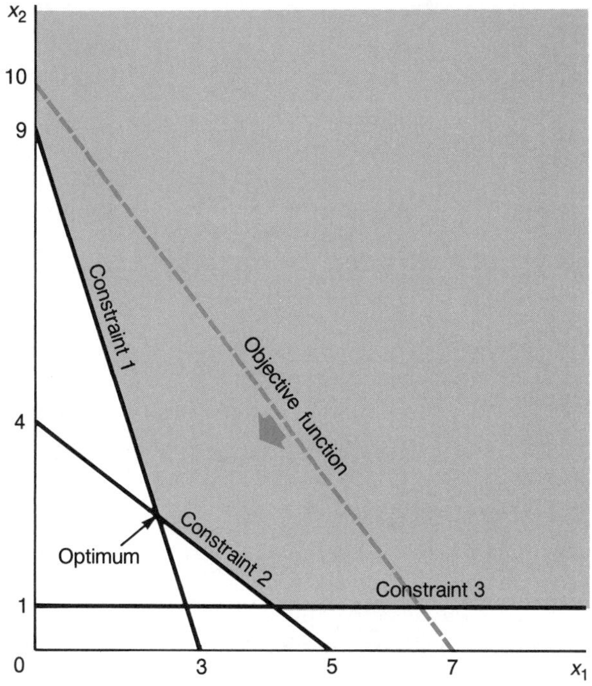

Subtracting the second constraint equation from this yields:

$$\begin{array}{rcl} 30x_1 + 10x_2 & = & 90 \\ -(\ 8x_1 + 10x_2 & = & 40) \\ \hline 22x_1 \qquad\quad & = & 50 \end{array}$$

Solving, we find $x_1 = 2.27$. Substituting this value into either of the two original constraint equations or the modified first equation will yield a value of $x_2 = 2.19$. For example, using the modified equation, we find:

$30(2.27) + 10x_2 = 90$. Then, $10x_2 = 90 - 30(2.27)$, or $10x_2 = 21.9$

Solving, $x_2 = 21.9/10 = 2.19$.

The optimum value of the objective function (i.e., the minimum cost) is determined by substituting these values into the objective function:

$\$.10(2.27) + \$.07(2.19) = \$.38$

TABLE 3–3 Summary of Extreme Point Analysis for Example 2

Extreme Point		How Determined	Value of the Objective Function
x_1	x_2		
0	9	Inspection (see Figure 3–14)	$.10(0) + $.07(9) = $.63
5	0	Inspection	$.10(5) + $.07(0) = $.50
2.27	2.19	Simultaneous equations (see Example 1)	$.10(2.27) + $.07(2.19) = $.38

■

EXAMPLE 2 Solve the preceding problem using the extreme point approach.

Solution

The extreme points can be determined either by inspection of Figure 3–14 or from simultaneous equations. The results are summarized in Table 3–3.

The minimum value of the objective function is $.38, which occurs when $x_1 = 2.27$ and $x_2 = 2.19$. This agrees with the solution found in Example 1 using the objective function approach.

Surplus

Surplus is the amount by which the optimal solution causes a ≥ constraint to *exceed* the required minimum amount. It can be determined in the same way that slack can: Substitute the optimal values of the decision variables into the left side of the constraint and solve. The difference between the resulting value and the original right-hand side amount is the amount of surplus. For instance, in Example 1, substituting the optimal values into each of the first two constraints would show that there is no surplus. We can also see from the graph (Figure 3–14) that the solution is *on* both lines, so there is no surplus. However, in the third constraint, with $x_2 = 2.19$, we find that the surplus is $2.19 - 1 = 1.19$.

Surplus can only occur in a ≥ constraint. Since surplus is defined as the amount by which the left-hand side of a constraint exceeds the right-hand side, surplus can be represented in a constraint by *subtracting* from the left-hand side. The result is an equality. Also, surplus variables must be accounted for in the objective function. As with slack variables, this is done by using a coefficient of zero for each surplus variable. For the problem illustrated in Example 1, the addition of surplus variables produces the following:

$$\begin{array}{llr}
\text{minimize} & .10x_1 + .07x_2 + 0s_1 + 0s_2 + 0s_3 & \\
\text{subject to} & & \\
1 & 6x_1 + 2x_2 - s_1 & = 18 \\
2 & 8x_1 + 10x_2 - s_2 & = 40 \\
3 & x_2 - s_3 & = 1 \\
 & \text{All variables} \geq 0 &
\end{array}$$

SOME SPECIAL ISSUES

This section points out some special issues that may arise during the formulation or solution of LP problems. These issues are:

1. Problems with no feasible solutions.
2. Unbounded problems.
3. Redundancy in constraints.
4. Problems with multiple optimal solutions.

No Feasible Solutions

It is possible to formulate a problem for which it is impossible to satisfy the set of all constraints. This situation sometimes occurs in problems that have a mix of greater than constraints and less than constraints, where in order to satisfy one of the constraints, another constraint must be violated. Consider the graph in Figure 3–15, where constraint A places an upper bound on feasible solutions and constraint B places a lower bound on feasible solutions. Since the two constraints do not touch or overlap, there is no combination of decision variable values that can satisfy both constraints at the same time.

Sometimes it happens that the problem has been formulated incorrectly (e.g., a constraint coefficient is incorrect, an inequality has the wrong direction). Therefore, when this situation occurs, the first step is to check for one of those errors. If it turns out that the formulation is correct, the manager or analyst might decide to revise some constraint(s), say, by obtaining additional scarce resources, or loosening restrictions. The chapter supplement illustrates that sort of analysis. The manager might decide that some constraints are more important than others and might focus on the important ones. Chapter 9 includes a discussion of *goal programming,* which might be of some use in such instances.

Unbounded Problems

An unbounded problem exists when the value of the objective function can be increased without limit. A graphical example of this is shown in Figure 3–16. This difficulty is usually due to either incorrectly maximizing when the real goal is to minimize an objective function or using greater than constraints when less than

FIGURE 3–15 No Combination of x_1 and x_2 Can Simultaneously Satisfy Both Constraints

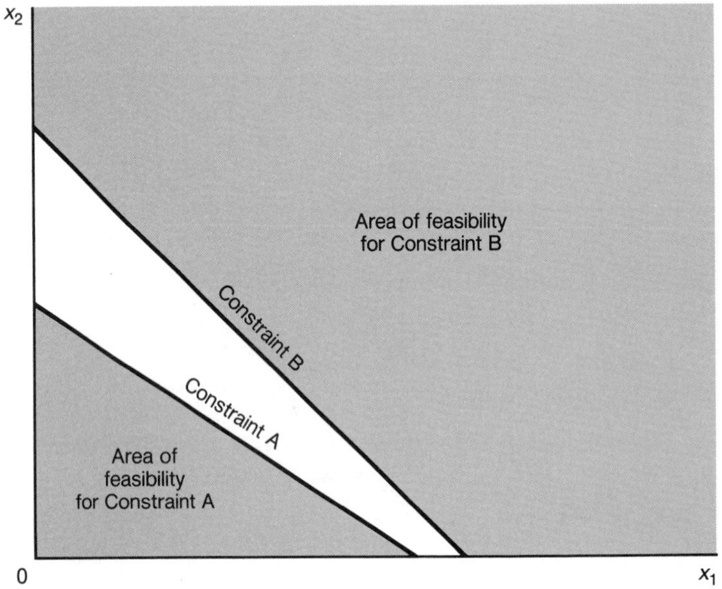

FIGURE 3–16 An Unbounded Solution Space

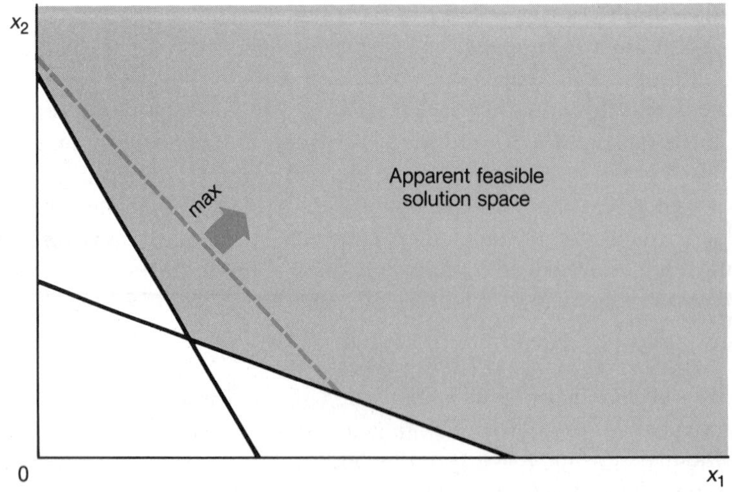

FIGURE 3–17 Examples of Redundant Constraints

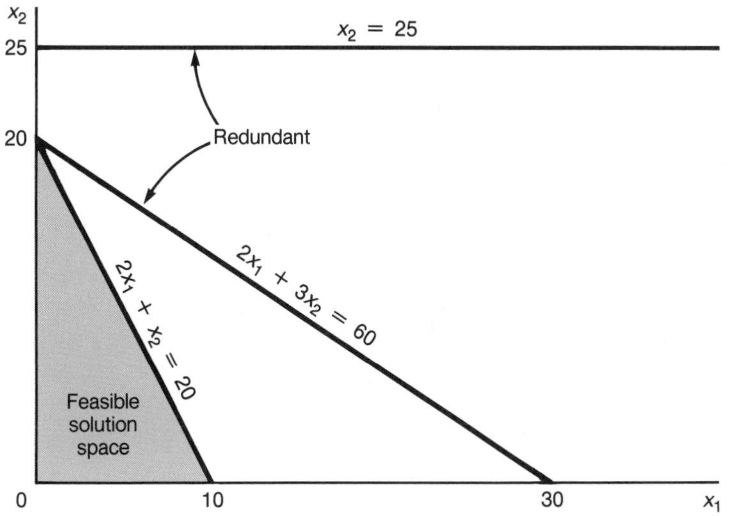

constraints are called for. Although the latter error also may occur in a minimization problem, the problem will not be unbounded because of the non-negativity constraints (i.e., the resulting solution will be 0,0). Again, checking equalities or rethinking the problem statement will resolve the problem. The latter case may uncover another constraint that should have been included in the original statement of the problem.

Redundant Constraints

In some cases, a constraint does not form a unique boundary of the feasible solution space. Such a constraint is called a **redundant constraint.** This constraint is illustrated in Figure 3–17. Note that a constraint is redundant if it meets the following test: Its removal would not alter the feasible solution space.

When a problem has a redundant constraint, at least one of the other constraints in the problem is more restrictive than the redundant constraint.

Multiple Optimal Solutions

Most linear programming problems have a single optimal solution. However, in some instances, a problem will have multiple optimal solutions, which is to say that different combinations of values of the decision variables will yield the same optimal value for the objective function.

Figure 3–18 illustrates how this happens in a two-variable problem. We can see

FIGURE 3–18 Some LP Problems Have Multiple Optimal Solutions

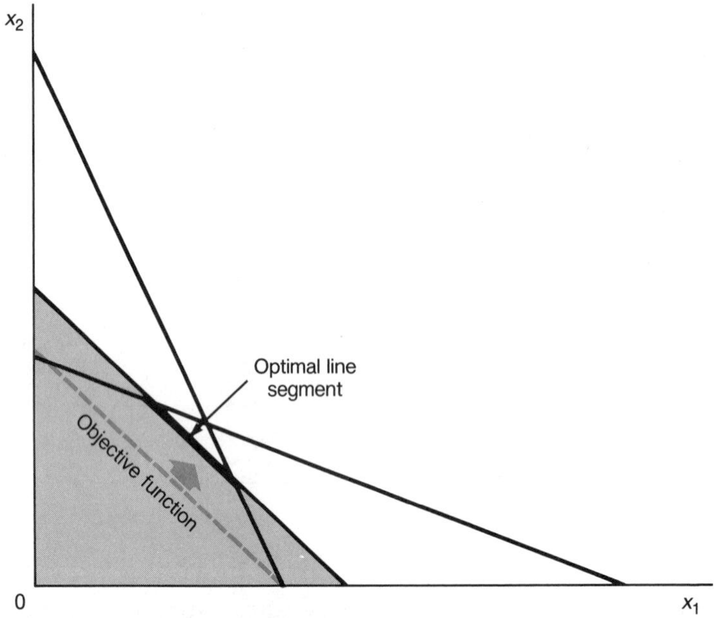

that the objective function is *parallel* to a portion of the boundary of the feasible solution space. Because of this, it ends up last touching an entire segment of the boundary. Hence, every combination of x_1 and x_2 on this line will yield the same (optimal) solution. Note, however, that this does not refute the earlier statement that the solution will always be at a corner point. In fact, we can see that there are two corner points that are optimal, one at either end of the line segment.

One benefit of having multiple optimal solutions is that for other (perhaps qualitative) reasons, a manager may prefer one of these solutions over the others, even though each would achieve the same value of the objective function. Furthermore, if non-integer solutions are acceptable, the manager has an infinity of optimal solutions to choose from. In practical terms, one of the two corner points is usually chosen because of ease in identifying those values.

SUMMARY

This chapter illustrates how two-variable linear programming problems can be approached using graphical techniques. Sometimes, the solution can be read directly from the graph, but usually it must be found algebraically using simultaneous equations.

The graphical technique can only handle problems involving two variables; therefore, its value as a general tool for solving LP models is rather limited. Nonetheless, as a vehicle for illustrating important concepts related to LP models and solutions, it is invaluable.

The chapter illustrates the solution of both maximization and minimization problems. In addition, the calculating of slack and surplus are demonstrated. Also, certain special issues that sometimes arise, including problems that have no feasible solutions, unbounded problems, problems with multiple optimal solutions, and redundant constraints are discussed.

GLOSSARY

Binding Constraints Constraints whose intersection determines the optimal solution to a problem.

Corner Point An extreme point of the feasible solution space; an intersection of two or more constraints that touches the feasible solution space.

Extreme Point See **Corner Point.**

Extreme Point Theorem If an LP problem has an optimal solution, at least one optimal solution will occur at a corner point of the feasible solution space.

Feasible Solution Space Determined by the set of constraints of a problem, it contains all feasible solutions to an LP problem, including the optimal solution.

Fundamental Theorem of LP If there is a solution to an LP problem, at least one optimal solution will occur at a corner point of the feasible solution space.

Optimal Solution A combination of decision variable amounts that yields the best possible value of the objective function and satisfies all constraints. There may be multiple combinations of decision variables that yield that same best value of the objective function.

Redundant Constraint A constraint that does not form a unique part of the boundary of the feasible solution space.

Simultaneous Equations Solving a set of two equations *simultaneously* for the values of the decision variables that will satisfy both equations.

Slack The amount of scarce resource or capacity that will be unused by a given feasible solution to an LP problem.

Standard Form A linear program in which all constraints are written as equalities.

Surplus The amount by which a $\geq$ constraint is exceeded by a given solution to an LP problem.

SOLVED PROBLEMS

Problem 1. Given this LP model:

maximize $10x_1 + x_2$

subject to

A	$3x_1 + x_2 \leq 12$
B	$2x_1 + 2x_2 \leq 16$
C	$x_1 - x_2 \leq 2$
	$x_1, x_2 \geq 0$

a. Graph the model.
b. Find the optimal point on the graph using the objective function method.
c. Use simultaneous equations to determine the optimal values of x_1 and x_2.
d. Determine the amount of slack for each constraint.

Solution

a. Plot each constraint by first setting one variable equal to zero and solving for the other, and then setting the other variable equal to zero and solving for the first. Then, connect those two points with a straight line. The last constraint is a bit different than the majority of constraints you will encounter in this chapter due to the negative value. Even so, we still follow the same procedure in determining the x_1 and x_2 intercepts. The result is that the x_2 intercept is -2, and the x_1 intercept is $+2$.

After all of the constraints have been plotted, shade in the feasible solution space. To determine which side of the third constraint represents less than 2, substitute 0,0 into the constraint.

The plot is shown in Figure 3–19.

b. The objective function can be plotted by first setting it equal to the product of the x_1 and x_2 coefficients (10) and solving for the x_1 and x_2 intercepts. The objective function is shown in Figure 3–19. It is apparent that the optimum point occurs at the intersection of constraint lines A and C.

c. The intersection of A and C is found as follows:

$$\begin{array}{lrl} \text{A} & 3x_1 + x_2 & = 12 \\ \text{C} & x_1 - x_2 & = 2 \\ \hline & 4x_1 & = 14 \quad \text{Solving, } x_1 = 3.5 \end{array}$$

Substituting $x_1 = 3.5$ into either of the constraints and solving for x_2 yields $x_2 = 1.5$. Then the optimal value of the objective function is found by substituting these values into the objective function: $10(3.5) + 1.5 = 36.5$.

d. There is no slack for the two constraints whose intersection determines the optimal solution because any point *on* the line means the left and right sides of

FIGURE 3–19 Constraints and Feasible Solution Space for Solved Problem 1

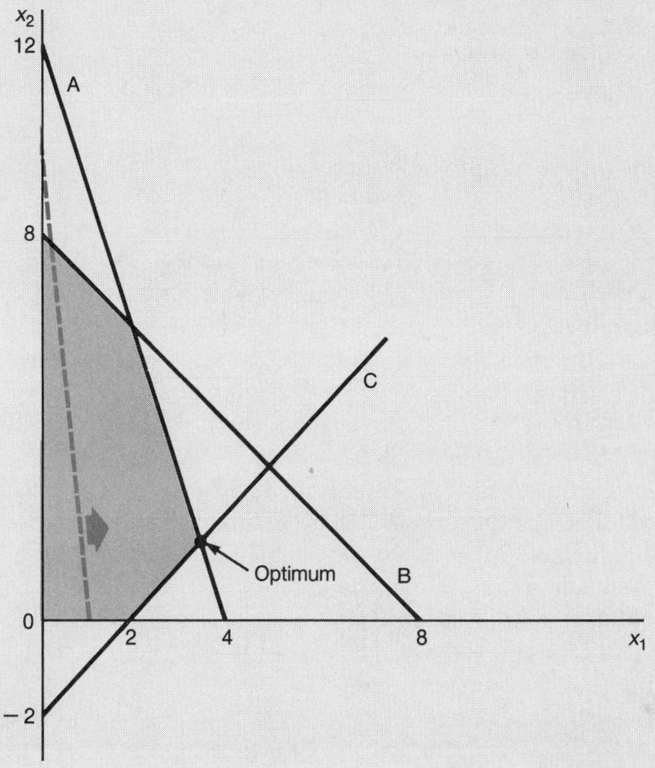

the constraint expression are *equal*. For constraint B, we can determine the amount of slack by substituting in the optimal values of x_1 and x_2 and solving:

$$2(3.5) + 2(1.5) = 10$$

The slack is the original value minus this amount. Thus, slack equals $16 - 10 = 6$.

Problem 2. Given this LP model:

minimize $\quad 3x_1 + 4x_2$

subject to

A	$6x_1 + 1x_2 \geq 120$
B	$4x_1 + 4x_2 \geq 320$
C	$3x_1 + 5x_2 \geq 300$
	$x_1, x_2 \geq 0$

a. Graph the model.

b. Determine the optimal point on the graph using the objective function method.

c. Use simultaneous equations to determine the optimal values of x_1 and x_2, and then find the minimum cost.

d. Determine the amount of slack or surplus for each constraint.

Solution

a. To plot the model, for each constraint:

(1) Make the constraint an equality.

(2) Alternately set one of the variables equal to zero and solve for the other. For example, for the first constraint, setting $x_1 = 0$ and solving for x_2, we find $x_2 = 120$; setting $x_2 = 0$ and solving for x_1, we find $x_1 = 20$. Thus, we have two points: $x_1 = 0$, $x_2 = 120$, and $x_1 = 20$, $x_2 = 0$.

(3) Mark the points on the graph and connect with a straight line. Label the line (i.e., A).

(4) After all constraints have been plotted, identify and shade in the feasible solution space. (See Figure 3–20.)

b. To plot the objective function, set it equal to any value, usually some multiple of the product of the x_1 and x_2 coefficients (i.e., 12), and then solve for the x_1 and x_2 intercepts in the same way as with a constraint. Connect the intercepts with a straight (dashed) line (see Figure 3–20). The objective function line was plotted using $3x_1 + 4x_2 = 360$.

c. The optimal solution is at the intersection of lines B and C. Solving these simultaneously, we find:

$$\begin{array}{ll} \text{B} & 4x_1 + 4x_2 = 320 \\ \text{C} & 3x_1 + 5x_2 = 300 \end{array}$$

Multiplying the B equation by 5 and the C equation by 4 and then subtracting the modified C equation form the modified B equation will cause the x_2 term to drop out:

$$\begin{array}{ll} \text{B}' & 20x_1 + 20x_2 = 1{,}600 \\ \text{C}' & \underline{12x_1 + 20x_2 = 1{,}200} \\ & 8x_1 \qquad\quad = \;\; 400 \;\text{Solving, } x_1 = 50 \end{array}$$

Substituting $x_1 = 50$ into either of the original equations or the modified equations will permit determination of x_2. For instance, using the original B:

$$4(50) + 4x_2 = 320$$

Multiplying and rearranging terms, we have:

$$4x_2 = 120. \text{ Thus, } x_2 = 30$$

The minimum cost is found by substituting the optimal values into the objective function: $3(50) + 4(30) = 270$.

FIGURE 3-20 A Graph of Solved Problem 2

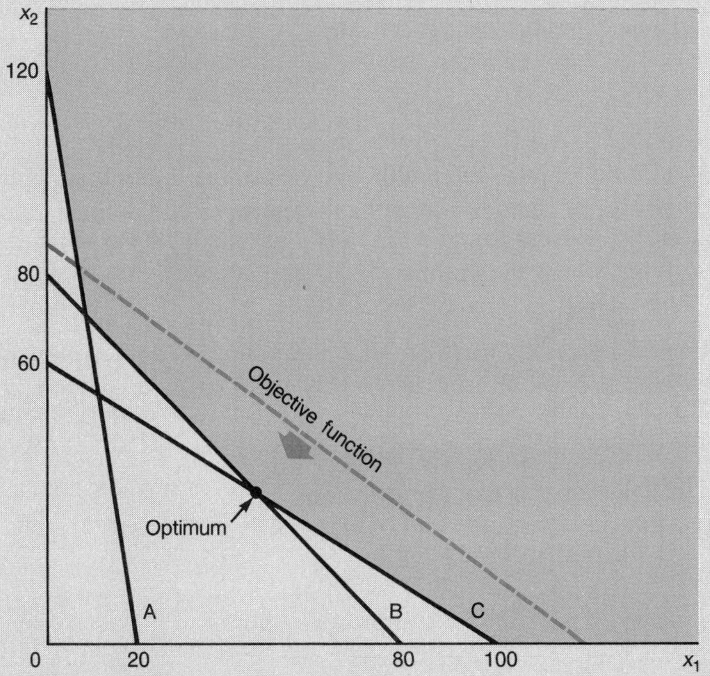

d. The term *slack* pertains to ≤ constraints; *surplus* pertains to ≥ constraints. Because the constraints in this problem are of the ≥ variety, *surplus* is the appropriate term.

Because the intersection of contraints B and C determines the optimal solution (i.e., they are binding constraints), they have no surplus. (You can verify this by substituting the optimal values into these two constraints.) For constraint A, substitution yields:

$$6(50) + 1(30) = 330$$

Because this *exceeds* the minimum requirement of 120 by 210 (i.e., 330 − 120 = 210), the surplus is 210.

PROBLEMS

1. Given this linear programming model:

maximize $10x_1 + 16x_2$ (profit)

subject to

A	$8x_1 + 20x_2 \leq 120$
B	$25x_1 + 20x_2 \leq 200$
	$x_1, x_2 \geq 0$

a. Graph the constraints.

b. Shade in the feasible solution space.

c. Plot the objective function and determine the optimal point on the graph.

d. Use simultaneous equations to determine the optimal values of the decision variables and the maximum value of the objective function.

e. What would the optimal values be if the objective function had been $6x_1 + 3x_2$?

2. For the preceding problem, determine the coordinates of each feasible corner point using the original objective function. Then, determine the profit at each of those corner points. Use that information to identify the optimal solution.

3. The manager of a construction project has formulated this LP model:

maximize $25x_1 + 30x_2$ (profit)

subject to

Time	$20x_1 + 15x_2 \leq 1{,}200$ hours
Materials	$8x_1 + 12x_2 \leq 600$ tons
	$x_1, x_2 \geq 0$

a. Graph the model.

b. Determine the optimal values of the decision variables using the objective function approach. What is the maximum profit?

4. For the previous problem, use the extreme point approach to determine the optimal solution.

5. The manager of a warehouse has developed this LP model:

maximize $50x_1 + 30x_2$ (revenue)

subject to

Time	$15x_1 + 12x_2 \leq 900$ minutes
Space	$8x_1 + 16x_2 \leq 800$ square feet
	$x_1 \geq 40$ units
	$x_1, x_2 \geq 0$

a. Graph the constraints and shade in the feasible solution space.

b. Determine the optimal solution and maximum revenue.

6. Answer the questions of the previous problem with this modification: Assume the objective function is $30x_1 + 50x_2$. (The manager had the coefficients of the objective function reversed.)

7. The owner of a telephone subscription service specializes in taking orders for two magazines, x_1 and x_2. She has formulated the following model that describes the unit contributions to profits and the use of scarce resources involved:

maximize $.60x_1 + .90x_2$

subject to

Telephone	$8x_1 + 12x_2 \le 480$	minutes per day
Paperwork	$10x_1 + 6x_2 \le 480$	minutes per day
	$x_1 \ge 20$	
	$x_1, x_2 \ge 0$	

a. Is there a unique optimal solution?

b. What is the maximum profit?

c. Can you find an optimal solution for which both decision variables are integer?

8. The manager of a food processing plant that specializes in potato chips has developed an LP model to reflect processing times.

x_1 = boxes of regular chips

x_2 = boxes of crinkle cut chips

maximize $.40x_1 + .30x_2$ (profit)

subject to

Cutting	$3.6x_1 + .8x_2 \le 144$	minutes
Frying	$3.2x_1 + 1.6x_2 \le 160$	minutes
Packing	$4.8x_1 + 7.2x_2 \le 576$	seconds
Crinkle	$x_2 \le 80$	boxes
Crinkle	$x_2 \ge 20$	boxes
	$x_1, x_2 \ge 0$	

a. Determine the combination of boxes of the two types of chips that will maximize profits.

b. Is any constraint redundant? Explain briefly.

9. For the previous problem, determine each of the following:

a. The amount of each resource that will be used.

b. The amount of slack for each resource.

c. The condition that would exist if the profit for crinkle cut chips dropped to $.20 per box.

10. (Refer to Problem 7 in Chapter 2.) Solve for the optimal quantities of each type of car and the optimal value of the objective function.

11. Given this model:

minimize $4x_1 + 2x_2$ (cost)

subject to

A	$16x_1 + 5x_2 \geq 80$
B	$18x_1 + 15x_2 \geq 180$
C	$24x_1 + 45x_2 \geq 360$
	$x_1 \geq 0,\ x_2 \geq 0$

a. Solve for the values of x_1 and x_2 that will minimize cost.

b. Which restriction is exceeded by the optimal solution to the model? By how much?

12. Given this model:

minimize $20x_1 + 30x_2$ (cost)

subject to

Town	$6x_1 + x_2 \geq 12$
County	$7x_1 + 7x_2 \geq 49$
State	$3x_1 + 11x_2 \geq 33$
	$x_1, x_2 \geq 0$

a. Find the optimal values of x_1 and x_2 and the minimum cost.

b. Determine the amount of surplus associated with each constraint.

13. The manager of a health store has formulated the following LP model, which describes parameters for a new product:

minimize $2.40x_1 + 1.50x_2$ (cost)

subject to

Vitamin A	$10x_1 + 6x_2 \geq 1{,}200$ mg.
Vitamin B_1	$10x_1 + 30x_2 \geq 1{,}800$ mg.
	$x_1, x_2 \geq 0$

a. Determine the optimal solution.

b. What is the minimum cost at the optimum?

14. The new manager of a food processing plant hopes to reduce costs by using linear programming to determine the optimal amounts of two ingredients it uses, x_1 and x_2. The manager has constructed this model:

minimize $.40x_1 + .40x_2$

subject to

Protein	$3x_1 + 5x_2 \geq 30$ grams
Carbohydrates	$6x_1 + 4x_2 \geq 48$ grams
	$x_1, x_2 \geq 0$

a. Determine the optimal solution.

b. Compute the minimum cost for the optimal solution.

15. There is a single optimal solution to Problem 14. However, if the objective function had been parallel to one of the constraints, there would have been two equally optimal solutions. If the cost of x_2 remains at \$.40, what cost of x_1 would cause the objective function to be parallel to the carbohydrate constraint? Explain how you determined this.

16. Graph this problem and briefly explain why it cannot be solved:

maximize $2.20x_1 + 2.35x_2$

subject to

A $6x_1 + 9x_2 \geq 108$
B $3x_1 + 5x_2 \leq 45$
$x_1, x_2 \geq 0$

17. Given this linear programming problem:

maximize $5x_1 + 3x_2$

subject to

1 $7x_1 + 4x_2 \geq 84$
2 $5x_1 + 8x_2 \geq 80$
$x_1, x_2 \geq 0$

a. Graph the problem.
b. Why is it impossible to obtain an optimal solution for the problem?
c. Can you suggest two different possible errors that might have occurred in formulating the problem that prevent a solution?

18. Explain why the following linear programming problem cannot be solved for an optimal solution.

minimize $7x_1 + 3x_2$

subject to

1 $6x_1 + 8x_2 \leq 48$
2 $4x_1 + 3x_2 \geq 24$
3 $x_2 \geq 5$
$x_1, x_2 \geq 0$

19. Explain why the following linear programming formulation is probably in error:

minimize $30x_1 + 33x_2$

subject to

1 $15x_1 + 18x_2 \leq 90$
2 $20x_1 + 12x_2 \leq 120$
$x_1, x_2 \geq 0$

20. A wood products firm uses leftover time at the end of each week to make goods for stock. Currently, there are two products on the list of items that are produced for stock: a chopping board and a knife holder. Both items require three operations: cutting, gluing, and finishing. The manager of the firm has collected the following data on these products:

Item	Profit per Unit	Time per Unit (minutes)		
		Cutting	Gluing	Finishing
Chopping board	$2	1.4	5	12
Knife holder	$6	.8	13	3

The manager has also determined that during each week 56 minutes are available for cutting, 650 minutes are available for gluing, and 360 minutes are available for finishing.

a. Determine the optimal quantities of the decision variables.

b. Which resources are not completely used by your solution? How much of each resource is unused?

21. The manager of an inspection department has been asked to help reduce a backlog of safety devices that must be inspected. There are two types of safety devices: one for construction workers and one for window washers. The manager will be permitted to select any combination of items because new testing equipment will soon be available that will handle the remaining items. However, in the short run, the manager has been asked to help generate revenue. The revenue for each construction device is $60, and the revenue for each window washing device is $40. The manager has obtained data on the necessary inspection operations, which are:

Operation	Time per Unit (minutes)		Total Time Available (minutes)
	Construction	Window Washing	
Test #1	3/4	1/3	75
Test #2	1/4	1/2	50
Test #3	1/2	1/4	40

a. Determine the optimum values of the decision variables and the revenue that will result.

b. Which testing operations will have slack time? How much?

c. Is any constraint redundant? Which one? Why?

22. A dietician has been asked by the athletic director of a university to develop a snack that athletes can use in their training programs. The dietician intends to mix two separate products together to make the snack. The following information has been obtained by the dietician:

Nutrient	Minimum Amount Required (grams)	Contribution per Ounce (grams)	
		Product A	Product B
Carbohydrates	20	2	5
Protein	12	6	1
Calories	450	90	50

Product A costs \$.20 per ounce and Product B costs \$.10 per ounce.

a. Determine the optimal quantities of the two products for cost minimization. What is the cost per snack?

b. Are any requirements exceeded? If so, which ones, and by how much?

23. The manager of the deli section of a grocery superstore has just learned that the department has 112 pounds of mayonnaise, of which 70 pounds is approaching its expiration date and must be used. In order to use up the mayonnaise, the manager has decided to prepare two items: a ham spread and a deli spread. Each pan of the ham spread will require 1.4 pounds of the mayonnaise and each pan of the deli spread will require 1.0 pound. The manager has received an order for 10 pans of ham spread and 8 pans of the deli spread. In addition, the manager has decided to have at least 10 pans of each spread available for sale. Both spreads will cost \$3 per pan to make, but ham spread yields revenue of \$5 per pan and deli spread yields \$7 per pan.

a. Determine the solution that will minimize cost.

b. Determine the solution that will maximize profit.

24. A production manager is faced with the question of how to allocate the manufacturing of a microwave oven between his own company and a subcontractor because neither firm can handle the demand alone. Fabrication costs are \$10 per unit within the company and \$20 per unit from the subcontractor; assembly costs are \$8 per unit within the company and \$5 from the subcontractor; and inspection costs are \$3 per unit within the company and \$1 per unit from the subcontractor. The company has a budget of \$120,000 for fabrication, \$40,000 for assembly, and \$12,000 for inspection. The contribution to profits is \$60 per unit regardless of which firm does the work.

a. What is the optimal solution? How much profit will it yield?

b. How much of the total budget will be unused by the optimal solution?

25. Determine the optimal solution and value of the objective function for Problem 3 in Chapter 2.

26. (Refer to Problem 4 in Chapter 2.)
   a. What are the optimal values of the decision variables and the objective function?
   b. What is the amount of slack for each resource?
   c. Which constraints are redundant?

27. An accountant has developed the following LP model:

maximize $4.0A + 3.6B$ (revenue)

subject to

$$
\begin{array}{lrcl}
1 & 11A + 5B & \geq & 55 \\
2 & 3A + 4B & \leq & 36 \\
3 & 4A - 9B & \leq & 0 \\
 & A, B & \geq & 0
\end{array}
$$

   a. Determine the optimal quantities of variables A and B and the maximum revenue.
   b. For the optimal solution, determine the slack or surplus that would result for each constraint.
   c. Are any constraints redundant? Explain.

28. In Chapter 2, Problem 9 involved formulating a model that would permit determination of the optimal quantities of two types of lawn mowers. Solve that model for the optimal solution. Then answer these questions:
   a. Is any constraint redundant? Which constraint(s)?
   b. Determine the amount of slack for each resource.

29. (Refer to Problem 12 in Chapter 2.) Determine the optimal quantities of spaghetti and sauce needed to minimize cost while meeting the nutritional requirements and other specified conditions.
   a. Are any of the nutritional requirements exceeded? By how much? Is that slack or surplus?
   b. How many calories are indicated by the optimal solution?
   c. What is the minimum cost per serving?

30. Given this LP model:

maximize $x_1 + 5x_2$

subject to

$$
\begin{aligned}
x_1 + 3x_2 &\leq 12 \\
3x_1 + 4x_2 &= 24 \\
x_1 \quad\quad &\leq 6 \\
x_1, x_2 &\geq 0
\end{aligned}
$$

a. Determine the optimal values of the decision variables.

b. Compute the optimal value of the objective function.

c. Is any constraint redundant? If so, which one?

31. Tom Smith is the manager of a discount store. He wants to maximize the total revenue from two furniture items, a bedroom set and a living room set. It is important that the showroom space of 40,000 square feet be *completely* filled with these sets, some of which will be in crates. Nonetheless, the manager wants to give the impression that the store is overstocked on these items. The bedroom sets will occupy an average of 400 square feet each, and the living room sets will occupy an average of 500 square feet each. The manager estimates that it requires approximately 14 minutes to unload a bedroom set and 7 minutes to unload a living room set. There are 980 minutes available for the unloading. The living room sets will produce a revenue of $500 each, and the bedroom sets will produce a revenue of $1,000 each. The manager has also decided that a minimum of 20 living room sets should be ordered.

    a. What question is to be answered by linear programming?

    b. Set up the problem in a linear programming format.

    c. Determine the optimal solution.

32. A real estate broker is responsible for selling homes in a new tract. There will be two types of floor plans: Model I and Model II. Each Model I will require .6 acres of land, and each Model II will require 1.0 acres of land. Twelve acres of land are available. The broker already has orders for three Model I and Model II homes, and the contractor has requested that no more than ten Model I homes be sold because of other circumstances. The broker also operates a tree nursery and wants to use at least 81 maple trees to landscape the tract. Each model home will receive nine maple trees. The broker estimates it will cost $300 to sell each Model I home and $400 to sell each Model II home.

    a. What question can be answered using linear programming?

    b. Set up this problem in an LP format.

    c. Determine the optimal solution graphically.

    d. If the broker had estimated a cost of $600 to sell each Model I and $400 to sell each Model II, what solution would be optimal?

Chapter 3 Case

Son, Ltd.

Son, Ltd., manufactures a variety of chemical products used by photoprocessors. Son was recently bought out by a conglomerate, and managers of the two organizations have been working together to improve the efficiency of Son's operations.

Managers have been asked to adhere to weekly operating budgets and to develop operating plans using quantitative methods whenever possible. The manager of one department has been given a weekly operating budget of $11,980 for production of three chemical products, which for convenience shall be referred to as Q, R, and W. The budget is intended to pay for direct labor and materials. Processing requirements for the three products, on a per unit basis, are:

Product	Labor (hours)	Material A (pounds)	Material B (pounds)
Q	5	2	1
R	4	2	—
W	2	½	2

The company has a contractual obligation for 85 units of Product R per week.

Material A costs $4 per pound, as does Material B. Labor costs $8 an hour.

Product Q sells for $122 a unit, Product R sells for $115 a unit, and Product W sells for $76 a unit.

The manager is considering a number of different proposals regarding the quantity of each product to produce. The manager is primarily interested in maximizing contribution. Moreover, the manager wants to know how much labor will be needed, as well as the amount of each material to purchase.

Required: Prepare a report that addresses the following issues:

1. The optimal quantities of products and the necessary quantities of labor and materials.
2. One proposal is to make equal amounts of the products. What amount of each will maximize contribution, and what quantities of labor and materials will be needed? How much less will total contribution be if this proposal is adopted?
3. How would you formulate the constraint for Material A if it was determined that there is a 5 percent waste factor for Material A and equal quantities of each product are required?

Chapter 3 Supplement Graphical Sensitivity Analysis

Supplement Outline

Learning Objectives

After completing this supplement, you should be able to:

1. Explain how sensitivity analysis can be useful to a decision maker.
2. Explain how to analyze and interpret the impact of a change in the value of an objective function coefficient.
3. Explain how to analyze and interpret the impact of a change in the right-hand side value of a constraint.

This supplement describes how graphical methods can be used for **sensitivity analysis:** determining the impact that a change in one of the parameters (numerical values) of an LP model will have on the optimal solution and on the optimal value of the objective function.

Sensitivity analysis is useful because it enables a decision maker to quickly assess the impact of a change. Graphical analysis is useful because it provides a visual portrayal of the process and the results.

A decision maker's interest in analyzing the impact of a change in the value of a parameter can come from a variety of sources. For example, changes in either costs or revenues can cause a change in the value of an objective function coefficient. Or, a decision maker might wonder what the impact would be if a change in cost or revenue *could* be made (i.e., would it be worth the time, cost, etc.?). Another example would be an opportunity to obtain additional amounts of a scarce resource (e.g., raw material). It could be very useful to know if acquiring additional amounts would be profitable, and how much more could be profitably used, given other constraints of the problem.

Sensitivity analysis pertains to a change in the value of one parameter *while all other parameters are held constant.* Thus, the procedure and interpretations described here do not apply to situations that involve changes to more than one parameter. (Multiple changes are addressed in Chapter 6.)

LP models have three kinds of parameters:

1. Objective function coefficients.
2. Constraint coefficients.
3. Right-hand side (RHS) values of constraints.

The discussion here will cover sensitivity analysis of the first and last on this list; it will not cover changes in constraint coefficients.

For purposes of illustration, the microcomputer problem from Chapters 2 and 3 will be used. That problem is repeated here for easy reference:

x_1 = quantity of Type 1 to produce
x_2 = quantity of Type 2 to produce

maximize $60x_1 + 50x_2$ (profit)

subject to

Assembly	$4x_1 + 10x_2 \leq 100$	hours
Inspection	$2x_1 + 1x_2 \leq 22$	hours
Storage	$3x_1 + 3x_2 \leq 39$	cubic feet
	$x_1, x_2 \geq 0$	

The graph of this problem and optimal solution are repeated in Figure 3S–1.

Let us begin with an analysis of changes in an objective function coefficient.

FIGURE 3S–1 A Graph of the Microcomputer Problem

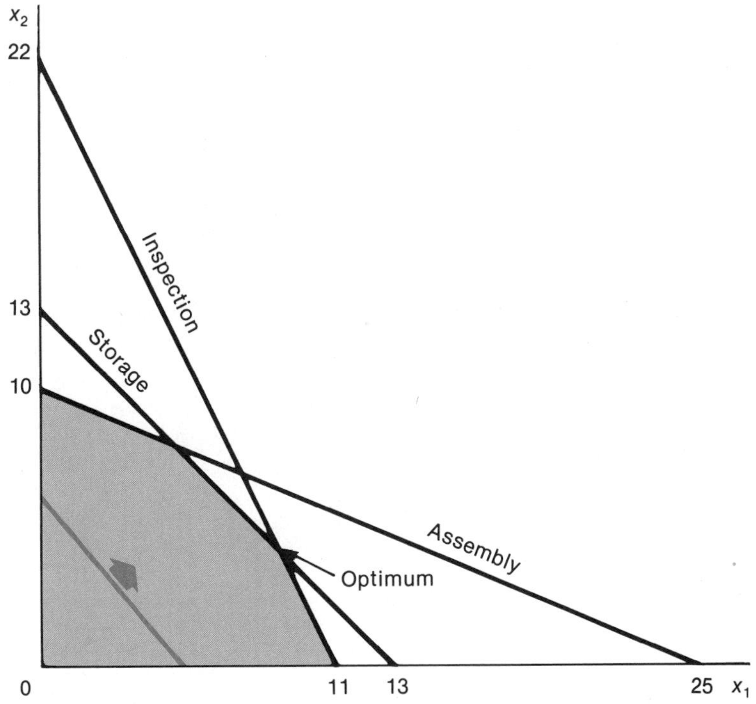

A CHANGE IN THE VALUE OF AN OBJECTIVE FUNCTION COEFFICIENT

If there is a change in the value of one of the objective function coefficients (while the other one remains fixed), this will cause the slope of the objective function line to change. However, if the change in slope is relatively small, the optimal corner point of the feasible solution space will not change. Of particular interest is the amount by which a coefficient can be changed without changing the optimal solution point. This is known as the **range of optimality.**

We can see graphically in Figure 3S–2 how much the slope of the objective function line can change and not change the optimal solution point. If the direction of change causes the slope to become less steep (see Figure 3S–2*a*), the same solution point will be optimal as long as the revised objective function line does not go beyond being parallel to the storage constraint. If it is just parallel to the storage line, multiple solutions are optimal, *including* the original solution point. But beyond that, the next intersection (storage and assembly) will become optimal.

FIGURE 3S-2

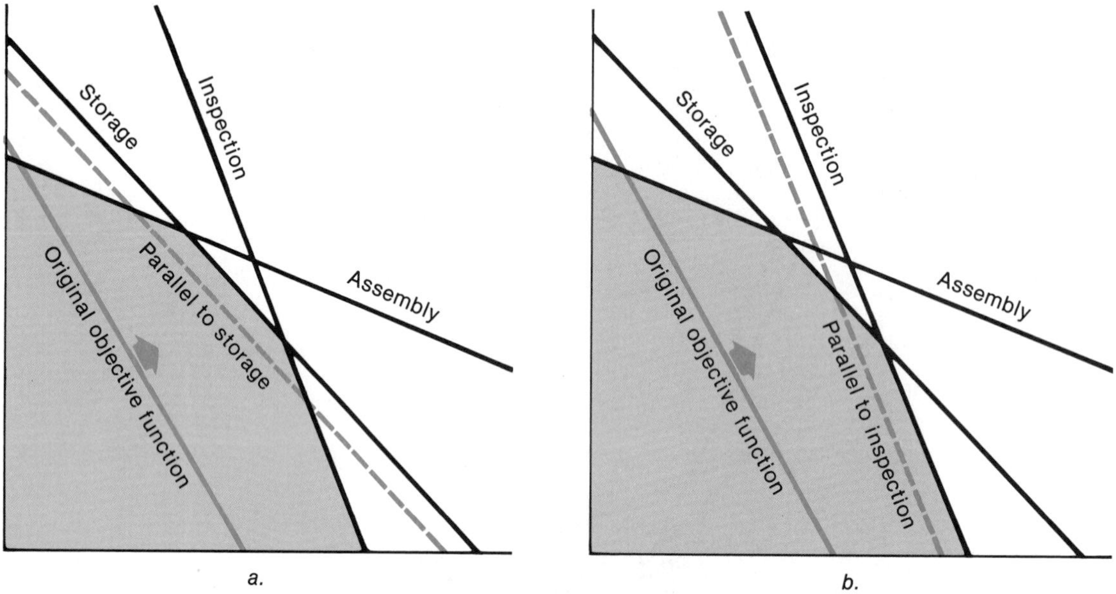

Similarly, if changing the coefficient results in a *steeper* slope (see Figure 3S-2*b*), the same solution will hold as long as the objective function line does not go beyond being parallel to the inspection constraint. If it does, the optimal solution will move to the intersection of the inspection constraint and the x_1 axis.

Thus, as long as a change in the coefficient does not cause the slope of the objective function line to exceed either of those parallel conditions, the same solution will be optimal.

A change in either of the objective function coefficients can cause its slope to change in either direction. In either case, a coefficient change in one direction will cause the slope to increase, while a change in the opposite direction will cause the slope to decrease. Let's take one of the coefficients at a time and see how we can determine its range of optimality.

Suppose we begin with the coefficient of x_1, which is 60. Let's determine what its value would have to be in order for the objective function line to be parallel to the storage line. Note that the two lines will be parallel if the ratio of the x_1 coefficient to the x_2 coefficient is the same for both lines. As they currently exist, the two sets of coefficients are:

Storage	$3x_1 + 3x_2$
Objective function	$60x_1 + 50x_2$

As you can see, the storage coefficient ratio (x_1 to x_2) is 3 to 3. Consequently, for the objective function line to be parallel to storage, its coefficients would have to be equal. If we are changing the x_1 coefficient while holding the x_2 coefficient constant at 50, this would mean the x_1 coefficient would also have to be equal to 50. Hence, the objective function would be $50x_1 + 50x_2$.

Similarly, to be parallel to the inspection line, the coefficients of the objective function would have to be such that the x_1 coefficient was double the x_2 coefficient, as you can see by comparing the two sets of coefficients as they are in the original problem:

Inspection	$2x_1 + 1x_2$
Objective function	$60x_1 + 50x_2$

In order to achieve the 2 to 1 ratio of the inspection constraint, the x_1 coefficient must be 100. Hence, the objective function would be $100x_1 + 50x_2$.

Thus, our analysis shows:

Parallel to storage	$50x_1 + 50x_2$
Parallel to inspection	$100x_1 + 50x_2$

Therefore, we can say that the range of optimality for the x_1 coefficient of the objective function is 50 to 100. (Note that the x_2 coefficient remained at 50.) This means that for *any* value of the x_1 coefficient in this range, including the endpoints, the same values of x_1 and x_2 will be optimal.

We can determine the range of optimality for the x_2 coefficient of the objective function in the same manner. First, determine what x_2 coefficient is needed to achieve parallelism with the storage line, with the x_1 coefficient held at 60.

Storage	$3x_1 + 3x_2$
Objective function	$60x_1 + 50x_2$

We can see that an x_2 coefficient of 60 would make the lines parallel:

Storage	$3x_1 + 3x_2$
Objective function	$60x_1 + 60x_2$

Similarly, in order for the objective function to be parallel to the inspection line, the ratio would have to be 2 to 1:

Inspection	$2x_1 + 1x_2$
Objective function	$60x_1 + 50x_2$

This can be achieved by making the x_2 coefficient 30:

Inspection	$2x_1 + 1x_2$
Objective function	$60x_1 + 30x_2$

Comparing these two objective functions will indicate the range of optimality for the x_2 coefficient of the objective function:

Parallel to storage	$60x_1 + 60x_2$
Parallel to inspection	$60x_1 + 30x_2$

Hence, the range of optimality for the x_2 coefficient is 30 to 60. Again, for any value of the x_2 coefficient in this range, the optimal solution will remain the same.

We have just seen that the optimal values of decision variables do not change if a change in the value of an objective function coefficient is within that coefficient's range of optimality. But what about the optimal value of the objective function? Does it change? The answer is yes, it does. The reason is that its value is determined by *both* the values of the decision variables and the values of the coefficients. Hence, if one of the coefficients changes, while everything remains the same, its value must change.

■

EXAMPLE S1 In Chapter 3, the optimal values for the decision variables and the objective function for the microcomputer problem were determined. They were:

$$x_1 = 9$$
$$x_2 = 4$$
$$Z = 740$$

In this supplement, we just found the range of optimality for each coefficient of the objective function for the microcomputer problem. They were:

For the x_1 coefficient, 50 to 100

For the x_2 coefficient, 30 to 60

Given this information, analyze the impact of a change in the x_1 coefficient of the objective function from 60 to 82.50. Specifically, what impact will there be on the optimal values of the decision variables and the objective function?

Solution

First, check to see if the new value of the x_1 coefficient is within the range of optimality. We can see that 82.50 is within the range of 50 to 100. Consequently, there will be no change in the optimal values of x_1 and x_2.

However, the optimal value of Z will change. To find its new value, we must substitute the new coefficient into the objective function with the optimal values of the decision variables and solve. Thus:

$$82.50(9) + 50(4) = 942.50$$

An interesting situation occurs when a decision variable has a value of zero in the optimal solution. For example, suppose in the microcomputer problem that

FIGURE 3S–3 Solution for Revised Microcomputer Problem

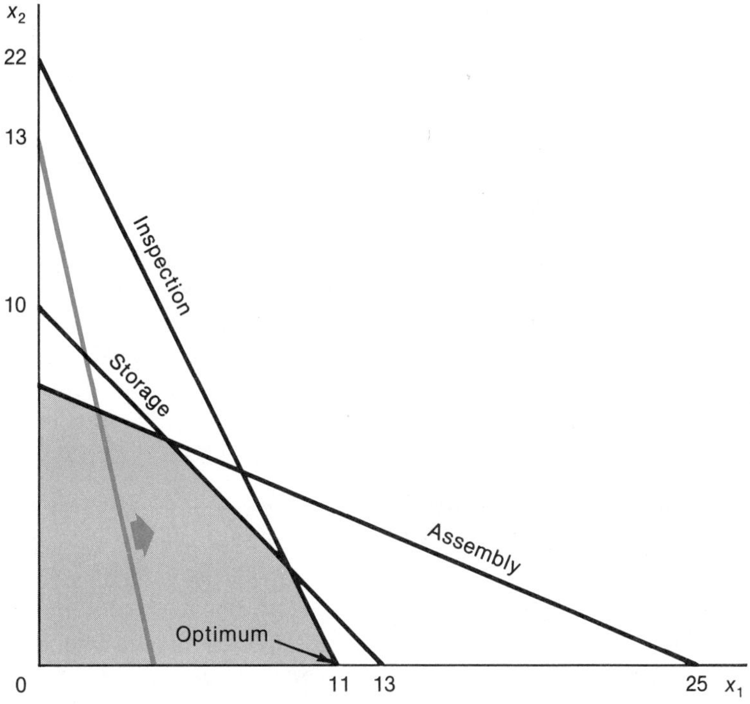

the x_2 coefficient in the objective function had been 20 instead of 50, so the objective would have been:

maximize $60x_1 + 20x_2$

The optimal solution would have been $x_1 = 11, x_2 = 0$. This is illustrated in Figure 3S–3. The slope of the objective function in this case is such that the lower right-hand corner of the feasible solution space is now optimal.

The reason that x_2 is zero is that it is not profitable enough relative to x_1. The question of interest then becomes, "What would the profit per unit (objective function coefficient) of x_2 have to be in order for it to have a nonzero optimal value?" The answer depends on the value of the x_2 coefficient of the objective function that would make the objective function just parallel to the inspection constraint, because then the solution would include nonzero values of x_2.

The objective function would be parallel to the inspection constraint if its coefficients were in the ratio of 2 to 1. With the x_1 coefficient held at 60, this would mean an x_2 coefficient of 30. Hence, we can say that the value of the x_2 coefficient must be at least 30 in order for x_2 to "come into" the solution. This is a special case of the range of optimality; it is sometimes referred to as the **range of insignificance,** meaning the range of values for which a decision variable will be zero. In this example, the range of insignificance for the x_2 coefficient of the objective function is less than 30; any value less than this will be too small to cause x_2 to have a nonzero value in the optimal solution.

In summary, in performing sensitivity analysis on objective function coefficients, we can determine the range of optimality for variables that are nonzero in the optimal solution, and we can determine the range of insignificance for variables that are zero in the optimal solution. For a change in the value of an objective function that is within its range of optimality, the optimal values of the decision variables will not change although the value of the objective function will change. For a variable that has a value of zero in the optimal solution, if a change in its objective function coefficient occurs that is within the range of insignificance, no change will occur in either optimal values of decision variables or the optimal value of the objective function.

A CHANGE IN THE RHS VALUE OF A CONSTRAINT

In analyzing the impact of a change in the right-hand side (RHS) value of a constraint, it is first necessary to observe if the constraint in question is a *binding constraint* (i.e., forms the intersection of the optimal corner point of the feasible solution space). There are two types of constraints, binding and nonbinding, and the procedure differs depending on which type of constraint we are dealing with.

Let's take the case of a nonbinding constraint first. The assembly constraint in the microcomputer problem is nonbinding on the optimal solution because it does not pass through the optimal corner point (see Figure 3S–1). The constraint is:

$$4x_1 + 10x_2 \le 100 \text{ hours}$$

Because it is nonbinding, and a less-than-or-equal-to constraint, it will have a certain amount of slack in the optimal solution. By substituting the optimal values of the decision variables into the left side of the constraint and then subtracting the result from the right side, we can determine the amount of slack. Recall that the optimal values in the microcomputer problem were $x_1 = 9$, $x_2 = 4$. Substituting into the assembly constraint gives us:

$$4(9) + 10(4) = 76$$

Subtracting 76 from the RHS value of 100 hours, we get

$$100 - 76 = 24 \text{ hours}$$

Thus, in the optimal solution, there are 24 hours of assembly time that are unused. Consequently, if additional hours of assembly time became available (say, by scheduling overtime in the assembly department), that would simply increase the amount of slack. So if an additional 10 hours of assembly time were scheduled, the amount of slack would increase by 10 to 34 hours. It would not make sense to schedule additional hours because the department already has excess capacity of 24 hours. Conversely, if there were fewer hours available (say, because of absenteeism), as long as the decrease did not exceed the 24 hours of slack, this would have no impact on the solution. Hence, no amount of increase would effect the optimal values of the decision variables, nor would a decrease that left at least 76 hours (i.e., 100 − 24 = 76). This range, from 76 to infinity (or 76 to no upper limit) is known as the **range of feasibility** for the assembly constraint. Because the assembly constraint is a nonbinding constraint, any change within this range will have no effect on the solution quantities or on the optimal value of the objective function.

Let us now consider how to determine the range of feasibility for a binding constraint. For the optimal solution in the microcomputer problem, both the storage and the inspection constraints were binding; the optimal corner point occurred at their intersection (see Figure 3S–1). Because each is a binding constraint, even a slight change in the RHS value of either constraint will cause the optimal corner point to shift, and consequently, cause the optimal values of the decision variables and the optimal value of the objective function to change. However, an interesting phenomenon occurs as long as the change in the RHS value of a binding constraint is within its range of feasibility: The change in the optimal value of the objective function is linearly related to the amount of change. For example, we will be able to determine that the value of the objective function will change by $10 for each one-unit change in the RHS value of the inspection constraint, increasing $10 for each additional hour of inspection time and decreasing $10 for each hour the inspection constraint is decreased from its original amount of 22 hours, as long as the increase or decrease is within the range of feasibility. At the end of this section, the issue of changes that go beyond the range of feasibility will be addressed.

For binding constraints, there are two pieces of information that are of interest. One relates to the procedure for determining the range of feasibility for the RHS value of the constraint, and the other relates to determining the amount by which the optimal value of the objective function will change for each one-unit change in the RHS value of the constraint within the range of feasibility. This amount is referred to as the **shadow price** of a constraint. We begin with the change in the optimal value of the objective function for a one-unit change in the RHS of a constraint.

We can determine the impact of a one-unit change in the RHS value of a constraint on the optimal value of the objective function by increasing (or decreasing) the RHS value of the constraint in question by one unit and solving this revised problem. For instance, for the inspection constraint, this would yield the following:

$$2x_1 + 1x_2 = 22 + 1 \text{ (i.e., } 2x_1 + 1x_2 = 23)$$

Although we could graph the problem again using this revised inspection constraint, we would find that the new graph would appear almost identical to the former graph; the solution point would move only slightly. It would still be at the intersection of the storage and inspection constraints. Therefore, we can simply avoid replotting the graph, and instead proceed to using a simultaneous solution of the two constraints to determine the new optimal values of x_1 and x_2:

$$\begin{array}{ll} \text{Inspection} & 2x_1 + 1x_2 = 23 \\ \text{Storage} & 3x_1 + 3x_2 = 39 \end{array}$$

One way to solve this is to multiply the entire inspection constraint by 3 and then subtract the storage constraint from it. Thus:

$$\begin{array}{ll} \text{Inspection} \times 3 & 6x_1 + 3x_2 = 69 \\ \text{Storage} & -(3x_1 + 3x_2 = 39) \\ \hline & 3x_1 \qquad\quad = 30 \end{array}$$

Solving, we find that $x_1 = 10$. Then, substituting this value into either the storage or the inspection constraint and solving, we can determine the new optimal value of x_2. For instance, using the inspection constraint, we find:

$$2(10) + 1x_2 = 23$$

Solving, $x_2 = 3$.

Now, if we substitute these new optimal values into the objective function, we obtain:

$$60(10) + 50(3) = 750$$

Previously, with $x_1 = 9$ and $x_2 = 4$, we found:

$$60(9) + 50(4) = 740$$

Thus, we see that the one-unit increase in inspection time produced an increase in the objective function of 10. Hence, the shadow price of the inspection constraint is 10, and for *each* one-unit increase or decrease that is within the range of feasibility for the RHS of the inspection constraint, the optimal value of the objective function will increase or decrease by 10. For example, an increase of 2 in the RHS of the inspection constraint will cause an increase of 20 in the optimal value of the objective function. This relationship holds as long as the amount of change in the RHS is within the range of feasibility for that particular constraint.

We can determine the shadow price of storage constraint in the same manner. Adding one unit to its RHS changes it to 40. Solving using simultaneous equations yields:

$$\begin{array}{ll} \text{Inspection} \times 3 & 6x_1 + 3x_2 = 66 \\ \text{Storage} + 1 & -(3x_1 + 3x_2 = 40) \\ \hline & 3x_1 \qquad\quad = 26 \end{array}$$

Solving, $x_1 = 8.67$. Substituting into the inspection constraint and solving for x_2, we find $x_2 = 4.67$. Using these new values in the objective function, we obtain the following (note that rounding will give a slightly larger value):

$$60(8.67) + 50(4.67) = 753.33$$

Compared to the original value of 740 for the objective function, we can see that an increase in one unit in the RHS of the storage constraint caused an increase of 13.33. Hence, the shadow price for the storage constraint is 13.33. This tells us that for a change in the amount of storage space that is within the range of feasibility, the value of the objective function will change by 13.33 times the amount of change in storage space. This shows the importance of knowing what the range of feasibility is: "Over what range of values is the shadow price valid?" That is our next topic.

The shadow price that is in effect at the optimal solution will remain in effect (i.e., it will not change) as long as the same constraints that are binding continue to be binding. Thus, as long as the optimal solution is at the point where the same constraints intersect, the shadow price will be the same.

A key factor in understanding analysis of the range of feasibility is recognizing that when the RHS value of a constraint is changed, the resulting graph of the revised constraint line will be *parallel* to the original line. The new line will be closer to the origin if the RHS has been decreased, or farther from the origin if the RHS value has been increased. Moreover, the larger the change, the farther apart the revised line and the original line will be.

In order to determine the range of feasibility for binding constraints using the graphical approach, we follow this procedure:

1. Place a straight edge along the constraint.
2. Slide it away from the origin, making sure to keep it parallel to the constraint. Continue until you come to the last point where your straight edge intersects the other binding constraint. Note that point on the graph.
3. Return the straight edge to the original line. Now move it parallel to the constraint, but in the direction of the origin until you get to the last point where the two binding constraints intersect. Note this point.
4. Determine the coordinates of the two points you identified. Substitute each set of values into the left-hand side of the constraint and solve. The resulting two values are the endpoints of the range of feasibility.

■

EXAMPLE S2 Determine the range of feasibility for each of these binding constraints in the microcomputer problem:

1. The inspection constraint.
2. The storage constraint.

FIGURE 3S–4 The Upper Limit on Using Additional Inspection Time

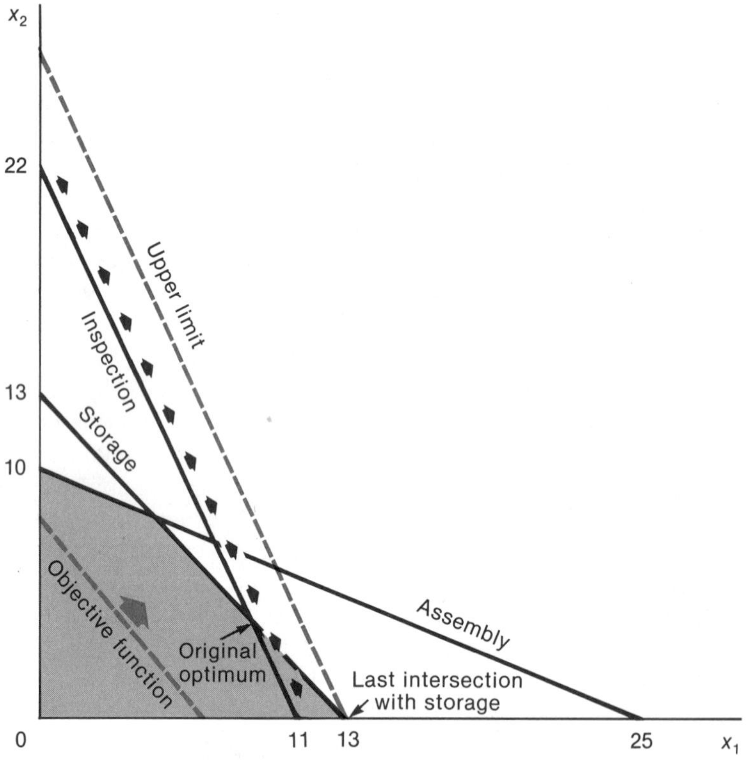

Solution

1. Following the above procedure, we determine the last point where the storage constraint intersects with the line that is parallel to the inspection line, moving away from the origin. See Figure 3S–4.

   Next, we repeat the procedure moving toward the origin. See Figure 3S–5.

   The coordinates of the upper line are easy to obtain directly from the graph: $x_1 = 13$, $x_2 = 0$. For the lower limit, note that at that last point, the storage and assembly lines intersect. Hence, we can determine the coordinates of that point by solving the equations of the storage and assembly lines simultaneously. This will yield $x_1 = 5$ and $x_2 = 8$.

   By substituting these two sets of coordinates into the left side of the inspection constraints, we obtain the upper and lower ends of the range of feasibility for the inspection constraint. For $x_1 = 13$, $x_2 = 0$, we get:

FIGURE 3S–5 The Lower Limit on Inspection Time

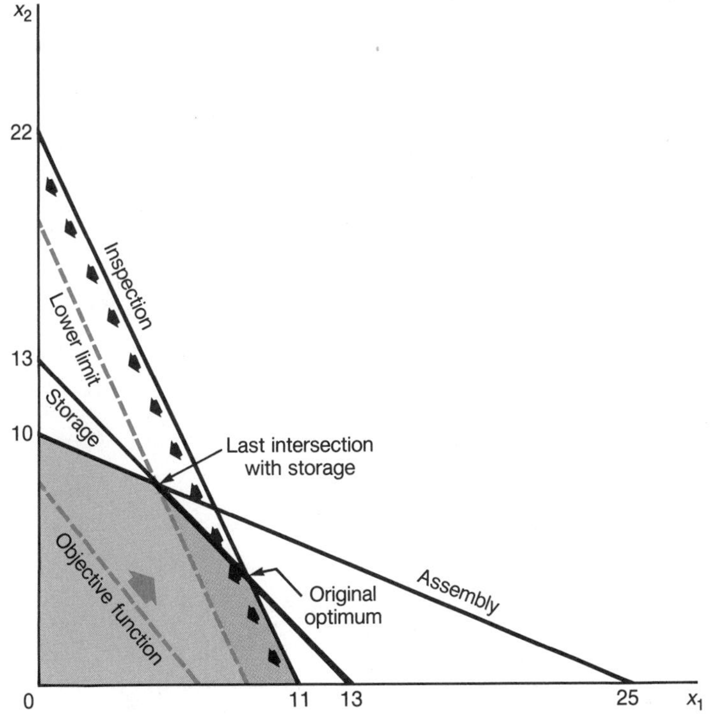

$$2(13) + 1(0) = 26 \quad \text{(upper limit)}$$

For $x_1 = 5$, $x_2 = 8$, we get:

$$2(5) + 1(8) = 18 \quad \text{(lower limit)}$$

Hence, the range of feasibility for the RHS of the inspection constraint is 18 to 26.

The range of feasibility is bordered by these two limits, as illustrated in Figure 3S–6.

2. Repeating the process for the storage constraint, we determine the last points (upper limit and lower limit) for which the line parallel to *storage* intersects the *inspection* constraint (see Figure 3S–7)

   We can see on the graph that the lower limit intersects at $x_1 = 11$, $x_2 = 0$, and that the upper intersection is where the inspection and assembly lines cross. Solving those two equations simultaneously yields $x_1 = 7.5$ and $x_2 = 7$.

FIGURE 3S–6 Range of Feasibility for Changes in Inspection Time

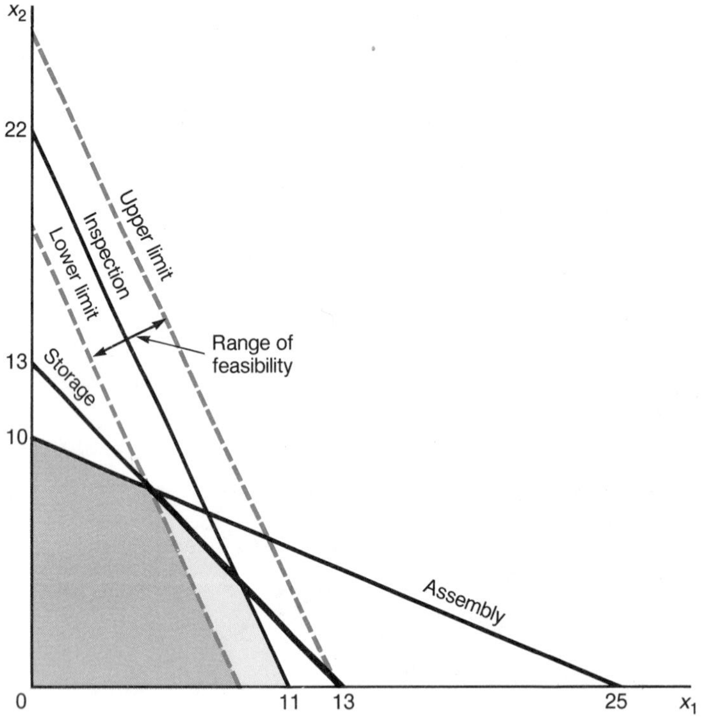

Substituting these two sets of values into the storage constraint gives us:

$$3(7.5) + 3(7) = 43.5 \quad \text{(upper limit)}$$
$$3(11) + 3(0) = 33 \quad \text{(lower limit)}$$

Hence, the range of feasibility for the RHS of the storage constraint is 33 cubic feet to 43.5 cubic feet.

As a final note, let us consider what happens if a change in the RHS value of a constraint takes it beyond its range of feasibility. There are two cases. One is a decrease that results in a RHS that is below the lower limit of the range of feasibility. Should this occur, it would be necessary to solve the modified problem in order to find the new optimal solution and find the new shadow prices. The other case occurs when the upper end of the range of feasibility is exceeded. In such instances, the excess beyond the upper limit becomes slack and the shadow price for that constraint becomes zero. For example, suppose analysis indicates

FIGURE 3S–7 Range of Feasibility for the Storage Constraint

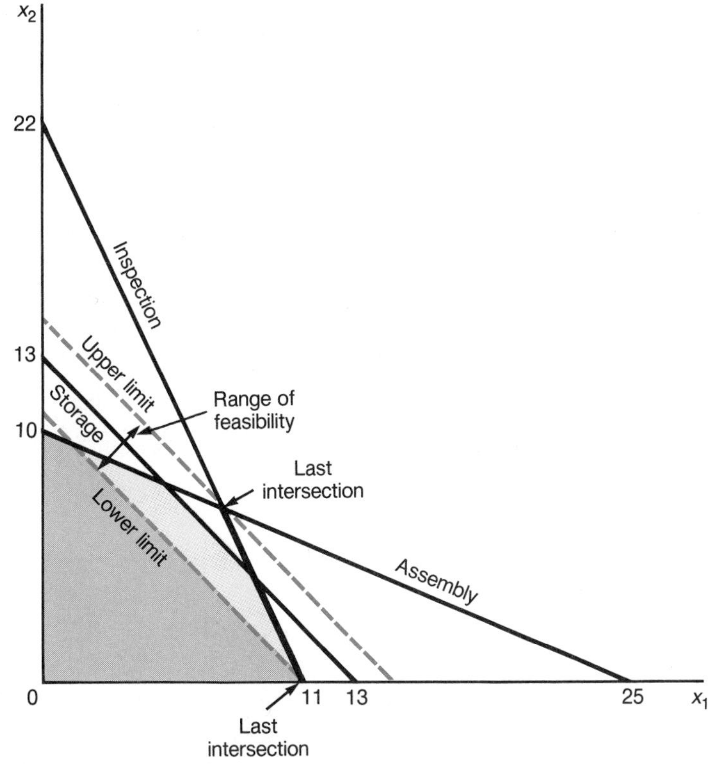

that the upper limit of the range of feasibility of a constraint is 200. If the RHS of this constraint is changed to, say, 210, the excess of 10 will become slack.

MINIMIZATION PROBLEMS

Minimization problems are handled in exactly the same way that maximization problems are, except that in finding the range of feasibility, *subtract* 1 from the RHS instead of adding 1 to the RHS. Note, too, that for the range of insignificance, the value will be *lower* than the current value, instead of higher.

SUMMARY

This supplement describes graphical sensitivity analysis of an optimal solution of a linear programming model. Sensitivity analysis enables an analyst to determine how a change in *one* of the numerical values of a model will impact the optimal solution and the optimal value of the objective function. Two types of changes are described in this supplement: a change in the value of an objective function coefficient and a change in the RHS value of a constraint.

Analysis of a change in the value of an objective function coefficient involves finding the range of values for which the optimal values of decision variables would not change. This is referred to as the range of optimality for that coefficient. Hence, a change that falls within the range of feasibility will not change the optimal solution, although the optimal value of the objective function will change. The same analysis can be used to determine the minimal value of an objective function coefficient necessary to cause the corresponding decision variable to be nonzero in the optimal solution.

Analysis of RHS changes begins with determination of a constraint's shadow price in the optimal solution. The range over which the RHS value can change without causing the shadow price to change is called its range of feasibility. Within this range, the same decision variables will remain optimal, although their values and the optimal value of the objective function will change.

GLOSSARY

Range of Feasibility The range in value over which the RHS of a constraint can change without changing its shadow price.

Range of Insignificance The range in value over which an objective function coefficient can change without causing the corresponding decision variable to take on a nonzero value. Applicable only to variables that have a value of zero in the optimal solution.

Range of Optimality The range in value over which an objective function coefficient can change without changing the optimal values of solution variables.

Sensitivity Analysis Analysis of the impact of a change in one of the numerical values of a linear programming model on the optimal solution and the optimal value of the objective function.

Shadow Price For a change in the RHS value of a constraint that is within its range of feasibility, the amount of change in the optimal value of the objective function per unit change of the RHS value (e.g., $2 per pound, $.53 per minute).

SOLVED PROBLEMS

Problem 1. Given this LP model:

maximize $3x_1 + 3x_2$

subject to

A $6x_1 + 4x_2 \leq 24$

B $10x_1 + 20x_2 \leq 80$

$x_1, x_2 \geq 0$

a. Find the range of optimality, or the range of insignificance, whichever is appropriate, for each objective function coefficient.

b. Find the shadow price and the range of feasibility for the RHS of each constraint.

Solution

Begin by plotting the graph and solving for the optimal solution:

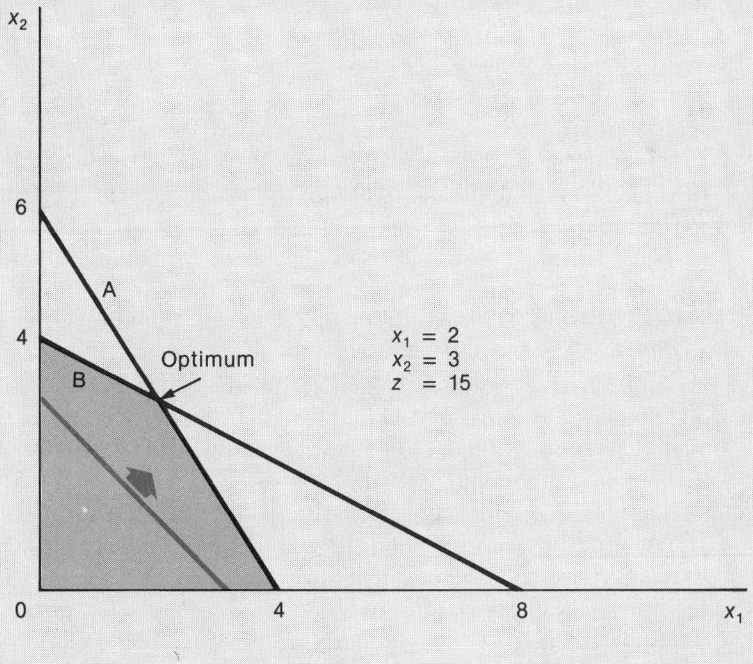

a. We can see that neither decision variable has a value of zero in the optimal solution. Therefore, the range of optimality is appropriate for both of their objective function coefficients. The range of optimality is the amount that an objective function coefficient can change (thereby changing the slope of the objective function line) and still not cause the solution to move to another corner point.

We can determine the range of optimality for each coefficient by determining the value it would need to cause the objective function line to be just parallel to each of the binding constraints. Thus, for the x_1 coefficient, for the objective function line to be parallel to the first constraint, its value would have to be $6/4 = 1.5$ times that of the x_2 coefficient, which would make it 4.5. Then, to be parallel to the second constraint, the x_1 coefficient would have to be $1/2$ (i.e., $10/20 = 1/2$) of the x_2 coefficient, which would make it 1.5. Hence, the range of optimality for the x_1 coefficient is 1.5 to 4.5

Similarly, for the x_2 coefficient, we must find the value that will make the objective function line parallel to the first constraint and then the second constraint. For the first constraint, we know that the ratio of the two coefficients must be $6/4 = 1.5$. Given that the x_1 coefficient is 3, the x_2 coefficient would then be 2 ($6/4 = 3/2$). And, to be parallel to the second constraint, the ratio must be $10/20 = 1/2$. So with the x_1 coefficient equal to 3, the x_2 coefficient must be 6 ($3/6 = 1/2$). Hence, the range of optimality for the x_2 coefficient is 2 to 6.

b. To find the shadow price of a constraint that is a binding constraint (both constraints here are binding constraints), increase its RHS by 1, and determine the new optimal values of the decision variables. Then substitute those new values into the objective function to find its new optimal value. Subtract the original Z from the new Z to obtain the shadow price. Note: If a constraint is not binding, its shadow price is 0.

Thus, adding 1 to the RHS of the first constraint and solving for the new intersection with the second constraint, we find $x_1 = 2.25$ and $x_2 = 2.875$. This yields $Z' = 15.375$. The original Z was 15. Therefore, the shadow price is $15.375 - 15 = .375$ for the first constraint.

Similarly, by adding 1 to the RHS of the second constraint (making it 81), and using the original first constraint, we obtain an intersection of $x_1 = 1.95$, $x_2 = 3.075$. Then $Z' = 15.075$, so the shadow price is $15.075 - 15 = .075$ for the second constraint.

Now, to find the range of feasibility for the RHS of a constraint, place a straight edge along the line on the graph. First, hold it parallel to the line while moving away from the origin. Stop when it reaches the last intersection with the other binding constraint in this quadrant. You can see from the graph that the upper limit is at 8, 0. Similarly, moving parallel to the first constraint but toward the origin, the lower limit is at 0, 4.

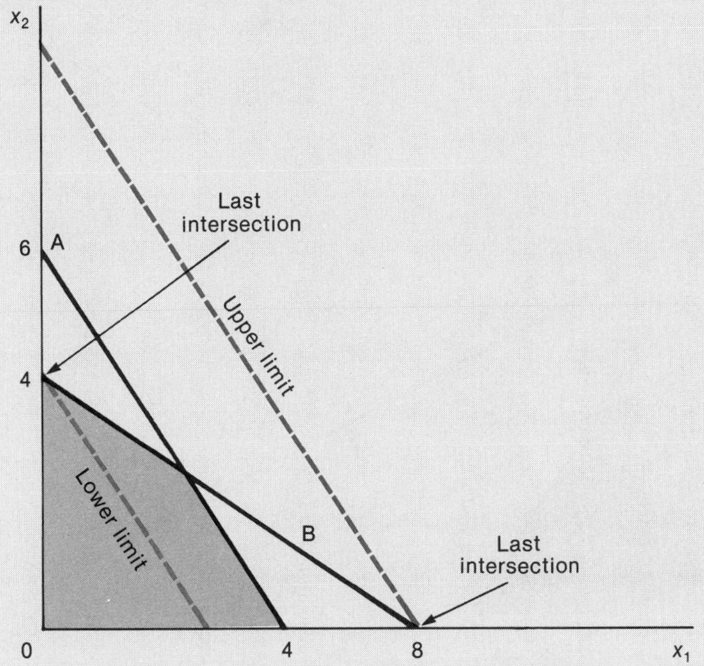

Substituting each of these sets of values into the first constraint will give us our range of feasibility:

8, 0: $6(8) + 4(0) = 48$

0, 4: $6(0) + 4(4) = 16$

Hence, the range of feasibility for the first constraint is 16 to 48.

Similarly, to find the range of feasibility for the second constraint, we hold a straight edge along its graph and move it parallel to the line away from the origin until we reach the last intersection (0, 6) and toward the origin until we reach the last intersection with the other binding constraint (4, 0). Substituting these sets of values into the second constraint, we find:

0, 6: $10(0) + 20(6) = 120$

4, 0: $10(4) + 20(0) = 40$

Hence, the range of feasibility for the second constraint is 40 to 120.

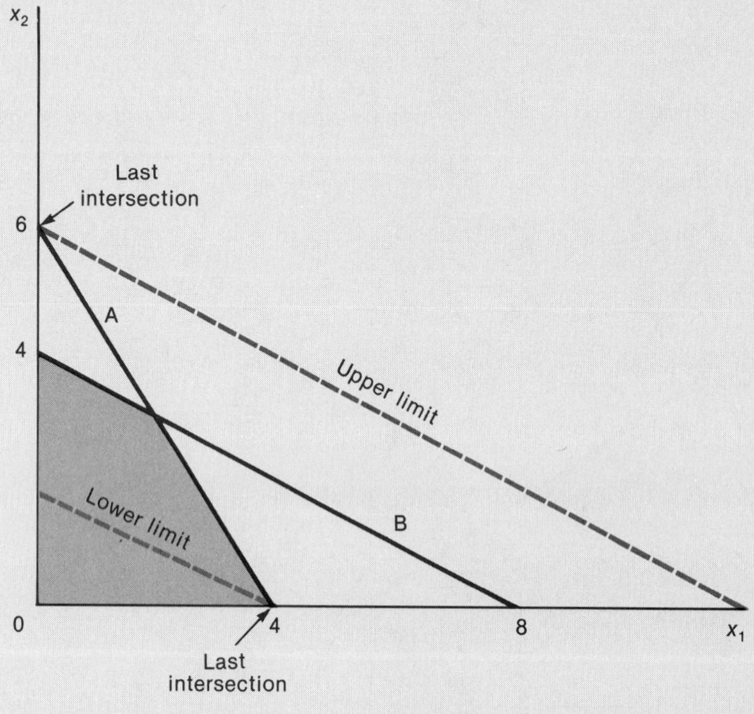

Problem 2. Suppose the objective function in a previous problem had been maximize $8x_1 + 2x_2$. The optimal solution would then have been $x_1 = 4$, $x_2 = 0$.

Find the range of insignificance for the x_2 coefficient in the objective function.

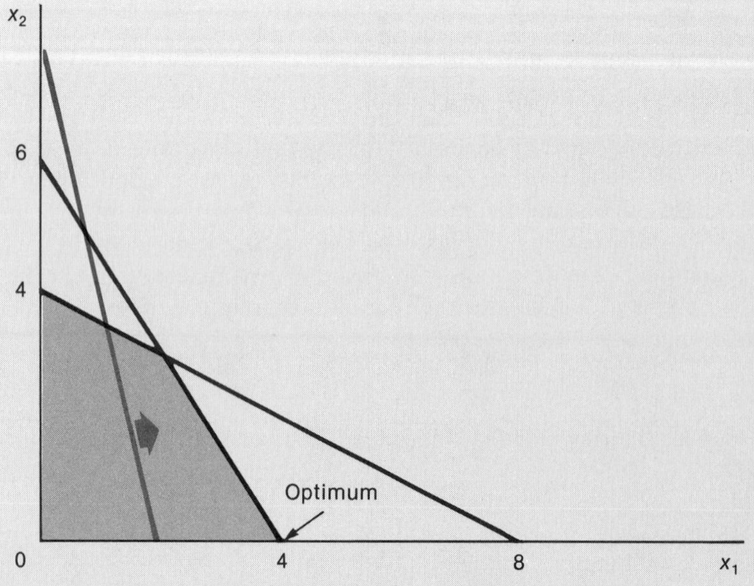

Solution

x_2 will have an optimal value of zero (i.e., it will be insignificant) unless its objective function coefficient becomes large enough for it to make a positive contribution to the objective. This would occur if its value increased to where it caused the objective function line to be at least parallel to the first constraint. Thus, the ratio of the x_1 and x_2 coefficients would have to be 6/4 = 1.5. With the x_1 coefficient equal to 8, this would require an x_2 coefficient of at least 12. Hence, the range of insignificance for the x_2 coefficient is a value of less than 12 in the objective function.

PROBLEMS

1. Sensitivity analysis can provide a decision maker with additional insights about an optimal solution to an LP model.
   a. Explain in general terms what sensitivity analysis accomplishes.
   b. Why might sensitivity analysis be useful to a decision maker?
   c. List the two types of parameters the discussion of sensitivity analysis in the supplement focused on.

2. Briefly define or explain each of these terms:
   a. Shadow price.
   b. Range of feasibility.
   c. Range of optimality.
   d. Range of insignificance.
   e. Binding constraint.

3. Given this LP model and its graph:

   maximize $5x_1 + 9x_2$

   subject to

   A $2x_1 + 1x_2 \leq 10$
   B $1x_1 + 3x_2 \leq 12$
   $x_1, x_2 \geq 0$

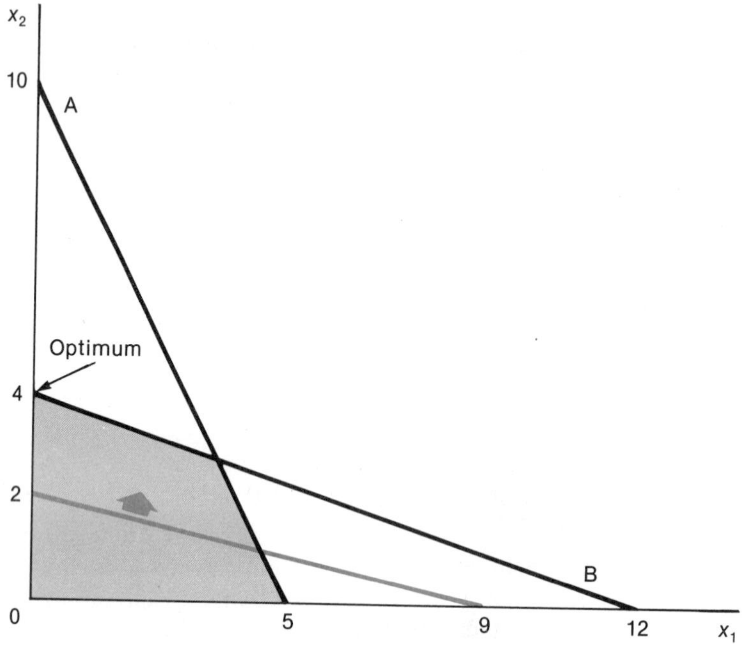

a. Find the range of optimality for the x_2 coefficient in the objective function.

b. Find the range of optimality for the x_1 coefficient of the objective function.

c. Find the shadow price for each constraint's RHS.

d. Determine the range of feasibility for each constraint's shadow price.

e. What impact would a change in the objective function coefficient of x_1 from 5 to 4 have on the optimal values of the decision variables? What effect would it have on the optimal value of the objective function?

f. What effect would a decrease of 1 in the value of the x_2 coefficient of the objective function have on the optimal values of the decision variables? What effect would it have on the optimal value of the objective function? Explain.

4. Given this LP model:

maximize $\quad 8x_1 + 3x_2$

subject to

Labor	$5x_1 + 2x_2 \leq 30$ hours
Equipment	$1x_1 + 2x_2 \leq 16$ hours
Material	$10x_1 + 7x_2 \leq 70$ pounds
	$x_1, x_2 \geq 0$

a. Plot the graph and determine the optimal solution.
b. Find the range of optimality or insignificance for each objective function coefficient.
c. Determine the shadow price of each constraint for the optimal solution.
d. Determine the range of feasibility for the RHS of each constraint.

5. Given this LP model:

minimize $4x_1 + 8x_2$

subject to

Fiber	$5x_1 + 8x_2 \geq 40$
Protein	$6x_1 + 4x_2 \geq 24$
	$x_1, x_2 \geq 0$

a. Find the range of optimality or insignificance for each objective function coefficient.
b. How would a decrease of \$1 in the x_1 coefficient of the objective function affect the optimal values of the decision variables? How would it affect the optimal value of the objective function?
c. What is the shadow price for the fiber constraint's RHS? Over what range of values is it valid?
d. What is the shadow price for the RHS of the protein constraint? Over what range of values is it valid?
e. What impact on cost would a decrease of 2 units in the RHS of the protein constraint have?

6. The manager of FYZ Incorporated has been presented with the following LP model:

minimize $30A + 45B$ (cost)

subject to

$$5A + 2B \geq 100$$
$$4A + 8B \geq 240$$
$$B \geq 20$$
$$A \text{ and } B \geq 0$$

The manager would like your assistance in answering her questions:
a. What are the optimal values of A and B? What is the minimum cost?
b. If the cost of B could be reduced to \$42 per unit, how many units of B would be optimal? What would the minimum cost be?
c. What is the shadow price for the RHS of the first constraint? Over what range is it valid?
d. By what amount would the cost change, and in what direction, if the first constraint was changed to 110?

7. The manager of the assembly department of IKW, Inc., has developed this LP model:

maximize	$12P + 10Q$	(profit)
subject to		
Line 1	$11P + 11Q \leq 121$	hours
Line 2	$8P + 15Q \leq 120$	hours
Inspection	$3P + 15Q \leq 60$	minutes
	$P, Q \geq 0$	

a. What are the optimal values of P, Q, and Z?

b. By how much can the profit per unit of P change without changing the optimal values of P and Q?

c. If the amount of inspection time could be increased, how much more could be used?

d. If Line 2 time was reduced by one hour, what impact would this have on profit?

e. If additional time for Line 1 could be obtained, how much could be effectively used. What would happen if more time than this was added to Line 1?

Chapter 4
Linear Programming
The Simplex Method

Chapter Outline

Learning Objectives

After completing this chapter, you should be able to:

1. Explain the ways in which the simplex method is superior to the graphical method for solving linear programming problems.
2. Solve small maximization problems manually using the simplex method.
3. Interpret simplex solutions.
4. Discuss the role computers play in solving simplex problems and the relevance of manual solutions.
5. Discuss unbounded solutions, degeneracy, and multiple optimal solutions in terms of the simplex method.

The preceding two chapters introduced the the topic of linear programming and illustrated how two-variable LP problems could be solved graphically. Linear programming problems represent a very important category of problems in management science, and graphical procedures are very helpful in developing a conceptual understanding of LP problems and their solutions. Nevertheless, in practice, graphical solutions do not represent a realistic approach to most LP problems because the majority of these problems involve more than two decision variables, whereas the graphical method is limited to problems with two decision variables.

This chapter introduces the simplex procedure, which is a general-purpose approach for solving LP problems regardless of the number of decision variables. The procedure is demonstrated for a maximization problem that has only $\leq$ constraints. The next chapter describes how to handle both minimization problems and maximization problems that have some constraints that are not of the $\leq$ variety.

For purposes of illustration, the microcomputer problem that was solved using the graphical approach in the preceding chapter is solved using the simplex method. An important benefit of using this example is that because the problem involves only two decision variables, it will be possible to illustrate the simplex counterparts to the graphical solution. This will help you to gain an intuitive grasp of the simplex technique.

The chapter concludes with a discussion of computer solutions and a discussion of some special issues that can arise in solving problems manually.

OVERVIEW OF THE SIMPLEX METHOD

The simplex method is an iterative technique that begins with a feasible solution that is not optimal, but serves as a starting point. Through algebraic manipulation, the solution is improved until no further improvement is possible; that is, until the optimal solution has been identified.

We learned in the last chapter that the optimal solution to a linear programming model will occur at an extreme point of the feasible solution space. This is true even if a model involves more than two variables; optimal solutions occur at these points. Extreme points represent intersections of constraints. Of course, not every intersection will result in an extreme point of the feasible solution space; some will be outside of the feasible solution space. Hence, not every solution will be a feasible solution. Solutions that represent intersections of constraints are called **basic solutions;** those that also satisfy all of the constraints, including the non-negativity constraints, are called **basic feasible solutions.** The simplex method is an algebraic procedure for systematically examining basic feasible solutions. If an optimal solution exists, the simplex method will identify it.

The simplex method is based on simultaneous solutions of linear equations. An LP model can be expressed in terms of an objective function and a system of linear equations. Recall the **standard form** of the microcomputer problem:

maximize	$60x_1 + 50x_2 + 0s_1 + 0s_2 + 0s_3$	
subject to		
Assembly	$4x_1 + 10x_2 + s_1$	$= 100$
Inspection	$2x_1 + x_2 + s_2$	$= 22$
Storage	$3x_1 + 3x_2 + s_3$	$= 39$
	All variables ≥ 0	

The constraints form a system of linear equations. As a rule, linear programming models have fewer equations than variables. For example, in this case there are three equations and five variables (two decision variables and three slack variables). When a system of equations has more variables than equations, unique solutions are not possible. Instead, the solution possibilities are infinite. For instance, consider the following case that has two variables, but only one equation:

$$x_1 + x_2 = 10$$

Both variables could equal 5; or one could equal 2 and the other could equal 8; or one could equal 8.5 and the other 1.5, and so on. In other words, there is no single solution. Now, consider this case:

$$x_1 + x_2 = 10$$
$$x_1 - x_2 = 0$$

A single solution exists: $x_1 = 5$, $x_2 = 5$. Thus, unless the number of equations *equals* the number of variables, a unique solution cannot be found.

In order to make the number of variables equal to the number of equations, enough variables can be set equal to zero so that the remaining number of nonzero variables equals the number of equations. In the case of the microcomputer model, if two of the variables were set equal to zero (in effect, dropping them from the equations), the result would be three equations and three variables. In general, if we have n variables and m equations, with $n > m$, we must set $n - m$ of the variables equal to zero in order to obtain a system of equations in which the number of variables equals the number of equations. And if we then solve the resulting system of equations for the values of the remaining variables, we will obtain a solution that represents an intersection of constraints. In other words, by setting $n - m$ variables equal to zero, we are able to determine a solution that occurs at one of the constraint intersections. The result is a basic solution. Moreover, the variables that have been set equal to zero are referred to as *nonbasic variables,* whereas the remaining variables are referred to as **basic variables.** And by setting different combinations of variables equal to zero, we end up with solutions at different intersections. Of course, there is no guarantee that a particular solution will be both basic and feasible; some of the constraint intersections will occur outside the feasible solution space. Naturally, the optimal solution to a problem must be one of the intersections that lie along the boundary of the feasible solution space, which are basic feasible solutions. They are the only solutions that are worthwhile to examine. Fortunately, the simplex procedure has a very desirable property that enables us to do just that: If we can supply a basic feasible solution to start with (called an *initial feasible solution*), the simplex method will generate other basic feasible solutions. You might think of it in this way: Imagine a house with many rooms, one of which contains all feasible solutions. If the simplex method is placed in that room, it will remain there, examining basic feasible solutions until it has identified the optimal solution. Thus, an important requirement for using the simplex method is to find a basic feasible solution to start the process.

Finding an Initial Feasible Solution

A basic feasible solution is a basic solution that satisfies all of the constraints in a model, including the non-negativity constraints. As noted in the preceding section, we can obtain a basic solution by setting $n - m$ of the variables equal to zero and solving for the remaining variables. For example, in the microcomputer problem (five variables, three constraints), we must set two variables equal to zero. Suppose we set the two decision variables equal to zero. They would drop out of the equations, and we would be left with the following very simple equations:

$$\begin{aligned} s_1 \qquad\qquad &= 100 \\ s_2 \qquad &= 22 \\ s_3 &= 39 \end{aligned}$$

Obviously, it is very easy to see what the values of the remaining variables are. Moreover, we can verify that this is a basic feasible solution because the equations are satisfied and no variable has a negative value. Hence, an easy way for us to obtain a basic feasible solution in this case was to set the decision variables equal to zero. In fact, in a maximization problem in which all constraints are of the $\leq$ variety, an initial basic feasible solution can be obtained by setting all of the decision variables equal to zero. Therefore, the initial solution will consist entirely of slack variables.

The variables that are solved for are the basic variables, and the other variables are the nonbasic variables. The complete solution consists of the basic and the nonbasic variables. Therefore, for the microcomputer problem, the complete initial feasible solution is:

$$\begin{aligned} x_1 &= 0 \\ x_2 &= 0 \\ s_1 &= 100 \\ s_2 &= 22 \\ s_3 &= 39 \end{aligned}$$

This basic feasible solution was simple to obtain because the system of equations we are working with has two important properties:

1. The right sides of the equations are non-negative.
2. Each of the basic variables appears in a single equation with a coefficient equal to 1. (In all other equations, the variable, essentially, has a coefficient of 0; i.e., it doesn't appear.)

A system with these properties is said to be in *tableau form*. We can assure ourselves of easily finding a basic feasible solution by making sure that our system of linear equations has these two properties.

If constraints have negative values on the right, these can be converted into positive values by multiplying both sides of the constraint by -1. This will cause every sign to be reversed, and it will also reverse the direction of an inequality sign. Once any right-side negatives have been eliminated, slack or surplus values can be added to convert any inequalities into equalities. Then, by setting the decision variables equal to zero, the resulting set of equations will easily yield a basic feasible solution. This then becomes the starting point for a simplex solution to the problem. From this point, the simplex procedure allows a sequence of adjacent extreme points of the feasible solution space to be examined. The mathematical characteristics of each extreme point are summarized in a table that is referred to as a **tableau.**

A tableau is useful because there are numerous calculations to keep track of: a tableau summarizes the results of each iteration. Among the information contained in a tableau are the values of all basic variables (the nonbasic variables have values of zero), the value of the objective function at that extreme point, and whether or not the solution is optimal. If a solution is not optimal, the numerical values in the tableau can be manipulated to obtain the values of a similar tableau for the next extreme point. The process continues in this manner, with ever-improving solutions, until the optimal extreme point has been identified.

In LP problems that have all less-than-or-equal-to constraints, the standard form and the tableau form are the same. That is not the case for problems that have equal-to or greater-than-or-equal-to constraints. The next chapter will address those kinds of constraints and show how to obtain the tableau form of the problem.

DEVELOPING THE INITIAL SIMPLEX TABLEAU

Once an LP model has been expressed in tableau form, the initial simplex tableau can be developed. In order to be able to refer in a general way to a simplex tableau, the following notation will be used:

c_j = coefficient of variable j in the objective function

a_{ij} = coefficient of variable j in constraint i

b_i = right-hand side value of constraint i

This notation can be illustrated by comparing the microcomputer LP model to a general version of the same model (see Figure 4–1).

FIGURE 4–1 Comparison of Microcomputer Model and General Simplex Notation

Microcomputer Model

maximize $60x_1 + 50x_2 + 0s_1 + 0s_2 + 0s_3$

subject to

$$\begin{array}{llllll} 4x_1 + & 10x_2 + & s_1 & & & = 100 \\ 2x_1 + & x_2 & & + s_2 & & = 22 \\ 3x_1 + & 3x_2 & & & + s_3 & = 39 \end{array}$$

Symbolic Model

maximize $c_1x_1 + c_2x_2 + 0s_1 + 0s_2 + 0s_3$

subject to

$$\begin{array}{llllll} a_{11}x_1 + & a_{12}x_2 + & a_{13}s_1 & & & = b_1 \\ a_{21}x_1 + & a_{22}x_2 & & + a_{24}s_2 & & = b_2 \\ a_{31}x_1 + & a_{32}x_2 & & & + a_{35}s_3 & = b_3 \end{array}$$

Now, let's see how the first tableau is developed. We begin by drawing the outline of our tableau and listing the variables in our model across the top of the tableau (see Table 4–1a). Next, we fill in the parameters of our model in the appropriate rows and columns. This is illustrated using general notation in Table 4–1b, and then, specifically, by using the numbers from the microcomputer problem in Table 4–1c. Note that there are three rows, one for each constraint.

Next, we add two columns to the left side of the tableau (see Table 4–1d). The first column is a list of the basic variables; it is called the **basis.** Recall that the initial feasible solution consists of the slack variables. The next column indicates the objective coefficient for the basic variable for each row. The *C* at the top of the second column indicates that the values in that column and the values in the top row are objective function coefficients. Note that the last column on the right is called the Quantity column; it refers to the right-hand side values of the constraints.

There are two more rows needed at the bottom of the tableau in order to complete it. The first is a *Z* row and the second a $C - Z$ row. The row *Z* values are determined column by column. For each column, the *Z* value is obtained by multiplying each of the numbers in the column by their respective row coefficients in column *C*. For example, the *Z* value for the x_1 column is computed in this way:

$$0(4) + 0(2) + 0(3) = 0$$

Similarly, the *Z* value for the x_2 column is:

$$0(10) + 0(1) + 0(3) = 0$$

For the s_1 column, the result is:

$$0(1) + 0(0) + 0(0) = 0$$

The remaining columns are computed in similar fashion.

TABLE 4–1

a.

List of variables →	x_1	x_2	s_1	s_2	s_3	

b.

Coefficients of objective function →	c_1	c_2	0	0	0	RHS values
	x_1	x_2	s_1	s_2	s_3	↓
1st constraint →	a_{11}	a_{12}	1			b_1
2nd constraint →	a_{21}	a_{22}		1		b_2
3rd constraint →	a_{31}	a_{32}			1	b_3

c.

	60	50	0	0	0	
	x_1	x_2	s_1	s_2	s_3	↓
	4	10	1			100
	2	1		1		22
	3	3			1	39

d.

	C→	60	50	0	0	0	
Basis	↓	x_1	x_2	s_1	s_2	s_3	Quantity
s_1	0	4	10	1	0	0	100
s_2	0	2	1	0	1	0	22
s_3	0	3	3	0	0	1	39

TABLE 4–2 Completed Initial Tableau for the Microcomputer Problem

Basis	C	60 x_1	50 x_2	0 s_1	0 s_2	0 s_3	Quantity
s_1	0	4	10	1	0	0	100
s_2	0	2	1	0	1	0	22
s_3	0	3	3	0	0	1	39
	Z	0	0	0	0	0	0
	$C - Z$	60	50	0	0	0	

Because each of the row coefficients is 0 this means all the row Z values will equal zero for the initial tableau. There is also a Z value for the Quantity column. It is computed in similar fashion:

$$0(100) + 0(22) + 0(39) = 0$$

The values in the bottom row are calculated column by column. For each column, the value in row Z is subtracted from the C value in the top row. Thus, for the x_1 column we have $60 - 0 = 60$, for the x_2 column we have $50 - 0 = 50$, and for each of the slack columns we have $0 - 0 = 0$. These values are shown in Table 4–2, which is the completed initial tableau.

Interpreting the Solution

Each tableau represents a basic feasible solution to the problem. Let's examine this particular tableau to see some of the kinds of information it contains.

As previously noted, this solution is comprised entirely of the slack variables. We can read the variables that are in the basis, or "in solution," down the left side of the table, and their values down the right side. This tells us that $s_1 = 100$, $s_2 = 22$, and $s_3 = 39$. If a variable is not included in the basis, its value is equal to zero. Therefore, because x_1 and x_2 are not listed, their values are zero. Hence, this solution corresponds to the origin.

A feature of **variables in solution** is that a 0 appears in the bottom row of the tableau in that variable's column. Thus, all three slack variables have a zero in the bottom row in their respective columns. Conversely, the two variables not in solution both have nonzero values in the bottom row. In addition, note the values in the column of every variable that is in solution. In each case, the column is made up of a single 1 and the rest 0's. For example, in column s_1 the values are

1
0
0

This is called a *unit vector*. Variables that are in solution will have unit vector columns (i.e., one 1 and the rest 0). Moreover, the 1 will appear in the same row that the variable appears in. Thus, s_1 is the first variable listed in the basis. Hence, a 1 appears at the intersection of the first row and the s_1 column. Similarly, s_2 appears in the second row. Therefore, a 1 appears in the second row of the s_2 column and an s_3 is listed in the third row, so a 1 appears in the third row of the unit vector for the s_3 column.

The unit vector concept is important because in developing subsequent tableaus, we will want to change the makeup of the list of variables that form the basis. That will require manipulating the system of equations in such a way that the variable we wish to bring into the basis ends up with a unit vector column. In other words, using algebraic operations, we will alter the system of equations so that they conform to a unit vector in the specific column. This will provide us with a tableau that contains a basic feasible solution with that variable. The procedure for doing this will be described shortly. Before moving to that discussion, let's consider other information the tableau provides.

The last value in the Z row (i.e., in the Quantity column) indicates that the value of the objective function for this solution is 0. (The other values in the Z row will be explained shortly.)

The values in the bottom row indicate any potential for improvement. For example, the 60 in column x_1 reveals that if one unit of x_1 could be brought into the solution (i.e., if $x_1 = 1$), the value of the objective function would increase by \$60, and that additional units of x_1 also would increase the value of the objective function by \$60 per unit. The other values in the bottom row have similar interpretation: Each unit of x_2 will contribute an increase of \$50, but because no additional units of slack exist (those variables are at their maximum levels because they are already in solution), there is no potential for increased profit in slack columns. Obviously, this solution is not optimal because potential improvement is possible. This leads us to the following rule:

A simplex solution in a maximization problem is optimal if the $C - Z$ row consists entirely of zeros and negative numbers (i.e., there are no positive values in the bottom row). When this has been achieved, there is no opportunity for improving the solution.

In order to find an improved solution, we must now develop another tableau.

DEVELOPING THE SECOND TABLEAU

As noted previously, the simplex approach is iterative. Each iteration moves one step closer to the optimal solution. At each iteration, one variable that is not in the solution is added to the solution and one variable that is in solution is removed from solution in order to keep the number of variables in the basis equal to the number of contraints. The first tableau has all slack variables in the basis and the decision variables are nonbasic. Hence, one of the decision variables will be brought into solution to replace one of the three slack variables currently in the solution mix. This leads us to two important questions:

1. Which variable should be brought into (enter) the solution mix (basis)?
2. Which variable should be replaced in the solution mix (basis)?

The answer to the first question is found in the $C - Z$ row: Bring the variable into solution that has the largest positive value in the $C - Z$ row, because it has the largest profit potential. The positive values are 60 and 50. The larger of these is 60, which is in the x_1 column. This indicates that x_1 should enter the basis. The x_1 column is now designated as the *pivot* column, and the numbers in that column in the body of the table (i.e., $\begin{matrix}4\\2\\3\end{matrix}$) will be key values for developing the second tableau. Let's see why.

The numbers in the body of the first tableau are the coefficients of the constraints. Thus, in the x_1 column, the numbers are 4, 2, and 3, which are the x_1 coefficients in the three constraints. Each number indicates how much of the basic variable for that row must be given up, or reduced, in order to get one unit of x_1. For instance, the 4 in the first row tells us that 4 units of slack will be required to obtain 1 unit of Model 1 microcomputer (x_1). Similarly, the 2 in the second row indicates that 2 units of slack s_2 must be used up to obtain that same 1 unit of x_1 and the 3 in the third row tells us that 3 units of s_3 must be used up to get the unit of x_1. Therefore, a unit of x_1 requires 4 units of s_1, 2 units of s_2, and 3 units of s_3. The numbers in the body of a simplex tableau are, therefore, referred to as *substitution rates* because they indicate how much each basic variable will be reduced in order to obtain 1 unit of the entering variable.

Because each unit of x_1 that can be brought into solution will increase profit by \$60, we naturally want to make as much x_1 as possible. The amount of x_1 that can be made will depend on the substitution rates and the amount of slack available, which is shown in the Quantity column. By dividing the substitution rates shown in the x_1 column into their respective row quantity amounts, we will be able to determine which variable in the basis is most limiting. Table 4–3 shows each of the three ratios. They are 25 for the first row, 11 for the second, and 13 for the third. Hence, if the *only* constraint was the first, we could make 25 units of x_1. However, there are three constraints, and the second one is the most restrictive because it reveals that there is only enough of the second resource to make 11 units of x_1. Hence, the smallest of the ratios governs how much x_1 we can make. Further, in making the 11 units of x_1, the second resource will be used up (i.e., s_2 will be reduced to zero). Thus, s_2 will drop out of the solution mix (basis) and its place will be taken by x_1.

It is interesting to note that the three ratios (25, 11, and 13) correspond to the intersections of the constraints with the x_1 axis (see Figure 4–2). Note that the

TABLE 4–3 Determining the Entering and Exiting Variables

	C	60	50	0	0	0			
Basis		x_1	x_2	s_1	s_2	s_3	Quantity		
s_1	0	4	10	1	0	0	100	100/4 = 25	Smallest
s_2	0	2	1	0	1	0	22	22/2 = 11 ←	non-negative
s_3	0	3	3	0	0	1	39	39/3 = 13	ratio
	Z	0	0	0	0	0	0		
	C − Z	60 ↑ Largest positive value	50	0	0	0			

FIGURE 4–2 The Next Corner Point Is Determined by the Most Limiting Constraint

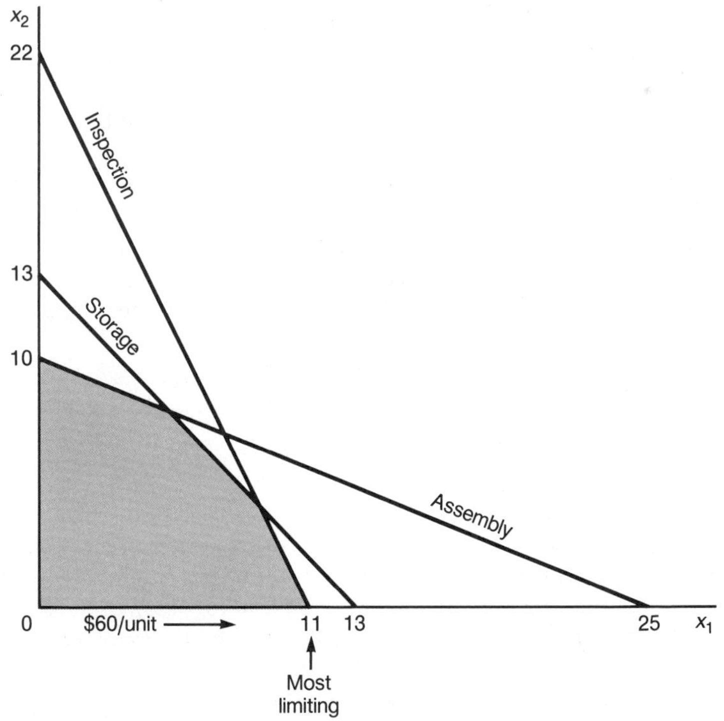

smallest of the ratios represents the extreme point of the feasible solution space; the other points lie beyond the feasible solution space. Hence, by selecting the smallest ratio, the simplex procedure stays within the feasible solution space.

It sometimes happens that some of the substitution rates for the variable we want to bring into solution are zero or negative. A zero would imply that no amount of the corresponding variables in the basis is required to obtain a unit of the entering variable. For instance, if there were a fourth constraint in this problem, and it was that $x_2 = 10$, x_1 does not appear in the constraint. Hence, bringing x_1 into solution would not affect this constraint. A negative substitution rate implies that bringing a variable into solution will *increase* the amount of a basic variable. In effect, the entering variable frees up additional resources. The point is the negative and zero substitution rates will not limit the amount of the entering variable that can be made. Therefore, we need only concern ourselves with positive substitution rates; there is no need to divide the Quantity column values by a negative or a zero substitution rate. Consequently, in determining the variable that will leave the basis, the rule is:

Select the leaving variable as the one that has the smallest non-negative ratio of quantity divided by substitution rate.

(Note, too, that dividing a number by zero results in an undefined value, not zero.)

Up to this point we have determined that variable x_1 will enter the basis (become a basic, or solution, variable), and that variable s_2 will leave the solution. The row of the variable that will leave the solution (in this case, s_2) is called the **pivot row.** Its values will be used to obtain values for the same row of the next tableau. Those values will then be used to determine values for the other constraint rows of the next tableau. The second tableau will provide us with an improved and, perhaps, optimal solution.

The top two rows of the tableau (the objective function coefficients and the list of variables) will stay the same (see Table 4–4). Now we must compute three sets of values:

1. Revised constraint equations.
2. Revised values for row Z.
3. Revised values for row $C - Z$.

Recall that in a simplex tableau, the variables that are in solution have a unit vector in their columns, with a 1 at the intersection of the column and the basis row containing the variable. What we want to accomplish by algebraic manipulation of the original system of equations is to obtain an equivalent system of equations that has a 1 in the second equation and a 0 in every other row. Although the resulting system of equations will be equivalent to the original system, a number of the coefficients of the equation will change, as will some (or all) of the

TABLE 4–4 Starting the Second Tableau

Basis	C	60 x_1	50 x_2	0 s_1	0 s_2	0 s_3	Quantity
s_1	0						
x_1	60						
s_3	0						
	Z						
	C − Z						

values in the Quantity column. However, this will enable us to easily find the values of the basis variables at the next feasible extreme point: We can read them from the last column of the new tableau. Also, the revised values will enable us to compute the appropriate values for the two bottom rows of the table. Among other things, this will enable us to determine if the solution is optimal; if it is not, it will enable us to identify the next variable that must be brought into solution.

The algebraic manipulations needed to obtain new row values are called *elementary row operations*. We will use two such operations:

1. Multiply (or divide) all of the elements in a row by a constant.
2. Add or subtract the multiple of a row to or from another row.

Again, it is emphasized that doing this will simply provide us with an equivalent system of equations. In fact, if you recall using simultaneous equations for graphical problems, you will realize that these two operations often were used to solve for intersections of constraints.

Let us begin our computations with the revised values for new row x_1. We want to force the 2, which is at the intersection of the x_1 column and the s_2 row of the initial tableau, to 1 (see Table 4–5). We can force the value to 1 by dividing the 2 by itself. We can do this and not really change the second equation if we divide every coefficient in the row by the same constant (or equivalently, multiply every element by the reciprocal of 2). Thus, the original equation can be transformed into an equivalent equation with a 1 and the x_1 coefficient by multiplying each element by ½:

2nd constraint	$2x_1 + 1x_2 + 0s_1 + 1s_2 + 0s_3 = 22$
Multiply by ½	$\frac{1}{2}(2x_1 + 1x_2 + 0s_1 + 1s_2 + 0s_3 = 22)$
Revised equation	$1x_1 + \frac{1}{2}x_2 + 0s_1 + \frac{1}{2}s_2 + 0s_3 = 11$

The revised coefficients can now be entered in the second tableau (see Table 4–6). The new pivot row will be used to transform the values of the other row equations into equivalent equations that can be used to easily identify the

TABLE 4–5 Initial Tableau

Basis	C	60 x_1	50 x_2	0 s_1	0 s_2	0 s_3	Quantity
s_1	0	4	10	1	0	0	100
s_2	0	(2)	1	0	1	0	22
s_3	0	3	3	0	0	1	39
	Z	0	0	0	0	0	0
	$C - Z$	60	50	0	0	0	

TABLE 4–6 The Pivot Row of the Second Tableau

Basis	C	60 x_1	50 x_2	0 s_1	0 s_2	0 s_3	Quantity
s_1	0						
x_1	60	1	½	0	½	0	11
s_3	0						
	Z						
	$C - Z$						

next solution. These will be obtained using the second of the above-mentioned elementary row operations.

We can easily see how the first constraint can be revised so that the x_1 coefficient is 0 by writing out the first constraint equation and the new pivot row equation:

1st constraint	$4x_1 + 10x_2 + 1s_1 + 0s_2 + 0s_3 = 100$
Pivot row	$1x_1 + \frac{1}{2}x_2 + 0s_1 + \frac{1}{2}s_2 + 0s_3 = 11$

If we multiply the pivot row by 4 (i.e., the coefficient of x_1 in the constraint we want to transform) and subtract the result, the x_1 term will drop out of the equation and become zero, which is what we want. Thus, the multiple of the pivot row is:

$$4x_1 + 2x_2 + 0s_1 + 2s_2 + 0s_3 = 44$$

TABLE 4–7 Revised First Row and Pivot Row of the Second Tableau

Basis	C	60 x_1	50 x_2	0 s_1	0 s_2	0 s_3	Quantity
s_1	0	0	8	1	−2	0	56
x_1	60	1	½	0	½	0	11
s_3	0						
	Z						
	$C - Z$						

Subtracting this from the 1st constraint gives us our new equation for the first constraint:

$$\begin{array}{lrcrcrcrcrcr}
\text{1st constraint} & 4x_1 & + & 10x_2 & + & 1s_1 & + & 0s_2 & + & 0s_3 & = & 100 \\
\text{Pivot multiple} & -(4x_1 & + & 2x_2 & + & 0s_1 & + & 2s_2 & + & 0s_3 & = & 44) \\
\hline
 & 0x_1 & + & 8x_2 & + & 1s_1 & - & 2s_2 & + & 0s_3 & = & 56
\end{array}$$

We can now enter the coefficients of this transformed constraint equation in the first row of the second tableau (see Table 4–7).

A similar operation can be performed on the third constraint equation. Note that in the first tableau (see Table 4–5) there is a 3 in the x_1 column. In order to reduce that value to 0, we can multiply the pivot row values by 3 and then subtract the resulting equation from the third constraint equation. Thus, we have:

$$\begin{array}{lrcrcrcrcrcr}
\text{3rd constraint} & 3x_1 & + & 3x_2 & + & 0s_1 & + & 0s_2 & + & 1s_3 & = & 39 \\
\text{Pivot row} & -3(1x_1 & + & \tfrac{1}{2}x_2 & + & 0s_1 & + & \tfrac{1}{2}s_2 & + & 0s_3 & = & 11) \\
\hline
 & 0x_1 & + & \tfrac{3}{2}x_2 & + & 0s_1 & - & \tfrac{3}{2}s_2 & + & 1s_3 & = & 6
\end{array}$$

These coefficients can now be entered in the third row of the second tableau (see Table 4–8). Note that the constraint equations always maintain their same row positions.

Now we are ready to compute the values for row Z. These are found by multiplying the values in each column by the corresponding coefficients in the C column and adding them. The computations are as follows:

Row	C	Column → x_1	x_2	s_1	s_2	s_3	Quantity
s_1	0	0(0) = 0	0(8) = 0	0(1) = 0	0(−2) = 0	0(0) = 0	0(56) = 0
x_1	60	60(1) = 60	60(½) = 30	60(0) = 0	60(½) = 30	60(0) = 0	60(11) = 660
s_3	0	0(0) = 0	0(3/2) = 0	0(0) = 0	0(−3/2) = 0	0(1) = 0	0(6) = 0
Z		60	30	0	30	0	660

TABLE 4–8 Partially Completed Second Tableau

Basis	C	60 x_1	50 x_2	0 s_1	0 s_2	0 s_3	Quantity
s_1	0	0	8	1	−2	0	56
x_1	60	1	½	0	½	0	11
s_3	0	0	3⁄2	0	−3⁄2	1	6
	Z						
	C − Z						

Now the row $C - Z$ values can be computed. Thus:

	x_1	x_2	s_1	s_2	s_3
C	60	50	0	0	0
−Z	−60	−30	−0	−30	−0
	0	20	0	−30	0

Entering the Z and $C - Z$ values in the tableau completes the second tableau (see Table 4–9).

Interpreting the Second Tableau

At this point, variables s_1, x_1, and s_3 are in solution. Not only are they listed in the basis, they also have a 0 in row $C - Z$. The solution at this point is: $s_1 = 56$, $x_1 = 11$, and $s_3 = 6$. Note, too, that x_2 and s_2 are not in solution. Hence, they are each equal to zero. The profit at this point is $660, which is read in the Quantity column in row Z. Also, note that each variable in solution has a unit vector in its column.

Checking the bottom row of the tableau, we note that there is a positive number (i.e., 20 in the x_2 column). This indicates that the solution can be improved. Because that is the only positive number, we will focus on it. The implication is that for every unit of x_2 (microcomputer, Model 2) that we can bring into the solution, profit will increase by $20.

Before moving on to developing the third tableau, let us pause to consider why producing units of x_2 will only increase the profit by $20 a unit when the x_2 coefficient in the objective function is $50. The reason is that in order to free up resources to produce some units of x_2, it will be necessary to produce fewer units of x_1. The $20 is the *net* profit increase that will result, taking into account the portion of a unit of x_1 that must be given up in order to be able to produce a

TABLE 4–9 Completed Second Tableau

Basis	C	60 x_1	50 x_2	0 s_1	0 s_2	0 s_3	Quantity
s_1	0	0	8	1	−2	0	56
x_1	60	1	½	0	½	0	11
s_3	0	0	3⁄2	0	−3⁄2	1	6
	Z	60	30	0	30	0	660
	$C - Z$	0	20	0	−30	0	

unit of x_2. In effect, it will be necessary to give up ½ of an x_1 (profit equals ½ of \$60) in order to be able to produce one unit of x_2 (profit of \$50). The net is \$50 − ½(\$60) = \$20. You can see where the ½ comes from; it appears in Table 4–9 at the intersection of the x_2 column and the x_1 row.

DEVELOPING THE THIRD TABLEAU

We have determined thus far that variable x_2 will enter the solution. Now, we must identify the variable that will leave the solution. To do this, we divide the constraint coefficients in the x_2 column into their corresponding Quantity column values. These computations are shown at the right side of Table 4–10.

The smallest non-negative ratio is in the third row. This tells us that variable s_3 must be taken out of solution (i.e., set equal to zero), and replaced with incoming variable x_2.

Before proceeding with the calculations, consider the graph shown in Figure 4–3. It shows the extreme point of the feasible solution space represented by the second tableau. It also illustrates that proceeding to the next tableau is conceptually the same as moving along the boundary of the feasible solution space to the adjacent corner point. Note, too, the number 4, 7, and 22 shown on the x_2 axis. These are the same numbers that were calculated as ratios in Table 4–10. They indicate the basic solution points in terms of the value of x_2 (i.e., the intersections of the inspection constraint with other constraints). The smallest of these ratios reveals the boundary of the feasible solution space and, hence, the basic feasible solution to investigate next.

Because x_2 will come into the solution, its coefficient in the x_2 column must be transformed to a 1. As before, if we note that the current value at that location (i.e., the intersection of the entering variable's columns and the exiting variable's row) is 3⁄2, we can accomplish this by dividing every element in the third row by 3⁄2. Equivalently, we can multiply every element by its reciprocal, ⅔. The resulting

TABLE 4–10 Determining the Exiting Variable

Basis	C	60 x_1	50 x_2	0 s_1	0 s_2	0 s_3	Quantity	
s_1	0	0	8	1	−2	0	56	56/8 = 7
x_1	60	1	½	0	½	0	11	11/½ = 22
s_3	0	0	3⁄2	0	−3⁄2	1	6	6/3⁄2 = 4 ← Smallest non-negative ratio
	Z	60	30	0	30	0	660	
	C − Z	0	20	0	−30	0	0	

FIGURE 4–3 Moving to the Next Corner Point

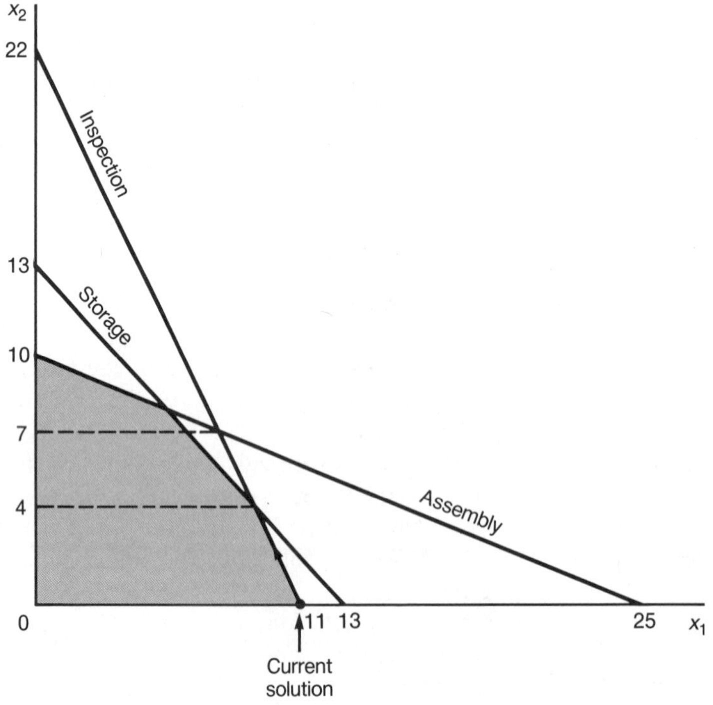

TABLE 4–11 Pivot Row Values for the Third Tableau

Basis	C	60 x_1	50 x_2	0 s_1	0 s_2	0 s_3	Quantity
s_1	0						
x_1	60						
x_2	50	0	1	0	−1	⅔	4
	Z						
	C − Z						

values become the pivot row for the third tableau. Omitting the variables from the list for convenience, we have:

$$\frac{2}{3}\left(0 \quad \frac{3}{2} \quad 0 \quad -\frac{3}{2} \quad 1 \quad 6\right) = 0 \quad 1 \quad 0 \quad -1 \quad \frac{2}{3} \quad 4$$

These values now can be entered into the third tableau (see Table 4–11).

The values in the remaining two constraint rows now must be transformed to equivalent equations in which the elements in the x_2 column are zero. This can be accomplished in the following way:

Multiply the values in the pivot row by the value in the entering variable's column for the row being transformed. Thus, to transform values in row 1, multiply the pivot row of the third tableau by 8. Then subtract the results from the values that appeared in the preceding tableau. Similarly, to obtain new row 2 values, multiply the pivot row in the third tableau by ½ and subtract the results from the row 2 values of the preceding tableau.

For the first row, multiplying the pivot row by 8, we obtain these values:

$$8\left(0 \quad 1 \quad 0 \quad -1 \quad \frac{2}{3} \quad 4\right) = 0 \quad 8 \quad 0 \quad -8 \quad \frac{16}{3} \quad 32$$

Subtracting these from the previous row 1 values, we obtain:

Previous values	0	8	1	−2	0	56
	−(0	8	0	−8	$\frac{16}{3}$	32)
	0	0	1	6	$-\frac{16}{3}$	24

For row 2, multiplying the pivot row values by ½, we obtain these values:

$$\frac{1}{2}\left(0 \quad 1 \quad 0 \quad -1 \quad \frac{2}{3} \quad 4\right) = \left(0 \quad \frac{1}{2} \quad 0 \quad -\frac{1}{2} \quad \frac{1}{3} \quad 2\right)$$

TABLE 4–12 Partially Completed Third Tableau

Basis	C	60 x_1	50 x_2	0 s_1	0 s_2	0 s_3	Quantity
s_1	0	0	0	1	6	$-16/3$	24
x_1	60	1	0	0	1	$-1/3$	9
x_2	50	0	1	0	-1	$2/3$	4
	Z						
	C − Z						

Subtracting these from the previous values for row 2, we obtain the transformed values for the second row of the third tableau:

$$\begin{array}{lcccccc} \text{Previous values} & 1 & \frac{1}{2} & 0 & \frac{1}{2} & 0 & 11 \\ & -(0 & \frac{1}{2} & 0 & -\frac{1}{2} & \frac{1}{3} & 2) \\ \hline & 1 & 0 & 0 & 1 & -\frac{1}{3} & 9 \end{array}$$

These values can now be entered in the third tableau (see Table 4–12).

We can use the values in Table 4–12 to compute values for row Z:

Row	x_1	x_2	s_1	s_2	s_3	Quantity
s_1	0(0) = 0	0(0) = 0	0(1) = 0	0(6) = 0	0(−16/3) = 0	0(24) = 0
x_1	60(1) = 60	60(0) = 0	60(0) = 0	60(1) = 60	60(−1/3) = −60/3	60(9) = 540
x_2	50(0) = 0	50(1) = 50	50(0) = 0	50(−1) = −50	50(2/3) = 100/3	50(4) = 200
Z	60	50	0	10	40/3	740

The Z values can now be used to compute the $C - Z$ row values:

	x_1	x_2	s_1	s_2	s_3
C	60	50	0	0	0
Z	−(60	50	0	10	40/3)
C − Z	0	0	0	−10	−40/3

Adding these two rows to the tableau completes the third tableau (see Table 4–13).

Interpreting the Third Tableau

In this tableau, all of the values in the bottom row are either negative or zero, indicating that no additional potential for improvement exists. Hence, this tableau contains the optimal solution, which is:

TABLE 4–13 Completed Third Tableau

Basis	C	60 x_1	50 x_2	0 s_1	0 s_2	0 s_3	Quantity
s_1	0	0	0	1	6	$-16/3$	24
x_1	60	1	0	0	1	$-1/3$	9
x_2	50	0	1	0	-1	$2/3$	4
	Z	60	50	0	10	$40/3$	740
	$C - Z$	0	0	0	-10	$-40/3$	

$$s_1 = 24$$
$$x_1 = 9$$
$$x_2 = 4$$

Note, too, that because they do not appear in the solution, variables s_2 and s_3 have values of zero. Thus, in order to achieve the maximum daily profit, the company should produce 9 units of Model 1 and 4 units of Model 2 microcomputers. This will leave no slack in either inspection ($s_2 = 0$) or in storage ($s_3 = 0$). However, there will be 24 hours of assembly time that is unused. The maximum profit will be \$740.

Notice that the variables in solution all have unit vectors in their respective columns for the constraint equations. Further, note that a 0 appears in row $C - Z$ in every column whose variable is in solution, indicating that its maximum contribution to the objective function has been realized.

SUMMARY OF THE SIMPLEX PROCEDURE FOR A MAXIMIZATION PROBLEM

The simplex procedure for a maximization problem *with all ≤ constraints* consists of these steps.

Initial Tableau

1. Write each constraint so that all variables are on the left side of the constraint and a non-negative constant is on the right. Then add a slack variable to the left side of the constraint, thereby making it an equality.
2. Develop the initial tableau.
   a. List the variables across the top of the table and write the objective function coefficient of each variable just above it.
   b. There should be one row in the body of the table for each constraint. List the slack variables in the basis column, one per row.

c. In the C column, enter the objective function coefficient of 0 for each slack variable.

d. Compute values for row Z.

e. Compute values for row $C - Z$.

Subsequent Tableaus

1. Identify the variable that has the largest positive value in row $C - Z$. This variable will come into solution next.
2. Using the constraint coefficients in the entering variable's column, divide each one into the corresponding Quantity column value. However, *do not divide by a 0 or a negative value*. The smallest non-negative ratio that results indicates which variable will leave the solution mix.
3. Compute replacement values for the leaving variable: Divide each element in the row by the row element that is in the entering variable column. These are the pivot row values for the next tableau. Enter them in the same row as the leaving variable and label the row with the name of the entering variable. Write the entering variable's objective function coefficient next to it in column C.
4. Compute values for each of the other constraint equations:

   a. Multiply each of the pivot row values by the number in the entering variable column of the row being transformed (e.g., for the first row, use the first number in the entering variable's column; for the third row, use the third number in the entering variable's column).

   b. Then subtract the resulting equation from the current equation for that row and enter the results in the same row of the next tableau.
5. Compute values for row Z: For each column, multiply each row coefficient by the row value in column C and then add the results. Enter these in the tableau.
6. Compute values for rows $C - Z$: For each column, subtract the value in row Z from the objective function coefficient listed in row C at the top of the tableau.
7. Examine the values in the bottom row. If all values are zero or negative, the optimal solution has been reached. The variables that comprise the solution are listed in the basis column and their optimal values can be read in the corresponding rows of the quantity column. The optimal value of the objective function will appear in row Z in the Quantity column.

   If the solution is not optimal, repeat steps 1–7 of this section until the optimal solution has been attained.

COMPUTER SOLUTIONS

The simplex procedure provides an all-purpose method for solving linear programming problems. Unfortunately, for all but the smallest problems, the computational burden imposed by the simplex procedure is considerable. This is true even for problems that are moderate in size; for larger problems, manual computations would require a herculean effort for solution. Fortunately, standard computer packages for solving linear programming problems using simplex are widely available. In practice, they are used almost exclusively instead of manual computations. Therefore, computer solutions represent the most realistic method for handling LP problems.

One of the most widely used linear programming packages is LINDO. Developed by Linus Schrage of the University of Chicago, it is available in both mainframe and personal computer versions. Also, there are many other packages available for mainframes and personal computers. Although these packages have a high degree of similarity in terms of input and output, they do have minor differences. Therefore, rather than describe a particular package, the discussion here will present a generic overview of how computers are used to obtain solutions to linear programming models.

Recall the microcomputer model:

$$\text{maximize} \quad 60x_1 + 50x_2$$

$$\text{subject to} \quad \begin{aligned} 4x_1 + 10x_2 &\leq 100 \\ 2x_1 + x_2 &\leq 22 \\ 3x_1 + 3x_2 &\leq 39 \\ x_1, x_2 &\geq 0 \end{aligned}$$

The problem, as input into the computer, would appear something like this:

```
MAX 60X1 + 50X2
SUBJECT TO
      4X1 + 10X2 < = 100
      2X1 + X2 < = 22
      3X1 + 3X2 < = 39
```

(Caps for letters may or may not be required. If not, the first constraint would look like this: 4x1 + 10x2 < = 100.) Note the key differences between this input and our basic model:

1. Two keystrokes are used for the $\leq$ constraints. (Some programs treat $<$ as the equivalent of $\leq$ and require only a single keystroke.)
2. The non-negativity constraints are not needed; they are automatically assumed by the computer code (program).
3. Slack and surplus variables are not used; the computer uses them automatically, as needed.
4. Although the microcomputer model does not involve any coefficients expressed as fractions (e.g., $\frac{1}{2}x_1$, $\frac{1}{4}x_2$), fractions are not allowed. Instead, all coefficients must be integers or decimals (e.g., $.5x_1$, $.25x_2$).

Often, users have the option of choosing the type of output they want. One option is to be given all of the tableaus; another is to be given only the final tableau; and still another is to be given only the final solution. Beyond that, most

TABLE 4–14 Sample Computer Output for the Microcomputer Problem

```
AFTER 2 ITERATIONS
THIS SOLUTION IS OPTIMAL:

VARIABLE      QUANTITY
   S1            24
   X1            9
   X2            4

OPTIMAL Z    =    740

VARIABLE    REDUCED COST
   X1             0
   X2             0
              DUAL PRICE
   S1             0
   S2           -10
   S3           -13.33
```

TABLE 4–15 A Second Sample of Computer Output

```
          LP OPTIMUM FOUND AT STEP 3
          OBJECTIVE FUNCTION VALUE
   1)            740.000

VARIABLE           VALUE          REDUCED COST
        X1        9.00000            0.00000
        X2        4.00000            0.00000

ROW         SLACK OR SURPLUS      DUAL PRICES
   2)            24.00000            0.00000
   3)             0.00000           10.00000
   4)             0.00000           13.33334
```

programs provide additional information called *sensitivity analysis*. Interpretation of that information is discussed in Chapter 6.

Table 4–14 presents an example of how the computer output might appear for the microcomputer problem. The output shows the optimal values of the variables in the basis and the optimal value of the objective function. The terms REDUCED COST and DUAL PRICE will be explained in Chapter 6. However, the numbers are those that appear in the bottom row of the final tableau.

See Table 4–15 for a different version of computer output. Aside from differing slightly in format, the main difference between the two sets of output is that one program reports the DUAL PRICES as negative amounts and the other as positives. However, the important thing is their values rather than their signs.

Computer packages generally have the capability of providing individual tableaus in addition to providing the optimal solution. For instance, a LINDO printout of the microcomputer problem tableaus would appear as follows:

```
MAX     60 X1 + 50 X2
SUBJECT TO
   2)    4 X1 + 10 X2 <=    100
   3)    2 X1 + X2<=    22
   4)    3 X1 + 3 X2 <=    39
END

THE TABLEAU
ROW   (BASIS)          X1         X2 SLK      2 SLK      3 SLK      4

   1 ART          -60.000    -50.000      0.000      0.000      0.000      0.000
   2 SLK     2      4.000     10.000      1.000      0.000      0.000    100.000
   3 SLK     3      2.000      1.000      0.000      1.000      0.000     22.000
   4 SLK     4      3.000      3.000      0.000      0.000      1.000     39.000

     X1 ENTERS AT VALUE         11.000     IN ROW    3 OBJ. VALUE=  660.00

THE TABLEAU
ROW   (BASIS)          X1         X2 SLK      2 SLK      3 SLK      4

   1 ART            0.000    -20.000      0.000     30.000      0.000    660.000
   2 SLK     2      0.000      8,000      1.000     -2.000      0.000     56.000
   3        X1      1.000      0.500      0.000      0.500      0.000     11.000
   4 SLK     4      0.000      1.500      0.000     -1.500      1.000      6.000

     X1 ENTERS AT VALUE         11.000     IN ROW    4 OBJ. VALUE=  740.00


THE TABLEAU
ROW   (BASIS)          X1         X2 SLK      2 SLK      3 SLK      4

   1 ART            0.000      0.000      0.000     10.000     13.333    740.000
   2 SLK     2      0.000      0.000      1.000      6.000     -5.333     24.000
   3        X1      1.000      0.000      0.000      1.000     -0.333      9.000
   4        X2      0.000      1.000      0.000     -1.000      0.667      4.000

      LP OPTIMUM FOUND AT STEP     2
            OBJECTIVE FUNCTION VALUE
   1)              740.000000

   VARIABLE             VALUE          REDUCED COST
           X1         9.000000             0.000000
           X2         4.000000             0.000000

   ROW             SLACK OR SURPLUS     DUAL PRICES
     2)             24.000000             0.000000
     3)              0.000000            10.000000
     4)              0.000000            13.333333

   NO. ITERATIONS=          2
```

The output is somewhat self-explanatory with few comments. The top row of each tableau has the label ART. This stands for artificial, and the values in the row are the negative of what ordinarily appears in the bottom row of a tableau. Thus, in the last tableau we saw 10.000 and 13.333 in the top row. Recall in the example earlier in the chapter these appeared as negatives. Hence, the top row is $Z - C$ rather than $C - Z$. Note, too, that row Z does not appear at all. Finally, SLK refers to a slack variable. However, LINDO begins numbering with the top row, so s_1 is labeled SLK 2, s_2 is SLK 3, and so on. Also, the spacing along the top labels is such that the number of each slack variable appears directly over the appropriate column, but its label is shifted a bit to the left. Thus, the third column is SLK 2.

Computers handle linear programming problems with such ease, speed, and accuracy that you may wonder why you should even bother to learn how to solve problems manually. Actually, there are several benefits of the manual approach. One is to gain insight into how solutions are generated. Without this knowledge, the computer becomes a black box that mysteriously comes up with solutions. People who use computers under those circumstances rarely fare as well as those who possess a basic understanding of the underlying process, either in formulating problems or in understanding the results. Therefore, solving a small number of manageable problems manually can provide valuable insight that is not readily obtainable another way. In addition, the opportunity to sharpen quantitative skills is important; the world is becoming increasingly quantitative, and those who have the ability to deal with quantitative information in a confident manner are less likely to be intimidated either by quantitative information or by computers. Still another benefit of manual solution is that other techniques for solving linear programming problems use procedures that are very similar to some of those used in simplex. Consequently, learning and understanding those techniques is easier after exposure to the simplex procedure.

SOME SPECIAL ISSUES

During the course of solving linear programming problems, various conditions can occur that make the problem unusual and, in some instances, impossible to solve. In this section, three of these special issues are examined: unbounded solutions, degeneracy, and multiple optimal solutions. Recall that unbounded solutions and multiple optimal solutions were discussed in the previous chapter.

Unbounded Solutions

A solution is unbounded if the objective function can be improved without limit. The condition is relatively easy to recognize in a simplex solution: An unbounded solution will exist if there are no positive values in the pivot column. Recall that the way to determine which variable will leave the interim solution is to compute the ratios of values in the Quantity column and values in the pivot column (see, for example, Table 4–10). The variable with the smallest positive ratio will leave the solution. The solution is unbounded if there are no positive ratios. A negative ratio means that increasing x_1 would increase resources! A zero ratio means that increasing x_1 would not use any resources. Since non-negative values cannot appear in the Quantity column, the only way to not have any positive ratios would be if there were no positive values in the pivot column (i.e., the solution is unbounded).

This condition generally arises because the problem is incorrectly formulated. If the constraints do not properly bound the solution, or the objective function is stated as a maximization when it should be a minimization, unbounded solutions will occur.

Degeneracy

In the process of developing the next simplex tableau for a tableau that is not optimal, the leaving variable must be identified. This is normally done by computing the ratios of values in the Quantity column and the corresponding row values in the entering variable column, and selecting the variable whose row has the smallest non-negative ratio. In some cases, there will be a tie for the lowest non-negative ratio. Such an occurrence is referred to as **degeneracy,** because it is theoretically possible for subsequent solutions to *cycle* (i.e., to return to previous solutions). There are ways of dealing with ties in a specific fashion; however, it will usually suffice to simply select one row (variable) arbitrarily and proceed with the computations.

Multiple Optimal Solutions

As we learned in the preceding chapter, some linear programming problems have multiple optimal solutions. That is, the same maximum value of the objective function might be possible with a number of different combinations of values of the decision variables. This occurs because the objective function is parallel to a binding constraint. In effect, the two corner points for the segment of the constraint that borders the feasible solution space and all points in between that lie on the constraint are optimal solutions.

In a graphical solution, this condition is readily apparent. With simplex, this condition can be detected by examining the $C - Z$ row of the final tableau. If a zero appears in the column of a nonbasic variable (i.e., a variable that is not in solution), it can be concluded that an alternate solution exists.

Consider this modified microcomputer problem:

maximize $\quad 60x_1 + 30x_2$

subject to

$$\begin{aligned} 4x_1 + 10x_2 &\le 100 \\ 2x_1 + 1x_2 &\le 22 \\ 3x_1 + 3x_2 &\le 39 \end{aligned}$$

Note that the only change is the x_2 coefficient of the objective function: It is 30 instead of 50. This change causes the objective function to be parallel to the second constraint because in both the objective function and the second constraint, the ratio of the x_1 coefficient to the x_2 coefficient is 2:1. The final tableau for this modified problem is shown in Table 4–16. The zero in row $C - Z$ in the x_2 column indicates that an **alternate optimal solution** exists. The presence of this

TABLE 4–16 Final Tableau for Modified Microcomputer Problem with an Alternative Optimal Solution

Basis	C	60	30	0	0	0	Quantity
		x_1	x_2	s_1	s_2	s_3	
s_1	0	0	8	1	−2	0	56
x_1	60	1	½	0	½	0	11
s_3	0	0	3/2	0	−3/2	1	4
	Z	60	30	0	30	0	660
	C − Z	0	0	0	−30	0	

TABLE 4–17 The Alternate Optimal Solution for the Modified Microcomputer Problem

Basis		60	30	0	0	0	Quantity
		x_1	x_2	s_1	s_2	s_3	
s_1	0	0	0	1	6	−16/3	24
x_1	60	1	0	0	1	−1/3	9
x_2	30	0	1	0	−1	2/3	4
	Z	60	30	0	30	0	660
	C − Z	0	0	0	−30	0	

zero tells us that the variable x_2 can be brought into solution without increasing or decreasing the value of the objective function, assuming one of the variables currently in solution is a candidate for leaving.

The other optimal corner point can be determined by entering the nonbasic variable with the $C - Z$ equal to zero (x_2 in this case) and, then, finding the leaving variable in the usual way. For the modified microcomputer problem, s_3 would leave the solution, and the optimal solution would be shown as in Table 4–17. As expected, the profit for the alternate solution is $660, which is the same as in the previous solution shown in Table 4–16.

There are, of course, other points that will yield the same optimal value for the objective function: All points that lie on the second constraint between these two alternate optimal solutions. Only the end points can be determined by simplex manipulations. Other points could be found algebraically. Conversely, a decision maker may have in mind other combinations that he or she wants to test as possible alternate optimal solutions. This can be accomplished by substituting those values into the objective function to see if they produce the same value for the objective function as the simplex-generated solutions. However, even if they do, it must also be determined if they satisfy each of the constraints. Those that meet both criteria represent alternate optimal solutions.

SUMMARY

This chapter introduces the simplex algorithm, which is a general-purpose method for obtaining solutions to linear programming problems. In contrast to the graphical approach that was described in the preceding chapter, the simplex approach is not limited to problems with two decision variables. Rather, it can handle any number of decision variables.

This chapter focuses on solutions to maximization problems that have all less than or equal to constraints. The following chapter deals with minimization problems and maximization problems with mixed constraints.

The simplex procedure involves developing a series of tableaus, each of which describes the solution at a corner point of the feasible solution space, beginning with the origin. Each solution is progressively better than the previous one. The process is continued until no further improvement can be realized, at which time the optimal solution can be identified.

Manual development of simplex solutions produces a certain degree of insight into understanding the simplex model and how solutions are interpreted. However, because of the effort required for all but the smallest problems, computer packages are generally relied on to perform the computations necessary to obtain solutions. The chapter ends with a brief discussion of three special issues: unbounded problems, degeneracy, and multiple optimal solutions.

GLOSSARY

Alternate Optimal Solution A feasible solution that will produce the same value of the objective function as a solution that has been determined to be optimal.

Basic Feasible Solution A basic solution that satisfies all the constraints.

Basic Solution A solution to a set of linear equations in which the number of variables equals the number of equations.

Basic Variable A variable included in a basic solution.

Basis A set of variables that are in solution at a given stage of a simplex analysis. These are listed in the *basis* column of each tableau.

C Unit contribution of each variable to the objective function. The *C* row of a tableau indicates the unit contribution for every decision variable and slack variable; the *C* column indicates the unit contributions for variables that are in the basis.

Degeneracy A condition in which there is a tie for the lowest ratio in the process of determining which variable should leave a particular nonoptimal solution. When one or more basic variables equal zero.

Optimal Simplex Solution Values in the Quantity column of the final simplex tableau (tableau for which there are no positive values in the $C - Z$ row).

Pivot Row The row of the leaving variable in a tableau and the row of the entering variable in the following tableau. Values are used to compute the values of the remaining *basis* rows of the following tableau.

Pivot Value Value at the intersection of the column of the variable that is entering the solution and the leaving variable row.

Standard Form Expressing the constraints of an LP problem as equalities, with all variables on the left side of the equation and a constant on the right side.

Tableau A table used to keep track of the results of each stage of a simplex analysis.

Variables in Solution Variables listed in the basis column of a tableau. Their values are shown in the Quantity column of the tableau.

SOLVED PROBLEM

Problem 1. Solve this problem using the simplex method:

maximize $7x_1 + 2x_2$

subject to

$$\begin{aligned} \tfrac{1}{2}x_1 + 3x_2 &\le 12 \\ x_1 &\le 10 \\ 4x_1 - 2x_2 &\ge -5 \\ x_1, x_2 &\ge 0 \end{aligned}$$

Solution

In order to use the simplex method, all variables must be on the left side of each equality and a non-negative constant on the right. The third constraint does not satisfy this requirement and, hence, must be modified. Multiplying the entire constraint by -1 will remove the negative sign from the right side and will yield this constraint:

$$-4x_1 + 2x_2 \le 5$$

Next, the slack variables must be added and the non-negativity constraints deleted:

maximize $7x_1 + 2x_2 + 0s_1 + 0s_2 + 0s_3$

subject to

$$\begin{aligned} \tfrac{1}{2}x_1 + 3x_2 + s_1 &= 12 \\ x_1 + s_2 &= 10 \\ -4x_1 + 2x_2 + s_3 &= 5 \end{aligned}$$

The coefficients and right-hand side constants can be placed in the initial tableau:

Basis	C	7	2	0	0	0	
		x_1	x_2	s_1	s_2	s_3	Quantity
		½	3	1	0	0	12
		1	0	0	1	0	10
		−4	2	0	0	1	5
	Z						
	C − Z						

Setting the decision variables equal to zero, the three constraint equations reduce to:

$$\begin{aligned} s_1 \quad\quad\quad &= 12 \\ s_2 \quad\quad &= 10 \\ s_3 &= 5 \end{aligned}$$

This becomes our initial feasible solution; the three slack variables can be listed in the basis column and their objective function coefficients can be listed in the C column (see the next tableau).

Next, the Z values can be computed:

Row	x_1	x_2	s_1	s_2	s_3	Quantity
s_1	0(½) = 0	0(3) = 0	0(1) = 0	0(0) = 0	0(0) = 0	0(12) = 0
	0(1) = 0	0(0) = 0	0(0) = 0	0(1) = 0	0(0) = 0	0(10) = 0
	0(−4) = 0	0(2) = 0	0(0) = 0	0(0) = 0	0(1) = 0	0(5) = 0
Z	0	0	0	0	0	0

Using these values, we now find values for the bottom row:

Row					
C	7	2	0	0	0
Z	0	0	0	0	0
$C - Z$	7	2	0	0	0

Adding these values to the table completes the initial tableau:

Basis	C	7 x_1	2 x_2	0 s_1	0 s_2	0 s_3	Quantity
s_1	0	½	3	1	0	0	12
s_2	0	1	0	0	1	0	10
s_3	0	−4	2	0	0	1	5
	Z	0	0	0	0	0	
	$C - Z$	7	2	0	0	0	

Because the values in the $C - Z$ row are not all zero or negative, the solution can be improved. Because the greatest improvement (the largest positive value) per unit will come from adding x_1 (\$7 per unit versus \$2 per unit for x_2), x_1 becomes the entering variable.

Because x_1 is the entering variable, we focus on the substitution rates in the x_1 column (i.e., ½, 1, and − 4). Since it is not acceptable to divide by a negative number, the − 4 is omitted. Dividing the other two numbers into the right-hand side Quantity values yields:

Basis	Quantity	Quantity/a_{i1}
s_1	12	12/½ = 24
s_2	10	10/1 = 10
s_3	5	

The smallest ratio is 10. This tells us that variable s_2 will go out of the solution and will be replaced by x_1.

Next, we must obtain the pivot row values for the next tableau. These are found by dividing each number of the leaving row by the value that is at the intersection of the entering variable column and the leaving variable row. In this case, it is the 1 in the x_1 column. Dividing each of the values in the second row by 1 produces the same values. These now can be entered in the second tableau:

Basis	C	7 x_1	2 x_2	0 s_1	0 s_2	0 s_3	Quantity	
s_1	0							
x_2	7	1	0	0	1	0	10	Pivot row
s_3	0							
	Z							
	$C - Z$							

Next, we use the pivot row values to compute revised coefficients for the other two constraint rows. (Previously, this was shown as a row operation. Another approach is to perform the computations in columnar from. Either is acceptable; the latter is demonstrated here.) In this approach, the term *row pivot* is used as one of the column headings. It refers to the value that is at the intersection of the entering variable's column and the basis row for which new values are to be computed. Thus, with x_1 the entering variable, we can see from the initial tableau that the row pivot value for row s_1 is ½ and for row s_3 it is −4.

s_1 row:

Column	Current value	−	Row pivot	×	Value in pivot row	=	New value
x_1	½	−	½	×	1	=	0
x_2	3	−	½	×	0	=	3
s_1	1	−	½	×	0	=	1
s_2	0	−	½	×	1	=	−½
s_3	0	−	½	×	0	=	0
Quantity	12	−	½	×	10	=	7

s_3 row:

Column	Current value	−	Row pivot	×	Value in pivot row	=	New value
x_1	−4	−	−4	×	1	=	0
x_2	2	−	−4	×	0	=	2
s_1	0	−	−4	×	0	=	0
s_2	0	−	−4	×	1	=	4
s_3	1	−	−4	×	0	=	1
Quantity	5	−	−4	×	10	=	45

These values can be added to the second tableau:

Basis	C	7 x_1	2 x_2	0 s_1	0 s_2	0 s_3	Quantity
s_1	0	0	3	1	−½	0	7
x_1	7	1	0	0	1	0	10
s_3	0	0	2	0	4	1	45
	Z						
	C − Z						

Next, the Z and $C - Z$ values can be computed. First, the row Z values:

Row	x_1	x_2	s_1	s_2	s_3	Quantity
s_1	0(0) = 0	0(3) = 0	0(1) = 0	0(−½) = 0	0(0) = 0	0(7) = 0
x_1	7(1) = 7	7(0) = 0	7(0) = 0	7(1) = 7	7(0) = 0	7(10) = 70
s_3	0(0) = 0	0(2) = 0	0(0) = 0	0(4) = 0	0(0) = 0	0(45) = 0
Z	7	0	0	7	0	70

Then row $C - Z$ values:

Row					
C	7	2	0	0	0
Z	7	0	0	7	0
C − Z	0	2	0	−7	0

Adding these to the table completes the second tableau:

Basis	C	7 x_1	2 x_2	0 s_1	0 s_2	0 s_3	Quantity
s_1	0	0	3	1	−½	0	7
x_2	7	1	0	0	1	0	10
s_3	0	0	2	0	4	1	45
	Z	7	0	0	7	0	70
	C − Z	0	2	0	−7	0	

Because a positive value appears in the bottom row of the tableau, the solution is not yet optimal. And because the positive value is in the x_2 column, we know that x_2 must be brought into solution. In order to determine which variable will leave the solution, we divide the values in the Quantity column by the corresponding positive values in the x_2 column, which yields:

Row	Quantity	Quantity/x_2
s_1	7	7/3 = 2.33
x_1	10	(can't divide by 0)
s_3	45	45/2 = 22.5

The smallest positive ratio is 2.33, which means that variable s_1 will leave the solution and be replaced by x_2. Hence, the new basis will consist of x_2, x_1, and s_3. The new values are calculated (not shown) in the same manner as previously demonstrated. The resulting values are:

Basis	C	7	2	0	0	0	
		x_1	x_2	s_1	s_2	s_3	Quantity
x_2	2	0	1	⅓	−⅙	0	2.33
x_1	7	1	0	0	1	0	10
s_3	0	0	0	−⅔	13⁄3	1	40.33
	Z	7	2	⅔	20⁄3	0	74.66
	$C - Z$	0	0	−⅔	−20⁄3	0	

Because there are no positive values in the $C - Z$ row, this tableau contains the optimal solution, which is:

$$x_1 = 10$$
$$x_2 = 2.33$$
$$s_3 = 40.33$$
$$Z = 74.66$$

Remember, too, that any variable not listed in the basis has a value of zero. Therefore, s_1 and s_2 are equal to zero.

PROBLEMS

1. Both the simplex and graphical techniques can be used to solve certain linear programming problems.
   a. What type of LP problems can both be used to solve?
   b. What advantages does the graphical approach have over the simplex approach in such cases?

c. What advantages does the simplex approach have in such cases?

d. What characteristic of an LP problem would require the use of simplex rather than the graphical approach?

2. The simplex technique makes use of slack variables.

   a. What is the purpose of slack variables?

   b. How does one know how many slack variables to use in a maximization problem such as those discussed in this chapter?

   c. Can a slack variable appear in the optimal solution? Explain.

   d. Could an optimal solution to a maximization problem be composed completely of slack variables? Explain.

3. The simplex technique uses a series of tableaus.

   a. In general terms, what does a tableau represent?

   b. How does one decide which variable should *enter* a given nonoptimal solution? What happens in the case of a tie?

   c. How does one decide which variable should *leave* a given nonoptimal solution? What happens in the case of a tie?

4. The final tableau contains the optimal solution to an LP problem.

   a. Where are the variables that are in solution listed in the final tableau?

   b. Where are the optimal values of the solution variables found?

   c. How many variables will be in the optimal solution?

   d. Where is the optimal value of the objective function found in the final tableau?

5. Consider the following simplex tableau:

Basis	C	20 x_1	12 x_2	0 s_1	0 s_2	0 s_3	Quantity
s_1	0	0	2	1	−3	0	30
x_1	20	1	0	0	1	0	50
s_3	0	0	1	0	0	1	50
	Z	20	0	0	20	0	1,000
	C − Z	0	12	0	−20	0	

   a. Is this the initial tableau? How do you know?

   b. What variables are in solution? What are their values?

   c. What is the value of the objective function?

   d. Is this solution optimal? How do you know?

   e. Which variable will enter the solution?

   f. Which variable will leave the solution?

   g. Determine the optimal solution. Indicate which variables are in solution, what their optimal values are, and the value of the objective function at the optimum.

6. Given this linear programming problem:

maximize $9x_1 + 6x_2$

subject to

1	$12x_1 + 5x_2 \leq 600$
2	$x_2 \leq 72$
	All variables ≥ 0

a. Graph this problem.

b. Write the problem in standard form.

c. Develop the initial tableau.

d. Determine the optimal solution using simplex. Identify the variables that are in solution at the optimum and their values.

Show the sequence of tableaus on your graph.

7. An analyst at a meat packing plant has formulated this LP problem:

maximize $5x_1 + 3x_2$

subject to

1	$1.5x_1 + 1x_2 \leq 45$
2	$x_1 \leq 25$
3	$x_2 \leq 40$
	All variables ≥ 0

a. Graph this problem.

b. Solve the problem graphically using the objective function approach.

c. Solve the problem using simplex.

d. Indicate the sequence of tableaus on the graph.

8. Given this linear programming problem:

maximize $9x_1 + 9x_2$

subject to

1	$6x_1 + 3x_2 \leq 42$
2	$4x_1 + 5x_2 \leq 40$
	All variables ≥ 0

a. Solve the problem for the optimal values of the decision variables using simplex.

b. Graph the problem and indicate the sequence of tableaus followed for the simplex solution.

9. Solve this problem for the optimal solution using simplex:

maximize $40x_1 + 30x_2$

subject to

Labor	$5x_1 + 1x_2 \leq 250$
Materials	$10x_1 + 9x_2 \leq 900$
Other	$x_1 \leq 40$
	All variables ≥ 0

10. Determine the optimal solution to this problem using simplex:

maximize $1.00x_1 + 1.20x_2$

subject to

Department 1	$5x_1 + 3x_2 \leq 120$
Department 2	$1x_1 + 3x_2 \leq 60$
	All variables ≥ 0

11. Ted Collins has developed this linear programming formulation of a problem. Use simplex to find the optimal solution for Ted's model.

maximize $.40x_1 + .44x_2$

subject to

Handling	$10x_1 + 20x_2 \leq 300$
Shipping	$5x_1 + 4x_2 \leq 100$
Storage	$x_2 \leq 20$
	All variables ≥ 0

12. Norm Stokes, the manager of a machine shop, must determine the optimal quantities of two products to make. He has formulated the problem as follows:

maximize $80x_1 + 70x_2$

subject to

Sanding	$9x_1 + 7x_2 \leq 63$
Painting	$4x_1 + 4x_2 \leq 32$
	All variables ≥ 0

Solve for the optimal solution using simplex.

13. Given this LP problem, solve for the optimal solution using simplex:

maximize $.60x_1 + .70x_2$

subject to

Mixing/forming	$.5x_1 + .4x_2 \leq 200$
Firing/cooling	$.2x_1 + .5x_2 \leq 360$

14. Solve this problem for the optimal solution:

maximize $.44x_1 + .41x_2 + .35x_3$

subject to

$$\begin{array}{lrcl}
\text{Supplies} & 3x_1 + 5x_2 + 5x_3 & \leq & 140 \\
\text{Time} & 100x_1 + 50x_2 & \leq & 2{,}100
\end{array}$$

All variables ≥ 0

15. Solve this problem for the optimal solution:

maximize $11x_1 + 10x_2 + 14x_3$

subject to

$$\begin{array}{lrcl}
\text{A} & 4x_2 - 1x_3 & \leq & 0 \\
\text{B} & 5x_1 + 2x_2 + 5x_3 & \leq & 72 \\
\text{C} & x_1 & \leq & 13
\end{array}$$

x_1, x_2, and $x_3 \geq 0$

16. Mary Arnold, the manager of a shop that installs commercial carpeting, has developed the following linear programming model:

maximize $10x_1 + 6x_2 + 7x_3$

subject to

$$\begin{array}{lrcl}
\text{Material} & 4x_1 + 8x_2 + 5x_3 & \leq & 860 \\
\text{Labor} & 2x_1 + 3x_2 + 1x_3 & \leq & 400
\end{array}$$

x_1, x_2, and $x_3 \geq 0$

Solve Mary's problem for the optimal solution.

17. Stu Holtz, the manager of an aircraft assembly shop, has formulated a linear programming model with the help of a consultant:

maximize $120x_1 + 100x_2 + 110x_3$

subject to

$$\begin{array}{lrcl}
\text{Material} & 16x_1 + 25x_2 + 20x_3 & \leq & 4{,}000 \\
\text{Labor A} & 2x_1 + 2x_2 + 2x_3 & \leq & 450 \\
\text{Labor B} & 5x_1 + 4x_2 + 3x_3 & \leq & 600
\end{array}$$

x_1, x_2, and $x_3 \geq 0$

Solve for the optimal solution. Is there an alternate optimal solution? If so, what is it?

18. The following LP model is based on data from a tree farm:

maximize $7x_1 + 8x_2 + 9x_3$

subject to

Fertilizer	$6x_1 + 4x_2 + 5x_3 \leq 210$
Land	$3x_1 + 2x_2 + 4x_3 \leq 180$
Equipment	$6x_2 + 5x_3 \leq 240$
	All variables ≥ 0

Determine the optimal solution to this problem.

19. Pete Smith, a project manager at Allied Aircraft, has formulated an LP model in order to identify the optimal set of product assignments for two staff members. The model is:

maximize $4x_1 + 3x_2 + 5x_3 + 2x_4$

subject to

A	$x_1 + x_2 \leq 1$
B	$x_1 + x_3 \leq 1$
C	$x_3 + x_4 \leq 1$
D	$x_2 + x_4 \leq 1$
	$x_1, x_2, x_3, x_4 \geq 0$

where

x_1 = assign Project 1 to Stan
x_2 = assign Project 2 to Stan
x_3 = assign Project 1 to Barb
x_4 = assign Project 2 to Barb

Solve for the optimal set of assignments.

20. The problem that generated the following tableau probably was incorrectly formulated. Explain why this is so.

	C	22	31	0	0	0	
Basis		x_1	x_2	s_1	s_2	s_3	Quantity
s_1	0	1/5	−4	1	0	0	146
s_2	0	1	0	0	1	0	93
s_3	0	5	0	0	0	1	19
	Z	0	0	0	0	0	0
	C − Z	22	31	0	0	0	

21. Consider the following simplex tableau:

Basis	C	7 x_1	8 x_2	10 x_3	0 s_1	0 s_2	Quantity
x_2	8	1.5	1	1.25	.25	0	52.5
s_2	0	0	0	−2.50	−.50	1	55
	Z	12	8	10	2	0	420
	C − Z	−5	0	0	−2	0	

a. Is the solution unbounded? How do you know?
b. Is the solution optimal? How do you know?
c. Is there an alternate optimal solution? If so, what is it?

22. The manager of a firm that assembles various electronic items wants to establish an optimal production plan for making tape decks. The manager has obtained the pertinent information, which is shown in the following table:

Item	Assembly (hours)	Inspection (hours)	Packaging (minutes)	Variable Cost	Selling Price
Type A	5	1.2	8	$70	$110
Type B	3	1.0	8	60	90
Type C	2	1.6	8	50	85
Time available	600 hours	144 hours	960 minutes		

Determine the quantity of each type of tape deck that should be made if the objective is to maximize the total contribution of the output to profit. In addition, determine if there is an alternate optimal solution. If there is, what is that solution?

23. Ace Advertising often uses linear programming to determine an optimal allocation of advertising budgets. Recently, a client asked for a plan that would allocate no more than $12,000 among radio, TV, and newspaper advertisements with the stipulation that no more than 40 percent of the budget be allocated to any one medium. The client wanted a plan that would maximize the effectiveness of advertisements.

The owner did some research that yielded an effectiveness index for each medium and also determined the cost for an ad for each medium, as shown:

Medium	Effectiveness	Cost per Ad
Radio	2.4	$200
TV	3.2	400
Newspaper	1.6	300

Determine the number of ads in each medium in order to maximize effectiveness.

24. The owner of Homewood Enterprises, a business that makes and sells wood products, intends to expand the work schedule by one-half day each week and wants to optimize the use of that additional time. The firm makes five different items: a chair, a table, a desk, a bookcase, and a food serving cart. The respective profits per unit are $16, $30, $40, $42, and $32. The products require essentially the same basic operations: cutting, sanding and finishing, and assembly. The times for these operations differ for the various items. However, the times are fairly standard. and are shown in the following table:

	Time per Operation (minutes)		
Item	Cutting	Sanding and Finishing	Assembly
Chair	8	12	4
Table	6	10	3
Desk	9	15	5
Bookcase	9	12	4
Food cart	12	8	6

There are 320 minutes available for cutting, 400 for sanding and finishing, and 270 for assembling. What combination of products should be produced in the additional period each week in order to maximize profits? What will the total profit be? What assumption(s) does the formulation of this problem require?

25. An investor has $135,000 to invest. After carefully investigating many alternatives, the investor has decided to diversify the investment by allocating it among money market funds, oil stocks, corporate bonds, and Treasury notes. The investor intends to keep the money invested for five years, after which time the money will be used to purchase a new home and fund the family's six children for college. The yields on the investment alternatives are as follows:

Type	Estimated Annual Yield
Money market	9%
Stocks	12
Bonds	11
Treasury notes	10

The investor has decided on certain restrictions that will be used to govern the investment of the funds. He wants no more than one-half of the total to be invested in stocks. However, he does not want the amount that is invested in stocks to exceed the amount that is invested in bonds. In addition, he does not want the amount that is invested in the money market to exceed the total that is invested in Treasury notes.

Given these conditions, how much should be invested in each alternative in order to maximize annual yield?

26. Midwest Manufacturing expects to acquire $1.2 million by issuing new comon stock. There are different uses for the funds, including purchasing new processing equipment, updating material handling equipment, purchasing electronic office equipment, and repaying an outstanding loan.

After considerable study and discussion, a committee composed of the plant manager, the vice president of finance, and the vice president of manufacturing has arrived at the following recommendations: No more than $.7 million should be allocated to the purchase of new equipment and no more than $.4 million should be allocated to the updating of material handling equipment. The outstanding loan is for $.3 million, and it can be repaid in whole or in part.

The committee has projected the rates of return for the various uses of the funds as shown in the accompanying table.

Use	Projected Annual Rate of Return
New processing equipment	18%
Updating material handling equipment	22
New office equipment	15
Repayment of loan	15

What allocation of the funds will achieve the largest return on the funds?

27. A chocolatier has contracted to operate a small candy counter in a fashionable store. To start with, the selection of offerings will be intentionally limited. The counter will offer a regular mix candy that is equal parts of

cashews, raisins, caramels, and chocolates and a deluxe mix that is one-half cashews and one-half chocolates. These will be sold in one-pound boxes. In addition, the candy counter will offer individual one-pound boxes of cashews, raisins, caramels, and chocolates.

A major attraction of the candy counter is that all candies are made fresh right at the counter. However, there is a limited storage space for supplies and ingredients. Bins are available that can hold the amounts shown in the table below:

Ingredient	Capacity (pounds per day)
Cashews	120
Raisins	200
Caramels	100
Chocolates	160

The profit per box for the various items has been determined to be as follows:

Item	Profit per Box
Regular	$.80
Deluxe	.90
Cashews	.70
Raisins	.60
Caramels	.50
Chocolates	.75

a. Set up the problem in a linear programming format.

b. Determine the optimal values of the decision variables and the maximum profit.

28. A financial adviser handles investment portfolios for individual investors and several credit unions. The adviser has employed a variety of different methods for designing portfolios, some more successful than others. Quite often, the adviser spends considerable effort using trial and error to determine a suitable mix of investments for each client. The adviser wonders if it would be possible to use linear programming to accomplish her objectives, and she has selected a new account to see how it might be handled using an LP approach.

The investor in question has total of $120,000 in his account. After discussions with the client, the adviser has formulated a list of requirements for the account that will provide a balance of growth opportunity, income, and safety. It has been decided that no more than 80 percent of the total amount will be invested in securities; the rest will be placed in a bank account that will yield 9.5 percent annually. In addition, the adviser has identified two growth stocks, A and B, that appear promising. Stock A has a projected annual return of 15 percent and stock B has a projected annual return of 12 percent. Because of the risk associated with the growth stocks, the adviser has decided that no more than 50 percent of the amount invested in securities should be allocated to growth stocks and no more than half in either stock. The adviser also has identified a pair of mutual funds, one an income fund based on short-term securities and the other a bond fund, that seem suited for this particular account. She has decided to limit the amount invested in the mutual funds to no more than 60 percent of the amount in the account. The income fund has a projected annual rate of return of 11 percent and the bond fund has a projected annual rate of return of 10 percent.

Determine how the money in the account should be allocated among the investment alternatives identified above in order to achieve the maximum rate of return. Also, determine what the expected annual return in dollars will be for the client.

29. (Refer to problem 8 in Chapter 2.) Determine the optimal quantities of regular blend, extra blend, and puppy delite.

30. (Refer to Problem 17 in Chapter 2.) Find the optimal quantity of each type of bag and the maximum profit.

31. (Refer to Problem 19 in Chapter 2.) Determine the optimal number of two-pound boxes of trail mix, and the optimal numbers of the various one-pound boxes, as well as the maximum revenue.

Chapter 5
Simplex
Maximization with Mixed Constraints and Minimization

Chapter Outline

Learning Objectives

After completing this chapter, you should be able to:

1. Convert = and ≥ constraints into standard form.
2. Solve maximization problems that have mixed constraints and interpret those solutions.
3. Solve minimization problems and interpret those solutions.
4. Recognize infeasibility in a simplex solution.

INTRODUCTION

In the last chapter, the simplex approach to the solution of linear programming problems was introduced. The technique was demonstrated by solving a maximization problem in which all of the constraints were of the $\leq$ variety.

In this chapter, the question of how to deal with problems that do not have all $\leq$ constraints is addressed. Such conditions can occur in the context of both maximization and minimization problems. The chapter begins with a discussion of how to modify $=$ constraints and $\geq$ constraints so that they are in a form that is compatible with a simplex solution. Next, a simplex solution of a maximization problem that has a mix of the three constraint types will be illustrated, followed by a simplex solution of a minimization problem.

= and ≥ Constraints

The simplex technique requires that all constraints be in *standard form:* equalities with variables on the left side of the equation and a constant on the right side. Constraints that are $\leq$ can be put into standard form by adding a slack variable to the constraint. Constraints with $=$ and $\geq$ signs are handled a bit differently.

Recall that the purpose of a slack variable is to allow for the fact that the amount of a scarce resource that is required by a particular combination of decision variables (i.e., a solution) may be less than the amount available. The slack variable assumes a value equal to the leftover amount. In the case of an equality constraint, slack is not acceptable; such constraints require a precise amount. However, we saw in the previous chapter that the origin serves as a convenient starting point for an initial solution. Thus, there is a conflict between using the origin as a starting point, with all decision variables set equal to zero, and equality constraints, which do not permit any slack. This disparity is circumvented in simplex by the introduction of **artificial variables.** These variables are somewhat analogous to slack variables in that they are added to equality constraints in the same way that slack variables are added to $\leq$ constraints. However, artificial variables have no physical interpretation, they merely serve as a device to enable us to use the simplex process. During the simplex process, any artificial variables are quickly eliminated from the solution. In fact, the optimal solution must never contain an artificial variable with a nonzero value.

The interim value of an artificial variable can range from the right-hand side value of the constraint down to zero; artificial variables have the same nonnegativity restriction that decision variables and slack variables have.

Consider this equality constraint:

$$3x_1 + 5x_2 = 40$$

In its standard form, ready for simplex solution, it becomes:

$$3x_1 + 5x_2 + A_1 = 40$$

where

A_1 = artificial variable for the first constraint

Note that if a problem has five constraints, and the fifth constraint listed is an equality constraint, its artificial variable would be designated as A_5.

Now consider this ≥ constraint:

$$8x_1 + 3x_2 \geq 50$$

Unlike a ≤ constraint, a ≥ constraint is never allowed to have a value that is less than the minimum amount designated by the constraint. However, it can have a value that exceeds the designated amount (50, in this case). In some situations, a solution will result in values of the decision variables that exceed the designated minimum level of a constraint. That excess can be thought of as a *surplus*. To allow for that possibility, a **surplus variable** is *subtracted from* each ≥ constraint to account for any excess over the minimum required amount of a constraint. Hence, with the surplus variable included, the above constraint becomes:

$$8x_1 + 3x_2 - s_1 = 50$$

where

s_1 = the surplus variable for the first constraint

Note that with the surplus variable subtracted, the constraint becomes an equality. As before, to allow for initial solutions that will be less than that amount, an artificial variable also must be added. Thus, in its tableau form, the constraint becomes:

$$8x_1 + 3x_2 - s_1 + A_1 = 50$$

If the *second* constraint in a problem is:

$$4x_1 + 2x_2 \geq 34$$

in its tableau form it is written as:

$$4x_1 + 2x_2 - s_2 + A_2 = 34$$

Thus, in dealing with problems that have mixed constraints, some combination of slack, surplus, and artificial variables will be called for. Table 5–1 summarizes the use of these variables.

A vital issue in incorporating surplus and artificial variables in problems is how they are represented in the *objective function*. Surplus variables are handled in exactly the same way that slack variables are: namely, they are assigned coefficients of zero in the objective function. Assignment of coefficients for *artificial* variables depends on whether the problem is a maximization or minimization problem. In either case, we are using artificial variables to facilitate solution and we do not want them to appear in the final solution. Consequently, assigning objective function coefficients to artificial variables depends on whether the goal is to maximize or minimize. In maximization problems, assigning a large *negative*

TABLE 5–1 Summary of Use of Slack, Surplus, and Artificial Variables

Type of Constraint	To Put into Standard Form
$\leq$	Add a slack variable
$=$	Add an artificial variable
$\geq$	Subtract a surplus variable and add an artificial variable

contribution will ensure that an artificial variable will not appear in the optimal solution. Conversely, in a minimization problem, assigning a large *positive* cost will have a similar effect. Although it would be acceptable to arbitrarily select a large negative or positive value for the artificial variable coefficients, it is more common to simply designate the coefficient with a large **M**. Thus, in a maximization problem, the objective function might be:

$$\text{maximize} \quad 10x_1 + 15x_2 + 0s_1 + 0s_2 - MA_2$$

Note that from the objective function we can tell that there must be two constraints: the first of which must be a $\leq$ constraint with s_1 as its slack variable and the second of which must be a $\geq$ constraint with s_2 as the surplus variable and A_2 as the artificial variable. If there had not been an s_2 in the objective function, we would have concluded that the second constraint was an equality.

Conversely, in a minimization problem, the objective function might be:

$$\text{minimize} \quad 6x_1 + 3x_2 + 0s_1 + 0s_2 + MA_2$$

Again, we can conclude that there are two constraints, the first a $\leq$ and the second a $\geq$.

The next section illustrates the solution of a maximization problem that has **mixed constraints,** and the section following that illustrates the solution of a minimization problem.

SOLVING MAXIMIZATION PROBLEMS THAT HAVE MIXED CONSTRAINTS

Chapter 4 introduced the simplex method and illustrated it for a maximization problem with all $\leq$ constraints. The previous section described how to put $=$ and $\geq$ constraints into a form that would be suitable for a *manual* simplex solution (computer solutions generally require only the original form of a problem, keeping $\leq$, $=$, and $\geq$ signs as is). In this section, a maximization problem that has all three kinds of constraints is solved. For the most part, the technique is identical to that illustrated in the previous chapter. What is new is the introduction of the $-M$ coefficients in the objective function and the use of the artificial variables. Their presence makes the simplex procedure a bit more complex than before.

EXAMPLE 1 Solve this problem using the simplex approach:

maximize $6x_1 + 8x_2$

subject to

$$\begin{aligned} &\text{Constraint 1} & x_2 &\le 4 \\ &\text{Constraint 2} & x_1 + x_2 &= 9 \\ &\text{Constraint 3} & 6x_1 + 2x_2 &\ge 24 \end{aligned}$$

$$x_1 \text{ and } x_2 \ge 0$$

For purposes of illustration, a graph of the problem is shown in Figure 5–1. Note that the feasible solution space lies along a segment of constraint 2.

Using the procedures established in the previous section, the problem can be rewritten in standard form, which results in the following:

$$\begin{aligned} &\text{Constraint 1} & x_2 + s_1 &= 24 \\ &\text{Constraint 2} & x_1 + x_2 + A_2 &= 9 \\ &\text{Constraint 3} & 6x_1 + 2x_2 - s_3 + A_3 &= 24 \end{aligned}$$

The objective function becomes:

maximize $6x_1 + 8x_2 + 0s_1 + 0s_3 - MA_2 - MA_3$

In order to develop the initial tableau, follow these guidelines: List the variables across the top of the tableau in order, beginning with the decision variables, then the slack/surplus variables, followed by any artificial variables. For the initial basis, use artificial variables for constraints that have them. Otherwise, use a constraint's slack variable. Hence, surplus variables will not appear in an initial solution. Using these guidelines, the tableau shown in Table 5–2 was developed.

The main body of the first tableau essentially reproduces the problem in standard form, as previously illustrated. However, unlike the procedure outlined in the previous chapter, the row Z values are not all zeroes because of the presence of the M's in the C column. Those values were computed in this way: Because the C value for the first row is zero, that row can be ignored. Using the second and third rows, for row Z we obtain:

Row	Multiplier	x_1	x_2	s_1	s_3	A_2	A_3	Quantity
A_2	$-M$	$1 = -M$	$1 = -M$	$0 = 0$	$0 = 0$	$1 = -M$	$0 = 0$	$9 = -9M$
A_3	$-M$	$6 = -6M$	$2 = -2M$	$0 = 0$	$-1 = M$	$0 = 0$	$1 = -M$	$24 = -24M$
Total		$-7M$	$-3M$	0	$+M$	$-M$	$-M$	$-33M$

FIGURE 5-1 Graph for Example 1

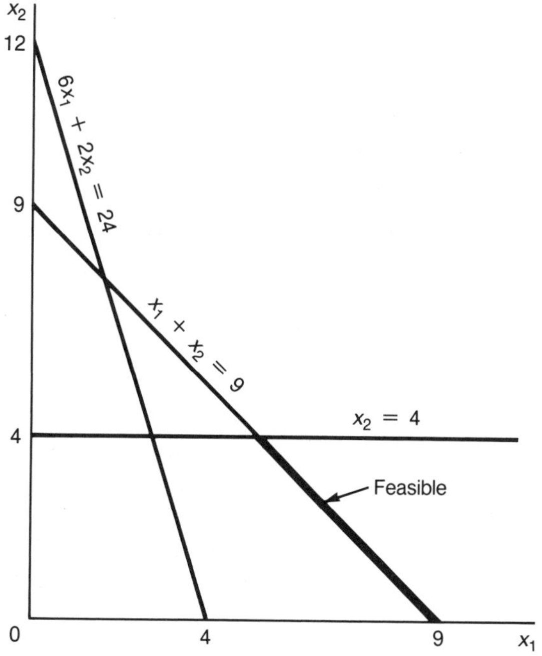

TABLE 5-2 Initial Tableau for Example 1

Basis	C	6 x_1	8 x_2	0 s_1	0 s_3	$-M$ A_2	$-M$ A_3	Quantity
s_1	0	0	1	1	0	0	0	4
A_2	$-M$	1	1	0	0	1	0	9
A_3	$-M$	6	2	0	-1	0	1	24
	Z	$-7M$	$-3M$	0	$+M$	$-M$	$-M$	$-33M$
	$C - Z$	$6 + 7M$	$8 + 3M$	0	$-M$	0	0	

Then for row $C - Z$, subtract these values from row C values to obtain:

	x_1	x_2	s_1	s_3	A_2	A_3
C	6	8	0	0	$-M$	$-M$
Z	$-7M$	$-3M$	0	$+M$	$-M$	$-M$
$C - Z$	$6 + 7M$	$8 + 3M$	0	$-M$	0	0

The initial solution can be interpreted in this way. The first constraint has a slack of 4 units, artificial variable A_2 has a value of 9, and artificial variable A_3 has a value of 24. The "profit" is $-\$33M$, where M is simply a very large number. You might wish to think of M as a million. This would mean a negative profit of 33 million.

As before, the entering variable will be the one with the largest positive value in row $C - Z$. The two positives are $6 + 7M$ for x_1 and $8 + 3M$ for x_2. Because M is so large relative to the 6 and 8, the latter can simply be ignored. Thus, we can easily see that $+ 7M$ is larger than $+3M$; therefore, we select variable x_1 to enter the solution. Next, dividing the values in the x_1 column into their respective Quantity column values, we obtain these ratios:

Row	Ratio
x_1	4/0 = (undefined)
A_2	9/1 = 9
A_3	24/6 = 4

Because A_3 yields the smallest *positive* ratio, it will be the leaving variable; dividing each value in the A_3 row by the pivot value of 6 will give us the values for the new pivot row for the second tableau. Table 5–3 shows the second tableau along with the calculations needed to obtain the values for row A_2. The values for row s_1 remain the same because that row has a pivot value equal to zero in the first tableau. The values for rows Z and $C - Z$ were computed in the same way as just shown for the initial tableau. Notice that no value is computed for column A_3. In fact, column A_3 has been omitted from the second tableau. Once an artificial variable leaves the basis, it is no longer needed for simplex computations. Moreover, its values would not provide any useful information. Consequently, there is no need to carry it along in subsequent tableaus; to do so would only add to the computational burden.

Because there are positive values in the $C - Z$ row, this solution is not optimal. The two positive values are essentially $\frac{2}{3}M$ and $\frac{1}{6}M$, the larger of which is $\frac{2}{3}M$. Therefore, the variable with that larger positive value, x_2, will enter the solution. Table 5–3 also shows the ratios needed to determine the variable that will leave the solution. Since the first row has the smallest ratio, s_1 will leave the solution. The pivot value for the leaving variable is 1, which means that the values for the

TABLE 5–3 The Second Tableau for Example 1

Values for A_2 row

Column	Original value	−	Row pivot	×	New pivot row value	=	New row value
x_1	1	−	1	×	1	=	0
x_2	1	−	1	×	1/3	=	2/3
s_1	0	−	1	×	0	=	0
s_3	0	−	1	×	−1/6	=	1/6
A_2	1	−	1	×	0	=	1
Quantity	9	−	1	×	4	=	5

Basis		6 x_1	8 x_2	0 s_1	0 s_3	$-M$ A_2	Quantity	Ratio
s_1	0	0	1	1	0	0	4	4/1 = 4 ←Minimum
A_2	$-M$	0	2/3	0	1/6	1	5	5/(2/3) = 7½
x_1	6	1	1/3	0	−1/6	0	4	4/(1/3) = 12
	Z	6	$2 - \frac{2}{3}M$	0	$-1 - \frac{1}{6}M$	$-M$	$24 - 5M$	
	$C - Z$	0	$6 + \frac{2}{3}M$ ↑ Largest positive	0	$1 + \frac{1}{6}M$	0		

new pivot row for the next tableau will be the same because we are dividing each value in the first row by 1.

Table 5–4 shows the third tableau and computations for rows A_2 and x_1.

Table 5–4 reveals that the solution is still not optimal: There is still a positive value in the $C - Z$ row of the table. The value is $1 + \frac{1}{6}M$, which is in the s_3 column. Hence, variable s_3 will enter the solution. Only variable A_2 has a positive ratio, so it will leave the solution.

The pivot value for A_2 in the third tableau is 1/6. Dividing each of the values in that row will yield values for the new pivot row of the fourth tableau. Thus:

x_1	x_2	s_1	s_3	Quantity
0 ÷ 1/6 = 0	0 ÷ 1/6 = 0	−2/3 ÷ 1/6 = −4	1/6 ÷ 1/6 = 1	7/3 ÷ 1/6 = 14

The fourth (and final) tableau is shown in Table 5–5 along with the computations for row x_1. No computations were necessary for row x_2 since its pivot value in the third tableau is 0; its values do not change. Also, there is no need to compute values for the A_2 column because that variable has left the solution.

TABLE 5–4 The Third Tableau for Example 1

	Values for row A_2							Values for row x_1						
Column	Original value	−	Row pivot	×	Value in pivot row	=	New row value	Original value	−	Row pivot	×	New pivot row value	=	New row value
x_1	0	−	2/3	×	0	=	0	1	−	1/3	×	0	=	1
x_2	2/3	−	2/3	×	1	=	0	1/3	−	1/3	×	1	=	1
s_1	0	−	2/3	×	1	=	−2/3	0	−	1/3	×	1	=	−1/3
s_3	1/6	−	2/3	×	0	=	1/6	−1/6	−	1/3	×	0	=	−1/6
A_2	1	−	2/3	×	0	=	0	0	−	1/3	×	0	=	0
Quantity	5	−	2/3	×	4	=	7/3	4	−	1/3	×	4	=	8/3

Basis	C	6 x_1	8 x_2	0 s_1	0 s_3	$-M$ A_2	Quantity	Ratio
x_2	8	0	1	1	0	0	4	—
A_2	$-M$	0	0	−2/3	1/6	1	7/3	7/3 ÷ 1/6 = 14 ← Only positive
x_1	6	1	0	−1/3	−1/6	0	8/3	8/3 ÷ −1/6 = −16
	Z	6	8	$6 + \frac{2}{3}M$	$-1 - \frac{1}{6}M$	$-M$	$48 - \frac{7}{3}M$	
	$C - Z$	0	0	$-6 - \frac{2}{3}M$	$1 + \frac{1}{6}M$	0		

TABLE 5–5 Final Tableau for Example 1

	New values for row x_1						
Column	Original value	−	Row pivot	×	New pivot row value	=	New row value
x_1	1	−	−1/6	×	0	=	1
x_2	0	−	−1/6	×	0	=	0
s_1	−1/3	−	−1/6	×	−4	=	−1
s_3	−1/6	−	−1/6	×	1	=	0
Quantity	8/3	−	−1/6	×	14	=	5

Basis	C	6 x_1	8 x_2	0 s_1	0 s_3	Quantity
x_2	8					4
s_3	0					14
x_1	6					5
	Z	6	8	2	0	62
	$C - Z$	0	0	−2	0	

FIGURE 5-2 Sequence of Tableaus for Example 1

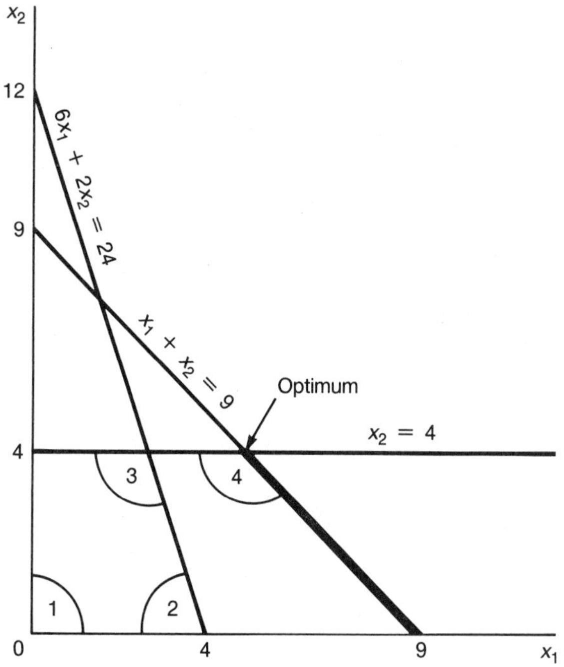

This solution is optimal because there are no positive values in row $C - Z$. The optimal solution can be obtained from the tableau. It is:

$$x_1 = 5$$
$$x_2 = 4$$
$$s_3 = 14$$
$$\text{Profit} = 62$$

Figure 5-2 illustrates the sequence of tableaus that were required to solve the problem in Example 1.

SOLVING MINIMIZATION PROBLEMS

For the most part, manual solution of minimization problems using simplex is handled in the same fashion as maximization problems with mixed constraints. The two key exceptions are that the M coefficients in the objective function are given positive signs instead of negative signs, as noted previously, and the selection of a variable to enter the solution is based on the largest *negative* value in row $C - Z$ of a tableau. In addition, you will discover that minimization

FIGURE 5-3 Graph of the Problem in Example 2

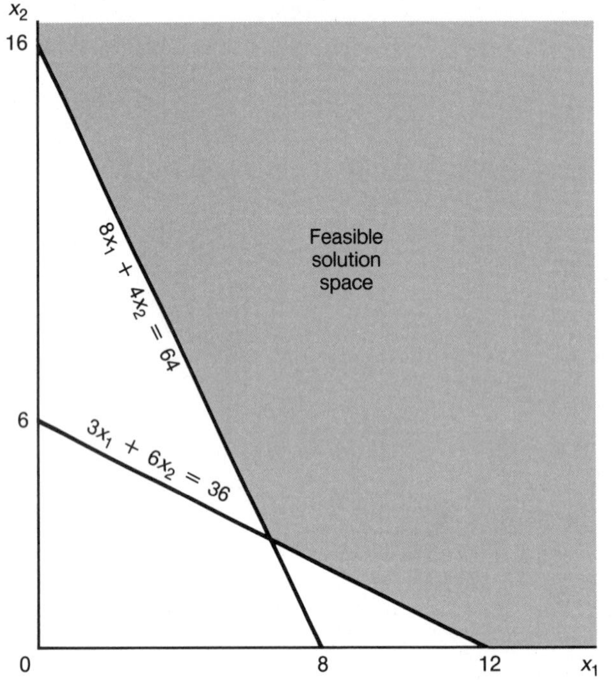

problems always require at least one artificial variable because of the nature of those problems: At least one constraint will be of the = or ≥ variety.

The following example illustrates a manual solution of a minimization problem. Again, note that artificial variables are required only for manual solution; computer codes do not require that you input artificial variables.

■

EXAMPLE 2 Solve this problem using the simplex method:

minimize $7x_1 + 9x_2$

subject to

Constraint 1 $3x_1 + 6x_2 \geq 36$

Constraint 2 $8x_1 + 4x_2 \geq 64$

x_1 and $x_2 \geq 0$

The problem is shown graphically in Figure 5-3 for purposes of illustration. Written in standard form, the problem becomes:

TABLE 5–6 Initial Tableau for Example 2

Basis	C	7 x_1	9 x_2	0 s_1	0 s_2	M A_1	M A_2	Quantity	Ratio	
A_1	M	3	6	−1	0	1	0	36	36/3 = 12	Smallest
A_2	M	8	4	0	−1	0	1	64	64/8 = 8 ←	non-negative ratio
	Z	11M	10M	−M	−M	M	M	100M		
	C − Z	7 − 11M ↑ Largest negative	9 − 10M	M	M	0	0			

$$\text{minimize} \quad 7x_1 + 9x_2 + 0s_1 + 0s_2 + MA_1 + MA_2$$

subject to

$$\begin{aligned} &\text{Constraint 1} \quad 3x_1 + 6x_2 - s_1 + A_1 = 36 \\ &\text{Constraint 2} \quad 8x_1 + 4x_2 - s_2 + A_2 = 64 \\ &\qquad\qquad \text{All variables} \geq 0 \end{aligned}$$

Table 5–6 shows the first tableau. As was the case with the problem illustrated in Example 1, when artificial variables are present, they are used as the basis for the initial solution. Further, the values for row Z must be computed for the first tableau as well as the others because they are nonzero even at this beginning stage.

The initial solution has no real meaning. Artificial variable A_1 assumes a value of 36 and A_2 assumes a value of 64, simply as a starting point. The cost of this solution is $100M$. Again, you might want to think of M as some real number, such as 1 million.

The variable that will enter the initial solution is x_1. We know this because x_1 has the largest *negative* value in row $C - Z$. Dividing the values in this pivot column into their respective row quantities reveals that variable A_2 will leave the solution because it has the smallest non-negative ratio. Moreover, dividing each value in row A_2 by the row pivot of 8 will give us the values for the revised pivot row (row x_1) in the second tableau.

The remaining values for the second tableau are computed as before. The completed second tableau and computations for row A_1 are shown in Table 5–7.

The solution contained in the second tableau is not optimal because negative values appear in the $C - Z$ row. The x_2 column has the largest negative, so x_2 will enter the solution. A_1 has the smallest positive ratio, so it will leave the solution.

The new pivot (x_2) row of the next tableau is obtained by dividing each value in the A_1 row of the second tableau by 9⁄2. The other values are computed in the usual way. The resulting tableau is shown in Table 5–8.

TABLE 5–7 Second Tableau for Example 2

Column	Original value	−	Row pivot	×	New pivot row value	=	New row value
	Values for row A_1						
x_1	3	−	3	×	1	=	0
x_2	6	−	3	×	$\frac{1}{2}$	=	$\frac{9}{2}$
s_1	1	−	3	×	0	=	−1
s_2	0	−	3	×	$-\frac{1}{8}$	=	$\frac{3}{8}$
A_1	1	−	3	×	0	=	1
Quantity	36	−	3	×	8	=	12

Basis	C	7 x_1	9 x_2	0 s_1	0 s_2	M A_1	Quantity	Ratio
A_1	M	0	$\frac{9}{2}$	−1	$\frac{3}{8}$	1	12	$12 \div \frac{9}{2} = \frac{24}{9}$ ←Smallest non-negative ratio
x_1	7	1	$\frac{1}{2}$	0	$-\frac{1}{8}$	0	8	$8 \div \frac{1}{2} = 16$
	Z	7	$\frac{7}{2} + \frac{9}{2}M$	−M	$-\frac{7}{8} + \frac{3}{8}M$	M	56 + 12M	
	C − Z	0	$\frac{11}{2} - \frac{9}{2}M$	M	$\frac{7}{8} - \frac{3}{8}M$	0		
			↑ Largest negative					

TABLE 5–8 Third Tableau for Example 2

Basis		7 x_1	9 x_2	0 s_1	0 s_2	Quantity
x_2	9	0	1	$-\frac{2}{9}$	$\frac{1}{12}$	$\frac{8}{3}$
x_1	7	1	0	$\frac{1}{9}$	$-\frac{1}{6}$	$\frac{20}{3}$
	Z	7	9	$-\frac{11}{9}$	$-\frac{5}{12}$	$\frac{212}{3}$
	C − Z	0	0	$\frac{11}{9}$	$\frac{5}{12}$	

Since there are no negative values in row $C - Z$, this tableau contains the optimal solution, which is:

$$x_1 = \frac{20}{3}, \text{ or } 6.67$$
$$x_2 = \frac{8}{3}, \text{ or } 2.67$$
$$\text{Cost} = \frac{212}{3}, \text{ or } 70.67$$

Figure 5–4 shows the sequence of tableaus that were used to obtain the optimal solution.

FIGURE 5–4 Sequence of Tableaus for Solution of Example 2

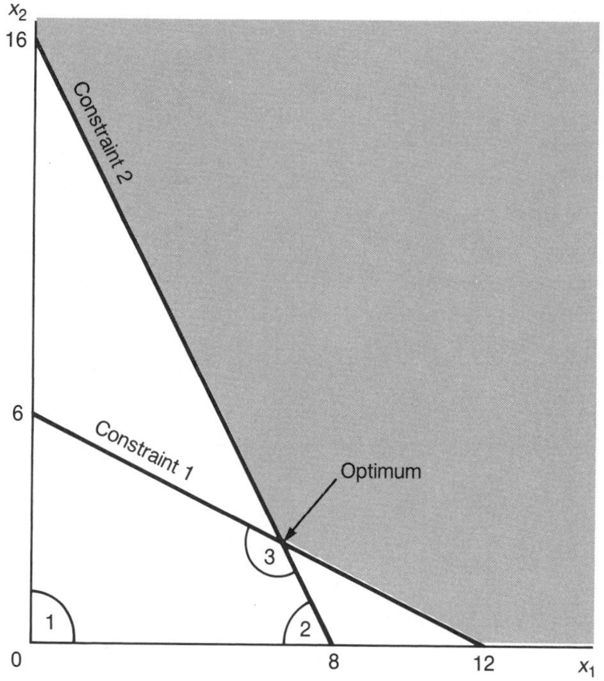

It should be noted that although the example here involved only ≥ constraints, minimization problems also may involve = and ≤ constraints. Such problems do not pose any particular difficulties. For a manual solution, the constraints must be put into standard form, after which the method illustrated in Example 2 can be followed.

Finally, an alternative approach to solving a minimization problem is to change the sign of each coefficient in the objective function and then solve it as a *maximization* problem.

SPECIAL ISSUE: INFEASIBILITY

The term **infeasibility** refers to a linear programming problem in which no combination of decision and slack/surplus variables will simultaneously satisfy all constraints. Infeasibility can be the result of an error in formulating a problem or it can be because the existing set of constraints is too restrictive to permit a solution. In the simplex approach, infeasibility can be recognized by the presence of an artificial variable in a solution that appears optimal (i.e., a tableau in which the signs of the values in row $C - Z$ indicate optimality), and it has a nonzero quantity. Thus, if A_2 appears in the basis of an optimal tableau, and has a value of zero in the Quantity column, that is okay. If it has a nonzero value, that would indicate infeasibility.

SUMMARY

This chapter describes how to convert = and ≥ constraints to standard form so that problems with those constraints can be solved manually using simplex. The solution of a maximization problem with mixed constraints is demonstrated along with the solution of a minimization problem. The issue of infeasibility (and how to recognize it in a tableau format) is also discussed.

GLOSSARY

Artificial Variable Represented by the symbol A. Added to = and ≥ constraints during the process of converting those constraints to standard form. Used to form an initial solution.

Infeasibility No feasible solution possible. Recognized by the presence of an artificial variable with a nonzero value in the final tableau.

M Symbol used to represent the coefficient of an artificial variable in the objective function; negative for a maximization problem and positive for a minimization problem. It also represents a very large value in the objective function.

Mixed Constraints LP problems in which the constraints are not all of the same form, but, instead, some combination of ≤, =, and ≥ constraints.

Surplus Variable Subtracted from a ≥ constraint in the process of converting the constraint to standard form. Represents the amount by which a minimum required constraint level is exceeded by a given solution.

SOLVED PROBLEM

Problem 1. Use the simplex technique to find the optimal solution to this problem:

maximize $5x_1 + 2x_2$

subject to

1 $x_1 + x_2 \leq 50$
2 $3x_1 + x_2 \geq 90$
3 $x_2 = 10$
$x_1, x_2 \geq 0$

Solution

a. Rewrite each constraint using slack, surplus, and artificial variables as needed so that they are in proper tableau form. Use these rules:

(1) For a $\leq$ constraint, add a slack variable.

(2) For an $=$ constraint, add an artificial variable.

(3) For a $\geq$ constraint, subtract a surplus variable and add an artificial variable.

Using these rules, we have:

1 $x_1 + x_2 + s_1 = 50$
2 $3x_1 + x_2 - s_2 + A_2 = 90$
3 $x_2 + A_3 = 10$

b. Add the slack, surplus, and artificial variables to the objective function using a zero for slack and surplus variables and $-M$ for artificial variables. Thus:

maximize $5x_1 + 2x_2 + 0s_1 + 0s_2 - MA_2 - MA_3$

c. Use these to start the first tableau:

Basis	C	5	2	0	0	$-M$	$-M$	Quantity
		x_1	x_2	s_1	s_2	A_2	A_3	
s_1	0	1	1	1	0	0	0	50
A_2	$-M$	3	1	0	-1	1	0	90
A_3	$-M$	0	1	0	0	0	1	10
	Z							
	$C - Z$							

Note that selection of variables for the initial basis is based on these rules:

(1) If an artificial variable appears in a constraint, the artificial variable will appear in the basis of the initial tableau.

(2) If there is no artificial variable, use the slack variable in the basis.

d. Obtain values for rows Z and $C - Z$. For Z, multiply the values in the C column by the values in the variable columns, and add the results. Thus, for the x_1 column, we have:

$$\begin{aligned} 0(1) &= 0 \\ -M(3) &= -3M \\ -M(0) &= \underline{\quad 0} \\ & \quad -3M \end{aligned}$$

Then, find the $C - Z$ value by subtracting the Z value from the C row value. For the x_1 column with $Z = -3M$ and $C = 5$, this becomes $5 - 3M$. The other values are computed in similar fashion. The completed tableau is:

	C	5	2	0	0	$-M$	$-M$	
Basis		x_1	x_2	s_1	s_2	A_2	A_3	Quantity
s_1	0	1	1	1	0	0	0	50
A_2	$-M$	3	1	0	-1	1	0	90
A_3	$-M$	0	1	0	0	0	1	10
	Z	$-3M$	$-2M$	0	$+M$	$-M$	$-M$	$-100M$
	$C - Z$	$5 + 3M$	$2 + 2M$	0	$-M$	0	0	

The appearance of positive values in rows $C - Z$ tells us that this solution is not optimal. The largest of these, $5 + 3M$, which is in column x_1, tells us that variable x_1 should be brought into the solution.

Dividing the *positive* values (only) into the Quantity values gives us:

$$\frac{50}{1} = 50$$

$$\frac{90}{3} = 30$$

The smaller of these is 30. This tells us that the second row (A_2) must be replaced. Therefore, x_1 will replace A_2 in the second row.

The value at the intersection of column x_1 and row A_2 is 3. Dividing every value in row A_2 by 3 gives us the revised pivot row values for the next tableau:

$$\frac{3}{3} = 1 \quad \frac{1}{3} \quad 0 \quad \frac{-1}{3} \quad \frac{1}{3} \quad 0 \quad \frac{90}{3} = 30$$

Using the relationship:

New value = Current value − (Row pivot value) (Revised pivot row value) gives us these values for row s_1:

$$1 - (1)(1) \quad = 0$$

$$1 - (1)(1/3) \quad = 2/3$$

$$
\begin{aligned}
1 - (1)(0) &= 1 \\
0 - (1)(-1/3) &= 1/3 \\
0 - (1)(1/3) &= -1/3 \\
0 - (1)(0) &= 0 \\
50 - (1)(30) &= 20
\end{aligned}
$$

For row A_3, the values remain the same in the next tableau because the row pivot value is zero.

The partial second tableau is thus:

Basis	C	5 x_1	2 x_2	0 s_1	0 s_2	$-M$ A_2	$-M$ A_3	Quantity
s_1	0	0	⅔	1	⅓	−⅓	0	20
x_1	5	1	⅓	0	−⅓	⅓	0	30
A_3	$-M$	0	1	0	0	0	1	10
	Z							
	$C - Z$							

Computing the Z and $C - Z$ values yields:

Basis	C	5 x_1	2 x_2	0 s_1	0 s_2	$-M$ A_2	$-M$ A_3	Quantity
								20
								30
								10
	Z	5	⅗ − M	0	−⅗	⅗	$-M$	150 − 10M
	$C - Z$	0	⅓ + M	0	⅗	$-M$ − ⅗	0	

The appearance of positive values in the $C - Z$ row tells us that this solution is not optimal. The largest positive is in column x_2. Hence, x_2 will come into solution. Dividing the values in the x_2 column into the Quantity values gives us these ratios:

$$\frac{20}{2/3} = 30$$

$$\frac{30}{1/3} = 90$$

$$\frac{10}{1} = 10$$

The smallest nonzero ratio is 10, which represents the third row. Therefore, variable A_3 will be replaced by variable x_2.

Dividing the values in row A_3 of the last tableau by the row pivot (which is the 1 at the intersection of row A_3 and column x_2) tells us that the values will remain the same for this row. The resulting values for the other two rows can be computed using the relationship that the New value = Current value − (Row pivot)(Revised pivot row). The resulting values are:

Basis	C	5 x_1	2 x_2	0 s_1	0 s_2	$-M$ A_2	$-M$ A_3	Quantity
s_1	0	0	0	1	⅓	−⅓	−⅔	40/3
x_1	5	1	0	0	−⅓	⅓	−⅓	80/3
x_2	2	0	1	0	0	0	1	10
	Z							
	$C - Z$							

The values for rows Z and $C - Z$ are:

	5 x_1	2 x_2	0 s_1	0 s_2	$-M$ A_2	$-M$ A_3	Quantity
Z	5	2	0	−5⁄3	5⁄3	⅓	153.3
$C - Z$	0	0	0	+5⁄3	$-M-5/3$	$-M-1/3$	

Because there is still a positive value in the bottom row, this solution is not optimal. In the next solution, s_2 will, therefore, come into the basis. And because only one positive value exists in the s_2 column (i.e., in row s_1), s_1 will come out of solution.

The next (and final) tableau (calculations not shown) is:

Basis	C	5 x_1	2 x_2	0 s_1	0 s_2	$-M$ A_2	$-M$ A_3	Quantity
s_2	0	0	0	3	1	−1	−2	40
x_1	5	1	0	1	0	0	−1	40
x_2	2	0	1	0	0	0	1	10
	Z	5	2	5	0	0	−3	220
	$C - Z$	0	0	−5	0	$-M$	$-M + 3$	

PROBLEMS

1. In order to solve simplex problems manually, constraints must be put into standard form.

   a. Describe how a ≤ constraint is put into standard form.

   b. Put these constraints into standard form:

   (1) $2x_1 + 6x_2 \leq 20$
   (2) $3x_1 + 2x_2 \leq 30$

   c. Describe how an = constraint is put into standard form.

   d. Put these constraints into standard form:

   (1) $3x_1 + 5x_2 = 16$
   (2) $4x_1 - x_2 = 18$

   e. Describe how a ≥ constraint is put into standard form.

   f. Put these constraints into standard form:

   (1) $6x_1 + 4x_2 \geq 24$
   (2) $5x_1 - 2x_2 \geq 14$

2. A maximization problem that has mixed constraints has two decision variables. The profit for x_1 is \$16 per unit and the profit for x_2 is \$11 per unit.

   a. Suppose that the *first* constraint in each of the three sets listed in the previous problem forms the set of constraints for an LP problem. Write out the appropriate objective function.

   b. Repeat part ***a*** using the second constraint in each set listed in the previous problem.

   c. How would your answer to part ***a*** change if the objective had been minimization rather than maximization?

3. Linear programming problems that have mixed constraints involve the use of slack, surplus, and artificial variables.

   a. Can you envision a constraint that would require the use of both a slack and a surplus variable? Explain why or why not.

   b. Can you envision a constraint that would require the use of both a slack variable and an artificial variable? Explain why or why not.

4. The initial tableau for a linear programming problem with mixed constraints is as follows:

Basis	C	4 x_1	6 x_2	0 s_1	0 s_2	$-M$ A_1	$-M$ A_3	Quantity
A_1	$-M$	0	1	-1	0	1	0	30
s_2	0	0	1	0	1	0	0	100
A_3	$-M$	2	1	0	0	0	1	140
	Z	$-2M$	$-2M$	$+M$	0	$-M$	$-M$	$-170M$
	C − Z	$4 + 2M$	$6 + 2M$	$-M$	0	0	0	

Reconstruct the original problem (i.e., write out the objective function and each of the constraints).

5. Given this linear programming problem:

maximize $8x_1 + 5x_2$

subject to

1 $4x_1 + 3x_2 \leq 240$

2 $x_2 \geq 50$

All variables ≥ 0

a. Graph the problem.

b. Write the problem in its standard form.

c. Solve the problem using simplex. What is the optimal solution?

d. Indicate the sequence of tableaus on your graph.

6. A manager has formulated this linear programming model:

maximize $1x_1 + 3x_2$

subject to

1 $5x_1 + 9x_2 \leq 90$

2 $10x_1 + 3x_2 \geq 60$

All variables ≥ 0

Supply the manager with this information:

a. A graph of the problem showing the feasible solution space and the optimal solution point.

b. The problem written in standard form.

c. A simplex solution to the problem along with an indication of what the optimal values of the decision variables are and the optimal value of the objective function.

d. Indicate the sequence of tableaus on the graph.

7. Suppose the manager in the previous problem has informed you that due to external conditions, the objective function must be changed to: $2x_2 + 1x_1$. Provide the manager with a simplex solution to this revised problem. What are the revised optimal values of the decision variables and the objective function?

8. The operations manager of an airport terminal has formulated this linear programming problem:

maximize $4x_1 + 6x_2$

subject to

1	$x_2 \geq 30$
2	$x_2 \leq 100$
3	$2x_1 + x_2 = 140$
	All variables ≥ 0

a. Graph the problem.

b. Write the problem in standard form.

c. Solve the problem using a simplex.

d. A 70 appears in Quantity column of the second tableau. Show on your graph what the number represents.

e. A 70 appears in the Quantity column of the final tableau. Show on your graph what the number represents.

f. What is the optimal solution?

9. Brad Johnson, the owner of Ann's Custom Dress Shop, must decide how many of each of two styles to produce next week. Each style requires five square yards of silk, and the shop has 450 square yards to work with. There are firm orders for 20 of Style 1 and 40 of Style 2. Both styles will yield a profit of $10 per dress. Labor and other materials are not restrictive.

a. Formulate the problem in linear programming format.

b. Write the problem in standard form, and develop the initial tableau.

c. Solve the problem using simplex. Hint: to start, be arbitrary.

d. How many of each style will yield the maximum possible profit? What is the maximum profit?

10. Karen Green, the manager of Party!, a firm that prepares and sells trays of party foods, is faced with the following problem. The firm offers two basic trays, which it lists in its brochure as Tray # 1 and Tray # 2. The firm has an order for 30 of Tray # 2. There is 120 square feet of refrigerated storage space. Both types of trays require refrigerated storage: Tray # 1 takes up 2 square feet per tray and Tray # 2 takes up 1 square foot per tray. The main difficulty, according to the manager, is that the firm has 240 pounds of a certain food product that must be used up. Tray # 1 uses 2 pounds per tray and Tray # 2 uses 6 pounds per tray. The remaining ingredients are in ample supply, but there is no reason to use up any of them. Profit per tray is $5 for Tray # 1 and $4 for Tray # 2. How many of each tray should the manager arrange to be produced in order to maximize profits, given the constraints?

11. Given this linear programming problem:

maximize $10x_1 + 20x_2 + 14x_3$

subject to

$$\begin{array}{lrrrl} \text{A} & 5x_1 + & 4x_2 + & 2x_3 & \leq 60 \\ \text{B} & & x_2 & & \leq 5 \\ \text{C} & & & x_3 & \geq 10 \end{array}$$
$$\text{All variables} \geq 0$$

Solve using simplex for the optimal quantities and the maximum profit.

12. The Forest Products Company must set its production schedule for the remainder of the week. Manager Terry Jackson wants to use the current equipment setup, which is conducive to three styles of interior panels: oak, walnut, and hickory. Oak panels yield a profit of \$6 each, walnut panels a profit of \$5 each, and hickory panels a profit of \$4 each. The company has enough raw material to make 120 panels. The manager has promised a retailer that an order of 40 walnut panels will be produced during this run. Determine the optimal quantities of each type of panel given the constraints, if profit maximization is the goal.

13. Suppose that Terry Jackson of the forest products company in the preceding problem has learned that because of equipment breakdown, production time for the period under consideration will be limited to 144 hours. Terry knows that each panel of oak requires 3 hours, whereas the other two types require 2 hours of production time. Determine the optimal quantities of each type of panel, given this additional information.

14. Solve Problem 14, Chapter 2, for the optimal quantities and the maximum annual return.

15. Wood Manufacturing makes two types of oak kitchen tables. One type yields a profit of \$50 a unit. The other type consists of two parts, a top and a bottom (which consists of the legs and table braces). Because these can be sold separately as replacement parts, each has its own profit. The top yields a profit of \$30 per unit and the bottom yields a profit of \$40 per unit. Currently, the firm has 10 bottom units on hand, but no tops and none of the first type, which is made as a single unit. Due to storage requirements, the manager wants to end up with the same number of table tops and bottoms for the second style of table, including those already on hand. Determine the optimal number of each table, top, and bottom to make in order to meet these requirements and maximize profit, given the information in the following table and the fact that there are 100 hours available:

Product	Hours per Unit
Single unit	8
Two-piece unit	
Top	4
Bottom	2

16. The manual solutions of maximization and minimization problems using simplex are very similar. There are, however, several key differences.

  a. Briefly describe the differences relative to the objective functions.

  b. Briefly describe the differences between maximization and minimization problems in terms of how it is determined which variable will enter the solution, given a nonoptimal tableau.

17. The production manager of Consolidated Manufacturing has developed this linear programming model:

minimize $6x_1 + 9x_2$

Subject to

$$\begin{array}{llr} 1 & 10x_1 + 4x_2 \geq & 400 \\ 2 & x_2 \geq & 14 \\ & \text{All variables} \geq & 0 \end{array}$$

  a. Graph the problem and determine where the optimal solution point is on the graph.

  b. Write the problem in standard form. Hint: remember that surplus variables have a negative sign in constraints.

  c. Determine the optimal solution using simplex.

  d. Indicate the sequence of tableaus on your graph.

18. A staff member who works for a hospital administrator has developed the following linear programming model:

minimize $8x_1 + 5x_2$

subject to

$$\begin{array}{llr} 1 & 15x_1 + 6x_2 \geq & 450 \\ 2 & x_1 \qquad \geq & 15 \\ 3 & x_2 \geq & 20 \\ & \text{All variables} \geq & 0 \end{array}$$

  a. Graph the problem and determine where the optimal solution is on the graph.

  b. Write the problem in standard form.

  c. Solve the problem using simplex. What are the optimal values of the decision variables?

  d. What other variable is in solution at the optimum? How is it interpreted? Show this on your graph.

19. The owner of a small business has formulated the following linear programming problem with the help of a consultant:

minimize $2x_1 + 3x_2$

subject to

$$\begin{array}{ll} 1 & 5x_1 + 2x_2 \geq 200 \\ 2 & x_2 \geq 20 \\ & \text{All variables} \geq 0 \end{array}$$

a. Graph the problem.

b. Solve the problem for the optimal values of the decision variables and the minimum cost, using simplex.

c. Indicate the sequence of tableaus on your graph.

20. Jennifer Perry is the manager of a firm that does electroplating. She has developed this linear programming model:

minimize $6x_1 + 3x_2$

subject to

$$\begin{array}{ll} 1 & 2x_1 + 1x_2 \geq 80 \\ 2 & 2x_1 + 4x_2 \geq 200 \\ & \text{All variables} \geq 0 \end{array}$$

a. Graph the model. Indicate the optimal solution on the graph.

b. Solve for the optimal values of the decision variables and the minimum cost using simplex.

c. Indicate the sequence of tableaus on the graph.

21. Rework the previous problem using as the objective function $10x_1 + 3x_2$.

22. Solve the following problem for the optimal solution using simplex:

minimize $20x_1 + 10x_2 + 14x_3$

subject to

$$\begin{array}{ll} 1 & 2x_1 + x_2 + 2x_3 \geq 72 \\ 2 & x_1 + x_2 - x_3 \geq 18 \\ & \text{All variables} \geq 0 \end{array}$$

23. Solve this cost minimization problem for the optimal solution:

minimize $20x_1 + 12x_2 + 16x_3$

subject to

$$\begin{array}{ll} 1 & x_1 + x_2 \geq 25 \\ 2 & x_2 - x_3 = 0 \\ 3 & x_3 \geq 5 \\ & \text{All variables} \geq 0 \end{array}$$

Hint: Artificial variable A_2 will leave the solution first.

24. A firm that manufactures dog food intends to offer its customers a new product that it will blend from raw materials it purchases from several suppliers. The owner of the firm believes that blending will produce a superior product at minimal cost. She has obtained the following information on the raw materials from the suppliers.

	Raw Material			Minimum
	A	B	C	Required, %
Protein, %	10	8	12	10
Fat, %	25	20	20	20
Fiber, %	5	8	6	6

The raw material costs are $1 per pound for A, $1.20 per pound for B, and $1.40 per pound for C. The product will sell for $1.65 per pound. Mixing and handling costs are the same for all three raw materials. Determine the optimal blend of the three raw materials.

25. (Refer to Chapter 2, Problem 10a.) Find the optimal values of the decision variables and the optimal value of the objective function.

26. (Refer to Chapter 2, Problem 12.) Determine the optimal quantities of spaghetti and sauce per serving and the cost per serving.

27. (Refer to Chapter 2, Problem 16.) Determine the optimal quantity of each ingredient and the cost per bottle.

28. (Refer to Chapter 2, Problem 15.) Find the optimal mix of ingredients and the cost *per pound*.

29. (Refer to Chapter 2, Problem 20.) Given the client's requests and the amount of funds available, how much money will be uninvested?

30. (Refer to Chapter 2, Problem 21.) Find the optimal quantities of wine, apple juice, and grape juice, and find the optimal value of the objective function.

Chapter 6
Postoptimality Analysis

Chapter Outline

Learning Objectives

After completing this chapter, you should be able to:

1. Explain in general terms why it can be useful for a decision maker to extend the analysis of an LP problem beyond determination of the optimal solution.
2. Use sensitivity analysis to evaluate a change in the value of an objective function coefficient.
3. Use sensitivity analysis to evaluate a change in the RHS of a constraint.
4. Explain what a dual is.
5. Formulate the dual of a problem.
6. Read and interpret the solution to a dual problem, and relate the dual solution to the primal solution.
7. Explain in economic terms the interpretation of dual variables and the dual solution.
8. Determine if adding another variable to a problem will change the optimal solution mix of the original problem.

This chapter describes **postoptimality analysis** of LP models; analysis that *begins* with the optimal solution in order to gain additional insights into how potential changes to the model would impact the optimal solution.

The material in the chapter is presented in two sections. The first section deals with sensitivity analysis and the last section deals with duality.

SENSITIVITY ANALYSIS

The purpose of **sensitivity analysis** is to explore the effects of potential changes in parameters of LP models on the optimal solution. The Chapter 3 Supplement describes graphical sensitivity analysis. If you have not yet read that material, you may want to do so now, because it illustrates in graphical form the mathematical concepts that are described in this section.

Introduction

Sensitivity analysis is designed to give a decision maker the ability to answer "what if . . . ?" questions about an LP model that involve changing the value of a model parameter, such as changing the right-hand side (RHS) value of a constraint, or changing the value of an objective function coefficient. For example, the decision maker may be considering a price change that will cause a change in a profit coefficient. Two obvious questions come to mind: Will the optimal values of the decision variables change? Will the optimal value of the objective function change? Sensitivity analysis enables the decision maker to easily answer these and similar questions concerning potential changes in values of parameters without having to re-solve an entire problem.

There are three categories of model parameters that might be subject to potential changes:

1. A change in the value of an objective function coefficient.
2. A change in the right-hand side (RHS) value of a constraint.
3. A change in a coefficient of a constraint.

The discussion here will be limited to the first two of these; it will not cover changes to coefficients of constraints. And unless otherwise noted, the discussion will assume that only *one* parameter is being changed, while all other parameters remain unchanged.

Sensitivity analysis involves identification of ranges of change for various parameters. A central concept in sensitivity analysis is that changes to parameters that fall within prescribed ranges either have no effect, or they have an easily determinable effect, on the optimal solution. There are three aspects of these ranges that are important for understanding sensitivity analysis:

1. Which range pertains to a given situation? For example, which range relates to a change in the RHS value of a constraint?

2. How can the range be determined?
3. What impact on the optimal solution does a change that is within the range have?

Two approaches to obtaining sensitivity ranges are described in this section. The first involves using the values contained in a final simplex tableau to compute the ranges and to obtain other useful information. The second approach involves use of a computer package to provide the ranges and other information.

In order to demonstrate sensitivity analysis, the microcomputer example used in several of the preceding chapters will be continued. That problem is repeated here:

x_1 = quantity of Model 1 Microcomputers
x_2 = quantity of Model 2 Microcomputers

maximize $60x_1 + 50x_2$

subject to

Assembly time	$4x_1 + 10x_2 \leq 100$
Inspection time	$2x_1 + 1x_2 \leq 22$
Storage space	$3x_1 + 3x_2 \leq 39$

A Change in an Objective Function Coefficient

A decision maker may want to know what impact a change in an objective function coefficient would have on the optimal solution and on the optimal value of the objective function. Such changes can occur because of cost changes, new pricing policies, product or process design changes, or other changes. Sometimes they reflect improved accuracy.

Even though the value of an objective function coefficient is changed, that will not necessarily cause the optimal solution to change. A change in an objective coefficient will cause a change in the slope of the objective function line (or plane). However, that change might not be enough to move the solution to another corner point of the feasible region. Generally, there is a range of possible values for an objective function for which the optimal solution will remain the same. This is referred to as the **range of optimality.** Within this range, the optimal values of solution variables (i.e., variables in the basis of the final tableau) will not change. For variables that are not in the basis, the term *range of insignificance* is sometimes used to indicate the range in objective function coefficient values that will not cause that variable to come into the basis. Hence, for values that are within a nonbasic variable's range of insignificance, the solution will not change.

Thus, if the value of an objective function coefficient is changed, and that change falls within the range of optimality of a basic variable, or within the range of insignificance of a nonbasic variable, the optimal values of the variables in solution (both decision variables and slack/surplus variables) will not change. However, the optimal value of the objective function *will* change for a change that

TABLE 6–1

Basis	C	60	50	0	0	0	
		x_1	x_2	s_1	s_2	s_3	Quantity
s_1	0	0	0	1	6	−16⅔	24
x_1	60	1	0	0	1	−⅓	9
x_2	50	0	1	0	−1	⅔	4
	Z	60	50	0	10	40⁄3	740
	C − Z	0	0	0	−10	−40⁄3	

is *within* the range of optimality because it is determined by the values of the decision variables and their objective function coefficients. By similar reasoning, the optimal value of the objective function *will not change* for a change to a nonbasic variable's coefficient that is within its range of insignificance because that variable will not come into the basis, and therefore, will not affect the value of Z.

The range of optimality can easily be computed using the values contained in the final tableau. The procedure is as follows. For a change in an objective function variable's coefficient:

1. Identify the *row* of the final tableau that corresponds to that variable. In the microcomputer problem, the second row of the tableau (see Table 6–1) is the x_1 row and the third row is the x_2 row.
2. Divide the row entries, column by column, into the bottom row of the table. For example, for the x_1 row we obtain:

Column	x_1	x_2	s_1	s_2	s_3
$\frac{C - Z \text{ value}}{x_1 \text{ value}}$	$\frac{0}{1} = 0$	$\frac{0}{0}$ = undefined	$\frac{0}{0}$ = undefined	$\frac{-10}{1} = -10$	$\frac{-40/3}{-1/3} = +40$

   We are interested in the smallest positive ratio and the smallest negative ratio (i.e., the negative ratio that is closest to zero). The smallest positive ratio is 40, and the smallest negative ratio is −10.
3. The smallest positive ratio indicates the amount by which the x_1 coefficient can be increased, and the smallest negative ratio indicates the amount by which the x_1 coefficient can be decreased. Use these amounts to determine the range of optimality for the x_1 coefficient. Note that its current value is 60. Thus, we find:

   $60 + 40 = 100$ (upper limit)
   $60 - 10 = 50$ (lower limit)

   Hence, the range of optimality for x_1 is 50 to 100.

EXAMPLE 1 Use the above procedure to determine the range of optimality for the x_2 objective function coefficient in the microcomputer problem.

Solution

The necessary steps are:

1. Identify the x_2 row of the final tableau.
2. Divide the row entries in the body of the table into entries in the $C - Z$ row. Thus, we find:

Column	x_1	x_2	s_1	s_2	s_3
$\frac{C - Z \text{ value}}{x_2 \text{ value}}$	$\frac{0}{0}$ = undefined	$\frac{0}{1} = 0$	$\frac{0}{0}$ = undefined	$\frac{-10}{-1} = +10$	$\frac{-40/3}{2/3} = -20$

3. Identify the smallest positive ratio and the smallest negative ratio (the negative ratio that is closest to zero). The ratios are $+10$ and -20.
4. Use the ratios and the current objective function coefficient (50) to determine the range of optimality:

$$50 + 10 = 60 \quad \text{(upper limit)}$$
$$50 - 20 = 30 \quad \text{(lower limit)}$$

Hence, the range of optimality for the x_2 coefficient is 30 to 60.
5. Interpret the range: Any value of the x_2 coefficient in the objective function from 30 to 60 will yield the same optimal variables of basic variables that the current coefficient of 50 yields. However, the optimal value of Z will change.

Now let us see how we can easily determine the range of insignificance for a nonbasic variable. Because both of the decision variables in the microcomputer problem are in the basis of the final tableau, we cannot use that example. However, the final tableau for another problem that has a nonbasic variable is shown in Table 6–2. Note that variable x_3 does not appear in the basis; hence, it is a nonbasic variable. Next, note that the two basic variables, x_1 and x_2, each have a zero in their respective columns in row $C - Z$, but that x_3 has -10.7 in row $C - Z$. These are the amounts by which their respective objective function coefficients would have to be increased in order for them to come into solution. Because x_1 and x_2 are already in solution, their values are zero. Thus, basic variables will always have a zero at their position in row $C - Z$. The -10.7 for x_3 tells us that its objective function coefficient would have to increase by 10.7 in order for it to cause that variable to come into solution. The current x_3 coefficient in the objective function is 112 (see the top row of Table 6–2). Therefore, an increase of 10.7 would make it:

TABLE 6–2 Final Simplex Tableau for Range of Insignificance Example

Basis	C	120 x_1	105 x_2	112 x_3	0 s_1	0 s_2	0 s_3	Quantity
x_1	120	1	0	.06	.14	−.08	0	16.8
x_2	105	0	1	1.1	−.1	.2	0	8
s_3	0	0	0	.88	−.28	.16	1	16.4
	Z	0	0	122.7	6.3	11.4	0	2,856
	$C - Z$	0	0	−10.7	−6.3	−11.4	0	

$$112 + 10.7 = 122.7$$

Notice that this is the same value that appears in row Z in the x_3 position. Thus, we can read directly from the tableau the amount by which a nonbasic variable's coefficient would have to increase (10.7) in order for it to become a basic variable (and, consequently, replace one of the current basic variables in the solution), and the minimum value of its objective function coefficient that would cause that to happen (122.7). The range of insignificance for the objective function coefficient of x_3 is *less than 122.7;* as long as its value does not equal or exceed that amount, x_3 will remain a nonbasic variable, and neither the optimal values of solution variables nor the optimal value of Z will change.

A Change in the RHS of a Constraint

A useful first step in analyzing a RHS change is to note whether a constraint is a binding or a nonbinding constraint. Recall that a binding constraint is one that determines the optimal solution; it therefore ends up with no slack or surplus. Generally, the optimal solution occurs at the intersection of two binding constraints. Conversely, a nonbinding constraint ends up with slack or surplus in the optimal solution. One way to determine which constraints are nonbinding is to check the list of variables in the basis of the final tableau; if a constraint's slack or surplus variable appears, that constraint is nonbinding. For the microcomputer problem (see Table 6–3), s_1 appears in the final basis; hence, the first constraint (assembly time) is nonbinding. And because the slack variables for the other two constraints do *not* appear, those two constraints *are* binding.

Another way that we can use to identify binding and nonbinding constraints in the final tableau is to examine the value in row $C - Z$ under the corresponding slack/surplus column of each variable: If the value is 0, the constraint is nonbinding; if the value is nonzero, the constraint is binding. Referring to the tableau in Table 6–3, we can see that s_1 has a 0 in row $C - Z$, indicating that the first constraint is nonbinding, and that s_2 and s_3 both have nonzero values, indicating that the second and third constraints are binding.

TABLE 6–3 Final Tableau for the Microcomputer Problem

Basis	C	60 x_1	50 x_2	0 s_1	0 s_2	0 s_3	Quantity
s_1	0	0	0	1	6	−16/3	24
x_1	60	1	0	0	1	−1/3	9
x_2	50	0	1	0	−1	2/3	4
	Z	60	50	0	10	40/3	740
	$C - Z$	0	0	0	−10	−40/3	

The issue that is of particular interest for a nonbinding constraint is the amount by which its RHS can be changed without causing it to become binding. That amount is simply the value of its slack or surplus variable in the optimal solution. For instance, in the microcomputer problem, $s_1 = 24$ in the optimal solution. Hence, the assembly constraint could be reduced by as much as 24 hours before assembly would become a binding constraint. Recall that the assembly constraint was:

$$4x_1 + 10x_2 \leq 100 \text{ hours}$$

Hence, it could be reduced to $100 - 24 = 76$ hours. On the other hand, if we were to increase the RHS of the assembly constraint, that would only *increase* the amount of slack, it would not cause assembly to be a binding constraint. Thus, if we were to increase the RHS of the assembly constraint by 10 hours, that would increase the amount of its slack by 10 hours. And the more we added to the RHS, the greater the amount of slack that would result.

What we have, then, is a range of values for the RHS of the assembly constraint for which that constraint would remain nonbinding (and hence, not contribute anything to profit). The range is from 76 to infinity. This is the **range of feasibility** for the assembly constraint; the range of RHS values for which the optimal value of the objective function would be unaffected by a change in the amount of assembly time available.

Note that if we had been dealing with a ≥ constraint that was nonbinding, it would have *surplus* rather than slack in the optimal solution, and that amount of surplus would be how much the RHS could be *increased* without the constraint becoming binding on the solution. For example, suppose this constraint:

$$2x_1 + 5x_2 \geq 20$$

has a surplus of 6 in the optimal solution. This would mean that its RHS could be increased by as much as 6 before it would become binding. Its range of feasibility would be 0 to 26, because zero would mean no constraint. Alternately, we could

TABLE 6–4 Shadow Prices in the Microcomputer Final Tableau

Basis	C	60 x_1	50 x_2	0 s_1	0 s_2	0 s_3	Quantity
s_1	0	0	0	1	6	$-16/3$	24
x_1	60	1	0	0	1	$-1/3$	9
x_2	50	0	1	0	-1	$2/3$	4
	Z	60	50	0	10	$40/3$	740
	C − Z	0	0	0	-10	$-40/3$	

Shadow prices (row Z, columns s_1, s_2, s_3)

say the lower limit of the range is (negative) infinity, or even that there was no limit. That is, we could write:

$-$infinity to 26   or   no limit to 26

What we can conclude about a nonbinding constraint is that within its range of feasibility, neither the optimal solution quantities will change (except for the slack/surplus amount of the nonbinding constraint) nor will the optimal value of the objective function change. The same cannot be said for a binding constraint; *both* the optimal solution quantities and the values of the objective function will change. However, the changed values will be fairly simple to determine.

Whenever a change in an RHS value is contemplated, it is useful to know the *marginal value* of that constraint. These marginal values are called *shadow prices*; there is one for each constraint. A **shadow price** indicates the amount that the objective function will change for a one-unit change in the RHS value of the corresponding contraint. The shadow prices are located in row *Z* of the final tableau in the slack/surplus columns. Table 6–4 illustrates the shadow prices for the microcomputer problem. Thus, we see that the shadow price is 0 for the first constraint (assembly time), 10 for the second constraint (inspection), and $40/3$, or 13.33, for the third constraint (storage space). Recall that the first constraint is not binding, so the 0 shadow price confirms what we already know: A change in the RHS of the first constraint will not have an impact on the optimal value of the objective function, as long as the change is within the range of feasibility for that constraint. The 10 for s_2 indicates that for each one-unit change in the RHS of the second constraint, the optimal value of the objective function will change by 10; increasing by $10 per unit if the RHS is increased, or decreasing by $10 per unit if the RHS is decreased. Similarly, an increase or decrease in the RHS of the third constraint will cause a corresponding increase or decrease in the optimal value of the objective function of $13.33.

It should be noted that this discussion assumes that any increase or decrease in cost associated with the change in the RHS is accounted for in the objective function. That is the case if the objective function involves profits rather than revenues, costs, or times. For example, if a shadow price is 10, and the objective function pertains to revenues, if an additional unit (RHS) of resource is to be added, the total revenue will increase by $10 minus the cost of the additional unit of resource. Consequently, if the cost of the unit exceeds the shadow price of $10, it would not make sense to add more of that resource. However, for an objective function related to unit profits (which would already account for the cost of resources), if an additional unit of resource could be added for the "regular" cost, the entire shadow price would go toward increasing the total profit. If the additional resource required payment of a premium above the regular amount, that premium would have to be subtracted from the shadow price to determine the *net* profit.

Finally, note that shadow prices are valid only within the range of feasibility of a constraint; outside that range, they are not valid. That is, a shadow price indicates the amount by which the optimal value of the objective function will change per unit change in the RHS value of a constraint, *as long as the change in the RHS value is within the range of feasibility*. Consequently, it is important to know what a constraint's RHS range of feasibility is in order to accurately assess the impact of RHS changes. Let us therefore turn our attention to establishing the range of feasibility for a binding constraint.

The key to computing the range of feasibility for the constraints lies in the final simplex tableau. More specifically, the values in the body of the final tableau in each slack column can be used to compute the range of feasibility for the corresponding constraint. The final tableau for the microcomputer problem is repeated in Table 6–5. The shaded portion of the table indicates the values needed to compute the ranges of feasibility.

For each constraint, the entries in the associated slack column must be divided into the values in the Quantity column. Because there are three in each column, there will be three ratios after the division. For example, for the Storage column values, the resulting ratios are:

s_3	Quantity	Quantity/s_3
$-16/3$	24	$\frac{24}{-16/3} = -4.5$
$-1/3$	9	$\frac{9}{-1/3} = -27$
$2/3$	4	$\frac{4}{2/3} = +6$

Unlike the simplex calculations, negative ratios are acceptable. Two of these ratios indicate the extent to which the constraint level can be changed and still have the current shadow price remain valid. The smallest positive ratio indicates how much the constraint level can be *decreased* before it reaches the lower limit of its range of feasibility. Thus, the storage constraint can be decreased by 6 cubic

TABLE 6–5 Final Tableau for the Microcomputer Problem

Basis	C	60 x_1	50 x_2	0 s_1 (Assembly)	0 s_2 (Inspection)	0 s_3 (Storage)	Quantity
s_1	0	0	0	1	6	$-16/3$	24
x_1	60	1	0	0	1	$-1/3$	9
x_2	50	0	1	0	-1	$2/3$	4
	Z	60	50	0	10	$40/3$	740
	$C - Z$	0	0	0	-10	$-40/3$	

feet before it hits the lower limit of its range of feasibility. Conversely, the smallest negative ratio (i.e., the negative ratio closest to 0) indicates how much the storage constraint can be *increased* before it reaches its upper limit of feasibility. Hence, the storage level can be increased by 4.5 cubic feet before it hits that upper limit.

Perhaps it seems strange that a positive ratio relates to a decrease and a negative ratio to an increase. However, the positive ratio indicates the amount that must be added to the lower limit to achieve the current constraint level (i.e., how much the current level is above the lower limit). Thus, knowing the current level, we must subtract that amount to obtain the lower limit. Thus, for the storage constraint, the current level is 39. Thus, we have:

$$\text{Lower limit} + 6 = 39, \text{ so Lower limit} = 39 - 6$$

Similarly, the smallest negative ratio reveals how much the current level is below the upper limit, so that amount must be added to the current level to determine the upper limit. For the storage constraint, that is:

$$\text{Upper limit} - 4.5 = 39, \text{ so Upper limit} = 39 + 4.5$$

The same general rule always applies when computing the upper and lower limits on the range of feasibility for a maximization problem:

Allowable decrease: The smallest positive ratio.
Allowable increase: The negative ratio closest to zero.

For a minimization problem, the rules are reversed: The allowable *decrease* is the negative ratio closest to zero, and the allowable *increase* is the smallest positive ratio.

■

EXAMPLE 2 Determine the range of feasibility for each of the constraints in the microcomputer problem.

Solution

Table 6–6 illustrates the computations and resulting ranges.

It is important to recognize when determining ranges of feasibility that each range is determined *under the assumption that the levels of the other constraints will not change*. Later in the chapter, a procedure for handling multiple changes will be described.

You are probably wondering why these ratios tell us how much latitude there is for feasible changes in a constraint level. Recall that the values in the body of any simplex tableau are *substitution rates*. They indicate how much, and in what direction, a one-unit change in a column variable will cause the current quantity value to change. For example, in the final tableau, the values in the s_3 column and the Quantity column are:

Basis	s_3	Quantity
s_1	$-16/3$	24
x_1	$-1/3$	9
x_2	$2/3$	4
Z	$40/3$	

The values in the s_3 (storage) column tells us the following: A one-unit increase in storage space will:

1. Cause s_1 (assembly slack) to decrease by $16/3 = 5.33$ units.
2. Cause x_1 to decrease by $1/3 = .33$ units.
3. Cause x_2 to increase by $2/3 = .67$ units.
4. Cause profit to increase by $40/3 = \$13.33$.

Because the Quantity column entries indicate how much of s_1, x_1, and x_2 are currently in solution, dividing each of those entries by the respective substitution rates in the s_3 column will indicate the limit on possible changes that will reflect the shadow price of $40/3$. Since the substitution rates apply in either direction (i.e., for a one-unit increase or a one-unit decrease in storage space), we can determine the potential for both changes at the same time: The smallest positive ratio reveals the amount that the current level of the constraint is above the lower limit, and the smallest negative ratio reveals the amount that the current level of the constraint is below the upper limit.

TABLE 6–6 Determining the Range of Feasibility for the Microcomputer Problem

(Right side of the final tableau)

Assembly	Inspection	Storage	
0	0	0	
s_1	s_2	s_3	Quantity
1	6	$-16/3$	24
0	1	$-1/3$	9
0	-1	$2/3$	4
0	10	$40/3$	740
0	-10	$-40/3$	

	Assembly	Inspection	Storage
	$\frac{24}{1} = +24$	$\frac{24}{6} = +4$	$\frac{24}{-16/3} = -4.5$
	$\frac{9}{0} =$ undefined	$\frac{9}{1} = +9$	$\frac{9}{-1/3} = -27$
	$\frac{4}{0} =$ undefined	$\frac{4}{-1} = -4$	$\frac{4}{2/3} = +6$
Original amount	100 hours	22 hours	39 cubic feet
Range: Upper limit	None	$22 + 4 = 26$	$39 + 4.5 = 43.5$
Range: Lower limit	$100 - 24 = 76$	$22 - 4 = 18$	$39 - 6 = 33$

When a decision maker becomes involved with changing constraint levels, that person wants to know not only the range over which the level can be changed, but also what impact a contemplated change would have on the optimal solution. Fortunately, when the proposed change is within the range of feasibility, very little effort is required to obtain the resulting optimal solution. Again, the key values are the substitution rates for the constraint in question, as the next two examples illustrate.

■

EXAMPLE 3 The manager in the microcomputer problem is contemplating one of two possible changes in the level of the storage constraint. One change would be an increase of 3 cubic feet in its level and the other would be an increase of 8 cubic feet in its level. Determine the revised optimal solution for each possible change.

Solution

The first step in analyzing the effect of a constraint level change is to check to see if the change is within the range of feasibility. We previously determined that the upper limit of that range for the storage constraint is $39 + 4.5$. Hence, an increase of 3 cubic feet is within the range, but an increase of 8 cubic feet is not.

The effect of an increase of 3 cubic feet can be computed in this way:

(Partial final tableau)

Basis	s_3	Quantity	Current solution		Change		Revised solution	
s_1	$-16/3$	24	24	+	$3(-16/3)$	=	8	(s_1)
x_1	$-1/3$	9	9	+	$3(-1/3)$	=	8	(x_1)
x_2	$2/3$	4	4	+	$3(2/3)$	=	6	(x_2)
Z	$40/3$	740	740	+	$3(40/3)$	=	780	(profit)

For an increase in storage space of 8 cubic feet, since the upper limit of the feasible range for storage is 4.5 cubic feet (see Table 6–3), the amount of increase above 4.5 cubic feet will be excess, or slack. The additional amount needed to achieve the upper limit is used to compute the revised solution. Thus:

Basis	Current solution		Change		Revised solution
s_1	24	+	$4.5(-16/3)$	=	0
x_1	9	+	$4.5(-1/3)$	=	7.5
x_2	4	+	$4.5(2/3)$	=	7
Z	740	+	$4.5(40/3)$	=	800

Note, however, that beyond the upper limit, s_3 would come into solution, reaplacing s_1, which would no longer be slack. The amount of slack would be $8 - 4.5 = 3.5$ cubic feet. Consequently, the revised solution would be:

$$s_3 = 3.5$$
$$x_1 = 7.5$$
$$x_2 = 7$$
$$\text{Profit} = 800$$

■

EXAMPLE 4 Suppose the manager in the microcomputer problem is contemplating a *decrease* in storage space due to an emergency situation. There are two possibilities being considered: a decrease of 6 cubic feet and a decrease of 9 cubic feet. Recall that the limit on a decrease is 6 cubic feet (see Table 6–6). Hence, the computation of the impact of a decrease in 6 cubic feet of storage space is relatively simple:

Basis	Current solution	Change		Revised solution
s_1	24	$-6(-16/3)$	=	56
x_1	9	$-6(-1/3)$	=	11
x_2	4	$-6(2/3)$	=	0
Profit	740	$-6(40/3)$	=	660

Now consider a decrease of 9 cubic feet. Note that this decrease in storage space is beyond the lower limit of the feasible range. In general, the substitution rates and the shadow prices do not hold when the lower limit is exceeded. Consequently, *for a decrease in the level of a constraint beyond its lower limit, a new simplex solution would need to be generated.*

Computer Analysis

Standard computer LP packages have the capability of performing sensitivity analysis of objective function coefficients and right-hand side values. They either do these automatically, or as an option. Although different computer packages do not necessarily present the result in exactly the same format, the differences among packages tend to be minor.

With that in mind, let us consider a sample of computer output. Table 6–7 repeats the final tableau of the microcomputer solution for reference, and Table 6–8 illustrates a computer printout of sensitivity analysis of the microcomputer problem.

The printout begins with the original problem and the optimal values of the variables. The optimal values of the decision variables are given first under the VARIABLE heading, followed by the optimal values of the slack variables, which are listed under the ROW heading. Just to the right of the optimal values of the decision variables are REDUCED COSTS, and to the right of the optimal slack values are DUAL PRICES. Here, ROW 2 refers to s_1, ROW 3 refers to s_2, and ROW 4 refers to s_3. The DUAL PRICES are equal to the values in row $C - Z$ of the final tableau (see Table 6–7). Recall that for variables that are in solution, the $C - Z$ values will be equal to zero. A nonzero reduced cost, then, would appear if a decision variable was not in solution; that nonzero reduced cost (e.g., 2) would indicate the amount that the variable's objective function coefficient could be increased without it coming into the solution. Thus, if a reduced cost was 2.00, that variable's objective function would have to be increased by at least 2.00 in order for it to be in solution if the problem were to be reworked with that one change.

The DUAL PRICES are the shadow prices for the slack or surplus variables (slack variables for the microcomputer problem).

In the remaining portion of the printout, sensitivity analysis results are shown. First, the OBJECTIVE COEFFICIENT RANGES (range of optimality) are shown, followed by the RIGHT-HAND SIDE RANGES (range of feasibility). For each decision variable, the CURRENT VALUE refers to its objective function coefficient, whereas the next column indicates the amount of possible increase and the next column the amount of possible decrease that will result in the same optimal values of the variables that are in solution. For the right-hand side ranges, the slack variables are listed (actually, row 2 refers here to s_1, row 3 to s_2, and row 4 to s_3). The CURRENT VALUE refers to the original right-hand side values of the constraints. The next two columns show the amount by which the right side of a constraint can be changed and still be within the range of feasibility.

TABLE 6–7 Final Tableau for the Microcomputer Problem

Basis	C	60 x_1	50 x_2	0 s_1	0 s_2	0 s_3	Quantity
s_1	0	0	0	1	6	$-16/3$	24
x_1	60	1	0	0	1	$-1/3$	9
x_2	50	0	1	0	-1	$2/3$	4
	Z	60	50	0	10	$40/3$	740
	C − Z	0	0	0	-10	$-40/3$	

TABLE 6–8 Computer Printout of Sensitivity Analysis of the Microcomputer Problem

```
MAX   60X1 + 50X2

SUBJECT TO
  2) 4X1 + 25X2 <= 100
  3) 2X1 + X2 <= 22
  4) 3X1 + 3X2 <= 39
END

      LP OPTIMUM FOUND AT STEP   3
           OBJECTIVE FUNCTION VALUE
                  740.00

VARIABLE         VALUE       REDUCED COSTS
      X1          9.00           0.00
      X2          4.00           0.00

ROW         SLACK OR SURPLUS   DUAL PRICES
      2          24.00           0.00
      3           0.00          10.00
      4           0.00          13.33

            SENSITIVITY ANALYSIS
                OBJECTIVE COEFFICIENT RANGES

VARIABLE   CURRENT     ALLOWABLE     ALLOWABLE
           VALUE       INCREASE      DECREASE
X1          60.00        40.00         10.00
X2          50.00        10.00         20.00

                   RIGHT-HAND SIDE RANGES
ROW        CURRENT     ALLOWABLE     ALLOWABLE
           VALUE       INCREASE      DECREASE
2          100.00      INFINITY       24.00
3           22.00        4.00          4.00
4           39.00        4.50          6.00
```

MANAGER DIALOGUE

Susan Frank is the operations manager of Small Manufacturing, Inc. She has developed a linear programming model to help her determine the product mix on one of her three production lines:

maximize $15x_1 + 20x_2 + 14x_3$ (profit)

subject to

Material A $5x_1 + 6x_2 + 4x_3 \leq 210$ lbs. per day
Material B $10x_1 + 8x_2 + 5x_3 \leq 200$ lbs. per day
Material C $4x_1 + 2x_2 + 5x_3 \leq 170$ lbs. per day
$x_1, x_2, x_3 \geq 0$

where

x_1 = quantity of Product 1 to produce
x_2 = quantity of Product 2 to produce
x_3 = quantity of Product 3 to produce

Susan has obtained the following computer printout for this model, and wants to use that information to answer a number of questions she has.

Question What is the maximum profit, and how much of each product should be produced each day in order to achieve the maximum profit?

Answer The maximum profit is $548, and the optimal values are $x_1 = 0$ units, $x_2 = 5$ units, and $x_3 = 32$ units.

Question What do the symbols R2, R3, and R4 represent?

Answer They correspond to the rows or lines in the model. R2 refers to the second row, R3 to the third, and R4 to the fourth. R2 represents the first constraint, R3 the second, and so on.

Question Are any materials unused in the solution?

Answer Yes. We can tell this by looking in the SLACK OR SURPLUS section in the center of the printout. R2 is 52.000000; this indicates 52 pounds a day of Material A will be unused by this solution.

Question What do the values in the REDUCED COST section represent?

Answer They indicate the amount by which each variable's unit profit would have to increase in order for that variable to be profitable enough to produce it. Hence, the profit on x_1 would have to increase by at least $10.60 a unit in order to make it profitable to produce it. The other two variables have REDUCED COSTS of 0.000000 because they are already included in the optimal solution.

Question What do the DUAL PRICES represent? How are they useful?

Answer They are the shadow prices for the constraints. For instance, Material A (R2) has a shadow price of zero, and Material B (R3) has a shadow price of $2.40. The shadow price tells us how much the optimal value of the objective function would increase if one additional unit of that resource (e.g., 1 pound per day) was available. The shadow price for Material A is zero because the optimal solution leaves some of this resource unused; the shadow price for Material B is nonzero because it is a binding constraint.

Question Does this mean that if 100 pounds per day of Material B were made available above the 200 pounds now available, profit would increase by $240?

(continues)

MANAGER DIALOGUE (*continued*)

Answer Not necessarily. The shadow price is only valid for a change in the amount of a resource such as Material B that is within the range of feasibility.

Question Does the printout tell us what range of feasibility is?

Answer From the information provided in the last section of the printout, we can easily determine the range of feasibility for each constraint. Note that the CURRENT RHS column shows the right-hand side amounts that were used to obtain the current solution. The next two columns indicate the amount that each of these values can be increased and decreased without exceeding the range of feasibility of the shadow prices. For instance, Material A has no upper limit, and can be decreased to 210 − 52 = 158. Hence, its range of feasibility is 158 to infinity. Similarly, Material B has a range of feasibility of 200 − 30 = 170 to 200 + 70.91 = 270.91, and Material C has a range of 170 − 120 = 50 to 170 + 30 = 200 pounds per day.

Question What does the OBJ COEFFICIENT RANGES section tell me?

Answer It enables you to determine the range of optimality for the objective function coefficient of each variable, which is the amount by which *one* of the coefficients can change without changing the optimal values of x_1, x_2, or x_3. For instance, the coefficient of x_3 can change from its CURRENT COEF value of 14 by as much as the ALLOWABLE INCREASE of 36 to 14 + 36 = 50, or decrease by as much as the ALLOWABLE DECREASE of 1.5 from 14 to 12.5 without causing the current optimal solution to change. The range of optimality for the coefficients of each of the other variables can be determined in the same way. Note, however, that x_1 has a value of zero in the optimal solution. An alternate term that is sometimes used for such variables in the *range of insignificance.* The range of x_1 is found by adding the ALLOWABLE INCREASE to the CURRENT COEF: 15 + 10.6 = 25.6. That is, as long as the profit per unit on x_1 is less than 25.60, x_1 will have a value of zero in the optimal solution, assuming all other values remain unchanged.

Question Does sensitivity analysis permit multiple changes, say changes to more than one RHS value, or is it strictly limited to one change?

Answer Generally speaking, sensitivity analysis can be applied when only one change is contemplated. However, in some instances, multiple changes can be handled, if certain requirements are met. Basically, there are two requirements. One is that all changes be of the same type (e.g., all changes involve RHS values). The other is that they meet what is sometimes called the 100 percent rule. In effect, each change is measured as a percentage of its ALLOWABLE INCREASE or DECREASE and then the percentages for all changes are added. If their sum does not exceed 100 percent, sensitivity analysis of the sort we have been discussing is permissible.

(concluded)

```
MAXIMIZE

OBJ      )   15 X1 + 20 X2 + 14 X3

SUBJECT TO

R2       )   5 X1 + 6 X2 + 4 X3 < = 210

R3       )   10 X1 + 8 X2 + 5 X3 < = 200

R4       )   4 X1 + 2 X2 + 5 X3 < = 170

END

                 LP OPTIMUM FOUND AT STEP 3

                 OBJECTIVE FUNCTION VALUE

1)                       548.0000

     VARIABLE            VALUE            REDUCED COST

     X1                0.000000            10.600000
     X2                5.000000             0.000000
     X3               32.000000             0.000000

     ROW          SLACK OR SURPLUS         DUAL PRICES

     R2   )           52.000000             0.000000
     R3   )            0.000000             2.400000
     R4   )            0.000000             0.400000

NO. ITERATIONS = 3

           RANGES IN WHICH THE BASIS IS UNCHANGED

                  OBJ COEFFICIENT RANGES

VARIABLE     CURRENT        ALLOWABLE        000.000000
              COEF          INCREASE          DECREASE

X1          15.000000       10.600000        15.000000
X2          20.000000        2.400000        10.600000
X3          14.000000       36.000000         1.500000

                  RIGHT-HAND SIDE RANGES
ROW          CURRENT        ALLOWABLE        ALLOWABLE
               RHS          INCREASE          DECREASE

R2          210.000000        INFINITY        52.000000
R3          200.000000       70.909091        30.000000
R4          170.000000       30.000000       120.000000
```

Multiple Changes

Up until this point, the discussion of sensitivity analysis has been restricted to cases that involve *one* change of either a coefficient of an objective function or the RHS value of a constraint. Ranges of optimality for objective function coefficients and ranges of feasibility for RHS values of constraints were said to be applicable to a change in one parameter only; multiple changes (e.g., values of two or more objective function coefficients are changed, or values of two or more of the RHS amounts of constraints are changed) were not discussed. Let us now address that issue.

In certain instances, the impact of multiple changes can be readily evaluated. It begins with a determination of the ranges of optimality (if objective function changes are involved) or a determination of the ranges of feasibility (if RHS values are involved). That reveals the amount that each parameter is allowed to change (the ALLOWABLE INCREASE or the ALLOWABLE DECREASE) and still be within the range of optimality or the range of feasibility. Next, a set of specific changes is analyzed by computing the percentage of the ALLOWABLE INCREASE or ALLOWABLE DECREASE that each change represents. For instance, suppose we want to evaluate multiple changes that involve two objective function coefficients, and we determine that the first coefficient's change would be 20 percent of its ALLOWABLE INCREASE and the second coefficient's change would be 40 percent of its ALLOWABLE INCREASE. As long as the total of these percentages does not exceed 100 percent, the impact of the combined changes will be very similar to the result of a single change that falls within its range of optimality. That is, the original optimal values of all basis variables will remain the same,[1] but the optimal value of the objective function would change, taking into account the new coefficients of the objective function.

Similarly, if, say, three RHS values were to be changed, and we determined that the first change would constitute an increase that was 30 percent of the ALLOWABLE INCREASE for that constraint's RHS, the second was an increase of 30 percent of *its* ALLOWABLE INCREASE, and the third was 30 percent of *its* ALLOWABLE *DECREASE,* the sum of these would be 90 percent (note that the percentages are *added* even though two are for increases and one for a decrease). Because the sum of the percentages does not exceed 100 percent, the changes satisfy the 100 percent requirement. In the case of RHS changes, this means that the shadow prices remain the same. Consequently, the impact on the optimal value of the objective function can be determined by taking into account the combined effects of RHS changes and the corresponding shadow prices. Similarly, revised Quantity values can be computed using values from the original final tableau.

---

[1] If the total percentage *equals* 100 percent, an alternate optimal solution may cause the optimal Quantity values to change.

■

EXAMPLE 5 Let us consider how the solution to the microcomputer problem would be affected by multiple changes to *either* its objective function coefficients *or* the RHS values of its constraints. Let's consider these changes:

1. A change in the objective function from maximize $60x_1 + 50x_2$ to maximize $70x_1 + 55x_2$.
2. A change in the RHS of the inspection constraint from 22 to 23 hours and a change in the storage constraint from 39 to 36 cubic feet.

Solution

(Values for ALLOWABLE INCREASES and DECREASES are taken from the printout shown in Table 6–8.)

1. The change in the x_1 coefficient is +10 (60 to 70) and the change in the x_2 coefficient is + 5. The ALLOWABLE INCREASE for the x_1 coefficient is 40; hence, the percentage increase is 10/40 = 25 percent. The ALLOWABLE INCREASE for the x_2 coefficient is 10; hence, its percentage increase is 5/10 = 50 percent. The total change is 25 percent + 50 percent = 75 percent. Because the total does not exceed 100 percent, it is within the range of sensitivity. Therefore, we can say that the optimal values of s_1, x_1, and x_2 remain the same as in the original problem. However, the optimal value of Z will increase by the sum of the increase in the x_1 coefficient multiplied by the optimal value of x_1 and the increase in the x_2 coefficient multiplied by the optimal value of x_2. Thus, the increase will be: 10(9) + 5(4) = 110; the new value will be 740 + 110 = 850.
2. The percentage change for each of the constraints would be:

Inspection	(23 − 22)/4.00 = 25 percent
Storage	(36 − 39)/6 = −50 percent

The total change would be 75 percent (treat the percentages as absolute values). Because this does not exceed 100 percent, it is within the range of sensitivity. Consequently, the shadow prices (10.00 and 13.33) do not change. The optimal value of Z will change. The amount of change will be:

$$+1(10.00) - 3(13.33) = -30$$

Hence, the optimal value of Z will be 740 − 30 = 710.

We can also compute revised value for the *decision variables* by using the substitution rates in the original final tableau (see Table 6–7).

	s_2	s_3
x_1	1	−⅓
x_2	−1	⅔

	Original quantity		Inspection change		Storage change		Revised quantity
x_1	9	+	1(1)	−	3(−⅓)	=	11
x_2	4	+	1(−1)	−	3(⅔)	=	1

The revised value of the slack variable (x_1) is not computed in this way. Instead, its value can be found by substituting the revised optimal values of the decision variables into the first constraint. Thus:

$$\text{Assembly} \quad 4x_1 + 10x_2 + s_1 = 100$$
$$4(11) + 10(1) + s_1 = 100$$

Solving, $s_1 = 46$.

Summary of Sensitivity Analysis

Sensitivity analysis is an extension of linear programming that goes beyond finding the optimal solution to a problem. It enables managers to answer "what if . . . ?" questions related to potential changes to parameters of a model.

The discussion pertained to two types of changes: changes to objective function coefficients and changes to the RHS values of constraints. Sensitivity analysis is always appropriate for situations in which *one* such change is being contemplated; multiple changes require changes to satisfy the 100 percent rule.

Sensitivity analysis can be performed using a computer package, or by performing simple computations using the information contained in the optimal simplex tableau.

Table 6–9 provides a summary of the impact of a change that falls within the range of optimality or within the range of feasibility.

DUALITY

Every linear programming problem can have two forms. The original formulation of a problem is referred to as its **primal** form. The other form is referred to as its **dual** form. As you will see, the dual is kind of a "mirror image" of the primal because in both its formulation and its solution, the values of the dual are flip-flop versions of the primal values.

The solution to the primal problem contains the solution to the dual problem, and vice versa. Consequently, once either the primal or the dual problem has been solved, the solution to the other is also apparent. You might wonder, then, why we even bother to discuss duality. The answer is mainly in the economic interpretation of the results of the dual solution. Analysis of the dual can enable a manager to evaluate the potential impact of a new product, and it can be used to

TABLE 6–9 Summary of Results of Changes That Are within Ranges

Objective Function Coefficient Change within the Range of Optimality

Factor	Result
Variables in solution	Same variables still in solution
Optimal values of solution variables	Don't change
Optimal value of Z	Will change

RHS Change within the Range of Feasibility

Factor	Result
Shadow price	Remains the same
List of basic variables	Remains the same
Values of basic variables	Change
Optimal value of Z	Changes

determine the marginal values of resources (i.e., constraints). Relative to a new product, a manager would want to know what impact adding a new product would have on the solution quantities and the profit; relative to resources, a manager can refer to a dual solution to determine how much profit one unit of each resource is equivalent to. This can help the manager to decide which of several alternative uses of resources is most profitable.

Formulating the Dual

All of the problems formulated in the preceding chapters can be classified as primal problems because they were formulated directly from descriptions of the problem. The dual, on the other hand, is an alternate formulation of the problem that requires the existence of the primal. Let's now consider how the dual can be formulated from the primal problem.

Consider this primal problem:

minimize $\quad 40x_1 + 44x_2 + 48x_3$

subject to

$$\begin{aligned} 1x_1 + 2x_2 + 3x_3 &\geq 20 \\ 4x_1 + 4x_2 + 4x_3 &\geq 30 \\ x_1, x_2, x_3 &\geq 0 \end{aligned}$$

The dual of this problem is:

maximize $\quad 20y_1 + 30y_2$

TABLE 6–10 Transforming the Primal into Its Dual

	Primal			Dual		
Objective function and right-hand side values	minimize	$40x_1 + 44x_2 + 48x_3$		maximize	$20y_1 + 30y_2$	
	subject to			subject to		
	1		≥ 20	1		≤ 40
	2		≥ 30	2		≤ 44
				3		≤ 48
	Primal			**Dual**		
Constraint coefficients	1	$1x_1 + \ 2x_2 + \ 3x_3 \geq$		1	$1y_1 + \ 4y_2 \leq$	
	2	$4x + \ 4x_2 + \ 4x_3 \geq$		2	$2y_1 + \ 4y_2 \leq$	
				3	$3y_1 + \ 4y_2 \leq$	

subject to

$$
\begin{aligned}
1y + \ 4y_2 &\leq 40 \\
2y_1 + \ 4y_2 &\leq 44 \\
3y_1 + \ 4y_2 &\leq 48 \\
y_1, y_2 &\geq 0
\end{aligned}
$$

A comparison of these two versions of the problem will reveal why the dual might be termed the "mirror image" of the primal. Table 6–10 shows how the primal problem is transformed into its dual.

We can see in Table 6–10 that the original objective was to minimize, whereas the objective of the dual is to maximize. In addition, the coefficients of the primal's objective function becomes the right-hand side values for the dual's constraints, whereas the primal's right-hand side values become the coefficients of the dual's objective function.

Note that the primal has three decision variables and two constraints, whereas the dual has two decision variables and three constraints.

The constraint coefficients of the primal are constraint coefficients of the dual, except that the coefficients of the first "row" of the primal become the coefficients of the first "column" of the dual, and the coefficients of the second "row" of the primal become the coefficients of the second "column" of the dual.

Finally, note that the $\geq$ constraints of the primal become $\leq$ constraints in the dual.

When the primal problem is a *maximization* problem with all $\leq$ constraints, the dual is a *minimization* problem with all $\geq$ constraints, as the next example illustrates.

EXAMPLE 6 Formulate the dual of the microcomputer problem.

Solution

The original (primal) problem was:

maximize $60x_1 + 50x_2$

subject to

$$\begin{aligned} 4x_1 + 10x_2 &\le 100 \\ 2x_1 + 1x_1 &\le 22 \\ 3x_1 + 3x_2 &\le 39 \end{aligned}$$

To formulate the dual, we can follow this sequence:

1. For the objective function:
   a. Because the primal is a maximization, the dual will be a minimization.
   b. The right-hand side values for the constraints become the coefficients of the objective function of the dual.
   Thus, the objective function of the dual is:

   minimize $100y_1 + 22y_2 + 39y_3$

   The variable names are *ys* for the dual, simply to differentiate them from the primal variables. There will be one dual variable for each constraint.
2. For the constraints:
   a. There will be one dual constraint for each primal decision variable. Hence, because the primal has two such variables, the dual will have two constraints.
   b. The right-hand side values of the dual constraints will equal the primal's objective function coefficients taken in order. That is, the right-hand side value of the first dual constraint will equal the first coefficient of the primal's objective function coefficient, and the right-hand side value of the second dual constraint will equal the second objective function coefficient of the primal.
   c. The coefficients of the first primal constraint will become the first coefficients in each of the dual constraints: The x_1 coefficient in the first primal constraint becomes the y_1 coefficient in the first dual constraint and the x_2 coefficient in the first primal constraint becomes the y_1 coefficient in the second dual constraint, and so on.
   Thus, the constraints of the dual are:

   1 $4y_1 + 2y_3 + 3y_3 \ge 60$
   2 $10y_1 + 1y_2 + 3y_3 \ge 50$

Putting these two parts together, the dual of the microcomputer problem is:

minimize $100y_1 + 22y_2 + 39y_3$

subject to

1 $4y_1 + 2y_2 + 3y_3 \geq 60$

2 $10y_1 + 1y_2 + 3y_3 \geq 50$

$y_1, y_2, y_3 \geq 0$

Formulating the Dual When the Primal Has Mixed Constraints

In order to transform a primal problem into its dual, it is easier if all constraints in a maximization problem are of the $\leq$ variety, and in a minimization problem, every constraint is of the $\geq$ variety.

To change the direction of a constraint, multiply both sides of the constraint by -1. For example:

$$-1(2x_1 + 3x_2 \geq 18) \text{ is } -2x_1 - 3x_2 \leq -18$$

If a constraint is an equality, it must be replaced with *two* constraints, one with a $\leq$ sign and the other with a $\geq$ sign. For instance:

$$4x_1 + 5x_2 = 20$$

will be replaced by

$$4x_1 + 5x_2 \leq 20$$
$$4x_1 + 5x_2 \geq 20$$

Then one of these must be multiplied by -1, depending on whether the primal is a maximization or a minimization problem.

■

EXAMPLE 7 Formulate the dual of this problem:

maximize $50x_1 + 80x_2$

subject to

$$3x_1 + 5x_2 \leq 45$$
$$4x_1 + 2x_2 \geq 16$$
$$6x_1 + 6x_2 = 30$$
$$x_1, x_2 \geq 0$$

Solution

Since this is a maximization problem, put constraints into the $\leq$ form.

The first constraint is already in that form. The second constraint can be converted to that form by multiplying both sides by -1. Thus:

$$-1(4x_1 + 2x_2 \geq 16) \text{ becomes } -4x_1 - 2x_2 \leq -16$$

The third constraint is an equality, and must be restated as two separate constraints. Thus, it becomes:

$$6x_1 + 6x_2 \leq 30 \text{ and } 6x_1 + 6x_2 \geq 30$$

The second of these two must now be multiplied by -1, which yields:

$$-6x_1 - 6x_2 \leq -30$$

Hence, the form of the primal is:

maximize $\quad 50x_1 + 80x_2$

subject to

$$\begin{aligned} 3x_1 + 5x_2 &\leq 45 \\ -4x_1 - 2x_2 &\leq -16 \\ 6x_1 + 6x_2 &\leq 30 \\ -6x_1 - 6x_2 &\leq -30 \\ x_1, x_2, &\geq 0 \end{aligned}$$

The dual is:

minimize $\quad 45y_1 - 16y_2 + 30y_3 - 30y_4$

subject to

$$\begin{aligned} 3y_1 - 4y_2 + 6y_3 - 6y_4 &\geq 50 \\ 5y_1 - 2y_2 + 6y_3 - 6y_4 &\geq 80 \\ y_1, y_2, y_3, y_4 &\geq 0 \end{aligned}$$

Comparison of the Primal and Dual Simplex Solutions

The flip-flopping of values between the primal and the dual carries over to their final simplex tableaus. Table 6–11 contains the final tableau for the dual and Table 6–12 contains the final tableau for the primal.

The primary concern with a simplex solution is often threefold:

1. Which variables are in solution?

TABLE 6–11 Final Tableau of *Dual* Solution to the Microcomputer Problem

Basis	C	100	22	39	0	0	M	M	
		y_1	y_2	y_3	s_1	s_2	a_1	a_2	Quantity
y_3	39	16/3	0	1	1/3	−2/3	−1/3	2/3	40/3
y_2	22	−6	1	0	−1	1	1	−1	10
	Z	76	22	39	−9	−4	9	4	740
	C − Z	24	0	0	9	4	9 − M	4 − M	

←Primal shadow prices

Primal solution quantities

TABLE 6–12 Final Tableau of *Primal* Solution to the Microcomputer Problem

Basis	C	60	50	0	0	0	
		x_1	x_2	s_1	s_2	s_3	Quantity
s_1	0	0	0	1	6	−16/3	24
x_1	60	1	0	0	1	−1/3	9
x_2	50	0	1	0	−1	2/3	4
	Z	60	50	0	10	40/3	740
	C − Z	0	0	0	−10	−40/3	

2. How much of each variable is in the optimal solution?
3. What are the shadow prices for the constraints?

Let's consider how we can obtain the answers to these questions from the dual solution. Notice that the *solution quantities* of the dual are equal to the *shadow prices* of the primal (i.e., 40/3 and 10). Next, notice that values of the solution quantities of the primal (i.e., 24, 9, and 4) can be found in the bottom row of the dual. Now, in the primal solution, s_1 equals 24. In the dual, the 24 appears in the y_1 column. The implication is that a slack variable in the primal solution becomes a real variable (i.e., a decision variable) in the dual. The reverse is also true: A real variable in the primal solution becomes a slack variable in the dual. Therefore, in the primal solution, we have $x_1 = 9$ and $x_2 = 4$; in the dual, 9 appears under s_1 in the bottom row and 4 appears under s_2. Thus, we can read the solution to the primal problem from the bottom row of the dual: In the first three columns of the dual, which equate to slack variables of the primal, we can see that the first slack equals 24 and the other two are zero. Under the dual's slack columns, we can read

TABLE 6–13 Cross-Referencing Primal and Dual Values in the Final Tableaus

Primal	How Labeled/ Where Found in the *Primal*	Correspondence in the *Dual*
Decision variable	$x_1, x_2, x_3, \ldots$	$s_1, s_2, s_3 \ldots$
Slack variable	$s_1, s_2, s_3, \ldots$	$y_1, y_2, y_3 \ldots$
Shadow price	*Z* row under slack columns	Quantity column in *decision variable* rows
Solution quantities	Quantity column	$C - Z$ row under slack and decision variable columns

the values of the primal's decision variables. In essence, then, the *variables* of the primal problem become the *constraints* of the dual problem, and vice versa.

The way in which primal and dual values are cross-referenced is summarized in Table 6–13.

Economic Interpretation of the Dual

In order to fully appreciate the correspondence between the primal and dual formulations of a problem, we shall now focus on the economic interpretation of the dual, using the microcomputer problem for purposes of illustration.

Suppose the microcomputer firm has been approached by a representative of a department store chain that wants the firm to make computers that will be sold under the store's brand name. The microcomputer company has only a limited capacity for producing computers, and therefore, must, decide whether to produce its own computers or produce computers for the department store.

For convenience, the original problem is repeated here:

x_1 = number of Model 1s

x_2 = number of Model 2s

maximize $\quad 60x_1 + 50x_2$

subject to

Assembly time	$4x_1 + 10x_2 \leq 100$
Inspection time	$2x_1 + 1x_2 \leq 22$
Storage space	$3x_1 + 3x_2 \leq 39$

The manager of the firm would reason in the following way: For each unit of Model 1 that the firm sacrifices to produce computers for the department store, it will gain 4 hours of assembly time, 2 hours of inspection time, and 3 cubic feet of storage space, which can be applied to the store computers. However, it will also give up a unit profit of \$60. Therefore, in order for the firm to realistically consider the store's offer, the amounts of scarce resources that will be given up must produce a return to the firm that is at least equal to the foregone profit. Hence, the value of 4 assembly hours + 2 inspection hours + 3 cubic feet of storage space should be ≥ \$60. By similar reasoning, giving up one unit of Model 2 will require that the value received by giving up 10 assembly hours + 1 inspection hour + 3 cubic feet of storage must equal or exceed the Model 2 profit of \$50 per unit. These, then, become the constraints of the dual problem. Thus:

Value Received per Unit of	Resources Freed Up	Minimum Profit Required
Model 1	$4y_1 + 2y_2 + 3y_3$	\$60
Model 2	$10y_1 + 1y_2 + 3y_3$	\$50

Hence, the constraints of the dual refer to the *value* of capacity (i.e., the scarce resources). The formulation indicates that in order to switch from the making units of Models 1 and 2 to making computers for the department store, the value received from that switch must be at least equal to the profit foregone on the microcomputer models. The variables y_1, y_2, and y_3 are the *marginal values* of scarce resources 1 (assembly time), 2 (inspection time), and 3 (storage space). Solving the dual will tell us the *imputed* values of the resources given our optimal solution.

Naturally, the department store would want to *minimize* the use of the scarce resources, because the computer firm almost certainly would base its charges on the amount of resources required. Consequently, the objective function for the dual problem focuses on minimizing the use of the scarce resources. Thus:

$$\text{minimize} \quad 100y_1 + 22y_2 + 39y_3$$

Looking at the optimal solution to the dual of the microcomputer problem (see Table 6–11), we can see the marginal values of y_2 and y_3 in the Quantity column, but not the value of y_1. This is because the optimal solution to the primal did not completely use up all of the assembly capacity. Consequently, no amount of either x_1 or x_2 would need to be given up to obtain one free hour of assembly time. Thus, the marginal value of one hour of assembly time is \$0.

Finally, the optimal dual solution always yields the same value of the objective function as the primal optimal. In this case, it is 740. The interpretation is that the imputed value of the resources that are required for the optimal solution equals the amount of profit that the optimal solution would produce.

Adding Another Variable

The concepts introduced in the preceding section also can be applied to evaluating the feasibility of adding another decision variable to the problem. For example, suppose the microcomputer firm is considering a third model of microcomputer that will yield a profit of \$70 per unit, and this will require resource requirements of 8 hours of assembly time, 4 hours of inspection time, and 5 cubic feet of storage space per unit. The dual constraint for this model would be:

$$8y_1 + 4y_2 + 5y_3 \geq 70$$

In order to determine if this new variable would come into the optimal (primal) solution, we can substitute the dual solution of $y = 0$, $y_2 = 10$, and $y_3 = 40/3$ (i.e., the *shadow prices,* or marginal values of the resources) into this constraint to see if it would be satisfied. Thus, we find, $8(0) + 4(10) + 5(40/3) = 106.67$. Because this amount is greater than the new dual constraint, *the original solution remains optimal*. Hence, the new variable (x_3) would not come into solution. Conversely, if the dual constraint has not been satisfied, the new variable would have come into solution. In this instance, the marginal value of scarce resources that would be required for the new model exceeds the marginal contribution to profit that the new model would provide. That is, \$106.67 > \$70.

The value of this approach is that it is not necessary to rework the entire problem in order to test the potential impact that adding a new decision variable would have on the optimal solution.

SUMMARY

This chapter discusses analysis of linear programming problems that use the optimal simplex solution as a starting point. The primary purpose of such analysis is to provide the decision maker with greater insight about the sensitivity of the optimal solution to changes in various parameters of a problem. Such changes might involve the specified levels of constraints or coefficients of the objective function. Interest in changes may arise due to improved information relating to a problem or because of the desire to know the potential impact of changes that are contemplated.

The chapter also discusses the concept of the dual, which is an alternate formulation of the LP problem. Either the original problem or its dual can be solved to determine the optimal solution. Awareness of the dual provides increased insight into LP problems. In particular, the dual variables have a different economic interpretation than the original decision variables. Further, the dual formulation can be easily used to determine if the addition of another variable to a problem will change the optimal solution mix.

GLOSSARY

Dual An alternate form of a linear programming problem.

Postoptimality Analysis Analysis of an LP solution to determine how sensitive the solution would be to possible changes in the various parameters of the original problem.

Primal The original formulation of an LP problem.

Range of Feasibility The range over which the right-hand side value of a constraint can change without changing the optimal solution mix of a problem.

Range of Insignificance The range over which the coefficient of a nonbasic decision variable can change without that variable coming into solution.

Range of Optimality The range over which the objective function coefficient of a variable that is in solution can change without causing the quantity values of the optimal solution to change.

Sensitivity Analysis See **Postoptimality Analysis.**

Shadow Price Indicates the impact on the value of the objective function that would result from a one-unit change in the right-hand side value of a constraint. Found in the slack or surplus columns in row Z of a simplex tableau.

SOLVED PROBLEMS

Problem 1. Given this LP model and its final simplex tableau:

maximize $10x_1 + 6x_2 + 5x_3$

subject to

$$2x_1 + 3x_2 + 4x_3 \leq 25$$
$$x_1 + 3x_2 + 2x_3 \leq 22$$
$$6x_1 + 3x_2 + 4x_3 \leq 32$$
$$x_1, x_2, x_3 \geq 0$$

Basis	C	10 x_1	6 x_2	5 x_3	0 s_1	0 s_2	0 s_3	Quantity
s_1	0	0	0	8/5	1	−4/5	−1/5	1
x_2	6	0	1	8/15	0	2/5	−1/15	6⅔
x_1	10	1	0	2/5	0	−1/5	1/5	2
	Z	10	6	36/5	0	2/5	8/5	60
	$C - Z$	0	0	−11/5	0	−2/5	−8/5	

a. Determine the range of feasibility for each RHS (i.e., original right-hand side value).

b. Determine the range of optimality for the coefficients of the decision variables that are in solution.

c. By how much would the objective function coefficient of x_3 have to increase before it would come into solution? What is the range of insignificance for x_3?

Solution

a. The *range of feasibility* refers to the range over which the RHS value of a constraint can be changed without changing the shadow price for that particular constraint.

The shadow price for the first constraint is 0 because s_1 is in solution. Therefore, the first constraint is slack ($s_1 = 1$ in the Quantity column). A constraint that is slack can be increased forever because any increase means that it will have even more slack. It can be decreased by 1 (the amount of slack), before it becomes a binding constraint. Hence, its range of feasibility is from 24 (i.e., 25 − 1) to $+\infty$.

For variables that are not in solution, such as s_2 and s_3 (note the nonzero values in row $C - Z$), the range of feasibility determination involves dividing the substitution rates in the s_2 and s_3 columns into the corresponding Quantity column values. Thus:

s_2 $\quad \dfrac{1}{-4/5} = -5/4 \text{ or } -1.25$ $\qquad$ s_3 $\quad \dfrac{1}{-1/5} = -5$

$\dfrac{6\frac{2}{3}}{2/5} = \dfrac{20/3}{2/5} = 16.67$ $\qquad$ $\dfrac{6\frac{2}{3}}{-1/15} = \dfrac{20/3}{-1/15} = -100$

$\dfrac{2}{-1/5} = -10$ $\qquad$ $\dfrac{2}{1/5} = +10$

In each case, we are interested in the smallest positive and smallest negative ratios. For s_2, the smallest negative ratio is -1.25 and the smallest (only) positive ratio is 16.67. For s_3, the smallest negative ratio is -5, and the (only) positive ratio is $+10$. The negative ratio indicates the *increase* needed to equal the upper end of the range of feasibility, and the positive ratio indicates the amount of *decrease* needed to equal the lower end of the range. Therefore, for the second constraint, we find:

Upper end = 22 + 1.25 = 23.25
Lower end = 22 − 16.67 = 5.33 $\qquad$ Range: 5.33 to 23.25

For the third constraint, we find:

Upper end = 32 + 5 = 37
Lower end = 32 − 10 = 22 $\qquad$ Range: 22 to 37

Thus, the range of feasibility for each constraint is:

Constraint	Current Value	Range of Feasibility
1	25	24 to $+\infty$
2	22	5.33 to 23.25
3	32	22 to 37

b. Decision variables x_2 and x_1 are in solution (they are listed in the *basis*). In each case, we must divide the substitution rates in the *row* that pertains to the variable in question into the corresponding values in the $C - Z$ row. For x_2 we find:

$$\frac{C - Z\text{ row}}{x_2\text{ row}}: \quad \frac{0}{0} = \text{und.} \quad \frac{0}{1} = 0 \quad \frac{-11/15}{8/15} = -1.375 \quad \frac{0}{0} = \text{und.} \quad \frac{-2/5}{2/5} = -1 \quad \frac{-8/5}{-1/15} = +24$$

where und. = undefined.
For x_1 we find:

$$\frac{C - Z\text{ row}}{x_1\text{ row}}: \quad \frac{0}{1} = 0 \quad \frac{0}{0} = \text{und.} \quad \frac{-11/5}{2/5} = -5.5 \quad \frac{0}{0} = \text{und.} \quad \frac{-2/5}{-1/5} = +2 \quad \frac{-8/5}{1/5} = -8$$

In each case, the smallest negative ratio (i.e., negative ratio closest to zero) will indicate the allowable *decrease* and the smallest positive ratio will indicate the allowable *increase*. For x_2, the ratios are -1 and $+24$. Thus, the x_2 coefficient of 6 in the objective function can be decreased by as much as 1 or increased by as much as 24. The range optimality for the x_2 coefficient in the objective function, therefore, is:

$$(6 - 1 = 5) \quad \text{to} \quad (6 + 24 = 30)$$

For x_1, the ratios are -5.5 and $+2$. Therefore, the range of optimality for x_1 is:

$$(10 - 5.5 = 4.5) \quad \text{to} \quad (10 + 2 = 12)$$

Thus, the range of optimality for each variable that is in solution is:

Variable	Range of Optimality
x_1	4.5 to 12
x_2	5 to 30

c. For variables that are not in solution, such as x_3 in this example, their contribution per unit (coefficient in the objective function) is too small (in a maximization problem) to cause them to have an optimal value that is nonzero. However, if the objective function coefficient is *increased* by more than the value in the variable's column in the $C - Z$ row ($^{11}/_{15}$ for x_3), and the original model solved using that value, the variable would come into solution. Hence, the answer is that the x_3 coefficient would have to be increased by more than $^{11}/_{5}$ or 2.2 in order to bring s_3 into solution. Thus, its coefficient must be more than 5 + 2.2 or 7.2 for it to come into solution. Therefore, its range of significance is ≤ 7.2.

Problem 2. (Refer to Solved Problem 1.) Manager Tom Oakley is considering making multiple changes to the original model. For each set of changes, decide (1) if the impact of the changes can be determined without re-solving the entire problem and (2) if so, determine revised values for the Quality column, including the optimal value of the objective function.

a. Increase every RHS value by 1.

b. Increase the objective function coefficient of x_1 by 1 and decrease the objective function coefficient of x_2 by 1.

c. Increase the objective function coefficient of x_1 by .80 and decrease the objective function coefficient of x_2 by .50.

Solution

a. Using the feasibility ranges for RHS changes from Solved Problem 1:

Constraint	RHS	Range of Feasibility
1	25	24 to +infinity
2	22	5.33 to 23.25
3	32	22 to 37

There is no limit on the first constraint, so we can ignore that increase. (Generally, there would be no benefit in increasing the RHS of a constraint that is currently slack.) The second constraint's increase as a percentage of the ALLOWABLE INCREASE would be 1/1.25 = 80 percent; the third constraint's percentage increase would be 1/5 = 20 percent. (Note: The 5 in the last computation is the difference between the 37 upper limit of the range of feasibility and the current RHS value of 32.) The sum of these two percentages is 100 percent. It just satisfies the requirement that the sum of the percentage changes must not exceed 100 percent. Therefore, the proposed changes are *within* the acceptable range.

The revised values of the *decision variables* that appear in the basis can be computed using the current Quantity values and substitution rates given in the final simplex tableau in the previous problem:

Basis	s_1	s_2	s_3	Quantity
x_2	0	2/5	−1/15	6 2/3
x_1	0	−1/5	1/5	2
Z	0	2/5	8/5	60

The revised values are:

Row	Amount of change: +1 s_1	+1 s_2	+1 s_3	Current quantity		Revised quantity
x_2	1(0) +	1(2/5) +	1(−1/15) +	6 2/3	=	7
x_1	1(0) +	1(−1/5) +	1(1/5) +	2	=	2
Z	1(0) +	1(2/5) +	1(8/5) +	60	=	62

To determine the revised Quantity for s_1, substitute the revised optimal values for x_1 and x_2 into the original constraint 1, which is:

$$2x_1 + 3x_2 + 4x_3 + s_1 = 25$$

Thus:

$$2(2) + 3(7) + 4(0) + s_1 = 25$$

Solving, $s_1 = 0$.

b. The ranges of optimality were determined in Solved Problem 1:

Variable	Current Value	Range of Optimality
x_1	10	4.5 to 12
x_2	6	5 to 30

Increasing the x_1 coefficient from 10 to 11 would be an increase of 50 percent of the ALLOWABLE INCREASE: 1/2 = 50 percent. Decreasing the x_2 coefficient by 1 would be 100 percent of the ALLOWABLE DECREASE: 1/1 = 100 percent. The total percentage would be 50 percent + 100 percent = 150 percent; this would exceed the 100 percent limitation. Consequently, these two changes would cause a change in the optimal solution quantities.

c. Increasing the objective function coefficient of x_1 by .80 would constitute 40 percent of its ALLOWABLE INCREASE, as determined in part (*b*). Decreasing the objective function coefficient of x_2 by .50 would constitute 50 percent of its ALLOWABLE DECREASE. The total percentage would be 90 percent. Because this total is less than the 100 percent limitation, the optimal values of variables in solution will not change. However, the *profit* will change. To find out what the revised profit would be, we can multiply the optimal quantities by their respective objective function changes and then adjust the optimal value of the objective function accordingly. Thus, with $x_1 = 2$ and $x_2 = 6\frac{2}{3}$, and $\Delta c_1 = .80$ and $\Delta c_2 = -.50$, we have:

$$\Delta Z = .80(2) - .50(6\tfrac{2}{3}) = -1.733$$

The revised value of Z is then:

$$Z' = 60 - 1.733 = 58.267$$

Problem 3. (Refer to Solved Problem 1.) The manager of the department for which the LP model was formulated would like to know the answers to certain questions:

a. If one additional unit of the third constraint could be obtained at the same cost as the previous units (so that the profits per unit in the objective function did not change), what impact would this have on profit?

Solution

The shadow price for the third constraint is $\frac{8}{5}$. Therefore, for one additional unit, profit would increase by $\frac{8}{5}$ or \$1.60.

b. If one additional unit of the third resource (constraint) could be obtained at a *premium* of \$.50, what impact would this have on profit?

Solution
The premium must be deducted from the shadow price. Hence, the net impact would be \$1.60 − \$.50 = \$1.10.

c. If 4 units of the third resource were obtained at the original cost per unit, what impact would this have on the optimal values in the Quantity column?

Solution
First, we must check to see if the specified change is within the range of feasibility. An additional 4 units would make the RHS of the third constraint 32 + 4 = 36; the upper end of the range of feasibility for the third constraint is 37 (see Solved Problem 1). Hence, the change is within the range of feasibility. Therefore, the new values can easily be computed using the substitution values in the s_3 column.

Row	Current Quantity		Additional Resource	×	s_3 Column		New Quantity
s_1	1	+	4	×	$(-1/5)$	=	1.8
x_2	6.67	+	4	×	$(-1/15)$	=	6.4
x_1	2	+	4	×	$(1/5)$	=	2.8
Z	60	+	4	×	$(8/5)$	=	66.4

d. What would happen if the RHS of the third constraint was increased from 32 to 39?

Solution
The upper end of the range of feasibility is 37. Any resource beyond that would be slack. Consequently, an increase from 32 to 39 units means that only 5 units could be used; 2 units would be left over. Consequently, s_3 would appear in the solution, and it would have a value of 2 in the Quantity column. Profit would increase to 60 + 5(8/5), rather than 60 + 7(8/5), because only 5 units could be used.

PROBLEMS

1. Sensitivity analysis can provide a decision maker with additional insights about a linear programming solution.
   a. Explain in general terms what sensitivity analysis accomplishes.
   b. Why might sensitivity analysis be useful to a decision maker?
   c. List the three types of parameters that sensitivity analysis might focus on. Which two are covered in this chapter?

2. Briefly define or explain each of these terms:
   a. Shadow price.
   b. Range of feasibility.
   c. Range of optimality.
   d. Range of insignificance.

3. Given this final tableau:

Basis	C	20 x_1	12 x_2	0 s_1	0 s_2	0 s_3	Quantity
x_2	12	0	1	½	−3/2	0	15
x_1	20	1	0	0	1	0	50
s_3	0	0	0	−½	3/2	1	35
	Z	20	15	6	2	0	1,180
	C − Z	0	0	−6	−2	0	

   a. Identify the shadow prices, and indicate the constraint with which each shadow price is associated.
   b. Interpret each shadow price.

4. The LP model for the preceding solution was:

   maximize $20x_1 + 12x_2$

   subject to

   1 $3x_1 + 2x_2 \leq 180$ (Raw material 1)
   2 $x_1 \leq 50$ (Raw material 2)
   3 $x_2 \leq 50$ (Raw material 3)

   a. Determine the range of feasibility for raw material 1 and interpret your answer.
   b. Determine the range of feasibility for raw material 2 and interpret your answer.
   c. Determine the range of feasibility for raw material 3 and interpret your answer.
   d. Which of these two possible changes would have the greater impact on the value of the objective function in the final solution?
   (1) Increase the second constraint by 10 units.
   (2) Increase the third constraint by 40 units.

5. Determine the range of optimality (or the range of insignificance, if appropriate) for the coefficient of each decision variable in Problem 3.

6. Given the following final tableau:

Basis	C	9 x_1	6 x_2	0 s_1	0 s_2	Quantity
x_1	9	1	0	1/12	−5/12	20
x_2	6	0	1	0	1	72
	Z	9	6	9/12	27/12	612
	$C - Z$	0	0	−9/12	−27/12	

a. Identify the shadow prices and indicate the constraint with which each shadow price is associated.

b. Interpret each shadow price.

7. The constraints for the preceding problem were:

1 $\quad 12x_1 + 5x_2 \leq 600$ hours
2 $\quad x_2 \leq 72$ hours

a. Determine the range of feasibility for the first constraint and interpret your answer.

b. Determine the range of feasibility for the second constraint and interpret your answer.

c. If the first constraint was revised to 450 hours, what impact would that have on the solution quantities and the value of Z?

8. (Refer to the solution shown in Problem 6.) Determine the range of optimality for each coefficient of the objective function.

9. Given the following LP problem and the final tableau for its simplex solution:

maximize $\quad 11x_1 + 10x_2 + 14x_3$

subject to

A $\quad 4x_2 - 1x_3 \leq 0$
B $\quad 5x_1 + 2x_2 + 5x_3 \leq 72$
C $\quad x_1 \leq 13$

Basis	C	11 x_1	10 x_2	14 x_3	0 s_1	0 s_2	0 s_3	Quantity
x_2	10	.227	1	0	.227	.045	0	3.27
x_3	14	.909	0	1	−.091	.182	0	13.09
s_3	0	1	0	0	0	0	1	13.00
	Z	15	10	14	1	3	0	215.96
	$C - Z$	−4	0	0	−1	−3	0	

a. Determine the range of feasibility for each of the constraints and interpret each range.

b. Determine the range of insignificance, or the range of optimality (whichever is appropriate), for each of the variables in the objective function.

10. Suppose that constraint A in the previous problem will be changed to 10. Determine the impact that this change would have on the following:

a. The quantities.

b. The value of the objective function.

11. (Refer to Problem 9.) Answer these questions concerning changes in the objective function coefficients:

a. By how much would the contribution of variable x_1 have to change, and in which direction, before x_1 would come into solution?

b. If the coefficient of variable x_2 were to increase by 5, what impact would this have on the value of the objective function?

c. If the coefficients of variables x_2 and x_3 were each decreased by 2, would that be within the range of sensitivity for multiple changes? If so, what would the values in the Quantity column be?

12. (Refer to Problem 9.) Suppose the RHS value of constraint A was 10 and the RHS value of constraint B was 80. Would this be within the range of sensitivity for multiple changes? If so, what would the values in the Quantity column be?

13. The manager of FGH, a small manufacturer of horseback riding accessories, has received a staff report that contains an LP model and final simplex tableau:

F = quantity of Product F
G = quantity of Product G
H = quantity of Product H

maximize $15F + 20G + 14H$

subject to

A $5F + 6G + 4H \leq 210$ pounds
B $10F + 8G + 5H \leq 200$ minutes
C $4F + 2G + 5H \leq 170$ square feet
$F, G, H \geq 0$

Basis	C	15 F	20 G	14 H	0 s_1	0 s_2	0 s_3	Quantity
s_1	0	−2.6	0	0	1	−.73	−.07	52
G	20	1	1	0	0	.17	−.17	5
H	14	.4	0	1	0	−.07	.27	32
	Z	25.6	20	14	0	2.40	.40	548
	$C - Z$	−10.6	0	0	0	−2.40	−.40	

Help the manager interpret each of the following:

a. The meaning of the 2.40 in row Z of the final tableau.

b. The meaning of the -10.6 in row $C - Z$.

c. The meaning of the 25.6 in row Z.

14. (Refer to Problem 13.)

a. What is the range of optimality for the 20 in the objective function? Interpret your result (i.e., what values do not change within this range?).

b. How would the value of Z change if the 20 in the objective function were decreased by 10? Increased by 2?

c. What is the range of feasibility for constraint A? Interpret your answer.

d. What is the range of feasibility for the RHS of the last constraint?

e. What would the values in the Quantity column be if the last constraint were increased by 20 units?

f. What Z would result if the RHS of the last constraint was 210?

15. The manager of a knitting department has developed the following LP model and optimal solution.

x_1 = units of Product 1
x_2 = units of Product 2
x_3 = units of Product 3

maximize $7x_1 + 3x_2 + 9x_3$ (profit)

subject to

Labor	$4x_1 + 5x_2 + 6x_3 \le 360$ hours
Machine	$2x_1 + 4x_2 + 6x_3 \le 300$ hours
Material	$9x_1 + 5x_2 + 6x_3 \le 600$ pounds
	x_1, x_2, and $x_3, \ge 0$

Basis	C	7 x_1	3 x_2	9 x_3	0 s_1	0 s_2	0 s_3	Quantity
x_1	7	1	0	0	−.2	0	.20	48
x_3	9	0	.83	1	.3	0	−.13	28
s_2	0	0	−1	0	−1.4	1	.40	36
	Z	7	7.5	9	1.3	0	.2	588
	$C - Z$	0	−4.5	0	−1.3	0	−.2	

a. Why isn't any Product 2 called for in the optimal solution? How much would the per unit profit of Product 2 have to be in order for it to enter into the optimal solution mix?

b. What is the range of optimality for the profit per unit of Product 1?

c. What would the values in the Quantity column be if the objective coefficient of x_1 were to increase by 3?

d. What is the range of feasibility of the labor constraint?

e. What would the values in the Quantity column be if the amount of labor available decreased by 10 hours?

f. If the manager could obtain additional material, how much more could be used effectively? What would happen if the manager obtained more than this amount?

16. (Refer to Problem 15.) The manager has some additional questions relative to the optimal solution:

a. If it is possible to obtain an additional amount of *one* of the resources, which one should be obtained, and how much can be effectively used? Explain.

b. If the manager is able to obtain an additional 100 pounds of material at the usual price, what impact would that have on the optimal value of the objective function?

c. If the manager is able to obtain an additional 100 pounds of material, but has to pay a premium of 5 cents a pound, what will the net profit be?

d. If knitting machines operate for 10 hours a day, and one of the machines will be out of service for two and a half days, what impact will this have on the optimal value of Z?

17. The A-B-C department of a large company makes three products (A, B, and C). The department is preparing for its final run next week, which is just before the annual two-week vacation during which the entire department shuts down. The manager wants to use up existing stocks of the three raw materials used to fabricate A, B, and C.

She has formulated the LP model and obtained optimal solutions:

A = quantity of Product A
B = quantity of Product B
C = quantity of Product C

maximize $12A + 15B + 14C$

subject to

Material 1	$3A + 5B + 8C \leq 720$ pounds
Material 2	$2A + 3C \leq 600$ pounds
Material 3	$4A + 6B + 4C \leq 640$ pounds
	A, B, and $C \geq 0$

Basis		12 A	15 B	14 C	0 s_1	0 s_2	0 s_3	Quantity
C	14	0	.1	1	.2	0	−.15	48
s_2	0	0	−3.1	0	−.2	1	−.35	232
A	12	1	1.4	0	−.2	0	.40	112
	Z	12	18.2	14	.4	0	2.7	2,016
	C − Z	0	−3.2	0	−.4	0	−2.7	

As a staff person, the manager has asked you to answer each of the following questions concerning the final solution:

a. Although Product B is the most profitable, and Product A the least profitable, the solution calls for making none of B but 112 of A. Why?

b. If B's profit per unit could be increased to $18, how much B would be produced? Explain how you obtained your answer.

c. What is the range of feasibility for the Material 3 RHS?

d. By how much would profit increase if an additional 100 pounds of material 3 could be obtained at its usual cost? What if the amount were an additional 400 pounds?

e. Do you see any difficulty in allowing the X-Y-Z department to take 200 pounds of material 2? Explain.

f. What would the values in the Quantity column be if 20 additional pounds of Material 1 could be obtained without paying a premium for it?

g. Suppose the manager wants to evaluate the effect of cost changes that would reduce each of the objective function coefficients by 1. Would these changes be within the range of sensitivity for multiple changes? If so, what would the optimal values in the Quantity column be?

h. If the manager can obtain an additional 20 pounds of Materials 1 and 3, is that within the range of sensitivity? If so, what would the optimal values in the Quantity column be?

18. The manager in the microcomputer problem (See Table 6–5) is considering scheduling overtime in either the assembly or the inspection departments.

a. Which department would be the best choice for overtime? Why?

b. Suppose overtime will cost $7 per hour over the current rate. Does it make sense to schedule overtime? If so, how much overtime, and what effect would there be on total profit by scheduling this overtime?

19. Given this problem and its final tableau:

minimize $10x_1 + 3x_2$

subject to

1 $2x_1 + 1x_2 \geq 80$

2 $2x_1 + 4x_2 \geq 200$

Basis	C	10 x_1	3 x_2	0 s_1	0 s_2	Quantity
s_2	0	6	0	−4	1	120
x_2	3	2	1	−1	0	80
	Z	6	3	−3	0	240
	C − Z	4	0	3	0	

Determine the range of feasibility for each of the constraints.

20. For the preceding problem, determine the range of optimality or the range of insignificance (whichever is appropriate) for each decision variable.

21. Given this problem and its final simplex tableau:

minimize $20x_1 + 12x_2 + 16x_3$

subject to

1 $x_1 + x_2 \geq 25$

2 $x_2 - x_3 = 0$

3 $x_3 \leq 5$

Basis	C	20 x_1	12 x_2	16 x_3	0 s_1	0 s_3	Quantity
x_1	20	1	0	1	−1	0	25
x_2	12	0	1	−1	0	0	0
s_3	0	0	0	1	0	1	5
	C	20	12	8	−20	0	500
	C − Z	0	0	8	20	0	

a. What impact on the solution would a decrease of 10 units in the first constraint have?

b. If the first constraint could be decreased 10 units at a cost per unit of \$15, would it be worthwhile to do so? Explain.

c. What change in the coefficient of x_3 in the objective function would cause it to come into solution?

d. If the cost coefficient of x_1 increased by \$5, what impact would that have on the quantities and on the value of the objective function in the final tableau?

22. The manager in the microcomputer problem analyzed in this chapter wants to reconsider adding a third computer model to the product line. After re-evaluating the third model, the manager now estimates that it will yield a profit of \$80 per unit, with resource requirements of 7 hours of assembly

time, 3 hours of inspection time, and 5 cubic feet of storage space. Determine if the third model would come into the solution.

23. For the preceding problem, given the resources requirements specified, what is the lowest profit that would cause the third model to come into solution?

24. (Refer to Problems 3 and 4.) It has been proposed that a new product be added. The manager has two possibilities, x_3 and x_4. Their resource requirements and unit contributions to profits would be:

	Raw Material Requirements			
Product	**1**	**2**	**3**	**Unit Profit**
x_3	2	—	1	15
x_4	—	4	1	10

If the manager decides to add a product, she must select only one of these, due to marketing considerations. Should one of these be added, or would it be better to produce only x_1 and x_2? Explain.

25. The manager of the department depicted in Problem 9 would like to know if a fourth variable would have a positive impact on profits. The new variable would have resource requirements of 3 units for B and a profit per unit of $12. Determine if the new variable would come into solution and, if so, what impact there would be on profits.

26. What is a dual problem? How is the dual useful?

27. Formulate the dual of this problem:

minimize $5x_1 + 7x_2 + 9x_3$

subject to

1 $20x_1 + 10x_2 + 30x_3 \geq 300$

2 $40x_1 + 5x_2 + 10x_3 \geq 200$

$x_1, x_2, x_3 \geq 0$

Which problem would you prefer to solve, the primal or the dual? Why?

28. Solve the dual of the previous problem. Interpret your solution in terms of the primal problem: What does the optimal (graphical) dual solution tell you?

29. Formulate the dual of this problem, but do not solve it:

maximize $30x_1 + 50x_2 + 40x_3$

subject to

1	$5x_1 + 7x_2 + 3x_3 \leq 1{,}000$
2	$4x_1 + 6x_2 + 8x_3 \leq 1{,}200$

$$x_1, x_2, x_3 \geq 0$$

30. As noted in this chapter, it is possible to extract information about either the primal or its dual from the other one's final simplex tableau. Suppose you have the final tableau for the dual of a certain problem. Indicate where in that tableau you would find each of the following pieces of information:

a. An indication of which variables are in solution.

b. The quantities for the variables in solution.

c. The shadow prices for the slack variables.

31. (Refer to Problem 19.) Suppose we want information about the dual.

a. What values would be in the quantity column of the dual?

b. What values would be in the $C - Z$ row of the dual?

c. What variables would be in solution in the dual?

32. Formulate the dual of the model given in Problem 3.

33. The manager of the Happy Dog Company, Sam Smart, has developed this LP model:

x_1 = quantity of regular blend
x_2 = quantity of extra blend
x_3 = quantity of puppy delite

maximize $.20x_1 + .18x_2 + .25x_3$

subject to

K9	$\frac{1}{3}x_1 + \frac{1}{2}x_2 \leq 1{,}500$ pounds
K8	$\frac{1}{3}x_1 + \frac{1}{4}x_2 + \frac{1}{10}x_3 \leq 1{,}000$ pounds
K1	$\frac{1}{3}x_1 + \frac{1}{4}x_2 + \frac{9}{10}x_3 \leq 1{,}000$ pounds

$$x_1, x_2, x_3 \geq 0$$

The final tableau for the model is:

Basis	C	.20 x_1	.18 x_2	.25 x_3	0 s_1	0 s_2	0 s_3	Quantity
x_2	.18	0	1	−3.6	4	0	−4	2,000
s_2	0	0	0	−.8	0	1	−1	0
x_1	.20	1	0	5.4	−3	0	6	1,500
	Z	.2	.18	.432	.12	0	.48	660
	$C - Z$	0	0	−.182	−.12	0	−.48	

a. What is the marginal value of a pound of K9? Over what range is that value valid?

b. By how much would profit decrease if there was one less pound of K1 available?

c. The manager believes it is possible to increase the profit per pound of puppy delite to $.40. Would that alter the optimal solution? Explain.

d. If the profit per unit of the extra blend dropped to $.16 a pound, would the optimal quantities of the variables in solution change? Would the optimal value of the objective function change? If so, what would its new value be?

e. If the unit profits were changed to .22 for regular blend, .20 for extra blend, and .26 for puppy delite, would these changes be within the range of sensitivity for multiple changes? If so, would that cause any of the values in the Quantity column to change? Explain.

34. A firm makes four products. Each product requires material, labor, and machine time. A linear programming model has been developed to describe the situation:

maximize $12x_1 + 10x_2 + 15x_3 + 11x_4$ (profit)

subject to

Material	$5x_1 + 3x_2 + 4x_3 + 2x_4 \leq 240$ pounds
Machine	$6x_1 + 8x_2 + 2x_3 + 3x_4 \leq 240$ hours
Labor	$2x_1 + 3x_2 + 3x_3 + 2x_4 \leq 180$ hours
	$x_1, x_2, x_3 \geq 0$

where

x_1 = quantity of Product 1
x_2 = quantity of Product 2
x_3 = quantity of Product 3
x_4 = quantity of Product 4

The optimal solution for this model is:

	C	12	10	15	11	0	0	0	
Basis		x_1	x_2	x_3	x_4	s_1	s_2	s_3	Quantity
x_3	15	−1.2	−1.4	1	0	0	−.4	.6	12
s_1	0	4.2	1.4	0	0	1	.4	−1.6	48
x_4	11	2.8	3.6	0	1	0	.6	−.4	72
	Z	12.8	18.6	15	11	0	.6	4.6	972
	C − Z	−.8	−8.6	0	0	0	−.6	−4.6	

a. The manager is concerned because none of Product 1 is called for in the optimal solution. At what profit per unit would Product 1 come into solution?

b. What is the marginal value of an hour of machine time? Over what range of machine time is this amount valid?

c. The manager can secure additional labor hours by the use of overtime. This involves paying a premium of $2 per hour. How much overtime can be effectively used, and what will the *net* total profit be in that amount of overtime is scheduled?

d. Using the original model, if the manager was able to secure another 40 hours of machine time, what would the revised Quantity values be?

e. Using the original model, if the manager was able to obtain an additional 10 hours of machine time and an additional 10 hours of labor, what would the revised Quantity values be?

35. A garden store prepares various grades of pine bark for mulch: nuggets (x_1), mini-nuggets (x_2), and chips (x_3). The process requires pine bark, machine time, labor time, and storage space. The following linear programming model has been developed:

maximize $9x_1 + 9x_2 + 6x_3$ (profit)

subject to

Bark	$5x_1 + 6x_2 + 3x_3 \le 600$ pounds
Machine	$2x_1 + 4x_2 + 5x_3 \le 660$ minutes
Labor	$2x_1 + 4x_2 + 3x_3 \le 480$ hours
Storage	$1x_1 + 1x_2 + 1x_3 \le 150$ bags
	$x_1, x_2, x_3 \ge 0$

In addition, this optimal tableau was obtained:

	C	9	9	6	0	0	0	0	
Basis		x_1	x_2	x_3	s_1	s_2	s_3	s_4	Quantity
x_1	9	1	1.5	0	.5	0	0	−1.5	75
s_2	0	0	3.5	0	1.5	1	0	−9.5	135
s_3	0	0	2.5	0	.5	0	1	−4.5	105
x_3	6	0	−.5	1	−.5	0	0	2.5	75
	Z	9	10.5	6	1.5	0	0	1.5	1,125
	C − Z	0	−1.5	0	−1.5	0	0	−1.5	

a. What is the marginal value of a pound of pine bark? Over what range is this value appropriate?

b. What is the maximum price the store would be justified in paying for additional pine bark?

c. What is the marginal value of labor? Over what range is this value in effect?

d. The manager obtained additional machine time through better scheduling. How much additional machine time can be effectively used for this operation? Why?

e. If the manager can obtain *either* additional pine bark *or* additional storage space, which one should be chosen and how much should be obtained (assuming additional quantities cost the same as usual)?

f. If a change in the chip operation would increase the profit on chips from \$6 per bag to \$7 per bag, would the optimal quantities change? Would the value of the objective function change? If so, what would the new value(s) be?

36. A firm produces jars of chilled fruit that are sold to restaurants. Three varieties of fruit are sold: California mix (x_1), Florida mix (x_2), and Hawaiian mix (x_3). A linear programming model for the process is:

$$\begin{array}{lrl} \text{maximize} & 4x_1 + 3x_2 + 6x_3 & \text{(profit)} \\ \text{subject to} & & \\ \quad \text{Oranges} & 3x_1 + 2x_2 + 1x_3 \le & 920 \text{ pounds} \\ \quad \text{Grapefruit} & 2x_1 + 2x_2 + 2x_3 \le & 900 \text{ pounds} \\ \quad \text{Pineapple} & 1x_1 + 2x_2 + 3x_3 \le & 930 \text{ pounds} \\ \quad \text{Peeling/cutting} & 1.2x_1 + 1.4x_2 + 1.5x_3 \le & 1{,}260 \text{ minutes} \\ \quad \text{Mixing/packaging} & 1x_1 + 2x_2 + 1x_3 \le & 600 \text{ minutes} \\ & x_1, x_2, x_3 \ge 0 & \end{array}$$

The optimal tableau for this model is:

Basis	C	4 x_1	3 x_2	6 x_3	0 s_1	0 s_2	0 s_3	0 s_4	0 s_5	Quantity
s	0	0	0	0	1	−2	1	0	0	50
x_1	4	1	.50	0	0	.75	−.50	0	0	210
x_3	6	0	.50	1	0	−.25	.50	0	0	240
s_4	0	0	.05	0	0	−.53	−.15	1	0	648
s_5	0	0	1	0	0	−.50	0	0	1	150
	Z	4	5	6	0	1.5	1	0	0	2,280
	$C - Z$	0	−2	0	0	−1.5	−1	0	0	

a. The equipment used for peeling and cutting must be replaced. The new equipment will have a capacity of only 1,200 minutes. What impact will this change have on the optimal values of the basis variables and on profit?

b. What would the unit profit on the Florida mix have to be before it would become profitable to produce?

c. If management had a choice of obtaining more oranges or more pineapples, which one should be chosen? Why?

d. Management has just learned that an additional 50 pounds of pineapple are on hand. What will the optimal values in the Quantity column change to?

e. Management is considering making changes that will cause the profit on the Hawaiian mix to be $8 per unit. Would this affect the solution? Will it affect the optimal value of the objective function?

f. Management is considering a change in equipment that would result in increasing the profit on the Hawaiian mix to $8 per unit, but result in decreasing the profit on the California mix by $1. Would these changes be within the range of sensitivity? If so, how much would the optimal profit change?

37. Use a computer package to perform sensitivity analysis on the LP model given in Problem 33, and then use that information to answer the questions listed in Problem 33.

38. Use a computer package to perform sensitivity analysis on the LP model given in Problem 34, and then use those results to answer parts (*a*)–(*c*) of Problem 34.

39. Use a computer package to perform sensitivity analysis on the LP model given in Problem 35, and then use the results to answer the questions for that problem.

40. Use a computer package to perform sensitivity analysis on the LP model given in Problem 36, and then use the results to answer the questions (except ***d***) for that problem.

41. Special D, Inc., is a new firm that is engaged in recycling. Its main facility uses a three-step system to process beverage containers. A consultant has developed the following LP model of the process:

maximize $14Q + 11R + 15T$ (revenue)

subject to

Sorting	$2.4Q + 3.0R + 4.0T \le 960$ minutes
Crushing	$2.5Q + 1.8R + 2.4T \le 607$ minutes
Packing	$12Q + 18R + 24T \le 3{,}600$ minutes

$$Q, R, \text{ and } T \ge 0$$

The consultant has also included a computer printout of postoptimality analysis:

```
MAXIMIZE

OBJ          14 Q +  11 R +  15 T

SUBJECT TO

R2          2.4 Q + 3.0 R + 4.0 T <=   960

R3          2.5 Q + 1.8 R + 2.4 T <=   607

R4           12 Q +  18 R +  24 T <=  3600

END

                         LP OPTIMUM FOUND AT STEP 3

                         OBJECTIVE FUNCTION VALUE

1)                            3485.000000

VARIABLE                        VALUE            REDUCED COST

Q                            190.000000              0.000000
R                              0.000000              0.250000
T                             55.000000              0.000000

ROW                       SLACK OR SURPLUS        DUAL PRICES

R2                           284.000000              0.000000
R3                             0.000000              5.000000
R4                             0.000000              0.125000

NO. OF ITERATIONS = 3

                   RANGES IN WHICH THE BASIS IS UNCHANGED

                         OBJ COEFFICIENT RANGES

VARIABLE          CURRENT          ALLOWABLE          ALLOWABLE
                  COEF             INCREASE           DECREASE

Q                 14.000000         1.625000           6.500000
R                 11.000000         0.250000          11.000000
T                 15.000000        13.000000           0.333333

                              RIGHT-HAND SIDE RANGES

ROW               CURRENT          ALLOWABLE          ALLOWABLE
                    RHS            INCREASE           DECREASE

R2               960.000000         INFINITY          284.000000
R3               607.000000       143.000000          247.000000
R4              3600.000000      2089.810000          686.400000
```

Answer these questions using this information:

a. Which variables are in the basis? What are their optimal values?

b. Find the range of optimality for the variables that are in the basis.

c. Find the range of insignificance for *R*.

d. Identify the shadow price for each constraint.

e. Determine the range over which each shadow price is valid.

f. By how much would revenue decrease if sorting time was reduced to 900 minutes? How much would revenue increase if sorting time was increased to 1,269 minutes?

g. What effect would an increase of $2 in the revenue per unit of *T* have on the optimal value of *T*? On the total revenue?

h. Would an increase of $1 in the revenue per unit of *R* have any impact on the optimal solution? Explain.

i. If you could obtain additional quantities of one resource (either sorting, crushing, or packing) at no additional cost, and your goal was to achieve the greatest increase in revenue, which resource would you add, and how much of it would you add? Explain.

42. Fashion Designs produces four clothing products in one of its factories. The following LP model has been developed and solved using a standard LP package.

x_1 = weekly quantity of slacks
x_2 = weekly quantity of dresses
x_3 = weekly quantity of skirts
x_4 = weekly quantity of blouses

maximize $15x_1 + 15x_2 + 12x_3 + 16x_4$ (profit)

subject to

Cutting	$x_1 + 2x_2 + 4x_3 + x_4$	$\leq$ 800 hours per week
Sewing	$4x_1 + 2x_2 + 3x_4$	$\leq$ 700 hours per week
Inspecting	$2x_1 + 2x_2 + x_3 + x_4$	$\leq$ 600 minutes per week
Packing	$3x_1 + 2x_2 + 2x_3$	$\leq$ 660 minutes per week

$$x_1, x_2, x_3, x_4, \geq 0$$

```
MAXIMIZE

OBJ         15 X1 + 15 X2 + 12 X3 + 16 X4

SUBJECT TO

R2          1 X1 + 2 X2 + 4 X3 + 1 X4 <= 800

R3          4 X1 + 2 X2          + 3 X4 <= 700
```

```
R4          2 X1 + 2 X2 + 1 X3 + 1 X4 <= 600

R5          3 X1 + 2 X2 + 2 X3        <= 660

END

                 LP OPTIMUM FOUND AT STEP 5

                 OBJECTIVE FUNCTION VALUE

1)                     5508.333333

     VARIABLE             VALUE            REDUCED COST

     X1                  0.000000            20.583333
     X2                225.000000             0.000000
     X3                 66.666666             0.000000
     X4                 83.333333             0.000000

     ROW             SLACK OR SURPLUS      DUAL PRICES

     R2                  0.000000             2.916666
     R3                  0.000000             4.250000
     R4                  0.000000             0.333333
     R5                 76.666666             0.000000

NO. ITERATIONS = 5

              RANGES IN WHICH THE BASIS IS UNCHANGED

                 OBJ COEFFICIENT RANGES

     VARIABLE     CURRENT       ALLOWABLE       ALLOWABLE
                  COEF          INCREASE        DECREASE

     X1           15.000000      5.583333       15.000000
     X2           15.000000     11.666666        0.333333
     X3           12.000000      1.000000        8.750000
     X4           16.000000      0.500000        6.700000

                 RIGHT-HAND SIDE RANGES

                 OBJ COEFFICIENT RANGES

     ROW          CURRENT       ALLOWABLE       ALLOWABLE
                  RHS           INCREASE        DECREASE

     R2          800.000000    460.000000      200.000000
     R3          700.000000    900.000000      153.333333
     R4          600.000000     57.500000      225.000000
     R5          660.000000     INFINITY        76.666666
```

a. Which departments have capacities that limit output? Explain.

b. The plant manager is considering scheduling overtime. Is there any department or departments that should be excluded from consideration? Why?

c. What is the marginal value of overtime scheduled in the cuttting department? How much overtime could be effectively used?

d. Overtime costs the company a premium of $3 per hour over regular costs. If one department is scheduled for overtime, which one should be scheduled, and how much overtime can be effectively used? What would the revised optimal value of the objective function be, including an allowance for the premium?

e. If the unit profit on x_3 dropped by 50 percent, how would that affect the optimal values of the decision variables and the optimal value of the objective function?

f. What would the profit per unit on slacks have to be before the company would want to begin producing them?

43. Serious Toys, Unlimited, produces three types of building blocks for preschoolers. Recently, the company underwent a major reorganization of its manufacturing facility and a restructuring of its prices. As a result, a new LP model has been formulated to describe the situation:

A = number of advanced sets
B = number of beginner sets
C = number of intermediate sets

maximize $1.2A + 1.6B + 1.4C$ (profit)

subject to

Plastic	$6A + 5B + 3C \leq 300$	pounds per hour
Labor	$9A + 4B + 5C \leq 280$	minutes per hour
Machine	$2A + 8B + 4C \leq 320$	minutes per hour
	$A, B, C \geq 0$	

The model has been processed through a computer package, with this output:

```
MAXIMIZE

OBJ             1.2 A  +  1.6 B  +  1.4 C

SUBJECT TO

R2              6 A  +  5 B  +  3 C <= 300

R3              9 A  +  4 B  +  5 C <= 280

R4              2 A  +  8 B  +  4 C <= 320

END
```

LP OPTIMUM FOUND AT STEP 3

OBJECTIVE FUNCTION VALUE

1) 88.000000

VARIABLE	VALUE	REDUCED COST
A	0.000000	0.800000
B	20.000000	0.C00000
C	40.000000	0.000000

ROW	SLACK OR SURPLUS	DUAL PRICES
R2	80.000000	0.000000
R3	0.000000	0.200000
R4	0.000000	0.100000

NO. ITERATIONS = 3

RANGES IN WHICH THE BASIS IS UNCHANGED

OBJ COEFFICIENT RANGES

VARIABLE	CURRENT COEF	ALLOWABLE INCREASE	ALLOWABLE DECREASE
A	1.200000	0.800000	1.200000
B	1.600000	0.740000	0.480000
C	1.400000	0.600000	0.300000

RIGHT-HAND SIDE RANGES

ROW	CURRENT RHS	ALLOWABLE INCREASE	ALLOWABLE DECREASE
R2	300.000000	INFINITY	80.000000
R3	280.000000	120.000000	120.000000
R4	320.000000	96.000000	147.690000

a. How would you interpret the DUAL PRICE of 0.200000 for R3?

b. What is the range of feasibility for the RHS of the labor constraint?

c. If the amount of labor available were to increase by 60 minutes per hour, would the optimal quantities of the decision variables change? Would the optimal profit change?

d. If machine time increased by 50 minutes per hour, by how much would profit increase?

e. If machine time increased by 100 minutes per hour, by how much would profit increase?

f. How much would another 10 pounds of plastic per hour be worth in terms of increased profit? Explain.

g. If the profit per unit on advanced sets increased by 70 percent, would that affect the optimal solution? Explain.

44. Dog Daze Manufacturing produces a variety of dog food products. These are made in batches, and then kept in inventory that is used to fill orders from kennels and pet stores. The manager has helped to develop an LP model of the process for the company's three raw material inputs: x_1, x_2, x_3:

x_1 = bags of Raw material 1
x_2 = bags of Raw material 2
x_3 = bags of Raw material 3

minimize $38x_1 + 19x_2 + 60x_3$ (cost)

subject to

$$\begin{array}{lrl} \text{Protein} & 2.5x_1 + 4x_2 + 3x_3 \geq 794 & \text{pounds} \\ \text{Fiber} & 3x_1 + 2x_2 + 4x_3 \geq 300 & \text{pounds} \\ \text{Fat} & 2x_1 + x_2 + 2x_3 \geq 600 & \text{pounds} \\ & x_1, x_2, x_3 \geq 0 & \end{array}$$

The manager has obtained a computer printout of sensitivity analysis for the model:

```
MINIMIZE

OBJ              38 X1 + 19 X2 + 60 X3

SUBJECT TO

R2              2.5 X1 + 4 X2 + 3 X3 >= 794

R3                3 X1 + 2 X2 + 4 X3 >= 300

R4                2 X1 + 1 X2 + 2 X3 >= 600

END

                    LP OPTIMUM FOUND AT STEP 6

                    OBJECTIVE FUNCTION VALUE

1)                       11400.000000

     VARIABLE                  VALUE          REDUCED COST

     X1                   292.000000              0.000000
     X2                    16.000000              0.000000
     X3                     0.000000            -22.000000

     ROW              SLACK OR SURPLUS         DUAL PRICES

     R2                     0.000000              0.000000
     R3                   608.000000              0.000000
     R4                     0.000000            -19.000000
```

RANGES IN WHICH THE BASIS IS UNCHANGED

OBJ COEFFICIENT RANGES

VARIABLE	CURRENT COEF	ALLOWABLE INCREASE	ALLOWABLE DECREASE
X1	38.00000	24.200000	26.220000
X2	19.00000	41.800000	19.000000
X3	60.00000	INFINITY	22.000000

RIGHT-HAND SIDE RANGES

ROW	CURRENT RHS	ALLOWABLE INCREASE	ALLOWABLE DECREASE
R2	794.000000	1606.000000	44.000000
R3	300.000000	608.000000	INFINITY
R4	600.000000	35.200000	401.500000

Use the printout to answer these questions about the model:

a. Which constraints are binding on the solution? How do you know?

b. What does the REDUCED COST of −22.000000 indicate?

c. How do you interpret the 608.000000 in the SLACK OR SURPLUS section?

d. Determine the range of optimality for the objective function coefficients of x_1 and x_2.

e. What does the DUAL PRICE of −19.000000 reveal?

f. What is the range of feasibility for the last constraint's RHS?

g. Would a decrease to 575 for the RHS of the last constraint affect the optimal value of the objective function? If so, by how much?

h. The manager is considering reducing each RHS by 6 percent, and may ask you to provide information on how that would impact the total cost. If you are asked, what would you need to do? Why?

Chapter 6 Case

Red Brand Canners

On Monday, September 13, Mr. Mitchell Gordon, Vice President of Operations, asked the Controller, the Sales Manager, and the Producation Manager to meet with him to discuss the amount of tomato products to pack that season. The tomato crop, which had been purchased at planting, was beginning to arrive at the cannery, and packing operations would have to be started by the following Monday. Red Brand Canners was a medium-sized company that canned and distributed a variety of fruit and vegetable products under private brands in the western states.

Mr. William Cooper, the Controller, and Mr. Charles Myers, the Sales Manager, were the first to arrive in Mr. Gordon's office. Dan Tucker, the Production Manager, came in a few minutes later and said that he had picked up Produce Inspection's latest estimate of the quality of the incoming tomatoes. According to their report, about 20 percent of the crop was Grade A quality, and the remaining portion of the 3-million pound crop was Grade B.

Gordon asked Myers about the demand for tomato products for the coming year. Myers replied that they could sell all of the whole canned tomatoes they could produce. The expected demand for tomato juice and tomato paste, on the other hand, was limited. The Sales Manager then passed around the latest demand forecast, which is shown in Table 1. He reminded the group that the selling prices had been set in light of the long-term marketing strategy of the company and that the potential sales had been forecast at these prices.

Bill Cooper, after looking at Myers' estimates of demand, said that it looked like the company ''should do quite well [on the tomato crop] this year.'' With the new accounting system that had been set up, he had been able to compute the contribution for each product, and according to his analysis the incremental profit on the whole tomatoes was greater than the incremental profit on any other tomato product. In May, after Red Brand had signed contracts agreeing to purchase the grower's production at an average delivered price of 6 cents per pound, Cooper had computed the tomato products' contributions (see Table 2).

Dan Tucker brought to Cooper's attention that although there was ample production capacity, it was impossible to produce all whole tomatoes since too small a portion of the tomato crop was ''A'' quality. Red Brand used a numerical scale to record the quality of both raw produce and prepared products. This scale ran from 0 to 10, the higher number representing better quality. According to this scale, ''A'' tomatoes averaged 9 points per pound and ''B'' tomatoes averaged 5 points per pound. Tucker noted that the minimum average input quality was 8 points per pound for canned whole tomatoes and 6 points per pound for juice. Paste could be made entirely from ''B''-grade tomatoes. This meant that whole tomato production was limited to 800,000 pounds.

TABLE 1 Demand Forecasts

Product	Selling Price per Case	Demand Forecast (cases)
24—2½ whole tomatoes	$4.00	800,000
24—2½ choice peach halves	5.40	10,000
24—2½ peach nectar	4.60	5,000
24—2½ tomato juice	4.50	50,000
24—2½ cooking apples	4.90	15,000
24—2½ tomato paste	3.80	80,000

TABLE 2 Product Item Profitability

Product	24—2½ Whole Tomatoes	24—2½ Choice Peach Halves	24—2½ Peach Nectar	24—2½ Tomato Juice	24—2½ Cooking Apples	24—2½ Tomato Paste
Selling price	$4.00	$5.40	$ 4.60	$ 4.50	$4.90	$3.80
Variable costs						
Direct labor	1.18	1.40	1.27	1.32	0.70	0.54
Variable overhead	0.24	0.32	0.23	0.36	0.22	0.26
Variable selling	0.40	0.30	0.40	0.85	0.28	0.38
Packaging material	0.70	0.56	0.60	0.65	0.70	0.77
Fruit*	1.08	1.80	1.70	1.20	0.90	1.50
Total variable costs	3.60	4.38	4.20	4.38	2.80	3.45
Contribution	0.40	1.02	0.40	0.12	1.10	0.35
Less allocated overhead	0.28	0.70	0.52	0.21	0.75	0.23
Net profit	0.12	0.32	(0.12)	(0.09)	0.35	0.12

* Product usage is as given below:

Product	Pounds per Case
Whole tomatoes	18
Peach halves	18
Peach nectar	17
Tomato juice	20
Cooking apples	27
Tomato paste	25

TABLE 3 Marginal Analysis of Tomato Products

Z = cost per pound of Grade A tomatoes in cents
Y = cost per pound of Grade B tomatoes in cents

$$(600{,}000 \text{ lb} \times Z) + (2{,}400{,}000 \text{ lb} \times Y) \quad (3{,}000{,}000 \text{ lb} \times 6) \qquad (1)$$

$$\frac{Z}{9} = \frac{Y}{5} \qquad (2)$$

Z = 9.32 cents per pound
Y = 5.18 cents per pound

Product	Canned Whole Tomatoes	Tomato Juice	Tomato Paste
Selling price	$4.00	$4.50	$3.80
Variable cost (excluding tomato cost)	2.52	3.18	1.95
	$1.48	$1.32	$1.85
Tomato cost	1.49	1.24	1.30
Marginal profit	($0.01)	$0.08	$0.55

Gordon stated that this was not a real limitation. He had been recently solicited to purchase 80,000 pounds of grade A tomatoes at 8½ cents per pound and at that time had turned down the offer. He felt, however, that the tomatoes were still available.

Myers, who had been doing some calculations, said that although he agreed that the company "should do quite well this year," it would not be by canning whole tomatoes. It seemed to him that the tomato cost should be allocated on the basis of quality and quantity rather than by quantity only, as Cooper had done. Therefore, he had recomputed the marginal profit on this basis (see Table 3), and from his results had concluded that Red Brand should use 2,000,000 pounds of the "B" tomatoes for paste, and the remaining 400,000 pounds of "B" tomatoes and all of the "A" tomatoes for juice. If the demand expectations were realized, a contribution of $48,000 would be made on this year's tomato crop.

Discussion questions

1. Explain why each of these is incorrect:
   a. Bill Cooper's statement to "use the entire crop for whole tomatoes. . . ."
   b. Charles Myer's reasoning, as described in the final paragraph.
2. Formulate the mathematical model that can be used to determine the optimal canning policy for this season's crop. Disregard Mitchell Gordon's idea of purchasing additional tomatoes. Define the decision variables in terms of pounds of tomatoes.

3. Solve your model and interpret the solution.

4. Given the solution to your model, would you recommend the purchase of additional tomatoes (up to 80,000 pounds)? If so, how much should be purchased?

5. Using your answer to the preceding question, reformulate the model, solve the reformulated model, and indicate how the additional tomatoes will be used.

6. (Refer to the model of Question 3.) Suppose Bill Cooper has just learned that the cost of grade B tomatoes should actually be double its current amount (due to an accounting error). Will this change alter the optimal values of the decision variables? Explain. Will it alter the value of the objective function? Explain.

Chapter 7
Transportation and Assignment Problems

Chapter Outline

Learning Objectives

After completing this chapter, you should be able to:

1. Describe the nature of transportation and assignment problems.
2. Use the transportation method to solve problems manually.
3. Deal with special cases of transportation problems.
4. Solve transportation problems using a computer.
5. Use the assignment method to solve problems manually.
6. Deal with special cases of assignment problems.
7. Solve assignment problems using a computer.

Certain types of linear programming problems can be solved using special-purpose algorithms instead of using the simplex method. Prior to the widespread use of computers to solve LP problems, special-purpose algorithms were particularly useful because they enabled practitioners to obtain solutions to these special cases with much less computational burden than simplex would have required. Now, these special-purpose algorithms provide further insight into LP problems and their solutions.

This chapter describes two special-purpose algorithms: the *transportation model* and the *assignment model*. Model formulation, manual solution of models, and formatting models for computer solution are covered for each of these classes of problems. The discussion begins with the transportation method.

TRANSPORTATION PROBLEMS

The transportation model is usually applied to distribution-type problems, in which supplies of goods that are held at various locations are to be distributed to other receiving locations. For example, a company may have 10 warehouses that are used to supply 50 retail stores. Obviously, there are many different combinations of warehouse-store supply lines that could be used. Generally, some of these combinations will involve transportation costs that are higher than others. The purpose of using an LP model would be to identify a distribution plan that would minimize the cost of transporting the goods from the warehouses to the retail stores, taking into account warehouse supplies and store demands as well as transportation costs. Other examples of transportation problems include shipments from factories to warehouses, shipments between departments within a company, and production scheduling. Moreover, some companies use the transportation method to compare location alternatives (i.e., to decide where to locate factories and warehouses in order to achieve the minimum-cost distribution configuration).

Formulating the Model

A transportation problem typically involves a set of sending locations, which are referred to as *origins*, and a set of receiving locations, which are referred to as *destinations*. In order to develop a model of a transportation problem, it is necessary to have the following information:

1. Supply quantity (capacity) of each origin.
2. Demand quantity of each destination.
3. Unit transportation cost for each origin-destination route.

The transportation algorithm requires the assumption that all goods be homogeneous, so that any origin is capable of supplying any destination, and the assumption that transportation costs are a direct *linear* function of the quantity shipped over any route. We shall add one additional requirement that will simplify the problem: The total quantity available for shipment is equal to the total quantity demanded. Later in the chapter we shall see how the problem can be modified to handle cases where this assumption is not met.

Let's consider an example. Harley's Sand and Gravel Pit has contracted to provide topsoil for three residential housing developments. Topsoil can be supplied from three different "farms" as follows:

Farm	Weekly Capacity (cubic yards)
A	100
B	200
C	200

Demand for the topsoil generated by the construction projects is:

Project	Weekly Demand (cubic yards)
1	50
2	150
3	300

The manager of the sand and gravel pit has estimated the cost per cubic yard to ship over each of the possible routes:

	Cost per Cubic Yard to		
From	Project #1	Project #2	Project #3
Farm A	$4	$2	$8
Farm B	5	1	9
Farm C	7	6	3

This constitutes the information needed to solve the problem. The next step is to arrange the information into a transportation table. This is shown in Table 7–1. The origins (farms) are listed down the left side of the table, and their respective supply quantities are listed down the right side of the table. The destinations (projects) are listed across the top of the table, and their respective demands are listed across the bottom of the table. The unit shipping costs are shown in the upper right-hand corner of each cell, which represents a shipping route. Hence, the cost per cubic yard to ship topsoil from Farm A to Project #1 is $4. (For convenience, dollar signs are not shown.)

TABLE 7–1 Transportation Table for Harley's Sand and Gravel

From: \ To:	Project #1	Project #2	Project #3	Supply
Farm A	4	2	8	100
Farm B	5	1	9	200
Farm C	7	6	3	200
Demand	50	150	300	

Overview of the Solution Technique

The transportation solution technique is similar in certain respects to the simplex technique because both involve an initial feasible solution that is evaluated to determine if it can be improved. Moreover, both involve displaying initial and improved solutions in a series of tableaus or tables. However, as noted earlier, the transportation method requires considerably less computational effort. Moreover, it is not unusual to discover that the initial feasible solution in a transportation problem is the optimum solution. Figure 7–1 gives an overview of the transportation method.

A solution to a transportation problem consists of *quantities* that are assigned to the various routes (i.e., cells in the table). These values can range from zero, which implies that no units will be shipped over that route, to a maximum that equals the smaller of two quantities: the row (supply) and column (demand) totals. The logic of the maximum quantity is simple: The quantity shipped cannot exceed the available supply in a row, and it should not exceed the amount demanded (column total). Such a solution is a *feasible* solution. The starting point of the transportation method is a feasible solution.

Finding an Initial Feasible Solution

A feasible solution is one in which assignments are made in such a way that all supply and demand requirements are satisfied. In general, the number of nonzero (occupied) cells should equal one less than the sum of the number of rows and the number of columns in a transportation table. In the case of a table with 3 rows and 3 columns, the number of occupied cells should be $3 + 3 - 1 = 5$ in order to be able to use the transportation algorithm. Sometimes, fewer occupied or completed cells appear in a solution. When that happens, the solution is referred to as a

FIGURE 7–1 Overview of the Transportation Method

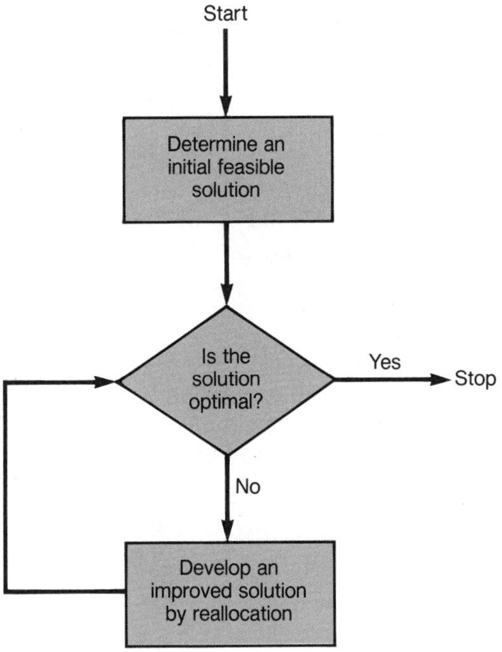

degenerate solution; such a solution requires modification in order to be able to determine if it is optimal. This topic is covered later in the chapter.

Aside from a degenerate case, the transportation method will generate solutions that have the number of completed cells equal to the number of rows plus number of columns minus 1. Other feasible solutions that use more of the cells are imaginable, but not really desirable. For instance, it may be possible to imagine a solution that uses all of the cells. However, the cell costs are *marginal* costs to transport single units. Often, there are fixed costs associated with the number of cells (routes) used. For example, in the Harley problem, consider that, undoubtedly, each route requires a separate truck, which represents, perhaps, a high fixed cost. Hence, the more routes, the more trucks, and the higher the fixed cost. Therefore, it would be desirable to devise a solution that used as few routes as possible. In general, such a solution will require the above-mentioned number of completed cells.

A number of different approaches can be used to find an initial feasible solution. Two of these are described here:

1. The northwest-corner method.
2. An intuitive approach.

Finding an Initial Feasible Solution: The Northwest-Corner Method

The **northwest-corner method** is a systematic approach for developing an initial feasible solution. Its chief advantages are that it is simple to use and easy to understand. Its chief drawback is that it does not take transportation costs into account. Consequently, such a solution may require much additional effort to obtain the optimal solution.

The northwest-corner method gets its name because the starting point for the allocation process is the upper left-hand (northwest) corner of the transportation table. For the Harley problem, this would be the cell that represents the route from Farm A to Project #1. The following set of principles guides the allocation:

1. Begin with the upper left-hand cell, and allocate as many units as possible to that cell. This will be the smaller of the row supply and the column demand. Adjust the row and column quantities to reflect the allocation.
2. Remain in a row or column until its supply or demand is completely exhausted or satisfied, allocating the maximum number of units to each cell in turn, until all supply has been allocated (and all demand has been satisfied because we assume total supply and demand are equal).

For the Harley problem, the sequence would be as follows (see Table 7–2):

1. Beginning in cell A–1, allocate 50 units, exhausting demand in column 1 and leaving 50 units of supply in row A.
2. Staying in row A, move to cell A–2, where supply is now 50 and demand is 150 units. Allocate 50 units to this cell, exhausting the supply of row A and leaving 100 units in column 2.
3. Staying in column 2, move down to cell B–2, where supply is 200 units. Allocate 100 units to this cell, exhausting demand in column 2 and leaving 100 units of supply in row B.
4. Staying in row B, move to cell B–3 and allocate 100 units, exhausting that row's supply and leaving 200 units in column 3.
5. Staying in column 3, move down to cell C–3 and allocate 200 units, exhausting both the row and column quantities.

In terms of minimizing total transportation cost, this solution may or may not be optimal. We shall make that determination very shortly. At this point, let's simply compute the total cost this solution would generate if it was implemented.

The total cost is found by multiplying the quantities in "completed" (i.e., nonempty) cells by the cell's unit cost, then summing those amounts. Thus:

Total cost =	50(4) =	$ 200
	50(2) =	100
	100(1) =	100
	100(9) =	900
	200(3) =	600
		$1,900

TABLE 7–2 Initial Feasible Solution for Harley Using Northwest-Corner Method

From: \ To:	Project #1	Project #2	Project #3	Supply
Farm A	[4] 50 (first)	[2] 50 (second)	[8]	100
Farm B	[5]	[1] 100 (third)	[9] 100 (fourth)	200
Farm C	[7]	[6]	[3] 200 (last)	200
Demand	50	150	300	500

As noted earlier, the main drawback of the northwest-corner method is that it does not consider cell (route) costs in making the allocation. Consequently, if this allocation is optimal, that can be attributed to chance rather than the method used.

Finding an Initial Feasible Solution: The Intuitive Approach

This approach, also known as the *minimum-cost method,* uses lowest cell cost as the basis for selecting routes. The procedure is as follows:

1. Identify the cell that has the lowest unit cost. If there is a tie, select one arbitrarily. Allocate a quantity to this cell that is equal to the lower of the available supply for the row and the demand for the column.
2. Cross out the cells in the row or column that has been exhausted (or both, if both have been exhausted), and adjust the remaining row or column total accordingly.
3. Identify the cell with the lowest cost from the remaining cells. Allocate a quantity to this cell that is equal to the lower of the available supply of the row and the demand for the column.
4. Repeat steps 2 and 3 until all supply and demand has been allocated.

Let's see how this method can be applied to the Harley problem. The cell with the lowest cost is B–2, in which the cost is $1 (see Table 7–3a). Farm B has a supply of 200 cubic yards of gravel, whereas Project #2 has a demand for only 150 cubic yards. Consequently, we allocate 150 cubic yards (the lesser of the two quantities) to cell B–2. Because this exhausts the demand of Project #2, we cross out the cells in that column and the demand, and we change the row total to 50 (see Table 7–3b).

Of the cells that remain, C–3 has the lowest cost (A–2 cannot be used because it has been crossed out). The supply of Farm C is 200 cubic yards, the demand of

TABLE 7–3a Find the Cell that has the Lowest Unit Cost

To: / From:	Project #1	Project #2	Project #3	Supply
Farm A	4	2	8	100
Farm B	5	1	9	200
Farm C	7	6	3	200
Demand	50	150	300	500

Lowest cell cost

TABLE 7–3b Allocate 150 Units to Cell B–2

To: / From:	Project #1	Project #2	Project #3	Supply
Farm A	4	2	8	100
Farm B	5	150 1	9	~~200~~ 50
Farm C	7	6	3	200
Demand	50	~~150~~	300	500

Project #3 is 300 cubic yards. The lesser of these is 200 cubic yards, so that quantity is placed in cell C–3. Since the supply of Farm C has been completely used, the cells in row 3 are crossed out along with the row total. The remaining demand for Project #3 is 100 units, so that column total must be adjusted accordingly (see Table 7–4).

Of the remaining cells, A–1 has the lowest cell cost. The column total is 50 and the row total is 100; hence, the quantity 50 is assigned to that cell. Because the demand of Project #1 has been satisfied, the cells in the column must be crossed out, and 50 units must be subtracted from the supply of Farm A (see Table 7–5).

At this point, only two remaining cells have not been crossed out: cells A–3 and B–3. Cell A–3 has the lower cost, so it is next in line for allocation. The remaining

TABLE 7–4 200 Units Are Assigned to Cell C–3

From: \ To:	Project #1	Project #2	Project #3	Supply
Farm A	[4]	[2]	[8]	100
Farm B	[5]	150 [1]	[9]	~~200~~ 50
Farm C	[7]	[6]	200 [3]	~~200~~
Demand	50	~~150~~	~~300~~ 100	500

TABLE 7–5 50 Units Are Assigned to Cell A–1

From: \ To:	Project #1	Project #2	Project #3	Supply
Farm A	50 [4]	[2]	[8]	~~100~~ 50
Farm B	[5]	150 [1]	[9]	~~200~~ 50
Farm C	[7]	[6]	200 [3]	~~200~~
Demand	~~50~~	~~150~~	~~300~~ 100	500

supply is 50 units, and the remaining demand is 100 units; consequently, the quantity 50 is placed in A–3. This completes the use of supply for Farm A, and it leaves a demand of 50 units for Project #3. The last remaining cell, then, receives a quantity of 50 units, canceling the remaining supply and demand for *both* its row and column (see Table 7–6).

We can easily verify that this is a feasible solution by checking to see that the row and column totals of the assigned cell quantities equal the supply and demand totals for the rows and columns. For example, 50 + 50, or 100 units have been allocated in the first row, which equals the supply of Farm A. Likewise, 50 units have been assigned in the first column, which equals the demand of Project #1.

This solution may or may not be optimal. In the next section, the procedure for testing for optimality will be described. For now, let us simply compute the total

TABLE 7–6 Completion of the Initial Feasible Solution for the Harley Problem Using the Intuitive Approach

From: \ To:	Project #1	Project #2	Project #3	Supply
Farm A	[4] 50	[2]	[8] 50	100
Farm B	[5]	[1] 150	[9] 50	200
Farm C	[7]	[6]	[3] 200	200
Demand	50	150	300	500

cost of this solution and compare it to that of the northwest-corner solution. Here we have:

Cell	Cost per Unit	Number of Units	Transportation Cost
A–1	$4	50	$ 200
A–3	8	50	400
B–2	1	150	150
B–3	9	50	450
C–3	3	200	600
		500	$1,800

Compared to the plan generated using the northwest-corner method, this one has a total cost that is $100 less. The fact that this plan is less costly than the previous one was expected: The previous one did not involve the use of cost information in allocating units. Whether this plan is optimal, or can be improved on, remains to be seen.

Evaluating a Solution for Optimality

The test for optimality for a feasible solution involves a cost evaluation of empty cells (i.e., routes to which no units have been allocated) to see if an improved solution is possible. We shall consider two methods for cell evaluation:

1. The stepping-stone method.
2. The MODI method.

The stepping-stone method involves a good deal more effort than the MODI method, as you will note. However, it provides an intuitive understanding of the

TABLE 7-7 **Initial Feasible Solution Obtained Using the Northwest-Corner Method**

From: \ To:	Project #1	Project #2	Project #3	Supply
Farm A	50 [4]	50 [2]	[8]	100
Farm B	[5]	100 [1]	100 [9]	200
Farm C	[7]	[6]	200 [3]	200
Demand	50	150	300	500

evaluation process. Moreover, when a solution is not optimal, the distribution plan must be revised by reallocating units into and out of various cells, and only the stepping-stone method can be used for the reallocation. It is, therefore, necessary to be able to use the stepping-stone approach, although the preferred choice is first to use the MODI method and, then, the stepping-stone method, if necessary.

Evaluation Using the Stepping-Stone Method

The **stepping-stone method** involves tracing a series of closed paths in the transportation table, using one such path for each empty cell. The path represents a shift of one unit into an empty cell, and it enables the manager or analyst to answer a "what if . . .?" question: What impact on total cost would there be if one unit were shifted into an unused route? The result is a cost change per unit shifted into a cell. If the shift results in a cost savings, the stepping-stone path also can be used to determine the maximum number of units that can be shifted into the empty cell, as well as modifications to other completed cells needed to compensate for the shift into the previously unused cell.

The name *stepping-stone* relates to an analogy of crossing a pond or stream by moving from stone to stone; in the case of a transportation solution, the "stones" are the completed cells.

The initial feasible solution we found using the northwest-corner method is reproduced in Table 7-7. We know it is not optimal because the intuitive method generated an initial solution that has a lower total cost. However, it will be instructive to analyze the northwest-corner solution in order to see how the stepping-stone method works and to gain some insight into the process of developing an improved solution.

Only the unoccupied cells need to be evaluated because the question at this point is *not* how many units to allocate to a particular route but only if converting

TABLE 7–8 Evaluation Path for Cell B–1

From: \ To:	Project #1	Project #2	Project #3	Supply
Farm A	[4] 50 −	[2] 50 +	[8]	100
Farm B	[5] +	[1] − 100	[9] 100	200
Farm C	[7]	[6]	[3] 200	200
Demand	50	150	300	500

a cell from zero units to nonzero (a positive value) would decrease or increase total costs. The unoccupied cells are A–3, B–1, C–1, and C–2. They must be evaluated one at a time, but in no particular order.

Let's begin with cell B–1. We start by placing a + in the cell being evaluated, which stands for the addition of one unit (e.g., a cubic yard of topsoil) to the cell. In order to maintain the column total of 50, we must subtract one unit from an occupied cell; cell A–2 is the only option. This is designated by placing a − in cell A–1 (see Table 7–8). Because we subtracted one unit from *row* A, we must compensate for this, which we can do by adding a unit (i.e., placing a + sign) in cell A–2. Similarly, we compensate for the addition of one unit to column 2 by subtracting a unit from cell B–2, and place a − in that cell to reflect this. Because we initially added one unit to row B in cell B–1, this last subtraction also compensates for that, and we have traced a completed path, which we can use to evaluate B–1. Before doing that, let's consider rules that will guide tracing these paths.

Rules for tracing stepping-stone paths:

1. All unoccupied cells must be evaluated. Evaluate cells one at a time.
2. Except for the cell being evaluated, only add or subtract in occupied cells. (It is permissible to skip over occupied cells to find an occupied cell from which the path can continue.)
3. A path will consist of only horizontal and vertical moves, starting and ending with the empty cell that is being evaluated.
4. Alternate + and − signs, beginning with a + sign in the cell being evaluated.

TABLE 7–9 Evaluation Path for Cell C–1

From: \ To:	Project #1	Project #2	Project #3	Supply
Farm A	[4] 50 −	[2] 50 +	[8]	100
Farm B	[5]	[1] 100 −	[9] 100 +	200
Farm C	[7] +	[6]	[3] 200 −	200
Demand	50	150	300	500

Note that it is not necessary to actually alter the quantities in the various cells to reflect the one-unit change; the + and − signs suffice.

The general implication of the plus and minus signs is that cells with a + sign mean one unit would be added, cells with a − sign indicate one unit would be subtracted. The net impact of such a one-unit shift can be determined by adding the cell costs with signs attached and noting the resulting value. Thus, for cell B–1, we have a net change of + 2:

B–1

+	−
5	4
2	1
+7	−5

$+7 - 5 = +2$

This means that for each unit shifted into cell B–2 in this way (which is the *only* way a shift could be made), the total cost would *increase* by $2. Consequently, such a shift would not be desirable.

Turning our attention to cell C–1, we begin its evaluation by placing a + sign in that cell (see Table 7–9). We can move horizontally or vertically to an occupied cell. Suppose we move to cell C–3 and place a − sign there. Next, we move vertically to cell B–3, place a + sign in it, then horizontally to B–2, place a − sign there, move up to cell A–2, place a + sign there, and, then, move horizontally to A–1 and place a − sign there. Coincidentally, some of the cells have + or − signs that are the same as in the previous evaluation path. However, this is not necessary; each evaluation path is independent of others in terms of assigning + and − signs. The evaluation of this path is +10.

C–1

+	−
7	3
9	1
2	4
+18	−8

+10

Hence, using this path for reallocation would *increase* total cost by \$10 per unit. Again, this would be undesirable.

Evaluation paths for empty cells A–3 and C–2 are shown in Table 7–10. Their net changes are:

A–3

+	−
8	2
1	9
+9	−11

− 2

C–2

+	−
6	1
9	3
+15	−4

+ 11

The negative value for cell A–3 indicates an improved solution is possible: For each unit we can shift into that cell, the total cost will decrease by \$2. The next question is, how many units can be reallocated into that cell?

Before addressing that question, let's consider an alternative method for cell evaluation that avoids having to trace all of the evaluation paths.

Evaluation Using the MODI Method

The **MODI** (MOdified DIstribution) method of evaluating a transportation solution for optimality involves the use of *index numbers* that are established for the rows and columns. These are based on the unit costs of the occupied cells. The index numbers can be used to obtain the cell evaluations for empty cells without the use of stepping-stone paths.

There is one index number for each column and one for each row. These can be conveniently displayed along the left and upper edges of a matrix. The index numbers are determined in such a way that for any occupied cell, the sum of the row index and the column index equals the cell's unit transportation cost:

$$\begin{array}{ccccc} \text{Row index} & + & \text{Column index} & = & \text{Cell cost} \\ r_i & + & k_j & = & c_{ij} \end{array} \qquad (7\text{–}1)$$

The index numbers are determined sequentially in a manner dictated by the position of occupied cells. The process always begins by assigning a value of zero as the index number of row 1.

TABLE 7–10 Evaluation Paths for Cells A–3 and C–2

From: \ To:	Project #1	Project #2	Project #3	Supply
Farm A	50 [4]	50 − [2]	+ [8]	100
Farm B	[5]	100 + − [1]	− + 100 [9]	200
Farm C	[7]	+ [6]	− 200 [3]	200
Demand	50	150	300	500

TABLE 7–11 Initial Feasible Solution Obtained Using the Northwest-Corner Method

Index numbers to be computed

	From: \ To:	Project #1 (k_1)	Project #2 (k_2)	Project #3 (k_3)	Supply
0	Farm A	50 [4]	50 [2]	[8]	100
r_2	Farm B	[5]	100 [1]	100 [9]	200
r_3	Farm C	[7]	[6]	200 [3]	200
	Demand	50	150	300	500

The method will be illustrated by developing index numbers for the initial feasible solution for the Harley problem generated by the northwest-corner method, which is repeated in Table 7–11.

We begin by assigning a value of zero as the index for row 1. Once a row index has been established, it will enable us to compute column index numbers for all occupied cells in that row. Similarly, once a column index number has been determined, index numbers for all rows corresponding to occupied cells in that column can be determined.

The index number for column 1 is based on the fact that the sum of its value and the row index number must equal the cell cost of \$4 for cell A–1. Thus,

TABLE 7-12 Index Numbers for Initial Northwest-Corner Solution to the Harley Problem

		+4	+2	+10	
	To: / From:	Project #1	Project #2	Project #3	Supply
0	Farm A	[4] 50	[2] 50	[8]	100
−1	Farm B	[5]	[1] 100	[9] 100	200
−7	Farm C	[7]	[6]	[3] 200	200
	Demand	50	150	300	500

$0 + k_1 = 4$, so $k_1 = +4$. Similarly, using occupied cell A–2, the index number for column 2 can be determined: $0 + k_2 = 2$, so $k_2 = +2$.

Knowledge of the index number for column 2 enables us to compute the index number for row B using the unit cost for occupied cell B–2: $r_2 + 2 = 1$, so $r_2 = -1$. The value of r_2 then enables us to compute the index number for column 3: $-1 + k_3 = 9$, so $k_3 = +10$. The remaining index number, that of row 3, can be determined using the unit cost of occupied cell C–3 and the column 3 index number, k_3: $r_3 + 10 = 3$, so $r_3 = -7$.

The complete set of row and column index numbers is shown in Table 7–12. Generally, it is advisable to do a quick check of the values by confirming that for all *occupied* cells, the sum of the row and the column index number equals the unit cell cost.

We can now readily determine the cell evaluations (improvement potentials) for each of the unoccupied cells using the relationship:

$$\begin{array}{ccccccc} \text{Cell evaluation} & = & \text{Cell cost} & - & \text{Row index} & - & \text{Column index} \\ e_{ij} & = & c_{ij} & - & r_i & - & k_j \end{array} \tag{7–2}$$

These determinations can be made in any order. For example, the cell evaluation for A–3 is $8 - 0 - 10 = -2$. This implies an improvement (decrease in total cost) of \$2 per unit for units that can be shifted into cell A–3. Similarly, for empty cell B–1, the improvement potential is $5 - (-1) - 4 = +2$, which indicates any units shifted into this cell would *increase* total cost by \$2 each. For unoccupied cell C–1, the evaluation is $7 - (-7) - 4 = +10$, and for cell C–2, the cell evaluation is $6 - (-7) - 2 = +11$. These values are summarized in Table 7–13. Note that they agree with the values we computed earlier using the stepping-stone method.

TABLE 7–13 Cell Evaluations for Northwest-Corner Solution for the Harley Problem

		+4	+2	+10	
	To: / From:	Project #1	Project #2	Project #3	Supply
0	Farm A	4 / 50	2 / 50	8 / (−2)	100
−1	Farm B	5 / (+2)	1 / 100	9 / 100	200
−7	Farm C	7 / (+10)	6 / (+11)	3 / 200	200
	Demand	50	150	300	500

When all evaluations are positive or zero, an optimal solution has been found. If one or more is negative, the cell with the *largest* negative should be brought into solution because that route has the largest potential for improvement *per unit*. In this case, we found that cell A–3 had an evaluation of −2, which represented an improvement potential of $2 per unit. Hence, an improved solution is possible.

Developing an Improved Solution

Developing an improved solution to a transportation problem requires focusing on the unoccupied cell that has the largest negative cell evaluation. In the Harley problem, the only negative evaluation was for cell A–3.

Improving the solution involves reallocating quantities in the transportation table. More specifically, we want to take advantage of the improvement potential of cell A–3 by transferring as many units as possible into that cell. The stepping-stone path for that cell is necessary for determining *how many* units can be reallocated while retaining the balance of supply and demand for the table. The stepping-stone path also reveals *which cells* must have quantity changes and both the *magnitude* and the *direction* of the changes. The stepping-stone path for cell A–3 is reproduced in Table 7–14. The + signs in the path indicate units to be added, the − signs indicate units to be subtracted. The limit on subtraction is *the smallest quantity in a negative position* along the cell path. There are two quantities in negative positions, 50 and 100. Because 50 is the smaller quantity, that amount will be shifted in the following manner: Subtract 50 units from each cell on the path with a − sign, and add 50 units to the quantity of each cell with a + sign in it. The result is shown in Table 7–15. A quick check reveals that the sums of quantities in each row and in each column are equal to original row and column totals.

TABLE 7–14 Stepping-Stone Path for Cell A–3

To: / From:	Project #1	Project #2	Project #3	Supply
Farm A	4 / 50	2 / 50 (−)	8 (+)	100
Farm B	5	1 / 100 (+)	9 / 100 (−)	200
Farm C	7	6	3 / 200	200
Demand	50	150	300	500

TABLE 7–15 Distribution Plan after Reallocation of 50 Units

To: / From:	Project #1	Project #2	Project #3	Supply
Farm A	4 / 50	2	8 / 50	100
Farm B	5	1 / 150	9 / 50	200
Farm C	7	6	3 / 200	200
Demand	50	150	300	500

With each iteration (new solution), it is necessary to evaluate the empty cells to see if further improvement is possible. This requires use of either the MODI or the stepping-stone method. Both will yield the same values. Suppose we use the MODI method.

We begin by setting the index number for row 1 equal to zero. The column 1 index number is found using the equality $0 + k_1 = 4$. Solving, we find $k_1 = +4$. Similarly, for column 3, $0 + k_3 = 8$, so $k_3 = +8$. Using cell B–3 as a "pivot," the index number for row 2 can be found from the equality $r_2 + k_3 = 9$. Because k_3 was found to equal $+8$, this means that $r_2 = +1$. This value now allows us to compute the index number for column 2 because $r_2 + k_2 = 1$: $1 + k_2 = 1$, so $k_2 = 0$. Lastly, the index number for row 3 can be determined on the basis of the

TABLE 7–16 Index Numbers and Cell Evaluations

		+4	0	+8	
	To: / From:	Project #1	Project #2	Project #3	Supply
0	Farm A	50 [4]	(+2) [2]	50 [8]	100
+1	Farm B	(0) [5]	150 [1]	50 [9]	200
−5	Farm C	(+8) [7]	(+11) [6]	200 [3]	200
	Demand	50	150	300	500

unit cost of cell C–3 and our finding that $k_3 = +8$. Thus, $r_3 + 8 = 3$, so $r_3 = +5$. These values provide the basis for computing evaluations for the empty cells using the relationship $e_{ij} = c_{ij} - r_i - k_j$:

Cell A–2: $2 - 0 - 0 = +2$
Cell B–1: $5 - 1 - 4 = 0$
Cell C–1: $7 - (-5) - 4 = +8$
Cell C–2: $6 - (-5) - 0 = +11$

Because none of these numbers is negative, this is an optimal solution.

The index numbers and the cell evaluations are summarized in Table 7–16. You may recall that this was the same solution obtained using the intuitive method for the initial feasible solution (see Table 7–6). At that point, it was determined that the total cost for the distribution plan was $1,800.

Special Issues

A number of special issues are discussed in this section in order to round out your understanding of the transportation model. They are:

1. Determining if there are alternate optimal solutions.
2. Recognizing and handling degeneracy (too few occupied cells to permit evaluation of a solution).
3. Avoiding unacceptable or prohibited route assignments.
4. Dealing with problems in which supply and demand are not equal.
5. Solving maximization problems.

Alternate optimal solutions Sometimes transportation problems have multiple optimal solutions. In such instances, it can be useful for a manager to be aware of alternate solutions, because this gives the manager an option of bringing nonquantitative considerations into the decision.

In the case of the transportation problem, the existence of an alternate solution is signaled by an empty cell's evaluation equal to zero. In fact, you may have noted that cell B–1 had an evaluation equal to zero in the final solution of the Harley problem (see Table 7–16). We can find out what that alternate solution is by reallocating the maximum number of units possible around the stepping-stone path for that cell. That path is shown in Table 7–17a. The smallest quantity in a negative position on that path is 50 units. Shifting those 50 units results in the distribution plan shown in Table 7–17b.

As a check, note that the total cost is the same as before, $1,800:

$$100(8) + 50(5) + 150(1) + 200(3) = \$1,800$$

Degeneracy In a transportation problem, **Degeneracy** occurs when there are too few occupied cells to enable all the empty cells to be evaluated. In the case of the stepping-stone method, this means that there will be at least one empty cell for which an evaluation path cannot be constructed. For the MODI method, it means that it will be impossible to determine all of the row and column index numbers.

It is relatively simple to determine if a solution is degenerate: A solution is degenerate if the number of occupied cells is less than the number of rows plus the number of columns minus 1.

Test for degeneracy:
Number of occupied cells must equal:

$$R + C - 1$$

where

R = number of rows
C = number of columns

A quick check of the alternate solution to the Harley problem developed in the preceding section will reveal that the solution was degenerate: The number of completed cells is 4, while the required number of completed cells is $3 + 3 - 1 = 5$. This presented no difficulty because we were not concerned with evaluating the empty cells; we simply were interested in comparing the total cost of that solution with the total cost of the original optimal solution to verify that the two yielded the same total cost.

However, try to trace a stepping-stone path for any of the empty cells and you will understand the nature of the problem. It should be mentioned that this

TABLE 7-17a Index Numbers and Cell Evaluations

From: \ To:	Project #1	Project #2	Project #3	Supply
Farm A	50 [4]	[2]	50 [8]	100
Farm B	[5]	150 [1]	50 [9]	200
Farm C	[7]	[6]	200 [3]	200
Demand	50	150	300	500

TABLE 7-17b Alternate Optimal Solution

From: \ To:	Project #1	Project #2	Project #3	Supply
Farm A	[4]	[2]	100 [8]	100
Farm B	50 [5]	150 [1]	[9]	200
Farm C	[7]	[6]	200 [3]	200
Demand	50	150	300	500

particular case is somewhat atypical in that usually *some* paths can be traced, but not all of them. Similarly, if you attempt to compute index numbers for the rows and columns, you will be unable to compute them for row B, column 1, or column 2.

Obviously, some modification has to be made in order to determine if a given solution is optimal. The modification is to treat some of the empty cells as occupied cells. This is accomplished by placing a delta (Δ) in one of the empty cells.[1] The delta represents an extremely small quantity (e.g., .001 unit); it is so small that supply and demand for the row and column involved will be unaffected

[1] Actually, the number of deltas needed will equal the difference between the number of completed cells and $R + C - 1$. However, you will only be exposed to the most common case in which one more completed cell is needed.

even without modifying other quantities in the row or column, and so small that total cost will not change.

The purpose of the delta is to enable evaluation of the remaining empty cells. The choice of location for the delta can be somewhat tricky: Some empty cells may be unsuitable if they do not enable evaluations of the remaining empty cells. Moreover, the delta cannot be placed in a cell that later turns out to be in a negative position of a cell path involved in reallocation because delta will be the "smallest quantity in a negative position" and shifting that minute quantity around the cell path will leave the solution virtually unchanged. Consequently, a certain amount of trial and error may be necessary before a satisfactory location can be identified for delta.

The technique can be demonstrated for the degenerate alternate solution of the Harley problem. Suppose that after some experimentation, cell A–1 has been selected for the location of delta. (Not all choices would be acceptable. For example, try placing the delta in cell C–2 and compute the improvement potentials for the empty cells. Remember that delta cannot be in a negative position of a negative cell.) The resulting index numbers generated using MODI and the improvement potential for empty cells based on delta in cell A–1 are shown in Table 7–18. This confirms that the solution is optimal.

Unacceptable routes In some cases, certain origin-destination combinations may be unacceptable. This may be due to weather factors, equipment breakdowns, labor problems, or skill requirements that either prohibit, or make undesirable, certain combinations (routes).

Suppose that in the Harley problem route A–3 was suddenly unavailable because of recent flooding. In order to prevent that route from appearing in the final solution (as it originally did), the manager could assign a unit cost to that cell that was large enough to make that route uneconomical and, hence, prohibit its occurrence. One rule of thumb would be to assign a cost that is 10 times the largest cost in the table. Thus, because the largest cost is \$9, a unit cost of \$90 could be assigned instead of the original cost of \$8 per unit. Then this revised problem could be solved using northwest-corner or intuitive for an initial solution and either stepping-stone or MODI to evaluate the initial solution and any possible reallocations.

The optimal solution is shown in Table 7–19. The prohibited route may appear in a nonoptimal solution, but it will be eliminated by the time the optimal solution is reached.

Unequal supply and demand Up to this point, examples have involved cases in which supply and demand were equal. As you might guess, there are situations in which the two are not equal. When such a situation is encountered, it is necessary to modify the original problem so that supply and demand are equal. This is accomplished by adding either a dummy column or a dummy row; a dummy row is added if supply is less than demand and a dummy column is added if

TABLE 7–18 Harley Alternate Solution Modified for Degeneracy

	From: \ To:	Project #1 (+4)	Project #2 (0)	Project #3 (+8)	Supply
0	Farm A	Δ [4]	(+2) [2]	100 [8]	100
+1	Farm B	50 [5]	150 [1]	(0) [9]	200
−5	Farm C	(+8) [7]	(+11) [6]	200 [3]	200
	Demand	50	150	300	500

TABLE 7–19 Solution to Harley Problem with a Prohibited Route

	From: \ To:	Project #1 (+4)	Project #2 (+2)	Project #3 (+10)	Supply
0	Farm A	50 [4]	50 [2]	(+80) [90] ← Prohibited route	100
−1	Farm B	(+2) [5]	100 [1]	100 [9]	200
−7	Farm C	(+10) [7]	(+11) [6]	200 [3]	200
	Demand	50	150	300	500

demand is less than supply. The dummy is assigned unit costs of zero for each cell, and it is given a supply (if a row) or a demand (if a column) equal to the difference between supply and demand. Quantities in dummy routes in the optimal solution are not shipped. Rather, they serve to indicate which supplier will hold the excess supply, and how much, or which destination will not receive its total demand, and how much it will be short.

Let's consider an example. Suppose that Farm C in the Harley problem has experienced an equipment breakdown, and it will be able to supply only 120 cubic yards of topsoil for a period of time. Therefore, total supply will be 80 units less

TABLE 7–20 A Dummy Origin Is Added to Make Up 80 Units

To: / From:	Project #1	Project #2	Project #3	Supply
Farm A	4	2	8	100
Farm B	5	1	9	200
Farm C	7	6	3	120
Dummy	0	0	0	80
	50	150	300	500

TABLE 7–21 Solution Using the Dummy Origin

To: / From:	Project #1	Project #2	Project #3	Supply
Farm A	50 [4]	[2]	50 [8]	100
Farm B	[5]	150 [1]	50 [9]	200
Farm C	[7]	[6]	120 [3]	120
Dummy	[0]	[0]	80 [0]	80
	50	150	300	500

than total demand. This will require adding a dummy origin with a supply of 80 units. The modified problem is shown in Table 7–20, and the final solution is shown in Table 7–21. We interpret the solution indicating that Project 3 will be short 80 units per week until the equipment is repaired. Note, though, that this analysis has considered only transportation costs, and that other factors, such as shortage costs or schedules of the projects, may dictate some other course of action.

If the intuitive approach is used to obtain the initial feasible solution when a dummy is involved, make assignments to the dummy *last*. Hence, begin by assigning units to the cell with the lowest *nonzero* cost, then the next lowest nonzero cost, and so on. For the Harley problem, this would mean that units would be assigned first to cell B–2 because its cost of $1 is the lowest nonzero cell cost.

Maximization Some transportation-type problems concern profits or revenues rather than costs. In such cases, the objective is to *maximize* rather than to minimize. Such problems can be handled by adding one additional step *at the start:* Identify the cell with the largest profit and subtract all the other cell profits from that value. Then replace the cell profits with the resulting values. These values reflect the *opportunity costs* that would be incurred by using routes with unit profits that are less than the largest unit profit. Replace the original unit profits with these opportunity costs and solve in the usual way for the *minimum* opportunity cost solution. This will be identical to maximizing the total profit. For example, suppose in the Harley problem, the cell values had been unit profits instead of unit costs. Cell B–3 had the largest dollar value: $9. Hence, each cell's dollar amount would be subtracted from 9. For cell A–1, the resulting opportunity cost would have been $9 - 4 = 5$, and so on. Cell B–3 would have an opportunity cost of 0, making it the most desirable route.

The remainder of the steps for developing an initial feasible solution, evaluation of empty cells, and reallocation are identical to those used for cost minimization. When the optimal distribution plan has been identified, use the *original cell values* (i.e., profits) to compute the total profit for that plan. (See Solved Problem 2.)

Other Applications

There are a number of other kinds of situations in which the transportation method has proved useful. They include the transshipment problem, which is a variation of a transportation problem, and location analysis.

Transshipment problems Certain transportation problems may involve the use of *intermediate* destinations where goods are temporarily stored before being shipped on to their final destinations. Thus, these intermediate points are both destinations and origins. These are called **transshipment problems.** The transportation method can be used to handle such problems. The goal generally is the same as with other transportation problems: to minimize total transportation cost.

Suppose the manager of Harley has decided to use Farm A and Project #2 as transshipment points for temporary storage of topsoil because those two sites are conveniently located and because both have ample storage capacity. In order to use the transportation method to handle this problem, the manager must modify the transportation table to reflect the transshipment locations. That is, a *column* must be added for Farm A and a *row* must be added for Project #2. In addition, the manager must determine the unit costs for each of the new routes (see Table 7–22) and the capacity of each location. Note that there will be no shipments from

TABLE 7–22 Revised Harley Problem with Transshipment Points

Receiving points

	From: \ To:	Project #1	Project #2	Project #3	Farm A	Capacity
Shipping points	Farm A	4	2	8	0	100 +400 500
	Farm B	5	1	9	6	200
	Farm C	7	6	3	5	200
	Project #2	2	0	3	2	350
		50	150 +350 500	300	400	1250

Farm A *to* Farm A, or from Project #2 to Project #2. Consequently, unit costs for those routes will be zero. Any units allocated to those routes would simply reflect unused capacity. The manager also must compute the transshipment capacities of the two locations. Logically, Farm A would receive shipments from the other two farms, which at most would be the sum of their supplies (200 + 200 = 400). Thus, its capacity would be that 400 units plus its own supply of 100, or 500 units. Similarly, the most units Project #2 would be called on to store would be its own demand of 150 units plus the sum of the demands of the other two projects (50 + 300 = 350), for a total of 500 units.

Once this additional information has been arranged in tabular form, the transportation method can be used, as it was previously, to determine the optimal allocation plan.

Location analysis Another use of the transportation method is to compare transportation costs for alternative locations. For instance, a company may be preparing to build a new warehouse, and there may be a number of potential locations under consideration. One aspect of the decision may be differences in transportation costs that would result from each alternative.

Suppose that currently the firm has three factories that supply four warehouses, and another warehouse will be added. Suppose that two separate locations for the new warehouse, Chicago and Detroit, are being studied. The impact of each of the two potential locations can be determined by solving *two* transportation problems, one for each location. In other words, one extra column would be

TABLE 7–23a System with Chicago Warehouse

	Warehouse #1	Warehouse #2	Warehouse #3	Warehouse #4	Warehouse Chicago
Factory A					9
Factory B					6
Factory C					5

TABLE 7–23b System with Detroit Warehouse

	Warehouse #1	Warehouse #2	Warehouse #3	Warehouse #4	Warehouse Detroit
Factory A					4
Factory B					10
Factory C					7

added to the transportation table, representing one of the warehouses, and the problem would be solved for the minimum total cost. That column, then, would be replaced in the table by a column representing the other warehouse, and again the problem would be solved for the minimum cost. This would give decision makers an opportunity to assess the impact of each warehouse location on the total distribution costs for the system (see Tables 7–23a and 7–23b).

It should be noted that transportation cost typically would be one of a number of variables that would be taken into account in making such a decision. Moreover, some other factor, such as nearness of the warehouse to a target market, might take precedence over transportation cost.

Computer Solution of Transportation Problems

Although the transportation problems presented in this chapter do not require a great deal of effort to obtain an optimal solution, it can be helpful to make use of a computer to solve problems. This is particularly true for larger problems.

TABLE 7–24 The Harley Problem with Cells Labeled

From: \ To:	Project #1	Project #2	Project #3	Supply
Farm A	x_{11} [4]	x_{12} [2]	x_{13} [8]	100
Farm B	x_{21} [5]	x_{22} [1]	x_{23} [9]	200
Farm C	x_{31} [7]	x_{32} [6]	x_{33} [3]	200
Demand	50	150	300	500

Use of the computer generally requires that transportation problems be arranged in the standard LP format, which consists of an objective function and a set of constraints. These can be readily derived from the information contained in a transportation table, such as the table for the Harley problem, which is repeated in Table 7–24 for convenience.

In order to reformulate the problem, it is necessary to assign a variable name to each cell of the table. These variables will represent the *quantities* to be shipped on the various routes in the problem. One way to do this is to use matrix notation. This is illustrated in Table 7–24.

The objective function is simply the sum of products of the cell costs and the decision variables for each cell. Therefore, for the Harley problem, the objective function is:

$$\text{minimize} \quad 4x_{11} + 2x_{12} + 8x_{13} + 5x_{21} + 1x_{22} + 9x_{23} + 7x_{31} + 6x_{32} + 3x_{33}$$

As for the constraints, there will be one constraint for each row and one for each column. Because there are three rows and three columns, there will be six constraints. We know that the sum of quantities in any row or column must equal the row or column total. Consequently, each of the constraints can be written as an equality. The constraint for any row or column consists of the sum of the decision variables in that row or column set equal to the row or column total. Hence, for the Harley problem, the constraints are:

$$\left.\begin{array}{ll} \text{Farm A} & x_{11} + x_{12} + x_{13} = 100 \\ \text{Farm B} & x_{21} + x_{22} + x_{23} = 200 \\ \text{Farm C} & x_{31} + x_{32} + x_{33} = 200 \end{array}\right\} \text{Supply}$$

$$\left.\begin{array}{ll} \text{Project \#1} & x_{11} + x_{21} + x_{31} = 50 \\ \text{Project \#2} & x_{12} + x_{22} + x_{32} = 150 \\ \text{Project \#3} & x_{13} + x_{23} + x_{33} = 300 \end{array}\right\} \text{Demand}$$

As always, the non-negativity constraints apply. However, they are not shown here because they are not necessary when using a computer solution.

Submitting the problem in this format to a computer code will produce the same set of values that manual solution produced.

ASSIGNMENT PROBLEMS

Assignment problems are a special case of linear programming problems. They lend themselves to manual solution using a special-purpose algorithm that is described in this section. Assignment problems are characterized by a need to pair items in one group with items in another group in a one-for-one matching. For example, a manager may be faced with the task of assigning four jobs to four machines, one job to a machine. Another manager may be faced with the task of assigning five projects to five staff members, with each staff member responsible for a single project.

Typically, the time or cost required to complete a job or a project will differ, depending on the machine used for the job or the staff member doing the project. The manager's goal in such cases is to develop a set of assignments that will *minimize* the total time or cost of doing the work. In other cases, the goal may be to minimize distance traveled, scrap, or some other measure of effectiveness. Moreover, some problems involve profit or revenue, and in those cases, the obvious goal would be to develop a set of assignments that would lead to the *maximum* total profit or revenue. Because minimization problems are more common, we begin with a minimization problem.

■

EXAMPLE 1 A manager has prepared a table that shows the cost of performing each of four jobs by each of four employees (see Table 7–25). According to this table, Job 1 will cost \$15 if done by Employee A, \$20 if it is done by Employee B, and so on. The manager has stated that his goal is to develop a set of job assignments that will minimize the total cost of getting all four jobs done. It is further required that the jobs be performed simultaneously, thus requiring one job being assigned to each employee.

Although the manager recognizes that this problem can be solved using the simplex routine, he also knows that he can solve the problem by hand using the *Hungarian method*.

The Hungarian Method

The Hungarian method is based on minimization of *opportunity costs* that would result from potential pairings. These are additional costs that would be incurred if the lowest-cost assignment is not made, either in terms of jobs (i.e., rows) or

TABLE 7–25 Job Costs for Each Possible Pairing

		Employee A	B	C	D
Job	1	$15	20	18	24
	2	12	17	16	15
	3	14	15	19	17
	4	11	14	12	13

TABLE 7–26 Row Reduction

Original costs

		Employee A	B	C	D	Row minimum
Job	1	15	20	18	24	15
	2	12	17	16	15	12
	3	14	15	19	17	14
	4	11	14	12	13	11

Row reduction →

Cost after the row reduction

		Employee A	B	C	D
Job	1	0	5	3	9
	2	0	5	4	3
	3	0	1	5	3
	4	0	3	1	2

employees (i.e., columns). For example, we can see in Table 7–25 that the lowest processing cost for Job 1 is $15 when done by Employee A. Therefore, if the job were assigned for some reason to Employee B, the additional (i.e., opportunity) cost would be $20 − $15 = $5. Similarly, if Job 1 were assigned to Employee C, the opportunity cost would be $18 − $15 = $3, and if it were assigned to Employee D, the opportunity cost would be $24 − $15 = $9. We can perform similar calculations for the other rows by identifying the lowest cost for each row, then subtracting that value from each of the other costs in that row to obtain *job* opportunity costs for all job assignments. This is usually referred to as a **row reduction.** The results of the row reduction for the costs are shown in Table 7–26. The procedure for a row reduction is summarized in the following.

Procedure for row reduction:

1. Identify the minimum value for each row.
2. Subtract the minimum value in each row from all the values in that row.
3. Use the resulting values to develop a new table.

Now, the same logic can be applied from the perspective of the employees; this is called **column reduction.** That is, because each employee will have a job, and

TABLE 7–27 Column Reduction of Opportunity (Row Reduction) Costs

Revised (row reduction) costs

		A	B	C	D
Job	1	0	5	3	9
	2	0	5	4	3
	3	0	1	5	3
	4	0	3	1	2
Column minimum		0	1	1	2

Column reduction
↓

		A	B	C	D
Job	1	0	4	2	7
	2	0	4	3	1
	3	0	0	4	1
	4	0	2	0	0

because there are cost differences among employees, there can be opportunity costs in that respect. These will be in addition to the job opportunity costs because the minimum-cost (column) assignments will not necessarily be the same as the minimum-cost row assignments. For instance, the lowest-cost assignment for Job 1 was Employee A. However, the lowest-cost assignment for Employee A would be Job 4, which has a cost of \$11. The opportunity costs for employees can be determined using the values obtained from the row reductions because they are in addition to those opportunity costs.

The procedure is similar to that for a row reduction:

Procedure for column reduction:

1. Identify the lowest-cost value in each column.
2. Subtract the lowest-cost value in each column for each of the values in that column.
3. Use the resulting values to form a new table.

The column reductions for this example are illustrated in Table 7–27. Notice that because the minimum cost in column A is zero, there is no change in costs with a column reduction. This will always be the case for a row or column with a minimum cost equal to zero. Since both the second and third columns have

TABLE 7–28 Determine the Minimum Number of Lines Needed to Cover the Zeros

	A	B	C	D
1	0	4	2	7
2	0	4	3	1
3	0	0	4	1
4	0	2	0	0

minimum costs of $1, the values in the new table are all one less in those columns than in the previous table. Similarly, the new values in the last column are $2 less than in the previous table.

Once both the row and column opportunity costs have been determined, we can attempt to make the minimum-cost assignments. Recognizing that assignments with opportunity costs of zero reflect minimum costs, it would be desirable to attempt to make assignments only with matches that have costs of zero. For instance, assigning any job to employee A would have a zero cost. However, once a job is assigned to A, no other job can be assigned to A (i.e., the other zero costs in that column become irrelevant). Consequently, even though it may appear on the surface that there are enough zeros to make zero-cost assignments, the fact that each assignment eliminates an entire row and column from further consideration (i.e., assignments) means that a complete set of zero-cost assignments might not be possible at this juncture.

A quick method of determining if a set of zero opportunity cost assignments can be made is to find the *minimum* number of lines needed to "cover" all the zero costs. That is, if we draw a line through the zero costs in column A, this will account for four of the seven zeros. How many such lines will be needed to cross out all zeros? The answer is two more (a line through row 3 and one through row 4), for a total of three (see Table 7–28). Now, if the minimum number of covering lines *equals* the number of rows (or columns, because this is a square table), an optimal assignment is possible. In this case, apparently, an optimal assignment is not possible because only three lines were necessary. (Note that there is another way of covering the second zero in row 3; a vertical line could have been drawn through column B. The point is that only three lines, however drawn, would be needed.)

We must, therefore, make further reductions. No further row or column reductions are possible because there is a zero in every row and column. To get around this, we do the following: Subtract the smallest uncovered cost ($1 in this case), from every other *uncovered* cost and adding that same amount to costs that lie at an intersection of two covering lines. This is done in Table 7–29. The rationale for this is: Subtracting the smallest uncovered cost reveals the next smallest increment in opportunity costs, whereas adding that amount to intersections removes those assignments from consideration. Because both are at an intersection means

TABLE 7–29 Further Revision of the Cost Table

	A	B	C	D
1	0	4	2	7
2	0	4	3	(1)
3	0	0	4	1
4	0	2	0	0

(1) Smallest uncovered cost

Revised costs

	A	B	C	D
1	0	3	1	6
2	0	3	2	0
3	1	0	4	1
4	1	2	0	0

TABLE 7–30 A Minimum of Four Lines Are Needed to Cover All Zero Costs

	A	B	C	D
1	0	3	1	6
2	0	3	2	0
3	1	0	4	1
4	1	2	0	0

that *another assignment* already exists in both that row and that column; hence, we can ignore those intersection possibilities.

We now can repeat the process of finding the minimum number of covering lines. With the revised table, a minimum of four lines is needed (see Table 7–30). Hence, an optimal assignment is now possible.

To avoid confusion in making the assignments, begin by identifying a row or column that has only a single zero. Candidates are columns B and C and rows 1 and 3 because each has only one zero. Suppose we take row 1. We can denote the assignment of Job 1 to Employee A by boxing in the 0 at that intersection, and because this assignment eliminates Job 1 and Employee A from further consideration, we can cross out both column A and row 1. Next, we might select row 3 because it has a single zero, and box that one. This eliminates row 3 and Employee B, and they can be crossed out. Similarly, we can box the zero in column C, and cross out that column and row 4. Finally, we can box the remaining zero in column D, row 2 to complete our assignments. These assignments are shown in Table 7–31.

The total cost of the assignments can be determined by referring to the original cost table (Table 7–25). The total cost is:

1–A	$15
2–D	15
3–B	15
4–C	12
	$57

TABLE 7–31 Optimal Assignments

		Employee			
		A	B	C	D
Job	1	[0]	3	1	6
	2	0	3	2	[0]
	3	1	[0]	4	1
	4	1	2	[0]	0

It is instructive to note that this cost is equal to the sum of the row and column reduction costs plus the reduction amount for the revised (final) cost table. That is, the row reduction amounts' total was \$15 + \$12 + \$14 + \$11 = \$52 (see Table 7–26); and the column reduction amounts' total was \$0 + \$1 + \$1 + \$2 = \$4 (see Table 7–27). The revised cost table involved an additional reduction of \$1 for all uncovered numbers. Hence, the total reduction was \$52 + \$4 + \$1 = \$57, which agrees with the amount just determined.

Summary of Procedure

1. Perform a *row reduction* on the cost table by subtracting the least cost in each row from all costs in that row.
2. Perform a *column reduction* on the cost table that results from the row reduction by subtracting the least cost in each column from all costs in that column.
3. Determine if an optimal assignment can be made by drawing the minimum number of horizontal and/or vertical lines necessary to cover all zero costs. If the number of lines equals the number of rows, go to step 5.
4. If the minimum number of lines is less than the number of rows, identify the smallest uncovered opportunity cost. Subtract that amount from all uncovered costs and add that amount to the covered costs that lie at line intersections. Repeat step 3.
5. Make the assignments. Begin with a row or column that has a single zero. Box that zero to indicate the assignment and eliminate that row and column from further consideration by drawing a line through the row and another line through the column. Continue assigning rows or columns with single zero-cost elements, then choose arbitrarily for assignments where multiple zero-cost elements exist.

Requirements for Use of the Hungarian Method

Situations in which the Hungarian method of linear programming can be used are characterized by the following:

1. There will be a one-for-one matching of two sets of items.

2. The goal is to minimize costs (or to maximize profits) or a similar objective (e.g., time, distance, etc.).
3. The costs or profits (etc.) are known or can be closely estimated.

Special Situations

Certain situations can arise in which the model deviates slightly from that previously described. Among those situations are the following:

1. The number of rows does not equal the number of columns.
2. The problem involves maximization rather than minimization.
3. Certain matches are undesirable or not allowed.
4. Multiple optimal solutions exist.

The procedure outlined previously for assignment problems requires an equal number of rows and columns. However, certain problems may not satisfy that requirement. For example, a situation might involve four jobs that need processing but there are only three machines available for processing. Consequently, one job will not be processed immediately. In order to perform the analysis, and to learn which job will not be processed, an extra "machine" must be added to the table. In analyzing the problem, one job will be assigned to the nonexistent machine. Hence, that will be the job that is not immediately processed.

■

EXAMPLE 2 Prepare this assignment table so that the optimal set of assignments can be made using the previously described procedure.

		Job			
		1	2	3	4
Machine	A	15	19	12	16
	B	23	21	18	17
	C	20	16	11	19

Solution

Compensate for too few machines by adding another machine (row) to the table. Because no such machine exists, there will be no cost for the assignment. Hence, use costs of 0 for this dummy row:

		Job			
		1	2	3	4
Machine	A	15	19	12	16
	B	23	21	18	17
	C	20	16	11	19
	D	0	0	0	0

Then, proceed as before. Note that the column reduction step will have no effect because each column already has a zero. Simply skip that step and go on to the next step.

If the goal is to *maximize* rather than to minimize, one extra step must be added to the start of the process: Identify the largest value in each column and, then, subtract all numbers in each column from the column maximum. Having done that, perform the same steps that would be required if the problem were minimization because the modified values represent *opportunity costs*. The set of assignments that minimizes the opportunity costs will also maximize the original values.

■

EXAMPLE 3 The following table contains *profits* that would be realized from various possible pairings. Prepare the table so that the optimal solution can be obtained using the Hungarian method for *minimization*.

	1	2	3
A	14	22	30
B	20	18	40
C	11	12	50

Solution

Identify the maximum value in each column and then subtract every value in a given column from the column maximum, as shown below:

Original values

	1	2	3
A	14	22	30
B	20	18	40
C	11	12	50
Column maximum	20	22	50

Opportunity costs

	1	2	3
A	6	0	20
B	0	4	10
C	9	10	0

In certain instances, a particular match or pairing may be either *undesirable* or otherwise unacceptable. For example, an employee may not have the skills necessary to perform a particular job or a machine may not be equipped to handle a particular operation. When such a restriction is present, a letter (e.g., a capital M) is often placed in the table in the position that would represent a pairing. Analysis is performed as usual except that the M is ignored throughout the analysis. That is, the M is not used in any reductions, nor is any value added to it or subtracted from it during the course of the analysis.

■

EXAMPLE 4 Determine the optimal set of pairings given the following cost table. Note that assignment B–3 is undesirable, as denoted by the M in that position.

	1	2	3
A	8	7	2
B	1	4	M
C	7	9	3

Solution

Notice how the M does not change throughout the analysis:

Original values

	1	2	3
A	8	7	2
B	1	4	M
C	7	9	3

After row reduction

	1	2	3
A	6	5	0
B	0	3	M
C	4	6	0

After column reduction

	1	2	3
A	6	(2)	0
B	0	0	M
C	4	3	0

After further reduction, optimal solution

	1	2	3
A	4	0	0
B	0	0	M
C	2	1	0

In some cases, there are multiple optimal solutions to a problem. This condition can be easily recognized when making the optimal assignments: No *unique* 0 will exist at some point, resulting in more than one choice for assignment and, hence, more than one optimal solution. It should be noted that *all* optimal solutions will yield the *same* value of the objective function (e.g., the same minimum cost).

■

EXAMPLE 5 Given this final assignment table, identify two optimal solutions.

	1	2	3
A	4	0	0
B	0	3	2
C	1	0	0

Solution

The first assignment must be B–1, because B–1 is the only 0 that appears in a single row or column. Having made that assignment, there are two choices for the remaining two rows, and two choices for the remaining two columns. This results in two possible solutions, as shown:

	1	2	3
A	4	[0]	0
B	[0]	3	2
C	1	0	[0]

	1	2	3
A	4	0	[0]
B	[0]	3	2
C	1	[0]	0

Computer Solution of Assignment Problems

If an assignment problem is to be solved using the simplex method (i.e., as a standard LP problem), it must be stated in terms of an objective function and a set of constraints. This is illustrated in the next example.

■

EXAMPLE 6 The time for each of three employees to perform each of three jobs is shown in the following table. Formulate an LP model that will minimize total processing time. Note that each employee must perform only one job (and each job must be performed by only one employee).

Processing times (hours)

		Job, *j*		
		1	2	3
Employee, *i*	1	3	5	6
	2	8	9	7
	3	9	2	4

Solution

Let x_{ij} stand for the assignment of Employee i to Job j. If no assignment is made, $x_{ij} = 0$; if an assignment is made, $x_{ij} = 1$. There are nine decision variables, one for each of the nine positions in the table. In tabular form, these are:

		Job, j		
		1	2	3
	1	x_{11}	x_{12}	x_{13}
Employee, i	2	x_{21}	x_{22}	x_{23}
	3	x_{31}	x_{32}	x_{33}

The objective function combines the decision variables with their respective processing times. Thus, the objective function is:

$$\text{minimize} \quad 3x_{11} + 5x_{12} + 6x_{13} + 8x_{21} + 9x_{22} + 7x_{23} + 9x_{31} + 2x_{32} + 4x_{33}$$

The constraints are that there must be only one assignment for each employee (row), and only one for each job (column). Consequently, there are six constraints, three for the rows and three for the columns, and each is equal to 1. Thus, the constraints are:

$$\left.\begin{aligned} x_{11} + x_{12} + x_{13} &= 1 \\ x_{21} + x_{22} + x_{23} &= 1 \\ x_{31} + x_{32} + x_{33} &= 1 \end{aligned}\right\} \text{Rows}$$

$$\left.\begin{aligned} x_{11} + x_{21} + x_{31} &= 1 \\ x_{12} + x_{22} + x_{32} &= 1 \\ x_{13} + x_{23} + x_{33} &= 1 \end{aligned}\right\} \text{Columns}$$

We also require that all values be either 0 or 1, which can be written as follows:

All $x_{ij} = 0$ or 1

In some cases, the number of rows and number of columns may not be equal. For those cases, use *equality* constraints for the rows if there are fewer rows than columns, or for the columns if there are fewer columns. For the remaining constraints, use $\leq$ inequalities.

SUMMARY

This chapter describes two types of problems that lend themselves to solution using linear programming techniques: the transportation problem and the assignment problem. Transportation-type problems often involve the distribution of goods, whereas assignment-type problems involve the matching or pairing of two sets of items. Usually, such problems have different costs for different distribution alternatives or different pairings, and the objective is to identify the plan that minimizes total cost.

For each type of problem, a procedure for formulating the problem in a way that lends itself to solution using a simple algorithm is described. Solving such problems manually provides additional insight into LP models and their solutions. In addition, procedures are described for setting up each type of problem in a format that lends itself to computer solution, which, in practice, is the most realistic way of handling such problems.

GLOSSARY

Assignment Problem A problem that requires pairing two sets of items given a set of paired costs or profits in such a way that the total cost (profit) of the pairings is minimized (maximized).

Column Reduction A step in the Hungarian method, whereby the smallest number in each column is subtracted from all of the numbers in that column.

Degeneracy A condition that can occur in a transportation model: The number of occupied cells is too small to permit evaluation for optimality without first modifying the solution.

MODI MOdified DIstribution method, used to evaluate a transportation solution for optimality. Involves the use of row and column index numbers.

Northwest-Corner Method A procedure for obtaining an initial feasible solution to a transportation problem that begins by allocating units to the upper left-hand corner of a transportation table.

Row Reduction A step in the assignment method, whereby the smallest number in each row of a table is subtracted from all of the numbers in its row.

Stepping-Stone Method A procedure for determining if a solution to a transportation problem is optimal that involves tracing closed paths from each empty cell through occupied cells.

Transshipment Problem A transportation problem in which some locations are used as intermediate shipping points, thereby serving both as origins and as destinations.

SOLVED PROBLEMS

Problem 1. Solve this transportation problem for the optimal solution. If there is an alternate optimal solution, identify it.

From: \ To:	1	2	3	Supply
A	[2]	[3]	[9]	61
B	[5]	[6]	[4]	61
Demand	50	55	17	

Solution

First, check to see if supply and demand are equal. Demand is 50 + 55 + 17 = 122; supply is 61 + 61 = 122. Hence, they are equal.

Next, determine an initial feasible solution. This can be done using either the northwest-corner method or the intuitive method. Because the question did not specify which one, either can be used. Suppose we use the intuitive method. The lowest cell cost is $2 in A–1, so we begin by allocating as many units as possible to that cell. With a supply of 61 and a demand of 50, the most we can allocate is 50 (which is the smaller of the two quantities). This exhausts the demand of column 1 and leaves 11 units still to be allocated in the first row. Because column 1 demand is exhausted, we draw a line through the costs in column 1 to remove them from further consideration.

From: \ To:	1	2	3	Supply
A	50 [2]	[3]	[9]	~~61~~ 11
B	[5]	[6]	[4]	61
Demand	~~50~~	55	17	122

The next lowest cost is the $3 in cell A–2, where demand is 55 and remaining supply is 11. Because 11 is the smaller of the two, allocate 11 units, and adjust the row and column totals accordingly. Cross out the costs in row 1, since that supply has been exhausted. This results in the following:

From: \ To:	1	2	3	Supply
A	[2] 50	[3] 11	[9]	~~61~~
B	[5]	[6]	[4]	61
Demand	~~50~~	~~55~~ 44	17	122

The remaining two cells are filled in the same manner, with the result:

From: \ To:	1	2	3	Supply
A	[2] 50	[3] 11	[9]	61
B	[5]	[6] 44	[4] 17	61
Demand	50	55	17	122

Because the row and column quantities allocated add to the row and column totals, this is a feasible solution.

Next, we must ensure that the minimum number of occupied cells exists, or else we will have to adjust for degeneracy. That number is one less than the sum of the number of rows and the number of columns. With two rows and three columns, the desired number of occupied cells is: $2 + 3 - 1 = 4$. Since this agrees with the number we have, we can proceed to the next step, which is evaluation for optimality.

We can use either the stepping-stone method or MODI because no method was specified. Since MODI is not as messy as stepping-stone, let's use MODI. We begin with an index of 0 for the first row, which we write at the left of the first row. Then, for any completed cells in the first row, the column index number is the sum of the cell cost + 0. Hence, for column 1 we have an index number of 2, and for column 2, the index number is 3. Once we have determined the index number for column 2, we can compute the index number for the second row. It is equal to the cell cost for B–2 minus the index for column 2. Hence, it is $6 - 3 = 3$. And with that row index, we can determine the column index for column 3. It is equal to the cell cost for B–3 minus the index for the second row: $4 - 3 = 1$. The following table shows these index numbers.

		2	3	1	
	From: \ To:	1	2	3	Supply
0	A	50 [2]	11 [3]	[9]	61
3	B	[5]	44 [6]	17 [4]	61
	Demand	50	55	17	122

Now, we can compute the cell evaluations for the *empty* cells, using the relationship: Cell evalution = Cell cost − Row index − Column index. For cell B–1, this is 5 − 3 − 2 = 0; for cell A–3 it is 9 − 0 − 1 = +8. These are shown in the following table.

		2	3	1	
	From: \ To:	1	2	3	Supply
0	A	50 [2]	11 [3]	(+8) (circled) [9]	61
3	B	(0) (circled) [5]	44 [6]	17 [4]	61
	Demand	50	55	17	122

Because there are no negative cell evaluations, this is the optimal solution. Thus, to minimize transportation cost, ship 50 units from A to 1, 11 units from A to 2, 44 units from B to 2, and 17 units from B to 3. The total cost will be:

Route	Cost per Unit	×	Quantity	=	Route Cost
A–1	$2		50		$100
A–2	3		11		33
B–2	6		44		264
B–3	4		17		68
					$465

The appearance of a cell evaluation of zero indicates that an *alternate solution* with the same total cost exists. To determine what that other solution is, we must trace the stepping-stone path for the cell that has the zero evaluation. It is:

To: / From:	1	2	3	Supply
A	50 [2]	11 [3]	[9]	61
B	[5]	44 [6]	17 [4]	61
Demand	50	55	17	122

The negative *positions* in the path are cells A–1 and B–2. The smallest quantity in a negative position is the 44 units in cell B–2. It is this amount that can be reallocated around the path, subtracting it from the quantity at each negative position and adding it at each positive position. After doing this, the alternate solution becomes apparent. It is:

To: / From:	1	2	3	Supply
A	6 [2]	55 [3]	[9]	61
B	44 [5]	[6]	17 [4]	61
Demand	50	55	17	122

If you compute the total cost, you will see that it is the same as the total cost of the original optimal solution. Hence, the two solutions are equivalent in that regard.

Problem 2. Solve this transportation problem for the *maximum* profit. The values in the upper right-hand corner of each cell represent profit per unit for that cell. Use the intuitive method for the initial solution and the MODI method to evaluate the empty cells.

To: / From:	A	B	C	Capacity
#1	[2]	[8]	[6]	40
#2	[9]	[7]	[5]	50
#3	[4]	[4]	[3]	60
Demand	60	30	60	150

Solution

a. Because this is a maximization problem, our first step is to convert it to a minimization problem so that we can solve it in the same way we solve all transportation problems. To do this, we note that the largest unit profit in the table is 9. Subtract all of the unit profits in the table from 9, and enter the resulting opportunity costs in a new table:

From: \ To:	A	B	C	Capacity
#1	7	1	3	40
#2	0	2	4	50
#3	5	5	6	60
Demand	60	30	60	150

b. Now solve this revised problem as a regular transportation problem where the objective is to minimize the (opportunity) costs. The resulting solution will maximize profits.

(1) Make the initial set of allocations using the intuitive method: Begin with cell 2–A because it has the lowest cell cost (0). Allocate the smaller of the row capacity (50) and the column demand (60). Thus, allocate 50 units, and adjust the row and column amounts accordingly. Cross out the costs in row 2 because its capacity is now exhausted. The next lowest cost is for cell 1–B. Allocate 30 units and cross out the costs in column B and the column total of 30. Continue in this manner until all units have been allocated to cells. The resulting shipping plan is:

From: \ To:	A	B	C	Capacity
#1	[7]	30 [1]	10 [3]	40
#2	50 [0]	[2]	[4]	50
#3	10 [5]	[5]	50 [6]	60
Demand	60	30	60	150

(2) Determine the index numbers for MODI: begin by assigning a row index number of zero to the first row. Then, you can determine column index numbers using the occupied cells in the first row. For column B, the index number is 1 and for column C, it is 3. (Recall that the sum of the row and column index numbers for an occupied cell must equal the cell cost.) Next, use the index number for column C and the cell cost for 3–C to obtain the index number for row 3. We can see that the sum of the row 3 index number (unknown at this point) and the column C index number (3) must equal 6. Hence, the row index number must equal 3. Continuing in this manner, we obtain index numbers for the remaining row and column. These are shown in the next table.

(3) Use the index numbers to evaluate the empty cells: for each empty cell, subtract the sum of the row and column index numbers for that cell from the cell's unit cost. The result is the cell evaluation. For cell 1–A, we have $7 - (0 + 2) = +5$. For cell 2–B, we have $2 - (-2 + 1) = +3$. For cell 2–C, we have $4 - (-2 + 3) = +3$. For cell 3–B, we have $5 - (3 + 1) = +1$. These are shown in the following table.

		+2	+1	+3	
		A	B	C	Capacity
0	#1	(+5) [7]	30 [1]	10 [3]	40
−2	#2	50 [0]	(+3) [2]	(+3) [4]	0
+3	#3	10 [5]	(+1) [5]	50 [6]	60
	Demand	60	30	60	150

(4) Because none of the cell evaluations are negative, this solution is optimal.

(5) Find the total profit by using the unit profits for the *original* transportation table, *not* the table containing the opportunity costs. This yields:

$$30(8) + 10(6) + 50(9) + 10(4) + 50(3) = \$940$$

Problem 3. The following table contains processing costs for two jobs on various machines. Each job must be processed on one machine. Determine a set of pairings that will minimize total processing costs.

		Job 1	Job 2
Machine	A	8	7
	B	5	4
	C	3	1

Solution

The problem requires a pairing, or matching, of jobs and machines. Thus, it is an assignment problem. Assignment techniques require square tables (i.e., in this case, an equal number of jobs and machines). Because there are three machines and only two jobs, a third (dummy) job must be added. Processing costs of zero are assigned to each of the possible pairings of the dummy job and the machines, resulting in this table:

		Job 1	Job 2	Job 3
Machine	A	8	7	0
	B	5	4	0
	C	3	1	0

Ordinarily, the next step would be to perform a row reduction. Note, however, that the smallest value in each row is a zero. Consequently, a row reduction (i.e., subtracting the smallest value in each row from the other values in the row) will result in the same values. Therefore, we move to the next step, which is a column reduction. The smallest value in the first column is 3, the smallest in the second column is 1, and the smallest in the third column is 0. The column reduction is illustrated in the next set of tables.

(Original values)

		Job 1	Job 2	Job 3
Machine	A	8	7	0
	B	5	4	0
	C	3	1	0
Smallest value:		3	1	0

(Values after the column reduction)

		Job 1	Job 2	Job 3
Machine	A	5	6	0
	B	(2)	3	0
	C	0	0	0

Now, we test to determine if the optimal solution can be found at this point. This involves crossing out the zeros in the table with as few (horizontal or vertical) lines as possible. As shown in the preceding table, only two lines are required. If the lines had equaled the number of rows (or columns, because we had a square table), the optimal set of assignments could be made. Because that is not the case, we move on to the next step.

Identify the smallest value that is not crossed out. It is the 2 in location B–1. Circle it, as in the preceding table, and then subtract it from any value that has not been crossed out. Also, add it to the intersection of the crossing lines. The results are shown in the next table.

		Job 1	Job 2	Job 3
Machine	A	3	4	0
	B	0	1	0
	C	0	0	2

At this point, three lines (not shown) would be needed to cross out all of the zero values. Therefore, we can identify the optimal solution. To do this, begin with a row or column that has only one zero. In this case, the first row has only one zero; so does the second column. Hence, either of those could be chosen for the initial assignment. Suppose we choose A–3. We indicate this by drawing a box around the 0 at A–3, and then cross out all of the values in row A and all of the values in column 3.

		Job 1	Job 2	Job 3
Machine	A	3	4	[0]
	B	0	1	0
	C	0	0	2

We must continue to make assignments to rows or columns that have only one zero, until none with unique zeros remain. Zeros that have been crossed out should be ignored. At this point, row B has only one remaining zero, and the second column also has one zero. Therefore, either of these could be chosen. Suppose we choose B–1. Drawing a box around that zero and crossing out all of the other values in row B and column 1 leaves only the 0 at C–2.

		Job 1	Job 2	Job 3
Machine	A	3	4	[0]
	B	[0]	1	0
	C	0	0	2

Thus, the last assignment is C–2, and our optimal set of assignments is A–3, B–1, and C–2. The (minimum) cost associated with this set of assignments can be determined by referring to the original table of values and noting the cost of each assignment. Thus:

Assignment	**Cost**
A–3	0
B–1	5
C–2	1
	6

Because Job 3 (the dummy) has been assigned to Machine A, this tells us that, in reality, Machine A will not have a job assigned to it.

PROBLEMS

1. Consider the transportation problem of the California Dishwasher Company:

From: \ To:	Store 1	Store 2	Store 3	Supply
Warehouse A	12	20	15	50
Warehouse B	9	11	4	15
Warehouse C	20	14	8	55
Demand	25	50	45	120

a. Develop an initial feasible solution using the northwest-corner method. Compute the total cost for this solution.

b. Evaluate the solution using the stepping-stone method. Is the solution optimal? Explain.

c. Repeat the evaluation using MODI and compare your cell evaluations to those obtained using the stepping-stone method.

d. Obtain an improved solution and evaluate it using MODI. Is it optimal?

e. What is the total cost for your optimal solution?

2. Consider the transportation problem of Sunbelt Heat Pumps:

From: \ To:	Cincinnati	Miami	Memphis	Tampa	Supply
Houston	12	5	7	2	98
Atlanta	11	3	6	1	80
Demand	35	50	25	68	

a. Develop an intuitive solution to this problem; evaluate it, and revise if necessary to obtain the minimum cost solution. Then, compute the total cost.

b. Solve the problem using the northwest-corner and stepping-stone methods. Are there alternate optimal solutions to this problem? How do you know?

3. Rod Steele, superintendent of Rochester Forging, has developed the following transportation model. Solve it for the minimum-cost solution using the intuitive method for the initial solution and MODI for evaluation. Is there an alternate optimal solution? What is it?

From: \ To:	Albany	Buffalo	Cleveland	Supply (tons per day)
Pittsburgh	14	8	3	40
Toronto	9	5	7	80
Philadelphia	6	12	4	60
Demand (tons per day)	70	60	50	

4. *a.* Find the minimum-cost solution to the following transportation problem using the northwest-corner method and stepping-stone. What is the total cost?

   b. Find the minimum-cost solution using the intuitive method and MODI.

From: \ To:	Detroit	Denver	Kansas City	Supply
Chicago	2	17	12	64
St. Louis	9	12	6	44
Omaha	7	5	10	36
Demand	48	48	48	

5. The manager of Home Office Supplies, Gigi Staples, has just received demand forecasts and capacity (supply) figures for next month. These are summarized along with unit shipping costs in the following transportation table.

To: / From:	D_1	D_2	D_3	D_4	D_5	Supply
O_1	8	4	12	11	9	220
O_2	7	6	10	5	6	260
O_3	12	13	9	16	9	200
Demand	140	180	150	140	195	

a. Using the intuitive method and MODI, find the minimum-cost solution.
b. Which destinations will not receive their entire demand? How many units short will each be?

6. Consider the transportation problem of Doors Plus, a producer of steel doors for public schools:

To: / From:	Charlotte	Columbus	Chicago	Supply
Rochester	26	15	22	160
Dallas	18	12	17	125
Buffalo	28	24	20	30
Demand	75	90	150	

a. Using the intuitive method and MODI, find the minimum-cost solution.
b. Now suppose that the Rochester–Chicago route is temporarily unavailable. Beginning with the solution from (*a*), determine a distribution plan that will avoid this route. How much extra does this plan cost compared to the plan when all routes are possible? Note: Costs are in $100s.

7. The Future Furniture company recently began construction of a new warehouse. During the construction period, several changes have occurred that require development of a new distribution plan. The current figures for supply are:

Plant	Capacity (pieces per week)
East L.A.	600
West L.A.	800
El Toro	400

Current figures for demand are:

Warehouse	Demand (pieces per week)
Orange County #1	300
Orange County #2	400
Long Beach	200
Los Angeles	900

Average shipping costs per unit are:

From: \ To:	Orange County #1	Orange County #2	Long Beach	Los Angeles
East L.A.	$8	$9	$6	$4
West L.A.	10	7	2	3
El Toro	5	7	9	12

a. Develop an initial feasible solution using the intuitive method.

b. Find the optimal solution. What are the total costs?

c. If the El Toro–Orange County #1 route becomes temporarily unavailable, what distribution plan would minimize total cost? How much more would it cost than if the El Toro–Orange County #1 route could be used?

8. Rework the Harley problem from the first section of this chapter, treating the cell values as unit profits instead of unit costs. Determine the optimal distribution plan and the total profit for that plan.

9. Assume in the preceding problem that route A–3 is temporarily unavailable.

a. Develop a solution that will maximize total profit without involving A–3.

b. What are the total profits for this plan?

10. Solve the transshipment problem presented in Table 7–22 for the minimum-cost distribution plan, then interpret your answer.

11. Solve Problem 1 treating the cell values as revenue per unit instead of cost per unit. Develop the initial solution using the intuitive approach. What is the total revenue associated with your optimal solution?

12. Consider the following transportation table:

From: \ To:	Warehouse #1	Warehouse #2	Warehouse #3	Supply
Plant A	50	32	40	700
Plant B	16	30	20	200
Plant C	35	28	42	200
Demand	300	400	400	

a. Develop a distribution plan that minimizes total shipping cost.

b. If route 3–A is unacceptable for some reason, what distribution plan would be optimal? What would its total cost be?

13. Suppose the cell values in the previous problem represent unit profits and that all routes are acceptable. What distribution plan would be best in terms of maximizing profits? What would be the total profit for that plan?

14. Reconsider the situation presented in Problem 6. Suppose that Chicago demand is temporarily reduced to 80 units.

a. Determine the optimal solution.

b. What is the total cost of the distribution plan?

c. Which location will have excess capacity? How much?

15. The owner of More Than Just a Name, Tom Selleck, projects that within three years, demand for riding mowers will exceed supply by approximately 550 units a month. Projected demand and current capacities and costs are:

From: \ To:	Warehouse #1	Warehouse #2	Warehouse #3	Warehouse #4	Supply (mowers per month)
Plant A	10	27	7	14	250
Plant B	12	20	8	30	270
Demand (mowers per month)	340	140	140	450	

The firm intends to build a plant with a capacity of 550 units per month, and has narrowed the choices of location to two sites, C1 and C2. Transportation costs for each potential origin are:

C1 to	Unit Cost
#1	13
#2	27
#3	17
#4	25

C2 to	Unit Cost
#1	24
#2	17
#3	15
#4	21

Determine the optimal shipping plan and the minimum total cost for each possible location. Which has the lower total cost? What would the annual savings be if the location with the lower cost is selected?

16. The distribution manager of the firm whose transportation problem was described in Problem 4 has decided that an intermediate location would be very useful to temporarily store goods bound for Denver from Chicago and St. Louis at Omaha. A storage depot with a capacity for 58 units has been constructed at Omaha for this purpose. Estimated shipping costs are $10 per unit from Chicago to Omaha and $4 per unit from St. Louis to Omaha. Determine the shipping plan that will minimize total costs for this revised problem.

17. Bob Bright, the manager of Sunbelt Heat Pumps, whose shipping costs are described in Problem 2 of this chapter, intends to use Atlanta and Cincinnati as points for temporary storage, each with a capacity of 50 units. Estimated costs are:

Cincinnati to	Cost per Unit
Miami	$5
Memphis	$2
Tampa	$4
Atlanta	$9

Houston to	Cost per Unit
Atlanta	$7

Determine an optimal shipping plan for this revised problem.

18. Using the information given in Problem 12, determine the optimal shipping plan, treating the problem as a transshipment one and using this additional information: Plant A and Warehouse 3 will be used as temporary storage points. Shipping costs will be $12 per unit from B to A and $20 per unit from C to A. Shipping costs from Warehouse 3 to Warehouse 1 will be $15 per unit, $18 per unit from Warehouse 3 to Warehouse 2, and $40 per unit from Warehouse 3 to Plant A.

19. Are there alternate solutions for Problem 17? If so, identify one.

20. A soft drink manufacturer, Sara Soda, Ltd., has recently begun negotiations with brokers in the areas where it intends to distribute its products. Before finalizing the agreements, however, Manager Dave Pepper wants to determine shipping routes and costs. The firm has three plants with capacities as shown below:

Plant	Capacity (cases per week)
Metro	40,000
Ridge	30,000
Colby	25,000

Estimated demands in each of the warehouse localities are:

Warehouse	Demand (cases per week)
SR1	24,000
SR2	22,000
SR3	23,000
SR4	16,000
SR5	10,000

The estimated shipping costs per case for the various routes are:

From: \ To:	RS1	RS2	RS3	RS4	RS5
Metro	.80	.75	.60	.70	.90
Ridge	.75	.80	.85	.70	.85
Colby	.70	.75	.70	.80	.80

Determine the optimal shipping plan that will minimize total shipping cost under these conditions:

a. Route Ridge–RS4 is unacceptable.

b. All routes are acceptable.

c. What is the additional cost of the Ridge–RS4 route not being acceptable?

21. Solve this LP problem using the transportation method. Find the optimal transportation plan and the minimum cost. Also, decide if there is an alternate solution. If there is one, identify it.

minimize $8x_{11} + 2x_{12} + 5x_{13} + 2x_{21} + x_{22} + 3x_{23} + 7x_{31} + 2x_{32} + 6x_{33}$

subject to

$$\begin{aligned} x_{11} + x_{12} + x_{13} &= 90 \\ x_{21} + x_{22} + x_{23} &= 105 \\ x_{31} + x_{32} + x_{33} &= 105 \\ x_{11} + x_{21} + x_{31} &= 150 \\ x_{12} + x_{22} + x_{32} &= 75 \\ x_{13} + x_{23} + x_{33} &= 75 \\ \text{All variables} &\geq 0 \end{aligned}$$

22. GuessTech is a small plastics company whose products may or may not be biodegradable. Three of its products can be manufactured on either of two machines. Neither machine has the capacity to handle all of the load; therefore, some of the work must be handled by one and the remainder by the other. The manager of the shop wants to minimize total cost. Cost information is given in the following table:

	Production Cost per Unit	
	Machine 1	Machine 2
Product A	$1.20	$1.40
Product B	1.50	1.30
Product C	1.60	1.50

Daily capacity of Machine 1 is 600 units and daily capacity of Machine 2 is 750 units. Production quotas are 400 units of each product per day.

Formulate this problem as a linear programming model, then solve for the optimal solution.

23. Write the information presented in Problem 17 in a more general LP format. Use a computer package to solve for the optimal solution and interpret the results (i.e., what shipping plan is optimal?).

24. Rewrite Problem 14 in a format more conducive to computer solution. Obtain the computer solution using an appropriate package and interpret the results.

25. Solve Problem 8 for the optimal solution using a computer package and interpret the results.

26. Use a computer package to solve Problem 7 for the optimal solution and interpret the results. Assume all routes are acceptable.

27. Solve for the optimal solution to Problem 6 using a computer package and interpret the results. Assume all routes are acceptable.

28. Solve Problem 5 for the optimal solution using a computer package and interpret the results.

29. Use a computer package to obtain the optimal solution to Problem 2 and then interpret the results.

30. Use a computer package to obtain the optimal solution to Problem 1 and interpret the results.

31. A shop foreman has prepared the following table, which shows the costs for various combinations of job-machine assignments.

		Machine		
		A	B	C
Job	1	20	35	22
	2	42	18	25
	3	6	23	15

a. Perform a row reduction on the cost table.

b. Perform a column reduction on the costs that resulted from the row reduction.

c. Can an optimal assignment be made? Why or why not?

d. What is the optimal (minimum-cost) assignment for this problem?

e. What is the total cost for the optimum assignment?

32. The foreman of a machine shop wants to determine a minimum-cost matching for operators and machines. The foreman has determined the hourly cost for each of four operators for the four machines, as shown in the following cost table.

		Machine			
		A	B	C	D
Operator	1	70	80	75	64
	2	55	52	58	54
	3	58	56	64	68
	4	62	60	67	70

a. Determine the minimum-cost assignment for this problem.

b. What is the total cost for the optimal assignment?

c. Is there an alternate optimal assignment? What is it? Calculate the total cost for the alternate optimal assignment.

d. Set up this problem in the form of an objective function and a set of constraints.

33. The approximate travel times for officiating crews for college basketball for four games scheduled for a weekend are shown in the following table:

		Game site			
		Syracuse	Buffalo	Rochester	Ithaca
Crew	A	1.2*	1.4	0.2	1.5
	B	1.0	2.0	0.5	1.0
	C	1.2	3.4	2.4	0.5
	D	2.1	3.1	1.1	0.8

* Time in hours.

a. What set of crew assignments will minimize travel time?

b. What is the total travel time required for the optimal assignment?

34. Suppose in the preceding problem that because of a previous conflict between Crew D and one of the teams playing at Ithaca, Crew D cannot be assigned to that location. With this in mind, determine an optimal set of assignments. What effect, if any, does this restriction have on the total travel time for all crews?

35. (Refer to Problem 33.) Suppose that a basketball game in Niagara Falls has been canceled, freeing up another crew to select from. The crew travel times to Syracuse, Buffalo, Rochester, and Ithaca are 1.8, .5, .6, and 2.0 hours, respectively. Assume, too, that the D–Ithaca assignment is undesirable.

a. Determine the set of assignments that will minimize total travel time.

b. Which crew will not be assigned?

c. Is there an alternate optimal solution? Explain.

36. An industrial engineer has prepared a table that shows the costs for each possible combination of job and machine for four jobs, as shown:

		Machine			
		A	B	C	D
Job	1	45	75	80	35
	2	55	60	60	65
	3	70	65	50	45
	4	60	75	70	65

a. Determine the set of assignments that will minimize total processing cost.

b. What is total processing cost?

c. Is there an alternate optimal solution? What is it?

37. If the numbers in the previous problem reflected profits rather than costs, what set of assignments would have been optimal?

38. (Refer to Problem 36.) Suppose that Job 1 could not be assigned to Machine D because of a technical problem. What set of assignments would

now minimize total cost? What additional cost is incurred because of the technical problem?

39. An analyst has kept track of the number of defectives produced by five workers on five different machines. The results are shown below for a run of 400 units per machine:

		Machine				
		A	B	C	D	E
Worker	1	9	7	4	6	2
	2	7	4	5	2	1
	3	3	4	3	2	3
	4	9	7	8	6	5
	5	0	3	2	4	3

a. Determine a set of assignments that will minimize the total number of errors for a given run size.

b. Is there an alternate optimal solution? If so, what is it?

c. What is the total number of defectives expected for the optimal assignment?

40. In the previous problem, if another machine was available and the number of defectives produced by the five workers for a run of 400 units was 4, 4, 2, 3, and 1, respectively, determine the following:

a. A set of assignments that will minimize the total number of expected defectives.

b. Which machine will not be used?

c. Is there an alternate optimal solution? If so, what is it?

41. A manager has four jobs that must be assigned. Estimated processing times for each of four employees are shown in the accompanying table.

		Employee			
		Smith	Jones	Green	Mehl
Job	1	6.2*	8.0	5.4	4.8
	2	6.0	7.2	5.8	4.4
	3	5.5	6.0	6.6	6.8
	4	6.3	6.6	7.0	7.3

* Time in hours.

a. Determine a set of assignments that will minimize total processing time.

b. What is the total processing time for the optimal assignments?

43. A company has four manufacturing plants and four warehouses. Each of the plants will supply one of the warehouses. The warehouses each have a demand that is equal to a factory's output for a given period. Assume that

all capacities and all demands are 300 units per period. The shipping costs for all routes are shown in the table below. The costs are in thousands.

		Warehouse			
		1	2	3	4
Plant	A	2.4	1.8	2.6	1.8
	B	2.0	1.9	2.2	2.2
	C	1.4	1.7	2.0	1.4
	D	1.6	2.1	2.1	1.6

a. Determine a set of assignments that will minimize total shipping cost for a period.

b. What is the total shipping cost for your plan?

c. Is there an alternate optimal solution? If so, what is it?

d. Would the optimal solution change if the values represented shipping *time* instead of shipping *cost?* Explain.

44. On Monday morning, the manager of a small print shop, Carri Fonts, finds that four jobs must be handled on a "rush" basis. Fortunately, there are four employees available to work on these jobs, and each will handle one of the jobs. Each employee has a slightly different estimated completion time for each job, as shown in the table below:

Completion time (hours)

		Job			
		A	B	C	D
Employee	Tom	4.2	4.1	5.4	5.0
	Dick	4.4	4.0	5.2	4.8
	Harry	4.3	4.2	5.0	4.9
	Jane	4.0	4.1	5.4	5.0

Carri wants to determine how to assign the employees to jobs so that the total completion time is as low as possible.

Formulate this as a linear programming model and solve by computer.

45. The accompanying table shows projected profits for all possible combinations of four workers and jobs awaiting processing. Formulate an LP model that will yield optimal pairings in terms of total profits and solve by computer.

		Job		
		1	2	3
Worker	A	$500	400	450
	B	800	300	200
	C	700	400	500
	D	900	500	799

46. Set up Problem 31 in the form of an objective function and a set of constraints and solve using a computer.

47. Set up Solved Problem 3 in the form of objective function and a set of constraints.

Chapter 8
Integer Programming

Chapter Outline

Learning Objectives

After completing this chapter, you should be able to:

1. Tell how integer programming problems differ from general linear programming problems.
2. Explain the differences among pure, mixed, and 0–1 problems.
3. Use graphical methods to solve two-variable integer problems.
4. Use the branch and bound method to solve integer problems.
5. Use the enumeration method to solve 0–1 problems.

In the preceding chapters, which dealt with linear programming solutions, the issue of noninteger solutions was largely ignored. This was done for a number of reasons. One was that to require integer solutions would have added considerably to the complexity of the models. Another was that numerous applications exist in which integer solutions are not necessary. This is especially true for problems that involve variables that are measured on a *continuous* scale (e.g., volume, weight, length, and time). In other cases, a rounded solution may be acceptable. For example, if a problem involved determining the numbers of various types of nails to produce, an answer of 9,200.7 could easily be rounded up to 9,201 with little or no consequence. Even if the solution turned out to be infeasible, reality would force a feasible solution (e.g., after making 9,200 nails, there might not be enough raw material to make one more nail).

On the other hand, there are important cases in which integer solutions are required. For instance, if a problem concerned the optimal number of cargo ships, apartment houses, or office buildings to build, a noninteger answer would not be acceptable. Similarly, simply rounding to the nearest integer will not necessarily produce an answer that is optimal or near optimal, especially if millions of dollars are involved. Obviously, in cases such as these, it is desirable to identify the optimal, *integer* values of decision variables. This chapter describes methods for doing that.

TYPES OF INTEGER PROGRAMMING PROBLEMS

Basically, there are three types of linear programming problems that involve integer solutions: pure-integer problems, mixed-integer problems, and 0–1 problems.

Pure-Integer Problems

Problems requiring that *all* decision variables have integer solutions are referred to as **pure-integer problems.** Examples include the number of each type of plane to produce, the number of each type of large machine to produce, the number of each type of house to construct, and so on.

Mixed-Integer Problems

In **mixed-integer problems,** some, but not all, of the decision variables are required to have integer values in the final solution, whereas others need not have integer values. For example, an investor may want to decide on a portfolio of investments that includes land and/or race horses. In general, land would be a continuous variable; an investor could conceivably purchase 25.37 acres. Conversely, the number of horses purchased would presumably be an integer.

0–1 Problems

A third kind of problem, a **0–1 problem,** relates to situations in which decision variables are of the yes-no type. For example, a bank may be considering possible locations for new branch offices. Sites that are chosen would receive a 1, whereas those not chosen would receive a 0. Similarly, in a problem requiring matching, say, of jobs and machines or workers and jobs, the optimal matches would receive a 1, and all others would receive a 0.

SOLVING INTEGER PROGRAMMING PROBLEMS

In practical terms, there are two methods that can be used to solve integer programming problems. One is called the **branch and bound method;** it involves solving a sequence of *subproblems* until the optimal solution has been identified. The other is **enumeration;** it involves preparing a list of *all* possible alternatives, weeding out the ones that are infeasible, then determining which of the feasible solutions is optimal. The enumeration approach is particularly well suited for 0–1-type problems because the possible outcomes are easily identified and fairly limited for small problems. The branch and bound approach is more general; it lends itself to all types of integer programming problems. Consequently, the discussion here will focus primarily on the branch and bound approach, although the enumeration approach will be illustrated in the context of 0–1 problems.

The branch and bound method will be illustrated graphically for instructional purposes. However, as a practical matter, branch and bound solutions rely on computer support—each subproblem must be solved using the computer. Manual solution of subproblems using simplex is theoretically possible, but the computational burden would be enormous. Graphical methods could be used, but only for two-variable problems. With that in mind, let's consider a graphical solution to a very simple problem in order to better understand the nature of integer programming problems and solutions.

Figure 8–1 shows a simple integer programming problem and a graph of the constraints and the objective function. Note that the feasible solution space consists entirely of integers (represented by the dark points) that satisfy the contraints. In an LP problem that did not require an integer solution, the objective function would be plotted, then moved manually away from the origin in order to determine the optimal intersection. We can see this in Figure 8–1, but we also can see that this is not one of the integer solutions. In order to obtain a feasible integer solution using the objective function, we must move it (parallel to the one shown) back toward the origin. Hence, in order to achieve a feasible integer solution, we must settle for a lower value of the objective function (because moving the objective function toward the origin decreases its value). In moving the line toward the origin, the *first* point we come to will be the optimal integer solution. As you can see in Figure 8–1, that point is 1,1. Thus, the optimal integer solution is $x_1 = 1, x_2 = 1$.

FIGURE 8–1 Graph of an Integer Programming Problem

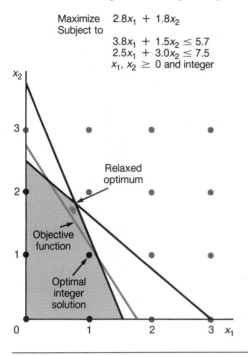

Maximize $2.8x_1 + 1.8x_2$
Subject to
$3.8x_1 + 1.5x_2 \leq 5.7$
$2.5x_1 + 3.0x_2 \leq 7.5$
$x_1, x_2 \geq 0$ and integer

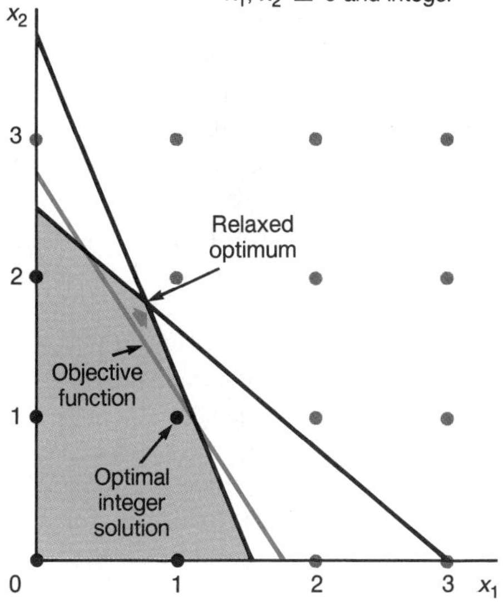

THE BRANCH AND BOUND METHOD

The simplex method is an efficient way of obtaining the optimal solution to linear programming problems. It incorporates a repetitive procedure that investigates adjacent points along the outer edge of the feasible solution region until no further improvements are possible. Unlike the general linear programming problem, optimal solutions to integer programming problems are not necessarily along the outer surface of the feasible solution region. Moreover, solutions are restricted to integer values for some or all of the variables. This means the simplex technique cannot be used *directly* to identify an optimal solution to an integer programming problem. In fact, there is *no* technique that will lead directly to the optimal solution. Consequently, obtaining an optimum requires an intelligent search approach.

The *branch and bound* method is such an approach. It begins with the solution of an integer problem as if it were a typical linear programming problem (i.e., the integer requirements are ignored). This is referred to as the **LP relaxation solution** because the integer aspect of the problem is relaxed or ignored temporarily. If this initial solution should happen to produce integer values for all of the decision variables, then the solution also is the optimal solution to the integer problem. Very often, this does not happen; one or more of the decision variables is noninteger. Even so, the LP relaxation solution performs two valuable functions. One is that it provides a standard of comparison against which other solutions can be judged. This is due to the fact that no other solution, integer or noninteger, can possibly yield a better value of the objective function. For a maximization problem, the initial LP solution is an *upper bound* on what may be possible to obtain with further analysis. The optimal *integer* solution will either equal this value, or be *less* than this. However, because the search process involves the use of *additional* contraints while keeping the original constraints, it is impossible to obtain a solution that yields a higher value of the objective function.

The other function of the relaxed solution is providing a starting point for the analysis. Should the LP relaxation solution fail to produce all integer values for the decision variables, the branch and bound method involves partitioning (branching) the feasible solution region into smaller and smaller subsets. For each subset, the optimal solution is identified using either simplex or graphical procedures. Noninteger solutions indicate that further branching may be required. However, some subsets will yield higher values of the objective function than others and, therefore, appear more promising. Consequently, branching from those solutions rather than from lower-valued subsets is advisable. Some subsets may yield integer solutions; however, these may or may not prove to be optimal when compared to other integer solutions for other subsets.

In order to have a basis for comparison, the value of the objective function for each subset is determined. That, then, becomes the upper bound for all subsequent subsets in that portion of the node diagram because no subset can yield a solution that will have a higher value of the objective function than the subset from which it was derived. The process continues until an integer solution is identified that has a higher objective function value than that possible in any other subset. This procedure is demonstrated in the following example.

A Pure-Integer Problem

Pure integer problems require that all variables have integer values.

■

EXAMPLE 1 Consider this all-integer problem:

maximize $6x_1 + 8x_2$ (millions)

subject to

$$4x_1 + 6x_2 \leq 36$$
$$10x_1 + 7x_2 \leq 70$$
$$x_1 \text{ and } x_2 \geq 0 \text{ and integer}$$

Solve for the optimal integer solution.

FIGURE 8–2 The LP Relaxation Solution

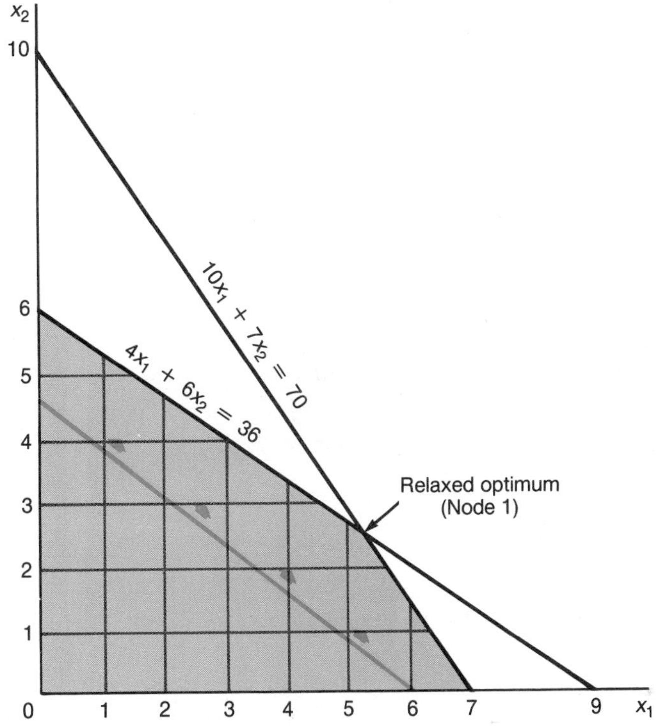

Solution

The first step is to find the LP relaxation solution. Because only two decision variables are involved, either the simplex method or the graphical method can be used. For purposes of illustration, the graphical method will be used.

The LP relaxation solution for Example 1 is shown in Figure 8–2. The values of the decision variables and the objective function at that point are:

$$x_1 = 5.25$$
$$x_2 = 2.50$$
$$Z = \$51.50$$

Note that neither of the two variables is an integer in this initial solution. Consequently, a search must now be conducted to find optimal integer values.

The results at each stage of the branch and bound procedure can be summarized by a node (circle) on a "tree" or **node diagram** that consists of branches (straight lines) and nodes. Each node contains the value of the objective function at that point in the analysis along with a listing of the values of the decision variables that produced this

FIGURE 8–3 Node 1 Summarizes the LP Relaxation Solution

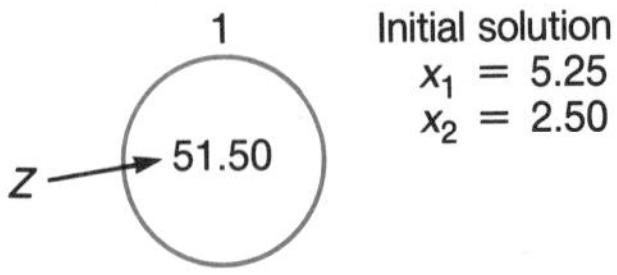

FIGURE 8–4 Branching from the First Node

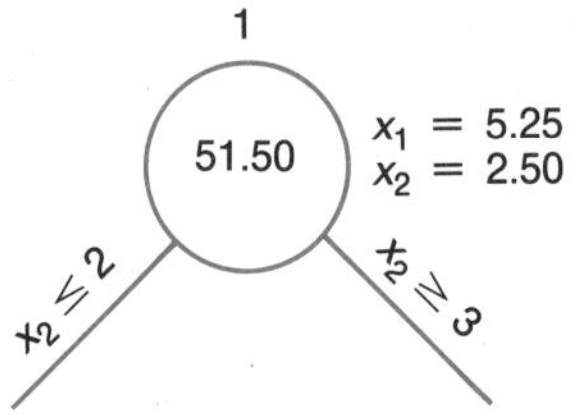

value. The initial node of the tree contains the results of the solution of the original problem. The initial node for this problem is shown in Figure 8–3.

The search for an integer solution begins by selecting one of the two variables to focus on. We shall use this rule of thumb:

Select the variable with the largest fractional part to branch on.[1]

The **fractional parts** of the two variables are $x_1 = .25$ and $x_2 = .5$. Hence, x_2 has the largest fractional part.

Because the value $x_2 = 2.5$ is not acceptable, we now explore two possible alternatives: either $x_2 \leq 2$ or $x_2 \geq 3$, since there is no integer value *between* 2 and 3. In effect, we are subdividing the feasible solution space into two regions that will be explored separately (see Figure 8–4). This results in two subproblems:

For $x_2 \leq 2$: (Node 2)

maximize $Z = 6x_1 + 8x_2$

subject to

$$4x_1 + 6x_2 \leq 36$$
$$10x_1 + 7x_2 \leq 70$$
$$x_2 \leq 2$$
$$x_1, x_2 \geq 0 \text{ and integer}$$

For $x_2 \geq 3$: (Node 3)

maximize $Z = 6x_1 + 8x_2$

subject to

$$4x_1 + 6x_2 \leq 36$$
$$10x_1 + 7x_2 \leq 70$$
$$x_2 \geq 3$$
$$x_1, x_2 \geq 0 \text{ and integer}$$

(The objective function and first two constraints are the original problem; $x_2 \leq 2$ and $x_2 \geq 3$ are the new constraints.)

Original problem

New constraint

The next step in the procedure is to solve each problem separately for its optimum. As noted previously, this ordinarily would be done using the simplex method. A graphical solution is used in order to better illustrate the concepts. Figure 8–5 indi-

[1] Choice of branching rule is somewhat arbitrary; branching on the smallest fractional part is another possibility. For consistency, branching on the largest fractional part will be used.

FIGURE 8–5 Subproblems and Solution Points for Nodes 2 and 3

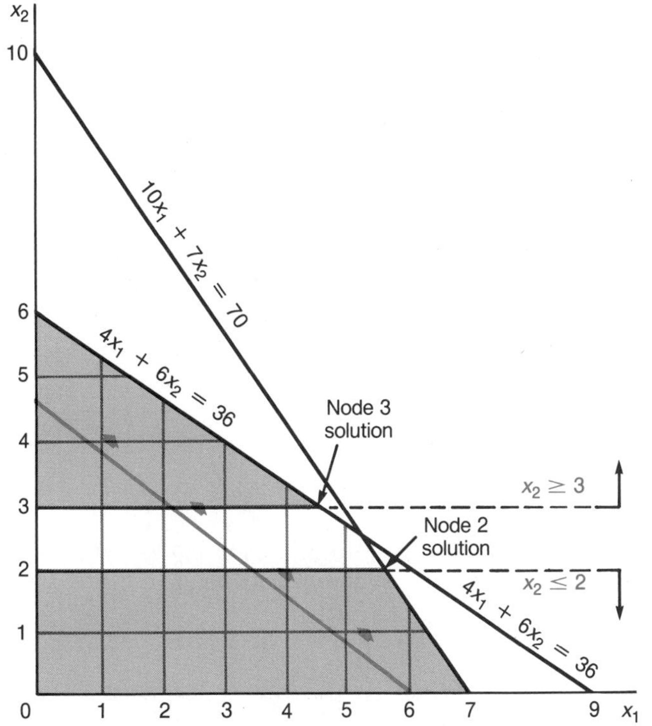

cates the two subregions for the two problems and each one's optimum, which was identified by sliding the objective function away from the origin. The exact values of the variables at those points can be determined by substitution:

Node 2: (substitute $x_2 = 2$)	Node 3: (substitute $x_2 = 3$)
$10x_1 + 7(2) = 70$	$4x_1 + 6(3) = 36$
Solving, $x_1 = 5.6$	Solving, $x_1 = 4.5$
$Z = 6(5.6) + 8(2) = 49.60$	$Z = 6(4.5) + 8(3) = 51.00$

Because neither of these solutions have both x_1 and x_2 integer, additional branching will be necessary. The Z values for each subproblem now become the upper bounds for their respective nodes: No subsequent branching from that node can produce a value of the objective function that exceeds this upper bound. The lower bound at each node *could* be determined, but that information would be of little use, so it is not computed. This new information is summarized in Figure 8–6.

Because neither solution involves only integer values, both nodes offer further branching possibilities. However, because the upper bound value of Node 3 ($51.00) is

FIGURE 8–6 Solutions for Nodes 2 and 3

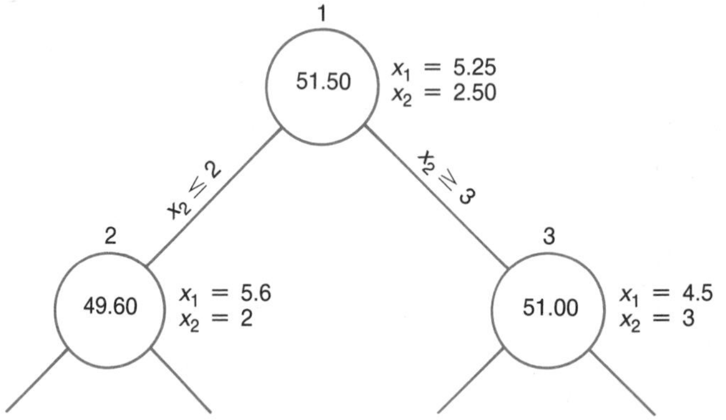

greater than the upper bound value of Node 2 ($49.60), it seems reasonable to explore branches from Node 3 first.

Since the only noninteger is $x_1 = 4.5$, we can branch on $x_1 \le 4$ and $x_1 \ge 5$ from Node 3. This produces two new subproblems, which are:

For $x_1 \le 4$: (Node 4)

maximize $Z = 6x_1 + 8x_2$

subject to

$$4x_1 + 6x_2 \le 36$$
$$10x_1 + 7x_2 \le 70$$
$$x_2 \ge 3$$
$$x_1 \le 4$$

$x_1, x_2 \ge 0$ and integer

For $x_1 \ge 5$: (Node 5)

maximize $Z = 6x_1 + 8x_2$

subject to

$$4x_1 + 6x_2 \le 36$$
$$10x_1 + 7x_2 \le 70$$
$$x_2 \ge 3$$
$$x_1 \ge 5$$

$x_1, x_2 \ge 0$ and integer

(The first three constraints: Node 3 problem; $x_1 \le 4$ ← New constraint → $x_1 \ge 5$)

Figure 8–7 shows the graphical representation of these two subproblems. For the case where $x_1 \le 4$, the solution point is designated as Node 4. There is no feasible solution region for the case where $x_1 \ge 5$ (designated as Node 5). The value of x_2 for Node 4 can be determined by substituting $x_1 = 4$ into the constraint $4x_1 + 6x_2 = 36$ and solving for x_2. Thus, $4(4) + 6x_2 = 36$, or $6x_2 = 36 - 16 = 20$. Thus, $x_2 = 3.33$, and the value of the objective function becomes $Z = \$6(4) + \$8(3.33) = \$50.64$. This new information is summarized in Figure 8–8.

Because Node 5 does not have a feasible solution, no further branching from that node is possible. At this point, Nodes 2 and 4 are candidates for further branching. Because Node 4 has the higher upper bound, it appears to offer more promise than branching from Node 2 at this time. Therefore, we shall continue from Node 4.

FIGURE 8–7 Subproblem and Solution Point for Node 4

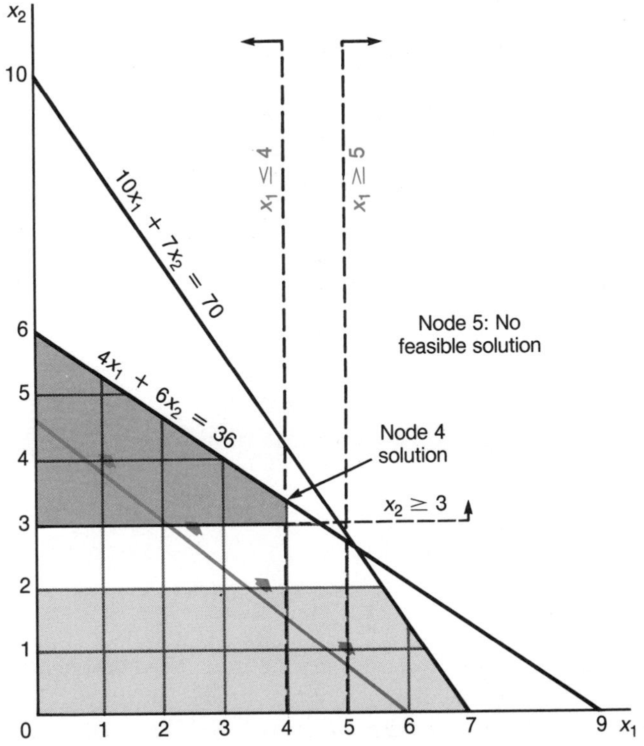

The noninteger variable is x_2, so we branch on x_2. The two new branches are $x_2 \leq 3$ and $x_2 \geq 4$, and we have two additional subproblems, which are:

For $x_2 \leq 3$: (Node 6)

maximize $Z = 6x_1 + 8x_2$

subject to

$$\left.\begin{aligned} 4x_1 + 6x_2 &\leq 36 \\ 10x_1 + 7x_2 &\leq 70 \\ x_2 &\geq 3 \\ x_1 \quad &\leq 4 \end{aligned}\right\}\text{ Node 4 problem}$$

$$x_2 \leq 3 \leftarrow \text{New constraint}$$

$$x_1, x_2 \geq 0 \text{ and integer}$$

For $x_2 \geq 4$: (Node 7)

maximize $Z = 6x_1 + 8x_2$

subject to

$$\begin{aligned} 4x_1 + 6x_2 &\leq 36 \\ 10x_1 + 7x_2 &\leq 70 \\ x_2 &\geq 3 \\ x_1 \quad &\leq 4 \end{aligned}$$

$$x_2 \geq 4$$

$$x_1, x_2 \geq 0 \text{ and integer}$$

FIGURE 8–8 Solutions for Nodes 4 and 5

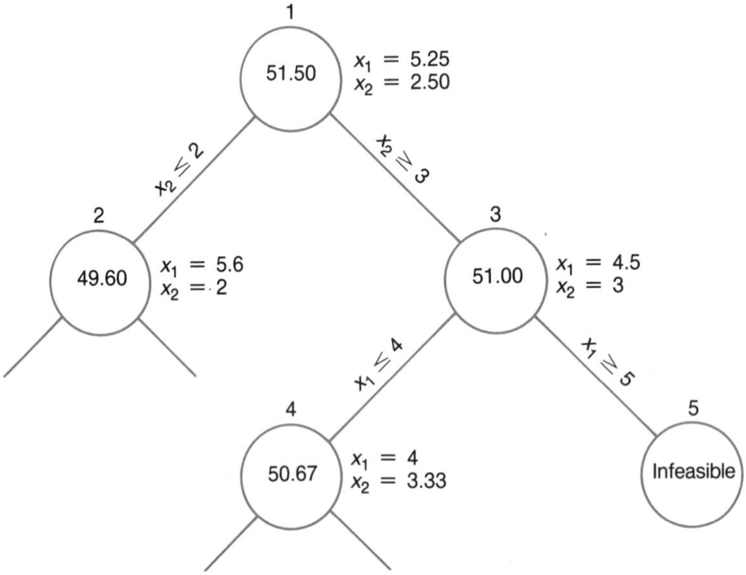

Notice that as we move down through the tree, the subproblems are getting larger and larger in terms of the number of constraints involved. This is because *the subproblem for each node consists of the original set of constraints plus all of the constraints of higher branches that lead to the node being considered.*

For the branch where $x_2 \leq 3$, we have an interesting situation. The initial branch from Node 1 was $x_2 \geq 3$. Coupled with the current branch of $x_2 \leq 3$, this implies only one possible value for x_2 at this node: $x_2 = 3$. Hence, the feasible solution region is the line $x_2 = 3$ from $x_1 = 0$ until it intersects with the constraint $x_1 = 4$. This is shown in Figure 8–9, along with the solution for the other subproblem where $x_2 \geq 4$. The values of x_1 and x_2 at each point are as follows: For $x_2 = 3$, $x_1 = 4$ (read directly from Figure 8–9). Then $Z = \$48$. For $x_2 = 4$, substituting this value into the equation $4x_1 + 6x_2 = 36$ and solving for $x_1 = 3$, and $Z = \$50$.

This new information is summarized along with previous information in the tree in Figure 8–10.

Note that at Node 6 and at Node 7 both decision variables are integer. This means that no additional branching will occur from either node: No lower node can produce a value of the objective function that will exceed the value at this point, and these solutions are both integer. At this point, we can determine that Node 7 contains the optimal solution for our problem. Let's see why. Comparing the solutions at Nodes 6 and 7, it is obvious that Node 7 is superior because it has a higher value of the objective function ($50 at Node 7 versus $48 at Node 6). The only other possibility is branching from Node 2. Node 2 cannot be the optimal because it is not all-integer.

FIGURE 8–9 Subproblems and Solutions for the Next Two Nodes

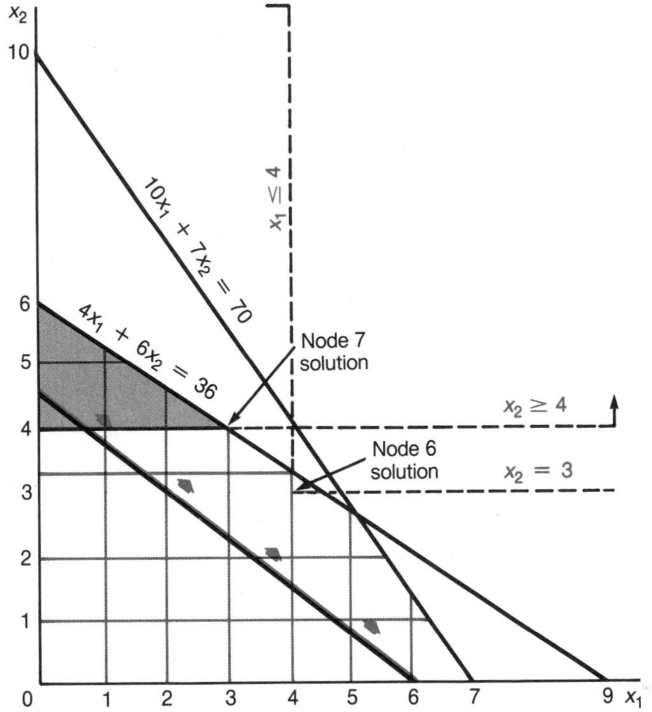

More important, its upper bound is less than that of Node 7, which is all-integer. Further, as noted above, no lower node obtained by branching from a given node (e.g., Node 2) can possibly yield a higher value of the objective function than the given node. Hence, no lower node stemming from Node 2 can have a higher value than \$49.60. And since \$49.60 is less than the value at Node 7, Node 7 contains the optimal solution.

It is interesting to note that although Node 6 consists of all integers, it is not the optimal solution. The implication is that it is not enough to simply reach an all-integer node in order to terminate the search for the optimum. Another all-integer node may exist that will yield a higher value of the objective function. Instead, the optimal solution is found when *two* conditions are satisfied:

1. A node consists of all integer values, or in the case of a mixed-integer problem, the variables that are required to be integer are all integers.
2. No other node at a branch end, whether all-integer or not, has a higher upper bound.

FIGURE 8–10 Solutions for Nodes 6 and 7

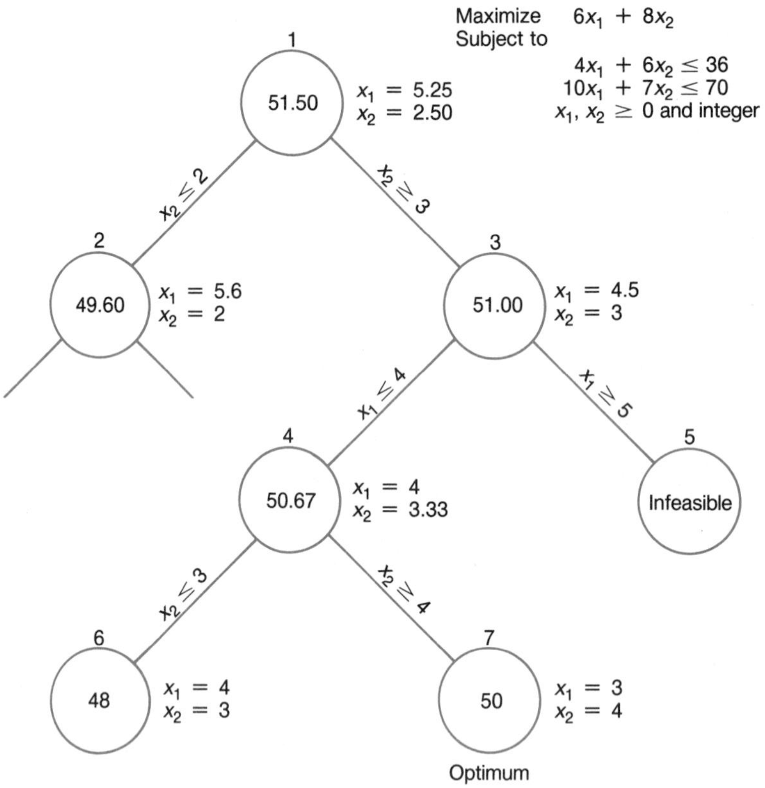

In effect, these two conditions mean that once an all-integer node is obtained, the value of the objective function of the node serves as a standard of comparison to use in deciding whether further branching from another, noninteger, node would be worthwhile.

At this point, let's pause for a moment to reflect on the nature of a branch and bound solution, as exemplified by the tree in Figure 8–10. First, notice that the values at the nodes (i.e., the values of the objective function) get smaller moving down the tree. Although in some problems a lower node may have a value *equal to* a higher node's value, the value at a node in a maximization problem can *never* exceed the value of the node it emanates from. This holds true because each subproblem is more restrictive than the preceding one.

Next, notice that after the first node, each node has at least one variable that is integer. Further, the branch variable (e.g., x_2 coming into Node 3, x_1 coming into Node 4) has a value equal to the branch integer. Thus, if the branch is $x_1 \leq 4$ (see Node 4), x_1 will have a value of 4 at this node.

Finally, notice that after obtaining solutions for Nodes 2 and 3, we explored the tree on the portion that had the higher upper bound. In this case, the tree was explored stemming from Node 3. If Node 4 had an upper bound that turned out to be less than the Node 2 value of $49.60, we would have elected to explore the two branches from Node 2 rather than from Node 4.

Keeping these thoughts in mind as you analyze problems using the branch and bound method should minimize the level of effort required to solve them.

Summary of the Branch and Bound Method for an All-Integer Maximization Problem

1. Solve the problem as if it were a standard LP problem: Ignore any integer requirements.
2. If all variables have integer values, this is the optimal integer solution. (For a mixed-integer problem, if all variables with integer requirements are integer, the solution is optimal.) If any variables with integer requirements are noninteger, this is not the optimal solution. Using the values of the variables for this solution, compute the value of the objective function. This is the *upper bound:* No feasible solution can yield a better value.
3. Examine the noninteger valued variables with integer requirements. Identify the one with the largest fractional part. In case of a tie, choose one arbitrarily. *Branch* on that variable: Round it both up and down to integer values. For the lower integer value, formulate a new constraint requiring that this variable cannot exceed this lower value. For the upper integer value, formulate a new constraint requiring that this variable must equal or exceed this upper value.
4. Solve two new problems, one consisting of the original problem and the lower integer constraint and the other consisting of the original problem and the upper integer constraint. (For subsequent nodes, include the constraints for all branches leading to the node being considered.) For each node (problem), one of three possibilities will materialize:
   a. All required variables will be integer. This *may* be the optimal solution. Compute the upper bound for this solution. Stop branching on this portion of the tree. This upper bound is now a standard of comparison for other nodes: Stop branching from any node if its upper bound does not exceed this node's value. For nodes with higher upper bounds, return to step 3.
   b. The solution will be infeasible. Again, stop branching on this portion of the tree, but consider other portions: Return to step 3.
   c. If some integer-required variables are still noninteger, compute the upper bound for this node. If any all-integer nodes exist, compare the upper bound of this node to the highest upper bound of the all-integer nodes. If it exceeds that value, return to step 3. Otherwise, stop branching from this node and consider other nodes using step 3.
5. The optimal integer solution is found when the value of the objective function at a node with all integer values is not exceeded by the upper bound of any other node, whether they represent all integers or not.

Mixed-Integer Problems

Mixed-integer problems occur in linear programming when some, but not all, of the variables are required to have integer values. This section presents two examples of mixed-integer problems and their solutions.

EXAMPLE 2 Suppose that the problem illustrated in Example 1 required that only x_1 be integer. Let us see how the branch and bound method could be used to find the optimal solution. The revised problem, then, is:

maximize $Z = 6x_1 + 8x_2$

subject to

$$\begin{aligned} 4x_1 + 6x_2 &\le 36 \\ 10x_1 + 7x_2 &\le 70 \\ x_1 \text{ integer} \end{aligned}$$

As before, the first step is to obtain the LP relaxation solution. This is the same as before:

$$\begin{aligned} x_1 &= 5.25 \\ x_2 &= 2.5 \\ Z &= 6(5.25) + 8(2.5) = 51.50 \end{aligned}$$

This solution point is indicated in the graph in Figure 8–11. Note that in the graph, the vertical lines represent the integer values of x_1. Hence, the final solution will be where one of those lines intersects the boundary of the feasible solution space.

The upper bound on the solution is the value of Z for the LP relaxation solution: 51.50.

The information obtained from the LP solution is summarized in Figure 8–12.

Because x_1 is required to be integer, we branch on that variable, rounding $x_1 = 5.25$ down and up to obtain two additional constraints: $x_1 \le 5$ and $x_1 \ge 6$. The two resulting subproblems are:

For $x_1 \le 5$: (Node 2)

maximize $Z = 6x_1 + 8x_2$

subject to

$$\begin{aligned} 4x_1 + 6x_2 &\le 36 \\ 10x_1 + 7x_2 &\le 70 \\ x_1 &\le 5 \\ x_1 \text{ integer} \end{aligned}$$

For $x_1 \ge 6$: (Node 3)

maximize $Z = 6x_1 + 8x_2$

subject to

$$\begin{aligned} 4x_1 + 6x_2 &\le 36 \\ 10x_1 + 7x_2 &\le 70 \\ x_1 &\ge 6 \\ x_1 \text{ integer} \end{aligned}$$

FIGURE 8–11 The LP Relaxation Solution Point

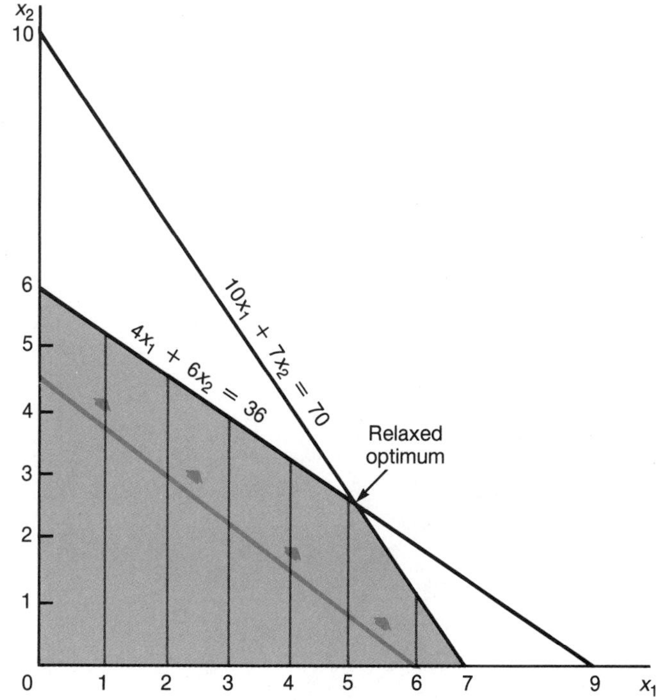

FIGURE 8–12 Solution at Node 1 for Example 2 and Branches to Nodes 2 and 3

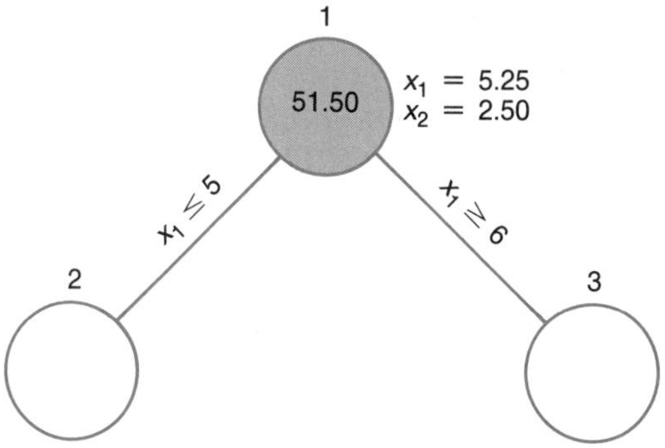

FIGURE 8–13 Subproblems and Solution Points for Nodes 2 and 3

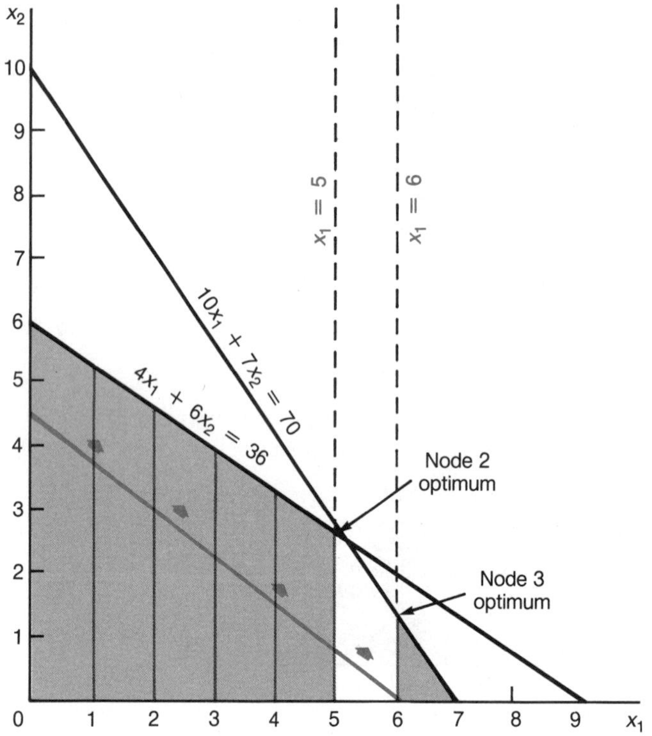

The solutions to these subproblems are illustrated in Figure 8–13. The solution at Node 2 can be obtained by substituting the value $x_1 = 5$ into the equation $4x_1 + 6x_2 = 36$ and solving for x_2. This results in:

$$x_1 = 5$$
$$x_2 = 2.67$$
$$Z = 6(5) + 8(2.67) = 51.33$$

Similarly, the solution at Node 3 can be obtained by substituting the value $x_1 = 6$ into the equation $10x_1 + 7x_2 = 70$ and solving for x_2. This results in:

$$x_1 = 6$$
$$x_2 = 1.43$$
$$Z = 6(6) + 8(1.43) = 47.44$$

These results are summarized in Figure 8–14. Note that at both Nodes, x_1 has an integer value, thus satisfying the requirement that it be integer. Moreover, the value of Z for each node represents an upper bound on the value of the objective function for

FIGURE 8–14 Solutions for Nodes 2 and 3

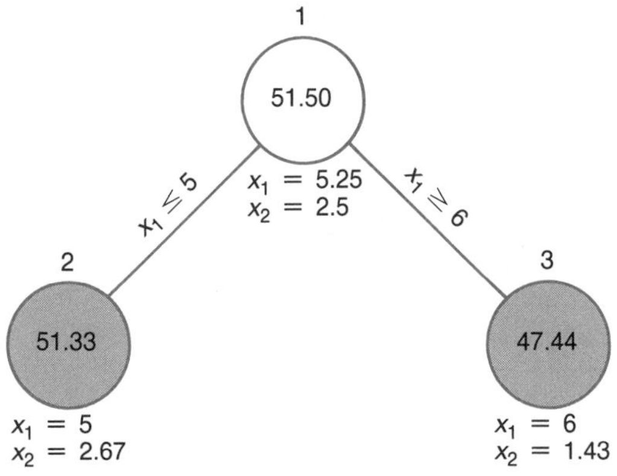

any further searching on those branches. Consequently, the optimal solution to the problem exists at either Node 2 or Node 3. Since Node 2 has the higher value of Z, it represents the optimal solution.

■

EXAMPLE 3 Now suppose that the problem stated in Example 1 requires only that x_2 be integer. The problem, then, becomes:

maximize $\quad Z = 6x_1 + 8x_2$

subject to

$$4x_1 + 6x_2 \leq 36$$
$$10x_1 + 7x_2 \leq 70$$
$$x_2 \text{ integer}$$

The problem is illustrated graphically in Figure 8–15, with the horizontal lines representing integer values of x_2 within the feasible solution space. As before, the LP relaxation solution is:

$x_1 = 5.25$

$x_2 = 2.5$

$Z = 51.5$ (upper bound)

This information is summarized in Node 1 of Figure 8–16, which also indicates the two branches from Node 1 based on rounding the noninteger value $x_2 = 2.5$ to $x_2 = 2$ and $x_2 = 3$.

FIGURE 8–15 The LP Relaxation Solution Point

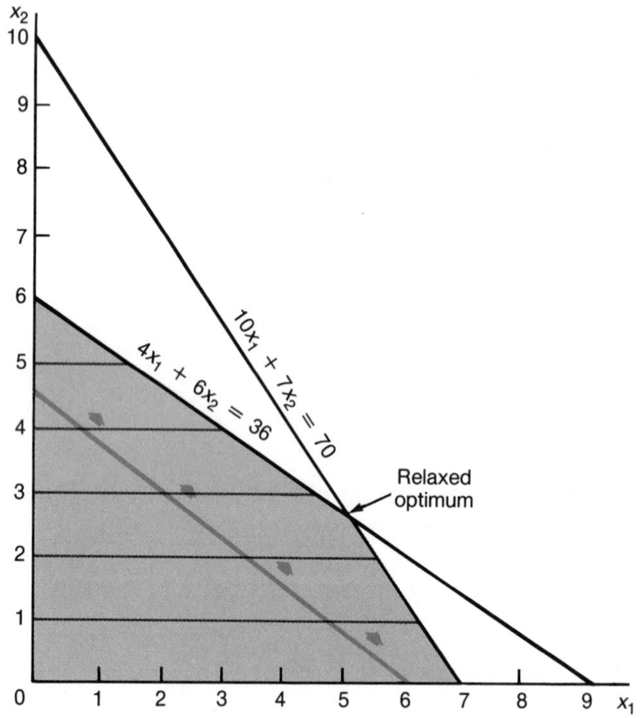

FIGURE 8–16 Node 1 Solution and Branches

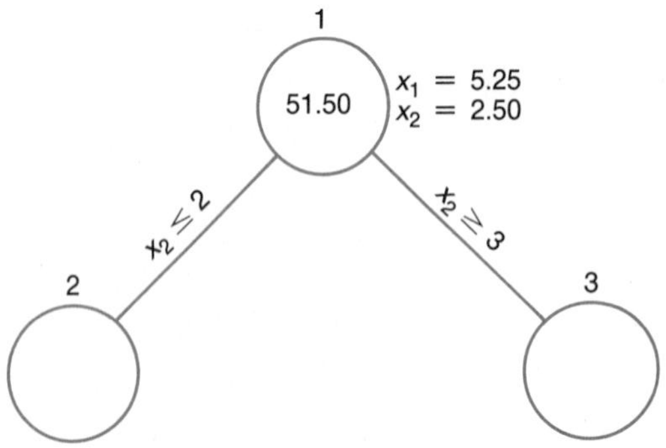

FIGURE 8–17 Subproblems and Solution Points for Nodes 2 and 3

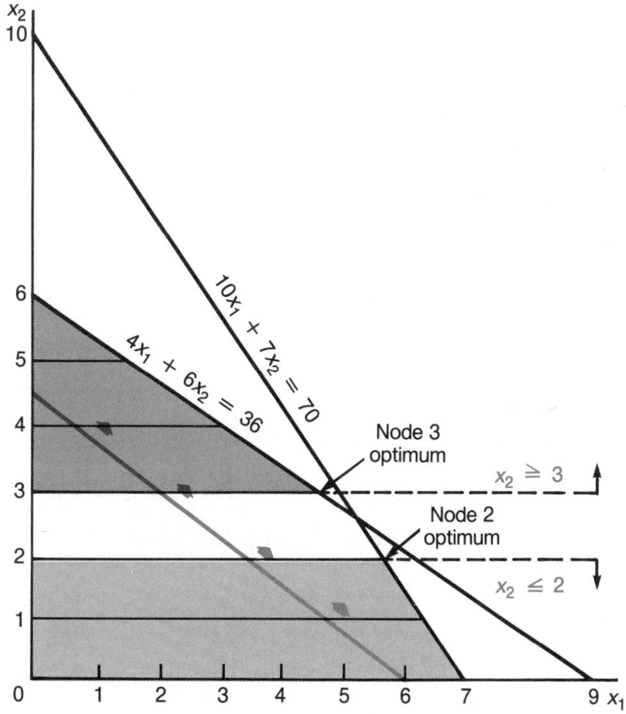

The two subproblems which emerge are:

For $x_2 \leq 2$: (Node 2)

maximize $Z = 6x_1 + 8x_2$

subject to

$$4x_1 + 6x_2 \leq 36$$
$$10x_1 + 7x_2 \leq 70$$
$$x_2 \leq 2$$
$$x_1, x_2 \geq 0 \text{ and } x_2 \text{ integer}$$

For $x_2 \geq 3$: (Node 3)

maximize $Z = 6x_1 + 8x_2$

subject to

$$4x_1 + 6x_2 \leq 36$$
$$10x_1 + 7x_2 \leq 70$$
$$x_2 \geq 3$$
$$x_1, x_2 \geq 0 \text{ and } x_2 \text{ integer}$$

The solutions to these subproblems are illustrated in Figure 8–17. The optimum value of x_1 for Node 2 can be obtained by substituting $x_2 = 2$ in the equation $10x_1 + 7x_2 = 70$. The result is $x_1 = 5.6$. The value of the objective function at Node 2 is then:

$$Z = 6(5.6) + 8(2) = 49.60$$

FIGURE 8–18 Solutions for Nodes 2 and 3 (Node 3 contains the optimal

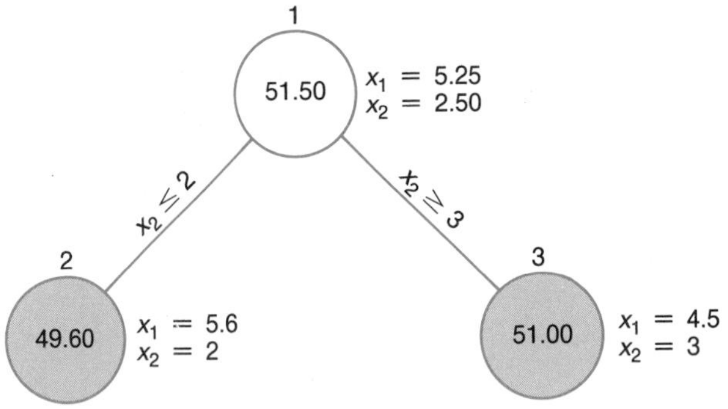

The optimum value of x_1 for Node 3 similarly can be determined by substituting $x_2 = 3$ into the equation $4x_1 + 6x_2 = 36$. Solving for x_1 yields $x_1 = 4.5$. The value of the objective function at Node 3 with these values is:

$$Z = 6(4.5) + 8(3) = 51$$

The results of these two subproblems are summarized in Figure 8–18. Note that x_2 has an integer value at both Node 2 and Node 3, satisfying that requirement. Thus, we can compare the values of Z at the two nodes and see that Z is higher at Node 3. Therefore, it contains the optimal solution: $x_1 = 4.5$ and $x_2 = 3$.

We have examined a pure-integer problem and two mixed-integer problems. In the next section, we look at 0–1 problems.

0–1 PROBLEMS

An important category of integer programming problems relates to *binary* decisions. These decisions involve choosing between *two* possible values for each decision variable. Often these can be thought of as yes-no decisions. For example, a manager may have to decide whether to fund a project (yes) or not (no), whether to hire a person or not, whether to replace an existing machine or not, and so on. Generally these problems involve multiple variables, such as the need to choose three locations for new convenience stores from a list of 20 potential sites. Even so, a yes-no decision must be made for each potential site (i.e., there are 20 decision variables).

Some 0–1 problems can be handled by special-purpose algorithms. One such algorithm is the *assignment model,* which is described in Chapter 7. In this chapter, two general-purpose algorithms are described: the branch and bound method and the enumeration method. The enumeration method is the simpler of the two. It is described first.

Enumeration Method

The enumeration method consists of these steps:

1. List all possible alternatives.
2. Determine which alternatives are feasible.
3. Find the value of the objective function for each feasible alternative.
4. Select the feasible alternative with the best value of the objective function.

The enumeration method is most useful when the number of alternatives is fairly small (say, no more than 16), and there are no more than 3 or 4 constraints. Otherwise, the process of evaluating alternatives becomes tedious. In general, the number of alternatives is equal to 2^n, where n is the number of decision variables. For instance, if a problem has three decision variables, the number of 0–1 alternatives is $2^3 = 8$. Similarly, if there are six decision variables, the number of alternatives is $2^6 = 64$.

An example will illustrate the simplicity of the enumeration approach.

■

EXAMPLE 4 Solve the following problem using the enumeration method:

maximize $65x_1 + 70x_2 + 40x_3 + 50x_4$

subject to

1 $10x_1 + 12x_2 + 6x_3 + 8x_4 \leq 30$

2 $3x_1 + x_2 + 2x_3 \leq 5$

All variables 0 or 1

Solution

There are four decision variables. Hence, the number of possible alternatives is $2^4 = 16$.

A tree diagram will aid in identifying each of these alternatives. (See Figure 8–19.) The logic of the tree is based on the fact that each variable will have a value of 0 or 1. The variables could be listed in any sequence, but simply listing them by order of subscript is easiest. Thus, x_1 can be either 0 or 1 to start the tree (from left to right).

FIGURE 8–19 Tree Diagram for Example 4

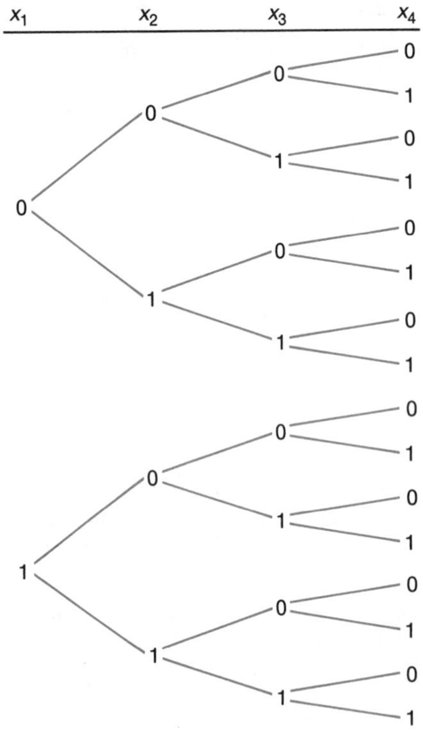

Each of these possibilities leads to two more based on the two possible values of x_2. Similar logic leads to a doubling of the branches for each of the remaining variables. Checking under variable x_4, we see that there are, indeed, 16 branch ends. The alternatives can be read by following each branch from left to right and listing the sequence. Thus, the uppermost branch yields 0–0–0–0, which means all variables are 0; the next sequence is 0–0–0–1, which means variables x_1, x_2, and x_3 are 0 and x_4 is 1; the next sequence is 0–0–1–0, which means variables x_1 and x_2 are 0, variable x_3 is 1, and variable x_4 is 0; and so on. All of the alternatives are listed in Table 8–1 in the order that they appear in the tree.

In order to evaluate the alternatives, the 0–1 values must be substituted into both constraints for each alternative and the values must be computed. If the value does not violate a constraint, the alternative is feasible for that constraint. If all constraints are sastisfied (in this case, *both* constraints) then the value of the objective function is calculated. For example, for alternative 8, the values $x_1 = 0$, $x_2 = 1$, $x_3 = 1$, and $x_4 = 1$ can be substituted into each constraint. The results are:

Constraint 1 $10(0) + 12(1) + 6(1) + 8(1) = 26$ (feasible because $26 < 30$)

Constraint 2 $3(0) + 1(1) + 2(1) = 3$ (feasible because $3 < 5$)

TABLE 8–1 Enumeration and Evaluation of Alternatives for Example 4

	Alternative				Constraint 1		Constraint 2		Both Feasible?	Value of Objective Function
	x_1	x_2	x_3	x_4	Value	Feasible?	Value	Feasible?		
1	0	0	0	0	0	√	0	√	√	0
2	0	0	0	1	8	√	0	√	√	50
3	0	0	1	0	6	√	2	√	√	40
4	0	0	1	1	14	√	2	√	√	90
5	0	1	0	0	12	√	1	√	√	70
6	0	1	0	1	20	√	1	√	√	120
7	0	1	1	0	18	√	3	√	√	110
8	0	1	1	1	26	√	3	√	√	160
9	1	0	0	0	10	√	3	√	√	65
10	1	0	0	1	18	√	3	√	√	115
11	1	0	1	0	16	√	5	√	√	105
12	1	0	1	1	24	√	5	√	√	155
13	1	1	0	0	22	√	4	√	√	135
14	1	1	0	1	30	√	5	√	√	185*
15	1	1	1	0	28	√	6	No	No	—
16	1	1	1	1	36	No	6	No	No	—

* Optimum.

Both are feasible, so this is a feasible alternative. The value of the objective function for this alternative would be:

$$Z = 65(0) + 70(1) + 40(1) + 50(1) = 160$$

As a second example, consider alternative 15, where $x_1 = 1, x_2 = 1, x_3 = 1$, and $x_4 = 0$. Substituting into the two constraints yields:

Constraint 1 $10(1) + 12(1) + 6(1) + 8(0) = 28$ (feasible because $28 < 30$)

Constraint 2 $3(1) + 1(1) + 2(1) = 6$ (not feasible because $6 > 5$)

Since both constraints are not feasible, this is not a feasible alternative; hence, there is no point here in computing the value of the objective function.

After checking the feasibility of all constraints and computing the value of the objective function for feasible alternatives, we find that alternative 14, with $x_1 = 1$, $x_2 = 1, x_3 = 0$, and $x_4 = 1$ would provide the maximum value of the objective function for this problem.

Branch and Bound Method

Now let's see how the branch and bound method can be used to solve the 0–1 problem presented in Example 4.

■

EXAMPLE 5 Solve this 0–1 problem using branch and bound:

maximum $65x_1 + 70x_2 + 40x_3 + 50x_4$

subject to

1	$10x_1 + 12x_2 + 6x_3 + 8x_4 \leq 30$
2	$3x_1 + x_2 + 2x_3 \leq 5$

All variables 0 or 1

Solution

That all variables must have values of 0 or 1 was taken into account in the enumeration approach by only listing 0 and 1 values for alternatives. However, using the branch and bound method, this information must be explicitly factored into the problem because generally the simplex method will be used to solve branch and bound problems. This is accomplished by specifically including the additional constraints for the 0–1 variables. For this problem, those constraints are:

3	$x_1 \leq 1$
4	$x_2 \leq 1$
5	$x_3 \leq 1$
6	$x_4 \leq 1$

The branch and bound method with simplex yielded the tree in Figure 8–20, where we see the optimum is at Node 7 with $x_1 = 1$, $x_2 = 1$, $x_3 = 0$, and $x_4 = 1$. The objective function has a value of 185. Although the tree is very similar to trees in preceding examples, observe that all branches are expressed as *equalities* rather than as *inequalities*. This reflects the 0–1 nature of the problem.

Let's consider a step-by-step analysis of the tree.

Node 1. The LP relaxation solution that has an objective function value of \$188.46. Because all of the variables are not equal to 0 or 1, this is not the optimal solution. Because x_1 has the larger fractional part, x_1 is the variable to branch on.

Node 2. An all 0 or 1 solution. This is a candidate for the optimum at this point. However, the branch $x_1 = 1$ must first be explored.

Node 3. The solution is not completely 0–1. However, the upper bound of \$188.33 is higher than at Node 2, so a continued search from Node 3 is indicated. Variables x_2 and x_3 have the same fractional parts, so variable x_2 was selected *arbitrarily* to branch on.

Node 4. All variables are 0 or 1, so no further branching will be done from this node. Moreover, because its objective function value of \$155 is less than the value at Node 2, this is not a candidate for the optimum. Consequently, Node 2 still exists as the standard against which to judge other solutions.

Node 5. Still not completely 0–1, but because the upper bound of \$186.25

FIGURE 8–20 Tree for Example 5

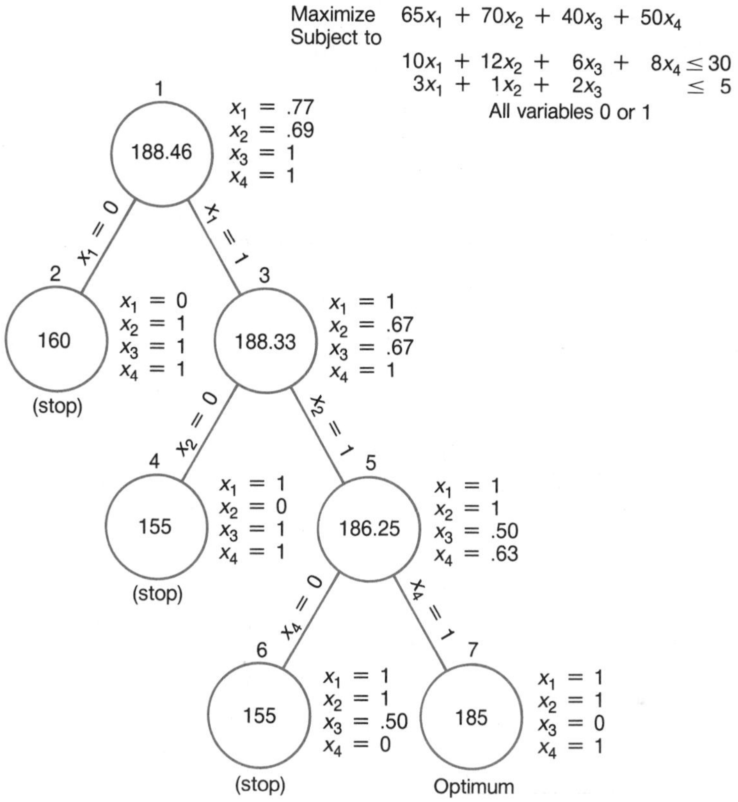

exceeds the value at Node 2, additional branching is called for. Because variable x_4 has the larger fractional part, it is branched on.

Node 6. Although not completely 0–1, its upper bound is less than the value at Node 2, so no further branching from Node 6 would be justified.

Node 7. This is the optimal solution because all variables are 0 or 1 and its value of $185 exceeds the only other possible optimum, that of Node 2.

A MINIMIZATION PROBLEM

This section illustrates the use of the branch and bound method for a minimization problem. The branching rule used for maximization problems of branching from a node on the variable with the largest fractional part also will be used for minimization problems. The main difference to keep in mind is that the objective function value at each node is being *minimized*. This means that the objective function value at the various nodes going down through the tree will get *larger* (or occasionally stay the same) rather than get smaller, as in a maximization problem. Thus, each new node will result in a value that is equal to, or greater than, the value at the node it emanated from.

■

EXAMPLE 6 Solve this problem using the branch and bound method:

minimize $15x_1 + 10x_2 + 12x_3$

subject to

1	$4x_1 + 6x_2 + 5x_3 \geq 60$
2	$3x_1 + x_2 + x_3 \geq 18$
	$x_1, x_2, x_3, \geq 0$ and integer

Solution

The tree for this problem is shown in Figure 8–21. A step-by-step analysis of the tree follows:

Node 1. The solution to the original problem. Because the values of some variables are noninteger, this is obviously not the optimal solution. The value of variable x_2 has the larger fractional part, so it forms the basis for branching.

Node 2. This is not the optimum because several variables are still noninteger. Branching from this node will be called for unless Node 3 is optimal. Otherwise, branch on x_3.

Node 3. Although noninteger, its objective function value is *lower* than that of Node 2. Hence, explore this portion of the tree before the portion stemming from Node 2. Branch on variable x_1 because it is the only noninteger variable.

Node 6. All-integer values, so this may be the optimum. However, the value of the objective function is higher than at Node 2, implying the need for further exploration from Node 2. We must also check out Node 7.

Node 7. Also all-integer, but with a higher objective function value than Node 6. Hence, this solution is nonoptimal, and because it is integer, no additional branching from this node would be called for; lower nodes would yield equal or higher values of the objective function.

Node 4. Noninteger. No additional branching will be done, though, because its value is higher than Node 6, which is all-integer. Check out Node 5.

Node 5. Not all integer, but with a value less than that at Node 6, continue searching from this node. Branch on variable x_2.

FIGURE 8–21 Node Diagram for Example 6

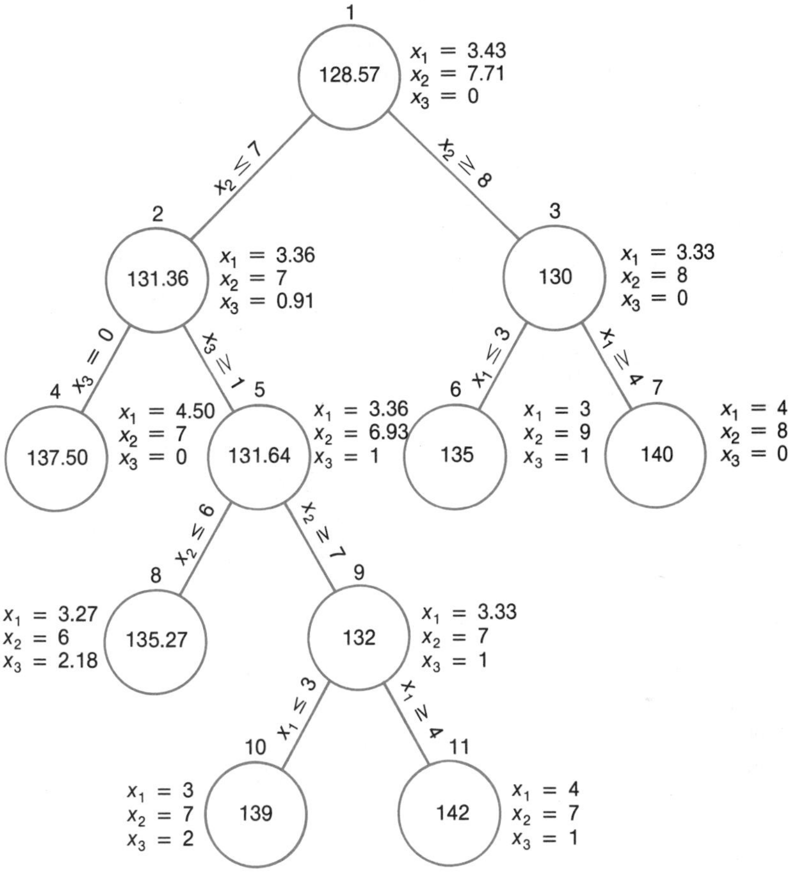

Node 8. Not all integer, but a node value higher than Node 6. Stop searching here.

Node 9. Not an all-integer solution, but it has lower value than at Node 6. Continue branching.

Node 10. All integer, but higher than the value at Node 6.

Node 11. All integer, but higher than the value of Node 6.

Consequently, the optimal solution appears at Node 6.

A COMMENT ABOUT SENSITIVITY

Integer programming problems do not readily lend themselves to the sort of sensitivity analysis that was described in Chapter 6. This stems from the fact that only a relatively few of the infinite solution possibilities in a feasible solution space will meet integer requirements. Unfortunately, there is no easy way to determine the extent to which changes in a right-hand side quantity will alter the choice of integer alternatives. The only way to accomplish that is to rework the problem with the changes and observe the effect. This is, indeed, unfortunate, because it often happens that relatively small changes in constraints can have large changes on the value of the objective function. If these amounts were known to management, it is highly likely that management would elect to take the necessary action to change the constraints. For this reason, it may make sense to explore a range of constraint quantities in order to ascertain if the value of the objective function would change materially. In cases in which it would change, say, for a slight increase in the right-hand side value of a constraint, this potential could then be presented to management for consideration.

Similarly, there is no simple way to determine the impact of changes to the objective function coefficients on the solution to a problem. Again, trial and error examination of a range of reasonable alternatives involving completely solving each revised problem is required.

MANAGER DIALOGUE

Marcos is a mid-level manager of a company that is just beginning to use integer programming models. The following describes a recent conversation between Marcos and the consultant who is instructing company managers and analysts on using the branch and bound method for solving integer problems.

Marcos Let me see if I understand the branch and bound method. To use it, I start with an LP model for which I desire an integer solution, and feed it to a computer. The computer will give me an initial solution, which may or may not satisfy the requirement that certain variables have integer values.

Consultant That is correct. The solution is called the *LP relaxation solution*. It becomes the first node of a diagram that is used to keep track of the search for the optimal integer solution. Each node of the diagram represents the solution to a slightly different version of the original problem. As you move down in the tree, you are increasing the level of constraints contained in the model.

Marcos Am I also correct in assuming that the solution for each node is generated by the computer rather than graphically or using the simplex method?

Consultant Yes you are. The purpose of illustrating graphical solutions was to provide some insight into the nature of the search for integer solutions. But as a practical matter, computer solutions are used almost exclusively unless you are dealing with small, 0–1-type problems that make enumeration a viable alternative.

Marcos Once the computer gives me the solution for a node, I write the optimal value of the objective function in the node and the optimal values of the decision variables alongside the node. If the computer indicates that the solution is infeasible, I indicate that on the diagram and terminate that portion of the search. I also stop the search at a node for which all variables have integer values. In either case, I would turn to another section of the tree for further analysis. Do you agree?

Consultant Yes. Note, though, that you may stop your search at a node for still another reason: The node in question may have a value of Z that is less desirable than that of another node. For instance, suppose you are solving a maximization problem and get an optimal Z of 22.4 for a node that has one or more variables with noninteger values. Before continuing your search, you must check other nodes to see if any one has a higher value for Z. If such a node exists, and if it is an all-integer node, terminate the search at the node where $Z = 22.4$. If another node with a higher value of Z exists, but it, too, is noninteger, *temporarily* discontinue searching from the node where $Z = 22.4$, and instead, move to the node with the higher value of Z. Repeat this procedure whenever you obtain a node where some variables have noninteger values.

(continues)

MANAGER DIALOGUE (*continued*)

Marcos Terminating the search at portions of the node diagram where infeasible or all-integer nodes appear seems simple enough, but the noninteger nodes still make me a little hesitant. Can you elaborate a bit more?

Consultant Let's digress just a bit. The typical integer solution process starts with the first three nodes: the first node, which is the LP relaxation solution, and the two branches from the first node, call them Nodes 2 and 3. You may have the solution at this point. That will be the case if one of these things happen:

1. Both nodes are all-integer. Pick the one with the best value of Z.
2. One node is all-integer, the other is infeasible.
3. One is all-integer and has a better value of Z than the other node, which is noninteger.

If one node is infeasible and the other noninteger, continue searching by branching from the noninteger node. If both nodes are noninteger, branch from the one that has the better value of Z (higher for a max problem, lower for a min problem). Continue until the optimal solution is found.

Marcos And how do I know when the optimal solution has been found?

Consultant The simplest answer I can think of is this—when no further branching is possible (all nodes are infeasible or all-integer), or when no noninteger node has a value of Z that is better than the best value of Z at an all-integer node. You should note that you must have at least one all-integer node before you can ever consider the possibility of finding the optimal solution, but that just because you obtain an all-integer node, that does not mean that you have actually found the *optimal* all-integer solution.

FORMULATING INTEGER PROGRAMMING PROBLEMS

Formulating a problem correctly is often the most important phase of decision analysis. In the case of integer programming, problem formulation sometimes requires a fair degree of ingenuity in order to correctly portray a situation. In this section, a variety of formulations are demonstrated that have proved very useful in setting up commonly encountered integer programming requirements.

Either-Or Alternatives

A manufacturer may need a machine to replace one that recently has failed. Two alternatives, x_1 and x_2, are being considered, but only one will be needed. The constraint that expresses this would be:

(*concluded*)

Marcos One last question. I've noticed that there are always exactly two branches from each node, regardless of the number of variables in a problem. It seems to me that I end up choosing one of the two branches to continue on, and never come back to the other. What I end up with is one main zigzag path through the node diagram with a bunch of little stubs along the way. Am I correct in believing that this is how these searches turn out?

Consultant Your observation is perceptive, but misleading. It is true that many problems do turn out like that. In fact, some of the software used to enable computers to solve the problem from start to finish rely on that apparent result to guide the solution. Unfortunately, the rule does not always hold. In fact, it is not very difficult to construct problems that cannot be solved by such software that always selects the better of the two branches and eliminates the other from further consideration. That is why you must always compare the solution at each node to those of other existing nodes, and always branch from the node that has the best value of Z at each step in the process.

But that is not as difficult as it might appear. Quite the opposite, because you will always have one node that is the second best, and you will compare each new node's Z value to that value. You continue on a given path as long as each new "challenger" continues to be better than the second best node. As soon as a challenger falls below the second best, the search from that challenger node ends. Note that each node will give rise to two such challengers. When both fail to best the "second best," it becomes the best and any additional searching (unless it is an all-integer node) will shift to that node.

$$x_1 + x_2 = 1$$

If there is a possibility that neither machine will be acquired, then the constraint would be written as:

$$x_1 + x_2 \leq 1$$

k-Out-of-n Alternatives

In many problems, a decision maker must choose a specified number of alternatives; say, choose two machines from a list of five alternatives. Or, the requirement may be to choose *at least two,* or, perhaps, *no more than two* machines from the list.

The formulation for exactly two machines out of five would be:

$$x_1 + x_2 + x_3 + x_4 + x_5 = 2$$

For at least two machines out of five, the formulation would be:

$$x_1 + x_2 + x_3 + x_4 + x_5 \geq 2$$

For no more than two out of five machines, the formulation would be:

$$x_1 + x_2 + x_3 + x_4 + x_5 \leq 2$$

Sometimes a problem will permit a range of choices. For example, a situation may call for the purchase of anywhere from two to four machines. The problem would then require two constraints, one for the upper bound and the other for the lower bound. Thus, for two to four machines, the constraints would be:

$$x_1 + x_2 + x_3 + x_4 + x_5 \geq 2$$
$$x_1 + x_2 + x_3 + x_4 + x_5 \leq 4$$

If-Then Alternatives

It sometimes happens that a decision to take some action necessitates another action that supports the initial decision. For example, the purchase of machine x_2 may necessitate the purchase of another machine, x_1. The formulation would be:

$$x_1 \geq x_2$$

Note that this formulation implies that the reverse case is not required: The purchase of x_1 does not require the purchase of x_2. In order to satisfy the requirement that the right-hand side consist solely of a numerical quantity, this can be rewritten as:

$$x_1 - x_2 \geq 0$$

If the purchase of either machine requires the purchase of the other, the appropriate formulation would be:

$$x_1 - x_2 = 0$$

Either-Or Constraints

Situations may arise in which a constraint will apply *only if* a particular alternative is chosen. For instance, the choice of a certain machine may necessitate special power requirements. Consequently, it can be useful to be able to "turn on" or "turn off" a constraint as appropriate. This can be accomplished by tieing the constraint to the decision variable that will govern its applicability. Suppose the machine in question is choice x_8, which will require the constraint $5x_4 + 3x_5 \geq 100$ if x_8 is chosen. This can be incorporated into the problem by writing the constraint as:

$$5x_4 + 3x_5 \geq 100x_8$$

Then, if x_8 is selected, $x_8 = 1$, and the constraint will stand. If x_8 is not selected, then $x_8 = 0$, and the constraint will, in effect, drop out. Rearranging terms so that all variables are on the left side and a constant on the right side results in:

$$5x_4 + 3x_5 - 100x_8 \geq 0$$

If there are two potential constraints, one of which will apply if a certain choice (say, x_8) is made, and the other if that choice is not made, the formulation would be slightly different. For example, suppose the constraints are $5x_4 + 3x_5 \geq 100$ if x_8 is chosen and $5x_4 + 3x_5 \geq 50$ for any other choice (i.e., x_8 is not chosen). This could be expressed as:

$$5x_4 + 3x_5 \geq 100x_8 \quad \text{(applies if } x_8 = 1\text{)}$$
$$5x_4 + 3x_5 \geq 50(1 - x_8) \quad \text{(applies if } x_8 = 0\text{)}$$

These can be written as:

$$5x_4 + 3x_5 - 100x_8 \geq 0 \quad \text{and}$$
$$5x_4 + 3x_5 + 50x_8 \geq 50$$

If the constraints relate to *upper limits* (i.e., the constraints are $\leq$), then a slightly different approach should be used. Suppose the constraints are either $4x_1 + 8x_2 \leq 40$, or $2x_1 + x_2 \leq 16$, depending on whether project y_1 is commissioned. Say, the first constraint applies if y_1 is not commissioned, and the second if it is. This can be handled by writing the constraints in this form:

1 $\quad 4x_1 + 8x_2 \leq 40 + My_1$ $\quad$ where M is a very large number

2 $\quad 2x_1 + x_2 \leq 16 + M(1 - y_1)$

In addition, we have:

$y_1 \leq 1$ $\quad$ where $\quad y_1 = 1$ indicates the project is commissioned

If y_1 is commissioned, then $y_1 = 1$ and the first constraint becomes so large that it is not binding. Conversely, if $y_1 = 0$, the reverse is true: The first constraint becomes binding, whereas the second becomes very large and, therefore, not binding.

Fixed Charge Problems

It very often happens that the contribution that a variable makes to profit is linear *after* a fixed charge has been deducted. For instance, the profit per unit produced on a machine may be \$20 per unit after a setup cost of \$80 has been allowed for. Suppose the product is x_1. Then without the setup charge the portion of the objective function with x_1 would be $20x_1$. It might seem that we could simply subtract the fixed charge from the objective function. However, this approach overlooks the possibility that the optimum value of the x_1 might be zero, in which case there would be *no* setup charge and, hence, no subtraction from the objective function value. To allow for this, we can introduce another variable, y_1, which can assume values of 0 or 1:0 if x_1 is 0, and 1 if x_1 is greater than 0.

The portion of the objective function for these two variables is:

$$20x_1 - 80y_1$$

In addition, the following constraints will be needed:

$x_1 \le My_1$ where M is a very large number

$y_1 \le 1$

The first constraint will force x_1 to be zero if y_1 is zero. If $y_1 = 1$, there will be no limit on x_1, assuming a very large value has been selected for M. To conform with having a constant on the right side, the first constraint can be written as:

$$x_1 - My_1 \le 0$$

Note that these constraints and the portion of the objective function shown would be in addition to any other constraints and other portions of the objective function that may be required by a problem.

■

EXAMPLE 7 A company makes two products, x_1 and x_2. Product x_1 generates a profit of \$20 per unit before a fixed charge of \$80 per batch for setup is allowed for; product x_2 generates a profit of \$30 per unit before a setup charge of \$90 is allowed for. Each product requires two hours of machine time, and 400 hours of machine time are available. Integer values of each product are required for technical reasons. The manager wants to maximize profits. Set up this all-integer problem.

Solution

x_1 = quantity of Product 1
x_2 = quantity of Product 2
y_1 = fixed charge variable for Product 1
y_2 = fixed charge variable for Product 2
M = a very large number

maximize $20x_1 + 30x_2 - 80y_1 - 90y_2$

subject to

Machine time	$2x_1 + 2x_2 \le 400$ hours
x_1 fixed charge	$x_1 - My_1 \le 0$
x_2 fixed charge	$x_2 - My_2 \le 0$
	$y_1 \le 1$
	$y_2 \le 1$
	All variables ≥ 0
	x_1 and x_2 integer

Variables That Have Minimum Level Requirements

In some cases, a variable either will have to be zero or an amount that exceeds a specified value. For instance, a minimum order size for a purchased part might be required by a vendor. Say the minimum quantity for x_1 is 200 units. This can be expressed using another variable, y_1, that is a 0–1 variable:

$$x_1 - 200y_1 \geq 0$$
$$y_1 \leq 1$$
$$x_1 \text{ and } y_1 \text{ integer}$$

Then, if $x_1 = 0$, the first constraint would cause y_1 to be zero as well. For completeness, the new variable, y_1, should be accounted for in the objective function. Because it is, in effect, a dummy variable, it will not contribute to the value of the objective function. Hence, it should be assigned a coefficient of zero in the objective function.

SUMMARY

Problems that lend themselves to a linear programming formulation are frequently encountered in practice. In many instances, some or all of the decision variables may also be required to be integer. In such cases, the goal is to identify the best solution that will meet the integer requirements. In general, the simplex method cannot be used to directly obtain integer solutions, although in a few rare cases a simplex solution may produce integer values. Instead, an intelligent search procedure usually must be employed to identify an optimal solution. This chapter illustrates a graphical solution for instructive purposes. However, the most realistic approach is to employ successive application of the simplex method until a solution is obtained. This involves use of the branch and bound method, a method that creates subproblems that are increasingly more restrictive until an optimal solution is uncovered.

An important class of integer programming problems involves situations in which decision variables can take on values of only 0 or 1, often synonymous with yes-no decisions. The branch and bound method can be used to solve 0–1 problems, although small problems often can be handled using enumeration and valuation of all possible solutions.

GLOSSARY

Bound An upper or lower limit on the value of the objective function at a given stage of the analysis of an integer programming problem.

Branch Selection of an integer value of a decision variable to examine for a possible integer solution to a problem.

Branch and Bound Method A method of analyzing integer programming problems that reduces a problem to smaller and smaller subsets through a succession of branches and bounds in the process of finding the optimal integer solution.

Enumeration Method A method used with 0–1 problems that involves listing every possible outcome in order to identify the optimal solution.

Fractional Part The noninteger portion of a number. For example, the fractional part of 8.72 is .72.

LP Relaxation Solution Solution of an integer programming problem that does not take into account the integer requirements. Used as a starting point for the branch and bound method.

Mixed-Integer Problem A problem that requires that some, but not all, decision variables have integer values.

Node Diagram A visual method for keeping track of the subsets of an integer problem that have been analyzed, their branches, and their bounds.

Pure-Integer Problem An integer programming problem requiring that all decision variables have integer values.

Zero-One (0–1) Problem An integer programming problem requiring that all decision variables have a value of either 0 or 1.

SOLVED PROBLEMS

Problem 1. Here is an all-integer problem and a portion of the node diagram of its solution:

maximize $5x_1 + 7x_2 + 4x_3$

subject to

$$7x_1 + 4x_2 + 9x_3 \leq 75$$
$$6x_1 + 7x_2 + 12x_3 \leq 91$$
$$4x_1 + 3x_2 \leq 25$$

All variables ≥ 0 and integer

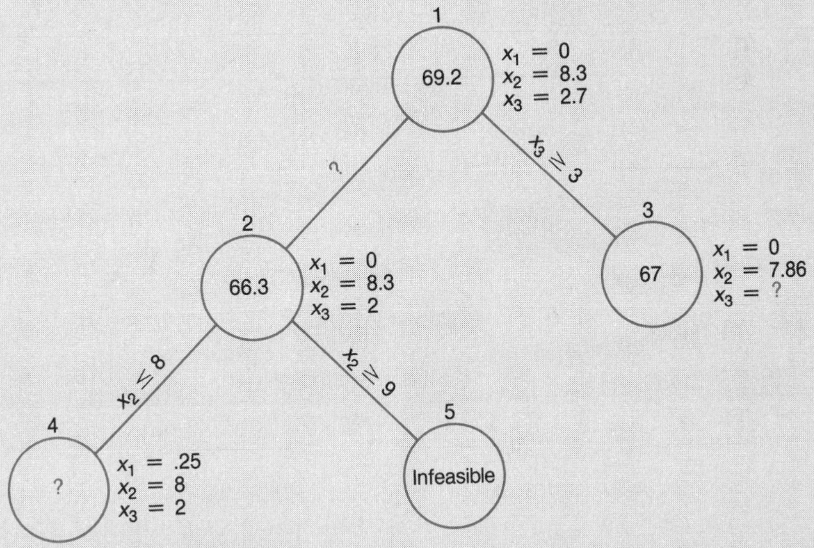

Do the following:

a. Determine the missing (?) values.

b. Explain why Node 5 is infeasible.

c. Does the optimal solution appear at one of the nodes shown, or is further branching necessary? If further branching is necessary, which node is the most promising to branch from? What branches should be used?

Solution

a. There are three missing values on the diagram: the branch (constraint) from Node 1 to Node 2; the value of variable x_3 at Node 3, and the value of the objective function at Node 4. Branching is done on the basis of the variable with the largest factional part. At Node 1, variable x_3 has the largest fractional part (.7); hence, the branches are $x_3 \leq 2$ and $x_3 \geq 3$. Because the latter is the branch to Node 3, the branch to Node 1 must be $x_3 \leq 2$.

The branch leading into a node determines the value of the branching variable at the node; it forces the branching variable to *equal* the branch value. Therefore: $x_3 = 3$ at Node 3.

The value of the objective function at a node is determined by the values of the decision variables at the node and their objective function coefficients. Thus, the value is:

$$5(.25) + 7(8) + 4(2) = 65.25$$

b. A node can be infeasible for a number of reasons. In this instance, the value of x_2 at Node 5 must equal 9 because the branch constraint forces that value. However, in the third constraint of the original problem, $x_3 = 9$ would mean that the upper limit of 25 would be exceeded for any non-negative value of x_1. Hence, the node is infeasible.

c. Nodes 4 and 3 are not all integers, so additional branching is possible and necessary. Because Node 3 has a higher objective function value (67) than Node 4 (65.25), branching from Node 3 is more promising at this point.

Problem 2. Solve this problem using enumeration:

minimize $\quad 3x_1 + 2x_2 + 4x_3$

subject to

$$\begin{aligned} 5x_1 + 2x_2 + 3x_3 &\geq 5 \\ x_1 + x_2 + 2x_3 &\geq 2 \\ x_1, x_2, x_3 \text{ } &0 \text{ or } 1 \end{aligned}$$

Solution

First determine the number of possible 0–1 solutions. With three variables, that number is $2^3 = 8$.

Next, develop a list of the possible solutions (see the following table). This can be done either by using a tree or by listing them directly. For instance, solution Number 5 (1 1 0) means $x_1 = 1, x_2 = 1, x_3 = 0$.

				Feasible?		
Number	x_1	x_2	x_3	Constraint 1	Constraint 2	Value of Objective Function
1	0	0	0	No	—	—
2	1	0	0	√	No	—
3	0	1	0	No	—	—
4	0	0	1	No	—	—
5	1	1	0	√	√	5
6	1	0	1	√	√	7
7	0	1	1	√	√	6
8	1	1	1	√	√	9

For each solution, first determine if it satisfies the first constraint. For example, the first solution (0 0 0) does not satisfy the first constraint; substituting those values into the left side of the constraint produces a value of zero, which does not satisfy the minimum required of 5. If the first constraint is not satisfied, go on to the next solution because all constraints must be satisfied in order to have a feasible solution. If the first constraint *is* satisfied, evaluate the second. If *both* are satisfied, determine the value of the objective function by substituting the values of the variables into the objective function and solving.

For each solution that satisfies both constraints, the value of the objective function has been computed. Since this is a minimization problem, the solution $x_1 = 1, x_2 = 1, x_3 = 0$ is optimal; it has the lowest value of the objective function.

PROBLEMS

1. Given the following problem:

x_1 = number of riding mowers
x_2 = number of tractors

maximize $50x_1 + 50x_2$

subject to

Labor	$14x_1 + 5x_2 \leq 70$ hours
Machine	$2x_1 + 3x_2 \leq 18$ hours
	x_1 and $x_2 \geq 0$ and integer

a. Graph this problem and identify the LP relaxation solution on the graph.
b. Determine the optimal LP solution algebraically.
c. What are the branches from Node 1 using branch and bound? Why?
d. Solve the remainder of the problem using branch and bound. Illustrate the subproblems on your graph.

2. Suppose the objective function in the previous problem had to be revised to reflect a price change to this: $120x_1 + 50x_2$. Solve the revised problem for the optimal integer values of x_1 and x_2 using the branch and bound method. Show the LP relaxation and subproblem solutions graphically.

3. Consider this all-integer problem:

maximize $Z = 5x_1 + 3x_2$ (thousands)

subject to

$$34x_1 + 30x_2 \leq 255$$
$$8x_1 + 20x_2 \leq 80$$
$$x_1 \text{ and } x_2 \geq 0 \text{ and integer}$$

Solve using the branch and bound method. Show the LP relaxation and subproblems graphically.

4. Show the previous problem with this modification: Only x_1 needs to be integer.

5. Solve this problem using branch and bound:

maximize $\quad 6x_1 + 5x_2$

subject to

$$18x_1 + 7x_2 \leq 126$$
$$12x_1 + 16x_2 \leq 192$$
$$x_1, x_2 \geq 0 \text{ and } x_2 \text{ integer}$$

6. Solve the previous problem under the stipulation that both x_1 and x_2 must be integer. Show the LP relaxation solution and subproblems graphically.

7. A manufacturer of executive jet aircraft is concerned with its profit picture over the short run. It produces two different models of planes, x_1 and x_2. Its profits are \$30,000 for each x_1 and \$20,000 for each x_2. It has orders for seven of each type of plane. There are two major constraints on production:

Labor	$4x_1 + 2x_2 \leq 17$ weeks
Materials	$5x_1 + 4x_2 \leq 21$ tons
	$x_1, x_2 \geq 0$ and integer

Also, assume that no more than 4 x_2's can be produced due to a prior union agreement.

Solve this problem using the branch and bound method. Illustrate the LP relaxation solution and subproblem solutions graphically.

8. A producer of pleasure boats wants to maximize revenue during the next month. Two types of boats are sold, x_1 and x_2. Type x_1 sells for \$40,000 and type x_2 sells for \$30,000. The x_1 boats require 10 weeks of labor and 600 board feet of lumber each. The x_2 boats need 3 weeks of labor and 1,000 board feet of lumber. There are 30 weeks of labor and 3,000 board feet of lumber available this season. Because of the desire to avoid ending up with uncompleted boats, the manager has specified that only integer solutions will be accepted. Use the branch and bound method to obtain the optimal solution. Illustrate the LP relaxation solution and the subproblems graphically and in a node diagram.

9. A janitorial service, Mother's Helpers, provides workers to clean office buildings during late evening hours using workers with two skill levels, 1 and 2. Each Level 1 person is paid \$12 per hour and each Level 2 person is paid \$8 per hour. The workers wash floors and vacuum offices. Each Level 1 can vacuum 9 offices per hour, whereas each Level 2 can vacuum only 2 offices per hour. Each Level 1 can wash 2 floors per hour and each Level 2 can wash 3 floors per hour. In order to complete a new job in the allotted time, 18 offices must be vacuumed per hour and 12 floors must be washed per hour. Determine the number of each type of person that will

be needed to complete the job within the allotted time and at minimum cost. Show the LP relaxation solution and the subproblems graphically.

10. Answer the previous problem with this modification: The objective is to minimize $5x_1 + 7x_2$.

11. Answer Problem 10 with this modification: x_1 need not be integer, but x_2 must be. This is due to the potential for using Level 1 people on a nearby job. For example, one person might be used for one-third time on this job.

12. Answer Problem 9 (janitorial service) for the case where only x_1 is required to be integer. Use the objective function $6x_1 + 4x_2$. Explain how x_2 could be non-integer.

13. Solve the following 0–1 problem for the optimal integer solution using:
    a. The enumeration method.
    b. the branch and bound method.

maximize $\quad 70x_1 + 40x_2 + 60x_3 + 80x_4$

subject to

$$5x_1 + 6x_2 + 8x_3 + 10x_4 \leq 20$$
$$4x_1 + 2x_2 + 2x_3 + 5x_4 \leq 6$$
All variables 0 or 1

14. All electronics manufacturer produces a toy robot that suddenly is in great demand. The firm can produce three versions of the robot. One version yields a contribution to profit of \$22 per unit, the second, a contribution to profit of \$18 per unit, and the third, a contribution to profit of \$25 per unit. The firm can produce and sell any of the versions, subject to these limitations for each hour: 40 pounds of raw material is available, four assembly workers are available, and there are two inspectors who work exclusively on this plus another who works 40 percent of the time on this. Each Version 1 robot requires 4 pounds of raw material, 12 minutes for assembly, and 12 minutes for inspection; whereas each Version 2 requires 8 pounds of raw material, 24 minutes for assembly, and 6 minutes of inspection; and each Version 3 requires 3 pounds of raw material, 18 minutes for assembly, and 12 minutes for inspection. Assuming that only integer values will be acceptable because the robots are packaged and shipped hourly, what quantity of each type will maximize total hourly contribution to profits?

15. A direct marketing manager wants to select prototypes of letters to send out to the company's customers. There are four prototypes to choose from. In previous trials, Type 1 had a response rate of 30 percent, Type 2 a response rate of 25 percent, Type 3 a response rate of 35 percent, and Type 4 a response rate of 40 percent. No more than three types will be chosen, however, due to other considerations. Type 1 will mean a cost of \$6,000, Type 2 a cost of \$4,000, Type 3 a cost of \$5,000, and Type 4 a cost of \$7,000. The manager has \$18,000 to spend. If the goal is to maximize total responses, which letter or letters should be sent out?

a. Solve using enumeration.

b. Solve using the branch and bound method.

16. A franchise operation that sells frozen custard intends to open one or more new stores in a medium-sized metropolitan area. Three sites are under consideration. Each site has a somewhat different projected profit contribution and different supervision requirements. The first site has an estimated daily profit of $200 and a weekly supervision requirement of 48 hours; the second site has a projected profit of $100 per day and a weekly supervision requirement of 30 hours; and the third site has a projected profit of $150 per day and a weekly supervision requirement of 20 hours. The firm will have 65 hours available per week for supervision. Which site or sites should be selected in order to obtain the highest projected daily profit? What projected daily profit will your solution produce?

    a. Solve this problem using complete enumeration.

    b. Solve this problem using the branch and bound method.

17. A vice president of finance of a bank holding company recently faced this problem. Proposals for four projects were submitted to her. Project A had an estimated total return to the company of $210,000, Project B had an estimated return of $180,000, Project C a return of $160,000, and Project D a return of $175,000. In weighing these proposals, the vice president had to take into account the cash requirements of the projects and the available cash for the time periods involved. This information is summarized below.

	Cash Needs			
Project	**Period 1**	**Period 2**	**Period 3**	**Period 4**
A	$8,000	$8,000	$10,000	$10,000
B	7,000	9,000	9,000	11,000
C	5,000	7,000	9,000	11,000
D	9,000	8,000	7,000	6,000

Cash availability is $22,000 for Period 1, $25,000 for Period 2, $38,000 for Period 3, and $30,000 for Period 4. Determine which projects to fund and the amount of cash that will be needed per period in order to maximize the total estimated return, using these approaches:

a. Enumeration.

b. The branch and bound method.

18. The operations manager of a power company must design a set of crew assignments for cleanup duties after a severe windstorm, which knocked out power in various spots throughout the county. At least 40 workers and 20 supervisors must be assigned. The operations manager is particularly determined to minimize the cost of operating the trucks assigned for cleanup. Three types of trucks are suitable: Type 1, with an hourly operating cost of $60, Type 2 with an hourly operating cost of $30, and Type 3, with an

hourly operating cost of $80. The Type 1 trucks have a crew of two workers and one supervisor, the Type 2 trucks have one worker and two supervisors, and the Type 3 trucks have four workers and one supervisor. How many of each truck type should be used in order to both minimize the total houly operating cost and satisfy the worker and supervisor requirements? Assume only integer solutions are acceptable. Also, determine the total cost of your solution.

19. Deregulation Airlines is planning to expand its fleet of aircraft. Four different models are under consideration: A, B, C, and D. The estimated annual contribution to profits of these models is $4.5 million, $6 million, $6.5 million, and $5 million respectively. Two important factors that must be taken into account are the fuel requirements and the maintenance requirements for each model. The weekly fuel requirements (in thousands of gallons) are 18, 25, 28, and 20, respectively, and the monthly maintenance requirements (in hours) are 20, 18, 28, and 30, respectively. Fuel availability will be 710,000 gallons per month and maintenance capacity is 900 worker-hours per month. Determine the number of aircraft of each model that the company should purchase if its goal is to achieve the greatest contribution to annual profits. Assume that only integer solutions are acceptable.

20. An investor must decide how to invest $70,000. After considerable research, the investor has narrowed the investment alternatives to four possibilities: Invest $25,000 in a real estate plan, invest $20,000 in a new product, invest $30,000 in a certificate of deposit, and invest $35,000 in a certain stock. The first three investments must be in the exact amounts listed, although the last can be in any amount up to $35,000. The expected returns for each dollar invested are $3 for the real estate, $2 for the new product, $4 for the CD, and $2.50 for the stock. Assume that stock amounts must be in multiples of $7,000. Solve for the optimum solution.

21. Solve the following problem using the branch and bound method:

maximize $5x_1 + 8x_2 + 4x_3$

subject to

1 $1.5x_1 + 2x_2 + 1.6x_3 \leq 10$

2 $25x_1 + 50x_2 + 20x_3 \leq 160$

$x_1, x_2, \text{ and } x_3 \geq 0$ and integer

22. The Rubber Blanket Company has recently undergone a reorganization. It must now decide on quantity levels for these products: x_1, x_2, and x_3. Their respective contributions to profits are estimated to be $10, $15, and $18 per unit, in thousands. The products are subject to the following constraints:

$$4x_1 + 6x_2 + 3x_3 \leq 70$$
$$90x_1 + 80x_2 + 100x_3 \leq 1{,}200$$

The variables do not need to be integer. In addition, there is a one-time cost associated with the production of each product. For x_1 the cost would be \$3,000, for x_2 the cost would be \$4,000, and for x_3 the cost would be \$6,000.

a. Formulate the problem.

b. Determine the optimal values for the decision variables and the maximum profit.

23. Manager Cheryl Carver is faced with this problem: A product can be made on either one of two machines: x_1 or x_2. However, the machines have different processing requirements and different profit and cost structures. These differences are summarized in the following table:

Machine	Profit per Unit	Setup Cost	Raw Material #1 per Unit	Raw Material #2 per Unit
x_1	\$50	\$250	2 pounds	4 quarts
x_2	40	210	3 pounds	2 quarts

Cheryl wants to determine whether all of the output should be produced on one of the machines (if so, which machine) or whether the output should be split between these two machines. The goal is to maximize the contribution to profit. Thirty pounds of raw material #1 and thirty-six quarts of raw material #2 will be available for this production run.

a. Set up her problem in a format suitable for integer programming.

b. Assuming that an integer solution is required, determine the optimal solution to Cheryl's problem.

24. (Refer to Problem 23.) Treat the unit profits in the previous problem as unit costs. In addition, suppose that the firm has an order for 10 units of the product.

a. Set up this problem in an integer programming format.

b. Solve for the optimal integer solution. Interpret your answer.

25. The product manager at a savings and loan must have a large mailing printed and sent out to customers. A previous mailing was delayed due to a problem at the printer's shop, and the product manager wants to reduce that risk by giving no more than ¾ of the job to one printer. The total job will consist of 400 pieces. The product manager has obtained cost quotations from the four local shops that she feels can handle the job and meet quality specifications. This information is summarized in the following table:

Printer	Cost per Piece	Base fee
A	\$.50	\$300
B	.40	350
C	.45	380
D	.47	320

Assume that the goal is to minimize the total cost of printing the mailing pieces. Determine the integer solution that will yield the lowest possible total cost.

26. The new manager of a plastics division must make a decision on shipping containers that will be used to ship products by truck. The main issue is to decide how many of each type container to use. Three types are available: A, B, and C. Type A has a loaded weight of 60 pounds and a volume of 16 cubic feet, Type B has a weight of 64 pounds and a volume of 20 cubic feet, and Type C has a weight of 48 pounds and a volume of 14 cubic feet. Each truck has a volume of 1,200 cubic feet and a weight limit of 2,000 pounds. The containers have profit contributions of $200 for each A, $220 for each B, and $240 for each C. How many of each container should be allocated per truck in order to maximize the total contribution to profit?

27. The owner of a new cab company wants to determine locations for cab waiting points. He has gathered the following information:

Location	Can Serve Areas	Cost per Day
1	A,E	$400
2	A,C,D	500
3	B,C,E	450
4	B,D	440
5	D,E	430

The owner wants to be sure that all areas can be served, yet he wants this done for as little cost as possible. What choice of locations will accomplish this?

28. A group of investors is contemplating opening a number of restaurants in a large metropolitan area. Some of these will offer full service and some take-out service only. The group has identified five potential locations for take-out restaurants, of which it will select at least three, and it has identified six potential locations for full-service restaurants, of which it will select at least two. Operating costs will be $15,000 per month for take-out service only and $25,000 per month for full-service restaurants. The group has a monthly budget of $195,000 for operating costs. Estimated profits are $5,000 per month for take-out service and $7,000 a month for full-service restaurants. The group needs to know how many of each type restaurant to select and the profit that will be generated.

a. Formulate a model for this problem.

b. Solve for the optimal solution.

c. How much of the operating budget will be unused?

29. Solve this all-integer problem for the optimal solution using branch and bound:

maximize $13x_1 + 26x_2 + 14x_3$

subject to

$$\begin{aligned} 16x_1 + 9x_2 + 4x_3 &\le 44 \\ 6x_2 + 10x_3 &\le 20 \\ x_1, x_2, \text{ and } x_3 &\ge 0 \text{ and integer} \end{aligned}$$

30. Find the optimal solution to this problem using branch and bound:

maximize $9x_1 + 5x_2 + 5x_3$

subject to

$$\begin{aligned} 20x_1 + 14x_2 + 19x_3 &\le 100 \\ 8x_1 + 4x_2 &\le 18 \\ x_1, x_2, \text{ and } x_3 &\ge 0 \text{ and integer} \end{aligned}$$

31. The manager of a stamping department is getting ready to begin a new operation. A single product is to be produced. It can be produced on any of three machines. Information concerning the machines is contained in the following table:

Machine	Setup Cost	Profit per Unit	Daily Capacity
A	$300	$10	500
B	250	12	450
C	325	13	450

Each machine requires an operator, and two operators are available. The profit per unit excludes setup cost, and setups must be done at the start of each new day.

a. Formulate this profit maximization problem.

b. Solve for the optimal quantities to produce per day on each machine.

32. A department has three machines available, and the new department manager must select one of the machines to assign to a new product line. The product line will consist of three slightly different products, A, B, and C. Production requirements, machine capacities, and setup costs are given in the following table:

Machine	Setup Cost	Production Time Per Piece A	B	C	Capacity (hours)
1	$150	4	3	5	1,000
2	120	3	2	4	800
3	110	2	4	2	700

The profit per pound on the three products is listed in the following table:

Product	Profit
A	$13
B	10
C	12

a. Formulate this problem taking into account an additonal factor: At least 40 pounds of each product must be made.

b. Solve for the optimal solution and profit.

33. Find the optimal solution to this problem using the branch and bound method.

maximize $12x_1 + 18x_2 + 14x_3$

subject to

$$6x_1 + 5x_2 + 5x_3 \leq 48$$
$$x_1,\ x_2, \text{ and } x_3 \geq 0 \text{ and integer}$$

34. Find the optimal solution to this problem using the branch and bound method. If there are multiple optimal solutions, identify each one.

maximize $5x_1 + 6x_2 + 5x_3 + 4x_4$

subject to

$$10x_1 + 11x_2 + 9x_3 + 7x_4 \leq 39$$
$$2x_1 + 3x_2 + 3x_3 + 2x_4 \leq 13$$
$$\text{All variables} \geq 0 \text{ and integer}$$

35. Find the optimal solution to this problem:

minimize $x_1 + x_2 + 2x_3 + x_4$

subject to

$$3x_1 + 2x_2 + 4x_3 + x_4 \geq 41$$
$$\text{All variables} \geq 0 \text{ and integer}$$

36. Determine the optimal solution to this all-integer problem:

minimize $10x_1 + 11x_2 + 12x_3$

subject to

$$8x_1 + 9x_2 + 10x_3 \geq 20$$
$$3x_1 + 4x_2 + 3x_3 \geq 13$$
$$\text{All variables} \geq 0 \text{ and integer}$$

Chapter 8 Case

Suburban Suntime

The Suburban Suntime Corporation manufactures a line of high-priced outdoor furniture consisting of a picnic table, a bench, an armchair, and a chaise lounge. The picnic table is sold in a set with two of the benches; the benches also may be sold separately. Here is information on prices and resource availability for next month.

	Picnic Table (set)	Bench (separate)	Armchair	Chaise Lounge	Available
Price	$725	$225	$275	$300	
Redwood (board ft.)	22	6	7	8	4,500
Cedar (board ft.)	12	4	4	0	3,600
12-inch fittings (number)	18	4	0	2	2,250
8-inch fittings (number)	12	4	6	6	2,075
Bolts (number)	48	12	12	20	5,925
Labor (hours)	20	5	8	12	4,800

Redwood costs $8 per board foot; cedar costs $6 per board foot; 12-inch fittings cost $2.50; 8-inch fittings cost $1.50; bolts cost $.50. The hourly wage rate and fringe benefits of the workers average $9.00 per hour.

Because of prior orders, at least 50 (separate) benches and at least 40 chaise lounges must be produced.

Discussion question

Determine the quantity of each product to be produced next month. Assume partial units are unacceptable.

Source: Written by Professor Paul Van Ness, College of Business, Rochester Institute of Technology. Reprinted by permission.

Chapter 9
Goal Programming

Chapter Outline

Learning Objectives

After completing this chapter, you should be able to:

1. Describe the type of problems that goal programming is designed to handle.
2. Explain what a goal is and how it is expressed in a goal programming model.
3. Discuss the similarities and differences between goal programming and linear programming models.
4. Formulate goal programming models.
5. Solve goal models that have two decision variables using a graphical approach.
6. Solve goal models using a computer-assisted approach.
7. Interpret solutions to goal programming problems.

Linear programming is a powerful analytical tool that can be applied to a wide range of problems. However, its use is limited to problems that can be expressed in terms of a single objective (e.g., maximize profits). To be sure, there are many instances in which a single objective is appropriate. Nonetheless, there also are many instances in which multiple objectives are appropriate. For example, a manager may have quality, productivity, *and* profit objectives. But unless these can be reduced to a common unit of measure, such as dollars of profit, standard linear programming models cannot be used. One alternative is to use goal programming.

Goal programming is a variation of linear programming that can be used for problems that involve multiple objectives. Goal programming (GP) models are quite similar to LP models. Both are formulated under the same requirements and assumptions (e.g., linearity, non-negativity, certainty). Moreover, graphical methods can be used to illustrate the basic concepts of goal programming, just as they were used to illustrate linear programming concepts, and computers can be used to handle problems that do not lend themselves to graphical solution.

When it was first introduced in the 1960s, goal programming was designed to handle linear problems. Since then, it has been extended to integer and nonlinear problems. However, the discussion here will focus exclusively on linear problems.

This chapter introduces the basic concepts of goal programming. It begins with a discussion of how GP differs from LP, then goes on to formulation and solution of GP models.

GOAL PROGRAMMING VERSUS LINEAR PROGRAMMING

Goal programming models differ from the previously described linear programming models in two key ways. One relates to constraints and the other to model objectives.

In the context of goal programming, multiple objectives are referred to as **goals.** Each goal relates to a target level of performance. For instance, a problem may involve a goal for labor utilization: The performance target may be to use 100 hours of labor on a job. Another goal may relate to an advertising budget: The target may be an expenditure of $25,000 on advertising.

In goal programming models, goals are expressed as *constraints*. However, **goal constraints** are somewhat different than the ones encountered in previous chapters. Recall that in linear programming models, a solution would not be considered feasible if it violated any of the constraints. Because of the absolute requirement that constraints be satisfied, you might think of those constraints as **hard constraints.** In contrast, goal constraints specify desirable levels of performance. These are treated as approximate rather than absolute amounts which should be achieved to the extent possible. Therefore, you might think of a goal constraint as a **soft constraint.**

Goal programming models may consist entirely of soft (goal) constraints or they may consist of a combination of soft and hard (nongoal) constraints. The solution to a goal programming model must satisfy any hard constraints, although it may not necessarily achieve the target levels of the goal (soft) constraints. When one or more goals are not achieved by a solution, it is because there are conflicts either between goals or between goals and hard constraints. For example, one constraint might specify that x_1 should be 10 units, whereas another constraint might specify that x_1 should be at least 20 units. Because these two cannot both be satisfied by a single solution, we say that they conflict. In linear programming terms, we would say that such a problem has no feasible solution space. However, this is the sort of problem goal programming is designed to handle. *Deviations* from goals are permitted if they are needed to obtain a solution. Thus, in goal programming, the objective is to satisfy the hard constraints (if any) and achieve reasonably *acceptable levels* for the goal constraints. This is referrred to as **satisficing.**

In order to obtain a solution that provides acceptable levels of satisfaction of goals when there are conflicts, it becomes necessary to make *trade-offs:* satisfying hard constraints and achieving higher levels of some goals at the expense of other goals. When goal programming was originally introduced, the approach used was to treat goals as equally important in terms of searching for an acceptable solution. Thus, a deviation from one goal was just as acceptable as a deviation from another goal. Later versions permitted weighting of deviations so that differences in importance in goals could be taken into account. However, this required decision makers to come up with a set of weights that truly reflected differences in importance. Some decision makers found this process to be difficult and somewhat artificial. More recently, interest has centered on **priority models,** wherein decision makers are merely required to *rank* deviations from the various goals in their order of importance. That approach seems to hold considerable promise. It is the one we shall focus on.

Deviation Variables

In order to account for possible deviation from a goal, **deviation variables** are incorporated into each goal to represent the differences between actual performance and target peformance. There are two possible kinds of deviations from a target: being under the targeted amount (*underachievement*), and being over the targeted amount (*overachievement*). Deviation variables are included in each goal constraint: u_i for underachievement and v_i for overachievement, where i is the number of the constraint ($i = 1,2,3, \ldots$). Adding these two deviation variables to a goal constraint creates an equality because the deviation variables account for any discrepancy between actual and target. We can readily see this by considering a goal constraint.

Suppose a manager has formulated a goal for labor hours. The mathematical expression of the goal constraint might look like this:

$$4x_1 + 2x_2 + u_1 - v_1 = 100 \text{ hours}$$

Variables x_1 and x_2 represent decision variables, whereas u_1 stands for the amount of underutilization of labor and v_1 stands for overtime hours. The subscripts for u and v indicate that this is the first constraint (in a list of goal constraints).

The right side of the equation indicates the target (goal) amount. In this case,„it is 100 hours. The left side of the equation contains both the decision variables and the deviation variables. The fact that both underachievement and overachievement variables are included in the goal indicates that a deviation in either direction is permissible (although not necessarily desirable). If a deviation is not permissible, it would not appear in the goal equation. For example, if overachievement were not permissible in the labor constraint, then v_1 would be omitted from the constraint.

Note the signs of the deviational variables and consider that the purpose of these variables is to indicate the amount of any discrepancy between the target level and the amount actually achieved by a particular solution. In effect, the deviation variables are equivalent to slack (amount of underachievement) and surplus (amount of overachievement). Hence, u is added and v is subtracted in a goal constraint. For instance, suppose that the quantity $4x_1 + 2x_2$ is equal to 80 hours, which is 20 hours less than the goal of 100 hours. Thus, utilization is *under* by 20 hours: $u_1 = 20$. Conversely, suppose the quantity $4x_1 + 2x_2$ is equal to 110. This is *over* the goal of 100 hours by 10 hours. Therefore, $v_1 = 10$. Now notice that in each of these cases, the other deviation variable would equal zero because it would be physically impossible to be over and under a goal simultaneously. Of course, if the quantity $4x_1 + 2x_2$ is exactly equal to 100, then both of the deviation variables would equal zero. Thus, at least one of the two deviation variables in each goal must equal zero in any solution.

MODEL FORMULATION

A goal programming model consists of an objective and a set of constraints. The constraints may be goal constraints or they may be a mix of goal and nongoal constraints. In addition, there is the non-negativity requirement that all variables (decision variables and deviation variables) must be non-negative.

In priority models, the **objective** indicates which deviation variables will be minimized and their order of importance. Thus, the objective is to minimize specified deviations from certain goals according to priority.

Consider this GP model:

subject to

$$\left.\begin{array}{lll} \text{A} & 4x_1 + 2x_2 & \leq 40 \\ \text{B} & 2x_1 + 6x_2 & \leq 60 \end{array}\right\} \text{Nongoal (hard)}$$

$$\begin{array}{lrl} 1 & 3x_1 + 3x_2 + u_1 - v_1 = 75 \\ 2 & x_1 + 2x_2 + u_2 - v_2 = 50 \end{array}\Big\} \text{Goal (soft)}$$

$$\text{All variables} \geq 0$$

There are three deviation variables specified in the objective: u_1, v_1, and u_2. Their subscripts indicate the goal to which they pertain. The P's represent priorities, and their subscripts indicate order of importance, with 1 being the highest priority. Hence, we can see in the objective that the highest priority is to minimize being under on the first goal. (Note that u_1 appears only in that goal.) The next highest priority is to minimize being over on the first goal, and the last priority is to minimize being under on the second goal. Note that not every deviational variable is specified in the objective. The second deviation variable in the second constraint, v_2, is not included in the objective. Evidently, the decision maker does not want to minimize being over on the second goal. If, for example, that second goal relates to profit, we could understand why a decision maker would not want to minimize being over on that goal.

In order to differentiate goal and nongoal constraints, the nongoal constraints have been assigned capital letters, whereas the goal constraints have been assigned numbers. Note that only the goal constraints have deviation variables and all goal constraints are expressed as equalities.

Having now examined the goal model, let's turn our attention to formulating such a model. One approach would be as follows:

1. Identify the decision variables.
2. Identify the constraints and determine which ones are goal constraints.
3. Formulate the nongoal constraints (if any).
4. Formulate the goal constraints.
5. Formulate the objective.
6. Add the non-negativity requirement statement.

The next example illustrates this process.

■

EXAMPLE 1 A company manufactures three products: x_1, x_2, and x_3. Material and labor requirements per unit are:

Product	x_1	x_2	x_3	**Availability**
Material (lb./unit)	2	4	3	600 pounds
Assembly (min./unit)	9	8	7	900 minutes
Packing (min./unit)	1	2	3	300 minutes

The manager has listed the following objectives in order of priority:

1. Minimize overtime in the assembly department.
2. Minimize undertime in the assembly department
3. Minimize both undertime and overtime in the packaging department.

Solution

Apparently, there are three constraints: material, assembly time, and packing time. Moreover, assembly and packing constraints should be expressed as goals because they are included in the priority list. Material is not included so it should be a nongoal constraint. The constraints are:

Material	$2x_1 + 4x_2 + 3x_3$	$\leq$ 600 pounds
Assembly	$9x_1 + 8x_2 + 7x_3 + u_1 - v_1$	= 900 minutes
Packing	$1x_1 + 2x_2 + 3x_3 + u_2 - v_2$	= 300 minutes
	All variables ≥ 0	

The objective is based on the listing and the deviation variables as defined in the constraints. It is:

minimize $P_1v_1 + P_2u_1 + P_3(u_2 + v_2)$

The third priority, P_3, expresses that fact that minimizing both under and over on the second goal are equally important. Thus, the complete model is:

minimize $P_1v_1 + P_2u_1 + P_3(u_2 + v_2)$

subject to

A	$2x_1 + 4x_2 + 3x_3$	$\leq$ 600 pounds
1	$9x_1 + 8x_2 + 7x_3 + u_1 - v_1$	= 900 minutes
2	$1x_1 + 2x_2 + 3x_3 + u_2 - v_2$	= 300 minutes
	All variables ≥ 0	

GRAPHICAL SOLUTIONS

Graphical solutions are limited to goal problems that have two decision variables. As you might suspect, many real problems involve more than two decision variables. Nonetheless, the graphical approach provides a visual illustration of certain goal programming concepts. For that reason, it is invaluable in terms of the insight it can produce.

The graphical approach involves plotting all of the constraints, both hard and soft. In order to plot a goal constraint, ignore the deviation variables and simply

FIGURE 9–1 A Plot of a Goal Constraint

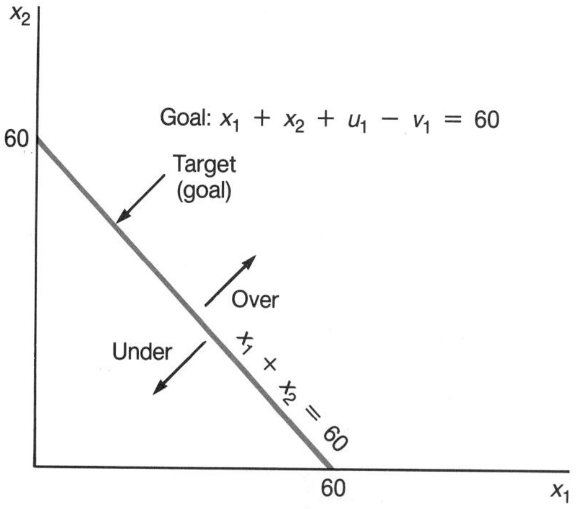

FIGURE 9–2 Designating Priority and Direction

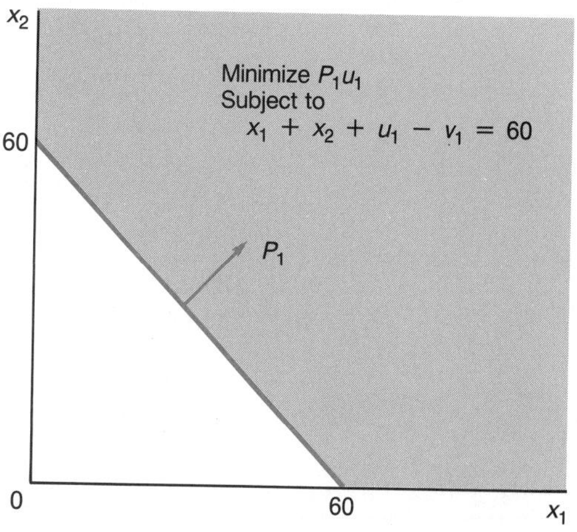

plot it as you would a constraint that has no deviation variables. Thus, the goal constraint:

$$x_1 + x_2 + u_1 - v_1 = 60$$

would be plotted as if it were:

$$x_1 + x_2 = 60$$

The deviation variables do not appear on the graph; instead their values are determined algebraically at the end of the analysis along with the optimal values of the decision variables. However, over- and underdeviations correspond to the regions on either side of the line, as illustrated in Figure 9–1.

After plotting a goal constraint, indicate the direction that will satisfy the objective, as illustrated in Figure 9–2. Notice that the region that will satisfy the objective (minimize P_1u_1) is the line itself plus the area *opposite* the deviation specified. In other words, we minimize being under by being *on or over* the goal.

Taken as a whole, the graphical approach to goal programming involves plotting all the nongoal constraints (if any), just as in LP, and identifying the feasible solution space. However, unlike LP, the objective is not plotted. Instead, the goals are plotted one at a time, according to the priorities given by the objective. After each is plotted, the best solution to that point is found. However, as successive goals are plotted, only solutions that do not require additional deviations from the higher level goals already plotted are considered. In effect, minimizing the deviation with the highest priority is treated as infinitely more desirable than minimizing the deviation with the next highest priority, and minimizing the next highest priority is treated infinitely more important than the next highest

FIGURE 9–3 Plot of the Hard Constraint and the Feasible Solution Space

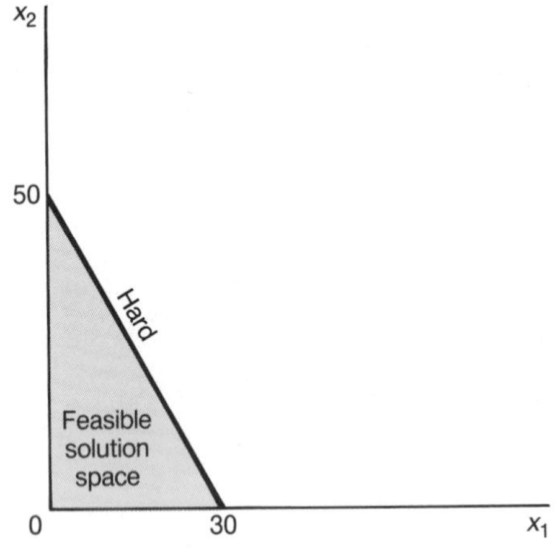

FIGURE 9–4 The Acceptable Region after Adding the First Goal Constraint

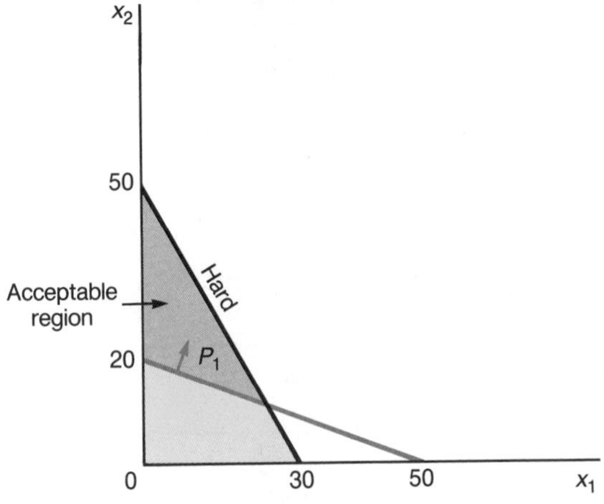

priority, and so on, as each additional goal is added to the graph. This solution procedure will become more apparent as we work through a number of examples.

Consider this goal programming model:

$$\text{minimize} \quad P_1u_1 + P_2u_2 + P_3u_3$$

$$\begin{aligned} \text{subject to} \quad 5x_1 + 3x_2 & \le 150 \\ 2x_1 + 5x_2 + u_1 - v_1 &= 100 \\ 3x_1 + 3x_2 + u_2 - v_2 &= 180 \\ x_1 + u_3 - v_3 &= 40 \\ \text{All variables} &\ge 0 \end{aligned}$$

In order to solve this graphically, we first identify and plot any hard constraints: the ones that do not have deviation variables. In this model, only the first is the hard type. It is plotted in Figure 9–3, and the feasible solution space is shaded in.

Next, we see in the objective that the highest priority is to minimize being under on the first goal constraint. So, we plot the first constraint and indicate that the desirable region is on the line and above it. (See Figure 9–4.) Now we can see that a portion of the feasible solution space also includes some of the desirable region. At this stage, any point in the overlap area would be acceptable.

Next, we see that the second highest priority relates to the second goal constraint (i.e., the subscript of u_2 tells us this). Hence, we plot the second goal constraint and indicate its area of desirability, which is on and above the line (see Figure 9–5). This region does not overlap the acceptable region as previously determined. However, we must not sacrifice a higher level priority for a lower

FIGURE 9–5 The Second Goal Is Added to the Graph

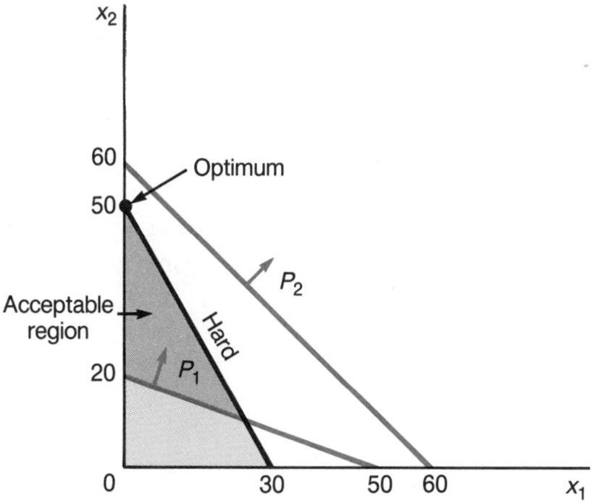

FIGURE 9–6 The Third Goal Is Added, but It Doesn't Change the Solution

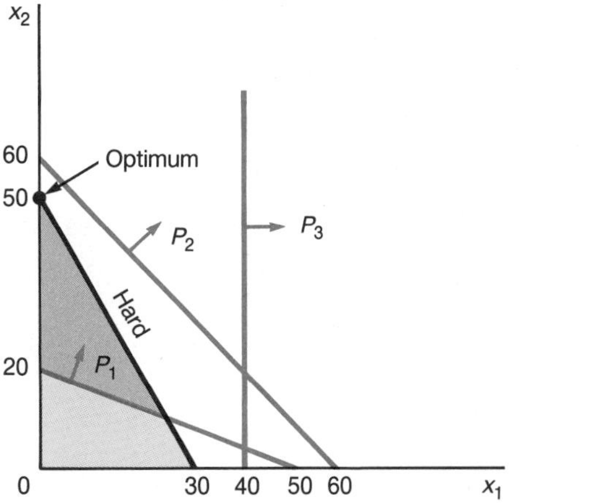

one. Therefore, there will be some underdeviation on the second goal. By inspecting the figure, we will find that the closest portion of the acceptable region to the second goal is the point $x_1 = 0, x_2 = 50$. This is the best point because it satisfies the first two constraints while minimizing the amount of underdeviation from the third (i.e., second goal) constraint.

Finally, we see in the objective that the last priority is to minimize being under on the third goal. Hence, we add the third goal to the graph (see Figure 9–6). The third goal does not overlap the acceptable region either. As with the second goal, we must not sacrifice a higher level priority (i.e., u_1) for a lower one (i.e., u_3). Therefore, adding the third goal does not change the previous solution because that solution satisfies the hard constraint and the highest priority (i.e., $u_1 = 0$) and it minimizes the amount of under deviation (u_2) on the second goal. To be sure, other points in the acceptable region would yield a lower value for u_3, but this would be at the expense of increasing u_2. Because higher level priorities are treated as infinitely more than lower level priorities (i.e., P_2 and P_3), we hold with our previous solution.

Thus, our solution is $x_1 = 0, x_2 = 50$. We see in Figure 9–6 that the solution satisfies P_1, so $u_1 = 0$. In order to find u_2, we simply substitute the optimum values of the decision variables into the second goal constraint and solve for u_2 after first omitting v_2 because it is apparent from the graph that the solution is not over the second goal constraint. Thus:

$$3x_1 + 3x_2 + u_2 - v_2 = 180$$

becomes

$$3(0) + 3(50) + u_2 = 180$$

Solving, $u_2 = 30$.

Similarly, we can compute the amount the solution is under on the third goal constraint:

$$x_1 + u_3 - v_3 = 40$$

becomes:

$$0 + u_3 = 40$$

Hence, $u_3 = 40$.

It is important to note that deviations generally cannot be read directly from the graph but, instead, must be computed using the appropriate goal constraints and the optimal values of the decision variables.

The next example illustrates a case in which there are no hard constraints, only goal constraints.

■

EXAMPLE 2 Solve this goal programming model for the optimal values of the decision variables using the graphical approach, then determine the optimal values of each deviation variable specified in the objective.

minimize $\quad P_1v_1 + P_2u_2 + P_3v_3$

subject to

Material	$5x_1 + 4x_2 + u_1 - v_1 =$	200 pounds
Profit	$2x_1 + x_2 + u_2 - v_2 =$	40 (\$000)
Machine	$2x_1 + 2x_2 + u_3 - v_3 =$	30 minutes
	All variables ≥ 0	

Solution

Because there are no hard constraints, we begin by noting that the highest priority is to minimize being over on the first goal constraint. Hence, we plot the first constraint and indicate the acceptable region (see Figure 9–7*a*).

The second highest priority refers to the second goal, so we plot the second goal and indicate the region that will satisfy both the first and second goals (see Figure 9–7*b*).

The third priority refers to the third goal, so we plot that and see that it does not have any points in common with the acceptable region. Consequently, some amount of overdeviation on the third will be unavoidable. We can see on the graph that this deviation can be minimized by the point $x_1 = 20$, $x_2 = 0$ (see Figure 9–7*c*), since this point is closest to the third goal.

Now we can determine the values of the deviation variables specified in the objective. By inspection of the graph, we can see that the solution satisfies the first

FIGURE 9–7

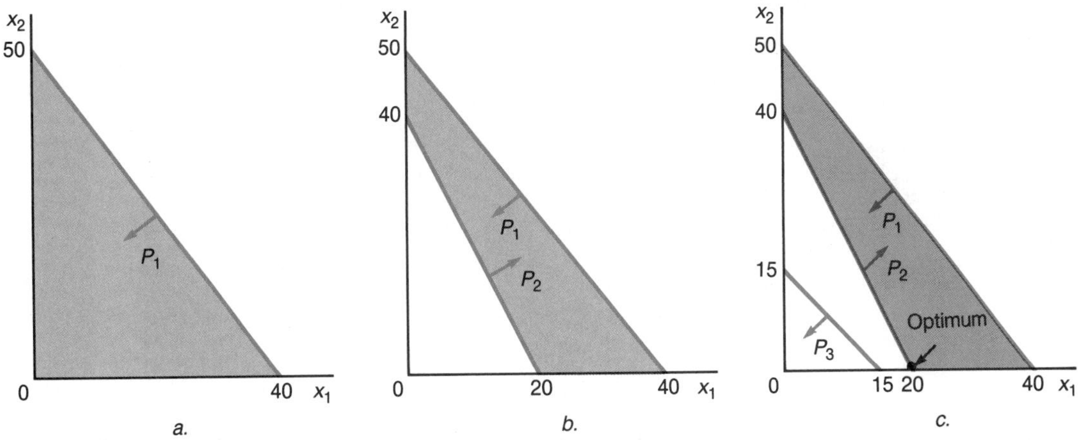

two priorities. Therefore, $v_1 = 0$ and $u_2 = 0$. We also can see that the solution is over on the third goal. We can determine this amount by substituting the optimal values of x_1 and x_2 into the third constraint and solving for v_3 (u_3 is omitted because we can see on the graph that the solution is not under on the third goal):

$$2(20) + 2(0) - v_3 = 30$$

Solving, $v_3 = 10$.

COMPUTER-ASSISTED SOLUTIONS

Goal programming problems can be solved using a standard LP package. The approach is conceptually similar to graphical solution, except that more than two decision variables can be handled with the computer approach. The computer-assisted approach adds goals sequentially according to priority and generates a solution after each goal is added. The computer approach differs from the graphical approach in three important ways. One is that the visual benefit of a graph is absent for problems that involve three or more decision variables. A second difference relates to the objective function: It changes as new goals are added to the model and the decision variables are now included in the objective. The third difference is that the results of each sequential solution may be used to modify a goal before proceeding to the next stage in the sequence.

The process begins by solving a model that includes any hard constraints and one goal constraint: The goal constraint that contains the deviation variable that has the highest priority. The solution for that model fixes the value of the deviation variable for the remainder of the analysis. Consequently, that variable is deleted from the model. This process is repeated using remaining deviation variable that has the highest priority, and so on, until all priorities have been considered. The following example illustrates the process.

Earlier in the chapter, this problem was solved using the graphical approach:

minimize $\quad P_1u_1 + P_2u_2 + P_3u_3$

subject to

$$\begin{aligned} 5x_1 + 3x_2 \quad\quad\quad\quad\quad\quad &\leq 150 \\ 2x_1 + 5x_2 + u_1 - v_1 &= 100 \\ 3x_1 + 3x_2 + u_2 - v_2 &= 180 \\ x_1 \quad\quad\quad + u_3 - v_3 &= 40 \\ \text{All variables} \geq 0 & \end{aligned}$$

For the computer-assisted approach, the first model must focus on the deviation variable with the highest priority, which is u_1 in this problem. That variable relates to the second constraint (i.e., the first goal constraint). Consequently, this first problem consists of the first (hard) constraint and the second (goal) constraint, and an objective function that includes all decision variables as well as the deviation variables in the first goal constraint. The model is:

minimize $\quad 0x_1 + 0x_2 + u_1 + 0v_1$

subject to

$$\begin{aligned} 5x_1 + 3x_2 \quad\quad\quad\quad &\leq 150 \\ 2x_1 + 5x_2 + u_1 - v_1 &= 100 \end{aligned}$$

Note that the decision variables are now represented in the objective function. Also, note that all of the variables except the highest priority deviation variable have coefficients of zero. Computer codes require that all variables in a problem be included in the objective function in order to be able to compute a value for them; the zero coefficients reflect the fact that the quantities of these variables will have no impact on the objective, which is to minimize the amount of under-deviation on the first goal.

The computer solution for this model is:

```
VARIABLE   QUANTITY
   S1         90
   X2         20

OPTIMAL Z      0
```

The computer indicates that the optimal solution at this point is $x_2 = 20$, and, because the other variables (x_1, u_1, and v_1) are not listed, their values are zero.

The fact that OPTIMAL Z = 0 and S1 = 90 is of no consequence for our purposes.

It can be useful to compare this solution with the initial graphical solution obtained in Figure 9–4, where we found an *area of feasibility* rather than a single optimal point. However, the computer uses the simplex approach and merely identifies one corner point.

Having determined that $u_1 = 0$, we substitute that value into the first goal constraint and delete u_1 from the model. This, essentially, fixes the value of u_1 at zero for the remainder of the analysis.

The next priority is to minimize u_2, which is in the second goal constraint. That constraint is now brought into the model, and the objective is modified accordingly. The revised model is:

$$\text{minimize} \quad 0x_1 + 0x_2 + 0v_1 + u_2 + 0v_2 \quad \text{(Note that } u_1 \text{ is omitted.)}$$

$$\begin{aligned} \text{subject to} \quad 5x_1 + 3x_2 \qquad\qquad &\le 150 \\ 2x_1 + 5x_2 \qquad - v_1 &= 100 \quad \text{(Note that } u_1 \text{ is omitted.)} \\ 3x_1 + 3x_2 + u_2 - v_2 &= 180 \end{aligned}$$

Again, all objective function coefficients are zero except for the deviation variable being minimized. Note that the previous deviation variable, u_1, is now removed from the objective function, although v_1 still remains. The u_1 also has been removed from the first goal constraint. Thus, the revised model consists of the previous model with one additional goal constraint added, the previous deviation variable of interest has been deleted, and the objective function has been revised accordingly.

The computer solution to the revised model is:

```
VARIABLE  QUANTITY
   V1        150
   X2         50
   U2         30

OPTIMAL Z     30
```

In this solution, $x_2 = 50$ and $x_1 = 0$. This corresponds to the graphical solution shown in Figure 9–5. The deviation variable of interest, u_2, has a value of 30. This information is used to modify the second goal constraint. Substituting the value of $u_2 = 30$ into the constraint and then subtracting this amount from both sides gives:

$$3x_1 + 3x_2 + 30 - v_2 = 180$$

and becomes

$$3x_1 + 3x_2 \qquad - v_2 = 150$$

TABLE 9–1 Summary of Computer Solutions

	Model	Values of Decision Variables	Values of Deviation Variables
1	Hard + First goal	$x_1 = 0, x_2 = 20$	$u_1 = 0$
2	Hard + First two goals	$x_1 = 0, x_2 = 50$	$u_1 = 0, u_2 = 30$
3	Hard + First three goals	$x_1 = 0, x_2 = 50$	$u_1 = 0, u_2 = 30, u_3 = 40$

This puts the constant on the right-hand side, and it fixes the value of u_2 at 30 (i.e., the value of u_2 cannot change as further solutions are generated).

The third and last priority relates to deviation variable u_3. Removing the previous variable, u_2, for the model and incorporating the deviation variables for the third goal, the revised model is now:

$$\text{minimize} \quad 0x_1 + 0x_2 + 0v_1 + 0v_2 + u_3 + 0v_3$$

subject to

$$\begin{aligned} 5x_1 + 3x_2 & & & \leq 150 \\ 2x_1 + 5x_2 & & - v_1 & = 100 \\ 3x_1 + 3x_2 & & - v_2 & = 150 \\ x_1 & + u_3 & - v_3 & = 40 \end{aligned}$$

Again, note that all variables in the objective function have coefficients of zero except the deviation variable that currently is being minimized, and all higher priority deviation variables that were previously minimized are eliminated for the revised model.

The computer solution for this model is:

```
VARIABLE  QUANTITY
   X1        0
   X2        50
   V1        150
   U3        40

OPTIMAL Z    40
```

Because all priorities have been accounted for at this point, this solution completes the analysis. The optimal values of the decision variables are: $x_1 = 0$ and $x_2 = 50$; and the optimal values of the three deviation variables specified in the objective are: $u_1 = 0$, $u_2 = 30$, and $u_3 = 40$. The fact that $Z = 40$ and $V_1 = 150$ in the final solution is not relevant to the problem.

The computer solutions are summarized in Table 9–1.

Note that once the value of a deviation variable is determined, subsequent solutions do not change it. The same is not necessarily true for the decision variables; they may or may not change in value in subsequent solutions.

SUMMARY

Goal programming is a variation of linear programming that can be used to handle problems that have multiple objectives. In goal programming, the objectives (goals) are expressed as "soft" constraints that reflect target levels to be achieved. In addition, some goal programming models also have constraints that specify upper or lower bounds rather than target levels. These are referred to as "hard" constraints; they are identical to the constraints encountered in the linear programming models of previous chapters.

In a goal programming model, the focus is on minimizing deviations from the various goals according to a priority ranking established by the decision maker: In the analysis of a goal programming model, the deviation with the highest priority is minimized disregarding the other goals. Then, the deviation with the second highest priority is minimized as long as it doesn't require any increase in the highest priority deviation. This process is continued until all priorities have been attended to.

Two solution approaches are demonstrated in the chapter: a graphical approach similar to graphical linear programming and a computer-assisted approach using a standard LP package.

The chapter also illustrates the formulation of goal programming models.

GLOSSARY

Deviation Variable A variable that is used to account for the amount by which a solution overachieves or underachieves a goal.

Goal A target level of performance (e.g., a profit of $30,000).

Goal Constraint A goal expressed as an equality, from which deviation is possible.

Goal Programming A variation of linear programming that allows multiple objectives.

Hard Constraint A nongoal constraint; specifies an upper or lower bound that cannot be exceeded or an equality that must be met exactly.

Objective A list of deviation variables that are to be minimized.

Priority Model A goal programming model that ranks deviations according to their importance.

Satisficing An analytical process in which trade-offs are made in order to find a satisfactory solution.

Soft Constraint A goal (target) constraint.

SOLVED PROBLEMS

Problem 1. Formulate a goal programming model and solve it graphically, given this information:

The manager of a company that makes quilted material that is sold by the yard wants to determine the mix of products to make during a week shortened by a holiday. Material supplies are plentiful, but labor is not. There are 24 hours of labor available; each yard of Colonial quilt requires 2 hours of labor and each yard of Southern Comfort quilt requires 3 hours.

The manager's priorities, in order of importance, are:

a. Minimize the underutilization of labor.

b. If there is any overtime, try to keep it to 12 hours or less.

c. Try to avoid making less than 10 yards of Southern Comfort.

d. Avoid using any overtime, if possible.

Solution

Start by identifying the decision variables:

x_1 = amount of Colonial quilt to produce

x_2 = amount of Southern Comfort quilt to produce

Begin formulation by listing the *names* of the constraints or goals. Thus, the constraints relate to:

a. Labor.

b. Overtime.

c. Amount of Southern Comfort.

d. Overtime (same as ***b***).

This suggests that there are three constraints.

For the labor constraint, apparently, it is possible to be either under ("minimize underutilization") or over ("avoid overtime if possible"). Hence, the labor constraint is a goal constraint:

$$2x_1 + 3x_2 + u_1 - v_1 = 24 \text{ hours}$$

The overtime constraint is a bit unusual because it pertains only to a deviation variable (being over on the labor goal). The overtime goal is:

$$v_1 + u_2 - v_2 = 12 \text{ hours}$$

The manager has listed as the third priority to try to avoid making less than 10 yards of Southern Comfort; it would seem that deviations in either direction are possible. That goal constraint is:

$$x_2 + u_3 - v_3 = 10 \text{ yards}$$

Next, the priorities can be arranged into the objective:

$$P_1u_1 + P_2v_2 + P_3u_3 + P_4v_1$$

FIGURE A

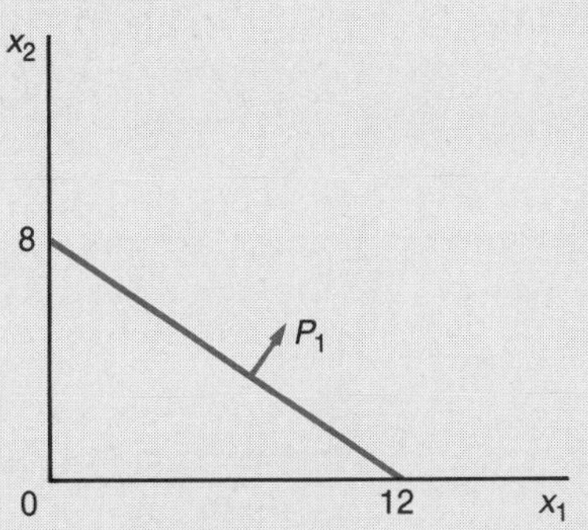

FIGURE B

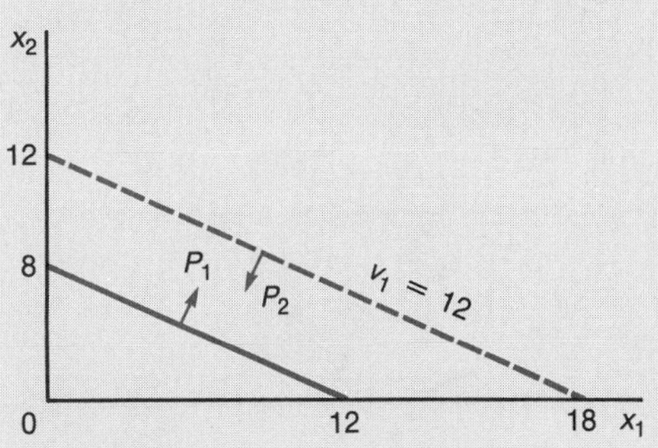

where

u_1 = amount of underutilization of labor
v_1 = amount of overtime above 12 hours of overtime
u_3 = amount of Southern Comfort under 10 yards
v_1 = amount of overtime

In summary, the model is:

minimize $\quad P_1u_1 + P_2v_2 + P_3u_3 + P_4v_1$

subject to

Labor	$2x_1 + 3x_2 + u_1 - v_1 = 24$ hours
Overtime	$v_1 \quad + u_2 - v_2 = 12$ hours
Southern	$x_2 + u_3 - v_3 = 10$ yards
	All variables ≥ 0

In order to solve this graphically, because there are no hard constraints, begin by plotting the goal constraint that contains the deviation variable with the highest priority (u_1) and indicate the direction of the priority (see Figure A).

Next, add the goal constraint containing the deviation variable (v_2) that has the second highest priority and indicate the direction of the priority (see Figure B). In order to plot a deviation goal, set $v_1 = 12$, then add the amount of overtime to the right side of the labor constraint (because v_1 is in that constraint). The result is:

$$2x_1 + 3x_2 + u_1 - v_1 = 36 \text{ hours}$$

Plotting this line produces the dashed line in Figure B. The dashes differentiate this *deviation constraint* from the other constraints.

At this point, any combination of x_1 and x_2 that lies on or between the two goal constraints would be acceptable.

The third priority refers to u_3. Hence, we add the third goal constraint to the plot (see Figure C). The shaded region indicates the area of acceptability.

FIGURE C

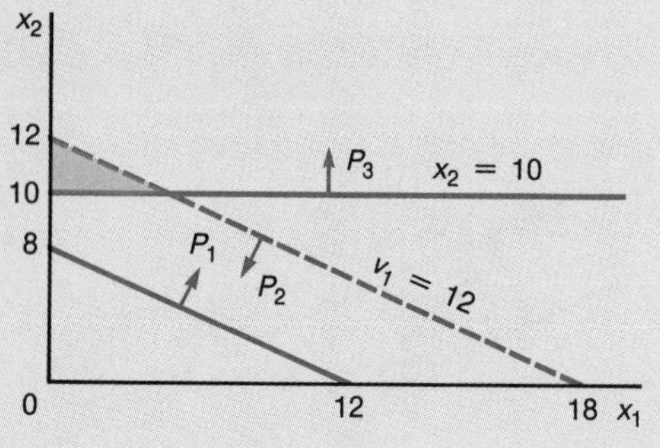

FIGURE D

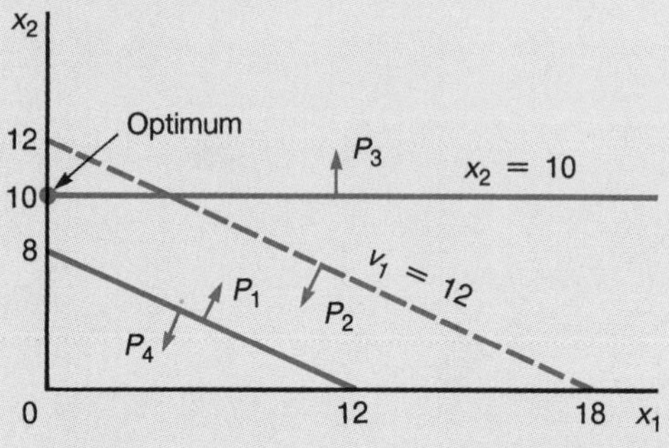

The fourth priority refers to v_1 and, thus, to the first goal constraint, which is already on the graph. Therefore, the only addition is an indication of the direction of P_4 (see Figure D). This makes the optimum point the point that is in the acceptable area that is closest to the first goal constraint (i.e., $x_2 = 10$).

In terms of the deviations, we see in Figure D that the optimum point lies in the area that is acceptable for the first three priorities. Hence, only the fourth will be nonzero. We can determine its value by submitting the optimal values of the decision variables (i.e., $x_1 = 0, x_2 = 10$) into the labor goal, omitting the deviation variables:

$$2(0) + 3(10) = 30$$

This is 6 above the original 24; hence, $v_1 = 6$.

Problem 2. Solve the following goal programming model for the optimal values of the decision variables and determine the optimal values of the deviation variables that are specified in the objective:

minimize $\quad P_1u_1 + P_2u_2$

subject to

$$\begin{aligned} 4x_1 + x_2 \quad\quad\quad\quad\quad &\leq 40 \\ x_1 + 2x_2 \quad\quad\quad\quad\quad &\leq 24 \\ x_1 + 2x_2 + u_1 - v_1 &= 30 \\ x_1 \quad\quad\quad + u_2 - v_2 &= 15 \\ \text{All variables} &\geq 0 \end{aligned}$$

Solution

We first note which ones are the hard constraints: the first two because they do not have any deviation variables. These are plotted, and the feasible solution space is identified (see part *a*).

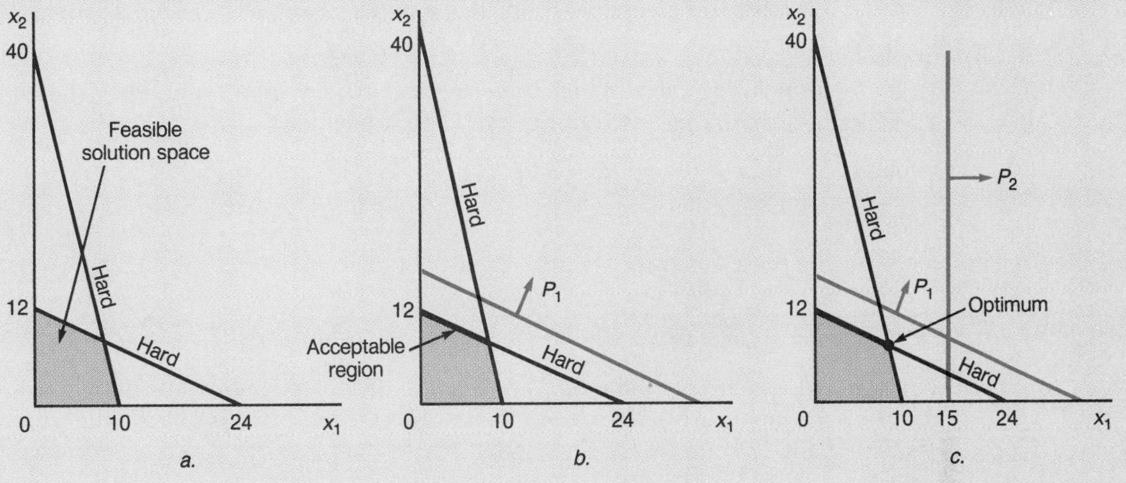

Next, we see that the highest priority is to minimize being under on the first goal. We add this to the graph and see that some amount of underdeviation is unavoidable because the goal does not have any points in common with the feasible solution space. In addition, note that the goal constraint is *parallel* to one of the hard constraints. Therefore, the portion of the feasible solution space that minimizes the underdeviation on the first goal is the line segment indicated in part *b*.

The other priority is to minimize being under on the second goal. Adding that goal to the graph (see part *c*) reveals that the best part of the line segment from *b* is the point where the two hard constraints intersect. Hence, that point is the optimum. Solving for that point using simultaneous equations (not shown) yields $x_1 = 8, x_2 = 8$.

Substituting these values into the first goal constraint (omitting v_1 because it is obviously zero) and solving for u_1 yields:

$$x_1 + 2x_2 + u_1 = 30$$

and becomes

$$8 + 2(8) + u_1 = 30$$

Thus, $u_1 = 6$.

Doing the same for the second constraint yields:

$$x_1 + u_2 = 15$$

and becomes

$$8 + u_2 = 15$$

Thus, $u_2 = 7$.

Problem 3. Solve the preceding problem using the computer-assisted approach.

Solution

Begin by formulating a model that contains the hard constraints and the deviation variable that has the highest priority (u_1). The model is:

minimize $\quad 0x_1 + 0x_2 + u_1 + 0v_1$

subject to

$$\begin{aligned} 4x_1 + x_2 &\leq 40 \\ x_1 + 2x_2 &\leq 24 \\ x_1 + 2x_2 + u_1 - v_1 &= 30 \end{aligned}$$

Note that all variables in the model are listed in the objective function and that all of their coefficients are zero except the deviation variable that is to be minimized.

The computer solution for this model is:

```
VARIABLE   QUANTITY
   S1         28
   X2         12
   U1          6

OPTIMAL Z=     6
```

The information primarily of interest is the value of u_1, which is 6. This is the optimal value of u_1, and we now fix that value for the remainder of the analysis by substituting it into the corresponding goal constraint. Thus:

$$x_1 + 2x_2 + u_1 - v_1 = 30$$

becomes

$$x_1 + 2x_1 + 6 - v_1 = 30$$

Then, moving the +6 to the right side of the equation, we end up with:

$$x_1 + 2x_2 - v_1 = 24$$

In the revised model, u_1 will be eliminated from the objective function.

In order to formulate the revised model, we note that the remaining deviation variable to be minimized is u_2. Hence, the deviation variables in the second goal constraint are now added to the objective function, and the second goal constraint is added to the model. Thus, the revised model is:

minimize $\quad 0x_1 + 0x_2 + 0v_1 + u_2 + 0v_2 \quad$ (u_1 has been eliminated)

subject to

$$\begin{aligned} 4x_1 + x_2 &\leq 40 \\ x_1 + 2x_2 &\leq 24 \\ x_1 + 2x_2 - v_1 &= 24 \quad \text{(revised goal constraint)} \\ x_1 + u_2 - v_2 &= 15 \end{aligned}$$

The computer solution is:

```
VARIABLE  QUANTITY
  X1          8
  X2          8
  U2          7

  OPTIMAL Z = 7
```

Because no other deviation variables remain, the optimal solution has been determined. The optimal values of the decision variables are $x_1 = 8$, $x_2 = 8$. The optimal values of the deviation variables are $u_1 = 6$ (from the initial model) and $u_2 = 7$. The results are summarized in the following table.

Model	Deviation Variable	Model Constraints	Solution: Decision Variables	Solution: Deviation Variables
Initial	u_1	2 hard + 1st goal	$x_1 = 0$, $x_2 = 12$	$u_1 = 6$
Revised	u_2	2 hard + 1st and 2nd goals	$x_1 = 8$, $x_2 = 8$	$u_1 = 6$, $u_2 = 7$

PROBLEMS

1. Manager Barney Bidwell has formulated the following LP model:

x_1 = amount of Product 1
x_2 = amount of Product 2
x_3 = amount of Product 3

$$\text{maximize} \quad 4x_1 + 2x_2 + 3x_3$$

subject to

$$\begin{aligned} &\text{Labor} && 2x_1 + x_2 + 4x_3 \le 160 \text{ hours} \\ &\text{Storage} && x_1 + 2x_2 + 3x_3 \le 150 \text{ square feet} \\ &\text{Product 1} && x_1 \ge 10 \text{ units} \\ & && x_1, x_2, x_3 \ge 0 \end{aligned}$$

After discussions with several colleagues, Barney now believes that a goal programming model would be more appropriate. Accordingly, the manager has decided on these priorities, which are listed in order of importance:

a. Minimize the underutilization of labor.

b. Achieve a satisfactory profit level of $300.

c. Try to avoid making less than 10 units of x_1.

Reformulate this as a GP model.

2. For the preceding problem, incorporate one additional priority:

   d. If overtime is used, try to avoid using more than 10 hours. Indicate how the model of the previous problem would *change*.

3. Given this goal programming model:

minimize $P_1u_2 + P_2v_1$

subject to

Labor	$10x_1 + 10x_2 + u_1 - v_1 = 600$ hours
Product 1	$x_1 + u_2 - v_2 = 80$ units
	All variables ≥ 0

   a. Is the first constraint a hard or a soft constraint? How do you know?

   b. What is the highest priority in this model?

   c. Solve the problem graphically for the optimal solution. What are the optimal values of the decision variables? What are the optimal values of the deviation variables u_2 and v_1?

   d. Suppose that the objective had been $P_1v_1 + P_2u_2$. What would your answers to the question posed in part *c* be?

4. Given this goal programming problem:

minimize $P_1u_1 + P_2v_2 + P_3u_3$

subject to

Newspaper advertising	$8x_1 + 15x_2 + u_1 - v_1 = 120$ lines
Budget	$2x_1 + 3x_2 + u_2 - v_2 = 12$ (\$000)
Direct marketing	$6x_1 + 18x_2 + u_3 - v_3 = 54$ hours
	All variables ≥ 0

   a. Plot the first constraint and indicate the direction that will satisfy the highest priority.

   b. Plot the second constraint and indicate the direction that will satisfy the second highest priority.

   c. What is the optimal solution at this point?

   d. Add the third constraint and indicate the direction that will satisfy the third priority. Does the addition of the third constraint and the third priority alter the solution? Why? Would changing the third priority to P_3v_3 alter the solution? Why?

   e. Compute the values of the deviation variables u_1, v_2, and u_3 for the optimal solution.

5. Find the values of the decision variables that will minimize the objective for the following goal model and also find the resulting values of each of the deviation variables that are listed in the objective:

minimize $P_1v_1 + P_2v_3 + P_3u_2 + P_4u_4$

subject to

Plastic	$2x_1 + 4x_2 + u_1 - v_1 =$	80 pounds
Cloth	$3x_1 + 6x_2 + u_2 - v_2 =$	180 square yards
Product 1	$x_1 + u_3 - v_3 =$	30 units
Painting	$5x_1 + u_4 - v_4 =$	250 minutes

All variables ≥ 0

6. Given the following goal model:

   a. Find the values of the decision variables that minimize the objective.

   b. Determine the values of the deviation variables that are in the objective that will result from your solution.

minimize $P_1v_1 + P_2u_2 + P_3u_3$

subject to

Budget	$2A + 4B + u_1 - v_1 =$	80 (\$000)
Profit	$2A + 4B + u_2 - v_2 =$	120 (\$000)
Product A	$A + u_3 - v_3 =$	30 barrels

All variables ≥ 0

7. Given this goal model:

minimize $P_1u_1 + P_2u_2 + P_3(u_3 + v_3)$

subject to

Sodium	$8N + 6L \leq$	48 grams
Carbohydrate	$N + 6L + u_1 - v_1 =$	24 grams
Protein	$5N + L + u_2 - v_2 =$	10 grams
Input L	$L + u_3 - v_3 =$	3 cubic centimeters

All variables ≥ 0

   a. Find the best values of the decision variables.

   b. Find the values of all deviation variables that are listed in the objective.

8. Given this goal model:

minimize $P_1v_1 + P_2u_2$

subject to

Product A	$A \leq$	30 units
Budget	$3A + 5B + u_1 - v_1 =$	300 (\$)
Revenue	$9A + 10B + u_2 - v_2 =$	900 (\$)

All variables ≥ 0

   a. Determine the optimal values of the decision variables and the resulting values of v_1 and u_2.

   b. How would your answers change if the first constraint was $A \geq 30$?

9. Solve this goal programming problem for the optimal solution.

minimize $P_1v_1 + P_2u_2 + P_3u_3 + P_4u_4$

subject to

$$
\begin{array}{lrrl}
\text{Profit} & 9S + 5T & & \geq 45 \quad (\$000) \\
\text{Budget} & 8S + 9T & + u_1 - v_1 & = 72 \quad (\$000) \\
\text{Material} & S + 5T & + u_2 - v_2 & = 5 \\
\text{T} & T & + u_3 - v_3 & = 10 \\
\text{S} & S & + u_4 - v_4 & = 9 \\
 & & \text{All variables} & \geq 0
\end{array}
$$

Then, indicate the optimal values of the decision variables *and* the values of each of the deviation variables that are listed in the objective. Solve using the graphical method.

10. Given this goal model, determine the optimal values of the decision variables and the resulting values of the deviation variables that are listed in the objective:

minimize $P_1v_1 + P_2v_2 + P_3u_2 + P_4v_3 + P_5u_3$

subject to

$$
\begin{array}{lrrl}
\text{Product 1} & x_1 & & \leq 100 \text{ units} \\
\text{Storage} & x_1 + x_2 & + u_1 - v_1 & = 80 \text{ square feet} \\
\text{Product 1} & x_1 & + u_2 - v_2 & = 40 \text{ units} \\
\text{Material} & 2x_1 + 4x_2 & + u_3 - v_3 & = 320 \text{ pounds} \\
 & & \text{All variables} & \geq 0
\end{array}
$$

11. Solve this goal problem for the optimal solution using a computer-assisted approach:

minimize $P_1v_1 + P_2u_2 + P_3v_3$

subject to

$$
\begin{array}{lrrl}
\text{Material} & 5x_1 + 4x_2 & + u_1 - v_1 & = 200 \text{ pounds} \\
\text{Profit} & 2x_1 + x_2 & + u_2 - v_2 & = 40 \ (\$000) \\
\text{Machine} & 2x_1 + 2x_2 & + u_3 - v_3 & = 30 \text{ minutes} \\
 & & \text{All variables} & \geq 0
\end{array}
$$

(This problem was solved in the chapter (Example 2) using the graphical approach. It would be helpful to compare the computer solution and the graphical solution.)

12. Solve Problem 6 using the computer-assisted approach.

13. Solve Problem 9 using the compter-assisted approach.

Part II
Decision Theory

Decision theory is a generalized approach for modeling situations in which a decision maker must choose one alternative from a list of alternatives when it is uncertain exactly which one of several conditions the alternatives must perform under. For instance, a young couple may be in the process of buying their first home. They expect the process to take about six months, as they visit prospective houses and read the classifieds. In the meantime, they must make a decision about buying a car, because their current car is just about to expire. Their decision problem involves selecting a car (and car payment schedule) without knowing what house (and house payments) they will end up with. The alternatives are the possible new and used cars they can buy now, and the future conditions are the house payments for the house they will eventually buy.

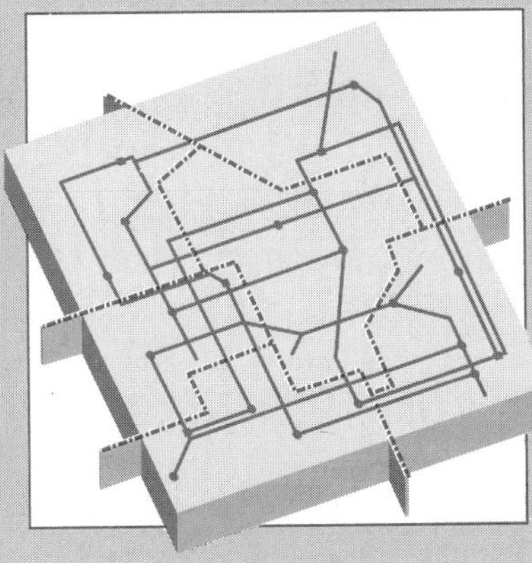

Chapter 10 describes decision theory approaches to making a decision given a set of alternatives and various conditions under which the alternatives might have to perform. A variety of methods are illustrated, ranging from situations in which there is _complete uncertainty_ as to how likely the various conditions are, to _partial uncertainty,_ where some assessment of the likelihood of the various conditions is possible. Tabular and graphical methods are illustrated for analyzing decision problems and selecting appropriate alternatives.

Part Outline

Chapter 10
Decision Theory

Chapter Outline

Learning Objectives

After completing this chapter, you should be able to:

1. Outline the characteristics of a decision theory approach to decision making.
2. Describe and give examples of decisions under certainty, risk, and complete uncertainty.
3. Construct a payoff table.
4. Make decisions using maximin, maximax, minimax regret, insufficient reason, and expected value criteria.
5. Determine the expected value of perfect information.
6. Use decision trees to lay out decision alternatives and possible consequences of decisions.
7. Determine whether acquiring additional information in a decision problem will be worth the cost.
8. Analyze the sensitivity of decisions to probability estimates.

Most decision makers are called on to make a variety of decisions. Very often they encounter situations in which they must choose one alternative from a list of alternatives. For instance, the president of a small manufacturing firm may have to select a site for a new warehouse from a list of potential sites. Similarly, a marketing manager may have to select a pricing strategy from a list of strategies.

Decision theory is important in these kinds of decisions because it provides decision makers with a rational way of making a selection; it provides a logical framework for analyzing the situation and coming up with a selection. Unlike optimizing approaches, such as linear programming, decision theory does not guarantee an "optimal" decision. This is because the type of problems that lend themselves to linear programming solutions involve complete *certainty*. Decision theory problems, on the other hand, are characterized by at least some uncertainty, and very often, by a considerable amount of uncertainty. But even though decision theory can not provide optimal solutions, it can indicate to the decision maker which alternative on a list is most suited to the decision maker's own philosophy, be it optimistic, pessimistic, or somewhere in between.

Applications of decision theory are widespread. They include selection of investment portfolios, oil and gas exploration (to drill or not to drill), contracting (to bid or not to bid), agriculture (which crops to plant, how much acreage, whether to use pest control), manufacturing (which technology to invest in, which machines, how much capacity, maintenance schedules), marketing (introduction of new products, advertising/trade promotion/couponing strategies), home buying (selection of mortgage type—conventional fixed or adjustable rate), retailing (strategies for buying, pricing, and inventories), and so on. Obviously, decision analysis is an important management science topic.

This chapter introduces the general approach of decision theory and two important tools of analysis: payoff tables and decision trees. These provide structure for organizing relevant information in a format conducive to rational decision making. The chapter begins with a description of the components of a decision model.

INTRODUCTION

Decision theory problems are characterized by the following:

1. A list of alternatives.
2. A list of possible future states of nature.
3. Payoffs associated with each alternative/state of nature combination.
4. An assessment of the degree of certainty of possible future events.
5. A decision criterion.

Let's examine each of these.

List of Alternatives

The list of alternatives must be a set of mutually exclusive and collectively exhaustive decisions that are available to the decision maker. (Sometimes, but not always, one of these alternatives will be to "do nothing.")

For example, suppose that a real estate developer must decide on a plan for developing a certain piece of property. After careful consideration, the developer has ruled out "do nothing" and is left with the following list of acceptable alternatives:

1. Residential proposal.
2. Commercial proposal #1.
3. Commercial proposal #2.

States of Nature

States of nature refer to a set of possible future conditions, or *events,* beyond the control of the decision maker, that will be the primary determinants of the eventual consequence of the decision. The states of nature, like the list of alternatives, must be mutually exclusive and collectively exhaustive. Suppose, in the case of the real estate developer, the main factor that will influence the profitability of the development is whether or not a shopping center is built, and the size of the shopping center, if one is built. Suppose that the developer views the possibilities as:

1. No shopping center.
2. Medium-sized shopping center.
3. Large shopping center.

Payoffs

In order for a decision maker to be able to rationally approach a decision problem, it is necessary to have some idea of the payoffs that would be associated with each decision alternative and the various states of nature. The payoffs might be profits, revenues, costs, or other measure of value. Usually the measures are financial. They may be weekly, monthly, or annual amounts, or they might represent *present values* of future cash flows.[1] Usually, payoffs are estimated values. The more accurate these estimates, the more useful they will be for decision-making purposes and the more likely it is that the decision maker will choose an appropriate alternative.

---

[1] A *present value* is a lump sum payment that is the current equivalent of one or a set of future cash amounts using an assumed interest rate.

The number of payoffs depends on the number of alternative/state of nature combinations. In the case of the real estate developer, there are three alternatives and three states of nature, so there are 3 × 3 = 9 possible payoffs that must be determined.

Degree of Certainty

The approach used by a decision maker often depends on the degree of certainty that exists. There can be different degrees of certainty. One extreme is complete certainty and the other is complete **uncertainty.** The latter exists when the likelihood of the various states of nature are unknown. Between these two extremes is **risk,** a term that implies that probabilities are known for the states of nature.

Knowledge of the likelihood of each of the states of nature can play an important role in selecting a course of action. Thus, if a decision maker feels that a particular state of nature is highly likely, this will mean that the payoffs associated with that state of nature are also highly likely. This enables the decision maker to focus more closely on probable results of a decision. Consequently, probability estimates for the various states of nature can serve an important function *if they can be obtained.* Of course, in some situations, accurate estimates of probabilities may not be available, in which case the decision maker may have to select a course of action without the benefit of probabilities.

Decision Criterion

The process of selecting one alternative from a list of alternatives is governed by a **decision criterion,** which embodies the decision maker's attitudes toward the decision as well as the degree of certainty that surrounds a decision. For instance, some decision makers tend to be optimistic, whereas others tend to be pessimistic. Moreover, some want to maximize gains, whereas others are more concerned with protecting against large losses.

One example of a decision criterion is: "Maximize the expected payoff." Another example is: "Minimize opportunity cost." A variety of the most popular decision criteria are presented in the remainder of this chapter.

THE PAYOFF TABLE

A **payoff table** is a device a decision maker can use to summarize and organize information relevant to a particular decision. It includes a list of the alternatives, the possible future states of nature, and the payoffs associated with each of the alternative/state of nature combinations. If probabilities for the states of nature are available, these can also be listed. The general format of a payoff table is illustrated in Table 10–1.

TABLE 10–1 General Format of a Decision Table

		State of Nature		
		s_1	s_2	s_3
	a_1	V_{11}	V_{12}	V_{13}
Alternative	a_2	V_{21}	V_{22}	V_{23}
	a_3	V_{31}	V_{32}	V_{33}

where

a_i = the *i*th alternative
s_j = the *j*th state of nature (event)
V_{ij} = the value of payoff that will be realized if alternative *i* is chosen and event *j* occurs

TABLE 10–2 Payoff Table for Real Estate Developer

		No center	Medium center	Large center
	Residential	$4	16	12
Alternative	Commercial #1	5	6	10
	Commercial #2	−1	4	15

A payoff table for the real estate developer's decision is shown in Table 10–2. The three alternatives under consideration are listed down the left side of the table and the three possible states of nature are listed across the top of the table. The payoffs that are associated with each of the alternative/state-of-nature combinations are shown in the body of the table. Suppose that those values represent profits (or losses) in hundred thousand dollar amounts. Hence, if the residential proposal is chosen and no shopping center is built, the developer will realize a profit of $400,000. Similarly, if the second commercial proposal is selected and no center is built, the developer will lose $100,000.

DECISION MAKING UNDER CERTAINTY

The simplest of all circumstances occurs when decision making takes place in an environment of complete certainty. For example, in the case of the real estate problem, an unexpected early announcement concerning the building of the shopping center could reduce the problem to a situation of certainty.

Thus, if there is an announcement that no shopping center will be built, the developer then can focus on the first column of the payoff table (see Table 10–3). Because the Commercial proposal #1 has the highest payoff in that column ($5), it would be selected. Similarly, if the announcement indicated that a medium-sized shopping center is planned, only the middle column of the table would be relevant, and the residential alternative would be selected because its estimated payoff of 16 is the highest of the three payoffs for a medium-sized shopping center; whereas if a large center is planned, the developer could focus on the last column, selecting the Commercial #2 proposal because it has the highest estimated payoff of 15 in that column.

In summary, when a decision is made under conditions of complete certainty, the attention of the decision maker is focused on the column in the payoff table that corresponds to the state of nature that will occur. The decision maker then selects the alternative that will yield the best payoff, given that state of nature.

DECISION MAKING UNDER COMPLETE UNCERTAINTY

Under complete uncertainty, the decision maker either is unable to estimate the probabilities for the occurrence of the different states of nature, or else he or she lacks confidence in available estimates of probabilities, and for that reason, probabilities are not included in the analysis. Still another possibility is that the decision is a one-shot case, with an overriding goal that needs to be satisfied (e.g., a firm may be on the verge of bankruptcy and this might be the last chance to turn things around).

Decisions made under these circumstances are at the opposite end of the spectrum from the certainty case just mentioned. We shall consider four approaches to decision making under complete uncertainty. They are:

1. Maximin.
2. Maximax.
3. Minimax regret.
4. Insufficient reason.

TABLE 10–3 If It Is Known that No Shopping Center Will Be Built, Only the First Column Payoffs Would Be Relevant

	No center	Medium center	Large center
Residential	$4	16	12
Commercial #1	5	6	10
Commercial #2	−1	4	15

TABLE 10–4 Maximin Solution for Real Estate Problem

	State of Nature				
	No center	Medium center	Large center	Worst payoff	
Residential	$4	16	12	4	
Commercial #1	5	6	10	5	← Maximum
Commercial #2	−1	4	15	−1	

Maximin

The **maximin** strategy is a conservative one; it consists of identifying the worst (minimum) payoff for each alternative and then selecting the alternative that has the best (maximum) of the worst payoffs. In effect, the decision maker is setting a floor for the potential payoff; the actual payoff cannot be less than this amount.

For the real estate problem, the maximin solution is to choose the second alternative, Commercial #1, as illustrated in Table 10–4.

Many people view the maximin criterion as pessimistic because they believe that the decision maker must assume that the worst will occur. In fact, if the minimum payoffs are all negative, this view is accurate. Others view the maximin strategy in the same light as a decision to buy insurance: Protect against the worst possible events, even though you neither expect them nor want them to occur.

Maximax

The **maximax** approach is the opposite of the previous one: The best payoff for each alternative is identified, and the alternative with the maximum of these is the designated decision.

For the real estate problem, the maximax solution is to choose the residential alternative, as shown in Table 10–5.

Just as the maximin strategy can be viewed as pessimistic, the maximax strategy can be considered optimistic; that is, choosing the alternative that could result in the maximum payoff.

Minimax Regret

Both the maximax and maximin strategies can be criticized because they focus only on a single, extreme payoff and exclude the other payoffs. Thus, the maximax strategy ignores the possibility that an alternative with a slightly smaller payoff might offer a better overall choice. For example, consider this payoff table:

	State of Nature		
	s^1	s_2	s_3
a_1	−5	16	−10
a_2	15	15	15
a_3	15	15	15

The maximax criterion would lead to selecting alternative a_1, even though two out of the three possible states of nature will result in negative payoffs. Moreover, both other alternatives will produce a payoff that is nearly the same as the maximum, regardless of the state of nature.

A similar example could be constructed to demonstrate comparable weakness of the maximin criterion, which is also due to the failure to consider all payoffs.

An approach that does take all payoffs into account is **minimax regret.** In order to use this approach, it is necessary to develop an *opportunity loss* table. The

TABLE 10–5 Maximax Solution for Real Estate Problem

	State of Nature				
	No center	Medium center	Large center	Best payoff	
Residential	$4	16	12	16	← Maximum
Commercial #1	5	6	10	10	
Commercial #2	−1	4	15	15	

opportunity loss reflects the difference between each payoff and the best possible payoff in a column (i.e., given a state of nature). Hence, opportunity loss amounts are found by identifying the best payoff in a column and then subtracting each of the other values in the column from that payoff. For the real estate problem, the conversion of the original payoffs into an opportunity loss table is shown in Table 10–6.

Hence, in column 1, the best payoff is 5; therefore, all payoffs are subtracted from 5 to determine the amount of payoff the decision maker would miss by not having chosen the alternative that would have yielded the best payoff *if that state of nature occurs*. Of course, there is no guarantee that it will occur. Similarly, the best payoff in the column 2 is 16, and all payoffs are subtracted from that number to reflect the opportunity losses that would occur if a decision other than Residential was selected *and* a medium-sized shopping center turned out to be the state of nature that comes to pass. And, for column 3, the opportunity costs evolve by subtracting each payoff from 15. Note that for every column, this results in a value of zero in the opportunity loss table in the same position as the best payoff for each column. For example, the best payoff in the last column of the payoff table is 15, and the corresponding position in the last column of the opportunity loss table is 0.

The values in an opportunity loss table can be viewed as potential **regrets** that might be suffered as the result of choosing various alternatives. A decision maker could select an alternative in such a way as to minimize the maximum possible regret. This requires identifying the maximum opportunity loss in each row and then choosing the alternative that would yield the best (minimum) of those regrets. As illustrated in Table 10–7, for the real estate problem, this leads to selection of the Residential alternative.

Table 10–6 Opportunity Loss Table for Real Estate Problem

Original Payoff Table

	No center	Medium center	Large center
Residential	$4	16	12
Commercial $1	5	6	10
Commercial #2	−1	4	15
Best Payoff in Column	5	16	15

Opportunity Loss Table

	No center	Medium center	Large center
Residential	5 − 4 =1	16 − 16 =0	15 − 12 =3
Commercial #1	5 − 5 =0	16 − 6 =10	15 − 10 =5
Commercial #2	5 − − 1 =6	16 − 4 =12	15 − 15 =0

Although this approach has resulted in the same choice as the maximax strategy, the reasons are completely different; therefore, it is merely coincidence that the two yielded the same result. Under different circumstances, each can lead to selection of a different alternative.

Although this approach makes use of more information than either maximin or maximax, it still ignores some information and, therefore, can lead to a poor decision. Consider, for example, the opportunity loss table illustrated in Table 10–8. Using minimax regret, a decision maker would be indifferent between alternatives a_2 and a_3, although a_1 would be a better choice because for all but one of the states of nature there would be *no* opportunity loss, and in the worst case, a_1 would result in an opportunity loss that exceeded the other worst cases by $1.

Table 10–7 Identifying the Minimax Regret Alternative

	Opportunity Losses				
	No center	Medium center	Large center	Maximum loss	
Residential	1	0	3	3	← Minimum
Commercial $1	0	10	5	10	
Commercial #2	6	12	0	12	

TABLE 10–8 Minimax Regret Can Lead to a Poor Decision

Opportunity Loss Table

	s_1	s_2	s_3	s_4	s_5	Worst in Row	
a_1	0	0	0	0	24	24	
a_2	23	23	23	23	0	23	Minimum regret
a_3	23	23	23	23	0	23	

Principle of Insufficient Reason

The minimax regret criterion weakness is the inability to factor row differences. Hence, sometimes the minimax regret strategy will lead to a poor decision because it ignores certain information.

The **principle of insufficient reason** offers a method that incorporates more of the information. It treats the states of nature as if each were equally likely, and it focuses on the average payoff for each row, selecting the alternative that has the highest row average.

The payoff table from which the opportunity losses of Table 10–8 were computed is shown in Table 10–9, along with the row averages. Note how a_1 now

Table 10–9 The Principle of Insufficient Reason

Payoff Table

	s_1	s_2	s_3	s_4	s_5	Row Average	
a_1	28	28	28	28	4	23.2	← Maximum
a_2	5	5	5	5	28	9.6	
a_3	5	5	5	5	28	9.6	

stands out compared to the others. In fact, we could have obtained a similar result by finding the row averages for the opportunity loss table and then choosing the alternative that had the lowest average. Thus, the row averages for the opportunity losses presented in Table 10–8 are:

Alternative	Row Average	
a_1	4.8	← Minimum
a_2	18.4	
a_3	18.4	

Note that in both cases, the difference between the average of a_1 and the average of the other two is the same (13.6). Hence, we could obtain the same result from *either* the payoff table *or* the opportunity loss table; they will both always lead to the same decision.

The basis for the criterion of insufficient reason is that under complete uncertainty, the decision maker should not focus on either high or low payoffs, but should treat all payoffs (actually, all states of nature) as if they were *equally likely*. Averaging row payoffs accomplishes this.

DECISION MAKING UNDER RISK

The essential difference between decision making under complete uncertainty and decision making under partial uncertainty is the presence of *probabilities* for the occurrence of the various states of nature under partial uncertainty. The term *risk* is often used in conjunction with partial uncertainty.

The probabilities may be subjective estimates from managers or from experts in

Table 10–10 Real Estate Payoff Table with Probabilities

Probabilities	.2	.5	.3		
	No center	Medium center	Large center	Expected payoff	
Residential	$4	16	12	$12.40	← Maximum
Commercial $1	5	6	10	7.00	
Commercial #2	−1	4	15	6.30	

a particular field, or they may reflect historical frequencies. If they are reasonably correct, they provide a decision maker with additional information that can dramatically improve the decision-making process.

The sum of the probabilities for all states of nature must be 1.00. Thus, the real estate developer might estimate the probability of no shopping center being built at .2, the probability of a medium-sized shopping center at .5, and the probability of a large shopping center at .3. (Note that .2 + .5 + .3 = 1.0.)

Expected Monetary Value

The **expected monetary value (EMV)** approach provides the decision maker with a value that represents an *average* payoff for each alternative. The best alternative is, then, the one that has the highest expected monetary value.

The average or expected payoff of each alternative is a weighted average: the state of nature probabilities are used to weight the respective payoffs. Thus, the expected monetary value is:

$$EMV_i = \sum_{i=1}^{k} P_j V_{ij} \qquad (10\text{–}1)$$

where

EMV_i = the expected monetary value for the *i*th alternative
P_j = the probability of the *j*th state of nature
V_{ij} = the estimated payoff for alternative *i* under state of nature *j*

For example, using the figures in Table 10–10, we can compute the expected payoffs for the real estate developer's alternatives. The expected monetary value of the residential alternative is:

$$EMV_R = .2(\$4) + .5(\$16) + .3(\$12) = \$12.40$$

Similarly, the expected monetary values of the other alternatives are:

$$\text{EMV}_{C1} = .2(\$5) + .5(\$6) + .3(\$10) = \$7.00$$
$$\text{EMV}_{C2} = .2(-\$1) + .5(\$4) + .3(\$15) = \$6.30$$

Because the residential alternative has the largest expected monetary value, it would be selected using this criterion.

Note that it does *not* necessarily follow that the developer will actually realize a payoff equal to the expected monetary value of a chosen alternative. For example, note that the possible payoffs for the residential proposal are 4, 16, and 12, whereas the expected payoff is $12.40, which is not equal to any of the payoffs. Similarly, the expected payoffs for either of the other alternatives do not equal any of the payoffs in those rows. What, then, is the interpretation of the expected payoff? Simply a long-run average amount; the approximate average amount one could reasonably anticipate for a large number of identical situations.

In contrast to the strategies outlined for decision making under complete uncertainty, which are realistically best used for one-time major decisions, the expected value approach is more suited to an ongoing decision strategy. Over the long run, taking probabilities into account will yield the highest payoff, even though in the short run actual payoffs will tend to be higher or lower than the expected amounts. Conversely, over the long run, a strategy that failed to take probabilities into account would tend to yield lower payoffs than one that does take the probabilities into account.

Expected Opportunity Loss

An alternate method for incorporating probabilities into the decision-making process is to use **expected opportunity loss (EOL).** The approach is nearly identical to the EMV approach, except that a table of opportunity losses is used rather than a table of payoffs. Hence, the opportunity losses for each alternative are weighted by the probabilities of their respective states of nature to compute a long-run average opportunity loss, and the alternative with the *smallest* expected loss is selected as the best choice.

For the real estate problem, the expected opportunity losses can be calculated as follows:

$$\text{EOL}_{R} = .2(1) + .5(0) + .3(3) = 1.1 \leftarrow \text{Minimum}$$
$$\text{EOL}_{C1} = .2(0) + .5(10) + .3(5) = 6.5$$
$$\text{EOL}_{C2} = .2(6) + .5(12) + .3(0) = 7.2$$

Note that the EOL approach resulted in the same alternative as the EMV approach. This is more than coincidence; the two methods will always result in the same choice because they are equivalent ways of combining the values; maximizing the payoffs is equivalent to minimizing the opportunity losses.

Expected Value of Perfect Information

It can sometimes be useful for a decision maker to determine the potential benefit of knowing for certain which state of nature is going to prevail. For instance, a decision maker might have the option of delaying a decision until it is evident which state of nature is going to materialize. The obvious benefit of waiting would be to move the decision into the realm of certainty, thereby allowing the decision maker to obtain the maximum possible payoff. Such delays typically will involve a cost of some sort (e.g., higher prices, the cost of an option, storage costs). Hence, the question is whether the cost of waiting outweighs the potential benefits that could be realized by waiting. Or, the decision maker might wonder if it would be worth the cost to refine or eliminate the probabilities of the states of nature (e.g., using marketing research or a better forecasting technique). Although such techniques may not completely eliminate uncertainty, the decision maker often can benefit from knowledge of the upper limit of the potential gain that perfect information would permit.

The **expected value of perfect information (EVPI)** is a measure of the difference between the certain payoff that could be realized under a condition of certainty and the expected payoff under a condition involving risk.

Consider the payoff that the real estate developer could expect under certainty. If the developer knew that no center would be built, Commercial #1 proposal would be chosen with a payoff of 5; if the developer knew a medium-sized shopping center would be built, the residential alternative would be chosen for a payoff of 16; and if the developer knew that a large center would be built, Commercial #2 proposal would be chosen for a payoff of 15. Hence, if it were possible to remove the uncertainty surrounding the states of nature, the decision maker could capitalize on the knowledge. Obviously, before investing time or money in eliminating the possibilities, it is impossible for the decision maker to say which state of nature will turn out to be the one that will occur. However, what can be said is that the probability that perfect information will indicate that no center will be built is .2, that the probability that perfect information will indicate a medium center will be built is .5, and the probability of perfect information indicating a large center is .3. Thus, these probabilities, which are the original state of nature probabilities, can be used to weight the payoffs, one of which will occur under certainty. This is called the **expected payoff under certainty** (EPC), and is computed in the following way for the real estate problem.:

$$\text{EPC} = .2(5) + .5(16) + .3(15) = 13.5$$

The difference between this figure and the expected payoff under risk (i.e., the EMV) is the expected value of perfect information. Thus:

$$\text{EVPI} = \text{EPC} - \text{EMV} \tag{10-2}$$

For the real estate problem, with EPC = 13.5 and EMV = 12.4, we find:

$$\text{EVPI} = 13.5 - 12.4 = 1.1.$$

The EVPI represents an *upper bound* on the amount of money the real estate developer would be justified in spending to obtain perfect information. Thus, the real estate developer would be justified in spending up to $110,000 to find out for certain which state of nature will prevail. Of course, it is not always possible to completely remove uncertainty. In such cases, the decision maker must weigh the cost to reduce the uncertainty (i.e., obtain better estimates of the probabilities) against the expected benefits that would yield.

Note that the EVPI is exactly equal to the previously computed EOL. In fact, these two quantities will always be equal. The EOL indicates the expected *opportunity loss* due to imperfect information, which is another way of saying the expected *payoff* that could be achieved by having perfect information. Hence, there are two equivalent ways to determine the expected value of perfect information: subtract the EMV from the expected payoff under certainty, or compute the EOL.

Comment

The expected value approach is particularly useful for decision making when a number of similar decisions must be made; it is a "long-run" approach. For one-shot decisions, especially major ones, other methods (perhaps maximax or maximin) may be preferable. In addition, nonmonetary factors, although not included in a payoff table, may be of considerable importance. Unfortunately, there is no convenient way to include them in an expected value analysis.

DECISION TREES

Decision trees sometimes are used by decision makers to obtain a visual portrayal of decision alternatives and their possible consequences. The term gets its name from the treelike appearance of the diagram (see Figure 10–1).

A tree is composed of squares, circles, and lines. The squares indicate decision points while the circles represent chance events. The lines or "branches" that emanate from a square represent alternatives, while the branches that emanate from a circle represent states of nature. The tree is read from right to left.

Decision trees are fairly simple to construct. The decision tree for the real estate developer's problem is shown in Figure 10–2. The dollar amounts alongside each chance node (circle) indicate the expected payoff of the alternative that leads into that particular chance node. The expected payoffs are computed in the same manner as previously described, and, as before, the decision maker will select the alternative with the largest expected payoff if maximizing expected payoff is the decision criterion.

It should be noted that although decision trees represent an alternative approach to payoff tables, they are not commonly used for problems that involve a

FIGURE 10–1 Decision Tree Format

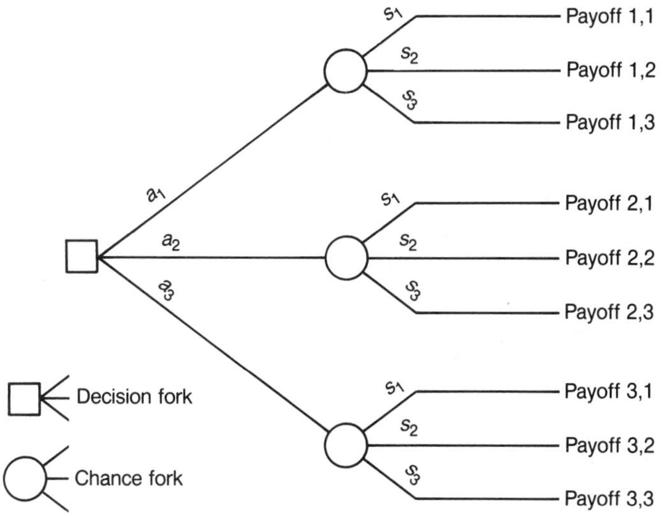

FIGURE 10–2 Decision Tree for Real Estate Developer Problem

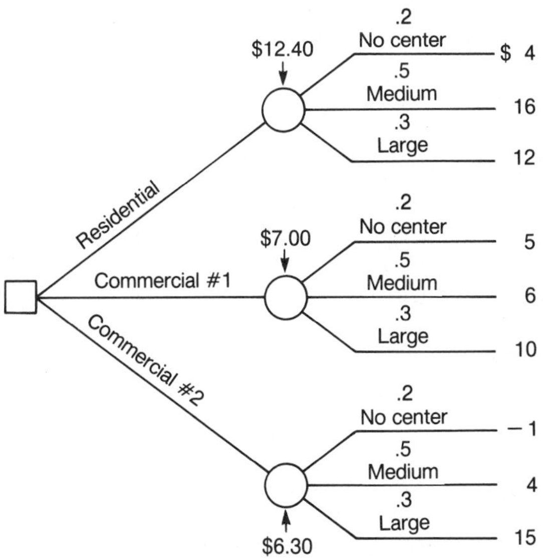

single decision. Rather, their greatest benefit lies in portraying *sequential* decisions (i.e., a series of chronological decisions). In the case of a single decision, constructing a tree can be cumbersome and time-consuming. For example, imagine the decision tree that would be necessary to portray a decision with 7 alternatives and 10 states of nature; there would be 70 payoffs, and, hence, 70 branch-ends on the right side of the tree. Conversely, situations that involve sequential decisions are difficult to represent in payoff tables.

As an example of a sequential decision, suppose that the real estate developer has several options that might be considered after the initial decision. For instance, regardless of which of the three alternatives he chooses, the worst payoff will result if no shopping center is built. Hence, it might be prudent for the developer to plan for that contingency. Thus, the developer might consider certain options. Suppose the developer states that he would consider these additional alternatives in the event that no center is built:

1. Do nothing.
2. Develop a small shopping center.
3. Develop a park.

The tree diagram of Figure 10–2 has been modified to include these additional options, along with their estimated payoffs as supplied by the real estate developer, and it is shown in Figure 10–3. Note that the payoffs for Do nothing are the same as in the original tree for the event no center is built.

In order to analyze this modified tree (i.e., to make a choice among the alternatives Residential, Commercial #1, and Commercial #2), the branches for each possible second decision must be reduced in each instance to a single branch. This is easily accomplished by recognizing that at each of those points, a rational decision maker would simply choose the alternative with the largest payoff. Hence, if Residential were chosen initially and no center was built, a park would be selected because it would have the largest payoff. Similarly, if Commercial #1 was chosen and no center was built, the small center option would be chosen because it offers the largest payoff, and if Commercial #2 were initially chosen and no center was built, the developer would choose the option of building a small center because its payoff is greater than either Do nothing or Park. Thus, in each case, the tree is pruned by cutting the undesirable options and keeping the one best option. This also is illustrated in Figure 10–3. Note that the payoff for the best option, then, becomes the payoff for each No center branch. The tree would then be analyzed as previously.

DECISION MAKING WITH ADDITIONAL INFORMATION

Decision makers can sometimes improve decision making by bringing additional information into the process. The additional information can come from a variety of sources. For example, either a market survey might be used to acquire addi-

FIGURE 10–3 Real Estate Problem with a Second Possible Decision

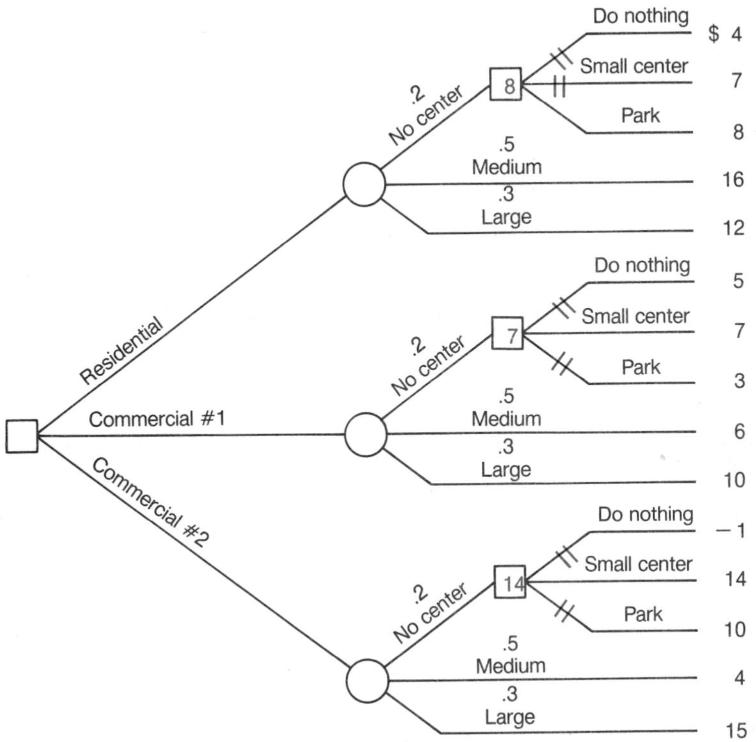

tional information or a forecasting technique might be employed. In certain situations, it may be possible to delay a decision; the passage of time often allows a decision maker to obtain a clearer picture of the future because it shortens the time horizon the decision maker must deal with. Whatever the source of information, the benefit is that *estimates of probabilities* of possible future events tend to become more accurate.

In general, obtaining additional (sample) information includes an associated cost. Consequently, a key question for a decision maker in such circumstances is whether the value of additional information is worth the cost of obtaining that information. The analysis of that type of problem is the subject of this section.

Let's take a look at an example.

An Example

Suppose an advertising manager is trying to decide which of two advertising proposals to use for an upcoming promotion. The manager has developed the following payoff table:

		Market	
		.70 Strong	.30 Weak
Alternative	Print media	40*	20
	Video media	50	10

* ($000)

At this point, the manager simply could make a decision using the expected value criterion with the information given. However, suppose that the manager has the option of testing the market, and this testing will provide *additional information* in the form of revised probabilities on whether the market will be strong or weak. If the manager chooses to test the market, it will cost $1,000; the manager, therefore, must decide whether the expected benefit from the test will offset the cost required to conduct the test.

If the manager conducts the test, this will undoubtedly alter the probabilities of a strong and weak market that were originally estimated. In fact, an integral part of the analysis in assessing the value of this sample information involves computing revised probabilities. However, in order to home in on what we are trying to accomplish, let's suppose that the revised probabilities have been calculated, and consider how the decision maker could use that new information to make a decision.

The market test can show one of two things: a strong market or a weak market. Each result would pertain to the payoff table, but with different probabilities for the states of nature. Suppose these are the two possible results:

If the Market Test Shows a Strong Market

	.95 Strong	.05 Weak
Print	40	20
Video	50	10

If the Market Test Shows a Weak Market

	.34 Strong	.66 Weak
Print	40	20
Video	50	10

Finally, suppose the manager is able to determine that the probability that the market test will show a strong market is .59 and the probability that it will show a weak market is .41.

The overall problem, given these probabilities, is shown conceptually in the tree diagram of Figure 10–4.

Analysis of the problem will result in determining an expected payoff for the two branches at the square node. This will enable the manager to select the branch (i.e., alternative) that has the higher expected payoff. Thus, if Use market test has the higher expected payoff, the manager would select that alternative, assuming the difference between its payoff and the payoff for Don't use market test is enough to cover the cost ($1,000) of the market test. Of course, if Don't use market test has the higher expected payoff, the manager would select that alternative because it would not require the cost of the market test.

FIGURE 10–4 Conceptual Portrayal of Market Test Example

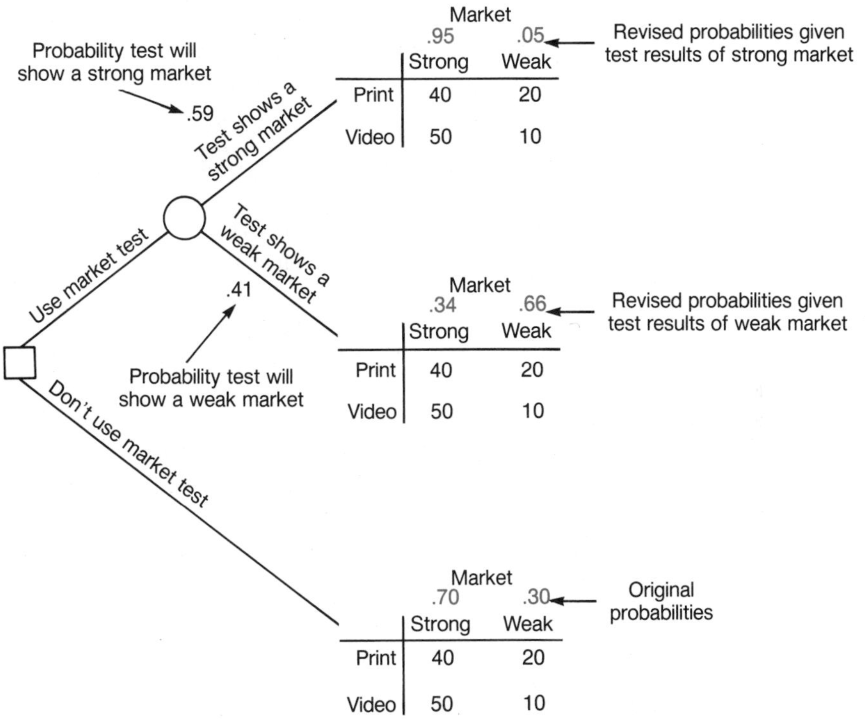

In order to determine the payoffs for those two branches, it is necessary first to compute the expected monetary value of each of the three payoff tables. These are computed as follows:

	Market .95 Strong	.05 Weak		
Print	40	20	$.95(40) + .05(20) = 39$	
Video	50	10	$.95(50) + .05(10) = 48$	(maximum expected payoff)

	Market .34 Strong	.66 Weak		
Print	40	20	$.34(40) + .66(20) = 26.8$	(maximum expected payoff)
Video	50	10	$.34(50) + .66(10) = 23.6$	

	Market			
	.70 Strong	.30 Weak		
Print	40	20	.70 (40) + .30 (20) = 34	
Video	50	10	.70 (50) + .30 (10) = 38	(maximum expected payoff)

Note that in each instance, we want the alternative (either *print* or *video*) that has the higher expected payoff.

The maximum expected payoff for the original table (i.e., the one with probabilities of .70 and .30) is 38 thousand. This, in effect, is the expected value of the branch Don't use the market test.

To find the expected payoff for the Use market test branch, we must combine the probability of each possible test result with the expected payoff for that result and then sum these. In other words, there is a probability of .59 that the market test will indicate a strong market, in which case the manager will choose the *video* alternative with an expected payoff of 48. Likewise, there is a probability of .41 that the test will show a weak market, and the manager will choose *print* with an expected payoff of 26.8. Hence, the overall or *combined* expected payoff for using the market test is:

$$.59(48) + .41(26.8) = 39.308$$

Thus, our analysis boils down to the results shown in Figure 10–5. Using the market test has an expected value of $39.308 thousand, or $39,308, whereas not using the market test has an expected value of $38 thousand, or $38,000. We can see that using the market test has an expected value that is $1,308 more than not using the test. Recall, though, that the test will involve an additional cost of $1,000. It would be prudent to spend $1,000 if the additional expected payoff is only $1,308. Hence, the manager should use the market test because to do so would lead to an expected gain of $308:

$$\$1,308 - \$1,000 = \$308$$

The preceding analysis illustrates how a manager can assess the value of additional (sample) information when such information is available. In this instance, we found that the expected gain that would result from using the additional information was outweighed by the cost that would be needed to acquire that additional information.

In sum, we can compute the **expected value of sample** (additional) **information,** or **EVSI,** as:

$$\text{EVSI} = \begin{array}{l}\text{Expected Value}\\ \textit{with}\text{ sample}\\ \text{information}\end{array} - \begin{array}{l}\text{Expected value}\\ \textit{without}\text{ sample}\\ \text{information}\end{array} \qquad (10\text{–}3)$$

Then, if the *cost* of obtaining the additional information is less than this amount, it would seem reasonable to spend the money to obtain the information. But if the

FIGURE 10–5 Summary of Analysis of Market Test Example

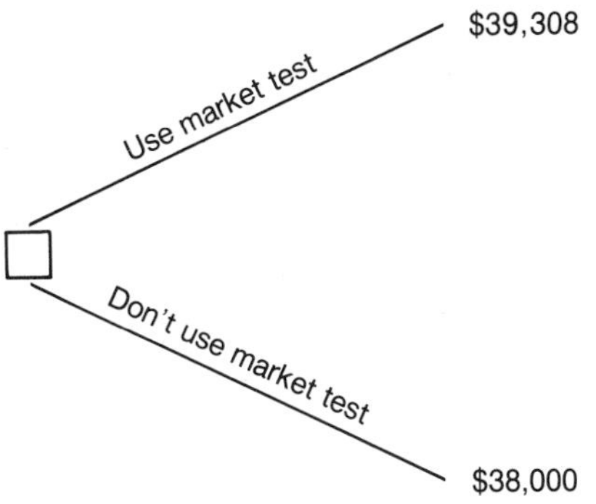

cost equals or exceeds the expected value of the information, it would seem reasonable to *not* spend the additional money needed to obtain the information.

In order to complete our discussion of decision making using additional information, we need to see how the revised probabilities are computed and how the probabilities for the test results are computed. Before doing that, let's take a brief look at a measure that sometimes is used to express the degree of increase in information from a sample (e.g., test results) relative to perfect information.

Efficiency of Sample Information

One way to judge how much information is generated by a sample is to compute the ratio of EVSI to EVPI. This is known as the *efficiency of sample information*. Thus:

$$\text{Efficiency of sample information} = \frac{\text{EVSI}}{\text{EVPI}} \qquad (10\text{–}4)$$

For the preceding example, the probabilities *without* additional information were .70 and .30, and the payoff table was:

	Market	
	.70 Strong	.30 Weak
Print	40	20
Video	50	10

The expected monetary value was 38 (i.e., $38,000). The expected profit under certainty (EPC) is:

$$.70(50) + .30(20) = 41, \text{ or } \$41{,}000$$

TABLE 10–11 Reliability of Market Test

Results of Market Test	Actual State of Nature	
	Strong Market	Weak Market
Shows strong market	.80	.10
Shows weak market	.20	.90

(To compute EPC, multiply the best payoff in each column by the column probability and sum the products.)

EVPI is the difference between EPC and EMV. Thus:

$$\text{EVPI} = \$41{,}000 - \$38{,}000 = \$3{,}000$$

In the preceding example, it was determined that the EVSI = $1,308. Hence, the efficiency of the sample information is:

$$\frac{\$1{,}308}{\$3{,}000} = .436$$

This number is interpreted as follows: The number can range from 0 to 1.00. The closer the number is to 1.00, the closer the sample information is to being perfect; the closer the number is to 0, the less the amount of information there is in the sample. Thus, a value such as .436 is mid-range, meaning that relative to perfect information, the information that could be gained from the market test is moderate.

Computing the Probabilities

Two sets of probabilities were used in the analysis of sample information: the probabilities of the test results (.59 and .41) and the revised probabilities for the states of nature (i.e., strong and weak markets) given the test results (i.e., .95, .05 and .34, .66). We now turn our attention to the calculation of those values.

A basic piece of information that is necessary to the procedure is the reliability of the source of sample information (in this case, the market test). In assessing this reliability, the manager might make use of historical data on test results versus actual results, expert opinion, or his or her personal judgment of the probabilities. Let's suppose that in this case, the manager was able to obtain the reliability information from past records. The reliability information pertains to every possible combination of test result and actual result. The reliability figures for the preceding example are shown in Table 10–11.

The figures indicate that in past cases when the market actually was strong, the market test correctly indicated this information 80 percent of the time, and incorrectly indicated a weak market 20 percent of the time. Moreover, when a weak market existed, the market test incorrectly indicated a strong market 10 percent of the time, while it correctly indicated a weak market 90 percent of the

TABLE 10–12 Probability Calculations Given the Market Test Indicates a Strong Market

Actual Market	Conditional Probabilities		Prior Probabilities		Joint Probabilities	Revised Probabilities
Strong	.80	×	.70	=	.56	.56/.59 = .95
Weak	.10	×	.30	=	.03	.03/.59 = .05
					.59	

TABLE 10–13 Probability Calculations Given the Market Test Indicates a Weak Market

Actual Market	Conditional Probabilities		Prior Probabilities		Joint Probabilities	Revised Probabilities
Strong	.20	×	.70	=	.14	.14/.41 = .34
Weak	.90	×	.30	=	.27	.27/.41 = .66
					.41	

time. (Note that the probabilities in each *column* add to 1.00.) These probabilities are known as *conditional* probabilities because they express the reliability of the sampling device (e.g., market test) *given* the condition of actual market type.

In order to calculate the desired probabilities, we must combine these conditional probabilities with the original (*prior*) probabilities (.70 and .30) that were associated with the original payoff table. We must do this for each of the possible test results.

For a strong market test result, the calculations are shown in Table 10–12.

The first column of the table lists the two possible actual market conditions: strong and weak. The next column shows the probability of a market test that will show a strong market, given each possible actual market condition. The prior probabilities are the initial estimates of each type of market condition. Multiplying the prior probabilities by the conditional probabilities yields the *joint* probability of each market condition. The sum of these (e.g., .59) is the probability that a test result will show a strong market. (Note that this one is one of the two types of probabilities we set out to compute.) The last column of the table illustrates the computation of the revised probabilities, given a market test that shows a strong market. The computation involves obtaining the ratio of the joint probability of each market condition to the total joint probability (in this case, .59). The resulting values of .95 and .05 are the ones shown in Figure 10–4 (top). (Note that these are two of the revised probabilities we set out to compute.)

Probabilities for a market test that shows a weak market are computed in a similar way. These are illustrated in Table 10–13. As in the preceding table, the sum of the joint probabilities indicates the probability of this test result (weak market), and the ratios in the last column are the revised probabilities, given this test result.

SENSITIVITY ANALYSIS

Analyzing decisions under risk requires working with estimated values: Both the payoffs and the probabilities for the states of nature are typically estimated values. Inaccuracies in these estimates can have an impact on choice of an alternative, and ultimately, on the outcome of a decision. Given such possibilities, it is easy to see that a decision maker could benefit from an analysis of the *sensitivity* of a decision to possible errors in estimation. If it turns out that a certain decision will be deemed optimal over a wide range of values, the decision maker can proceed with relative confidence. Conversely, if analysis indicates a low tolerance for errors in estimation, additional efforts to pin down values may be needed.

In this section, sensitivity to *probability* estimates is examined. Sensitivity to payoff estimates is not covered; that topic is beyond the scope of this text.

Probabilities estimates are particularly interesting because it is not unusual to find instances in which managers are reluctant to attempt to pinpoint probabilities. This may stem from a desire to avoid having to justify those estimates, or it may be that certain managers are uncomfortable with making such estimates. The approach described here enables decision makers to identify a *range* of probabilities over which a particular alternative would be optimal. In other words, the manager or decision maker is presented with ranges of probabilities for various alternatives, and he or she need only decide if a probability is within a range, rather than decide on a specific value for the probabilities of a state of nature.

Let's consider an example that has two states of nature. Because only two states of nature can occur, this permits us to use *graphical analysis*. Suppose a decision maker has prepared this profit payoff table:

		State of Nature	
		#1	#2
Alternative	*a*	3	9
	b	12	1
	c	9	6

The analysis is designed to provide ranges for the probability of State of nature #2, merely because it is convenient to do so. Nonetheless, these ranges can easily be converted into ranges for State of nature #1, as you will see. We will use a graph that has two vertical axes and one horizontal axis, as shown in Figure 10–6. The left vertical axis pertains to payoffs if State of nature #1 occurs, whereas the right vertical axis pertains to payoffs if State of nature #2 occurs. The horizontal axis represents the probability of State of nature #2, P(#2). Each alternative can be represented on the graph by plotting its payoff for State of nature #1 on the left side and its payoff for State of nature #2 on the right side and then connecting those two points with a straight line. This is illustrated for Alternative *a* in Figure 10–7. The line represents the expected value of Alternative *a* for the entire range

FIGURE 10–6 Format of Graph for Sensitivity Analysis

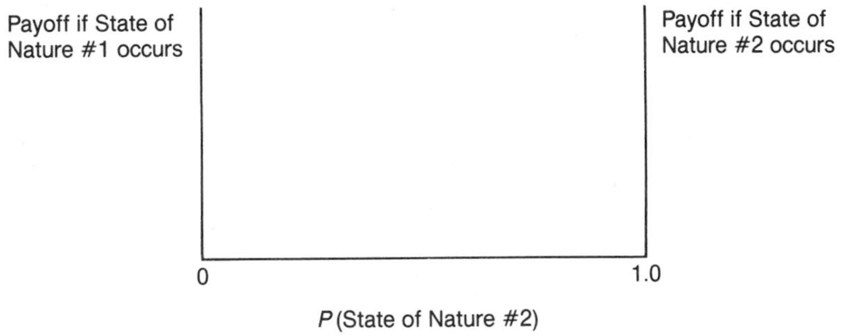

FIGURE 10–7 The Expected Value Line for Alternative *a*

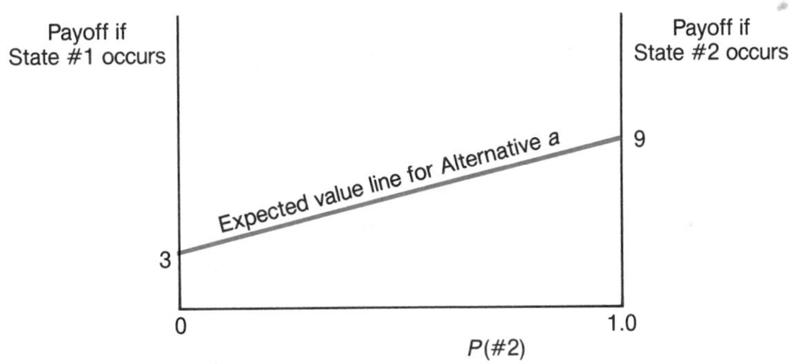

of $P(\#2)$. Thus, for any value of $P(\#2)$, the expected value of Alternative *a* can be found by running a vertical line from the value of $P(\#2)$ on the horizontal axis up to the point where it intersects the line. By running a horizontal line to either axis from that intersection, the expected value for that probability can be determined. An example is illustrated in Figure 10–8.

Of course, different values of $P(\#2)$ would produce different expected values. In general, you should be able to see from the graph that the nearer $P(\#2)$ is to 0, the closer the expected value of Alternative *a* will be to the payoff for State of nature #1, whereas the nearer $P(\#2)$ is to 1.0, the closer the expected value will be to the payoff for State of nature #2.

Our analysis of sensitivity requires that all the alternatives be plotted on the same graph. Adding the other two alternatives produces the graph shown in Figure 10–9. You will recall that plotting the line for an alternative involves connecting its payoff for #1 (left axis) and its payoff for #2 (right axis.)

FIGURE 10–8 Example of Finding the Expected Value for Alternative *a* when *P*(#2) Is .50

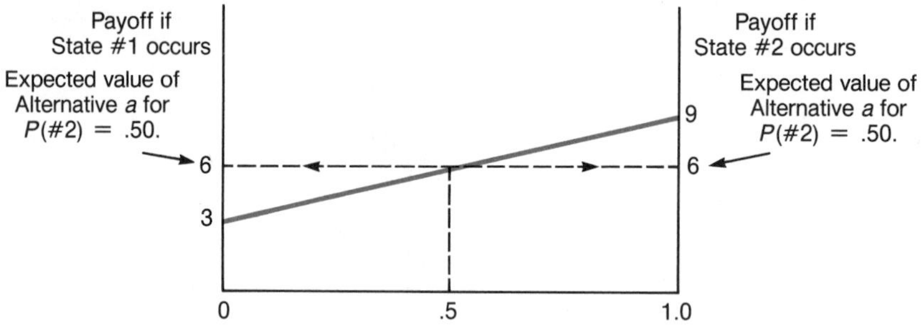

FIGURE 10–9 All Three Alternatives Are Plotted on a Single Graph

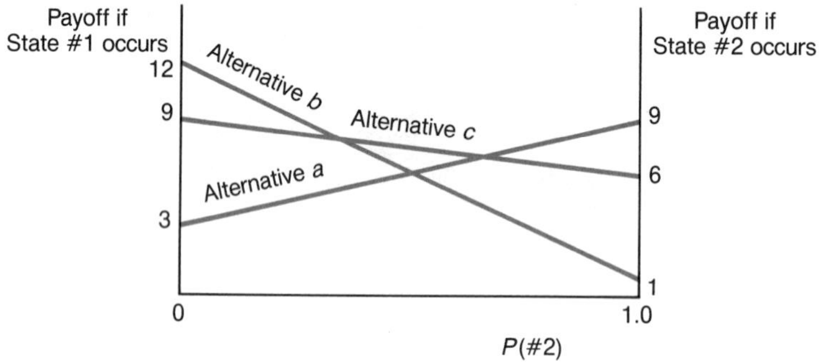

Because higher expected profits are more desirable than lower expected profits, the highest line for any given value of $P(\#2)$ represents the optimal alternative for that probability. Thus, referring to Figure 10–9, for low values of $P(\#2)$, Alternative *b* would give higher expected profits than either Alternative *a* or *c*. However, for values of $P(\#2)$ close to 1.0, Alternative *a* would have higher expected profits than either *b* or *c*, whereas for values of $P(\#2)$ somewhere in the middle, Alternative *c* would yield the highest expected profits. What we want to determine is the *range* of $P(\#2)$ for which each alternative is the best.

We can see in Figure 10–10 that Alternative *b* is best up to the point (probability) where lines *b* and *c* intersect because the *b* line is highest from $P(\#2) = 0$ up to that probability. Then, line *c* is highest from that point until it intersects with line *a*; after that, line *a* is highest all the way to $P(\#2) = 1.0$. Hence, the values of $P(\#2)$ at these intersections are the key values in our analysis because they

FIGURE 10–10 The Line with the Highest Expected Profit Is Optimal for a Given Value of *P*(#2)

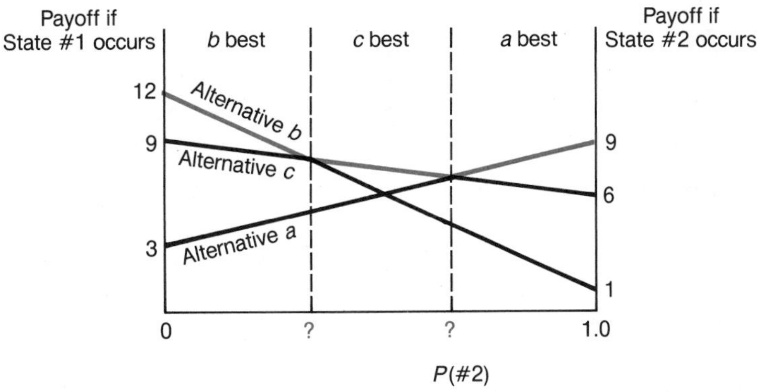

represent the end points of the ranges. These concepts are illustrated in Figure 10–10.

In order to be able to determine the $P(\#2)$ values at the line intersections, it is necessary to first develop equations of the lines in terms of $P(\#2)$. This

$$EV = \text{Payoff \#1} + (\text{Payoff \#2} - \text{Payoff \#1})P \qquad (10\text{–}5)$$

where

EV = expected value of alternative
$P = P(\#2)$

Thus, for Alternative *a*, the equation is:

$EV_a = 3 + (9 - 3)P$, which is $EV_a = 3 + 6P$

Similarly, for *b* and *c* we have:

$EV_b = 12 + (1 - 12)P$, which is $EV_b = 12 - 11P$
$EV_c = 9 + (6 - 9)P$, which is $EV_c = 9 - 3P$

Now, to find the values of P at the intersections, we can set two equations equal to each other and solve for P. Thus, for the intersection of lines *b* and *c*, we have:

$$12 - 11P = 9 - 3P$$

Solving for P yields:

$8P = 3$, so $P = 3/8$, or .375

For the intersection of lines *a* and *c*, we set $EV_a = EV_c$:

$$3 + 6P = 9 - 3P$$

Solving for P, we find:

$$9P = 6, \text{ so } P = 6/9 \text{ or } .67$$

Thus, lines b and c intersect at $P(\#2) = .375$. So, Alternative b is best over the range of $P(\#2)$ from 0 to less than .375 (note that for $P(\#2) = .375$, b and c are equivalent). Similarly, Alternative c is best from $P(\#2) > .375$ to $P(\#2) < .67$, and from there up to $P(\#2) = 1.0$, Alternative a is best.

In sum, the range of $P(\#2)$ over which each alternative is best is:

For Alternative *a:* $.67 < P(\#2) \leq 1.0$

For Alternative *b:* $0 \leq P(\#2) < .375$

For Alternative *c:* $.375 < P(\#2) < .67$

These ranges give the decision maker important insight on probability estimates. For example, a decision maker may be reluctant to specify an exact probability for State of nature #2. However, with this information, the decision maker merely has to identify the most appropriate *range* for $P(\#2)$. Thus, if the decision maker believes that $P(\#2)$ is somewhere in the range of, say, .80 to .90, according to the preceding calculations, Alternative a would be best. Or, if the decision maker believes that $P(\#2)$ lies close to .50, then Alternative c would be best.

A similar analysis can be performed if the payoffs are costs or other values that are to be minimized rather than maximized. In such cases, the *lowest* line for a given value of $P(\#2)$ would be most desirable. An example of this is illustrated in the Solved Problems section at the end of this chapter.

One final comment regarding the use of $P(\#2)$. It was mentioned previously that $P(\#2)$ is used for convenience. It happens that the equations of the lines are a bit easier to develop using $P(\#2)$ rather than $P(\#1)$. However, should a problem refer to $P(\#1)$ ranges rather than $P(\#2)$, you can proceed by finding the ranges in terms of $P(\#2)$ and then converting these into $P(\#1)$ ranges as the final step. This merely involves recognizing that $P(\#1)$ and $P(\#2)$ are complements. For example, if $P(\#2) = 0$, then $P(\#1) = 1.0$; if $P(\#2) = .40$, then $P(\#1) = .60$; and so on. Hence, if Alternative a is optimal for the range $0 \leq P(\#2) < .40$, then in terms of $P(\#1)$, Alternative a is optimal for the range $.60 < P(\#1) \leq 1.00$. Figure 10–11 further illustrates this concept using the previous example.

UTILITY

Throughout this chapter decision criteria have been illustrated that use monetary value as the basis of choosing among alternatives. Although monetary value is a common basis for decision making, it is not the only basis, even for business decisions. In certain instances, decision makers use *multiple criteria,* one of which is the potential *satisfaction* or *dissatisfaction* associated with possible payoffs.

For example, a great many people participate in state lotteries. However, the

FIGURE 10–11 Converting $P(\#2)$ Ranges into $P(\#1)$ Ranges

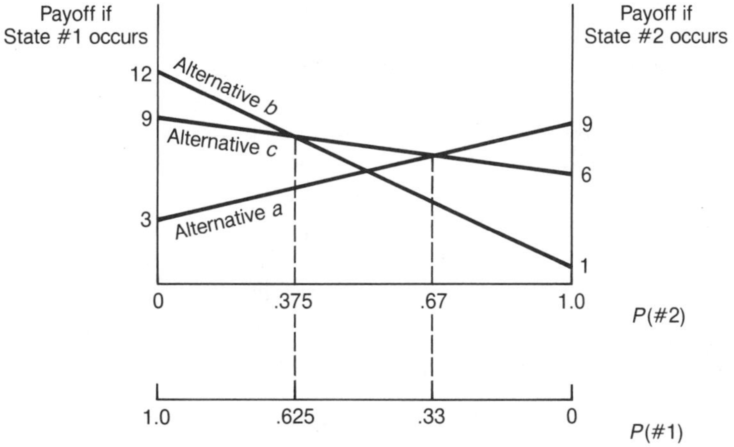

fact is lotteries have a *negative* expected value; the *expected* return is less than the cost of the lottery. If it were not, the states would lose money by running lotteries. Why do people play lotteries, then? The answer is that they are hoping to win a large amount of money, and they are willing to sacrifice a relatively small amount of money to have that chance. In other words, even though their chances of winning are close to zero, they have a greater **utility** for the potential winnings, despite a negative expected value, than for the amount of money they have to give up (pay) to participate in the lottery. Similar arguments can be made for other forms of wagering. People who behave in this fashion, whether for purposes of wagering or in other forms of decision making, are sometimes referred to as *risk takers*.

Just the opposite happens when a person buys insurance, giving up a fixed dollar amount to insure against an event (e.g., a fire) that has very little chance of occurring. Even so, if a fire or other insured event did occur, the consequences would be so catastrophic that an individual would not want to be exposed to that degree of risk. Thus, even though buying insurance carries a negative monetary value, most individuals recognize the merit of doing so. We refer to such individuals as *risk averters*. Of course, some individuals exhibit both forms of behavior in their decision making; they are risk takers for certain kinds of decisions but risk averters for others. A lottery player who owns a life insurance policy would be an example of this.

Thus, *utility* is a measure of the potential satisfaction derived from money. Although utility can be an important factor in certain kinds of decision making, assessing and using utility values can be rather complex. Not only does utility vary within an individual for different types of situations, but it also seems to vary among individuals for the same situations. That is, different people might choose different alternatives in a given instance because of utility considerations.

SUMMARY

Decision theory is a general approach to decision making. It is very useful for a decision maker who must choose from a list of alternatives, knowing that one of a number of possible future states of nature will occur and that this will have an impact on the payoff realized by a particular alternative.

Decision models can be categorized according to the degree of uncertainty that is assigned to the occurrence of the states of nature. This can range from complete knowledge about which state will occur, to partial knowledge (probabilities), to no knowledge (no probabilities, or complete uncertainty). When complete uncertainty exists, the approach a decision maker takes in choosing among alternatives depends on how optimistic or pessimistic he or she is, and it also depends on other circumstances related to the eventual outcome or payoff. Under complete certainty, decisions are relatively straightforward. Under partial uncertainty, expected values often are used to evaluate alternatives. An extension of the use of expected values enables decision makers to assess the value of improved or perfect information about which state of nature will occur.

Problems that involve a single decision are usually best handled through payoff tables, whereas problems that involve a sequence, or possible sequence, of decisions, are usually best handled using tree diagrams.

Sometimes, decision makers can improve the decision process by taking into account additional (sample) information, which enables them to modify state of nature probabilities. Because there is almost always an additional cost associated with obtaining that sample information, the decision maker must decide whether the expected value of that information is worth the cost necessary to obtain it.

Sensitivity analysis can sometimes be useful to decision makers, particularly for situations in which they find it difficult to accurately assess the probabilities of the various states of nature. Sensitivity analysis can help by providing ranges of probabilities for which a given alternative would be chosen, using expected monetary value as the criterion. Hence, the problem of specifying probabilities is reduced to deciding whether a probability merely falls within a range of values.

Although expected monetary value is a widely used approach to decision making, certain individuals and certain situations may require consideration of utilities, which reflect how decision makers view the satisfaction associated with different monetary payoffs.

GLOSSARY

Decision Criterion A standard or rule for choosing among alternatives (e.g., choose the alternative with the highest expected profit).

Decision Tree A schematic representation of a decision problem that involves the use of branches and nodes.

Expected Monetary Value (EMV) For an alternative, the sum of the products of each possible payoff and the probability of that payoff.

Expected Opportunity Loss (EOL) For an alternative, the sum of the products of each possible regret and the probability of that regret.

Expected Payoff under Certainty (EPC) For a set of alternatives, the sum of products of the best payoff for each state of nature and that state's probability.

Expected Regret See **Expected Opportunity Loss.**

Expected Value of Perfect Information (EVPI) The maximum additional benefit attainable if a problem involving risk could be reduced to a problem in which it was certain which state of nature would occur. Equal to the minimum expected regret. Also equal to EPC minus best EMV.

Expected Value of Sample Information (EVSI) The expected benefit of acquiring sample information. Equal to the difference between the best EMV without information and the best EMV with information.

Maximax A decision criterion that specifies choosing the alternative with the best overall payoff.

Maximin A decision criterion that specifies choosing the alternative with the best of the worst payoffs for all alternatives.

Minimax Regret A decision criterion that specifies choosing the alternative that has the lowest regret (opportunity loss).

Opportunity Loss For an alternative given a state of nature, the difference between that alternative's payoff and the best possible payoff for that state of nature.

Payoff Table A table that shows the payoff for each alternative for each state of nature.

Principle of Insufficient Reason A decision criterion that seeks the alternative with the best average payoff, assuming all states of nature are equally likely to occur.

Regret See **Opportunity Loss.**

Risk A decision problem in which the states of nature have probabilities associated with their occurrence.

State of Nature Possible future events.

Uncertainty Refers to a decision problem in which probabilities of occurrence for the various states of nature are unknown.

Utility Of a payoff, a measure of the personal satisfaction associated with a payoff.

SOLVED PROBLEMS

Problem 1. Given this *profit* payoff table:

		State of Nature #1	#2	#3
Alternative	*a*	12	18	15
	b	17	10	14
	c	22	16	10
	d	14	14	14

Determine which alternative would be chosen using each of these decision criteria:

a. Maximax.

b. Maximin.

c. Minimax regret.

d. Principle of insufficient reason.

Solution

a. The maximax approach seeks the alternative that has the best overall payoff. Because these are profits, the best payoff would be the largest value, which is the payoff 22. Thus, in order to have a chance at that payoff, the decision maker should choose Alternative *c*.

b. The maximin approach is to choose the alternative that will provide the best of the worst possible payoffs. To find this, first identify the worst profit possible for each alternative:

Alternative	Worst Payoff
a	12
b	10
c	10
d	14 (best)

Because Alternative *d* has the best of the worst payoffs, it would be chosen using maximin.

c. In order to find the minimax regret decision, we must first obtain the opportunity loss, or regret, table. This is a two-step process. First, identify the best payoff in each *column*. Then subtract every payoff in each column from the best payoff in the column. Hence, the best payoffs are: 22 in column #1, 18 in column #2, and 15 in column #3. The resulting regret table is:

		State of Nature			Worst	
		#1	#2	#3	Regret	
Alternative	*a*	10	0	0	10	
	b	5	8	1	8	
	c	0	2	5	5	(minimum regret)
	d	8	4	1	8	

(Notice that none of the regrets is negative. This will *always* be the case.) Because Alternative *c* has the lowest of the worst regrets, it would be chosen.

d. Using the principle of insufficient reason, we must determine the average payoff for each alternative. We do this by summing the payoffs for each and then dividing by the number of payoffs (three). The resulting averages are:

Alternative	**Average Payoff**
a	15
b	13.67
c	16 (best)
d	14

Because Alternative *c* yields the highest average profit using the principle of insufficient reason, it would be chosen.

Problem 2. Suppose the payoffs in the preceding problem had been *costs* rather than profits. Determine which alternative would be chosen, using these decision criteria:

a. Maximax.

b. Maximin.

c. Minimax regret.

d. Principle of insufficient reason.

Solution

a. The maximax approach seeks the best overall payoff. Because these are now costs, the smallest value is the best. The smallest value in the table given in Solved Problem 1 is 10. It appears both as a possible cost for Alternative *b* and for Alternative *c*. Hence, using maximax, the decision maker would be indifferent between those two alternatives.

b. For maximin, we must determine the worst payoff for each alternative. Because the values are now *costs*, the *largest* value for each alternative is listed:

Alternative	Worst Payoff
a	18
b	17
c	22
d	14 (lowest cost)

Because Alternative *d* has the best of the worst payoffs, it would be chosen.

c. To obtain the regret table, we must identify the best payoff for each column. Because costs are involved, we want the lowest payoff in each column. For column #1, 12 is the lowest; for column #2, 10 is the lowest; and for column #3, 10 is the lowest. When costs are involved, the regrets are obtained by subtracting the lowest cost in the column *from* all of the payoffs in the column. Again, this results in all positive and zero regrets:

		State of Nature			Worst
		#1	#2	#3	Regret
Alternative	*a*	0	8	5	8
	b	5	0	4	5
	c	10	6	0	10
	d	2	4	4	4 (minimum regret)

Because Alternative *d* had the lowest of the worst regrets, it would be chosen.

d. Using the principle of insufficient reason, we find the average payoff for each alternative. These averages are the same as determined in the preceding problem:

Alternative	Average Cost
a	15
b	13.67 (best)
c	16
d	14

Because Alternative *b* has the lowest average payoff, it would be chosen.

Problem 3. For the payoff table given in Solved Problem 1, suppose the manager has assigned probabilities of .2 to the occurrence of State #1, .5 to the occurrence of State #2, and .3 to the occurrence of State #3.

a. Which alternative would be chosen using maximum expected value as the criterion, treating the payoffs as profits?

b. Calculate the expected value of perfect information using (1) the expected payoff under certainty approach and (2) the expected regret approach.

Solution

a. Compute the expected value of each alternative:

EV_a: .2(12) + .5(18) + .3(15) = 15.9 (best)
EV_b: .2(17) + .5(10) + .3(14) = 12.6
EV_c: .2(22) + .5(16) + .3(10) = 15.4
EV_d: .2(14) + .5(14) + .3(14) = 14.0

Because Alternative *a* has the largest expected profit, it would be selected using expected monetary value as the decision criterion.

b. (1) The expected payoff under certainty approach is:

$$\text{EVPI} = \begin{matrix}\text{Expected payoff}\\ \text{under certainty}\end{matrix} - \begin{matrix}\text{Expected}\\ \text{monetary value}\end{matrix}$$

The expected payoff under certainty is found by taking the best payoff in each column, multiplying that by the column probability, and summing the results for all columns. Thus:

EPC: .2(22) + .5(18) + .3(15) = 17.9

Then:

EVPI: 17.9 − 15.9 = 2.0

(2) Using the regret approach, find the expected regret for each alternative: Using the regrets obtained in Solved Problem 1*c*, we have:

Alternative		Expected Regret
a	.2(10) + .5(0) + .3(0) =	2.0 (lowest)
b	.2(5) + .5(8) + .3(1) =	5.3
c	.2(0) + .5(2) + .3(5) =	2.5
d	.2(8) + .5(4) + .3(1) =	3.9

The lowest expected regret is equal to 2.0. This amount is the expected value of perfect information, EVPI. Note that this agrees with the answer obtained in 1*b*.

Problem 4. Given this table of estimated *costs:*

		State of Nature #1	State of Nature #2
Alternative	*a*	10	1
	b	2	8
	c	7	6

Find the range of $P(\#2)$ for which each alternative has the best expected value.

Solution

First, plot each alternative's expected value line on a graph. To do this, mark the payoff for #1 on the left vertical axis and the payoff for #2 on the right vertical axis, then connect these two points with a straight line. Then label each line (e.g., Alternative *a*).

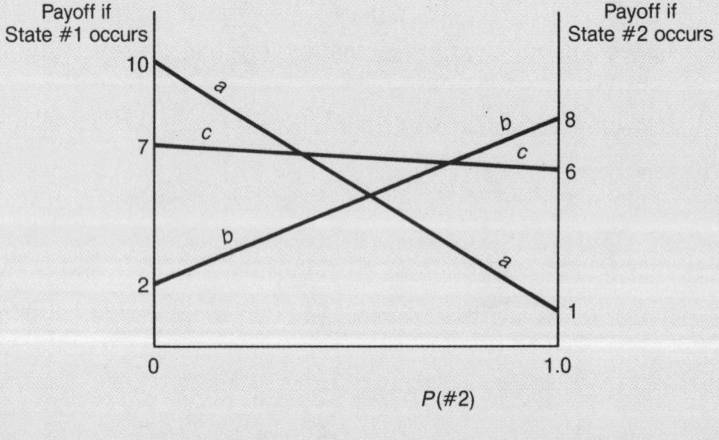

Because costs are involved rather than profits, the *lower* the expected value (i.e., the expected *cost*), the better. Consequently, it is the lowest line for given values of $P(\#2)$ that is most desirable. The following figure shows this. We can see, then, that for values of $P(\#2)$ near 0, Alternative *b* has the lowest expected cost, whereas for values of $P(\#2)$ close to 1.0, Alternative *a* is best. Note that Alternative *c* is never best. In order to find the value of $P(\#2)$ for which Alternative *b* and Alternative *a* are equivalent, we must formulate equations for lines *a* and *b*. Recall that each line has the form:

$$EV = \#1 \text{ Payoff} + (\#2 \text{ Payoff} - \#1 \text{ Payoff}) \times P(\#2)$$

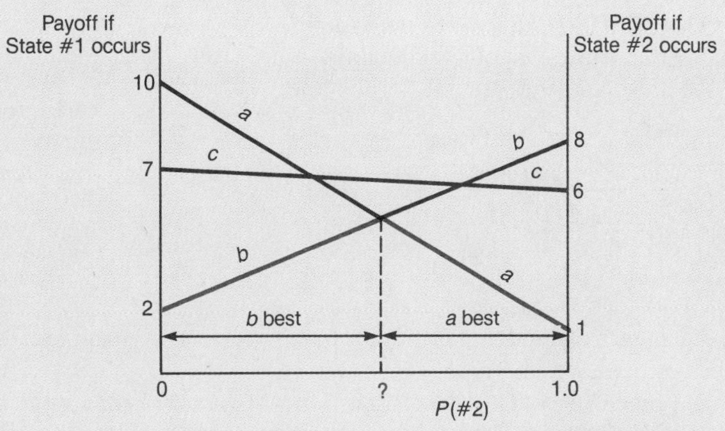

Thus, for line a we have:

$$EV_a = 10 + (1 - 10)P, \text{ which reduces to } EV_a = 10 - 9P$$

For line b, we have:

$$EV_b = 2 + (8 - 2)P, \text{ which reduces to } EV_b = 2 + 6P$$

Setting these equal to each other and solving for P gives us:

$$10 - 9P = 2 + 6P$$

Rearranging terms produces:

$$15P = 8$$

Solving for P:

$$P = 8/15, \text{ or } .533$$

Thus, when $P(\#2) = .533$, the decision maker would be indifferent between choosing Alternative a or b. For values of $P(\#2)$ from 0 to less than .533, Alternative b will give the lowest expected cost, whereas for values of $P(\#2)$ larger than .533, Alternative a has the lowest expected cost. Hence, the ranges over which each alternative is best are:

Alternative	**Best Over Range of**
b	$0 \leq P(\#2) < .533$
a	$.533 < P(\#2) \leq 1.0$
c	Never

Problem 5. *Decision making with sample information* A manager has developed a table that shows payoffs ($000) for a future store. The payoffs depend on the size of the store and the strength of demand:

		Demand	
		Low	High
Store Size	Small	30	50
	Large	10	80

The manager estimates that the probability of low demand is .50, and the probability of high demand is .50.

The manager could request that a local research firm conduct a survey (cost: $2,000) that would better indicate whether demand will be low or high. In discussions with the research firm, the manager has learned the following about the reliability of surveys conducted by the firm:

		Acutal Result Was	
		Low	High
Survey Showed	Low	.90	.30
	High	.10	.70

a. If the manager should decide to use the survey, what would the revised probabilities be for demand, and what probabilities should be used for survey results (i.e., survey shows Low and survey shows High demand)?

b. Construct a tree diagram for this problem.

c. Determine the EVSI.

d. Would you recommend that the manager use the survey? Explain.

Solution

a. The following are revised probabilities if the survey shows Low demand:

Actual Demand	Conditional Probability		Prior Probability		Joint Probability	Revised Probability
Low	.90	×	.50	=	.45	.45/.60 = .75
High	.30	×	.50	=	.15	.15/.60 = .25
					.60	1.00

The following are revised probabilities if survey shows High demand:

Actual Demand	Conditional Probability		Prior Probability		Joint Probability	Revised Probability
Low	.10	×	.50	=	.05	.05/.40 = .125
High	.70	×	.50	=	.35	.35/.40 = .875
					.40	1.000

Hence, the revised probabilities are *P*(Low) = .75 and *P*(High) = .25 if the survey shows Low demand; and *P*(Low) = .125 and *P*(High) = .875 if the survey shows High demand. Further, the probability that the survey will show Low demand is .60 (the sum of joint probabilities) and the probability the survey will show High demand is .40.

b.

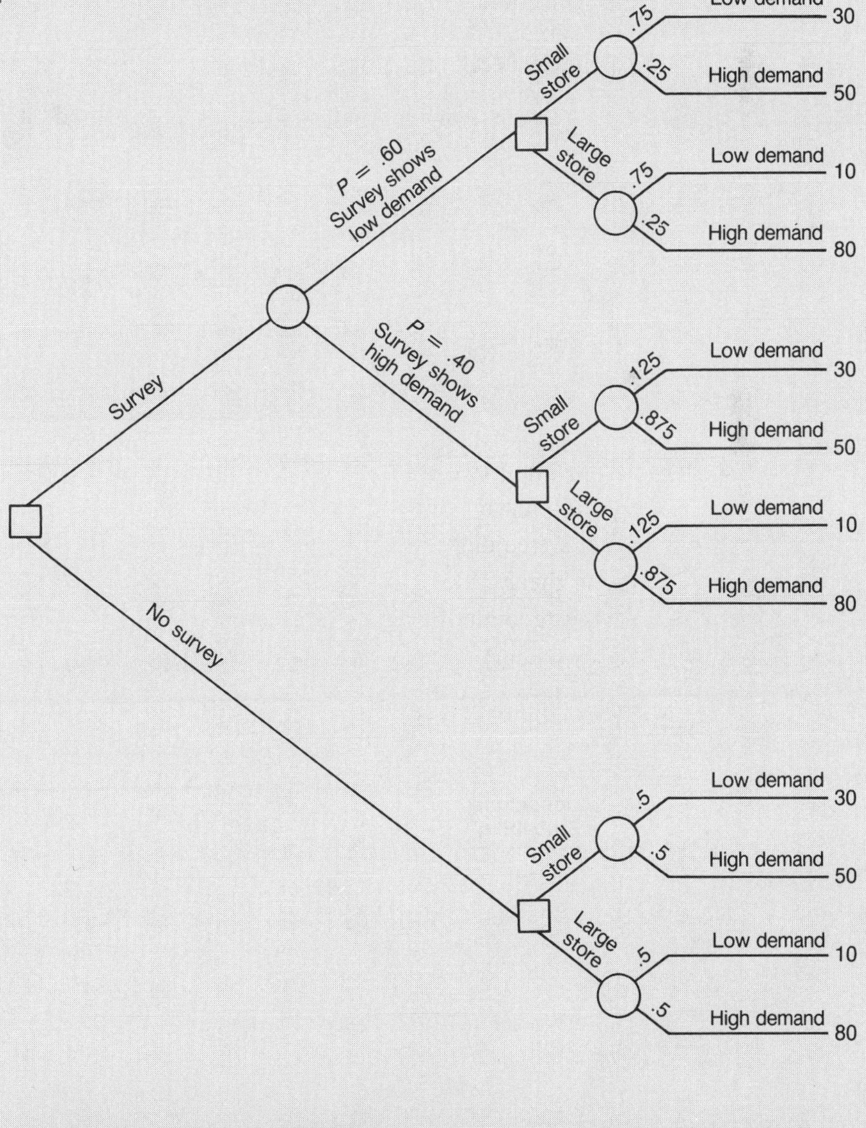

c. In order to find EVSI, first find the expected payoffs for store size for each of the following: Survey shows Low Demand, Survey shows High Demand, and No survey. Thus:

Survey shows Low:

Small store .75(30) + .25(50) = 35.00
Large store .75(10) + .25(80) = 27.50

Survey shows High:

Small store .125(30) + .875(50) = 47.50
Large store .125(10) + .875(80) = 71.25

No survey:

Small store .50(30) + .50(50) = 40.00
Large store .50(10) + .50(80) = 45.00

These then can be placed on a tree diagram as expected payoffs for store size decisions:

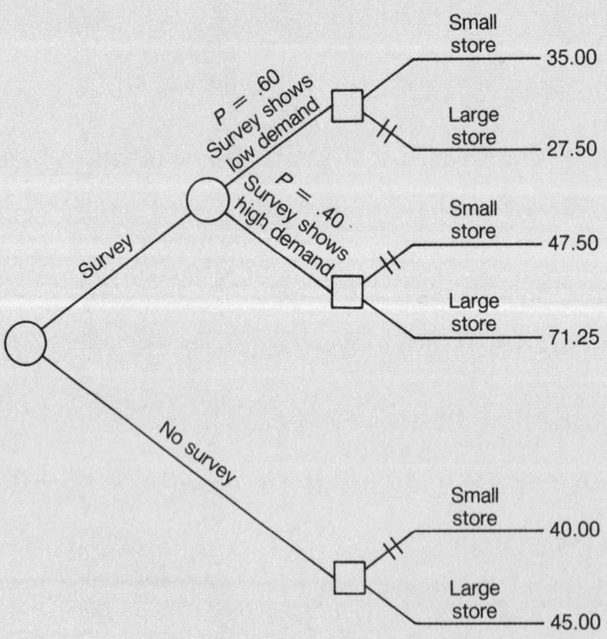

Next, the branch at each ending decision node with the smaller expected payoff can be "cut" or eliminated, as shown by the two slashes on appropriate branches.

Then, the expected payoff for using the survey can be computed using the remaining branches and their expected payoffs. Thus:

$.60(35.00) + .40(71.25) = 49.50$

The expected payoff for No survey is shown on the tree. It is 45.00.

The expected value of sample information is the difference between these two. Thus:

$EVSI = 49.50 - 45.00 = 4.50$ thousand, or $4,500

d. Because the EVSI is $4,500, whereas the cost of the survey is $2,000, it would seem resonable for the manager to use the survey; the expected gain would be $2,500.

PROBLEMS

1. Consider the following payoff table (profits in $100,000):

		State of Nature			
		s_1	s_2	s_3	s_4
Alternative	a_1	7	14	13	10
	a_2	3	6	12	15
	a_3	−8	−1	11	22

Which alternative would be chosen for each of the following decision criteria?

a. Maximin.

b. Maximax.

c. Minimax regret.

d. Principle of insufficient reason.

2. Suppose that probabilities were available for the states of nature in the previous problem. Which alternative would maximize expected payoff if the probabilities were $P(s_1) = .2$, $P(s_2) = .1$, $P(s_3) = .4$, and $P(s_4) = .3$?

3. Farah Fashion, an assistant buyer of a sportswear department in a New York store, must decide on clothes orders for the winter season. Two new styles of coats were introduced at a recent show. The styles are quite different, and the assistant buyer must decide whether to fill the entire order with

one of the styles or to split the order between the two. The profits for various states of nature have been estimated by the head buyer, and are shown in the following payoff table:

		Market Acceptance		
		Style A	Style B	Split
	Style A	80	30	45
Alternative	Style B	20	90	55
	Split	60	70	96

Determine which alternative would be selected for each of these decision criteria:

a. Maximin.

b. Maximax.

c. Minimax regret.

d. Principle of insufficient reason.

4. Suppose that the assistant buyer in the preceding problem is able to estimate that the probability for market acceptance of Style A is .30, the probability for market acceptance of Style B is .20, and the probability of a market split is .50.

   a. Which alternative would maximize the expected profit?

   b. Determine the expected value of perfect information using the expected payoff under certainty approach.

   c. Verify that using the opportunity loss table results in the same expected value of perfect information found in part *b*.

   d. Construct a decision tree. Indicate expected branch profits.

5. Suppose that the amounts given in the payoff table of Problem 3 were costs rather than profits. Determine the appropriate decision for each of the following criteria:

   a. Maximin.

   b. Maximax.

   c. Minimax regret.

   d. Principle of insufficient reason.

6. If the data in Problem 3 were costs, and market acceptance probabilities are estimated to be .3 for A, .2 for B, and .5 for split, determine which alternative will minimize expected cost.

7. Anabelle Lee, the director of social services of Down County, has just learned of additional information requirements mandated by the state. This will place an additional burden on the agency. The director has identified three acceptable alternatives to handle the increased workload. One is to reassign present staff members, another is to hire and train two new workers, and the third is to redesign current practice so that workers can readily collect the information with little additional effort. An unknown factor is the caseload for the coming year, during which time the new data will be collected on a trial basis. The estimated costs for various options and caseloads are shown in the table that follows:

	Caseload		
	Moderate	High	Very high
Reassign staff	$50*	60	85
New staff	60	60	60
Redesign collection	40	50	90

* Cost in thousands.

Assuming that probabilities of various caseloads are unreliable, based on past experience, what decision would be appropriate using each of the following criteria?

a. Maximin.

b. Maximax.

c. Minimax regret.

d. Principle of insufficient reason.

8. After contemplating the caseload question, Annabelle (see Problem 7) has decided that reasonable caseload probabilities are .10 for moderate, .30 for high, and .60 for very high.

a. Which alternative will yield the minimum expected cost?

b. Construct a decision tree for this problem. Indicate the expected costs for the three decision branches.

c. Determine the expected value of perfect information using an opportunity loss table.

9. Suppose the director of social services will have the option of hiring an additional staff member if one staff member is hired initially and the caseload turns out to be high or very high. Under that plan, the first entry in row 2 of the cost table (see Problem 7) will be 40 instead of 60, the second entry

will be 75, and the last entry will be 80. Assume the caseload probabilities are noted in Problem 8. Construct a decision tree that shows the sequential nature of this decison, and determine which alternative will minimize expected cost.

10. The owner of the Danish Pastry Baking Company, Fred Butterfield, recently submitted two bids, one to the county to supply baked goods to various county buildings for two years, and the other to supply baked goods to the city school district, again for two years. The owner estimates the probabilities of receiving the contracts as follows:

Outcome	Probability
No contracts	.20
City only	.20
County only	.50
City and county	.10

Fred has just learned that a bakery in a nearby county is about to close, and that two delivery trucks will be for sale. These trucks can be bought for a very reasonable price compared to the cost of new trucks, but Fred is unsure of whether to buy one truck, two trucks, or no trucks.

If Fred does not buy any trucks and no contracts are awarded, the net profit will be zero. If the city contract alone is awarded, a profit of $14,000 will be realized even without any trucks because the firm has some excess capacity at present. If the county contract alone is awarded, the profit will be only $10,000. If both contracts are awarded, Fred can buy either one new truck, two new trucks, or no trucks. The estimated profits considering salvage and depreciation are $12,000 for one truck, $15,000 for two trucks, and a loss of $2,000 for no trucks.

If one of the used delivery trucks is purchased, the estimated profits are −$3,000 for no contract, $8,000 for City only, $6,000 for County only, and $11,000 for City and County. However, in the event that both contracts are awarded to the bakery, Fred has the option of buying another truck and realizing a net profit of $16,000.

If two used trucks are initially bought, the estimated profits are −$7,000 for No contract, $9,000 for City only, $5,000 for County only, and $25,000 for both. If No contract is awarded, the owner has the option of selling one or both trucks. For one truck, the net profit would be $3,000, whereas if two are sold, the net profit would be $6,000. If Fred uses maximum expected profits as the decision criterion, which alternative should be chosen? Explain your reasoning.

11. The owner of a small business is considering three options: buying a computer, leasing a computer, or getting along without a computer. From information obtained from the firm's accountant, the following payoff table was developed:

	s_1	s_2
Do nothing	4	2
Buy	8	1
Lease	5	3

The owner would like to use the expected value criterion to make a decision, but she is hesitant because her probability estimates are quite rough.

a. Eliminate the alternative that is dominated by another alternative.

b. Determine $P(s_1)$ and $P(s_2)$ such that the owner would be indifferent between the two remaining alternatives.

c. For what range of probability would Lease have a higher expected payoff than the other alternative?

d. If probabilities are ignored, which alternative would offer the more conservative choice in this situation? Why?

12. Given the payoff table that follows, determine the value of P(low) and P(moderate) that would make a decision maker indifferent between London and Tokyo.

	Low	Moderate
London	10	8
Tokyo	6	12

13. Analyze the tree diagram shown in Figure 10–3 using expected monetary value as the decision criterion. What alternative is recommended?

14. A manufacturer produces and sells chilled, ready-to-eat pasta salad in round lots of 50 serving units each. These items have a very limited shelf life; therefore, if items are made but not sold, they have no value. Conversely, if demand exceeds supply during the week (regular production runs are made on Friday of each week for sales the following week), an extra production run can be made. The cost per unit for a regular run is $5 per unit, whereas the cost of an extra production run is $7 per unit. All items are sold for $10 per unit, regardless of production cost. Historically, demand has been for 50, 100, or 150 units each week, so the company makes one of those run sizes. In the past, the manager of the department has made 100 units per week for regular production.

a. Prepare a payoff table showing profits for each of the lot sizes.

b. If probability of demand for 50 units is .40, probability of demand for 100 units is .50, and probability of demand for 150 units is .10, what lot size would you recommend if the goal is to maximize expected profit?

c. What is the EVPI?

d. Answer questions *a*, *b*, and *c* given this additional consideration: Suppose that disposal cost for unsold items is $1 per unit.

15. For Solved Problem 5, determine the EVSI, and decide if you would recommend using the survey if the reliability of surveys conducted by the firm was *changed* to:

		Actual Result Was	
		Low	High
Survey Showed	Low	.75	.15
	High	.25	.85

Assume that all other information remains unchanged. What is the efficiency of sample information in this instance?

16. An attorney is preparing a case for trial. In an attempt to decide whether to follow an aggressive approach or a conservative approach in presenting his client's case, the attorney has developed this payoff table:

	Win	Lose
Aggressive	$40,000	−10,000
Conservative	20,000	−6,000

The attorney believes there is a probability of .30 that he can win the case. However, for a fee of $2,000, he can consult with an expert who is familiar with this type of case and can provide another opinion on whether the case will be won. Previous experience with using that expert can be summarized by the following table:

		Outcome	
		Won	Lost
Expert Predicted	Win	.85	.05
	Lose	.15	.95

Is the expected value of the expert's advice worth the fee? Illustrate your analysis using a decision tree.

17. Barry Greene, the manager of a commercial loan department of a bank, must decide how to allocate loans among various loan proposals. The manager has the following payoff table, which shows profits for various loan strategies and economic scenarios:

	Economy	
	Stable	Changing
Strategy A	$50,000	20,000
Strategy B	10,000	80,000

Barry believes that a stable economy is four times as likely as a changing economy. However, the manager is somewhat uncomfortable with this personal assessment and would like to take advantage of a governmental research agency's services regarding the probability of each type of economy.

According to the agency, its reliability for such forecasts in the past has been:

		Actual	
		Stable	Changing
Forecast	Stable	.88	.08
	Changing	.12	.92

a. Using the criterion of maximizing expected payoff, what strategy would Barry select without using the agency?

b. If Barry decides to use the agency, what would be the revised probabilities for the economy for each forecast possibility?

c. Prepare a tree diagram that illustrates the problem.

d. Determine the EVSI.

e. If the agency fee is \$3,000, would you recommend using the agency? Explain. What is the efficiency of sample information?

18. Annabelle Lee, the director of social services (see Problems 7 and 8), has just learned about a consulting firm that has worked with similar departments throughout the country in making similar assessments. After discussing the matter with a representative of the firm, the following table was produced to summarize the firm's reliability in terms of this problem:

		Actual Caseload		
		Moderate	High	Very high
Predicted Caseload	Moderate	.80	0	0
	High	.10	.90	.10
	Very high	.10	.10	.90

The firm's fee to handle this prediction problem would be \$8,000.

a. Determine the EVSI and the efficiency of sample information.

b. Do you recommend that the consulting firm be used? Explain.

19. Given this payoff table:

	Demand low	Demand high
Build small	20	20
Build large	10	40

a. Suppose the values in the table are profits. In terms of the probability that demand will be high, over what range of probability will each alternative action be best?

b. Now suppose that the values in the payoff table are costs. Over what range of values for *P*(Demand high) will each alternative be best?

20. Manager Sara Stern has compiled estimated profits for various alternative courses of action, but she is reluctant to assign probabilities to the states of nature. The payoff table is:

		State of Nature	
		#1	#2
Alternative	A	20	140
	B	120	80
	C	100	40

a. Plot the expectecd value lines on a graph.

b. Is there any alternative that would never be appropriate in terms of maximizing expected profit? Explain on the basis of your graph.

c. For what range of $P(\#2)$ would Alternative B be the best choice if the goal is to maximize expected profit?

d. For what range of $P(\#1)$ would Alternative B be the best choice if the goal is to maximize expected profit?

21. Repeat all parts of the preceding question assuming the values in the payoff tables are estimated *costs* and the goal is to minimize expected cost.

22. The research staff of a marketing agency has assembled the following payoff table of estimated profits:

		Receive contract	Not receive contract
Proposal	#1	10	−2
	#2	8	3
	#3	5	5
	#4	0	7

Relative to the probability of not receiving the contract, determine the range of probability for which each of the proposals would maximize expected profit.

23. Although he has prepared a payoff table for a decision problem, manager John Burns is reluctant to assign probabilities to the two states of nature he has determined will occur (i.e., one of these two will definitely occur). Given his payoff table, and his feeling that the probability of receiving the job is between .45 and .50, which alternative should John choose if it is his intention to maximize expected profits?

		Receive job	Do not receive job
Alternative	A	90	30
	B	40	70
	C	10	80

24. Given this payoff table:

		State of Nature #1	#2
Alternative	A	120	20
	B	60	40
	C	10	110
	D	90	90

a. Determine the range of $P(\#1)$ for which each alternative would be best, treating the payoffs as profits.

b. Answer part *a* treating the payoffs as costs.

Part III
Forecasting and Inventory Models

The models described in the three chapters in this part are among the most widely used of all of the management science models. Some of the inventory models were the earliest of management science models.

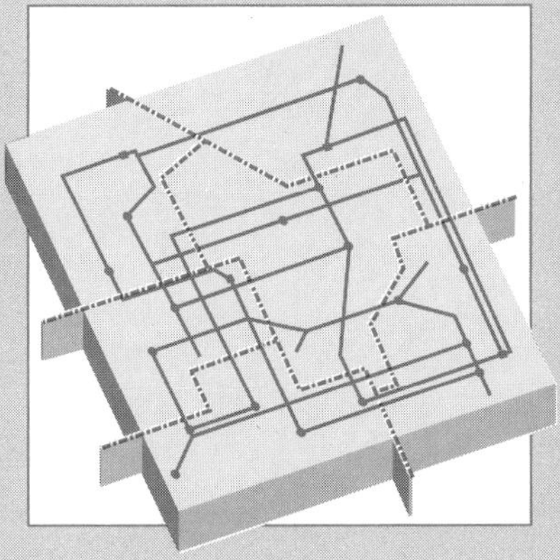

Chapter 11 describes forecasting models. Forecasting is one of the most basic tools of managers, since managers have a continuing need to plan for the future and forecasting helps them to remove some of the uncertainty about the future. The chapter covers basic forecasting methodology, as well as suggestions for choosing an appropriate technique and methods for evaluating and controlling forecast errors.

Chapter 12 is the first of two chapters on inventory models. It provides a basic introduction to inventories, their functions, information requirements for managing inventories, objectives of inventory management, and basic models for ordering inventories, including order quantity models, when to reorder, and safety stock considerations. Chapter 13 expands the description of inventory models. It describes models that can be used when ordering at fixed intervals (e.g., weekly), models for ordering perishable items, models for ordering component parts for assembled items (such as lawn mowers, typewriters, or radios), and just-in-time systems that operate on very little inventory.

Part Outline

Chapter 11
Forecasting

Chapter Outline

Learning Objectives

After completing this chapter, you should be able to:

1. Explain the importance of forecasting in organizations.
2. Describe the three major approaches to forecasting.
3. Use a variety of techniques to make forecasts.
4. Measure the accuracy of a forecast over time.
5. Determine when a forecast can be improved.
6. Discuss the main considerations in selecting a forecasting technique.

INTRODUCTION

Planning and implementing decisions are tasks performed by virtually all decision makers. Sometimes these tasks are carried out smoothly and successfully, with very satisfactory consequences. But sometimes, they are not. Very often, the degree of success is dependent on the amount of uncertainty surrounding some future event. If there is considerable uncertainty, it is much more difficult to formulate plans that will produce the desired results than when there is little or no uncertainty involved. Forecasts are important because they can help to reduce some of the uncertainty. That is, forecasts provide decision makers with an improved picture of probable future events and, thereby, enable decision makers to plan accordingly. For example, if a forecast indicates that an organization can expect an increase in demand for its products or services, plans may focus on the best way to meet those increases. Conversely, a forecast of decreasing demand may trigger attempts to overcome this by pricing strategy, advertising, or design improvements.

In fact, forecasts are vital inputs for almost all planning processes. Forecasts are used for *planning the system* (e.g., product and service design, process design, capacity planning, and equipment investment decisions) as well as for *planning the use of the system* (e.g., advertising, production and inventory planning and scheduling, purchasing commitments, planning the size of the work force, budgeting, and cost estimation).

Forecasts have the potential to greatly affect the success or failure of an organization's plans. Good forecasts can enable an organization to take advantage of future opportunities; poor forecasts can result in missed opportunities, inefficient operations, customer dissatisfaction, and costs associated with attempts to compensate for inappropriate actions or failure to act.

Good forecasts are more likely to result using this process:

1. Determine the purpose of the forecast. This will generally govern the amount of resources that can be justified for developing and maintaining the forecast.
2. Determine the time horizon. Some techniques work better in the short term, others for intermediate range applications, and still others work better for the long range.
3. Select an appropriate technique.
4. Identify the necessary data, and gather it if necessary. Special-purpose forecasts may require special collection efforts, whereas more repetitive forecasting requires ongoing, routine data collection.
5. Make the forecast.
6. Monitor forecast errors in order to determine if the forecast is performing adequately. If it is not, take appropriate corrective action.

It is important to recognize that *all* forecasts have the tendency to be inaccurate; there is no technique in existence that will provide perfect forecasts outside of the carefully controlled conditions that are possible in a laboratory. In the real world, the important question is not, "Will the forecast be perfect?" but rather, "How far off might the forecast be?"

There are many different forecasting techniques from which to choose. For purposes of discussion, the techniques described in this chapter are arranged into three categories: qualitative techniques, times series techniques, and explanatory models. Qualitative techniques are those that rely on judgment and experience. Time series techniques involve smoothing historical data and projecting past experience into the future. There is no attempt in time series models to explain certain patterns in historical data. Rather, the assumption is that future experience will be similar to past experience. Explanatory models involve identifying one or more variables whose values can be used to predict future experience. The presumption is that a logical relationship exists between the variables that can be expressed mathematically.

This chapter describes forecasting methods under each of these three categories, beginning with qualitative models. That is followed by a discussion of accuracy, which includes measuring and evaluating forecast accuracy. The chapter ends with a brief discussion of factors that should be considered when selecting a forecasting technique.

QUALITATIVE FORECASTS

Qualitative forecasts are based on judgment and/or opinion rather than on the analysis of "hard" data, such as weekly sales figures. Sometimes qualitative techniques are used because there is not time enough to gather and analyze data (e.g., an emergency situation calling for immediate action), whereas other times data may be nonexistent (e.g., for a new product or service), and still other times existing data may be obsolete (e.g., due to changing conditions such as consumers' buying behaviors or the introduction of a technological breakthrough by a competitor).

Among the advantages of qualitative forecasting techniques are that such forecasts can be made quickly and permit inclusion of "soft" factors (i.e., those that are difficult to quantify) that are ordinarily excluded by quantitative techniques. This might include hunches and intuition as well as insight acquired over a lengthy period of time. Conversely, qualitative forecasts may suffer from personal biases, confusion of desired results with probable results, and overly optimistic or pessimistic attitudes.

The qualitative techniques described in this chapter are typical of those commonly used and are intended to illustrate the variety of forecasting methods that are available to decision makers.

Inputs for qualitative forecasts can be obtained from a variety of sources, including consumers, salespeople, managers, technical staff members, and outside experts. Each of these potential sources is discussed briefly in the following paragraphs.

Customers and Consumers

In sales forecasting it usually is desirable to differentiate between those who purchase from us and those who purchase from competitors. In particular, knowledge of why a customer purchased our product or service, instead of another's, can be useful for determining the strength of customer loyalty. Moreover, it may be possible to uncover information that will be useful in improving the product or service in question. Similar kinds of information can be obtained from consumers in general—information that could improve the ability of a firm to predict future buying patterns and, perhaps, to increase its market share.

Questionnaires and interviews are often used to obtain the desired information. In the case of customers, a questionnaire is often attached to a warranty card or included in follow-up mailings. Although both techniques are widely used, a considerable amount of care and expertise generally is required in order to obtain meaningful information in all phases of an investigation. This includes careful construction and administration of questions, analysis of the data, and interpretation of results. Misjudgments in any of these areas can lead to erroneous forecasts.

Because data obtained from questionnaires and interviews are often analyzed by computer, it would be easy to conclude that using such data makes these approaches quantitative instead of qualitative. Nonetheless, such data are based on judgments and opinions, thus making them qualitative in nature.

Salespeople

Salespeople can be an important source of information for forecasting, as well as for feedback on products and services, because of their direct contact with present and potential customers. For example, they may be aware of certain buying tendencies and customers' plans for future buying.

On the other hand, salespeople exhibit a tendency to be overly influenced by recent successes or failures; they tend to overestimate future sales when current sales are high and underestimate future sales when current sales are low. Further, it is important not to use forecasts to set sales quotas, because that would present an incentive for salespeople to underestimate future sales.

Analogous sources of information are other personnel who have direct contact with consumers, even though their jobs are not viewed as "sales." This would include ticket agents, bank tellers, service attendants, repairers, librarians, cashiers, and so forth.

Managers and Technical Staff

Managers and technical staff members can sometimes provide insight about future demand that is not readily available from other sources. Such information can be obtained informally, in group meetings, or more formally, perhaps, through use of a questionnaire. One such approach that uses a *series of anonymous questionnaires* is the **Delphi technique.** It involves several rounds of questions, with information obtained from each preceding round used to develop the next set of questions. The fact that responses are anonymous tends to encourage openness and creativity. Successive questionnaires enable information uncovered at one stage of the process to be shared with others who may not have been previously aware of it, and who can then use the new information in responding to the questionnaire.

The Delphi technique also has been used for purposes not related specifically to forecasts, such as in new product development, the planning of future directions for organizational development and growth (e.g., in deciding if a firm should move into cancer research, or if a holding company should attempt a takeover of a regional bank).

It should be noted that the Delphi technique has received a certain amount of criticism. Accuracy has been questioned, the process sometimes fails certain testing criteria, and the questions may lead to a false consensus.

Executives

In some cases, a small group of upper-level managers (e.g., marketing, operations, financial) may collaborate on a forecast. Whereas surveys of managers, salespeople, and consumers may be used to develop short- and intermediate-range forecasts, executives may be used to develop long-range plans and to evaluate potential new directions or other opportunities for the firms and forecast their possible benefits.

The advantage of using this group of people stems mainly from their overall knowledge of the organization, their talents and perspectives, and their ability to make the necessary resources available in order to support efforts to match product and services with forecast expectations. The disadvantages of group forecasts relate to the risk of diffusing responsibility for the forecast, the high cost represented by the time the group spends in developing a forecast, and the risk that strong personalities will dominate the process.

Outside Experts

In some instances, an organization can benefit from the expertise of outside experts. This may be the case if a firm is entering a new market or undertaking a new business venture that is quite different from its current one. In those cases, experts may provide better forecasts than people within the organization. It should be noted, however, that these cases are more the exception than the rule.

Importance of Qualitative Forecasting

Qualitative forecasting approaches are important for a number of different reasons. Speed in making a forecast sometimes is a factor in choosing a qualitative approach over a quantitative one, especially if data acquisition for a quantitative approach will be time-consuming. The ability to incorporate experience and judgment are sometimes given as important reasons for using qualitative methods. However, the two are not necessarily mutually exclusive; quantitative forecasts can be modified by users in order to incorporate judgment and experience. Thus, qualitative reasoning can be used to supplement (and hopefully, improve) quantitative forecasts.

FORECASTS THAT USE TIME SERIES DATA

Time series data are historical values of a variable that have been recorded at periodic intervals (e.g., daily demand, weekly sales, quarterly revenues, annual demand). Forecasting techniques that use time series data typically involve the assumption that past experience reflects probable future experience (i.e., the past movements or *patterns* in the data will persist into the future).

Some of the most commonly observed patterns in historical data are trends, seasonal variations, and cyclical variations. **Trends** are long-term upward or downward movements; **seasonal variations** are recurring movements often related to such things as work, culture, or climate; and **cyclical variations** are long-term up and down movements in data. Identifying and using these patterns to forecast is sometimes difficult because of the presence of random and irregular variations in the data. **Random variations,** the net result of a large number of minor factors, are almost always present in time series data. Irregular variations are the result of unusual factors (e.g., severe weather conditions that disrupt supply or demand, equipment breakdowns, fire). When possible, irregular variations should be identified and their effects removed from the data because they tend to distort it.

Figure 11–1 illustrates the different possible patterns that might be observed in time series data. These patterns might exist separately or in combinations. For example, Figure 11–2 illustrates data that include both seasonality and trend.

Selecting a technique to use with time series data requires some knowledge of what pattern or patterns a series tends to exhibit. For that reason, it is a good idea to *plot the data* before selecting a technique, especially since certain techniques perform better on trends, whereas others work best with seasonality or cycles, and still others work best when a series varies around an average.

When working with time series data, a distinction should be made between "demand" and "sales." Because stockouts sometimes artificially constrain sales, unless it can be established that stockouts have not occurred, demand rather than sales data should be used for forecasting. It should be noted that sales figures may be much easier to obtain than demand, and in some cases demand figures either may be quite difficult to determine or may require a system designed specifically to collect the necessary data.

Techniques for Averaging

Averaging techniques generate a forecast that reflects recent values of a time series (e.g., the average value over the last several periods). These techniques

FIGURE 11–1 Examples of Simple Patterns Sometimes Found in Time Series Data

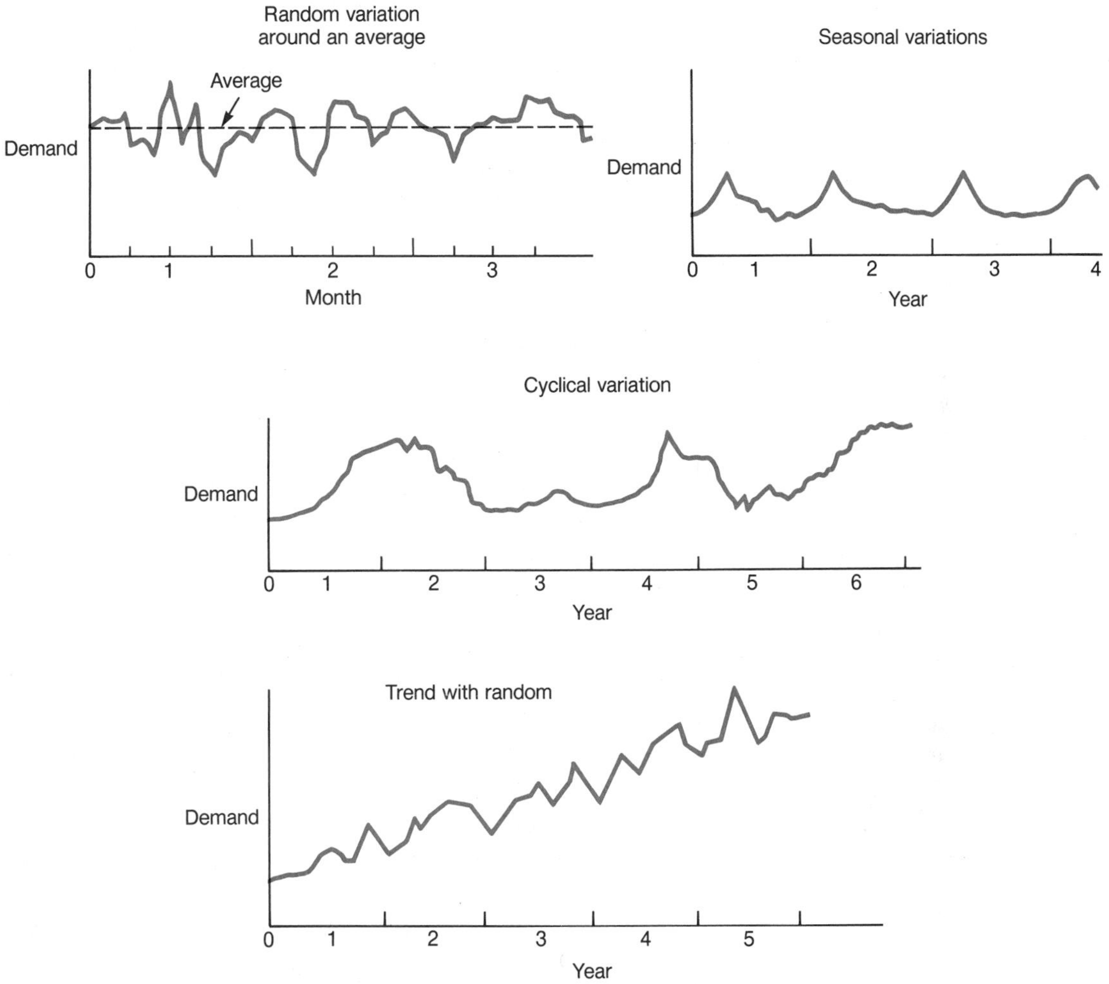

work best when a series tends to vary around an average, although they can handle step changes or *gradual* changes in the level of the series. A forecast based on an average tends to exhibit less variability than the original data because the averaging smooths out some of the up/down movements in the series (see Figure 11–3). This can be advantageous because many of these movements merely reflect random variability rather than a true change in level, or trend, in the series. Moreover, because response to changes in expected demand often can represent considerable cost (e.g., changes in production rate, changes in the size of a work force, inventory changes, etc.), it can be desirable to avoid reacting to minor

FIGURE 11-2 Data with Trend and Seasonal Variations

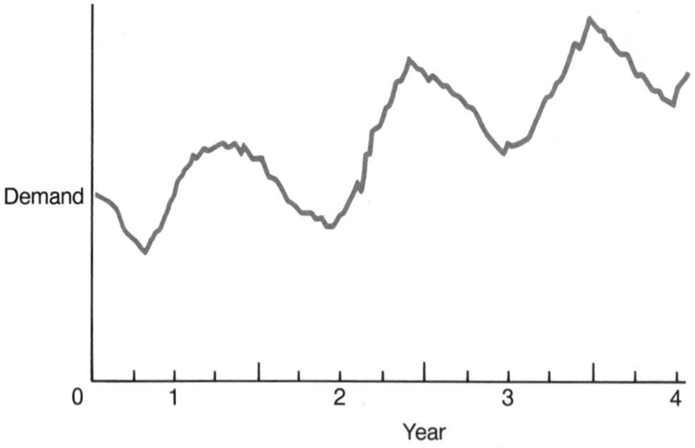

FIGURE 11-3 Averaging Applied to Three Possible Patterns

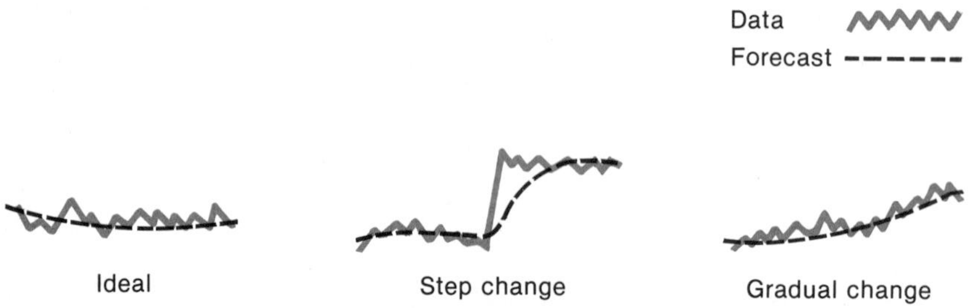

variations. In effect, minor variations are treated as random variations, whereas larger variations are viewed as more likely to reflect "real" changes, although these, too, are smoothed to a certain degree.

We examine three techniques for averaging in this section:

1. Naive forecasts.
2. Moving averages.
3. Exponential smoothing.

Naive The simplest forecasting technique is the *naive* method. A **naive forecast** for any period equals the previous period's actual value. For example, if demand last week was 50 units, the forecast for the upcoming week is 50 units. Similarly, if demand in the upcoming week turns out to be 54 units, the forecast for the following week would be 54 units.

Although at first glance the naive approach may appear *too* simplistic, nonetheless, it is a legitimate forecasting tool. Consider the advantages: It has virtually no cost, it is quick and easy to prepare a forecast because data analysis is nonexistent, and it is easy for users to understand. The main objection to this method is its inability to provide highly accurate forecasts. However, if resulting accuracy is acceptable, this approach deserves serious consideration. Moveover, even if other forecasting techniques offer better accuracy, they will almost always involve a greater cost. The accuracy of a naive forecast can serve as a *standard of comparison* against which to judge the cost and accuracy of other techniques. Hence, managers must answer the question: Is the increased accuracy of another method worth the additional resources required to achieve that accuracy?

The naive concept can also be applied to a series that exhibits seasonality or trend. For example, if monthly sales exhibit a seasonal pattern, demand for the current December can be based on demand for the preceding December, demand for January can be based on demand from the preceding January, and so on. Similarly, if trend is present, the increase (or decrease) from this period's actual demand to the period's demand can be estimated as the same as the change observed between the last two periods. For instance, if June's demand is 90 units higher than May's demand, a naive forecast that allowed for trend would be June's actual demand plus an additional 90 units. Then, if July's demand was only 85 greater than June's, August's forecast would be July's actual plus 85 units.

Moving averages One weakness of the naive method is that it causes the forecast to *trace* the actual data, with a lag of one period; it does not smooth at all. But by expanding the amount of historical data a forecast is based on, this difficulty can be overcome. A **moving average forecast** uses a number of the most recent actual data values in generating a forecast. The moving average forecast can be computed using the following equation:

$$MA_n = \frac{\sum_{i=1}^{n} A_i}{n} \tag{11-1}$$

where

i = the "age" of the data, $i = 1, 2, 3 \ldots$

n = the number of periods in the moving average

A_i = actual value with age "i"

For example, MA_3 would imply a three-period moving average.

■

EXAMPLE 1 Compute a three-period moving average forecast given demand for shopping carts for the last five periods:

Period	"Age"	Demand
1	5	40
2	4	44
3	3	36
4	2	42
5	1	40

$$MA_3 = \frac{36 + 42 + 40}{3} = 39.33$$

If actual demand in period 6 turns out to be 41, the moving average forecast for Period 7 would be:

$$MA_3 = \frac{42 + 40 + 41}{3} = 41.00$$

Note that in a moving average, as each new actual value becomes available, the forecast is updated by adding the newest value and dropping the oldest and then recomputing the average. Consequently, the forecast "moves" by reflecting only the most recent values.

In computing a moving average, the "age" column shown in the preceding example would not be included; it was shown merely to illustrate the concept. Instead, it would simplify computation to include a *moving total* column, which gave the sum of the n most current values from which the average will be computed. It is relatively simple to update the moving total: Subtract the oldest value from the newest value, and add that amount to the moving total for each update.

Figure 11–4 illustrates a three-period moving average forecast plotted against actual demand over 31 periods. Note how the moving average forecast lags the actual values and how smooth the forecasted values are compared to the actual values.

The moving average can incorporate as many data points as desired, beginning with the latest value and working backward. Hence, a 10-period moving average forecast would be the average of the latest 10 actual values. In selecting the number of periods to include in a moving average, the decision maker must take into account that the number of data points in the average determines its sensitivity to each new data point: The fewer the data points in an average, the more responsive the average tends to be, as depicted in Figure 11–5. Hence, if responsiveness is important, a moving average with relatively few data points should be used. This will permit quick adjustment to, say, a step change in the data, but it will also cause the forecast to be somewhat responsive, even to random variations. Conversely, moving averages based on more data points will smooth more but be less responsive to "real" changes. Hence, the decision maker must weigh the cost of responding more slowly to changes in the data against the cost of responding to what might simply be random variations.

The advantages of a moving average forecast are that it is easy to compute and

FIGURE 11-4 A Moving Average Forecast Tends to Smooth and Lag Changes in the Data

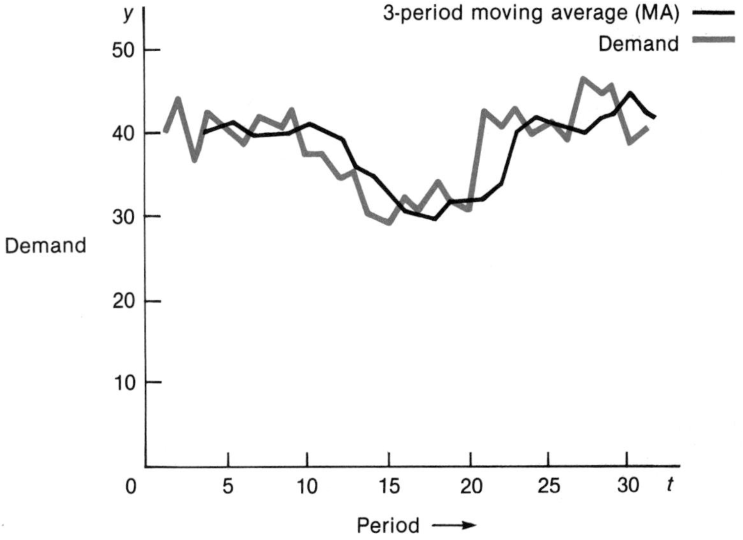

11-5 The More Periods in a Moving Average, the Greater the Forecast Will Lag Changes in the Data

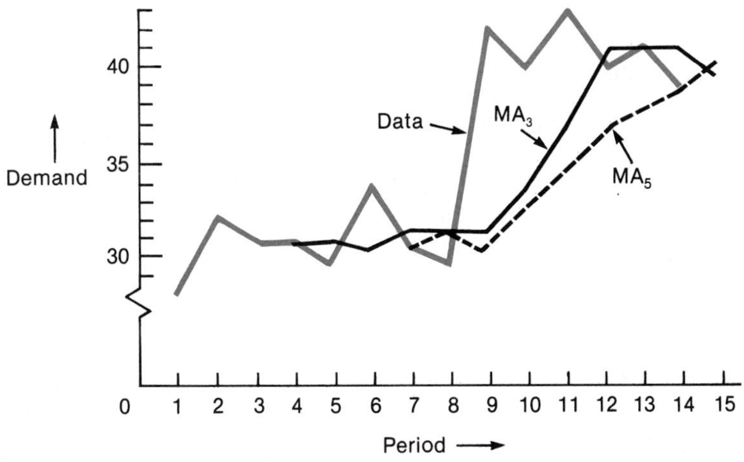

FIGURE 11–6 Relative Weights in Exponential Smoothing

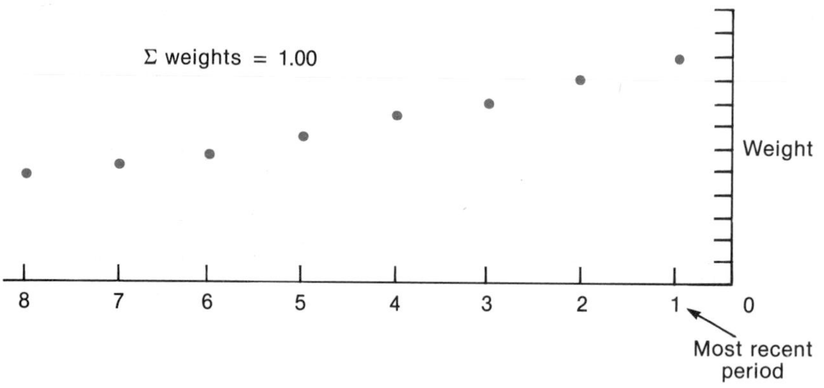

easy to understand. A disadvantage is that data storage requirements can be significant, especially if large numbers of moving average forecasts are being made. This is because individual values that comprise the average must be separately identified so that with each new forecast, the oldest value can be discarded. A more serious consideration is that all values in the average are weighted equally. Hence, in a 10-period moving average, each value is given a weight of 1/10; the oldest value is given the *same* weight as the most recent value. Decreasing the number of values in the average will increase the weight of more recent values, but this will be at the expense of losing potential information from less recent values.

Exponential smoothing **Exponential smoothing** is an averaging technique that reduces these difficulties. Data storage requirements are minimal (only the most recent actual value must be stored), even though the forecast is based on many of the values in the series. In addition, the weights given to previous values are not equal; instead, they decrease with the age of the data, as illustrated in Figure 11–6.

The exponentially smoothed forecast can be computed using this formula:

$$F_t = F_{t-1} + \alpha(A_{t-1} - F_{t-1}) \tag{11-2}$$

where

F_t = the forecast for Period t
F_{t-1} = the forecast for Period $t - 1$
α = smoothing constant (Greek alpha)
A_{t-1} = actual demand or sales for Period $t - 1$

The **smoothing constant, α,** represents a percentage of the forecast error. Each new forecast is equal to the previous forecast plus a percentage of the previous error. For example, suppose the previous forecast was 100 units, actual demand was 90 units, and $\alpha = .10$. The new forecast would be computed as follows:

FIGURE 11-7 A Small Value of α Will Smooth More than a Larger Value

t	Actual	α = .10		α = .40	
Period	Demand	Forecast	Error	Forecast	Error
1	42	—	—	—	—
2	40	42	−2	42	−2
3	43	41.8	1.2	41.2	1.8
4	40	41.92	−1.92	41.92	−1.92
5	41	41.72	−0.78	41.15	−0.15
6	39	41.65	−2.65	41.09	−2.09
7	46	41.39	4.61	40.25	5.75
8	44	41.85	2.15	42.55	1.45
9	45	42.06	2.94	43.13	1.87
10	38	42.35	−4.35	43.88	−5.88
11	40	41.92	−1.91	41.53	−1.53
12		41.73		40.92	

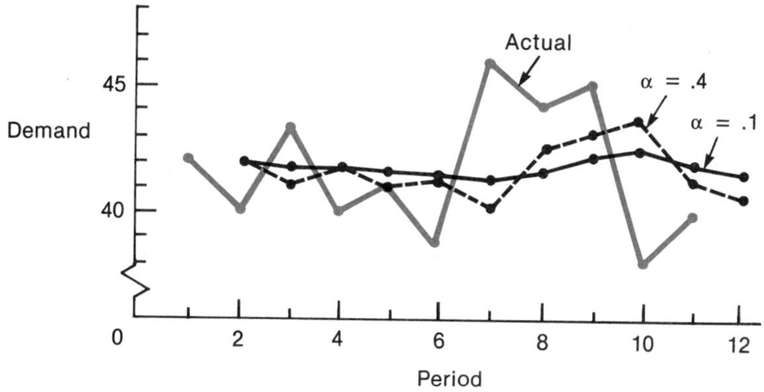

$$F_t = 100 + .10(90 - 100) = 99$$

Then, if the next actual demand turns out to be 102, the next forecast would be:

$$F_t = 99 + .10(102 - 99) = 99.3$$

A number of different approaches can be used to obtain a *starting forecast* (e.g., average first several periods, subjective estimate). For simplicity, use the first actual as the forecast for the following period and then begin the exponential smoothing.

The sensitivity of forecast adjustment to error is determined by the smoothing constant, alpha. The closer its value is to zero, the slower the forecast will be to adjust to forecast errors (i.e., the greater the smoothing). Conversely, the closer the value of alpha is to 1.00, the greater the sensitivity and the less the smoothing. This is illustrated in Figure 11-7.

Selecting a smoothing constant is, basically, a matter of judgment or trial and error. The goal is to select a smoothing constant that will balance the benefits of smoothing random variations with the benefits of responding to real changes if, and when, they occur. Commonly used values range from .05 to .50.

Some computer packages include a feature that permits automatic modification of the smoothing constant if the forecast errors become unacceptably large.

Exponential smoothing is one of the most widely used techniques in forecasting, partly because of its minimal data storage requirements and ease of calculation and partly because of the ease with which the weighting scheme can be altered (i.e., by simply changing the value of α).

Techniques for Trend

Trend is a persistent upward or downward movement in a time series. The trend may be linear or nonlinear. The discussion here will focus exclusively on linear trends because linear trends are fairly common and because they are the easiest to work with.

There are two important techniques that can be used to develop forecasts when trend is present. One involves use of a trend equation and the other is an extension of exponential smoothing.

Trend equation A *linear trend equation* has the form:

$$y_t = a + bt \qquad (11\text{–}3)$$

where

t = a specified number of time periods from $t = 0$
y_t = the forecast for Period t
a = value of y_t at $t = 0$
b = slope of the line

For example, consider the trend equation $y_t = 45 + 5t$. The value of y_t when $t = 0$ is 45, and the slope of the line is 5, which means that the value of y_t will increase by five units for each one unit increase in t. If $t = 10$, the forecast, y_t, is $45 + 5(10) = 95$ units. The equation can be plotted by finding two points on the line. One can be found by substituting some value of t into the equation (e.g., $t = 10$) and then solving for y_t. The other is a (i.e., y_t at $t = 0$). Plotting those two points and drawing a line through them will yield a graph of the linear trend line.

The coefficients of the line, a and b, can be computed from historical data using these two equations:

$$b = \frac{n\Sigma ty - \Sigma t \Sigma y}{n\Sigma t^2 - (\Sigma t)^2}$$

$$a = \frac{\Sigma y - b\Sigma t}{n} \qquad (11\text{–}4)$$

TABLE 11–1 Values of Σt and Σt^2

n	Σt	Σt^2	n	Σt	Σt^2
1	2	1	11	66	506
2	3	5	12	78	650
3	6	14	13	91	819
4	10	30	14	105	1,015
5	15	55	15	120	1,240
6	21	91	16	136	1,496
7	28	140	17	153	1,785
8	36	204	18	171	2,109
9	45	285	19	190	2,470
10	55	385	20	210	2,870

where

n = the number of periods
y = a value of the time series

Note that these equations are identical to those that are used for computing a linear regression line, except that t replaces x in the equations. Manual computation of the coefficients of a trend line can be simplified by use of Table 11–1, which lists values of Σt and Σt^2 for up to 20 ($n = 20$) periods.

■

EXAMPLE 2 Monthly demand for Dan's Doughnuts over the past nine months for trays (six dozen per tray) of sugar doughnuts was:

Mar	112
Apr	125
May	120
Jun	133
Jul	136
Aug	146
Sept	140
Oct	155
Nov	152

1. Plot the data to determine if a linear trend equation is appropriate.
2. Obtain a trend equation.
3. Forecast demand for the next two months.

Solution

1. The data seem to show an upward, roughly linear trend:

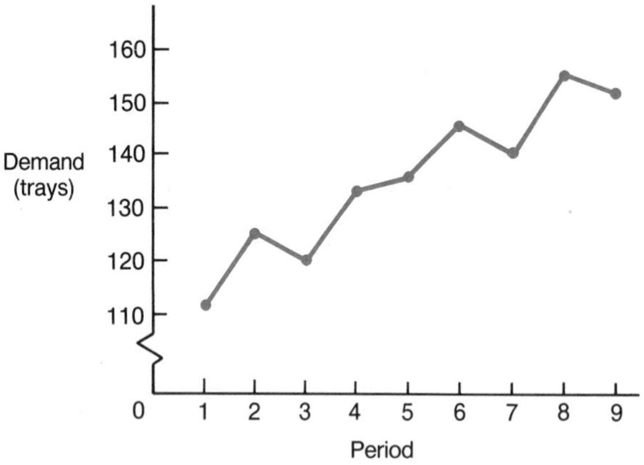

2.

Month	t	y	ty
Mar	1	112	112
Apr	2	125	250
May	3	120	360
Jun	4	133	532
Jul	5	136	680
Aug	6	146	876
Sep	7	140	980
Oct	8	155	1,240
Nov	9	152	1,368
		1,219	6,398

From Table 11–1, for $n = 9$, $\Sigma t = 45$, and $\Sigma t^2 = 285$. Using Formula 11–4, we find:

$$b = \frac{9(6{,}398) - 45(1{,}219)}{9(285) - 45(45)} = \frac{2{,}727}{540} = +5.05$$

$$a = \frac{1{,}219 - 5.05(45)}{9} = 110.19$$

The resulting equation is: $y_t = 110.19 + 5.05t$.

3. The next two months represent $t = 10$ and $t = 11$. Hence:

$$y_{Dec} = 110.19 + 5.05(10) = 160.69$$
$$y_{Jan} = 110.19 + 5.05(11) = 165.74$$

Owner Dan T. may decide to round these forecasts to the nearest full tray.

Trend-adjusted exponential smoothing A variation of simple exponential smoothing can be used when a time series includes trend. It is called *trend-adjusted* exponential smoothing, or sometimes *double* smoothing, to differentiate it from simple exponential smoothing, which is only appropriate when data vary around an average or have step or ramp changes. If a series exhibits trend, and simple smoothing is used on it, the forecasts will all *lag* the trend. For example, if the data are increasing, each forecast will be too low. Conversely, decreasing data will result in forecasts that are too high. Again, plotting the data can indicate when trend-adjusted smoothing would be preferable to simple smoothing.

The trend-adjusted forecast (TAF) is comprised of two elements: a smoothed error and a trend factor:

$$\text{TAF}_{t+1} = S_t + T_t \tag{11-5}$$

where

$$S_t = \text{smoothed error}$$
$$T_t = \text{current trend estimate}$$

and

$$S_t = \text{TAF}_t + \alpha_1(A_t - \text{TAF}_t)$$
$$T_t = T_{t-1} + \alpha_2(\text{TAF}_t - \text{TAF}_{t-1} - T_{t-1})$$

where α_1 and α_2 are smoothing constants.

In order to use this method, one must select values of α_1 and α_2 (usually through trial and error) and make a starting forecast and an estimate of trend.

Suppose a manager estimates a trend of +10 units, based on observed changes in the first four data points, and uses a starting forecast of 250, and $\alpha_1 = .5$ and $\alpha_2 = .4$. If the next actual value is 255, the TAF for the following period would be computed in this manner:

$$S_t = 250 + .5(255 - 250) = 252.5$$
$$T_t = 10 + .4(0)^*$$

* Since this is the initial forecast, no previous error is available, so a value of zero is used.

$$\text{TAF} = S_t + T_t = 252.5 + 10 = 262.5$$

If the next actual value is 265, the next TAF would be:

$$S_t = 262.5 + .5(265 - 262.5) = 263.75$$
$$T_t = 10 + .4(262.5 - 250 - 10) = 11.00$$
$$\text{TAF} = 263.75 + 11.00 = 274.75.$$

These values are the first few values in the following example.

■

EXAMPLE 3 After plotting demand for four periods, the aforementioned manager has concluded that a trend-adjusted exponential smoothing model would be appropriate to predict future demand. Calculations are shown for next five periods. The initial estimate of trend is based on the net change of 28 for the *three* periods from 1 to 4, for an average of approximately +10 units.

	t Period	A_t Actual	TAF_t	TAF_t	$+ \alpha_1(A_t$	$- TAF_t)$	$= S_t$	T_{t-1}	$+ \alpha_2(TAF_t$	$- TAF_{t-1}$	$- T_{t-1})$	$= T_t$
Model development	1	212										
	2	224										
	3	229										
	4	240										
Model test	5	255	250*	250	+ .5(255	− 250)	= 252.5	10	+ .4(0)			= 10
	6	265	262.5	262.5	+ .5(265	− 262.5)	= 263.75	10	+ .4(262.5	− 250	− 10)	= 11.00
	7	272	274.75	274.75	+ .5(272	− 274.75)	= 273.37	11.00	+ .4(274.75	− 262.5	− 11.00)	= 11.50
	8	285	284.87	284.87	+ .5(285	− 284.87)	= 284.94	11.50	+ .4(284.87	− 274.75	− 11.50)	= 10.95
	9	294	295.89	295.89	+ .5(294	− 295.89)	= 294.95	10.95	+ .4(295.89	− 284.87	− 10.95)	= 10.98
Next forecast →	10 →		305.93									

* Estimated by the manager.

A plot of the actual data and predicted values is shown below.

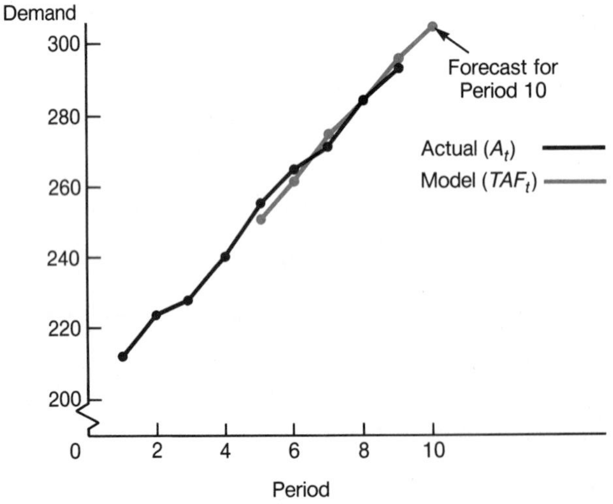

In choosing smoothing constants, it is usually prudent to use an α_1 of .5 if the trend is apt to change or if the initial estimate is uncertain because this will enable fairly rapid adjustment as opposed to values of α_1 that are closer to zero.

Compared to a linear trend line, trend-adjusted exponential smoothing is a more flexible technique because it can handle changes in trend more readily. A linear trend line would have to be recomputed periodically in order to accomplish the same flexibility. On the other hand, the linear trend line does not require the amount of computation that trend-adjusted smoothing does. Further, it can be used to forecast more than simply one period ahead, whereas exponential smoothing cannot.

Techniques for Seasonality

Seasonal variations in time series data are regularly repeating upward or downward movements in series values that can be tied to recurring events. Familiar examples of seasonality relate to weather variations (e.g., sales of winter and summer sports equipment) and vacations or holidays (e.g., airline travel, greeting card sales, visitors at tourist and resort centers). Seasonality often is used to refer to regular annual variations. However, the term *seasonal variation* also is applied to daily, weekly, monthly, and other regularly recurring patterns in data. For example, rush hour traffic occurs twice a day: incoming in the morning and outgoing in the late afternoon. Theaters and restaurants often find weekly demand patterns, with demand higher later in the week than earlier. Banks may experience daily seasonal variations (heavier traffic during the noon hour and just before closing), weekly variations (heavier toward the end of the week), and monthly variations (heaviest around the end of the month because of social security checks, payrolls, and welfare checks being cashed or deposited). Mail volume; sales of toys, beer, automobiles, and turkeys; highway usage; hotel registrations; and gardening are common examples of activities that show seasonal variations.

Seasonality in data is expressed relative to the *average* value of a time series (i.e., to the value if seasonality were not present). Most often, seasonal variations are stated as *percentages* of the series average at a particular point in time. For example, the **seasonal relative** for November for toy sales may be 1.20, or 120 percent. This tells us that November toy sales are 20 percent *above* average. If the seasonal relative for March is .92, this means that March sales are 92 percent of average, or 8 percent *below* the average if seasonality were not present. Thus, a seasonal relative reflects the amount by which a value differs from the expected average for that time period.

Knowledge of seasonal variations is an important factor in planning and scheduling in many retail businesses. Moreover, seasonality can be an important factor in capacity planning for systems that must be designed to handle peak loads (e.g., public transportation, electric power plants, highways and bridges, and so on). Knowledge of the extent of seasonality in a time series can enable one to *remove* seasonality from the data (i.e., to "seasonally adjust" data) in order to discern

FIGURE 11–8 Naive Approaches with Seasonality

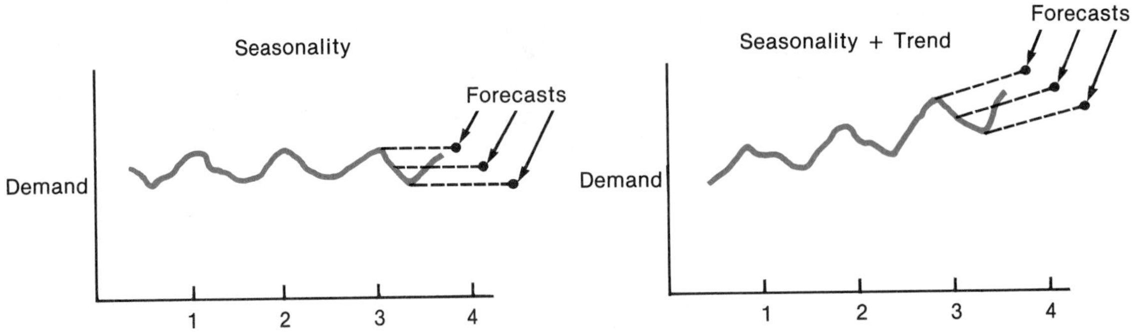

other movement, or lack of movement, in the series. Thus, we frequently read or hear about "seasonally adjusted unemployment," and "seasonally adjusted personal income."

The simplest seasonal model is a variation of the naive technique described for averages. Instead of using the last *period's* actual demand as the forecast amount, the seasonal naive model uses last *season's* actual amount for the forecast. Hence, our forecast of theater attendance this Friday evening would equal last Friday's attendance using the seasonal naive model, and November toy sales in one year might be estimated based on toy sales in November of the preceding year. If trend and seasonal variations are present, the naive model might be: last season's demand plus 10 percent, or whatever increase or decrease is appropriate. (See Figure 11–8.)

Again, the naive approach either can be used as such or it can serve as a standard of comparison against which other, more refined, techniques can be judged.

Centered moving average A commonly used method for representing the trend portion of a time series involves a **centered moving average.** Computations are identical to a moving average *forecast,* as are the resulting values. However, the values are *not projected* as in a forecast, but, instead, they are *positioned in the middle* of the periods used to compute the moving average. The implication is that the average is most representative of that point in the series. For example, suppose we have the following time series data:

Period	Demand	Three-Period Centered Average
1	40	
2	46	42.67
3	42	

$$\text{Average} = \frac{40 + 46 + 42}{3} = 42.67$$

A three-period average is 42.67. As a centered average, it would be positioned at Period 2; the average is most representative of the series at that point. The *ratio* of demand at Period 2 to this centered average at Period 2 is an estimate of the seasonal relative at that point.

Because the ratio is 46/42.46 = 1.08, the series is about 8 percent above average at this point. In order to achieve a reasonable estimate of seasonality for any season (e.g., Friday attendance at a theater), it is usually necessary to compute seasonal ratios for a number of seasons and then average these ratios. For instance, in the case of theater attendance, average the relatives of five or six Fridays for the Friday relative, average five or six Saturdays for the Saturday relative, and so on. As a rule of thumb, at least three seasons of data should be available in order to obtain reasonable estimates of seasonal relatives.

■

EXAMPLE 4 The manager of a parking lot has computed daily relatives for the number of cars per day for his lot. The computations are repeated here (about three weeks are shown for illustration). A seven-period centered moving average is used because there are seven days (seasons) per week.

Day	Volume	Moving Total	Centered MA_7	Volume/MA
Tues	67			
Wed	75			
Thur	82			
Fri	98		71.86	98/71.86 = 1.36 (Friday)
Sat	90		70.86	90/70.86 = 1.27
Sun	36		70.57	36/70.57 = 0.51
Mon	55	503 ÷ 7 =	71.00	55/71.00 = 0.77 (Monday)
Tues	60	496 ÷ 7 =	71.14	60/71.14 = 0.84
Wed	73	494 etc.	70.57	73/70.57 = 1.03
Thur	85	497 .	71.14	85/71.14 = 1.19
Fri	99	498 .	70.71	99/70.71 = 1.40 (Friday)
Sat	86	494 .	71.29	86/71.29 = 1.21
Sun	40	498	71.71	40/71.71 = 0.56
Mon	52	495	72.00	52/72.00 = 0.72 (Monday)
Tues	64	499	71.57	64/71.57 = 0.89
Wed	76	502	71.86	76/71.86 = 1.06
Thur	87	504	72.43	87/72.43 = 1.20
Fri	96	501	72.14	96/72.14 = 1.33 (Friday)
Sat	88	503	73.00	88/73.00 = 1.21
Sun	44	507	73.57	44/73.57 = 0.60
Mon	50	505	72.71	50/72.71 = 0.69 (Monday)
Tues	70	511		
Wed	80	515		
Thurs	81	509		

The estimated Friday relative is: $\frac{1.36 + 1.40 + 1.33}{3} = 1.36$. Relatives for other days can be computed in a similar manner. For example, the estimated Monday relative is: $\frac{0.77 + 0.72 + 0.69}{3} = 0.73$.

The number of periods used in a centered moving average is equal to the number of data points between seasons. Hence, with monthly data, a 12-period moving average would be used. When the number of periods is even instead of odd, as in the preceding example, one additional step is needed because the middle of an even set falls *between* two periods. The additional step involves taking a centered 2-period moving average of the even-numbered centered moving average, which results in averages that "line up" with data points and, hence, permit determination of seasonal ratios.

The reason that a centered moving average is used to obtain representative values is that because it "looks forward" and it "looks backward" by virtue of its centered position, it is able to closely follow data movement, regardless of whether they involve trends, cycles, or random variability alone. Figure 11–9 illustrates how a centered moving average closely tracks data that has moderate variability.

If both trend and seasonality appear in a series, each component can be determined separately, as described previously, and then combined to obtain a forecast.

■

EXAMPLE 5 A furniture manufacturer wants to predict quarterly demand for a certain loveseat for Periods 15 and 16, which happen to be the second and third quarters of a particular year. The series consists of both trend and seasonality. The trend portion of demand can be projected using the equation $y_t = 124 + 7.5t$. Quarter relatives are $Q_1 = 1.20$, $Q_2 = 1.10$, $Q_3 = .75$, and $Q_4 = .95$. Use this information to predict demand for Periods 15 and 16.

Solution

The trend values at $t = 15$ and $t = 16$ are:

$$y_{15} = 124 + 7.5(15) = 235.5$$
$$y_{16} = 124 + 7.5(16) = 244.0$$

Multiplying the trend value by the appropriate quarter relative will yield a forecast that includes both trend and seasonality. Since we are told that $t = 15$ is a second quarter and $t = 16$ a third quarter, the forecasts are:

FIGURE 11–9 A Centered Moving Average Closely Tracks the Data

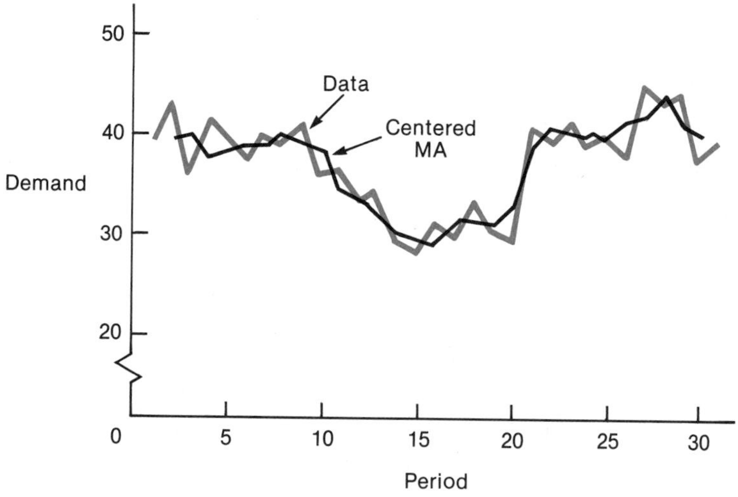

Period 15	235.5(1.10)	= 259.05
Period 16	244.0(0.75)	= 183.00

Techniques for Cycles

When cycles (up and down movements similar to seasonal variations, but of longer duration, say, two to six years between peaks) occur in time series data, they often are so irregular that it is difficult or impossible to project them from past data because turning points are difficult to identify. A short moving average or a naive approach may be of some value, although both will produce forecasts that lag cyclical movements by one or several periods.

The most commonly used approach is explanatory: Search for another variable that relates to, and leads, the variable of interest. For example, the number of housing starts (permits to build houses) in a given month often is an indicator of demand for certain products and services a few months later that are directly tied to construction of new homes (e.g., landscaping, sales of washers and dryers, sales of carpeting and furniture, new demands for shopping, transportation, schools, etc.). Thus, if an organization is able to establish a high correlation between such a *leading* variable (i.e., changes in the variable precede changes in the variable of interest), an equation that describes the relationship can be developed that will enable forecasts to be made. It is important that there be a persistent relationship between the two variables. Moreover, the higher the correlation, the better the chances that the forecast will be on target.

EXPLANATORY MODELS

Explanatory forecasting models incorporate one or more variables that are *related* to the variable of interest and, therefore, they can be used to predict future values of that variable. The most widely used explanatory models in forecasting are called *regression models,* and the discussion here will concentrate on them, with particular emphasis on simple linear regression models.

Simple Linear Regression

A simple linear regression model consists of two variables that are thought to be related. One of these is the variable to be forecasted, and it is referred to as the *dependent* variable; its value "depends" on (is a function of) the value of another variable. The other variable, which will be used to "explain" or predict the value of the dependent variable, is referred to as an *independent* variable. In order to make a forecast, the two variables must be expressed in a linear equation of the form:

$$y = a + bx \tag{11-6}$$

where

y = the dependent variable
x = the independent variable
a = value of y when $x = 0$
b = slope of the line

For example, the marketing manager of a paper products company has developed the following equation to predict demand for paper towels (dependent variable) based on the amount of television advertising (independent variable) during the same week:

$$y = 3.57 + 3.78x$$

where

x = television advertising in millions of dollars in preceding week
y = sales of paper towels in millions of dollars

Thus, the marketing manager must feel that advertising expenditure is a major factor in determining sales of this product. According to the equation, if advertising expenditure is \$1.0 (million), sales will be about $3.57 + 3.78(1.0) = \$7.35$ (million).

In order to successfully use this approach, it is necessary to be able to:

1. Identify an appropriate independent variable or variables.
2. Obtain a sample of at least 10 observations.
3. Develop an equation.
4. Identify any restrictions on predictions.
5. Measure accuracy in a given forecast.

To begin with, selecting the explanatory variable requires some knowledge of factors that might *logically* be related to the variable of interest. For example, the miles per gallon that a car gets would seem to be somewhat related to its weight; the yield from a home garden may depend on the amount of fertilizer used; and the cost of a textbook may depend on the number of pages it has. If two variables seem related (e.g., changes in one appear to be related to changes in the other), but no reasonable explanation for the relationship can be found, the relationship may simply be due to chance and, therefore, it would be highly unreliable. If it is decided that *more than one* explanatory variable is important, then *multiple regression analysis* is required. This topic will be considered after simple regression analysis is discussed.

Once an independent variable has been identified, it will be necessary to obtain enough observations to construct a model. (One rule of thumb is to observe at least 10.) These can come from historical data or they can be observations taken specifically for the purpose of estimating the relationship. The observations represent *paired values*. That is, for each observation of the dependent variable there must be a corresponding value for the independent variable.

Consider, for example, 10 paired observations about sales and advertising (all figures are in millions of dollars):

Observation	Advertising Expenditure, x	Sales, y
1	\$1.1	\$ 7
2	1.4	8
3	1.4	10
4	2.0	10
5	0.9	7
6	1.6	10
7	2.0	11
8	1.7	11
9	1.2	9
10	0.8	6

The data can be plotted on a graph to determine if a linear relationship is appropriate (see Figure 11–10). It appears that a linear relationship would reasonably represent the data, if we allow for some variability around a straight line.

The next step is to determine the one line that best fits these points. The line is called a *least squares* regression line because the method used to compute the

FIGURE 11–10 A Linear Relationship Appears to Exist

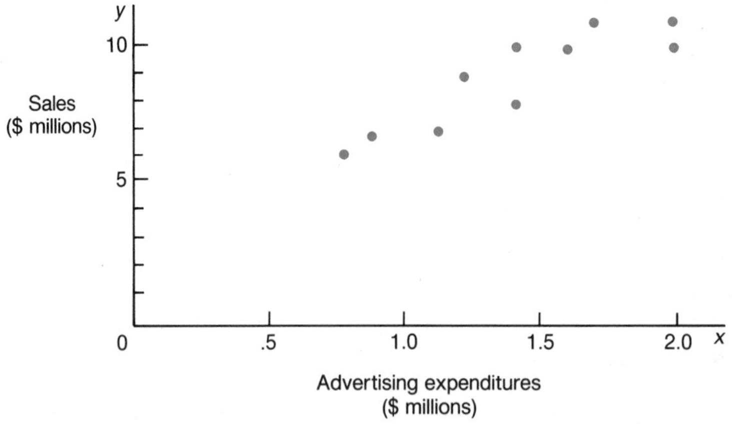

coefficients of the equation is designed to minimize the sum of the *squared* vertical deviations of points from the line. The equations used for this are essentially the same as those used to compute a linear trend line, except that x replaces t in the equations. Thus:

$$b = \frac{n\Sigma xy - \Sigma x \Sigma y}{n\Sigma x^2 - (\Sigma x)^2}$$

$$a = \frac{\Sigma y - b\Sigma x}{n} = \bar{y} - b\bar{x} \qquad (11\text{–}7)$$

where

n = number of observations

The necessary summations needed to compute these regression coefficients are obtained in Table 11–2, along with the Σy^2, which will be used later.

The regression equation can be used to predict a value of y for a given value of x. However, the equation is valid only for values of x that lie within the range of the original x values (which was .8 to 2.0). We have no knowledge of whether the relationship holds beyond that range of values. In fact, if predictions are required for x values outside this range, additional observations should be made, taking care to obtain measurements of y for values of x at desired points.

An indication of how well the line fits the points can be obtained by computing the *correlation coefficient*, which measures the strength of the relationship between the two variables. It can be calculated using this equation:

$$r = \frac{n\Sigma xy - \Sigma x \Sigma y}{\sqrt{n(\Sigma x^2) - (\Sigma x)^2} \times \sqrt{n(\Sigma y^2) - (\Sigma y)^2}} \qquad (11\text{–}8)$$

TABLE 11–2 Calculations for Regression Coefficients

Observation	x	y	xy	x^2	y^2
1	1.1	7	7.7	1.21	49
2	1.4	8	11.2	1.96	64
3	1.4	10	14.0	1.96	100
4	2.0	10	20.0	4.00	100
5	0.9	7	6.3	0.81	49
6	1.6	10	16.0	2.56	100
7	2.0	11	22.0	4.00	121
8	1.7	11	18.7	2.89	121
9	1.2	9	10.8	1.44	81
10	0.8	6	4.8	0.64	36
	14.1	89	131.5	21.47	821 (used later)

$$b = \frac{10(131.5) - 14.1(89)}{10(21.47) - 14.1(14.1)} = \frac{60.1}{15.89} = 3.78$$

$$a = \frac{89 - 3.782(14.1)}{10} = 3.57$$

Thus, the equation is $y = 3.57 + 3.78x$. See Figure 11–11.

FIGURE 11–11 Graph of Regression Line

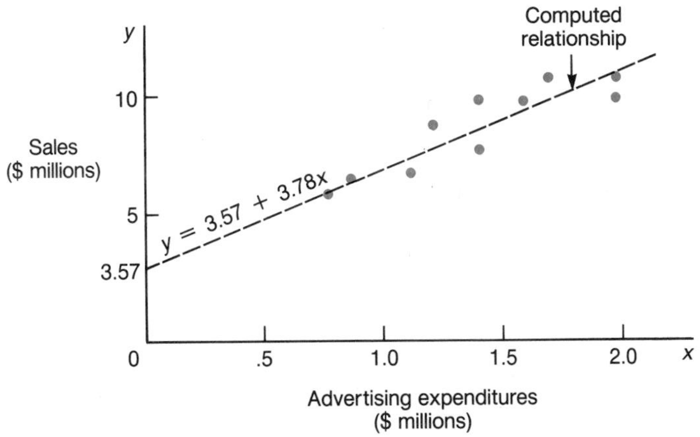

For the data shown in Table 11–2, the correlation is +.887. Note that the sign of the correlation is the same as the sign of the slope of the line. Correlation can range from −1.00 (perfect negative relationship) to +1.00 (perfect positive relationship). A positive correlation implies that the lowest values of x generally are paired with the lowest values of y and the highest x and y values are paired. Conversely, a negative correlation implies low x values are paired with high y values and vice versa. A correlation coefficient that is close to zero implies that points do not tend to line up but, instead, tend to scatter randomly.

The square of the correlation coefficient, r^2, can be used as a measure of goodness of fit; the closer the value is to 1.00, the better the fit. If $r^2 = 1.00$, the fit is perfect—all points fall on the line. For the advertising data, $r^2 = .787$. This tells us that about 79 percent of the sum of the squared deviations of y values around the mean of the y values can be eliminated by taking the relationship between x and y into account. We say that the independent variable "explains" 79 percent of the variation. Evidently, 21 percent of the variation cannot be explained by x. This is probably due to other factors that have not been included in our model. More shall be said on that matter very shortly.

There are a number of important questions that must be answered if a regression equation is to be used for forecasting. The major ones are:

1. Is the relationship significant (i.e., more than could be expected by chance)?
2. How accurate will a particular forecast probably be?

These and other questions depend in part on the extend to which the points scatter around the regression line. This is measured by the *standard error of estimate*, s_e, which is computed using the equation:

$$s_e = \sqrt{\frac{\Sigma y^2 - a\Sigma y - b\Sigma xy}{n - 2}} \qquad (11\text{–}9)$$

The $n - 2$ in the denominator reflects that two coefficients, a and b, were estimated. For the data in Table 11–2, we have:

$$s_e = \sqrt{\frac{821 - 3.57(89) - 3.78(131.5)}{10 - 2}} = .880$$

If the value of r^2 is less than, say .40, the computed relationship will not be strong enough to yield acceptable forecast accuracy. To test for the existence of relationship (i.e., that the true slope is nonzero), compute the ratio:

$$t_{test} = \frac{b}{s_b} \qquad (11\text{–}10)$$

where

b = slope of regression line

$$s_b = s_e\sqrt{\frac{1}{x^2 - [(x)^2/n]}}$$

Using the values computed in Table 11–2, and this value of s_e, we find:

$$s_b = .880\sqrt{\frac{1}{(21.47)^2 - [14.1(14.1)/10]}} = .880\sqrt{.629} = .698$$

$$t_{test} = \frac{3.78}{.698} = 5.42$$

TABLE 11-3 Selected Values of $t_{.025}$ for $n - 2$

n	t	n	t
10	2.31	17	2.13
11	2.26	18	2.12
12	2.23	19	2.11
13	2.20	20	2.10
14	2.18	21	2.09
15	2.16	22	2.09
16	2.15		

This value can be compared to the appropriate value from Table 11-3. For $n = 10$, that table value is 2.31. If the t_{test} value is greater than the table value, as it is in this case, it can be concluded that the relationship is significant (i.e., probably not due to chance alone). Thus, the computed equation can be used to make predictions.

The next question is: How accurate will a given prediction be? One approach to the answer is to use the regression equation to compute the *expected* value of the dependent variable for a selected, or *given*, value of x and then construct a 95 percent confidence interval around that expected value. That is:

$$y \pm t\, s_{\text{reg}} \tag{11-11}$$

where

$$y = a + bx$$

t = appropriate value from Table 11-3

$$s_{\text{reg}} = s_e \sqrt{1 + \frac{1}{n} + \frac{(x_g - \bar{x})^2}{\Sigma x^2 - [(\Sigma x)^2/n]}}$$

x_g = value of x being used in the regression equation to predict y.

Say $x = 1.3$. From Table 11-2, $\bar{x} = \dfrac{14.1}{10} = 1.41$. Then:

$$s_{\text{reg}} = .880 \sqrt{1 + \frac{1}{10} + \frac{(1.3 - 1.41)^2}{21.47 - [14.1(14.1)/10]}} = .880\sqrt{1.108} = .926$$

The significance of this last equation is that the variability of a forecast based on a simple linear regression model depends on the amount of scatter around the regression line (as reflected by s_e) and the extent to which the desired value of x varies from the mean of the x values. For the case where $x_g = 1.3$, a 95 percent confidence interval for the predicted value of y is:

$$y = a + bx = 3.57 + 3.78(1.3) = 8.48$$

$$\text{95 percent interval} = 8.48 \pm 2.31(.926) = 8.48 \pm 2.14 \text{ or } 6.34 \text{ to } 10.62$$

FIGURE 11–12 The Conditional Distributions of *y*'s Are Assumed to be Normal

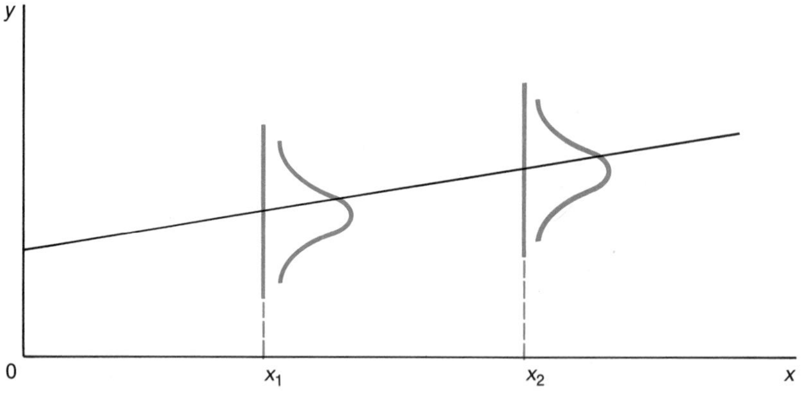

Thus, if advertising expenditure is \$1,300,000, expected sales would be \$8,480,000, and the marketing manager could place a 95 percent confidence interval around that amount that ranges from \$6,340,000 to \$10,620,000.

Regression Assumptions

There are a number of assumptions that underlie the use of linear regression. If all are not reasonably satisfied, using the regression equation as a forecasting tool may be inappropriate. Briefly, the major assumptions are:

1. For any given value of x, there is a distribution of possible y values that has a mean equal to the expected value (i.e., $y = a + bx$) and the distribution is normal. (See Figure 11–12.) These are called *conditional distributions*. This assumption usually is satisfied if the points cluster around the line.
2. The conditional distributions for all values of x have the same dispersion (i.e., the scatter of points around the line is the same for all sections of the line). This often can be judged visually. An example of a case that does not satisfy this assumption is presented in Figure 11–13. Uniform scatter is called *homoscedasticity*.
3. The requirement of uniform scatter also means that there should not be any patterns around the line (e.g., cycles, as illustrated in Figure 11–14). The existence of such a pattern implies that the model is incomplete. For example, squared and cubed terms may be needed to adequately describe the relationship (e.g., $y = 12 + x + 2.4x^2 - 1.3x^3$).
4. Values of y should not be correlated over time. If they are, it may be more appropriate to use a time series model. This can be checked by

FIGURE 11–13 The Scatter around the Line Is Not Uniform

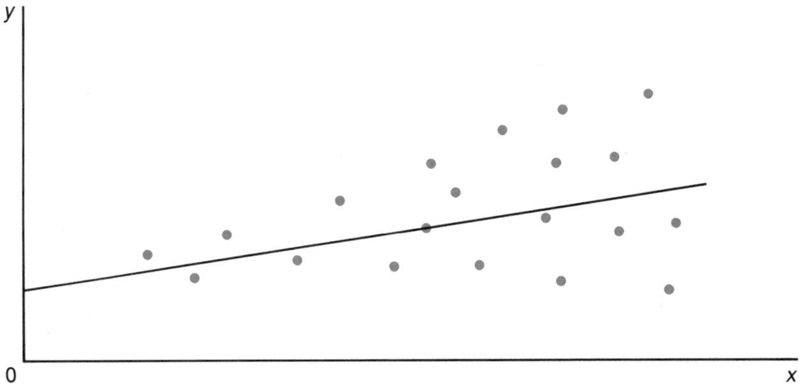

FIGURE 11–14 There Should Not Be Any Patterns around the Line

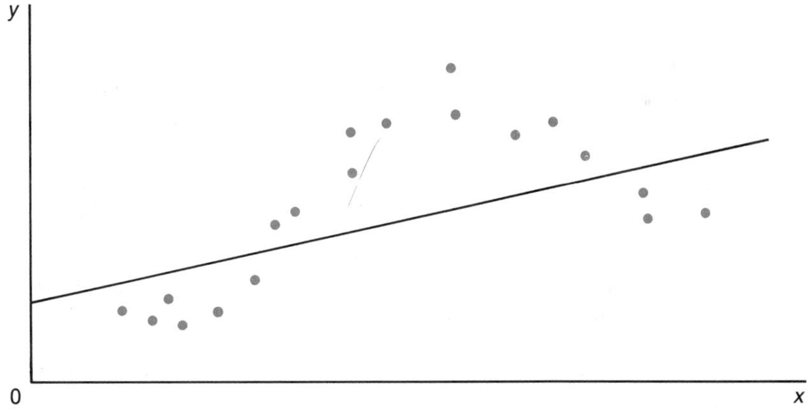

plotting *y* values in the order of observation (e.g., June sales, July sales, August sales).

5. It is permissible to select values of the independent variable and then observe the resulting values of the dependent variable. However, the reverse is not permissible; *y* is assumed to be a random variable conditional on the value of *x*.

TABLE 11–4 Expansion of Data Used in Simple Regression Section

Observation	Advertising Expenditure, x_1	Price per Unit, x_2	Sales, y
1	$1.1	$22	$ 7
2	1.4	22	8
3	1.4	19	10
4	2.0	21	10
5	0.9	23	7
6	1.6	20	10
7	2.0	18	11
8	1.7	19	11
9	1.2	22	9
10	0.8	22	6

Multiple Regression

In certain situations, an explanatory model with one predictor variable will not provide an acceptable level of accuracy for forecasts. For instance, in Table 11–3, advertising expenditures were used to predict sales. The resulting coefficient of determination was .787, which meant that the unexplained variation (i.e., the variation in sales that could not be explained by variations in advertising expenditure) was about 21 percent. Management may desire a smaller unexplained variation, thereby achieving greater accuracy in forecasts. An increased value of r^2 can be attained by incorporating other explanatory variables in the model. For example, one might suspect that *unit price* of a product would have some influence on sales: Sales usually are inversely related to price. One additional variable may provide the desired increase in r^2, such as unit price, or other variables may need to be investigated. In each case the question of adding more variables to the model is whether the added r^2 achieved is worth the increase in costs (of data collection, analysis, etc.). Thus, the simple regression model, $y = a + bx$, is replaced by the multiple regression model, say, with two explanatory variables:

$$y = a + b_1x_1 + b_2x_2 \tag{11–12}$$

where

b_i reflects the change in y for a one-unit change in x_i

Suppose an analyst collected price data for the preceding example just in case the simple linear regression model proved unsatisfactory. Those values are shown in Table 11–4, along with the original values.

A computer analysis of the data in Table 11–4 produced the following multiple regression equation:

$$y = 15.2 + 2.41x_1 - 0.465x_2$$

TABLE 11–5 Computer Printout for the Advertising/Price Data

VARIABLE	COEFFICIENT	STD DEV. OF COEF.	T-RATIO
X0	15.180	5.279	2.88
X1	2.412	0.839	2.88
X2	−0.465	0.209	−2.23

STD. DEV. OF Y AROUND REGRESSION LINE IS: S = 0.718

R-SQUARED = 87.5 PERCENT

THE REGRESSION EQUATION IS: Y = 15.2 + 2.41 X1 − 0.465 X2

In addition, r^2 for the data was .875, leaving only about 12 percent unexplained variation, compared to the original analysis which had $r^2 = .787$ and an unexplained variation of about 21 percent.

At this point, management must decide if the level of explained variation is acceptable. If it is not, an effort should be made to identify other possible predictor variables and to determine if they can improve the relationship. Now, it may turn out that although there are many other variables that have a logical relationship to sales of the product in question, none has a major influence on sales, so that inclusion of other variables may not improve the relationship. Then again, some of the other variables may be closely correlated with either advertising expenditures or with price, and for that reason they would add little or nothing in terms of reducing the unexplained variation. Furthermore, the cost of developing and using a model is often a function of the number of explaining variables being used: The greater the number of variables, the greater the cost. Consequently, a decision must be made about whether the cost to achieve a certain level of explained variation is worth the increased accuracy.

As you might guess, much more can be said about multiple regression. However, such a discussion is beyond the scope of this text. For those who are interested, there are many statistics textbooks that provide the necessary details. There are, however, a few points that can be mentioned to enrich the limited discussion here. Most solutions to multiple regression forecasting problems are obtained using a computer package such as SAS (Statistical Analysis System), BMDP (Biomedical Computer Programs, P Series), and SPSS (Statistical Package for the Social Sciences). Your computer may have one of these or another similar package that can be used to handle multiple regression problems. It will be instructive to consider a typical computer output in order to understand how such output is interpreted (see Table 11–5).

In addition to the regression equation, the output from a typical multiple regression computer run includes information on the strength of the relationship (as measured by R^2) and whether or not each of the explanatory variables contributes to the relationship.

In Table 11–5, three variables are listed. X0 is "a" in the equation $Y = a + b_1X_1 + b_2X_2$; it is the value of y when both X_1 and X_2 are equal to zero. The coefficients are the values a, b_1, and b_2 in the equation. The standard deviation of the coefficients indicates a measure of chance variability for each coefficient. A rule of thumb is to compute the t-ratio (which is the ratio of the coefficient to its standard deviation) for each variable and then compare that to 2.00: If the t-ratio is greater than $\pm$ 2, conclude that the variable is a valid explanatory variable. Note that the t-ratio for each variable is given in Table 11–5, and in each case, it is greater than $\pm$ 2. Hence, we can conclude that each is useful in predicting values of y. Had one of the t-ratios been less than $\pm$ 2, we would have concluded that it did not contribute information to explaining the relationship, and we would eliminate it from the regression analysis.

Table 11–5 also lists a value for R-squared. The value of R-squared indicates the percent of explained variation. The standard deviation of y around the regression line can be used to determine the probable accuracy of predictions obtained using the analysis.

ACCURACY AND CONTROL

Accuracy and control of forecasts is a vital aspect of forecasting. To begin with, the complex nature of most real-world variables makes it almost impossible to correctly predict future values of those variables on a regular basis. Consequently, it is essential to include an indication of the extent to which the forecast might deviate from the value of the variable that actually occurs, along with the forecast itself. This will provide the forecast user with a better perspective on how far off a forecast might be.

Moreover, because some techniques will provide more accuracy than others in a given situation, in choosing among different techniques, the decision maker needs a measure of accuracy that can be used as a basis for comparison.

Finally, some forecasting applications involve a series of forecasts (e.g., weekly revenues), whereas others involve a single forecast that will be used for a one-time decision (e.g., deciding on the size of a power plant). When periodic forecasts are made, it is important to monitor forecast errors in order to determine if the errors are within reasonable bounds. If they are not, it is necessary to take corrective action. This involves controlling the forecast.

Forecast Errors

Forecast error is the difference between the value that occurs and the value that was predicted for a given time period. Hence, Error = Actual − Forecast:

$$e_t = A_t - F_t \tag{11–13}$$

Positive errors result when the forecast is too *low* and negative errors result when the forecast is too *high*. For example, if actual demand for a week is 100 units, while forecasted demand was 90 units, the forecast was too low: the error is $100 - 90 = +10$.

There are a variety of possible reasons for forecast errors. Among the primary sources of forecast errors are the following:

1. The model may be inadequate due to (*a*) the omission of an important variable, (*b*) a change or shift in the variable that the model cannot deal with (e.g., sudden appearance of a trend or cycle), or (*c*) the appearance of a new variable (e.g., new competitor).
2. Irregular variations due to severe weather or other natural phenomena, temporary shortages or breakdowns, catastrophes, or similar events may occur.
3. The forecasting technique may be used incorrectly or the results may be misinterpreted.
4. There are random variations in the data. Randomness is the inherent variation that remains in the data after all causes of variation have been accounted for.

A forecast is generally deemed to perform adequately when the errors exhibit only random variations. Hence, the key to judging when to reexamine the validity of a particular forecasting technique is whether forecast errors are random. If they are not random, an investigation must be made to determine which of the other sources of error is present and to correct the problem.

Summarizing Forecast Accuracy

Evaluating and controlling forecast accuracy requires the use of one or more summary measures of forecast errors. Two measures commonly used for these purposes are the mean absolute deviation and the mean squared error.

The **mean absolute deviation (MAD)** measures the average forecast error over a number of periods, without regard to the sign of the error: For computation, all errors are treated as positive. The **mean squared error (MSE)** is the average squared error experienced over a number of periods. The following formulas are used in their computation:

$$\text{MAD} = \frac{\Sigma|e|}{n} = \frac{\Sigma|A - F|}{n} \tag{11–14}$$

$$\text{MSE} = \frac{\Sigma e^2}{n - 1} = \frac{\Sigma(A - F)^2}{n - 1} \tag{11–15}$$

The MSE is a variance, and the $n - 1$ in its denominator is used instead of n for essentially the same reason that $n - 1$ is used to compute a *sample* standard deviation.

The basic difference between the two summary measures of accuracy is that the MSE, by using the square of each error, tends to emphasize large errors more than the MAD measure does. The computation of each summary measure is illustrated in the following example.

■

EXAMPLE 6 Both MAD and MSE are relatively easy to compute:

Period	*A* Demand	*F* Forecast	*A* − *F* Error	|*A* − *F*|	$(A-F)^2$
1	45	—	—	—	—
2	50	48	+2	2	4
3	53	50	+3	3	9
4	52	55	−3	3	9
5	56	55	+1	1	1
6	58	62	−4	4	16
			−1	13	39

$$\text{MAD} = \frac{\Sigma|A-F|}{n} = \frac{13}{6} = 2.17 \qquad \text{MSE} = \frac{\Sigma(A-F)^2}{n-1} = \frac{39}{6-1} = 7.80$$

A manager can use either measure to compare the relative accuracies of alternative forecasts. For instance, suppose a manager must decide on which of three smoothing constants to use for exponential smoothing. The manager could use historical data to test each of the smoothing constants, and by using either MAD or MSE, select the one that yields the best accuracy. Suppose the manager focuses on MAD, with these results:

Alternative	MAD
#1	26.3
#2	18.2
#3	37.0

Because Alternative #2 has the best accuracy, the manager probably would decide to use that alternative rather than either of the others. Of course, the manager may decide that none of these alternatives provides an acceptable degree of accuracy. Subsequently, an attempt might be made to identify another alternative that would provide an acceptable level of accuracy.

FIGURE 11–15 Monitoring Forecast Errors

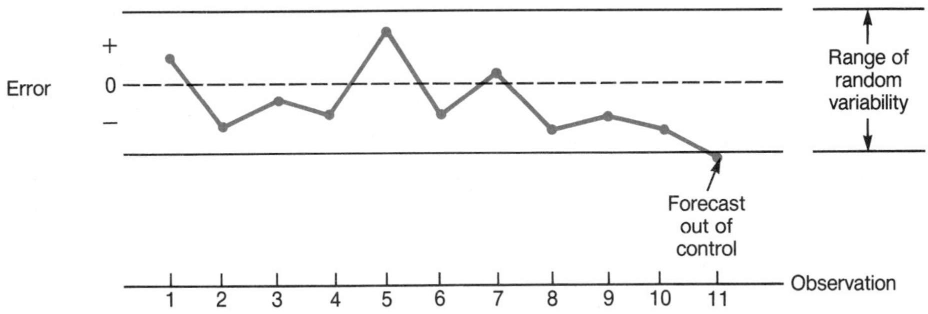

Monitoring and Controlling the Forecast

In order to control a forecast, it is necessary to monitor the forecast errors over a period of time. The purpose of such monitoring is to attempt to distinguish between random errors, which are inherent and cannot be eliminated, and nonrandom errors, which can be eliminated (e.g., by modifying a technique, improving data collection or analysis, or switching to another technique). Thus, monitoring the forecast errors is intended to answer the question: "Is it time to reexamine the validity of the forecasting technique being used?"

Two somewhat similar methods are commonly used to monitor forecast errors, one involving MAD and the other involving MSE. In both cases, upper and lower bounds or *limits* are determined, which serve as a standard against which forecast errors can be judged: They indicate a range of *random* variability. Thus, points falling within that range are suggestive of random variability, whereas points falling outside that range are suggestive of the presence of nonrandomness. This concept is illustrated in Figure 11–15.

Tracking signal A popular method for monitoring forecast errors is the **tracking signal**. This is the ratio of cumulative forecast error at any point in time to the corresponding MAD at that point in time. Thus, the formula for computing the tracking signal for a period is:

Tracking signal

$$\text{T.S.}_t = \frac{\Sigma(A - F)_t}{\text{MAD}_t} \qquad (11\text{–}16)$$

For example, using the data and calculations for Example 6, the tracking signal for Period 6 is $-1/21.7 = -.46$. Such a small value would be suggestive of random variation. In practice, values that range from ±4 to ±7 are used as action limits. A value of a tracking signal that is beyond the action limits would suggest the need for corrective action. Generally, a manager or analyst will set limits based on experience with the variable in question as well as on the relative costs of falsely concluding the errors are unacceptable when they are not.

It is a good idea to use a value for the MAD that is current because it will tend to reflect the latest behavior of errors. This can be accomplished by using a limited number of only the most recent errors (e.g., the last seven or so) in computing the MAD. Another alternative is to update the value of MAD with exponential smoothing using the formula:

$$MAD_t = MAD_{t-1} + \alpha(|e|_{t-1} - MAD_{t-1}) \tag{11-17}$$

With either approach, a decision must be made regarding the number of periods to include in the average. The greater the number of data points used to compute MAD, or the lower the value of alpha, the lower the response rate of the updated MAD, and vice versa. The choice of rate of response is largely a matter of experience with a particular series and costs of misjudging what is happening.

■

EXAMPLE 7 A tracking signal is used to monitor the forecast errors in this example with an exponentially smoothed MAD using $\alpha = .2$. An initial MAD is computed using the first five errors.

t Period	Error	Cumulative Error	$\|e_t\|$	Cumulative $\|e\|$	MAD_t	Tracking Signal
1	−5	−5	5	5		
2	7	+2	7	12		
3	2	+4	2	14		
4	4	+6	4	18		
5	−2	+4	2	20	4.00*	+1.00
6	0	+4	0		3.20†	+1.25
7	−3	+1	3		3.16	+0.32
8	6	+6	6		3.73	+1.61
9	−8	−2	8		3.38	−0.59
10	1	−1	1		2.90	−0.34

* Computed using $MAD = \frac{\Sigma|e|}{5}$ for first five periods.

† All values from this point on are computed using $MAD_t = MAD_{t-1} + \alpha(|e_t| - MAD_{t-1})$. For example, for Period 7, $MAD = 3.20 + .2(3 - 3.20) = 3.16$.

Because the tracking signal is reasonably small in every period (compared to limits of, say +4), it can be concluded that the forecast is performing adequately.

Control charts **Control charts** are another technique for monitoring forecast errors. In contrast to a tracking signal, which focuses on *cumulative* error, a

FIGURE 11–16 Conceptual Representation of a Control Chart

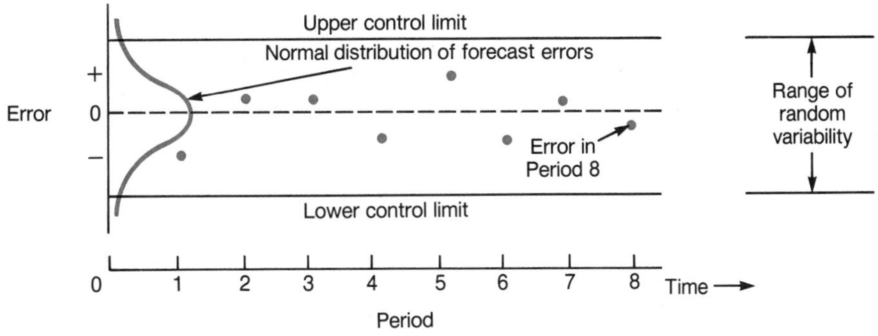

control chart focuses on *individual* errors. Like a tracking signal, the control chart has upper and lower limits, which define the range of acceptability of errors. In the case of the control chart, these limits serve as decision rules for each new error; a value beyond either limit is taken as probable evidence that the errors are no longer random. In effect, a statistical test of significance is being performed on each error. The test is based on the assumption that the distribution of random errors is normal with a mean of zero and a standard deviation equal to the square root of the MSE, as illustrated in Figure 11–16.

Control limits are set at a multiple of the square root of the MSE: common limits are plus and minus two times the square root of MSE. Occasionally, limits of plus and minus three standard deviations are used.[1] Limits of ± 2 standard deviations are more sensitive to nonrandom errors, but are also more apt to imply nonrandomness when only random variations are present. Conversely, limits of ± 3 standard deviations are less sensitive to nonrandom variations, but are also less likely to imply nonrandomness when only random variations are present. Based on a normal distribution of errors, approximately 95 percent of random errors would be expected to fall within ± 2 standard deviation control limits and about 99.7 percent within ± 3 standard deviation limits.

Thus, like the tracking signal, a control chart focuses attention on deviations that lie outside predetermined limits. However, the control chart approach also involves checking for possible patterns in the errors, even if all errors are within the control limits. Some of the most common patterns are illustrated in Figure 11–17. Checking is usually done by visual inspection, although statistical tests are sometimes used. Visual inspection is enhanced by plotting the errors on a control chart. If a pattern is discovered, this means that errors are *predictable* and, thus, nonrandom. The implication is that the forecast can be improved. For example, trend in the errors means the errors are getting progressively worse. In time series

[1] A standard deviation, $s = \sqrt{\text{MSE}}$.

FIGURE 11-17 Examples of Possible Patterns

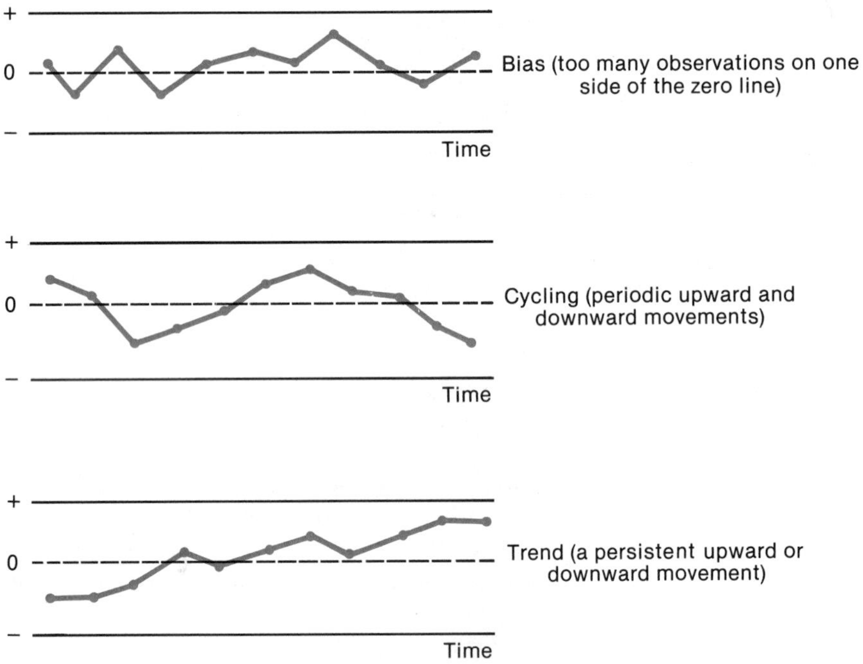

data, adding or increasing a trend response may be needed. In an explanatory model, recomputing the slope or other adjustment may be called for.

■

EXAMPLE 8 On the basis of historical data, the MSE of forecast errors has been calculated as 11.56. Determine 95 percent control limits and decide if the forecast errors listed reflect errors that are random.

Period	Actual	Forecast	Error
1	65	67	−2
2	72	71	+1
3	80	75	+5
4	82	79	+3
5	84	83	+1
6	85	87	−2
7	88	91	−3
8	94	95	−1
9	101	99	+2

FIGURE 11–18 The Errors Seem to Cycle

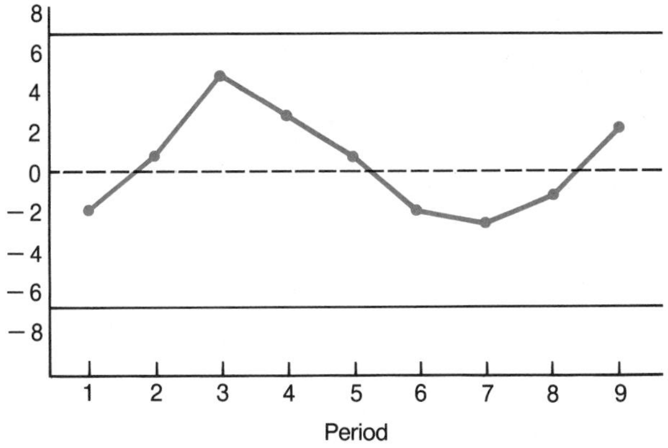

Solution

Ninety-five percent control limits require two standard deviations on either side of zero. Hence, with MSE = 11.56, we have:

$$\text{Upper control limit} = 0 + 2\sqrt{11.56} = 2(3.4) = +6.8$$
$$\text{Lower control limit} = 0 - 2\sqrt{11.56} = 2(3.4) = -6.8$$

Because all of the errors are within the range of ±6.8, it initially appears that the errors are random. However, a plot of the errors on a control chart reveals that there is a cyclical pattern in the errors; therefore, we must conclude that the errors are not random. (See Figure 11–18.)

Because historical errors are used to define randomness in control charts, whenever a chart is deemed to be out of control and the forecasting model is modified, a new set of upper and lower limits must be computed. These new limits must be based on data obtained using the modified model rather than any previous data. An example of using new data to obtain new limits is illustrated in Figure 11–19, in which the removal of a cyclical pattern results in narrower control limits.

Comment The control chart approach is generally superior to the tracking signal approach. A major weakness of the tracking signal approach is its use of cumulative errors: Individual errors can be obscured so that large positive and negative values can cancel out each other. Conversely, with control charts, every error is judged individually. Hence, it can be misleading to rely on a tracking signal approach to monitor errors. In fact, the historical roots of the tracking signal approach relate to a time when using computers in business was just

FIGURE 11–19 Removal of a *Pattern* Usually Results in Narrower Control Limits

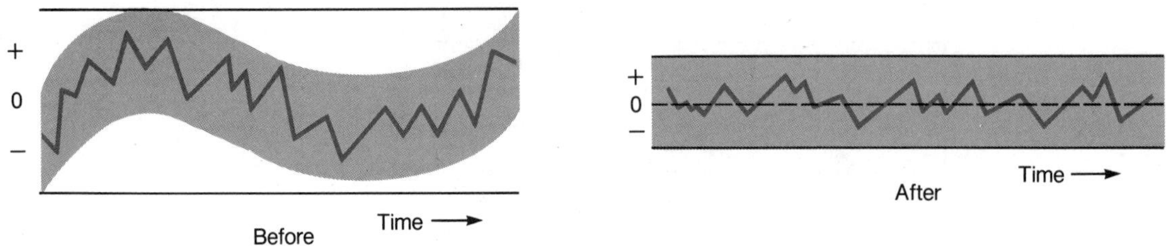

beginning. At that time, it was much more difficult to compute standard deviations than it was to compute average deviations; *for that reason*, the concept of a tracking signal was developed. Now, of course, modern computers and calculators can easily provide standard deviations. Nonetheless, the use of tracking signals has persisted, probably because users are unaware of its inferiority relative to a control chart approach.

Runs Tests

Plotting and visually inspecting forecast errors is a good way to detect nonrandomness. Another, more formal approach to the problem is to use **runs tests.** Generally speaking, a **run** is an uninterrupted string of like occurrences in time-ordered data. For example, if the first three forecast errors are positive and the next two negative (i.e., + + + – –), we could count the runs of pluses and minuses. In this case, there would be two runs: The first consists of the three pluses and the second consists of the two minuses.

Now the *order* of occurrence is the focal point. Thus, if the sequence had been + + – – + there would have been three runs, and if the sequence had been + – + – + there would have been five runs. In counting runs, it can be helpful to underline each run, such as $\underline{+\ +\ +}\ \ \underline{-\ -}\ \ \underline{+\ +}\ \ \underline{-\ -\ -\ -}$.

The concept of runs tests is that the number of runs in random data will have an expected value, which is a function of the number of observations in the data set and the type of runs being counted. We shall be concerned with two types of runs: pluses and minuses, and up/down movements in the data. If the data are random, then it is likely that the observed number of runs (i.e., the runs actually counted in the data) will not vary by more than a certain amount from the expected value. The test itself is based on a normal distribution. If the observed number of runs does not vary by more than two standard deviations from the expected number of runs, it can be reasonably concluded that the data are random. The two standard deviation limit provides a probability of about 4.5 percent of concluding a sequence is nonrandom when, in fact, it is random. The test involves a determina-

FIGURE 11–20 The Concept of a Runs Test

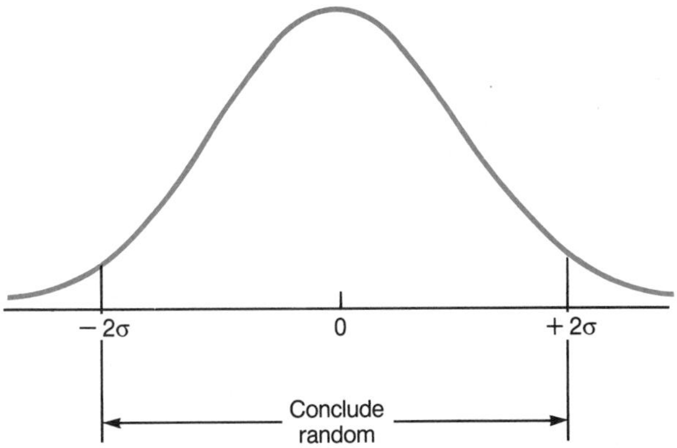

tion of the number of standard deviations that the observed number of runs differs from the expected:

$$z = \frac{\text{Observed number of runs} - \text{Expected number of runs}}{\text{Standard deviation of runs}} \qquad (11\text{–}18)$$

If this quantity is in the range $-2.00 \le z \le +2.00$, you can conclude that the sequence is random. This concept is illustrated in Figure 11–20.

There are a number of different runs tests. Each is a little different than the others in terms of the types of patterns it is sensitive to. We shall limit ourselves to two such tests, one that counts runs of pluses and minuses and the other that counts up and down movements in the data. The up/down test involves coding each observation's value with respect to the previous value. Consider the sequence +2, +4, +1, −2. Because +4 is greater than +2, the second value receives a U indicating the movement was up. Next, the +1 receives a D because it is down from the previous value, and the −2 also receives a D because it is down from +1. The first value does not receive any designation because it is not preceded by another value.

■

EXAMPLE 9 Given these forecast errors:

Observation	1	2	3	4	5	6	7	8	9
Error	+1	−4	−2	+2	−4	+5	−3	+4	+7

Code the data with respect to both +/− and up/down, and then determine the number of runs of each type.

Solution

	1	2	3	4	5	6	7	8	9	
Observation	1	2	3	4	5	6	7	8	9	
Error	+1	−4	−2	+2	−4	+5	−3	+4	+7	
Coding										
+/−	+	−	−	+	−	+	−	+	+	7 runs
U/D		D	U	U	D	U	D	U	U	6 runs

In order to evaluate the runs counted in a sequence, it is necessary to compute the expected number of runs and the standard deviation of number of runs. The general formulas for this are:

+/− runs $$E(r) = \frac{n}{2} + 1, \sigma = \sqrt{\frac{n-1}{4}} \tag{11-19}$$

Up/down runs $$E(r) = \frac{2n-1}{3}, \sigma = \sqrt{\frac{16n-29}{90}} \tag{11-20}$$

where

$E(r)$ = the expected number of runs

■

EXAMPLE 10 Determine if the data in the previous example are random using +/− and up/down runs tests.

Solution

$n = 9$

+/− test $$E(r) = \frac{9}{2} + 1 = 5.5, \sigma = \sqrt{\frac{9-1}{4}} = 1.41$$

$$z = \frac{\text{observed} - \text{expected}}{\sigma} = \frac{7-5.5}{1.41} = +1.06$$

Up/down test $$E(r) = \frac{2(9)-1}{3} = 5.7, \sigma = \sqrt{\frac{16(9)-29}{90}} = 1.13$$

$$z = \frac{6-5.7}{1.13} = +.27$$

Because the calculated values of z are both within the acceptable range of −2.00 to +2.00, we conclude that the series is random.

In general, we would conclude a series to be nonrandom if either or both z values were outside the −2.00 to +2.00 range.

If any zeros occur in +/− data, assign a + to the first one, a − to the second, and + to the third, and so on. Likewise, if *ties* occur in the up/down data (e.g., +3, +3), assign a U to the first, a D to the second, and so on, alternating U and D.

USING FORECAST INFORMATION

Organizations may regard the information provided by forecasts in either a *reactive* or a *proactive* manner. A reactive approach views forecast values as probable descriptions of future demand, and it attempts to respond to meet that demand (e.g., build up inventories, work overtime, retrain workers, scale down operations, lay off workers). Conversely, a proactive approach attempts to influence or create demand (e.g., through advertising, pricing policy, product and service innovation).

A reactive approach is usually associated with forecasts that use historical data, and a proactive approach is usually associated with explanatory models. Nonetheless, a manager who is confronted with an unfavorable forecast based on historical data may decide to adopt a proactive approach toward the future. However, in order to effectively do that, some sort of explanatory model must be used because time series models do not include a mechanism for incorporating explanatory variables.

Qualitative forecasts can sometimes be helpful. For example, a Delphi questionnaire can be designed to elicit ideas for the best way to *create* demand, or it can be designed to elicit ideas on how to *respond to* a probable future event.

SELECTING A FORECASTING APPROACH

Successful forecasting begins with careful thought about the choice of a forecasting approach. This section outlines the major considerations in making that choice.

The *importance of the forecast* is a prime consideration because it will give some indication of the resources that could be devoted to preparing the forecast and the degree of accuracy that is necessary. Essentially, the importance of the forecast is determined by the *use* to which the forecast will be put. Is the purpose of the forecast to obtain rough estimates, or will the forecast be used to develop very detailed plans? To what extent might profits and/or opportunity costs be affected? Is there a risk that plans based on forecasts will result in errors that are costly or difficult to overcome?

The *cost* of developing a forecast is an obvious factor, although the cost factor should be weighed against the potential benefits of a particular technique. For example, a relatively costly forecasting technique might be justifiable because of the importance of obtaining a good forecast.

Perhaps, the most obvious factor is the expected *accuracy* of a forecast. However, the person selecting a forecasting approach must strike a balance

TABLE 11-6 Comparison of Types of Forecasts

Factor	Type: Short Range	Intermediate Range	Long Range
Frequency	Often	Occasional	Infrequent
Techniques	Averaging Projection Regression Judgment	Projection Seasonal Regression Judgment	Regression Judgment
Degree of management involvement	Low	Moderate	High
Cost per forecast	Low	Moderate	Moderate to high
Level of aggregation	Item	Product family	Product family Total output

between cost and accuracy because the highest accuracy usually, but not always, is delivered by approaches that tend to cost the most.

The *planning horizon* is usually a consideration, for two reasons. One is that some techniques lend themselves more to long-term forecasts (e.g., trend analysis), whereas others perform best, or are limited to, short-term forecasts (e.g., averaging techniques). The other involves the time necessary to prepare a forecast: Some techniques require more time and effort than others. Consequently, if a forecast is needed almost immediately, certain techniques will be ruled out at the start because they cannot be developed during the required time frame.

The *resources* (computer software, data collection, and interpretation, and other expertise) that are required vary considerably among the different forecasting approaches, so it is important to match requirement with available resources.

A factor that is often overlooked is the *user* or *users*. Users are the ones who will make the forecast operational. It is important to consider the level of sophistication of the users and then to select an approach that corresponds to that level. The danger in selecting a technique that is beyond the level of the user's sophistication is that users may tend to mistrust the forecast and they may modify the forecast to suit their own needs or perceptions. Further, forecasts typically have certain assumptions that underlie their use. Highly sophisticated techniques tend to embody assumptions that are beyond the ability of users to appreciate them: Users either may fail to check to see that assumptions are met or they may not grasp the importance of certain assumptions. Because of such factors, they may employ a technique incorrectly and, subsequently, lose faith in the model after getting burned a few times. A good rule is to *choose the simplest technique that gives acceptable results*. It also is prudent to include users in the selection process, whenever possible, to increase their confidence about the approach. Finally, in cases in which it is decided that a certain technique is best, even though the technique is somewhat beyond the level of user sophistication, it is important that a quantitative analyst, who is familiar with the technique, present it to users

TABLE 11-7 Forecasting Approaches

Approaches	Brief Description
Qualitative	
Judgmental methods	
Consumer surveys	Questioning consumers on future plans
Sales force composites	Joint estimates obtained from salespeople
Executive opinion	Finance, marketing, and manufacturing managers join to prepare forecast
Delphi technique	Series of questionnaires answered anonymously by managers and staff; successive questionnaires are based on information obtained from previous surveys
Outside opinion	Consultants or other outside experts prepare the forecast
Quantitative	
Time series	
Naive	Next value in a series will equal the previous value
Moving averages	Forecast is based on an average of recent values
Exponential smoothing	Sophisticated form of averaging
Trend	Trend equation used to forecast
Associative models	
Simple regression	Values of one variable are used to predict values of another variable
Multiple regression	Two or more variables are used to predict values of another variable

so that it appears trustworthy. This analyst also can alert users to potential dangers of the technique and can explain how to spot troubles and what action should be taken if troubles arise.

Finally, if historical data are available, it can be exceedingly informative to *plot the data;* trend, seasonal, or cyclical patterns tend to be much more apparent when data are graphed.

Table 11-6 presents a comparison of forecast types according to frequency, degree of management involvement, and cost.

SUMMARY

Decision makers rely on forecasts to reduce uncertainty about the future. For this reason, forecasts play a vital role in planning.

Decision makers have a wide variety of forecasting models to choose from. These can be classified as qualitative, projection of historical patterns, and explanatory models. The qualitative models use judgment and experience; the historical projection models simply extend past experience, as reflected by movements of a series over time, into the future; and explanatory models incorporate one or more variables whose movements are related to movements of the variable of interest and, hence, serve as predictor variables. Table 11-7 provides a summary of the forecasting techniques discussed in the chapter.

Measuring forecast error and controlling errors are important aspects of forecasting because forecast errors provide feedback about how well a forecast is performing. The errors either may be random or they may be some combination of random and correctable variation. The purpose of controlling the forecast is to distinguish between these two types in order to know when to take corrective action.

Choosing a forecasting technique depends on the purpose of the forecast, the desired accuracy, the cost, previous experience, sophistication of users, and planning horizon.

GLOSSARY

Centered Moving Average A moving average with values positioned at the center of the data that each average is derived from.

Control Chart A statistical device used to decide if the magnitude of forecast errors is small enough to be consistent with random variation.

Cyclical Variations Semi-regular variations in time series data that occur at intervals that are longer than a year.

Delphi Technique Uses a series of anonymous questionnaires in an attempt to achieve a consensus forecast.

Explanatory Forecasting Model A model that uses predictor variables to "explain" values of a dependent variable.

Exponential Smoothing A weighted average technique used to smooth time series data.

MAD (Mean Absolute Deviation) The average magnitude of forecast error.

Moving Average Forecast A forecast based on the average of the most recent values (e.g., last 3, last 4) of a time series.

MSE (Mean Squared Error) The average of the squares of forecast errors (uses $n - 1$ instead of n in computing the average).

Naive Forecasts Forecasts based on the last value in a time series (e.g., last period's demand, the change between the last two periods, demand for the same season the last time around).

Random Variation No predictable pattern of variation.

Run A sequence of like observations in time series data.

Runs Test A statistical technique used to decide if the number of runs counted in a time series is within limits that would imply chance variation.

Seasonal Variation Variability in time series data that can be attributed to events related to weather, cultural, or other, regularly occurring, events.

Seasonal Relatives Show up at the lake every summer. Also, relative deviation from the average or trend.

Smoothing Constant (Alpha) Percentage of forecast error that is used to update the forecast in exponential smoothing.

Time Series A time-ordered sequence of observations.

Tracking Signal A technique for monitoring forecast error based on cumulative forecast error.

Trend A long-term movement in time series data, often linear, but not necessarily.

SOLVED PROBLEMS

Problem 1. For each of these data sets, plot the data, then suggest an appropriate forecasting technique:

Period	1	2	3	4	5	6	7	8	9	10	11
Set #1	64	63	65	69	68	72	76	73	76	79	79
Set #2	79	83	86	82	91	86	80	85	79	88	78

Solution

The plots are:

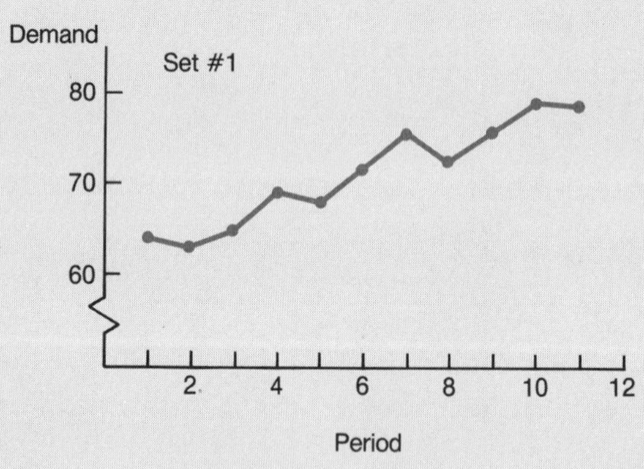

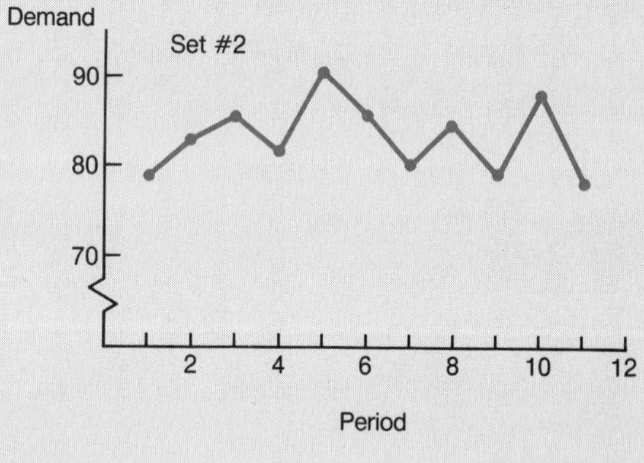

The plot of Set #1 indicates a trend is present. Appropriate techniques include a linear trend line and trend-adjusted exponential smoothing. The plot of Set #2 seems to show variation around an average. Appropriate techniques include a moving average and exponential smoothing.

Problem 2. Given this time series, make a forecast for Period 5 using each of these techniques:

a. Naive.

b. A three-period moving average.

c. Exponential smoothing with alpha equal to .20.

Period	1	2	3	4
Demand	15	13	17	19

Solution

a. The naive forecast for Period 5 is equal to the actual demand for Period 4. Hence, the naive forecast is 19.

b. A three-period moving average forecast is equal to the average of the three preceding demands. Hence, this forecast is:

$$MA_3 = \frac{13 + 17 + 19}{3} = 16.33$$

c. An exponential smoothing forecast incorporates historical data into a forecast. In order for this to occur, we begin with data prior to the point of the forecast. In this instance, we can begin by using the first actual demand as a forecast for Period 2, then continue through forecasts for Periods 3 and 4 before developing the forecast for Period 5. The exponential forecast is:

$$F_{\text{next}} = F_{\text{last}} + \alpha(\text{Last actual} - F_{\text{last}})$$

Using Period 1 demand of 15 as the forecast for Period 2, we have:

Period 3	15	+ .20(13 − 15)	= 14.6
Period 4	14.6	+ .20(17 − 14.6)	= 15.08
Period 5	15.08	+ .20(19 − 15.08)	= 15.86

Problem 3. Given this data on predicted and actual demand for 10 periods:

Period	Demand	Predicted
1	145	142
2	144	145
3	146	146
4	158	146
5	151	150
6	148	150
7	155	149
8	142	151
9	152	147
10	144	150

a. Determine the forecast error for each period.

b. Compute a tracking signal beginning in Period 5. Update MAD using Formula 11–17 with alpha = .3. Use limits of ±5.

c. Construct a control chart for the errors.

d. Perform +/− and U/D runs tests.

e. Based on the preceding analyses, what can you conclude about how well the forecast is performing?

Solution

a: and *b*. (See next page.)

Period	*D* Demand	*F* Forecast	*D − F* Error	Cum. Error	Absolute Error	Cum. Abs. Error	MAD	Tracking Signal $\left[\frac{\text{Cum. Error}}{\text{MAD}}\right]$
1	145	142	+3	+3	3	3		
2	144	145	−1	+2	1	4		
3	145	146	0	+2	0	4		
4	158	146	+12	+14	12	16		
5	151	150	+1	+15	1	17	17 ÷ 5 = 3.40	4.41
6	148	150	−2	+13	2		3.40 + .3(2 − 3.40) = 2.98	4.36
7	155	149	+6	+19	6		2.98 + .3(6 − 2.98) = 3.89	4.88
8	142	151	−9	+10	9		3.89 + .3(9 − 3.89) = 5.42	1.85
9	152	147	+5	+15	5		5.42 + .3(5 − 5.42) = 5.29	2.84
10	144	150	−6	+9	6		5.29 + .3(6 − 5.29) = 5.50	1.64

Note that all tracking signal values are within ±5 limits.

c. The sum of the squares of forecast errors is:

$$(+3^2) + (-1^2) + \cdots + (-6^2) = 427$$

The MSE is:

$$\frac{427}{10 - 1} = 47.44, \text{ and } \sqrt{\text{MSE}} = 6.89$$

Although no specific control limits were mentioned, ±2 are typical. Using those limits, we find the acceptable error range to be:

$$0 \pm 2(6.89) = 0 \pm 13.78$$

Plotting the errors on a control chart with these limits yields:

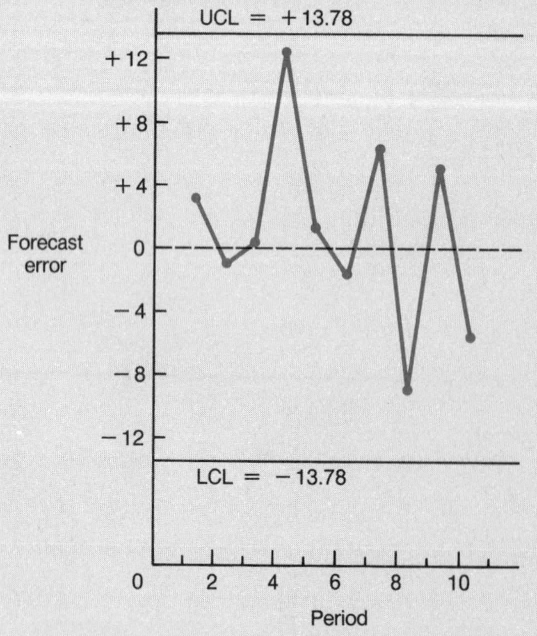

Although all of the errors are within the control limits, the plot reveals a possible downward trend that will bear watching.

d. First, code the data (+/− and U/D):

Period	1	2	3	4	5	6	7	8	9	10	
Error	+3	−1	0	+12	+1	−2	+6	−9	+5	−6	
+/−	+	−	*	+	+	−	+	−	+	−	8 runs
U/D		D	U	U	D	D	U	D	U	D	7 runs

* Assign a + to the first 0.

The computations for the runs tests are:

1. Expected number of runs ($n = 10$ observations):

$$+/-\qquad E(r) = \frac{n}{2} + 1 = \frac{10}{2} + 1 = 6$$

$$\text{U/D}\qquad E(r) = \frac{2n - 1}{3} = \frac{2(10) - 1}{3} = 6.33$$

2. Standard deviation of expected number of runs:

$$+/-\qquad \sigma = \sqrt{\frac{n - 1}{4}} = \sqrt{\frac{10 - 1}{4}} = 1.50$$

$$\text{U/D}\qquad \sigma = \sqrt{\frac{16n - 29}{90}} = \sqrt{\frac{16(10) - 29}{90}} = 1.21$$

3. The test statistic:

$$z = \frac{E(r) - \text{Number counted in data}}{\text{Standard deviation}}$$

$$+/-\qquad z = \frac{8 - 6}{1.50} = +1.33$$

$$\text{U/D}\qquad z = \frac{7 - 6.33}{1.21} = +.55$$

Usual limits for the test statistic are ±2. Both tests fall within these limits.

e. The forecast errors were evaluated using a tracking signal, a control chart, and runs tests. In all instances, the results fell within acceptable limits although a plot of errors revealed a possible downward trend. Consequently, we can conclude that the forecast is performing adequately; but with some reservation about the possible trend in errors. (In practice, *either* a tracking signal *or* a control chart would be used, but not both. Conversely, *both* runs tests should be employed on a given set of forecast errors.)

PROBLEMS

1. The number of bushels of apples sold at a roadside fruit stand over a 12-day period were as follows:

Day	Number Sold	Day	Number Sold
1	25	7	35
2	31	8	32
3	29	9	38
4	33	10	40
5	34	11	37
6	37	12	32

a. If a two-period moving average had been used to forecast sales, what would the daily forecasts have been starting with the forecast for Day 3?

b. If a four-period moving average had been used, determine what the forecasts would have been for each day, starting with Day 5.

c. Plot the original data and each set of forecasts on the same graph. Which forecast has the greater tendency to smooth? Which forecast has the better ability to respond quickly to changes?

d. What does use of the term *sales* instead of the term *demand* imply?

2. If exponential smoothing with $\alpha = .4$ had been used to forecast daily sales for apples in the preceding problem, determine what the daily forecasts would have been. Then, plot the original data, the exponential forecasts, and a set of naive forecasts on the same graph. Based on a *visual* comparison, can you say that the naive would have been more accurate or less accurate than the exponential smoothing method, or would they have been about the same?

3. A jeweler wants to forecast sales of one carat diamond rings. Sales data for the previous 15 weeks have been obtained:

Week	1	2	3	4	5	6	7	8	9	10	11	12	13	14	15
Sales	25	19	24	28	30	35	32	36	34	30	32	25	29	32	30

a. Develop a series of forecasts, beginning in Week 4, that would have resulted if a three-period moving average forecast had been used.

b. Using a starting forecast for Week 4 of 23 rings, develop the forecasts that would have resulted if an exponential smoothing model with $\alpha = .20$ had been used.

4. An electrical contractor's records during the last five weeks indicate the number of job requests:

Week	1	2	3	4	5
Requests	20	22	18	21	22

Predict the number of requests for Week 6 using each of these methods:

a. Naive.

b. A four-period moving average.

c. Exponential smoothing with $\alpha = .30$.

5. Sales of waterbeds at a specialty store during the past seven weeks were:

Week	1	2	3	4	5	6	7
Number sold	26	24	29	33	32	37	36

a. Use two different, but appropriate methods to predict the number of units that will be sold during Week 8. Explain why these methods are appropriate.

b. If actual sales during the next five weeks turn out to be 40, 45, 44, 50, and 53, which of the two methods would have provided a better forecast? Explain what probably occurred based on a comparison of the new data with the original data.

6. A gift shop in a tourist center is open on weekends (Friday, Saturday, and Sunday). The owner-manager hopes to improve scheduling of part-time employees by determining seasonal relatives for each of these days. Data on recent activity at the store (sales transactions per day) have been tabulated and are shown below. Develop seasonal relatives for the shop.

	Week					
	#1	#2	#3	#4	#5	#6
Friday	149	154	152	150	159	163
Saturday	250	255	260	268	273	276
Sunday	166	162	171	173	176	183

7. Use a naive trend approach to predict sales transactions for the gift shop in the previous problem for the following week.

8. An analyst must decide between two different forecasting techniques, a linear trend equation and the naive approach. The linear trend equation is $y_t = 124 + 2t$, and it was developed using data from periods 1 through 10. Based on data for Periods 11 through 20 as shown, which of these two methods has the greater accuracy? The data are for daily sales of trail bikes.

t	Units Sold	*t*	Units Sold
11	147	16	152
12	148	17	155
13	151	18	157
14	145	19	160
15	155	20	165

9. Terri Trendy, the manager of a fashionable restaurant that is open Wednesday through Saturday, has commented that the restaurant does about 30 percent of its business on Friday night, 35 percent on Saturday night, and 20 percent on Thursday night. What seasonal relatives would describe this situation?

10. A pharmacist has been monitoring sales of Quick, an over-the-counter pain reliever. Daily sales during the last 15 days were:

Day	1	2	3	4	5	6	7	8	9	10	11	12	13	14	15
Number sold	36	38	42	44	48	49	50	49	52	48	52	55	54	56	57

Without doing any calculations, which method would you suggest using to predict future sales, a linear trend equation, or trend-adjusted exponential smoothing? Why?

11. If you now learn that on some of the days in the previous problem the store ran out of the pain reliever in question, would that knowledge cause you any concern? Explain.

12. Assume that the data in Problem 10 refer to demand rather than sales. Using trend-adjusted smoothing with an initial forecast of 50 for Week 8 and an initial trend estimate of 2, and $\alpha_1 = \alpha_2 = .30$, develop forecasts for Days 9 through 16. What is the MSE for the eight forecasts for which there are actual data?

13. A quality control analyst has kept a record of the defective rate of a process he has been trying to improve during a period of about four weeks. The following data (percentages) were recorded:

	Week			
	1	2	3	4
Monday	10.2	9.4	8.4	7.8
Tuesday	8.2	7.3	7.0	6.5
Wednesday	7.2	6.8	6.3	5.0
Thursday	6.8	6.0	5.4	4.8
Friday	9.4	9.0	8.2	7.1

a. Determine daily relatives for the defective rate.

b. Compute a linear trend equation for the defective rate.

c. Use your answers from the preceding two parts to predict the defective rate for each day of Week 5.

14. A TV repair shop located near a large hospital provides rental TVs to hospital patients. According to shop invoices, the number of TVs rented out per day for the last 12 days were:

Day	Rentals	Day	Rentals
Sunday	14	Sunday	18
Monday	17	Monday	20
Tuesday	18	Tuesday	13
Wednesday	10	Wednesday	16
Thursday	15	Thursday	16
Friday	16		
Saturday	14		

Which approach, naive or exponential smoothing with alpha = .2, would have produced the greater accuracy had it been used for forecasting? Use a starting forecast of 14 for the first Monday for exponential smoothing.

15. An automobile dealer wants to forecast demand for a certain model car for the first week in March using the following data from recent sales:

January	Sales	February	Sales
Week 1	42	Week 1	32
2	38	2	28
3	38	3	26
4	34	4	25

a. Make the forecast on the basis of a linear trend equation.

b. Use trend-adjusted smoothing to make the forecast. Use an average of the first two weeks for the third week forecast to start, and an initial trend estimate of -3. Also, use $\alpha_1 = .2$ and $\alpha_2 = .3$.

16. A commuter airline operates five days a week. The general manager of the company wants to determine seasonal relatives for passenger traffic. She has compiled the following data:

	Week				
	#1	#2	#3	#4	#5
Monday	212	219	215	218	210
Tuesday	175	180	170	176	174
Wednesday	180	190	194	184	190
Thursday	190	186	188	194	190
Friday	231	225	246	232	240

Estimate daily relatives for passenger traffic.

17. A farming cooperative manager wants to estimate quarterly relatives for grain shipments, based on the data shown here (quantities are in metric tons):

	Quarter			
Year	**1**	**2**	**3**	**4**
1	200	250	210	340
2	210	252	212	360
3	215	260	220	358
4	225	272	233	372
5	232	284	240	381

Determine quarter relatives. (Hint: use a centered four-period moving average initially, then a centered, two-period moving average of the four-period moving average.)

18. The vice president of operations for a frozen food company estimates quarterly earnings using a model that has both a seasonal component and a trend component. The seasonal relatives used are: $Q_1 = 1.2$, $Q_2 = 1.0$, $Q_3 = .7$, and $Q_4 = 1.1$. The trend equation is: $y_t = \$144{,}000 + \$15{,}000t$, where $t = 0$ in the last quarter of last year. Predict earnings for each quarter of *next* year (not *this* year) using this information.

19. Determine an appropriate linear trend equation based on the historical data shown, and forecast the next two values of the series.

Month	Units Demanded
March	445
April	461
May	489
June	505
July	530
August	544

20. For each of the following data sets, decide if a linear regression model would be appropriate for predictive purposes. If you feel such a model is acceptable, determine the least squares equation for the line.

a.

x	y
7	34
9	60
3	30
3	65
6	60
6	35
12	70
15	70
16	75
2	50
14	65
4	55
5	30

b.

x	y
20	160
120	75
80	125
130	80
160	90
180	80
200	70
100	100
40	155
120	80
125	60

c.

x	y
72	88
90	80
65	75
35	110
55	95
64	90
82	70
40	98
65	80
85	110
40	60

21. A production manager has collected data on job times. She wants to learn if there is any relationship between the production time per piece and the number of pieces in a job. The following data were collected from shop records:

Job	Time (minutes per piece)	Number of Pieces
1	3.1 min.	15
2	1.1	75
3	2.2	45
4	1.6	62
5	2.5	40
6	1.5	70
7	4.2	12
8	1.8	50
9	1.0	90
10	3.4	18
11	2.8	32

a. Which variable is the independent variable in this situation?

b. Plot the data on a graph. Does it appear that a linear relationship exists?

c. Develop a regression equation for the relationship. What does the slope imply?

d. Over what range of values can the regression equation be used for predictive purposes? Explain.

22. The managing partner of a chain of dry cleaning stores wants to determine how the volume of suits the chain cleans in a week relates to the price charged. Records on prices and volume have been kept, and the data have been reproduced here:

Week	Price	Volume (thousands of suits)
1	$2.20	2.3
2	2.10	2.4
3	2.30	1.9
4	2.20	1.8
5	2.20	2.0
6	2.30	2.2
7	2.00	2.5
8	2.15	2.3
9	2.25	2.1
10	2.30	1.8

For what reasons would you not recommend using simple linear regression to predict the volume of suits based on the price charged per suit?

23. A financial planner wants to develop a linear regression model that he can use to evaluate clients' portfolios. He has collected relevant data on 20 clients, and he has used his microcomputer to analyze the data. The computer output included the following information:

$$y = 470.4 + 25.1x \quad \text{where} \quad x = \text{beginning portfolio value}$$
$$s_e = 4.30 \qquad y = \text{portfolio value 2 years later}$$
$$s_b = 6.21$$
$$r = +.924$$

a. Is the relationship significant? Explain.

b. How well does the regression equation "fit" the data? Explain.

c. If the planner determines that s_{reg} for a certain new client's portfolio of 98 is 3.70, develop a 95 percent confidence interval for the dependent variable and interpret your answer.

24. An appliance manufacturer wants to know if there is a relationship between percentage change in disposable personal income (DPI), which is reported quarterly by the government, and the percentage change in gross

orders during the following quarter for appliances sold by the manufacturer. An analyst has obtained data for the past 10 quarters:

Quarter	Percent Change, DPI	Percent Change in Orders (following quarter)
1	−2.3	−2.5
2	−1.5	1.0
3	2.8	7.4
4	0.5	2.6
5	4.6	8.5
6	−1.0	1.0
7	0.7	1.4
8	5.2	3.4
9	−2.5	−0.5
10	1.7	1.8

a. Compute the correlation coefficient for this data. Is the correlation strong enough, in your opinion, to base a predictive linear model on it? Explain.

b. Develop a linear regression equation for the data. Which is the dependent variable?

c. Test the relationship for significance. What can you conclude?

d. Develop a 95 percent confidence interval for percent change in orders when the percent change in DPI for the preceding quarter is 2.0.

25. A company gives a standardized test to all of its new recruits. At the end of the first year of employment, each of these people is given a performance rating. Test scores and performance ratings for a randomly selected sample of recruits yielded these values:

Person	Test Score	Performance Rating
1	78	6.7
2	112	9.4
3	95	9.1
4	82	8.8
5	104	9.5
6	84	8.6
7	89	9.0
8	110	9.8
9	93	9.1
10	95	9.2
11	86	7.7
12	90	9.2
13	107	9.6

a. Develop a linear regression equation for this data.

b. What percent of the performance rating variability can be explained by test scores?

c. Is the relationship between these two measures significant?

d. Determine a 95 percent confidence interval for the predicted performance rating an employee will receive, given the employee had a test score of 86.

26. Under what conditions might a manager choose to use a multiple regression model for forecasting rather than a simple regression model? What trade-offs might influence the decision one way or the other? Explain.

27. Analyst Anita Anton has gathered sales data on Fax machines in preparation for developing a multiple regression predictive model. The computer printout is reproduced below, where X1 = unit price of product, X2 = store location (miles from the home office), and X3 = unit price of main competitor.

VARIABLE	COEFFICIENT	STD. DEV OF COEF.	T-RATIO
X0	68.45	14.70	4.656
X1	−8.20	2.63	−3.118
X2	2.04	1.23	1.659
X3	−4.56	1.95	−2.338

a. Write the apparent regression equation.

b. Are all of the variables valid predictors? Explain.

28. Using his new computer, the manager of a small business has obtained the following printout for an explanatory forecasting model.

VARIABLE	COEFFICIENT	STD. DEV. OF COEF.
X1	217.92	44.42
X2	12.30	3.15
X2	20.14	13.45
X3	−4.45	1.02

R-SQUARED = 92.71 PERCENT

a. Write the apparent regression equation.

b. What percent of variation is unexplained?

c. Which variables are valid predictors? Explain.

d. Predict demand for the case where X1 = 5.4, X2 = .79, and X3 = 10.3.

29. Suppose you have collected the following data and must now do a multiple regression analysis.

Period	Demand	Advertising	Unit Price
1	140	23	34
2	163	25	33
3	152	25	33
4	158	25	32
5	168	28	31
6	174	28	31
7	170	28	30
8	181	30	30
9	177	30	31
10	183	30	31
11	189	30	30
12	189	32	29

a. Using a computer package, obtain the regression equation and other relevant statistics to predict demand on the basis of advertising and unit price. Are both price and advertising valid predictors? Explain.

b. Make Period an "explanatory" variable, and include it in the analysis: Rerun the problem using Period as the third independent variable. Which variables are valid predictors? Explain.

c. What percent of variation is unexplained?

d. What model would be best to predict demand?

30. The manager of a computer store has been using a certain forecasting model to predict sales of personal computers, and he has monitored forecast errors during the past 13 weeks, with these results:

Week	Error (rounded)	Week	Error (rounded)
1	+3	8	−2
2	+5	9	−3
3	−4	10	+1
4	+1	11	−6
5	+2	12	−4
6	0	13	−4
7	−3		

Is the forecasting model performing adequately in terms of errors? Explain why or why not, using a control chart and runs tests.

A small, private university has been using an exponential smoothing model to predict applications for certain programs for the past 12 semesters, with forecast errors as shown below:

Semester	1	2	3	4	5	6	7	8	9	10	11	12
Actual	201	205	190	210	214	187	180	184	195	190	182	173
Forecast	190	210	200	195	210	208	182	182	188	192	188	180

a. Use the first four periods to compute MAD, then update it with exponential smoothing using $\alpha = .40$.

b. Develop a tracking signal starting in the fifth period. If limits of ± 5 are used, is the forecast tracking properly?

c. Use runs tests to evaluate the 12 forecast errors. Are they random?

32. The credit manager of a bank has been forecasting mortgage applications using a moving average model. Results for the previous 16 weeks were:

Week	1	2	3	4	5	6	7	8	9	10	11	12	13	14	15	16
Error	+6	−2	−1	+5	−4	+7	−5	−5	+4	+3	+4	−2	−2	+5	−5	0

a. Compute MAD for the first six weeks, then update it using exponential smoothing with $\alpha = .5$.

b. Begin a tracking signal in Week 7. Using limits of ± 5, is the forecast working properly? Explain.

c. Construct a control chart using the first 10 weeks of the data. With limits of ± 2, use the control chart to evaluate the forecast for the remaining weeks.

33. A textbook publishing company has compiled data on total annual sales of its business texts for the preceding nine years:

Year	1	2	3	4	5	6	7	8	9
Sales (000)	40.2	44.5	48.0	52.3	55.8	57.1	62.4	69.0	73.7

a. Using an appropriate model, forecast textbook sales for each of the next five years.

b. Prepare a control chart for the forecast using the original data.

c. Suppose actual sales for the next five years turn out as follows:

Year	10	11	12	13	14
Sales (000)	77.2	82.1	87.8	90.6	98.9

Is the forecast performing adequately? Explain.

34. The owner of a catering company wants to use exponential smoothing to forecast demand for the catering service. These historical values reflect recent experience:

Week	1	2	3	4	5	6	7	8	9	10	11	12	13	14
Demand	8	10	10	12	9	7	8	7	9	10	13	12	11	10

a. Use the first half of the data to develop a model. Choose between a smoothing constant of .10 and one of .30.

b. Test your choice of a smoothing constant on the remainder of the data, using a control chart with two standard deviation limits.

c. Forecast the expected demand for Week 15.

d. If actual demand turns out to be 8, is the forecast in control? Forecast the demand for the following week. If actual demand turns out to be 13, is the forecast in control? Explain.

35. Use runs tests on the errors in the preceding problem. Can you conclude that the sequence is random? Explain.

36. The owner of a flower shop has been using a certain forecasting model to predict weekly demand for long-stemmed red roses. Forecast errors during the last 20 weeks were:

Week	Error	Week	Error
1	+3	11	+1
2	−4	12	−4
3	−1	13	0
4	−2	14	+3
5	+4	15	+2
6	+2	16	−4
7	−6	17	−3
8	+4	18	+5
9	+1	19	−1
10	+7	20	−2

Compute the MAD for the first five weeks, and begin a tracking signal in Week 6, updating MAD with alpha = .3. Is the forecast working properly? Explain. Use limits of ±4 for the tracking signal.

37. Evaluate the data in the previous problem using runs tests. What can you conclude?

38. The graph below reflects forecast errors for 20 days for a moving company. Use runs tests to evaluate the errors. What can you conclude?

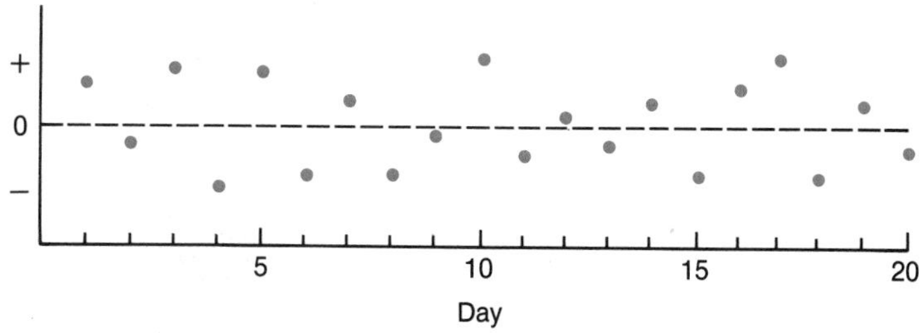

39. Forecast errors for the last 23 weeks for a motel are shown in the following graph. Use runs tests to determine if the errors are random.

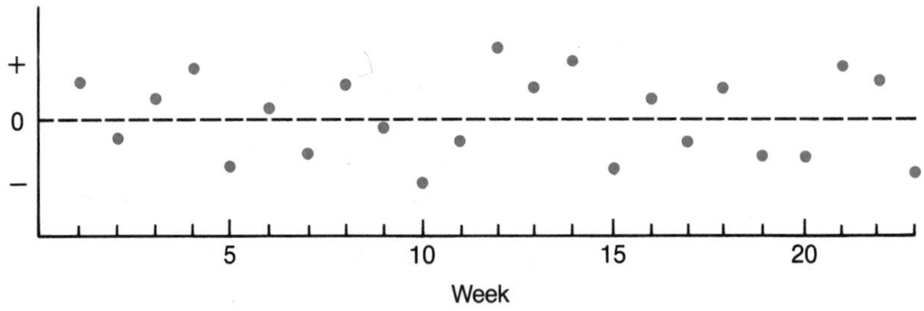

Chapter 11 Case

Gnomial Functions, Inc.

Gnomial Functions, Inc. (GFI) is a medium-sized consulting firm in San Francisco which specializes in developing various forecasts of product demand, sales, consumption, or other information for its clients. To a lesser degree, it has also developed ongoing models for internal use by client companies. When contacted by a potential client, GFI usually establishes a basic agreement with the firm's top management that sets out the general goals of the end product, primary contact personnel in both firms, and an outline of the project's overall scope (including any necessary time constraints for intermediate and final completion and a rough price estimate for the contract). Following this step, a team of GFI personnel is assembled to determine the most appropriate forecasting technique and to develop a more-detailed work program to be used as the basis for final contract negotiations. This team, which may vary in size according to the scope of the project and the client's needs, will perform the tasks established in the work program in conjunction with any personnel from the client firm who would be included in the team.

Recently, GFI has been contacted by a rapidly growing regional firm that manufactures, sells, and installs active solar water-heating equipment for commercial and residential applications. DynaSol Industries has seen its sales increase by more than 200 percent during the last 18 months and wishes to obtain a reliable estimate of its sales during the next 18 months. The company management expected that sales should increase substantially because of competing energy costs, tax-credit availability, and fundamental shifts in the attitudes of the regional population towards so-called exotic solar systems. They also faced increasing competition within the burgeoning market. This situation requires major strategic decisions concerning the company's future. At the time when GFI was contacted, DynaSol had almost reached the manufacturing capacity of its present facility and, if it were to continue growing with the market, would have to expand either by relocating to a new facility entirely or by developing a second manufacturing location. Each involved certain known costs and each had its own advantages and disadvantages. The major unknown, as far as management was concerned, was the growth of the overall market for this type of product and how large a share the company would be able to capture.

Table 1 contains the preliminary information available to GFI on DynaSol's past sales.

Discussion questions

1. Given the information available and your knowledge of different forecasting techniques, your role as a team member is to develop a recommendation for utilizing a specific forecasting technique in the subsequent study. The final

Source: James A. Fitzsimmons and Robert S. Sullivan, *Service Operations Management* (New York: McGraw-Hill, 1982).

TABLE 1

Month	DynaSol Industries Sales (units)	Sales ($000)	Regional Market Sales (units)	Sales ($000)
September	24	$ 44.736	223	$ 396.048
October	28	52.192	228	404.928
November	31	59.517	230	408.480
December	32	61.437	231	422.564
January	30	57.998	229	418.905
February	35	67.197	235	429.881
March	39	78.621	240	439.027
April	40	80.637	265	484.759
May	43	86.684	281	529.449
June	47	94.748	298	561.479
July	51	110.009	314	680.332
August	54	116.480	354	747.596
September	59	127.265	389	809.095
October	62	137.748	421	931.401
November	67	148.857	466	1,001.356
December	69	153.300	501	1,057.320
January	74	161.121	529	1,057.320
February	79	172.007	573	1,145.264

contract negotiations are pending, so it is essential that you take into account the advantages and disadvantages of your preferred technique as they would apply to the problem at hand and point out any additional information you would like to have.

2. Assume that you are a member of DynaSol's small marketing department and the contract negotiations with GFI have fallen through irrevocably. The company's top management has decided to use your expertise to develop a forecast for the next six months (and perhaps for the six-month period following that one as well) because it must have some information on which to base a decision to expand its operations. Develop such a forecast and note, for the benefit of top management, any reservations or qualifications you feel are vital to its understanding and use of the information.

Chapter 12

Inventory Models I
Independent Demand

Chapter Outline

Learning Objectives

After completing this supplement, you should be able to:

1. List and briefly explain the major reasons that organizations hold inventories.
2. List and briefly describe the information requirements of inventory management.
3. State the objectives of inventory management.
4. Describe the A-B-C approach to inventory management.
5. Use appropriate formulas to compute order quantities.
6. Use appropriate formulas to determine when to reorder, the necessary amount of safety stock to hold, service levels, and expected amounts of shortages.

INTRODUCTION

Inventories are stocks of goods held for expected future use or for potential future use. Most business organizations carry some forms of inventory. Depending on the nature of the organization's business, these might include raw materials, purchased parts, work-in-process, finished goods, supplies, and spare parts. Obviously, the kinds of items carried in inventory by, say, a manufacturing firm would differ from those carried by a supermarket, and both would differ from the kinds of items carried by a hospital. Nonetheless, the reasons for carrying inventories, and the way that they are managed, are similar regardless of the specific items. Consequently, the discussion presented in this chapter pertains to inventory management in all types of business organizations.

The key questions to be answered in inventory management are the following:

1. How much to order?
2. When to order?
3. How much control is appropriate?

This chapter is designed to show how these questions can be answered.

The chapter begins with a brief discussion of the functions of inventory followed by a discussion of the information requirements of inventory management. The remainder of the chapter is devoted to a description of the various models that are available to managers for effective inventory management.

The models described in this chapter are best suited for inventory items that have **independent demand.** In general, independent demand items are the end items (final products) rather than components of end items. Examples include items that are sold in supermarkets, department stores, appliance stores, automobile dealerships, hardware stores, drugstores, and so on. **Dependent demand** occurs in items that are assembled from multiple components; demand for the various components is *derived* from the number of finished items desired. For instance, if the assembled item is an automobile, and each one has four tires, then an order for 100 automobiles will require 400 tires. Thus, the demand for tires is derived from the demand for automobiles. Appropriate models for dependent demand situations are described in the next chapter.

FUNCTIONS OF INVENTORIES

Organizations hold inventories for a variety of reasons. Among the most important reasons are the following:

1. To meet anticipated demand.
2. To be able to buy or produce in economic lot sizes.
3. To separate stages of operations.

4. To guard against stockouts.
5. To maintain flexibility in scheduling.
6. To display items in order to accommodate customer selection.
7. To allow for goods in transit (pipeline).

A brief discussion of these functions will be helpful.

1. *To meet anticipated demand* When standard products are involved, organizations keep inventories in order to respond quickly to customer demand. For instance, retail customers expect to buy items "off the shelf." Organizations may experience fairly steady demand for products or seasonal variations, and in response to the latter, they periodically plan for a buildup of inventory to meet seasonal demands.

2. *To be able to buy or produce in "economic" lot sizes* Organizations typically buy more than is currently needed because there are usually certain economies involved, one of which may be quantity discounts.

3. *To decouple (separate) various stages of operations* Unexpected varations in supply or demand rates, equipment breakdowns, and human error can wreak havoc with smooth and orderly operations, unless a certain amount of "buffer" stock is maintained between stages. Thus, keeping a stock of finished goods will enable a factory to produce at a constant rate even though demand tends to vary because the fluctuations can be absorbed by inventory. Similarly, keeping a stock of raw materials will enable a factory to continue operating, even though a delivery from a supplier is delayed, say, by inclement weather; and inventories between successive steps in the manufacturing process would enable production to continue for a while despite an equipment failure. Many manufacturing firms find it more economical to maintain a constant work force and steady rate of output than to permit output and employment to vary. They accomplish this by using inventories to absorb much of the fluctuations. Similarly, retail stores, hospitals, and other businesses use inventories to absorb variations in supply and demand.

4. *To guard agains stockouts* In many instances, demand rates and delivery times are subject to variability. Higher than average demand rates, and/or longer than usual delivery times can lead to **stockouts** (shortages) of goods, unless additional stock is carried to offset these possibilities.

5. *To maintain flexibility in scheduling* Costs and complexities related to scheduling personnel and equipment sometimes make it desirable to produce at times and in quantities that do not directly correspond to current demand. The ability to produce goods for inventory instead of directly for customers' orders gives managers greater flexibility in scheduling.

6. *To display items* Most retail establishments benefit from displaying their goods because this allows customers to examine and compare the items. This is true for supermarkets, appliance stores, department stores, and many other types

of retail outlets. Manufacturers may also have showrooms where customers and potential customers can examine products.

7. *To allow for pipeline goods* After goods are produced, they are usually stored at least temporarily before being loaded onto trucks or trains for shipment to distributors, stores, and so on. These goods in transit are one form of inventory.

INFORMATION REQUIREMENTS

Successful inventory management is predicated on accurate information about demand, lead times needed to replenish inventories, the costs associated with ordering and holding inventory, and quantities of inventory on hand.

Demand

Inventory decisions rely heavily on demand forecasts. Required information includes expected demand over a planning horizon (often a year), whether demand is steady or variable, and if it is variable, whether the variation is random or whether time-varying components (e.g., seasonal) are present. The models presented in this chapter assume either a steady demand or one that can be described by a probability distribution. The time-varying case is discussed in the next chapter.

Lead Time

As in the case of demand, it is necessary to have information on the length of time it will take to order and receive a quantity of inventory, whether that time is reasonably constant or tends to vary, and if it does vary, its distribution.

Lead time includes the time necessary to decide how much should be ordered, the time to prepare an invoice, the time to send mail or telephone a supplier, the supplier's time to package and ship the order, delivery time, the time to unload and inspect the order for quality and quantity, and the time it takes to otherwise prepare the items for use.

Inventory Costs

Generally, four costs are associated with inventories:

1. Holding.
2. Replenishment.
3. Purchase.
4. Shortage.

Holding cost, or **carrying cost,** involves the cost of maintaining an inventory, which includes storage costs, the opportunity cost of the money invested in inventory, obsolescence, spoilage, deterioration, pilferage, and in some locales, taxes.

Typically, the largest part of the holding cost is composed of opportunity costs. Theoretically, opportunity cost is the return on investment that could be earned if the money were not invested in inventory. In practical terms, that amount may be subject to frequent change. Rather than attempt to continually revise that amount, an approximate amount is decided on, and it is updated infrequently, unless conditions change dramatically.

Holding costs often are expressed in terms of cost per unit on an annual basis. Some organizations prefer to specify a fixed dollar amount (e.g., $2 per unit), whereas others prefer to specify holding costs relative to unit price (e.g., 30 percent of unit cost). In either case, it is important to include in the holding costs only those elements that are *avoidable* (i.e., those costs that vary with the amount of inventory that is actually carried). Thus, warehouse space costs that are charged on the basis of square footage of floor space actually used would truly reflect a part of the holding cost, whereas warehouse cost charged without taking space into account should not be used for purposes of assessing holding costs.

Replenishment, or **ordering costs,** relates to the *transaction cost* required to replenish an inventory. If the inventory is *ordered* either internally or externally, ordering costs include the paperwork necessary for ordering and receiving, some part of the salaries of those in the purchasing department, telephone and fax charges, postage costs, and receiving and inspection (for quality and quantity) costs. Again, only avoidable costs should be included (i.e., those costs that depend on the *frequency* of restocking). In general, replenishment costs are independent of the quantity ordered. Although that might not be strictly true, most of the components are, in fact, independent of order size. Moreover, the assumption of a fixed stocking cost is not a major one.

From a producer's standpoint, replenishment costs relate to *setup* of an operation for production. Typical costs include cleaning, adjusting or attaching special tools to equipment, or the positioning of special equipment. Although machines may require some resetting and adjustment over the course of large runs, these costs can be treated as independent of the size of a production run.

Purchase price is the amount a buyer must pay for inventory items. In some instances, purchasing in large quantities can result in *quantity discounts.*

Shortage costs may reflect the cost of lost sales as a result of customers buying from other sources because a supplier is out of stock or there is a cost for backordering (e.g., rush orders, interrupted production, rescheduling).

Many of these costs are not readily obtainable from existing accounting records. In particular, holding and shortage costs generally are rough estimates. In the case of holding costs, it was mentioned previously that opportunity costs may change frequently, perhaps daily, and it would be exceedingly difficult to continually revise holding costs to reflect this. In addition, it can be quite difficult to make an accurate determination of the amount of handling and storage costs that should be assigned to each different group of items in inventory. Similarly, shortage costs often are difficult to assess with a high degree of accuracy. For example, although it is a relatively simple matter to determine the lost *profit* on a sale due to a stockout, it is far more complex to measure the effects this will have on goodwill and customer dissatisfaction, and whether this dissatisfaction will cause the customer to switch to another supplier either temporarily or permanently. Compounding the problem is the fact that some customers may tend to buy *other* items, so a shortage of one type of good (e.g., daily newspaper in a drugstore) may spill over into lost sales of other items (e.g., candy, film, aspirin, toothpaste, etc.) even though these items are available.

It is important, then, to recognize that holding and shortage costs are estimates, perhaps *rough* estimates, of actual costs. consequently, inventory models that involve these costs tend to yield *approximate* order sizes and restocking points. Also, it will be beneficial to examine the *sensitivity* of the various models to errors in cost estimates.

Quantity on Hand

In order to make a decision on when and how much to order, it is essential to know how much is currently in stock. Unlike information on demand rates, lead times, and costs, which may only need to be updated infrequently, information on quantity of inventory on hand must be updated regularly. This can take the form of either a *perpetual* system, or a *periodic* system.

Under a perpetual system, records are updated *continuously* (i.e., each time one or more units are removed from inventory). This involves counting, or otherwise measuring, the amount being removed or added and adjusting inventory records accordingly. Many drugstores and supermarkets use laser scanning of Universal Product Codes (UPC), which are a series of wide and narrow lines on individual items, to update records. Similarly, many discount and other department stores use another form of scanning device, which "reads" product tags and automatically updates inventory records.

Periodic systems require periodic physical counts of the amount of inventory on hand, at which time records are updated. The growth in the use of scanning devices has caused a decline in the use of the periodic approach. Nonetheless, for a variety of reasons, periodic systems remain an important way for many organizations to review their existing inventories. For instance, small grocery stores, drugstores, and other small businesses tend not to have scanning devices, so they must rely on actual inspection and counts. Manufacturing firms generally do not have methods of automatically updating their systems, although many monitor items as they are withdrawn from storage. Note, too, that even with automatic updating, firms must periodically *validate* records using physical inspection because theft, obsolescence, or deterioration can reduce the amount of usable inventory. In addition, physical inspection is required for accounting purposes, and commercial banks conduct their own inventory inspections for the purpose of analyzing requests for loans.

OBJECTIVES OF INVENTORY MANAGEMENT

In general, the objective of inventory management is to minimize the total cost of carrying, ordering, and purchasing inventories, and shortage costs. More often than not, these costs are computed for one year. Thus, the goal is to minimize total annual cost, where:

$$\begin{array}{lllllllll} \text{Total} & & \text{Annual} & & \text{Annual} & & \text{Annual} & & \text{Annual} \\ \text{annual} & = & \text{holding} & + & \text{replenishment} & + & \text{purchase} & + & \text{shortage} \\ \text{cost} & & \text{cost} & & \text{cost} & & \text{cost} & & \text{cost} \end{array} \qquad (12\text{–}1)$$

As it turns out, not all of these costs pertain to every situation. In fact, as a general rule, usually only two or three of these costs are involved. For example, if quantity discounts are not a factor, purchase price is independent of order size, and order size decisions need not involve unit price. Likewise, shortages may be avoidable in certain cases, making it unnecessary to include that component in the decision. At other times, management will opt for a specified *customer service level,* thereby avoiding the issue of directly including the shortage cost in an analysis.

THE A-B-C APPROACH

In designing inventory control systems, it is important to recognize that all inventory items do not have the same importance. Items can differ in terms of holding costs, shortage costs, price, annual volume, the need for security, and so on. Thus, in a department store, for example, small but expensive items such as cameras generate more profit and carry a higher loss due to theft than, say, children's socks. Consequently, some items should get more control than others.

The **A-B-C approach** provides a rational way of allocating control dollars. It involves classifying inventory items according to one or several measures of importance, then allocating control efforts and dollars on that basis.

The letters A, B, and C refer to different classes of items. A items are the most important, B items are moderately important, and C items are least important. Quite often, items are classified on the basis of annual dollar value (i.e., Unit price × Annual volume).

Figure 12–1 illustrates a fairly typical condition that exists in most inventories: A small *number* of items account for a large portion of the *dollar value* of the inventory. These are usually classified as A items. At the other end of the scale, there are usually a large number of items that together represent only a small fraction of the dollar value of the inventory. These are the C items. The remaining

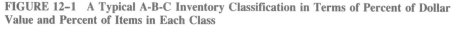

FIGURE 12–1 A Typical A-B-C Inventory Classification in Terms of Percent of Dollar Value and Percent of Items in Each Class

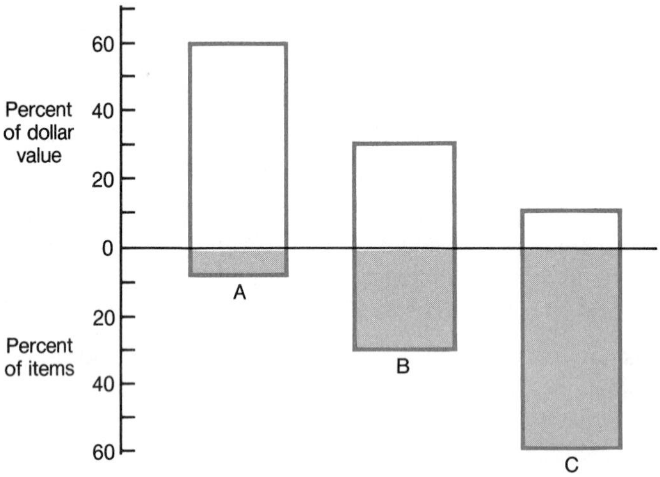

items, which account for roughly 30 to 40 percent of both the number of items and the dollar value of the inventory, are the B items.

A further illustration of A-B-C classification using dollar values is given in Table 12–1. For each item, the annual dollar value is computed by multiplying the unit price by the annual volume.

It is useful to note that there are both high and low volume items in every category. Thus, a high-volume low price item can be an A as can a high price, low-volume item. Conversely, even with a high volume, an inexpensive item such as *t* in Table 12–1, with a price of 1 cent per unit, will be placed in the C category.

It should be noted that although dollar value is commonly used in classifying items, in effect, dollar value is a surrogate for inventory costs. That is, the goal of classification is to direct control efforts to where they will have the most impact on inventory costs and profit potential. Because holding costs often are stated as a percentage of unit price, classification on the basis of dollar values is probably quite satisfactory from the standpoint of holding costs. Similarly, profit potential and dollar volume may be closely correlated. However, shortage costs, especially on items stocked for the buyer's use (e.g., spare parts), may not correspond to dollar values. Consequently, it usually is necessary for management to review the items assigned to each category and, perhaps, shift certain "critical" items from a B or C classification into the A category, even though some may be low-volume, inexpensive items. Typical examples include parts that are vital for a production operation, lifesaving equipment, and spare parts for critical machines.

These decisions are not necessarily obvious. Among the factors that might be taken into account are length of lead time (short lead time would decrease the

TABLE 12–1 An Illustration of A-B-C Classification Based on Dollar Value

Item	Annual Volume	×	Unit Price	=	Annual Dollar Value	Category
a	28,000		$ 6.00		$168,000	A
b	100		1,500.00		150,000	A
c	14,000		3.00		42,000	B
d	8,000		5.00		40,000	B
e	30,000		1.00		30,000	B
f	400		60.00		24,000	B
g	2,000		4.50		9,000	C
h	4,000		2.20		8,800	C
i	6,000		1.20		7,200	C
j	18,000		.30		5,400	C
k	40,000		.10		4,000	C
l	600		4.00		2,400	C
m	700		2.00		1,400	C
n	1,000		.70		700	C
o	800		.50		400	C
p	1,800		.20		360	C
q	2,000		.15		300	C
r	1,000		.20		200	C
s	70		2.00		140	C
t	13,000		.01		130	C

need to place some items in the A category), the possibility of A-C pairings in customer orders (an important customer typically may order both A and C items, and a shortage of a C item might then receive more attention than without the pairing), and the estimated shortage cost.

It should be noted that the A-B-C scheme is not limited to three categories, although three categories seem to be the minimum. Because the classes are intended to reflect different degrees of control, the number of classes used should reflect the ability and intention of management to differentiate control efforts.

Some organizations use a two-tiered approach to A-B-C classification; they subdivide each category into fast- and slow-moving items. The implication is that the analysis of items can differ depending on rate of turnover. For example, demand for fast-moving items can often be modeled by a normal distribution, whereas demand for slow-moving items might be more appropriately modeled by a Poisson, or an empirical, distribution.

Once items have been assigned to the various categories of control, the manager must designate methods of control for the items with each group. Although some managers tend to control all items within a given category in the same way, others prefer to differentiate control efforts even further.

Regardless of whether or not a two-tiered approach is used, a manager must identify models for replenishment and must determine safety stock. Very often an economic order quantity model is used for items in the B category as well as for some items in the bottom of the A category and items at the top of the C category. In the case of the A items, there should be more frequent reviews of reorder points and evaluation of the effectiveness of a given reordering policy than with B items. The remaining A items would receive even more careful and individualized attention (e.g., more frequent inventory checks and evaluations). The remaining items in the C category would tend to have very loose control. Infrequent large orders with large safety stocks may be used to allow minimal attention to those items. One common approach is the use of a two-bin system for triggering reorders. A supply of a C item may be physically or conceptually placed into two containers or "bins," one of which contains an amount equal to expected usage up to the reorder point. When that stock is exhausted, the second bin is opened. It contains enough stock to meet expected demand during lead time, plus safety stock. In addition, at the top of this second bin there can be an order card, which will be submitted to a designated person to request additional stock. When the order arrives, any remaining stock may be removed or added to the supply, which consists of two bins' worth of stock, and the process begins anew.

ECONOMIC ORDER QUANTITY MODELS

Economic order quantity (EOQ) models answer the question of how much to order. In this section three EOQ models are described:

1. Economic order size.
2. Economic run size.
3. Economic order size with quantity discounts.

The discussion begins with the economic order size model.

Economic Order Size

The economic order size model, introduced in 1915, is now one of the most widely used decision models for independent demand ordering. From a learning standpoint, this model is particularly instructive because it is simple, it illustrates the trade-offs involved in inventory decisions, and it demonstrates the robustness of inventory models.

Assumptions of the model are:

1. Annual demand is known, either through a forecast or because of customer orders.
2. Items will be withdrawn from inventory at a uniform rate.
3. A constant order size, Q, will be used.
4. Unit cost is independent of order size. Hence, quantity discounts are not a consideration.
5. Orders will be received in their entirety rather than piecemeal.

FIGURE 12–2 Amount of Inventory on Hand under EOQ Assumptions

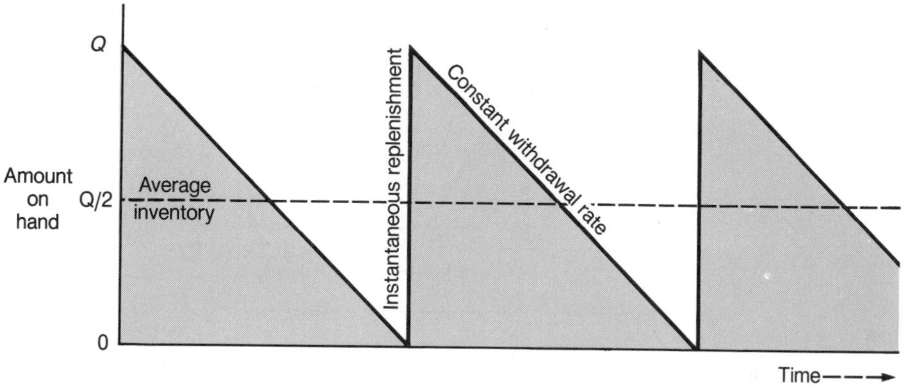

6. Replenishment lead times are known and constant.
7. No shortages will be permitted.

At first glance, you are probably wondering how a model that has so many "unrealistic" assumptions could be useful, let alone widely used. Although it is true that some of the assumptions represent oversimplifications, a number of them do not. Moreover, much of the value of this basic model is in conceptualizing the inventory problem. Later models will illustrate how the model can easily be modified to permit different conditions (e.g., quantity discounts, noninstantaneous receipts, and so on).

The amount of an item on hand when these assumptions are satisfied is illustrated in Figure 12–2. If the system starts with Q units (the order quantity) on hand, and these are withdrawn at a constant rate, the amount on hand will decrease steadily towards zero inventory. Average inventory will equal $Q/2$. And because lead time and withdrawal are constant, replenishment can easily be timed to coincide with depletion to zero, so that a new order immediately restores the amount on hand to Q units. This is commonly referred to as the *sawtooth* model.

The purpose of the assumptions of constant withdrawal rate and constant replenishment lead time is merely to avoid the necessity of dealing with shortages at this time. In practice, the EOQ model is used in conjunction with a reorder point model: the EOQ model indicates *how much* to order and the reorder point model indicates *when* to order. The reorder point model can handle variations in both withdrawal rate (i.e., demand) and lead time, so those assumptions regarding constant demand and lead time are merely for convenience here. Figure 12–3 illustrates the contrast between constant demand and demand with some (random) variability.

The objective of an EOQ analysis is to identify the order size that will minimize the sum of annual holding and ordering (replenishment) costs. Purchase costs are

FIGURE 12–3 Comparison of Constant and Variable Withdrawal of Inventory

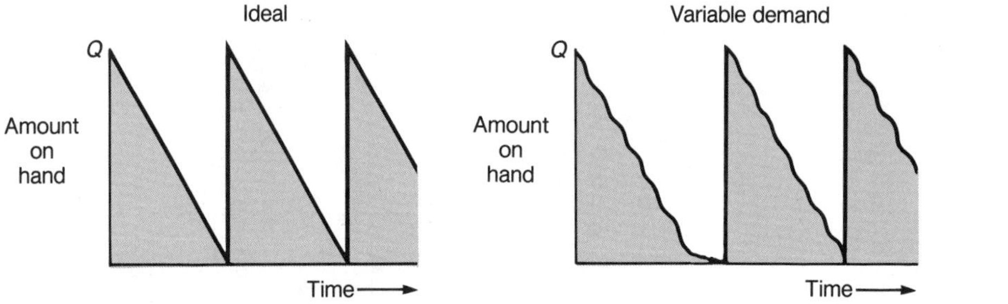

not included in the analysis because they are the same regardless of order size, and shortage costs need not be considered because it is assumed shortages can be avoided.

Annual holding cost is the product of average inventory, $Q/2$, and unit holding cost, H (i.e., the cost to hold a unit in inventory for a year). Hence, annual holding cost is: $\frac{Q}{2}H$. The implication of this is that holding cost is zero if Q is zero, and holding cost increases *linearly* as Q increases.

Annual ordering cost is the product of stocking cost per order, S, and the number of orders per year. With annual demand $= D$ and order size $= Q$ the number of orders per year will be $\frac{D}{Q}$ and the annual stocking or ordering cost will be $\frac{D}{Q}S$.

For a given annual demand, D, and given stocking cost, S, increasing the size of Q causes the annual ordering cost to decrease because the larger Q is, the fewer the number of orders needed. Note, however, that the decrease is not linear.

The total annual cost of holding and ordering inventory, TC, is the sum of these two, which is:

$$TC = \begin{matrix}\text{Annual}\\ \text{holding}\\ \text{cost}\end{matrix} + \begin{matrix}\text{Annual}\\ \text{ordering}\\ \text{cost}\end{matrix}$$

$$= \frac{Q}{2}H + \frac{D}{Q}S \qquad (12\text{-}2)$$

where

D = annual demand
Q = order quantity
H = unit holding cost per year
S = ordering cost for one order

FIGURE 12–4 Total Cost Is Minimized at Q_o

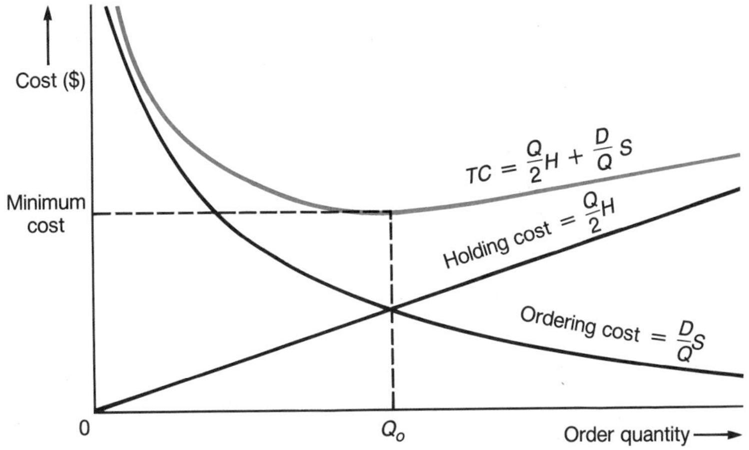

Strictly speaking, D and H do not need to be annual amounts. For example, they could both be in monthly amounts. However, they *do* have to both refer to the *same time period*, whether it is years, months, or weeks.

These cost relationships are illustrated in Figure 12–4. The optimum order quantity, Q_o, is the order size at which the total cost curve is a minimum. Note that this occurs at the point where ordering cost equals holding cost.

An expression for the economic order quantity, Q_o, can be determined either algebraically[1] or through the use of calculus.[2] The result is the following formula:

$$Q_o = \sqrt{\frac{2DS}{H}} \tag{12–3}$$

where Q_o = optimum order quantity.

---

[1] The minimum occurs where holding cost equals ordering cost. Thus: $\frac{Q}{2}H = \frac{D}{Q}S$

Solving for Q yields Formula 12–3.

[2] The following steps are required:

1. Obtain the first derivative of total cost: $TC = \frac{Q}{2}H + \frac{D}{Q}S \quad \frac{dC}{dQ} = \frac{H}{2} - \frac{DS}{Q^2}$
2. Setting this equal to zero and solving for Q, we find $Q_o = \sqrt{\frac{2DS}{H}}$.
3. Because the second derivative is positive, this indicates the function is a minimum at Q_o.

$$\frac{d^2C}{dQ^2} = +\frac{2DS}{Q^3} > 0 \text{ for } Q > 0$$

EXAMPLE 1 A camera shop manager expects to sell approximately 450 cameras of a certain style next year. She estimates that it costs $12 to carry a camera in inventory for one year, and that the stocking cost is $48 for each order.

1. Determine the EOQ.
2. Compute annual holding costs and annual stocking costs.
3. How many times per year will this camera be ordered?

Solution

D = $450 cameras per year
S = $48
H = $12 per unit-year

1. $Q_o = \sqrt{\frac{2DS}{H}} = \sqrt{\frac{2(450 \text{ cameras per year})(\$48)}{\$12 \text{ per camera per year}}} = 60 \text{ cameras.}$

2. Annual holding cost $= \frac{Q}{2}H = \frac{60 \text{ cameras}}{2}(\$12 \text{ per camera per year}) =$ $360 per year.

   Annual stocking cost $= \frac{D}{Q}S = \frac{450 \text{ cameras per year}}{60 \text{ cameras}}(\$48) = \$360 \text{ per year.}$

3. Number of orders per year $= \frac{D}{Q} = \frac{450 \text{ cameras per year}}{60 \text{ cameras}} = 7.5 \text{ per year}$ (i.e., 15 orders in two years).

Notice in the preceding example that at the EOQ, annual holding cost and annual stocking cost are equal, as depicted in Figure 12–4.

In some instances, holding cost is expressed as a percentage of unit price instead of as a constant, or fixed, dollar amount (e.g., the holding cost may be 20 percent of unit price, P). H is then $.20P$, and this amount is used in the various calculations. For instance, if $P = \$60$ and holding costs are 20 percent, $H = .20(\$60) = \$12$ per unit on an annual basis. Once determined, the value of H is used in exactly the same way that a constant H is used.

Sensitivity of the EOQ Model

The EOQ computation is based on *estimates* (rather than known values) of demand, replenishment costs, and holding costs. Once they recognize this, some managers are reluctant to use the EOQ model because they think it follows that the resulting order size will be off by a considerable margin. However, most of those fears are groundless because the model compensates for this: It is relatively *insensitive* to what might seem like large errors. We can get a feel for the sensitivity of the model by postulating various errors in the estimates in the preceding camera example, and examining the effects of those errors on both the EOQ and the total cost.

Suppose first that the estimates of both D and S are 20 percent too high, meaning the true (but unknown) values are $D = 375$ and $S = \$40$, but H is correct at \$12. Then the true values of Q and TC are:

$$Q_o = \sqrt{\frac{2DS}{H}} = \sqrt{\frac{2(375)(40)}{12}} = 50 \text{ units}$$

$$TC = \frac{Q_o}{2}H + \frac{D}{Q_o}S = \frac{50}{2}(12) + \frac{375}{50}(40) = \$600$$

If our incorrect estimates of D and S lead us to an order size of 60 (see Example 1) instead of 50, the order size would be 20 percent more than the optimal order size. Let's see what effect that would have on TC. Using the true values of D and S, but the incorrect estimate of 60 for Q, we find:

$$TC = \frac{60}{2}(12) + \frac{375}{60}(40) = \$610$$

Comparing the \$610 to the \$600 that would result if the optimal order size of 50 units had been used, we can see that the total cost has increased by a relatively small amount (less than 2 percent), even though the order size was off by +20 percent!

Now, suppose D and S in the camera example were too low by about 20 percent, but H was correct; suppose the true value of D was 562 and the true value of S was \$60. This would make the true value of Q about 75. Then the TC, using the correct values of D, S, and H, and the correct Q of 75, would be \$900. Using the incorrect value of $Q = 60$, which is 20 percent below the true value, the TC would be \$922. This is only about 2.4 percent above optimal, even though the order size is 20 percent below optimal.

The calculations reveal that even though the order size is off by as much as ± 20 percent, the impact on total cost is relatively minor. This might make you wonder what impact a larger deviation in order size, such as ± 40 percent, might have on total cost.

Suppose, then, that because of incorrect estimates of D, S, and H, Q was 40 percent above the true amount (i.e., the true optimal order size is 43). If the correct order size is used, the TC would be about 6 percent less than if an order size of 60 is used. On the other hand, if Q was 40 percent *below* the optimal quantity, the TC would be about 13 percent above what the optimal order size would yield.

Table 12–2 summarizes the preceding sensitivity comparisons. The results seem to suggest that errors of ±20 percent in the EOQ produce only minimal

TABLE 12–2 Summary of Sensitivity Comparisons

Deviation of Q from Q_o	−40%	−20%	0%	+20%	+40%
Deviation of TC from minimum	13%	2.4%	0%	1.7%	6%

increases in total cost, and that even errors as large as ±40 percent in the EOQ produce relatively small increases in total cost. The results also suggest that positive deviations in Q have less of an impact on total costs than negative deviations of equal magnitudes.

It is interesting to note that the percentages in Table 12–2 are not simply due to the set of figures used in the illustration. Rather, those percentages hold for *any* case that results in the deviations of Q shown. In fact, by examining various deviations of Q from Q_o, it is possible to construct a curve that conveniently summarizes the increase in total cost as a function of the deviation of Q from Q_o. That curve is presented in Figure 12–5. It confirms that the curve is relatively flat over a considerable range in the vicinity of the EOQ. Hence, the EOQ formula is fairly *robust;* relatively large errors in Q, which might be caused by rough estimates in D, S, and H, produce relatively small increases in total cost. Thus, there is a *zone* of order quantities that will produce an approximate minimum total cost. In addition, as suggested by the calculations summarized in Table 12–2, the curve rises more slowly to the right (i.e., for positive deviations) than to the left of Q_o. The implication is that when in doubt, it would be better to order in larger rather than smaller quantities.

Because the EOQ is based on estimates, computing it to the nearest tenth or hundredth would imply a precision that does not exist. Instead, *the EOQ should be rounded to a whole number.* In fact, we have just seen that even moderate deviations in the EOQ from its optimum size tend to have only minor impact on total cost, and a manager might even prefer to round the computed value to a more convenient quantity. For example, if the computed EOQ is 489, and 500 units constitutes a "round lot" or a full shipment, the manager could easily take advantage of whatever benefits this might present without materially affecting total cost. Note that if a rounded EOQ is used, the annual ordering cost and the annual holding cost will not be exactly equal.

Economic Production Run Quantity

A variation of the basic EOQ model can be used to determine optimal production run quantities. Whether goods are ordered or produced, holding costs are a factor. Moreover, whereas ordering involves ordering costs, production involves an analogous factor—setup costs. Setup cost consists of costs related to preparing equipment for a production run. And, just as ordering cost is independent of the size of an order so, too, is setup cost independent of the size of a production run.

FIGURE 12-5 Deviation of Total Cost from Its Minimum as a Function of Deviation of Order Quantity from the EOQ

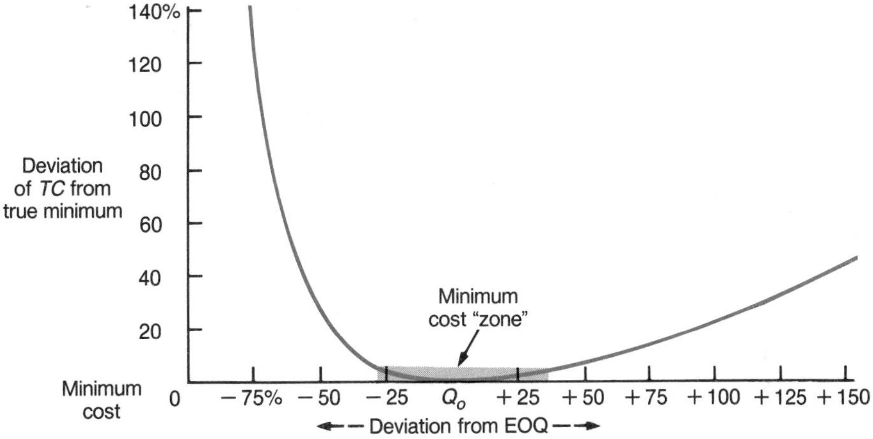

There is, however, one basic difference between ordering and producing with respect to inventory. The nature of production is that it typically occurs *over a period of time* rather than at one point in time. Consequently, inventory tends to build up over time, unlike the EOQ case in which an entire order is received as a single delivery. (If ordered goods are received unit by unit over a period of time, the model described in this section would be appropriate instead of the basic EOQ model.)

The sawtooth diagram used to illustrate inventory on hand for the EOQ case can be modified to show the case in which inventory is replenished over time (see Figure 12–6). Note that the inventory cycle now has two distinct phases. In the first phase, both production and demand take place, with the net result of inventory building up at a rate that is equal to the difference between the demand and production rates. For example, a production rate of 80 units per day and a demand rate of 10 units per day would result in a buildup rate of 70 units per day. This buildup will continue as long as production continues; when production ceases, inventory will begin to drop at a rate equal to the demand rate. This inventory reduction is the second phase. When inventory is depleted, the cycle repeats. Moreover, under the assumptions of constant production and demand rates, the two phases can be described by straight lines.

The optimum run quantity can be computed using the previously described EOQ formula modified to allow for production and demand rates. It is:

$$Q_{\text{run}} = \sqrt{\frac{2DS}{H}} \times \sqrt{\frac{p}{p - d}} \qquad (12\text{–}4)$$

FIGURE 12–6 A Profile of Amount of Inventory on Hand under Noninstantaneous Replenishment

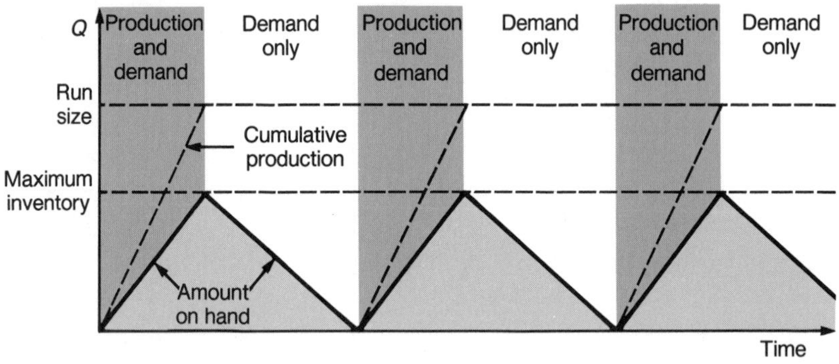

where

D = annual demand
S = setup cost
H = annual cost to hold one unit
p = production rate
d = demand rate

The length of a run (say, in days) is equal to the run size divided by the production rate:

$$\text{Run time} = \frac{Q_{\text{run}}}{p} \tag{12–5}$$

The maximum inventory is equal to the buildup rate $(p - d)$ times the run time:

$$I_{\max} = (p - d)\frac{Q_{\text{run}}}{p} \tag{12–6}$$

The average amount of inventory on hand is $\frac{I_{\max}}{2}$.

The total cost is:

$$TC = \text{Holding cost} + \text{Setup cost}$$

$$= \frac{I_{\max}}{2}H + \frac{D}{Q_{\text{run}}}S \tag{12–7}$$

As with the EOQ model, holding costs may be stated as a dollar amount or as a percentage of cost (or price). In the latter case, multiply the percentage and the cost or price to obtain a value of H in dollars per unit.

■

EXAMPLE 2 Pure 'n Sweet Candies makes and sells a variety of chocolates in a theme park shop. During the summer months, the shop sells an average of 60 pounds of chocolate-covered peanuts per day. The chocolate-covered peanuts can be produced at a rate of 210 pounds per day. These peanuts sell for \$5 per pound. The shop is open seven days per week, and the weekly carrying cost, according to manager Candy Kane, is approximately 1 percent of the selling price per pound. Setup cost is \$7.50. Determine the following:

1. The optimum run size and the number of runs per week.
2. The maximum amount of chocolate-covered peanuts on hand.
3. The weekly total of holding and setup costs.
4. The length of a production run in days.

Solution

D = 7 days per week × 60 pounds per day = 420 pounds per week

S = \$7.50

H = .01 per week × \$5.00 = \$.05 per pound/week

p = 210 pounds per day

d = 60 pounds per day

Note that both D and H refer to the *same time frame*.

1. $$Q_{run} = \sqrt{\frac{2DS}{H}}\sqrt{\frac{p}{p-d}} = \sqrt{\frac{2(420)(\$7.50)}{\$.05}}\sqrt{\frac{210}{210-60}} = 420 \text{ pounds.}$$
   Hence, there should be one run per week.

2. $$I_{max} = (p-d)\frac{Q_{run}}{p} = (210-60)\frac{420}{210} = 300 \text{ pounds.}$$

3. $$TC = \frac{I_{max}}{2}H + \frac{D}{Q_{run}}S = \frac{300}{2}(\$.05) + \frac{420}{420}(\$7.50) = \$7.50 + \$7.50 = \$15.00$$
   (Note the equality of holding and setup costs.)

4. $$\text{Run time} = \frac{Q_{run}}{p} = \frac{420 \text{ pounds}}{210 \text{ pounds per day}} = 2 \text{ days.}$$

TABLE 12–3 Sample Price List

Order Quantity	Unit Price
1 to 119	$42
120 to 164	41
165 or more	40

As was the case with the EOQ, the production run size is robust in terms of reasonably small errors having relatively small impact on the total cost.

Quantity Discounts

Quantity discounts are reductions in unit prices offered by sellers to encourage customers to buy in large quantities. The price reductions usually are offered as a series of ranges, as in the price list illustrated in Table 12–3.

The manager must decide whether the benefits of an order size large enough to obtain a price discount (namely, lower unit costs and lower annual ordering cost due to fewer orders) will outweigh the higher inventory carrying costs that will result from larger order sizes. Hence, the goal of the decision maker is to minimize the sum of three annual costs: holding, ordering, and purchasing. Purchasing cost is the product of unit price, P, and annual demand, D. The total cost with these three costs taken into account can be computed using the following formula.

$$\begin{aligned} TC &= \text{Holding cost} + \text{Ordering cost} + \text{Purchasing cost} \\ &= \frac{Q}{2}H + \frac{D}{Q}S + PD \end{aligned} \qquad (12\text{–}8)$$

where

P = unit price

Adding purchase cost to the total cost equation simply increases the total cost by the amount $P \times D$, regardless of order size. In terms of the graph of total cost, adding purchasing cost raises the total cost curve at every point by the same amount. However, neither the shape of the curve nor the quantity at which it reaches its minimum change, as illustrated in Figure 12–7. As a matter of fact, this explains why there was no need to involve unit price in the basic EOQ model, where only one price prevailed regardless of order size. However, all of that changes when quantity discounts are available.

With the presence of quantity discounts, price obviously becomes a very real consideration. The heart of the issue is the way in which discounts affect the total cost curve. Because adding price to the total cost equation raises the curve at every point by $P \times D$, the amount of increase depends on the size of P. Hence,

FIGURE 12–7 Adding *PD* Doesn't Change the EOQ or the Slope of the *TC* Curve

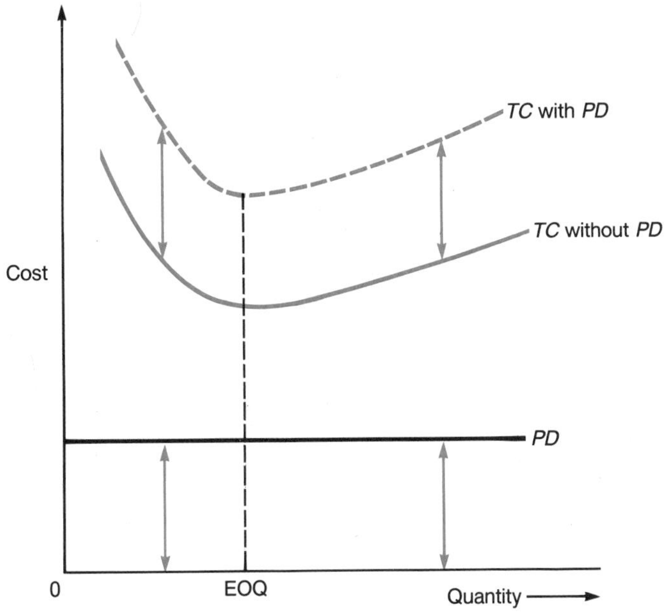

different prices will raise the curve by different amounts. In fact, the lower the value of P, the lower the total cost curve. With three possible unit prices, one might imagine three total cost curves, one for each price. The highest curve would reflect the largest unit price, and the lowest curve would reflect the lowest unit price. Note, however, that each total cost curve would only be valid for the range of quantities specified in the price list. Thus, referring to Table 12–3, for quantities of 119 or less, the highest price curve would be appropriate, for quantities of 120 units to 164, the total cost curve reflecting $41 per unit would be appropriate, and for quantities of 165 or more, the cost curve for $40 per unit would be appropriate. Because the price changes are in steps, the total cost curve, which represents the entire range of possible quantities, will itself have steps that occur at the *price breaks,* or quantities where unit price decreases. These concepts are illustrated in Figure 12–8. The solid portions of each total cost curve indicate the range over which that particular curve reflects the *valid* total cost (i.e., where quantity and price are matched according to the price list).

The analysis of quantity discounts for a given situation will proceed along one of two slightly different paths, depending on whether holding costs are specified relative to unit price or whether they are specified independently of price (i.e., they are constant per unit).

FIGURE 12–8 With Quantity Discounts, the Total Cost Curve Becomes a Series of Steps at the Price Break Quantities

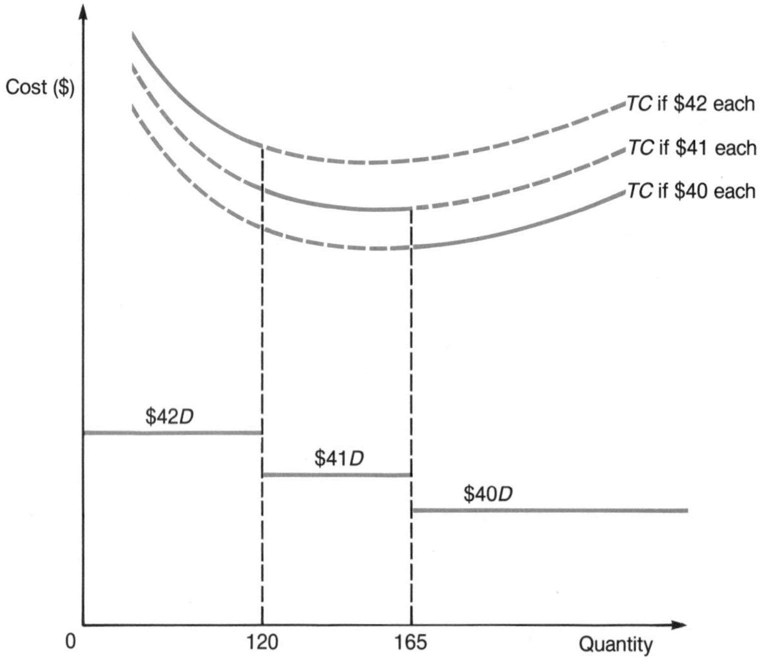

When holding costs are constant, the various total cost curves (there will be a different TC curve for each different unit price) will line up. That is, all curves will reach their minimum points at the same quantity. In contrast, when holding costs are expressed as percentages of unit price, the EOQs for each total cost curve will move to the right as price decreases. Hence, each curve will reach its minimum at a different quantity than the others. Figure 12–9 reveals the reason for this basic variation between constant and percentage holding cost TC curves with discounts.

The general procedure, then, is to find the lowest total cost curve that has a valid or "feasible" EOQ (i.e., the EOQ falls within the quantity range for that price).

If that quantity is valid for the lowest TC curve, it is a "global" or overall optimum, and no further computation is required. If the quantity is not valid for the lowest curve, the next highest curve must be examined, and so on, until a valid EOQ–price range match is found. Once that is achieved, the total cost must be computed for that EOQ and for all higher price break quantities using their

FIGURE 12–9

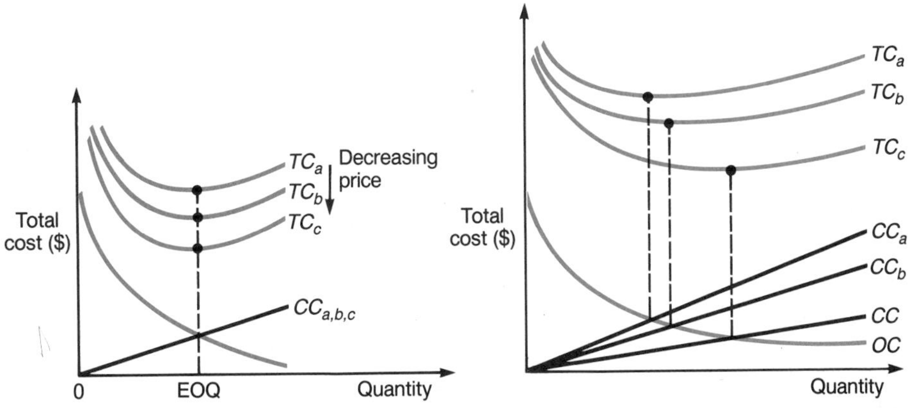

A. When carrying costs are constant, all curves have the same EOQ

B. When carrying costs are given as a percentage of unit price, price decreases carrying costs and that causes an increase in the EOQ

respective unit prices. The quantity that results in the lowest total cost is the optimum order quantity.

Because constant holding cost situations produce EOQs that are independent of price, all TC curves for a given situation will have the same EOQ. Consequently, a single calculation will reveal that quantity. The approach for constant holding costs can be summarized as follows:

1. Compute the EOQ.
2. Find which price range it falls in.
3. If it is large enough to obtain the lowest unit price, it is the optimum order quantity; it will minimize total cost.
4. If it falls in a range associated with a higher unit price, compute the total cost using that price and the total cost for the minimum quantity needed to qualify for a lower unit price. Do this for all lower-price breaks.
5. The quantity (valid EOQ or price break) that produces the lowest total cost is the optimum.

Let's take a look at some examples.

■

EXAMPLE 3 Given the price list below, determine the order size that will minimize the total of annual holding, ordering, and purchasing costs. Annual demand is 500 units, ordering cost is \$25, and holding cost is \$10 per unit a year.

Quantity	Unit Price
1 to 20	$180
21 to 30	178
31 to 40	175
41 or more	174

Solution

Note that holding cost is constant. Therefore, all curves have the same EOQ. Compute the EOQ:

$$\sqrt{\frac{2DS}{H}} = \sqrt{\frac{2(500)(\$25)}{\$10}} = 50 \text{ units}$$

Because this quantity falls in the range associated with the lowest unit price, it will yield a lower total cost than any other possible quantity. Therefore, it is unnecessary to compare the total cost of the EOQ with total costs of other quantities.

EXAMPLE 4 Determine the order quantity that will minimize total annual inventory cost for the price schedule below. Annual demand is 1,200 units, ordering cost is $41, and holding cost is $2 per unit per year.

Quantity	Unit Price
1 to 199	$27
200 to 299	26
300 to 399	25
400 or more	24

Solution

Compute the EOQ:

$$\sqrt{\frac{2DS}{H}} = \sqrt{\frac{2(1{,}200)(\$41)}{\$2}} = 222 \text{ units}$$

Note that this quantity doesn't qualify for the lowest unit price; an order size of 222 units would mean a price of $26 per unit. It may or may not result in the lowest total cost. To find out, it is necessary to compare its total cost to that of all *larger* price breaks (i.e., 300 and 400).

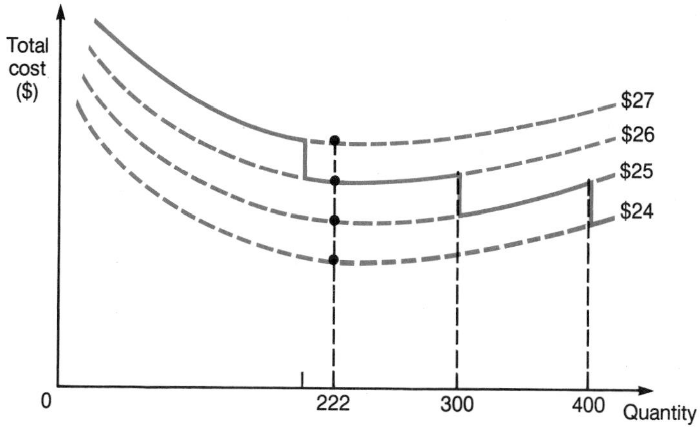

Total cost is computed as follows:

$$TC = \frac{Q}{2}H + \frac{D}{Q}S + PD$$

$$TC_{222} = \frac{222}{2}(\$2) + \frac{1,200}{222}(\$41) + \$26(1,200) = \$31,644$$

$$TC_{300} = \frac{300}{2}(\$2) + \frac{1,200}{300}(\$41) + \$25(1,200) = 30,464$$

$$TC_{400} = \frac{400}{2}(\$2) + \frac{1,200}{400}(\$41) + \$24(1,200) = 29,323$$

Hence, the best order size is 400 units because it will yield the lowest total annual cost.

You might be wondering why only the price break quantities are considered. If you check the graph in the preceding example, you will see that for all points to the right of the EOQ, the curves are rising. Thus, the further up the curve, the higher the total cost. Because the EOQ is not valid on these curves, the price break is the best point on each curve because it is the closest to the EOQ on the curve; therefore, its *TC* is less than quantities to its right.

Analysis of quantity discounts when the holding cost is a percentage of price is a little more involved than when *H* is constant because each curve has a different EOQ. The approach involves finding the lowest *TC* curve that has a valid EOQ. If it is the lowest curve, the EOQ is the optimum quantity. If it is on a higher curve, its total cost must be compared to the total costs of all larger price breaks, as is the case with *H* constant. Thus, the procedure is:

1. Compute the EOQ of each curve, beginning with the lowest cost curve, until a valid EOQ is found.
2. If it is on the lowest cost curve, that quantity is optimum.
3. If it is on a higher cost curve, compare its total cost and the total cost of all larger price breaks. The one with the lowest total cost is the optimum order quantity.

   Let's take a look at an example.

EXAMPLE 5 The billing department of the Apple of the Month Company expects to use 4,500 reams of paper during the coming 12 months. Annual carrying cost per unit is 30 percent of unit price. Ordering cost is $24. The price list below applies. What order quantity will minimize total inventory costs for the year?

Quantity	Unit Price
1 to 150	$8.30
151 to 499	8.00
500 or more	7.50

Solution

$D = 4{,}500$ reams per year

$S = \$24$

$H = .30P$

1. Compute the EOQ for the lowest price:

$$\sqrt{\frac{2DS}{H}} = \sqrt{\frac{2(4{,}500)(\$24)}{.30(\$7.50)}} = \$310$$

2. That order size is not valid at a unit price of $7.50, so disregard it.
3. Compute the EOQ for the next higher price:

$$\sqrt{\frac{2DS}{H}} = \sqrt{\frac{2(4{,}500)(\$24)}{.30(\$8.00)}} = 300 \text{ reams}$$

   This quantity is valid. No further EOQs need be computed.
4. Compare the total annual cost of an order size of 300 reams with the total annual cost of ordering at any larger price breaks. In this instance, there is only one larger break; it is at 500 reams. The total costs can be computed using this formula:

$$TC = \frac{Q}{2}(.30P) \quad + \frac{D}{Q}S \quad + PD$$

$$TC_{300} = \frac{300}{2}(.30)(\$8.00) + \frac{4,500}{300}(\$24) + \$8.00(4,500) = \$36,720$$

$$TC_{500} = \frac{500}{2}(.30)(\$7.50) + \frac{4,500}{500}(\$24) + \$7.50(4,500) = \$34,529$$

An order size of 500 reams would be optimum; total costs would be about $2,200 less than an order size of 300 reams.

Note that in each of the preceding three examples, the optimum order quantity was at the largest price break. Although this will not always be the case, it frequently turns out that the largest price break yields the minimum cost. Why? Because in most instances, the purchasing cost represents a major portion of the total cost, say, between 60 and 98 percent. Consequently, even a small percentage change in purchasing cost (due to a price discount) will usually offset any increase in carrying cost caused by ordering larger amounts.

Finally, you may be wondering why computation of EOQs stops when the lowest valid one is found. The answer lies in the fact that no upper level EOQ could possibly have a total cost that is less than one on the lower curve because the lower unit price means the entire curve at every point will be lower by an amount equal to the difference between the two prices multiplied by the annual volume, *D*.

Figure 12–10 presents a flowchart that summarizes the analysis of quantity discount problems.

DETERMINING WHEN TO REORDER

EOQ models provide managers with a rational basis for deciding *how much* to order, but they do not answer the question of *when* to order. That is the purpose of **reorder point (ROP)** models. However, EOQ models often are used in conjunction with ROP models.

A *reorder point* is a *quantity* of inventory: When the amount on hand falls to that level, this is a signal to reorder. For example, an ROP might be 50 units for a certain item. Consequently, when the amount on hand falls to that level, an order is triggered. The implication, of course, is that *perpetual* knowledge of the amount of stock on hand exists so that the order can be made at the appropriate time.

The size of the ROP is a function of the expected demand during lead time and the extent of variability in lead time demand. The greater the expected demand and the greater the variability in that amount, the greater will be the ROP. Determination of the ROP involves consideration of both expected demand and

FIGURE 12–10 Flowchart for Analysis of Quantity Discount Problems

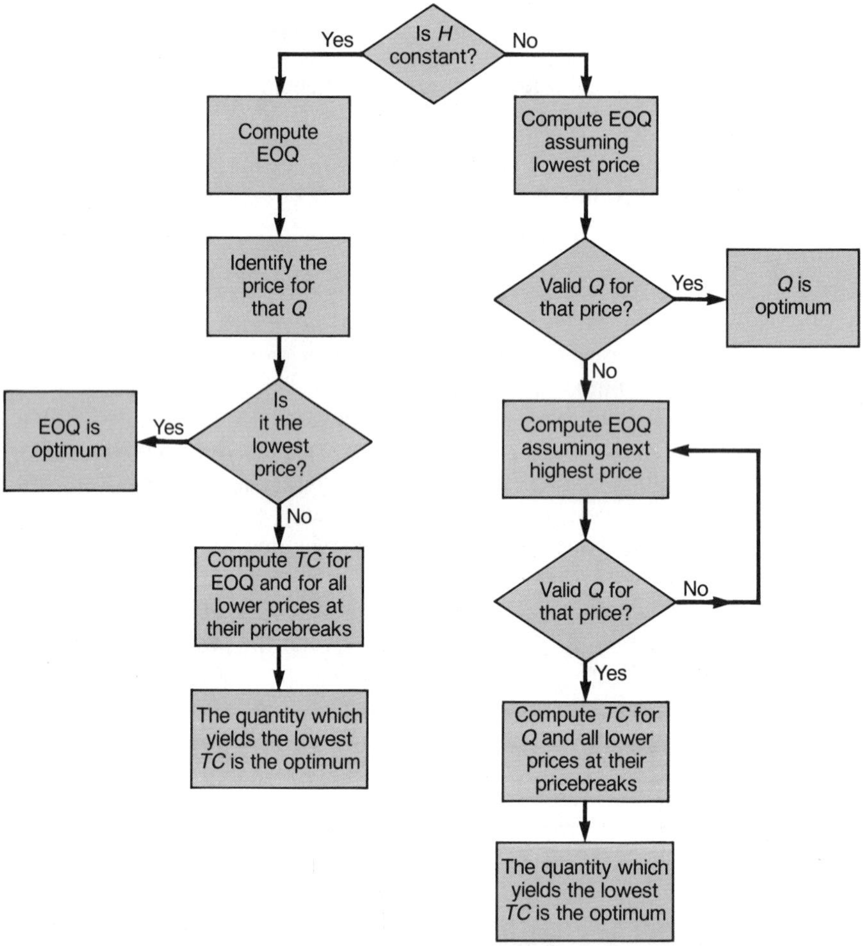

demand variability as well as the **risk of a stockout** that management is willing to tolerate.

Safety Stock and Service Level

If demand and lead time can both be assumed to be constant, the ROP level is simply equal to lead-time demand. Thus, if lead-time demand is known to be *exactly* 50 units, the ROP is 50 units. In practical terms, such cases are the exception rather than the rule. It is more common to encounter situations in which variability exists. The presence of variability gives rise to potential stockouts because it is not completely certain how much inventory will be depleted during lead time. The source of the variability might be fluctuations in demand, fluctuations in the length of lead time, or both. Temporary increases in demand and/or lead time tend to put pressure on available supplies, and this may lead to a shortage or stockout. In order to lessen that possibility, it is common to include in the ROP an additional amount of stock beyond expected demand requirements, called **safety stock.** Hence, the reorder point quantity includes both expected demand and some additional stock to offset possible increases in lead-time demand. A general expression for the ROP is:

$$ROP = \begin{matrix}\text{Expected demand} \\ \text{during lead time}\end{matrix} + \begin{matrix}\text{Safety} \\ \text{stock}\end{matrix} \qquad (12\text{–}9)$$

Including safety stock in the ROP increases its size above expected demand, so that orders are triggered with a larger amount of inventory on hand.

What the manager must decide is *how much safety stock is needed?* Although large amounts of safety stock lessen the chance of stockouts, they add to holding costs. Consequently, the manager must attempt to achieve a balance between shortage costs and holding costs in establishing a level of safety stock. However, because managers often find it difficult to assess shortage costs, many prefer to set safety stock amounts in terms of a **customer service level,** which is the probability that a stockout will not occur (i.e, that demand will not exceed the amount on hand). A manager may decide that a service level of 95 percent is adequate. This would imply a stockout risk of 5 percent (i.e., 1.00 − .95).

Service levels may be specified relative to lead time or on an annual basis:

Lead-time service level is the probability that demand will not exceed supply during lead time.

Annual service level is the percentage of expected annual demand that can be satisfied from stock on hand.

In general, the two service levels will not be the same. That is, a given amount of safety stock will result in a certain lead-time service level and usually in a *different* annual service level. However, the two values are related, and either one can be determined if the other's value is known or specified, as you will see.

Practically speaking, the risk of a stockout exists only during lead time. At other times, the amount of stock on hand greatly exceeds expected (short-term) demand fluctuations. Moreover, when the supply of inventory falls to a predetermined level, inventory is reordered and the lead-time interval begins. As time passes and additional units are withdrawn from inventory, the risk of a stockout increases until either a stockout occurs or the order is received, at which point the risk again becomes negligible.

Because stockouts tend to occur only during lead time, some managers focus

FIGURE 12-11 Service Level, Risk, ROP, and Safety Stock

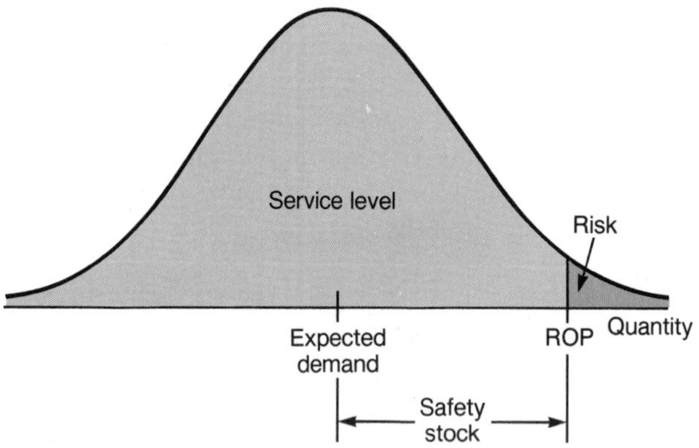

on service levels and safety stock relative to lead times. Determining the ROP (and hence, safety stock) needed to achieve a desired service level requires some knowledge of the distribution of lead-time demand. Very often, lead-time demand can be described by a normal distribution, although for low-volume items, a Poisson distribution is often used.

When lead-time demand is described by a normal distribution, the service level achieved by a particular ROP is equivalent to the area under the curve to the left of the ROP, as illustrated in Figure 12-11. Risk, then, is the area under the curve to the right of the ROP, and safety stock is the difference (on the horizontal axis) between expected demand and the ROP. Increasing the ROP (i.e., moving it to the right) causes the service level to increase and the risk to decrease because it increases safety stock. Note, though, that as the ROP gets farther and farther out in the right tail of the distribution, equal increments of increase in the ROP achieve smaller and smaller increases in the service level. Consequently, the manager must decide the point at which additional increases in service level are no longer worth the cost of the added safety stock that would be needed.

Another perspective on lead-time demand is presented in Figure 12-12, where we see how the daily demands sum over the lead time to form a lead-time distribution of demand.

Computing the Reorder Point

In order to compute the ROP, it is necessary to know the distribution of lead-time demand and its mean. Moreover, if the distribution is normal, it is also necessary to know its standard deviation. For the present, let us assume that the distribution of lead-time demand is normal.

FIGURE 12–12 Lead-Time Demand

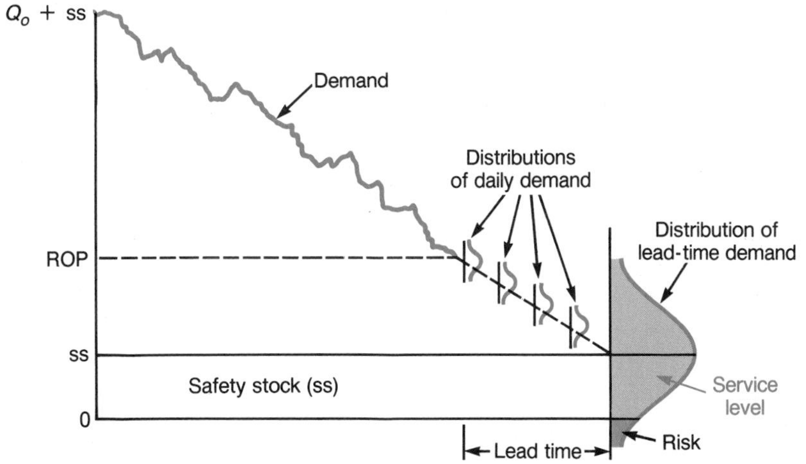

The mean and standard deviation of the distribution can be obtained in two ways. One is by direct estimates, based on historical lead-time demand. Hence, the manager can gather data from previous lead times, which will enable the mean and standard deviation to be estimated. An indirect approach would be to gather data on both short-term demand (e.g., daily) and length of lead times and then combine that information to obtain the mean and standard deviation of lead-time demand. The advantage of directly estimating the mean and standard deviation of lead-time demand is that it is easier to comprehend; the advantage of the indirect approach is that it facilitates examination of the separate effects of lead-time and demand variability on the ROP. The latter may be important in terms of any attempt to find ways of reducing inventory levels (e.g., would it make more sense to try to reduce lead-time variability, the length of lead time, or demand variability?).

Regardless of how they are derived, once the mean and standard deviation of lead-time demand have been obtained, the ROP can be computed using the formula

$$ROP = \begin{array}{c}\text{Expected demand}\\ \text{during lead time}\end{array} + z\sigma_{dL} \qquad (12\text{–}10)$$

where

Expected demand = distribution mean

z = number of standard deviations from the mean

σ_{dL} = standard deviation of lead-time demand

EXAMPLE 6 After reviewing previous lead-time experience, theater manager Fred Farkle feels reasonably confident that lead-time demand for popcorn can be adequately modeled using a normal distribution that has a mean of 60 pounds and a standard deviation of 8 pounds. What ROP will yield a service level of 95 percent?

Solution

Expected demand = 60 pounds

σ_{dL} = 8 pounds

z = 1.65 [from Appendix Table B2]

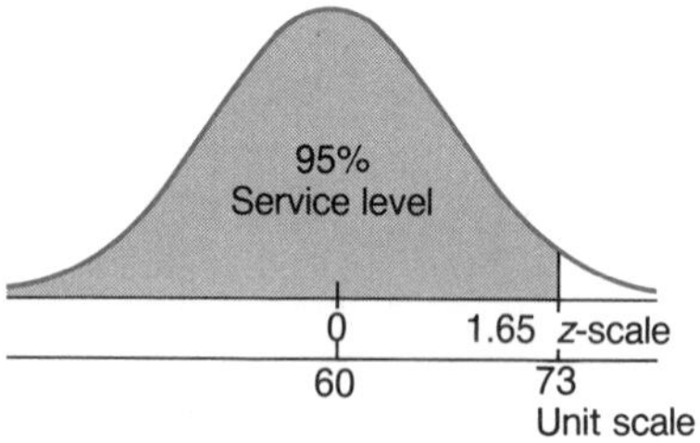

$$ROP = \text{Expected demand} + z\sigma_{dL}$$
$$= 60 \text{ pounds} + 1.65(8 \text{ pounds})$$
$$= 73.2, \text{ or approximately 73 pounds}$$

Two points are worth noting in the previous example. One is the rounding of the ROP to the nearest integer. One reason for this is because computations are based on estimates, stating the ROP to the nearest tenth would imply more precision than there actually is. Another reason is that many items are discrete units. On the other hand, if a situation involved large units of measure (e.g., tons), it may make sense to either not round or to round to the nearest tenth.

A second point is that a manager would want to make sure that lead time is *stable* (i.e., no seasonal patterns were present). If seasonal variations are expected, an allowance would have to be made for them in the ROP.

Now let's consider the indirect approach to determining the ROP. The variability of lead-time demand may come solely from demand, with lead time constant; solely from lead time, with daily demand constant; or from both. Consequently, there are three formulas from which to choose.[3] If demand is variable and lead time constant, the ROP is:

$$ROP = \bar{d}L + z\sigma_d\sqrt{L} \qquad (12\text{–}11)$$

where

$\bar{d}$ = average daily demand

L = lead time in days

[3] All formulas in this section assume that demand and lead time are *independent*, and that distributions of demand and/or lead time are *normal*.

σ_d = standard deviation of daily demand

$\sigma_d\sqrt{L} = \sigma_{dL}$

The logic of this formula is that the variance of lead-time demand is the sum of L daily demand variances, or $\sigma_d^2(L)$, so that the standard deviation of lead-time demand is the square root of this, or $\sigma_d\sqrt{L}$.

■

EXAMPLE 7 Average daily demand for the house wine at a restaurant is 10 gallons per day. Demand can be described by a normal distribution with a standard deviation of 2 gallons per day. Determine the ROP that will give a 95 percent service level if lead time is six days. How much of this is safety stock?

Solution

$\bar{d}$ = 10 gallons per day

σ_d = 2 gallons per day

L = 6 days

Because demand is variable and lead time is constant, Formula 12–11 is appropriate:

$$\begin{aligned} ROP &= \bar{d}L + z\sigma_d\sqrt{L} \\ &= 10(6) + 1.65(2)\sqrt{6} \\ &= 60 + 8.08 \text{ or about 68 gallons} \end{aligned}$$

Safety stock is 8.08 gallons, or about 8 gallons.

If daily demand is constant and lead time is variable, the appropriate formula is:

$$ROP = d\bar{L} + zd\sigma_L \qquad (12\text{–}12)$$

where

$\bar{L}$ = average lead time

σ_L = standard deviation of lead time

■

EXAMPLE 8 Suppose that daily demand for the house wine is constant at 10 gallons per day. Lead time is variable and can be described by a normal distribution that has a mean of six days and a standard deviation of 1.5 days. Determine the ROP for a service level of 95 percent.

Solution

$d = 10$ gallons per day
$\overline{L} = 6$ days
$\sigma_L = 1.5$ days
$z = 1.65$ [from Appendix Table B2]

$$ROP = d\overline{L} + zd\sigma_L$$
$$= 10(6) + 1.65(10)(1.5)$$
$$= 84.75 \text{ units, which rounds to 85 units.}$$

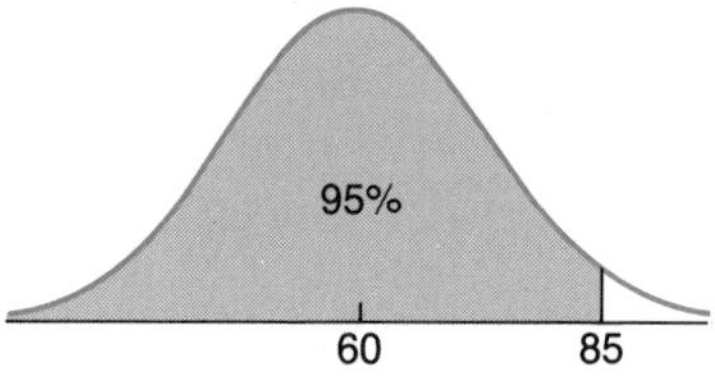

If demand and lead time are independent of each other, and if both are roughly normally distributed, the ROP can be computed using the formula:

$$ROP = \overline{d}\,\overline{L} + z\sqrt{\sigma_d^2\overline{L} + \overline{d}^2\sigma_L^2} \qquad (12\text{–}13)$$

As in the previous formulas, the portion of the equation after z represents the amount of safety stock. In this case, the standard deviation of lead-time demand is the square root of the variances of the previous two formulas.

■

EXAMPLE 9 Suppose daily demand for the house wine is normally distributed with a mean of 10 gallons per day and a standard deviation of 2 gallons per day, and that lead time is normally distributed with a mean of six days and a standard deviation of 1.5 days. What ROP will provide a service level of 95 percent?

Solution

$\overline{d} = 10$ gallons per day
$\sigma_d = 2$ gallons per day
$\overline{L} = 6$ days
$\sigma_L = 1.5$ days

$$ROP = \overline{d}\overline{L} + z\sqrt{\sigma_d^2\overline{L} + \overline{d}^2\sigma_L^2}$$
$$= 10(6) + 1.65\sqrt{2^2(6) + 10^2(1.5)^2}$$
$$= 60 + 26.04$$
$$= 86 \text{ gallons (rounded)}$$

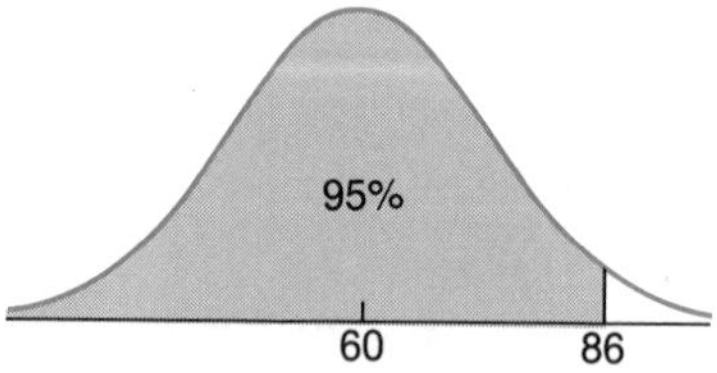

These formulas also can be used to determine the service level (or risk of a stockout) that a given ROP will provide. In order to do that, solve for z and use that value to find the service level in Appendix Table B2.

■

EXAMPLE 10 A manager uses an ROP of 70 gallons for the house wine that has a daily demand that can be described by a normal distribution with a mean of 10 gallons per day and a standard deviation of 2 gallons per day, and the lead time is constant at six days. What is the risk of a stockout during lead time?

Solution

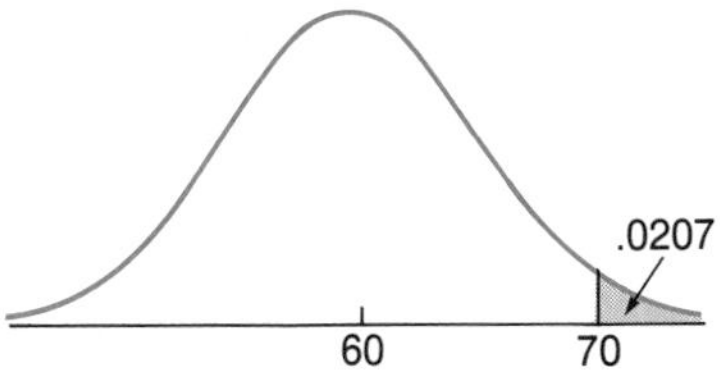

$$ROP = 70 \text{ gallons}$$
$$\bar{d} = 10 \text{ gallons per day}$$
$$\sigma_d = 2 \text{ gallons per day}$$
$$L = 6 \text{ days}$$

In order to determine the risk, solve the ROP equation for z. Thus:

$$ROP = \bar{d}L + z\sigma_d\sqrt{L}$$
$$70 = 10(6) + z(2)\sqrt{6}$$

Solving, $z = 2.04$.

From Appendix Table B2, this gives a service level of .9793 and a stockout risk of $1 - .9793 = .0207$.

Comment The preceding discussion focused on using the standard deviation of *demand* for reordering for cases in which demand is variable. Another possibility is to use the standard deviation of *forecast error*. Using that approach, a manager would substitute the standard deviation of forecast error for the standard deviation of demand in the ROP formulas. Now, the important question is: Which one should be used? The answer is: It depends. In many instances, formal forecasts are not used (even though they should be). Often, this is the case for small retail businesses. Consequently, there is no variability of forecast error to refer to. Hence, demand variability should be used. Also, if it happens that demand is truly random (i.e., with no trends or other patterns), the standard deviation of forecast error will be equal to the standard deviation of demand. Therefore, the standard deviation of demand would be acceptable. However, if demand either tends to change over time (e.g., trend) or is influenced by identifiable factors (e.g., price, packaging, advertising), then, it would be more realistic to use the standard deviation of forecast error in ROP calculations.

If forecast error variability is used, and *daily* standard deviation of forecast error is available, that should be substituted directly into ROP formulas. If the standard deviation of forecast error for *lead time* is available, that quantity should be substituted in ROP formulas in place of the entire portion of the ROP formula to the right of z. And if the standard deviation of forecast error is available only for some other time frame (e.g., weekly, monthly, annually), square that figure (to obtain the variance) and then divide this by the number of days in the time frame (e.g., 5 working days per week). The result will be the *daily variance* of forecast error. If you obtain the square root of this variance, that value will be the standard deviation of forecast error on a daily basis.

Finally, a word about the assumption of a normal lead-time demand distribution. Aside from a normal distribution being relatively simple to work with, you may wonder how realistic the assumption is. For the two cases in which demand is variable, the assumption is quite reasonable, even if the distribution of *daily* demand is not normal. In each of those cases, lead-time demand represents the *sum* of daily demands, and sums of random variables (e.g., daily demands) tend to be normally distributed even though the distribution that produced the daily demands is not normal. Moreover, this tendency depends on two factors: the degree to which daily demand approaches a unimodal distribution and the number of values being summed. The greater the number of values being summed, the less need there is for a distribution of daily demand that is normal, and vice versa.

For the case in which demand is constant and lead time is variable, the requirement for a normal distribution (of lead time) is more important because there is no summing of random variables involved. Even in this case, however, moderate departure from a normal distribution can be tolerated. Also, in practice, this case seems to be much less prevalent than the other two, which concern variable demand.

For low-volume items, lead-time demand may be more adequately described by a discrete distribution (e.g., Poisson) than by the normal distribution, which is continuous. One peculiarity of discrete distributions is the frequently encountered inability to match a specified service level, as illustrated in the following example.

■

EXAMPLE 11 Lead-time demand for spare parts for a machine used to harvest grapes can be described by a Poisson distribution with a mean of 1.5 parts. The service manager wants a service level of 95 percent for these parts. What ROP is appropriate?

Solution

Cumulative Poisson probabilities are found in Appendix Table C. Probabilities for a mean of 1.5 are reproduced below for purposes of discussion:

	Lead-Time Demand							
	0	1	2	3	4	5	6	7
Mean = 1.5	.223	.558	.809	.934	.981	.996	.999	1.000

Note that the cumulative probability corresponds to service level, and the .95 is not a possible service level. Instead, the closest values are .934 if an ROP of three parts is used, or .981 if an ROP of four parts is used. The service manager would have to choose between these two alternatives.

Sensitivity

A reasonable question for management concerns the possible benefits of a deliberate effort to reduce lead time and/or lead-time variability, in terms of decreasing the amount of safety stock held. This would be desirable because annual holding cost for safety stock is the product of safety stock and holding cost per unit, H. Hence, a 20 percent reduction in safety stock would produce a 20 percent reduction in the cost of holding safety stock. Since there are many possible ways to increase ordering efficiency, such as standardizing paperwork, telephoning orders instead of mailing them, inspecting merchandise promptly upon receipt, and working more closely with suppliers, lead-time reductions are often quite feasible.

Suppose a 20 percent reduction in *both* the average lead time and lead-time variability could be achieved. The decrease in safety stock this would produce, using the figures from Examples 7, 8, and 9, is shown in Table 12–4.

Note that the largest reductions occur where lead time is variable (i.e., Examples 8 and 9). Similar analyses could be made for other reductions in either average lead time or lead-time variability, either alone or together, and for changes in demand. Presumably, in the case of demand, management's concern would focus more on reduction of demand *variability* and, perhaps, on increases in safety stock needed to support increased demand.

Amount of Shortage

It can be useful for management to know the average or expected *number* of units short in a given inventory cycle because total shortage cost generally is a function of the amount of a shortage.

TABLE 12–4 Decrease in Safety Stock that Would Result from a 20 Percent Decrease in the Mean and Standard Deviation of Lead Time

Example	Safety Stock	Safety Stock with Reduced Lead Time	Percent Decrease in Safety Stock
7	8 units	7 units	12.5
8	25	20	20.0
9	26	21	19.2

Although the ROP models do not reveal this quantity, it can be obtained from the information used to compute the ROP. More specifically, the manager needs to know the standard deviation of lead-time demand and the normal z that corresponds to the desired service level, assuming that lead-time demand can be represented adequately by a normal distribution. The expected number of units short during lead time is given by the formula:

$$E(n) = E(z)\sigma_{dL} \tag{12–14}$$

where

$E(n)$ = the expected number of units short during lead time
$E(z)$ = standardized number short
σ_{dL} = standard deviation of lead-time demand

Values of $E(z)$ can be obtained from the unit normal loss function table (Table 12–5), which relates $E(z)$ and z, the number of standard deviations the ROP is from the mean of the lead-time demand distribution.

■

EXAMPLE 12 Determine the average number of units short for a cycle in which lead-time demand is normal, with a standard deviation of 14 units and the desired customer service level is 95 percent.

Solution

z = 1.65 for 95%
σ_{dL} = 14 units
$E(z)$ = 0.21 [from Table 12–5 with $z = +1.65$]

Thus:

$$E(n) = E(z)\sigma_{dL}$$
$$= .021(14) = .294 \text{ units short per cycle.}$$

It should be noted that the value of $E(n)$ indicates an average over many cycles, and that for any *one* cycle, the number of units short would be an integer (e.g., 0, 1, 2 . . .) if inventory is counted in number of units.

A related question involves the number of units short per year or other convenient time frame. That quantity is simply a function of $E(n)$ and the number of orders per year, which is D/Q. Thus:

$$E(N) = E(n) \times \frac{D}{Q} \tag{12–15}$$

TABLE 12–5 Normal Distribution Service Levels and Unit Normal Loss Function

z	Service Level	E(z)	z	Service Level	E(z)	z	Service Level	E(z)	z	Service Level	E(z)
−2.40	.0082	2.403	−0.80	.2119	.920	0.80	.7881	.120	2.40	.9918	.003
−2.36	.0091	2.363	−0.76	.2236	.889	0.84	.7995	.112	2.44	.9927	.002
−2.32	.0102	2.323	−0.72	.2358	.858	0.88	.8106	.104	2.48	.9934	.002
−2.28	.0113	2.284	−0.68	.2483	.828	0.92	.8212	.097	2.52	.9941	.002
−2.24	.0125	2.244	−0.64	.2611	.798	0.96	.8315	.089	2.56	.9948	.002
−2.20	.0139	2.205	−0.60	.2743	.769	1.00	.8413	.083	2.60	.9953	.001
−2.16	.0154	2.165	−0.56	.2877	.740	1.04	.8508	.077	2.64	.9959	.001
−2.12	.0170	2.126	−0.52	.3015	.712	1.08	.8599	.071	2.68	.9963	.001
−2.08	.0188	2.087	−0.48	.3156	.684	1.12	.8686	.066	2.72	.9967	.001
−2.04	.0207	2.048	−0.44	.3300	.657	1.16	.8770	.061	2.76	.9971	.001
−2.00	.0228	2.008	−0.40	.3446	.630	1.20	.8849	.056	2.80	.9974	.0008
−1.96	.0250	1.969	−0.36	.3594	.597	1.24	.8925	.052	2.84	.9977	.0007
−1.92	.0274	1.930	−0.32	.3745	.576	1.28	.8997	.048	2.88	.9980	.0006
−1.88	.0301	1.892	−0.28	.3897	.555	1.32	.9066	.044	2.92	.9982	.0005
−1.84	.0329	1.853	−0.24	.4052	.530	1.36	.9131	.040	2.96	.9985	.0004
−1.80	.0359	1.814	−0.20	.4207	.507	1.40	.9192	.037	3.00	.9987	.0004
−1.76	.0392	1.776	−0.16	.4364	.484	1.44	.9251	.034	3.04	.9988	.0003
−1.72	.0427	1.737	−0.12	.4522	.462	1.48	.9306	.031	3.08	.9990	.0003
−1.68	.0465	1.699	−0.08	.4681	.440	1.52	.9357	.028	3.12	.9991	.0002
−1.64	.0505	1.661	−0.04	.4840	.419	1.56	.9406	.026	3.16	.9992	.0002
−1.60	.0548	1.623	0.00	.5000	.399	1.60	.9452	.023	3.20	.9993	.0002
−1.56	.0594	1.586	0.04	.5160	.379	1.64	.9495	.021	3.24	.9994	.0001
−1.52	.0643	1.548	0.08	.5319	.360	1.68	.9535	.019	3.28	.9995	.0001
−1.48	.0694	1.511	0.12	.5478	.342	1.72	.9573	.017	3.32	.9995	.0001
−1.44	.0749	1.474	0.16	.5636	.324	1.76	.9608	.016	3.36	.9996	.0001
−1.40	.0808	1.437	0.20	.5793	.307	1.80	.9641	.014	3.40	.9997	.0001
−1.36	.0869	1.400	0.24	.5948	.290	1.84	.9671	.013			
−1.32	.0934	1.364	0.28	.6103	.275	1.88	.9699	.012			
−1.28	.1003	1.328	0.32	.6255	.256	1.92	.9726	.010			
−1.24	.1075	1.292	0.36	.6406	.237	1.96	.9750	.009			
−1.20	.1151	1.256	0.40	.6554	.230	2.00	.9772	.008			
−1.16	.1230	1.221	0.44	.6700	.217	2.04	.9793	.008			
−1.12	.1314	1.186	0.48	.6844	.204	2.08	.9812	.007			
−1.08	.1401	1.151	0.52	.6985	.192	2.12	.9830	.006			
−1.04	.1492	1.117	0.56	.7123	.180	2.16	.9846	.005			
−1.00	.1587	1.083	0.60	.7257	.169	2.20	.9861	.005			
−0.96	.1685	1.049	0.64	.7389	.158	2.24	.9875	.004			
−0.92	.1788	1.017	0.68	.7517	.148	2.28	.9887	.004			
−0.88	.1894	.984	0.72	.7642	.138	2.32	.9898	.003			
−0.84	.2005	.952	0.76	.7764	.129	2.36	.9909	.003			

where

$E(N)$ = expected number of units short per year

$E(n)$ = expected number of units short per order cycle

D = annual demand

Q = order quantity

EXAMPLE 13 Determine the expected number of units short per year if $E(n) = .294$ units, $D = 1{,}000$ units per year, and $Q = 100$ units.

Solution

There are 10 order cycles per year: $\frac{D}{Q} = \frac{1{,}000}{100} = 10$. Thus, the expected number of units short per year is $E(n)(10) = .294(10) = 2.94$, or about 3 units.

Sometimes, it is useful to refer to the *annual service level,* which is defined as 1.0 minus the fraction of units short per year:

$$\text{Annual service level} = 1.0 - \frac{E(N)}{D} \tag{12–16}$$

This relationship can be used to interpret lead-time service level in terms of annual service level, and vice versa, and to answer related questions such as the amount of safety stock needed to achieve a specified annual service level.

EXAMPLE 14 Given $D = 1{,}000$ units per year, $Q = 100$ units, $\sigma_{dL} = 14$ units, and $E(N) = 10$ units, determine the following:

1. The lead-time service level implied by an expected annual shortage of 10 units.
2. A quantity of safety stock that will be consistent with an annual shortage of 10 units.

Solution

1. Find $E(n)$: $E(N) = E(n)\frac{D}{Q}$

   $$10 = E(n)\frac{1{,}000}{100}$$

   Solving, $E(n) = 1$
   Find $E(z)$: $E(n) = E(z)\sigma_{dL}$
   $1 = E(z)(14)$
   Solving, $E(z) = .071$
   Use Table 12–5 to determine the value of the service level. Thus, for $E(z) = .071$, the service level is .8599, or .86.
2. For a lead-time service level of .86, $z = +1.08$. Safety stock $= z\sigma_{dL} = 1.08(14) = 15.12$, or 15 units.

In a situation in which the ROP is set on the basis of an annual service level, it is entirely possible that the resulting value of z will be negative. This means that the ROP is less than expected lead-time demand, and that in more than half of the order cycles, shortages will occur. Also, it means that there is *no* safety stock. Although such cases are unusual, they are not illogical. The implication is that shortage costs are relatively low in comparison to holding costs.

SUMMARY

Inventories are stores of goods held for future use. Organizations maintain inventories because the inventories *decouple* the stages in a production process, allow for economic lot sizes in the buying and selling of goods, and allow for flexibility in planning and scheduling of operations.

The main questions that must be addressed in inventory management are: When to order? and How much to order? Various EOQ models can be used to answer the question of order quantities. The question of when to order is frequently handled using ROP models, which can incorporate variability in both usage rates and lead times in order to achieve desired service levels. The various models are summarized in Table 12–6.

The A-B-C model of inventory management underscores that the types of items carried in a typical inventory differ in terms of their importance to the overall goals of the organization, and for that reason, suggests that resources used to order, hold, and control inventories be allocated according to a priority system that recognizes the differing degrees of importance.

The techniques described in this chapter pertain to *independent demand* items, which usually are end items of a production process. The next chapter deals with dependent demand items, which typically are component parts whose demand is derived from demand for the finished product.

GLOSSARY

A-B-C Approach A classification system for inventory management that groups items according to importance.

Carrying Costs Costs associated with holding inventories, such as obsolescence, deterioration, opportunity costs, and pilferage.

Customer Service Level A measure of effectiveness of inventory management. *Cycle* service level refers to the *probability* that demand during lead time will not exceed the amount on hand; *annual* service level refers to the *percentage* of demand that is satisfied from stock on hand.

Dependent Demand Derived demand, such as the demand for components that will be needed for a specified output of assembled products.

EOQ (Economic Order Quantity) The order quantity that minimizes the sum of annual carrying and ordering costs.

TABLE 12–6 Summary of Inventory Formulas

Model	Formula	Symbols
1. Basic EOQ	$Q_o = \sqrt{\frac{2DS}{H}}$	Q_o = economic order quantity D = annual demand S = order cost H = annual carrying cost per unit
2. Economic run size	$Q_o = \sqrt{\frac{2DS}{H}}\sqrt{\frac{p}{p-d}}$ $I_m = \sqrt{\frac{2DS}{H}}\sqrt{\frac{p-d}{p}}$	Q_o = optimum run size p = production or delivery rate d = demand rate I_m = maximum inventory level
3. Reorder point under *a.* Constant demand and lead time	$ROP = d(L)$	ROP = quantity on hand at reorder point d = demand rate L = lead time
b. Variable demand rate	$ROP = \bar{d}L + z\sqrt{L}(\sigma_d)$	$\bar{d}$ = average demand rate σ_d = standard deviation of demand rate z = standard normal deviation
c. Variable lead time	$ROP = d\bar{L} + zd(\sigma_L)$	$\bar{L}$ = average lead time
d. Variable lead time and demand	$ROP = \bar{d}\bar{L} + z\sqrt{\bar{L}\sigma_d^2 + \bar{d}^2\sigma_L^2}$	σ_l = standard deviation of lead time
4. Expected number of units short	$E(N) = E(z)\sigma_{dL} \times \frac{D}{Q}$	$E(N)$ = expected number short per year $E(z)\sigma_{dL}$ = expected number short per cycle $E(z)$ from Table 12–5

Holding Costs See **Carrying Costs.**

Independent Demand Demand that is not derived from demand for an end item (e.g., the demand for finished goods).

Lead Time The interval of time between ordering and receipt of goods.

Ordering Costs Costs associated with placing an order for inventory, such as preparing the invoice and inspecting an order for quality and quantity.

Risk of a Stockout The probability that demand will exceed supply during lead time.

ROP (Reorder Point) The quantity of inventory needed to meet expected demand during lead time plus safety stock. When stock on hand falls to this level, a reorder is triggered.

Safety Stock Inventory carried in excess of expected demand to offset possible increased demand and/or increased lead time.

Stockout An out-of-stock condition created when demand exceeds supply on hand.

SOLVED PROBLEMS

Problem 1. *EOQ* Mayflour Manufacturing uses approximately 40 packing crates per day for shipping. The firm ships 250 days per year. Annual holding costs are $1 per crate and ordering cost is $100.

a. What order size will minimize total annual holding and ordering cost?

b. How many times a year will Mayflour order using this order size?

c. Determine the total annual holding and ordering cost for packing crates.

Solution

a. The EOQ will minimize total annual cost. In order to compute it we must know annual demand (D), annual holding cost per unit (H), and ordering cost (S). S = $100 and H = $1. D must be computed:

$$D = 40 \text{ crates per day} \times 250 \text{ days} = 10{,}000 \text{ crates per year}$$

Thus:

$$Q_o = \sqrt{\frac{2DS}{H}} = \sqrt{\frac{2(10{,}000)(100)}{1}} = 1414.21, \text{ or } 1{,}414 \text{ rounded}$$

(Because D, S, and H usually are *estimated*, the EOQ should be stated as a whole number, so as not to give the impression that it is a precise value.)

b. The number of orders per year is equal to the annual demand divided by order size:

$$\begin{aligned} D/Q &= 10{,}000 \text{ crates per year}/1{,}414 \text{ per order} \\ &= 7.07 \text{ orders per year (i.e., approximately 7)} \end{aligned}$$

c.
$$\begin{aligned} TC &= \text{Annual holding cost} + \text{Annual ordering cost} \\ &= \frac{Q_o}{2}H + \frac{D}{Q_o}S \\ &= \frac{1{,}414}{2}(1) + \frac{10{,}000}{1{,}414}(100) \\ &= 707 + 707.21 = \$1{,}414.21 \end{aligned}$$

(Note: At the EOQ, both costs are equal. However, due to rounding the EOQ in part (a), the costs are slightly different: 707 versus 707.21.)

Problem 2. *Economic run size* A furniture manufacturer, Wooding, Inc., cuts wood for desk tops it produces. The wood can be cut and sanded at the rate of 300 tops per day. Desks are assembled at the rate of 80 per day. Setup cost for cutting is $200 and holding cost is $20 per year. Annual demand is 16,000 desks.

a. What run size is most economical for desks?

b. How many runs per year will be made?

c. What will be the maximum inventory?

Solution

a.
$$p = 300 \text{ tops per day}$$
$$d = 80 \text{ tops per day}$$
$$D = 16{,}000 \text{ desks per year}$$
$$S = \$200$$
$$H = \$20 \text{ per year}$$

$$Q_o = \sqrt{\frac{2DS}{H}}\sqrt{\frac{p}{p-d}}$$
$$= \sqrt{\frac{2(16{,}000)(200)}{20}}\sqrt{\frac{300}{300-80}} = 660.58, \text{ or } 661 \text{ rounded}$$

b. Runs per year $= D/Q_o$: $\frac{16{,}000}{661} = 24.21$, or about 24.

c. $$I_{max} = \sqrt{\frac{2DS}{H}}\sqrt{\frac{p-d}{p}} = \sqrt{\frac{2(16{,}000)(200)}{20}}\sqrt{\frac{300-80}{300}}$$
$$= 484.4, \text{ or } 484 \text{ rounded}$$

Problem 3. *Quantity discount* The Mountainview Motel replaces about 800 sheets every year. The supplier charges a price that depends on quantity ordered: for 1 pair to 99 pairs, the price is \$20 a pair; for 100 to 199 pairs, the price is \$18 a pair, and for larger quantities, the price is \$17 a pair. Holding cost is \$3 per pair per year and ordering cost is \$65 for each order. If the owner, Bob Mountainview, wants to minimize the sum of holding, ordering, and purchasing costs, what order size is optimal?

Solution

Because holding cost is constant rather than a percentage of price, all total cost curves will have the *same* Q_o. If $D = 800$ pairs per year, $S = \$65$, and $H = \$3$, Q_o is:

$$Q_o = \sqrt{\frac{2DS}{H}} = \sqrt{\frac{2(800)(65)}{3}} = 186.20, \text{ or } 186 \text{ rounded}$$

The prices and quantity ranges are:

Range	Price
1 to 99	\$20
100 to 199	18
200+	17

A sketch of the total cost curves looks like this:

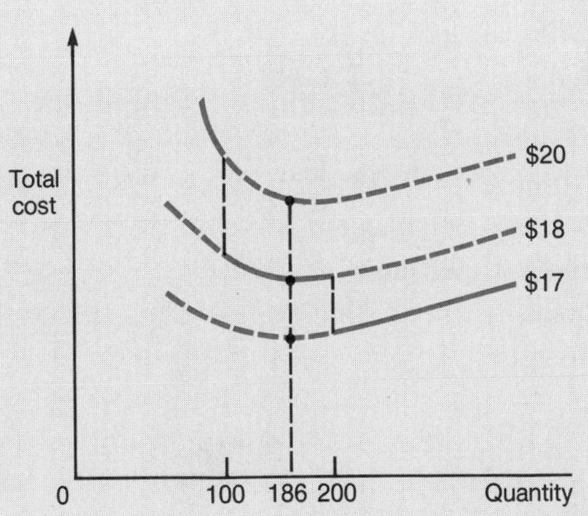

The EOQ quantity is feasible on the \$18 curve (i.e., 186 falls in the range 100 to 199, which has a price per pair of \$18).

Consequently, if the optimal quantity is on the \$18 curve, it will be at 186. If it is on the lowest curve, it will be at 200 pairs. Thus, once we find the range in which the EOQ is feasible, we identify the price breaks of any lower cost curve and make a total cost comparison:

$$TC = \frac{Q}{2}H + \frac{D}{Q}S + PD$$

$$TC_{186} = \frac{186}{2}(3) + \frac{800}{186}(65) + 18(800)$$

$$= 279 + 279.57 + 14{,}400 = \$14{,}958.57$$

$$TC_{200} = \frac{200}{2}(3) + \frac{800}{200}(65) + 17(800)$$

$$= 300 + 260 + 13{,}600 = \$14{,}160$$

Because the total cost for 200 is lower than the total cost for 186, 200 is the optimal order quantity.

Problem 4. *ROP* A small shop sells fresh-made caramel corn. Because of the desire to offer the freshest product possible (and because of severe storage limitations), the manager of the shop, Tom Sweet, wants to determine when to reorder (i.e., prepare) another batch. Because processing time is one hour, a stockout would mean lost business because customers are not willing to wait more than a few minutes for this product.

Demand averages 30 pounds of carmel corn per hour. This can be approximated by a normal distribution with a mean of 30 and a standard deviation of 4 pounds. Tom wants a service level of 96 percent.

a. What ROP will achieve Tom's desired service level?

b. How much safety stock will be needed?

c. What is the risk of a stockout?

d. What is the expected amount of shortage?

Solution

In this problem, demand is variable and lead time is constant.

$$\bar{d} = 30 \text{ pounds per hour}$$
$$\sigma_d = 4 \text{ pounds per hour}$$
$$L = 1 \text{ hour}$$
$$\text{Service level} = 96 \text{ percent}$$

a. $\text{ROP} = \bar{d}LT + z\sigma_d\sqrt{L}$

For a service level of 96 percent, $z = 1.75$ [Appendix Table B2]

Thus:

$$\begin{aligned}\text{ROP} &= 30(1) + 1.75(4)\sqrt{1}\\ &= 30 + 7\\ &= 37 \text{ pounds}\end{aligned}$$

b. The safety stock is the amount of stock in excess of expected demand. Expected demand is 30 pounds (see part *a*), and the safety stock is 7 pounds.

c. The risk of a stockout is:

$$1.00 - \text{Service level}$$

Thus, the risk is $1.00 - .96 = .04$, or 4%.

d. The expected amount of shortage is:

$$E(n) = E(z)\sigma_{dL}$$

From Table 12–5, with $z = 1.75$, $E(z)$ is approximately equal to .016. And $\sigma_{dL} = \sigma_d\sqrt{L}$, which is $4\sqrt{1} = 4$. Therefore, $E(n) = .016(4) = .064$ pounds, or about 1 ounce. Obviously, this amount of shortage is quite small. The manager may want to reconsider the amount of safety stock being carried (i.e., the manager could use a smaller ROP, such as 35 or 36 pounds).

PROBLEMS

1. A food processor expects to use 54,000 glass jars per year for a new line of fruit juices that have recently been introduced. Because of breakage and special handling requirements, annual holding cost is 6 cents per jar. Reordering procedures are fairly standard and have a cost of \$20. Determine the following:

   a. The economic order quantity.

   Average inventory if the EOQ is used.

c. The optimum number of orders per year.

d. Total annual holding and ordering cost.

2. A municipal lighting department replaces 10 obsolete street lights each week, 50 weeks per year. Each light costs $60. Ordering cost is $75 per order, and annual holding cost is 20 percent of the price per light.

   a. What order quantity will minimize total annual holding and ordering costs?

   b. What annual cost will result if the EOQ is used?

   c. The commissioner of public works has suggested that lights be ordered in round lots of 100 units. What effect would that policy have on annual holding and ordering costs?

3. An oil drilling company, AccuDrill, wears out drill bits at a rate of 4 per day. The drill is operated 5 days a week, 50 weeks a year. The bits cost $70 each, and the annual holding cost is 18 percent of purchase price. Ordering cost is $10 for each order. Assume the usage rate of drill bits is constant. Determine the following:

   a. Annual demand for drill bits.

   b. The economic order quantity.

   c. Maximum inventory of bits, assuming no safety stock.

   d. The frequency with which drills are reordered.

   e. Suppose a review of this process indicates that holding costs have increased to 25 percent due to increased opportunity costs, and that ordering cost is $12. What EOQ would now be appropriate? What cost penalty would the company incur by staying with the former EOQ?

4. The new manager of One Hour Cleaners, a dry cleaning firm, is reevaluating ordering policies for metal hangers. After careful consideration, the manager has decided that the holding cost is $10 per box annually and the ordering cost is $15 for each order. Monthly usage of hangers is approximately 70 boxes. How often should hangers be ordered and in what quantity if the goal is to minimize the annual total of holding and ordering costs?

5. Dairy Creme, an ice cream producer, has the capacity to make 400 gallons of ice cream per day. The firm has negotiated an agreement to supply 100 gallons of strawberry ice cream per day to a local distributor for 250 days per year. Cleaning and adjusting the equipment prior to each run costs $35, and the annualized cost of carrying a gallon of ice cream is $2.15. Determine the following:

   a. Annual demand.

   b. The optimum run size.

   c. The inventory buildup rate.

   d. Length of a run in days.

   e. Maximum inventory of strawberry ice cream.

f. The number of runs per year.

g. Total annual holding and setup cost.

6. Healthy Pet, Inc. produces a variety of canned and dry food for dogs and cats. One of its products is Gourmet Mix, which it can produce at a rate of 2,000 cases per week. Weekly demand for this product is quite stable, generally within a few cases of 800 cases. The firm operates 52 weeks a year.
   The Gourmet Mix sells wholesale for $24 per case, and the holding cost is 20 percent of the wholesale price. Setup cost for a run is $48. The company is now producing 1,600 cans per run.
   a. Given this information, what run size would minimize the annual cost of holding and setup for the Gourmet Mix?
   b. How much could the company save annually in holding and setup costs by using the economic run size?

7. A small firm has received a contract to supply photoelectric cells to a large manufacturing company, at a stated rate of 45 per day. The firm has the capacity to produce 70 per day. Setup cost is $60 and holding cost is $2 per unit. Both firms operate 250 days a year.
   a. What run size will minimize holding and setup costs?
   b. The manager has some concern about the belated discovery that the warehouse can store only 525 of these photoelectric cells at one time. How would you respond to that concern (i.e., will there be a problem)? Explain.

8. How would you respond to the criticism that EOQ models tend to provide misleading order sizes and do not really minimize inventory costs because holding and ordering costs and annual demand are, at best, educated guesses?

9. Upon returning from an unexciting vacation, Tom Dooley, the manager of the Commuter Travel Agency, discovers a revised price list for itinerary packets, which is reproduced below. The agency uses approximately 3,000 packets per year. Because the packets are used mainly for business travelers, demand is relatively stable throughout the year. After conferring with his fiancee, who is completing her MBA at a nearby university, the manager estimates the holding cost to be $2 per year for a packet, and ordering cost to be $7.

Quantity	Unit Price
1–139	$6.60
140–299	6.40
300+	6.00

   a. What order size would minimize the annual sum of holding, ordering, and purchasing costs?
   b. How frequently will reordering be necessary using your order size?

10. A print shop handles orders for 12,000 rolls of admission tickets per year, which it delivers at a rate of 1,000 rolls per month. Reordering blank rolls entails a cost of approximately $100, according to the manager, Bob Pressman, and the carrying cost is estimated to be 20 cents per roll on a yearly basis. Order quantities of less than 3,000 rolls have a price of $1.90 per roll, quantities of 3,000 rolls to 5,999 rolls cost $1.82 per roll, and larger amounts cost $1.70 per roll.

   a. What order size would minimize the sum of carrying, ordering, and purchasing costs?

   b. What other factors might be considered by the manager in deciding whether to use the minimum cost order size or whether to use another quantity, such as 3,464 rolls?

11. Pure 'n Simple, a leading producer of bottled apple juice, uses about 41,000 cartons of 2-liter plastic bottles per year. Because juice is processed from cold storage fruit, production and distribution are uniform throughout the year. A recent emphasis on cost reduction requires a review of order quantities for the plastic bottles. Currently, 2,000 cartons are ordered at a time. Ordering cost is $50 and holding cost is 25 percent of unit purchase price per carton per year. Purchase price depends on order quantities: 1 to 1,199 are $3.70 per carton, 1,200 to 2,199 are $3.50 per carton, and larger quantities are $3.40 per carton.

   a. What order size will result in the minimum annual cost of holding, ordering, and purchasing of the plastic bottles?

   b. Suppose the manager favors the current order quantity of 2,000 because it represents exactly five truckloads. Assuming only full truckloads will be used, is there a more economical order size? If so, what is it?

12. An automotive assembly plant is implementing a purchasing policy of buying from local suppliers whenever possible. One item that can be bought locally is a head gasket. The plant uses 3,000 boxes of gaskets per year. Ordering cost is $60 and holding cost is 30 percent of unit price per year. There are two local vendors from which to choose. Their price lists are shown below. Assuming the goal is to minimize inventory costs, which vendor and what order quantity would you recommend? Why?

Vendor A		Vendor B	
Number of Boxes	**Price per Box**	**Number of Boxes**	**Price per Box**
1 to 399	$3.97	1 to 500	$4.00
400 to 549	3.80	501 to 1,399	3.80
550 or more	3.66	1,400 or more	3.60

13. Metro Transit expects to replace 3,600 fan belts during the coming year. The cost to place and receive an order is $30, and annual holding cost is $1.67 per unit, based on average inventory. The usage of fan belts during

lead time can be described by a normal distribution that has a mean of 60 fan belts and a standard deviation of 11 fan belts.

a. What order quantity will minimize the sum of annual ordering and holding costs?

b. If an acceptable risk of stockout is 10 percent, how many belts should be on hand when an order is placed?

c. How much safety stock is being carried?

14. The traffic bureau of Gothamville uses an average of 15 books of traffic citations per day. Daily usage is approximately normal with a mean of 15 books and a standard deviation of 2.5 books. Processing of reorders takes four days, and it is relatively constant. Because of the income generated by the citations, the chief has requested a low risk of stockout. If books are reordered when the quantity on hand is 70 books, what is the risk that a stockout will occur? What is the expected number of books short for any given lead-time interval?

15. Robo Tech., Inc., specializes in assembling pick-and-place robots for materials handling. Daily production is essentially stable because assembly robots are used. A recent design change requires the use of an oil-impregnated bearing. The firm will use these bearings at the rate of 50 per day. Lead time for the bearings is normal with a mean of 3 days and a standard deviation of 1 day. Bearings are shipped by truck from a regional warehouse. What reorder point would provide a service level for lead time of 99 percent?

16. A professional football team uses large quantities of adhesive tape during and immediately preceding the football season. Daily usage tends to be normal with a mean of 40 rolls and a standard deviation of 6 rolls. Ordering lead time is also approximately normal, and it has a mean of 3 days and a standard deviation of ½ day. The front office wants a stockout risk of 2 percent.

a. What ROP is appropriate?

b. By how much could safety stock be reduced if there were some way to reduce the lead-time variability to zero? What effect on safety stock would result if a constant lead time of 1 day could be achieved?

17. Because of theft, vandalism, abuse, and normal wearouts, a large hotel replaces approximately 260 color television sets per year. Ordering cost is $65 for each order, and annual holding cost is $40 per set. Lead-time demand can be described by a normal distribution with a mean of 8 and a standard deviation of 3.5 sets. The manager of housekeeping, Lilly May, is willing to accept an average shortage of 2 sets per lead time due to the ability to transfer sets among rooms, except for a relatively few times when the rooms are completely booked.

a. What is the economic order quantity of televisions?

b. How many orders per year will be made?

c. What is the expected number of units short per year?

d. What ROP should be used to achieve the desired protection?

e. What is the risk of a stockout during lead time for that ROP?

18. A firm that sells smoke alarms expects annual demand to be 3,000 units next year. The firm sells exclusively to building contractors, and the smoke detectors are shipped at a fairly constant rate, although there is some variability in demand. In fact, daily demand can be described by a normal distribution that has a mean of 12.6 detectors per day and a standard deviation of 5 per day. The firm orders the detectors from a manufacturer in Hong Kong. Lead time for orders is normal with a mean of 43 days and a standard deviation of 3 days. Ordering and receiving costs are $93.75 per order and holding cost is $1 per unit a year.

a. The sales manager wants an annual service level of .999. What ROP would meet this objective?

b. What is the expected annual cost of carrying safety stock?

19. Manager Barry Hardy wants to establish an ROP for safety harnesses used by construction workers. Occasionally, harnesses wear out and must be replaced. However, because of their high cost, the manager does not want to tie up a great deal of money needlessly. After analyzing use over the past several years, Barry has concluded that usage during lead time can be described by a Poisson distribution that has a mean of 1.3 harnesses.

a. If the current ROP is 3 harnesses, what is the effective service level? What is the risk of a shortage?

b. What ROP would provide a risk of shortage of approximately 1 percent?

20. During the winter months, the Twisting Slopes ski resort must replace blades on snow removal equipment. The wearout rate can be described by a Poisson distribution that has a mean of two blades per week. Manager Sam Summers usually tries to keep a two-week supply of blades on hand, and he reorders whenever the supply drops to two blades. Additional blades can be obtained from a distributor, and delivery takes about one week.

a. What is the risk of a stockout under this arrangement?

b. What ROP would achieve a service level of approximately 98 percent?

21. An illustration of A-B-C classification of inventory items was given in Table 12–1. Refer to that table and use the data provided to determine the percentage of items in each category and the percentage of dollar volume in each category.

22. Below is a partial listing of the items on a firm's computer printout of inventory. Using annual dollar value as the criterion, arrange these items into an A-B-C classification. Assign three items to the B category.

Part Number	Unit Price	Annual Volume
C150	$ 1	30,000
C175	2	7,000
MM09	200	400
TL44	4	6,000
MT45	70	3,000
T418	30	3,000
C110	3	5,000
UN04	3	6,000
UN12	4	4,000
BA28	60	2,000
T400	5	4,000

Chapter 12 Case

Elysian Cycles

Elysian Cycles (EC), located in a major southwestern city, is a wholesale distributor of bicycles and bicycle parts. Its primary retail outlets are located in eight cities within a 400-mile radius of the distribution center. These retail outlets generally depend on receiving orders for additional stock within two days after notifying the distribution center (if the stock is available). The company's management feels this is a valuable marketing tool that aids survival in a highly competitive industry.

EC distributes a wide variety of finished bicycles, but these are all based on five different frame designs, each of which may be available in several sizes. Table 1 gives a breakdown of the product options available to the retail outlets.

EC receives these different styles from a single manufacturer overseas, and shipments may take as long as four weeks from the time an order is made by telephone or telex. With the cost of communication, paperwork, and customs clearance included, EC estimates that each time an order is placed it incurs a cost of $65. The cost per bicycle is roughly 60 percent of the suggested list price for any of the styles available.

Demand for the bicycles is somewhat seasonal in nature, heavier in the spring and early summer and tapering off through the fall and winter seasons (except for a heavy surge during the six weeks prior to Christmas). A breakdown of the previous year's business with the retail outlets usually forms the basis for EC's yearly operations plan. A growth factor (either positive or negative) is used to refine further the demand estimate by reflecting the upcoming yearly market for bicycle sales. By developing a yearly plan and updating it when appropriate, EC can establish some reasonable basis for obtaining any necessary financing from the bank. Last year's monthly demand for the different bicycle styles EC distributes is shown in Table 2.

Because of the increased popularity of bicycles for recreational purposes and the supplanting of some automobile usage, EC believes that its market may grow by as much as 25 percent during the upcoming year. However, because there have been years when the full amount of expected growth did not materialize, EC has decided to base its plan on a more conservative 15 percent growth factor to allow for variations in consumer buying habits and to ensure that it is not excessively overstocked if the full market does not occur. Holding costs associated with inventory of any bicycle style is estimated to be about 0.75 percent of the unit cost of a bicycle per month.

Source: James A. Fitzsimmons and Robert S. Sullivan, *Service Operations Management* (New York: McGraw-Hill, 1982).

TABLE 1 Bicycles Stocked

Frame Style	Available Sizes	Number of Gears	Suggested List Price (complete bicycle)
A	18, 21, 23	3	$ 99.95
B	18, 21, 23	10	124.95
C	18, 21, 23, 24.5	10	169.95
D	21, 23, 24.5	10	219.95
E	21, 23, 24.5	10 or 15	349.95

TABLE 2 Monthly Demand

	Frame Style					
Month	A	B	C	D	E	Total
January	0	3	5	2	0	10
February	2	8	10	3	1	24
March	4	15	21	12	2	54
April	4	35	40	21	3	103
May	3	43	65	37	3	151
June	3	27	41	18	2	91
July	2	13	26	11	1	53
August	1	10	16	9	1	37
September	1	9	11	7	1	29
October	1	8	10	7	2	28
November	2	15	19	12	3	51
December	3	30	33	19	4	89
Total	26	216	297	158	23	720

Discussion question

Develop an inventory control plan for Elysian Cycles to use as the basis for its upcoming yearly plan. Be sure to justify your reasons for choosing a particular type (or combination of types) of inventory system(s). On the basis of your particular plan, specify the safety stock requirements if EC institutes a policy of maintaining a 95 percent service level.

Chapter 12 Case

Harvey Industries

Background

Harvey Industries, a Wisconsin company, was incorporated in 1950 and specializes in the assembly of high-pressure washer systems and in the sale of repair parts for these systems. The products range from small portable high-pressure washers to large industrial installations for snow removal from vehicles stored outdoors during the winter months. Typical uses for high-pressure water cleaning include:

Automobiles
Airplanes
Building maintenance
Barns
Engines
Ice cream plants
Lift trucks
Machinery
Swimming pools

Industrial customers include General Motors, Ford, Chrysler, Delta Airlines, United Parcel Service, and Shell Oil Company.

Although the industrial applications are a significant part of its sales, Harvey Industries is primarily an assembler of equipment for coin operated self-service car wash systems. The typical car wash is of concrete block construction with an equipment room in the center, flanked on either side by a number of bays. The cars are driven into the bays where the owner can wash and wax the car, utilizing high-pressure hot water and liquid wax. A dollar bill changer is available to provide change for the use of the equipment and the purchase of various products from dispensers. The products include towels, white wall cleaner, and upholstery cleaner.

In recent years Harvey Industries has been in financial difficulty. The company has lost money for three of the last four years, with the last year's loss being $17,174 on sales of $1,238,674. Inventory levels have been steadily increasing to their present levels of $124,324.

The company employs 23 people with the management team consisting of the following key employees: president, sales manager, manufacturing manager, con-

Source: This case was prepared by Donald F. Condit of the Lawrence Technological University, Southfield, Michigan, as a basis for class discussion rather than to illustrate either effective or ineffective organizational practices. Presented at Midwest Case Writers Association Workshop, 1984, and accepted by referees of the Midwest Case Writers Association for international distribution. Reprinted by permission.

troller, and purchasing manager. The abbreviated organization chart reflects the reporting relationship of the key employees and the three individuals who report directly to the manufacturing manager.

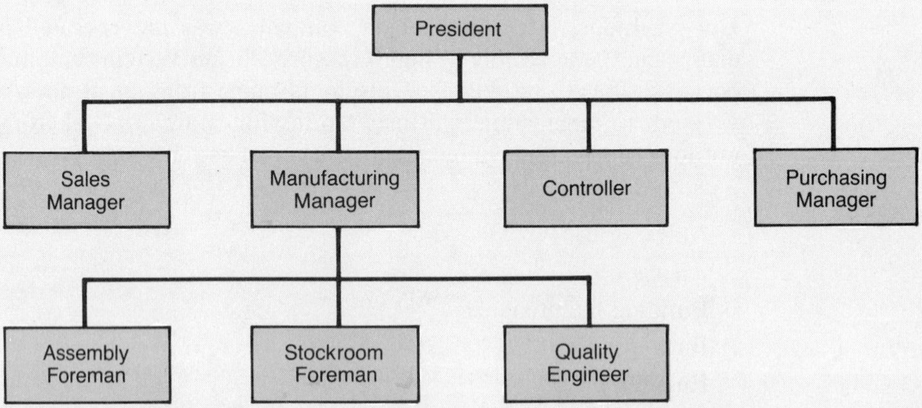

Current Inventory Control System

The current inventory control "system" consists of orders for stock replenishment being made by the stockroom foreman, the purchasing manager, or the manufacturing manager whenever one of them notices that the inventory is low. An order for replenishment of inventory is also placed whenever someone (either a customer or an employee in the assembly area) wants an item and it is not in stock.

Some inventory is needed for the assembly of the high-pressure equipment for the car wash and industrial applications. There are current and accurate bills of material for these assemblies. The material needs to support the assembly schedule are generally known well in advance of the build schedule.

The majority of inventory transactions are for repair parts and for supplies used by the car washes, such as paper towels, detergent, and wax concentrate. Because of the constant and rugged use of the car wash equipment, there is a steady demand for the various repair parts.

The stockroom is well organized, with parts stored in locations according to each vendor. The number of vendors is relatively limited, with each vendor generally supplying many different parts. For example, the repair parts from Allen Bradley, a manufacturer of electrical motors, are stocked in the same location. These repair parts will be used to provide service for the many electrical motors that are part of the high-pressure pump and motor assembly used by all of the car washes.

Because of the heavy sales volume of repair parts, there are generally two employees working in the stockroom—a stockroom foreman who reports to the manufacturing manager and an assistant to the foreman. One of these two employees will handle customer orders. Many customers stop by and order the parts and supplies they need. Telephone orders are also received and are shipped by United Parcel Service the same day.

The assembly area has some inventory stored on the shop floor. This inventory consists of low value items that are used every day, such as nuts, bolts, screws, and washers. These puchased items do not amount to very much dollar volume throughout the year. Unfortunately, often times the assembly area is out of one of these basic items and this causes a significant amount of downtime for the assembly lines.

Paperwork is kept to a minimum. A sales slip listing the part numbers and quantities sold to a customer is generally made out for each sale. If the assembly department needs items that are not stocked on the assembly floor, someone from that department will enter the stockroom and withdraw the necessary material. There is no paperwork made out for the items needed on the assembly floor.

There were 973 different part numbers purchased for stock last year and those purchases amounted to $314,673. Although the company does not utilize a computer, it does have some accurate records on how much money was spent on each part number last year. An analysis of the data shows that $220,684 was spent on just 179 of the part numbers.

Fortunately for Harvey Industries, most of the items they purchase are stocked by either the manufacturer or by a wholesaler. When it is discovered that the company is out of stock on an item, it generally takes only two or three days to replenish the stock.

Due to the company's recent losses, its auditing firm became concerned about the company's ability to continue in business. Recently the company sold off excess vacant land adjoining its manufacturing facility to generate cash to meet its financial obligations.

New President

Because of the recent death of the owner, the Trust Department of a Milwaukee Bank (as trustee for the estate) has taken over the company's affairs and has appointed a new company president. The new president has identified many problem areas—one of which is improper inventory control. He has retained you as a consultant to make speific recommendations concerning a revised inventory control system. What are your recommendations and their rationale?

Chapter 13
Inventory Models II

Chapter Outline

Learning Objectives

After completing this chapter, you should be able to:

1. Compare and contrast fixed interval ordering with ordering fixed quantities and solve typical fixed interval problems.
2. Describe the circumstances under which the single period model is appropriate and solve typical problems.
3. For the major elements of MRP:
   a. Compare and contrast independent and dependent demand and the implications of their differences.
   b. List and briefly describe MRP inputs.
   c. Describe MRP processing.
   d. Briefly discuss safety stocks, lot sizing, and capacity planning.
   e. Describe MRP II and relate it to MRP.
4. Prepare an MRP plan.
5. Describe just-in-time systems and compare these to more traditional approaches to production and inventory control.

The preceding chapter introduced the subject of inventory management and some basic inventory models. This chapter describes some additional models. The models in this chapter cover ordering at fixed intervals (fixed-interval model), ordering items that have limited shelf lives (the single-period model), and ordering items that have dependent demand (MRP). The discussion begins with ordering at fixed intervals.

ORDERING AT FIXED INTERVALS

Inventory ordering using the EOQ/ROP approach involves ordering a predetermined amount (the EOQ) whenever the quantity of inventory on hand falls to a predetermined level (the ROP). In such cases, the order *size* is fixed, although the length of order cycles tends to vary if demand is variable. In contrast to this is ordering that occurs only at fixed *intervals* (e.g., once a week, once a month, etc.). If demand is variable in these situations, it is the order *size* that will vary, because the length of the order cycle remains constant. The **fixed interval model** addresses this condition.

Fixed order intervals either can occur as the result of a supplier's policy of delivering at prescribed times (e.g., every Tuesday morning) or it may reflect a buyer's policy that is based on the economics of the situation. For example, in some instances, if a buyer orders a variety of items from the same supplier, there can be economies in both transportation costs and ordering costs achieved by grouping orders instead of ordering items separately using a reorder point approach.

Examples of types of firms that have the tendency to use a fixed interval approach to reordering include drugstores, supermarkets, department stores, and other retail businesses. Moreover, many other nonretail businesses order office and cleaning supplies and other items at fixed intervals.

The basic requirement in fixed ordering is determining the order size. Determination is done in each order cycle just prior to ordering. It generally involves counting or measuring the quantity of inventory on hand and subtracting that amount from the projected amount needed based on expected usage and safety stock. If demand is variable, the amount on hand at the reordering time will tend to vary from cycle to cycle, resulting in differing order sizes.

Unlike the ROP model, the protection interval that must be covered extends beyond the lead time. In fact, under the fixed interval system, the risk of a stockout (and, hence, the need to protect against such an occurrence) extends over *two* order cycles. This concept is illustrated in Figure 13–1. The reason for this is that even though stocks may be depleted much earlier than expected, as a general rule, another order cannot be placed until the fixed reorder time. Of course, once the first of the two orders is received, the risk of a stockout is greatly diminished. However, a temporary (or permanent) increase in demand could cause the amount on hand to fall below a desirable level without being able to

FIGURE 13–1 Fixed Interval Ordering

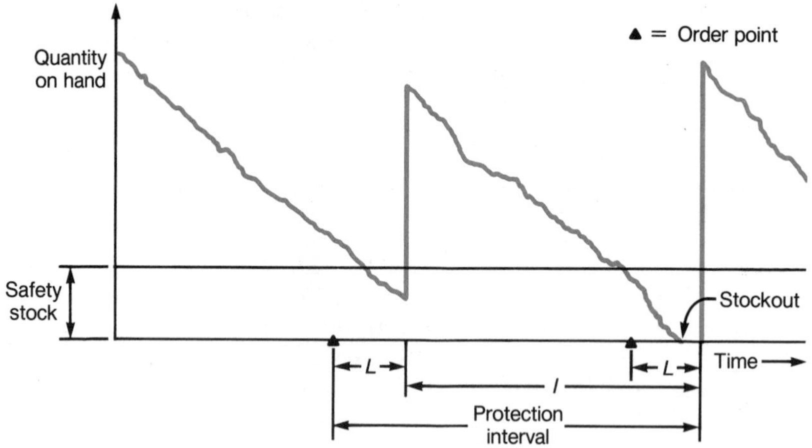

reorder. Consequently, when determining the amount to order, this possibility must be taken into account.

Although both demand and lead time might vary in a given case, perhaps, the most common case is when lead time is constant and demand varies. For purposes of illustration, only that case will be described. The appropriate order quantity can be calculated using this formula:

$$Q_o = \bar{d}(L + I) + z\sigma_d \sqrt{L + I} - A \qquad (13\text{–}1)$$

where

σ_d = standard deviation of demand
I = length of fixed interval
L = length of lead time
A = amount on hand

It is assumed that demand is approximately normal, although this is not a strict requirement.

■

EXAMPLE 1. A hospital orders surgical supplies using a fixed interval system. Suppose that just prior to ordering, a check of the supply of rolls of gauze bandages shows that there are 40 currently on hand. Suppose also that these rolls have a daily usage that is approximately normal with a mean of 9 rolls and a standard deviation of 4 rolls. Lead time is 2 days and the desired risk of a stockout is 1 percent. What order size is appropriate if the order interval is 12 days? How much of that is safety stock?

Solution

$\bar{d}$ = 9 rolls per day   For a risk of 1 percent, z = +2.33 (from Appendix Table B)

σ_d = 4 rolls per day

I = 12 days

L = 2 days

A = 40 rolls

$$Q_o = \bar{d}(I + L) + z\sigma_d\sqrt{I + L} - A$$
$$= 9(12 + 2) + 2.33(4)\sqrt{12 + 2} - 40$$
$$= 126 + 34.87 - 40 = 120.87, \text{ or } 121 \text{ rolls}$$

Safety stock is 34.87, which rounds to 35 rolls.

The formula can also be used to determine the amount of protection afforded by a particular order quantity, given the amount on hand.

EXAMPLE 2 In the preceding example, what risk of stockout would there be if an order quantity of 121 rolls is submitted when the amount on hand is 30 rolls?

Solution

Q_o = 121 rolls

A = 30 rolls

Risk = ?

Solve for z, then determine the risk:

$$121 = \bar{d}(I + L) + z\sigma_d\sqrt{I + L} - A$$
$$= 126 + z(4)\sqrt{12 + 2} - 30$$

Solving, z = 1.67, which reflects a risk of 1 − .9525 (from Appendix Table B) = .0475.

Note that although the fixed interval approach seems to imply that periodic reviews of inventory are necessary, there is no reason that fixed intervals cannot be used with perpetual inventory systems. However, it is advisable to occasionally perform a physical count in order to check the validity of the system because theft, spoilage, or some other factor might have a significant impact on the amounts on hand.

THE SINGLE PERIOD MODEL

The fixed interval model and the EOQ/ROP models are useful for situations in which leftover inventory can be carried over into the following order cycle without penalty (i.e., the inventory does not deteriorate or lose value). There are, however, items that either cannot be carried over or that have a penalty for the carryover. They include perishables (e.g., fresh fruits and vegetables, baked goods, meats and poultry, fast foods, and fresh cut flowers) and dated materials (e.g., newspapers, magazines, stock reports, tax forms, and textbooks). In addition, items held for a specific, limited use (e.g., spare parts for a machine, special attachments for equipment, and custom-made tools or equipment) also fall under this heading. The rationale is that their useful lives are equal to the life of the equipment they are held for.

The objective in deciding on order sizes for the **single period model** is to balance the cost of possible oversupply against the possible cost of undersupply. The cost of undersupply is a shortage cost, and it either may be the lost profit per unit short or it may involve a penalty, such as the cost of lost production because of the lack of a spare part. The cost of oversupply can reflect holding costs, the difference between purchase cost and salvage value, and even disposal costs incurred at the end of the order cycle. If shortage costs reflect only the profit potential, then:

$$C_{\text{shortage}} = C_s = \text{Revenue per unit} - \text{Cost per unit}$$

Excess cost is usually computed in the following manner:

$$C_{\text{excess}} = C_e = \text{Cost per unit} + \text{Holding cost per unit} - \text{Salvage value per unit}$$

Note that disposal costs would amount to *negative* salvage value. For example, if an item initially cost \$5, had a holding cost of \$1, and a disposal cost of \$2, the cost of excess would be \$5 + \$1 + \$2 = \$8 per unit. Also, in most cases, holding cost is excluded from the analysis. This is especially true if *incremental* costs of holding are small.

The objective of balancing expected shortage and excess costs is achieved when the order quantity is such that the service level equals the ratio of unit shortage cost to the sum of unit shortage and excess cost:

$$\text{Service level}_{\text{optimum}} = \frac{C_s}{C_s + C_e} \qquad (13\text{–}2)$$

If stocking levels are *continuous* (e.g., amount of fresh cider), an order size that precisely achieves the computed service level can be specified. However, if stocking quantities are *discrete* (e.g., the *number* of spares stocked), the optimum stocking level is the lowest one for which the resulting service level equals or exceeds the computed service level (i.e., it is usually necessary to *round up*).

■

EXAMPLE 3 Mack the Knife sells shark steaks at a small shop along the seashore. Mack buys the steaks for \$2.50 a pound from a local supply house and sells them for \$3.25 a pound. Holding costs are negligible, according to Mack, Jr. Leftover steaks are sold at \$1 per pound for bait. Daily demand can be described by a normal distribution that has a mean of 150 pounds and a standard deviation of 20 pounds. The order interval is 1 day. What order size is optimal?

Solution

$$C_s = \text{Revenue per unit} - \text{Cost per unit} = \$3.25 - \$2.50 = \$.75 \text{ per pound}$$

$$C_e = \text{Cost per unit} - \text{Salvage value per unit} = \$2.50 - \$1.00 = \$1.50 \text{ per pound}$$

$$\text{Service level} = \frac{C_s}{C_s + C_e} = \frac{\$.75}{\$.75 + \$1.50} = .33$$

This implies $z = -.44$ (from Appendix Table B).
In general, the order quantity is expected demand plus $z\sigma_d$. Thus:

$$Q_o = 150 - .44(20) = 141.2 \text{ lb.}$$

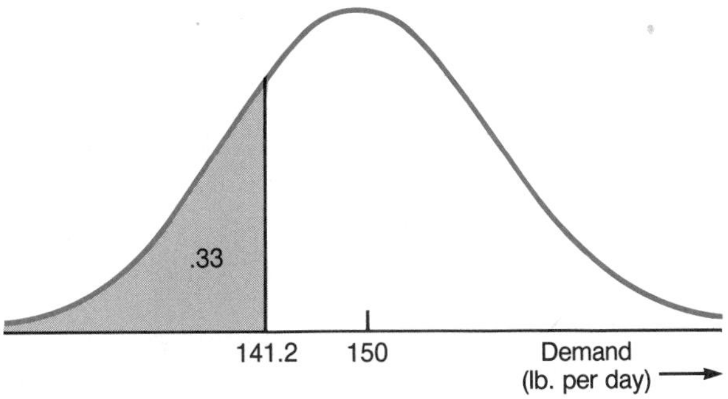

It is interesting to note that the optimum stocking level is less than the expected demand of 150 pounds per day. In fact, two thirds of the time, demand will exceed supply, causing a stockout. Nevertheless, because unit excess cost is twice unit shortage cost, undersupply is preferable to oversupply.

At times, the source of a demand distribution will be historical data. (It is important that this data reflect *demand* and not simply *sales* because sales data can never exceed actual supply and, thus, sales has an arbitrary upper limit.) In general, historical data usually will result in discrete demand categories, in which case it is often necessary to round up from the computed service level to determine the optimum stocking level.

■

EXAMPLE 4 The manager of a bakery counter in a small supermarket has kept a record of demand for lemon chiffon pies. It is shown below. In addition, the manager has indicated that shortage cost is \$1.20 per pie and that excess cost is \$.40, including salvage value, per pie. How many pies per day should be prepared?

Number of Pies Demanded	Frequency	Cumulative Frequency
0	.05	.05
1	.15	.20
2	.30	.50
3	.35	.85
4	.10	.95
5	.05	1.00
6 or more	.00	

Solution

$$\text{Service level} = \frac{C_s}{C_s + C_e} = \frac{\$1.20}{\$1.20 + \$.40} = .75$$

Note that this service level falls *between* .50 and .85 in the *cumulative* frequency distribution (between stocking levels of 2 or 3 pies). Rounding up gives a stocking level of 3 pies. In doing this, the resulting service level becomes .85.

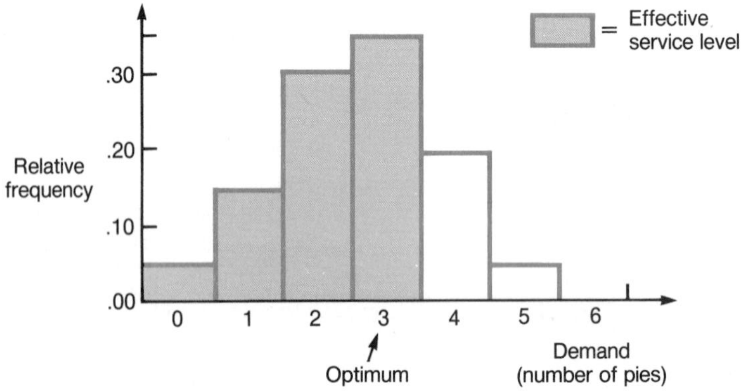

If demand can be described by a theoretical distribution, such as a Poisson distribution, the cumulative probabilities can be obtained from the appropiate probability table.

EXAMPLE 5 The manager in the preceding example also is interested in order quantities for Bavarian cream pies. Unit shortage and excess costs are the same as for the lemon pies. However, demand can be described by a Poisson distribution that has a mean of 6.0 pies per day.

Solution

Service level = .75 (from preceding example)

Portion of Poisson distribution (from Appendix Table C):

	Demand									
Mean	**0**	**1**	**2**	**3**	**4**	**5**	**6**	**7**	**8**	**9**
6.0	.003	.017	.062	.151	.285	.446	.606	.744	.847	.916

Because the service level falls between .744 (stock 7) and .847 (stock 8), round up and stock 8 Bavarian cream pies.

Sensitivity Analysis

A common difficulty in setting stocking levels concerns estimation of shortage cost because shortage cost includes not only the opportunity cost of missed profits but also the possibility of customer dissatisfaction, which might manifest itself in temporary or permanent loss of that customer. Moreover, a customer may purchase other items along with the one in question, and if that item is out of stock, the customer may purchase all of the items from a competitor. For these reasons, managers have difficulty in pinpointing the amount of shortage cost.

One way around this problem that works for discrete demand is to determine the *range* of shortage cost for which a given stocking level will provide an optimum order size. This concept is illustrated in the following example.

EXAMPLE 6 Suppose the manager in the preceding example was concerned about basing the decision to stock 8 Bavarian cream pies on what he considers to be a very shaky estimate of shortage cost. He wonders how much that estimate could vary and still have 8 pies be optimum.

Solution

Eight pies will be optimum for any service level between the cumulative probabilities for 7 (i.e., .744) and 8 (i.e., .847). We can solve the equation for the values of C_s that will cause the service level to just equal those extremes. This will give us the range of shortage costs that will make 8 pies the optimum. Thus:

$$.744 = \frac{C_s}{C_s + \$.40} \quad \text{and} \quad \frac{C_s}{C_s + \$.40} = .847$$

Solving the first of these for C_s yields \$1.16, and solving the second yields C_s = \$2.21. Hence, a shortage cost that falls within the range \$1.16 to \$2.21 will make 8 pies the optimum stocking quantity.

One final note: If the service level ratio in a given situation should happen to *equal* a cumulative probability such as .744 in Example 5, there will be two equivalent solutions: stock 7 and stock 8. Both will yield the same minimum cost.

If stocking levels are continuous, this approach will not apply because even the slightest change in C_s will alter the optimum stocking level. Note, though, that the optimum stocking level will tend to be more sensitive to errors in the estimate of C_s the farther out in either tail that stocking level is, because small changes in the service level will cause greater changes in the stocking level.

MATERIAL REQUIREMENTS PLANNING (MRP)

In an assembly environment, the items carried in inventory generally consist of raw materials, parts, subassemblies, and assemblies that will be used in the manufacture or assembly of end items such as automobiles, appliances, and a host of other products. What sets inventories of these items apart from inventories of retail items or finished goods is that demand for finished goods can be characterized as *independent demand,* whereas demand for items that become a part of another product can be characterized as *derived,* or **dependent, demand. Material requirements planning (MRP)** has been developed to handle the ordering and scheduling of dependent-type inventories.

Dependent Demand

When a producer of automobiles, for example, makes a decision on how many automobiles to produce during a given month, this automatically fixes the quantities of the materials and parts that go into making the autos. Thus, if 700 cars will be produced, and each is to have a compact spare tire, then exactly 700 compact spare tires will be required. Similarly, each car will need 4 wheels; hence, the 700 cars will require exactly 2,800 wheels. The same can be said for all the nuts and bolts, screws, bumpers, shock absorbers, rear windows, and so on. Because each car will require the same quantity of each material or part, the total quantity needed is simply a function of the number of cars that will be produced. Thus, the demand (requirements) for each different part or material is *derived* from knowledge of the components of each car and the number of cars to be produced. Thus, it is possible to determine almost exactly how much of each component will be required (defective parts and damaged items may require ordering a slightly larger amount).

This dependent nature of derived demand is one of the two major differences between dependent and independent demand. With independent demand, which generally applies to *end items* or *finished goods,* there is an element of randomness that is absent with dependent demand. When randomness is present, demand cannot be predicted exactly. Consequently, whereas independent demand necessitates safety stocks to reduce the threat of stockouts because of random variability in demand, dependent demand items have much less need for safety stock, and often no safety stock is carried.

The second major difference between independent and dependent demand items relates to how demand tends to be distributed over time. Independent demand tends to be fairly stable over time, whereas dependent demand tends to be "lumpy" because usage (demand) tends to occur over relatively narrow time intervals with periods of no intervening usage. This is because in many kinds of assembly operations, assembly occurs in stages or cycles rather than on a continuous basis. For example, an automobile assembly plant may produce 200 cars with one type of engine, then 500 cars with another type, and so on. Consequently, although similar *activities* are performed on a continual basis (e.g., installing engines), the *components* may change periodically. Inventory requirements for components, then, tend to be *periodic*. Under such conditions, savings in holding costs can be realized by scheduling components to arrive just prior to the time they will be needed instead of maintaining a continual inventory of them.

Figure 13–2 provides a comparison of the two types of demand. Note that independent demand is variable and continual, whereas dependent demand is "lumpy" but precise.

As noted in the preceding chapter, two basic questions in inventory management are when to order and how much to order. In comparing how these questions are dealt with in dependent and independent demand, consider that with dependent demand, managers can determine very closely how much is needed and when. In contrast, independent demand's variability makes the timing of orders more difficult, although order size is generally based on economic order quantity. In another sense, though, determining requirements for all of the components that go into any but the simplest of assembled products can amount to a formidable task.

You can get some idea of the interrelationships that exist in assembled products by considering the *product tree* shown in Figure 13–3. Product trees show, in hierarchical form, what an end product is composed of (i.e., the quantity of each component needed to make *one* unit of the end item). Reading the tree from the top down, we can see that the hypothetical end item in this case is composed of three assemblies (A1, A2, and A3) and Part P1, which probably is a connector. The numbers in parentheses indicate the quantity of each component needed to

FIGURE 13–2 A Comparison of Independent Demand

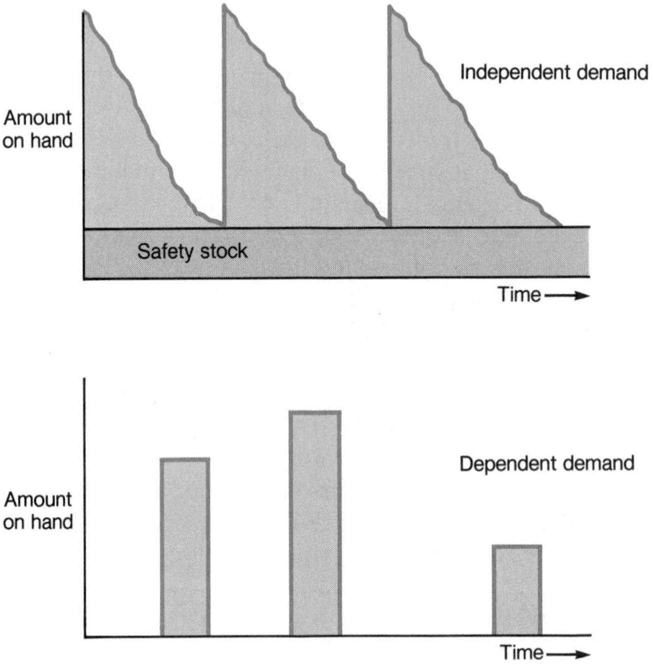

make *one* of the next higher component on that same branch. When no number in parentheses appears, this means that only one unit of the component is required for the next higher component (its "parent"). Thus, the end item in Figure 13–3 requires 2 of Assembly A1, 1 each of Assemblies A2 and A3, and 4 of Part P1. Assembly A1, in turn, requires 2 of Part P2 and 1 of Subassembly SA1, and so on. Note that 2 of Part P2 are needed for *each* unit of assembly A1, and another unit of P2 is used in Subassembly SA1. Therefore, the 2 units of Assembly A1 needed for 1 end item will necessitate $2 \times 3 = 6$ of Part P2. Thus, if 10 units of the end item are needed, this will require 20 of Assembly A1 and 60 of Part P2.

When the component in question is a raw material, the numbers in parentheses refer to the *weight* or *volume* of raw material needed to make one unit of the immediate parent. For example, Part P4 requires 1.2 pounds of Raw Material 1. Three units of Part 4 will, therefore, require $3 \times 1.2 = 3.6$ pounds of Raw Material 1.

■

EXAMPLE 7 Given the product tree shown in Figure 13–3, determine the quantities of Raw Material and Part P7 needed to make 10 units of the end item.

FIGURE 13–3 A Hypothetical Product Tree

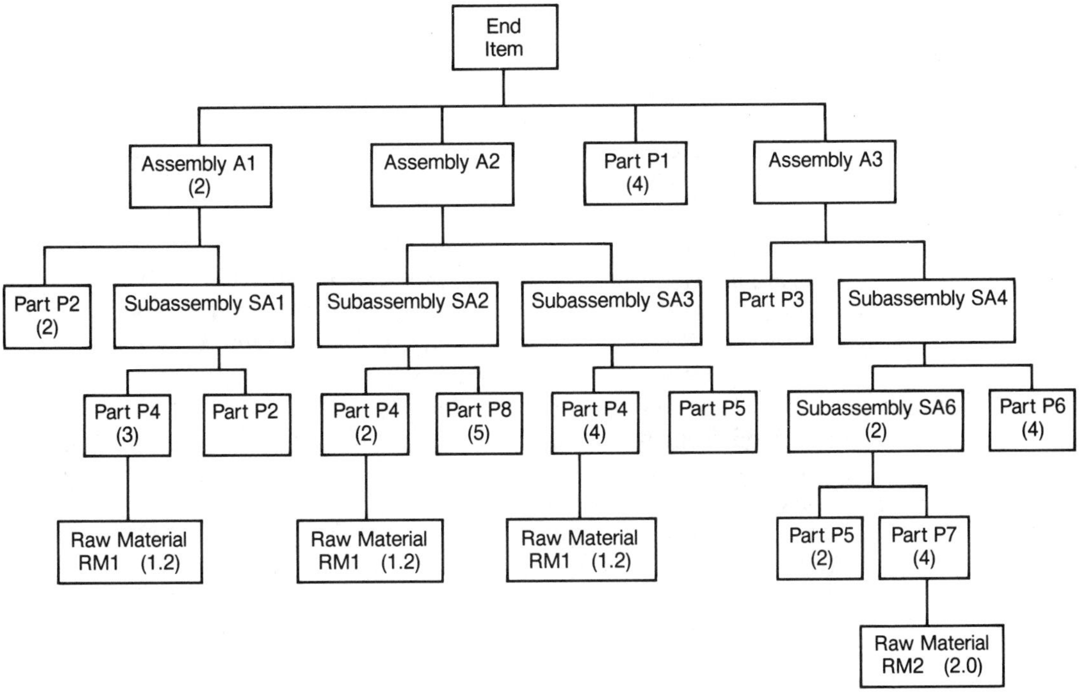

Solution

First, notice that both of these components appear *only* in the lower right portion of the tree. Consequently, only that portion of the tree must be considered in determining the quantities.

Beginning at the top of the tree, the quantities needed at the next lower level can be found by multiplying the quantity needed of the parent (e.g., the parent of Subassembly SA4 and Part P3 is Assembly A3, the parent of Raw Material 2 is Part P7, and so on) by the number of units of its immediate component parts.

Thus, for 10 units of the end item, we will need 10 units of Assembly A3, and that, in turn, will require 10 units of Part P3 and 10 units of Subassembly SA4. Ten units of Subassembly SA4 will require $10 \times 2 = 20$ units of Subassembly SA6 and $10 \times 4 = 40$ units of Part P6. The 20 units of Subassembly SA6 will mean $20 \times 2 = 40$ units for Part P5 and $20 \times 4 = 80$ units of Part P7; and the 80 units of Part P7 will require $80 \times 2.0 = 160$ pounds of Raw Material 2. Hence, for 10 units of the end item, we will need 160 pounds of Raw Material 2 and 80 units of Part P7.

FIGURE 13–4 A Master Schedule for End Item P

Week Number

Item: P	1	2	3	4	5	6	7	8	9
Quantity						200		100	

The calculations in the preceding example would have to be modified if any components are in inventory. For instance, we found that 80 units of Part P7 were needed. Suppose that 75 units are available from inventory. This would mean that only 5 *additional* units would be needed, and these would require 2.0 pounds each of Raw Material 2. Hence, we would need $5 \times 2.0 = 10$ pounds of Raw Material 2 instead of the 160 pounds calculated previously. Thus, the requirements at any level are derived from requirements at the previous level *after* deducting any amount already on hand in inventory, and that *net* amount is used to determine requirements for the next lower level.

The determination of requirements illustrated in Example 7 was relatively straightforward. However, when *timing* of orders is needed and lead times are taken into account, the process is much more complex. A more formal approach is then called for. The next section illustrates such an approach.

MRP Inputs

Basically, MRP is a formal system for ordering and scheduling dependent-demand inventories. There are three primary inputs to MRP:

1. A master schedule.
2. A bill of materials.
3. Inventory records.

A *master schedule* indicates the desired quantity and timing of an end item (e.g., a finished product such as a refrigerator or a microwave oven). Figure 13–4 illustrates how a master schedule for End Item P might appear. It shows that 200 units of P will be needed *at the start of* Week 6 and that another 100 units of P will be needed at the start of Week 8.

The quantities in the master schedule combine actual customer orders with forecasts and any orders from warehouses. Although there is no standard time horizon that master schedules cover, it is important for the master schedule to extend far enough into the future to cover the cumulative lead time needed to produce the end item. This would include procurement of raw materials and parts, fabrication time, and assembly time. Often these are sequential, as illustrated in Figure 13–5.

FIGURE 13–5 The Master Schedule Must Cover the Cumulative Lead Time

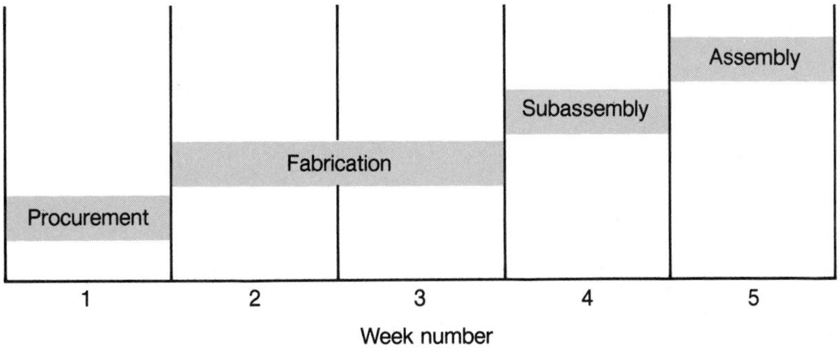

The *bill of materials* (BOM) file contains a list of all the components (subassemblies, parts, etc.) needed to assemble *one* unit of the end item. Thus, each end item will have a separate bill of materials file. The bill of materials in visual form is a product tree such as the one illustrated in Figure 13–3.

The *inventory records file* contains information on the status of each component on a period by period basis. This includes quantity on hand, quantity on order, changes due to canceled orders, who the vendor is, the lead time, and the lot size.

MRP Processing

The essence of material requirements planning is determining the quantity and timing necessary for each component in order to achieve the quantity and timing of end items in the master schedule. The process, then, begins with the master schedule. Then, each end item is "exploded" into its component parts using the bill of materials file, indicating the assemblies, subassemblies, parts, and raw materials that will be needed. Conceptually, this is the same as identifying an end item's product tree. Next, the actual amounts—the **net requirements**—of each component are determined, level by level, beginning at the top of the tree and working down. This is the heart of MRP; it involves determining the quantity of each item called for—the **gross requirements**—then subtracting out inventory **available,** which consists of any inventory on hand from previous periods plus orders scheduled to be available—**scheduled receipts.**

Net requirements are deemed **planned order receipts** until the orders are actually executed, at which time they become scheduled receipts. In order to meet the quantity and timing of net requirements, orders are planned for execution (**planned order release**) prior to planned order receipt according to the *lead time* needed.

FIGURE 13–6 Format of a Material Requirements Plan

	1	2	3	4	5	6
Gross requirements						
Scheduled receipts						
Available						
Net requirements						
Planned order receipt						
Planned order release						

FIGURE 13–7 Product Tree for End Item

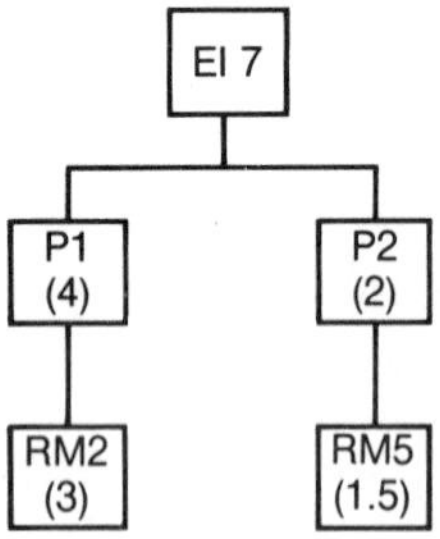

The computation of net requirements of each component is based on this formula:

$$\text{Net requirements} = \text{Gross requirements} - \text{Available} \tag{13–3}$$

In order to keep track of the computations of the quantities and timing of gross requirements, scheduled receipts, net requirements, and so on, a format such as the one shown in Figure 13–6 can be used. Once the appropriate quantities are filled in, this becomes the material requirements plan for a given component. Each component will have its own material requirements plan. Thus, if an end item has four different components, there will be five separate plans, one for each of the four components and one for the end item itself.

Consider the product tree shown in Figure 13–7 for End Item 7. The set of requirements plans for the end item and its components reflects the hierarchical form of the product structure tree. Conceptually, this can be portrayed as in Figure 13–8. The point is that requirements are determined from the top down,

FIGURE 13-8 Conceptual Portrayal of the Development of a Material Requirements Plan for End Item 7

Master schedule: End item 7

Week	1	2	3	4	5	6
Quantity						

End item 7	1	2	3	4	5	6
Gross requirements						
Scheduled receipts						
Available						
Net requirements						
Planned order receipt						
Planned order release						

Part P1	1	2	3	4	5	6
Gross requirements						
Scheduled receipts						
Available						
Net requirements						
Planned order receipt						
Planned order release						

Part P2	1	2	3	4	5	6
Gross requirements						
Scheduled receipts						
Available						
Net requirements						
Planned order receipt						
Planned order release						

Raw material RM2	1	2	3	4	5	6
Gross requirements						
Scheduled receipts						
Available						
Net requirements						
Planned order receipt						
Planned order release						

Raw material RM5	1	2	3	4	5	6
Gross requirements						
Scheduled receipts						
Available						
Net requirements						
Planned order receipt						
Planned order release						

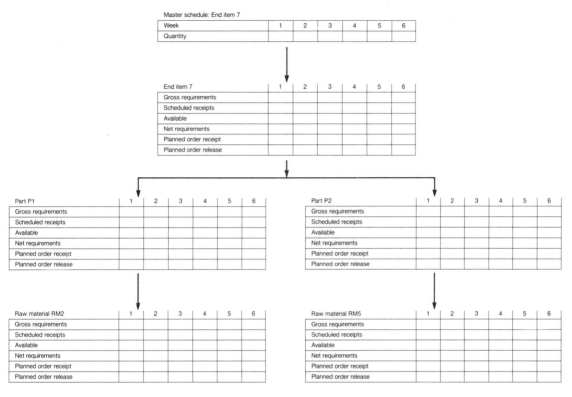

beginning with the master schedule, and the requirements of any component are determined (derived) from the requirements of the component (or end item) that is immediately above it in the product tree.

As a practical matter, the material requirements plan for the end item and its components is not displayed in the tree format of Figure 13-8; even a simple product would involve so many components that the tree format would be unwieldy. Instead, a plan is printed out and displayed in a vertical (one column) format, ideally with as much of the hierarchical order as possible. The next example illustrates this along with a sample requirements plan for End Item 7.

■

EXAMPLE 8 Discuss the material requirements plan for End Item 7 that is shown in Figure 13-9. The numbers in parentheses indicate the quantity of each component needed to make one unit of the next higher component on that same branch (i.e., its parent). The letters LT indicate the lead time in weeks for each particular component or end item.

FIGURE 13–9

Master schedule: End item 7

Week	1	2	3	4	5	6
Quantity					100	

End item 7 LT = 1	1	2	3	4	5	6
Gross requirements					100	
Scheduled receipts					—	
Available					—	
Net requirements					100	
Planned order receipt					100	
Planned order receipt				100		

x 4

Part P1 (4) LT = 1	1	2	3	4	5	6
Gross requirements				400		
Scheduled receipts		150				
Available		150	150			
Net requirements				250		
Planned order receipt				250		
Planned order receipt			250			

x 3

Raw material RM2 (3) LT = 1	1	2	3	4	5	6
Gross requirements			750			
Scheduled receipts			—			
Available	100	100				
Net requirements			650			
Planned order receipt			650			
Planned order receipt	650					

x 2

Part P2 (2) LT = 1	1	2	3	4	5	6
Gross requirements				200		
Scheduled receipts				—		
Available	40	40	40			
Net requirements				160		
Planned order receipt				160		
Planned order receipt			160			

x 1.5

Raw material RM5 (1,5) LT = 1	1	2	3	4	5	6
Gross requirements			240			
Scheduled receipts			40		—	
Available	200	200			—	
Net requirements			0			
Planned order receipt						
Planned order receipt						

Solution

The plan begins with the master schedule. We can see that 100 units are needed at the start of Week 5. This means that gross requirements for End Item 7 also are 100 units at the start of Week 5. Then, because there are no scheduled receipts or available inventory of End Item 7, the net requirements are 100 units in Week 5. Hence, there is a planned receipt of 100 units in Week 5. Then, because lead time (for assembly) of the end item is 1 week, there is a planned order release of 100 units one week ahead of this (i.e., in Week 4).

Each end item will use 4 of Part P1. Therefore, the planned order release of 100 units of Each Item 7 in Week 4 will create a requirement of $4 \times 100 = 400$ of Part P1, also in Week 4. But Part P1 has a scheduled receipt of 150 units in Week 2, making 150 units available in Weeks 2 and 3. So, net requirements become $400 - 150 = 250$ units in Week 4. Thus, there is a planned order receipt of 250 units of Part P1 in Week 4. Because lead time is one week, there is a planned order release of 250 units (i.e., fabricate 250 of Part P1) one week earlier (i.e., Week 3).

Because each Part P1 will require 3 units (pounds) of Raw Material RM2, the 250 units will require $3 \times 250 = 750$ units of Raw Material RM2. There are no scheduled receipts, but 100 units of Raw Material RM2 will be available (i.e., are now on hand). Hence, net requirements will be 650 units, in Week 3. Because lead time is two weeks, the planned order release is for 650 units in Week 1.

Gross requirements for Part P2 are derived from the quantity of the end item needed (i.e., 100 in this case). Because two of Part P2 are needed for each unit of the end item, a total of $2 \times 100 = 200$ units will be needed. There are no scheduled receipts, but 40 units will be available, so net requirements become 160 units. Thus, a planned order receipt of 160 units in Week 4 is needed and a planned order release of the same amount in Week 3 is needed because lead time is, again, one week.

The 160 units of Part P2 will require $1.5 \times 160 = 240$ pounds of Raw Material RM5 in Week 3. There is a scheduled receipt of 40 pounds in Week 3. Added to the previously available quantity of 200 pounds, 240 pounds will be available in Week 3. Because that just equals gross requirements of Raw Material RM5, no additional ordering will be needed. (Note that lead time is 3 weeks for Raw Material RM5. In order to receive the 40 units in Week 3, an order must be placed one week earlier, say, in Week 0. Once an order is placed, it is no longer a planned order; rather, the quantity becomes a scheduled receipt.)

Other Issues

Management of dependent-demand inventories is an important concern for manufacturing and assembly operations. Much has been written about the subject. Unfortunately, space limitations do not permit an in-depth coverage of it. Nonetheless, there are a few additional issues that must at least be mentioned:

1. Safety stock.
2. Lot sizing.
3. Capacity planning.

Let's briefly examine each of these issues.

Safety stock Under independent demand, safety stocks are held to offset variabilities in demand and/or lead time. Under dependent demand, demand quantities tend to be less variable, although lead times may vary. Consequently, under those circumstances it may make more sense to include some *safety time* in ordering; that is, when lead times tend to vary, order a bit earlier to allow for this rather than hold additional stock. In some cases, safety stock may be held; this usually occurs at the lowest levels of product structure (e.g., raw materials) or for purchased parts that are used on a more or less continual basis. Also, if assemblies or subassemblies are used in several products (e.g., engines for several different lawn mower models), safety stocks may represent a reasonable approach to variations in lead times. In practical terms, however, safety stocks should be viewed as exceptions rather than the general rule for dependent demand situations.

Lot sizing Selecting order (or production) quantities is referred to as *lot sizing*. In general, the primary goal in choosing a lot size is to minimize the sum of ordering (or setup) costs and inventory carrying costs. When demand tends to be lumpy, as it often does with dependent-demand items, the task of identifying an appropriate lot size is more difficult than when demand tends to be uniformly distributed over time. A variety of different approaches are used in practice, none of which is necessarily better than the others. Judgment and experience often are factors in choosing a particular approach.

Economic order quantity (EOQ) models (covered in the preceding chapter) sometimes are employed. The closer demand is to being uniformly distributed, the better such models work. EOQ models seem to work best either for components at lower levels of product trees or for purchased parts that are used in multiple products, for which demand tends to be the most uniform. For other components and for end items, demand tends to be too lumpy to use an EOQ approach to ordering. When demand is lumpy and/or uneven, the average inventory is less likely to equal one half the order quantity, and the EOQ logic breaks down.

Lot-for-lot ordering often is used. It involves using an order size that is equal to demand. This method was illustrated in the preceding example. It is by far the simplest approach; no computations are needed. It has the advantage of holding inventory only for a short period, unlike the EOQ approach, which would result in carrying inventories on a continual basis. One disadvantage is the inability to take advantage of economies related to a fixed order size, such as standard container sizes.

Fixed period ordering involves ordering enough inventory for a set number of periods (e.g., one-month supply). The number of periods may be arbitrary or it may reflect an effort to incorporate knowledge of demand patterns, such as cycles of demand.

A fairly sophisticated approach, the *Wagner-Whitin algorithm,* uses dynamic programming to try to minimize the sum of ordering and carrying costs. It involves identifying and examining a small number of strategies and then choosing the one that minimizes total costs. The complexity of the technique limits the willingness of many managers to adopt it.

Capacity requirements planning When a master schedule is being developed, usually it is in terms of what will be needed and when it will be needed, not what is possible. It is not until those needs have been exploded and compared to available amounts of inventories and production capabilities that the feasibility of a requirements plan can be determined. Consequently, it may be necessary to go through a number of iterations of revising the master schedule until a schedule that does not exceed capacity limitations is obtained.

Requirements and Benefits of MRP

Among the benefits of material requirements planning are the following:

1. Relatively low holding costs.
2. The ability to keep track of material requirements.
3. The ability to determine capacity requirements related to a given master schedule.

In order for MRP to be truly effective, it is necessary to have a *computerized* processing system because of the enormous record-keeping requirements. This includes the appropriate software. In addition, it is necessary to have accurate and timely master schedules, bills of materials, and inventory records.

In some instances, companies have attempted to install MRP systems without carefully checking on the accuracy of their bills of materials and inventory records. This has led to serious difficulties in adopting MRP because of the need to correct records; substantial amounts of time and human resources had to be invested. Also, employees sometimes resist new methods, leading to additional difficulties.

Even without these problems, MRP has not been the panacea many had hoped it would be. In part, this has caused manufacturers and consultants to take a more comprehensive view of resource planning. Some have adopted MRP II.

Manufacturing Resource Planning (MRP II)

Manufacturing resource planning (MRP II) is an expanded approach to planning and scheduling. It has not replaced MRP; instead, it expands the scope of resource planning, as can be seen in Figure 13–10.

FIGURE 13-10 An Overview of MRP II

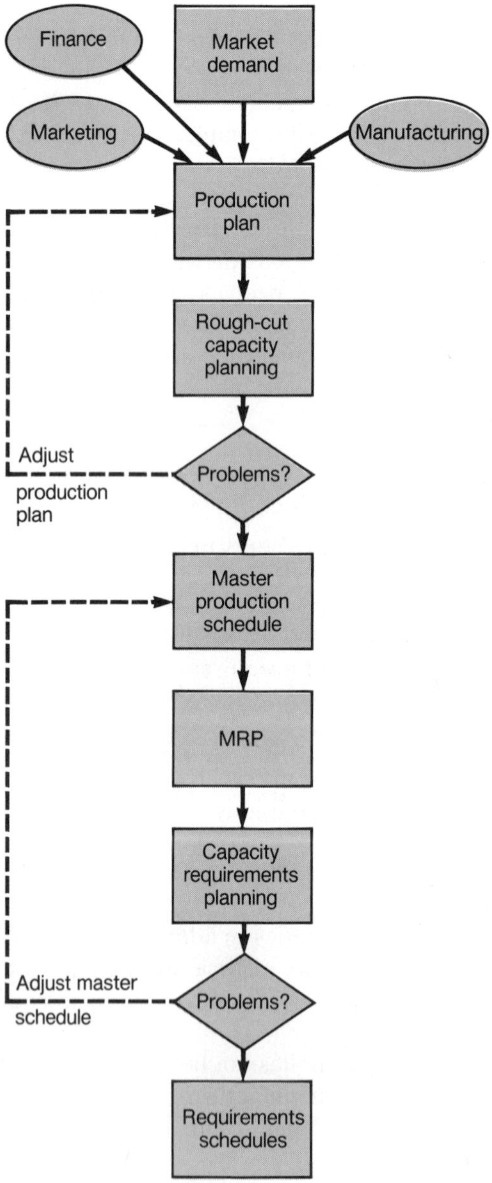

The primary input consists of market demand (mainly actual orders, but also some forecasts). Marketing, finance, and production people working together then develop a production plan. The purpose is to achieve a plan that everyone can live with, and one that all of these areas will be familiar with and will support. After an initial plan is developed, its (rough) requirements are compared to project capacity. This is known as *rough-cut capacity planning*. Any obvious discrepancies will generate modifications to the production plan. Once a satisfactory plan has been achieved, the more traditional MRP processing is done, generating more realistic material requirements. Even so, capacity requirements planning must still be done, although on a much finer level than the pre-master schedule rough-cut planning.

An obvious contribution of MRP II is this preplanning stage. Another is the ability to do simulation, allowing managers to evaluate a variety of production plans before actually committing to one.

JUST-IN-TIME (JIT)

Japanese manufacturers are becoming increasingly well known for their success in productivity and quality improvements, particularly in the area of repetitive manufacturing (e.g., automobiles, appliances, electronic equipment, and cameras). This is especially interesting because the Japanese approach to production planning and control in repetitive manufacturing tends to differ quite a bit from the approach used by many American manufacturers. Hence, it will be useful to examine the Japanese approach and to consider the lessons it provides for American manufacturing.

A major innovator of the Japanese approach has been Toyota Motor Company. In fact, we can learn a good deal about Japanese methods by taking a look at Toyota's methods. The following article, reprinted from *The Wall Street Journal,* presents an overview of those methods.

■ THE NUTS AND BOLTS OF JAPAN'S FACTORIES

Urban C. Lebner

"If American automobile king Henry Ford I were alive today, I am positive he would have done what we did with our Toyota production system."

—Taiichi Ohno in his 1978 book
The Toyota Production System

Toyota City, Japan—Groping to explain "how Japan does it," experts have made much of the close ties between business and government and of the loyalty of Japan's highly skilled workers to their employers. They've noted the fierce competitiveness of

Japanese companies in their home market, the nation's high savings rate, even the relative scarcity of lawyers.

Doubtless these are among the pieces needed to solve the puzzle. But some management consultants who've studied how Japan makes such high-quality, competitively priced products say there's another piece often overlooked. The Japanese, they say, have proved themselves increasingly adroit at organizing and running manufacturing operations. Japanese managers may lack the MBAs or the ability to plot big-picture business strategy of their American counterparts. But they know how to run factories.

"There's a growing acceptance that Japanese success is based at least in part on the development of manufacturing techniques that often tend to outrun our own," says management consultant Rex Reid, head of A. T. Kearney's Toyota office.

One of the most interesting examples of Japanese production-management skills is a concern quite familiar to Americans: Toyota Motor Co., the largest-selling foreign automaker in the U.S.

Believe in Their System

Toyota officials resist claiming that their way of building autos is better than anyone else's. They're somewhat embarrassed by the exuberant projections of Henry Ford's behavior essayed by their former chief production executive, Taiichi Ohno, in his 1978 book. But Toyota men clearly remain believers in what Mr. Ohno called "the Toyota production system."

For a first-hand look at the system, take a walk through the Tsutsumi plant here in Toyota City, a town of 280,000 in central Japan that's the site of eight of Toyota's 10 factories. Over here, Muneo Nakahara, 26 years old and an eight-year Toyota veteran, is doing his job. With the help of an overhead crane that Mr. Nakahara controls from a hand-held device, he hoists auto engines onto a conveyor belt that will take them to be matched up with auto bodies.

Mr. Nakahara is lifting the engines onto the conveyor from a small flat-bed truck that has brought them from the engine plant. Only two trucks carrying only 12 engines apiece park at Mr. Nakahara's post at any given time, so every few minutes an empty truck drives back to the engine plant and a new one takes its place.

That's the first feature of the Toyota system: no inventories. Toyota's factories keep on hand only that amount of parts needed for immediate production, from a few minutes' worth up to a few hours' worth depending on the part. When fresh parts are needed—and only when they're needed—they're delivered from other Toyota plants or from outside suppliers directly to the production line.

Outsiders who've seen Toyota in action often call this the "kanban system," kanban being the Japanese word for the piece of paper enclosed in clear plastic that accompanies each bin of parts. (When a worker on the line begins drawing from a new bin, he removes the kanban and routes it back to the supplier, for whom it serves as an order for a new bin of parts.) But Toyota officials say the pieces of paper are just tools. They call this inventory-control aspect of their broader system the "just-in-time" system.

The same philosophy guides the meshing of operations within each plant. An assembly line that is building subcomponents makes just that number of subcomponents immediately needed at the next stage of production. When it's made enough, it's changed over to build some other kind of subcomponent for awhile. Likewise, the final assembly line builds first one kind of car, then another, in small lots—only as much as called for in actual orders from Toyota's sales unit. Toyota engineers "average" and "level" production among the lines to coordinate output without building inventories. They compare auto assembly to rowing a boat: Everybody has to be pulling on the oars at the same rate.

"They concentrate very heavily on avoiding end-item and intermediate-item storage," says a Ford official in Detroit who's seen the system at work. "They throw out the whole concept of mass production."

The benefits are substantial. Toyota doesn't need space for inventory, people to handle and control inventory, or borrowed money to finance inventory. "It cuts costs in a lot of ways," says an official of Nissan Motor Co., Japan's second-largest automaker, which has adopted an inventory-control system similar to its rival's in some plants.

Then there are the side benefits. Because Toyota is constantly changing over its machines to make new things, its workers have become fast at repair and changeover. In his book, Mr. Ohno cites a mold on a press that took two to three hours to change in the 1940s. Today "it takes only three minutes to change the mold," Mr. Ohno says.

Aside from its emphasis on holding down inventories Toyota's system stresses quality controls. Throughout the Tsutsumi plant are boards with electric lights to indicate conditions on each assembly line. A red light means a line has been stopped because of a problem. Every worker has a button or cord with which he can stop the line, and he's told to use it whenever he thinks something's wrong with the operation of the line or when he spots defects in the product.

"We lose production temporarily this way," concedes Fujio Cho, manager of the production control department at Toyota's headquarters. "But in our experience stopping lines helps us detect problems early and avoid bad practices."

Another feature that becomes clear is the company's penchant for training workers to do more than one job. The man who runs one machine switches off every few moments to run another. The man who feeds rear windows to a robot also "tags" car shells with instructions telling workers farther down the line what to install in them. This versatility allows Toyota to realign its work force more efficiently when business is bad.

Indeed, "recession" thinking underlies a big part of Toyota's system. Much of the system originated in the late 1940s and early 1950s, when Toyota was producing exclusively for a domestic market that wasn't very strong. The company has been operating on the conventional assumption that it's most efficient to produce in large lots, "but that kind of thinking has pushed us close to bankruptcy, because the large lots we were producing couldn't be sold," says Mr. Cho. Toyota couldn't lay off workers—Japan's a "lifetime" employment system—so Toyota executives hit upon the simple yet radical idea that still pervades its operations: Overproduction is waste.

Special Relationship

It is, of course, open to question whether Toyota's is the best way to make cars, and Toyota officials themselves doubt whether other automakers could adopt it readily. They note among other problems that it takes a special kind of relationship with suppliers to make the system work.

Fully 50 of Toyota's 250 suppliers are headquartered in Toyota City, and almost all have plants here. They have to be close to make all those deliveries every day. It still shocks Toyota officials to be told that American automakers buy parts from suppliers all over the U.S. and even from suppliers in Europe and Japan. Toyota's most distant supplier is a five-hour drive away.

Then, too, suppliers must have close working relations with Toyota to adjust to Toyota's peculiar needs. It isn't surprising that many of Toyota's suppliers do all or most of their business with Toyota, and that Toyota owns large blocks of the stock of some of its most important suppliers. Many suppliers, even those Toyota doesn't own, have adopted Toyota's production system for their own operations. It improves coordination with Toyota, and helps them avoid getting stuck with the inventory buildup that Toyota refuses to get stuck with.

The point isn't whether Toyota's system is best. The point is that it's very good, and that Toyota is in many ways typical of Japanese manufacturers in its continual striving to improve production techniques. When experts talk about the competitiveness of Japanese products in international markets, that's something that shouldn't be forgotten.

Source: *The Wall Street Journal,* March 31, 1981. Reprinted by permission of *The Wall Street Journal.*

This article provides a number of very important insights on the **just-in-time (JIT)** approach to manufacturing along with some reasons for the successes the Japanese manufacturers have achieved. Let's take a closer look at the important points of the article.

The just-in-time approach attempts to minimize inventories. It accomplishes this by ordering and producing very small batches. Ideally, as each order of raw material arrives from a vendor, it goes directly into production, and as each batch is finished at one work center, it is moved to the following work center where the previous order has just been completed, and work is begun on the new order. Hence, inventories of raw materials and purchased parts are purposely kept as small as possible, as are inventories of partially completed goods between operations. Naturally, this means that a disruption anywhere in the system can easily cause the entire system to come to a halt because there is little slack between operations. However, the Japanese see this as an opportunity to learn where the weak points are in the system *and to correct those problems* so they do not recur. By way of contrast, most U.S. manufacturers carry safety stock "just in

FIGURE 13-11 JIT versus Large Lot Run Sizes

JIT Approach

AAA BBBBBBB CC AAA BBBBBBB CC AAA BBBBBBB CC AAA BBBBBBB CC

Time →

Large Lot Approach

AAAAAAAAAAAAAA BBBBBBBBBBBBBBBBBBBBBBBBBBBBBBBB CCCCCCCCC AAAAAAAAAAAA

Time →

case. . . .'' According to the JIT philosophy, buffers of inventory tend to cover up or hide problems that keep recurring and are never resolved, partly because they aren't always obvious and partly because the presence of inventory seems to make the problems less serious. Needless to say, the additional inventory carries a burden in terms of holding costs.

In order to maintain a JIT system with little inventory and small run sizes, it is necessary to have quick, low-cost changeovers and setups. That is, the basic concept of an economic run size is not refuted by the JIT approach. Rather, by driving down setup costs, the run size that minimizes total cost is decreased. Setup costs are driven down through research that leads to improved methods and equipment and through such approaches as group technology, where families of similar items are processed in sequence. The similarities result in the need for only partial teardowns and setups between runs of different items within the family.

Another factor that enables JIT users to keep in-process inventories low is small run sizes. Unlike most U.S. manufacturers, who use large run sizes to reduce the setup cost per unit, the Japanese produce a small number of one item, then a small number of another, and so on. The ability to quickly change over equipment and have relatively low-cost setups permits them to do this and keep inventories low in the process. This contrast between large and small run sizes is illustrated in Figure 13-11.

One potential source of disruption in a JIT system is problems with quality. When these sorts of problems appear, they must be investigated and corrected in order to eliminate recurrence. Again, the willingness to commit the time, effort, and money to correct problems at the source is essential to the success of the system. Eliminating quality problems is essential in JIT systems.

Toyota uses a *kanban* system for production control. Kanbans are manually prepared cards that authorize either the movement of parts or materials (conveyance kanbans) or production operations (production kanbans). There are also vendor kanbans, which authorize shipments of materials or parts from suppliers. Each kanban is a card roughly 4 inches by 8 inches that contains all the information pertinent to a batch or lot of parts. This includes the origin and destination of the lot, part name and number, the kind of part, a kanban number, the quantity of parts or material per parent item, and a workstation number, if applicable. The kanbans function as an integral part of the control system. No part or lot can be moved or worked on without one of these authorization cards. Roughly, the system works as follows. A kanban card is affixed to each container. When a workstation needs to replenish its supply of parts, a worker goes to the area where these parts are stored and withdraws one container of parts. Each container holds a predetermined quantity (i.e., the economic lot size). The worker removes the kanban card from that container and posts it in a designated spot where is will be clearly visible, and the worker then moves the lot to the workstation. The posted kanban is then picked up by a stock person who replenishes the stock with another container, and so on down the line. In effect, then, the kanban system is a "pull" system: Demand for parts triggers a replenishment, and parts are supplied only as usage dictates. Similar withdrawals and replenishments occur up and down the line from finished-goods inventory to vendors, and all are controlled by kanbans. In fact, if supervisors decide the system seems too tight, additional kanbans may be introduced to bring the system into balance.

The just-in-time system has yet another mechanism for maintaining balance: It is designed to identify bottlenecks and potential bottlenecks. In addition to carefully balancing the system prior to production, each workstation is equipped with a light system (*andon*) that is used to signal problems. A green light means no problem, an amber light indicates a worker is falling a bit behind, and a red light indicates the worker has a problem (e.g., an equipment breakdown or a quality problem). Workers are cross-trained, so that if one falls behind, others are able to assist until the system is back on track. Moreover, workers are also trained to handle many equipment repairs, thereby reducing the impact of equipment failures on the length of a disruption. In addition, because of the cross-training, workers can fill in for others in the case of illness or other problems. Hence, teamwork is an important part of the JIT approach.

Close vendor relationships are also important. Typically, manufacturers use only one or a few vendors, who are often located nearby. Vendors generally also use a JIT system. That, plus their nearby locations, enables them to frequently ship small lot sizes to the producing firm, which fits into the producer's JIT system.

The overall JIT philosophy can be summed up this way: Inventories are costly and they hide problems; they must be kept to a minimum. Lot sizes and order sizes should be geared to immediate needs only, with frequent reordering as needed. Machine setups and changeovers should be rapid, with efforts to reduce the costs associated with changeovers. Quality efforts should aim for zero defects so that quality problems do not disrupt production. Vendors should be thought of as part of the team rather than as adversaries. Machine breakdowns are to be avoided. Workers are a vital resource; management by consensus and worker participation in changes are desirable.

Hidden costs that can be associated with JIT systems are transportation costs and traffic congestion costs related to small delivery batches.

SUMMARY

This chapter covers four inventory models: fixed interval ordering, single period ordering, material requirements planning, and just-in-time.

When ordering is done at fixed intervals, the quantity to order must be determined anew with each new order; hence, order size tends to vary but the interval between orders remains constant. Because ordering can take place only at the fixed points in time, continuous monitoring of inventory is not required. Instead, periodic counts of stock on hand can be made just prior to ordering to determine the amount on hand. Fixed order points also mean that greater care must be taken to avoid stockouts: Even if stock runs low, there is no provision for replenishment except in accordance with the fixed interval schedule.

The single period model is used in situations in which inventory items generally cannot be carried over from one period to the next. A typical example is perishable items. The main concern in determining order size is to balance the probable costs of overstocking and the probable costs of understocking. Unlike in the fixed interval model, the determination of order size need be made only once, rather than repeated for each new order cycle.

Material requirements planning is a computerized approach for planning and scheduling inventory items that have dependent demand. Such situations arise in fabrication and assembly operations where the demand for subassemblies, parts, and/or raw materials is *derived* from the planned quantities of the finished goods they comprise. Computerized systems are required because of the enormous recordkeeping task and calculational burden imposed by assembled products.

Just-in-time systems reflect the influence of certain Japanese manufacturers. With these systems, typically, relatively small order quantities are scheduled to arrive just at the time the items are needed in the production process. The effect is to substantially reduce the amount of inventory being held to maintain operations.

GLOSSARY

Available Projected amount of inventory on hand.

Dependent Demand Inventory demand that is *derived* from requirements for other items; demand for *components* of final products.

Fixed Interval Model An inventory model in which replenishment orders are placed at fixed *time* intervals.

Gross Requirements The quantity of a dependent demand item that will be needed before taking into account amounts currently on hand or scheduled to be received.

Just-In-Time (JIT) An inventory ordering system that attempts to reduce the amount of inventory on hand by frequently reordering small quantities and timing the orders to arrive just when they are needed for production.

MRP (Material Requirements Planning) An inventory ordering and scheduling system for *dependent* demand items that attempts to match inventory levels with "lumpy" demand requirements.

MRP II (Manufacturing Resource Planning) Includes MRP, but expands the scope of resource planning and scheduling.

Net Requirements Inventory requirements for a dependent demand item after taking into account any quantities that are projected to be on hand when the item will be needed.

Planned-Order Receipt Planned quantity to be received.

Planned-Order Release Planned order quantity.

Scheduled Receipts Orders that have been executed but not yet received.

Single Period Model An inventory ordering model used to determine an optimal order size for items with limited shelf lives.

SOLVED PROBLEMS

Problem 1. *Fixed order interval* A machine operation uses an average of 150 pounds of a certain raw material each day. Usage can be described by a normal distribution with a mean of 150 pounds and a standard deviation of 6 pounds per day. Stock is ordered at 10-day intervals and lead time is 1 day. Establish a decision rule that will provide a service level of 95 percent.

Solution

$$\bar{d} = 150 \text{ pounds per day}$$
$$\sigma_d = 6 \text{ pounds per day}$$
$$OI = 10 \text{ days}$$
$$L = 1 \text{ day}$$
$$z = +1.65 \text{ for 95\% service level (from Appendix Table B)}$$

$$\begin{aligned} Q_o &= d(OI + L) + z(\sigma_d)\sqrt{OI + L} - A \\ &= 150(10 + 1) + 1.65(6)\sqrt{10 + 1} - A \\ &= 1650 + 32.83 - A \end{aligned}$$

Rounding the 32.83 *up* to 33, and adding it to 1650, $Q_o = 1683 - A$. Hence, the decision rule is: Order 1683 pounds minus the amount on hand.

Problem 2. *Single period model* The manager of a newsstand, Ed Stockingham, must make a decision on stocking levels for two items. One is a local newspaper and the other an out-of-town newspaper. Coincidently, the shortage and excess costs are the same for both items: $C_s = \$.12$ and $C_e = \$.05$.

a. Demand for the local newspaper can be modeled by a normal distribution that has a mean of 40 papers per day and a standard deviation of 5 papers per day. What stocking level would be optimal for Ed?

b. Demand for the out-of-town newspaper can be modeled by a Poisson distribution that has a mean of 3.8 papers per day. What stocking level would be optimal for Ed?

Solution

The service level ratio for either case is:

$$\frac{C_s}{C_s + C_e} = \frac{.12}{.12 + .05} = .706$$

a. For the local newspaper, with normally distributed demand, we find the service level ratio in Appendix Table B as close as we can. The closest value is .7054, which has a z of $+.54$. Using this value, along with the given values of the mean and standard deviation, we can compute the optimal stocking level.

$$\begin{aligned}\text{Optimal Stocking Level} &= \text{Mean} + z\sigma_d \\ &= 40 + .54(5) \\ &= 42.7\text{, or 43 rounded } \textit{up}\end{aligned}$$

Hence, Ed should stock 43 local newspapers each day.

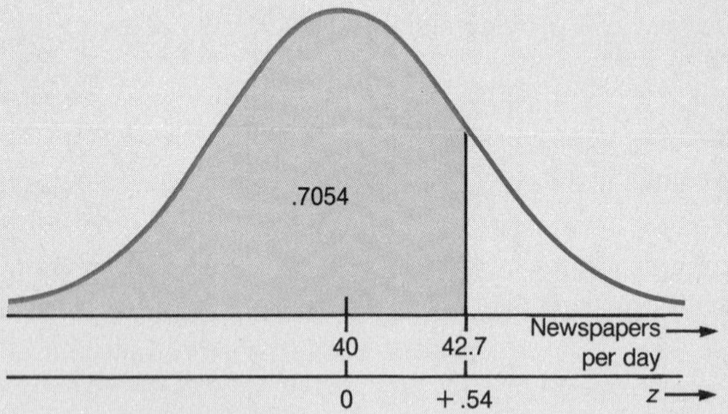

b. For the out-of-town newspaper, with Poisson distributed demand, we find the service level ratio in Appendix Table C as close as we can. Using the specified mean of 3.8, the service level ratio of .706 falls between .668 and .816. Rounding *up* leads us to .816, which corresponds to a stocking level of 5 newspapers per day. Hence, Ed should order 5 newspapers each day.

Problem 3. The product tree shown is incomplete. Explain why, and correctly draw the tree.

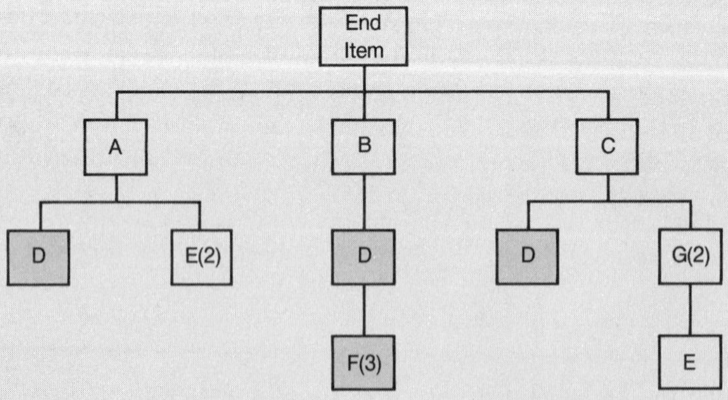

Solution

The composition of each component must be the same wherever it appears in the tree. Component D appears three times, once showing it is made of 3 units of F, twice showing no component parts. If we can assume that it is indeed composed of 3 units of F, the correct tree would be:

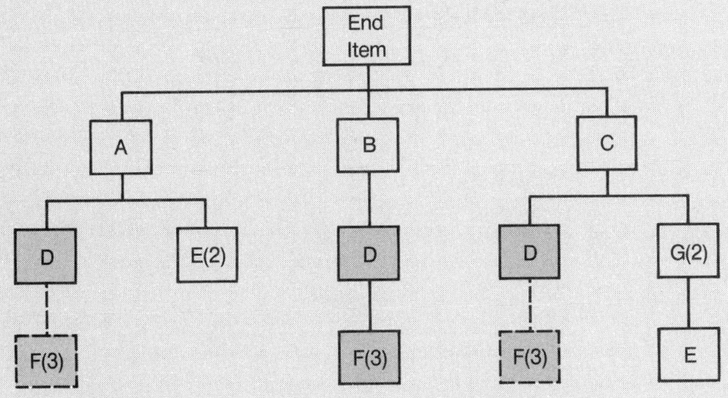

Problem 4. Given the product structure tree in the preceding problem, prepare a material requirements plan for component E using this additional information:

a. 300 units of the end item are needed in Period 6.

b. On-hand inventory consists of: 60 units of the end item, 100 units of Component C, 100 units of Component E.

c. Scheduled receipts are 40 units of Component A in Period 3.

d. Lead times are two periods for the end item and for Component A, and one period for all other components.

e. Lot-for-lot ordering is used, except for Component G, which has order sizes in multiples of 300 units and Component E, which has order sizes that are multiples of 400 units.

Solution

In order to prepare a material requirements plan for Component E, it is first necessary to prepare plans for the end item and for Components A, C, and G. These are shown on the next page, along with the plan for Component E.

First, the master schedule is prepared, with 300 units scheduled for the start of Period 6. This generates gross requirements of 300 units for the end item in Period 6. Because 60 units will already be available, net requirements are 240 units in Period 6. With a lead time of two periods, this means a planned order release of 240 units in Period 4. This, in turn, creates gross requirements of 240 units in Period 4 for both A and C because 1 of each of those components is needed for each unit of the end item.

Component A has a scheduled receipt of 40 units in Period 3, which results in 40 units being available in Period 3, leaving net requirements of 200 units and a planned order receipt of 200 units in Period 4. With a lead time of two periods, there is a planned order release of 200 units in Period 2.

Component C has 100 units available, leaving net requirements of 140 units in Period 4, a planned order receipt of 140 units, and a planned order release of 140 units in Period 3. That will generate gross requirements of $2 \times 140 + 280$ units of

Master schedule: End item

Week	1	2	3	4	5	6
Quantity						300

End item LT = 2	1	2	3	4	5	6
Gross requirements						300
Scheduled receipts						—
Available	60	60	60	60	60	
Net requirements						240
Planned order receipt						240
Planned order release				240		

A LT = 2	1	2	3	4	5	6
Gross requirements				240		
Scheduled receipts			40	—		
Available			40			
Net requirements				200		
Planned order receipt				200		
Planned order release		200				

C LT = 1	1	2	3	4	5	6
Gross requirements				240		
Scheduled receipts						
Available	100	100	100			
Net requirements				140		
Planned order receipt				140		
Planned order release			140			

Q = 300

G (2C) LT = 1	1	2	3	4	5	6
Gross requirements			280			
Scheduled receipts			—			
Available			20	20	20	20
Net requirements			280			
Planned order receipt			300			
Planned order release		300				

Q = 400

E (2A, 1G) LT = 1	1	2	3	4	5	6
Gross requirements		700				
Scheduled receipts		—				
Available	100	200	200	200	200	200
Net requirements		600				
Planned order receipt		800				
Planned order release	800					

Component G in Period 3 because each unit of C uses 2 units of G. Net requirements are 280 units, but the order size must be in multiples of 300 units. Hence, 300 units is the planned order receipt and planned order release quantity, leaving an excess of 20 units, which will be available beginning in Period 3.

Gross requirements for E equal 2 units for each A ordered plus 1 unit for each G ordered. Thus, $2 \times 200 + 1 \times 300 = 700$ units. With 100 units of E available, net requirements equals 600 units in Period 2. Because the order size must be in multiples of 400 units, 800 units will be ordered, leaving an excess of 200 units, which then becomes available, beginning in Period 2 and continuing through successive periods.

PROBLEMS

1. Due to a change in supplier policy, ordering of rock salt at Sam's Ski Slope will change from the current system to a fixed interval system. The following information is available: Assume demand is normally distributed and:

$\bar{d} = 20$ pounds per day	Order interval = 15 days
$\sigma_d = 5$ pounds per day	Lead time = 2 days
	Stockout risk not to exceed 3 percent

   a. Determine an appropriate decision rule for Sam's.

   b. Determine the order size for these cases:

   (1) There is no stock on hand at order time.

   (2) Twenty-five pounds of stock is on hand at order time.

2. (Refer to the information given in Problem 1.) What service level would be achieved if 320 pounds is ordered when the amount of stock on hand at order time is 10 pounds?

3. The manager of Thurgood Grocery Store, Tom Byrite, is preparing the weekly order sheet. Two of the items on the sheet are 12-ounce and 16-ounce cans of cocktail peanuts. Average daily demand is ten 12-ounce cans and seven 16-ounce cans. These amounts tend to be normally distributed with a standard deviation of 2.5 cans per day for 12-ounce cans and 2 cans per day for 16-ounce cans. Assume that demands for the two sizes are independent.

   a. If the order interval is seven days, lead time is two days, and a 5 percent stockout risk is acceptable, determine an appropriate decision rule for Tom for the 12-ounce cans and a decision rule for the 16-ounce cans.

   b. If both sizes come in boxes of 12 cans, how many *boxes* of each type should Tom order if there are 20 of each type on hand at order time?

   c. How reasonable is the assumption that demand for these two items is independent? What are some factors that could affect this?

4. The manager of a soda fountain must decide how many cans of maraschino cherries to order. Weekly usage can be described by a normal distribution that has a mean of 2 cans and a standard deviation of ½ can. Lead time is 2 days and an order interval is 10 days. The shop is open 5 days a week. (Hint: Work in terms of weeks, not days.)

   a. For a service level of 97 percent, establish a decision rule.

   b. What is the probability that a stockout will occur before an order is received for the case where 3 cans are on hand at order time?

5. Three former high-tech specialists decided to eschew the security and low pay of their jobs and form their own firm. They recently opened their fifth restaurant, which specializes in hot'n sweet barbecued chicken wings. The wings are bought fresh, twice weekly: on Tuesday and Friday mornings. The restaurant operates Tuesday through Saturday and is closed Sunday and Monday. Demand for the period Tuesday through Thursday is approximately normal with a mean of 300 pounds and a standard deviation of 50 pounds. Demand for Friday and Saturday also is approximately normal, but with a mean of 420 pounds and a standard deviation of 45 pounds. The wings are bought at a cost of $.60 per pound, and any leftover wings on Friday morning or Sunday morning are sold to a local high school at $.40 per pound. The estimated profit on wings sold in the restaurant is $.70 per pound. What order quantities for the two periods will minimize shortage and excess costs?

6. The manager of an automobile dealership, Lois Le Price faces the same problem each new model year: How many of a very expensive model should she order? The cars are so rare that she must order at the beginning of the year in order to receive any. It will cost the dealership $2,000 in holding costs and $1,700 in selling price if the car is not sold during the model year. If the car is sold during the model year, it will yield a profit of $2,500. Suppose that demand for these cars can be modeled by a Poisson distribution with a mean of one per year. How many cars should the manager order? What nonquantitative considerations might cause the manager to order at least one car?

7. Discouraged by the prices he was receiving from a local dairy cooperative, farmer Bill Barnes decided to open his own roadside stand to sell cottage cheese and other products. Although the stand, called Curds-to-Go, has been quite successful during its first six months of operation, Bill is somewhat concerned because in some weeks he ends up with surplus cottage cheese whereas in other weeks he runs out. His daughter, Billie Jean Barnes, who is a business major in college, studied the buying patterns during her spring break and concluded that demand is approximately normal with a mean of 200 pounds per week and a standard deviation of 30 pounds per week. According to farmer Bill Barnes, processing cost for labor and materials is $.45 per pound. The final product sells for $.99 a pound. Leftover cottage cheese at the end of each week is sold to neighboring farmers for feed at a price of $.15 per pound. How much cottage cheese should Bill prepare each week? Assume holding cost is negligible.

8. The Family Bakery prepares a certain number of birthday cakes each weekend for last-minute shoppers who neglect to order ahead. Each cake costs \$3.40 for labor and materials and sells for \$8.00. Leftover cakes are sold the following Monday at half-price, and usually 60 percent are sold and the rest are scrapped. Holding cost is \$.20 per cake for leftovers because of the need to refrigerate them. How many cakes should be prepared if historical demand is as shown below?

Number Demanded	Frequency
0	.10
1	.25
2	.20
3	.27
4	.10
5	.05
6	.03

9. Marvin Merkle, a recent college graduate, has purchased an exercise machine in order to help him to lose weight and keep in shape. The firm that sold Marvin the machine is about to go out of business, and he will be unable to buy a critical part, should it fail. Consequently, the question is how many spares to buy before the firm closes its doors permanently. The parts cost \$30 each, and according to the Florida-bound owner, the failure rate can be described by a Poisson distribution with a mean of 2.0 parts over the expected life of the machine.

a. For what range of shortage cost would buying two spare parts be appropriate, if spare parts have no holding cost or salvage value?

b. For what range of shortage costs would not buying any spares be most appropriate for Marvin?

10. A marina owner maintains three outboard boats to rent. Daily demand can be described by the following distribution:

x	P(x)
0	.10
1	.20
2	.20
3	.20
4	.10
5	.10
6	.10

The owner estimates that if a customer wants to rent a boat and none is available, the marina loses \$35 in profit.

a. For what range of excess cost is the current stocking level optimum?

b. Suppose that your range of excess cost is presented to the owner, who says that although she cannot provide an exact figure, your range is too high. Would this imply that the current stocking level is too high or too low? Explain.

11. Given the accompanying product structure tree, find the number of each component needed to make 20 units of the end item, assuming there are no on-hand inventories.

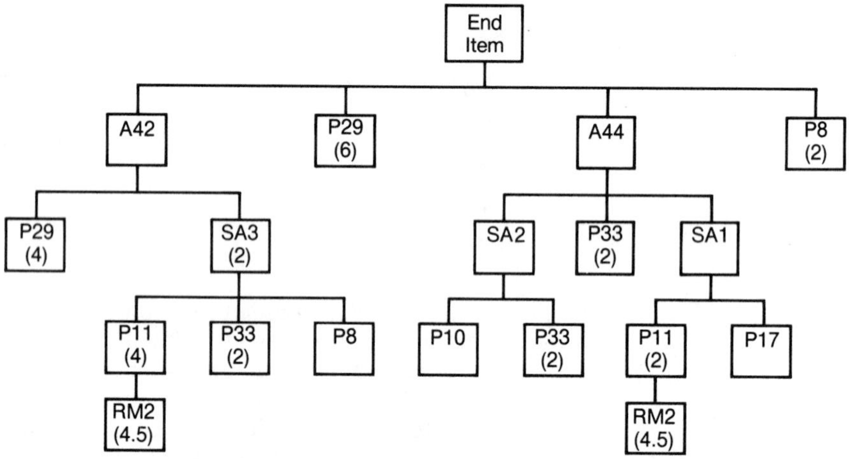

12. (Refer to the tree in Problem 11.) Determine the number of each component that must be ordered if 20 units of the end item will be made and the following on-hand inventories exist: 100 of P29, 30 of SA3, 162 or P11, 83 of P33, and 400 pounds of RM2.

13. The product structure tree shown has some missing components. Redraw the tree adding the missing components.

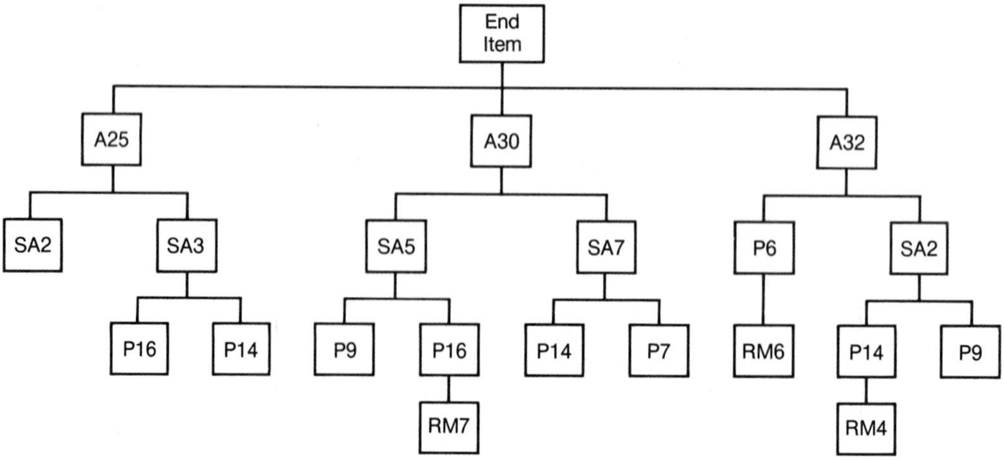

14. Construct a product structure tree using this information: End Item 8 is composed of Assemblies A1, A2, and A5 and Parts P3 and P7. Assembly A1 is composed of Subassembly SA3, Part P5(2), and Part P8(4); Assembly A2 is composed of Subassemblies SA1(2) and SA4 and Part P5(2); and Assembly A5 is composed of Subassemblies SA1 and SA6. Subassembly SA1 consists of Parts P2(4) and P6; Subassembly SA3 consists of Parts P1(2), P2, and P3(4); and Subassembly SA4 consists of Parts P1(4), P4(2), and P6. Part P1 requires 2.5 pounds of Raw Material RM4 and 1.5 pounds of Raw Material RM7; Part P3 requires 3.2 pounds of Raw Material RM3; and Part P4 requires 1.4 pounds of Raw Material RM4 and 2.0 pounds of Raw Material RM5.

15. (Refer to Problem 14.) Determine the quantities of each raw material that would be needed to make 40 units of End Item 8 under each of these circumstances:

a. No on-hand inventories are available.

b. There are 10 units of Parts P1, 15 of Part P3, and 85 pounds of Raw Material RM4.

16. Construct a product structure tree for End Item 10 given this information: It is composed of A(2), B, and C; A is composed of E(4) and F; B is composed of D(2) and E; C is composed of G(3) and H(2); E is composed of M(2) and N; F is composed of R and W(2); and G is composed of E, R, and K(4). Seven pounds of J is needed for each unit of K, and 5 pounds of S is needed per unit of W.

17. (Refer to Problem 16.) Determine the quantities of each component that would be needed to make 12 units of End Item 10 under each of these circumstances:

a. No on-hand inventories are available.

b. Twenty-five pounds each of Raw Material S and J are available, along with 20 units of W, 5 units of G, 50 units of K, and 10 units of B.

18. Prepare a material requirements plan for End Item 4 and its components given the information presented below:

Component	Lead Time	On-Hand
EI 4	1 week	0
A	1	0
B	2	0
C	1	20
D	2	60

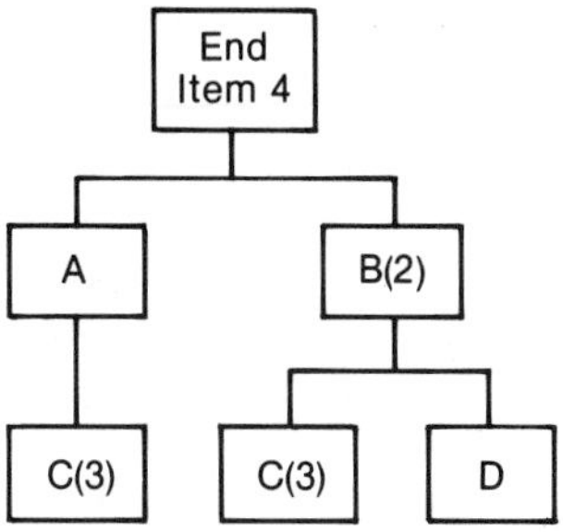

Thirty units of EI 4 are needed at the start of Week 6. There is a scheduled receipt of 70 units of C in Week 1 and 30 units of D in Week 2. Use lot-for-lot ordering.

19. A manufacturer of office furniture has an order for 150 three-drawer file cabinets. For this size order, two weeks are required to cut and form the drawers, and one week is required to form the cabinet. Final assembly involves placing the drawers in the cabinet and installing the hardware (handles, lock, decorative strip). One week is needed for final assembly.

    a. Prepare a list of the components of a file cabinet and indicate the quantity of each needed for one file cabinet.

    b. Draw a product structure tree for the file cabinet.

    c. Suppose the cabinets are due at the start of Week 5. Sufficient locks, decorative strips, and material from which the drawers and cabinets are formed are on hand for this order. Handles must be ordered, and lead time is two weeks. Prepare a material requirements plan for the file cabinets and components. Use lot-for-lot ordering.

20. One of the products Tables Unlimited assembles is mahogany tables. The tables consist of a top, a wooden brace, and four legs. Assembly involves fastening the brace to the top, then attaching the legs.

    a. Draw a product structure tree for the tables.

    b. The firm has an order for 200 tables in Week 6. There are currently 90 legs on hand and a scheduled receipt of 160 legs in Week 2. Also, 100 braces are on hand. Prepare a material requirements plan for the table and its components that will result in 200 tables at the start of Week 6. Lead time for purchasing of wood parts (top, braces, legs) is 1 week, and assembly times for this size order are 1 week for top/brace and 1 week to add the legs. (Hint: Prepare a separate material requirements plan for ordering the tops and another plan for the top/brace assembly.) Use lot-for-lot ordering for assembly operations and the tops. Use round lots that are 160 or multiples thereof for legs and 50 or multiples for braces.

21. End Item 22 is composed of two assemblies, B and D. Two units of B and one of D are needed for each EI 22. Assembly D is made for one C and four E's; assembly B is made from one G, one H, and four E's. There are currently 1,000 E's on hand and a scheduled receipt of 600 due in Week 1. E is purchased in round lots of 600 units. All other components are ordered on a lot-for-lot basis. There also is a current inventory of 150 units of C and a scheduled receipt of 200 units of G in Week 1 and 100 units of H in Week 4.

    Management wants 100 units of EI 22 at the start of Week 4 and 100 units at the start of Week 7. Prepare a material requirements plan for EI 22 and its components, assuming that sufficient capacity will exist to permit your plan. All lead times are one week.

Part IV
Networks

A network is a system of interconnected paths. Examples of such systems include highway systems, transportation systems (for example, subway or plane), communication systems, distribution systems (pipelines), and production systems. Networks are popular tools in management science because they are graphical (i.e., they provide a picture of a problem), and they are fairly easy to construct. There are also a number of computer codes that can be used to solve network problems.

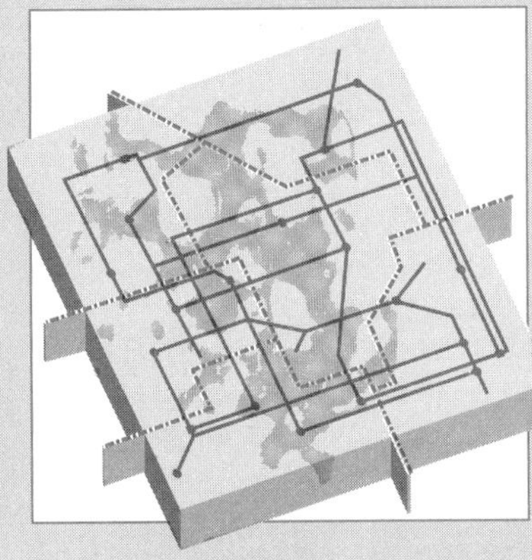

Chapter 14 describes three network models that are useful in solving three frequently encountered categories of problems. One relates to finding the shortest route from one point in a network to one or more other points in the network. Another describes a procedure for interconnecting the various points in a network (e.g., cities) using as little connecting material (e.g., cable lines for cable television) as possible. The third category involves a method for finding the maximal amount of flow that can pass through a network, such as the flow of petroleum through a network of pipelines and storage tanks.

Chapter 15 illustrates the use of networks to portray projects, which are focused efforts designed to accomplish specific objectives within a limited time frame (e.g., introduce a new product, launch a space station). Projects can be thought of as unique, one-time situations when compared with more routine work that occurs on a regular basis in organizations. The use of a technique known as PERT is illustrated for dealing with project networks.

Part Outline

Chapter 14
Networks

Chapter Outline

Learning Objectives

After completing this chapter, you should be able to:

1. State why network models are important tools for problem solving.
2. Describe the kinds of problems that can be solved using the shortest route algorithm and use it to solve typical problems.
3. Describe the kinds of problems that can be solved using the minimum spanning tree algorithm and use the algorithm to solve typical problems.
4. Describe the kinds of problems that can be solved using the maximal flow algorithm and use the algorithm to solve typical problems.

INTRODUCTION

This chapter explores three **network** models. Network models consist of a set of circles, or **nodes,** and lines, which are referred to as either **arcs** or *branches,* that connect some nodes to other nodes. Figure 14–1 illustrates a simple network diagram. This network has four nodes and five branches. Notice that the branches meet only at nodes; the nodes are *intersections* of the branches. For purposes of reference, the nodes are numbered. Moreover, a branch can be referred to by specifying the nodes on each of its ends (e.g., branch 1–2).

Networks are important tools of management science. Not only can networks be used to model a wide variety of problems, they can often be solved more easily than other models of the same problem, and they present models in a visual format.

The three network models described in this chapter are:

1. Shortest route.
2. Minimum spanning tree.
3. Maximal flow.

In the first of these, shortest route, networks are used to represent the distance, time, or cost of getting from one location (node) to various other locations, with the branches representing those distances, costs, or times. The objective is to determine the shortest route (distance, time, or cost) from one location to each of the other locations.

Spanning trees are concerned with interconnecting the nodes of a network using as little of the branch "material" as possible. Typical examples include linking towns and villages to a cable TV network, connecting electrical motors or appliances to a network, and so on.

Flow networks represent flow through a system, and the objective is to achieve as much flow as possible. Examples include flow through a system of pipelines, a flow of traffic through a system of highways, and a flow of products through a production system.

As you can see, many different kinds of problems seem to lend themselves to network models. Moreover, the solutions to many of the problems described in this chapter are quite simple. In fact, many of the problems presented in this chapter could be solved by inspection. Nonetheless, it is important to be able to use the algorithms described in the chapter to solve these problems. This relates to the fact that more complex problems are less amenable to solution by inspection; the simple problems are designed to facilitate learning solution techniques. Furthermore, the algorithms are the basis for computer solution of the problems. Fortunately, the algorithms involve very few steps, and they are intuitively appealing.

The first model we shall explore involves solving the shortest route problem.

FIGURE 14–1 A Simple Network Diagram

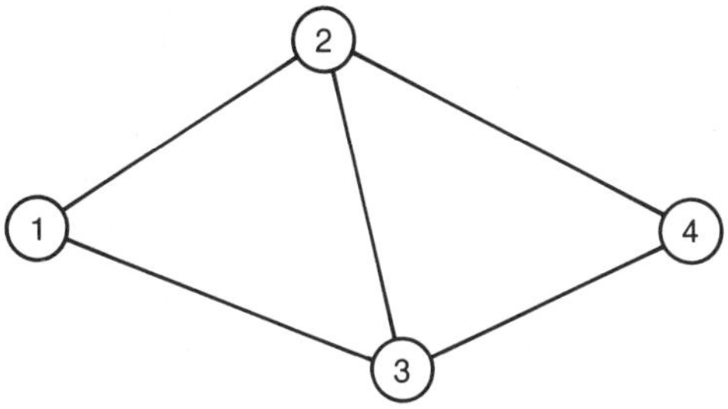

THE SHORTEST ROUTE PROBLEM

In the **shortest route problem,** the objective is to find the shortest distance from one location (origin) to another location (destination) through a network. Very often, the total distance traveled is the measure of effectiveness. Delivery systems and transportation systems are typical examples of where such problems occur. Other measures of effectiveness could be cost or time.

The Shortest Route Algorithm

The algorithm used to solve for the shortest routes assumes that all node distances are non-negative. The algorithm finds the shortest route from a specified node (usually Node 1) to every node in a network. The algorithm requires $n - 1$ steps, where n equals the number of nodes in a network.

The analysis uses a *labeling procedure,* wherein a label is developed for each node. The labels consist of two numbers separated by a comma: The first number refers to the distance from Node 1 to the labeled node along a certain path, while the second number refers to the node that immediately precedes this node along that path. Thus, if Node 5, say, has the label 18,3, this tells us that there is a path from Node 1 to Node 5 that has a distance of 18 from Node 1 and that the preceding node on that path is Node 3. (In order to find out which node precedes Node 3, we would have to refer to the label at Node 3. Hence, once the analysis has been completed, the shortest route to any given node from Node 1 can be found by tracing the node labels back through the network.)

The labeling procedure begins with the originating node (e.g., home base, central office, starting point). Usually this is Node 1. Its label is 0,S. The 0 indicates the distance from Node 1 to this node; because this is Node 1, the distance is 0. The S indicates that this is starting node. This node is considered to be *permanently labeled,* a term used to indicate that no shorter route to a node exists. Obviously, since Node 1 is the starting point, we can be sure that there is no "shorter route" to this node. In general, once we have determined the shortest distance to a node, we give that node a permanent label. We signify this by shading in the node.

Initially, none of the nodes are labeled. Then, as the analysis progresses, certain nodes are assigned *temporary* labels, which may be revised as part of the analysis. The label remains temporary until it can be ascertained that no shorter route to a node exists. At that point, the label becomes permanent, and the node is shaded in to reflect this. When all nodes have received permanent labels, the shortest routes can be determined by inspection of the permanent labels on the nodes.

The essence of the analysis is to determine permanent labels for the nodes, one at a time. Once a node receives its permanent label, the analysis focuses on that section of the network for assigning temporary labels. The following example will illustrate this simple procedure.

An Example

Given this network that shows the distance in miles between delivery destinations, find the shortest route to each destination from Node 1. Travel between nodes can be in either direction.

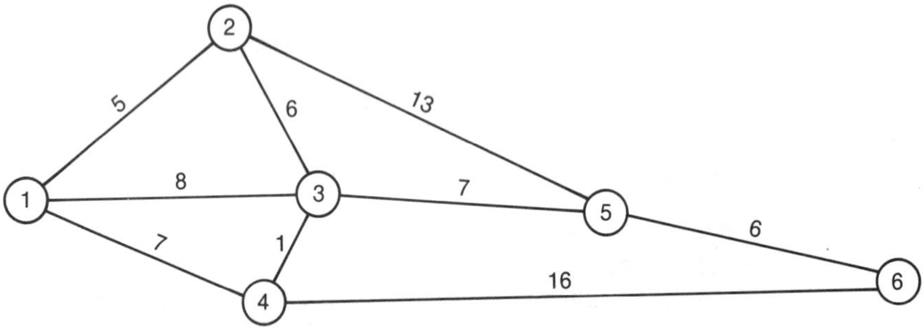

Note: Distances are not drawn to scale.

Begin by permanently labeling Node 1 with 0,S. Indicate that the label is permanent by shading in Node 1. Then, obtain temporary labels for every node that can be reached *directly* from Node 1 (i.e., Nodes 2, 3, and 4). The label should show the distance from Node 1 and indicate that Node 1 is the predecessor node. Thus, the temporary label for Node 2 is 5,1 because it is 5 miles from Node 1, and Node 1 precedes it. Similarly, the temporary label for Node 3 is 8,1 and the temporary label for Node 4 is 7,1.

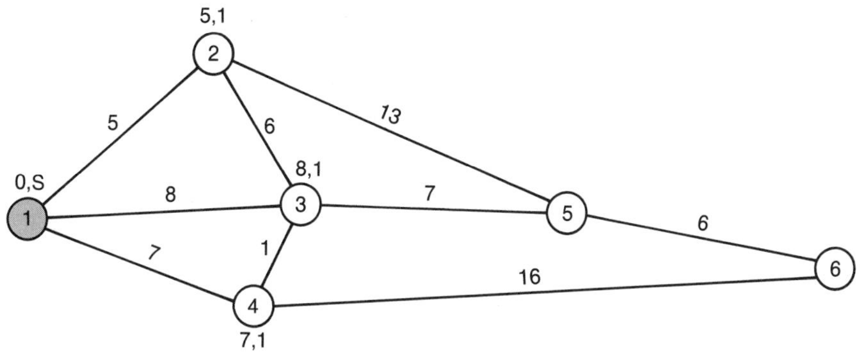

First iteration Determine which temporary label has the *smallest* distance from Node 1. It is the label for Node 2, with a distance of 5. Make this label permanent, and shade in Node 2. Now determine temporary labels for each node that can be reached directly from this latest permanent node *unless* a node already has a permanent label (e.g., Node 1), or unless a current temporary label already exists that cannot be improved on. For example, the current temporary label for Node 3 is 8,1; the distance from Node 1 along path 1–2–3 would be 5 + 6 = 11. Hence, the current label is shorter, so we should keep that label. Node 5, however, does not have a label. Its cumulative distance from Node 1 through Node 2 is 18; hence, its temporary label is 18,2 because Node 2 is its predecessor.

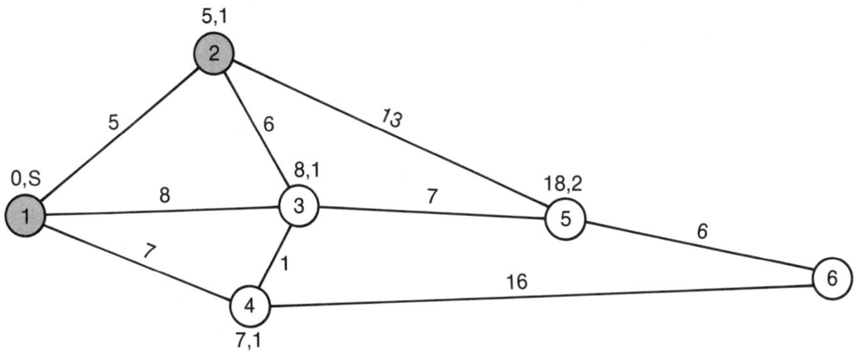

Second iteration Identify the node that has the smallest temporary label. (The choices are: Node 3, with a label of 8,1; Node 4 with a label of 7,1; and Node 5 with a label of 18,2.) Because 7 is the smallest distance, Node 4 has the smallest temporary label. Make this label permanent (shade in). Next, find each nonpermanent node that can be reached directly from this newest permanent node. These are Nodes 3 and 6. Node 6 has no temporary label; its temporary label will now be 23,4, indicating that its distance from Node 1 is 23 miles (the Node 4 label of 7 plus

16 miles from Node 4 to Node 6). Node 3 already has a temporary label of 8,1, indicating that it can be reached directly from Node 1 with a distance of 8 miles. We can see that it can also be reached in 8 miles by Route 1–4–3. Hence, there is a tie, so *either* label can be used. For simplicity then, suppose we retain the current label.

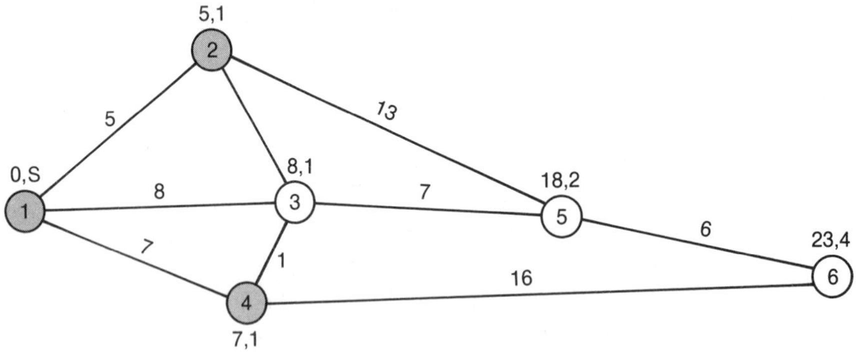

Third iteration The node with the smallest temporary label is Node 3. Therefore, its label now becomes a permanent label, and Node 3 is shaded in. It can also be helpful to indicate that a tie exists at this point, meaning that an alternate route exists to this node. Next, find each nonpermanent node that can be reached directly from Node 3. We see that Node 5 is the only such node. It has a temporary label of 18,2. However, we can see that by following a route from Node 3 to Node 5 directly, the cumulative distance from Node 1 will be only 15 (i.e., 8 + 7 = 15). Because the route through Node 3 is shorter, we *update* the temporary label of Node 5 to reflect this shorter route.

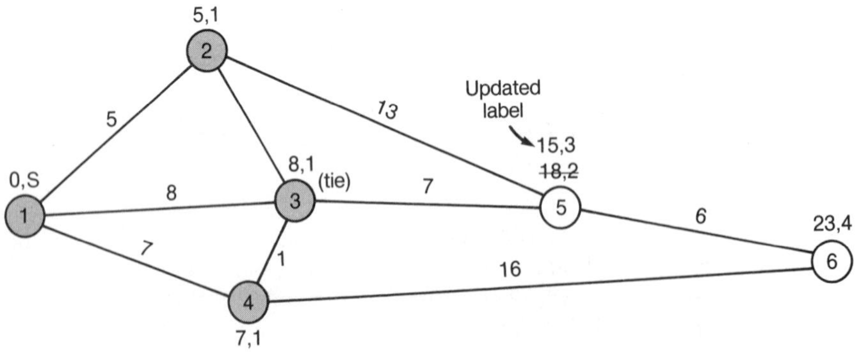

Fourth iteration Identify the Node with the smallest temporary label. Node 5 has a label of 15,3 and Node 6 has the label 23,4. Because 15 is smaller than 23, Node 5 is selected and converted to a permanent label.

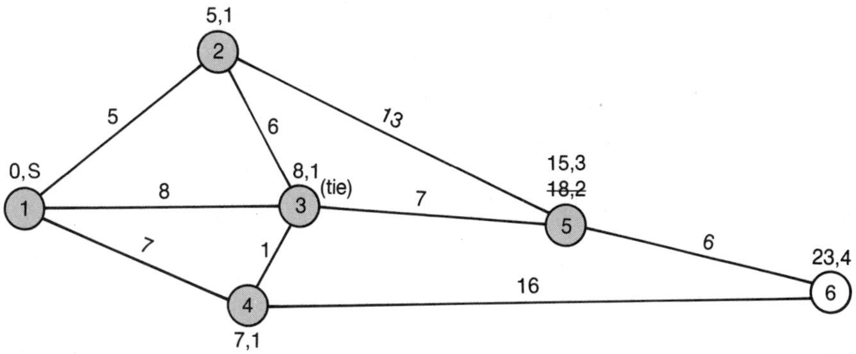

Fifth iteration The only node with a nonpermanent label, and the only such node that can be reached directly from the newest permanent node, is Node 6. Using this route, its cumulative distance from Node 1 would be 15 + 6 = 21. Because this is less than its current label shows, we update the label to 21,5. And because this is the only node without a permanent label, we can now permanently label it, using 21,5.

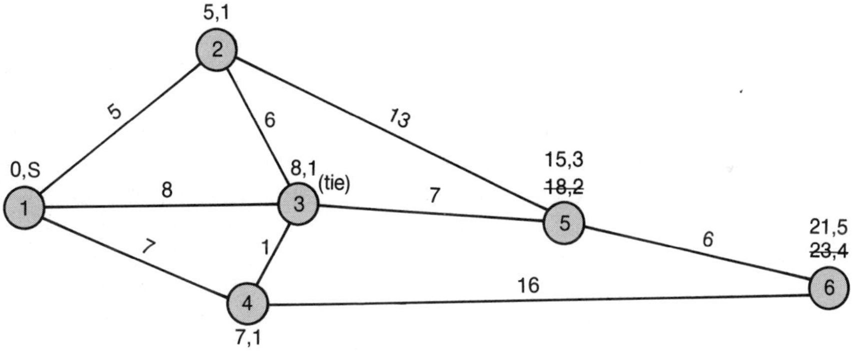

This completes the analysis of the routes. Using the final network, we can read the distances from Node 1 to each node from each node's permanent label. For example, the shortest distance from Node 1 to Node 5 is 15 miles, and the shortest distance from Node 1 to Node 6 is 21 miles.

In order to identify the route that yields the shortest distance to a particular node, it is necessary to work backwards through the network. This is sometimes referred to as *backtracking*. Here is how it is done. Begin with the node in question (say, Node 6). The second part of the label indicates the previous node in the shortest path. Hence, the previous node for Node 6 is Node 5. Turning our attention to Node 5, we see that its predecessor node is Node 3. Hence, so far we have 3–5–6. At Node 3, we note that there was a tie, meaning that either of two routes (1–3 or 1–4–3) will yield the same distance. Thus, we can choose either of these as our route and identify the other as an alternate route. Thus, we can say 1–3–5–6 is the route, but that 1–4–3–5–6 is an alternate route.

All of the routes can be obtained in this manner. They are summarized in the following table.

Node	Distance	Shortest Route	Alternate Route
2	5	1-2	
3	8	1-3	1-4-3
4	7	1-4	
5	15	1-3-5	1-4-3-5
6	21	1-3-5-6	1-4-3-5-6

Summary of Procedure

The procedure for determining the shortest routes and their lengths can be summarized by these steps:

Step 1 Begin at Node 1. Find the distance from Node 1 to each node that can be reached *directly* from Node 1. Temporarily label each of these nodes with their distance from Node 1 followed by a comma, and number 1. Then select the node that has the smallest distance from Node 1, and make its label permanent. Do this by shading in the node.

Step 2 Find the distance from the new permanent node to each nonpermanent node that can be reached directly from this node. Temporarily label each of these nodes with the cumulative distance from Node 1 if a node has no label, or if its current temporary label is greater than the cumulative distance from Node 1 obtained by going through the new permanent node. Then, consider all nodes that have temporary labels, and permanently label (shade in) the node that has the smallest cumulative distance from Node 1.

Step 3 Repeat the preceding step until all nodes have permanent labels.

Step 4 Identify the shortest route to each node from Node 1 by working backwards through the tree, according to the nodes specified in the node labels.

MINIMUM SPANNING TREE PROBLEM

One of the simplest of all management science techniques is the *minimum spanning tree* technique. The **minimum spanning tree problem** is to connect all of the nodes of a network using as little of the connecting "material" as possible. For instance, the nodes might represent oil storage tanks, and the arcs might represent pipelines that are used to carry the oil between tanks. The cost of the pipeline would be proportional to the length of pipeline used. Hence, the objective would be to connect all of the tanks using as little pipeline as possible. Similar applications include connecting outlying communities for cable television service using

FIGURE 14–2 Network for Oil Pipeline Problem

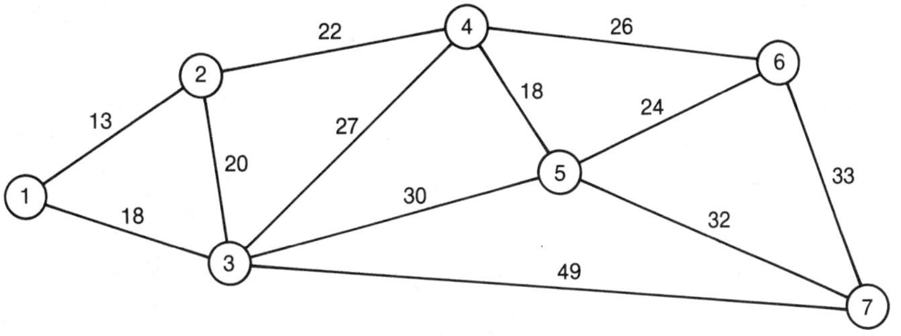

Note: Arc lengths are not precisely proportional to the distances shown on the arcs.

minimal cable wiring, designing communications systems using minimal amounts of electrical wiring, designing highway networks using minimal amounts of road materials, and so on. Alternative measures of effectiveness that lead to even broader applications involve minimizing cost or time instead of distance or quantity of material.

Consider the network shown in Figure 14–2, where the nodes represent fuel storage tanks and the connecting arcs represent possible pipeline connections. The numbers on the arcs indicate the distance in meters for a particular pipeline connection. The purpose of the analysis is to obtain the shortest system of pipeline that will interconnect all of the storage tanks.

Algorithm for Minimum Spanning Tree Solution

The algorithm is quite simple:

1. Start at any node. (Generally, Node 1 is used as the starting point.) Identify the shortest connecting arc to another node. Shade in the starting node and the other node, and make the connecting arc a jagged line.
2. Find the shortest arc from the existing portion of the tree (i.e., the shaded nodes) to a node that is not yet connected. Shade in that node. If a tie occurs, break it arbitrarily. Make the connecting arc jagged.
3. Continue until all nodes have been connected to the tree.
4. To find the total (minimal) length of the connecting arcs, sum their values.

An Example

Suppose the manager of the fuel depot wants to determine the minimum spanning tree for the network of storage tanks given in Figure 14–2 and the amount of pipe that will be needed to make the connections.

Let's begin at Node 1. Two arcs are potential connectors with other nodes; one is 13 meters in length and the other is 18 meters. Choose 13 because it is the smaller of the two. Darken that arc and shade in Nodes 1 and 2.

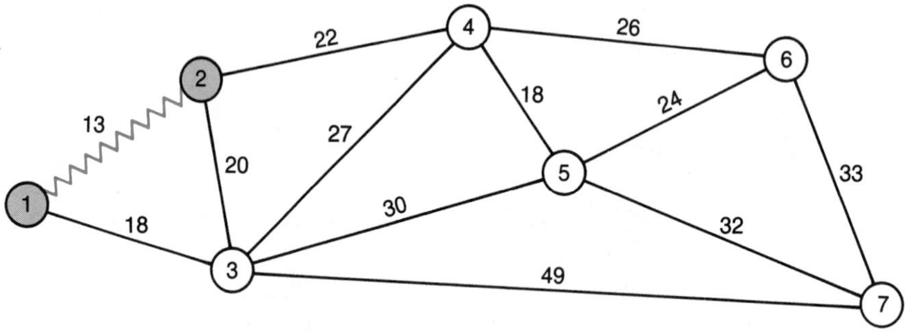

Now compare all possible arcs that could connect the existing portion of the tree (i.e., Nodes 1 and 2) to another node. The arcs are 18 (Node 1 to Node 3), 20 (Node 2 to Node 3), and 22 (Node 2 to Node 4). Select 18 because it is the smallest, and add Arc 1–3 and Node 3 to the tree.

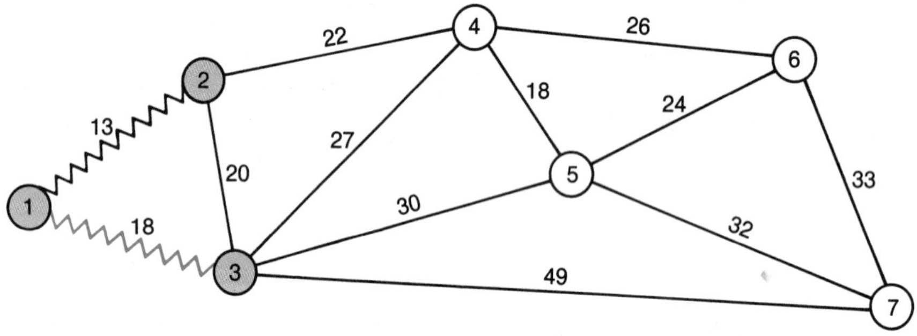

Again, find the arcs that lead from the current tree to nodes that are not currently connected. The arcs are 22 (Node 2 to Node 4), 27 (Node 3 to Node 4), 30 (Node 3 to Node 5), and 49 (Node 3 to Node 7). Because 22 is the smallest, it becomes the next link, and Node 4 becomes part of the tree.

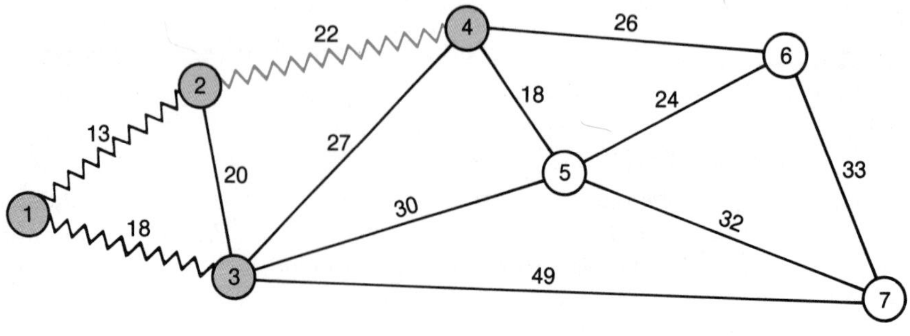

The possible arcs from the completed portion of the tree to unconnected nodes are 49, 30, 18, and 26. Because 18 is the shortest, make Arc 4–5 and Node 5 part of the tree.

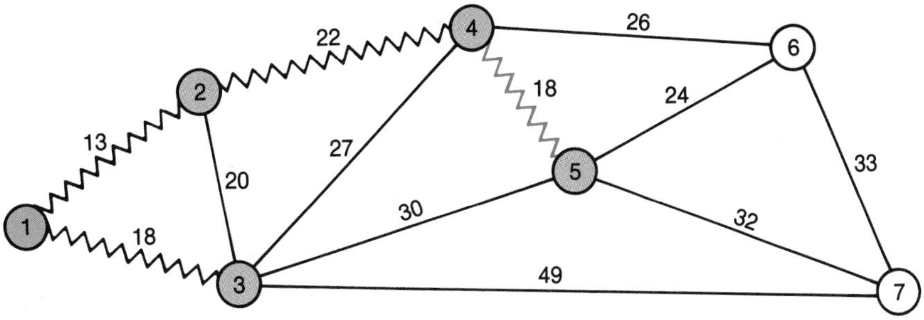

The possible arcs now are 26, 24, 32, and 49. Because 24 is the smallest, make Arc 5-6 and Node 6 part of the tree.

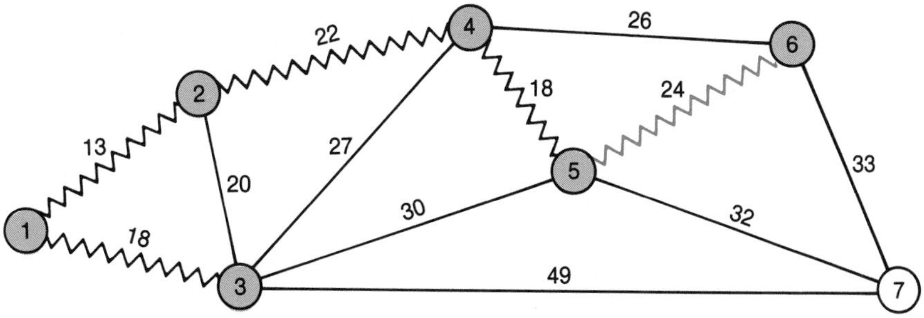

One node remains unconnected. Taking a slightly different perspective, we can see that the shortest link for this node and the completed portion of the tree is Arc 5–7. Hence, the minimum spanning tree is now complete. The last diagram shows the completed tree with the unused arcs omitted.

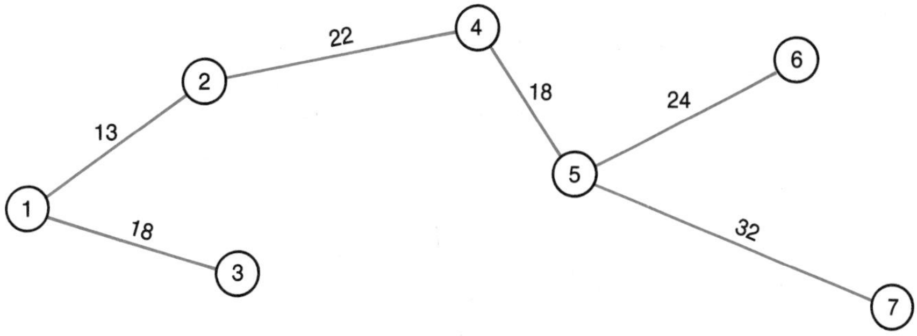

The length of pipe that will be needed for this system can be found by summing the arc lengths: 18 + 13 + 22 + 18 + 24 + 32 = 127 meters.

FIGURE 14–3 A Flow Network

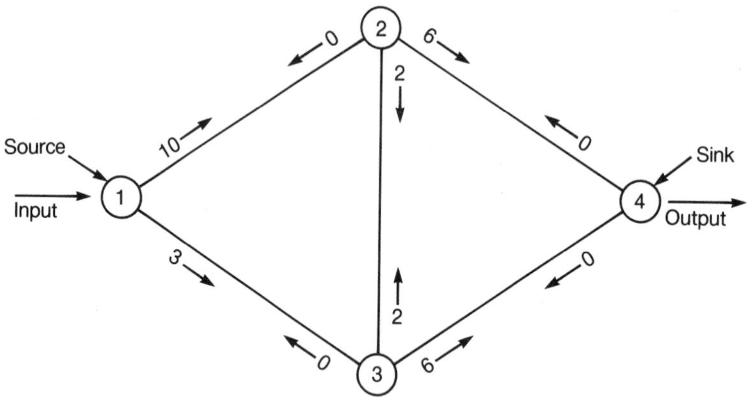

THE MAXIMAL FLOW PROBLEM

In a **maximal flow problem,** the objective is to maximize flow through a network. For example, a network might represent a system of roads and highways, and the objective might be to maximize the rate of flow of vehicles through the system. Other examples of maximal flow networks can be systems of pipelines that carry natural gas, oil, or water, paperwork systems, airline routes, production systems, and distribution systems.

In order to determine the maximal flow of a system, it is necessary to take into account the *flow capacities* of the various branches of a network. Branch capacities limit the rate of flow through a branch (arc) of the network. Hence, the objective is to determine the amount of flow through each branch that will achieve the maximum possible flow for the system as a whole.

It is assumed that there is a single input node (called a **source**) and a single output node (called a **sink**). It is also assumed that there is *flow conservation*, which means that the flow of any node is equal to the flow into that node.

As an example of a maximal flow network, consider the network shown in Figure 14–3. As you can see, Node 1 is the input node; therefore, all flow entering the system must come through that node. Node 4 is the output node; therefore, all flow leaving the system must go through that node. The numbers of the branches indicate the flow capacity of a branch *in a given direction*. For example, the 10 on Branch 1–2 indicates a maximum possible flow rate of 10 coming out of Node 1 along that branch. Now some branches permit flow in either direction. However, that is not the case for Branch 1–2; the 0 on Branch 1–2 indicates that no flow is possible *from* Node 2 to Node 1. Now consider Branch 2–3. We can see that the maximum flow rate along this branch is 2, and that flow can be in *either* direction.

However, it is important to recognize that in such a branch flows cannot occur simultaneously in both directions. Consequently, for any branch, flow can occur in one direction only (i.e., it must be *unidirectional*), even though it may be allowable in both directions. The determination of which direction, or if there should be any flow at all, is a matter for analysis to resolve.

Maximal Flow Algorithm

The algorithm for the maximal flow problem is quite simple, and it consists of relatively few steps. These are:

1. Find any path from the source node to the sink node that has a positive flow capacity. (Flow capacity of a path is determined by the smallest branch capacity along the path chosen in the direction of flow.) If no such path can be found, the current solution is optimal. If no such path can be found at the start, no flow is possible (i.e., there is no feasible solution). If a path with positive flow is found, continue the analysis.
2. Adjust the flow capacities of branches on the chosen path in the following manner. For each branch, at the end where the flow enters the branch, reduce the capacity by the amount of flow; at the end of the branch where flow leaves, increase the capacity by the amount of flow. For instance, consider Branch 1–3:

Suppose we decide to assign a flow of 3 to this branch, flowing from Node 1 to Node 3. According to the preceding rule, we must reduce the left capacity of the branch to 0 and the right side to 3. Hence, the revised branch would look like this:

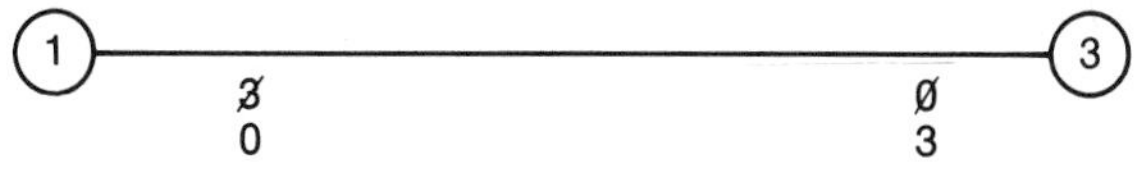

For clarity, we could also show the amount and direction of flow through this branch:

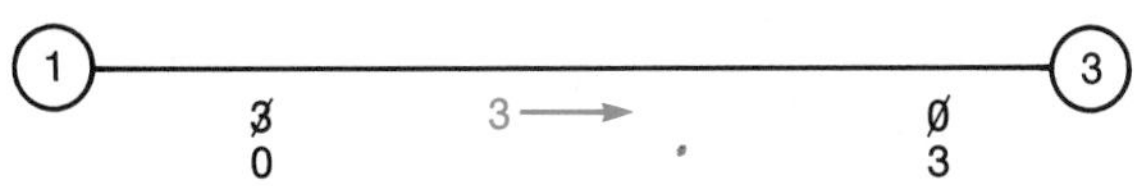

The interpretation of the information on the left end of the revised branch is that originally a maximal flow of 3 was possible; now, no additional flow is possible because the maximal flow is being used. If the revised value was positive (say, 2) this would indicate that additional flow from left to right in this branch is possible. On the right side of Branch 1–3, we see that, originally, *no* flow was possible from Node 3 to Node 1 through this branch. That is still true, even though the revised value is a 3. The 3 indicates how much of the current flow *can be reversed*. For example, at some point in the analysis of this network, we may assign a flow of 3 from Node 1 to Node 3 through this branch, and end up with the numbers shown. However, that assignment might not be optimal; at a later point in the analysis, we might want to undo some, or all, of this flow assignment. The revised value on the right end of the branch (i.e., 3) indicates the extent to which the current flow can be reduced. Had the original value on the right end been nonzero, we might well wish to consider flow in the other direction. Hence, as a matter of course, we always revise the values on both ends of a branch at the same time. Note, too, that the sum of the revised values will *always* equal the sum of the original values.

3. Return to step 1.

An Example

In order to demonstrate the algorithm, let's analyze the network shown in Figure 14–3. We can begin by choosing *any* path that will allow a positive flow from the source (Node 1) to the sink (Node 4). Obviously, there are a number of paths, such as 1–2–4, 1–2–3–4, 1–3–2–4, and 1–3–4. Suppose we arbitrarily select 1–2–4.

The maximum flow from Node 1 to Node 2 is 10, whereas the maximum flow from Node 2 to Node 4 is 6. Thus, the limiting capacity along this path is the 6 for Branch 2–4, so we can assign a flow of 6 for each branch on this path. This requires that the capacities at the end of each branch on the path be adjusted accordingly. Thus, we have:

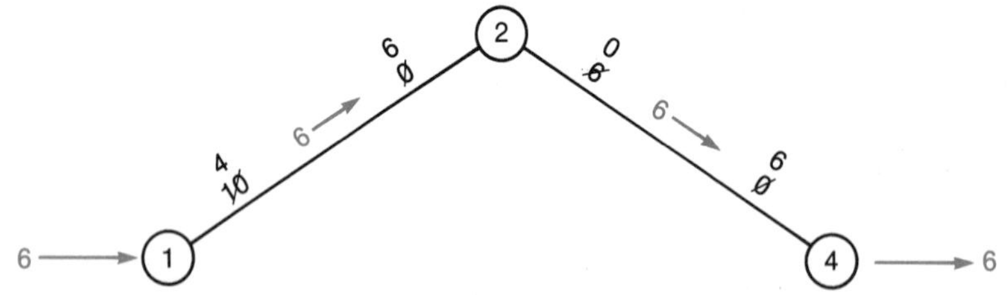

Branch 2–4 is fully loaded; no additional flow can be sent in the 2–4 direction. However, Branch 1–2 can still accept an additional flow of 4. In selecting our next path, either we might want to explore additional flow through Branch 1–2 or we might investigate some other path. Suppose we elect to further explore flow through 1–2, say by examining Path 1–2–3–4.

The revised network, as it now stands, is shown in Figure 14–4. By scanning Path 1–2–3–4, we can see that Branch 2–3 is the most restrictive: its flow capacity from Node 2 to Node 3 is 2. Hence, we can only assign a flow of 2 along this path. For Branch 1–2, this will add 2 to the current flow, making a total flow of 8 for that

FIGURE 14–4 Updated Flow Network

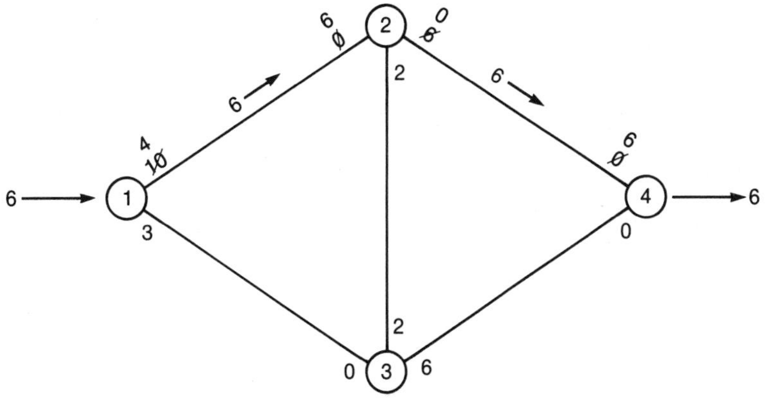

FIGURE 14–5 Second Revision of the Network

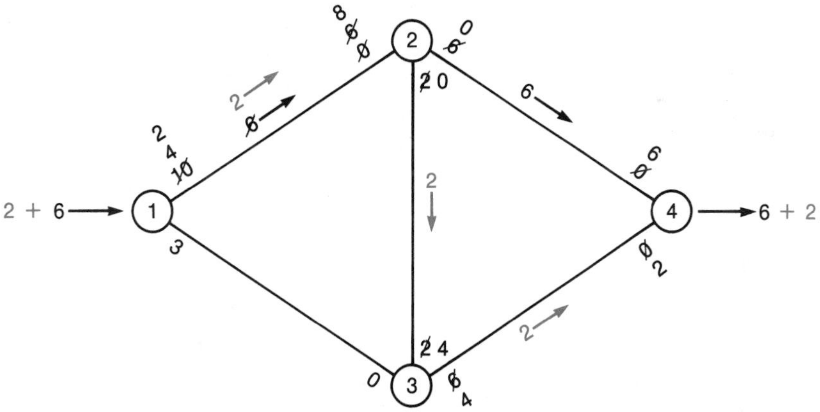

branch. For Branch 2–3, the flow will be 2, and for Branch 3–4, which now has no flow, the assigned flow will also be 2. The revised network is shown in Figure 14–5.

If no further positive flow from the source to the sink is possible, an optimal solution has been found. That is not the case, here, though. Path 1–3–4 can still accept some flow: Branch 1–3 can accept a flow of 3, whereas Branch 3–4 can accept a flow of 4. Hence, the limiting branch is 1–3; therefore, a flow of 3 can be assigned to this path. The resulting network is shown in Figure 14–6.

FIGURE 14–6 Third Revision of Flow Network

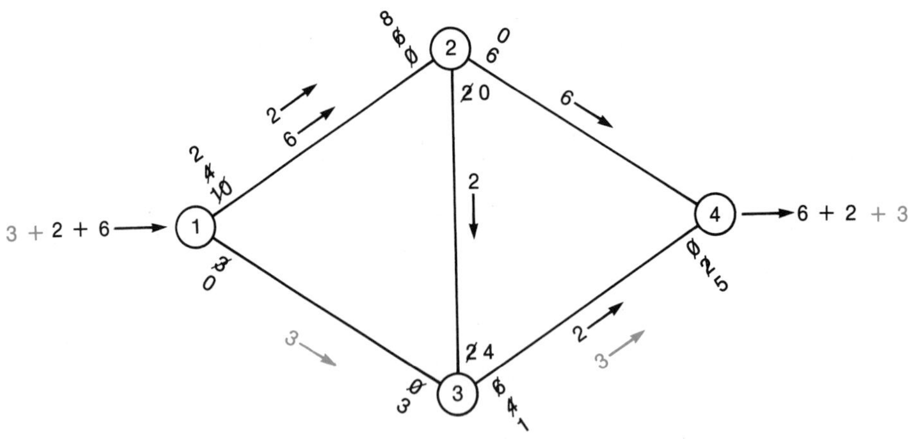

FIGURE 14–7 Final Solution for Flow Network Example

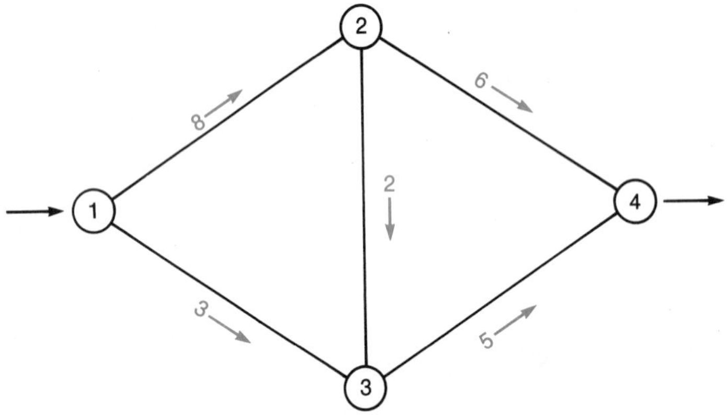

At this point, no additional flow is possible because no path has a positive flow capacity. Hence, this solution is optimal; the maximal flow rate is 11, which is shown as both the sum of the inputs and as the sum of the outputs. Moreover, the flow through the various branches of the network is also shown. These values are summarized in Figure 14–7.

For a network as small as this, it often is possible to determine the maximal rate of flow by inspection. However, for larger, more complicated networks, the more formal approach outlined here is prudent. In that regard, when trying to determine if a path exists that has a positive flow rate during the analysis, note the total capacity of branches leaving the source as well as the total capacity of the branches entering the sink. The flow capacity of the network cannot exceed either of these.

Comment

Sometimes it can be difficult to decide on the most appropriate representation of a problem; this is often the most difficult part of the process. Once the *type* of network problem has been identified, several computer codes are available to solve network problems.

SUMMARY

Network models are an important approach for problem solving. Not only can they be used to model a wide range of problems, they also are relatively simple to work with and provide a visual portrayal of a problem.

This chapter describes three frequently used algorithms: the shortest route algorithm, which is useful for determining the shortest distance (cost, etc.) from an origin to a destination through a network; the minimum spanning tree algorithm, which is useful in determining the minimum distance (cost, time) needed to connect a set of locations into a single system; and the maximal flow algorithm, which is useful for determining the greatest amount of flow that can be transmitted through a system in which various branches, or connections, have specified flow capacity limitations.

GLOSSARY

Arc A branch, or line, in a network.

Maximal Flow Problem Determining the maximum amount of flow that can be obtained for a system of pipes, roads, and so on.

Minimum Spanning Tree Problem Finding the shortest set of arcs that will connect all of the nodes of a network.

Network A set of nodes and connecting arcs or branches. Can be useful in representing various systems, such as distribution systems, production systems, and transportation systems.

Node A circle in a network. It may represent a location or a switching point.

Path A connected sequence of nodes and branches from one node (usually the source or origin) to another node (usually the sink or destination). Also, a route.

Shortest Route Problem Determining the shortest path from an origin to a destination through a network.

Sink The one node in a flow network to which all flow is directed; the exit point of a system.

Source The one node in a flow network through which all flow enters the system.

Spanning Tree A set of branches, or arcs, that connects all of the nodes in a network.

SOLVED PROBLEMS

Problem 1. *Shortest route* Given this network, which shows the distance in miles between each of five delivery locations, find the shortest route from the home office (Node 1) to each delivery location.

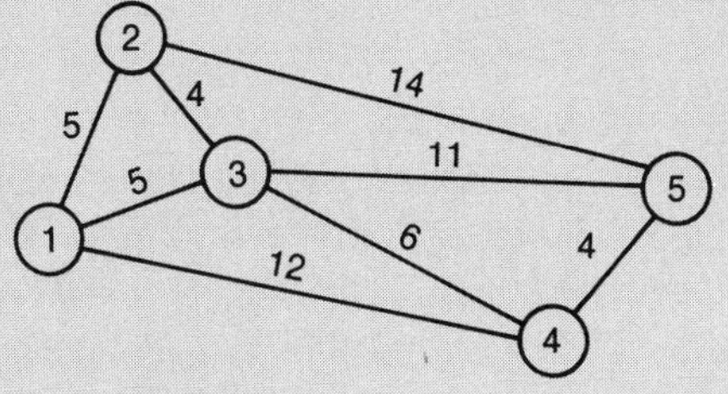

Solution

Using a single diagram for the entire analysis, begin by assigning the permanent label of 0,S to Node 1, then shade in the node to indicate that its label is permanent. Then, assign a temporary label to each node that can be reached directly from Node 1. The label should consist of two numbers: the first number will indicate the distance from Node 1 and the second number will indicate that Node 1 is the predecessor node:

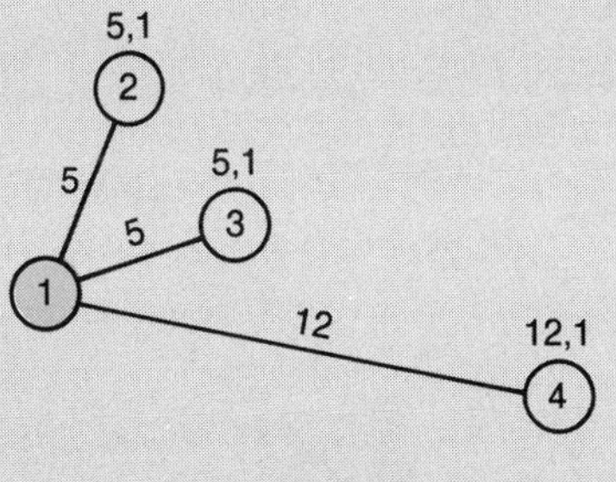

Determine which node shows the shortest temporary label distance. In this instance, there is a tie between Nodes 2 and 3. Both show a distance of 5, whereas Node 4 shows a distance of 12. Choose either Node 2 or Node 3 arbitrarily. Suppose we choose Node 2. Its label now becomes permanent, which we indicate by shading in Node 2. Now identify each nonpermanently labeled node that can be reached directly from this newest permanently labeled node. These are Nodes 3 and 5. The cumulative distance from Node 1 through Node 2 to Node 3 is 9. Because this distance exceeds the current temporary label of Node 3, no change should be made to the label at Node 3. Because Node 5 has no label, it will now get a temporary label of 19,2: The 19 is the cumulative distance for Path 1–2–5, and the 2 indicates that Node 2 is the next node before 5 on that path.

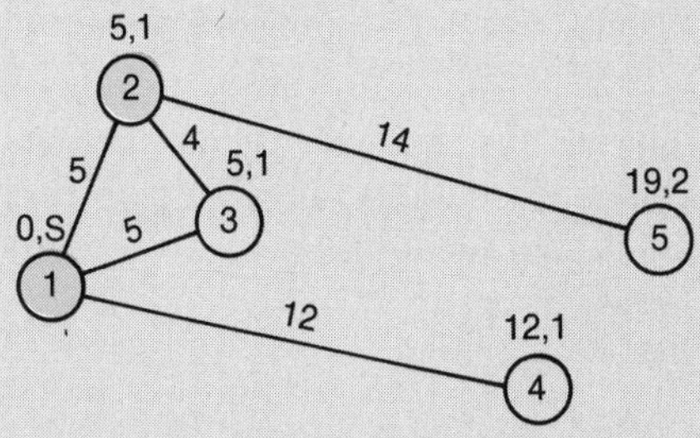

The smallest temporary label is now at Node 3, which has a distance from Node 1 of 5 (Node 4 has a distance of 12 and Node 5 has a distance of 19). Convert the label at Node 3 to a permanent label and shade in the node. Now find the cumulative distance from Node 1 through Node 3 to each nonpermanent node. The distance to Node 4 is 5 + 6 = 11. Because this distance is *less than* the current temporary label at Node 4, update the label with this smaller value. The cumulative distance to Node 5 through Node 3 is 5 + 11 = 16. Again, this amount is less than the temporary label, so the label at Node 5 must be updated to 16,3, showing a distance of 16 miles achieved with Node 3 as the previous node on the route.

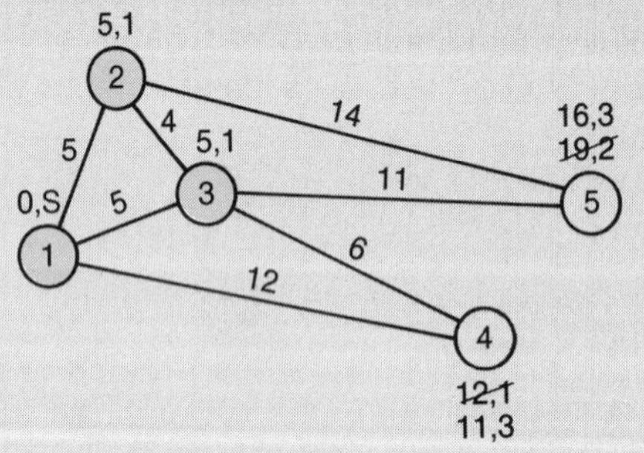

At this point, Node 4 has the smaller temporary label of the two remaining nodes. Hence, its label becomes permanent. Next, we see that the cumulative distance to Node 5 through Node 4 is equal to the 11 miles at Node 4 plus 4 miles from Node 4 to Node 5, which is 15 miles. Because this amount is less than the temporary label at Node 5, the label at Node 5 is updated to show this. And since that is the last node, the analysis is complete.

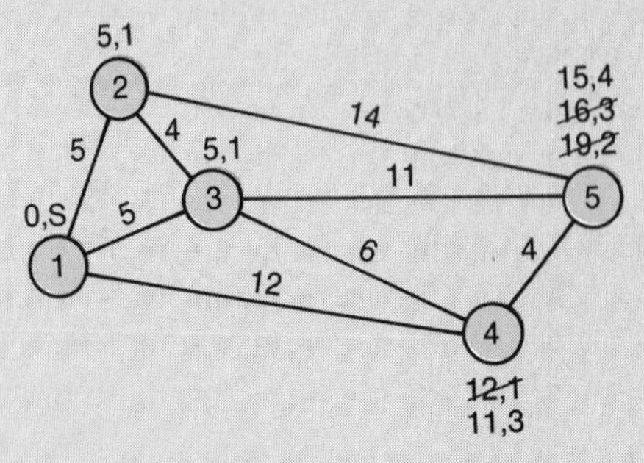

Backtracking through the network, using the sequence indicated by the node labels, and obtaining the distances from the node labels, we get:

Node	Distance	Route
2	5	1–2
3	5	1–3
4	11	1–3–4
5	15	1–3–4–5

Problem 2. *Minimum Spanning Tree* Given this network that shows distances in miles for potential node connections, find the minimum spanning tree and the minimum total of the connections.

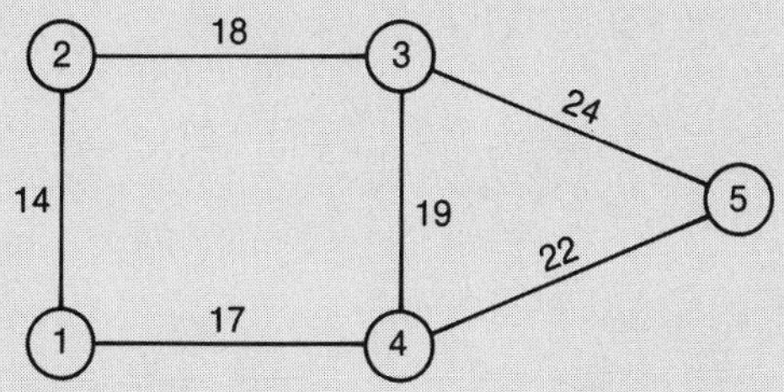

Solution

Start at Node 1 and choose the shortest arc to another node. There are two arcs to choose from: 1–2, which is 14, and 1–4, which is 17. Hence, choose 1–2. Indicate this by making Arc 1–2 a jagged line and shade in Nodes 1 and 2.

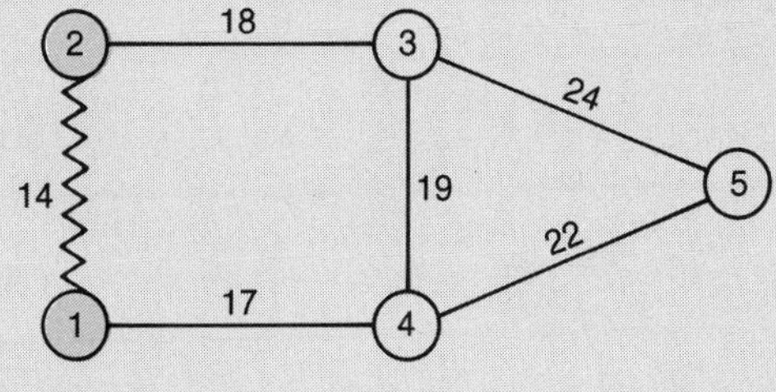

At this point, the (partial) tree consists of Nodes 1 and 2 and the arc between them. Find the smallest arc that will connect the partial tree with another node. There are two arcs to choose from: 1–4, which is 17, and 2–3, which is 18. Because 17 is the smaller of the two, Arc 1–4 is chosen. Indicate this by making Arc 1–4 a jagged line and shade in Node 4.

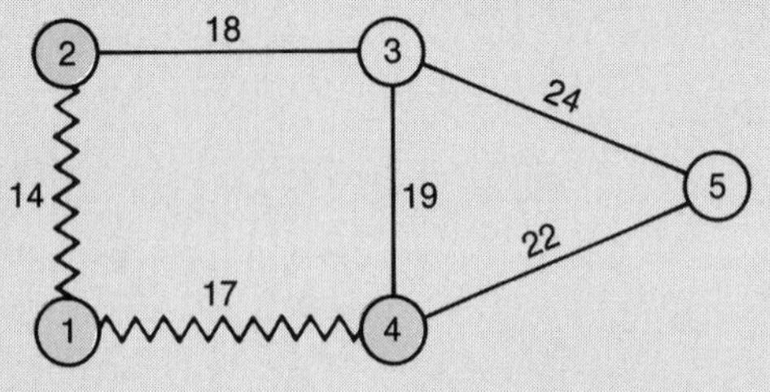

Now the tree consists of Nodes 1, 2, and 4 and their connecting links. The possible direct links to other nodes from this partial tree are 2–3, which is 18, 4–3, which is 19, and 4–5, which is 22. Because 18 is the smallest distance, Arc 2–3 is selected and a jagged line is drawn between nodes 2 and 3. Also, Node 3 is shaded in.

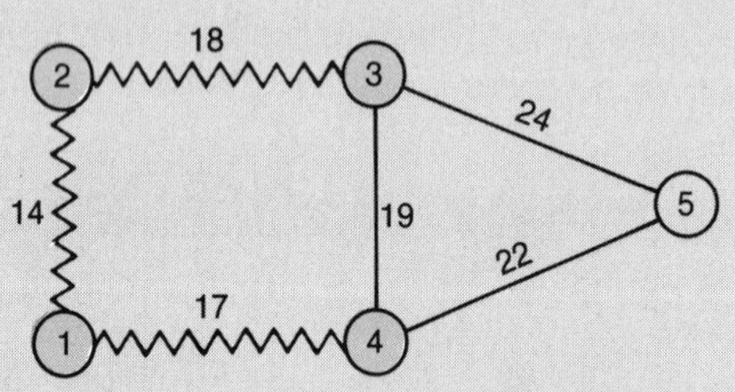

Only one node remains to be linked to the spanning tree, Node 5. It can be linked at Node 4 for a distance of 22, or at Node 3 for a distance of 24. Because 22 is the smaller distance, Arc 4–5 is chosen and represented using a jagged line. (Note that although Arc 3–4 has a value of only 19, it isn't considered because it does not offer a link with a node not already in the tree; both Nodes 3 and 4 are in the tree.) This completes the tree.

The minimum distance is: 14 + 17 + 18 + 22 = 71 miles.

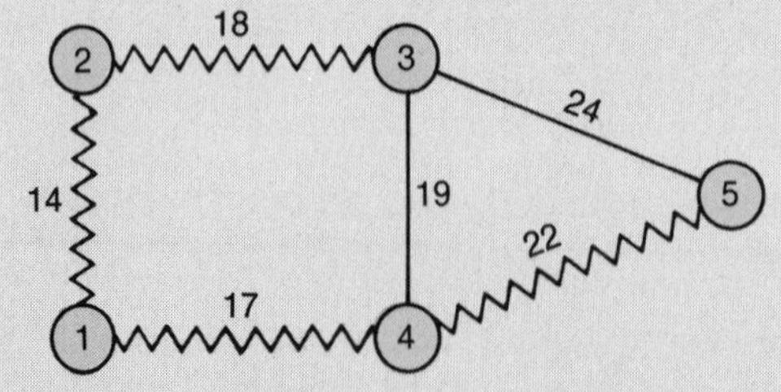

Problem 3. *Maximal flow* Determine the maximal flow through this system of pipelines from Node 1 to Node 5.

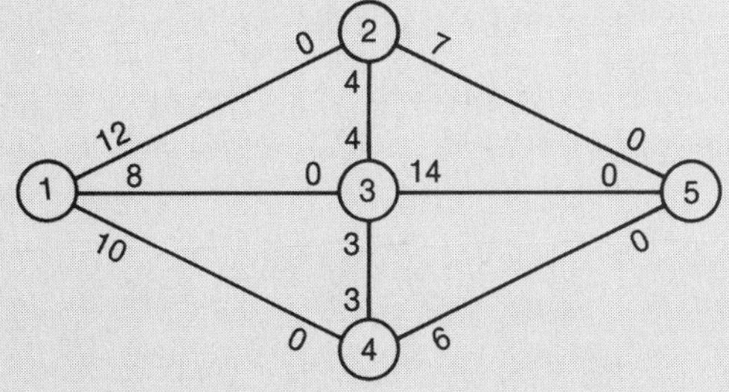

Solution

Begin by selecting *any* path through the network that has a positive flow capacity. One such path is 1–2–5, where Branch 1–2 has a capacity of 12, and Branch 2–5 has a capacity of 7. The limiting capacity is the smallest capacity along the path, which is 7.

Assign 7 to each branch on this path and revise the flow capacities accordingly.

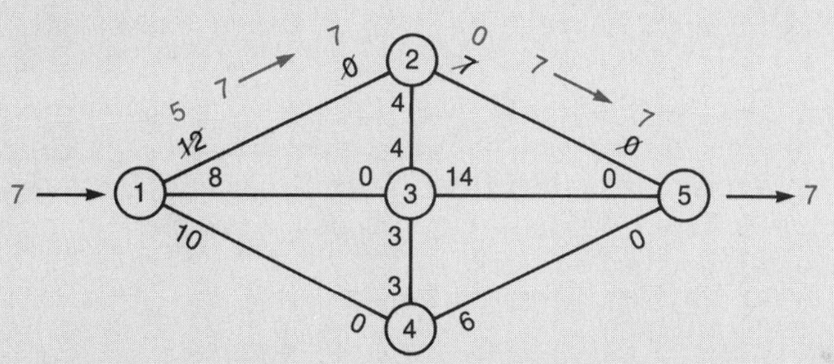

Find another path that has a positive flow capacity from Node 1 to Node 5. For simplicity, suppose we continue with Branch 1–2, using Path 1–2–3–5. The flow capacities of the branches on this path are 5 on 1–2, 4 on 2–3, and 14 on 3–5. Hence, 4 is the limiting capacity. Assigning 4 to each branch on the path and adjusting the branch capacities yields this updated network:

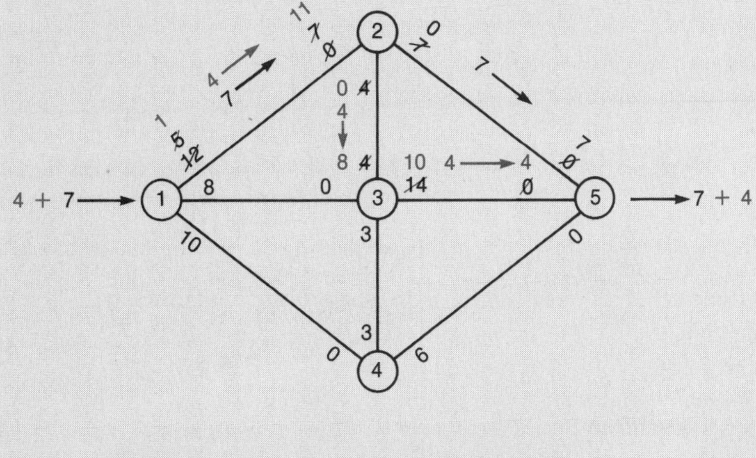

At this point, no further flow can pass through Node 2 because both branches that exit from it are loaded to capacity. However, Path 1–3–5 has a positive flow capacity of 8 (1–2 has 8 and 3–5 has 10). Assigning a flow of 8 to each branch on 1–3–5 yields this updated network:

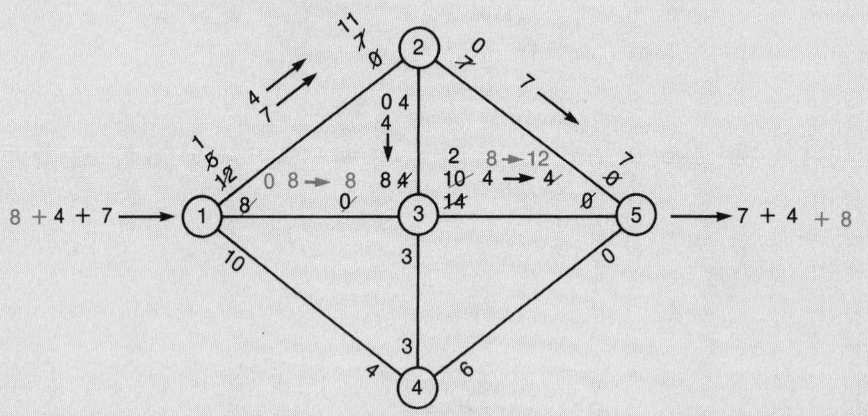

The only remaining branch from Node 1 that has a path with positive flow capacity is 1–4. Path 1–4–5 has a capacity of 6. Assigning 6 to the branches on this path yields this updated network.

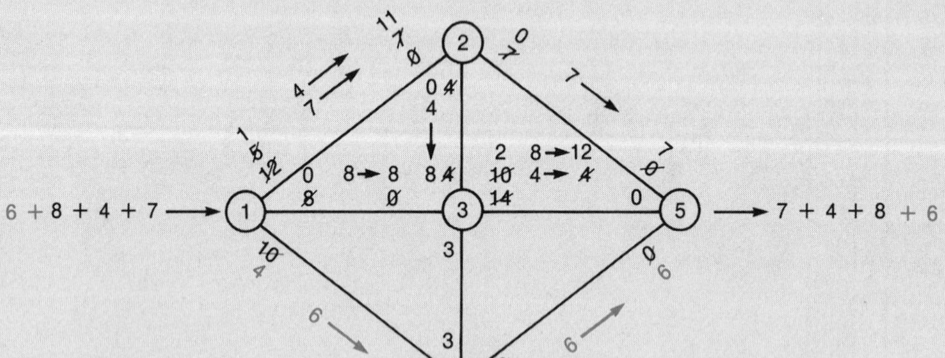

Only one path that has a positive flow capacity remains: 1–4–3–5, with a capacity of 2. Asssigning 2 to each branch on this path yields this updated network:

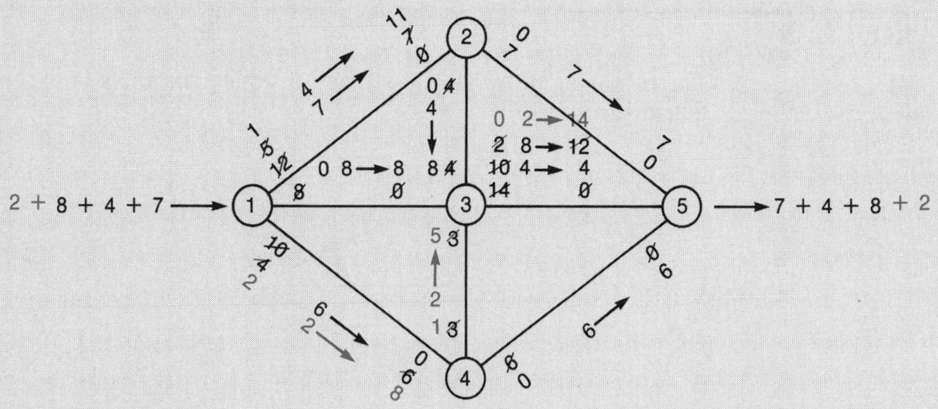

Since no paths from Node 1 to Node 5 have positive flow capacity, the analysis is complete. The maximal flow rate equals the sum of the entering flows at Node 1: 2 + 6 + 8 + 4 + 7 = 27. This, of course, equals the flow leaving the system at Node 5.

The final results are summarized in the following network:

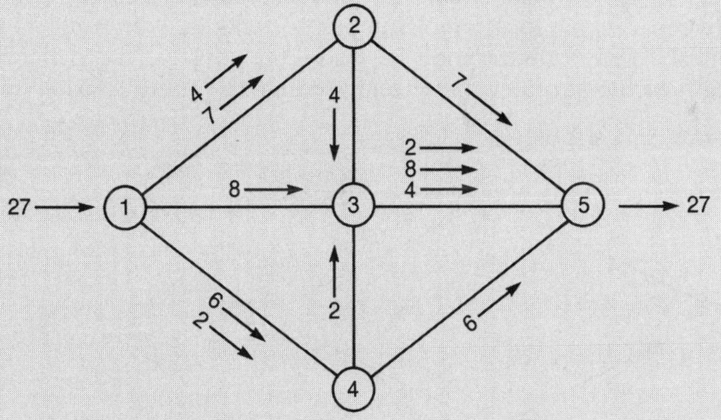

The flows through each branch are shown according to the way they were derived, simply for purposes of illustration and clarity. Thus, the total flow through Branch 1–2 is 11, and the total flow through Branch 3–5 is 14.

Finally, it should be noted that in many instances, slightly different branch assignments are possible that will produce the same maximal flow. Often, many alternative solutions are possible. However, as long as no path with a positive flow capacity can be found, the maximal flow solution has been found.

PROBLEMS

1. The following network shows road distances in miles between a firm's warehouse locations.

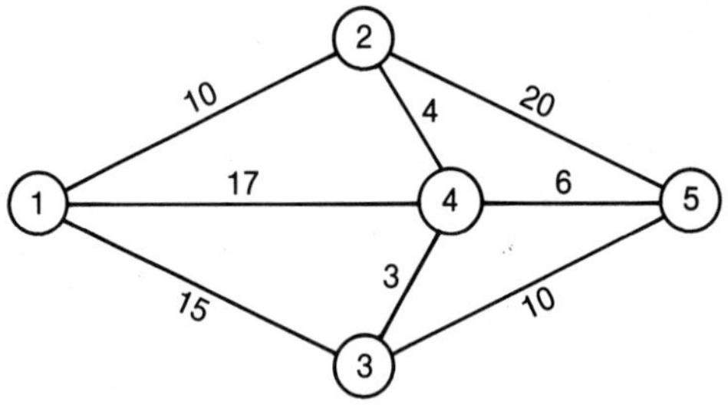

a. Using the shortest route algorithm, find the shortest route to each location from the central warehouse, which is located at Node 1.

b. List the shortest distance to each of the warehouse locations and the route that will result in the shortest distance traveled.

2. The following network represents construction sites (nodes) and access roads (arcs) to those sites. The numbers on the arcs show distances in miles between various locations. Company trucks deliver supplies to the sites from the main office (Node 1). Using the shortest route algorithm, find the length of the shortest route, and identify the route to each construction site.

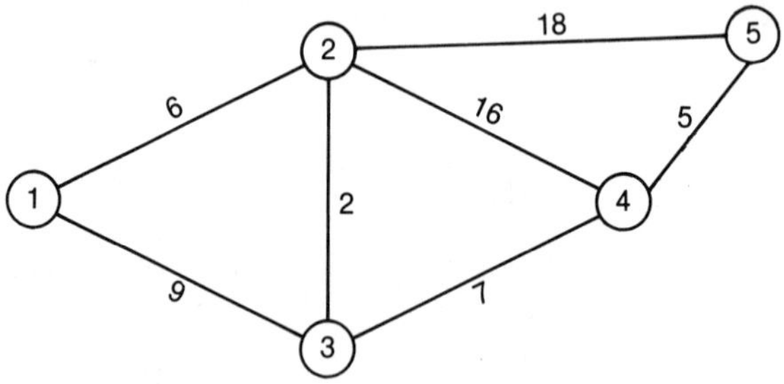

3. A taxi company dispatches cabs from a satellite office to any of five pickup points (airport, shopping mall, medical arts building, etc.). A system of roads and highways connects some of the locations, as shown in the following network diagram. Node 1 represents the satellite office. Use the shortest route algorithm to find the shortest route and distance to each of the pickup points.

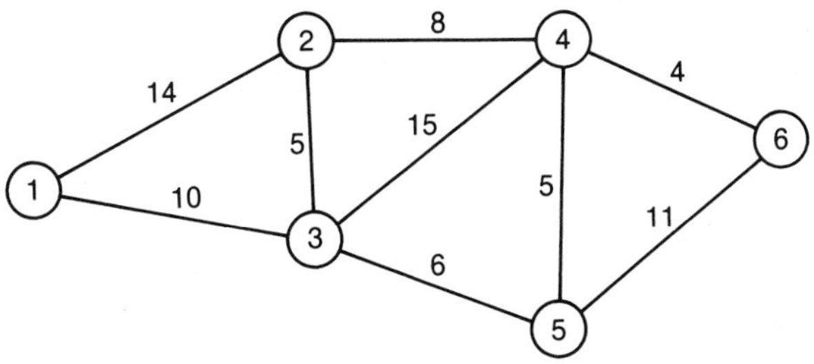

4. The network shown represents points of interest at a popular historic village and the approximate walking time (in minutes) along certain pathways. Assuming that Node 1 represents the main lodge and the other nodes the points of interest, find the shortest walking time to each point of interest from the main lodge, and indicate which points of interest will be encountered along that path.

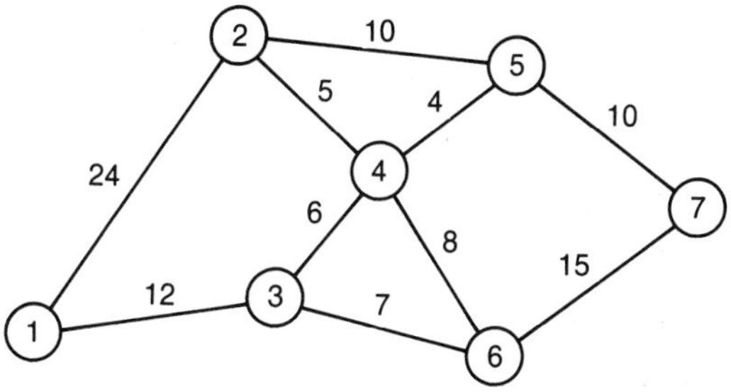

5. The values on the arcs connecting in various nodes represent the distance between nodes in miles for the following network.
   a. Find the shortest route to each node from Node 1 using the shortest route algorithm.
   b. Find the *round trip* distance to each node from Node 1, assuming the shortest route is used in both directions.
   c. Would another route for the return trip yield a shorter total round trip? Explain.

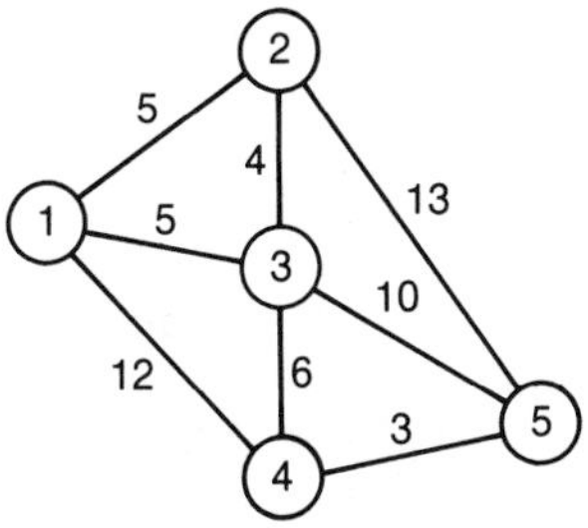

6. Distances shown on the arcs of the following network are in meters. Find the shortest route from Node 1 to each of the other nodes. If any alternate routes exist, identify them.

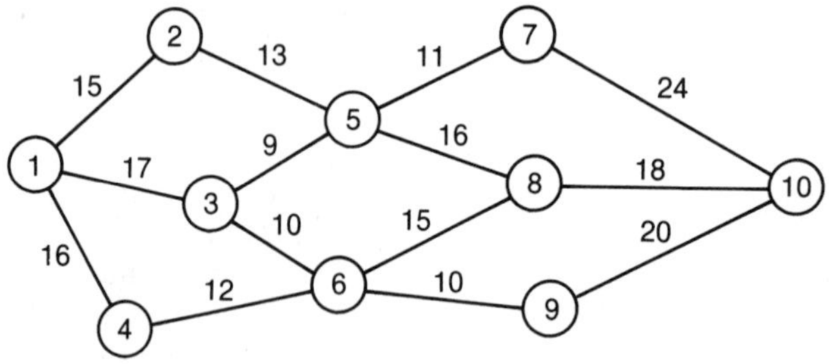

7. Approximate travel time between various customer locations are shown on the accompanying network. Assuming all delivery trucks leave from Node 1, find the shortest travel time to each customer location. If trucks could make multiple stops and, thereby, reduce the number of trucks required for this system, and assuming truck capacity is not a factor, how many trucks would be needed if the shortest travel times are used?

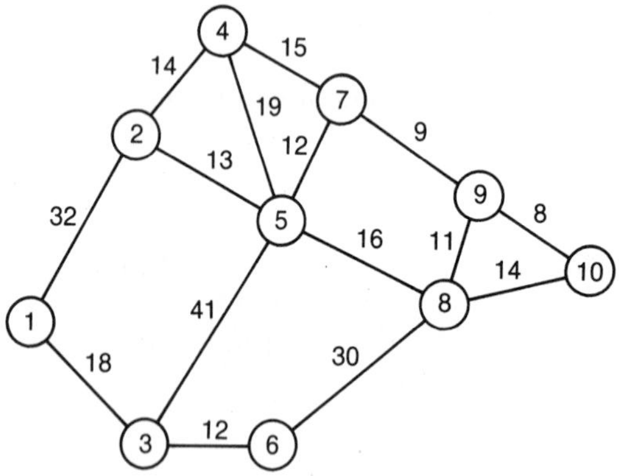

8. The following network shows distances in miles between villages and hamlets in a certain area of New York State. A dealer must decide on the route to use to send weekly shipments to a new customer located at Node 12. The dealer is located at Node 1. Using the shortest route algorithm, find the shortest route and the distance for a round trip.

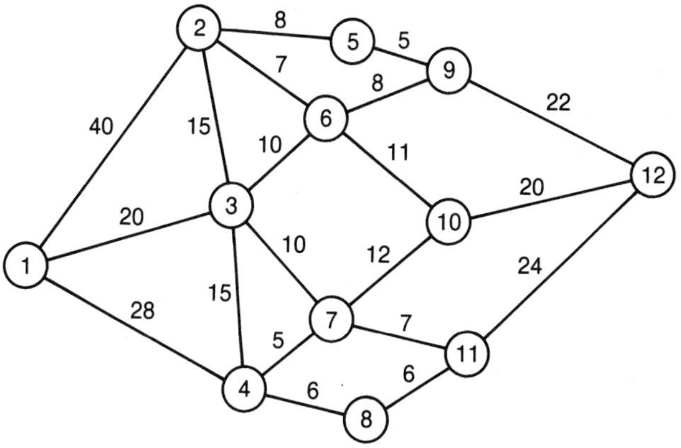

9. Find the minimum spanning tree for this network:

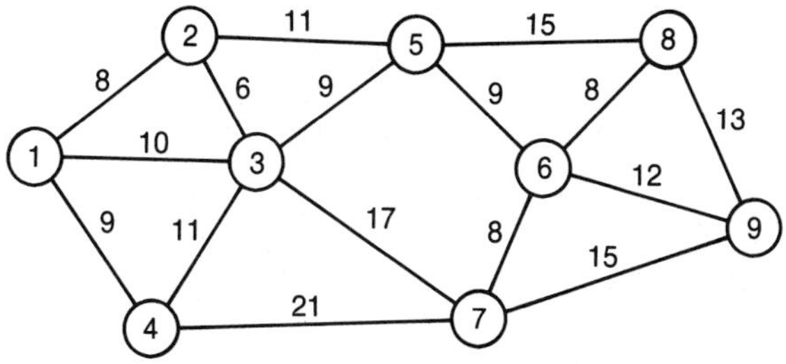

10. Find the set of arcs that will interconnect all of the nodes in this network using as little of the arc material as possible.

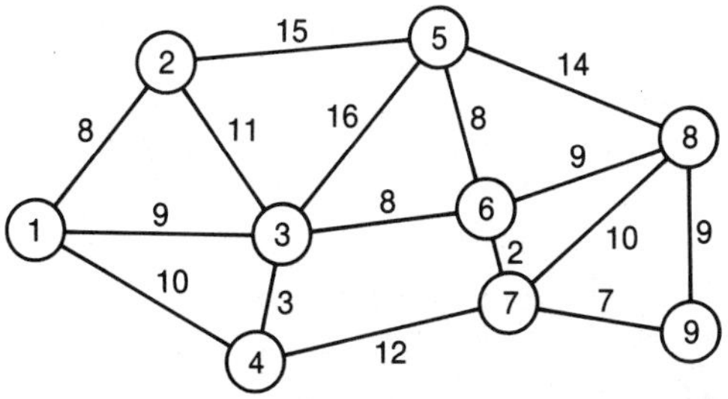

11. A cable television firm wants to connect a number of towns and villages to its cable system. The firm has identified various alternatives for connections and the cost of each potential connecting link, as shown in the accompanying network. Determine the set of connections that will minimize the total cost of linking these towns and villages to the system.

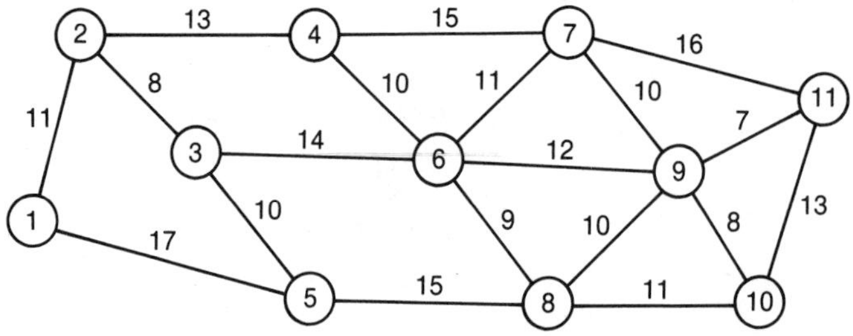

12. A company is in the process of designing a security system that will monitor key locations of its facilities. The locations are represented by the nodes in the accompanying network. The firm wants to minimize the cost of connecting these points to one and another to form a system. Determine the set of connections that will accomplish this. Cost figures for the connections are shown on the arcs.

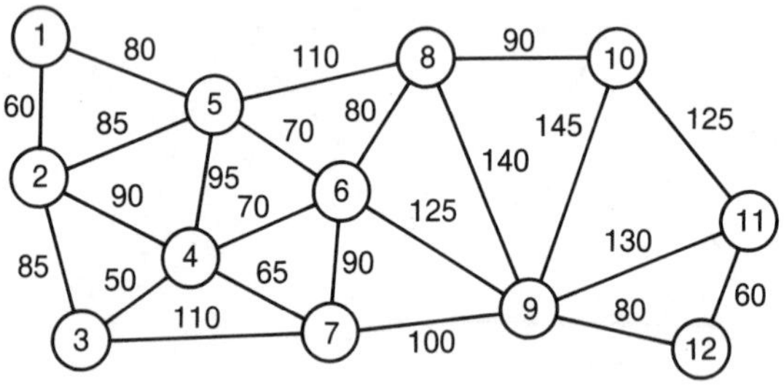

13. A designer involved in a project to construct access roads to a new park wants to minimize roadways, while still connecting key areas (e.g., lodges, picnic sites, boat launch). The key areas are designated by nodes on the accompanying diagram, and the figures on the arcs reflect distance between certain locations in miles. Determine the system of roadways that will accomplish these objectives.

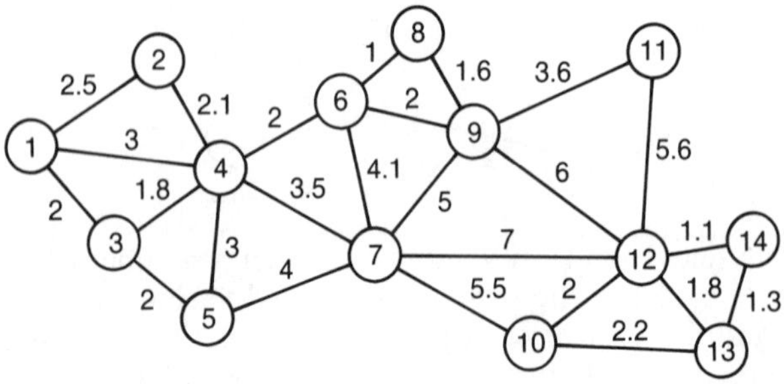

14. A system that will interconnect a set of storage tanks is in the design stages. The issue at present is to determine which connectors to use in order to minimize the amount of pipeline used. The different possibilities

can be seen in the accompanying diagram, which shows distances in meters. Find the least amount of pipeline and a set of connections that will accomplish this. Also, identify any alternate connections.

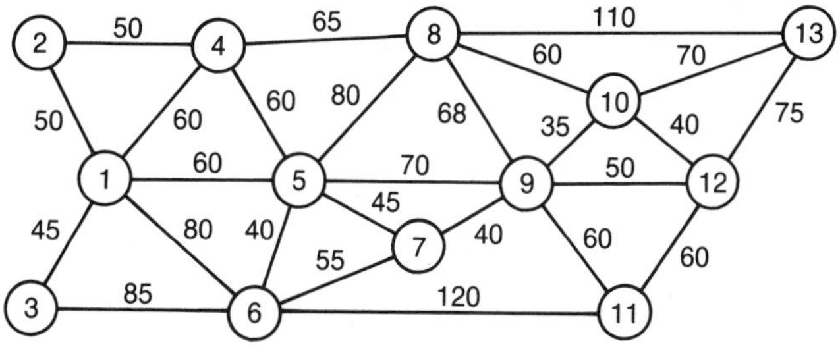

15. A manufacturer wants to install air conditioning in an existing plant. Various alternatives are being considered for laying the ducts that will connect desired locations of outlets. Locations of outlets are represented by nodes in the accompanying diagram. The arcs connecting various nodes represent the ducts, and the figures on the arcs show the cost of particular connections. Find the system of connections that will minimize the total cost of the system.

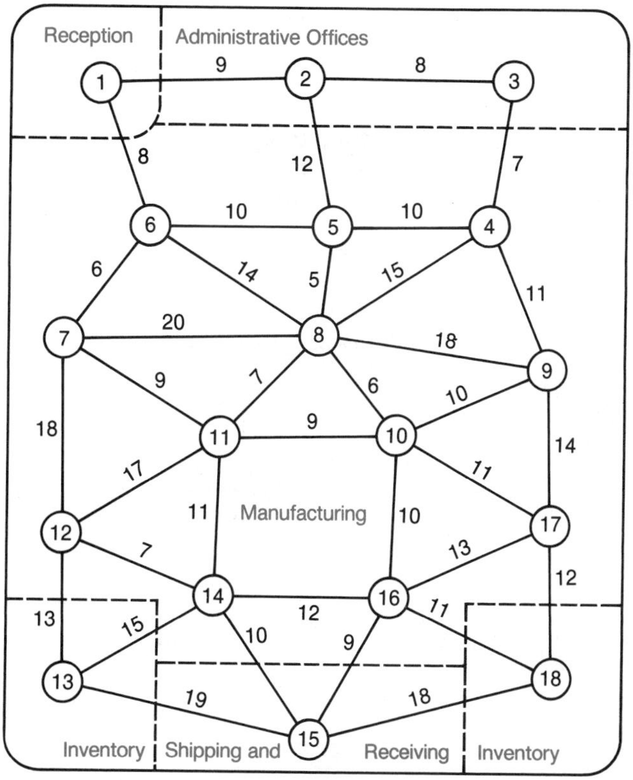

16. Find the maximal flow for this network:

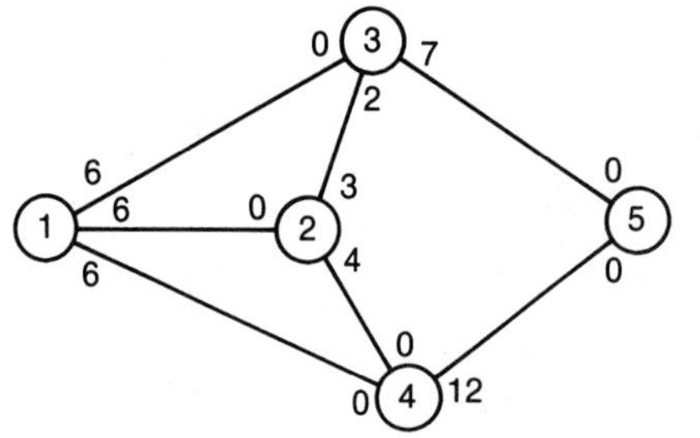

17. Determine the maximal flow for this network:

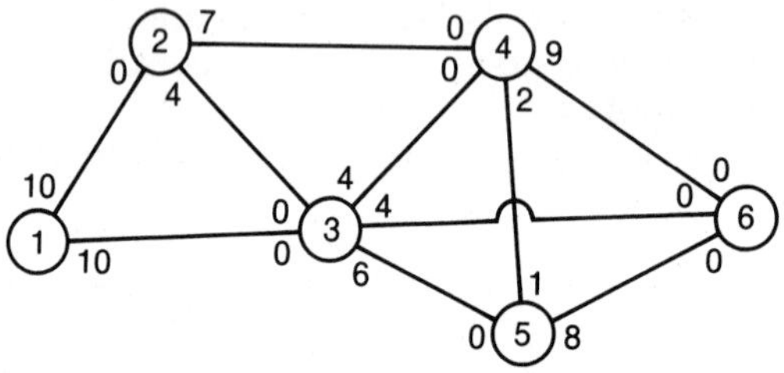

18. The network shows traffic capacity for a system of roads, all of which are one way. What is the peak load the system can handle, assuming flow is from Node 1 to Node 5? Figures on arcs represent hundreds of cars per hour.

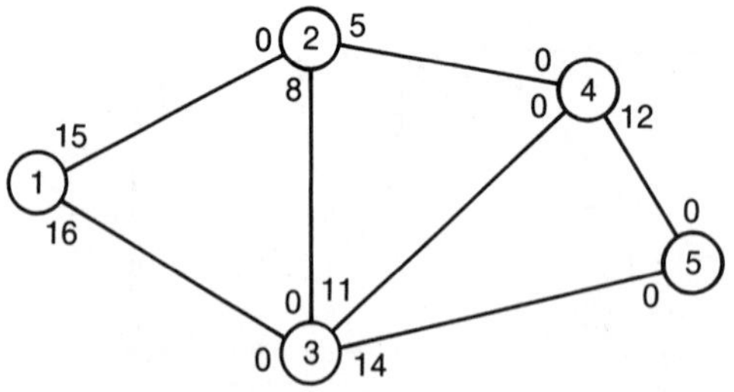

19. Given this flow network with arc capacities in units per minute, do the following:

a. Determine the maximal flow rate of the system.

b. If capacity of *one* of the arcs could be increased, which arc would you select and by how much would you increase its capacity? Explain.

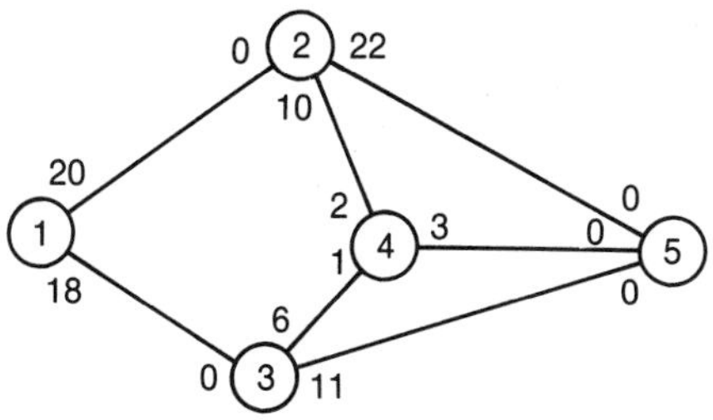

20. During the summer months, major construction projects are planned for a metropolitan area. This will result in closing certain bridges and reducing lanes open to traffic on some streets. Planners have developed the following network that shows major intersections (nodes), streets and bridges (arcs), and flow capacities in cars per minute.

a. Find the maximal flow rate of the system, assuming cars enter at Node 1 and leave at Node 7.

b. Are there alternate flows that would accomplish the same result? If so, identify one of these.

c. If the capacity of one arc could be increased, which arc would you choose, and how much increase would be usable? Explain.

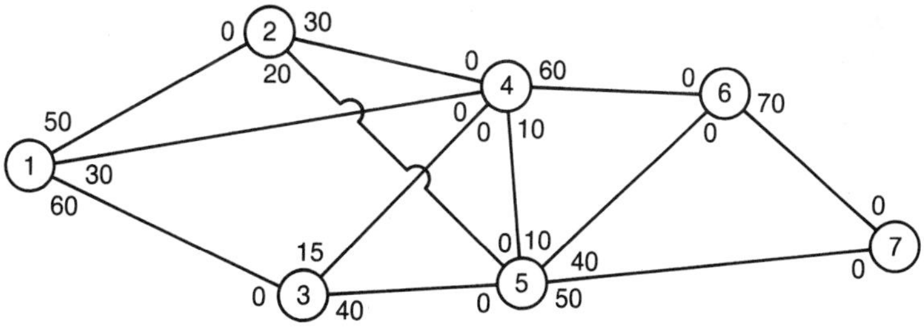

21. The accompanying network represents a possible design for a system of pipelines and storage tanks.

a. Determine the maximal flow rate for the network assuming Node 1 is the source and Node 7 the sink.

b. Suppose now there is an additional requirement: Flows in the pipelines leaving the source node should be approximately equal. What is the flow pattern and its maximal rate given this additional requirement?

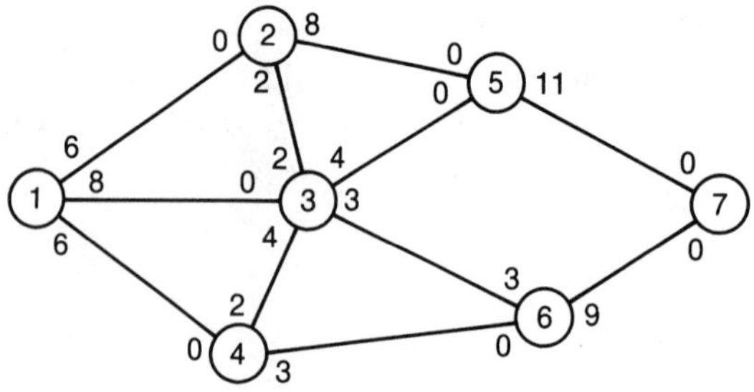

22. Determine the maximal flow rate for this system of bicycle paths, given the flow rates shown on the diagram. Assume Node 1 is the source node and Node 13 the sink node.

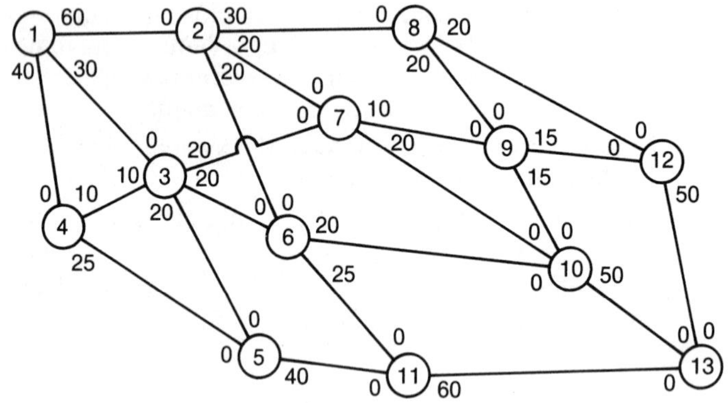

Chapter 15
PERT/CPM

Chapter Outline

Learning Objectives

After completing this chapter, you should be able to:

1. Give a general description of PERT/CPM techniques.
2. Construct simple network diagrams.
3. List the kinds of information that a PERT or CPM analysis can provide the manager.
4. Analyze networks that have deterministic times.
5. Analyze networks that have probabilistic times.
6. Describe activity ''crashing'' and solve simple problems.

This chapter describes techniques that are widely used to *plan and schedule projects*. A key tool in such endeavors is a *network* diagram. The chapter illustrates how network diagrams are used and why they are important for project management.

INTRODUCTION

Managers typically oversee a variety of operations. Some of these involve routine, repetitive activities, whereas others tend to vary with the task. **Projects** fall under the latter heading; they are unique, one-time operations designed to accomplish a specific set of objectives during a limited time frame. Examples of projects include constructing a shopping complex, installing a new computer system, moving a firm to a new location, launching a space shuttle, and introducing a new product or service to the marketplace.

Most projects have certain elements in common. Often they involve considerable cost. They usually have a long time horizon, and they involve a large number of activities that must be carefully planned and coordinated in order for the project to be completed within time, cost, and performance guidelines. Goals must be established, and priorities must be set. Tasks must be identified, and time estimates must be made. Resource requirements must also be projected, and budgets must be prepared. Once underway, progress must be monitored to assure that project goals and objectives will be achieved.

The project approach enables an organization to focus attention and concentrate efforts on accomplishing a narrow set of objectives within a limited time and budget framework. This can produce significant benefits relative to other approaches that might be considered. Even so, projects present a manager with a host of problems that differ in many respects from those encountered with more routine types of activities. The problems of planning and coordinating project activities can be quite formidable for large projects, which typically have hundreds or even thousands of activities that must be carefully planned and monitored if a project is to proceed according to schedule and at a reasonable cost.

PLANNING AND SCHEDULING WITH GANTT CHARTS

The **Gantt chart** is a popular tool for planning and scheduling *simple* projects. It enables a manager to initially schedule project activities and then monitor progress over time by comparing planned progress to actual progress. For example, consider the case of a bank that planned to create a new direct marketing department. Due to lack of space in its present facilities, the bank president decided to find a different facility to house the new department. He developed a

FIGURE 15–1 Gantt Chart for Bank Examples

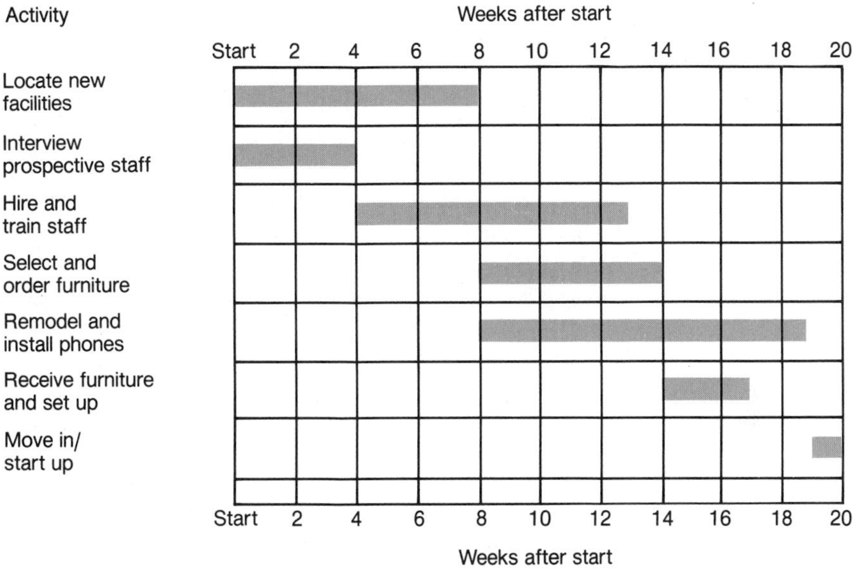

list of the major activities that would be required, as well as starting times and estimates of completion times for the activities:

Activity	Time to Accomplish (in weeks)	Weeks after Project Start
Locate new facilities	8	Immediate
Interview prospective staff	4	Immediate
Hire and train staff	9	4
Select and order furniture	6	8
Remodel and install phones	11	8
Receive furniture and set up	3	14
Move in/start up	1	19

The bank president's assistant was then asked to prepare a Gantt chart for this project. The chart is shown in Figure 15–1. Once completed, the chart indicated which activities were to occur, their planned duration, and when they were to occur. Then, as the project progressed, the manager was able to see which activities were ahead of schedule and which activities were delaying the project. This enabled the manager to direct attention where it was needed most to speed up the project in order to finish on schedule.

The obvious advantage of a Gantt chart is its simplicity, and this accounts for its popularity. However, Gantt charts fail to reveal certain relationships among activities that can be crucial to effective project management. For instance, if one of the early activities in a project suffers a delay, it would be important for the manager to be able to easily determine which later activities would have to be delayed *because they could not start until that activity was completed.* Conversely, some activities may safely be delayed without affecting the overall project schedule. Again, a Gantt chart does not directly reveal this. Consequently, Gantt charts are most useful for simple projects, say where activities are simultaneous or where a string of sequential activities is involved. On more complex projects, Gantt charts can be useful for initial project planning, which then gives way to the use of **networks,** the subject of the following sections.

PERT AND CPM

PERT (Program Evaluation and Review Technique) and **CPM (Critical Path Method)** are two of the most widely used techniques for planning and coordinating large-scale projects. By using PERT or CPM, managers are able to obtain:

1. A graphical display of project activities.
2. An estimate of how long the project will take.
3. An indication of which activities are the most critical to timely completion of the project.
4. An indication of how long any activity can be delayed without lengthening the project.

PERT and CPM were developed independently during the late 1950s. PERT evolved through the joint efforts of Lockheed Aircraft, the U.S. Navy Special Projects Office, and the consulting firm of Booz, Allen & Hamilton in an effort to speed up the Polaris missile project. At the time, there was considerable concern on the part of the U.S. government that the Soviet Union might be gaining nuclear superiority over the United States, and early completion of the project was given top priority by the Department of Defense. The project was a huge one, with over 3,000 contractors involved, and many thousands of activities. The use of PERT was quite successful: PERT is generally credited for shaving two years off the length of the project. Partly for that reason, PERT or a similar technique is now required on all large government projects.

CPM was developed by J. E. Kelly of the Remington Rand Corporation and M. R. Walker of Du Pont to plan and coordinate maintenance projects in chemical plants.

Although these two techniques were developed independently, they have a great deal in common. Moreover, many of the initial differences between the two techniques have disappeared as users borrowed certain features from one tech-

FIGURE 15–2 A Simple Project Network Diagram

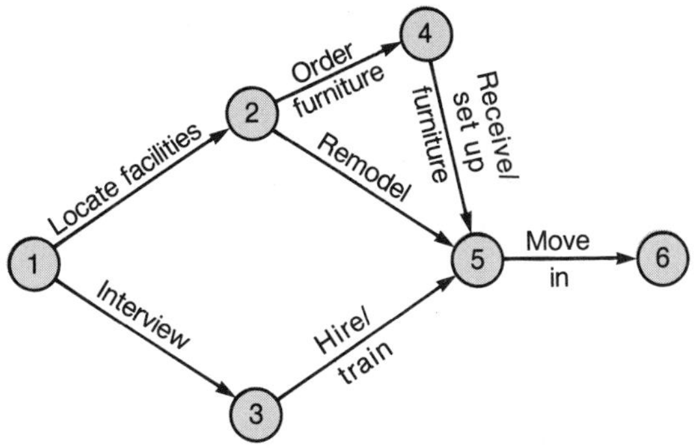

nique for use with the other. For example, PERT originally stressed probabilistic activity time estimates because the environment in which it was developed was typified by high uncertainty. In contrast, the tasks for which CPM was developed were much less uncertain, so CPM originally made no provision for variable time estimates. At present, either technique can be used with deterministic or probabilistic times. Other initial differences concerned the mechanical aspects of developing project networks. However, from a conceptual standpoint, most of these differences were relatively minor. In order to avoid confusion, we shall not delve into the differences here. For purposes of illustration, the discussion will proceed along the lines of PERT, particularly with respect to construction of precedence networks. Nonetheless, as a general rule, the comments and procedures described will apply to CPM analysis as well as to PERT analysis of projects.

The Network Diagram

One of the main features of PERT and related techniques is their use of a *network* or **precedence diagram** to depict major project activities and their sequential relationships. Recall the bank example that used a Gantt chart (see Figure 15–1). A network diagram for that same problem is shown in Figure 15–2. The diagram is composed of a number of arrows and nodes. The *arrows* represent the project **activities.** The *nodes* represent both beginnings and endings of activities. Notice how much clearer the sequential relationship of activities is with a network instead of a Gantt chart. For example, it is apparent that ordering and receiving the furniture and remodeling both require that a location for the office have been identified. Likewise, interviewing and hiring must precede training. However, interviewing and training can take place independently of activities associated with locating a facility, remodeling, and so on. Hence, a network diagram is generally the preferred approach for visual portrayal of project activities.

You should know that there are two slightly different conventions for constructing these network diagrams. Under one convention, the *arrows* are used to designate activities, whereas under the other convention, the *nodes* are used to designate activities. These conventions are referred to as *activity-on-arrow* (A-O-A) and *activity-on-node* (A-O-N). In order to avoid confusion, the discussion here will focus primarily on the activity-on-arrow convention. Then, later in the chapter, a comparison of the two conventions will be given. For now, we shall use the arrows for activities. The nodes in the A-O-A approach represent either the starting and finishing of activities, which are called **events.** The activities have associated time estimates, whereas the events do not.

The chart describes sequential relationships among major activities on a project. For instance, Activity 2–4 cannot be started, according to the chart, until Activity 1–2 has been completed. A **path** is a sequence of activities that leads from the starting node to the finishing node. Thus, the sequence 1–2–4–5–6 is a path. There are two other paths in this network: 1–2–5–6 and 1–3–5–6. The length (of time) of any path an be determined by summing the expected times of the activities on that path. The path with the longest time is of particular interest because it governs project completion time. In other words, expected project duration equals the expected time of the longest path. Moreover, if there are any delays along the longest path, there will be corresponding delays in project completion time. Conversely, attempts to shorten project completion must focus on the longest sequence of activities. Because of its influence on project completion time, the longest path is the **critical path** and its activities are referred to as **critical activities.**

Paths that are shorter than the critical path can experience some delays and still not affect the overall project completion time as long as the ultimate path time does not exceed the length of the critical path. The allowable slippage for any path is called the path **slack,** and it reflects the difference between the length of a given path and the length of the critical path. The critical path, then, has zero slack time.

Network Conventions

Developing and interpreting network diagrams requires some familiarity with networking conventions. Although there are many things that could be mentioned, the discussion here will concentrate on some of the most basic, and most common, features of network diagrams. This will provide sufficient background for understanding the basic concepts associated with precedence diagrams and it will allow you to solve typical problems.

One of the main features of a precedence diagram is that it reveals which activities must be performed in *sequence* (i.e., there is a precedence relationship) and which can be performed independently of each other. For example, in this diagram, Activity *a* must be completed before Activity *b* can begin, and Activity *b*

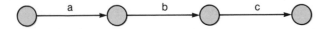

must be completed before Activity *c* can begin. If the diagram had looked like this, both Activity *a* and Activity *b* would have to be completed before Activity *c* could begin, but *a* and *b* could be performed at the same time; performance of *a* is independent of performance of *b*.

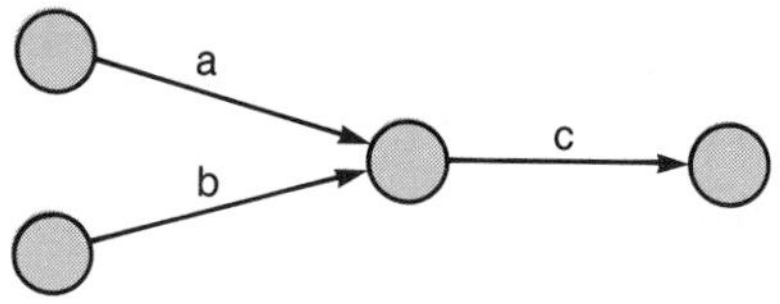

If Activity *a* must precede *b* and *c*, the appropriate network would look like this:

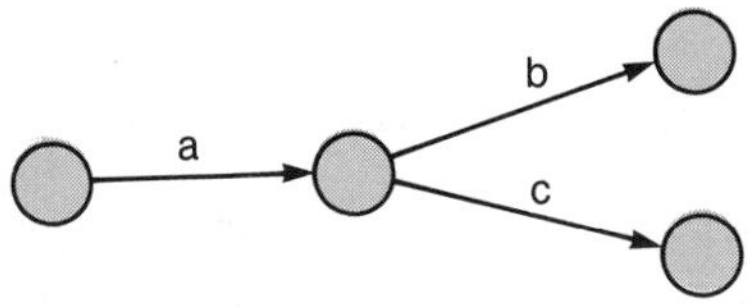

When multiple activities enter a node, this implies that all those activities must be completed before any activities that are to begin at that node can start. Therefore, in this diagram, both Activities *a* and *b* must be finished before either Activity *c* or Activity *d* can start.

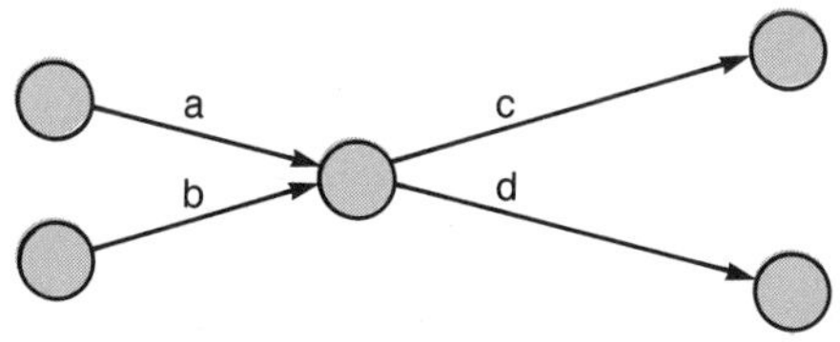

When two activities have the same beginning and ending nodes, a *dummy* node and **dummy activity** are used in order to preserve the separate identity of each activity. In the diagram below, Activities *a* and *b* must be completed before

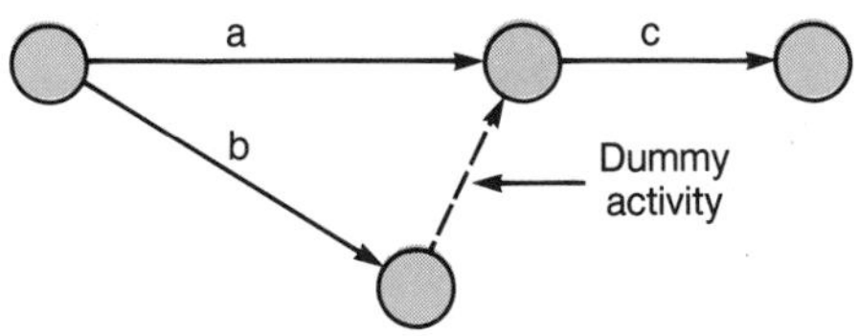

Activity *c* can be started. Separate identities are particularly important for computer analysis because most computer programs identify activities by their endpoints; activities with the same endpoints could not be distinguished from each other, although they might have quite different expected times.

Actually, there are a number of different uses for dummy activities. Another common use is depicted below:

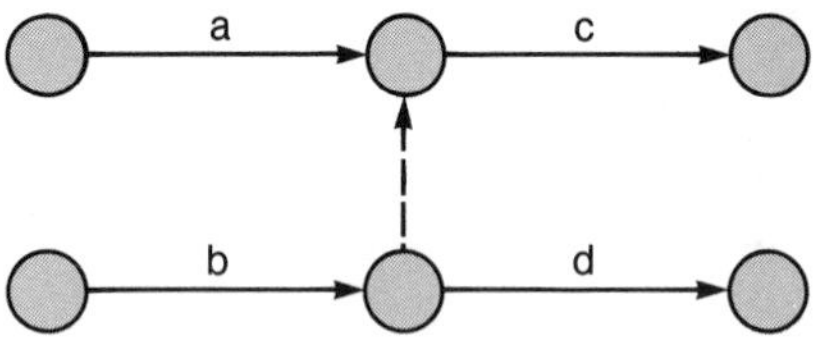

In this situation, both Activities *a* and *b* must precede Activity *c*. However, *d*'s start is dependent only on the completion of Activity *b*, and *not* on the completion of Activity *a*.

The primary function of dummy activities is to clarify relationships. As far as time is concerned, a dummy activity has an activity time equal to zero.

For reference purposes, nodes typically are numbered from left to right:

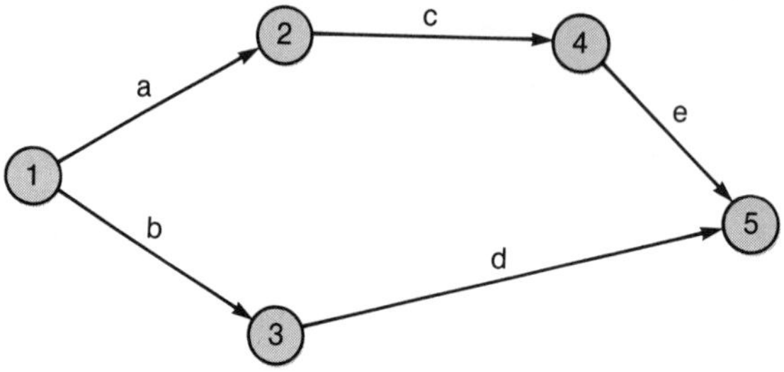

Starting and ending arrows are sometimes used during development of a network for increased clarity.

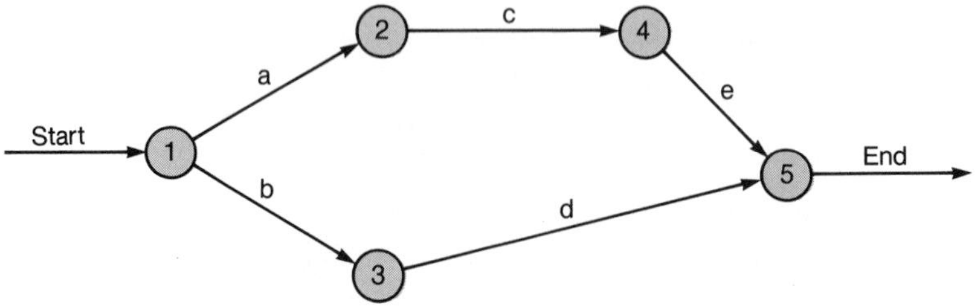

DETERMINISTIC TIME ESTIMATES

A major consideration in the way PERT and CPM networks are analyzed and interpreted is whether activity time estimates are *probabilistic* or *deterministic*. If time estimates can be made with a high degree of confidence that actual times will not differ significantly, we say the estimates are *deterministic*. On the other hand, if estimated times are subject to variation, we say the estimates are *probabilistic*. Probabilistic time estimates must include an indication of the extent of probable variation.

This section describes analysis of networks with **deterministic time estimates.** A later section deals with probabilistic times.

One of the best ways to gain an understanding of the nature of network analysis is to consider a simple example.

■

EXAMPLE 1 Given the information provided in the accompanying network diagram, determine each of the following:

1. The length of each path.
2. The critical path.
3. The expected length of the project.
4. The amount of slack time for each path.

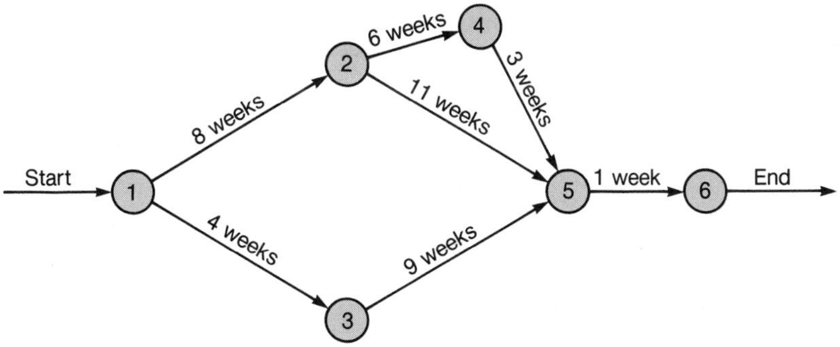

Solution

(The start and end "activities" have no times—they merely serve as reference points.)

1. As shown in the table below, the path lengths are 18 weeks, 20 weeks, and 14 weeks.
2. The longest path (20 weeks) is 1–2–5–6, so it is the critical path.
3. The expected length of the project is equal to the length of the critical path (i.e., 20 weeks).

4. The slack of each path is found by subtracting its length from the length of the critical path, as shown in the last column of the table. Note: Sometimes it is desirable to know the slack time associated with individual activities. The next section describes a method for obtaining those slack times.

Path	Length (weeks)	Slack
1-2-4-5-6	8 + 6 + 3 + 1 = 18	20 − 18 = 2
1-2-5-6	8 + 11 + 1 = 20*	20 − 20 = 0
1-3-5-6	4 + 9 + 1 = 14	20 − 14 = 6

* Critical path length.

A COMPUTING ALGORITHM

Many real-life project networks are much larger than the simple network illustrated in the preceding example; they often contain hundreds, or even thousands, of activities. Because the necessary computations can become exceedingly complex and time-consuming, large networks are generally analyzed by computer programs rather than manually. The intuitive approach just demonstrated does not lend itself to computerization because in many instances, path sequences are not readily apparent. Instead, an algorithm is used to develop four pieces of information about the network activities:

ES, the earliest time the activity can start, assuming all preceding activities start as early as possible.

EF, the earliest time the activity can finish.

LS, the latest time the activity can start and not delay the project.

LF, the latest time the activity can finish and not delay the project.

Once these values have been determined, they can be used to find:

1. Expected duration of the project.
2. Slack time.
3. Which activities are on the critical path.

The three examples that follow illustrate how these values are computed using the precedence diagram of Example 1, which is repeated as Figure 15–3 for convenient reference.

Computing ES and EF Times

Computation of earliest starting and finishing times is aided by two simple rules:

FIGURE 15–3

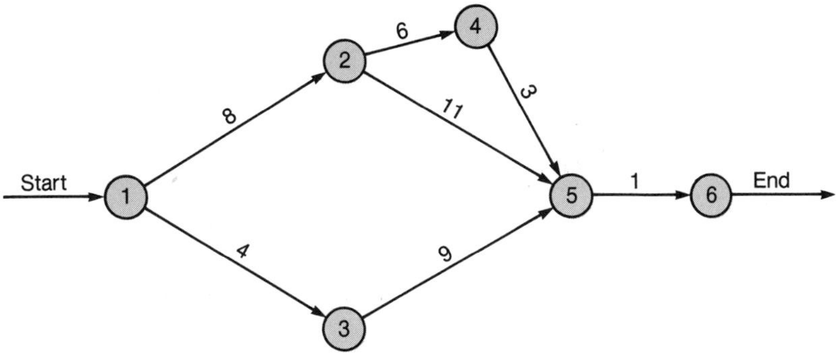

1. The earliest finish time for any activity is equal to its earliest start time plus its expected duration, t:

$$EF = ES + t \tag{15–1}$$

2. For nodes with one entering arrow: ES for activities at such nodes is equal to EF of entering arrow. For nodes with multiple entering arrows: ES for activities leaving such nodes equals the largest EF of entering arrows.

EXAMPLE 2 Compute the earliest starting time and earliest finishing time for each activity in the diagram shown in Figure 15–3.

Solution

Assume an ES of 0 for activities without predecessors. Thus, Activities 1-2 and 1-3, as initial activities, are assigned early starting times equal to zero. The earliest finishing times for these activities are:

$$EF_{1\text{-}2} = 0 + 8 = 8 \quad \text{and} \quad EF_{1\text{-}3} = 0 + 4 = 4$$

The EF of Activity 1-2 becomes the ES for the two activities that follow it: 2–4 and 2-5. Likewise, the EF of Activity 1-3 becomes the ES for Activity 3-5. Thus:

$$ES_{2\text{-}4} = 8,\ ES_{2\text{-}5} = 8, \quad \text{and} \quad ES_{3\text{-}5} = 4$$

The corresponding EF times for these activities are:

$$EF_{2\text{-}4} = 8 + 6 = 14$$
$$EF_{2\text{-}5} = 8 + 11 = 19$$
$$EF_{3\text{-}5} = 4 + 9 = 13$$

Activity 4–5 has an early starting time equal to EF_{2-4}, or 14, and an early finish time of 14 + 3 = 17. Finally, Activity 5–6, with three predecessors, has an early starting time equal to the *largest* EF of the three activities that precede. Hence, it has an ES of 19. Its EF time is 19 + 1 = 20.

These results are summarized in the table below.

Activity	Duration	ES	EF
1-2	8	0	8
1-3	4	0	4
2-4	6	8	14
2-5	11	8	19
3-5	9	4	13
4-5	3	14	17
5-6	1	19	20

Note that the last EF is the project duration. Thus, the expected length of the project is 20 weeks.

Computing LS and LF Times

Computation of the latest starting and finishing times is aided by the use of two rules:

1. The latest starting time for each activity is equal to its latest finishing time minus its expected duration:

$$LS = LF - t \tag{15-2}$$

2. For nodes with one leaving arrow: LF for arrows entering that node equals the LS of the leaving arrow. For nodes with multiple leaving arrows: LF for arrows entering that node equals the smallest LS of leaving arrows.

Finding ES and EF times involves a "forward pass" through the network; finding LS and LF times involves a "backward pass" through the network. Hence, we must begin with the EF of the last activity and use that time as the LF for the last activity. Then we obtain the LS for the last activity by subtracting its expected duration from its LF.

■

EXAMPLE 3 Compute the latest finishing and starting times for each activity shown in Figure 15–3.

Solution

Set LF of the last activity equal to the EF of that activity. Thus:

$$LF_{5-6} = EF_{5-6} = 20 \text{ weeks}$$

Next, compute the latest starting time:

$$LS_{5-6} = LF_{5-6} - t$$
$$= 20 - 1 = 19$$

In order for Activity 5–6 to be able to start no later than Week 19, all immediate predecessors must finish no later than that time. Thus:

$$LF_{4-5} = LF_{2-5} = LF_{3-5} = 19$$

The respective LS times for each activity are:

$$LS_{4-5} = 19 - 3 = 16$$
$$LS_{2-5} = 19 - 11 = 8$$
$$LS_{3-5} = 19 - 9 = 10$$

Similarly, $LF_{2-4} = LS_{4-5} = 16$, and $LS_{2-4} = 16 - 6 = 10$. Therefore, there are two arrows leaving Node 2: 2–4 with LS $= 10$ and 2–5 with LS $= 8$. The latest finish for Activity 1–2 thus becomes 8, which is the smallest LS for a leaving arrow. The LF for 1–3 is equal to the LS for 3–5:

$$LF_{1-3} = LS_{3-5} = 10$$

The LS for Activity 1–3 is:

$$LS_{1-3} = 10 - 4 = 6$$

The LS for Activity 1–2 is:

$$LS_{1-2} = LF_{1-2} - t$$
$$= 8 - 8 = 0$$

The LS, LF computations are summarized in the table below.

Activity	Duration	LF	LS
5–6	1	20	19
4–5	3	19	16
2–5	11	19	8
3–5	9	19	10
2–4	6	16	10
1–2	8	8	0
1–3	4	10	6

Computing Activity Slack Times

The slack time for any activity can be computed in either of two ways:

$$\text{Activity slack} = LS - ES \quad \text{or} \quad LF - EF \tag{15-3}$$

EXAMPLE 4 Compute activity slack times for the precedence diagram of Figure 15-3.

Solution

We have the option of using either the starting times or the finishing times. Suppose we choose the starting times. Using ES times computed in Example 2 and LS times computed in Example 3, slack times are:

Activity	LS	ES	(LS − ES) Slack
1-2	0	0	0
1-3	6	0	6
2-4	10	8	2
2-5	8	8	0
3-5	10	4	6
4-5	16	14	2
5-6	19	19	0

The critical path using this computing algorithm is denoted by activities with zero slack time. Thus, the table in the preceding example indicates that Activities 1-2, 2-5, and 5-6 are all critical activities, which agrees with the results of the intuitive approach demonstrated in Example 1.

Knowledge of individual slack times provides managers with greater detail for planning allocation of scarce resources and for directing control efforts toward those activities that might be most susceptible to delaying the project than the more simplistic intuitive approach does. In this regard, it is important to recognize that the activity slack times are based on the assumption that all other activities on the same path will be started as early as possible and will not exceed their expected times. In other words, if two activities are both on the same path (e.g., Activities 2-4 and 4-5 in the preceding example) and have the same slack (e.g., two weeks), this will be the total slack *available to both*. Hence, if the first activity uses all this slack, there will be zero slack for the other activity, and that much less slack for all following activities on that same path.

As noted above, this algorithm lends itself to computerization. A computer printout for this problem would appear something like the one shown in Table 15-1.

PROBABILISTIC TIME ESTIMATES

The preceding discussion assumed that activity times were known and not subject to variation. Although that assumption is appropriate in some situations, there are

TABLE 15–1 Computer Printout

		STARTING SCHEDULE				
		EARLY		LATE		
ACTIVITY	TIME	ES	EF	LS	LF	SLACK
1--2	8.00	0.00	8.00	0.00	8.00	0.00
1--3	4.00	0.00	4.00	6.00	10.00	6.00
2--4	6.00	8.00	14.00	10.00	16.00	2.00
2--5	11.00	8.00	19.00	8.00	19.00	0.00
3--5	9.00	4.00	13.00	10.00	19.00	6.00
4--5	3.00	14.00	17.00	16.00	19.00	2.00
5--6	1.00	19.00	20.00	19.00	20.00	0.00

THE CRITICAL PATH SEQUENCE IS:

SNODE	FNODE	TIME
1	2	8.00
2	5	11.00
5	6	1.00
		20.00

many others in which it is not. Consequently, those situations require a probabilistic approach.

Probabilistic time estimates use *three* time estimates for each activity instead of one:

1. *Optimistic time:* The length of time required under optimum conditions. It is represented by the letter a.
2. *Pessimistic time:* The amount of time that will be required under the worst conditions. It is represented by the letter b.
3. *Most-likely time:* The most probable amount of time that will be required. It is represented by the letter m.

These time estimates should be made by managers, or others, who have knowledge about the project.

The **beta distribution** is commonly used to describe the inherent variability in time estimates (see Figure 15–4). Although there is no theoretical justification for using the beta distribution, it has certain features that make it attractive in practice: The distribution can be symmetrical or skewed to either the right or left according to the nature of a particular activity, the mean and variance of the distribution can be readily obtained from the three time estimates listed above, and the distribution is unimodal with a high concentration of probability surrounding the most-likely time estimate.

Of special interest in network analysis are the average or expected time for

FIGURE 15–4 A Beta Distribution Is Used to Describe Probabilistic Time Estimates

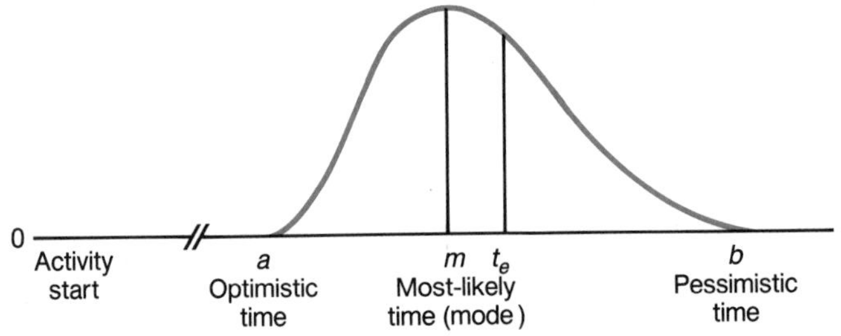

each activity, t_e, and the variance of each activity time, σ_i^2. The expected time is computed as a *weighted average* of the three time estimates:

$$t_e = \frac{a + 4m + b}{6} \tag{15–4}$$

The standard deviation of each activity's time is estimated as one sixth of the difference between the pessimistic and optimistic time estimates. (Analogously, essentially all of the area under a normal distribution lies within ±3 standard deviations of the mean, which is a range of *six* standard deviations.) The variance is found by squaring the standard deviation. Thus:

$$\sigma^2 = \left[\frac{(b - a)}{6}\right]^2 \quad \text{or} \quad \frac{(b - a)^2}{36} \tag{15–6}$$

The size of the **variance** reflects the degree of uncertainty associated with an activity's time: The larger the variance, the greater the uncertainty. Hence, an activity with a variance of 16 would have more uncertainty as to its eventual duration than one with a variance of, say, 6.

It is also desirable to compute the standard deviation of the expected time for *each path*. This can be accomplished by summing the variances of the activities on a path and then taking the square root of that number. That is:

$$\sigma_{\text{path}} = \sqrt{\Sigma(\text{variances of activities on path})} \tag{15–6}$$

■

EXAMPLE 5 The network diagram for a project is shown in the accompanying figure, with three time estimates for each activity. Activity times are in months. Do the following:

1. Compute the expected time for each activity and the expected duration for each path.
2. Identify the critical path.
3. Compute the variance for each activity and the variance for each path.

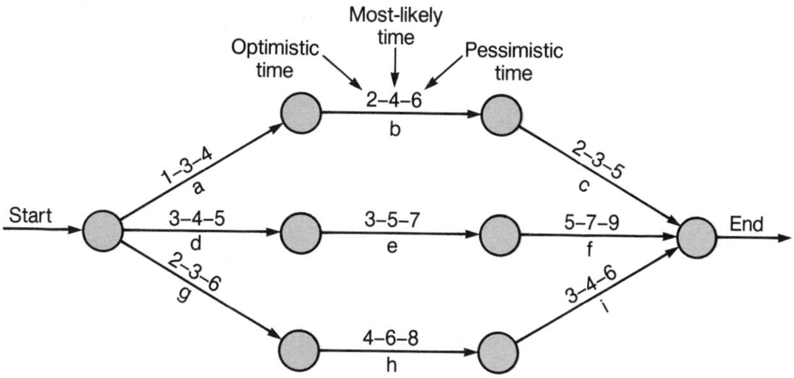

Solution

1.

Path	Activity	Times a	m	b	$t_e = \frac{a + 4m + b}{6}$	Path Total
	a	1	3	4	2.83	
a-b-c	*b*	2	4	6	4.00	10.00
	c	2	3	5	3.17	
	d	3	4	5	4.00	
d-e-f	*e*	3	5	7	5.00	16.00
	f	5	7	9	7.00	
	g	2	3	6	3.33	
g-h-i	*h*	4	6	8	6.00	13.50
	i	3	4	6	4.17	

2. The path that has the longest expected duration is the critical path. Since Path d–e–f has the largest path total, it is the critical path.

3.

Path	Activity	Times a	m	b	$\sigma^2_{act.} = \frac{(b - a)^2}{36}$	σ^2_{path}	σ_{path}
	a	1	3	4	$(4 - 1)^2/36 = 9/36$		
a-b-c	*b*	2	4	6	$(6 - 2)^2/36 = 16/36$	34/36 = .944	.97
	c	2	3	5	$(5 - 2)^2/36 = 9/36$		
	d	3	4	5	$(5 - 3)^2/36 = 4/36$		
d-e-f	*e*	3	5	7	$(7 - 3)^2/36 = 16/36$	36/36 = 1.00	1.00
	f	5	7	9	$(9 - 5)^2/36 = 16/36$		
	g	2	3	6	$(6 - 2)^2/36 = 16/36$		
g-h-i	*h*	4	6	8	$(8 - 4)^2/36 = 16/36$	41/36 = 1.139	1.07
	i	3	4	6	$(6 - 3)^2/36 = 9/36$		

Knowledge of the expected path times and their standard deviations enables a manager to make probabilistic estimates of the project completion time, such as:

> The probability that the project will be completed within 17 months of its start is about 84 percent.
>
> The probability that the project will take longer than 18 months is approximately 2 percent.

Statements of this sort are based on the assumption that the duration time of a path is a random variable that is normally distributed around the expected path time. The rationale for a normal distribution is that we are summing activity times (random variables), and sums of random variables tend to be normally distributed when the number of items being summed is large. However, even when the number of items is relatively small, the normal distribution is reasonable because the distributions being summed are unimodal.

The next example illustrates the use of a normal distribution to determine the probabilities for various completion times. Before we look at that example, it is important to make note of two points. One relates to *independence*. It is assumed that path duration times are independent of each other. In essence, this requires two things: Activity times are independent of each other, and each activity is only on one path. In order for activity times to be independent, the time for one must not be a function of another's time; if two activities were always early or late together, they would not be considered independent. The assumption of independent *paths* is usually considered to be met if only a *few* activities in a large project are on multiple paths. Even then, common sense should govern the decision of whether the independence assumption is justified.

A second important point is that a project is not completed until all of its activities, not just those on the critical path, have been completed. It sometimes happens that another path requires more time than the critical path, in which case the project runs longer than expected. Therefore, it can be risky to focus exclusively on the critical path. Instead, one must consider the possibility that at least one other path will delay the timely completion of the project. This requires determining the probability that *all* paths will finish by a specified time. To do that, find the probability that each path will finish by the specified time and multiply the resulting probabilities. Note that only paths with expected times that are relatively close to that of the critical path need to be considered because it would be highly unlikely that a path with a much shorter expected time would exceed the critical path's time. A simple rule of thumb is to ignore any path if its expected time plus 2.5 of *its* standard deviations is less than the specified time. These concepts are illustrated in the following example.

■

EXAMPLE 6 Using the information from the preceding example, answer the following questions:

1. Can the paths be considered independent? Why?

2. Determine the probability that the project will be completed within 17 months of its start.
3. Determine the probability that the project will be completed within 15 months of its start.
4. What is the probability that the project will not be completed within 15 months of its start?

Solution

1. Yes, the paths can be considered independent because no activity is on more than one path, and we have no information that would suggest that any activity times are interrelated.
2. In order to answer questions of this nature, we must take into account the degree to which the path distributions ''overlap'' the specified completion time. This concept is illustrated in the accompanying figure, which shows the three path distributions, each centered on that path's expected duration, and the specified completion time of 17 months.

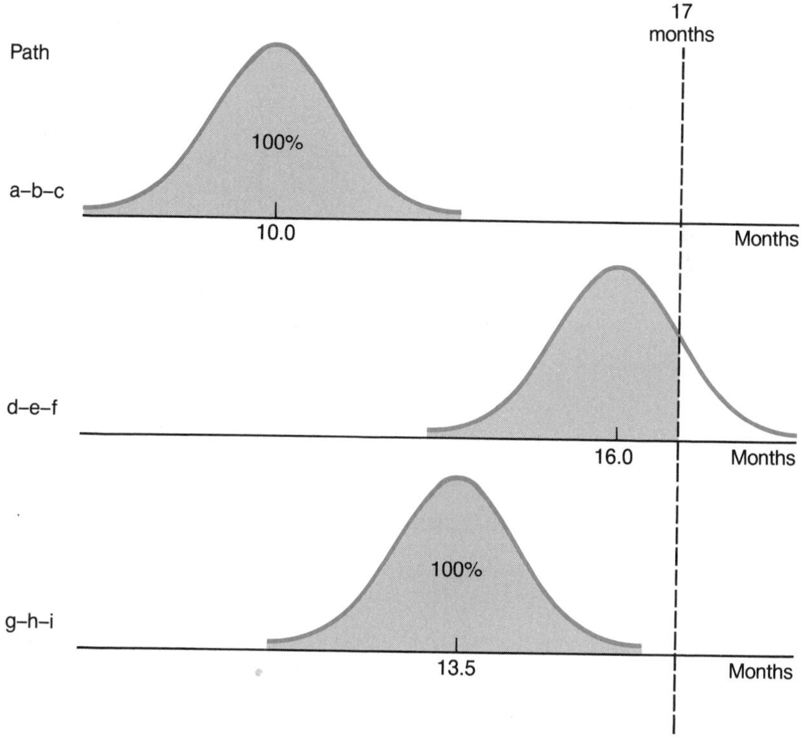

The shaded portion of each distribution corresponds to the probability that the part will be completed within the specified time. Observe that Paths a–b–c and g–h–i are far enough to the left of the specified time that it is highly likely that both will be finished by month 17 but that the critical path overlaps the specified completion time. Hence, we need only consider the distribution of Path d–e–f in assessing the probability of completion by month 17. To do so, we must first compute the value of z using the relationship:

$$z = \frac{\text{Specified time} - \text{Expected time}}{\text{Path standard deviation}} \tag{15-7}$$

In this instance, the expected time for Path d–e–f is 16.0; and we find:

$$z = \frac{17 - 16}{1.00} = +1.00$$

Turning to Appendix Table B with $z = +1.00$, we see that the area under the curve to the left of z is .8413. Hence, the probability of the project finishing within 17 months of its start is 84.13 percent.

3. This question illustrates how to handle a problem in which more than one of the distributions overlaps the specified time. Note in the accompanying figure that Paths d–e–f and g–h–i overlap month 15. This means that both paths have the potential for delaying the project beyond the 15 month.

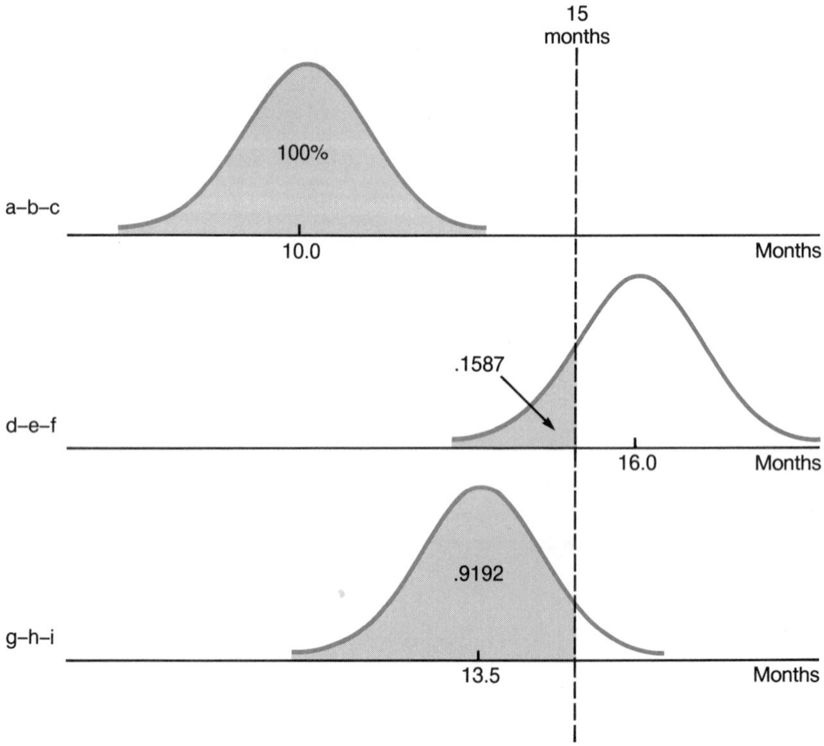

Although the figure is useful for expressing the concept of overlapping paths, we need a more rigorous approach to determine which paths to consider and each path's probability of completion. This requires computing a value of z using the formula for each path. Then, any path with a z of more than $+2.50$ is assigned a probability of 1.00. For this problem, with a specified time of 15 months, the z-values are:

Path	$z = \dfrac{15 - \text{Expected path duration}}{\text{Path standard deviation}}$	$P(z)$
a-b-c	$\dfrac{15 - 10.00}{.97} = +5.15$	1.0000
d-e-f	$\dfrac{15 - 16.00}{1.00} = -1.00$	.1587
g-h-i	$\dfrac{15 - 13.50}{1.07} = +1.40$	.9192

From Appendix Table B, the area to the *left* of $z = -1.00$ is .1587, and the area to the *left* of $z = +1.40$ is .9192. The joint probability of finishing before month 15 is the product of these probabilities: .1587(.9192) (1.00) = .1459.

ACTIVITIES ON NODES DIAGRAMS

Earlier in the chapter it was mentioned that network diagrams can be drawn with the activities on nodes (A-O-N) rather than on arrows. The result is a slightly different diagram. We can begin to get an appreciation for the differences by comparing the two approaches to a given problem. Consider this set of project activities:

Activity	Precedes
start	a,b
a	c
b	d,e
c	f
d	g
e	g
f	end
g	end

Figure 15–5 illustrates both types of networks.

One obvious difference in the two approaches is that there are more nodes in the A-O-N approach. In general this will be the rule. A second difference is that

FIGURE 15–5 A Comparison of the A-O-A and A-O-N Methods of Network Representation

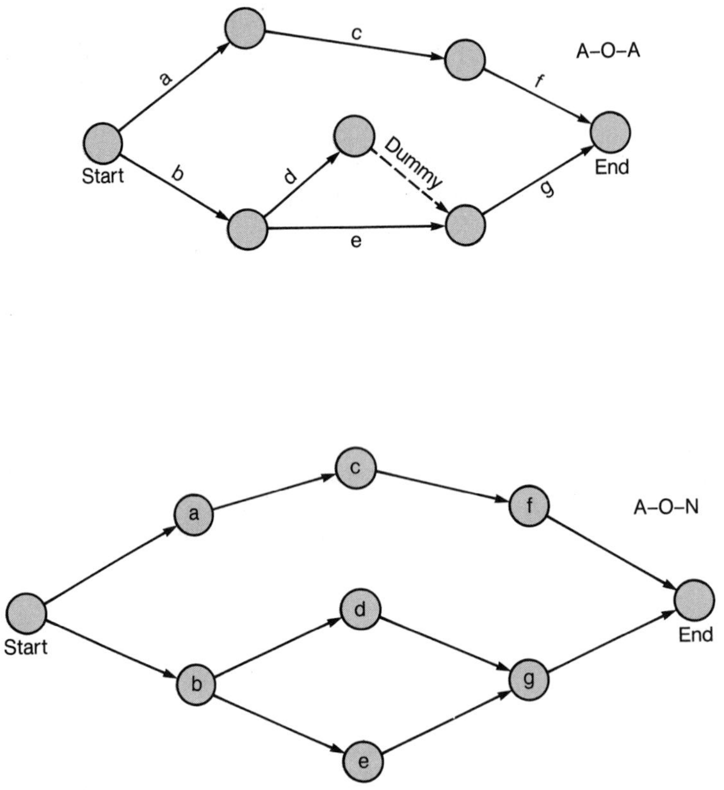

the A-O-N network has a dummy arrow that is necessary in order to correctly show the precedence relationship that exists. The dummy is not necessary in the A-O-N network; A-O-N networks eliminate the need for dummy activities, which is an advantage of having activities on nodes.

In practice, both approaches are used. Usually, PERT/CPM computer programs can handle either convention, but some require one or the other. Often the choice of method depends more on personal preference or established procedures.

SIMULATION

The preceding section illustrated a method for computing the probability that a project would be completed in a specified length of time. That discussion assumed that the paths of the project were *independent;* that is, that the same activities were not on more than one path. If an activity was on more than one path, and it happened that the completion time for that activity far exceeded its expected time, all paths that included that activity would be affected and, hence, their times would not be independent. In situations in which activities are on multiple paths, one must consider if the preceding approach can be used. For example, if only a few activities are on multiple paths, and particularly if the paths are *much* shorter than the critical path, that approach may still be reasonable. Moreover, for purposes of illustration, as in the text problems and examples, we treat the paths as being independent when, in fact, they may not be.

In practice, when *dependent* cases occur, often a *simulation* approach is used. It amounts to a form of repeated sampling wherein many passes are made through the PERT network. In each pass, a randomly selected value for each activity time is made based on the characteristics of the activity's probability distribution (e.g., its mean, standard deviation, and distribution type). After each pass, the expected project duration is determined by adding the times along each path and designating the time of the longest path as the project duration. After a large number of such passes (say, several hundred), there is enough information to prepare a frequency distribution of the project duration times. This distribution can be used to make a probabilistic assessment of the actual project duration that allows for the fact that some activities are on more than one path.

ADVANTAGES AND LIMITATIONS OF PERT

PERT and similar project-scheduling techniques can provide important services for the project manager. Among the most useful features are:

1. Use of these techniques forces the manager to organize and quantify available information and to recognize where additional information is needed.
2. The techniques provide a graphical display of the project and its major activities.
3. The techniques identify (*a*) activities that should be closely watched because of the potential for delaying the project and (*b*) other activities that have slack time and, therefore, can be delayed without affecting project completion time. This raises the possibility of reallocating resources in order to shorten the project.

No analytical technique is without limitations. Among the more important limitations of PERT are the following:

1. In developing the project network, one or more important activities may be omitted.
2. Precedence relationships may not all be correct as shown.
3. Time estimates usually include a fudge factor: Managers feel uncomfort-

able about making time estimates because they appear to commit themselves to completion within a certain time period.

4. The use of a computer is essential for large projects.

TIME-COST TRADE-OFFS—CRASHING

Estimates of activity times for projects are usually made for some given level of resources. In many situations, it is possible to reduce the length of a project by injecting additional resources. The impetus to shorten projects may reflect efforts to avoid late penalties, to take advantage of monetary incentives for timely completion of a project, or to free resources for use on other projects. In many cases, however, the desire to shorten the length of a project merely reflects an attempt to reduce the indirect costs associated with running the project, such as facilities and equipment costs, supervision, and labor and personnel costs. Managers often have certain options at their disposal that allow them to shorten, or **crash,** certain activities. Among the most obvious options are using additional personnel or more efficient equipment and relaxing work specifications. Hence, a project manager may be able to shorten a project, thereby realizing a savings on indirect project costs by increasing *direct* expenses to speed up the project. The goal in evaluating **time-cost trade-offs** is to identify a plan that will minimize the sum of the indirect and direct project costs.

In order to make a rational decision about which activities (if any) to crash and the extent of crashing desirable, a manager needs the following information:

1. Regular time and crash time estimates for each activity.
2. Regular cost and crash cost estimates for each activity.
3. A list of activities that are on the critical path.

Activities on the critical path are potential candidates for crashing because shortening noncritical activities would not have an impact on total project duration. From an economic standpoint, activities should be crashed according to crashing costs: Crash those with the lowest costs first. Moreover, crashing should continue as long as the cost to crash is less than the benefits received from crashing. These benefits might take the form of incentive payments for early completion of the project as part of a government contract, or they might reflect savings in the indirect project costs, or both. Figure 15–6 illustrates the basic relationships between indirect, direct, and total project costs due to crashing. The general procedure for crashing is:

1. Obtain estimates of regular and crash times and costs for each activity.
2. Determine the lengths of all paths and path slack times.
3. Determine which activities are on the critical path.
4. Crash critical activities, in order of increasing costs, as long as crashing costs do not exceed benefits. (Note that two or more paths may become critical as the original critical path becomes shorter, so that subsequent

FIGURE 15-6 Crashing Activities*

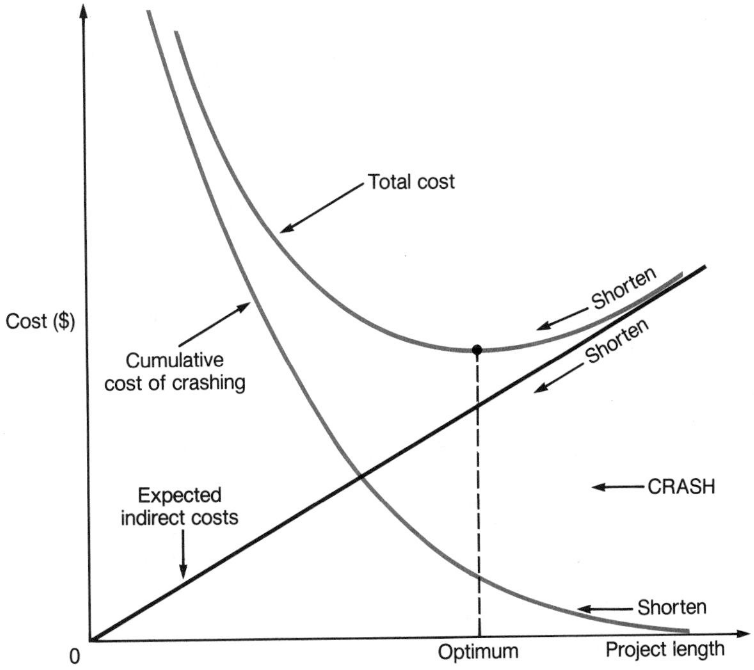

* Crashing activities reduce indirect project costs while increasing direct costs: The optimum amount of crashing results in minimizing the sum of these two types of costs.

improvements will require simultaneous shortening of two or more paths.) In some cases it will be most economical to shorten an activity that is on two or more of the critical paths. This is true whenever the crashing cost for a joint activity is less than the sum of crashing one activity on each separate path.

■

EXAMPLE 7 Using the information below, develop an optimum time-cost solution. Assume that indirect project costs are $1,000 per day.

Activity	Normal Time	Crash Time	Cost per Day to Crash
1–2	6	6	—
2–5	10	8	$500
1–3	5	4	300
3–4	4	1	700
4–5	9	7	600
5–6	2	1	800

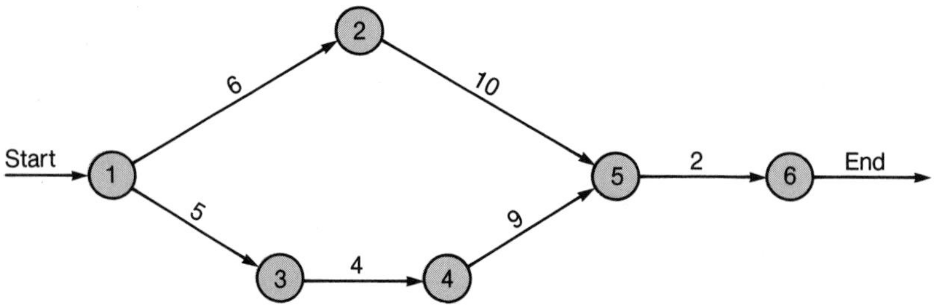

Solution

1. Determine which activities are on the critical path, its length, and the length of the other path:

Path	Length
1-2-5-6	18
1-3-4-5-6	20—critical path

2. Rank the critical path activities in order of lowest crashing cost and determine the number of days each can be crashed.

Activity	Cost per Day to Crash	Available Days
1-3	$300	1
4-5	600	2
3-4	700	3
5-6	800	1

3. Begin shortening the project, one day at a time, and check after each reduction to see which path is critical. (After a certain point, another path may equal the length of the shortened critical path.) Thus:

4. *a.* Shorten Activity 1–3 one day at a cost of $300. The length of the critical path now becomes 19 days.

   b. Activity 1–3 cannot be shortened any more. Shorten Activity 4–5 one day at a cost of $600. The length of Path 1–3–4–5–6 now becomes 18 days, which is the same as the length of Path 1–2–5–6.

   c. Since the paths are now both critical, further improvements will necessitate shortening one activity on each.

   The remaining points for crashing and their costs are:

Path	Activity	Crash Cost (per day)
1-2-5-6	1-2	No reduction possible
	2-5	$500
	5-6	800
1-3-4-5-6	1-3	No further reduction possible
	3-4	$700
	4-5	600
	5-6	800

At first glance, it would seem that crashing Activity 5–6 would not be advantageous because it has the highest crashing cost. However, Activity 5–6 is on both paths, so shortening Activity 5–6 by one day would shorten *both* paths (and, hence, the project) by one day for a cost of $800. The option of shortening the least expensive activity on each path would cost $500 for Activity 2–5 and $600 for Activity 4–5, or $1,100. Thus, shorten Activity 5–6 by one day. The project duration is now 17 days.

d. At this point, no additional improvement is feasible. The cost to crash Activity 2–5 is $500 and the cost to crash Activity 4–5 is $600 for a total of $1,100, and that would exceed the project costs of $1,000 per day.

e. The crashing sequence is summarized below:

	Length after Crashing *n* Days			
Path	***n* = 0**	**1**	**2**	**3**
1-2-5-6	18	18	18	17
1-3-4-5-6	20	19	18	17
Activity crashed		1-3	4-5	5-6
Cost		$300	$600	$800

MANAGER DIALOGUE

Jim Barney has been given a six-month assignment that will involve the development and installation of a computerized inventory system for his company. Jim has scheduled a meeting with a consultant because he is uncertain about how to proceed. He expects to use PERT, but he wants to use it effectively. The following paragraphs report on the essence of his conversation with the consultant.

Jim: I hope to be able to use PERT for the project I've described to you, but I am unsure of how to begin.

Consultant: The project you describe is fairly complex, with many different activities that need to be coordinated. It is certainly a good application for PERT. Using PERT will help in both planning and coordinating the project.

One of the first things you must do is assemble a list of the major activities that will comprise the project. In all likelihood, you will want to talk with key individuals within your company who will be involved in the project, and perhaps to others in other companies who have been involved in similar types of projects. Next, you must decide on the sequence of activities: Certain activities must precede other activities, but some sequences of activities will be unrelated to others. Using a network, or precedence diagram, to achieve a visual portrayal of the project can be extremely useful.

You will also need to make time estimates for each activity. If you believe that actual times will be close to estimated times, one time estimate for each activity will suffice. However, if you think that more than a few activities may have times that will vary significantly from a single time estimate, obtain three time estimates (optimistic, pessimistic, and most-likely) for each activity. If you decide to use single time estimates, you will be able to use them along with the network you have developed to obtain information about project duration and the activities that are critical to timely project completion. If you find that the expected project completion time is longer than you want, then you will want to consider shortening (crashing) the project.

Jim: Okay, that gives me a general idea of how to proceed, but it also raises several other questions. One relates to crashing, and a couple relate to multiple time estimates.

With regard to crashing, am I correct in my belief that the only activities I should consider crashing are those on the critical path?

Consultant: That is correct. Of course, in order to be able to use crashing, you will have to gather information on the cost to shorten each activity. You probably will find that the cost to crash increases disproportionately as the amount of crashing increases. For instance, you may find that it costs $100 to shorten an activity one day; $150 to shorten it a second day, and $275 to shorten it a third day. In order to obtain crash data, you will un-

(concluded)

doubtedly have to talk with those most familiar with the work about alternative ways of accomplishing tasks and the costs involved.

Once you have assembled data on crashing costs, and have identified the critical path length as well as the lengths of other paths, you can begin a crashing analysis. You should crash critical activities, beginning with the least expensive. After each crashing pass (e.g., shortening the project by one day), redetermine path lengths so as to be sure you are focused solely on the critical path. Of course, at some point, there may be a tie among two or more paths; multiple critical paths may exist. If you want to continue crashing, you will have to simultaneously shorten all critical paths.

Jim: That seems pretty clear. Let me ask my questions about using multiple time estimates for activities. My first question is: Once I've collected the estimates, what do I do next?

Consultant: You need to obtain a mean and variance for each activity based on those estimates. Then, obtain the mean and variance for each path in the network using those values. A path mean is the sum of the means of all of the activities on the path; and a path variance is the sum of the variances of all activities on the path. Next, convert each path variance to a path standard deviation by taking the square root of the variance.

Jim: And how do I use that information?

Consultant: It will enable you to determine the probability of completing the project within a certain length of time, such as 20 weeks, 25 weeks, and so on, depending on your requirements. To do this, you will have to specify a length of time, and then compute the value of z for each path. For each path that has a value of z that is $+2.50$ or less, obtain the appropriate probability from a normal table; it is the probability that this path will not take longer than the specified time. For paths with values of z that are greater than $+2.50$, assign a probability of 1.00 to completion within the specified time.

Multiplying all of the path probabilities together will give you the probability that the project will finish no later than the specified time. And subtracting that probability from 1.00 will give you the probability that the project will go beyond the specified time.

Jim: What if the value of z is negative, say -3.00, can I also assign a probability of 1.00 to that path?

Consultant: Absolutely not; a negative value of z indicates that the path's expected time *exceeds* the specified time. Consequently, there will be a low probability that the path will be completed in time, and hence, a low probability that the project will be completed by the specified time.

Jim: Thank you. You have been very helpful.

FORMULATING PERT PROBLEMS AS LP MODELS

PERT networks can be formulated and solved as linear programming models. Generally, that approach is not as efficient as solving PERT problems either manually or using a computer package designed specifically for PERT problems. However, one particularly useful application of LP to PERT problems relates to crashing (shortening) problems, because a linear programming formulation can greatly simplify finding a solution.

Let's consider a simple example of this. Suppose we have the following network:

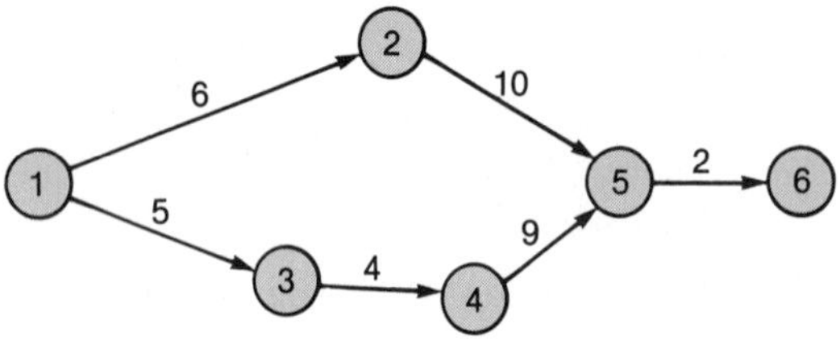

We can formulate this as an LP model that will minimize project completion time. We begin by defining variables in terms of the earliest starting time for an activity: x_1 is the earliest starting time at Node 1, x_2 is the earliest starting time at Node 2, and so on. It is apparent that the difference between the earliest starting times at two successive nodes must be at least equal to the activity time that connects the two nodes. (It can be greater if more than one activity converges at a node, but never less.) Thus, for Activity 1–2, we require that:

$$x_2 - x_1 \geq 6$$

A similar condition must exist for each successive pair of nodes. Thus, we require that $x_3 - x_1 \geq 5$, $x_4 - x_3 \geq 4$, and so on for the entire network. These inequalities become the constraints of our LP model. Our objective is to minimize the earliest "starting time" at the last node (Node 6 in this case). Hence, the LP model is:

minimize[1] x_6

subject to

Activity 1–2	$x_2 - x_1 \geq 6$
Activity 2–5	$x_5 - x_2 \geq 10$
Activity 1–3	$x_3 - x_1 \geq 5$

[1] Some LP packages require that every variable that appears in any constraint must also be accounted for in the objective function. Otherwise, an error message such as "undefined variable" occurs. If that is the case, use this objective function:

minimize $0x_1 + 0x_2 + 0x_3 + 0x_4 + 0x_5 + 1x_6$

Activity 3–4	$x_4 - x_3 \geq 4$
Activity 4–5	$x_5 - x_4 \geq 9$
Activity 5–6	$x_6 - x_5 \geq 2$
	All variables ≥ 0

The computer solution to this model (in abbreviated form) is:

```
X1 =  0.000000
X2 =  6.000000
X3 =  5.000000          OBJECTIVE FUNCTION VALUE IS 20.000000
X4 =  9.000000
X5 = 18.000000
X6 = 20.000000
```

These are the earliest starting times at each node. Note that the first node has a starting time of 0, and that the last node has a time of 20. The 20 is the project duration; hence, completion time for the project is 20. The OBJECTIVE FUNCTION VALUE of 20.000000 also gives us the project completion time.

Now let us extend the formulation to incorporate project crashing. Suppose that we have this information about activity crashing:

Activity	Normal Time	Crash Time	Cost per Day to Crash	Allowable Days of Crashing
1-2	6	6	–	0
2-5	10	8	$500	2
1-3	5	4	300	1
3-4	4	1	700	3
4-5	9	7	600	2
5-6	2	1	800	1

The allowable days of crashing is the difference between the normal time and the crash time. These become additional constraints in the LP model. Suppose y_{1-2} represents the possible crashing of Activity 1–2. Using the above information, we would write:

$$y_{1-2} \leq 0$$

Similarly, we would write:

$$y_{2-5} \leq 2$$
$$y_{1-3} \leq 1$$
$$y_{3-4} \leq 3$$
$$y_{4-5} \leq 2$$
$$y_{5-6} \leq 1$$

We must also recognize that shortening an activity by an amount represented by y will decrease the right-hand side of the constraint for the earliest starting times at the nodes. For instance, we previously saw that the constraint for Activity 1–2 was $x_2 - x_1 \geq 6$. Shortening this by y_{1-2} would give us $x_2 - x_1 \geq 6 - y_{1-2}$. However, recall that we must have all variables on the left side of the inequality. Adding y_{1-2} to both sides of this inequality achieves the desired result: $x_2 - x_1 + y_{1-2} \geq 6$. Similarly, for Activity 2–5, the result is $x_5 - x_2 + y_{2-5} \geq 10$, for Activity 1–3 the result is $x_3 - x_1 + y_{1-3} \geq 5$, and so on.

So far, we have two kinds of constraints. The first set of constraints relates to the limit on how much each activity can be shortened; the second set of constraints relates to the fact that the difference between the earliest starting time for two successive nodes cannot be less than the activity time for the activity that connects the two nodes. Notice that every activity must have one of each kind of constraint; the number of each kind of constraint will be equal to the number of activities. Hence, if there are six activities, there will be six constraints for limits on crashing time, and six constraints for earliest starting times.

There is still another kind of constraint. It relates to project completion time. We must specify the project completion time we want. This is often the result of an initial (noncrashing) analysis that provides us with the project completion time. For instance, suppose the initial analysis revealed a completion time of 20 days, and that management now wants to shorten the project time to 17 days. We use this information to set the earliest starting time at the last node to 17 days: $x_6 = 17$.

This completes our discussion of the constraints. Let's turn our attention to the objective function. The purpose of the model is to achieve the desired project time (17 days) by crashing at minimum cost. Hence, the variables and coefficients of the objective function relate to crashing. Using cost data from the preceding table, we have:

$$\text{minimize} \quad 0y_{1-2} + 500y_{2-5} + 300y_{1-3} + 700y_{3-4} + 600y_{4-5} + 800y_{5-6}$$

Note that the first coefficient in the objective function is 0; there is no crashing cost per day because Activity 1-2 cannot be shortened. This poses no particular problem, however, because one of our constraints is $y_{1-2} \leq 0$, and due to non-negativity requirements, it means that y_{1-2} will equal zero in the solution.

Our model, then, including definition of symbols used, is:

Node	Earliest Start Time	Activity	Days Shortened
1	x_1	1-2	y_{1-2}
2	x_2	2-5	y_{2-5}
3	x_3	1-3	y_{1-3}
4	x_4	3-4	y_{3-4}
5	x_5	4-5	y_{4-5}
6	x_6	5-6	y_{5-6}

minimize[2] $\quad 0y_{1-2} + 500y_{2-5} + 300y_{1-3} + 700y_{3-4} + 600y_{4-5} + 800y_{5-6}$

subject to

Allowable crashing
- Activity 1–2 $\quad y_{1-2} \leq 0$
- Activity 2–5 $\quad y_{2-5} \leq 2$
- Activity 1–3 $\quad y_{1-3} \leq 1$
- Activity 3–4 $\quad y_{3-4} \leq 3$
- Activity 4–5 $\quad y_{4-5} \leq 2$
- Activity 5–6 $\quad y_{5-6} \leq 1$

Difference in earliest start times
- Activity 1–2 $\quad x_2 - x_1 + y_{1-2} \geq 6$
- Activity 2–5 $\quad x_5 - x_2 + y_{2-5} \geq 10$
- Activity 1–3 $\quad x_3 - x_1 + y_{1-3} \geq 5$
- Activity 3–4 $\quad x_4 - x_3 + y_{3-4} \geq 4$
- Activity 4–5 $\quad x_5 - x_4 + y_{4-5} \geq 9$
- Activity 5–6 $\quad x_6 - x_5 + y_{5-6} \geq 2$

Desired project completion time $\quad x_6 \leq 17$

Non-negativity $\quad$ All variables ≥ 0

The (abbreviated) computer solution for this problem is:

```
X2 = 6      Y12 = 0
X3 = 4      Y25 = 0
X4 = 8      Y13 = 1      Z = 1700
X5 = 16     Y45 = 1
X6 = 17     Y56 = 1
```

We can interpret the solution in the following manner. The solution values for the y's tell us which activities are to be crashed (those that have y values that are nonzero: Activity 1–3, Activity 4–5, and Activity 5–6), and the number of days each is to be crashed (one day each). The x values indicate the revised earliest starting times for the crashed project. The total crashing cost is indicated by Z = 1700.

---

[2] If the computer package you are using requires every variable to appear in the objective function, the modified objective function would be:

minimize: $0x_1 + 0x_2 + 0x_3 + 0x_4 + 0x_5 + 0x_6 + 0y_{1-2} + 500y_{2-5} + 300y_{1-3} + 700y_{3-4} + 600y_{4-5} + 800y_{5-6}$

Note that this problem is the same as the one solved manually in Example 7, and that the solution is the same. There is, however, one important difference between the two solutions. In Example 7, the objective was to obtain the optimal crashed time, whereas in this example, we *specified* a shortened time of 17 days. But we did not know in advance that 17 would be optimal. In fact, if we want to obtain the optimal crashed time using the LP approach, we would either have to modify the model to incorporate indirect costs, or else do repeated runs, each one specifying one less time unit (day, week, etc.) and examine the resulting values of Z compared to indirect costs in order to identify the optimal solution.

SUMMARY

Projects are comprised of a unique set of activities established to achieve a given set of objectives during a limited life span. The nonroutine nature of project activities places a set of demands on the project manager, which are different in many respects than those required for the manager of more traditional operations activities, both in planning and coordinating the work.

PERT and CPM are two commonly used techniques for developing and monitoring projects. Although each technique was developed independently and for expressly different purposes, time and practice have erased most of the original differences so that now little distinction can be made between the two. Either one provides the manager with a rational approach to project planning along with a graphical display of project activities. Both depict the sequential relationships that exist among activities and reveal to managers which activities must be completed on time in order to achieve timely completion of the project. Managers can use that information to direct their attention toward the most critical activities.

Two slightly different conventions can be used when constructing a network diagram. One designates the arrow as activities, the other designates the nodes as activities. To avoid confusion, this chapter emphasized only one approach, activities-on-arrows.

The task of developing and quickly updating project networks becomes complex for projects of even moderate size, so that the task is often handled through the use of a computer, which involves a computing algorithm.

A deterministic approach is used for determining project duration estimates when activity times can be fairly well established. However, when activity times are subject to some uncertainty, a probabilistic approach is more realistic, and estimates of the length of such projects should be couched in probabilistic terms.

In some instances, it may be possible to shorten the length of a project by shortening one or more of the project activities. Typically, such gains are achieved by the use of additional resources, although in some cases it may be possible to transfer resources among project activities. Generally, projects are shortened either to the point where the cost of additional reduction would exceed the benefit of additional reduction or to the point where further improvements, although desirable, would be physically impossible.

PERT networks can be formulated and solved as linear programming models. Although that approach is generally inefficient for regular PERT problems, it can be a useful alternative method for solving PERT problems that involve crashing.

GLOSSARY

Activity A task.

Beta Distribution A convenient distribution used to describe variability in activity completion times.

CPM (Critical Path Method) PERT and CPM were developed separately at about the same time in the late 1950s. Both techniques are concerned with integrating and managing a project consisting of a number of different tasks.

Crashing Accelerating a project by speeding up those critical-path activities that have the lowest ratio of incremental cost to incremental time saved.

Critical Activity An activity on the critical path.

Critical Path The path in a network diagram that takes the longest time for completion.

Deterministic Time Estimate A single time estimate for an activity, with no alternative estimates or probability distribution of estimates.

Dummy Activity An artificial activity on an A-O-A network diagram to facilitate distinguishing between two or more activities that begin and end at the same nodes.

Early Finish (EF) For an activity, the early start plus the time required for completion of the activity.

Early Start (ES) For an activity, the earliest possible starting time.

Event A node in a precedence diagram showing both the completion of one or more activities and the start of another task or set of tasks.

Late Finish (LF) For an activity, the latest finish time without delaying the project.

Late Start (LS) For an activity, the late finish *minus* the time required for completion of the activity.

Network A graph that shows the interconnections between all the elements of a system. See also **Precedence Diagram.**

Normal Distribution Used to describe path completion time variability. Its parameters are obtained by summing the means and variances of the activity completion times.

Path A sequence of activities or nodes from the beginning to the end of a network.

PERT (Program Evaluation and Review Technique) See **CPM.**

Precedence Diagram A type of directed network graph that shows the sequential relationships for activities in a project.

Probabilistic Time Estimate A weighted average of three time estimates.

Project A set of diverse tasks that are organized to achieve a common objective.

Slack For an activity, the additional time, over and above completion time, that could be used for the activity without delaying the project.

Time-Cost Trade-Off See **Crashing.**

Variance With three time estimates for completion of an activity, the variance is the square of the difference between optimistic time and pessimistic time divided by 6; for a path, the variance is the sum of the variances of completion times for all of the activities on the critical path.

SOLVED PROBLEMS

Problem 1. The table below contains information related to the major activities of a research project. Use the information to do the following:

a. Draw a precedence diagram.

b. Find the critical path.

c. Determine the expected length of the project.

Activity	Precedes	Expected Time (days)
Start	*a,e,g*	—
a	*c,b*	5
c	*d*	8
d	*i*	2
b	*i*	7
e	*f*	3
f	*j*	6
i	*j*	10
j	End	8
g	*h*	1
h	*k*	2
k	End	17

Solution

a. In constructing networks these observations can be useful:

(1) Activities with no predecessors are at the beginning (left side) of the network.

(2) Activities with multiple predecessors are located at path intersections.

Start the network diagram by identifying and charting all activities with no predecessors:

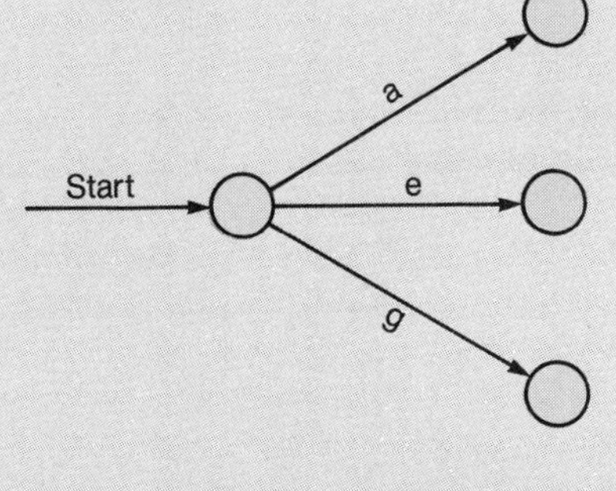

Next, complete the diagram in sections. Go down the activity list in order, when possible, to avoid overlooking any activities. The process is illustrated in the following diagram.

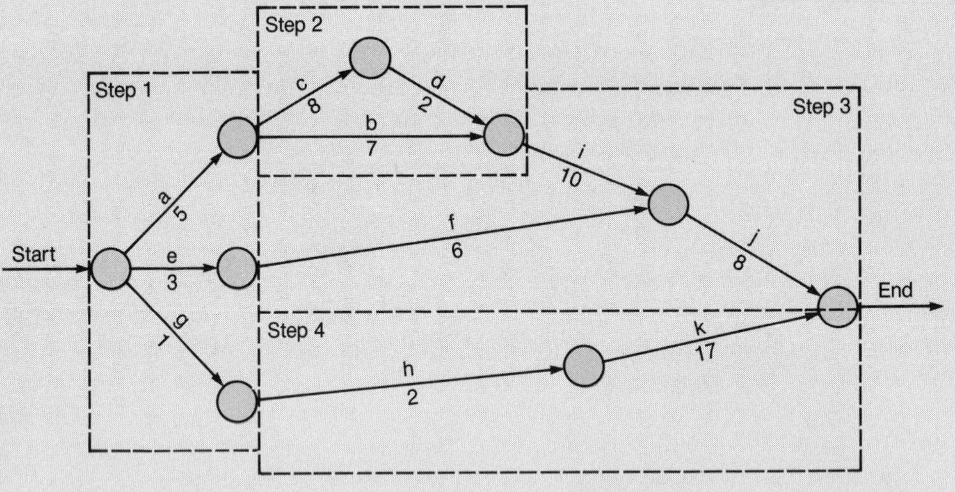

Here are some additional hints for constructing a precedence diagram:

(1) Use pencil.
(2) Start with a single node and end with a single node.
(3) Try to avoid having paths cross each other.
(4) Number nodes from left to right.
(5) Have activities going from left to right.
(6) Use only one arrow between any pair of nodes.

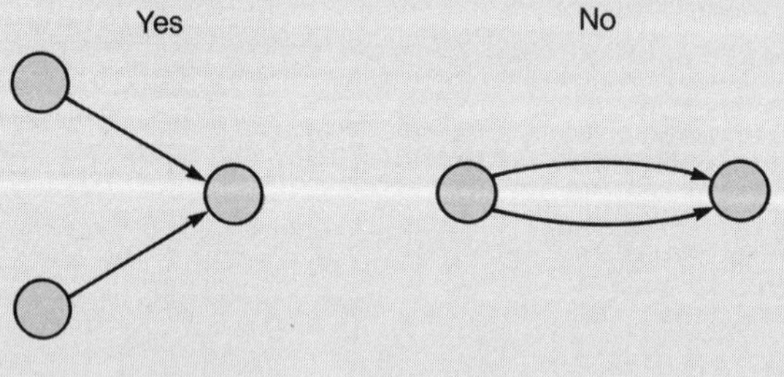

b. and *c.*

Path	Length (days)
a–c–d–i–j*	5 + 8 + 2 + 10 + 8 = 33†
a–b–i–j	5 + 7 + 10 + 8 = 30
e–f–j	3 + 6 + 8 = 17
g–h–k	1 + 2 + 17 = 20

* Critical path.

† Expected project duration.

Problem 2. Using the computing algorithm, determine the slack for each activity for the following diagram. Identify the activities that are on the critical path.

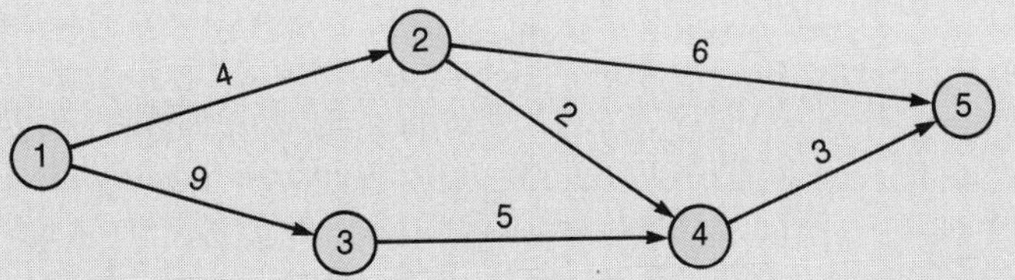

Solution

The task of determining ES, EF, LS, and LF times can be greatly simplified by setting up two brackets for each activity, as illustrated below:

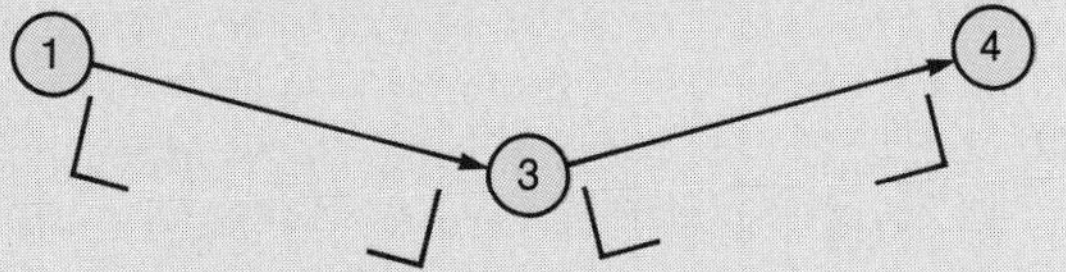

The bracket at the left end of each activity eventually will be filled in with the earliest and latest *starting* times, and the bracket at the right end of each activity will be filled in with the earliest and latest *finishing* times, as symbolized below:

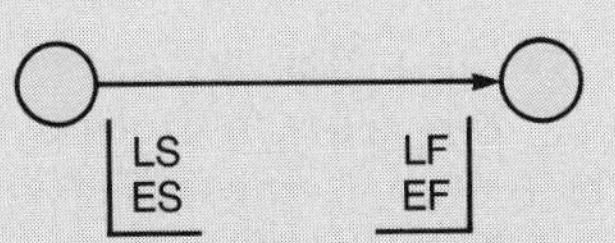

This is accomplished in a two-step process. First, the earliest starting times and earliest finishing times are determined, working from left to right, as shown in the diagram below.

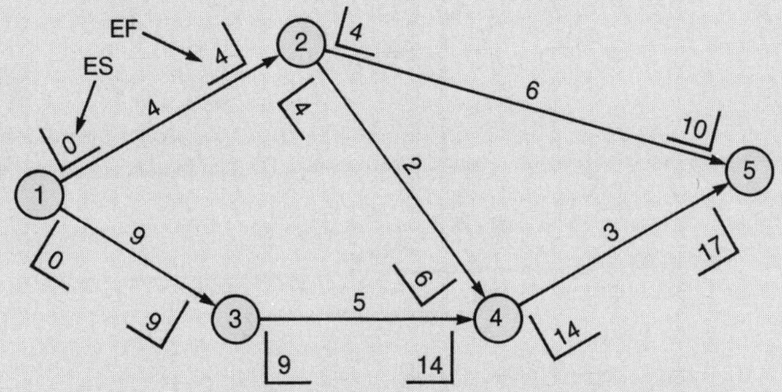

Thus, Activity 1–2 can start with 0. With a time of 4, it can finish at 0 + 4 = 4. This establishes the earliest start for all activities that begin at Node 2. Therefore,

2–5 and 2–4 can start no earlier than 4. Activity 2–5 has an early finish of 4 + 6 = 10, and Activity 2–4 has an early finish of 4 + 2 = 6. At this point, it is impossible to say what the earliest start is for 4–5—that will depend on which activity, 3–4 or 2–4, has the latest EF. Consequently, it is necessary to compute ES and EF along the lower path. Assuming an ES of 0 for 1–3, its EF will be 9, so 3–4 will have an ES of 9 and an EF of 9 + 5 = 14.

Considering that the two activities entering Node 4 have EF times of 6 and 14, the earliest that Activity 4–5 can start is the *largest* of these, which is 14. Hence, Activity 4–5 has an ES of 14 and an EF of 14 + 3 = 17.

Now compare the EFs of the activities entering the final node. The largest of these, 17, is the expected project duration.

The LF and LS times for each activity can now be determined by working backward through the network (i.e., from right to left). The LF for the two activities entering Node 5 is 17, the project duration. In other words, in order for the project to finish in 17 weeks, these last two activities must both finish by that time.

In the case of Activity 4–5, the LS neccessary for an LF of 17 is 17 − 3 = 14. This means that both 2–4 and 3–4 must finish no later than 14. Hence, their LF times are 14. Activity 3 has an LS time of 14 − 5 = 9, making the LF of Activity 1–3 equal to 9 and its LS equal to 9 − 9 = 0.

Activity 2–4, with an LF time of 14, has an LS time of 14 − 2 = 12. Activity 2–5 has an LF of 17 and, therefore, an LS of 17 − 6 = 11. Thus, the latest 2–5 can start is 11, and the latest 2–4 can start is 12 in order to finish by week 17. Since Activity 1–2 precedes *both* of these activities, it can finish no later than the *smaller* of these, which is 11. Therefore, 1–2 has an LF of 11 and an LS of 11 − 4 = 7.

The ES, EF, LF, and LS times are shown on the network below.

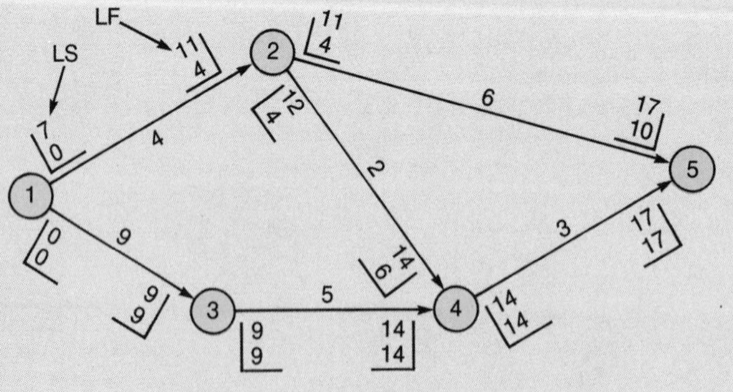

The slack time for any activity is the difference between *either* LF and EF *or* LS and ES. Thus:

Activity	LS	ES	Slack or	LF	EF	Slack
1–2	7	0	7	11	4	7
2–5	11	4	7	17	10	7
2–4	12	4	8	14	6	8
1–3	0	0	0	9	9	0
3–4	9	9	0	14	14	0
4–5	14	14	0	17	17	0

The activities with zero slack times indicate the critical path. Thus, the critical path is 1–3–4–5.

When working problems of this nature, keep in mind the following:

a. For nodes with multiple entering activities, the ES time for leaving activities of that node is the *largest* EF of the entering activities.

b. For nodes with multiple leaving activities, the LF for an entering activity for that node is the *smallest* LS of the leaving activities.

Problem 3. Expected times and variances for the major activities of an R&D project are depicted in the PERT chart below. Determine the probability that the project completion time will be:

a. Less than 50 weeks.

b. More than 50 weeks.

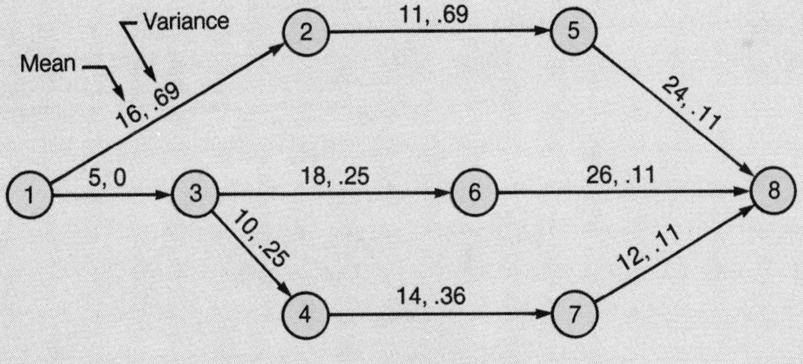

Solution

a. Compute the mean and standard deviation for each path:

Path	Expected Time (weeks)	Standard Deviation (weeks)
1-2-5-8	16 + 11 + 24 = 51	$\sqrt{.69 + .69 + .11} = 1.22$
1-3-6-8	5 + 18 + 26 = 49	$\sqrt{.00 + .25 + .11} = .60$
1-3-4-7-8	5 + 10 + 14 + 12 = 41	$\sqrt{.00 + .25 + .36 + .11} = .85$

b. Compute the z-score for each path for the length specified. Assign a probability of 1.00 to any path that has a score of more than $z = +2.50$. Use:

$$z = \frac{50 - t_{path}}{\sigma_{path}}$$

The probability that each path will be completed in 50 weeks or less is shown in the corresponding diagram. (Probabilities are from Appendix Table B.)

The probability that the project will be completed in 50 weeks or less depends on all three paths being completed in that time. Because the z for Path 1–3–4–7–8 is greater than $+2.50$, it is assigned a probability of completion of 1.00. It is less certain that the other two paths will be completed in that time. The probability that all will *not* exceed 50 is the *product* of their individual probabilities *of* completion. Thus, .2061 (.9525)(1.00) = .1963.

The probability that the project will *exceed* 50 weeks is the complement of this number, which is 1.00 − .1963 = .8037. (Note that it is *not* the product of the complements of the path probabilities.)

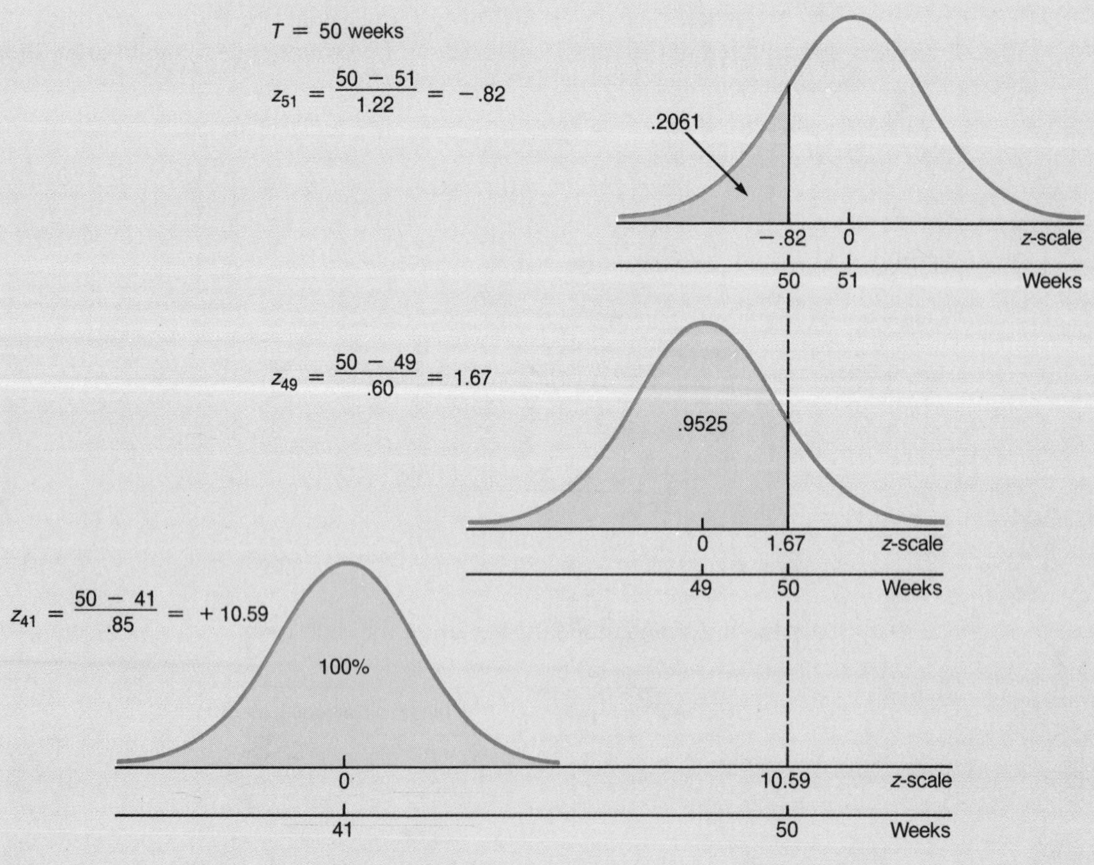

Problem 4. Indirect costs for a project are $12,000 per week for as long as the project lasts. The project manager has supplied the cost and time information shown below. Use the information to:

a. Determine an optimum crashing plan.

b. Graph the total costs for the plan.

Activity	Crashing Potential (weeks)	Cost per Week to Crash
a	3	$11,000
b	3	3,000 first week, $4,000 others
c	2	6,000
d	1	1,000
e	3	6,000
f	1	2,000

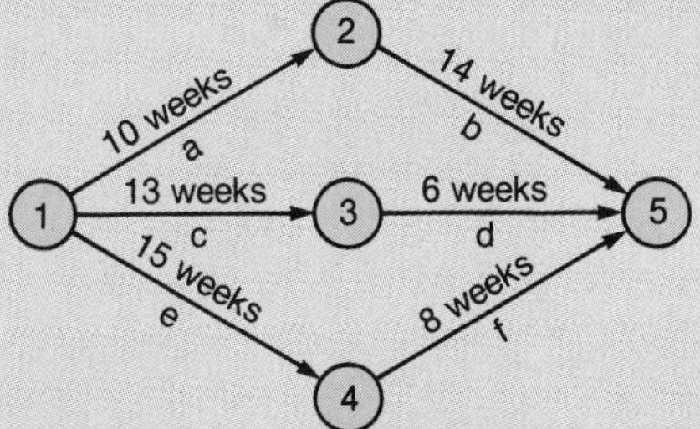

Solution

a. (1) Compute path lengths and identify the critical path:

Path	Duration (weeks)
a–b	24 (critical path)
c–d	19
e–f	23

(2) Rank critical activities according to crashing costs:

Activity	Cost per Week to Crash
b	$ 3,000
a	11,000

Activity *b* should be shortened one week because it has the lowest crashing cost. This would reduce indirect costs by $12,000 at a cost of $3,000, for a net savings of $9,000. At this point, Paths a–b and e–f would both have a length of 23 weeks: Therefore, both would be critical.

(3) Rank activities by crashing costs on the two critical paths:

Path	Activity	Cost per Week to Crash
a–b	*b*	$ 4,000
	a	11,000
e–f	*e*	6,000
	f	2,000

Choose one activity on each path to crash: *b* on a–b and *f* on e–f for a total cost of $4,000 + $2,000 = $6,000 and a net savings of $12,000 − $6,000 = $6,000.

(4) Check to see which path(s) might be critical: a–b and e–f would be 22 weeks in length, and c–d would still be 19 weeks.

(5) Rank activities on the critical paths:

Path	Activity	Cost per Week to Crash
a–b	*b*	$ 4,000
	a	11,000
e–f	*e*	6,000
	f	(no further crashing possible)

Crash *b* on Path a–b and *e* on e–f for a cost of $4,000 + $6,000 = $10,000, for a net savings of $12,000 − $10,000 = $2,000.

(6) At this point, no further improvement would be possible: Paths a–b and e–f would be 21 weeks in length, and one activity from each path would have to be shortened. This would mean *a* at $11,000 and *e* at $6,000 for a total of $17,000, which would exceed the $12,000 potential savings in indirect costs.

b. A summary of the crashing sequence follows, showing the length of the project after crashing *n* weeks:

Path	n = 0	1	2	3
a–b	24	23	22	21
c–d	19	19	19	19
e–f	23	23	22	21
Activity crashed		*b*	*b,f*	*b,e*
Crashing costs ($000)		3	6	10

A summary of costs for the preceding schedule would look like this:

Project Length	Cumulative Weeks Shortened	Cumulative Crashing Costs ($000)	Indirect Costs ($000)	Total Costs ($000)
24	0	0	24(12) = 288	288
23	1	3	23(12) = 276	279
22	2	3 + 6 = 9	22(12) = 264	273
21	3	9 + 10 = 19	21(12) = 252	271
20	4	19 + 17 = 36	20(12) = 240	276

The graph of total costs is shown below.

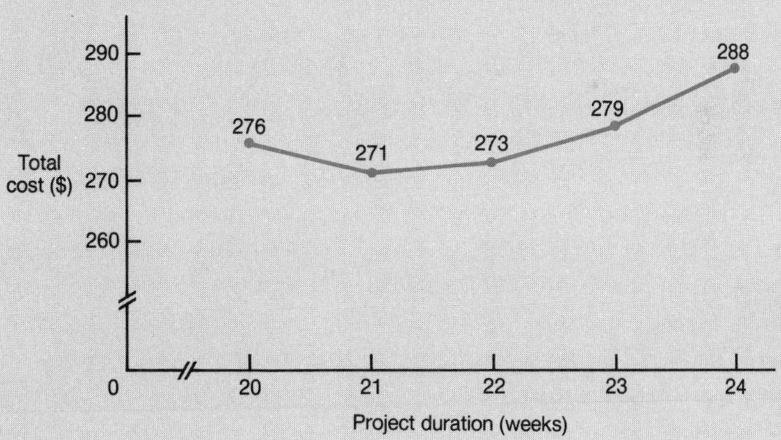

PROBLEMS

1. For each of the network diagrams below, determine both the critical path and the expected project duration. The quantities on the arrows represent expected activity times.

a.

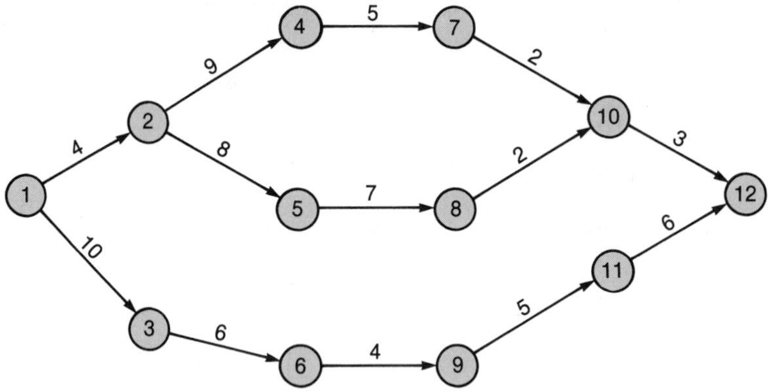
4
5
7
9
2
2
10
4
8
2
3
1
5
7
8
2
12
10
6
11
5
3
6
6
4
9

b.

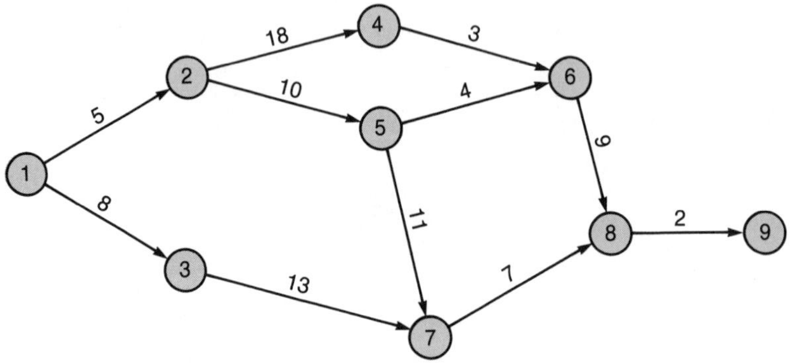
18
4
3
2
10
4
6
5
5
9
1
8
11
2
8
9
7
3
13
7

c.

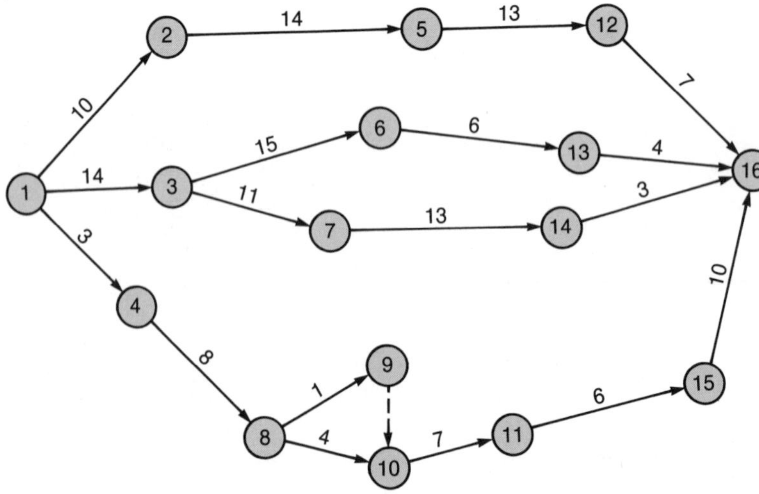
14
5
13
12
2
7
10
6
6
15
13
4
16
1
14
3
11
3
7
13
14
3
10
4
8
9
1
6
15
8
4
7
11
10

2. Using the information provided in the table below, do the following:
   a. Construct a network diagram.
   b. Determine which activities are on the critical path.
   c. Compute the length of the critical path.

Activity	Estimated Time (days)
1–2	5
2–3	6
2–4	4
3–6	9
6–7	2
4–5	4
4–7	18
5–7	10

3. The information shown pertains to a project that is about to commence. As the project manager, which activities would you be concerned with in terms of timely project completion? Explain.

Activity	Precedes	Estimated Time (days)
Start	*a,f*	—
a	*b*	15
b	*c,d*	12
c	*e*	6
d	End	5
e	End	3
f	*g,h*	8
g	*i,j*	8
h	*j*	9
i	End	7
j	*k*	14
k	End	6

4. Use the computational alogrithm to determine the slack time for each activity in the problems listed below:
   a. Problem 1*a*.
   b. Problem 1*b*.

5. For each of the problems listed below, determine the following quantities for each activity: earliest start time, latest start time, earliest finish time,

latest finish time, and slack. list the activities that are on the critical path and determine the expected duration of the project.

a. Problem 2.

b. Problem 3.

6. Reconsider the network diagram of Problem 1*a*. Suppose that after 12 weeks, Activities 1–2 and 2–4 have been finished, 2–5 is 75 percent finished, and 3–6 is 50 percent finished. How many weeks after the original start time should the project be finished?

7. Three recent college graduates have formed a partnership and have opened an advertising firm. Their first project consists of the activities listed below.

   a. Draw the precedence diagram.

   b. What is the probability that the project can be completed in 24 days or less? In 21 days or less?

   c. Suppose it is now the end of day 7 and that Activities *a* and *b* have been completed, while *d* is 50 percent completed. Time estimates for the completion of *d* are 5, 6, and 7. Determine the probability of finishing the project by the 24th day and the probability of finishing by the 21st day.

		Time in Days		
Activity	**Precedes**	**Optimistic**	**Most Likely**	**Pessimistic**
Start	*a,b,d*	—	—	—
a	*c*	5	6	7
b	*h*	8	8	11
c	*e*	6	8	11
d	*f*	9	12	15
e	End	5	6	9
f	*g*	5	6	7
g	End	2	3	7
h	*i*	4	4	5
i	End	5	7	8

8. The new director of special events at a large university has decided to completely revamp graduation ceremonies. Toward that end, a PERT chart of the major activities has been developed. The chart has five paths with expert completion times and variances as shown in the table below. Graduation day is 17 weeks from now. Assuming the project begins now, what is the probability that the project will be completed before:

a. Graduation time?
b. Week 16?
c. Week 13?

Path	Expected Duration (weeks)	Variance
A	10	1.21
B	8	2.00
C	12	1.00
D	15	2.89
E	14	1.44

9. The precedence diagram shown below reflects three time estimates for each activity. Determine:

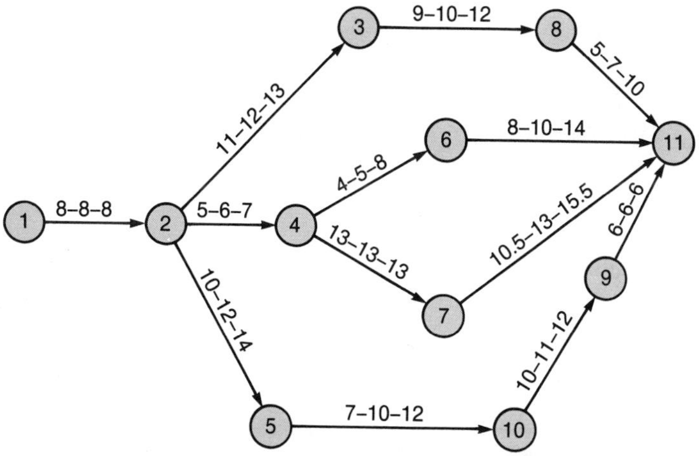

a. The expected completion time for each path and its variance.
b. The probability that the project will require more than 49 weeks.
c. The probability that the project will be completed in 46 weeks or less.

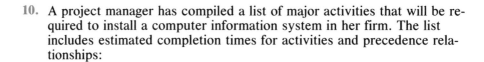

10. A project manager has compiled a list of major activities that will be required to install a computer information system in her firm. The list includes estimated completion times for activities and precedence relationships:

Activity	Precedes	Estimated Times (weeks)
Start	*a,b,c*	—
a	*d,f*	2–4–6
d	*e*	6–8–10
e	*h*	7–9–12
h	End	2–3–5
f	*g*	3–4–8
g	End	5–7–9
b	*i*	2–2–3
i	*j*	2–3–6
j	*k*	3–4–5
k	End	4–5–8
c	*m*	5–8–12
m	*n*	1–1–1
n	*o*	6–7–11
o	End	8–9–13

If the project is finished within 27 weeks of its start, the project manager will receive a bonus of $1,000; if the project is finished within 28 weeks of its start, the bonus will be $500. Find the probability of each bonus.

11. Construct an activity-on-node diagram for the set of activities listed in Problem 3.

12. Construct an activity-on-node diagram for the set of activities listed in Problem 2. In order to facilitate this, replace the activity designations (1–2, 2–3, etc.) with letters (*a*, *b*, *c*, etc.).

13. The project manager of a task force planning the construction of a domed stadium had hoped to be able to complete construction prior to the start of the next college football season. After reviewing construction time estimates, it now appears that a certain amount of crashing will be needed to ensure that the project is completed before the season opener. Given the time and cost estimates below, determine a minimum-cost crashing schedule that will shave five weeks off the project length.

Activity	Normal Time (weeks)	Cost to Crash One Week: First Crash	Cost to Crash One Week: Second Crash
1–2	12	$15,000	$20,000
2–3	14	10,000	10,000
1–4	10	5,000	5,000
4–5	17	20,000	21,000
4–6	18	16,000	18,000
4–7	12	12,000	15,000
5–8	15	24,000	24,000
6–9	8	—	—
7–10	7	30,000	—
10–11	12	25,000	25,000
3–12	9	10,000	10,000
8–12	3	—	—
9–12	11	40,000	—
11–12	8	20,000	20,000

14. A construction project has indirect costs totaling $40,000 per week. Major activities in the project and their expected times are shown in the precedence diagram below. Crashing costs for each activity are listed in the table below.

	Crashing Costs for One Week (000)		
Activity	First Crash	Second Crash	Third Crash
1–2	$18	$22	$44
2–5	24	25	25
5–7	30	30	35
7–11	15	20	—
11–13	30	33	36
1–3	12	24	26
3–8	—	—	—
8–11	40	40	40
3–9	3	10	12
9–12	2	7	10
12–13	26	—	—
1–4	10	15	25
4–6	8	13	—
6–10	5	12	—
10–12	14	15	—

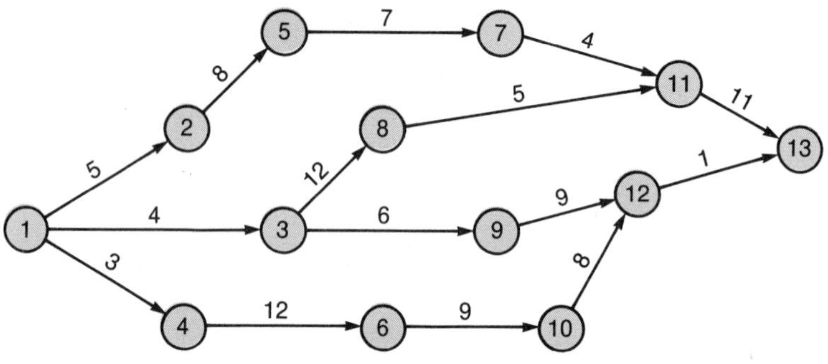

a. Determine the optimum time-cost crashing plan.

b. Plot the total-cost curve that describes the least expensive crashing schedule that will reduce the project length by six weeks.

15. The project manager of a major undertaking for Projects International, has assembled the following data for the undertaking:

		Cost per Week to Crash ($000)		
Activity	**Normal Time**	**First Week**	**Second Week**	**Third Week**
1–2	6	$40	40	40
2–3	5	16	20	24
2–4	6	18	20	22
3–5	7	21	21	21
4–5	6	17	20	25
5–6	6	44	—	—
6–10	6	20	41	42
1–7	4	47	—	—
7–8	8	34	36	38
8–9	7	25	30	36
9–10	12	37	—	—

Operating costs for the project average $75,000 per week. Determine the optimal crashing plan for the project and the total cost of operating and crashing for the project.

16. Formulate a linear programming model for the project described in Problem 2 and solve it using a computer package. Interpret the solution.

17. Write a linear programming model for the project described in Problem 1*b* and solve it using a computer package. Interpret your solution.

18. Formulate a linear programming model for Problem 15 and solve it assuming a desired project duration of 29 weeks. (Hint: use first-week crashing costs only; crash the project one week.) Indicate how your model could be revised to shorten the project one additional week, given a solution to the original (29-week) model.

19. Write a linear programming model that can be used to shorten the project described in Problem 14 by one week, and obtain the solution to your model. What is the crashing cost? Rewrite your model so that the project can be shortened a second week, and obtain the solution for the revised model. What is the crashing cost?

20. Write a linear programming model that can be used to shorten the project described in Problem 13 by one week, and obtain the solution to your model. Then, use linear programming to determine the optimal amount of time for the project.

Chapter 15 Case

Shale Oil Company

The Shale Oil Company contains several operating units that comprise its Aston, Ohio, manufacturing complex. These units process the crude oil that is pumped through and transform it into a multitude of hydrocarbon products. The units run 24 hours per day, seven days per week, and must be shut down for maintenance on a predetermined schedule. One such unit is Distillation Unit No. 5, or DU5. Studies have shown that DU5 can operate only 3½ years without major equipment breakdowns and excessive loss of efficiency. Therefore, DU5 is shut down every 3½ years for cleaning, inspection, and repairs.

DU5 is the only distillation unit for crude oil in the Aston complex, and its shutdown severely affects all other operating units. Some of the production can be compensated by Shale refineries in other locations, but the rest must be processed before the shutdown and stored. Without proper planning, a nationwide shortage of Shale gasoline could occur. The timing of DU5's shutdown is critical, and the length of time the unit is down must be kept to a minimum to limit production loss. Shale uses PERT as a planning and controlling tool to minimize shutdown time.

The first phase of a shutdown is to open and clean the equipment. Inspectors can then enter the unit and examine the damage. Once damages are determined, the needed repairs can be carried out. Repair times can vary considerably depending on what damage the inspection reveals. Based on previous inspection records, some repair work is known ahead of time. Thorough cleaning of the equipment is also necessary to improve the unit's operating efficiency. Table 1 lists the many maintenance activities and their estimated completion times.

Discussion questions

1. Determine the expected shutdown time and the probability the shutdown can be completed one week earlier.
2. What are the probabilities that Shale finishes the maintenance project one day, two days, three days, four days, five days, or six days earlier?
3. Shale Oil is considering increasing the budget to shorten the shutdown. How do you suggest the company proceed?

Source: By Professor Barry Render, University of New Orleans, in *Cases and Readings in Quantitative Analysis for Management* by Barry Render and Ralph M. Stair, Jr. (Boston: Allyn & Bacon, 1982).

TABLE 1 Preventive Maintenance of DU5

Activities		Time Estimates (in days) Optimistic	Most-Likely	Pessimistic
1–2	Circulate wash water throughout unit	1	2	2.5
2–3	Install blinds	1.5	2	2.5
3–4	Open and clean vessels and columns	2	3	4
3–5	Open and clean heat exchangers, remove tube bundles	1	2	3
3–6	Open and clean furnaces	1	2	4
3–7	Open and clean mechanical equipment	2	2.5	3
3–8	Inspect instrumentation	2	4	5
4–9	Inspect vessels and columns	1	2	3
5–10	Inspect heat exchanger shells	1	1.5	2
5–11	Inspect tube bundles	1	1.5	2
6–12	Inspect furnaces	2	2.5	3
6–17	Retube furnaces	15	20	30
7–13	Inspect mechanical equipment	1	1.5	2
7–18	Install new pump mechanical seals	3	5	8
8–19	Repair instrumentation	3	8	15
9–14	Repair vessels and columns	14	21	28
10–16	Repair heat exchanger shells	1	5	10
11–15	Repair tube bundles, retube	2	5	10
12–17	Repair furnaces	5	10	20
13–18	Repair mechanical equipment	10	15	25
14–20	Test and close vessels and columns	4	5	8
15–16	Install tube bundles into heat exchanger shells	1	2	3
16–20	Test and close heat exchangers	1	2	2.5
17–20	Test and close furnaces	1	2	3
18–20	Test and close mechanical equipment	1	2	3
19–20	Test instrumentation	2	4	6
20–21	Pull blinds	1.5	2	2.5
21–22	Purge all equipment with steam	1	3	5
22–23	Start up unit	3	5	10

Chapter 15 Case Fantasy Products

Company Background

The Fantasy Products Company is a manufacturer of high-quality small appliances intended for home use. Their current product line includes irons, a small hand-held vacuum, and a number of kitchen appliances such as toasters, blenders,

Source: Used with permission from Robert J. Thieraus, Margaret Cunningham, and Melanie Blackwell, Xavier University, Cincinnati, Ohio.

waffle irons, and coffee makers. Fantasy Products has a strong research and development department that continually searches for ways to improve existing products as well as developing new products.

Currently, the research and development department is working on the development of a new kitchen appliance that will chill foods quickly much as a microwave oven heats them quickly, although the technology involved is quite different. Tentatively named The Big Chill, the product will initially carry a price tag of around $125 and therefore the target market consists of upper income groups. At this price, it is expected to be a very profitable item. R&D engineers now have a working prototype and are satisfied that, with cooperation from the production and marketing people, the product can be ready in time for the all important Christmas buying season. A target date has been set for product introduction that is 24 weeks away.

Current Problem

Fantasy Products Marketing Vice President Vera Sloan has recently learned from reliable sources that a competitor is also in the process of developing a similar product that it intends to bring out at almost exactly the same time. In addition, her source indicated that the competitor plans to sell its product, which will be smaller than The Big Chill, for $99 in the hope of appealing to upper-middle as well as upper income groups. Vera, with the help of several of her key people who are to be involved in marketing The Big Chill, has decided that in order to compete, the selling price for The Big Chill will have to be lowered to within $10 of the competitor's price. At this price level, it will still be profitable, although not nearly as profitable as originally anticipated.

However, Vera is wondering whether it would be possible to expedite the usual product introduction process in order to beat the competition to the market. If possible, she would like to get a six-week jump on the competition; this would put the product introduction date only 18 weeks away. During this initial period, Fantasy Products could sell The Big Chill for $125, reducing the selling price to $109 when the competitor's product actually enters the market. Since forecasts based on market research show that sales during the first six weeks will be about 2,000 per week, there is an opportunity for considerable extra profit if the early introduction can be accomplished. In addition, there is a certain amount of prestige involved in being first to the market. This should help enhance The Big Chill's image during the anticipated battle for market share.

Data Collection

Since Fantasy Products has been through the product introduction process a number of times, the R&D department has developed a list of the tasks that must be accomplished and the order in which they must be completed. Although the

TABLE 1 List of Activities and Precedence Relationships

Activity	Description	Immediate Predecessor
A	Select and order equipment	—
B	Receive equipment from supplier	A
C	Install and set up equipment	A
D	Finalize bill of materials	B
E	Order component parts	C
F	Receive component parts	E
G	First production run	D,F
H	Finalize marketing plan	—
I	Produce magazine ads	H
J	Script for TV ads	H
K	Produce TV ads	J
L	Begin ad campaign	I,K
M	Ship product to customers	G,L

TABLE 2 Time and Cost Estimates

Activity	Normal Time	Normal Cost	Crash Time	Crash Cost
A	3	$ 2,000	2	$ 4,500
B	8	9,000	6	12,000
C	4	2,000	2	7,000
D	2	1,000	1	2,000
E	2	2,000	1	3,000
F	5	0	5	0
G	6	12,000	3	24,000
H	4	3,500	2	8,000
I	4	5,000	3	8,000
J	3	8,000	2	15,000
K	4	50,000	3	70,000
L	6	10,000	6	10,000
M	1	5,000	1	5,000

times and costs vary depending on the particular product, the basic process does not. The list of activities involved and their precedence relationships are presented in Table 1. Time and cost estimates for the introduction of The Big Chill are presented in Table 2. Note that some of the activities can be completed on a crash basis, with an associated increase in cost.

Discussion questions

Fantasy Products needs to decide whether to bring The Big Chill to market 18 weeks from now as Vera Sloan is recommending. As the management science specialist in the R&D department, you have been asked to answer the following questions:

1. When would the project be completed using normal times?
2. Is it possible to complete the project in 18 weeks? What would the associated additional cost be? Which activities would need to be completed on a crash basis?
3. Is the additional cost justified in terms of the increased profits expected?
4. The estimated demand is very uncertain; how much can this number vary without changing the recommendations you are making?
5. Is there some time frame other than the 18 weeks Vera has recommended that would make more sense in terms of profits?

Part V
Stochastic Models

Stochastic models are used to handle problems that involve *random variability*. Unlike optimizing models, which are based on input values that are assumed to be known and constant, stochastic models use values that are subject to random variability. Probabilities must be incorporated in the models to account for randomness, and solutions or other outputs of stochastic models take the form of *expected values*, which can be thought of as approximations rather than exact values.

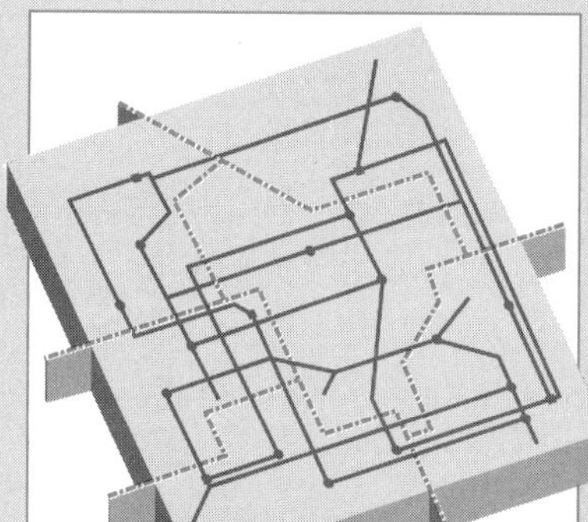

Queuing models, which are useful for making capacity decisions for service operations that must contend with customers that request service on a random basis are described in Chapter 16. Examples of such systems include checkout counters in supermarkets, waiting lines at stop signs, banks, and post offices, and telephone calls to reservation centers (e.g., airlines).

Simulation models are used to model and study certain behaviors of systems, often with the goal of exploring "what is . . . ?" type questions for systems in which random variability affects behaviors. They are discussed in Chapter 17.

Chapter 18 describes Markov analysis, used to model probabilistic switching behaviors of certain systems. These models are often used for problems involving customer loyalty and brand switching, machine breakdown and repair, and accounts receivable changes over time.

Part Outline

Chapter 16
Queuing Models

Chapter Outline

Learning Objectives

After completing this chapter, you should be able to:

1. Explain why waiting lines can occur in service systems.
2. Identify typical goals for design of service systems with respect to waiting.
3. Read the description of a queuing problem and identify the appropriate queuing model needed to solve the problem.
4. Solve typical problems using the formulas and tables presented in this chapter.
5. Outline the psychological aspects of waiting lines.
6. Explain the value of studying queuing models for managers and others who are concerned with service systems.

INTRODUCTION

An important class of management science problems involves situations in which waiting lines occur. Examples abound. In our daily lives, we commonly encounter waiting lines at gas stations, stop signs, supermarkets, restaurants, newsstands, and other places. We often experience waiting lines in transportation systems, such as planes circling an airport awaiting clearance from the control tower, trucks waiting to load or unload cargo, buses backed up waiting to enter a terminal, cabs queuing up at airports and train stations waiting for passengers (or passengers queuing up waiting for cabs), and ferrys queuing up waiting to off-load passengers and autos. Frequently, there are waiting lines at banks and post offices. In factories, jobs queue up awaiting processing, orders need to be filled, machines need repairs or need to be loaded after a job, and employees wait to punch the time clock or to eat in the cafeteria.

Most of these systems are characterized by highly variable arrival and service rates. Consequently, even though overall system capacity exceeds processing requirements, lines tend to form from time to time because of temporary system overloads caused by this variability. At other times, the reverse is true; variability in demand for service results in idle servers or idle service facilities because of a temporary absence of customers.

In general, then, the systems on which our interest centers are *under-loaded, highly variable* systems. Waiting lines tend to form in these systems due to temporary overloads created by variability in either the service or the arrival rates. This chapter provides an overview of models that are useful in describing and analyzing such systems. The concept of queuing models and queuing analysis can be particularly useful to decision makers who must make *capacity decisions*.

GOALS OF QUEUING SYSTEM DESIGN

Queuing models are *predictive* models of the expected behavior of a **system** in which waiting lines form. As such, queuing analysis forms a basis for the design of system capacity. The **queuing system** might be one that is in existence, but is not performing satisfactorily. In this case, the emphasis is on deciding how to modify the system so that it does perform in a satisfactory manner. Also, the system might be in the design stage, in which case the emphasis would be placed on achieving a design that will produce the desired system performance.

A very common goal in queuing design is to attempt to balance the cost of providing service capacity with the cost of customers waiting for service. These two costs are in direct conflict: a decrease in customer waiting cost can be achieved by increasing the amount of capacity (either by increasing the *number* of servers or by increasing the service rate). However, increasing the service capacity means an increase in the cost of the service. The combined cost of service capacity and customer waiting cost is U-shaped because of this trade-off rela-

FIGURE 16–1 The Total Cost Curve Is U-Shaped

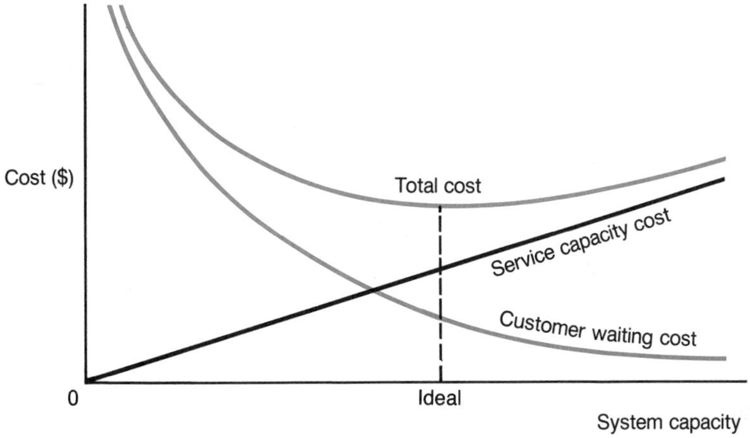

tionship, as depicted in Figure 16–1. The total cost is minimized at the lowest point of the total cost curve. Finding the minimum point often involves successively incrementing service capacity until there are no further decreases. Because increments of service capacity often are discrete (e.g., one server, two servers, etc.), it may be more realistic to represent the cost of service capacity through a series of steps, rather than through a straight line, and therefore, the total cost curve would not be as smooth as the one shown. Nonetheless, the purpose of the graph is merely to illustrate the general nature of the cost-minimization goal in system design.

Another approach, sometimes called for in designing or redesigning queuing systems, is to satisfy desired specifications. For example, a bank manager may request that the average number of customers kept waiting in line should be below seven. In this case, the question would involve determining the number of tellers needed to satisfy that objective. Similarly, the manager of a new restaurant may want to know what size waiting area will be needed to accommodate customers who are waiting to be seated.

ELEMENTS AND CHARACTERISTICS OF QUEUING SYSTEMS

Queuing systems can be differentiated by certain characteristics, such as the number of servers or whether access to the system is unrestricted or limited. Knowledge of such characteristics can help an analyst first to model the system and then to select an appropriate method for analyzing the system.

The major elements of queuing systems are outlined in Figure 16–2. Each of the elements are discussed briefly in this section.

FIGURE 16–2 Major Elements of Queuing Systems

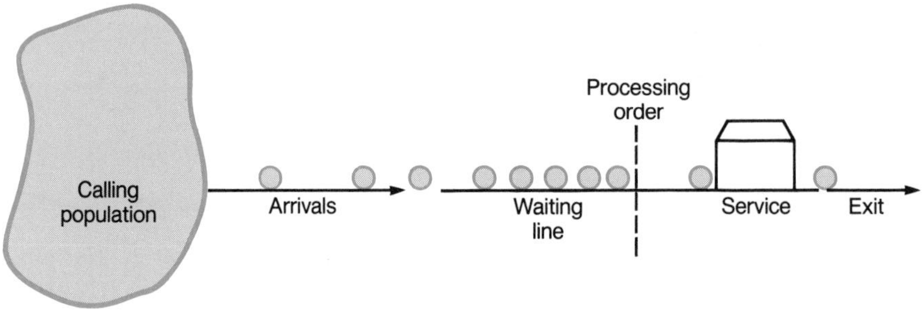

Calling Population

The **calling population** refers to the pool of potential arrivals to the system. In queuing terminology, it is often called the *customer source*. If the source is large enough that the probability of an arrival is not significantly influenced by the fact that some of the customers are waiting in line, we say that the calling population is **infinite.** Examples of such systems are those open to the general public (gas stations, theaters, restaurants, supermarkets, banks, post offices, ticket counters, and so on). Although none of these populations are truly infinite, the fact that some customers are waiting in line does not diminish the potential of others in the population entering the system. On the other hand, there are systems that have limited access for service. For example, a machine operator may be responsible for loading and unloading five presses in a factory. Therefore, there is a limit to the number of presses waiting to be loaded or unloaded. Similarly, a repairman may be responsible for emergency calls to fix a limited number of machines, a sales rep may handle a limited number of customers, and usually, a secretary works for a limited number of people. If the number of jobs that require service or the number of customers waiting for services causes the probability of another arrival to decrease (because the percentage in the population is substantially reduced), the calling population, or population source, is described as **finite** or *limited.*

Customer Arrivals

Customers are considered units that request or require service. In some systems the customers are people, and in others they are not. Examples of nonpeople systems include automobiles arriving at intersections, trucks arriving at a loading dock, machines awaiting repair, orders waiting to be filled, planes waiting to land, animals waiting for veterinarian attention, telephone calls waiting to be answered, and so on.

FIGURE 16–3 A Poisson Distribution Is Usually Used to Describe the Variability in Arrival Rate

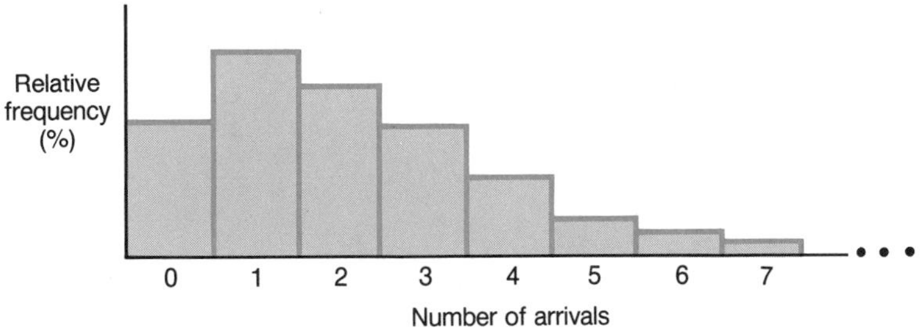

One key question is whether customers arrive at the system in single units (i.e., one at a time) or whether they arrive in batches. For instance, cars usually arrive at a car wash singly, whereas an entire busload of customers may arrive at a fast-food restaurant. Some situations might be called borderline cases: Theater patrons sometimes arrive in groups of two or more, as do diners at restaurants. For cases in which some arrivals are single units and others are small groups, we often treat them as single-unit arrivals for convenience. In fact, all of the models described in this chapter assume single unit arrivals.

A second key question relates to the distribution of customer arrivals. Generally, the models require that the arrival *rate* variability follow a *Poisson* distribution. A typical distribution is illustrated in Figure 16–3. An equivalent distribution that describes the **interarrival time** (i.e., the average time between arrivals) when the arrival rate is Poisson, is the *negative exponential* distribution. A typical distribution is illustrated in Figure 16–4. Note that the Poisson distribution describes a *discrete* random variable, which is the number of customers per unit of time, whereas the exponential distribution describes a *continuous* random variable, which is the time between arrivals. Perhaps the relationship between these two distributions can be understood better through an example. Suppose that the mean arrival rate of cars at a car wash is four cars per hour and this arrival rate can be described by a Poisson distribution. Therefore, the mean time between arrivals is 15 minutes (i.e., the *reciprocal* of the arrival rate of four per hour, which is ¼ hour), and this can be described by a negative exponential distribution.

Poisson arrival rates are commonly used in practice, and all of the models described in this chapter assume a Poisson distribution for the arrival rate. In practice, it may be necessary to determine if this assumption is true by using a Chi-square goodness-of-fit test.[1] For cases in which the assumption of a Poisson distribution does not hold, simulation (see the next chapter) may be the most reasonable alternative.

[1] Although beyond the scope of this text, Chi-square tests are commonly described in most basic statistics textbooks.

FIGURE 16–4 If the Arrival *Rate* Is Poisson, the Interarrival *Time* Is a Negative Exponential

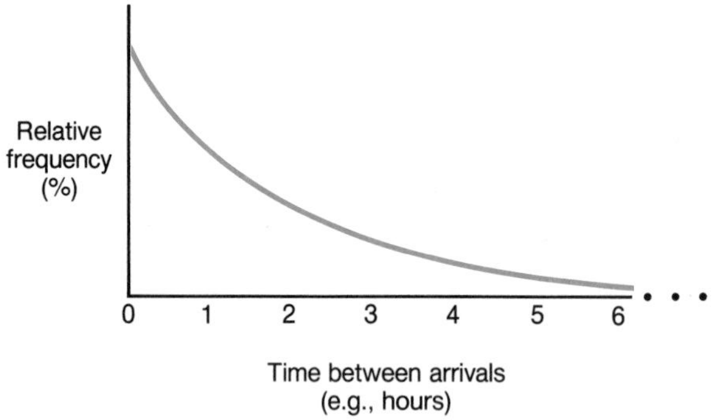

The Waiting Line

The waiting line consists of customers who have been admitted to the system and are awaiting service. In the car wash illustration, the waiting line would consist of cars lined up waiting to be washed. Some key issues are whether arriving customers may refuse to enter the system **(balking),** say, because of a long waiting line; whether customers may arrive, wait for a while, but then leave without being served **(reneging),** or whether customers may switch lines (e.g., checkout lines at supermarkets) in an attempt to lessen waiting time **(jockeying).** The models in this chapter do not deal with these interesting, but somewhat complex, situations. Instead, all models assume that once customers enter the queue, they remain there until they have been served. Moreover, a single waiting line is assumed in which customers are directed to the next available server.

Processing Order

A commonly encountered **queue discipline** (processing order) rule is *first-come, first-served*. When people are involved, this rule is widely perceived as "fair." In some instances, customers take a number when they enter the line (e.g., at a bakery, at a delicatessen takeout counter, or at a catalog sales desk in a department store); in other instances, customers actually wait in a single line (e.g., at many banks and post offices). Another approach is to assign arriving customers a **priority** classification, and process waiting customers according to those priorities. A hospital emergency room is an example of such a system; seriously ill or injured persons are treated before those with lesser illnesses or injuries. Similarly, time-sharing computer systems usually have priority classifications for jobs (e.g., the shortest job first), factories may process rush jobs ahead of routine jobs, and at many firms, orders of important customers may be processed ahead of orders of less important customers.

Both priority and first-come, first-served (FCFS) systems are presented in this chapter; however, most models use the first-come, first-served rule.

Service

The key issues for service concern the number of servers, the number of steps in the service process, and the distribution of service time.

A service center can have one server (**single channel**) or more than one server (**multiple channel**). Unless otherwise specified, we will assume that servers work *independently,* so that if a system has three servers, for example, this implies that as many as three customers could be handled simultaneously. Conversely, if you are told that the three servers work together as a crew, they would be treated as a single-channel system. Both single-channel and multiple-channel models are described in this chapter.

Service may consist of one or a few steps that are handled together (e.g., a banking transaction that consists of making a deposit and cashing a check, or simply making a deposit). This is called **single phase.** Converely, some systems involve a series of steps (e.g., multiple-step manufacturing processes, registration at a university where students move through a sequence of checkpoints, loan processing that requires multiple steps before final approval or rejection). Such service systems are called **multiple phase.** All models in this chapter assume single-phase systems.

A comparison of single- and multiple-channel, and single- and multiple-phase systems is presented in Figure 16–5.

The third important issue is the *distribution* of processing or service time. The most common assumption is that service time can be described by a negative exponential distribution[2] (see Figure 16–6). The implication of this sort of distribution is that most customers require short service times, a small proportion require moderate service times, and a few may require relatively long service times. In practice, exponential service times seem less pervasive than Poisson arrival rates. However, for simplicity, most of the models described in this chapter assume an exponential service time distribution.

Again, testing the assumption of a distribution would involve the use of a Chi-square goodness-of-fit test. If the assumption does not hold, either another queuing model, which does not require this assumption, should be used, or simulation could be used.

Exit

The final consideration is what customers do after leaving the system. For them, possible choices include rejoining the source pool immediately, rejoining the

[2] Exponentially distributed service *times* are equivalent to Poisson-distributed service rates. So, if the service rate is Poisson with mean μ, then the service time is exponential with mean $1/\mu$, and vice versa.

FIGURE 16–5 Comparison of Single- and Multiple-Channel Queuing Systems

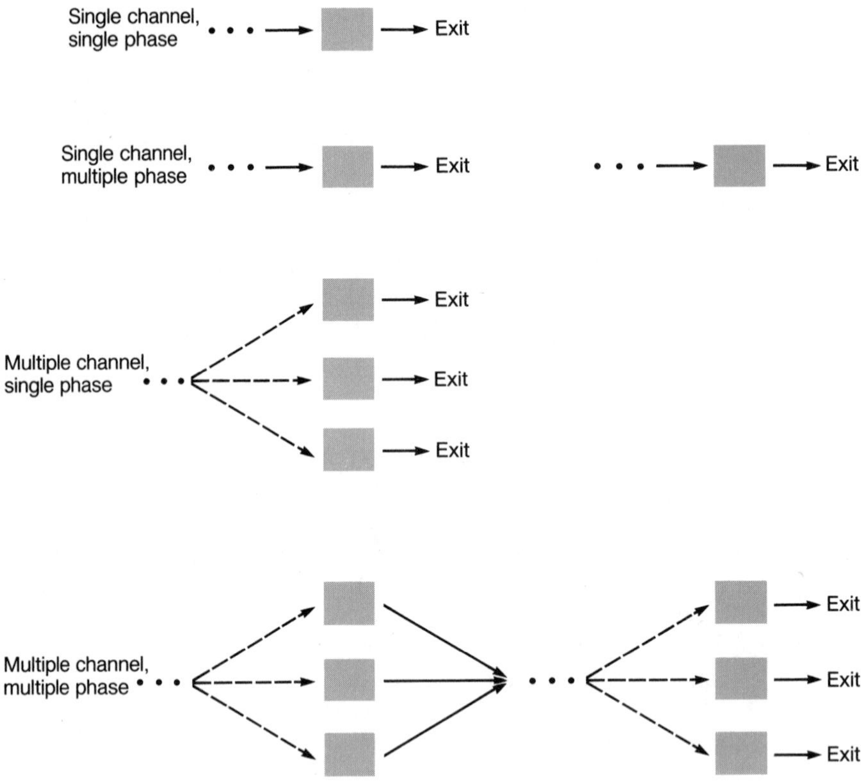

FIGURE 16–6 An Exponential Service-Time Distribution

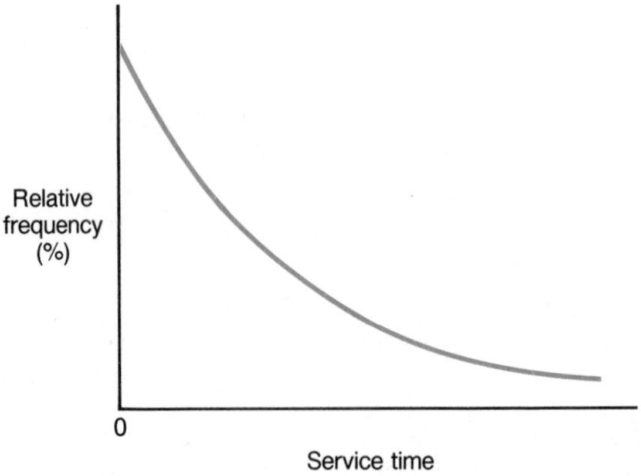

source pool after a delayed interval (e.g., hospital patients recovering at home, car wash customers not immediately returning for another wash, and so on), and permanent departure from the pool (e.g., patients who develop a permanent immunity to a disease). The models presented here assume either an immediate return to the pool (especially with limited calling populations) or a population that is large enough so that delayed returns or permanent departures have almost no impact on the arrival rate.

MEASURES OF SYSTEM PERFORMANCE

A number of different performance measures can be computed that summarize queuing behavior given the customer arrival rate, the number of servers, the service rate, and certain other information. Among the most commonly used measures are the following:

L_q = the average number waiting for service
L = the average number in the system (i.e., waiting or being served)
P_0 = the probability of zero units in the system
ρ = the system utilization (percentage of time servers are busy serving customers)
W_q = the average time customers must wait for service
W = the average time customers spend in the system (i.e., waiting for service and service time)
M = the expected maximum number waiting for service for a given level of confidence

One additional measure is the total cost of the system, which is generally based on the cost of customer waiting time and the cost of server time.

For example, the future owner of a proposed car wash may want to know the following:

1. On the average, how many cars/customers will be waiting for a wash?
2. How long, on the average, will a customer have to wait in line?
3. What proportion of the time will no customers be in the system?
4. What will be the upper limit on the number of cars waiting that will not be exceeded, say, 99 percent of the time?
5. How sensitive are the peformance measures to changes in either the number of servers or the service rate? How sensitive is the system to changes in the arrival rate?
6. What level of capacity will minimize the sum of capacity costs and customer waiting costs?

Two key parameters in any queuing system are the mean arrival rate, which is represented by the Greek letter λ (lambda), and the mean service rate, which is represented by the Greek letter μ (mu). Table 16–1 presents the symbols for number waiting and time waiting in an easy to remember format.

TABLE 16–1 Line and Service Symbols for Average Number Waiting, and Average Waiting and Service Times

	System: In the waiting line	System: Being served	In the system
Average number	L_q	$\frac{\lambda}{\mu}$	$L_q + \frac{\lambda}{\mu}$
Average time	W_q	$\frac{1}{\mu}$	$W_q + \frac{1}{\mu}$

where

λ = mean arrival rate
μ = mean service rate

In the following pages, models are presented that provide formulas and tables enabling one to determine values for various measures of system performance. All of these formulas and table values pertain to a system that is in a *steady state*. In a steady state, various measures, such as the average number waiting in line, or the average waiting time, are *independent* of a particular time. That is not always the case, though. Very often, when a system begins operating after a period of inactivity (e.g., a bank opens in the morning, repair crews arrive for work after a long weekend, and so on), a system goes through a transient state before it settles down. For instance, there may already be a line of customers waiting outside the bank before it opens. Then, too, when human servers are involved, they often go through a warmup period before they reach their usual operating efficiency. Once the system moves into its normal operating pattern, it is usually considered to be in a steady state, and that condition is the one to which the various models apply.

Basic Relationships

There are certain fundamental relationships that hold for all infinite source models. These relationships can be valuable for converting performance measures from *number* waiting to *time* waiting, and vice versa. The most useful of these relationships are:

1. The average number being served:

$$r = \frac{\lambda}{\mu} \quad \text{where} \quad \begin{aligned} \lambda &= \text{customer arrival rate} \\ \mu &= \text{service rate} \end{aligned} \qquad (16\text{–}1)$$

2. The average number in the system:

$$L = L_q + r \qquad (16\text{–}2)$$

where

$$L = \text{average number in the system}$$
$$L_q = \text{average number in line}$$

3. The average time in line:

$$W_q = \frac{L_q}{\lambda} \tag{16–3}$$

4. The average time in the system, including service:

$$W_s = W_q + \frac{1}{\mu} \tag{16–4}$$

5. System utilization (proportion of time servers are busy)

$$\rho = \frac{\lambda}{s\mu} \tag{16–5}$$

where

$$s = \text{number of channels or servers}$$

In order for a system to be feasible (i.e., underloaded), system utilization must be less than 1.00.

■

EXAMPLE

The owner of a car wash franchise intends to construct another car wash in a suburban location. Based on experience, the owner estimates that the arrival rate for the proposed facility will be 20 cars per hour and the service rate will be 25 cars per hour. (Let's assume, for the sake of illustration, that the arrival rate is Poisson and the service time is exponential). Service time will be variable because all cars are washed by hand rather than by machine. Cars will be processed one at a time (hence, this is a single-channel, or one-servicer, system). Determine the following:

1. The average number of cars being washed.
2. The average number of cars in the system (i.e., either being washed or waiting to be washed), for a case where the average number waiting in line is 3.2.
3. The average time in line (i.e., the average time cars wait to get washed).
4. The average time cars spend in the system (i.e., waiting in line and being washed).
5. The system utilization.

Solution

Arrival rate, λ, = 20 cars per hour

Service rate, μ, = 25 cars per hour

Number of servers, s, = 1

$L_q = 3.2$

1. $r = \frac{\lambda}{\mu} = \frac{20}{25} = .80$ cars being served

2. $L = L_q + r$
   $= 3.2 + .8 = 4.0$ cars

3. $W_q = \frac{L_q}{\lambda}$
   $= \frac{3.2}{20 \text{ cars per hour}} = .16$ hour, which is .16 hour × 60 minutes/hour
   $= 9.6$ minutes

4. $W_s = W_q + \frac{1}{\mu}$
   $= .16 \text{ hour} + \frac{1}{25} \text{ hour} = .20$ hour, which is .20 hour × 60 minutes/hour
   or 12 minutes

5. $\rho = \frac{\lambda}{s\mu} = \frac{20 \text{ cars per hour}}{(1)(25 \text{ cars/per hour})} = .80$, or 80 percent

---

QUEUING MODELS

In this section, the following queuing models are described:

1. Basic single-channel.
2. Multiple-channel.

Basic Single-Channel Model

This model pertains to situations in which there is one channel or server that processes all customers. Note that if a group of servers works as a single team, that situation would be considered a single-channel system.

A single-channel model is appropriate when these conditions exist:

1. One server or channel.
2. A Poisson arrival rate.
3. A negative exponential service time.
4. Processing order is first-come, first-served.
5. The calling population is infinite.
6. There is no limit on queue length.

The necessary formulas for the single-server model are presented in Table 16–2. The formulas enable us to compute various measures of system performance. For the most part, the meaning of each measure is readily apparent. One exception may be the last measure: Average waiting time for an arrival that is not immediately served.

TABLE 16–2 Formulas for Basic Single Server Model

Performance Measure	Formula	Formula Number
System utilization	$\rho = \frac{\lambda}{\mu}$	(16–6)
Average number in line	$L_q = \frac{\lambda^2}{\mu(\mu - \lambda)}$	(16–7)
Average number in system	$L = L_q + \frac{\lambda}{\mu}$	(16–8)
Average time in line	$W_q = \frac{L_q}{\lambda}$	(16–9)
Average time in system	$W = W_q + \frac{1}{\mu}$	(16–10)
Probability of zero units in the *system*	$P_0 = 1 - \left(\frac{\lambda}{\mu}\right)$	(16–11)
Probability of *n* units in the *system*	$P_n = P_0\left(\frac{\lambda}{\mu}\right)^n$	(16–12)
Probability the waiting line won't exceed *k* units	$P_{n \le k} = 1 - \left(\frac{\lambda}{\mu}\right)^{k+1}$	(16–13)
Average waiting time for an arrival not served immediately	$W_a = \frac{1}{\mu - \lambda}$	(16–14)

Let us consider that measure somewhat further. Suppose we observe a system for a period of time, and that during that time, five customers arrive. Suppose, further, that their waiting times (in minutes) are 2.1, 0, 1.4, 0, and .8. We can determine their average waiting time by summing their waiting times and dividing by 5. This would be analogous to W_q. Now suppose we focus on just those who actually waited (the 0 times mean that those customers went directly into service; they did not have to wait in line). Hence, the average time for those who had to wait would be the three nonzero times divided by 3. Note that in both cases, the numerator (the sum of times) would be the same. By eliminating those who did not wait, we obtain a higher average waiting time than we did with all arrivals included. Hence, if we are truly concerned with the waiting times of those who actually wait, we should then focus on W_a rather than on W_q.

With that in mind, let us take a moment to see how the formula for W_a can be derived. We have just seen that W_q is made up of two parts; actual waiting and nonwaiting. In fact, W_q is the *weighted average* of W_a and 0. That is, the proportion of customers that don't wait is $1 - \frac{\lambda}{\mu}$ (i.e., P_0), and the proportion that do wait is $1 - \left[1 - \frac{\lambda}{\mu}\right] = \frac{\lambda}{\mu}$ W_q is equal to the proportion that wait multiplied by W_a plus the proportion that don't wait multiplied by 0, divided by the sum of the weights:

$$W_q = \frac{\frac{\lambda}{\mu} W_a + \left(1 - \frac{\lambda}{\mu}\right) 0}{\frac{\lambda}{\mu} + \left(1 - \frac{\lambda}{\mu}\right) = 1} = \frac{\lambda}{\mu} W_a$$

Now refer to Table 16–2 for the formula for W_q. You can see that it is L_q divided by λ. Referring to Formula 16–7, we can see that $W_q = \frac{\lambda}{\mu(\mu - \lambda)}$. We just found that $W_q = \frac{\lambda}{\mu} W_a$. Substituting the equation for W_q here, we can solve for W_a:

$$W_q = \frac{\lambda}{\mu(\mu - \lambda)} = \frac{\lambda}{\mu} W_a \quad \text{so} \quad W_a = \frac{\frac{\lambda}{\mu(\mu - \lambda)}}{\frac{\lambda}{\mu}} = \frac{1}{\mu - \lambda}$$

■

EXAMPLE 2 The mean arrival rate of customers at a ticket counter with one server is 3 per minute, and the mean service rate is 4 customers per minute. Calculate each of the performance measures listed in Table 16–2. Suppose that $n = 2$ and $k = 5$.

Solution

1. $\rho = \frac{3}{4} = .75$, or 75 percent
2. $L_q = \frac{3^2}{4(4 - 3)} = 2.25$ customers.
3. $L = 2.25 + \frac{3}{4} = 3.00$ customers.
4. $W_q = \frac{2.25}{3} = .75$ minutes.
5. $W = .75 + \frac{1}{4} = 1.00$ minute.
6. $P_0 = 1 - \frac{3}{4} = .25$. This means that the probability is 25 percent that an arriving unit will not have to wait for service. Hence, the probability that an arrival *will* have to wait for service is 75 percent.
7. $P_{n=2} = .25 \left(\frac{3}{4}\right)^2 = .1406$.
8. $P_{n \leq 5} = .1 - \left(\frac{3}{4}\right)^{5+1} = .822$.
9. $W_a = \frac{1}{4 - 3} = 1.0$ minute.

TABLE 16–3

λ	μ	λ/μ	L_q Using Formula 16–7
3.00	5	.60	.900
3.50	5	.70	1.633
4.00	5	.80	3.200
4.50	5	.90	8.100
4.75	5	.95	18.050

FIGURE 16–7 As Utilization Approaches 100 percent, L_q and W_q Rapidly Increase

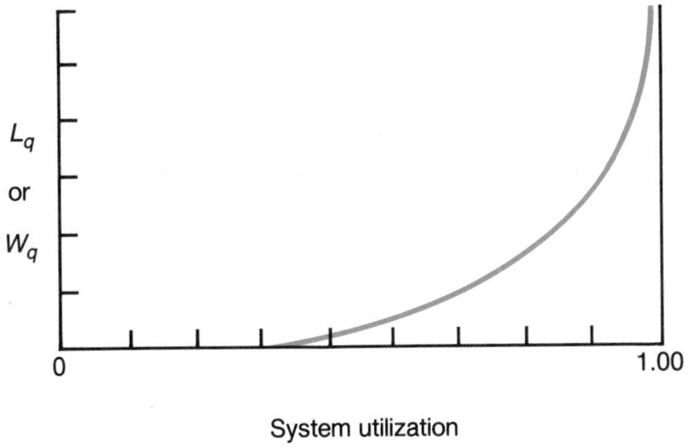

An important characteristic of queuing systems with variable arrival and service rates can be illustrated by noting what happens to the average number waiting for service as the utilization ratio increases. Table 16–3 lists values of L_q for a sequence of increases in **system utilization.** You can see that as utilization increases, the average number waiting in line increases. Note, too, that as the utilization ratio gets closer and closer to the maximum of 100 percent, the average line length increases rapidly, as illustrated in Figure 16–7. The moral is obvious: Heavily loaded systems will tend to have a disproportionate amount of waiting time. By the same token, when a system is heavily loaded, a disproportionate reduction in both the average number waiting and the time they wait can be achieved by modest reductions in the utilization (say, by increasing the service rate or reducing the arrival rate).

Multiple-Channel Model

The multiple-server, or multiple-channel model, as it is sometimes referred to, is very similar to the single-server model, except that the number of servers is not limited to one. The multiple-channel model is appropriate when these conditions exist:

1. A Poisson arrival rate.
2. A negative exponential service time.
3. The processing order is first-come, first-served.
4. The calling population is infinite.
5. There is no upper limit on queue length.
6. All servers have the same mean service rate.

In order to achieve first-come, first-served processing, some systems may have customers wait in a single line (e.g., most post offices). Other systems record order of arrival (e.g., busy restaurants) or have customers take a number on arrival (e.g., some bakeries and deli counters). Usually, supermarket checkouts would not fall into the multiple-channel category, even though they have multiple checkouts, because customers do not form a single line (i.e., they are not necessarily served in order of arrival at the checkout area).

Note that with the multiple-server model, s must be large enough that the condition $s\mu > \lambda$ is satisfied. Otherwise, the system will not be feasible because it is overloaded.

The multiple-server formulas are presented in Table 16–4.

EXAMPLE 3 The management of a grocery chain plans to open a new store. The store will have a bakery counter with a projected mean arrival rate during the evening hours of 1.2 customers per minute. Three clerks will be employed, and each will have an average service rate of one customer per minute. Compute each of the performance measures listed in Table 16–4 using the formulas. Additional information will be given where necessary in order to illustrate the solution.

Solution

$\lambda = 1.2$ customers per minute

$\mu = 1.0$ customer per minute

$s = 3$ servers

1. $$\rho = \frac{1.2}{3(1.0)} = .40.$$

2. $$L_q = \frac{1.2(1.0)\left(\frac{1.2}{1.0}\right)^3}{(3-1)!(3(1.0)-1.2)^2} P_0$$
$$= .32P_0$$

TABLE 16–4 Multiple-Channel Formulas

Performance Measure	Formula	Formula Number
System utilization	$\rho = \dfrac{\lambda}{s\mu}$	(16–15)
Average number in line	$L_q = \dfrac{\lambda\mu\left(\frac{\lambda}{\mu}\right)^s}{(s-1)!(s\mu-\lambda)^2} P_0$	(16–16)
Average number in the system	$L = L_q + \dfrac{\lambda}{\mu}$	(16–17)
Average time in line	$W_q = \dfrac{L_q}{\lambda}$	(16–18)
Average time in the system	$W = W_q + \dfrac{1}{\mu}$	(16–19)
Probability of zero units in the system	$P_0 = \left[\sum_{n=0}^{s-1} \dfrac{\left(\frac{\lambda}{\mu}\right)^n}{n!} + \dfrac{\left(\frac{\lambda}{\mu}\right)^s}{s!\left(1-\frac{\lambda}{s\mu}\right)}\right]^{-1}$	(16–20)
Probability of n units in the system, where $n \leq s$	$P_n = P_0 \dfrac{\left(\frac{\lambda}{\mu}\right)^n}{n!}$	(16–21)
Probability of n units in the *system,* where $n > s$	$P_n = \dfrac{P_0\left(\frac{\lambda}{\mu}\right)^n}{s!(s^{n-s})}$	(16–22)
Average waiting time for an arrival not immediately served	$W_a = \dfrac{1}{s\,\mu - \lambda}$	(16–23)
Probability that an arrival will have to wait for service	$P_w = \left(\dfrac{\lambda}{\mu}\right)^s \dfrac{P_0}{s!\left(1-\frac{\lambda}{s\mu}\right)}$	(16–24)

s = number of servers or channels

$$P_0 = \frac{1}{\left[\frac{\left(\frac{1.2}{1.0}\right)^0}{0!} + \frac{\left(\frac{1.2}{1.0}\right)^1}{1!} + \frac{\left(\frac{1.2}{1.0}\right)^2}{2!}\right] + \frac{\left(\frac{1.2}{1.0}\right)^3}{3!\left(1 - \frac{1.2}{3(1.0)}\right)}} = .294$$

$L_q = .32(.294) = .094$ customers

3. $L = .094 + \dfrac{1.2}{1.0} = 1.294.$

4. $W_q = \dfrac{.094}{1.2} = .078$ minutes.

5. $W = .078 = \dfrac{1}{1.0} = 1.078$ minutes.

6. P_0 (see part 2 above).

7. Suppose $n = 2$.

$$P_2 = \frac{.294\left(\frac{1.2}{1.0}\right)^2}{2!} = .212$$

8. Suppose $n = 4$.

$$P_4 = \frac{.294\left(\frac{1.2}{1.0}\right)^4}{3!(3^{4-3})} = \frac{.60964}{18} = .034$$

9. $$W_a = \frac{1}{3(1.0) - 1.2} = .556 \text{ minutes.}$$

10. $$P_w = \left(\frac{1.2}{1.0}\right)^3 \frac{.294}{3!\left(1 - \frac{1.2}{3(1.0)}\right)} = .141.$$

The computations for some of the multiple-server performance measures can be quite formidable, particularly for large values of s. Fortunately, there is an easier method for obtaining values for two key performance measures, L_q and P_0. Table 16–5 contains those values for selected values of λ/μ. The advantage of having a table that can provide values of L_q and P_0 can be seen from these two lists of performance measures that can be computed from them:

L_q : L, W, and W_q
P_0 : P_n and P_w

The remaining measures do not involve the computational burden that the listed measures do. Thus, obtaining performance measures for many multiple-channel problems is, indeed, simplified. The exception would be for situations in which the ratio λ/μ is not listed in the table, although, even then, rounding to a listed value is often reasonable.

To use the table, determine the value of λ/μ and read L_q and P_0 for s. For instance, in the preceding example with $\lambda/\mu = 1.2$, we found the value of L_q to be .094 after considerable effort. That same value can be read from Table 16–5. At the same time, we can read the value $P_0 = .294$, which agrees with the previous calculated value. We can further appreciate the value of having this table by considering this question: What are the values of L_q when $\lambda/\mu = 1.2$ for $s = 2$, 3, 4, and 5? We can quickly read all of the values from the table. Thus, we find $L_q =$ .675 for $s = 2$, .094 for $s = 3$, and .016 for $s = 4$.

The table also allows us to gain some insight into how sensitive a queuing system is to changes in the utilization. For example, suppose $\lambda/\mu = 2.9$. With three servers, the utilization is $2.9/3 = .967$, a fairly high load. This results in a high average number waiting (27.193). Adding one server reduces the utilization to $2.9/4 = .725$, and the average waiting line is reduced to 1.234. Thus, modest changes to a heavily loaded system can produce rather sizeable improvements in such performance measures as the average number waiting in line and in the system, and the associated average waiting times in line and system. For lighter system loads, the improvements become less and less: Adding a fifth server yields a reduction of about 1.0 in the average number waiting, and adding a sixth server yields a reduction of only about .20.

Finally, note that the single-channel model is a special case of the more general multiple-channel model. Therefore, single-channel problems can also be handled using Table 16–5.

Determining Maximum Line Lengths

An important issue in queuing system design relates to the amount of space that will be needed to accommodate waiting customers. This, naturally, is a function of the maximum expected length of the waiting line. Theoretically, for infinite source systems, the line can be infinitely long. However, in practical terms, it is possible to determine a figure for the number of customers waiting that will not be exceeded a specified percentage of time. For example, we could determine the line length that probably will not be exceeded 95 percent of the time or 99 percent of the time.

An approximate line length that will satisfy any stated probability can be determined by solving the following equation for n:

$$\rho^n = K \qquad (16\text{–}25)$$

where

$$K = \frac{1 - \text{Probability}}{L_q(1 - \rho)}$$

and L_q is from Table 16–5.

The equation can be readily solved using logarithms (either to the base 10, or to the base e):

$$n = \frac{\log K}{\log \rho} \quad \text{or} \quad \frac{\ln K}{\ln \rho} \qquad (16\text{–}26)$$

The resulting value of n usually will not be an integer. In general, *round up* to the next higher integer and use that value as n_{max}.

TABLE 16–5 Infinite Source Values for L_q and P_0 given λ/μ and s

λ/μ	s	L_q	P_0
.15	1	.026	.850
	2	.001	.860
.20	1	.050	.800
	2	.002	.818
.25	1	.083	.750
	2	.004	.778
.30	1	.129	.700
	2	.007	.739
.35	1	.188	.650
	2	.011	.702
.40	1	.267	.600
	2	.017	.667
.45	1	.368	.550
	2	.024	.633
	3	.002	.637
.50	1	.500	.500
	2	.033	.600
	3	.003	.606
.55	1	.672	.450
	2	.045	.569
	3	.004	.576
.60	1	.900	.400
	2	.059	.538
	3	.006	.548
.65	1	1.207	.350
	2	.077	.509
	3	.008	.521
.70	1	1.633	.300
	2	.098	.481
	3	.011	.495
.75	1	2.250	.250
	2	.123	.455
	3	.015	.471
.80	1	3.200	
	2	.152	.429
	3	.019	.447
.85	1	4.817	.150
	2	.187	.404
	3	.024	.425
	4	.003	.427
90	1	8.100	.100
	2	.229	.379
	3	.030	.403
	4	.004	.406
.95	1	18.050	.050
	2	.277	.356
	3	.037	.383
	4	.005	.386
1.0	2	.333	.333
	3	.045	.364
	4	.007	.367

λ/μ	s	L_q	P_0
1.1	2	.477	.290
	3	.066	.327
	4	.011	.367
1.2	2	.675	.250
	3	.094	.294
	4	.016	.300
	5	.003	.301
1.3	2	.951	.212
	3	.130	.264
	4	.023	.271
	5	.004	.272
1.4	2	1.345	.176
	3	.177	.236
	4	.032	.245
	5	.006	.246
1.5	2	1.929	.143
	3	.237	.211
	4	.045	.221
	5	.009	.223
1.6	2	2.844	.111
	3	.313	.187
	4	.060	.199
	5	.012	.201
1.7	2	4.426	.081
	3	.409	.166
	4	.080	.180
	5	.017	.182
1.8	2	7.674	.053
	3	.532	.146
	4	.105	.162
	5	.023	.165
1.9	2	17.587	.026
	3	.688	.128
	4	.136	.145
	5	.030	.149
	6	.007	.149
2.0	3	.889	.111
	4	.174	.130
	5	.040	.134
	6	.009	.135
2.1	3	1.149	.096
	4	.220	.117
	5	.052	.121
	6	.012	.122
2.2	3	1.491	.081
	4	.277	.105
	5	.066	.109
	6	.016	.111

λ/μ	s	L_q	P_0
2.3	3	1.951	.068
	4	.346	.093
	5	.084	.099
	6	.021	.100
2.4	3	2.589	.056
	4	.431	.083
	5	.105	.089
	6	.027	.090
	7	.007	.091
2.5	3	3.511	.045
	4	.533	.074
	5	.130	.080
	6	.034	.082
	7	.009	.082
2.6	3	4.933	.035
	4	.658	.065
	5	.161	.072
	6	.043	.074
	7	.011	.074
2.7	3	7.354	.025
	4	.811	.057
	5	.198	.065
	6	.053	.067
	7	.014	.067
2.8	3	12.273	.016
	4	1.000	.050
	5	.241	.058
	6	.066	.060
	7	.018	.061
2.9	3	27.193	.008
	4	1.234	.044
	5	.293	.052
	6	.081	.054
	7	.023	.055
3.0	4	1.528	.038
	5	.354	.047
	6	.099	.049
	7	.028	.050
	8	.008	.050
3.1	4	1.902	.032
	5	.427	.042
	6	.120	.044
	7	.035	.045
	8	.010	.045
3.2	4	2.386	.027
	5	.513	.037
	6	.145	.040
	7	.043	.040
	8	.012	.041

TABLE 16–5 *(continued)*

λ/μ	s	L_q	P_0
3.3	4	3.027	.023
	5	.615	.033
	6	.174	.036
	7	.052	.037
	8	.015	.037
3.4	4	3.906	.019
	5	.737	.029
	6	.209	.032
	7	.063	.033
	8	.019	.033
3.5	4	5.165	.015
	5	.882	.026
	6	.248	.029
	7	.076	.030
	8	.023	.030
	9	.007	.030
3.6	4	7.090	.011
	5	1.055	.023
	6	.295	.026
	7	.091	.027
	8	.028	.027
	9	.008	.027
3.7	4	10.347	.008
	5	1.265	.020
	6	.349	.023
	7	.1099	.024
	8	.034	.025
	9	.010	.025
3.8	4	16.937	.005
	5	1.519	.017
	6	.412	.021
	7	.129	.022
	8	.041	.022
	9	.013	.022
3.9	4	36.859	.002
	5	1.830	.015
	6	.485	.019
	7	.153	.020
	8	.050	.020
	9	.016	.020
4.0	5	2.216	.013
	6	.570	.017
	7	.180	.018
	8	.059	.018
	9	.019	.018
4.1	5	2.703	.011
	6	.668	.015
	7	.212	.016
	8	.070	.016
	9	.023	.017

λ/μ	s	L_q	P_0
4.2	5	3.327	.009
	6	.784	.013
	7	.248	.014
	8	.083	.015
	9	.027	.015
	10	.009	.015
4.3	5	4.149	.008
	6	.919	.012
	7	.289	.130
	8	.097	.013
	9	.033	.014
	10	.011	.014
4.4	5	5.268	.006
	6	1.078	.010
	7	.337	.012
	8	.114	.012
	9	.039	.012
	10	.013	.012
4.5	5	6.862	.005
	6	1.265	.009
	7	.391	.010
	8	.133	.011
	9	.046	.011
	10	.015	.011
4.6	5	9.289	.004
	6	1.487	.008
	7	.453	.009
	8	.156	.010
	9	.054	.010
	10	.018	.010
4.7	5	13.382	.003
	6	1.752	.007
	7	.525	.008
	8	.181	.008
	9	.064	.009
	10	.022	.009
4.8	5	21.641	.002
	6	2.071	.006
	7	.607	.008
	8	.209	.008
	9	.074	.008
	10	.026	.008
4.9	5	46.566	.001
	6	2.459	.005
	7	.702	.007
	8	.242	.007
	9	.087	.007
	10	.031	.007
	11	.011	.077

λ/μ	s	L_q	P_0
5.0	6	2.938	.005
	7	.810	.006
	8	.279	.006
	9	.101	.007
	10	.036	.007
	11	.013	.007
5.1	6	3.536	.004
	7	.936	.005
	8	.321	.006
	9	.117	.006
	10	.042	.006
	11	.015	.006
5.2	6	4.301	.003
	7	1.081	.005
	8	.368	.005
	9	.135	.005
	10	.049	.005
	11	.017	.006
5.3	6	5.303	.003
	7	1.249	.004
	8	.422	.005
	9	.155	.005
	10	.057	.005
	11	.021	.005
	12	.007	.005
5.4	6	6.661	.002
	7	1.444	.004
	8	.483	.004
	9	.178	.004
	10	.066	.004
	11	.024	.005
	12	.009	.005
5.5	6	8.590	.002
	7	1.674	.003
	8	.553	.004
	9	.204	.004
	10	.077	.004
	11	.028	.004
	12	.010	.004
5.6	6	11.519	.001
	7	1.944	.003
	8	.631	.003
	9	.233	.004
	10	.088	.004
	11	.033	.004
	12	.012	.004

TABLE 16–5 *(continued)*

λ/μ	s	L_q	P_0
5.7	6	16.446	.001
	7	2.264	.002
	8	.721	.003
	9	.266	.003
	10	.102	.003
	11	.038	.003
	12	.014	.003
5.8	6	26.373	.001
	7	2.648	.002
	8	.823	.003
	9	.303	.003
	10	.116	.003
	11	.044	.003
	12	.017	.003
5.9	6	56.300	.000
	7	3.113	.002
	8	.939	.002
	9	.345	.003
	10	.133	.003
	11	.051	.003
	12	.019	.003
6.0	7	3.683	.001
	8	1.071	.002
	9	.392	.002
	10	.152	.002
	11	.059	.002
	12	.022	.002
6.1	7	4.394	.001
	8	1.222	.002
	9	.445	.002
	10	.173	.002
	11	.068	.002
	12	.026	.002
6.2	7	5.298	.001
	8	1.397	.002
	9	.504	.002
	10	.197	.002
	11	.078	.002
	12	.030	.002
6.3	7	6.480	.001
	8	1.598	.001
	9	.571	.002
	10	.223	.002
	11	.089	.002
	12	.035	.002
6.4	7	8.077	.001
	8	1.831	.001
	9	.645	.002
	10	.253	.002
	11	.101	.002
	12	.040	.002
6.5	7	10.341	.001
	8	2.102	.001
	9	.730	.001
	10	.285	.001
	11	.115	.001
	12	.046	.001
6.6	7	13.770	.000
	8	2.420	.001
	9	.825	.001
	10	.285	.001
	11	.130	.001
	12	.052	.001
6.7	7	19.532	.000
	8	2.796	.001
	9	.932	.001
	10	.363	.001
	11	.147	.001
	12	.060	.001
6.8	7	31.127	.000
	8	3.245	.001
	9	1.054	.001
	10	.409	.001
	11	.167	.001
	12	.068	.001
6.9	7	66.055	.000
	8	3.786	.001
	9	1.191	.001
	10	.460	.001
	11	.188	.001
	12	.077	.001
7.0	8	4.447	.001
	9	1.347	.001
	10	.517	.001
	11	.212	.001
	12	.088	.001
7.1	8	5.270	.000
	9	1.525	.001
	10	.581	.001
	11	.238	.001
	12	.099	.001
7.2	8	6.314	.000
	9	1.729	.001
	10	.652	.001
	11	.268	.001
	12	.112	.001
7.3	8	7.675	.0003
	9	1.963	.0005
	10	.732	.0006
	11	.300	.0007
	12	.126	.0007
7.4	8	9.511	.0003
	9	2.233	.0005
	10	.820	.0006
	11	.337	.0006
	12	.142	.0006
7.5	8	12.109	.0002
	9	2.546	.0004
	10	.920	.0005
	11	.377	.0005
	12	.160	.0005
7.6	8	16.039	.0002
	9	2.912	.0004
	10	1.031	.0004
	11	.421	.0005
	12	.179	.0005
7.7	8	22.636	.0001
	9	3.343	.0003
	10	1.157	.0004
	11	.471	.0004
	12	.201	.0004
7.8	8	35.898	.0001
	9	3.856	.0002
	10	1.298	.0004
	11	.525	.0004
	12	.224	.0004

TABLE 16–5 *(concluded)*

λ/μ	s	L_q	P_0	λ/μ	s	L_q	P_0	λ/μ	s	L_q	P_0
7.9	8	75.827	.00003	8.1	9	6.161	.00017	8.4	9	10.9960	.00009
	9	4.474	.00023		10	1.841	.00025		10	2.647	.00017
	10	1.457	.00031		11	.728	.00028		11	1.006	.00020
	11	.586	.00035		12	.312	.00029		12	.429	.00021
	12	.251	.00036								
				8.2	9	7.344	.00014	8.5	9	13.891	.00007
8.0	9	5.227	.00020		10	2.074	.00022		10	3.003	.00015
	10	1.637	.00028		11	.811	.00025		11	1.121	.00018
	11	.653	.00031		12	.347	.00026		12	.476	.00019
	12	.280	.00033								
				8.3	9	8.884	.00011				
					10	2.341	.00019				
					11	.903	.00022				
					12	.386	.00024				

EXAMPLE 4 Determine the maximum number of customers waiting in line for probabilities of both 95 percent and 99 percent for this situation:

$s = 1$

$\lambda = 4$ per hour

$\mu = 5$ per hour

Solution

$$\rho = \frac{\lambda}{s\mu} = \frac{4}{1(5)} = .80 \text{ and } \frac{\lambda}{\mu} = \frac{4}{5} = .80$$

From Table 16–5 with $\frac{\lambda}{\mu} = .80$ and $s = 1$, $L_q = 3.2$.

$$\text{For 95 percent, } K = \frac{1 - .95}{3.2(1 - .80)} = .078$$

$$n = \frac{\log .078}{\log .80} = 11.43 \quad \text{Hence, } n_{\max} = 12$$

$$\text{For 99 percent, } K = \frac{1 - .99}{3.2(1 - .80)} = 0.156$$

$$n = \frac{\log .0156}{\log .80} = 18.64 \quad \text{Hence, } n_{\max} = 19$$

In some instances, the solution to Formula 16–26 will yield a negative value for n. If that happens, round up to zero. That happens when a system is only very lightly loaded and, in effect, most of the time there will not be a waiting line; hence, the zero.

A related question of interest is the number of channels needed to achieve a specified n_{max}. For example, the platform manager of a commercial bank may want to know how many tellers will be needed to hold the maximum number of waiting customers to 7. The solution to this question requires successively solving Formula 16–26, incrementing s each time, until the desired n_{max} is achieved.

EXAMPLE 5 Suppose that during a noon hour at a bank, the arrival rate is 8 customers per minute and the service rate is 2 customers per minute. This produces λ/μ of $8/2 = 4.0$. Using Table 16–5, we obtain the following:

s	L_q
5	2.216
6	.570
7	.180
8	.059

Using Formula 16–26 with appropriate values of ρ (as shown), n_{max} for, say, 95 percent and 99 percent can be determined:

s	ρ	$n_{.95}$	$n_{.99}$
5	.80	10	17
6	.67	4	8
7	.57	1	4
8	.50	0	

Therefore, 6 servers would achieve a probability of at least 95 percent that the number waiting would not exceed 4, while 7 servers would achieve a probability of at least 99 percent that the line would not exceed 4 waiting customers.

COST CONSIDERATIONS

The design of a service system often reflects the desire of management to balance the cost of capacity with the expected cost of customers waiting in the system. For example, in designing loading docks for a warehouse, the cost of docks plus loading crews must be balanced against the cost of trucks and drivers that will be in the system, both while waiting to be unloaded and while actually being unloaded. Similarly, the cost of having a mechanic wait for tools at a tool crib must be balanced against the cost of servers at the crib.

The optimal capacity (usually in terms of number of channels) is that which minimizes the sum of customer waiting costs and capacity or server costs. Thus, the goal would be:

$$\text{Minimize} \quad \begin{matrix}\text{Total}\\ \text{cost}\end{matrix} = \begin{matrix}\text{Customer}\\ \text{waiting cost}\end{matrix} + \begin{matrix}\text{Capacity}\\ \text{cost}\end{matrix}$$

The simplest approach to a cost analysis involves computing *system* costs; that is, computing costs for customers in the system and total capacity cost.

In order to identify the capacity size that will minimize total costs, an iterative process is used: Capacity is incremented one unit at a time (e.g., increase the number of channels by one) and the total cost is computed at each increment. Because the total cost curve is U-shaped (see Figure 16–1), usually the total cost will initially decrease as capacity is increased and then it will eventually begin to rise. Once it begins to rise, additional increases in capacity will cause it to continue to rise. Hence, once that occurs, the optimal capacity size can be readily identified.

The computation of customer waiting costs is based on the average *number* of customers in the *system*. This is, perhaps, not intuitively obvious; beginners usually feel that customer waiting *time* in the system would be more appropriate. However, that approach would pertain to only *one* customer—it would not convey information concerning *how many* customers would wait that long. Obviously, an average of 5 customers waiting would involve a lower waiting cost than an average of, say, 10 customers waiting. Therefore, it is necessary to focus on the number waiting. Moreover, if, say, an average of 2 customers are in the system, this is equivalent to having *exactly* two customers in the system at all times, even though in reality there will be times when there are 0, 1, 2, 3, or more customers in the system.

EXAMPLE 6 Trucks arrive at a warehouse at a rate of 15 per hour during business hours. Crews can unload the trucks at a rate of 5 per hour. The high unloading rate is due to cargo being containerized. Recent changes in wage rates have caused the warehouse manager to reexamine the question of how many crews to use. The new rates are: crew and dock cost is \$100 per hour; truck and driver cost is \$120 per hour.

Solution

(L_q values are from Table 16–5 using $\frac{\lambda}{\mu} = \frac{15}{5} = 3.0$.)

Crew Size	Crew/Dock Cost	$\left[L = L_q + \frac{\lambda}{\mu}\right]$ Average number in System	Driver/Truck Cost @ $120 per hour	Total Cost
4	$400	1.528 + 3.0 = 4.528	$543.36	$ 943.36
5	500	.354 + 3.0 = 3.354	402.48	902.48 (minimum)
6	600	.099 + 3.0 = 3.099	371.88	971.88
7	700	.028 + 3.0 = 3.028	363.36	1,063.36

Two crews will minimize the total cost. Note that because the total cost will continue to increase once the minimum is reached, it is not really necessary to compute total costs for crew sizes larger than 6, because total cost increased as the crew size was increased from 5 to 6, indicating that a crew size of 5 is optimal.

One additional point should be made concerning cost analysis. Because both customer waiting costs and capacity costs often reflect estimated amounts, the apparent optimal solution may not, in fact, represent the true optimum. One ramification of this is that when computations are shown to the nearest penny, or even the nearest dollar, the total cost figures may seem to imply a higher degree of precision than is really justified by the cost estimates. This is compounded by the fact that arrival and service rates may be either approximations or not be exactly represented by the Poisson/exponential distributions. Another ramification is that if cost estimates can be obtained as *ranges* (e.g., customer waiting cost is estimated to range between $40 and $50 per hour), total costs should be computed using both ends of the range to see if the optimal solution is affected by this. If it is, management must decide whether additional effort should be expended to obtain more precise cost estimates or else choose one of the two indicated optimal solutions. For instance, the latter strategy would most likely be employed if there were little disparity between total costs of various capacity levels close to the indicated optimal solutions.

OTHER QUEUING MODELS

The two previously described models—the single-channel and the multiple-channel, infinite source queuing models—represent what might be thought of as the "mainstream" queuing models. This stems partly from the conceptual understanding of queuing systems that they convey and partly from the ease with which system performance measures can be obtained. However, the field of queuing contains a rich variety of models. This section is designed to illustrate some of that richness, and to enlarge your appreciation for modeling queuing systems.

TABLE 16-6 Formulas for Poisson Arrivals, Any Service Distribution

Performance Measure	Formula	Formula Number
Average number waiting in line	$L_q = \dfrac{\left(\frac{\lambda}{\mu}\right)^2 + \lambda^2 \sigma^2}{2\left(1 - \frac{\lambda}{\mu}\right)}$	(16-27)
Average number in the system	$L = L_q + \dfrac{\lambda}{\mu}$	(16-28)
Average time waiting in line	$W_q = \dfrac{L_q}{\lambda}$	(16-29)
Average time in the system	$W = W_q + \dfrac{1}{\mu}$	(16-30)
System utilization	$\rho = \dfrac{\lambda}{s\mu}$	(16-31)

Each of the models presented in this section offers a slight variation in the assumptions that underlie the two basic models. For example, one model allows for any service time distribution; one pertains to constant service time; one has Poisson arrivals and exponential service times, but limits the potential length of the waiting line; one has Poisson arrivals and exponential service but a finite calling population; and one has priority service instead of first-come, first-served. Each of these models is presented briefly. Note that all of the models except the priority service one pertain to a single-server situation.

Poisson Arrival Rate with Any Service Distribution

The assumptions of this model are identical to the basic single-server model, except that service time need not be exponential. In order to use this model, however, it is necessary to have an estimate of the variance, σ^2, of the service time distribution. Some key formulas are presented in Table 16-6.

EXAMPLE 7 Joe's Tailor Shop is a one-man operation, and owner Fred White does all of the work. The customer arrival rate is Poisson with a mean of .25 per minute. Service time has a mean of 2.0 minutes and a standard deviation of 0.9 minutes. Compute each of the performance measures listed in Table 16-6.

Solution

$\lambda = .25$ per minute

$\mu = .50$ per minute

$\sigma = 0.9$ minutes

1. $L_q = \dfrac{\left(\dfrac{.25}{.50}\right)^2 + .25^2(0.9)^2}{2\left(1 - \dfrac{.25}{.50}\right)} = .301$ customers.

2. $L = .301 + \dfrac{.25}{.50} = .801$ customers.

3. $W_q = \dfrac{.301}{.25} = 1.204$ minutes.

4. $W = 1.204 + 2.0 = 3.204$ minutes.

5. $\rho = \dfrac{.25}{.50} = .50.$

Poisson Arrival Rate, Constant Service Time

The assumptions of this model are identical to those of the basic single-server model (and the preceding model), except that the service time is constant.

$$L_q = \frac{\left(\frac{\lambda}{\mu}\right)^2}{2\left(1 - \frac{\lambda}{\mu}\right)} = \frac{\lambda^2}{2\mu(\mu - \lambda)} \tag{16–32}$$

The basis for this formula can be seen by referring to the formula for L_q with any service distribution (see Table 16–6). Because the service time is constant, $\sigma^2 = 0$, the second term in the numerator drops out, reducing to the above formula. The formulas for performance measures other than L_q are the same as those shown in Table 16–6.

■

EXAMPLE 8 A video arcade game is designed to operate for exactly three minutes, during which time a player attempts to capture as many purple monkeys as possible. Customer player arrivals can be described by a Poisson distribution with a mean arrival rate of 12 per hour. Compute each of the performance measures listed in Table 16–6.

Solution

$\lambda = 12$ per hour

$\mu = 20$ per hour

1. $L_q = \dfrac{12^2}{2(20)(20 - 12)} = .45$ customers.

2. $L = .45 + \dfrac{12}{20} = 1.05$ customers.

TABLE 16–7 Single-Server, Finite Queue Length Formulas

Performance Measure	Formula	Formula Number
System utilization	$\rho = \frac{\lambda}{\mu}$	(16–33)
Probability of zero units in the system	$P_0 = \frac{1 - \rho}{1 - \rho^{m+1}}$	(16–34)
Probability of n units in the system	$P_n = P_0 \rho^n$	(16–35)
Average number of units in the system	$L = \frac{\rho}{1 - \rho} - \frac{(m + 1)\rho^{m+1}}{1 - \rho^{m+1}}$	(16–36)
Average number of units waiting in line	$L_q = L - (1 - P_0)$	(16–37)
Average time in system	$W = \frac{L_q}{\lambda(1 - P_m)} + \frac{1}{\mu}$	(16–38)
Average time waiting in line	$W_q = W - \frac{1}{\mu}$	(16–39)

m = maximum number permitted in the system.

3. $W_q = \frac{.45}{12} = .0375$ hour or $.0375 \times 60 = 2.25$ minutes.
4. $W = 2.25 + 3.00 = 5.25$ minutes.
5. $\rho = \frac{12}{20} = .60.$

Finite Queue Length

This model incorporates all of the assumptions of the basic single-server model. In addition, it allows for a limit on the maximum length of the line. The implication is that once the line reaches its maximum length, no additional customers will be allowed to join the line. New customers will be allowed on a space-available basis. The necessary formulas are shown in Table 16–7.

■

EXAMPLE 9 A single-bay car wash has a driveway that can only hold 4 cars. Because the car wash is on a busy highway, when there are 5 cars in the system, no additional cars can enter. The arrival and service rates are Poisson, the mean arrival rate is 9 per hour, and the mean service rate is 15 per hour. Compute each of the performance measures listed in Table 16–7.

Solution

$\lambda = 9$ per hour
$\mu = 15$ per hour
$m = 5$

1. $\rho = \dfrac{9}{15} = .60.$

2. $P_0 = \dfrac{1 - .6}{1 - .6^{5+1}} = .420.$

3. (Find P_5.) $P_5 = .434(.6^5) = .033.$

4. $L = \dfrac{.6}{1 - .6} - \dfrac{(5 + 1)(.6^{5+1})}{1 - .6^{5+1}} = 1.5 - .294 = 1.206$ cars.

5. $L_q = 1.206 - (1 - .420) = .63$ cars.

6. $W = \dfrac{.64}{9(1 - .033)} + \dfrac{1}{15} = .139$ hours.

7. $W_q = .139 - \dfrac{1}{15} = .072$ hours.

Finite Calling Population

This model has the same assumptions as the basic single-server model except that there is a limited calling population. A typical example of such a queuing system would be a machine operator who is responsible for loading and unloading five machines. Hence, the calling population is five.

Some appropriate formulas are listed in Table 16–8. Note that λ is defined as the mean arrival rate *per unit*.

EXAMPLE 10 One person handles adjustments for four machines. The machines run an average of 60 minutes before adjustments are needed, and the average adjustment time is 15 minutes. Service time can be described by a negative exponential distribution, and the call rate for each machine can be described by a Poisson distribution. Compute each of the performance measures listed in Table 16–8.

Solution

$\lambda = 1$ call per hour per machine
$\mu = 4$ machines per hour
$N = 4$
$\dfrac{\lambda}{\mu} = \dfrac{1}{4} = .25$

TABLE 16–8 Finite Calling Population Formulas

Performance Measure	Formula	Formula Number
Probability of no units in the system	$P_0 = \dfrac{1}{\sum_{i=0}^{N}\left(\dfrac{\lambda}{\mu}\right)^i\left[\dfrac{N!}{(N-i)!}\right]}$	(16–40)
Probability of n units in the system	$P_n = \dfrac{N!}{(N-n)!}\left(\dfrac{\lambda}{\mu}\right)^n P_0$	(16–41)
Average number waiting in line	$L_q = N - \dfrac{\lambda+\mu}{\lambda}(1-P_0)$	(16–42)
Average number in the system	$L = L_q + (1-P_0)$	(16–43)
Average waiting time in line	$W_q = \dfrac{L_q}{\lambda(N-L)}$	(16–44)
Average time in the system	$W = W_q + \dfrac{1}{\mu}$	(16–45)

N = number in calling population.
λ = mean arrival rate *per unit* in the population.

1. $P_o = \dfrac{1}{.25^0\dfrac{4!}{(4-0)!} + .25^1\dfrac{4!}{(4-1)!} + .25^2\dfrac{4!}{(4-2)!} + .25^3\dfrac{4!}{(4-3)!} + .25^4\dfrac{4!}{(4-4)!}}$

   $= \dfrac{1}{3.219} = .311$

2. (Suppose $n = 4$): $P_5 = \dfrac{4!}{(4-4)!}.25^4(.311) = .0012$

   Therefore, it is highly unlikely that no machines will be running (i.e., that all will be awaiting adjustments).

3. $L_q = 4 - \dfrac{1+4}{1}(1 - .311) = .555$ machines.

4. $L = .555 + (1 - .311) = 1.24$ machines.

5. $W_q = \dfrac{.555}{1(5-1.24)} = .148$ hours.

6. $W = .148 + .25 = .398$ hours.

Multiple-Server, Priority Servicing Model

This model incorporates all of the assumptions of the basic multiple-server model except that priority serving is used rather than first-come, first-served. Arrivals to the system are assigned a priority as they arrive (e.g, highest priority = 1, next

TABLE 16–9 Multiple-Server, Priority Service Model

Performance Measure	Formula	Formula Number
System utilization	$\rho = \dfrac{\lambda}{s\mu}$	(16–46)
Intermediate values: (L_q from Table 16-5)	$A = \dfrac{\lambda}{(1-\rho)L_q}$	(16–47)
	$B_k = 1 - \sum_{c=1}^{k} \dfrac{\lambda c}{s\mu}$	(16–48)
	$(B_0 = 1)$	
Average waiting time in line for units in kth priority class	$W_k = \dfrac{1}{A(B_{k-1})(B_k)}$	(16–49)
Average time in the system for units in the kth priority class	$W = W_k + \dfrac{1}{\mu}$	(16–50)
Average number waiting in line for units in the kth priority class	$L_k = \lambda_k \times W_k$	(16–51)

priority class = 2, next priority class = 3, and so on). An existing queue might look something like this:

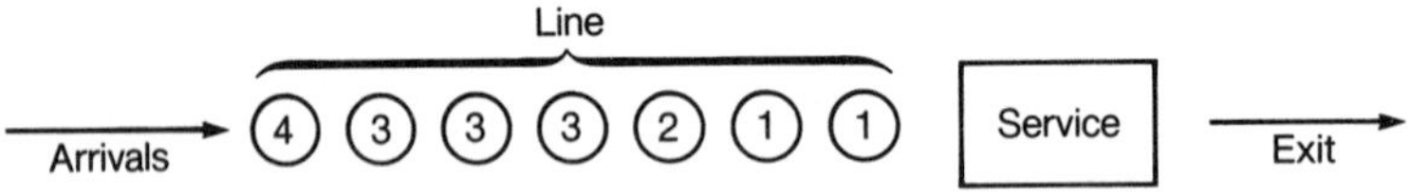

Within each class, waiting units are processed in the order they arrived (i.e., first-come, first-served). Thus, in this sequence, the first #1 would be processed as soon as a server was available. Then, the second #1 would be processed when that server, or another one, became available. If, in the interim, another #1 arrived, it would be next in line *ahead of the first #2*. If there were no new arrivals, the only #2 would be processed by the next available server. At that point, if a new #1 arrived, it would be processed ahead of the #3s and the #4. Similarly, a new #2 would be processed ahead of the #3s and the #4. Conversely, if a new #4 arrived, it would take its place at the end of the line.

Obviously, a unit with a low priority could conceivably wait a rather long time for processing. In some cases, units that have waited more than some specified time are reassigned a higher priority.

This model assumes that service is not **preemptive**. This means that service on a low priority unit is not interrupted even though a higher priority unit arrives after service has begun.

The appropriate formulas for this multiple-channel, priority service model are given in Table 16–9.

■

EXAMPLE 11 A machine shop handles tool repairs in a large company. Each job is assigned a priority when it arrives in the shop that is based on the urgency for that tool. Requests for repair can be described by a Poisson distribution. Arrival rates are: $\lambda_1 = 2$ per hour, $\lambda_2 = 2$ per hour, and $\lambda_3 = 1$ per hour. The service rate is 1 tool per hour for each server, and there are six servers in the shop. Determine the following information:

1. The system utilization.
2. The average time a tool in each of the priority classes will wait for service.
3. The average time a tool spends in the system for each priority class.
4. The average number of tools waiting for repair in each class.

Solution

$\lambda = \Sigma\lambda_k = 2 + 2 + 1 = 5$ per hour

$s = 6$ servers

$\mu = 1$ customer per hour

1. $\rho = \dfrac{\lambda}{s\mu} = \dfrac{5}{6(1)} = .833$

2. Intermediate values: $\dfrac{\lambda}{\mu} = \dfrac{5}{1} = 5$, from Table 16–5, $L_q = 2.938$

$$A = \frac{5}{(1 - .833)2.938} = 10.19$$

$$B_0 = 1$$

$$B_1 = 1 - \frac{2}{6(1)} = \frac{2}{3} = .667$$

$$B_2 = 1 - \frac{2 + 2}{6(1)} = \frac{1}{3} = .333$$

$$B_3 = 1 - \frac{2 + 2 + 1}{6(1)} = \frac{1}{6} = .167$$

$$W_1 = \frac{1}{A(B_0)(B_1)} = \frac{1}{10.19(1)(.667)} = .147 \text{ hours}$$

$$W_2 = \frac{1}{A(B_1)(B_2)} = \frac{1}{10.19(.667)(.333)} = .442 \text{ hours}$$

$$W_3 = \frac{1}{A(B_2)(B_3)} = \frac{1}{10.19(.333)(.167)} = 1.765 \text{ hours}$$

3. Average time in system $= W_k + \dfrac{1}{\mu}$. In this case, $\dfrac{1}{\mu} = \dfrac{1}{1} = 1$.

   Thus, we have:

Class	$W_k + 1 = W$ (hours)
1	.147 + 1 = 1.147
2	.442 + 1 = 1.442
3	1.765 + 1 = 2.765

4. The average number of units waiting in each class is $L_k = \lambda_k \times W_k$. Thus, we have:

Class	$\lambda_k \times W_k = L_k$ (units)
1	2(.147) = .294
2	2(.442) = .884
3	1(1.765) = 1.765

Revising Priorities

If any of the waiting times computed in the preceding example are deemed as too long by management (e.g., a waiting time of .147 hours for tools in the first class might be too long), there are several options. One would be to increase the number of servers. Another would be to attempt to increase the service rate, say, by introducing new methods. If such options are not feasible, another approach would be to reexamine the membership of each of the priority classifications. The reason for this is that if some repair requests, say, in the first priority class can be reassigned to the second priority class, this will tend to decrease the average waiting times for repair jobs that retain the highest priority classification simply because the arrival rate of those items will be lower.

■

EXAMPLE 12 Suppose the manager of the repair shop, after consulting with the managers of the departments that use the shop's services, has been able to revise the list of tools that are given the highest priorities. This would be reflected by revised arrival rates. Suppose that the revised rates are $\lambda_1 = 1.5$, $\lambda_2 = 2.5$, and λ_3 remains unchanged at 1.0. Determine the following information:

1. The system utilization.
2. The average waiting time for units in each priority class.

Solution

$$\lambda = \Sigma\lambda_k = 1.5 + 2.5 + 1.0 = 5.0$$

$s = 6$

$\mu = 1$

(Note that these values are the same as in the previous example.)

1. $\rho = \dfrac{5.0}{6(1)} = .833$, which is the same as in the previous example.
2. The value of A, since it is a function of s, μ, and λ, is the same as in the preceding example because these values are the same. Therefore, $A = 10.19$, and:

$$B_0 = 1\text{(always)}$$

$$B_1 = 1 - \frac{1.5}{6(1)} = .75$$

$$B_2 = 1 - \frac{1.5 + 2.5}{6(1)} = .333$$

$$B_3 = 1 - \frac{1.5 + 2.5 + 1.0}{6(1)} = .167$$

Then:

$$W_1 = \frac{1}{10.19(1)(.75)} = .131 \text{ hours}$$

$$W_2 = \frac{1}{10.19(.75)(.333)} = .393 \text{ hours}$$

$$W_3 = \frac{1}{10.19(.333)(.167)} = 1.765 \text{ hours}$$

Here, we find several interesting results. One is that by reducing the arrival rate of the highest priority class, the average waiting time for units in that priority class decreased. Hence, removing some members of the highest class and placing them into the next lower priority class reduced the average waiting time for units that remained in the highest class. Note, though, that the average waiting time for the *second* priority class also was reduced, even though units were added to that class. Although this may appear counterintuitive, it is necessary to recognize that the *total* waiting time (when all arrivals are taken into account) will remain unchanged. We can see this by noting that the average *number* waiting in the preceding example (see part *d*) was .294 + .884 + 1.765 = 2.943. In this example, using the average waiting times just computed, the average number waiting in all three classes is:

$$\sum_{k=1}^{3} \lambda_k W_k = 1.5(.131) + 2.5(.393) + 1.0(1.765) = 2.944$$

Aside from a slight difference due to rounding, the totals are the same.

Another interesting observation is that the average waiting time for customers in the third priority class did not change from the preceding example. The reason for this is that the *total* arrival rate for the two higher priority classes did not change, and its own average arrival rate did not change. Hence, units assigned to that lowest class must still contend with a combined arrival rate of 5 for the two higher priority classes.

THE PSYCHOLOGY OF WAITING

The emphasis in this chapter has been on mathematical analysis of systems in which waiting lines tend to form. The underlying theme was predicting performance characteristics in order to make decisions relating to system capacity. In certain instances, especially those in which a system is currently in operation and capacity changes would be either difficult or impossible, reduction of waiting times may not be feasible. Nonetheless, in many instances it is possible to diminish the *effects* of waiting, even though the length of a wait cannot be shortened. Some of these approaches are described in this section.

Two costs are generally associated with waiting. One is an economic cost, related to factors such as the cost of space that must be provided for potential waiting customers; the cost of employee time spent waiting (e.g., for tools, for repairs); the cost of machines waiting for service (e.g., loading/unloading, repairs); and the cost of idle servers and service capacity. These costs usually can be estimated with a fair degree of accuracy. Another economic cost is related to the potential for lost business due to customers failing to join a line that they perceive as too long. Other customers may wait in line for a while, then leave. In either case, customers may return to the line at a later time, may decide to forego the service, or may go elsewhere for it. If the customer returns, the impact on profits may be negligible; but if the customer does not return, the loss can be more significant, particularly if potential profit on *additional* products or services the customer may have bought also are taken into account. However, estimating such additional lost sales or profits may be difficult, at best. Consequently, taking such costs into account may be problematic.

A cost that is closely related to customers leaving a line is the *psychological* cost associated with the waiting customer's perception of the waiting time. For example, if customers believe that their time could be better spent elsewhere, they are apt to resent waiting, especially if they feel that management could remedy the length of wait (e.g., simply by adding additional servers). Conversely, if customers are occupied during the waiting period, either in a constructive way or through some form of distraction, they are less likely to resent the waiting experience. Examples of situations in which the psychological aspects of waiting are attended to include: doctors' and dentists' offices providing magazines to help patients pass the time; airlines providing music or in-flight movies on long flights; retail stores positioning mirrors near elevators, allowing those who are waiting to check their appearance; asking people to fill out forms while waiting (e.g., unemployment office, doctor, dentist), thus making the wait somewhat constructive.

Oddly enough, in certain retail situations, a moderate amount of waiting time is desirable. For instance, supermarkets place an array of impulse-purchase items at checkouts (e.g., candy, gum, cigarettes, magazines, batteries). Waiting customers may add these to their other purchases; the waiting period provides the opportunity for them to consider additional spending.

THE VALUE OF QUEUING MODELS

Queuing analysis is sometimes criticized on the grounds that the assumptions required by the models are not satisfied in many real-life situations. Among the more common complaints are the following:

1. Often, service times are not negative exponential.
2. The system is not in steady state, but tends to be dynamic.
3. "Service" is difficult to define because service requirements can vary considerably from customer to customer.

To be sure, it is important that the assumptions of arrival and service distributions be reasonably satisfied. A Chi-square goodness-of-fit test should be used for that purpose. Note that one of the special-purpose models described in this chapter allows *any* service distribution.

The second criticism is true in many cases. For example, the customer arrival rates at banks, supermarkets, and post offices, and highway and telephone traffic intensities vary by time of day and day of week. In some of these situations it may be possible to restrict the analysis to a narrow time interval for which the system is stable (e.g., for the lunch hour, the morning rush hour, and so on).

The last criticism may or may not be as important. Even if service requirements vary, taken as a whole, those times may exhibit an exponential distribution. Conversely, the times may be so disparate (e.g., some jobs require a few minutes and some a day or more) that two or more distributions are represented. In such cases, more elaborate modeling may be called for.

In any case in which the assumptions of the basic models are not met, the analyst must decide whether to search for, or develop, a more complex model, whether to use simulation, or whether to simply rely on intuition and experience. The choice will depend on time and cost considerations as well as on the abilities of the analyst.

Certainly the pervasiveness of waiting lines justifies some formal study of queuing systems and their characteristics. The basic models presented here, along with the several tables, enable beginners to grasp the important concepts associated with such systems without the need to deal with the fairly complex mathematics that are generally associated with queuing models. Thus, performance measures could be readily calculated, and the sensitivity of those measures to

TABLE 16–10 Summary of Queuing Models Described in This Chapter

Model	Number of Servers	Calling Population	Arrival Distribution	Service Distribution	Maximum Queue	Processing Order
Single-channel	1	∞	Poisson	Exponential	∞	FCFS
Multiple-channel	s	∞	Poisson	Exponential	∞	FCFS
Any service	1	∞	Poisson	Any	∞	FCFS
Constant service	1	∞	Poisson	Constant	∞	FCFS
Finite queue	1	∞	Poisson	Exponential	*m*	FCFS
Priority discipline	s	∞	Poisson	Exponential	∞	FCFS by priority
Limited population	1	*N*	Poisson	Exponential	*N*	FCFS

changes in system parameters (arrival and service rates, number of servers) could also be readily assessed.

SUMMARY

Waiting line problems represent an important class of management science models. Waiting lines are commonly found in a wide range of production and service systems that encounter variable arrival rates and service times. Management science interest in these problems centers on predicting system performance for the purpose of capacity design. The most common goal is to design systems that minimize the combined costs of providing capacity and customer waiting. An alternative goal is to design systems that attain specific performance criteria (e.g., keep the average waiting time to under five minutes).

Performance measures for queuing systems include the average number of customers waiting, the average waiting time, system utilization, and the maximum number waiting in line.

Important characteristics of queuing systems in terms of system modeling include the calling population, the arrival distribution, line features, the order of selection for processing, and the service distribution. In general, the models presented in this chapter assumed an infinite calling population, an arrival rate that can be adequately described by a Poisson distribution, that customers arrive individually rather than in batches, that customers funnel into a single waiting line when more than one server is used, that service is on a first-come, first-served basis, and that service time can be adequately described by a negative exponential distribution.

The models described in this chapter and some of their main features are summarized in Table 16–10.

GLOSSARY

Balking Potential customers refuse to enter a waiting line, usually because they feel the line is too long.

Calling Population Pool of potential customers.

Finite Calling Population A system in which the pool of potential customers is limited in size.

Infinite Calling Population A system in which the pool of potential customers is relatively large or unlimited.

Interarrival Time Length of time between customer arrivals.

Jockeying In systems that have multiple waiting lines when waiting customers switch from one waiting line to another.

Multiple-Channel System A queuing system with more than one server or service facility.

Multiple Phase System A system with multiple processing steps.

Preemptive Service In a priority serving model, this exists if service can be interrupted to handle a customer who has a higher priority than the one who is being served.

Priority Servicing Model Arriving customers are assigned to a priority class according to a predetermined rule and then they are serviced in order of priority class, using first-come, first-served within each class.

Queue Discipline (Processing Order) Order in which waiting customers are served. Usually by order of arrival, except for priority servicing models.

Queuing System System in which waiting lines tend to develop.

Reneging Occurs when a customer, after a period of waiting in line, leaves the waiting line before being serviced.

Single-Channel System A system with one server or one service facility.

Single-Phase System A system with one processing step.

System A queuing system consists of a waiting line and a service facility.

System Utilization The proportion of time that servers are busy (i.e., serving customers).

SOLVED PROBLEMS

Note: This chapter covers a wide range of queuing models. Rather than attempt to illustrate all of those models and variations, which would merely duplicate the examples presented in the chapter, this section is devoted to emphasizing a few of the basic concepts that underlie applying the queuing models presented in this chapter.

Problem 1. Customers arrive at the checkout area of a large supermarket during the early afternoon hours at the rate of 4 per minute. Checkout time averages 2 minutes per customer. There are six cashiers on duty. Assume that the arrival and checkout rates can be modeled by Poisson distributions. After arriving at the checkout area, customers select one of the six checkouts by choosing the one that appears to have the shortest line, and they wait in that line.

Answer these questions about this queuing system:

a. What is the significance of the phrase "during the early afternoon hours"?

b. What is the service rate, and why is it necessary to know it?

c. Is the system underloaded? Why is it important for a system to be underloaded?

d. We are told to assume the service rate can be modeled by a Poisson distribution. Is this any different than being told that the service time can be modeled by an exponential distribution?

e. How important is it to be able to assume either that the arrival and service rates are Poisson or that interarrival and service times are exponential? How could these be checked in practice?

f. What requirement of the queuing models presented in this chapter is violated if customers can select their own checkout lines? In order for the system to satisfy this requirement, what change would have to be made to the system?

Solution

a. In many queuing systems, the average customer arrival rate tends to vary by time of day. For example, lunch-hour traffic is higher in restaurants, banks, shops near office buildings, and the like, than during, say, the midmorning hours. Thus, performance measures will differ depending on the time of day. Consequently, performance measures should be related to specific time and/or day intervals.

b. The service rate is the reciprocal of the service time. Here, the service time is 2 minutes. Therefore, the service rate is:

$$\frac{1 \text{ customer}}{2 \text{ minutes}} = .5 \text{ customers per minute}$$

It is important to know the service rate because many of the formulas in the chapter require the service rate rather than the service time.

c. This question involves the concept of system utilization, which can be calculated as follows:

$$\rho = \frac{\lambda}{s\mu} = \frac{4 \text{ per minute}}{6(.5 \text{ per minute})} = 1.33$$

An underloaded system is one in which the system utilization is less than 1.00. In this case, the system is overloaded. The majority of queuing models require that the system be underloaded. If a system is overloaded, waiting lines will tend to grow longer and longer. Thus, overloaded systems are somewhat unrealistic. The exception would be a finite source system because the arrival rate would decrease as a larger and larger percentage of the population waited in line.

d. No, a Poisson *rate* is equivalent to an exponential *time*.

e. The majority of the models require these assumptions. Hence, if the assumptions are not valid, strictly speaking, the models will not provide results that will be realized (i.e., the calculated values will not reflect reality). Obtaining data (if possible) and using a Chi-square goodness-of-fit test would be a good way to test this.

f. The models require that service be done on a first-come, first-served basis (with the exception of the multiple priority model). In order to achieve this, customers could be asked either to wait in a single line, as is often done in banks and post offices, or could be given numbers when they arrive, and serviced in that order. Both would seem to be impractical; some other queuing model (or simulation) would be needed to handle this situation.

PROBLEMS

1. Relative to queuing models:

   a. What is meant by the terms *single-channel system* and *multiple-channel system?* If a crew of four workers operates as a team in servicing a customer, how many channels does the system have?

   b. Contrast the terms *service time* and *service rate*. Explain how one can convert from time to rate. Why is this important?

   c. Explain the terms *calling population, infinite source,* and *finite source.*

   d. How does the phrase first-come, first-served apply in queuing? Which models described in the chapter assume this?

   e. What does the phrase *the number in the system* refer to?

   f. Why do waiting lines form in systems that are underloaded?

   g. Which of these are assumptions of most or all of the models presented in this chapter?

      (1) Underloaded system.

(2) Variable arrival rate.
(3) Variable service rate.
(4) Processing is first-come, first-served.

h. What are the major elements of a queuing system?

2. An infinite source queuing system has an arrival rate of 45 customers per hour and an average service time of 2 minutes per customer. The arrival rate can be described as Poisson, and the service time distribution can be described as negative exponential. Suppose it has been determined that the average number of customers waiting for service is 1.929. There are two servers. Determine (hint: see Example 1):
   a. The average number of customers being served.
   b. The average number of customers in the system.
   c. The average time customers wait in line before being served.
   d. The average time customers spend in the system.
   e. System utilization.

3. One clerk is on duty during evening hours at the customer service desk of a supermarket. The clerk can process customer requests in an average time of 3 minutes, and this can be described by a negative exponential distribution that has a mean of 3. Customers arrive at a rate of 15 per hour (Poisson). Find:
   a. The expected number of customers waiting to be served.
   b. The average time customers spend waiting in line for service.
   c. The proportion of time that the clerk is not busy with customers.

4. For the preceding question, determine:
   a. The probability of no customers in the system.
   b. The probability of two customers at the service counter.
   c. The probability that a customer will have to wait for service.

5. Customers in a cafeteria line during lunch on weekdays arrive at the cashier's booth at a mean rate of 2.6 per minute. The cashier can process 4 customers per minute. Both rates are Poisson. Compute each of the performance measures listed in Table 16–2 for this system. For Formula 16–12, use $n = 2$, and for Formula 16–13, use $k = 3$.

6. A lawn mower repair service employs one repairperson, who takes an average of one hour to service a lawn mower. A mower is brought in for service on the average of one every 90 minutes. Assume that arrival and service rates can be described by Poisson distributions. Determine the following:
   a. The average number of mowers awaiting service.
   b. The average time a mower waits for service.

c. The probability that the number waiting for service will exceed 4 mowers.

d. The probability that the repairperson will be without a mower to service.

7. Customers at a bank wait in a single line for the next available teller. Customer arrivals can be modeled by a Poisson distribution that has a mean of 70 per hour during the midmorning hours. A teller can process an average of 100 customers per hour, which also can be modeled by a Poisson distribution. If there is one teller on duty, determine:

a. The average time a customer must wait in line for the teller.

b. The average number of customers waiting in line.

c. Average service time.

d. System utilization.

e. The probability of no customers waiting in line.

8. What values would be appropriate for the performance measures listed in the preceding problem for the case in which two tellers are available?

9. A supermarket deli counter has a ticket dispenser from which customers take tickets that maintain first-come-first-served processing. The mean arrival rate during the morning hours is 84 per hour. Each server can handle an average of 30 customers per hour. Both rates can be reasonably well described by Poisson distributions. Assume that 3 clerks are on duty. Compute each of the performance measures for this system using the formulas listed in Table 16–4. For Formula 16–21, use $n = 2$, and for Formula 16–22, use $n = 4$.

10. For the preceding problem, use Table 16–5 as the basis for determining values of the performance measures represented by Formulas 16–16 through 16–20.

11. For Problem 9, how many clerks would be necessary to keep the average time customers spend waiting *in line* to no more than 2.5 minutes? How many clerks would be needed to keep the average time customers spend *in the system* to under 2.5 minutes?

12. The owner of a bakery is thinking about installing a system of poles and chain links that will make customers wait in a single waiting line, instead of having them mill about the store waiting to be served. During evening hours there are two clerks on duty, and the mean customer arrival rate is .8 per minute. Service time averages 2.375 minutes per customer, and this can be reasonably described by an exponential distribution. The arrival rate can be described by a Poisson distribution. Compute each of the performance measures in Table 16–4, beginning with Formula 16–17, but omitting Formula 16–20. Use Table 16–5 to find L_q and P_0. For Formula 16–21, assume $n = 2$, and for Formula 16–22, assume $n = 6$.

13. Answer these additional questions concerning the previous problem:

   a. For the information given, what line length will not be exceeded with a probability of 95 percent?

   b. How many servers would be needed to keep the maximum line length to under 5 with a probability of 95 percent?

   c. How many servers would be needed to keep the average number waiting to be served (line only) to under 3?

14. Library users request assistance in locating items at an information desk at a mean rate of 13.8 requests per hour. Each assistant librarian can handle a request in an average of 10 minutes. Suppose that students from a nearby college have studied this system and found arrival and service rates to be Poisson.

   a. How many assistants would be needed to keep the average time in the system to 16 minutes or less?

   b. Determine the maximum number of persons waiting to submit a request for probabilities of 95 percent and 99 percent, if 5 assistants will be used.

   c. How many assistants would be needed to have a probability of 95 percent that line length would not exceed 7 persons?

15. In a large plant, a centralized tool crib is used in order to dispense tools to mechanics on a per need basis. Mechanics request tools at a mean rate of 40 per hour (Poisson). Clerks can handle requests in a mean time of 4.5 minutes each, including the paperwork that is involved. Service time can be described by an exponential distribution. Mechanics represent a cost of $25 per hour each, and clerks represent a cost of $15 each. Determine the number of clerks that will be needed in order to minimize the total cost of mechanics and clerks in the system.

16. In the parts department of a large automobile dealership there is a counter that is used exclusively for mechanics' requests for parts. It has been determined that such requests occur once every 5 minutes, on the average, and the time between the requests can be modeled by a negative exponential distribution that has a mean of 5 minutes. A clerk can handle requests at a rate of 15 per hour, and this can be modeled by a Poisson distribution that has a mean of 15. Suppose there are two clerks at the counter.

   a. On the average, how many mechanics would be at the counter, including those being served?

   b. What is the probability that a mechanic would have to wait for service?

   c. If a mechanic has to wait, how long, on the average, would the wait be?

   d. If clerks represent a cost of $20 per hour and mechanics represent a cost of $30 per hour, what number of clerks would be optimal in terms of minimizing cost?

17. During the daytime hours, calls for paramedics come into an emergency switchboard at the rate of two per hour. The operations chief can schedule two, three, or four crews to work this shift. The average time required to complete a trip and return to base is 40 minutes. Arrival and service rates are both Poisson.

   a. If the chief wants to maintain an average time of no more than 20 minutes between the time a call comes in and the time a crew is dispatched, how many crews should be scheduled?

   b. Suppose that two crews are used. What would the average time to dispatch be? What would the system utilization be?

   c. Suppose three crews are used. What would the average time to dispatch be? What would the system utilization be?

18. One aspect of designing an industrial plant concerns the number of loading docks to include in the design. Driver and truck cost will be $200 per hour, while equivalent dock cost will be $140 per hour. Average loading time is expected to be three hours, and trucks will arrive randomly at a rate of one truck every two hours. Arrival and service rates can be assumed to be Poisson distributed. Determine the number of loading docks that will minimize dock and truck/driver costs.

19. Certain automated equipment needs part replacement on a random basis. This can be described by a Poisson distribution that has a mean of one part every other hour. When a break occurs, a technician diagnoses the problem, then goes to the parts counter to obtain the appropriate part. The average time for a clerk to obtain the part is 30 minutes because of the need to check various parts catalogs and retrieve the part from storage. Assume arrival and service rates are Poisson. Clerk time represents a cost of $30 per hour per clerk. Equipment downtime and technician time represent $400 per hour.

   a. If two clerks are used, what would be the average number of machines (i.e., automated equipment) waiting for parts? Assume there is a large number of machines in service (i.e., treat as infinite source).

   b. What number of clerks would be optimal for minimizing cost?

20. A clerk in the children's shoes department of a large store waits on customers in the order that they arrive. Each customer signs in when entering the department. A recent study shows that the customer arrival rate on Wednesday mornings can be represented adequately by a Poisson distribution with a mean of 8 per hour. The clerk can handle customers at a mean rate of 12 per hour. Determine the mean number of customers in the system, and the mean time they spend in the system, under each of the following conditions:

   a. The service rate is exponential.

   b. The service rate is constant.

   c. The service time is neither exponential nor constant, but it is known that service time has a standard deviation of 3.5 minutes per customer.

21. A vending machine dispenses apples at a constant rate of 4 per minute. Apple eaters arrive to purchase apples at a mean rate of 3.4 per minute during breaks from classes held in the same building.

   a. Compute the mean number of persons waiting to buy an apple.

   b. Compute each of the remaining performance measures using the formulas in Table 16–6.

22. If the apple machine in the previous problem was temporarily out of order and apples were sold by one server who had the same 15 seconds service time but with a standard deviation of 2 seconds, what values would each of the performance measures in Table 16–6 have?

23. Calls come into the reservations desk of a resort motel during the morning hours (weekdays only) at a rate of 15 per hour (Poisson). In this telephone system, as many as two calls can be automatically placed on hold if the reservations clerk is busy with another call. Compute each of the performance measures in Table 16–7 with $\mu = 25$ per hour (Poisson).

24. One librarian is on duty at the reference desk of a branch of the public library during the morning hours. The librarian gets a request for assistance approximately once every 4 minutes. The time between requests can be modeled using a negative exponential distribution with a mean of 4 minutes. Each request requires an average of 3 minutes of the librarian's time. This can be modeled using a normal distribution with a mean of 3 minutes and a standard deviation of 1 minute. Determine each of the following performance measures:

   a. The average number of people waiting for the librarian, not including the person being helped.

   b. The average time needed for a person to make a request and to be helped.

   c. The proportion of time the librarian is not working on requests.

25. Many of a bank's customers use its automatic teller machine to transact business after normal banking hours. During the early evening hours in the summer months, it has been determined that customers arrive at a certain location at the rate of one every other minute. This can be modeled using a Poisson distribution. Each customer spends an average of 90 seconds completing his or her transactions. This time has a standard deviation of 20 seconds. Determine:

   a. The average time customers spend at the machine, either waiting in line or completing transactions.

   b. The probability that a customer will not have to wait upon arriving at the automatic teller machine.

   c. The average number waiting to use the machine.

26. In an automatic car wash, it takes 4 minutes to wash each car. Suppose cars arrive at the car wash at the rate of 12 per hour (Poisson). Determine the following:

a. The average number of cars waiting to be washed.

b. The average time between the car's arriving and leaving.

c. The probability that a car will not have to wait in line.

27. The service department of an automobile dealership can handle only six transmission repair jobs per day. Customers who need transmission repairs come in at the rate of one per hour during the morning and early afternoon. Repair time averages 50 minutes. The arrival and service rates can be modeled by Poisson distributions. One repairperson handles all transmission work. Compute each of the performance measures listed in Table 16–7.

28. A telephone reservation system can accept a maximum of two calls waiting. The reservationist processes calls in an average of four minutes. Average time between calls is five minutes. Both times can be modeled by exponential distributions. Determine each of the following measures:

a. The average number of calls waiting.

b. The probability of two or more calls waiting.

c. The probability that a caller will not have to wait for the reservationist.

29. An operator handles loading/unloading a group of three machines. The machines operate an average of 30 minutes per job, and loading/unloading time averages 5 minutes. Both times can be modeled by exponential distributions. Compute each of the performance measures listed in Table 16–8. Use $n = 3$ for Formula 16–41.

30. A repair crew handles equipment breakdowns of construction equipment. There is one piece of equipment at each of five construction sites. When a request for repair comes in, the crew travels to the site, repairs the equipment, and returns to its base. Travel and repair time can be described by an exponential distribution with a mean of 3.5 hours. Equipment breakdowns occur at the rate of one every five hours (Poisson).

a. What is the probability that at any given instant, none of the equipment is being serviced due to breakdowns?

b. On the average, how long does it take from the time a call comes in until the crew leaves to repair that piece of equipment?

c. On the average, how many machines are out of service?

d. What is the probability that the crew will be idle?

31. Customers arriving at a service center are assigned to one of three categories (1, 2, or 3, with Category 1 given the highest priority) for servicing. Records indicate that an average of nine customers arrive per hour, and that one third are assigned to each category. There are two servers, and each can process customers at the rate of five per hour. Arrival and service rates can be described by Poisson distributions.

a. What is the utilization rate for this system?

b. Determine the average waiting time for units in each class.

c. Find the average number of customers in each class that are waiting for service.

32. A manager must determine requirements for waiting space for customers. A priority system is used to process customers who are assigned to one of two classes when they enter the processing center. The highest priority class has an arrival rate of four per hour, while the other class has an arrival rate of two per hour. Both can be described as Poisson distributed. There are two servers, and each can process customers in an average of six minutes.

a. What is the system utilization?

b. Determine the number of customers of each class that are waiting for service.

c. Determine the average waiting time for each class.

d. If the manager was able to alter the assignment rules so that arrival rates of the two classes were equal, what would be the revised average waiting times for each priority class?

33. A priority waiting system assigns arriving customers to one of four classes. Arrival rates (Poisson) of the classes are shown in the following table:

Class	Arrivals per Hour
1	2
2	4
3	3
4	2

Five servers process the customers, and each can handle three customers per hour.

a. What is the system utilization?

b. On the average, how long do customers in the various classes wait for service? How many are waiting in each class, on the average?

c. If the arrival rate of the second priority class could be reduced to three units per hour by shifting some arrivals into the third priority class, how would your answers to part *b* change?

d. What observations can you make based on your answers to part *c*?

34. Referring to the preceding problem, suppose that each server could handle four customers per hour. Answer the questions posed in the preceding problem. Explain why the impact of reassigning customers is much less than in the preceding problem.

Chapter 17 Simulation

Chapter Outline

Learning Objectives

After completing this chapter, you should be able to:

1. Explain what the term *simulation* means and how simulation differs from analytical techniques.
2. Explain the difference between discrete and continuous simulations, between fixed-interval and next-event simulations, and between deterministic and probabilistic simulations.
3. List and briefly describe the steps in simulation.
4. Use the Monte Carlo Method to generate random numbers.
5. Conduct manual simulations using various distributions.
6. List the advantages and limitations of simulations.

INTRODUCTION

Simulation represents a marked departure from the other tools of analysis described in this book, such as linear programming, inventory analysis, and queuing. All of those other techniques were directed toward helping decision makers to identify an *optimal solution* to a problem. This is not the case with simulation; it is not an optimizing tool. Instead, its purpose is to enable a manager or analyst to *experiment* with a system—to **simulate**—in order to better understand its behavior, and as a result, to make better decisions with regard to the system.

Simulation involves the use of a model that exhibits the important behavioral characteristics of a real system. Studying the behavior of the model under various conditions can lead to tremendous insights with broad applications. Consider these examples:

1. Medical researchers use various animals to *simulate* the effects of certain drugs on human beings.
2. Aircraft designers use wind tunnels to *simulate* the effect of air turbulence on wings and other structural parts of an airplane.
3. NASA trains astronauts in environments that *simulate* the conditions they are likely to encounter on future space missions.
4. Football teams conduct contact drills to prepare their members for upcoming games by *simulating* playing conditions.
5. Training programs for commercial pilots put trainees through a relatively large number of *simulated* takeoffs and landings on the ground before exposing them to the reality of performing actual takeoffs and landings.
6. Automotive safety experts crash test cars to *simulate* accidents.

In each of these examples, an important benefit of simulation is the ability to *experiment* with a situation under *controlled conditions*. Thus, simulation is used to answer "What if . . . ?" questions. For example: What if the drug dosage is increased by a factor of two? What if the curvature of the wing is changed slightly? What would happen if a new pass defense is used by the other team? Decision makers can use simulation not only to obtain answers to such questions, but also to redesign a system that will perform in a more desirable way. The redesigned system, then, can be simulated to test its behavior under realistic conditions.

Obviously, there are many different kinds of simulations. One important class of simulation models, especially in business, is *mathematical* simulations. These involve modeling the key aspects of *events* (e.g., use of spare parts, demand for a product, machine breakdowns) in mathematical terms. Then, the model can be studied and modified in roughly the same manner as physical simulations. Because they are mathematical, such simulations lend themselves to computerization. This is important because many simulations are fairly complex and require numerous calculations, and computers offer the only feasible approach to handling such problems.

The simulations that we shall study are mathematical. They can be applied to a wide range of business problems. However, although most real-life simulations tend to be fairly complex, the discussion here will be limited to situations that are not very complex. In fact, many of the problems presented in this chapter lend themselves to *analytical* solutions rather than repeated *simulation runs,* which yield only approximate results. Nonetheless, there are several important reasons for limiting our study to fairly simple problems. One is that such problems lend themselves to *manual* procedures, which will produce identical results across the board. This means that everyone who tries a certain problem will come up with the same result, and this allows for discussion of that result. More important, the simple problems permit illustrating the basic concepts of simulation without being obscured by unnecessary, albeit realistic, complexity.

The discussion begins with a simple example of a simulation that will give you a feel for the descriptive nature of simulation. Next, some of the different types of simulation are outlined, followed by a description of how to actually do a simulation. The remainder of the chapter includes a broader discussion of simulation techniques, validation of simulation models, computer simulation, and the advantages and limitations of simulation as a management tool.

REPLACEMENT PARTS EXAMPLE

The manager of a repair shop in a large manufacturing firm had recently been informed that a new type of processing equipment would soon be installed in the plant. The manager was concerned about what level of replacement parts to maintain for a certain vital part that needs frequent replacement. If the part was overstocked, the shop would be needlessly tying up funds and space that could be better used for other purposes. Conversely, understocking the item would have serious consequences in terms of equipment downtime while replacement parts were rush-ordered. Moreover, rush-ordered parts tend to be more costly than those that are not rush-ordered.

In order to better understand the demands this new equipment will put on the shop's inventory, the manager decided to do a simulation analysis of potential usage. Because the equipment was new, there was no historical data on usage. Nonetheless, on the basis of usage of replacement parts for a similar piece of equipment plus discussions with engineers who were familiar with the new equipment, the manager was able to construct a model of usage of replacement parts. The manager then used the model to simulate usage for a 10-day period. The results of the simulation were as follows:

Day	1	2	3	4	5	6	7	8	9	10
Usage	1	0	1	1	0	0	0	2	1	0

Thus, simulated usage was 1 part on Day 1, no parts on Day 2, 1 part on Day 3, and so on. From this, the manager could see that daily usage of spares is typically 0 or 1. Also, a simple computation would show that average daily usage is .60 parts.

This example has a relatively small number of simulated days. As a practical matter, the number is too small to enable the manager to gain much insight into the situation. However, the purpose of the example was to illustrate the kind of results one might obtain from a simulation. Had the number of observations been larger, the manager could have learned a number of things about potential usage of replacement parts. For instance, suppose that 10 days constitutes an order cycle. The manager could have run many 10-day simulations. The resulting values could have indicated such information as the average number of parts used over a 10-day cycle as well as information on the *sequence* of daily usage (e.g., the strings of days with no usage, the occurrence of heavy usage on sequential days, and so on). This information would be helpful for establishing a reorder policy and setting stocking levels.

TYPES OF SIMULATION

There are various ways of classifying simulation types. Some of those ways are presented in this section. The purpose in contrasting the approaches to simulation is to help you gain some additional perspective on simulation.

Simulations can be classified as discrete or continuous, fixed-interval or next-event, and as deterministic or probabilistic. Let's take a look at each of these contrasting pairs, beginning with discrete versus continuous simulations.

Discrete versus Continuous Simulations

The replacement parts example involved a variable with integer outcomes: The number of parts used per day could be 0, 1, 2, 3, or 4. Hence, the outcomes were *discrete*. There are many similar situations that involve discrete variables. For the most part, such situations can be described by a *count* of the *number of occurrences* (e.g., number of cars serviced, number of items sold, number of complaints received, and so on).

In certain instances, the variable of interest is *continuous:* It can assume both integer and noninteger values over a range of values. Recall that quantities that are *measured* rather than counted have this characteristic, such as time, weight, distance, and length. The distinction between discrete and continuous variables is important for simulation design. Both cases are illustrated in the following pages.

Fixed-Interval versus Next-Event Simulations

In certain instances, an analyst will be interested in simulating the value of a variable over a given or *fixed interval*. For example, the situation may involve sales of a product, and the analyst may want to simulate the number of units sold *per day,* or *per week.* Hence, the analyst would design the simulation to indicate the sales over one of these intervals. Although time intervals are the most typical intervals, distance and area are two other possible intervals. For instance, a problem may involve the number of defects *per mile* of roadway, or the number of breaks *per square yard* of cloth. In such cases, interest usually centers on *how many* occurrences there are rather than the *where* or *when* of an occurrence. Hence, a manager of an automobile dealership will be mainly concerned with *how many* cars were sold on a particular day rather than whether a car was sold at 1:30 P.M. or 1:40 P.M. Similarly, the superintendent of a mill will often be more concerned with keeping track of the number of defects in cloth that the mill produces rather than exactly where defects occurred; his or her main interest will be deciding if there is a major problem, and number of defects would be an indicator of a potential problem.

When interest centers on the accumulated value of a variable over a length of time or other interval, we say that the simulation is a **fixed-interval simulation,** and we design the simulation to generate results that correspond to the interval of interest (e.g., sales per day).

Another type of simulation focuses on *when* something happens, or *how much time* is required to perform a task. For instance, a simulation of machine breakdowns may involve information on how long a machine operated before a breakdown and, perhaps, on how much time was required to repair the machine. This sort of information can be very useful for choosing among alternative machines, for deciding how many machines will be needed to meet production quotas, and for scheduling maintenance and repair crews.

When interest centers on *an occurrence* of an event (e.g., a breakdown, a fire alarm, an accident) and, perhaps, how much time or effort is required for the event (e.g., repair time, response time), we refer to the simulation of these situations as **next-event simulations.** Both types of simulations are illustrated in this chapter.

Deterministic versus Probabilistic Simulations

Another important aspect of a simulation is whether it involves a deterministic or a probabilistic situation. The former pertains to cases in which a specific outcome is *certain,* given a set of inputs; the latter pertains to cases that involve *random* variables and, therefore, the exact outcome cannot be predicted with certainty, given a set of inputs.

Consider a case in which an employer is contemplating changes in pay rates and working times for his employees. Although there may be many employees that would be affected, given the pay rates and projected hours of work, the total payroll can be determined right down to the penny. That would not be the case for, say, projecting the amount of time required to repair a complex piece of equipment that has malfunctioned. Because each case would differ somewhat from other cases, the time would be more appropriately modeled as a random variable. The resulting simulation would then have to be *probabilistic* in order to incorporate that feature. This chapter focuses exclusively on probabilistic simulations, which both tend to have broad application and are commonly encountered in managerial environments. This is not to say that deterministic cases are not encountered, but rather that they typically do not involve the level of insight or understanding that probabilistic simulations require.

All probabilistic simulations have a certain feature in common: They incorporate some mechanism for mimicking random behavior in one or more variables.

STEPS IN SIMULATION

Now that we have considered some of the different types of simulations, let us turn our attention to how to do a simulation study. Simulation studies typically involve these steps:

1. Defining the problem and setting objectives.
2. Gathering data.
3. Developing the model.
4. Validating the model.
5. Designing experiments.
6. Performing simulation runs.
7. Analyzing and interpreting the results.

These steps are illustrated in Figure 17–1.

Let's take a brief look at each of these steps.

Defining the Problem and Setting Objectives

The first step in simulation is to clearly define the problem that is to be studied. This involves a determination of what is to be accomplished (i.e., objectives of the simulation) and the reasons for using simulation. Once the objectives have been established, a means of measuring the degree to which objectives are met by the simulation study must be established. Unless the objectives are determined at the outset, there is the danger that the results of the study will be used to determine them. In general, the goal of a simulation study is to ascertain how a system will behave under certain conditions. However, it is important to specify in as much detail as possible what information is desired. This will help in evaluating the success of the simulation, and it also will provide guidance for model development and the design of simulation experiments.

In the problem definition phase, the *scope* of the study and the *level of detail* that is needed to obtain desired results must also be decided. For example, if a simulation study is to be made of a bus system's passenger ridership patterns, will its scope encompass all routes and all times of the day, or just certain routes

FIGURE 17-1 Steps in Simulation

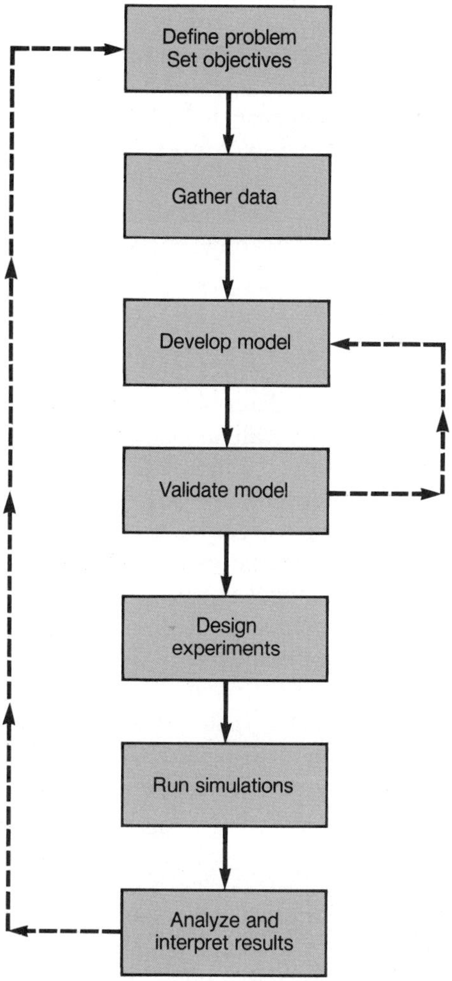

and/or certain hours? Will its scope cover all days of the week, or just certain peak days? Will it extend to different seasons, holiday travel, and so on? Will the level of detail include such factors as weather conditions, road conditions, traffic patterns, vehicle breakdowns, department store sales, community events, accidents, and the like? Moreover, will demographic information on riders (e.g., age, income, and occupation) be included? These questions are important because they have a bearing on model design and development, as well as the cost and time needed to accomplish this phase of the simulation.

Gathering Data

The amount and type of data needed are a function of the scope of the simulation and the level of detail that was decided on in the problem definition stage. The data will be needed both for model development and for evaluating and testing the model. Data may come from direct observation of a system, or they may come from existing historical records. In either case, it is important that the data capture the essence of the system being simulated so they will provide a realistic representation for modeling purposes. Thus, it is usually prudent to varify that this is the case before proceeding with model development. This may involve observation and/or checking with individuals who are knowledgeable about the system.

Developing a Model

The second step in simulation is to develop a model that will accomplish the intended results. Usually, this involves determining the structure of the model, then writing a computer program that will actually perform the simulations. Because manual simulations are employed in the text examples and accompanying chapter problems, writing computer programs will not be necessary in order to learn the concepts. Nevertheless, most practical applications of simulation do have that requirement. The structure of the model refers to the elements of a problem that are to be included in the model as well as their interrelationships. As in data gathering, capturing those interrelationships is an important aspect of model design, because unless they are realistically portrayed in the model, the results probably will not adequately reflect reality.

Finally, the model must be designed so that it will enable key decision alternatives to be tested. For instance, if bus size or maneuverability have alternatives with related consequences, the model must allow for those possibilities.

Validating the Model

This phase of simulation is closely related to model development. The purpose of **validation** is to check to determine if the model adequately reflects real system performance. There are two aspects of the validation procedure. The first is to compare the results of the model with known system performance under identical circumstances. Ideally, the model should generate the same results as the real system. Discrepancies should be noted, and the model should be revised as needed in order to achieve this goal. Naturally, this assumes that there is an existing system that can be used for this purpose. If this is not the case, validation must rely on a second aspect: a test of reasonableness.

The test of reasonableness refers to testing the performance of the model under conditions that relate to questions that are to be answered by the simulation. For instance, in the bus simulation, the question of the impact of different size buses may be important. Presumably, historical data on this are not available, because if they were, there would be no reason to employ simulation. Even though there has been no experience with certain conditions, it should be possible for individuals who are closely associated with the real system, or similar systems, to make meaningful assessments about the reasonableness of simulation results under such modified conditions.

Another aspect of this phase involves careful checking of both the assumptions that underlie the model and the values of the parameters used in the model. The judgment of those who will be using the results of the simulation is a key factor. Not only are those persons apt to be very knowledgeable about such matters, but by being asked for their inputs, they also become an integral part of model design. If those people are not consulted, there is a real possibility that the value of the simulation results will suffer. Either the users will not undertand the model and, therefore, will not "buy into" the results, or they will resent having been left out of the development of something that they will be expected to make work.

Notice the feedback loop between validation and model development. The validation phase often uncovers deficiencies in the model that must be corrected, and the ensuing results must then be validated. In fact, it is not unusual to go around this loop a number of times before the final model is obtained.

Designing Experiments

The fourth step in simulation is designing experiments. The experiments are the heart of a simulation study. They are intended to answer the "what if . . . ?" questions posed to the model. It is through this process of exploring the model's response to issues of concern that the manager or analyst learns about system behavior. The person who is designing the experiments must look to the objectives of the simulation for guidance. Hence, the more completely those objectives have been spelled out, the better the chances will be for designing experiments that will provide the desired answers to management's questions.

Running Simulations

The fifth step in the simulation process is actually "running" or performing the simulations. If a simulation is deterministic, runs that are made under identical sets of conditions will produce exactly the same result. Consequently, only one run is required for each set of conditions in a deterministic simulation. Probabilistic simulations, on the other hand, tend to produce different results with successive runs, even though the set of conditions under which the simulations are run are unchanged. Therefore, a probabilistic simulation will require a number of runs—perhaps a large number—in order to "average out" the variability that is inherent in such a simulation.

Probabilistic simulation amounts to a form of sampling, and each run represents one observation. Therefore, the same concepts used in random sampling to determine how large a sample to take apply to deciding how many simulation runs to make. In general, the higher the amount of variation observed in values of variables of primary interest in repeated runs, the greater the number of runs needed to estimate the expected values of those variables. If the variability is higher among certain variables, that higher variability will be the main determinant of the number of runs needed. Further, the greater the variability obtained during simulation for a particular variable, the greater the likelihood that the behavior exhibited by the real system will differ from the expected value based on the simulation study. If the observed variability is deemed excessive, management may want to devote some effort to redesigning the system to reduce the variability to a more acceptable level or, perhaps, to better cope with the variability. For example, flexible systems due to multipurpose equipment and/or personnel that are capable of performing different tasks can offset some of the effects of variability in demand for services. Flexible scheduling and selective pricing policies also are possible solutions.

Analyzing and Interpreting the Results

The final step in the simulation process is to analyze and interpret the results. Probabilistic simulations tend to require more effort in this phase than deterministic simulations. Due to the presence of random variability, one can never be completely sure that the observed results are completely representative. Statistical analysis of probabilistic simulations provides the key for dealing with random variability; expected values, confidence intervals, and tests of significance are vital tools of analysis. Thus, analysis of simulation results should provide the decision maker with both an expected value for a given variable and a range of values in which the actual value may fall. Moverover, significance tests can be used to help decide whether observed differences among alternatives are indicative of real, or simply chance, factors.

Interpreting simulation results depends to a certain extent on the degree to which the simulation model correctly portrays the real system. Obviously, if the simulation model is a crude approximation of the system, for whatever reason, applying those results to the real system will present a greater challenge, and greater risk, than if the model is a close approximation of reality. Hence, it is essential to take the degree of closeness between the model and the real system into account when interpreting the results.

THE MONTE CARLO METHOD

The central feature of probabilistic simulations is the incorporation of *random behavior* for the variable or variables of interest. Random behavior is exemplified by many games of chance, such as drawing cards from a well-shuffled deck, rolling dice, and spinning roulette wheels. In each case, the outcome of a particular draw, or roll, or spin has a *numerical value*. And while the probability of the occurrence of any particular value can be readily computed, it is impossible to predict precisely which value will occur next.

TABLE 17–1 Random Numbers

	1	2	3	4	5	6	7	8	9	10	11	12
1	18	20	84	29	91	73	64	33	15	67	54	07
2	25	19	05	64	26	41	20	09	88	40	73	34
3	73	57	80	35	04	52	81	48	57	61	29	35
4	12	48	37	09	17	63	94	08	28	78	51	23
5	54	92	27	61	58	39	25	16	10	46	87	17
6	96	40	65	75	16	49	03	82	38	33	51	20
7	23	55	93	83	02	19	67	89	80	44	99	72
8	31	96	81	65	60	93	75	64	26	90	18	59
9	45	49	70	10	13	79	32	17	98	63	30	05
10	01	78	32	17	24	54	52	44	28	50	27	68
11	41	62	57	31	90	18	24	15	43	85	31	97
12	22	07	38	72	69	66	14	85	36	71	41	58

These same characteristics are exhibited in a wide range of situations that are of interest to decision makers, such as the occurrence of accidents, fires, equipment breakdowns, the rate of demand for products and services, and service times. It is convenient to use an approach based on the type of random behavior that games of chance exhibit in order to *simulate* behavior of variables in these other situations because of the ease and simplicity with which randomness can be generated.

A commonly used approach for achieving randomness is the **Monte Carlo Method,** which derives its name from its similarity to games of chance. Conceptually, this approach is analogous to placing consecutively numbered chips (0, 1, 2, . . .) in a large bowl, mixing the chips, and then drawing a chip from the bowl and recording that number. By returning the chip to the bowl and repeating the process, a series of randomly generated numbers could be obtained. However, the process would be tedious and inefficient. Moreover, there are much better ways of obtaining random numbers. For manual simulation of the sort described in this chapter, a **random number table** is very useful. Computer simulations generally rely on internally generated random numbers.

Table 17–1 is the table of random numbers that we will use for many of the problems and examples in this chapter. It has been constructed to conform to these following characteristics when numbers are read in any order (e.g., across rows, up or down columns):

1. All numbers are equally likely.
2. No patterns appear in *sequences* of numbers.

The numbers are grouped in sets of two for convenience. However, they can be read in sets of one, two, three, or more as needed. The first characteristic—that the numbers are equally likely—means that if one-digit numbers are read, each number has a probability of one tenth (there are 10 one-digit numbers, 0 through 9) of occurring at any point. Therefore, knowing that a 3 has just been read has no relevance on predicting the next number; the probability of a 3 or any other number occurring next is still 1 in 10. Similarly, the probability for any two-digit number is one-hundredth because there are one hundred two-digit numbers (00, 01, 02, . . . , 99), and the probability is one-thousandth for any three-digit number.

When we say that no patterns will appear, this means, for example, that high values won't have a tendency to follow high values or low values won't have a tendency to follow high values. In other words, it will not be possible to predict which values will occur next in a sequence of values read from the table on the basis of previous values.

The obvious question at this point is: How can random numbers be used to simulate the behavior of a random variable? The answer lies in the way in which the random numbers are interpreted. How the numbers are interpreted is largely a function of the nature of the variable whose behavior is to be simulated. For instance, consider simulating the results of a series of coin tosses. For each toss, we want to know whether the result is a head or a tail. The values we obtain from the random number table are *numerical*. Consequently, they cannot be used *directly* to generate the desired results. Instead, we must first decide on a plan for transforming the numerical values we obtain from the table into "heads" and "tails." Actually, the approach is quite simple. Suppose we want to simulate results for a fair coin [i.e., $P(\text{heads}) = P(\text{tails}) = .50$]. There are 100 two-digit numbers. If we assign half of those to the result "heads" (say, 00 to 49) and the other half to the result "tails," (i.e., 50 to 99) we can simulate results that will generate "heads" about half the time and "tails" about half the time. Moreover, the sequence of heads and tails will behave in a random manner.

■

EXAMPLE 1 Simulate eight flips of a fair coin. Read two-digit numbers from Table 17–1, column 1 going down. Treat the numbers 00 to 49 as "heads" and 50 to 99 as "tails."

Solution

The first random number is 18. Because it falls in the range 00 to 49, it is treated as a head. The next number, 25, also falls in this range, so it too becomes a head. The third number is 73, which falls in the range 50 to 99, so it is treated as a tail. The remaining values are treated similarly. These results are summarized in Table 17–2.

Three out of eight trials produced tails, and five trials produced heads. Although we would expect to get approximtely 50 percent of each over the long run, this result seems reasonable for the relatively small number of observations taken.

The essence of using random numbers, then, is to establish a set of rules that can be used to convert the random numbers to simulated results. In general, problems will involve either *theoretical distributions* or *empirical distributions*

TABLE 17–2 Simulating a Coin Toss

Trial	Random Number*	Simulated Result	
1	18	Heads	Heads = 00 to 49
2	25	Heads	
3	73	Tails	Tails = 50 to 99
4	12	Heads	
5	54	Tails	
6	96	Tails	
7	23	Heads	
8	31	Heads	

* Taken from Table 17–1, column 1.

(i.e., based on historical data). Hence, there will be the need to assign random numbers to outcomes that relate to a specified distribution for the random variable in question.

Consider the replacement parts example that was described at the beginning of this chapter. Demand for spare parts was simulated for a 10-day period. Let's see how that simulation was accomplished. To begin with, the manager needed to obtain a distribution for demand. Recall that the manager did this through consultation with engineers and on the basis of his experience with other equipment. As a result, the manager developed the following distribution for demand frequency:

Parts per Day, x	$f(x)$
0	.60
1	.25
2	.10
3	.04
4	.01
	1.00

In order to assign random numbers to this distribution, it was convenient to first develop the *cumulative* distribution. Thus:

Parts per Day, x	$f(x)$	Cumulative $f(x)$
0	.60	.60
1	.25	.85
2	.10	.95
3	.04	.99
4	.01	1.00

TABLE 17–3 Assigning Random Numbers for the Replacement Parts Example

Demand per Day, x	Cumulative f(x)	Random Ranges
0	.60	00 to 59
1	.85	60 to 84
2	.95	85 to 94
3	.99	95 to 98
4	1.00	99

Because the cumulative probabilities are two-digit, it made sense to assign two-digit random number ranges because then there could be exact correspondence between the cumulative frequencies and the random numbers. The assignments for the random numbers are shown in Table 17–3. Note that the assignments begin at the low end of the distribution (i.e., demand of 0), with the smallest possible random number at that end. It will be helpful to note that after the first class, the left (lower) end of each range is equal to the cumulative frequency (ignoring the decimal point) of the preceding class, whereas the right (upper) end of each range is equal to 1 less than the cumulative probability for its class. For instance, for the second class (i.e., demand = 1), the range of two-digit random numbers that will correspond to that class is 60 to 84; the 60 equals the cumulative probability for the preceding class and the 84 is 1 less than the cumulative probability for the second class. Other ranges are similarly determined.

Now, daily usage of replacement parts can be simulated by obtaining a series of random numbers from Table 17–1 and, by noting in which range each random number falls, translating the numbers into number of parts demanded per simulated day. This is illustrated in Table 17–4 using two-digit random numbers from column 10.

These results are identical to those presented in the replacement parts example at the beginning of the chapter, and they illustrate how those results were obtained. Moreover, we have seen how a random number table can be used in conjunction with a frequency distribution to simulate the behavior of a random variable.

Although the Monte Carlo method is relatively simple to understand and to use, it provides the manager or analyst with a powerful tool by enabling that person to study the behavior of random variables over any desired number of periods, in a very short "real" time frame. Thus, experience can be quickly built up on paper using simulation, as opposed to going through the process of waiting that would be required if the experience were to come from observing reality.

TABLE 17–4 Simulation of Replacement Parts Usage

Demand per Day, x	Random Number Range	Day	1	2	3	4	5	6	7	8	9	10
		Random Number	67	40	61	78	46	33	44	90	63	50
0	00 to 59	→		0			0	0	0			0
1	60 to 84	→	1		1	1					1	
2	85 to 94	→								2		
3	95 to 98											
4	99											

Simulation Using a Theoretical Distribution

We have seen how frequency distributions based on historical data can be used to conduct a simulation. It is also possible to employ a theoretical distribution, such as a Poisson distribution or a normal distribution, for a simulation. In this section, use of a Poisson distribution is demonstrated; in the following section, the use of a normal distribution and two other theoretical distributions are demonstrated.

■

EXAMPLE 2 Distress calls are received at a coast guard station at a rate that can be modeled using a Poisson distribution with a mean of .50 calls per hour during weekends. Simulate three hours of experience.

Solution

We must first obtain cumulative Poisson probabilities for the stated mean of .50 from Appendix Table C. Those probabilities must then be used to develop ranges for random number interpretation. Thus:

x	Cumulative Probability	Number Ranges
0	.607	000–606
1	.910	607–909
2	.986	910–985
3	.998	986–997
4	1.000	998–999

Note that the number ranges are expressed to three digits. This will make it easier to use the Poisson table, which also is expressed in three-digit numbers. Suppose we want to use numbers from columns 1 and 2 of Table 17–1. We can use the two digits from column 1 plus the first digit from column 2 to obtain a three-digit random number. Thus, reading down the top of columns 1 and 2, we would obtain these three-digit numbers:

182
251
735
124
.
.
.

To simulate three hours of calls, we can use the first three numbers. The first number, 182, falls in the range 000 to 606, so it corresponds to no calls in the first hour. Similarly, the second number, 251, falls in the same range, so it corresponds to no calls in the second hour. The third number, 735, falls in the range 607 to 909, so it corresponds to one call in the third hour. These results can be summarized as follows:

Hour	Random Number	Simulated Number of Calls
1	182	0
2	251	0
3	735	1

In each of the preceding examples, the random variable of interest was discrete: Only certain distinct values were possible. In many cases, the random variable is continuous rather than discrete: It can assume *any* value, integer or noninteger, over some range. Service time would be an example of such a variable. For example, the time to repair a piece of equipment could be 53.28 minutes.

Simulations that involve continuous variables typically are next-event simulations, or they are otherwise concerned with *how much* value (time, distance, area, etc.) a random variable assumes.

Three distributions that are commonly encountered in such simulations are the uniform distribution, the exponential distribution, and the normal distribution. The generation of random numbers based on each of these distributions is described in the following sections, beginning with the uniform distribution.

The Uniform Distribution

In the case of a uniform distribution, a random variable can assume any value over a certain specified range, and all values in that range have an equal probability of

FIGURE 17–2 Conversion of a Random Number to a Uniform Distribution

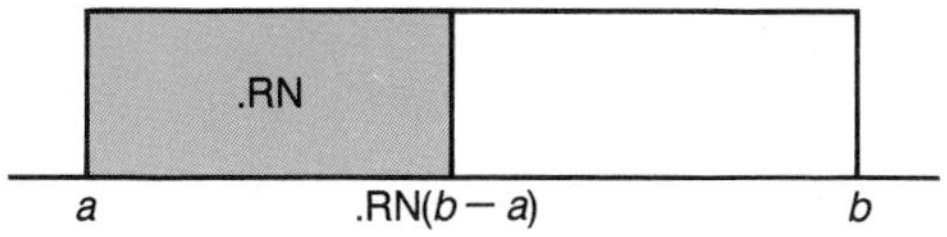

being selected. For instance, suppose that service time for a particular process varies uniformly between 2 and 3 minutes. This means that any value in this range is possible, and no value is any more likely than any other.

To simulate values of such a random variable, use the following procedure:

1. Obtain a two-digit random number (RN) from Table 17–1. Place a decimal in front of it (.RN).
2. Treat the lower end of the range as a and the upper end of the range as b. Compute the simulated value using the equation:

$$\text{Simulated value} = a + .\text{RN}(b - a) \tag{17–1}$$

3. For each simulated value, repeat steps 1 and 2.

Figure 17–2 illustrates this concept.

EXAMPLE 3 The time needed to process a job order can be modeled using a uniform distribution with endpoints of $a = 2$ minutes and $b = 5$ minutes. Simulate two processing times. Use random numbers from Table 17–1, row 3.

Solution

The random numbers are 73 and 57. The simulated times are:

For 73: $2 + .73(5 - 2) = 4.19$ minutes
For 57: $2 + .57(5 - 2) = 3.71$ minutes

The Exponential Distribution

In the negative exponential distribution, the probability is relatively high that the variable will assume a small value. Moreover, the probability decreases as the value in question increases. The probability that a random variable will take on a value greater than T given that the variable can be described by an exponential distribution with mean equal to $\frac{1}{\lambda}$ is given by the equation:

$$P(t > T) = e^{-\lambda T} \tag{17–2}$$

FIGURE 17–3 Simulating Exponentially Distributed Random Numbers

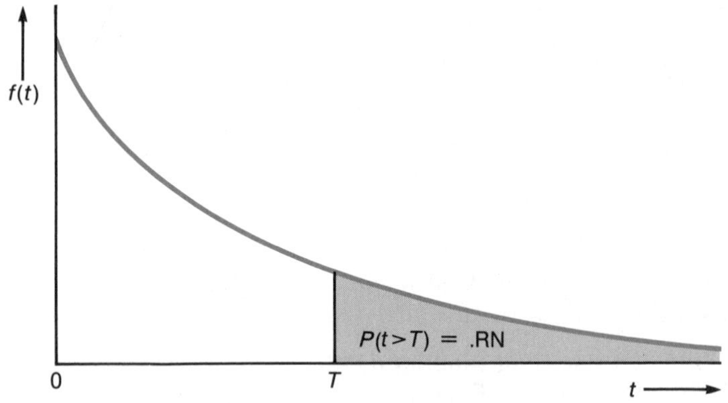

To simulate exponential values, we let the random number serve as this probability, $P(t > T)$, and then solve the equation for T. The result will be a simulated value from the exponential distribution with the given mean, λ. We can obtain an expression for T by taking the natural logarithm (ln) of both sides of the equation. Thus, with $P(t > T) = .\text{RN}$, we have:

$$\ln(.\text{RN}) = \ln(e^{-\lambda T}) = -\lambda\, T$$

$$\text{Then } T = -\frac{1}{\lambda}\ln(.\text{RN}) \qquad (17\text{–}3)$$

The effect of Formula 17–3 is that small random numbers produce large time values. This concept is illustrated in Figure 17–3.

■

EXAMPLE 4 An analyst has found that the length of time needed to repair a certain type of equipment when it fails can be described by a negative exponential distribution with a mean of 4 hours. Simulate two repair times for this type of equipment.

Solution

$$\frac{1}{\lambda} = 4 \text{ hours}$$

Suppose the two random numbers are 45 and 81. The simulated repair times are, using Formula 17–3:

For 45: $T = -4\ln(.45) = 3.194$ hours

For 81: $T = -4\ln(.81) = .843$ hours

TABLE 17–5 Normally Distributed Random Numbers

	1	2	3	4	5	6	7	8	9	10
1	1.46	0.09	−0.59	0.19	−0.52	−1.82	0.53	−1.12	1.36	−0.44
2	−1.05	0.56	−0.67	−0.16	1.39	−1.21	0.45	−0.62	−0.95	0.27
3	0.15	−0.02	0.41	−0.09	−0.61	−0.18	−0.63	−1.20	0.27	−0.50
4	0.81	1.87	0.51	0.33	−0.32	1.19	2.18	−2.17	1.10	0.70
5	0.74	−0.44	1.53	−1.76	0.01	0.47	0.07	0.22	−0.59	−1.03
6	−0.39	0.35	−0.37	−0.52	−1.14	0.27	−1.78	0.43	1.15	−0.31
7	0.45	0.23	0.26	−0.31	−0.19	−0.03	−0.92	0.38	−0.04	0.16
8	2.40	0.38	−0.15	−1.04	−0.76	1.12	−0.37	−0.71	−1.11	0.25
9	0.59	−0.70	−0.04	0.12	1.60	0.34	−0.05	−0.26	0.41	0.80
10	−0.06	0.83	−1.60	−0.28	0.28	−0.15	0.73	−0.13	−0.75	−1.49

The Normal Distribution

It is not unusual to find simulation problems that involve the normal distribution. In fact, the normal distribution is probably the most frequently encountered distribution in practice. This is due, in part, not only to the fact that many natural phenomena can be well-represented by a normal distribution, but also to the fact that the normal distribution is an important theoretical distribution in statistical sampling.

There are a number of different ways to achieve random numbers that are normally distributed. For instance, such random numbers can be easily generated by computers. For hand simulations, an extremely simple approach is to use a special table of normally distributed random numbers. This approach will be demonstrated here.

Table 17–5 contains normally distributed random numbers. Numbers can be obtained from this table in essentially the same manner that we obtained random numbers from Table 17–1. Thus, numbers can be read one by one, in either rows or columns. The numbers represent z, which measures the number of standard deviations an observation is from the mean of the normal distribution. For example, a value of −2.13 would indicate a simulated value that is 2.13 standard deviations *below* the distribution mean. This concept is illustrated in Figure 17–4.

In order to determine the value of the observation, the following formula can be applied:

$$\text{Simulated value} = \text{Mean} + \text{RN} \times \text{Standard deviation} \quad (17\text{–}4)$$

■

EXAMPLE 5 Simulate two values from a normal distribution that has a mean of 200 and a standard deviation of 10. Use the first two random numbers in column 5 of Table 17–5.

FIGURE 17–4 Simulation Using Normally Distributed Random Numbers

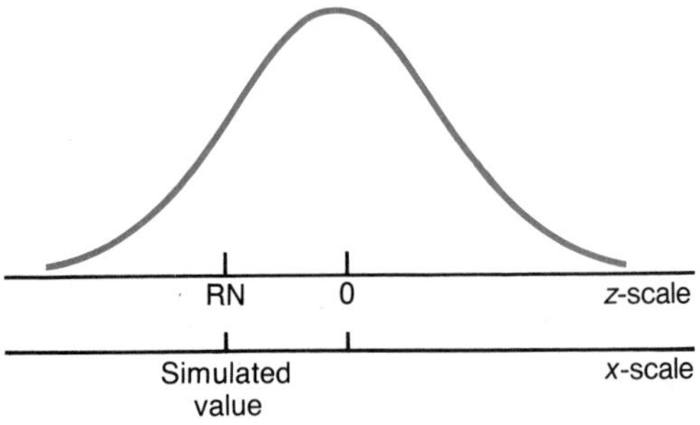

Solution

The random numbers are -0.52 and 1.39. Using Formula 17–4, the simulated values are:

$$\text{For } -0.52\text{: } 200 - 0.52(10) = 194.8$$
$$\text{For } 1.39\text{: } 200 + 1.39(10) = 213.9$$

MULTIPLE-VARIABLE SIMULATIONS

The preceding examples illustrate situations in which the behavior of a single variable is being simulated, such as the usage of parts per day, or the length of the repair time. In order to simulate the occurrence of an event, or the experience of one period of time (e.g., a day), in a single variable problem, one random number is required. Single-variable examples are useful for illustrating important simulation concepts. Moreover, there are many applications of single-variable problems in real life. Nevertheless, there also are many cases in real life that involve *multiple* variables, and we now turn our attention to that class of simulations.

A multiple-variable problem has at least two variables. For example, we might want to simulate a situation in which there are a number of machines that need a variety of services from time to time. The simulation might involve these phases: which machine needs service, what service is needed, and how much time is required to perform the service. Hence, *three* variables are involved, and *three* sets of random numbers will be needed, one to simulate each of the variables. Another example of a multiple-variable situation would be a case in which the first variable of interest was type of job to be processed and the second was length of processing time. One set of random numbers would be needed to simulate the type of job and a second set for processing time. Such a simulation may involve two

FIGURE 17–5 Two Common Types of Multiple-Variable Simulations

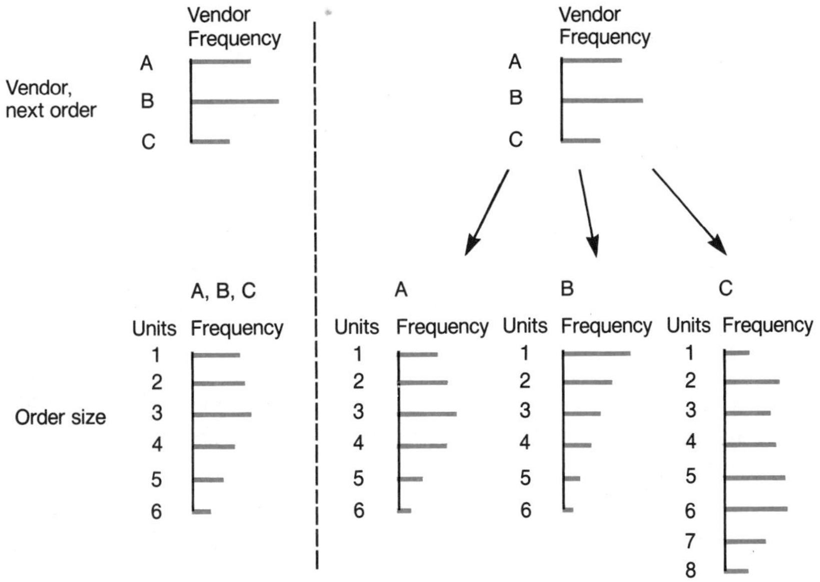

distributions, the first for type of job and the second for length of processing time. However, if different jobs had processing times that were described by *different* frequency distributions, then simulation of the processing time would depend on which type of job was generated by the simulation of job type.

A similar situation might involve order sizes that were dependent on which vendor was ordering. Figure 17–5 presents a comparison of these two types of multiple-variable simulations using this last example.

EXAMPLE 6 An analyst wants to simulate ordering stock from each of three departments, A, B, and C. The percentage of orders by department is shown in the following distribution:

Department	Frequency
A	.35
B	.25
C	.40

The order sizes for these departments can be described by these frequency distributions:

A: Order Size	Frequency	B: Order Size	Frequency	C: Order Size	Frequency
10	.15	20	.20	15	.25
15	.45	25	.25	20	.55
20	.25	30	.30	25	.15
25	.15	35	.15	30	.05
		40	.10		

Simulate four orders. For each order, indicate which department has placed the order and the size of the order. Read two-digit numbers from Table 17–1, column 2 for department and two-digit numbers from column 4 of the same table for order size.

Solution

The first step is to develop ranges for random number interpretations using the frequency distributions. Thus, for department we have:

Department	Frequency	Cumulative Frequency	Number Range
A	.35	.35	00–34
B	.25	.60	35–59
C	.40	1.00	60–99

For order size, each department has its individual distribution,

A: Order Size	Frequency	Cumulative Frequency	Number Range
10	.15	.15	00–14
15	.45	.60	15–59
20	.25	.85	60–84
25	.15	1.00	85–99

B: Order Size	Frequency	Cumulative Frequency	Number Range
20	.20	.20	00–19
25	.25	.45	20–44
30	.30	.75	45–74
35	.15	.90	75–89
40	.10	1.00	90–99

C: Order Size	Frequency	Cumulative Frequency	Number Range
15	.25	.25	00–24
20	.55	.80	25–79
25	.15	.95	80–94
30	.05	1.00	95–99

Next, we obtain random numbers from the specified columns of Table 17–1. Using numbers from column 2 for *departments* and numbers from column 4 for *order size,* we have the following:

Order Number	RN	Simulated Department	RN	Simulated Order Size	
1	20	A	29	15	(Using Department A distribution)
2	19	A	64	20	(Using Department A distribution)
3	57	B	35	25	(Using Department B distribution)
4	48	B	09	20	(Using Department B distribution)

Thus, the first random number in column 2 is 20. Referring to the frequency distribution for departments, this corresponds to Department A. Next, the order size is found by selecting the first random number from column 4 and referring to *Department A's* frequency distribution. Hence, the interpretation of the order size random number is dependent on the department, so we must first determine (simulate) the department and then determine (simulate) order size.

COMPUTER SIMULATION

The emphasis in this chapter is on manual simulation. The primary reason for this is to focus on understanding the *concepts* of simulation, and a "hands on" approach is usually the best way to accomplish that goal. Nevertheless, most real-life applications of simulation involve the use of computers. In order to get meaningful results, a large number of runs may have to be made. Sometimes, the required number of runs can be very large, say in the hundreds. This alone would militate against manual simulation. Beyond that, however, is the fact that many applications involve a great deal of complexity because of the need to simulate the interactions of multiple stages and numerous variables. Again, this militates against a manual approach.

Simulation Languages

Over the years, a number of simulation languages have been developed that make the task of writing simulation programs much more straightforward than working with a standard programming language such as FORTRAN or BASIC. Some of the most widely used of these specialty languages are SIMSCRIPT, GPSS, GASP, and DYNAMO. In addition, there are a number of other simulation languages, some of which are particularly suited to a narrow application such as simulation of queuing systems or networks.

Most of the simulation packages have certain features in common. In general, they provide for random number generation from different statistical distributions, collection and tabulation of simulation results, time keeping, and printouts of results.

Some managers prefer to write their own simulations, or have their staff do so, using one of the standard programming languages such as FORTRAN, Pascal, or BASIC rather than a simulation language. In cases where simulation is used infrequently, this approach may be practical; it may not be worth the time and effort to learn how to use a special simulation language. Conversely, if simulation is used fairly regularly to analyze problems, use of a simulation language is the expedient choice.

Pseudo-Random Numbers

Although computers could be programmed to read random numbers from a table of numbers that has been put into memory, such an approach would not be an efficient use of computer storage. Instead, computer codes usually incorporate a random number generator based on an algorithm that produces a string of digits that exhibit the characteristics of randomness. The resulting numbers, for all practical purposes, can be regarded as random numbers. However, they are referred to as **pseudo-random numbers** because the "next" number at any point in the series can be determined by using the same algorithm used by the computer. In that sense, the numbers are not truly random. Nevertheless, this condition does not impair the usefulness of computer-generated random numbers.

ADVANTAGES AND LIMITATIONS OF SIMULATION

Simulation has proven to be a valuable tool for exploring complex problems. Among the major advantages of simulation are the following:

1. It is particularly well-suited for problems that are difficult or impossible to solve mathematically.
2. It allows an analyst or decision maker to experiment with system behavior in a controlled environment instead of in a real-life setting that has inherent risks.
3. It enables a decision maker to compress time in order to evaluate the long-term effects of various alternatives.
4. It can serve as a mode for training decision makers by enabling them to observe the behavior of a system under different conditions.

Despite the obvious benefits of simulation, decision makers must exercise a certain amount of care in deciding when to use a simulation approach. The reasons for this are varied. Among the main reasons are the following:

1. Probabilistic simulation results are *approximations,* rather than optimal solutions.
2. Good simulations can be costly and time-consuming to develop properly;

they can also be time-consuming to run, especially in cases in which a large number of trials is indicated.

3. A certain amount of expertise is required in order to design a good simulation, and this may not be readily available.
4. Analytical techniques may be available that can provide better answers to problems.

WHEN TO USE SIMULATION

Because of the time, effort, and cost associated with simulation studies, and because probabilistic simulations only provide approximate answers to "What if . . . ?" questions, simulation is generally not the first choice of a decision maker who is faced with a problem. Instead, other approaches must first be examined: Simulation may be used if other approaches are deemed inappropriate. In most instances, an intuitive solution to a problem based on judgment and experience should be considered. If that does not provide a satisfactory solution, suitable analytical techniques should be considered. If none are suitable, simulation may be a reasonable alternative. The decision maker must still weigh the costs and benefits of simulation before using that route, and be fully cognizant that simulation will not guarantee an optimal decision to a problem.

SUMMARY

Simulation can be an important tool for managerial decision making. Unlike analytical techniques such as linear programming, however, it is not an optimizing technique. Instead, simulation is a *descriptive* tool. The goal in simulation is to create a model that will reflect the behavior of some real-life system in order to be able to observe how it may behave when certain inputs or parameters are changed.

The chapter focuses on manual simulations using the Monte Carlo method. Simulations are illustrated for both fixed-interval and next-event simulations, using a variety of discrete and continuous distributions. In addition, single-variable and multiple-variable simulations are described.

Simulation is useful for problems that are too complex to be handled by either intuitive approaches or analytical models. Simulation models enable decision makers to compress time and to observe system behaviors under a variety of different circumstances (i.e., to answer "What if . . . ?" questions). However, simulations sometimes yield only approximate results, they can be costly and/or time-consuming, and they often require considerable expertise to achieve satisfactory models.

GLOSSARY

Fixed-Interval Simulation A simulation in which the value of a variable is counted at the end of an interval.

Monte Carlo Method A method for generating random numbers that duplicates chance variability.

Next-Event Simulation A simulation in which the time or distance between event occurrences is simulated.

Pseudo-Random Number A random number generated by a computer based on an algorithm.

Random Number Table A table of randomly distributed digits used in Monte Carlo simulations.

Simulate Use a model to obtain observations that represent the behavior of a system.

Simulation A study of the behavior of a system under various conditions.

Validation Checking the output of a simulation model to determine if it approximates the known or expected behavior of its real-life counterpart.

SOLVED PROBLEMS

Problem 1. Simulate the number of calls per day to a fire station for a five-day interval, given the following information that was obtained from station records. Read two-digit numbers across row 11.

Calls	Number of Days
0	21
1	15
2	12
3	9
4	3
	60

Solution

If the frequency (number of days) is in actual counts rather than relative frequencies (i.e., relative frequencies would add to 1.00), the frequencies must be converted to relative frequencies. To do this, divide each count by the total (e.g., 21/60 = .35, 15/60 = .25, etc.). Next, obtain the cumulative relative frequencies by successively summing the relative frequencies (see the third and fourth column below). Then, obtain the random number range for each cumulative frequency (see the fifth column below). For example, the first range is 00 to 1 less than the cumulative frequency of .35. Thus, the range is 00 to 34. The second range is from 35 to 1 less than the second cumulative frequency, which is .60. Therefore, that range is 35 to 59, and so on.

Calls	Number of Days	Relative Frequency	Cumulative Relative Frequency	Random Number Range
0	21	.35	.35	00 to 34
1	15	.25	.60	35 to 59
2	12	.20	.80	60 to 79
3	9	.15	.95	80 to 94
4	3	.05	1.00	95 to 99
	60	1.00		

The first random number in row 11 is 41. Comparing this to the random number ranges, we can see that it falls in the second range, which corresponds to 1 call. Hence, the simulated number of calls on the first day is 1. The second random number is 62, which falls in the range 60 to 79. This corresponds to 2 calls on Day 2. The third random number is 57. It falls in the range 35 to 59, which corresponds to 1 call on Day 3. The fourth number is 31, which falls in the range 00 to 34. This corresponds to 0 calls on day 4. Lastly, the fifth number is 90, which corresponds to 3 calls on day 5. These results can be summarized as follows:

Day	1	2	3	4	5
Random number	41	62	57	31	90
Simulated number of calls	1	2	1	0	3

Problem 2. Travel time to fire calls can be modeled by a normal distribution that has a mean of 6 minutes and a standard deviation of 2 minutes. Simulate travel time for 3 calls using values from row 2.

Solution
The random numbers are: -1.05, 0.56, and -0.67. Using Formula 17–4, we obtain the following:

Call	Random Number	Calculation		Simulated Travel Time
1	−1.05	6 − 1.05(2)	=	3.90 minutes
2	0.56	6 + 0.56(2)	=	7.12
3	−0.67	6 − 0.67(2)	=	4.66

Problem 3. *Multi-event* Telephone company repair trucks require emergency repairs on a random basis. The company has three different types of emergencies, which it has classified as A, B, and C. They occur with these frequencies.

Type	Frequency
A	.35
B	.45
C	.20

Repair times tend to be *uniformly* distributed within these ranges:

Type	Repair Time
A	20 to 40 minutes
B	30 to 60 minutes
C	10 to 50 minutes

Simulate repair for 5 emergencies. Read two-digit numbers across row 2 for type of emergency and two-digit numbers across row 3 for repair time.

Solution

a. Prepare a cumulative distribution for type of emergency and establish ranges:

Type	Frequency	Cumulative Frequency	Random Number Ranges
A	.35	.35	00 to 34
B	.45	.80	35 to 79
C	.20	1.00	80 to 99
	1.00		

b. As specified in the question, obtain random numbers from row 2 for type emergency and random numbers from row 3 for repair time. These result in the following:

Emergency	Row 2 Random Number	Simulated Type	Row 3 Random Number	Calculation	Simulated Repair Time
1	25	A	73	20 + .73(40 − 20) =	34.6
2	19	A	57	20 + .57(40 − 20) =	31.4
3	05	A	80	20 + .80(40 − 20) =	36.0
4	64	B	35	30 + .35(60 − 30) =	40.5
5	25	A	04	20 + .04(40 − 20) =	20.8

Note that the calculation of simulated repair time *depends* on the simulated type of emergency; each emergency type has a different repair time distribution. In this instance, the first three simulated emergencies involved Type A, the fourth involved Type B, and the fifth involved Type A again. The A calculations are based on a uniform distribution of 20 to 40 minutes, whereas the B calculation is based on its uniform repair distribution of 30 to 60 minutes. And, it happened that no Cs occurred.

Problem 4. A consultant for a regional planning commission has developed a model for the purpose of studying population growth in a certain community. As part of the investigation, the consultant intends to simulate population growth in order to assess community demand for energy. The model to be used is the following:

$$P = 200{,}000 + 100t + 30e$$

where

P = total population

t = year t

e = error term

The error term, e, is expected to be normally distributed with a mean of zero and a standard deviation of 40. Simulate population totals for years $t = 3$ to $t = 5$, using values from column 2 of Table 17–5, reading down.

Solution
The values from Table 17–5 are:

0.09
0.56
−0.02

The first value corresponds to e for $t = 3$, the second corresponds to e for $t = 4$, and the third for e with $t = 5$. Therefore, the simulated population totals are:

$$P_{t=3} = 200{,}000 + 100(3) + 30[40(0.09)] = 200{,}408$$
$$P_{t=4} = 200{,}000 + 100(4) + 30[40(0.56)] = 201{,}072$$
$$P_{t=5} = 200{,}000 + 100(5) + 30[40(-0.020)] = 200{,}476$$

Problem 5. The time between mechanics' requests for tools in a large plant is normally distributed with a mean of 10 minutes and a standard deviation of 1 minute. The time to fill requests is also normal with a mean of 9 minutes per request and a standard deviation of 1 minute. Mechanics' waiting time represents a cost of $2 per minute, and servers represent a cost of $1 per minute. Simulate arrivals for the first nine mechanic requests and their service times, and determine the mechanics' waiting time, assuming one server. Would it be economical to add another server? Explain. Use Table 17–5, column 8 for requests and column 9 for service.

Solution
a. Obtain random numbers and convert to times (see columns a and b in the following table for requests and columns f and g for service).

Customer Arrivals				Service			
(a)	(b)	(c)	(d)	(e)	(f)	(g)	(h)
Random → Number	Time between Arrivals	Cumulative Arrival Time	(e − c) Customer Waiting Time	Service Begins	Random → Number	Service Time	(e + g) Service Ends
−1.12	8.88	8.88	0.00	8.88	1.36	10.36	19.24
−0.62	9.38	18.26	0.98	19.24	−0.95	9.05	28.29
−1.20	8.80	27.06	1.23	28.29	0.27	9.27	37.56
−2.17	7.83	34.89	2.67	37.56	1.10	10.10	47.66
0.22	10.22	45.11	2.55	47.66	−0.59	8.41	56.07
0.43	10.43	55.54	0.53	56.07	1.15	10.15	66.22
0.38	10.38	65.92	0.30	66.22	−0.04	8.96	75.18
−0.71	9.39	75.31	0.00	75.31	−1.11	7.89	83.20
−0.26	9.74	85.05	0.00	85.05	0.41	8.59	93.64
			8.62				

b. Determine arrival times (column c) by successive adding to times between arrivals in column b.

c. Use arrival times for service start *unless service is still in progress on a previous request*. In that case, determine how long the arrival must wait (e − c). Column e values are the sum of starting time and service time (column g), which is the time service ends (column h). Thus, service on each new request begins (column e) at the same time that service on the previous request ends (column h).

d. The simulation and resulting waiting times for the first nine arrivals are shown in the table. Total waiting time is 8.26 minutes.

e. The total cost for the 93.64 minutes (end of service on the ninth request) of the simulation is:

Waiting cost	8.26 minutes at \$2 per minute =	\$ 16.52
Server cost	93.64 minutes at \$1 per minute =	93.64
		\$110.16

f. Usually, a second simulation with two servers would be needed (but with the same arrival times so that the results would be comparable). However, in this case it is apparent that a second server would increase server cost by about \$93 but could not eliminate more than \$16.52 of waiting cost. Hence, the second server would not be justified.

PROBLEMS

(Unless otherwise specified, read random numbers *down* columns and from left to right *across* rows.)

1. Simulation has proven to be a valuable tool for decision makers over a wide range of problems.
   a. Explain what the term *simulation* means as employed in this chapter.
   b. Explain why simulation usually is the approach of last resort.
   c. What main characteristic did each of the simulation examples in this chapter possess?

2. The cumulative frequency distribution for the number of birthday cakes ordered per day at a bakery is as follows:

Number of Cakes	Cumulative Frequency
0	.01
1	.08
2	.18
3	.32
4	.51
5	.73
6	.89
7	.97
8	1.00

a. Establish random number ranges for each possible order size.

b. Using two-digit random numbers reading down column 9 of Table 17–1, simulate orders for a six-day period.

c. Simulate a second six-day period, continuing in column 9. How different are these results than those of part *b*? Why are the results different? What is the implication of this?

3. The number of wide screen television sets sold per day at a department store can be described by this frequency distribution:

Number of Sets	Frequency
0	.16
1	.24
2	.22
3	.15
4	.10
5	.08
6	.05

a. Indicate how random numbers could be assigned to this distribution.

b. Simulate the number of sets sold for a five-day period. Use random numbers from Table 17–1, row 2.

c. Repeat part *b* continuing in row 2 of the random number table.

d. Why do the weekly totals vary? How do the totals compare to expected sales?

4. The number of typographical errors in letters typed by a certain secretary can be described by this frequency distribution:

Number of Errors per Page	Frequency
0	.75
1	.18
2	.05
3	.02

a. Indicate how random numbers could be assigned to this distribution.

b. Simulate the number of errors in four two-page letters, reading two-digit numbers from row 7 of Table 17–1.

c. Based on the results of part *b,* compute the average number of errors per letter.

5. The manager of an auto service center has compiled data on the number of cars per day that need transmission work. The numbers are repeated here:

Number of Cars	Frequency
0	6
1	14
2	18
3	10
4	2

a. Indicate how random numbers could be assigned to this distribution.

b. Simulate experience for a five-day period. Read two-digit numbers going down column 8, Table 17–1.

6. The number of days beyond the promised date that customers leave their dry cleaning at a certain store can be summarized by this data, which was obtained from the store's records:

Days beyond Date Promised	Frequency
0	104
1	46
2	16
3	6
4	14
5	10
6	0
7	4

Simulate the days beyond the promised date that the next seven customers leave their clothes. Use two-digit numbers from column 6 of Table 17–1, reading down. Compute the average number of days clothes are left beyond schedule for the simulation.

7. The night manager of a resort hotel has asked the telephone operator to keep track of the nature of all calls received from outside of the hotel. The results for 100 calls are shown below:

Nature of Call	Number of Calls
R: Make a reservation	42
C: Confirm/cancel	27
A: Check availability	14
P: Price inquiry	7
O: Other	10

The manager knows that the amount of time spent by the operator in responding to the calls differs depending on the nature of the call. The manager is, therefore, particularly interested in getting an idea of the sequence of calls, in order to gain insight into how the operator's time might be spent with the calls. To do this, the manager wants to simulate 10 calls.

a. Keeping the list of call types in the order shown, indicate how random numbers would be assigned to each call type.

b. Reading two-digit numbers from row 8 of Table 17–1, simulate the 10 calls.

c. What proportion of calls involve making a reservation? Does this proportion seem reasonable? Explain why it is different than the data collected by the telephone operator.

d. Repeat parts *b* and *c* reading two-digit numbers from row 9 of Table 17–1.

8. A company that sells canoes fills orders from independent retailers from a single warehouse. The manager of the warehouse has collected data on the number of canoes sold per day. That distribution is:

Number Sold	Frequency
1	.02
2	.13
3	.20
4	.25
5	.15
6	.10
7	.10
8	.05

The same distribution holds for each day. The warehouse is open five days a week. The manager wants to simulate daily demand for four five-day periods, in order to test the merits of beginning each week with 20 canoes on hand. Canoes are received from the factory once a week.

a. Read two-digit numbers from row 4 then row 5 of Table 17–1 to simulate daily demand for the four weeks. Use this format to record your results:

		Day	1	2	3	4	5
	1	RN					
		Demand					
	2	RN					
Week		Demand					
	3	RN					
		Demand					
	4	RN					
		Demand					

b. Estimate the proportion of weeks that demand will exceed supply if supply equals 20 canoes.

c. Comment on how accurate you believe your estimate is and why.

9. The managing partner of a construction firm has determined from company records that a certain piece of heavy equipment has a breakdown frequency that can be described by a Poisson distribution with a mean of 2 per month.

a. Simulate one year of breakdown experience for this equipment. Read three-digit numbers from columns 2 and 3 of Table 17–1 (e.g., 208, 190, . . .).

b. How many months experienced no breakdowns? Does this result seem reasonable? Explain.

c. There are no instances where there were two months in a row without a breakdown. How plausible is this? Explain.

10. The fire chief in a certain city has been told by a consultant that the occurrence of three-alarm fires can be described by a Poisson distribution that has a mean of 0.4 fires per day. The chief is concerned because it requires approximately two days after fighting a major fire to return equipment to good working order, and she wonders if additional equipment should be

requested from the planning board. The consultant has suggested a simulation study of the problem.

a. Simulate 24 days of experience using columns 10 and 11 of Table 17–1 (e.g., 675, 407, . . .) for the first 12 days and columns 11 and 12 (e.g., 540, 733, . . .) for the second 12 days.

b. For each fire, determine if there was adequate time to prepare the equipment for the next fire.

c. Determine the proportion of fires for which there was not sufficient time to prepare for the next fire.

11. Demand for pineapple juice at a theme park can be described by a uniform distribution that ranges between 50 and 130 gallons per day. Simulate daily demand for pineapple juice for 10 consecutive days. Read two-digit random numbers from column 5 of Table 17–1. For what proportion of days is simulated demand greater than expected demand? Does this seem reasonable? Explain.

12. The amount of insecticide dispensed by a crop duster has been found to vary uniformly between 60 and 80 gallons per run. Simulate 12 runs reading two-digit random numbers from row 6 of Table 17–1.

13. A design engineer has estimated that the time to perform a service using state-of-the-art equipment will vary uniformly between 5 and 7 minutes. Simulate service times for eight requests using two-digit random numbers from column 9 of Table 17–1.

14. After reviewing processing times, the manager of a computer service agrees that computer processing times for a certain class of jobs can be described by a negative exponential distribution with a mean of 1.2 minutes of CPU. Using two-digit numbers from row 3 of Table 17–1, simulate the processing times for the next 10 jobs. Then, compute the mean processing time for the simulated jobs. Explain why it does not equal the distribution mean.

15. The manager of a shop that repairs telephone equipment has determined that repair time can be modeled by a negative exponential distribution with a mean repair time of one hour. Simulate repair times for a sequence of seven jobs, using two-digit numbers from column 4 of Table 17–1.

16. In a study of the length of telephone calls, an analyst found that account representatives in a stockbroker's office spent an average of 5 minutes per call, and that call length could be modeled using a negative exponential distribution with that mean. Using Table 17–1, row 6, simulate the time for 12 calls. Compute the mean simulated time and compare it to the theoretical mean. Does the difference seem reasonable?

17. A consultant found that the time a doctor spent with a patient who was recovering from major surgery could be modeled by a normal distribution with a mean of 7 minutes and a standard deviation of 2 minutes. Simulate

the times doctors might spend with a sequence of five patients using random numbers from row 2 of Table 17–5.

18. The time it takes a typist to type a letter in a certain office can be modeled by a normal distribution that has a mean of 4 minutes and a standard deviation of 1 minute. Using values from column 2 of Table 17–5, simulate the times for six letters and then determine the total time required to type those six letters.

19. After careful study of operating room procedures, an analyst concluded that the amount of time required to perform a certain type of surgery could be modeled using a normal distribution with a mean of 120 minutes and a standard deviation of 10 minutes. The analyst wants to simulate times for nine operations. Using random numbers for column 4 of Table 17–5, simulate the times for the nine operations. Compare the average simulated time with the model average. How do they compare?

20. On the basis of historical data, a manager concluded that the length of time between failures for a certain piece of food processing equipment could be modeled by an exponential distribution that has a mean of 8 hours. In addition, the manager found that repair times could be modeled by a normal distribution with a mean of 4 hours and a standard deviation of 1.1 hours. For the next five breakdowns, simulate the length of time between breakdowns and the time needed for repairs. Then, find the waiting time for each breakdown (i.e., the length of time equipment waited for repair because the repairperson was busy working on a previous breakdown). Read values from Table 17–1, row 3 for breakdowns and values from Table 17–5, column 6 for repair times. For each breakdown, indicate operating time before breakdown, waiting time, and repair time.

21. A small supplier receives orders from three different companies for a certain piece of electrical equipment. Forty-five percent of the orders come from Firm A, 35 percent from Firm B, and the remainder from Firm C. Order sizes vary, depending on the firm involved. In the past, orders were as follows:

	Relative Frequency		
Order Size	**A**	**B**	**C**
4	.15	.05	.25
8	.30	.25	.35
12	.40	.35	.25
16	.13	.25	.12
20	.02	.10	.03

Using two-digit numbers from rows 5 and 6 of Table 17–1, simulate the next six orders: For each order, determine which firm ordered (row 5), then the size of the order (row 6).

22. A firm that replaces windshields receives from 0 to 4 calls per day for a midsized windshield that fits GM cars. The manager of the firm has compiled a frequency distribution for such calls and a distribution of replacement times. The daughter of a friend is currently enrolled in a business program. She examined the replacement time distribution and concluded that a normal distribution with a mean of 1.30 hours and a standard deviation of .20 hours would adequately describe the situation. The distribution of calls for the windshields is:

Calls	Frequency
0	7
1	10
2	15
3	10
4	8

Simulate four days' worth of experience. Read two-digit numbers from Table 17–1, column 4 for calls, and values from Table 17–5, column 4 for times for each call. Determine the total time per day for replacements of this type.

23. A recent graduate of a prominent school's college of business encounters 6 traffic lights on the way to work in the morning. The traffic lights have a two-minute cycle: red for one minute and yellow/green for one minute. This person stops only for a red light. Assume the lights operate independently of each other.

    a. What is the probability that any particular light will be red when the motorist in this problem approaches it?

    b. What probability distribution, normal, exponential, or uniform, would best describe the length of time the motorist would have to wait for a red light? What are the parameters of the distribution?

    c. Simulate four trips for this motorist. For each light's color, use two-digit numbers from Table 17–1, columns 5 and 6. If a light is red (00–49), determine the length of wait the motorist has before the light turns green using two-digit numbers from Table 17–1, column 8. For each light, indicate its condition. For red lights, indicate the amount of waiting time.

    d. Based on the results of part *c*, compute an estimate of the average amount of time per trip the motorist waits at red lights.

24. The motorist in the preceding problem wonders if an alternate route would result in a shorter waiting time. The alternate route has only two stoplights with the same two-minute cycle previously described. It also has two stop signs. The number of cars waiting at each can be described by a Poisson distribution with a mean of 2.0. The wait at a stop sign is approximately 30

seconds, if no cars are waiting. For each car that is waiting, an additional 30 seconds is added to the waiting time of the motorist.

a. Simulate four trips on the alternate route. For each light, read a two-digit number from Table 17–1, column 7. For light waiting time, read a two-digit number from column 10 of Table 17–1. For stop signs, read a three-digit number from Table 17–1, columns 5 and 6, to determine the number of cars waiting.

b. Compute the waiting time for each trip, then the average waiting time. How does this compare to the results of the preceding problem? Which route seems to offer the shortest waiting time? Is that necessarily the best route? Explain.

25. The owner of a firm that installs blacktop driveways wants to simulate weekly revenues. He notes that 70 percent of the jobs the firm receives are for residential work and the rest are for commercial work. The revenue for residential work tends to be uniformly distributed between $400 and $1,000. The revenue for commercial work tends to be normally distributed with a mean of $1,800 and a standard deviation of $500. The number of jobs per week can be modeled by a Poisson distribution with a mean of 2. Simulate total revenue for four weeks using random numbers as follows: For number of jobs per week, read a three-digit random number from Table 17–1, column 7; for type of work, read a two-digit number from Table 17–1, column 8; for residential income, read a two-digit number from row 4 of Table 17–1; and for commercial income, read a number from row 3 of Table 17–5. Indicate the revenue per week from each type of work and the total combined weekly revenue.

26. A service department in a manufacturing firm handles requests for service from a machine center that has five machines. The service requests can be for cleaning/adjustment, minor repair, or major repair. Records indicate that 25 percent of the requests are for Machine 1, 15 percent for Machine 2, 30 percent for Machine 3, 10 percent for Machine 4, and 20 percent for Machine 5. The nature of the requests is summarized in the following table:

	Machine				
Service	**1**	**2**	**3**	**4**	**5**
Cleaning/adjustment	.20	.30	.25	.40	.50
Minor repair	.45	.55	.35	.25	.28
Major repair	.35	.15	.40	.35	.22

Cleaning and adjustment time is uniformly distributed between 20 minutes and 40 minutes for all machines. Minor repair times are exponential with a mean of ½ hour for all machines, and major repair times are normal with a mean of 5 hours and a standard deviation of 1 hour for all machines. Use random number tables in this way: two-digit numbers from Table 17–1, column 5 for machine, two-digit numbers from Table 17–1, column 7 for type of service, and random numbers from Table 17–5, row 1, for service time. Simulate five requests for service. For each request indicate (*a*) which machine, (*b*) what service is requested, and (*c*) the service time required. Read random numbers from the appropriate tables in order, and simulate each request completely before moving on to the next request.

27. The manager of a building supply company has constructed a model that portrays monthly demand for exterior plywood. The model is:

$$\text{Demand for } 4 \times 8 \text{ sheets} = 2{,}000 + 20t + e$$

where

e = forecast error
t = period number

The manager is reasonably comfortable with a forecast error that is normally distributed with a mean of zero and a standard deviation of 100. Using values from Table 17–5, column 5, simulate demand for periods 10 through 15. Then, on a single graph, plot the model without the e term and the simulated values for the periods indicated.

28. The owner of a fruit farm sells peaches at two roadside stands. Based on past experience and the aid of a retired professor, the owner has developed two models that portray weekly revenue generated by each of the two locations. The models are:

Hillside location	$4{,}500 + 80t - 10t^2 + e$
Farmdale location	$3{,}000 + 90t - 10t^2 + e$

For the Hillside location, e is normally distributed with a mean of zero and a standard deviation of 100; for the Farmdale location, e is uniformly distributed with endpoints of -50 and $+50$. Simulate the revenue generated at each location for weeks $t = 2$ through $t = 9$. For the Hillside simulation, use values from Table 17–5, column 2, reading down. For the Farmdale location, read two-digit numbers from Table 17–1, column 4, reading up from the bottom.

29. John Stewart designs video games for a toy manufacturer. John has recently been working on a video pinball game. He has established a set of probabilities for the movements of the "ball" during a game. The player receives points depending on the positions the ball strikes during a game. These are shown below, along with probabilities for ball paths. Simulate the paths for three balls, and determine the number of points received for each ball. Use row 1 of Table 17–1 for Ball 1, row 9 for Ball 2, and row 3 for Ball 3. Read from left to right.

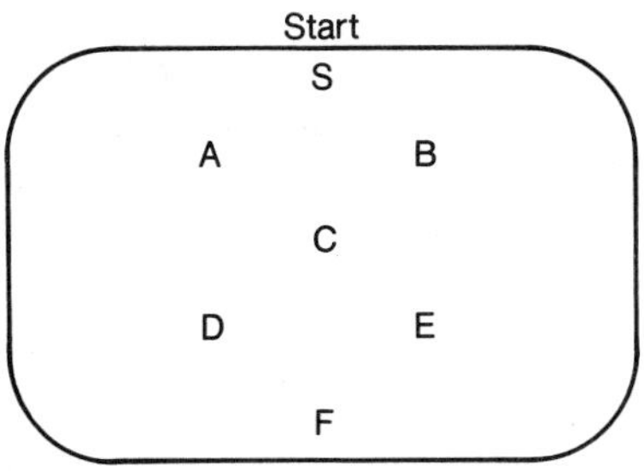

Position	Points
A	500
B	400
C	300
D	200
E	100
F	50

Path	Probability	Path	Probability
S to A	.30	C to A	.10
B	.30	B	.15
C	.25	C	.20
D	.10	D	.10
E	.04	E	.30
F	.01	F	.15
A to A	.25	D to A	.10
B	.25	B	.05
C	.25	C	.25
D	.10	D	.15
E	.10	E	.30
F	.05	F	.15
B to A	.30	E to A	.05
B	.20	B	.10
C	.20	C	.15
D	.15	D	.15
E	.10	E	.20
F	.05	F	.35

30. A distributor supplies pool chemicals to three firms that handle swimming pool maintenance. The distributor maintains an inventory of sodium bisulfate for the three firms. The distributor wants to limit the amount of supplies on hand due to storage problems. Nevertheless, the distributor would like to have a probability of at least 90 percent of not running out of stock during the week. Stocks are replenished every Monday and then picked up during the week by the three firms as needed. The chemicals are sold in multiples of five bags. Historical demand distributions for these firms are:

Weekly Demand	Relative Frequencey		
	Firm A	Firm B	Firm C
5	.10	.15	.20
10	.20	.25	.30
15	.20	.30	.25
20	.20	.20	.20
25	.30	.10	.05

Simulate demand for 10 weeks. Use row 1 of Table 17–1 for Firm A, row 2 for Firm B, and row 3 for Firm C. Based on your results, how many bags of sodium bisulfate should the distributor plan to have on hand at the beginning of each week to have a probability of 90 percent of satisfying weekly demand? Explain how you arrived at your answer.

31. Jobs are delivered to a workstation at random intervals. The time between job arrivals tends to be normally distributed with a mean of 15 minutes and a standard deviation of 1 minute. Job processing time is also normally distributed with a mean of 14 minutes per job and a standard deviation of 2 minutes.

    a. Using Table 17–5, simulate the arrival and processing of five jobs. Use column 4 of the table for job arrival times and column 3 for processing times. *Start each column at row 4.* Find the total times jobs wait for processing.

    b. The company is considering the use of new equipment that would result in processing time that is normal with a standard deviation of 1 minute. Job waiting represents a cost of $3 per minute, and the new equipment would represent an additional cost of $.50 per minute. Would the equipment be cost justified? (Note: Use the same arrival times and the same random numbers for processing times.)

32. Customers arrive randomly at a catalog department of a large store. The time between arrivals varies uniformly between 10 and 20 minutes. Service time is normal with a mean of 15 minutes and a standard deviation of 2 minutes.

    a. Simulate processing and waiting times for nine customers. Read three-digit numbers going down columns 9 and 10 of Table 17–1 for arrivals (e.g., 156, 884, 576). Use column 8, Table 17–5, for processing time.

    b. If management can reduce the range of arrival times to between 13 and 17 minutes, what would the impact be on customer waiting times? (Use the same service times and the same random numbers for arrival times from part *a*.) Round arrival times to two decimal places.

Chapter 17 Case

Krohler Supermarkets

The management of Krohler Supermarkets, a national chain, has become aware of decreasing profit margins from its stores during the previous year. Three factors contributed to this earnings decline: (1) rapidly increasing labor costs, (2) increasing costs of wholesale merchandise and inability to increase retail prices because of governmental controls and consumer resistance, and (3) increasing price competition from their major national competitors. Even though earnings have declined significantly, sales volume has been increasing from year to year, but at a lower rate in the immediate past year than in previous years.

Merchandise typically accounted for the largest proportion of a store's operating costs (roughly 80 percent), with the inventory control and stocking functions being critical to this aspect of managing operations. Inventory was ordered each week from a central warehouse by means of a fixed-interval system. Stocking consisted primarily of placing the commodities on display, pricing each item, controlling pilferage, and removing damaged goods.

Labor costs were the second largest factor in supermarket operations (roughly 10 percent). More than 40 percent of the store's wages went to people manning the "front end," which include cashiers and baggers. About 33 percent of the wages went to the stockers, and the balance went to people in the meat, produce, bakery, or deli departments or to the store supervisors. Krohler management personnel felt that a prime area in which to reduce overall operating costs would be the labor requirements, but they were unwilling to reduce their service level to the consumer because of the negative effect it would have on their competitive stance in the supermarket industry.

Krohler's small industrial engineering department had recommended to the management that an investigation be made of the potential savings associated with implementing automatic point-of-sale (APOS) systems at the checkout counters. These APOS systems combined electronic cash registers and optical scanning devices that interact with an in-store minicomputer, and they could substantially boost labor productivity and provide greater control over inventory levels and ordering requirements. Since almost every commodity Krohler carried was labeled with a unique manufacturing code (called the Universal Product Code), the system functioned by having a checker pull an item across the optical scanner so the code could be read. The price of the item would be obtained immediately from the minicomputer's memory, displayed on the register, and tallied into the customer's bill. At the same time, the computer would compute any applicable sales tax and note the sale of all items in its inventory control program for later summarization of daily stock levels and order requirements. If a particular item did not have the code attached to it (for example, a bag of apples, deli specialties, or nonuniform packages of meats), the cashier would enter the price and an item

Source: James A. Fitzsimmons and Robert S. Sullivan, *Service Operations Management* (New York: McGraw-Hill, 1982).

code manually into the register. In addition to the time savings anticipated in checking out individual customers, the industrial engineering department pointed out that a significant amount of time would be saved in closing out a register (counting the cash and reconciling opening and closing balances with the intervening sales) and also in not having to price each item on the shelves.

With the existing manual system in place, the basic function of front-end personnel, including cashiers and baggers, were: (1) enter the merchandise cost into the register, (2) enter applicable sales taxes, (3) total the cost of purchases and taxes, (4) receive payment (cash, check, food stamps, discount coupons, etc.) and make change, (5) bag the items purchased, and (6) assist a customer in removing the bag(s) from the store. Miscellaneous tasks also included check cashing, looking up prices on unmarked items, weighing and pricing produce, and responding to any customer questions.

In a typical Krohler Supermarket, there would be 10 checkout counters placed in a row at the store front, with one designated as an "express" lane to serve customers with 10 items or less. However, because sales fluctuated greatly by day and by hour, management tried very hard to match the number of counters open with expected demand so that both a high level of customer service and a high level of checkout-counter productivity would be maintained. Customer-service level was defined as the percentage of time that more than a certain number of customers were either being served or waiting in line to be checked out. A general rule of thumb used by Krohler management was that the percentage of time that more than three customers waited in line (including the person being served) should be held to 5 percent or less. Checkout-counter productivity was measured on the basis of sales dollars per manned checkout-counter hour.

As one means of examining the possible savings associated with an APOS system versus the existing manual system, Krohler's industrial engineering department was given the task of simulating the store operations with two systems. Assume you are part of the study team and develop responses to the following questions:

1. What specific questions should a simulation of the two different systems address?
2. What data must be collected before a simulation could be performed?

Discussion question

Given your responses to the above questions, develop a flowchart of a simulation model that could be used to study the operation of an APOS system at a typical Krohler supermarket.

Chapter 18
Markov Analysis

Chapter Outline

Learning Objectives

After completing this chapter, you should be able to:

1. Give examples of systems that may lend themselves to description by a Markov model.
2. Explain the meaning of transition probabilities.
3. Describe the kinds of system behaviors that Markov analysis pertains to.
4. Use a tree diagram to analyze system behavior.
5. Use matrix multiplication to analyze system behavior.
6. Use an algebraic method to solve for steady-state values.
7. Analyze accounts receivable using a Markov model.
8. List the assumptions of a Markov model.

INTRODUCTION

This chapter describes the analysis of *Markov* systems. A Markov system has these characteristics:

1. It will operate or exist for a number of periods.
2. In each period, the system can assume one of a number of states or conditions.
3. The states are both mutually exclusive and collectively exhaustive.
4. System changes between states from period to period can be described by *transition probabilities,* which remain constant.
5. The probability of the system being in a given state in a particular period depends only on its state in the preceding period and the transition probabilities. It is independent of all earlier periods.

Table 18–1 gives some illustrations of systems that may lead themselves to Markov analysis.[1]

The use of Markov analysis on such systems can help decision makers understand how the systems behave over time. This sort of knowledge can be useful for *short-term* decisions such as scheduling a work force, stocking inventory, and budgeting, and for *long-term* decisions such as determining locations for new facilities and capacity planning. These decisions may simply involve dealing with expected system behaviors or they may involve strategies for favorably altering the system (e.g., through price changes, advertising, and so on).

The chapter begins with an illustration of transition probabilities, which are the foundation of a Markov analysis. Then, three methods of analysis are illustrated: graphical and matrix, which are useful for describing short-term behavior; and the algebraic method, which is useful for describing long-term behavior patterns.

TRANSITION PROBABILITIES

A system whose behavior can be described as a **Markov process** can be summarized by a set of conditional, or *transition probabilities,* which indicate the tendencies of the system to change from one period to the next. An example will help to clarify this important concept.

Consider a car rental agency that has rental offices at each of a city's two airports. Customers are allowed to return a rented car to either airport, regardless of which airport they rented from. (It is assumed that this is a closed system: All cars must be returned to one of the two airports.) If some cars will be used for one-way rentals to another city, or if some cars are dropped off from other cities, they

[1] In order for a system to be considered Markov, it must satisfy certain assumptions that are described later in the chapter.

TABLE 18–1 Examples of Systems that May Be Described as Markov

System	Possible System States	Transition Probabilities
Brand switching	Proportion of customers who buy Brand A, Brand B, Brand C, etc.	Probability that a customer will switch from Brand A to Brand B, etc.
TV market share	Proportion of viewers who watch Channel 8, Channel 10, etc.	Probability that a viewer who watched Channel 8 news will switch to Channel 10 news, etc.
Rental returns	Porportion who return rentals to various locations.	Probability that a renter will return item to a different location than the one it was rented from.
Machine breakdowns	Proportion of machines running, proportion not running.	Probability that a machine's condition running/not running will change in the next period.

can be excluded from the system and treated separately. In addition, it is assumed that all rentals will be for only one day, and that at the end of the day, every car will be returned to one of the two rental offices. Suppose that the manager of the rental agency has made a study of return behavior and has found the following information: 70 percent of the cars rented from Airport A tend to be returned to that airport, and 30 percent of the Airport A cars tend to be returned to Airport B; 10 percent of the cars rented from Airport B are returned to Airport A, and 90 percent of the cars are returned to Airport B. This information is summarized in the **transition matrix** illustrated in Table 18–2.

Because it is assumed that all of the rentals will be returned to one of the two airports, the *row* totals are 1.00, or 100 percent. The same does not apply to the column totals, because these *conditional* probabilities are stated in terms of *renting* locations rather than return locations. That is, the first value in the table, .70, represents the proportion of cars that can be expected to be returned to Airport A, *given* that they were rented at Airport A. Similarly, the .30 represents the proportion of cars expected to be returned to Airport B, *given* that they were rented at Airport A.

The manager has several questions concerning the system:

1. What proportion of cars will be returned to each airport in the *short run* (e.g., over the next several days)? This information will help the manager in scheduling counter help at each location.
2. What proportion of cars will be returned to each location over the *long run*? This information will be helpful in deciding which of the two locations should be chosen for construction of a facility for servicing and repair of the cars.

In general, managers may be interested in either the short-run or the long-run behavior of a system, or in both. The following section gives an overview of these two behaviors.

TABLE 18–2 Transition Probabilities for Car Rental Example

		Returned to: Airport A	Returned to: Airport B	
Rented from	Airport A	.70	.30	/1.00
	Airport B	.10	.90	/1.00

SYSTEM BEHAVIOR

Both the long-term behavior and the short-term behavior of a system are completely determined by the system's transition probabilities. Short-term behavior is solely dependent on the system's **state** in the current period and the transition probabilities. Thus, in the case of the car rental system, it can be seen from the transition matrix that 70 percent of the cars rented at Airport A are expected to be returned to Airport A and that 30 percent are expected to be returned to Airport B. Likewise, 10 percent of the cars rented from Airport B are expected to be returned to Airport A and 90 percent to Airport B. These proportions are expected to remain in effect. Consequently, the *number* of cars returned to each location in any given period is simply a function of the transition probabilities and the number rented from each location in the preceding period. Knowledge of the number of cars at each location at a given point in time can be used to track the short-term behavior of the system. Moreover, the number of cars at each location in the preceding period is normally a significant factor that affects the number of cars at each location in the next several periods. However, the long-term behavior of the system will be unaffected by the initial number of cars at each location; the proportion of cars returned to each location over the long run will be the same, regardless of initial conditions. The long-run proportions are referred to as the **steady-state** proportions, or probabilities, of the system. Not every system has a tendency to stabilize, though. Some tend to cycle back and forth, and some tend to converge on a single state called an *absorbing state*. More will be said about these cases later. Because such systems are less common than steady-state systems, the discussion here will emphasize steady-state systems.

These short-term and long-term tendencies of steady-state systems can be seen in Figure 18–1, which shows the proportion of returns to Airport A as a function of where they were rented in Period 0. Notice that in the first few periods, the original starting point (Airport A or Airport B) has a marked effect on the proportions, but that effect becomes less and less as time goes by, and that after about 10 periods, the original (Period 0) renting location is immaterial. A similar graph could be constructed showing the proportion of original rentals from each location returned to Airport B. It would show a long-run proportion of 75 percent of those Period 0 rentals ending up at Airport B.

FIGURE 18–1 Expected Proportion of Period 0 Rentals Returned to Airport A

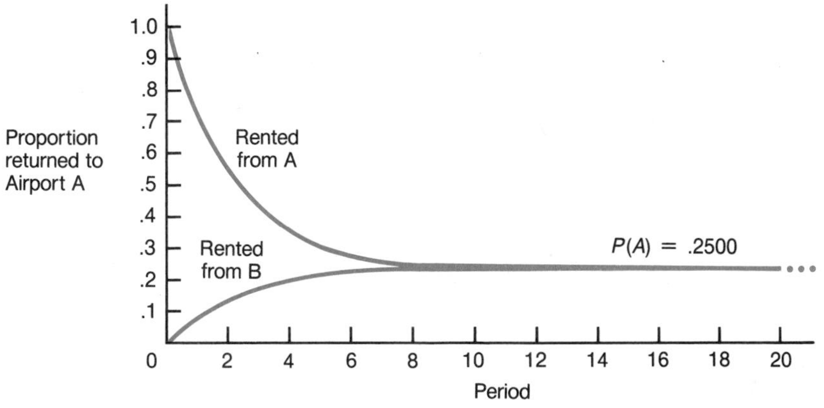

METHODS OF ANALYSIS

As previously noted, a manager's interest in system behavior can be related to either short-term considerations or long-term considerations, and often it is related to both. Methods for analyzing system behaviors relate to either the short term or the long term. Short-term behavior can be described using either a tree diagram or matrix multiplication. Long-term behavior could theoretically be analyzed by either of those approaches, but for practical reasons related to the amount of effort that would be involved, an algebraic method is used.

Each of these methods is presented below, beginning with a tree diagram for describing short-term system behavior.

Tree Diagram

A tree diagram is a visual portrayal of a system's transitions. It is composed of a series of branches, which represent the possible choices at each stage (period) and the conditional probabilities of each choice being selected. For example, a car rented from Airport A can be returned to either Airport A or Airport B. Thus, there are two choices, the first with a probability of .70 and the second with a probability of .30. Similarly, a car rented at Airport B has two possible return locations, Airport A with a probability of .10 and Airport B with a probability of .90. Hence, each possible starting point (rental location) has two possible return locations. Moreover, we can represent the choices for each with separate tree diagrams. The two diagrams are illustrated in Figure 18–2.

If two or more periods are involved, the tree becomes more involved, but it is also more informative, particularly if the *joint* probabilities are shown for each branch. These reflect the proportion of members of the system (e.g., rental cars)

FIGURE 18–2 Tree Diagrams for the Car Rental Example for One Period

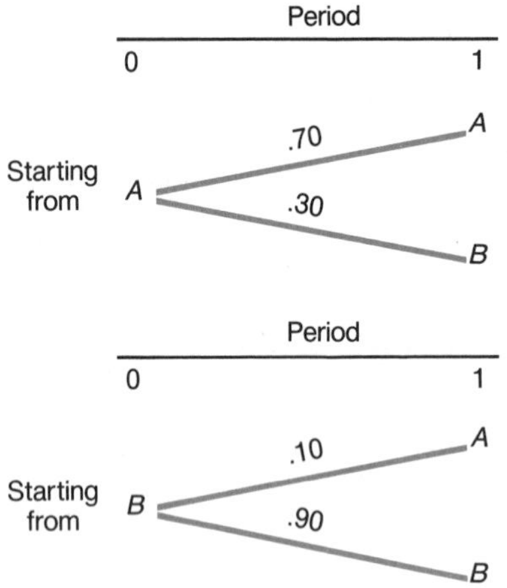

that can be expected to follow a certain path (series of branches) through the tree diagram. The next example illustrates this.

EXAMPLE 1 Prepare a tree diagram that shows the choices for two periods of the car rental system using the information contained in Table 18–2. Then, compute joint probabilities and use them to determine *how many* cars will be at Location A if A originally has 100 cars and Location B has 80 cars.

Solution

The two tree diagrams (one for a car rented from Airport A and the other for a car rented from Airport B) are shown in Figure 18–3. The joint probabilities are computed by multiplying the probabilities along each particular branch. Therefore, the proportion of cars rented from A in Period 0 that can be expected to be returned to A in Period 1 and then rented out and returned a second time to A is $.70 \times .70 = .49$. Similarly, the proportion of cars first rented from A in Period 0, then returned to B in Period 1, and finally rented from B in Period 1 and returned to A in Period 2 is $.30 \times .10 = .03$. Then, the *total* proportion of cars rented from A in Period 0 and expected back at A in Period 2 is $.49 + .03 = .52$, as shown. The other joint probabilities have a similar interpretation.

In effect, the joint probabilities reveal that 52 percent of the cars originally rented from A in Period 0 and 16 percent of the cars originally rented from B in Period 0 will end up at A in Period 2. Multiplying these probabilities by the number of cars originally at each location will yield the *expected number* of cars at Airport A at the

FIGURE 18–3 Two-Period Tree Diagrams for Car Rental Example

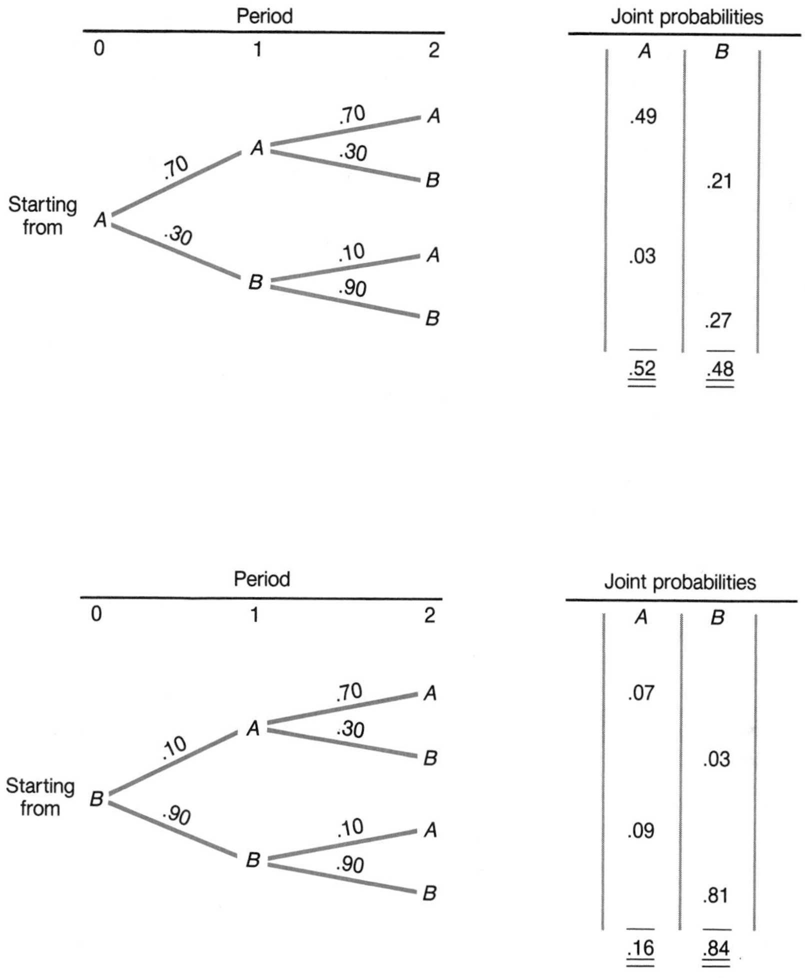

end of Period 2. Because Airport A had 100 cars in Period 0 and Airport B had 80 cars, we find:

$$\overset{A}{100(.52)} + \overset{B}{80(.16)} = 64.8 \text{ cars}$$

The fractional value of .8 does not imply that one of the cars may be returned with a missing door or bumper. The 64.8 represents an *average* number of cars. The actual number of cars would be an *integer* value reasonably close to that number (e.g., 64, 65, 66).

Advantages of a tree diagram are that it is simple to construct and it provides us with a visual model that illustrates how the transition probabilities combine to determine system behavior over the short run. However, as the number of periods covered by a tree increases beyond two or three, the number of branch ends tends to become too large to make this method practical. For example, to portray 5 periods would require 32 branch ends, and 6 periods would require 64 branch ends.

A more compact method for generating the short-term probabilities involves the use of matrix multiplication, which is covered in the next section.

Matrix Multiplication

A fairly simple method for obtaining expected state proportions over the short run is to use matrix multiplication. It is based on state proportions for any period being equal to the product of the proportions in the preceding period multiplied by the matrix of transition probabilities. Because the proportions, at any time, can be expressed in matrix form, this approach involves the multiplication of the "current" proportions, which is referred to as a *probability vector,* by the transition matrix. The vector has one row and the same number of columns as the transition matrix. For instance, the initial "current" vector for a case with two possible states of nature, and starting from State A, would be [1 0]. For the car rentals, this would mean all cars are at Airport A at the start. Conversely, starting in Period 0 from State B would be represented by [0 1]. For the car rentals, this would mean that all cars are at Airport B at the start. If there are three states of nature, Period 0 would be expressed in the following way, depending on the starting state:

Starting from	Current Matrix
A	[1 0 0]
B	[0 1 0]
C	[0 0 1]

Matrix multiplication requires that the elements of the row of the first matrix be matched with (multiplied by) the elements of the first column and summed to obtain the first state proportion for the next period, matched with the elements of the second column and summed to obtain the second state proportion, and so on. For example, we can calculate the state proportions for Period 1 for the car rental example for an A start as follows:

$$[1 \quad 0]\begin{bmatrix} .70 & .30 \\ .10 & .90 \end{bmatrix} = \begin{array}{cc} 1(.70) & 1(.30) \\ +0(.10) & +0(.90) \\ \hline [.70 & .30] \end{array}$$

These values are, of course, simply the elements of the first row of the transition matrix. This is because the transition matrix describes the proportion of system members that are expected to end up in each state in Period 1, given an A start (the first row), and given a B start (the second row). The main point, here, though, is how to complete the matrix multiplication in order to obtain those values, so that values for subsequent periods can be calculated. You might find it helpful to think of the initial matrix as *vertical* rather than horizontal. That is:

$$\begin{bmatrix}1\\0\end{bmatrix} \rightarrow \begin{bmatrix}.70 & .30\\ .10 & .90\end{bmatrix} \quad \text{or} \quad \begin{bmatrix}1 \times .70 & 1 \times .30\\ 0 \times .70 & 0 \times .90\end{bmatrix}$$

■

EXAMPLE 2 Use matrix multiplication for the car rental example to find the state proportions for Periods 2 and 3, assuming an A start.

Solution

Because Period 1 proportions are .70 and .30, for Period 2 we have:

$$[.70 \quad .30] \begin{bmatrix}.70 & .30\\ .10 & .90\end{bmatrix} = \begin{matrix} .70(.70) = .49 & .70(.30) = .21\\ .30(.10) = \underline{.03} & .30(.90) = \underline{.27}\\ .52 & .48\end{matrix}$$

Thus, the Period 2 matrix is [.52 .48], which means that 52 percent are expected to be in State A and 48 percent are expected to be in State B. Now, we can calculate the proportions for Period 3:

$$[.52 \quad .48] \begin{bmatrix}.70 & .30\\ .10 & .90\end{bmatrix} = \begin{matrix} .52(.70) = .364 & .52(.30) = .156\\ .48(.10) = \underline{.048} & .48(.90) = \underline{.432}\\ .412 & .588\end{matrix}$$

Note that in each period, the state proportions sum to 1.00, and that the calculation for any period using this approach requires the proportions from the preceding period.

If we continued this sequential multiplication of each period's matrix and the transition matrix we would discover that after a time the state proportions would not change significantly. That is, multiplying the state proportions by the transition matrix would result in the same state proportions. This condition is referred to as the *steady-state,* and the proportions indicate the expected percentage of system members in each state over the long run. Moreover, these steady-state values will be the same irrespective of which starting state is used, although the number of periods required to reach the steady-state may vary, depending on which state is used as a start. Table 18–3 illustrates the results of matrix multi-

TABLE 18–3 Period-by-Period Proportions for the Rental Example, and the Steady-State Proportions Based on Matrix Multiplications

	Starting from A		Starting from B	
Period	*P(A)*	*P(B)*	*P(A)*	*P(B)*
0	1.0	0.0	0.0	1.0
1	.70	.30	.10	.90
2	.52	.48	.16	.84
3	.412	.588	.196	.804
4	.3472	.6528	.2176	.7824
5	.3083	.6917	.2306	.7694
6	.2850	.7150	.2384	.7616
7	.2710	.7290	.2430	.7570
8	.2626	.7374	.2458	.7542
9	.2576	.7424	.2475	.7525
10	.2546	.7454	.2485	.7515
11	.2528	.7472	.2491	.7509
12	.2517	.7483	.2495	.7505
13	.2510	.7490	.2497	.7503
14	.2506	.7494	.2498	.7502
15	.2504	.7496	.2499	.7501
16	.2502	.7498	.2499	.7501
17	.2501	.7499	.2500	.7500
18	.2501	.7499		
19	.2500	.7500		

plications from each starting point and the eventual steady-state proportions for each state. Thus, starting from State A, the steady-state values were obtained in approximately 19 periods, while starting from State B, the steady-state proportions were obtained in approximately 17 periods.

As you can surmise, considerable effort would be required to obtain these values manually. A computer could remove this burden. However, the primary concern is with the *values* at steady-state, rather than with how many periods would be required to obtain the values. And for that purpose, there is a much simpler method for deriving these steady-state proportions. It is described in the next section.

Algebraic Solution

An algebraic approach provides the most efficient method for obtaining the steady-state probabilities. The basis for an algebraic solution is a set of equations developed from the transition matrix. Moreover, because the states are mutually exclusive and collectively exhaustive, the sum of the state probabilities must be 1.00, and another equation can be developed from this requirement. The result is a set of equations that can be used to solve for the steady-state probabilities.

FIGURE 18–4 Development of Algebraic Equations

From: \ To:	A	B
A	.70	.30
B	.10	.90

$A = .70A + .10B$ ←

$B = .30A + .90B$ ←

$1 = A + B$

EXAMPLE 3 Develop the equations needed for an algebraic solution to the steady-state of a Markov process and then use the equations to determine the steady-state probabilities.

Solution

The steady-state equations for the car rental example can be developed in the following manner. Because the ending states are represented by the *columns* of the transition matrix, the *probabilities in each column* supply the necessary information for that state's long-term probabilities. Thus, the equation for Airport A is:

$$A = .70A + .10B$$

where

A = proportion of cars at Airport A

B = proportion of cars at Airport B

In effect, it expresses that the expected proportion of system members (or, equivalently, the proportion of time the system is expected to be in that state) is comprised of 70 percent from A and 10 percent from B. Similarly, the equation for Airport B is:

$$B = .30A + .90B$$

This equation is derived from the fact that the expected proportion in B is 30 percent of A's "output" and 90 percent of B's "output." Still a third equation can be developed since the total of the two probabilities must be 1.00:

$$1 = A + B$$

The development of these equations is illustrated in Figure 18–4.

Because there are two unknowns and three equations, one of the equations is superfluous and can be eliminated. As a general rule, it will be most efficient to eliminate either of the state equations while retaining the other state equation as well as the last equation. Suppose that we arbitrarily eliminate the equation for B. We are then left with these two equations:

$$A = .70A + .10B$$
$$1 = A + B$$

From the second equation, we can express B in terms of A:

$$A = .70A + .10(1 - A)$$
$$= .70A + .10 - .10A$$
$$= .60A + .10$$

$$B = 1 - A$$

We can then substitute this for B in the equation for A and solve for A:

Collecting terms yields:

$$A - .60A = .10$$
$$.40A = .10$$
$$A = \frac{.10}{.40} = .25$$

Since $B = 1 - A$, $B \doteq 1 - .25 = .75$

Taking the example one step further, if there were initially 400 cars at Airport A and 300 at Airport B, determine the expected number of cars at each airport once the system has reached steady-state. Assume that all cars remain in the system, no new cars are added, and there is no transporting of cars between locations. The expected number for each airport is the product of the *total* number of cars (i.e., 700) and the steady-state probability of that airport. Thus, for A we have 700(.25) = 175 cars, and for B we have 700(.75) = 525 cars.

ANALYSIS OF A 3 × 3 MATRIX

The same methods that were used to analyze a transition matrix with two states can be readily adapted to handle larger problems. The following examples illustrate this. They refer to the transition matrix shown in Table 18–4.

TABLE 18–4 Transition Matrix for Examples 4, 5, and 6

To:	X	Y	Z
X	.70	.20	.10/1.00
Y	.40	.50	.10/1.00
Z	.30	.10	.60/1.00

Tree Diagram

EXAMPLE 4 Construct two tree diagrams for the transition matrix in Table 18–4, each showing two periods. Have one show a start at *X* and the other show a start at *Y*. In both cases, use the tree diagram to determine the probability that the system will be in state *X*, state *Y*, or state *Z* given each start in Period 0.

Solution

See the two tree diagrams and the desired probabilities in Figures 18–5 and 18–6.

FIGURE 18–5 Tree Diagram for Example 4, Starting from *X*

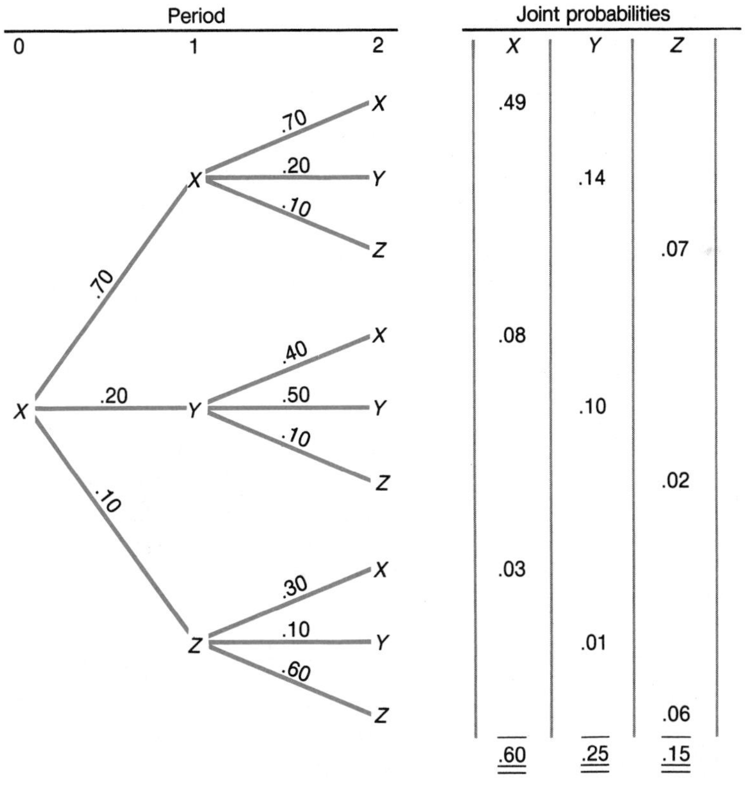

FIGURE 18–6 Tree Diagram for Example 4, Starting from *Y*

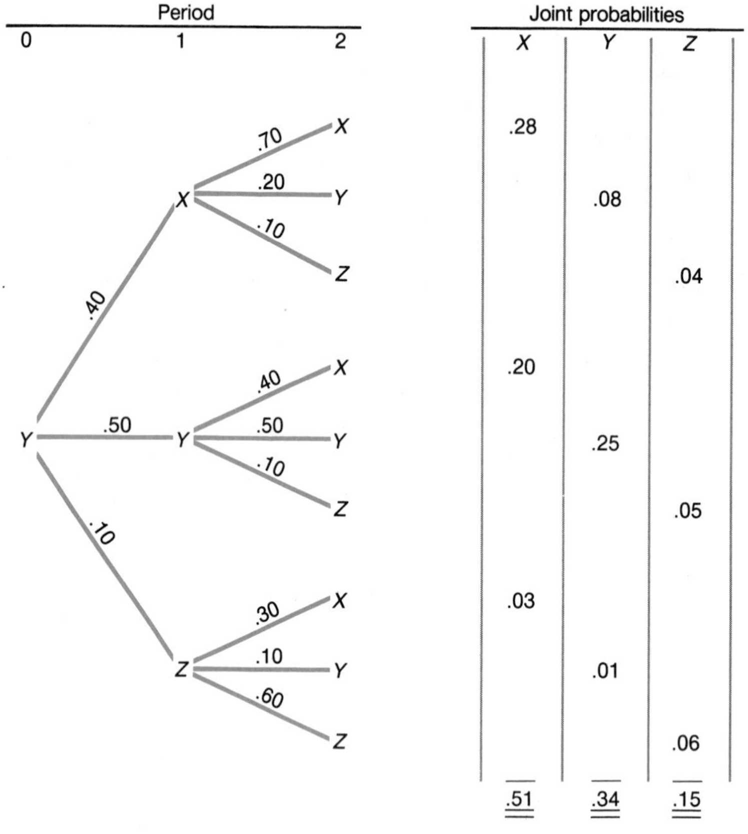

Matrix Multiplication

■

EXAMPLE 5 Use matrix multiplication to determine the probability that the system described in Table 18–4 will be in each of the various possible states (X, Y, and Z) for Periods 0, 1, 2, and 3, given a start of X in Period 0.

Solution

Period	
0	[1 0 0]
1	$[1\ \ 0\ \ 0]\begin{bmatrix}.70 & .20 & .10\\ .40 & .50 & .10\\ .30 & .10 & .60\end{bmatrix} = \begin{matrix}1(.70) & 1(.20) & 1(.10)\\ 0(.40) & 0(.50) & 0(.10)\\ \underline{0(.30)} & \underline{0(.10)} & \underline{0(.60)}\\ [\ .70 & .20 & .10]\end{matrix}$
2	$[.70\ \ .20\ \ .10]\begin{bmatrix}.70 & .20 & .10\\ .40 & .50 & .10\\ .30 & .10 & .60\end{bmatrix} = \begin{matrix}.70(.70) & .70(.20) & .70(.10)\\ .20(.40) & .20(.50) & .20(.10)\\ \underline{.10(.30)} & \underline{.10(.10)} & \underline{.10(.60)}\\ [\ .60 & .25 & .15]\end{matrix}$
	(Note that this agrees with the answer for an *X* start in the preceding example.)
3	$[.60\ \ .25\ \ .15]\begin{bmatrix}.70 & .20 & .10\\ .40 & .50 & .10\\ .30 & .10 & .60\end{bmatrix} = \begin{matrix}.60(.70) & .60(.20) & .60(.10)\\ .25(.40) & .25(.50) & .25(.10)\\ \underline{.15(.30)} & \underline{.15(.10)} & \underline{.15(.60)}\\ [\ .565 & .260 & .175\ ]\end{matrix}$

Algebraic Solution

■

EXAMPLE 6 For the transition matrix given in Table 18–4, complete each of the following:

a. Determine the long-run proportions for each state.

b. If there are 900 members in the system, with 400 in State *X* in Period 0, 300 in State *Y*, and 200 in State *Z*, determine the expected number in each state in the long run.

Solution

a. 1. Develop the state equations:

$$X = .70X + .40Y + .30Z$$
$$Y = .20X + .50Y + .10Z$$
$$Z = .10X + .10Y + .60Z$$
$$1 = X + Y + Z$$

2. Eliminate one of the equations arbitrarily, but not the last one. Suppose the third equation is eliminated. Because it is the state equation for Z, solve for Z in the last equation:

$$Z = 1 - X - Y$$

3. Substitute for Z in the first and second equations:

$$X = .70X + .40Y + .30(1 - X - Y)$$
$$Y = .20X + .50Y + .10(1 - X - Y)$$

4. Simplify each equation with the constant term on the right:

$$.60X - .10Y = .30$$
$$-.10X + .60Y = .10$$

5. Solving, we find:

$$X = .543,\ Y = .257$$

Using $Z = 1 - X - Y$ and these values of X and Y, we find:

$$Z = .200$$

b. Using the answers from part *a* we find the expected number in each state at steady-state, given 900 system members:

$$\begin{aligned} X &= 900(.543) = 488.7 \\ Y &= 900(.257) = 231.3 \\ Z &= 900(.200) = \underline{180.0} \\ & \qquad\qquad\quad\; 900.0 \end{aligned}$$

(It should be noted that the results are independent of the initial conditions.)

CYCLICAL AND ABSORBING SYSTEMS

Cyclical and absorbing systems offer a contrast to the ones described so far in this chapter. **Cyclical systems** are those that have a tendency to move from state to state in a definite pattern or cycle. An example of a cyclical system is presented in the transition matrix in Table 18–5.

Let's see why this is a cyclical system. Suppose the system begins in State *A*. Because of the transition probability of 1 for *A* to *B*, the system will be in State *B* in the following period. Then in the next period, it will move from *B* to *C* and then back to *A* and so on. Consequently, we can say with certainty which state the system will be in at any future period (e.g., Period 42) if we know its state in any earlier period (e.g., Period 1).

An **absorbing system** is one in which the system gravitates to one or more

TABLE 18–5 An Example of a Cyclical System

From: \ To:	*A*	*B*	*C*
A	0	1	0
B	0	0	1
C	1	0	0

TABLE 18–6 An Example of a System with Absorbing States

From: \ To:	*A*	*B*	*C*	*D*
A	.5	.2	.1	.2
B	.3	.2	.1	.4
C	0	0	1.0	0
D	0	0	0	1.0

states. In effect, once a member of such a system enters one of the absorbing states, it becomes trapped and can never exit that state. An example of a transition matrix for an absorbing system is shown in Table 18–6.

States *C* and *D* are absorbing states. We can readily observe this by noting that probabilities for exiting to other states from either of these states are equal to zero, whereas the probability of remaining in the state is 1.0, or 100 percent. Note that even though a system may begin with members in nonabsorbing states such as *A* or *B*, eventually the system will be reduced to members only in the absorbing states.

Analysis of Accounts Receivable

One example of absorbing states occurs when using Markov analysis for accounts receivable. The states of interest are possible classifications of accounts such as paid, one month overdue, two months overdue, and bad debt. The states paid and bad debt are absorbing states because once an account achieves either status, the passage of time will not change its classification; a paid bill will not become unpaid, and a bad debt will be turned over to a collection agency. Even though the bad debt eventually may be collected, the costs associated with collecting it may offset all or a good part of the amount collected. Therefore, it would be misleading to label the bill as "paid" in the sense we are talking about here. Analysis of accounts receivable can provide management with an estimate of the proportion of current accounts receivable that will end up in each of the two absorbing states: *paid* and *bad debt.*

Consider this example. A firm has a one-month billing cycle. At the end of each month, outstanding bills are classified into one of the following categories: paid, less than one-month old, one- and two-months old, and bad debt. Now, suppose that a transition matrix has been developed that contains probabilities for the accounts:

		Next state			
		Paid	1	2	Bad debt
	Paid	1	0	0	0
Current state	1	.80	0	.20	0
	2	.60	0	0	.40
	Bad debt	0	0	0	1

Let's examine the logic of this matrix. As previously noted, the paid category is an absorbing state. Hence, the probability that an account in this category will move to another category is 0; the probability it will remain as paid is 1. Similarly, *bad debt* is an absorbing state; the probability is 1 that it will retain that classification; any other state (in that row), therefore, has a probability of 0. For an account that is less than one-month old (i.e., State 1), there is some probability that it will be paid. Management may have determined this to be .80. Because the firm is on a one-month billing cycle, though, the accounts in this category must either move to the paid category or move to the two-month category; they cannot remain less than one-month old and neither can they become bad debts because the latter category is reserved for accounts that are more than two months overdue. Therefore, there is a zero probability of staying in State 1 and a zero probability of moving to the *bad debt* state. State 2 accounts, similarly, have a zero probability of remaining there and a zero probability of becoming one-month old. Instead, either these accounts will end up paid (for which management has assigned a probability of .60) or they will become bad debts (for which management has assigned a probability of .40).

For purposes of analysis, it is desirable to rearrange the matrix so that the extreme states (*paid* and *bad debt*) are listed first, followed by the other two states. Thus:

	Paid	Bad debt	1	2
Paid	1	0	0	0
Bad debt	0	1	0	0
1	.80	0	0	.20
2	.60	.40	0	0

Next, we partition this transition matrix into four parts:

	Paid	Bad debt	1	2
Paid	1	0	0	0
Bad debt	0	1	0	0
1	.80	0	0	.20
2	.60	.40	0	0

We, then, label the parts as follows:

	Paid / Bad debt	1 / 2
Paid / Bad debt	I	O
1 / 2	R	Q

In this way, we can see that:

$$I = \begin{array}{r} \\ \text{Paid} \\ \text{Bad debt} \end{array} \begin{array}{c} \begin{array}{cc} \text{Paid} & \text{Bad debt} \end{array} \\ \begin{bmatrix} 1 & 0 \\ 0 & 1 \end{bmatrix} \end{array}$$

$$O = \begin{array}{r} \\ \text{Paid} \\ \text{Bad debt} \end{array} \begin{array}{c} \begin{array}{cc} 1 & 2 \end{array} \\ \begin{bmatrix} 0 & 0 \\ 0 & 0 \end{bmatrix} \end{array}$$

$$R = \begin{array}{r} 1 \\ 2 \end{array} \begin{bmatrix} .80 & 0 \\ .60 & .40 \end{bmatrix}$$

$$Q = \begin{array}{r} \\ 1 \\ 2 \end{array} \begin{array}{c} \begin{array}{cc} 1 & 2 \end{array} \\ \begin{bmatrix} 0 & .20 \\ 0 & 0 \end{bmatrix} \end{array}$$

Matrix I is an *identity matrix:* It has 1s on the diagonal and 0s everywhere else. Matrix O is simply a matrix of all 0s. Matrix R contains the transition probabilities of absorptions in the next period, and matrix Q contains the transition probabilities of movement between nonabsorbing states.

Partitioning the matrix in this way allows us to compute the *fundamental matrix, F:*

$$F = (I - Q)^{-1} \qquad (18\text{–}1)$$

The -1 refers to the *inverse* of a matrix. Hence, to obtain the fundamental matrix, we must subtract matrix Q from matrix I, then find the inverse of the result. Therefore, we subtract Q from I:

$$(I - Q) = \begin{bmatrix} 1 & 0 \\ 0 & 1 \end{bmatrix} - \begin{bmatrix} 0 & .20 \\ 0 & 0 \end{bmatrix}$$

$$= \begin{vmatrix} 1 & -.20 \\ 0 & 1 \end{vmatrix}$$

Then, we find the inverse of this matrix.

In general, the inverse of a matrix is found in the following way. If matrix M is defined as:

$$M = \begin{bmatrix} m_{11} & m_{12} \\ m_{21} & m_{22} \end{bmatrix} \tag{18–2}$$

then, its inverse is:

$$M^{-1} = \begin{bmatrix} m_{22}/d & -m_{12}/d \\ -m_{21}/d & m_{11}/d \end{bmatrix}$$

where

$$d = m_{11}m_{22} - m_{21}m_{12}$$

For our accounts receivable problem, the inverse of the matrix (I − Q) is found in the following way:

$$(I - Q) = \begin{bmatrix} 1 & -.20 \\ 0 & 1 \end{bmatrix}$$

Using Formula 18–4, $d = 1(1) - 0(-.20) = 1.$

$$\text{Then } F = (I - Q)^{-1} = \begin{bmatrix} 1/1 & -(-.20)/1 \\ -0/1 & 1/1 \end{bmatrix} = \begin{bmatrix} 1 & .20 \\ 0 & 1 \end{bmatrix}$$

Thus, the fundamental matrix, F, is:

$$F = \begin{matrix} & 1 & 2 \\ 1 & 1 & .20 \\ 2 & 0 & 1 \end{matrix}$$

The fundamental matrix indicates the expected number of times the system will be in any of the nonabsorbing states before absorption occurs. Hence, if an account is in State 1, the expected number of times the customer would move to State 2 is .20.

The fundamental matrix can be used to determine the probability that an account eventually will move to the various absorbing states (i.e., paid or bad debt). This can be accomplished by multiplying matrix R by the fundamental matrix. The result in our example is:

$$FR = \begin{array}{c} \\ 1 \\ 2 \end{array}\begin{array}{c} \begin{array}{cc} 1 & 2 \end{array} \\ \begin{bmatrix} 1 & .20 \\ 0 & 1 \end{bmatrix} \end{array} \times \begin{array}{c} \\ 1 \\ 2 \end{array}\begin{array}{c} \begin{array}{cc} \text{Paid} & \text{Bad debt} \end{array} \\ \begin{bmatrix} .80 & 0 \\ .60 & .40 \end{bmatrix} \end{array}$$

$$= \begin{array}{c} \\ 1 \\ 2 \end{array}\begin{array}{c} \begin{array}{cc} \text{Paid} & \text{Bad debt} \end{array} \\ \begin{bmatrix} .92 & .08 \\ .60 & .40 \end{bmatrix} \end{array}$$

The interpretation of this matrix is that if an account is currently less than one-month overdue (i.e., in State 1), the probability is .92 that it will end up being paid and .08 that it will end up a bad debt. Similarly, if an account is currently in State 2 (more than one month overdue, but less than two months overdue), there is a probability of .60 that it will be paid and a probability of .40 that it will end up a bad debt.

If we know the value of the accounts in each state, we can use the FR matrix to determine the expected amount that will be paid and the expected amount of bad debt. For example, suppose that the amount owed for accounts in State 1 is currently \$30,000 and the amount owed for accounts in State 2 is currently \$45,000. Then, the expected paid and bad debt amounts can be calculated in the following way:

$$\begin{array}{c} \begin{array}{cc} 1 & 2 \end{array} \\ [30{,}000 \quad 45{,}000] \end{array} \begin{array}{c} \\ 1 \\ 2 \end{array}\begin{array}{c} \begin{array}{cc} \text{Paid} & \text{Bad debt} \end{array} \\ \begin{bmatrix} .92 & .08 \\ .60 & .40 \end{bmatrix} \end{array} = \begin{array}{c} \begin{array}{cc} \text{Paid} & \text{Bad debt} \end{array} \\ [54{,}600 \quad 20{,}400] \end{array}$$

ASSUMPTIONS

Markov analysis is predicated on a number of important assumptions. These are:

1. The probability that an item in the system either will change from one state (e.g., Airport A) to another or remain in its current state is a function of the transition probabilities only.
2. The transition probabilities remain constant.
3. The system is a closed one; there will be no arrivals to the system or exits from the system.

As you might surmise, these assumptions are fairly restrictive; not very many real-life systems completely satisfy them. For this reason, Markov analysis is not as useful, nor as widely used, as most of the other techniques described in this book. Even so, there are some uses of this technique, making the study of Markov analysis worthwhile. Moreover, analysis of systems that can be described in

Markov terms can provide some insight into system behaviors, and this knowledge can be generalized to other systems.

SUMMARY

Markov analysis can be useful for describing the behavior of a certain class of systems that change from state to state on a period-by-period basis according to known transition probabilities. Consumer buying patterns, market shares, and equipment breakdowns sometimes lend themselves to description in Markov terms.

Markov analysis uses tree diagrams, matrix multiplication, and an algebraic approach. The first two approaches are especially useful for describing short-term system behavior, whereas the third approach is more appropriate for describing long-term, or steady-state, behavior.

The assumptions required of Markov systems limit the extent to which practical applications can be found. Consequently, the use of Markov analysis is much less than it is for the majority of the techniques discussed in this text. Nevertheless, there are just enough applications to merit some understanding of the Markov approach.

GLOSSARY

Absorbing System A system in which members gravitate to one or a few states; eventually all members end up in those states.

Cyclical System A system that moves from state to state in a repetitive pattern.

Markov Process A closed system that changes from state to state according to stable transition probabilities.

State One of a set of mutually exclusive and collectively exhaustive conditions or postures a system can assume.

Steady-state The long-term tendencies of a Markov system to be in its various states.

Transition Matrix A matrix that shows the probability of a Markov system changing from its current state to each possible state in the next period.

SOLVED PROBLEMS

Problem 1. *Tree diagram* Given this transition matrix, find the probabilities of the system being in State 1 and State 2, if in Period 3 the system begins in State 1 in Period 0:

From: \ To:	1	2
1	.80	.20
2	.40	.60

Solution

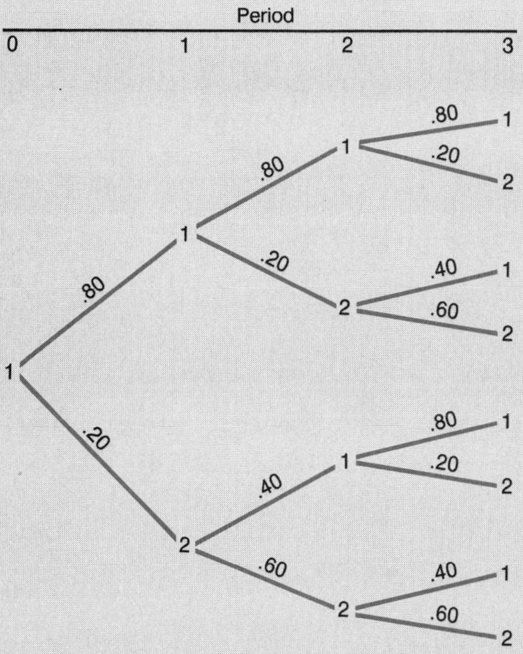

Joint probabilities: 1	Joint probabilities: 2
.80(.80)(.80) = .512	
	.80(.80)(.20) = .128
.80(.20)(.40) = .064	
	.80(.20)(.60) = .096
.20(.40)(.80) = .064	
	.20(.40)(.20) = .016
.20(.60)(.40) = .048	
	.20(.60)(.60) = .072
.688	.312

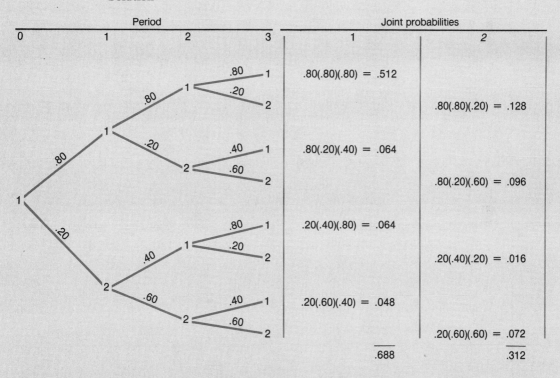

For each branch end, multiply the probabilities of the branches that lead to it, separating by 1 or 2, then add the results as shown. Thus, the probability is .688 that the system will be in State 1 and .312 that it will be in State 2.

Problem 2. *Matrix multiplication* For the transition matrix of the previous problem, find the probabilities that the system will be in State 1 and State 2 in Period 3 if the system begins in State 1 at Period 0.

Solution

Period		P(State 1)	P(State 2)
0		1	0
1	[1 0] $\begin{bmatrix} .80 & .20 \\ .40 & .60 \end{bmatrix}$	1(.80) = .80 0(.40) = .00 .80	1(.20) = .20 0(.60) = .00 .20
2	[.80 .20] $\begin{bmatrix} .80 & .20 \\ .40 & .60 \end{bmatrix}$	.80(.80) = .64 .20(.40) = .08 .72	.80(.20) = .16 .20(.60) = .12 .28
3	[.72 .28] $\begin{bmatrix} .80 & .20 \\ .40 & .60 \end{bmatrix}$	.72(.80) = .576 .28(.40) = .112 .688	.72(.20) = .144 .28(.80) = .168 .312

Problem 3. *Steady-state equations* Find the steady-state probabilities for this transition matrix:

From: \ To:	A	B	C
A	.5	.4	.1
B	.2	.5	.3
C	.3	.1	.6

Solution

The steady-state equations are derived from *column* probabilities of each state. Thus, we have:

$$A = .5A + .2B + .3C$$
$$B = .4A + .5B + .1C$$
$$C = .1A + .3B + .6C$$

In addition, we know that the three probabilities must sum to 1.00:

$$1 = A + B + C$$

We can use this to solve for one of the three probabilities in terms of the other two. For convenience, let's choose C. Then we have:

$$C = 1 - A - B$$

With three unknowns, we need only three equations. We can eliminate a steady-state equation for C and then substitute this last equation for C in the first two steady-state equations. That is:

$$A = .5A + .2B + .3(1 - A - B)$$
$$B = .4A + .5B + .1(1 - A - B)$$

Expanding the first of these yields:

$$A = .5A + .2B + .3 - .3A - .3B$$

Combining terms and moving the variables to the left side of the equation yields:

$$.8A - .1B = .3$$

Expanding the steady-state equation for B yields:

$$B = .4A + .5B + .1 - .1A - .1B$$

Combining terms and moving the variables to the left side of the equation yields:

$$-.3A + .6B = .1$$

Thus, the two resulting equations are:

$$\begin{aligned} .8A - .1B &= .3 \\ -.3A + .6B &= .1 \end{aligned}$$

Solving simultaneously, we find:

$$\begin{aligned} A &= .422 \\ B &= .376 \end{aligned}$$

Given these values and that $A + B + C = 1$, we can determine that:

$$C = .202$$

Problem 4. *Accounts receivable* A manager has developed the following transposition matrix for a firm's accounts receivable:

$$\begin{array}{c} \\ p \\ 1 \\ 2 \\ b \end{array} \begin{array}{c} \begin{array}{cccc} p & 1 & 2 & b \end{array} \\ \begin{bmatrix} 1 & 0 & 0 & 0 \\ .5 & .3 & .2 & 0 \\ .3 & 0 & .4 & .3 \\ 0 & 0 & 0 & 1 \end{bmatrix} \end{array}$$

where

p = paid
1 = 1 to 30 days overdue
2 = 31 to 60 days overdue
b = bad debt

(Note: accounts are billed weekly, but classified in terms of months overdue. Consequently, it is possible for an account to remain in either the 1 or 2 category for several periods. Therefore, there is a nonzero probability of remaining in either 1 or 2.)

a. Obtain the fundamental matrix.

b. If there is currently \$10,000 in accounts in the 1 category and \$6,000 in the 2 category, determine the expected amount of bad debt.

Solution

a. Begin by rearranging the transition matrix so that the two absorbing states (p and b) are listed first, followed by the two nonabsorbing states. This yields the matrix:

$$\begin{array}{c} \\ p \\ b \\ 1 \\ 2 \end{array}\begin{array}{c} \begin{array}{cccc} p & b & 1 & 2 \end{array} \\ \begin{bmatrix} 1 & 0 & 0 & 0 \\ 0 & 1 & 0 & 0 \\ .5 & 0 & .3 & .2 \\ .3 & .3 & 0 & .4 \end{bmatrix} \end{array}$$

Then, partition the matrix into four parts that are defined as I, O, R, and Q:

$$\begin{array}{c} \\ p \\ b \\ 1 \\ 2 \end{array}\begin{array}{c} \begin{array}{cc:cc} p & b & 1 & 2 \end{array} \\ \left[\begin{array}{cc:cc} 1 & 0 & 0 & 0 \\ 0 & 1 & 0 & 0 \\ \hdashline .5 & 0 & .3 & .2 \\ .3 & .3 & 0 & .4 \end{array}\right] \end{array} \quad \text{where} \quad \begin{array}{c} p \; b \; 1 \; 2 \\ \begin{array}{c} p \\ b \\ 1 \\ 2 \end{array}\left[\begin{array}{c:c} \text{I} & \text{O} \\ \hdashline \text{R} & \text{Q} \end{array}\right] \end{array}$$

Next, compute (I − Q):

$$\begin{bmatrix} 1 & 0 \\ 0 & 1 \end{bmatrix} - \begin{bmatrix} .3 & .2 \\ 0 & .4 \end{bmatrix} = \begin{bmatrix} .7 & -.2 \\ 0 & .6 \end{bmatrix}$$

Find the inverse of (I − Q). Recall that for matrix M, where M is:

$$\begin{bmatrix} m_{11} & m_{12} \\ m_{21} & m_{22} \end{bmatrix}$$

the inverse is:

$$\begin{bmatrix} m_{22}/d & -m_{12}/d \\ -m_{21}/d & m_{11}/d \end{bmatrix} \text{ where } d = m_{11}m_{22} - m_{21}m_{12}$$
$$= .7(.6) - 0(-.2) = .42$$

Thus:

$$(\text{I} - \text{Q})^{-1} = \begin{bmatrix} .6/.42 & .2/.42 \\ -0/.42 & .7/.42 \end{bmatrix} = \begin{bmatrix} 1.429 & .476 \\ 0 & 1.667 \end{bmatrix}$$

This is the fundamental matrix, F.

b. First, multiply matrix R by the fundamental matrix:

$$\text{FR} = \begin{array}{c} \\ 1 \\ 2 \end{array}\begin{array}{c} \begin{array}{cc} 1 & 2 \end{array} \\ \begin{bmatrix} 1.429 & .476 \\ 0 & 1.667 \end{bmatrix} \end{array} \begin{array}{c} \\ 1 \\ 2 \end{array}\begin{array}{c} \begin{array}{cc} p & b \end{array} \\ \begin{bmatrix} .5 & 0 \\ .3 & .3 \end{bmatrix} \end{array}$$

$$= \begin{array}{c} \\ 1 \\ 2 \end{array}\begin{array}{c} \begin{array}{cc} p & b \end{array} \\ \begin{bmatrix} .857 & .143 \\ .500 & .500 \end{bmatrix} \end{array}$$

Then, find the expected amounts of *paid* and *bad debt* categories:

$$\begin{matrix} 1 & 2 \\ [10{,}000 & 6{,}000] \end{matrix} \begin{matrix} \\ 1 \\ 2 \end{matrix} \overset{\begin{matrix} p & & b \end{matrix}}{\begin{bmatrix} .857 & .143 \\ .500 & .500 \end{bmatrix}} = \begin{matrix} p & b \\ [11{,}570 & 4{,}430] \end{matrix}$$

The expected amount of bad debt is $4,430. Note that in the last matrix the sum of the amounts in the two categories is equal to the amounts currently in the two categories, 1 and 2. Thus, all of the amounts have been accounted for.

PROBLEMS

1. The following table contains transition probabilities for two products, A and B:

		Next period	
		A	B
This period	A	.70	.30
	B	.20	.80

   a. What percentage of customers who purchased Product A this period can be expected to purchase Product A next period? What percentage who purchased A this period can be expected to purchase Product B next period?

   b. Use a tree diagram to determine the proportion of customers who can be expected to purchase Product A in Period 2, given that they purchased Product B in Period 0.

2. Repeat part *b* of the previous problem using matrix multiplication to determine the answer.

3. Find the steady state proportions for Products A and B in Problem 1 by means of simultaneous equations.

4. The weather on an island in the Caribbean can be described by the following transition probabilities:

		Tomorrow	
		Sunny	Cloudy/rainy
Today	Sunny	.90	.10
	Cloudy/rainy	.80	.20

a. Use a tree diagram to determine the probability of sunny weather on the third day from now, given that today's weather is cloudy.

b. Repeat part *a* using matrix multiplication.

c. Determine the proportion of sunny days using simultaneous equations.

5. After careful study, an analyst has determined that the probability that a certain machine will have a breakdown is dependent on whether it had a breakdown on the previous day and was repaired. The relevant probabilities are:

		Tomorrow	
		No breakdown	Breakdown
Today	No breakdown	.88	.12
	Breakdown	.96	.04

a. Given that the machine has a breakdown today, what is the probability that it will also experience a breakdown tomorrow?

b. What is the probability that the machine will experience a breakdown two days in a row?

c. Use a tree diagram to determine the probability that a machine will have a breakdown on the day after tomorrow, given that no breakdown occurs today.

d. Repeat part *c* using matrix multiplication.

e. Determine the proportion of days the machine can be expected to experience a breakdown using simultaneous equations.

6. Find the steady-state proportions for this transition matrix:

	1	2
1	.75	.25
2	.40	.60

7. A market researcher for Know Your Market, Inc., has studied consumer buying patterns in a situation in which consumers purchase one of three competing brands each week. The researcher found that Brand A retains 50 percent of its customers each week while giving up 30 percent to Brand B and 20 percent to Brand C. The researcher found that B gave up 50 percent to A and 20 percent to C, and that C gave up 50 percent to A and 30 percent to B.

a. Develop a table of transition probabilities.

b. What are the steady-state proportions for the three brands?

8. A bank manager at Country Bank has compiled the following table of transition probabilities for the customers' use of various bank offices:

		Next period		
	Office	Main	East	South
This period	Main	.60	.10	.30
	East	.20	.70	.10
	South	.25	.15	.60

a. Which office tends to have the highest "loyalty"? Why?

b. What proportion of customers who banked at the Main office this time can be expected to bank at the East office two periods later? Solve using a tree diagram.

c. Repeat the previous part using matrix multiplication.

9. Determine the steady-state proportions for the previous problem.

10. If the transition probabilities for the South office in Problem 8 change from .25, .15, and .60 to .20 for Main, .10 for East, and .70 for South, what impact will this have on the steady-state proportions for each office?

11. After studying a brand-switching problem, an analyst concluded that Brand A loses 20 percent of its customers each period to Brand B and 10 percent to Brand C; Brand B loses 10 percent of its customers each period to Brand A and 30 percent to Brand C; and that Brand C loses 30 percent to Brand A and 20 percent to Brand B.

a. Develop a table of transition probabilities for this situation.

b. If Brand A initially has 400 customers. Brand B has 250 customers, and Brand C has 350, what average number of customers will each brand have in the long run?

12. A small, rural town has two movie theaters. Transition probabilities for weekly attendance for Sunday matinees are shown in the following table:

		Next week	
		Cameo	Strand
This week	Cameo	.60	.40
	Strand	.40	.60

a. Determine the steady-state proportion of theatergoers for each theater.

b. A group of local investors plans to open a new theater. A consultant has projected transition probabilities for the three theaters for Sunday matinees as follows:

	Next week		
	Cameo	Strand	Cine
Cameo	.50	.30	.20
Strand	.30	.60	.10
Cine	.25	.25	.50

Determine the steady-state proportion of customers for each chapter.

c. Which original theater, the Cameo or the Strand, stands to suffer the greater loss of customers based on the projected probabilities?

13. Residents of a Vermont community buy their Christmas trees from one of three local dealers. The following switching probabilities have been determined:

		This year		
		A	B	C
Last year	A	.65	.25	.10
	B	.35	.60	.05
	C	.40	.30	.30

a. Determine the steady-state proportion of customers for each dealer.

b. Suppose that Dealer C is now considering advertising as a means of increasing his market share, since each customer represents a profit of $4. The dealer projects the following transition probabilities:

		This year		
		A	B	C
Last year	A	.60	.20	.20
	B	.30	.50	.20
	C	.30	.20	.50

If the cost of advertising will be $375, would you recommend that Dealer C advertise? Explain, assuming that there are 800 customers in the "system."

14. A firm that rents video equipment has three stores. Customers are allowed to return rental equipment to any of the stores, regardless of which store they rented the equipment from. A study of rental returns has produced the following probabilities.

		Returned to		
		A	B	C
	A	.84	.09	.07
Rented at	B	.20	.70	.10
	C	.14	.06	.80

a. Determine the steady-state proportion for the stores.

b. Using matrix multiplication, determine the expected proportion of customers returning equipment to each store for the next three periods, assuming a rental at store B.

15. The following table gives a breakdown of customers staying and switching brands for two periods:

		This period		
		Brand A	Brand B	Brand C
Last period	A	350	80	70
	B	240	480	80
	C	210	140	350

Assume that these figures accurately reflect period-to-period behaviors.

a. Find the transition probabilities.

b. Determine the steady-state proportions for each brand.

16. A serviceperson is responsible for handling breakdowns of three robots at Global Mfg. Management is concerned about the number of robots waiting for repair, and the service manager has developed the following table that describes recent experience:

		Number waiting next period		
		0	1	2
Number waiting this period	0	.50	.50	0
	1	.25	.50	.25
	2	0	.50	.50

a. What is the probability that 1 robot will be waiting for repair next period, given 2 are waiting this period?

b. What is the probability that 1 robot will be waiting for repair in Period 3, given none are waiting this period (Period 0)?

c. What proportion of time will there be a waiting line in this system?

17. A machine breaks down and is repaired according to the following transition matrix:

		Next day: Operating	Next day: Down
Current	Operating	.85	.15
	Down	.35	.65

The cost for machine downtime is $800 per day. The manager has been presented with a proposal for preventive maintenance that will alter Operating transition probabilities from .85 and .15 to .95 and .05. The other probabilities will remain the same. The cost of the preventive maintenance program would be $500 per day. Is the improvement in the steady-state probability of operating enough to justify the cost of the program? Explain.

18. (Refer to Problem 17.) Suppose the manager has a second proposal that relates to repair time. This proposal would change Down probabilities from .35 and .65 to .45 and .55, while not affecting the Operating probabilities. The cost of this proposal would be $700 per day. If the manager could choose only one proposal, which should it be?

19. Find the inverse of each matrix.

a. $\begin{bmatrix} .6 & -.2 \\ -.3 & .8 \end{bmatrix}$

b. $\begin{bmatrix} .7 & -.1 \\ 0 & .5 \end{bmatrix}$

c. $\begin{bmatrix} .8 & -.1 \\ 0 & .4 \end{bmatrix}$

20. Given this transition matrix for accounts receivable for GGM, Inc.:

$$\text{Current}\quad \begin{array}{c} \\ p \\ 1 \\ 2 \\ b \end{array} \overset{\text{Next period}}{\begin{array}{cccc} p & 1 & 2 & b \\ \hline \end{array}}$$

$$\begin{array}{c|cccc} & p & 1 & 2 & b \\ \hline p & 1 & 0 & 0 & 0 \\ 1 & .7 & 0 & .3 & 0 \\ 2 & .8 & 0 & 0 & .2 \\ b & 0 & 0 & 0 & 1 \end{array}$$

where

p = paid
1 = 1 to 30 days late
2 = 31 to 60 days late
b = bad debt

a. Interpret each of the values in Row 1.

b. Rearrange the matrix so the row and column headings follow the sequence *p b* 1 2.

c. Partition the new matrix into I, O, R, and Q matrices, and identify each.

d. Obtain the matrix (I − Q) and then find its inverse.

e. What is the fundamental matrix in this problem?

f. Determine the proportion of current accounts receivable that will end up as bad debt.

g. If there is currently \$5,000 in Category 1 and \$8,000 in Category 2, what is the expected amount that will end up as bad debt? What is the expected amount that will end up as paid?

21. A manager has prepared this transition matrix for the accounts receivable of a firm. However, some of the values are missing.

$$\text{Current}\quad \begin{array}{c} \\ p \\ 1 \\ 2 \\ b \end{array} \overset{\text{Next period}}{\begin{array}{cccc} p & 1 & 2 & b \\ \hline \end{array}} \hspace{-1em}$$

$$\text{Current}\quad \begin{array}{c|cccc} & p & 1 & 2 & b \\ \hline p & 1 & & & \\ 1 & .8 & 0 & & 0 \\ 2 & .8 & & 0 & \\ b & & & & 1 \end{array}$$

where

p = paid
1 = 1 to 30 days late
2 = 31 to 60 days late
b = bad debt

a. Fill in the missing values.

b. Obtain the fundamental matrix.

c. Determine the proportion of accounts that will end up as paid.

d. If there is currently \$50,000 in accounts that are 1 to 30 days late and double that amount that are 31 to 60 days late, determine the expected amount that will end up as paid.

22. Suppose the following transition matrix pertains to a food brokerage that has \$40,000 in accounts receivable that are 1 to 30 days overdue and \$20,000 in accounts receivable that are 31 to 60 days overdue. How much should be allowed for bad debt? (Note: Accounts are billed weekly.)

Next period

$$\text{Current}\quad \begin{array}{c} p \\ 1 \\ 2 \\ b \end{array} \overset{\begin{array}{cccc} p & 1 & 2 & b \end{array}}{\begin{bmatrix} 1 & 0 & 0 & 0 \\ .6 & .3 & .1 & 0 \\ .7 & 0 & .2 & .1 \\ 0 & 0 & 0 & 1 \end{bmatrix}}$$

where

p = paid
1 = 1 to 30 days overdue
2 = 31 to 60 days overdue
b = bad debt

23. A manager has developed the following transition matrix for accounts receivable:

$$\text{Current}\quad \begin{array}{c} \\ p \\ 1 \\ 2 \\ b \end{array} \overset{\text{Next period}}{\begin{array}{cccc} p & 1 & 2 & b \end{array}} \hspace{-6em} \begin{array}{c} \\ \left[\begin{array}{cccc} 1 & 0 & 0 & 0 \\ .6 & .2 & .2 & 0 \\ .5 & .2 & .1 & .2 \\ 0 & 0 & 0 & 1 \end{array}\right] \end{array}$$

where

p = paid
1 = 1 to 30 days overdue
2 = 31 to 60 days overdue
b = bad debt

A typical situation is to have approximately \$30,000 in accounts receivable that are 1 to 30 days overdue and \$10,000 in accounts receivable that are 31 to 60 days overdue. The manager has received a proposal from the marketing department for increasing the collection rate. Estimated probabilities under the proposal for Row 1 are .7, .2, .1, and 0 and for Row 2, .6, .2, .1, and .1. It will cost \$1,000 per period to maintain this new system. Can the proposal be justified on a cost basis? Explain.

Part VI
Nonlinear Models

Many of the problems encountered in business can be modeled using linear relationships. Linear relationships are desirable because they lend themselves to efficient solution procedures. However, there are problems encountered in business that involve nonlinear relationships. Many of these can be solved using calculus-based procedures.

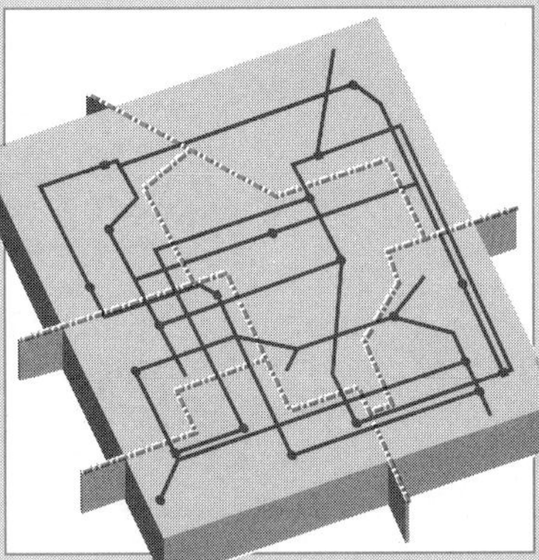

In Chapter 19 you will learn how to use differential calculus to obtain solutions to models that involve nonlinear relationships.

Part Outline

Chapter 19
Calculus-Based Optimization

Chapter Outline

Learning Objectives

After completing this chapter, you should be able to:

1. Explain the difference between optimization problems that can be solved using linear programming methods and those that require calculus-based methods.
2. Find the optimal values of the decision variable and the objective function in problems that involve one decision variable.
3. Find the optimal values of decision variables and the objective function in problems that involve two decision variables.
4. Use a Lagrange multiplier to find the optimal values of two decision variables and the objective function in problems that involve equality constraints.

Many of the chapters in this book describe models that involve only linear relationships. The widespread use of linear models in practice necessitates devoting substantial coverage to linear models. However, an important class of problems involve nonlinear relationships. This chapter illustrates methods that can be used to find optimal solutions for simple models that involve nonlinear relationships.

INTRODUCTION

The models described in this chapter are in some ways similar to the *linear programming* models described in Chapters 2 through 9. For example, all of the models have an objective function that is to be maximized or minimized. Some also have one or more constraints, but others involve only an objective function. However, all of the models in this chapter involve one or more *nonlinear relationships*.

There are many real-life examples of problems that involve nonlinear relationships. For instance, the inventory EOQ model's objective is to minimize the cost function:

$$TC = \frac{Q}{2}H + \frac{D}{Q}S$$

where

TC = total annual cost
Q = order quantity
H = annual holding cost per unit
D = annual demand
S = ordering cost

A graph of this U-shaped cost function is illustrated in Figure 19–1. Similar U-shaped cost curves can be used to describe other inventory cost functions as well as costs in forecasting models, waiting line models, and quality control. Moreover, cost-profit-volume models may also involve nonlinear relationships.

Nonlinear relationships occur because one or more of the causes of linearity is absent. For example, there may be a nonproportional relationship between two variables (such as price and quantity demanded; the relationship may only be linear over a limited range of price), or the relationship may be nonadditive (if you add one cup of sugar to one cup of water, the resulting volume will be less than two cups).

The difficulty with nonlinear models in general is that they can be significantly harder to solve than linear models. Moreover, linear models often provide reasonably good approximations to nonlinear models. Thus, the efficiency of solution techniques for linear models and the fact that they perform well as approximations

FIGURE 19–1 A U-Shaped Cost Function

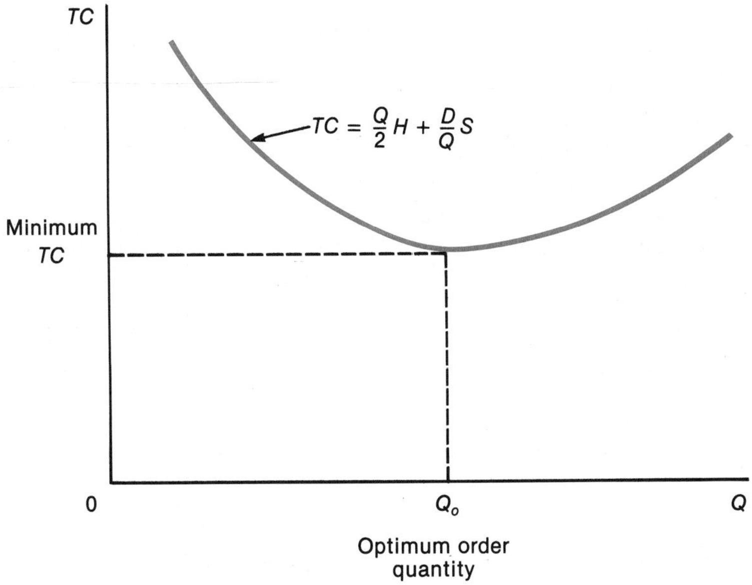

in many cases that involve nonlinear relationships explain the popularity of linear models. Nonetheless, there are many instances for which linear approximations are not acceptable. Judgment and experience on the part of the decision maker are necessary to determine when linear approximations are suitable and when they are not. For those cases that are deemed unsuitable for linear models, the methods described in this chapter may be of use if the model is fairly simple.

The chapter begins with a discussion of models that have one decision variable, including both unconstrained models (i.e., models that have only an objective function) and constrained models. It then moves on to a discussion of unconstrained models with two decision variables. For the special case of equality-constrained models, the use of *Lagrange multipliers* is demonstrated.

MODELS WITH ONE DECISION VARIABLE

In this section, the use of first and second derivatives for identifying maximum and minimum values of a mathematical function is illustrated. The section is presented in two parts. The first part illustrates the procedure for an *unconstrained function,* while the second part illustrates the procedure for a *constrained function.*

Unconstrained

Consider the case of Larry Brown, manager of a small manufacturing company. Larry has ordered a new machine that will increase the productivity of an existing machine. Larry must now select a location for the new machine. He knows that the closer the new machine is to the existing machine, the lower the cost of transporting work in process between the two machines. On the other hand, the closer the two machines are, the greater the cost to remodel the area to accommodate the new machine.

With the help of the accounting department, Larry developed a model that expressed the combined cost of remodeling and transporting work on a per unit basis:

$$\text{Cost per piece} = 1.5(\text{Distance})^2 - 42(\text{Distance}) + 300$$

In mathematical terms, this can be expressed as:

$$y = 1.5x^2 - 42x + 300$$

where

y = cost per unit
x = distance between the two machines in feet

Larry's problem is to determine the value of x that will minimize this cost function. He can do this by using differential calculus.[1] By taking the first derivative of the cost function and setting that equal to zero, he can solve for the value(s) of x for which the function reaches a local maximum or a local minimum. Then, by finding the second derivative of the function, he will be able to determine that at that value of x the function is a minimum. Let's see how this is accomplished.

There are two conditions that must be satisfied:

Condition 1 (*necessary*): The first derivative of a function must equal zero at every point that is a local maximum or a local minimum.
Condition 2 (*sufficient*): If the first condition is satisfied at a point, then it can be concluded that:

1. The point will be a local minimum *if* the sign of the second derivative is positive.
2. The point will be a local maximum *if* the sign of the second derivative is negative.

---

[1] The appendix to this chapter illustrates rules that can be used to differentiate frequently encountered simple mathematical expressions.

FIGURE 19–2 Illustrations of Local Maximum and Local Minimum Points

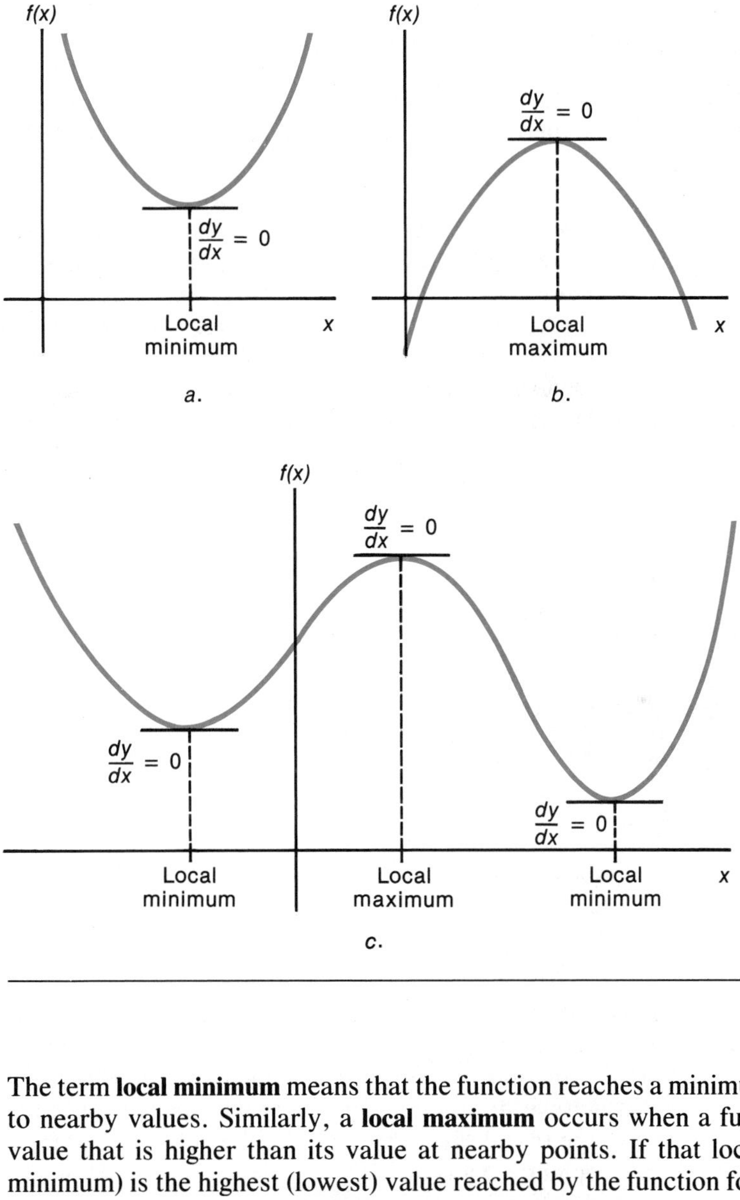

The term **local minimum** means that the function reaches a minimum value *relative* to nearby values. Similarly, a **local maximum** occurs when a function reaches a value that is higher than its value at nearby points. If that local maximum (or minimum) is the highest (lowest) value reached by the function for any value of x, then that value is also a **global maximum** (or **minimum**).

Consider the functions shown in Figure 19–2. In 19–2*a*, we see a function that is convex; it has a single minimum, so the local minimum is also the global minimum. Similarly, in 19–2*b*, we see a function that is strictly concave, with a single maximum that is a global maximum. Figure 19–2*c* shows a more complex function; it has a number of turns. The function has two minimum points and one maximum. The lower of the two minimum points is both a local minimum and a global minimum (assuming that these three turning points are the only ones the function has). Similarly, if the maximum is the only maximum point for the function, then it is also the global maximum. In the case of a function with more turning points, there would be an even greater number of local maxima and local minima.

It is generally not practical to plot the graph of a function in order to determine the point(s) at which it achieves a local maximum or local minimum. Instead, the procedure involves finding the first derivative of the function and setting it equal to zero. (Condition 1 requires that the first derivative equal zero at a local maximum or a local minimum.) The solution (or solutions, if there are more than one) that makes the first derivative equal to zero is the point that must be evaluated to determine if it is a local maximum or a local minimum. That is accomplished by taking the second derivative of the function and noting its sign; a plus sign indicates a local minimum and a minus sign indicates a local maximum. Note that if there are multiple solutions for the second derivative (e.g., $x = 2, x = -2$), each of these would be substituted into the second derivative in order to obtain the sign of the second derivative.

Not let's see how we can use calculus and the two conditions mentioned previously to determine the solution to Larry's problem. Recall that the cost function was:

$$y = 1.5x^2 - 42x + 300$$

The first derivative of this function is:

$$\frac{dy}{dx} = 3x - 42$$

Setting this equal to zero (Condition 1) and solving for x, we find:

$$3x - 42 = 0$$
$$x = 14$$

This indicates that the slope of the function (i.e., the first derivative) is zero at only one point, where $x = 14$. We must now determine whether this one point is a maximum or a minimum. To do this, we must obtain the second derivative of the function, which we do by applying the same procedure used to obtain the first derivative to the first derivative (i.e., take the derivative of the first derivative to obtain the second derivative).

The second derivative is:

$$\frac{d^2y}{dy^2} = +3$$

The positive sign tells us that the function has a local minimum at the point where $x = 14$. Because there is only one value of x for which the first derivative equals zero, we can say that the local minimum is also the *global* minimum. Hence, to minimize cost, Larry should position the new machine at a distance of 14 feet from the existing machine.

By substituting $x = 14$ into the original (cost) function, we can determine the cost per piece that will result from locating the new machine at a distance of 14 feet from the existing machine. Thus:

$$y = 1.5(14)^2 - 42(14) + 300 = 6$$

Hence, the cost will be \$6 per piece to move pieces between the two machines.

The procedure for finding the optimal solution of an unconstrained model with one decision variable can be summarized as follows:

1. Obtain the first derivative of the function.
2. Set the first derivative equal to zero and solve for the value(s) of the decision variable that will make the first derivative equal to zero.
3. Obtain the second derivative. If it is a constant (e.g., +5, −2), its sign will indicate whether the function achieves a local maximum (the sign of the second derivative is negative) or a local minimum (the sign of the second derivative is positive). If the second derivative includes the decision variable (e.g., $4x$, $x + 6$), substitute the value(s) found in step 2 and note the resulting sign(s) to determine if the function achieves a local max (−) or a local min (+) at each value.

■

EXAMPLE 1 Given this function:

$$y = \frac{1}{3}x^3 - 5x^2 + 21x + 100$$

a. Determine the value of x for which the function is a maximum.

b. Compute the value of the function at its maximum.

Solution

a. 1. Obtain the first derivative of the function:

$$\frac{dy}{dx} = x^2 - 10x + 21$$

2. Set the first derivative equal to zero and solve for x:

$$x^2 - 10x + 21 = 0$$

This can be factored into:

$$(x - 3)(x - 7) = 0$$

Solving, $x = +3$ or $x = +7$, in order for this to equal zero.

3. The second derivative is:

$$\frac{d^2y}{dx^2} = 2x - 10$$

At $x = +3$, this is $2(3) - 10 = -4$

At $x = +7$, this is $2(7) - 10 = +4$

The *negative* result (-4) indicates a local maximum, the positive result ($+4$) indicates a local minimum. Hence, the function reaches a local maximum at $x = +3$.

b. To find the value of the function at its maximum, substitute the value of x for which it is a maximum into the original function and solve. Thus:

$$y = \frac{1}{3}(3)^3 - 5(3)^2 + 21(3) + 100 = 127$$

Constrained

The procedure for finding the optimal value of a constrained decision variable is very similar to the procedure for an unconstrained decision variable. The key difference between the two is that the existence of a constraint means that there is a *feasible solution space* that must be taken into account. The feasible solution space may or may not include the optimum that would be indicated if the function were not constrained. In order to understand the consequences of this, consider the two cases depicted in Figure 19–3.

Figure 19–3a illustrates a case where the function attains its optimum *within* the feasible solution space. In Figure 19–3b, the function attains its optimum *outside* of the feasible solution space. In the first case, the optimum is unaffected by the constraint; in the second case, the optimum is determined by the constraint. It occurs at the point where the decision variable equals the constraint. Note, too, an important difference between nonlinear models and linear models: The optimal solution is not always on the boundary of the feasible solution space, although it may be.

The procedure for constrained optimization is to proceed as in the case of unconstrained optimization to identify local maximum and local minimum points. Then, check to see if the solution satisfies the constraint. For instance, suppose you find $x = 5$, and the constraint is that $x \leq 7$. Obviously, the solution satisfies the constraint, so $x = 5$ *may be* the optimal solution. The other possibility is that the value of x equal to the constraint (e.g., $x = 7$) may yield a better solution. In order to complete the analysis, substitute that value into the objective function and compare the result to the value of the objective function with the apparent

FIGURE 19–3a The Optimal Point Lies within the Feasible Solution Space

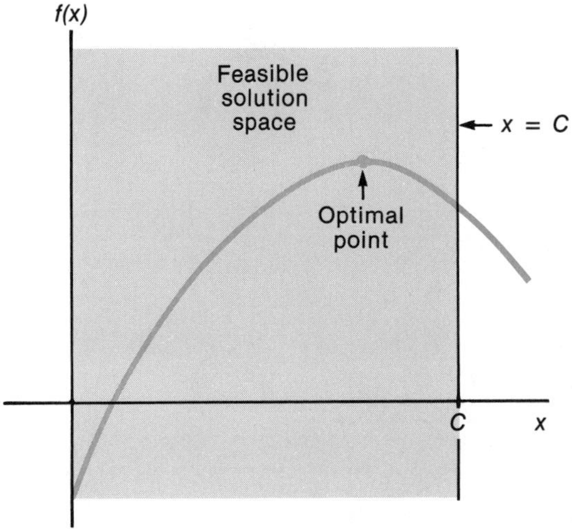

FIGURE 19–3b The Optimal Point Is on the Boundary of the Feasible Solution Space

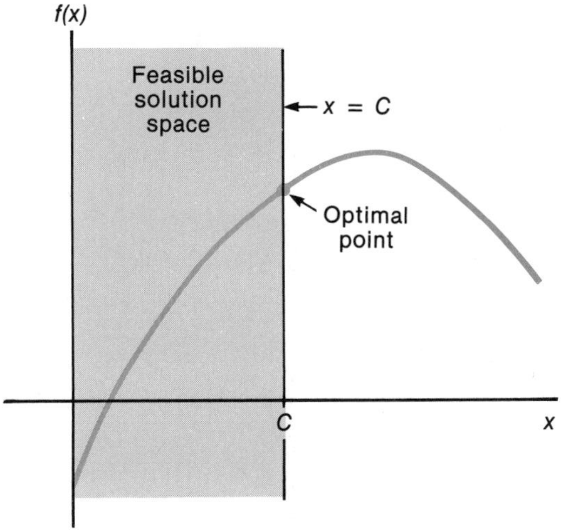

optimum (e.g., $x = 5$) to see which actually gives the better solution. Figure 19–4 illustrates a case for which the constraint provides a better solution than the apparent (local) optimum.

■

EXAMPLE 2 Determine the minimum cost for this model:

minimize $2x^2 - 20x + 60$

subject to $x \leq 8$

Solution

1. Obtain the first derivative and set it equal to zero:

$$\frac{dy}{dx} = 4x - 20 = 0$$

Solving, $x = 5$. Note that this value *satisfies* the constraint $x \leq 8$.

2. Obtain the second derivative and note its sign:

$$\frac{d^2y}{dx^2} = +4$$

The plus sign indicates that at $x = 5$, the function $2x^2 - 20x + 60$ reaches a local minimum.

FIGURE 19–4 The Global Maximum Can Be at the Point Where $x = C$

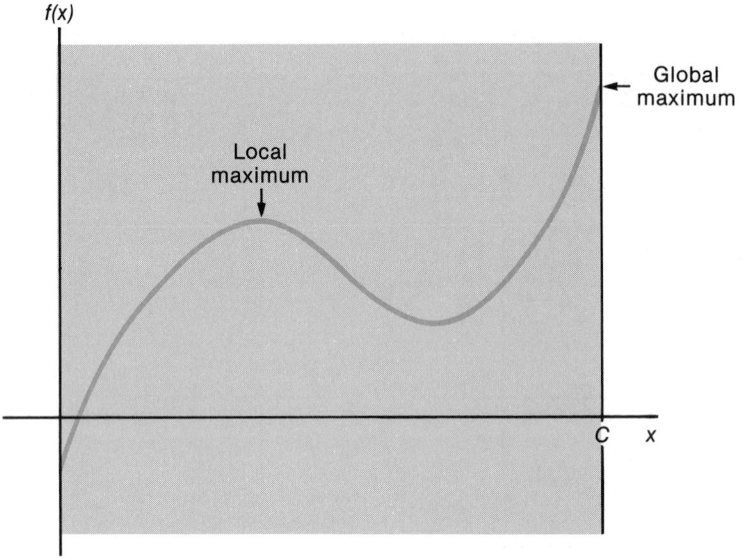

3. Compute the value of the function at $x = 8$ (the constraint):

$$2(8)^2 - 20(8) + 60 = 28$$

4. Compute the value of the function at its local minimum, $x = 5$:

$$2(5)^2 - 20(5) + 60 = 10$$

5. Comparing the results at steps 3 and 4, we can see that the function is lower at $x = 5$ than at $x = 8$. Hence, we can say that the function is minimized at $x = 5$, and the minimum cost (see step 4) is 10.

MODELS WITH TWO DECISION VARIABLES

Solution of models that involve two decision variables parallels the procedure used for models with one decision variable, except that the analysis is a bit more complicated, owing to the presence of a second decision variable. It becomes necessary to obtain the **partial derivative** of a function (i.e., the derivative of the function with respect to one variable, treating the other variable as a *constant*), as well as the second partial derivative of a function with respect to each of the variables. As before, the first derivatives are set equal to zero and solved, and second derivative conditions are checked to determine the nature of the function at the values obtained from the first derivative results.

Consider the case of a company that makes imaging equipment that it sells primarily to hospitals. The company makes two different models. Suppose we let x_1 = the quantity of Model 1, and x_2 = the quantity of Model 2. Model 1 sells for \$64(000) and Model 2 sells for \$72(000). The fixed cost of producing Model 1 equipment is \$500(000) and the fixed cost of producing Model 2 is \$600(000). The variable cost to produce each model (c_1, c_2) is complex and dependent on the quantity of each model that is produced.

$$c_1 = .4x_1 + .2x_2 \quad \text{(in thousands of dollars)}$$
$$c_2 = .3x_2 + .2x_1 \quad \text{(in thousands of dollars)}$$

Variable cost is then

$$x_1c_1 = .4x_1^2 + .2x_1x_2$$
$$x_2c_2 = .3x_2^2 + .2x_1x_2$$

The manager of the company wants to determine the values of x_1 and x_2 that will maximize profit, where profit is:

$$\begin{aligned} P &= \text{Total revenue} - (\text{Variable cost} - \text{Fixed cost}) \\ &= 64x_1 + 72x_2 - [x_1c_1 + x_2c_2 - (500 + 600)] \\ &= 64x_1 + 72x_2 - .4x_1^2 - .2x_1x_2 - .3x_2^2 - .2x_1x_2 - 1{,}100 \end{aligned}$$

Combining the two x_1x_2 terms, we have:

$$P = 64x_1 + 72x_2 - .4x_1^2 - .4x_1x_2 - .3x_2^2 - 1{,}100$$

In order to solve problems of this type, it is necessary to obtain the partial derivative of the function (i.e., P) with respect to each of the decision variables, and then set these equal to zero.

Condition 3 (*necessary*): The partial derivatives of an unconstrained function of two variables must both equal zero at a local maximum or a local minimum of the function.

Finding the partial derivatives and setting them equal to zero, we obtain:

$$\frac{\partial P}{\partial x_1} = 64 - .8x_1 - .4x_2 = 0$$

$$\frac{\partial P}{\partial x_2} = 72 - .4x_1 - .6x_2 = 0$$

Rearranging terms, we can write:

$$\frac{\partial P}{\partial x_1} : .8x_1 + .4x_2 = 64$$

$$\frac{\partial P}{\partial x_2} : .4x_1 + .6x_2 = 72$$

We can solve this by multiplying the second equation by 2 and then subtracting the first equation from the revised second equation. Thus:

$$\begin{array}{rcl} .8x_1 + \ \ .4x_2 &=& 64 \\ .8x_1 + 1.2x_2 &=& 144 \\ \hline .8x_2 &=& 80, \quad x_2 = 100 \end{array}$$

Substituting this value into either equation and solving for x_1, we obtain $x_1 = 30$. Hence, the optimal values *appear* to be $x_1 = 30$ and $x_2 = 100$.

Once these values have been obtained, we can check the second-order conditions to determine what sort of point they represent.

First, compute D, where:

$$D = \left(\frac{\partial^2 f}{\partial x_1^2}\right)\left(\frac{\partial^2 f}{\partial x_2^2}\right) - \left(\frac{\partial^2 f}{\partial x_1 \partial x_2}\right)^2$$

Then check the second-order conditions:

Condition 4 (*sufficient*). If Condition 3 is satisfied, and:

a. $D > 0$

1. The point is a local minimum if $\frac{\partial^2 f}{\partial x_1^2} > 0$.
2. The point is a local maximum if $\frac{\partial^2 f}{\partial x_1^2} < 0$.

b. $D < 0$

The point is neither a local minimum nor a local maximum. Instead, it is a **saddle point,** which means one of the variables reaches a local maximum at the same point that the other variable reaches a local minimum.

In this example, the second partials and the mixed partial, are:

$$\frac{\partial^2 f}{\partial x_1^2} = -.8, \ \frac{\partial^2 f}{\partial x_2^2} = -.6, \text{ and } \frac{\partial^2 f}{\partial x_1 \partial x_2} = +.4$$

Hence, $D = (-.8)(-.6) - (.4)^2 = +.33$. Because $D > 0$, and $\frac{\partial^2 f}{\partial x_1^2} < 0$, this point ($x_1 1 = 30$, $x_2 = 100$) is a local maximum (see Condition 4).

By substituting the optimal values into the original profit function, we can also determine the maximum profit:

$$P = 64(30) + 72(100) - .4(30^2) - .4(30)(100) - .3(100^2) - 1{,}100$$
$$= 3{,}460, \text{ or } \$3{,}460{,}000$$

EQUALITY CONSTRAINTS: LAGRANGE MULTIPLIERS

The solution to a problem that involves two variables and one or more equality constraints when either the function or the constraints (or both) are nonlinear can be handled using the *Lagrangian method*. For example, consider this problem:

maximize $\quad -2.5x_1^2 - x_2^2 - 3x_1x_2 + 18x_1 + 6x_2 + 100$

subject to

$$x_1^2 + x_2 = 10$$

The procedure involves setting the constraint equal to zero:

$$x_1^2 + x_2 - 10 = 0$$

and multiplying this by λ, the **Lagrange multiplier:**

$$\lambda\,(x_1^2 + x_2 - 10)$$

Then this new expression is added to the objective function to obtain a **Lagrangian function** that consists of the original decision variables and the Lagrangian multiplier, λ:

$$L(x_1, x_2, \lambda) = -2.5x_1^2 - x_2^2 - 3x_1x_2 + 18x_1 + 6x_2 + 100 + \lambda(x_1^2 + x_2 - 10)$$

Note that adding this new term does not really change the objective function because the new term is equal to zero.

Once we have obtained the Lagrangian function, we can analyze the problem in a way that is very similar to the procedure described in the preceding section for two-variable, unconstrained models. The only difference is that we now have a third variable to deal with.

As before, we obtain the partial derivative of the objective function with respect to each of the variables (x_1, x_2, and λ):

$$\frac{\partial L}{\partial x_1} = -5x_1 - 3x_2 + 18 + \lambda = 0$$

$$\frac{\partial L}{\partial x_2} = -2x_2 - 3x_1 + 6 + \lambda = 0$$

$$\frac{\partial L}{\partial \lambda} = x_1 + x_2 - 10 = 0$$

We can solve this system of equations for the values of x_1, x_2, and λ by first eliminating λ from the first two equations (e.g., subtract the first equation from the second). The result is:

$$(5x_1 - 3x_1) + (3x_2 - 2x_2) + (-18 + 6) + (-\lambda + \lambda) = 0$$
$$2x_1 + x_2 - 12 = 0$$

Then, using this new equation and the third partial derivative, we have:

$$\begin{array}{ll} \text{(new)} & 2x_1 + x_2 - 12 = 0 \\ \text{(third)} & x_1 + x_2 - 10 = 0 \end{array}$$

Subtracting the (third) from the (new), we find:

$$x_1 - 2 = 0$$

Thus, $x_1 = +2$. And substituting this into the (third) equation, we find that $x_2 = +8$.

We can now determine the value of λ, using $x_1 = 2$ and $x_2 = 8$, and either of the first two partial derivative equations. For example, using the first partial derivative equation, we find:

$$-5(2) - 3(8) - 18 + \lambda = 0$$

Solving, $\lambda = 16$.

At this point, we have found what appear to be optimal values of x_1 and x_2. However, instead of *maximizing* the original function, it may be that they actually *minimize* the function. Or, they may constitute a *saddle point*. The same conditions that applied in the previous section apply here. In order to check them, we must first substitute the value of $\lambda = 16$ into the first partial derivatives of L with respect to x_1 and x_2. Thus:

$$\frac{\partial L}{\partial x_1} = -5x_1 - 3x_2 + 18 + 16$$

$$\frac{\partial L}{\partial x_2} = -2x_2 - 3x_1 + 6 + 16$$

The second partials and the mixed partial are:

$$\frac{\partial^2 L}{\partial x_1^2} = -5, \frac{\partial^2 L}{\partial x_2^2} = -2, \text{ and } \frac{\partial^2 L}{\partial x_1 \partial x_2} = -3$$

As before, we compute the value of D:

$$D = \left(\frac{\partial^2 L}{\partial x_1^2}\right)\left(\frac{\partial^2 L}{\partial x_2^2}\right) - \left(\frac{\partial^2 L}{\partial x_1 \partial x_2}\right)^2$$

Because $D > 0$ and $\frac{\partial^2 L}{\partial x_1^2} < 0$, we do, in fact, have a local maximum. We can determine the value of the function at its local maximum by substituting the values we found for x_1 and x_2 into the original function. Thus:

$$-2.5(2^2) - (8^2) - 3(2)(8) + 18(2) + 6(8) + 100 = 62$$

Let's take a moment to recap the Lagrange procedure:

1. Form the Lagrange function. Do this by making the constraint equal to zero, multiply it by λ, and add the result to the original objective function.
2. Obtain the partial derivative of the Lagrange function with respect to each of the decision variables and to λ. Set these equal to zero.
3. Find the solution(s) for the decision variables. Do this by eliminating λ from the partials of x_1 and x_2, and then using the partial of the Lagrange multiplier. Then find the value of λ.
4. Treating the value of λ as fixed, find the second partials of x_1 and x_2, and the mixed partial.
5. Determine if the solution(s) is (are) a local maximum, local minimum, or a saddle point, according to Condition 4 that was described in the previous section.

Interpreting λ

The Lagrange multiplier, λ, has an important economic interpretation, analogous to dual variables in linear programming. Its value indicates the (sometimes approximate) amount that the objective function will change for a one-unit change in the right-hand side value of the constraint. For instance, in the preceding example, we found $\lambda = +16$. This means that if the right-hand side value of the constraint were to be increased by one unit (from 10 to 11), the resulting optimal value of the objective function would decrease by 16. Conversely, if the right-hand side value of the constraint were to be decreased by one unit, the optimal value of the objective function would increase by 16. Moreover, if the sign of λ had been negative (say, -22), the opposite would have been true: A one-unit decrease in the right-hand side value of the constraint would have caused a *decrease* of 22 in the optimal value of the objective function, and a one-unit increase in the right-hand side value of the constraint would have caused an *increase* of 22 in the right-hand side value of the objective function.

COMPUTER SOLUTIONS

For nonlinear models that are more complex than those presented in this chapter, solutions become considerably more challenging to obtain. One option is to make use of a computer code for solving the model. Unfortunately, most management science computer packages are not equipped to handle these sorts of problems, so more specialized software must be obtained. One such package, GINO, is offered by LINDO Systems, Inc., Chicago.

It should be pointed out, however, that formulating and solving nonlinear problems may require considerable expertise, and many such problems do not truly lend themselves to solution, even with a computer package.

SUMMARY

The models presented in this chapter are similar to the linear programming models presented in earlier chapters. The essential difference is that the models presented in this chapter have one or more *nonlinear* components. These models generally cannot be handled using conventional linear programming techniques. Instead, calculus-based solution procedures must be used.

The calculus-based procedures typically involve obtaining the first derivative of the objective function, finding all solutions for which the first derivative is equal to zero, and then checking second derivative conditions to ascertain the nature of the zero points (e.g., a local maximum or a local minimum). If two or more decision variables are involved, partial derivatives are used. If equality constraints and two or more decision variables are involved, a method that involves a *Lagrange multiplier* is used.

The models presented in this chapter are relatively simple. More complex models are more challenging to deal with. Some lend themselves to computer solutions.

GLOSSARY

Global Maximum The highest value attained by a function over its entire range.

Global Minimum The lowest value attained by a function over its entire range.

Lagrangian Function In models that have equality constraints, a modified objective function that incorporates the constraint(s) as part of the objective function.

Lagrange Multiplier, λ An additional variable used to incorporate the constraint(s) into the objective function in a model that has equality constraints.

Local Maximum The highest point of a function relative to nearby values. It may or may not be the highest point overall.

Local Minimum The lowest point of a function relative to nearby values. It may or may not be the lowest point overall.

Partial Derivative When a function has more than one decision variable, a derivative of the function with respect to one of the decision variables with all other variables treated as constants.

Saddle Point A point that is neither a maximum nor a minimum; with two variables, the function attains a maximum with respect to one variable while attaining a minimum with respect to the other variable.

SOLVED PROBLEMS

Problem 1. *One variable, unconstrained* Given the following function:

$$y = \frac{1}{3}x^3 - 6x^2 + 27x$$

a. Determine the value of x for which the function reaches (1) a local maximum and (2) a local minimum.
b. Determine the value of the function at the local maximum and local minimum.

Solution

a. **1.** Obtain the first derivative of the function:

$$\frac{dy}{dx} = x_2 - 12x + 27$$

2. Set the first derivative equal to zero and solve for x:

$$x^2 - 12x - 27 = 0$$

Factoring, we obtain:

$$(x - 3)(x - 9) = 0$$

Hence, the roots are $x = +3$ and $x = +9$.

3. Obtain the second derivative:

$$\frac{d^2y}{dx^2} = 2x - 12$$

Substitute the roots obtained in step 2 into the second derivative:

At $x = +3$, the second derivative equals -6
At $x = +9$, the second derivative equals $+6$

We can conclude that the function reaches a local maximum at $x = 3$ because the sign of the second derivative is negative for $x = +3$; and we can conclude that the function reaches a local minimum at $x = 9$ because the sign of the second derivative is positive for that value of x.

b. Substituting $x = 3$ and $x = 9$ into the original function, we find:

At $x = 3$, the value of the function equals 36
At $x = 9$, the value of the function equals 0

Problem 2. *Constrained optimization with one variable* Find the optimal profit for this model, and the value of the decision variable that will produce the optimal profit:

maximize $\quad -10x^2 + 5x + 1{,}000$

subject to $\quad x \leq 12$

Solution

1. Obtain the first derivative of the function, set it equal to zero, and solve for x:

$$\frac{dy}{dx} = -20x + 5 = 0$$

Solving, $x = 1/4$. Note that this value *satisfies* the constraint $x \leq 12$.

2. Obtain the second derivative, and note its sign:

$$\frac{d^2y}{dx^2} = -20$$

The negative sign indicates that the function reaches a local maximum at $x = 1/4$.

3. Compute the value of the function at the local maximization point and compare the result to the result obtained when $x = 12$ (the constraint):

$$\text{At } x = 1/4,\ f(x) = -10(1/4)^2 + 5(1/4) + 1{,}000 = 1{,}000.625$$
$$\text{At } x = 12,\ f(x) = -10(12)^2 + 5(12) + 1{,}000 = -380$$

The value of the function at $x = 1/4$ is greater than the value of the function at $x = 12$. Hence, the maximum value of the function (the optimal profit) is 1,000.625, which a value of $x = 1/4$ will produce.

Problem 3. *Unconstrained optimization with two decision variables* Given this model:

$$f(x_1,x_2) = 4x_1^2 + 15x_2^2 + 16x_1x_2 - 40x_1 - 76x_2 + 33$$

determine the optimal values of the decision variables and determine whether the optimal solution is a maximum, a minimum, or a saddle point.

Solution

1. Obtain the partial derivative of the function with respect to each of the decision variables:

$$\frac{\partial f}{\partial x_1} = 8x_1 + 16x_2 - 40$$
$$\frac{\partial f}{\partial x_2} = 30x_2 + 16x_1 - 76$$

2. Set the partials equal to zero and solve for x_1 and x_2:

$$8x_1 + 16x_2 - 40 = 0$$
$$30x_2 + 16x_1 - 76 = 0$$

Rearranging terms, we can write these two equations:

$$8x_1 + 16x_2 = 40$$
$$16x_1 + 30x_2 = 76$$

Multiplying each term of the first equation by 2 and subtracting the second equation from the result gives us:

$$2x_2 = 4$$

Solving, $x_2 = 2$. Substituting $x_2 = 2$ into $8x_1 + 16x_2 = 40$ yields $x_1 = 1$.

3. Next, obtain the second partials of the function with respect to each variable and the mixed partial:

$$\frac{\partial^2 f}{\partial x_1^2} = +8, \frac{\partial^2 f}{\partial x_2^2} = +30, \frac{\partial^2 f}{\partial x_1 \partial x_2} = +16$$

4. Compute the value of D:

$$D = \left(\frac{\partial^2 f}{\partial x_1^2}\right)\left(\frac{\partial^2 f}{\partial x_2^2}\right) - \left(\frac{\partial^2 f}{\partial x_1 \partial x_2}\right)^2$$
$$= (+8)(+30) - (+16)^2 = -16$$

Comparing this result to Condition 4, we find that a negative value for D indicates a *saddle point,* which is neither a local maximum nor a local minimum. Thus, the values $x_1 = 1$ and $x_2 = 2$ yield a point at which the function is a maximum with respect to one of these variables but a minimum with respect to the other variable.

Problem 4. *Equality constraints: Lagrange multiplier* Solve this problem for the optimal values of the decision variables and determine if the optimal values produce a point that is a local maximum, a local minimum, or a saddle point:

$$f(x_1,x_2) = -6x_1^2 - 4x_2^2 - 9x_1x_2 + 17x_1 + 10x_2$$

subject to $x_1 + x_2 = 3$

Solution

1. Let $\lambda = x_1 + x_2 - 3$.
2. Form a Lagrangian function incorporating λ:

$$L(x_1,x_2, \lambda) = -6x_1^2 - 4x_2^2 - 9x_1x_2 + 17x_1 + 10x_2 + \lambda (x_1 + x_2 - 3)$$

3. Obtain partial derivatives for x_1, x_2, and λ; and set each equal to zero:

$$\frac{\partial L}{\partial x_1} = -12x_1 - 9x_2 + 17 + \lambda = 0$$
$$\frac{\partial L}{\partial x_2} = -8x_2 - 9x_1 + 10 + \lambda = 0$$
$$\frac{\partial L}{\partial \lambda} = x_1 + x_2 - 3 = 0$$

4. Subtract the first partial from the second partial to obtain an equation without λ:

$$\begin{aligned} &(12x_1 - 9x_1) + (9x_2 - 8x_2) + (-17 + 10) + (-\lambda + \lambda) = 0 \\ = \quad & 3x_1 \quad + \quad x_2 \quad + \quad -7 \quad = 0 \end{aligned}$$

5. Use the third partial equation and this new equation to solve for x_1 and x_2. Subtract the third partial from the new equation:

$$\begin{array}{ll} \text{(new)} & 3x_1 + x_2 - 7 = 0 \\ \text{(third)} & \underline{x_1 + x_2 - 3 = 0} \\ & 2x_1 \qquad - 4 = 0 \end{array}$$

Solving, $x_1 = 2$. By substituting this into the (third) equation, we obtain $x_2 = 1$.

6. Substituting $x_1 = 2$ and $x_2 = 1$ into either of the first two partial derivative equations, we can solve for λ. Using the first equation, we find:

$$-12(2) - 9(1) + 17 + \lambda = 0$$

Solving, $\lambda = 16$.

7. With λ fixed at 16, the first partial derivatives of x_1 and x_2 become:

$$\frac{\partial L}{\partial x_1} = -12x_1 - 9x_2 + 17 + 16, \text{ or } -12x_1 - 9x_2 + 33$$

$$\frac{\partial L}{\partial x_2} = -8x_2 - 9x_1 + 10 + 16, \text{ or } -8x_2 - 9x_1 + 26$$

8. The second partials, and the mixed partial, are:

$$\frac{\partial^2 L}{\partial x_1^2} = -12, \frac{\partial^2 L}{\partial x_2^2} = -8, \frac{\partial^2 L}{\partial x_1 \partial x_2} = -9$$

9. Computing D, we find:

$$\begin{aligned} D &= \left(\frac{\partial^2 L}{\partial x_1^2}\right)\left(\frac{\partial^2 L}{\partial x_2^2}\right) - \left(\frac{\partial^2 L}{\partial x_1 \partial x_2}\right)^2 \\ &= (-12)(-8) - (-9^2) = +15 \end{aligned}$$

10. According to Condition 4, with the second partial derivative with respect to x_1 negative, and $D > 0$, this is a local maximum.

PROBLEMS

1. Find the minimum of this function and then answer the following questions:

   $$y = 4x^2 - 30x + 40$$

   a. At what value of x does the function have its minimum?

   b. How do you know that this is a minimum rather than a maximum?

2. Find the maximum of the following function, then answer the questions:

   $$y = -5x^2 + 4x + 2$$

   a. At what value of the decision variable does the function attain its maximum value?

   b. How can you be sure that the value you have found is a maximum?

3. The manager of a small plastics company has developed the following cost function and determined its minimum value to be 68. Explain why you agree or disagree with this finding.

   $$y = \tfrac{1}{2}x^2 - 8x + 90$$

4. For the following function, determine the value of x at which it attains a local maximum value, the value of x at which it attains a local minimum value, and the value of the function at each of those points.

   $$y = \frac{1}{3}x^3 - 4.5x^2 + 18x + 10$$

5. Determine the point at which the following function attains its local maximum, its local minimum, and the value of the function at each of those points.

   $$y = x^3 - 12x^2 + 36x + 3$$

6. A manager has developed the following cost function:

   $$y = \frac{1}{3}x^3 - 3x^2 + 70$$

   where x = amount spent on preventive maintenance of equipment (in thousands of dollars)

   Find the optimal amount of preventive maintenance in thousands of dollars.

7. Find the local maximum and local minimum points of this function:

   $$y = 2x^3 - 18x^2 + 48x$$

8. Find the optimal solution to this problem:

   maximize $\quad -2x^2 + 20x + 15$

subject to

$$x \le 4$$

9. Find the optimal solution to this problem:

minimize $5x^2 - 20x + 18$

subject to

$$x \ge 4$$

10. Find the optimal value of x:

maximize $-10x^2 + 40x - 1$

subject to

$$x \ge 3$$

11. Given this model:

$$f(x_1,x_2) = 2x_1^2 + 6x_2^2 - 10x_1 - 10x_2 + 3x_1x_2 + 80$$

find the optimal values of the decision variables, and decide whether the solution is a local minimum, a local maximum, or a saddle point.

12. Given the following model, find the optimal values of x_1 and x_2 and determine if the result is a local maximum, local minimum, or saddle point:

$$f(x_1x_2) = 5x_1^2 + 4x_2^2 - 8x_1x_2 - 6x_1 - 8x_2 + 7$$

where

x_1 = setting on machine control 1
x_2 = setting on machine control 2

13. For the following model, find the optimal values of the decision variables and determine whether those values refer to a local maximum, a local minimum, or a saddle point.

$$f(x_1x_2) = -10x_1^2 - 6x_2^2 + 50x_1 + 40x_2 - x_1x_2 + 100$$

14. The cost to produce each of two products is dependent on the quantity of each product (x_1, x_2) that is produced:

$c_1 = x_1 + x_2$ (in thousands of dollars)
$c_2 = 2x_2 + x_1$ (in thousands of dollars)

The manager of the department wants to determine the quantity of each product to produce in order to maximize profits. Product 1 sells for $10,000 a unit, and Product 2 sells for $12,000 a unit. Fixed cost is $2,000 for each product.

15. Find the optimal values of x_1 and x_2 for this model, and determine if the solution constitutes a local maximum, a local minimum, or a saddle point.

$$f(x_1,x_2) = -4x_1^2 - 2x_2^2 - 6x_1x_2 + 33x_1 + 22x_2 + 40$$

subject to

$$x_1 + 2x_2 = 8$$

16. Find the values of the decision variables that will minimize the value of this function:

$$f(x_1,x_2) = 3x_1^2 + 3x_2^2 - 20x_1 - 20x_2 + 2x_1x_2 - 100$$

subject to

$$x_1 + x_2 = 5$$

17. Given this model:

$$f(x_1,x_2) = -2x_1^2 - 2x_2^2 + 3x_1x_2 + 10x_1 - 10x_2$$

subject to

$$x_1 + 2x_2 = 7$$

a. Find the maximum solution to this model.

b. How much would you expect the optimal value to change if the constraint was changed from 7 to 8?

18. Given this model:

minimize $x_1^2 + 3x_2^2 + 2x_1x_2 - 6x_1 - 14x_2 + 2$

subject to

$$x_1 + x_2^2 = 12$$

a. Find the minimum value of the function and the optimal values of x_1 and x_2.

b. How much would you expect the optimal value to change if the constraint was changed from 12 to 13?

APPENDIX: RULES OF DIFFERENTIATION

This appendix describes rules for finding the derivatives of various types of algebraic functions.

A function may be expressed as:

$$y = f(x)$$

This is a general expression used to represent the function. Some examples of functions are:

$$y = x$$
$$y = 4x$$

$$y = 3x^2$$
$$y = x^2 + 2x^3$$
$$y = \frac{x + 1}{x^2}$$

The derivative of such a function may be expressed as:

$$\frac{dy}{dx} = f'(x)$$

The left side of the expression is read as "the derivative of y with respect to x."

The following rules provide simple guidelines for obtaining derivatives for functions like those illustrated above.

Case 1 y equals a constant.

Example: $y = 25$.

Rule: The derivative of a constant is equal to zero.

Hence, the derivative of $y = 25$ is:

$$\frac{dy}{dx} = 0$$

Case 2 y is equal to a variable.

Example: $y = x$.

Rule: The derivative of a variable is equal to 1.

Hence, the derivative of $y = x$ is:

$$\frac{dy}{dx} = 1$$

Case 3 y is equal to a variable raised to the power n.

Example: $y = x^3$.

Rule: The derivative of a variable raised to the power n is equal to:

$$\frac{dy}{dx} = nx^{n-1}$$

Hence, the derivative of x^3 is:

$$\frac{dy}{dx} = 3x^2$$

Case 4 y is equal to a function in which a variable is multiplied by a constant.

Example: $y = 5x^3$.

Rule: The derivative of a function that consists of a variable multiplied by a constant, k, is equal to:

$$\frac{dy}{dx} = nkx^{n-1}$$

Hence, the derivative of $y = 5x^3$ is:

$$\frac{dy}{dx} = 3(5)x^2 = 15x^2$$

Case 5 y is equal to the sum (or difference) of two (or more) functions, which could be expressed as:

$$y = f(x) + g(x)$$

Example: $y = x + 5x^3$.

Rule: When y is equal to the sum or difference of two or more functions, find the derivative of each function; the derivative of y is equal to the sum (or difference) of the resulting derivatives.

Hence, the derivative of $y = x + 5x^3$ is:

$$\frac{dy}{dx} = 1 + 15x^2$$

Case 6 y is equal to the product of two functions, expressed as:

$$y = f(x)g(x)$$

Example: $y = x^3(x + 1)$

Rule: The derivative of a product is equal to the derivative of the first function multiplied by the second function plus the derivative of the second function multiplied by the first function. This can be expressed as:

$$\frac{dy}{dx} = f'(x)g(x) + g'(x)f(x)$$

Hence, the derivative of $y = x^3(x + 1)$ is:

$$\frac{dy}{dx} = 3x^2(x + 1) + 1(x^3)$$

We may want to combine terms, which would give us:

$$3x^3 + 3x^2 + x^3 = 4x^3 + 3x^2$$

Case 7 y is equal to one function divided by another function, which can be expressed as:

$$y = \frac{f(x)}{g(x)}$$

Example: $y = \dfrac{(x^2 + 1)}{x^3}$

Rule: The derivative of two functions when one is divided by the other is equal to the denominator multiplied by the derivative of the numerator, minus the numerator multiplied by the derivative of the denominator, divided by the denominator squared.

Hence, the derivative of $y = \dfrac{(x^2 + 1)}{x^3}$ is:

$$\frac{dy}{dx} = \frac{x^3(2x) - (x^2 + 1)3x^2}{x^3(x^3)} = \frac{2x^4 - 3(x^2 + 1)x^2}{x^6} = \frac{-x_2 - 3}{x_4}$$

Case 8 *Partial derivatives.* If y is a function of two (or more) variables, we can obtain the partial derivative of y with respect to each of the variables.

Example: $y = x_1^2 + 3x_1x_2 + 2x_2^2$

Rule: To find the partial derivative of y with respect to a particular variable when multiple variables comprise the function, differentiate the function treating all other variables as *constants*.

Hence, we can obtain the partial derivative with respect to x_1, and the partial derivative with respect to x_2. Thus (note the symbol for partial derivatives, ∂):

$$\frac{\partial y}{\partial x_1} = 2x_1 + 3x_2$$

$$\frac{\partial y}{\partial x_2} = 3x_1 + 4x_2$$

Case 9 *Mixed partial derivative.* A partial derivative with respect to two variables.

Rule: To obtain the mixed partial derivative of a function, find the partial derivative of the function with respect to the first variable, and then find the partial derivative of that result with respect to the second variable.

Using the first partial derivative from Case 8, the mixed partial derivative of the function $y = x_1^2 + 3x_1x_2 + 2x_2^2$ is:

$$\frac{\partial^2 y}{\partial x_1 \partial x_2} = \frac{\partial}{\partial x_2}\left(2x_1 + 3x_2\right) = 3$$

Part VII
Decision Making and Information Systems

The preceding chapters of this book cover a broad range of techniques that are designed to aid managerial decision making. In this last part, another aid to managerial decision making, information systems, is briefly examined. These systems are intended to give managers pertinent knowledge about the operation of their organizations, in terms of both routine and special reports. Beyond that, some firms are exploring the use of artificial intelligence in the form of expert systems to assist them in decision making.

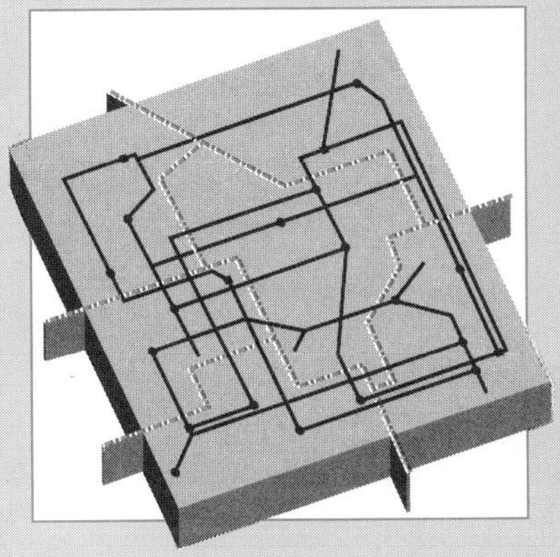

The theory and application of management science techniques benefited greatly from the capabilities of modern computers. So, too, has the theory and application of information systems. Both of these have had a tremendous influence on managerial decision making and, in all likelihood, both will have an increasing influence on the decision-making process in the future.

Part Outline

Chapter 20
Decision Making and Information Systems

Chapter Outline

Learning Objectives

After completing this chapter, you should be able to:

1. Contrast the terms *data* and *information*.
2. Explain the nature and importance of recordkeeping systems and give examples of these kinds of systems.
3. Explain what a management information system is and the various kinds of reports that such systems can supply to decision makers.
4. Explain what a decision support system is and how it differs from a management information system.
5. Explain what an expert system is, the purpose of such a system, and how it differs from a decision support system.

INTRODUCTION

Information is an integral part of decision making. Other things being equal, the better informed a decision maker is, the better decisions he or she will make. One aspect of this is having ready access to accurate, up-to-date information. Another is the ability to obtain information in ways that are most suitable to the needs of the decision maker. Beyond these, decision makers are finding new and better ways to use the power of computers to enhance the decision-making process. The purpose of this chapter is to describe some of the ways decision makers are doing this.

The chapter begins with a brief description of the recordkeeping function and a discussion of the difference between data and information. Next, management information systems are discussed, followed by decision support systems. The chapter ends with a description of expert systems, systems that combine reasoning power for problem solving with the speed and accuracy of computers.

TRANSACTION RECORDING SYSTEMS

Recording transactions provides the most basic level of information in a business organization. Transactions include the following:

1. Orders.
2. Sales.
3. Billings.
4. Accounts receivable.
5. Payroll.

Ideally, computers are used to keep track of transactions because of volume and accuracy requirements. And, in fact, the large majority of firms use them. Nevertheless, many small firms still process transactions manually, either out of ignorance or because of the cost and time and potential disruption they perceive will result from the conversion to a computerized system. One drawback of manual recordkeeping is that records often are less accessible for decision making because of the time and effort required to retrieve and distill the information they contain.

In and of themselves, recordkeeping systems are data processing systems rather than information systems. They do not directly provide decision makers with information in a form suitable for decision making.

Data versus Information

Data and information are different, although they are closely related. Data can be thought of as the raw material, and information can be thought of as the finished product. Information is obtained from data by *processing* the data into forms that are suitable for decision-making purposes.

Data consist of numbers that represent such things as costs, profits, production rates, deliveries, sales, and so on. However, in their raw or unprocessed form, data can be almost meaningless, and even misleading. This is because large volumes of numbers present an enormous amount of detail, so much so that they tend to give rise to confusion rather than illumination. Processing data helps by reducing the amount of detail that a decision maker must contend with. Moreover, processing arranges data into forms that are more conducive for the manager to recognize relationships and to draw conclusions. Processing transforms data into information by *organizing* and *condensing* data into tables, graphs, charts, or summary numerical measures (e.g., means, percentages, etc.), which more readily lend themselves to human interpretation. In effect, major details are brought out, while minor details are reduced or eliminated. Graphs and charts are particularly useful because they supply visual images, which often help managers to conceptualize problems. Tables provide organization, and numerical measures facilitate computerization. Because there are many ways of organizing, summarizing, and presenting data, a decision maker must devote a certain amount of thought to identifying the ways that are most appropriate for the kinds of decisions he or she will want to make, and to designing a system that will accomplish this.

MANAGEMENT INFORMATION SYSTEMS

A **management information system (MIS)** is a system designed to dispense various information to particular decision makers within an organization. In fact, decision makers depend on the flow of accurate and timely information to make informed decisions. Most systems provide reports that fall into one of the following categories:

1. Standard reports.
2. Exception reports.
3. Special reports.

In addition, most systems are designed to be able to answer specific inquiries.

Standard reports are routine reports issued at regular intervals. These might include weekly reports on sales and production, biweekly reports on payroll, monthly inventory reports, annual financial reports, and so on. These reports provide the basis for routine decision making. They enable managers to monitor important aspects of a company's operations and to confirm that expectations are being met.

Exception reports are produced to inform decision makers of an unusual occurrence or situation, one that falls outside of expected results. This generally requires nonroutine decision making. Examples might include an unusual number of customer complaints about a particular product or service, quality problems on a production line, unusually large forecasting errors, late deliveries from suppliers, and so on. The implication of an exception report is that special managerial attention is called for.

Special reports typically are prepared in response to a request for additional, nonroutine information on a particular topic. Although these may involve assembling information in a database in a special way, they often require collection of additional information. Examples might include special forecasts; information about conversion to a different production system (e.g., computerized, MRP, JIT, etc.) that involves estimates of time, cost, worker resistance, benefits, and so on; information on expansion; information pertaining to relocation of certain facilities; and the introduction of new products or services. In such instances, the nature of the request will dictate the types and sources of information that will be needed.

In addition to these various kinds of reports, management information systems usually are designed so that decision makers can obtain answers to specific inquiries. For example, a manager may want to know either how much of a particular item is in inventory or the number of customer complaints that have been received about a certain product. Some types of businesses find this capability more useful than others. For example, in the travel and hotel industry, such requests represent a major use of an information system. Thus, airlines, travel agents, and motels must repeatedly query the system about flight schedules, prices, availabilities, special packages, and so on. Not surprisingly, these and similar businesses depend on the ability to rapidly receive answers to specific inquiries from a database that contains accurate and up-to-date information.

DECISION SUPPORT SYSTEMS

A **decision support system (DSS)** is software that enables a decision maker to have access to current knowledge of a decision environment in such a way that the decision maker can evaluate, analyze, and reason with the knowledge for the purpose of decision making. A decision support system incorporates various kinds of models (e.g., linear programming models, financial models, regression models), algorithms for solving the models, and a database. It also makes the decision maker an *internal* component of the system by incorporating the decision maker's judgment in the process. Moreover, decision support systems place emphasis on "whole system" solutions as opposed to optimizing a narrow segment of a problem. For example, use of an LP algorithm alone might suggest a solution for production that would minimize related production costs, but one that would suboptimize another segment (e.g., delivery schedules) of the system. The goal of the DSS would be to identify a solution that would achieve an overall result that is optimal, or at least satisfactory, even if certain portions of the system could *individually* achieve solutions that were better in terms of their narrower reference frames.

A key feature of a DSS is its ability to help decision makers deal with unstructured decision activities. In order to do this, the system must be able to handle nonstandard requests from the decision maker and conduct nonstandard analyses, in addition to being able to handle standard requests and analyses.

A typical DSS system has three major components: A language component, a knowledge component, and a problem-processing component. The language component facilitates communication between the DSS and the decision maker, enabling the decision maker to communicate requests of the system and to understand communications from the DSS (e.g., requests for additional information, results of analyses). The knowledge component consists of a database, procedural knowledge, and any results obtained from analyses using models or algorithms. The problem-processing component is the central element of a DSS. It provides the link between the decision maker and the knowledge component. Thus, it has the ability to understand the decision maker's requests and to relate these requests to the appropriate elements of the knowledge component in order to satisfy the decision maker's request for information or analysis.

EXPERT SYSTEMS

One of the most advanced concepts in information and decision systems is the expert system. An **expert system** is one that uses artificial intelligence to enable users to obtain expert reasoning for problem solving. That is, an expert system incorporates human expertise that can be used to solve a particular problem or a class of similar problems. The term **artificial intelligence** refers to the ability of a machine, such as a computer, to exhibit humanlike reasoning behaviors. Two major aspects of this are the machine's ability to be able to work with a natural language system and its ability to reason.

A natural language system promotes communication between a user and the machine. The less esoteric a language system is, the more easily even casual users can access it. Ideally, a natural language system will enable users to type messages (say, in English) to the computer, and it will understand them. Moreover, such a system ought to have the ability to accept new terms that will be absorbed into its list of recognizable words for future use.

A reasoning system enables the computer to perform the necessary logic for solving a problem. In general, reasoning systems consist of three elements: A language system in which problems are stated, a knowledge system that contains facts and assertions about a problem area, and a problem-processing system that interacts with the knowledge system using a set of rules to solve a problem. A **rule set** consists of a collection of rules that contain knowledge about how to analyze specific aspects of a particular problem.

An expert system generally consists of a user interface, problem-processing software, and a rule set. The user interacts with the system via the user interface. Thus, the user starts the process by entering a specific request through the user interface, which interprets the request and then reformulates it in a manner consistent with the problem processor. The processor may find that there is insufficient information to solve the problem, in which case the user is asked for specific additional information. In actually solving the problem, the problem processor draws on the expertise contained in the rule set. Once the problem is solved, the solution is presented to the user, and if it is requested, the reasoning process can also be reported to the user.

Currently, much research on expert systems is underway. In fact, the probable impact that expert systems will have on management in the foreseeable future is great. To date, the expert systems with the best track records are those designed to handle specific types of problems that can be narrowly defined. The quest for perfecting general-purpose expert systems is continuing, however, and it is reasonable to expect that such systems will someday be commonplace in business organizations.

SUMMARY

Information plays a vital role in decision making. There are a variety of ways in which business organizations acquire and use information. In the simplest sense, recordkeeping systems provide a base of data from which information can be obtained. Management information systems provide managers with standard reports, exception reports, and the ability to handle special requests for information. Decision support systems are designed to help decision makers by incorporating decision models, algorithms for solving models, and a database. Emphasis in such systems is placed on whole system solutions rather than on narrowly focused problems. A key feature is the ability to help decision makers deal with unstructured problems. Expert systems reflect the latest development in information and decision systems. They incorporate artificial intelligence in systems that are designed to give decision makers access to problem solving based on expert reasoning.

GLOSSARY

Artificial Intelligence The ability of a computer to exhibit humanlike reasoning ability in problem solving.

Decision Support System Software that uses models and algorithms to help a decision maker solve problems. Can handle unstructured problems.

Expert System Uses artificial intelligence to enable users to take advantage of expert reasoning in problem solving.

Management Information System (MIS) A system designed to dispense information in the form of standard reports, exception reports, special reports, and as responses to special requests for information.

Rule Set A collection of rules that guide the reasoning process of an expert system.

DISCUSSION AND REVIEW QUESTIONS

1. Contrast the terms *data* and *information*.
2. What advantages do computers provide for recordkeeping when compared to manual systems?
3. What is a management information system? What are some of the different ways such a system can provide information to decision makers?
4. Contrast a decision support system and a management information system.
5. Explain the term *expert system*.
6. Explain the importance of a natural language system in an expert system.
7. Why do you suppose that expert systems that have a narrow focus have been more successful than general-purpose expert systems?
8. How does an expert system differ from a decision support system?
9. What factors will influence the rate at which expert systems are developed and used by business organizations?

Chapter 20 Case

Lemon County Commission's Court

Within Lemon County, there are 28 primary and secondary agencies or charity organizations providing various services to many different segments of the populace. For example, some of the agencies that received funding in previous years include the Better Business Bureau, the local chamber of commerce, Planned Parenthood, Inc., the local housing authority, several senior-citizen activity centers, an organization which counsels and aids rape victims, a drug-abuse counseling service, the Red Cross, a local community theater group, the Salvation Army, and a legal-aid clinic. Almost all of these service organizations are eligible to receive a portion of federal funds from several revenue-sharing programs created to channel funds to the local level in ways deemed appropriate at the local level. This is done by having annual blocks of federal money allocated to a local political body for further distribution at the discretion of that local body. The Lemon County Commissioner's Court has acted as this dispensing agent for several years.

Ned Kelly, one of the most budget-conscious commissioners, annually asks the county staff to compile a report containing the status of each funded-agency's progress in meeting its current goals with a cost-effectiveness analysis of the service. Applications from agencies that wish to be considered for funding from the next-year's block allocation are also included. The applications from each organization must include a requested funding level, goals for the upcoming year, and a proposed budget.

In the previous years, the staff relied heavily on individual reports from each agency, developed annually in response to the request for information on the numbers of people and types of aid or assistance rendered, the organization's current goals and degree of success in achieving those goals, and the organization's personnel structure and operating budget. In addition, the agencies receiving funds from this program were required to submit quarterly reports on their use of the funds, giving information on the number of clients and types of aid given. Both the annual and quarterly reports were used to prepare a summary overview and interpretation of the organizations' capabilities for the commissioner's court.

It has become evident to Kelly that the existing procedure was not well equipped to suit his major purpose in asking for valid, comparable information on all of the applicants. There had been instances in which clients of some funded organizations had publicly complained of long waiting times between applying for and receiving assistance, mishandled paperwork, excessive interview requirements, and inconsistent standards for granting assistance among the agencies. For the most part, Kelly was sympathetic to these complaints, but he usually preferred to avoid judging the merits of each organization's approach solely on the

Source: James A. Fitzsimmons and Robert S. Sullivan, *Service Operations Management* (New York: McGraw-Hill, 1982).

basis of the personal opinions of the clients. Yet at the same time, it was necessary to make some judgments for the purpose of allocating the available funds.

Some months prior to the time of year when the county usually requested information and grant applications from the local service agencies, the county auditor's assistant had come to see Kelly about problems her staff perceived in the current method of collecting information. Ruth Leslie pointed out to the commissioner that there was no standard means of reporting the information Kelly wanted on service quality, productivity, and cost. Each agency either responded with wordy descriptions of general types of service, rendered to present the most optimistic viewpoint possible, or simply provided poorly written and unsubstantiated reports on their level of performance. In addition, the agencies complained vociferously to the commissioner's court every year on the amount of time they were spending to develop the annual reports, and in some cases, the quarterly reports as well. Finally, Ms. Leslie noted that the process her staff went through to compile, to verify (to some degree), and to analyze the information in the reports was very time-consuming in itself, and it resulted in a product that was often criticized by Kelly for its incompleteness. As a result, Ms. Leslie observed that no one seemed to be satisfied with the current approach, and she suggested that the county initiate an integrated accounting and data collection system for the allocation and distribution of these funds.

Kelly was intrigued by the idea, but wanted to know more about the approach and how it would function to better serve the spectrum of interested parties. Consequently, he asked Ms. Leslie to prepare a short, *general* report outlining the concept of such a system as applied to the present circumstances. In particular, he wants her to address the potential effects upon the relationships among these service agencies (both private and public nonprofit in nature) and the county if such a system were put into practice. He is not interested in hardware requirements or any cost details until he is convinced that this approach is sound.

Discussion questions

1. Consider yourself to be in Ms. Leslie's position and develop an appropriate response to Kelly's request. Be sure to establish what a management information system should accomplish under the circumstances described above.
2. Describe how your concept would improve the quality of information available to the different participants of the system; speculate on how well it would be received by the service agencies and how successful it could be if implemented.
3. What potential stumbling blocks might impede the implementation of the system? Suggest priorities of activities for system implementation.

Appendix Tables

TABLE A Areas under the Normal Curve, 0 to z

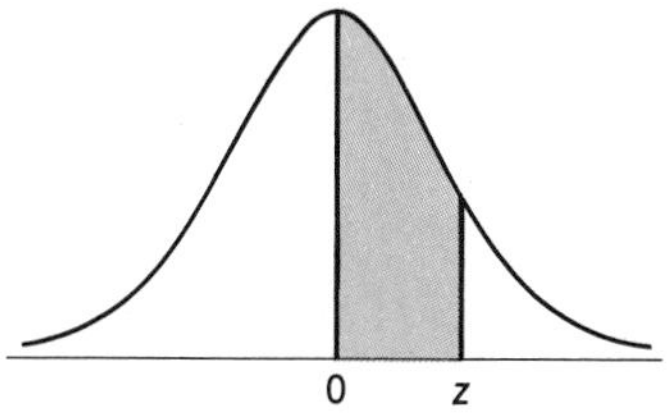

z	.00	.01	.02	.03	.04	.05	.06	.07	.08	.09
0.0	.0000	.0040	.0080	.0120	.0160	.0199	.0239	.0279	.0319	.0359
0.1	.0398	.0438	.0478	.0517	.0557	.0596	.0636	.0675	.0714	.0753
0.2	.0793	.0832	.0910	.0910	.0948	.0987	.1026	.1064	.1103	.1141
0.3	.1179	.1217	.1255	.1293	.1331	.1368	.1406	.1443	.1480	.1517
0.4	.1554	.1591	.1628	.1664	.1700	.1736	.1772	.1808	.1844	.1879
0.5	.1915	.1950	.1985	.2019	.2054	.2088	.2123	.2157	.2190	.2224
0.6	.2257	.2291	.2324	.2357	.2389	.2422	.2454	.2486	.2517	.2549
0.7	.2580	.2611	.2642	.2673	.2703	.2734	.2764	.2794	.2823	.2852
0.8	.2881	.2910	.2939	.2967	.2995	.3023	.3051	.3078	.3106	.3133
0.9	.3159	.3186	.3212	.3238	.3264	.3289	.3315	.3340	.3365	.3389
1.0	.3413	.3438	.3461	.3485	.3508	.3531	.3554	.3577	.3599	.3621
1.1	.3643	.3665	.3686	.3708	.3729	.3749	.3770	.3790	.3810	.3830
1.2	.3849	.3869	.3888	.3907	.3925	.3944	.3962	.3980	.3997	.4015
1.3	.4032	.4049	.4066	.4082	.4099	.4115	.4131	.4147	.4162	.4177
1.4	.4192	.4207	.4222	.4236	.4251	.4265	.4279	.4292	.4306	.4319
1.5	.4332	.4345	.4357	.4370	.4382	.4394	.4406	.4418	.4429	.4441
1.6	.4452	.4463	.4474	.4484	.4495	.4505	.4515	.4525	.4535	.4545
1.7	.4554	.4564	.4573	.4582	.4591	.4599	.4608	.4616	.4625	.4633
1.8	.4641	.4649	.4656	.4664	.4671	.4678	.4686	.4693	.4699	.4706
1.9	.4713	.4719	.4726	.4732	.4738	.4744	.4750	.4756	.4761	.4767
2.0	.4772	.4778	.4783	.4788	.4793	.4798	.4803	.4808	.4812	.4817
2.1	.4821	.4826	.4830	.4834	.4838	.4842	.4846	.4850	.4854	.4857
2.2	.4861	.4864	.4868	.4871	.4875	.4878	.4881	.4884	.4887	.4890
2.3	.4893	.4896	.4898	.4901	.4904	.4906	.4909	.4911	.4913	.4916
2.4	.4918	.4920	.4922	.4925	.4927	.4929	.4931	.4932	.4934	.4936
2.5	.4938	.4940	.4941	.4943	.4945	.4946	.4948	.4949	.4951	.4952
2.6	.4953	.4955	.4956	.4957	.4959	.4960	.4961	.4962	.4963	.4964
2.7	.4965	.4966	.4967	.4968	.4969	.4970	.4971	.4972	.4973	.4974
2.8	.4974	.4975	.4976	.4977	.4977	.4978	.4979	.4979	.4980	.4981
2.9	.4981	.4982	.4982	.4983	.4984	.4984	.4985	.4985	.4986	.4986
3.0	.4987	.4987	.4987	.4988	.4988	.4989	.4989	.4989	.4990	.4990

TABLE B 1. Areas under the Standardized Normal Curve from $-\infty$ to $-z$

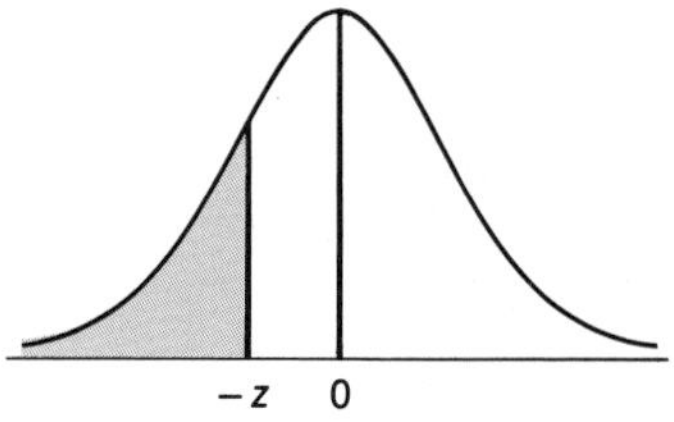

.09	.08	.07	.06	.05	.04	.03	.02	.01	.00	z
.0002	.0003	.0003	.0003	.0003	.0003	.0003	.0003	.0003	.0003	−3.4
.0003	.0004	.0004	.0004	.0004	.0004	.0004	.0005	.0005	.0005	−3.3
.0005	.0005	.0005	.0006	.0006	.0006	.0006	.0006	.0007	.0007	−3.2
.0007	.0007	.0008	.0008	.0008	.0008	.0009	.0009	.0009	.0010	−3.1
.0010	.0010	.0011	.0011	.0011	.0012	.0012	.0013	.0013	.0013	−3.0
.0014	.0014	.0015	.0015	.0016	.0016	.0017	.0018	.0018	.0019	−2.9
.0019	.0020	.0021	.0021	.0022	.0023	.0023	.0024	.0025	.0026	−2.8
.0026	.0027	.0028	.0029	.0030	.0031	.0032	.0033	.0034	.0035	−2.7
.0036	.0037	.0038	.0039	.0040	.0041	.0043	.0044	.0045	.0047	−2.6
.0048	.0049	.0051	.0052	.0054	.0055	.0057	.0059	.0060	.0062	−2.5
.0064	.0066	.0068	.0069	.0071	.0073	.0075	.0078	.0080	.0082	−2.4
.0084	.0087	.0089	.0091	.0094	.0096	.0099	.0102	.0104	.0107	−2.3
.0110	.0113	.0116	.0119	.0122	.0125	.0129	.0132	.0136	.0139	−2.2
.0143	.0146	.0150	.0154	.0158	.0162	.0166	.0170	.0174	.0179	−2.1
.0183	.0188	.0192	.0197	.0202	.0207	.0212	.0217	.0222	.0228	−2.0
.0233	.0239	.0244	.0250	.0256	.0262	.0268	.0274	.0281	.0287	−1.9
.0294	.0301	.0307	.0314	.0322	.0329	.0336	.0344	.0351	.0359	−1.8
.0367	.0375	.0384	.0392	.0401	.0409	.0418	.0427	.0436	.0446	−1.7
.0455	.0465	.0475	.0485	.0495	.0505	.0516	.0526	.0537	.0548	−1.6
.0559	.0571	.0582	.0594	.0606	.0618	.0630	.0643	.0655	.0668	−1.5
.0681	.0694	.0708	.0721	.0735	.0749	.0764	.0778	.0793	.0808	−1.4
.0823	.0838	.0853	.0869	.0885	.0901	.0918	.0934	.0951	.0968	−1.3
.0985	.1003	.1020	.1038	.1056	.1075	.1093	.1112	.1131	.1151	−1.2
.1170	.1190	.1210	.1230	.1251	.1271	.1292	.1314	.1335	.1357	−1.1
.1379	.1401	.1423	.1446	.1469	.1492	.1515	.1539	.1562	.1587	−1.0
.1611	.1635	.1660	.1685	.1711	.1736	.1762	.1788	.1814	.1841	−0.9
.1867	.1894	.1922	.1949	.1977	.2005	.2033	.2061	.2090	.2119	−0.8
.2148	.2177	.2206	.2236	.2266	.2396	.2327	.2358	.2389	.2420	−0.7
.2451	.2483	.2514	.2546	.2578	.2611	.2643	.2676	.2709	.2743	−0.6
.2776	.2810	.2843	.2877	.2912	.2946	.2981	.3015	.3050	.3085	−0.5
.3121	.3156	.3192	.3228	.3264	.3300	.3336	.3372	.3409	.3446	−0.4
.3483	.3520	.3557	.3594	.3632	.3669	.3707	.3745	.3783	.3821	−0.3
.3859	.3897	.3936	.3974	.4013	.4052	.4090	.4129	.4168	.4207	−0.2
.4247	.4286	.4325	.4364	.4404	.4443	.4483	.4522	.4562	.4602	−0.1
.4641	.4681	.4721	.4761	.4801	.4840	.4880	.4920	.4960	.5000	−0.0

TABLE B 2. Areas under the Standardized Normal Curve from $-\infty$ to $+z$

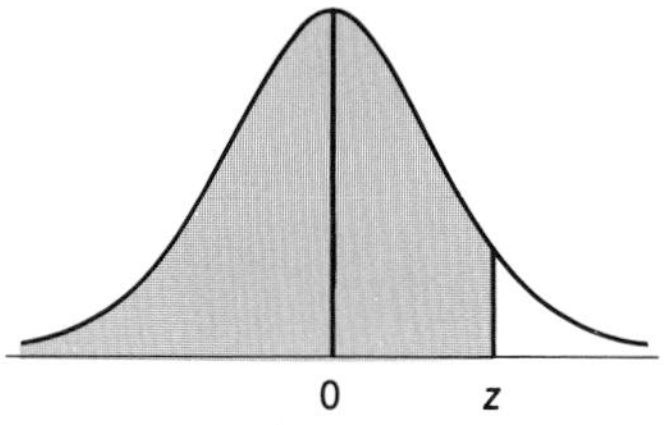

z	.00	.01	.02	.03	.04	.05	.06	.07	.08	.09
.0	.5000	.5040	.5080	.5120	.5160	.5199	.5239	.5279	.5319	.5359
.1	.5398	.5438	.5478	.5517	.5557	.5596	.5636	.5675	.5714	.5753
.2	.5793	.5832	.5871	.5910	.5948	.5987	.6026	.6064	.6103	.6141
.3	.6179	.6217	.6255	.6293	.6331	.6368	.6406	.6443	.6480	.6517
.4	.6554	.6591	.6628	.6664	.6700	.6736	.6772	.6808	.6844	.6879
.5	.6915	.6950	.6985	.7019	.7054	.7088	.7123	.7157	.7190	.7224
.6	.7257	.7291	.7324	.7357	.7389	.7422	.7454	.7486	.7517	.7549
.7	.7580	.7611	.7642	.7673	.7704	.7734	.7764	.7794	.7823	.7852
.8	.7881	.7910	.7939	.7967	.7995	.8023	.8051	.8078	.8106	.8133
.9	.8159	.8186	.8212	.8238	.8264	.8289	.8315	.8340	.8365	.8389
1.0	.8413	.8438	.8461	.8485	.8508	.8531	.8554	.8577	.8599	.8621
1.1	.8643	.8665	.8686	.8708	.8729	.8749	.8770	.8790	.8810	.8830
1.2	.8849	.8869	.8888	.8907	.8925	.8944	.8962	.8980	.8997	.9015
1.3	.9032	.9049	.9066	.9082	.9099	.9115	.9131	.9147	.9162	.9177
1.4	.9192	.9207	.9222	.9236	.9251	.9265	.9279	.9292	.9306	.9319
1.5	.9332	.9345	.9357	.9370	.9382	.9394	.9406	.9418	.9429	.9441
1.6	.9452	.9463	.9474	.9484	.9495	.9505	.9515	.9525	.9535	.9545
1.7	.9554	.9564	.9573	.9582	.9591	.9599	.9608	.9616	.9625	.9633
1.8	.9641	.9649	.9656	.9664	.9671	.9678	.9686	.9693	.9699	.9706
1.9	.9713	.9719	.9726	.9732	.9738	.9744	.9750	.9756	.9761	.9767
2.0	.9772	.9778	.9783	.9788	.9793	.9798	.9803	.9808	.9812	.9817
2.1	.9821	.9826	.9830	.9834	.9838	.9842	.9846	.9850	.9854	.9857
2.2	.9861	.9864	.9868	.9871	.9875	.9878	.9881	.9884	.9887	.9890
2.3	.9893	.9896	.9898	.9901	.9904	.9906	.9909	.9911	.9913	.9916
2.4	.9918	.9920	.9922	.9925	.9927	.9929	.9931	.9932	.9934	.9936
2.5	.9938	.9940	.9941	.9943	.9945	.9946	.9948	.9949	.9951	.9952
2.6	.9953	.9955	.9956	.9957	.9959	.9960	.9961	.9962	.9963	.9964
2.7	.9965	.9966	.9967	.9968	.9969	.9970	.9971	.9972	.9973	.9974
2.8	.9974	.9975	.9976	.9977	.9977	.9978	.9979	.9979	.9980	.9981
2.9	.9981	.9982	.9982	.9983	.9984	.9984	.9985	.9985	.9986	.9986
3.0	.9987	.9987	.9987	.9988	.9988	.9989	.9989	.9989	.9990	.9990
3.1	.9990	.9991	.9991	.9991	.9991	.9992	.9992	.9992	.9993	.9993
3.2	.9993	.9993	.9994	.9994	.9994	.9994	.9994	.9995	.9995	.9995
3.3	.9995	.9995	.9995	.9996	.9996	.9996	.9996	.9996	.9996	.9997
3.4	.9997	.9997	.9997	.9997	.9997	.9997	.9997	.9997	.9997	.9998

TABLE C Cumulative Poisson Probabilities

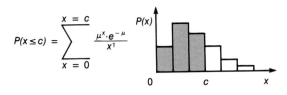

$$P(x \leq c) = \sum_{x=0}^{x=c} \frac{\mu^x \cdot e^{-\mu}}{x^1}$$

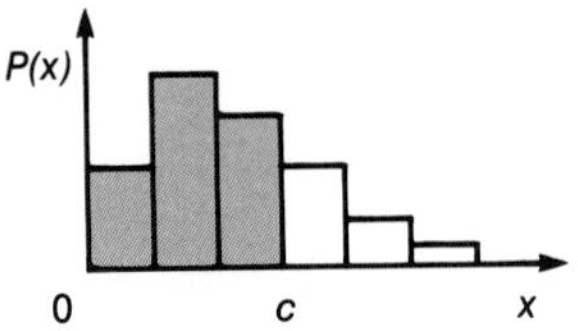

μ/x	0	1	2	3	4	5	6	7	8	9
0.05	.951	.999	1.000							
0.10	.905	.995	1.000							
0.15	.861	.990	.999	1.000						
0.20	.819	.982	.999	1.000						
0.25	.779	.974	.998	1.000						
0.30	.741	.963	.996	1.000						
0.35	.705	.951	.994	1.000						
0.40	.670	.938	.992	.999	1.000					
0.45	.638	.925	.989	.999	1.000					
0.50	.607	.910	.986	.998	1.000					
0.55	.577	.894	.982	.998	1.000					
0.60	.549	.878	.977	.997	1.000					
0.65	.522	.861	.972	.996	.999	1.000				
0.70	.497	.844	.966	.994	.999	1.000				
0.75	.472	.827	.960	.993	.999	1.000				
0.80	.449	.809	.953	.991	.999	1.000				
0.85	.427	.791	.945	.989	.998	1.000				
0.90	.407	.772	.937	.987	.998	1.000				
0.95	.387	.754	.929	.984	.997	1.000				
1.0	.368	.736	.920	.981	.996	.999	1.000			
1.1	.333	.699	.900	.974	.995	.999	1.000			
1.2	.301	.663	.880	.966	.992	.998	1.000			
1.3	.273	.627	.857	.957	.989	.998	1.000			
1.4	.247	.592	.833	.946	.986	.997	.999	1.000		
1.5	.223	.558	.809	.934	.981	.996	.999	1.000		
1.6	.202	.525	.783	.921	.976	.994	.999	1.000		
1.7	.183	.493	.757	.907	.970	.992	.998	1.000		
1.8	.165	.463	.731	.891	.964	.990	.997	.999	1.000	
1.9	.150	.434	.704	.875	.956	.987	.997	.999	1.000	
2.0	.135	.406	.677	.857	.947	.983	.995	.999	1.000	
2.2	.111	.355	.623	.819	.928	.975	.993	.998	1.000	
2.4	.091	.308	.570	.779	.904	.964	.988	.997	.999	1.000
2.6	.074	.267	.518	.736	.877	.951	.983	.995	.999	1.000
2.8	.061	.231	.470	.692	.848	.935	.976	.992	.998	.999

TABLE C *(concluded)*

μ/x	0	1	2	3	4	5	6	7	8	9	10	11	12	13	14	15	16	17	18	19	20
3.0	.050	.199	.423	.647	.815	.916	.966	.988	.996	.999	1.000										
3.2	.041	.171	.380	.603	.781	.895	.955	.983	.994	.998	1.000										
3.4	.033	.147	.340	.558	.744	.871	.942	.977	.992	.997	.999	1.000									
3.6	.027	.126	.303	.515	.706	.844	.927	.969	.988	.996	.999	1.000									
3.8	.022	.107	.269	.474	.668	.816	.909	.960	.984	.994	.998	.999	1.000								
4.0	.018	.092	.238	.433	.629	.785	.889	.949	.979	.992	.997	.999	1.000								
4.2	.015	.078	.210	.395	.590	.753	.868	.936	.972	.989	.996	.999	1.000								
4.4	.012	.066	.185	.359	.551	.720	.844	.921	.964	.985	.994	.998	.999	1.000							
4.6	.010	.056	.163	.326	.513	.686	.818	.905	.955	.980	.992	.997	.999	1.000							
4.8	.008	.048	.143	.294	.476	.651	.791	.887	.944	.975	.990	.996	.999	1.000							
5.0	.007	.040	.125	.265	.441	.616	.762	.867	.932	.968	.986	.995	.998	.999	1.000						
5.2	.006	.034	.109	.238	.406	.581	.732	.845	.918	.960	.982	.993	.997	.999	1.000						
5.4	.005	.029	.095	.213	.373	.546	.702	.822	.903	.951	.978	.990	.996	.999	1.000						
5.6	.004	.024	.082	.191	.342	.512	.670	.797	.886	.941	.972	.988	.995	.998	.999	1.000					
5.8	.003	.021	.072	.170	.313	.478	.638	.771	.867	.929	.965	.984	.993	.997	.999	1.000					
6.0	.003	.017	.062	.151	.285	.446	.606	.744	.847	.916	.957	.980	.991	.996	.999	.999	1.000				
6.2	.002	.015	.054	.134	.259	.414	.574	.716	.826	.902	.949	.975	.989	.995	.998	.999	1.000				
6.4	.002	.012	.046	.119	.235	.384	.542	.687	.803	.886	.939	.969	.986	.994	.997	.999	1.000				
6.6	.001	.010	.040	.105	.213	.355	.511	.658	.780	.869	.927	.963	.982	.992	.997	.999	.999	1.000			
6.8	.001	.007	.030	.082	.173	.301	.450	.599	.729	.830	.915	.955	.978	.990	.996	.998	.999	1.000			
7.0	.001	.007	.030	.082	.173	.301	.450	.599	.729	.830	.901	.947	.973	.987	.994	.998	.999	1.000			
7.2	.001	.006	.025	.072	.156	.276	.420	.569	.703	.810	.887	.937	.967	.984	.993	.997	.999	.999	1.000		
7.4	.001	.005	.022	.063	.140	.253	.392	.539	.676	.788	.871	.926	.961	.980	.991	.996	.998	.999	1.000		
7.6	.001	.004	.019	.055	.125	.231	.365	.510	.648	.765	.854	.915	.954	.976	.989	.995	.998	.999	1.000		
7.8	.000	.004	.016	.048	.112	.210	.338	.481	.620	.741	.835	.902	.945	.971	.986	.993	.997	.999	1.000		
8.0	.000	.003	.014	.042	.100	.191	.313	.453	.593	.717	.816	.888	.936	.966	.983	.992	.996	.998	.999	1.000	
8.2	.000	.003	.012	.037	.089	.174	.290	.425	.566	.692	.796	.873	.926	.960	.979	.990	.995	.998	.999	1.000	
8.4	.000	.002	.010	.032	.079	.157	.267	.400	.537	.666	.774	.857	.915	.952	.975	.987	.994	.997	.999	1.000	
8.6	.000	.002	.009	.030	.074	.150	.256	.386	.523	.653	.763	.849	.909	.949	.973	.986	.993	.997	.999	1.000	
8.8	.000	.002	.007	.024	.062	.128	.226	.348	.482	.614	.729	.822	.889	.935	.964	.981	.990	.995	.998	.999	1.000
9.0	.000	.001	.006	.021	.055	.116	.207	.324	.456	.587	.706	.803	.876	.926	.959	.978	.989	.995	.998	.999	1.000
9.5	.000	.001	.004	.015	.040	.089	.165	.269	.392	.522	.645	.752	.836	.898	.940	.967	.982	.991	.996	.998	.999

Answers to Selected Problems

Chapter 1 supplement: Break-even analysis

1. *a.* Loss of $4,000.
   b. Profit of $20,000.
   c. 8,000 cases.

2. *a.* 334.45 [335].
   b. $606.25.

3. *a.* Total cost = $13,000; Total revenue = $21,900; Profit = $8,900.
   b. 2,521 bottles.

4. *a.* 67 jobs.
   b. Loss of $1,476.75.

5. *a.* Profit of $79,600.
   b. 22,272 cases.
   c. Profit of $169,400.

6. *a.* First option: 8 events; second option: 12.8 [13] events.
   b. First option: profit of $400; second option: loss of $700.
   c. First option: profit of $400; second option: profit of $300.

7. *a.* In-house: Total cost = $2,900; subcontract: Total cost = $2,700.
   b. Ten months.

8. *a.* Profit = $8,500.
   b. Loss of $90,000.
   c. 145.45 [146] clients.

Chapter 2: Introduction to linear programming

1. *a.* The main purpose of the model is to determine the quantities of tables, chairs, and bookcases to produce in order to maximize the profit on those items.
   b. The decision variables are the quantities of tables, chairs, and bookcases.
   c. The system constraints are labor hours, machine hours, and wood.
   d. Each bookcase requires 2.5 hours of labor.
   e. At least 10 tables must be produced.
   f. The amount of profit that will be realized from tables.

2. *a.* Decision variables. x_1 represents the quantity of small window fans to produce, x_2 represents the quantity of medium fans to produce, and x_3 represents the quantity of large window fans to produce.
   b. The profit per unit on small window fans.
   c. The amount of profit that will be realized from medium window fans.
   d. System constraints.
   e. The amount of labor needed to produce one small window fan.

3. *a.* x_1 = the quantity of 3.5-ounce chocolate bars

x_2 = the quantity of 6-ounce chocolate bars

b. The constraints are: a supply of chocolate, the minimum quantity of 3.5-ounce bars to produce, and the minimum quantity of 6-ounce bars to produce.

maximize	$.13x_1 + .15x_2$
subject to	
Chocolate	$3.5x_1 + 6x_2 = 15{,}000$ ounces
3.5-oz. bars	$x_1 \geq 1{,}000$ bars
6-oz. bars	$x_2 \geq 1{,}200$ bars
	$x_1, x_2 \geq 0$

4. x_1 = quantity of softballs
x_2 = quantity of baseballs

maximize	$17x_1 + 15x_2$ (revenue)
subject to	
Leather	$6x_1 + 4x_2 \leq 6{,}000$ ounces
Nylon	$8x_1 + 3x_2 \leq 5{,}000$ yards
Wood chips	$10x_1 + 2x_2 \leq 5{,}000$ ounces
Labor	$3x_1 + 2x_2 \leq 3{,}600$ minutes
Machine	$1x_1 + 1x_2 \leq 2{,}000$ minutes
	x_1 and $x_2 \geq 0$

6. x_1 = quantity of Model A
x_2 = quantity of Model B
x_3 = quantity of Model C

maximize	$8.25x_1 + 7.50x_2 + 7.80x_3$ (profit)
subject to	
Station 1	$2.5x_1 + 1.8x_2 + 2.0x_3 \leq 2{,}250$ minutes
Station 2	$3.0x_1 + 1.6x_2 + 2.2x_3 \leq 2{,}250$ minutes
Model A	$x_1 \geq 20$ units
Model B	$x_2 \geq 20$ units
Model C	$x_3 \geq 20$ units
	$x_1, x_2,$ and $x_3 \geq 0$

9. x_1 = quantity of push mowers
x_2 = quantity of self-propelled mowers

maximize	$45x_1 + 70x_2$
subject to	
Assembly	$9x_1 + 12x_2 \leq 720$ minutes
Engines	$1x_1 + 1x_2 \leq 75$ engines
Packing	$2x_1 + 6x_2 \leq 300$ minutes
	x_1 and $x_2 \geq 0$

10. x_1 = acres of corn
x_2 = acres of soybeans
x_3 = acres of wheat

$$\text{minimize} \quad 20x_1 + 15x_2 + 12x_3$$

subject to

Land	$x_1 +$	$x_2 +$	x_3	$=$	500 acres
Corn	x_1			$\geq$	250 acres
Soybeans		x_2		$\leq$	200 acres
Corn/wheat	x_1		$- \; 2x_3$	$=$	0 acres

$$x_1, x_2, \text{ and } x_3 \geq 0$$

11. x_1 = number of shares of oil stock
x_2 = number of shares of auto stock
x_3 = number of shares of health stock

$$\text{maximize} \quad 11x_1 + 4x_2 + 2x_3$$

subject to

Invest	$120x_1 +$	$52x_2 +$	$18x_3$	$=$	\$100,000
40% Oil	$120x_1$			$\leq$	\$ 40,000
40% Auto		$52x_2$		$\leq$	\$ 40,000
40% Health			$18x_3$	$\leq$	\$ 40,000
Min. in oil	$120x_1$			$\geq$	\$ 10,000

$$x_1, x_2, \text{ and } x_3 \geq 0$$

14. x_1 = amount invested in Treasury notes
x_2 = amount invested in municipal bonds
x_3 = amount invested in blue chip stocks

$$\text{maximize} \quad .09x_1 + .08x_2 + .10x_3$$

subject to

Portfolio	$x_1 +$	$x_2 +$	x_3	$=$	\$120,000
Policy	$x_1 +$	$x_2 -$	x_3	$\geq$	0

$$x_1, x_2, \text{ and } x_3 \geq 0$$

15. x_1 = quantity of pork
x_2 = quantity of beef
x_3 = quantity of filler

$$\text{minimize} \quad 2.50x_1 + 1.80x_2 + 1.00x_3$$

subject to

Batch	$x_1 +$	$x_2 +$	x_3	$=$	2,000 lb.
Pork	x_1			$\geq$	800 lb.
Filler			x_3	$\leq$	600 lb.
Beef		x_2		$\geq$	300 lb.

$$x_1, x_2, \text{ and } x_3 \geq 0$$

19. x_1 = number of 2-lb. boxes of trail mix
x_2 = number of 1-lb. boxes of subway mix
x_3 = number of 1-lb. boxes of dried bananas
x_4 = number of 1-lb. boxes of dried apricots
x_5 = number of 1-lb. boxes of coconut pieces
x_6 = number of 1-lb. boxes of raisins
x_7 = number of 1-lb. boxes of walnuts

maximize $7.00x_1 + 3.00x_2 + 2.80x_3 + 3.25x_4 + 3.60x_5 + 3.50x_6 + 5.50x_7$

subject to

Dried bananas	$.4x_1 + .2x_2 + x_3$	≤ 400 lb.
Dried apricots	$.4x_1 + x_4$	≤ 300 lb.
Coconut pieces	$.4x_1 + .2x_2 + x_5$	≤ 250 lb.
Raisins	$.4x_1 + .2x_2 + x_6$	≤ 350 lb.
Walnuts	$.4x_1 + .4x_2 + x_7$	≤ 450 lb.
Mixes	$1.4x_1 + .7x_2 - .3x_3 - .3x_4 - .3x_5 - .3x_6 - .3x_7$	≤ 0

$x_1, x_2, x_3, x_4, x_5, x_6, \text{ and } x_7 \geq 0$

Chapter 3: Linear programming: Graphical solutions

1.

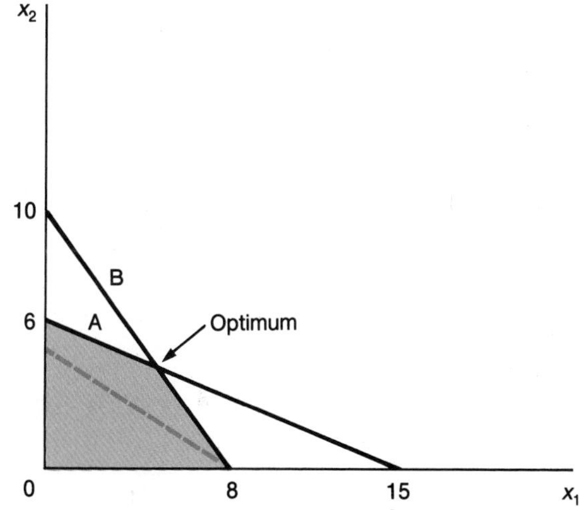

d. $x_1 = 4.71$
$x_2 = 4.12$
$Z = 113$

e. $x_1 = 8$
$x_2 = 0$
$Z = 48$

2. 0, 6: $Z = 96$; 4.71, 4.12: $Z = 113$; 8, 0: $Z = 80$.

3.

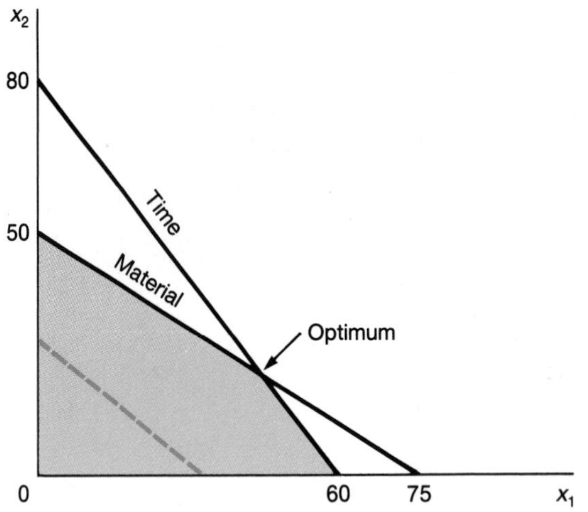

$x_1 = 45$
$x_2 = 20$
$Z = 1{,}725$

4. 0, 50: $Z = 1{,}500$
45, 20: $Z = 1{,}725$
60,0: $Z = 1{,}500$

5. *a.*

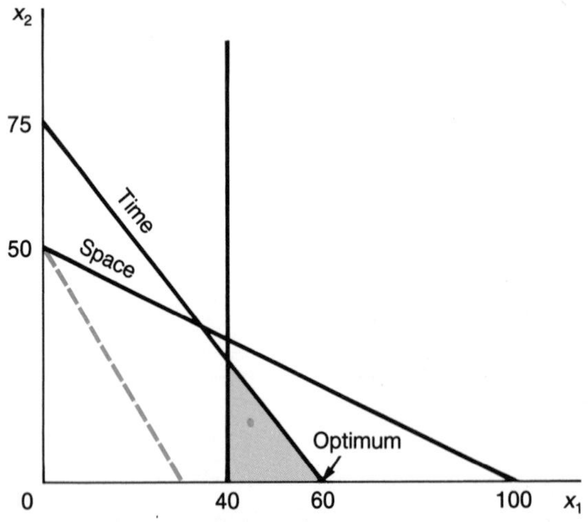

b. $x_1 = 60$
$x_2 = 0$
Profit = $3,000

6. *b.* $x_1 = 40$
$x_2 = 25$
Profit = $2,450

7. 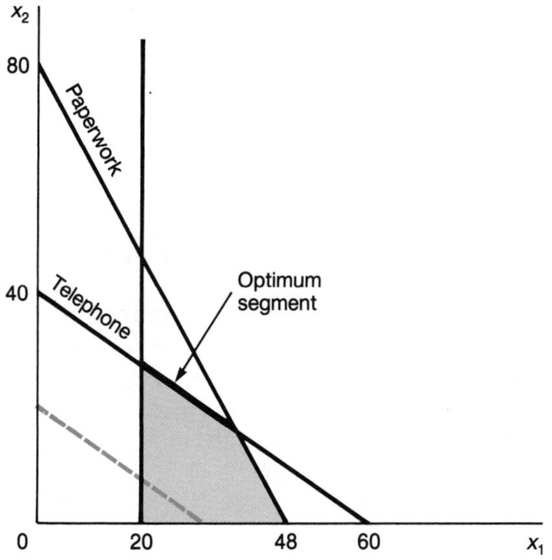

Profit = \$36

8. *a.* x_1 = 15 boxes; x_2 = 70 boxes; Z = \$27.

9. *a.* Cutting: 110 minutes
   Frying: 160 minutes
   Packing: 576 seconds
   b. Cutting: 34 minutes
   Frying: 0 minutes
   Packing: 0 seconds
   c. Multiple optimal solutions.

10. $x_1 = 50$; $x_2 = 40$; Z = \$41,000.

11. $x_1 = 2$; $x_2 = 9.6$; Cost = \$27.20.

13. $x_1 = 105$; $x_2 = 25$; Cost = \$289.50.

15. \$.60.

16. [Make A ≥ 108.]

19. Optimum is $x_1 = 0$, $x_2 = 0$.

20. *a.* $x_1 = 0$; $x_2 = 50$.
   b. Cutting: 16 minutes; Gluing: 0; Finishing: 210 minutes.

21. *a.* $x_1 = 40$; $x_2 = 80$; Z = \$5,600.

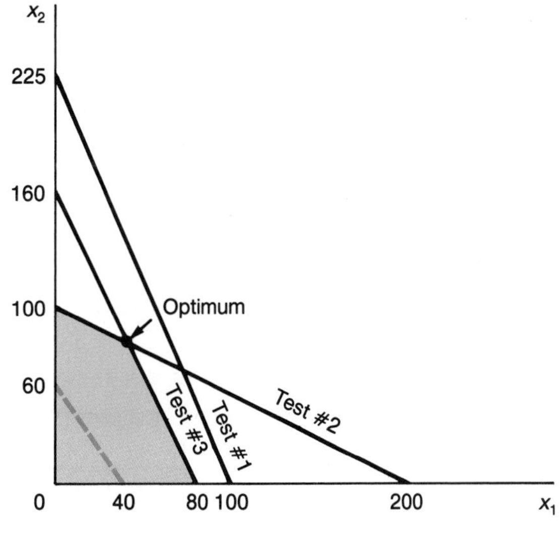

b. Test #1: 18.33 minutes.
c. Test #1.

22.

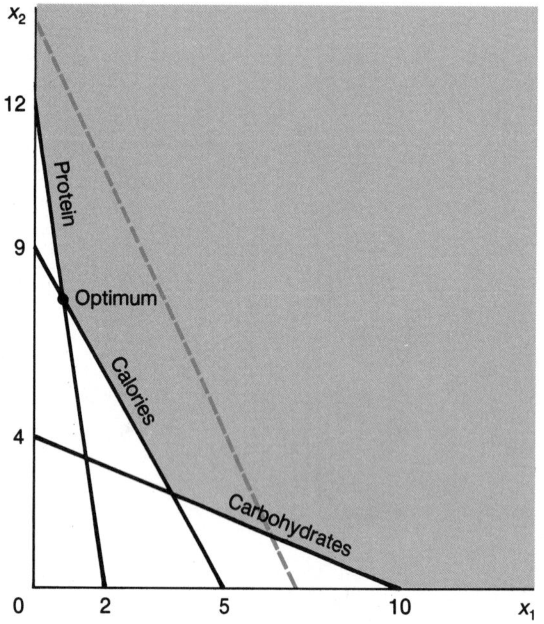

a. $x_1 = .7143$
$x_2 = 7.7143$
Cost = \$.91

b. Carbohydrates is exceeded by 20 gr.

23. x_1 = quantity of ham spread
x_2 = quantity of deli spread
Profit = \$376
Cost = \$165.42

25. $x_1 = 2{,}228.6$; $x_2 = 1{,}200$; $Z = \$469.72$.

26. Baseballs = 1,500.

28. $x_1 = 24$, $x_2 = 42$.

29. 1.67 cups of spaghetti; .42 cups of sauce.
a. Carbohydrates; 15.44 surplus.
b. 309 calories.

31. *c.* 50 bedroom sets; 40 living room sets; Revenue = \$70,000.

Chapter 3 Supplement: Graphical sensitivity analysis

3. *a.* 6 to infinity.
b. $c_1 \geq 3$.
c. A is 0, B is 3.
d. A is 4 to infinity.
B is 0 to 30.
e. None; none.
f. None; decrease by 4.

4. *a.* $x_1 = 6$, $x_2 = 0$.
b. c_1 is 7.5 to infinity.
c_2 is 0 to 3.20.
c. Labor is 1.6, Equipment is 0, and Material is 0.
d. Labor is 0 to 35, Equipment is 6 to infinity, and Material is 60 to infinity.

5. *a.* c_1 is 0 to 4.375; c_2 is 6.4 to infinity.
b. No effect; decrease by \$8.
c. −.80; 20 to infinity.
d. No limit to 48.
e. None.

6. *a.* A = 10, B = 25.
b. 25; \$1,350.
c. −1.875; 60 to 140.
d. Increase by \$18.75.

7. *a.* 11, 0, and \$132.
b. Decrease by 2, no limit on increase.
c. None.
d. 44; it would become slack.

Chapter 4: Linear programming: The simplex method

5. *b.* s_1, x_1, and x_3.
d. No, because there is a positive value in the $C - Z$ row.
e. x_2.
f. s_1.
g.

	C	20	12	0	0	0	
Basis		x_1	x_2	s_1	s_2	s_3	Quantity
x_2	12	0	1	½	−3/2	0	15
x_1	20	1	0	0	1	0	50
s_3	0	0	0	−½	3/2	1	35
	Z	20	12	6	2	0	1,180
	$C - Z$	0	0	−6	−2	0	

6. *c.*

Basis	C	9	6	0	0	Quantity
		x_1	x_2	s_1	s_2	
s_1	0	12	5	1	0	600
s_2	0	0	1	0	1	72
	Z	0	0	0	0	0
	C − Z	9	6	0	0	

d.

Basis	C	9	6	0	0	Quantity
		x_1	x_2	s_1	s_2	
x_1	9	1	5/12	1/12	0	50
s_2	0	0	1	0	1	72
	Z	9	15/4	3/4	0	450
	C − Z	0	9/4	−3/4	0	

Basis	C	9	6	0	0	Quantity
		x_1	x_2	s_1	s_2	
x_1	9	1	0	1/12	−5/12	20
x_2	6	0	1	0	1	72
	Z	9	6	3/4	9/4	612
	C − Z	0	0	−3/4	−9/4	

$x_1 = 20, x_2 = 72, Z = 612$

e.

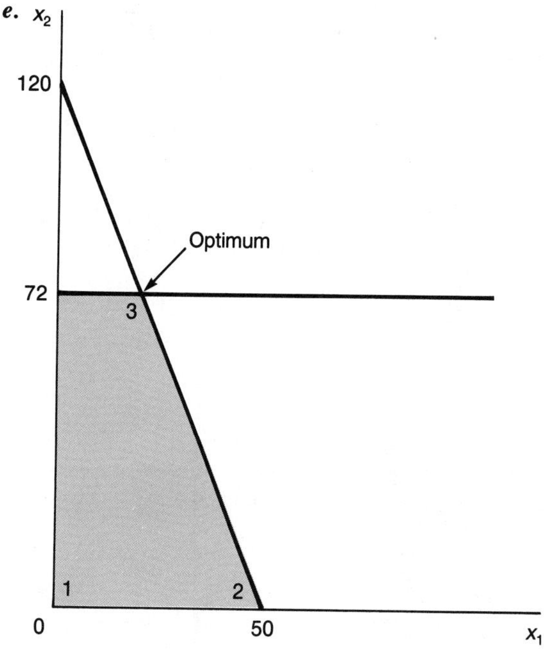

7.

Basis	C	5	3	0	0	0	Quantity
		x_1	x_2	s_1	s_2	s_3	
s_1	0	1.5	1	1	0	0	45
s_2	0	1	0	0	1	0	25
s_3	0	0	1	0	0	1	40
	Z	0	0	0	0	0	0
	C − Z	5	3	0	0	0	

Basis	C	5	3	0	0	0	Quantity
		x_1	x_2	s_1	s_2	s_3	
s_1	0	0	1	1	−1.5	0	7.5
x_1	5	1	0	0	1	0	25
s_3	0	0	1	0	0	1	40
	Z	5	0	0	5	0	125
	C − Z	0	3	0	−5	0	

Basis	C	5 x_1	3 x_2	0 s_1	0 s_2	0 s_3	Quantity
x_2	3	0	1	1	−1.5	0	7.5
x_1	5	1	0	0	1	0	25
s_3	0	0	0	−1	1.5	1	32.5
	Z	5	3	3	.5	0	147.5
	$C - Z$	0	0	−3	−.5	0	

$x_1 = 25, x_2 = 7.5, Z = 147.5$

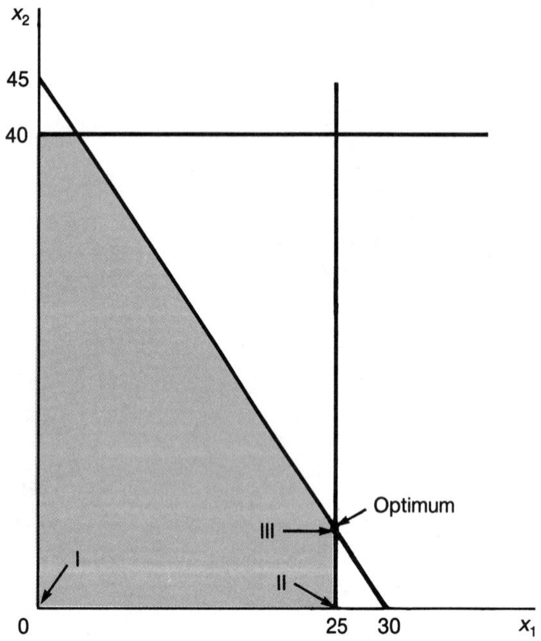

8.

Basis	C	9 x_1	9 x_2	0 s_1	0 s_2	Quantity
s_1	0	6	3	1	0	42
s_2	0	4	5	0	1	40
	Z	0	0	0	0	0
	$C - Z$	9	9	0	0	

Basis	C	9 x_1	9 x_2	0 s_1	0 s_2	Quantity
x_1	9	1	$1/2$	$1/6$	0	7
s_2	0	0	3	$-2/3$	1	12
	Z	9	$9/2$	$3/2$	0	63
	$C - Z$	0	$9/2$	$-3/2$	0	

Basis	C	9 x_1	9 x_2	0 s_1	0 s_2	Quantity
x_1	9	1	0	$5/18$	$-1/6$	5
x_2	9	0	1	$-2/9$	$1/3$	4
	Z	9	9	$1/2$	$3/2$	81
	$C - Z$	0	0	$-1/2$	$-3/2$	

$x_1 = 5, x_2 = 4, Z = 81$

9. Optimal tableau:

Basis	C	40 x_1	30 x_2	0 s_1	0 s_2	0 s_3	Quantity
x_2	30	0	1	$-2/7$	$1/7$	0	$400/7$
s_3	0	0	0	$-9/35$	$1/35$	1	$10/7$
x_1	40	1	0	$9/35$	$-1/35$	0	$270/7$
	Z	40	30	$12/7$	$22/7$	0	$22800/7$ = 3257.14
	$C - Z$	0	0	$-12/7$	$-22/7$	0	

$x_1 = 38.57, x_2 = 57.14, Z = 3257.14$

10. Optimal tableau:

	C	1.0	1.2	0	0	
Basis		x_1	x_2	s_1	s_2	Quantity
x_1	1.0	1	0	1/4	−1/4	15
x_2	1.2	0	1	−1/12	5/12	15
	Z	1.0	1.2	3/20	1/4	33
	$C - Z$	0	0	−3/20	−1/4	

14. Optimal tableau:

	C	.44	.41	.35	0	0	
Basis		x_1	x_2	x_3	s_1	s_2	Quantity
x_3	.35	0	7/10	1	1/5	−3/500	15.4
x_1	.44	1	1/2	0	0	1/100	21
	Z	.44	.465	.35	.07	.002	14.63
	$C - Z$	0	−.055	0	−.07	−.002	

15.

	C	11	10	14	0	0	0	
Basis		x_1	x_2	x_3	s_1	s_2	s_3	Quantity
s_1	0	0	4	−1	1	0	0	0
s_2	0	5	2	5	0	1	0	72
s_3	0	1	0	0	0	0	1	13
	Z	0	0	0	0	0	0	0
	$C - Z$	11	10	14	0	0	0	

	C	11	10	14	0	0	0	
Basis		x_1	x_2	x_3	s_1	s_2	s_3	Quantity
s_1	0	1	22/5	0	1	1/5	0	14.4
x_3	14	1	2/5	1	0	1/5	0	14.4
s_3	0	1	0	0	0	0	1	13
	Z	14	28/5	14	0	14/5	0	201.6
	$C - Z$	−3	22/5	0	0	−14/5	0	

	C	11	10	14	0	0	0	
Basis		x_1	x_2	x_3	s_1	s_2	s_3	Quantity
x_2	10	5/22	1	0	5/22	1/22	0	3.273
x_3	14	10/11	0	1	−1/11	2/11	0	13.091
s_3	0	1	0	0	0	0	1	13.000
	Z	15	10	14	1	3	0	216.000
	$C - Z$	−4	0	0	−1	−3	0	

16.

	C	10	6	7	0	0	
Basis		x_1	x_2	x_3	s_1	s_2	Quantity
s_1	0	4	8	5	1	0	860
s_2	0	2	3	1	0	1	400
	Z	0	0	0	0	0	0
	$C - Z$	10	6	7	0	0	

	C	10	6	7	0	0	
Basis		x_1	x_2	x_3	s_1	s_2	Quantity
s_1	0	0	2	3	1	−2	60
x_1	10	1	3/2	1/2	0	1/2	200
	Z	10	15	5	0	5	2,000
	$C - Z$	0	9	−2	0	−5	

	C	10	6	7	0	0	
Basis		x_1	x_2	x_3	s_1	s_2	Quantity
x_3	7	0	2/3	1	1/3	−2/3	20
x_1	10	1	7/6	0	−1/6	5/6	190
	Z	10	49/3	7	2/3	11/3	2,040
	$C - Z$	0	−31/3	0	−2/3	−11/3	

18. Optimal tableau:

Basis	C	7 x_1	8 x_2	9 x_3	0 s_1	0 s_2	0 s_3	Quantity
x_3	9	3.6	0	1	.6	0	−.4	30
s_2	0	−5.4	0	0	−1.4	1	.6	30
x_2	8	−3.0	1	0	−.5	0	.5	15
	Z	8.4	8	9	1.4	0	.4	390
	C − Z	−1.4	0	0	−1.4	0	−.4	

19. $x_1 = 0$; $x_2 = 1$; $x_3 = 1$; $x_4 = 0$.

22. A = 120; B = 0; C = 0; Z = $4,800.

23. Radio = 24; TV = 12; Newspaper = 8.

26. New equipment = $700,000; Updating material handling = $400,000; New office equipment = 0; Repayment of loan = $100,000.

28. Stock A = $24,000; Stock B = $24,000; Income fund = $72,000.

29. Regular = 1,501.5; Extra = 2,000; Puppy delite = 0.

30. Mix = 1,500; Peanuts = 0; Cashews = 60; Walnuts = 200; Pecans = 100; Profit = $3,378.

5. *c.*

Basis	C	8 x_1	5 x_2	0 s_1	0 s_2	−M A_2	Quantity
s_1	0	4	3	1	0	0	240
A_2	−M	0	1	0	1	1	50
	Z	0	−M	0	−M	−M	−50M
	C − Z	8	5+M	0	M	0	

Basis	C	8 x_1	5 x_2	0 s_1	0 s_2	Quantity
s_1	0	4	0	1	3	90
x_2	5	0	1	0	−1	50
	Z	0	5	0	−5	250
	C − Z	8	0	0	5	

Basis	C	8 x_1	5 x_2	0 s_1	0 s_2	Quantity
x_1	8	1	0	¼	¾	22.5
x_2	5	0	1	0	−1	50
	Z	8	5	2	1	430
	C − Z	0	0	−2	−1	

Chapter 5: Simplex: Maximization with mixed constraints and minimization

1. *a.* Add a slack variable.
c. Add an artificial variable.

2. *a.* maximize $16x_1 + 11x_2 + 0s_1 - MA_2 + 0s_3 - MA_3$

subject to

$$\begin{aligned} 2x_1 + 6x_2 + s_1 &= 20 \\ 3x_1 + 5x_2 + A_2 &= 16 \\ 6x_1 + 4x_2 - s_3 + A_3 &= 24 \end{aligned}$$

6. *c.*

Basis		1 x_1	3 x_2	0 s_1	0 s_2	$-M$ A_2	Quantity
s_1	0	5	9	1	0	0	90
A_2	$-M$	10	3	0	-1	1	60
	Z	$-10M$	$-3M$	0	M	$-M$	$-60M$
	$C-Z$	$1+10M$	$3+3M$	0	$-M$	0	

Basis	C	1 x_1	3 x_2	0 s_1	0 s_2	Quantity
s_1	0	0	$15/2$	1	$1/2$	60
x_1	1	1	$3/10$	0	$-1/10$	6
	Z	1	$3/10$	0	$-1/10$	6
	$C-Z$	0	$27/10$	0	$1/10$	

Basis	C	1 x_1	3 x_2	0 s_1	0 s_2	Quantity
x_2	3	0	1	$2/15$	$1/15$	8
x_1	1	1	0	$-1/25$	$-3/25$	$18/5$
	Z	1	3	$9/25$	$2/25$	27.6
	$C-Z$	0	0	$-9/25$	$-2/25$	

7. $x_1 = 3.6$; $x_2 = 8$; $Z = 19.6$.

8. *f.* $x_1 = 20$; $x_2 = 100$; $Z = 680$.

9. *d.* $x_1 = 50$; $x_2 = 40$; $Z = 900$.

10. Tray #1 = 30; Tray #2 = 30; $Z = 270$.

11. $x_3 = 30$; $Z = 420$.

12. Oak = 80; Walnut = 40; Hickory = 0; $Z = 680$.

13. Oak = 0; Walnut = 72; Hickory = 0; $Z = 360$.

15. Single = 0; Top = 20; Bottom = 10; $Z = 1{,}000$.

18. $x_1 = 22$; $x:_2 = 20$; $Z = 276$.

22. $x_1 = 0$; $x_2 = 36$; $x_3 = 18$; $Z = 612$.

23. $x_1 = 20$; $x_2 = 5$; $x_3 = 5$; $Z = 540$.

26. Spaghetti = 1.67 cups; Sauce = .417 cups; Cost = $.67 per serving.

28. $x_1 = 800$; $x_2 = 600$; $x_3 = 600$; $Z = 3{,}680$.

29. $x_1 = 94{,}117.67$; $x_2 = 0$; $x_3 = 23{,}529.41$; $Z = 117{,}647.10$.

30. Wine = 50 gallons; Apple juice = 107.14 gallons; Grape juice = 42.86 gallons; $Z = 546.29$.

Chapter 6: Postoptimality analysis

3. *a.* First constraint, 6; Second constraint, 2; Third constraint, 0.

5. c_1: 18 to infinity.
c_2: 0 to 13.33.

6. 1st constraint: $9/12$.
2nd constraint: $27/12$.

7. *a.* 360 to infinity. *b.* 0 to 120.

8. c_1: decrease by 9, increase by 5.4; c_2: decrease by 2.25, no limit on increase.

9. *a.* First constraint, −14.41 to 143.85; Second constraint, 0 to infinity; Third constraint, 0 to infinity.
b. x_1 is insignificant for $c_1 < 15$; range of optimality is 5.6 to infinity for c_2 and 9.6 to 25 for c_3.

10. *a.* $x_2 = 5.54$, $x_3 = 12.18$, $s_3 = 13.00$.
b. $z = 225.96$.

11. *a.* Increase by at least 4.
b. 16.35.

18. *a.* Inspection.
b. Yes, 4 hours. Profit will increase by $12.

19. First constraint, lower limit is 50, no upper limit; Second constraint, no lower limit, upper limit is 320.

20. x_1 will remain out of solution for c_1 equal to 6 or more; the range of optimality for c_2 is 0 to 5.

21. *a.* Revised values: $x_1 = 15$, $x_2 = 0$, $s_2 = 5$, $Z = 300$.
b. Yes, the net savings would be $50.
c. Decrease unit cost by $8.
d. No impact of quantities, but an increase in Z of $125.

24. Add Product 3.

25. Yes.

33. *a.* $.12; 1,000 pounds to 2,000 pounds.
b. $.48.
c. No, the profit on puppy delite would have to be more than $.43 for it to come into the solution mix.
d. The optimal quantities would not change, but Z would decrease by $40.
e. Z = $730.

Chapter 7: Transportation and assignment problems

1. *a.* A1 = 25; A2 = 25; B2 = 15; C2 = 10; C3 = 45; TC = $1,465.
b. Not optimal; B3 evaluation = −1.
d. A1 = 25; A2 = 25; B3 = 15; C2 = 25; C3 = 30.
e. TC = $1,450.

2. *a.* TC = $851.

4. Chicago/Detroit = 48, Chicago/Denver = 12, Chicago/Kansas City = 4, St.Louis/Kansas City = 44, Omaha/Denver = 36. TC = $792.

5. $O_1/D_1 = 40$, $O_1/D_2 = 180$, $O_2/D_4 = 140$, $O_2/D_5 = 120$, $O_3/D_3 = 150$, $O_3/D_5 = 50$, Dummy/D_1 = 100, Dummy/D_5 = 25. TC = $4,260.

6. *a.* Rochester/Columbus = 90, Rochester/Chicago = 70, Dallas/Charlotte = 75, Dallas/Chicago = 50, Buffalo/Chicago = 30. TC = $5,690.
b. Rochester/Charlotte = 70, Rochester/Chicago = 0, others unchanged. TC = $5,900.

7. *b.* TC = $8,000.
c. $600.

8. Profit = $3,850.

10. A–1 = 50; A–2 = 50; A–A = 400; B–2 = 200; C–3 = 200; 2–2 = 250; 2–3 = 100. TC = $1,400.

11. A–2 = 5; A–3 = 45; B–2 = 15; C–1 = 25; C–2 = 30; Profit = $1,860.

13. Profit = $43,800.

14. *b.* TC = $4,150.
c. Rochester, 70 units.

15. For C1, TC = $16,910; for C2, TC = $16,330.

17. TC = $851.

18. TC = $35,100.

21. TC = $1,050.

22. TC = $1,605.

31. 1–C, 2–B, 3–A, TC = $46.

32. *a.* 1–D, 2–C, 3–B, 4–A.
b. $240.
c. 1–D, 2–C, 3–A, 4–B; $240.

33. *a.* A–Buffalo, B–Rochester, C–Syracuse, D–Ithaca.
b. 3.9 hours.

34. A–Buffalo, B–Syracuse, C–Ithaca, D–Rochester. Time = 4.0 hours.

36. *a.* 1–D, 2–B, 3–C, 4–A.
b. $205.

37. 1–C, 2–D, 3–A, 4–B.

38. 1–A, 2–B, 3–C, 4–D or 1–A, 2–B, 3–D, 4–C. Additional cost is $15.

39. *a.* 1–E, 2–D, 3–C, 4–B, 5–A.
b. 1–C, 2–E, 3–D, 4–B, 5–A.
c. 14.

40. *a.* 1–C, 2–E, 3–D, 4–new, 5–A; 10 errors.
b. B.
c. 1–E, 2–D, 3–C, 4–new, 5–A.

41. *b.* 21.9 hours.

42. Profit = $27.90.

43. *a.* A–2, B–3, C–4, D–1.
b. 7.
c. A–2, B–3, C–1, D–4.

Chapter 8: Integer programming

1. *d.*

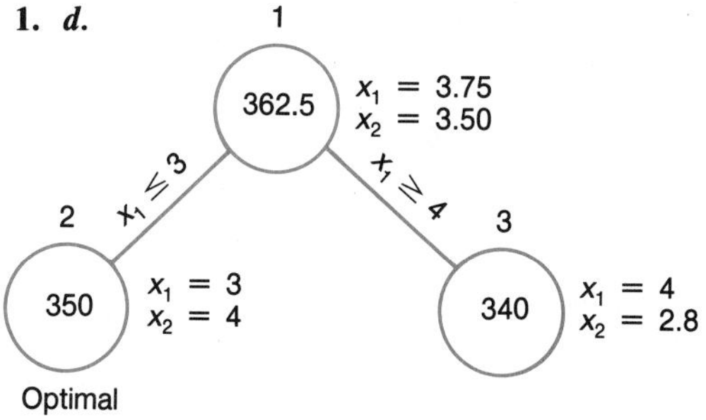

2.

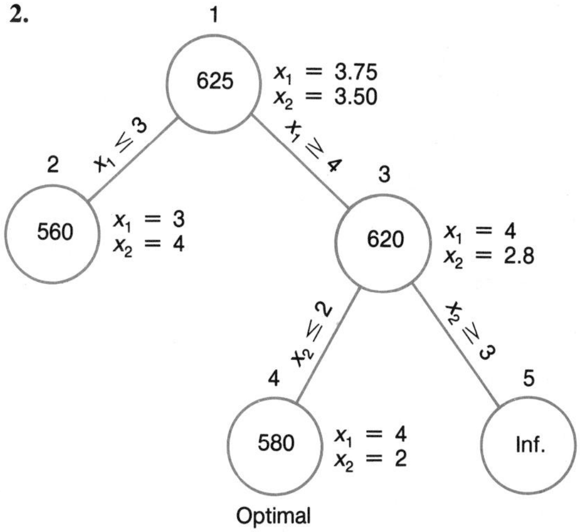

3.

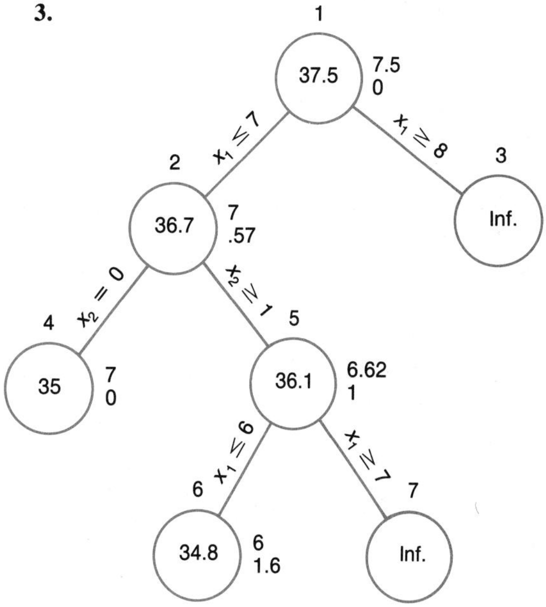

5. Optimum is $x_1 = 2.67$, $x_2 = 10$, $Z = 66$.

6. Optimum is $x_1 = 9$, $x_2 = 3$, $Z = 63$.

8. Optimum is $x_1 = 3$, $x_2 = 0$, $Z = 120{,}000$.

10. Optimum is $x_1 = 3$, $x_2 = 2$, $Z = 29$.

11. Optimum is $x_1 = 3$, $x_2 = 2$, $Z = 29$.

12. Optimum is $x_1 = 2$, $x_2 = 2.67$, $Z = 22.68$.

13. *a.* Optimum is $x_1 = 1$, $x_2 = 0$, $x_3 = 1$, $x_4 = 0$, $Z = 130$.
b.

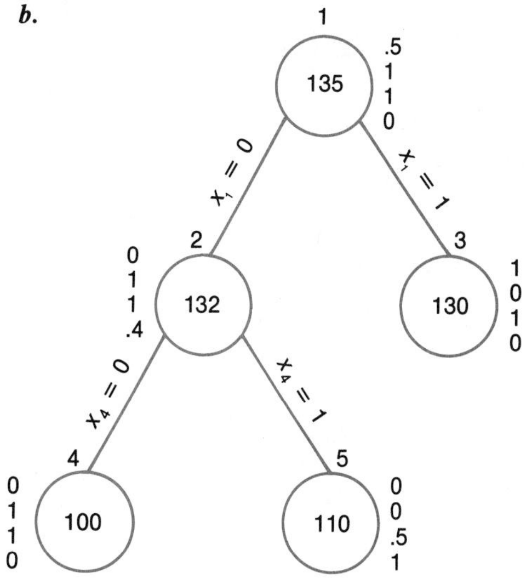

14. Optimum is $x_1 = 0, x_2 = 0, x_3 = 12$, $Z = 300$.

16. Optimum is $x_1 = 0, x_2 = 1, x_3 = 1$, $Z = 250$.

18. Optimum is $x_1 = 1, x_2 = 6, x_3 = 8$, $Z = 880$.

20. Optimum is $x_1 = 1, x_2 = 0, x_3 = 1, x_4 = 2$, $Z = 230$.

22. Optimum is $x_1 = 0, x_2 = 9.44, x_3 = 3.44$, $Z = 211.52$.

24. Optimum is $x_1 = 0, x_2 = 10, Z = 610$.

26. Optimum is $C = 41, Z = 9{,}840$.

28. Optimum is 3 takeouts, 6 full service.

30. Optimum is $x_1 = 2, x_2 = 0, x_3 = 3$.

34. Optimum is $x_1 = 0, x_2 = 1, x_3 = 0, x_4 = 4$; alternate: $x_1 = 0, x_2 = 0, x_3 = 2, x_4 = 3$.

36. Optimum is $x_1 = 3, x_2 = 1, x_3 = 0$.

Chapter 9: Goal programming

3. *a.* Soft.
b. Minimize being under on the second constraint.
c. $x_1 = 80, x_2 = 0; u_2 = 0, v_1 = 200$.
d. $x_1 = 60, x_2 = 0; v_1 = 0, u_2 = 20$.

4. *c.* $x_1 = 0, x_2 = 8$.
d. No.
e. $u_1 = 0, v_2 = 12, u_3 = 0$.

5.

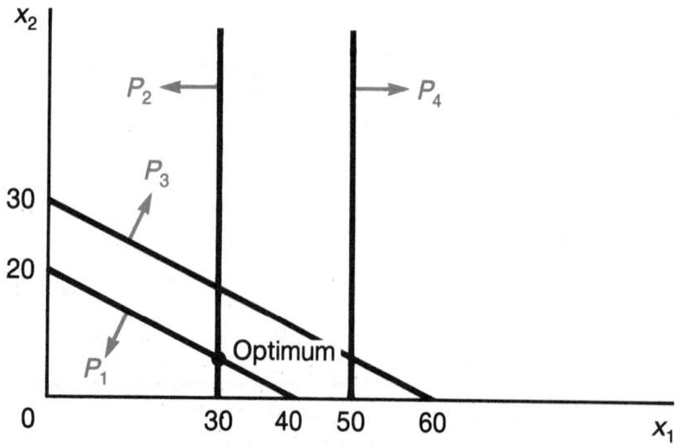

$x_1 = 30$ $\quad v_1 = 0$
$x_2 = 5$ $\quad v_3 = 0$
$u_2 = 60$
$u_4 = 100$

6. $v_1 = 0, u_2 = 40, u_3 = 0$.

8. *a.* $x_1 = 30, x_2 = 42, v_1 = 0, u_2 = 210$.

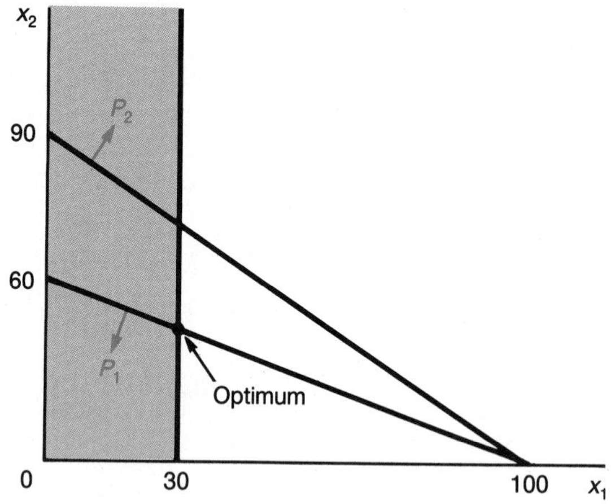

Chapter 10: Decision theory

1. *a.* a_1.
b. a_3.
c. a_2.

2. a_1: \$11.

3. *a.* Split.
b. Split.
c. Split.
d. Split.

4. *a.* Split.
b. \$10.

5. *a.* Style A.
b. Style B.
c. Split.
d. Style A.

6. Style B: \$51.5.

7. *a.* New staff.
b. Redesign.
c. New staff.
d. Tie: New staff or Redesign.

8. *a.* New staff: \$60.
c. \$5.

9. New staff, hire 2 initially: \$60.

10. Do nothing initially; if both contracts are awarded, buy 2 new trucks.

11. *a.* Eliminate Do nothing.
b. $P(s_1) = .40, P(s_2) = .60$.
c. Greater than .60.

12. .50.

13. Residential.

14. *b.* 50 units.
c. $70.

15. EVSI = 5.26, Efficiency = .526.

16. EVSI = 1.75.

17. *a.* A.
b. Stable: .978, .022; Changing: .343, .657.
d. 7.2.
e. Yes.

18. *a.* EVSI = 2.93, Efficiency = .73.

19. *a.* Build small for $P(\text{H})$ less than ⅓, build large for $P(\text{H})$ greater than ⅓, indifferent between small and large at $P(\text{H})$ = ⅓.
b. For $P(\text{H})$ < ⅓, build large, for $P(\text{H})$ > ⅓, build small, indifferent at ⅓.

20. *b.* C.
c. $P(\#2) > .625$.
d. $P(\#1) < .375$.

23. A.

24. *a.* A: $.70 < P(\#1) \leq 1.00$.
B: Never.
C: $0 \leq P(\#1) < .20$.
D: $.20 < P(\#1) < .70$.
b. A: $0 \leq P(\#1) < .25$.
B: $.25 < P(\#1) < .583$.
C: $.583 < P(\#1) \leq 1.00$.
D: Never.

Chapter 11: Forecasting

1.

Day	Ma$_2$	MA$_4$
3	28	
4	30	
5	31	29.5
6	33.5	31.75
7	35.5	33.25
8	36	34.75
9	33.5	34.5
10	35	35.5
11	39	36.25
12	38.5	36.75
13	34.5	36.75

2.

Day	Exponential Smoothing	Naive
1		
2	25	25
3	27.4	31
4	28.04	29
5	30.02	33
6	31.61	34
7	33.77	37
8	34.26	35
9	33.36	32
10	35.21	38
11	37.13	40
12	37.08	37
13	35.05	32

4. *a.* 22.
b. 20.75.
c. 20.72.

6. Friday 0.79
Saturday 1.34
Sunday 0.87

7. 163, 276, 183.

8. MSE (or MAD) is lower for trend than for naive.

9. Wednesday = 0.60, Thursday = 0.80, Friday = 1.40, Saturday = 1.20.

13. *a.* Monday = 1.17, Tuesday = .97, Wednesday = .86, Thursday = .80, Friday = 1.19.
b. $Y_t = 8.88 + .1469t$.
c. Monday = 6.77, Tuesday = 5.48, Wednesday = 4.73, Thursday = 4.28, Friday = 6.20.

16. Monday = 1.07, Tuesday = .87, Wednesday = .94, Thursday = .95, Friday = 1.17.

18. $Q_1 = 262.8$, $Q_2 = 234$, $Q_3 = 174.3$, $Q_4 = 290.4$.

19. $Y_t = 423.9 + 20.5t$; $Y_7 = 567.4$, $Y_8 = 587.9$.

21. *a.* Number of pieces.
c. $y = 4.02 - .037x$. For each one-unit increase in job size, the time per piece decreases an average of .037 minutes.
d. For job sizes ranging from 12 pieces to 90 pieces.

23. *a.* Yes.
b. $r^2 = .854$.
c. 293 ± 28.77.

27. *a.* $y = 68.45 - 8.20x_1 + 2.04x_2 - 4.56x_3$.
b. x_2 is not.

30. Control limits are 0 ± 6.98.

Run Tests	Number Counted	Number Expected	z	Conclusion
+/−	6	7.5	−.87	Random
U/D	9	8.33	.34	Random

37.

Test	Number Counted	Number Expected	z	Conclusion
+/−	10	11	−.46	Random
U/D	13	13	0	Random

38.

Test	Number Counted	Number Expected	z	Conclusion
+/−	18	11	3.2	Nonrandom
U/D	17	13	2.2	Nonrandom

39.

Test	Number Counted	Number Expected	z	Conclusion
+/−	16	12.5	1.49	Random
U/D	17	15	1.03	Random

Chapter 12: Inventory models I: Independent demand

1. *a.* 6,000.
b. 3,000.
c. 9.
d. $360.

2. *a.* 79.
b. $948.68.
c. Increase by $26.32.

3. *a.* $1,000.
b. 40.
c. 40.
d. 25 times per year.
e. 37, $2.

5. *a.* 25,000.
b. 1,042.
c. 300 per day.
d. 2.6 days.
e. 781.5.
f. 24.
g. $1,680.

6. *a.* $1,178.
b. $160.

7. *a.* 1,375.

9. *a.* 300.
b. 5.2 weeks.

10. *a.* 6,000.

11. *a.* 2,200.

12. Vendor A, 572.

13. *a.* 360.
b. 74.

14. .0228, .4 units.

15. 267.

16. *a.* 166.
b. 25 units, another 9 units.

17. *a.* 29.
b. 9.
c. 18.
d. 7.
e. .614.

18. *a.* 631 units.
b. $89.

19. *a.* .957.
b. 4.

20. *a.* .323.
b. 5.

21. A: 10%; B: 20%; C: 70%.

22. B: C150, MM09, T418.

Chapter 13: Inventory models II

1. *a.* Order 379 minus supply on hand.

2. Approximately .3140.

3. *a.* 16 oz.: 73 − *A*; 12 oz.: 102 − *A*.
b. 16 oz.: 5; 12 oz.: 7.

4. *a.* Order 6.25 cans minus the amount on hand.
b. .0606 (use $Q = 3$).

5. Tuesday–Thursday: 338.5 lb.; Friday–Saturday: 454.65 lb.

6. One.

7. 211 lb.

8. 3 cakes.

9. *a.* \$20.51 to \$62.88
b. \$4.70 or less.

10. *a.* \$15 to \$35.
b. Too low.

11.

Component:	A42	A44	SA3	SA2	SA1	P29	P8	P33	P11	P10	P17	RM2
Quantity:	20	20	40	20	20	200	80	160	200	20	20	900

12.

Component:	A42	A44	SA3	SA2	SA1	P29	P8	P33	P11	P10	P17	RM2
Quantity:	20	20	30	20	20	100	50	17	0	20	20	0

15. *a.* RM3 = 640
RM4 = 712
RM5 = 160
RM7 = 360

b. RM3 = 592
RM4 = 602
RM5 = 160
RM7 = 345

17. *a.*

Component:	A	B	C	D	E	F	G	H	J	K	M	N	R	S	W
Quantity:	24	12	12	24	144	24	36	24	1008	144	288	144	60	240	48

b.

Component:	A	B	C	D	E	F	G	H	J	K	M	N	R	S	W
Quantity:	24	2	12	4	129	24	31	24	493	74	258	129	55	115	28

19. *c.*

Master schedule for: File cabinets

Week	1	2	3	4	5	6	7	8
Quantity					150			

Cabinet (Week)	1	2	3	4	5	6	7	8
Gross requirements					150			
Scheduled receipts								
Available								
Net requirements					150			
Planned order receipt					150			
Planned order release				150				

Locks (Week)	1	2	3	4	5	6	7	8
Gross requirements				150				
Scheduled receipts								
Available				150				
Net requirements				0				
Planned order receipt								
Planned order release								

Handles	1	2	3	4	5	6	7	8
Gross requirements				450				
Scheduled receipts								
Available								
Net requirements				450				
Planned order receipt				450				
Planned order release		450						

Decorative Strip	1	2	3	4	5	6	7	8
Gross requirements				150				
Scheduled receipts								
Available				150				
Net requirements				0				
Planned order receipt								
Planned order release								

Drawers	1	2	3	4	5	6	7	8
Gross requirements				450				
Scheduled receipts								
Available								
Net requirements				450				
Planned order receipt				450				
Planned order release		450						

Frame	1	2	3	4	5	6	7	8
Gross requirements				150				
Scheduled receipts								
Available								
Net requirements				150				
Planned order receipt			150					
Planned order release			150					

Chapter 14: Networks

2.

Node	Distance	Route
2	6	1-2
3	8	1-2-3
4	15	1-2-3-4
5	20	1-2-3-4-5

3.

Node	Distance	Route
2	14	1-2
3	10	1-3
4	21	1-3-5-4
5	16	1-3-5
6	25	1-3-5-4-6

5.

Node	Distance	Route
2	5	1-2
3	5	1-3
4	11	1-3-4
5	14	1-3-4-5

8. 1-3-6-9-12; 60 miles.

9. Minimum distance = 69.

10. Minimum material = 54.

11. Minimum cost = 96.

12. Minimum cost = 805.

13. Minimum distance = 29.5.

15. 146.

16. 17.

17. 20.

18. 26.

19. *a.* 36.

22. 125.

Chapter 15: PERT/CPM

1. *a.* 1-3-6-9-11-12: 31.
b. 1-2-4-6-8-9: 37.
c. 1-2-5-12-16: 44.

2. 1-2-4-7: 27.

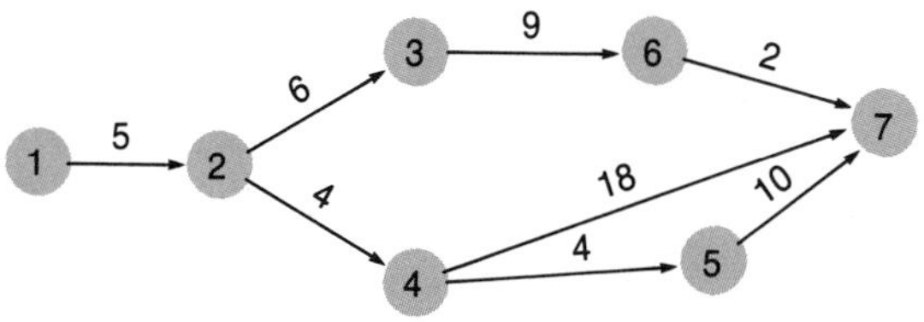

4. *a.* Summary:

Activity	ES	EF	LF	LS	Slack
1-2	0	4	11	7	7
2-4	4	13	21	12	8
4-7	13	18	26	21	8
7-10	18	20	28	26	8
10-12	21	24	31	28	7
2-5	4	12	19	11	7
5-8	12	19	26	19	7
8-10	19	21	28	26	7
1-3	0	10	10	0	0
3-6	10	16	16	10	0
6-9	16	20	20	16	0
9-11	20	25	25	20	0
11-12	25	31	31	25	0

b. Summary:

Activity	ES	EF	LF	LS	Slack
1-2	0	5	5	0	0
2-4	5	23	23	5	0
4-6	23	26	26	23	0
6-8	26	35	35	26	0
8-9	35	37	37	35	0
2-5	5	15	17	7	2
5-6	15	19	26	22	7
5-7	15	26	28	17	2
7-8	26	33	35	28	2
1-3	0	8	15	7	7
3-7	8	21	28	15	7

7. *b.* 24 days: .9686; 21 days: .235.

8. *a.* .8755.
b. .6881.
c. .0204.

9. *b.* .0262.
c. .2396.

10.

Path	Mean	Standard Deviation
a-d-e-h	24.34	1.354
a-f-g	15.50	1.258
b-i-j-k	14.83	1.014
c-m-n-o	26.17	1.658

d. 27 weeks: .6742; 28 weeks: .8643.

13. Crash schedule (1 wk. each): *c, c, f, f, e,* and *p*.

14. *a.* Crash 4 weeks:
(1) 7–11, (2) 1–2, (3) 7–11 and 6–10,
(4) 11–13 and 4–6.

Chapter 16: Queuing models

2. *a.* $r = 1.5$.
b. $L = 3.429$.
c. $W_q = 2.57$ minutes.
d. $W_s = 4.57$ minutes.
e. .75.

3. *a.* 2.25.
b. 9 minutes.
c. 25 percent.

4. *a.* 25 percent.
b. 14 percent.
c. 75 percent.

6. *a.* 1.33.
b. 2.
c. .132.
d. .33.

9. *a.* .933.
b. 12.273.
c. 15.07.
d. 8.77 minutes.
e. 10.77 minutes.
f. .016.
g. .063.
h. .055.
i. .167.
j. .878.

11. Line: 4; system: 5.

13. *a.* 56.
b. 3.
c. 3.

14. *a.* 4.
b. 95 percent: 0; 99 percent: 2.
c. 4.

15. 5 clerks.

16. *a.* .952.
b. .229.
c. .056 hour.
d. 2 clerks.

18. 3 docks

20.

	Number	Time (hours)
a.	2.00	.25
b.	1.34	.17
c.	1.66	.21

21. *a.* L_q 2.41.
b. $L = 3.26$, $W_q = .71$ min., $W = .96$ min., $\rho = 85\%$.

22. *a.* L_q 2.45.
b. $L = 3.30$, $W_q = .72$ min., $W = .97$ min., $\rho = 85\%$.

24. *a.* 1.25.
b. 8 min.
c. 25%.

26. *a.* 1.6.
b. .20 hour.
c. .20.

28. *a.* .56.
b. .39.
c. .34.

31. *a.* .90.
b. $W_1 = .1218$ hr., $W_2 = .3045$ hr., $W_3 = 2.1313$ hr.
c. 1: .3654, 2: .912, 3: 6.394.

32. *a.* .30.
b. 1: .034, 2: .025.
c. $W_1 = .0086$ hr., $W_2 = .0123$ hr.
d. $W_1 = .008$, $W_2 = .0116$.

Chapter 17: Simulation

2. *a.*

Number of Cakes	Cumulative Frequency	Random Number Range
0	.01	00
1	.08	01 to 07
2	.18	08 to 17
3	.32	18 to 31
4	.51	32 to 50
5	.73	51 to 72
6	.89	73 to 88
7	.97	89 to 96
8	1.00	97 to 99

b.

Day	1	2	3	4	5	6
RN	15	88	57	28	10	33
Simulated orders	2	6	5	3	2	4

c.

Day	1	2	3	4	5	6
RN	80	26	98	28	43	36
Simulated orders	6	3	8	3	4	4

3. *b.*

Day	1	2	3	4	5
RN	25	19	05	64	26
Simulated sales	1	1	0	3	1

c.

Day	1	2	3	4	5
RN	41	20	09	88	40
Simulated sales	2	1	0	5	2

4.

Letter	1		2		3		4	
Page	#1	#2	#1	#2	#1	#2	#1	#2
RN	23	55	93	83	02	19	67	89
Errors	0	0	2	1	0	0	0	1

Average errors per letter = 1.0.

6. Average days beyond schedule = .43.

8. *b.* ½.

9*a*.

Month	1	2	3	4	5	6	7	8	9	10	11	12
No. of breakdowns	1	1	2	2	4	2	2	5	2	3	2	0

11.

Day	1	2	3	4	. . .
Simulated demand	122.8	70.8	53.2	63.6	. . .

12.

Run	1	2	3	5	. . .
Simulated amount	79.2	68.0	73.0	75.0	. . .

14.

Job	1	2	3	4	5	. . .
Simulated processing time	.26	.46	.18	.87	2.68	. . .

15.

Job	1	2	3	4	. . .
Simulated repair time	1.23	0.44	1.05	2.41	. . .

17.

Patient	1	2	3	4	5
RN	−1.05	0.56	−0.67	−0.16	1.39
Simulated time	4.9	8.12	5.66	6.68	9.78

18.

Letter	1	2	3	4	5	6
Simulated time (min.)	4.09	4.56	3.98	5.87	3.56	4.35

21.

Order	1	2	3	4	5	6
Supplier	B	C	A	B	B	A
Order size	20	8	12	16	8	12

22.

Day	1	2	3	4
Calls	1	3	2	0
Times	1.338	1.268	.948	
		1.282	1.196	
		1.366		

27.

Period	10	11	12	13	14	16
Simulated demand	2,148	2,359	2,179	2,228	2,281	2,186

Chapter 18: Markov analysis

1. *a.* A: 70 percent; B: 30 percent.
b. 30 percent.

3. A = .40, B = .60.

4. *a.* .888.
c. 889.

6. 1 = .615, 2 = .385.

9. $M = .362$, $E = .293$, $S = .345$.

11. *b.* $A = 389$, $B = 333$, $C = 278$.

12. *a.* Each has 50 percent.
b. Cameo = .361, Strand = .412, Cine = .227.

14. *a.* $A = .508$, $B = .209$, $C = .283$.

16. *c.* 75 percent.

19. *a.* $\begin{bmatrix} 1.905 & .476 \\ .714 & 1.429 \end{bmatrix}$

20. *d.* $(I - Q) = \begin{bmatrix} 1 & -.3 \\ 0 & 1 \end{bmatrix}$

$(I - Q)^{-1} = \begin{bmatrix} 1 & .3 \\ 0 & 1 \end{bmatrix}$

f. 6 percent of Category 1 and 20 percent of Category 2.
g. $1,900

21. *d.* $128,000

Chapter 19: Calculus

1. *a.* 3.75.

2. *a.* .40.

4. minimum (28) at $x = 6$
maximum (32.5) at $x = 3$

5. maximum (35) at $x = 2$
minimum (3) at $x = 6$

6. \$6,000.

7. maximum is 40
minimum is 32

8. $x = 4, f = 63$.

9. $x = 4, f = 18$.

10. $x = 3, f = 29$.

11. $x_1 = 2, x_2 = 2/3$.

12. $x_1 = 7, x_2 = 8$; minimum.

13. $x_1 = 2.343, x_2 = 3.138$.

14. $x_1 = 1, x_2 = 2$; local maximum.

15. $x_1 = 3, x_2 = 2.5$; saddle point.

17. $x_1 = 2.333, x_2 = 2.333, \lambda = 12.333$
local maximum.

18. *a.* $x_1 = 10, x_2 = 2, \lambda = -18$
local minimum.
b. Increase by 18.

Index

J-K

L

M

N

O

P